◆ UK GAAP ◆

GENERALLY ACCEPTED ACCOUNTING PRACTICE

IN THE UNITED KINGDOM

◆ UK GAAP ◆

GENERALLY ACCEPTED ACCOUNTING PRACTICE

IN THE UNITED KINGDOM

Principal authors and editors

Mike Davies

Ron Paterson

Allister Wilson

Arthur Young
A MEMBER OF ARTHUR YOUNG INTERNATIONAL

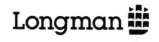

ISBN 0 85121 4851

Published by

Longman Professional and Business Communications Division
Longman Group UK Limited
21-27 Lamb's Conduit Street, London WC1N 3NJ

Associated Offices

Australia	Longman Professional Publishing (Pty) Limited 130 Phillip Street, Sydney, NSW 2000
Hong Kong	Longman Group (Far East) Limited Cornwall House, 18th Floor, Taikoo Trading Estate Tong Chong Street, Quarry Bay
Malaysia	Longman Malaysia Sdn Bhd No 3 Jalan Kilang A, Off Jalan Penchala Petaling Jaya, Selangor, Malaysia
Singapore	Longman Singapore Publishers (Pte) Ltd 25 First Lok Yang Road, Singapore 2262
USA	Longman Group (USA) Inc 500 North Dearborn Street, Chicago, Illinois 60610

A CIP catalogue record for this book is
available from the British Library

Printed in Great Britain by
Bell & Bain Ltd, Scotland.

Foreword

I warmly welcome the publication of this book. I expect it to become a standard work of reference for accountants, and people interested in accounting, in all kinds of occupations — people in practice, in industry, in government, researchers, students and their teachers.

In some ways, the present state of accounting is unsatisfactory. Accountants are very likely to disagree about the solution to an accounting problem — but that is a phenomenon that occurs in many subjects. More seriously, accountants have little shared understanding of ways of choosing among accounting options, of what work needs to be done to identify preferable means of reporting.

The aim must be to reach agreement about the purpose of accounting and about ways of collecting and evaluating evidence to assess which options satisfy the purposes most effectively. This book will make a contribution to that aim. It deals with purposes and concepts as well as more detailed reporting rules. It synthesises an enormous body of literature, drawing on authoritative international as well as British sources, research studies as well as standards. It gives illustrations and discusses difficulties. Most readers will disagree with some things that it says, but all should find that it helps to mark the path for improving accounting, as well as providing useful information.

My job as regulator of the telecommunications industry makes me particularly aware of the importance of good accounting in setting prices that are fair to customers and suppliers — and of the deficiencies in current accounting. It also makes me aware of the power of competition in bringing benefits to people, competition in products, services and ideas. This book will stimulate competition in ideas in accounting. I welcome it; and I wish it success in providing effective competition.

Bryan Carsberg
May 1989

Preface

In producing this book, we have aimed to provide a comprehensive review of all significant aspects of financial reporting practice in the UK. On a chapter by chapter basis, we have addressed the theoretical and historical background to each main area of accounting; however, more importantly and, in our view, more usefully, we have tried to translate theory into practice, by illustrating the disclosures and methods currently being applied in financial statements by prominent listed companies, by discussing various problem areas encountered in practice, and by offering our own recommendations on how the relevant rules on accounting should be interpreted and applied.

It will be clear from many of the comments in the book that we do not look on present accounting practice in the UK with complete satisfaction. Although we think that the standard of financial reporting in this country is generally high, and compares favourably with that of most other countries, we think that significant room for improvement still exists in certain areas. Accordingly, it has been our policy not to shrink from being opinionated on these matters, but rather to be critical of the existing rules where we thought criticism was due. We hope that our comments will form a constructive contribution to the further development of these rules, whether they lie in accounting standards or in legislation.

We have also attempted to illustrate how certain accounting problems are dealt with outside the UK, by looking at practice elsewhere, notably in the United States. We should make it clear that in doing so we have not aimed to give a full picture of GAAP in any other country or of the ways in which it differs from the UK; we have simply observed, in relation to individual topics, how these countries have responded to similar financial reporting issues. In addition, we have frequently referred to the requirements of International Accounting Standards. We support the initiative of the IASC in seeking to narrow the areas of difference between the GAAP of different countries, and we believe that the makers of accounting rules in the UK should also espouse the cause of international harmonisation more enthusiastically than has sometimes been done in the past.

This book is the product of a considerable team effort, and could not have been completed without the invaluable contributions made by a number of people — primarily the members of the Technical Department of Arthur Young, but also a number of partners and managers throughout the Firm.

The book's other contributing authors, all from the Firm's Technical Department, who devoted considerable time and effort towards researching particular areas of UK GAAP, including an extensive survey of published annual reports and related US and International accounting requirements, were as follows:

Alison Brown
Margaret Dougal
Carol Hawthorn
Steven Lindsay
Stuart MacDonald
John McMillan
Eugene Mitchell
Claire Newton
Vivian Pereira
Steve Reeves
Hedy Richards
Andrew Simmonds
David York.

We are particularly grateful to Derek Foster, who fulfilled the roles of mentor, consulting editor and sounding-board, and who cheerfully waded through many hundreds of pages of draft manuscript. Individual chapters also benefited materially from the comments of the following members of Arthur Young: Richard Findlater, Barbara Hadfield, Roger Housechild, Gavin James, Russi Javeri, Paula Moore, Steve Parkinson, Trevor Pijper, Andy Pollock, Paul Rutteman, Allan Siva, Garth Tweedale and David Whitaker. We would also like to thank Patrick Cross of Clay & Partners and Geoff Everingham of the University of Cape Town for their helpful comments on Chapters 22 and 2, respectively, as well as Richard Keeling and Kirk Robinson of the New York office of Arthur Young for reviewing certain aspects of the book.

Special thanks are due to Professor Sir Bryan Carsberg for agreeing to write the foreword to the book.

Lastly, our thanks go to: Derek Ashley, Trevor Pijper and Hedy Richards, for their work on the specimen financial statements; Anthony Morris and Elizabeth Lee for checking some of the figures; Cheryl Gillan, who handled the marketing and administrative aspects of the book with superb efficiency; Richard Smith who provided invaluable assistance with the layout and technology for the production of the book; Larissa Connor, who provided research assistance; and Samantha Ferrey for her contribution towards the book's word processing.

In summary, very many people have made a major contribution to the book, and they deserve the recognition for whatever merit it possesses; conversely, the blame for any deficiencies which remain must be laid at the door of the editors.

London, May 1989

Mike Davies
Ron Paterson
Allister Wilson

List of chapters

Detailed contents

Chapter 3   Revenue   recognition   79

Chapter 4   Group financial statements 111

Chapter 10   Fixed assets and depreciation 437

Chapter 15 Statements of cash and funds flow.............. 581

Chapter 20   Segmental reporting 811

Chapter 23 Directors' and officers' loans and transactions.... 915

Abbreviations

The following abbreviations are used in this book:

Professional and regulatory bodies:

AICPA   American Institute of Certified Public Accountants
APB   Accounting Principles Board (of the AICPA)
ASC   Accounting Standards Committee (a committee of the CCAB)
ASSC   Accounting Standards Steering Committee (the ASC's original name)
CCAB   Consultative Committee of Accountancy Bodies
CICA   The Canadian Institute of Chartered Accountants
DTI   Department of Trade and Industry
FASB   Financial Accounting Standards Board (successor to the APB)
IASC   International Accounting Standards Committee
ICAEW   The Institute of Chartered Accountants in England and Wales
ICAS   The Institute of Chartered Accountants of Scotland
SEC   Securities and Exchange Commission

Accounting related terms:

CA 85   The Companies Act 1985
CCA   Current cost accounting
E   Exposure Draft (of an IAS)
ED   Exposure Draft (of a SSAP)
EPS   Earnings per share
FIFO   The first-in, first-out basis of valuation
GAAP   Generally accepted accounting practice (as it applies to the UK), or generally accepted accounting principles (as it applies to the US)
IAS   International Accounting Standard (issued by the IASC)
LIFO   The last-in, first-out basis of valuation
NRV   Net realisable value
R&D   Research and development
SFAC   Statement of Financial Accounting Concepts (issued by the FASB as part of its conceptual framework project)
SFAS   Statement of Financial Accounting Standards (issued by the FASB)
SSAP   Statement of Standard Accounting Practice
TR   Technical Release (issued by the ICAEW)

Authoritative literature

The content of this book does not take into account authoritative literature and company law published subsequent to:

- SSAP 24 and ED 46 in the UK.

- The Companies Act 1985 and the Companies Bill published on 21st December 1988.

- SFAS 102 and SFAC No. 6, issued by the FASB.

- IAS 28 and E33, issued by the IASC.

Chapter 1

The development of UK GAAP

1 THE HISTORY OF THE ACCOUNTING STANDARDS COMMITTEE

1.1 The need for accounting standards

Prior to 1970, there were no mandatory requirements in the UK outside company law governing the presentation of financial statements of companies; and even those company law provisions which did exist comprised only the basic minimum, which was inadequate for the purpose of achieving a satisfactory standard of financial reporting. Consequently, accounting practices were varied, inconsistent and sometimes inappropriate; inter-firm and inter-period comparisons were difficult as companies altered accounting treatments and resorted to such practices as 'window-dressing' and 'reserve accounting' to achieve desired results in order to present a picture of profitability and growth. Certain professional accounting bodies (such as the ICAEW) had issued a series of recommendations on accounting principles — but these recommendations were not mandatory.

By 1969 it had become apparent that the basic accounting requirements contained in company law needed the support of more authoritative pronouncements than the recommendations that were being issued. Consequently, the Council of the ICAEW issued a 'Statement of intent on accounting standards in the 1970s',[1] wherein they indicated their intention to advance accounting standards along the following lines:

(a) narrowing the areas of difference and variety in accounting practice by publishing authoritative statements on best accounting practice which would, whenever possible, be definitive;

(b) requiring that when financial statements included significant items which depended substantially on judgements of value, or on the estimated outcome of future events or uncompleted transactions, rather than on ascertained amounts, the accounting bases adopted in arriving at their amount should be disclosed;

(c) recommending that departures from definitive standards should be disclosed in company financial statements;

(d)   providing an opportunity for appropriate representative bodies to express their views by giving wide exposure to Council's draft proposals for new accounting standards;

(e)   continuing its programme for encouraging improved accounting standards in legal and regulatory measures.[2]

As a result, the Accounting Standards Steering Committee was established in 1970 by the Council of the ICAEW as the means for the implementation of the above proposals. The Institute of Chartered Accountants of Scotland and the Institute of Chartered Accountants in Ireland became co-sponsors of the Committee almost immediately afterwards; the Chartered Association of Certified Accountants and the Chartered Institute of Management Accountants[3] joined subsequently in 1971 and the Chartered Institute of Public Finance and Accountancy in 1976. With effect from February 1, 1976, the Committee became the Accounting Standards Committee (ASC) and was reconstituted as a joint committee of these six accountancy bodies who now comprise the Consultative Committee of Accountancy Bodies (CCAB). Since January 1, 1986, the ASC has been a Committee of CCAB Limited.

1.2   The objects and terms of reference of the ASC

The Board of CCAB Limited has agreed that the objects of the ASC are 'to define accounting concepts, to narrow differences of financial accounting and reporting treatment, and to codify generally accepted best practice in the public interest. These objects encompass:

(a)   fundamentals of financial accounting and their application to financial statements;

(b)   definition of terms used;

(c)   questions of measurements of reported results and financial position; and

(d)   the content and form of financial statements.'[4]

In order to achieve these objects, the ASC was given the following terms of reference:

(a)   to keep under review standards of financial accounting and reporting;

(b)   to propose to the Councils of each of the CCAB members statements of standard accounting practice and interpretations of such statements;

(c)   to publish consultative documents, discussion papers and exposure drafts and submit to the Councils of each of the CCAB members non-mandatory guidance notes with the object of maintaining and advancing accounting standards;

(d)   to consult, as appropriate, with representatives of finance, commerce, industry and government, and other bodies and persons concerned with financial reporting; and

(e)   to maintain close links with the International Accounting Standards Committee and the accountancy profession in Europe and throughout the world.[5]

1.3   The Watts Report

In the light of the eight years' experience gained since its formation, a Review Group was set up in 1978 by the ASC, under the chairmanship of Mr. T. R. Watts, to review the standard-setting process and to consider what improvements in that process could be effected. The Review Group submitted a draft consultative document to the ASC in May 1978. The document was adopted by the ASC and published as a basis for public discussion and comment.[6] Following extensive public consultations and debate, the ASC made a number of recommendations in a report to the CCAB which was published in 1981 (the Watts Report).[7] Many of the recommendations of the Watts Report concern fundamental issues which are still, as yet, unresolved and have consequently been revisited by the Dearing Committee (see 5 below). These include such issues as the need for a conceptual framework; the establishment of a supervisory body to ensure compliance with accounting standards; the application of certain standards only to large companies; a full-time paid ASC chairman; and the need for more resources.

1.4   The McKinnon Report

A further review of the standard-setting process was carried out by an ASC working party in 1983. The reasons for the review were:

(a)   to develop certain recommendations contained in the Watts Report;

(b)   to seek ways by which the standard-setting process could be shortened; and

(c)   to consider whether there was a need for alternative or new types of pronouncement.

The findings of this working party were published in a report entitled 'Review of the Standard Setting Process' (the McKinnon Report). However, the report did not address the more fundamental issues raised in the Watts Report, and instead focused on the procedural aspects relating to the development of SSAPs. The report did, however, recommend that a new category of final pronouncement be introduced, namely the Statement of Recommended Practice (SORP).

2   ACCOUNTING STANDARDS AND THE CONCEPT OF 'TRUE AND FAIR'

2.1   The introduction of the true and fair concept

The requirement that all financial statements, which are prepared for the purpose of compliance with the Companies Act, should 'give a true and fair view' was first introduced in the Companies Act 1947.[8] This amended the former requirement of 'true and correct', a change considered necessary on the grounds that there was no clear distinction between the two adjectives when used to describe financial statements. Was it possible for financial statements to be 'true' yet 'incorrect'; or 'untrue' yet 'correct'?

The concept of true and fair was adopted by the EC Council in its Fourth Directive.[9] In terms of the Directive, annual accounts are defined as a 'composite whole' comprising a balance sheet, profit and loss account and notes; the accounts should be drawn up in accordance with the Directive's detailed provisions and 'give a true and fair view of the company's assets, liabilities, financial position and profit or loss'.[10] However, to obviate a potential conflict between its detailed provisions and the achievement of truth and fairness, the Directive declared the obligation to give a true and fair view to be overriding. Consequently, where the application of the provisions of the Directive would not be sufficient to give a true and fair view, additional information must be given, and where the application of a provision of the Directive is incompatible with the presentation of a true and fair view, that provision must be departed from (with appropriate disclosure in the notes of the departure).[11]

The provisions of the Fourth Directive were implemented in the UK through the enactment of the Companies Act 1981. Following the consolidation of the various Companies Acts 1948—1983 into the Companies Act 1985, the detailed requirements of the Directive are contained in Schedule 4 of that Act, and the requirement that financial statements should give a true and fair view is contained in section 228 for individual companies and section 230 for group financial statements. It is therefore clear that the concept of true and fair is a legal one, and the question as to whether or not a particular company's financial statements comply with sections 228 or 230 can ultimately only be decided by the courts.

2.2   What authority do SSAPs have?

The Explanatory Foreword to accounting standards states that 'statements of standard accounting practice ("accounting standards") are developed in the public interest by the ASC as being authoritative statements on accounting practice. Their primary aim is to narrow the areas of difference and variety in the accounting treatment of the matters with which they deal.'[12] It goes on to say that 'accounting standards are applicable to all financial statements whose purpose is to give a true and fair view of financial position and of profit and loss for the period'.[13] The question which therefore arises is what is the legal relationship between the Companies Act requirement of true and fair and the accounting standards issued by the ASC? Since the ASC claim that their standards are authoritative pronouncements on what is true and fair, does non-compliance with a SSAP result in financial statements not being true and fair? Conversely, since true and fair is a legal concept which can only be interpreted by the courts, does compliance with the SSAPs constitute compliance with the Companies Act?

These and other issues were discussed in the legal opinion obtained by the ASC in 1983 from Mr. Leonard Hoffman QC and Miss Mary Arden.[14] This opinion states that 'the courts will treat compliance with accepted accounting principles as prima facie evidence that the accounts are true and fair. Equally, deviation from accepted principles will be prima facie evidence that they are not. ... The function of the ASC is to formulate what it considers should be generally accepted accounting principles. Thus the value of a SSAP to a court which has to decide whether accounts are true and fair is two-fold. First, it represents an important statement of professional opinion about the standards which readers may reasonably expect in accounts which are intended to be true and fair. ... Secondly, because accountants are professionally obliged to comply with a SSAP, it creates in the readers an expectation that the accounts will be in conformity with the prescribed standards. This is in itself a reason why accounts which depart from the standard without adequate justification or explanation may be held not to be true and fair.'[15]

This view is supported in the judgment given by Woolf J in *Lloyd Cheyham & Co Ltd v Littlejohn & Co,* in which he stated that 'while they [SSAPs] are not conclusive, ... and they are not as the explanatory forward makes clear, rigid rules, they are very strong evidence as to what is the proper standard which should be adopted'.[16]

Clearly, therefore, SSAPs have no direct legal authority or effect — in fact they are little more than rules of professional conduct for the members of the professional bodies which make up the CCAB. However, it appears highly probable that they will have a very persuasive effect in the courts' interpretation as to whether or not a company's accounts present a true and fair view. This situation may, however, change in the near future should the recommendations of the Dearing Committee be implemented (see 5.2.5 below).

2.3   The role of International Accounting Standards

The International Accounting Standards Committee (IASC) came into existence in 1973 as a result of an agreement by various accountancy bodies around the world. The IASC is now sponsored by well over 50 countries, and its business is conducted by a Board comprising representatives of up to 13 countries and up to four organisations having an interest in financial reporting.[17] The objectives of the IASC as set out in its constitution are:

(a)   to formulate and publish in the public interest accounting standards to be observed in the presentation of financial statements and to promote their world-wide acceptance and observance; and

(b)   to work generally for the improvement and harmonisation of regulations, accounting standards and procedures relating to the presentation of financial statements.[18]

In the UK, the Councils of the six accountancy bodies which act collectively through the CCAB support the IASC in promoting world-wide harmonisation of accounting standards. This is achieved, inter alia, through seeking to incorporate the provisions of International Accounting Standards (IASs) within the body of the SSAPs.

When IASs were first issued, they permitted several alternative accounting treatments. The principal reason for this was that the IASC viewed its initial function as prohibiting undesirable accounting practices, whilst acknowledging that there might be more than one acceptable solution to a specific accounting issue. However, the Board of the IASC has now stated that it believes that the time is right to eliminate some of these permitted alternative accounting options, thereby taking a significant step towards the achievement of a truly international set of accounting standards which has world-wide acceptance.

To this end, the IASC has set up a Steering Committee to investigate ways of reducing or eliminating alternatives. This committee has published its proposals in an exposure draft[19] which lists the alternative treatments which are currently permitted under certain of the IASs, indicating those which should be eliminated and justifying the retention of the remainder. The committee is also investigating the desirability of developing a 'reconciling standard', which would indicate preferences for certain treatments without actually eliminating the alternatives. Companies could then present their financial statements in accordance with the reconciling standard in order to give comparability with other companies. This approach would prove especially useful for international securities offerings.

In general terms, because of the wide range of permissible options contained in the IASs, compliance with the SSAPs ensures compliance with the corresponding IASs. However, there are some matters which are covered in IASs but not yet addressed in the SSAPs; furthermore, the elimination of alternative accounting treatments is likely to have an effect on UK standards, since either significant differences between IASs and SSAPs will arise and/or the ASC will act to amend SSAPs to comply.

2.4   The US experience

The US equivalent of a 'true and fair view' is 'fair presentation in conformity with GAAP'. However, the ASC and the Financial Accounting Standards Board (FASB) in the US take rather different approaches to accounting standard setting. The ASC has adopted a broad fundamental approach which, on one hand, allows a high degree of flexibility, thereby requiring a considerable measure of judgement to be exercised in the application of many of the standards; on the other hand, the looseness (or complete lack) of detailed rules results in similar transactions being accounted for in ways which produce materially different effects. Conversely, some commentators have stated that the FASB has generated a plethora of highly detailed legalistic rules which have, to a large extent, obscured the concept of fair presentation.

A further significant difference between the UK and US is that for more than 50 years, the standard form audit report in the US has referred to fair presentation in accordance with 'generally accepted accounting principles'. From the outset, the Securities and Exchange Commission (SEC) has relied on the accounting profession to set accounting standards, and has viewed generally accepted accounting principles as those which have 'substantial authoritative support'. This term was first introduced in the SEC's Accounting Series Release (ASR) No. 4, which was issued in 1938 and stated that 'in cases where financial statements filed with the Commission ... are prepared in accordance with accounting principles for which there is no substantial authoritative support, such financial statements will be presumed to be misleading or inaccurate despite disclosures contained in the certificate of the accountant or in footnotes to the statements provided the matters involved are material'.

In 1964, the Council of the AICPA adopted a Special Bulletin entitled *Disclosure of Departures From Opinions of Accounting Principles Board*, which contained, inter alia, the following recommendations:

(a) 'Generally accepted accounting principles' are those principles which have substantial authoritative support.

(b) Opinions of the Accounting Principles Board constitute 'substantial authoritative support'.

(c) 'Substantial authoritative support' can exist for accounting principles that differ from Opinions of the Accounting Principles Board.[20]

In 1973, the SEC updated ASR 4 to recognise the establishment of the FASB by stating that 'principles, standards and practices promulgated by the FASB in its Statements and Interpretations will be considered by the Commission as having substantial authoritative support, and those contrary to such FASB promulgations will be considered to have no such support'.[21] This ties in with the AICPA's Code of Professional Conduct, which states that 'a member shall not (1) express an opinion or state affirmatively that the financial statements or other financial data of an entity are presented in conformity with generally accepted accounting principles or (2) state that he or she is not aware of any material modifications that should be made to such statements or data in order for them to be in conformity with generally accepted accounting principles, if such statements or data contain any departure from an accounting principle promulgated by bodies designated by Council to establish such principles that has a material effect on the statements or data taken as a whole'.[22]

2.5   The Canadian experience

In Canada, in addition to there being a federal corporations act (the Canada Business Corporations Act), the individual provinces each have their own separate corporations acts. Consequently, Canadian companies have the option of incorporating either under the legislation of the province in which they are based, or under the federal Act, although in practice most of the larger Canadian corporations are federally incorporated.

Canadian accounting standards have evolved from merely representing guidance as to good practice, through to becoming standards with full statutory backing. The landmarks in this evolutionary process are as follows:[23]

•   In 1953, when the Ontario Business Corporations Act was completely revised, the profession persuaded the government of the day to incorporate into the Act virtually all of the provisions of the first CICA bulletin on financial disclosure. As a result of the companies acts of other provinces and in the federal jurisdiction picking up these provisions, the legal impact of the CICA recommendations spread throughout the country.

•   In 1968, when the CICA *Handbook* was adopted, the committee followed the precedent set by the AICPA and established a requirement that 'where the accounting treatment or statement presentation does not follow the recommendations in this Handbook, the practice used should be explained in notes to the financial statements with an indication of the reason why the recommendation concerned was not followed'.[24]

- In 1972, the securities administrators of several Canadian provinces announced that they would regard the CICA *Handbook* pronouncements as 'generally accepted accounting principles'. As a result of this, the CICA *Handbook* took on quasi-legal status with respect to most filings under the jurisdiction of provincial securities acts. In 1975, as a result of the inclusion of a reference to the CICA *Handbook* in the regulations to the Canada Business Corporations Act, the same result was brought about in respect of the financial statements of companies which were under federal jurisdiction. Several provinces have also amended their companies legislation to this effect.

- In December 1988, the CICA published *Handbook* Section 1000 which, inter alia, defines 'generally accepted accounting principles' as the term used to describe the basis on which financial statements are normally prepared; this encompasses not only specific rules, practices and procedures relating to particular circumstances but also broad principles and conventions of general application, including the underlying financial statement concepts described in Section 1000. More specifically, generally accepted accounting principles comprise the Accounting Recommendations in the *Handbook*; however, for matters not covered by them, the principles that apply are either generally accepted by virtue of their use in similar circumstances by a significant number of entities in Canada, or are consistent with the Recommendations and developed through the exercise of professional judgment, by consulting other informed accountants, where appropriate, and by applying the concepts outlined in Section 1000.[25]

From time to time, the question is raised as to whether or not the UK should follow the Canadian model of giving accounting standards increased legal backing by incorporating them in the law. This issue was again addressed by the Dearing Committee, and is discussed at 5 below.

2.6   Germany

The incorporation of the EC Fourth Directive (Accounting Directive), the Seventh Directive (Consolidated Accounts Directive) and the Eighth Directive (Auditor Directive) was achieved in Germany through the enactment on January 1, 1986 of the Accounting Directives Law. One of the most important aspects of this modification of German law was the revision of the Commercial Code, which included the addition of a Third Book containing accounting rules applicable to all businesses.

In terms of the Commercial Code, company financial statements must, in compliance with *required accounting principles* (GoB), present a true and fair view of the net worth, financial position and results of the company.[26] GoB has been interpreted as meaning 'those principles which are not comprehensively codified but which, by application in specific cases, lead to a correct accounting treatment by reference to the objectives of financial statements. They can be determined deductively by making full use of statute and case law, accounting theory, pronouncements of the Institute of German Qualified Accountants as well as accounting practice'.[27] Since the concept of true and fair is relatively new to Germany's Commercial Code, its relationship to GoB is not entirely clear; however, it would appear that the general GoB rule would only be brought into play if, in the preparation of company financial statements, uncertainties in the interpretation and application of the specific rules of the laws and ordinances need to be resolved. Therefore, it seems that GoB will not impose any disclosure requirements additional to those contained in the law, unless the financial statements would not otherwise not show a true and fair view.

3   WHAT IS UK GAAP?

3.1   'Principles' or 'practice'?

In the UK, the expression 'GAAP' is used far more loosely than in most other countries; the reason for this is that GAAP does not have any statutory or regulatory authority or definition, as is the case in the US or Canada. Consequently, references to GAAP are rarely found in the literature in the UK, and where the expression is used, it is done so without adequate explanation or definition. The only instance where generally accepted accounting principles are referred to in the Companies Act is in the context of realised profits; Schedule 4, para. 91 states that realised profits are 'such profits of the company as fall to be treated as realised profits for the purposes of those accounts in accordance with principles generally accepted with respect to the determination for accounting purposes of realised profits at the time when those accounts are prepared'.[28] Although the legislation does not define the term 'principles generally accepted', the CCAB issued a Technical Release (TR 481) in September 1982 which gave guidance on the determination of realised profits.[29] TR 481 stated that 'principles generally accepted' for the determination of realised profits 'should be considered in conjunction with, inter alia, the legal principles laid down in the new Schedule 8 [now Schedule 4], statements of standard accounting practice ("SSAPs"), and in particular the fundamental accounting concepts referred to in SSAP 2'.[30] This interpretation, however, applies purely to the determination of realised profits; as will be seen below, it is our view that GAAP should be more widely interpreted.

In their opinion referred to in 2.2 above, Hoffman and Arden cited the decision in *Odeon Associated Theatres Ltd v Jones (Inspector of Taxes)*[31] as an illustration of the relationship between 'generally accepted accounting principles' and the legal concept of true and fair, and in so doing reached the conclusion that 'the function of the ASC is to formulate what it considers should be generally accepted accounting principles'.[32] Nevertheless, whilst most would agree that the SSAPs represent 'generally accepted accounting principles', what about those areas of accounting which are not addressed in the SSAPs? Furthermore, what about the accounting and disclosure requirements of the Companies Act and Stock Exchange — do they constitute 'generally accepted accounting principles'?

Our view is that GAAP is a dynamic concept which requires constant review, adaptation and reaction to changing circumstances. We believe that use of the term 'principle' gives GAAP an unjustified and inappropriate degree of permanence. GAAP changes in response to changing business and economic needs and developments. As circumstances alter, accounting practices are modified or developed accordingly. This is recognised in the Explanatory Foreword to the SSAPs which states that accounting standards 'are not intended to be a comprehensive code of rigid rules'.[33] Furthermore, the Explanatory Foreword refers to SSAPs as being 'authoritative statements of accounting practice'.[34] We therefore believe that GAAP goes far beyond mere rules and principles, and encompasses contemporary permissible accounting *practice*.

Accordingly, the boundaries of UK GAAP extend far beyond the accounting principles contained in the SSAPs; it includes the requirements of the Companies Act and of the Stock Exchange, as well as any other acceptable accounting treatments not incorporated in the official literature.

3.2   What is 'generally accepted'?

It is often argued that the term 'generally accepted' implies that there must exist a high degree of practical application of a particular accounting practice. However, this interpretation raises certain practical difficulties. For example, what about new areas of accounting which have not, as yet, been generally applied? What about different accounting treatments for similar items — are they all generally accepted?

It is our view that 'generally accepted' does *not* mean 'generally adopted or used'. We believe that, in the UK context, GAAP refers to accounting practices which are regarded as permissible by the accounting profession. The extent to which a particular practice has been adopted is, in our opinion, not the overriding consideration. Any accounting practice which is legitimate in the circumstances under which it has been applied should be regarded as GAAP. The decision as to whether or not a particular practice is permissible or legitimate would depend on one or more of the following factors:

(a)   Is the practice consistent with the needs of users and the objectives of financial reporting?

(b)   Is the practice addressed either in the accounting standards, statute or other official pronouncements?

(c)   If the practice is not addressed in UK accounting standards, is it dealt with in International Accounting Standards, or the standards of other countries such as the US?

(d)   Does the practice have authoritative support in the accounting literature?

(e)   Is the practice being applied by other companies in similar situations?

(f)   Is the practice consistent with the fundamental concept of 'true and fair'?

The aim of this book is to analyse existing UK GAAP on the basis of the above six criteria.

4   GAAP FOR SMALL COMPANIES

4.1   The Big GAAP/Little GAAP debate

The administrative and legislative burdens which have been imposed on small businesses have been a controversial issue for many years. In particular, issues such as the retention of the small company audit and the application of accounting standards to small companies have been the subject of numerous studies in the UK and around the world.[35] With the increasing number of accounting standards, owners of small companies have complained about the cost and inconvenience of applying accounting requirements which were designed for large public companies. Some hold the view that accounting standards should apply equally to all financial statements which purport to present a true and fair view; others believe that small companies should be exempted from the requirements of certain standards which are unduly burdensome; whilst there is yet a further contention that small companies should have a completely different set of accounting standards altogether.

Whilst it is beyond the scope of this book to discuss all the issues surrounding differential reporting for small companies, it is noteworthy that there has been an almost unanimous reluctance to pursue the development of two GAAPs. This is reflected, for example, in a Report to the Council of the Institute of Chartered Accountants of British Columbia, wherein the Task Force on Big GAAP/Little GAAP concluded that 'any attempt to develop two separate sets of generally accepted accounting principles ... raises insurmountable difficulties'.[36] Amongst the reasons offered for these difficulties was that 'defining in a meaningful fashion Big GAAP/Little GAAP principles would appear to be unattainable given that the accounting profession has been unable to adequately define generally accepted accounting principles'.[37]

In a research study carried out in 1985 by Professor B.V. Carsberg et al. on small company financial reporting in the UK, the conclusion was reached that 'the burden imposed by accounting standards and other reporting requirements does not seem to be a matter for primary concern among people in small companies'.[38] In attempting to explain this finding, the report suggested that 'perhaps small company managers have little awareness of what is involved in complying with standards because they leave this aspect of their accounting to their professional advisers'.[39]

4.2   Exemptions for 'small companies'

In October 1986, the ASC commissioned a working party to investigate the application of accounting standards to small companies. The findings of the working party, which were set out in TR 690,[40] were that 'there is no evidence to suggest that, in general, small companies find compliance with accounting standards unduly burdensome, given that they have to prepare financial statements that give a true and fair view'.[41] TR 690 did, however, indicate that the ASC would consider exempting small companies from certain future standards.[42]

This announcement has since been followed up by TR 706, which outlines the basis on which the ASC intends to judge whether exemptions are appropriate, defines the class of entities to which any exemption will normally apply and indicates the way in which the exemption will be formulated.[43] In TR 706, the ASC states that it 'accepts that there is a case, in specific circumstances, for exempting small entities from certain provisions of accounting standards'; however, 'such exemptions are likely to relate more often to disclosure requirements, rather than to recognition or measurement rules'.[44] Where the ASC is satisfied that exemption is merited in a specific instance, it will propose a relaxation for a class of entities which excludes:

(a)   public limited companies (plcs);

(b)   companies that have a plc as a subsidiary; and

(c)   other reporting entities, required to prepare true and fair accounts, which exceed ten times the qualifying conditions for a company to be treated as a medium-sized company under section 248 of the Companies Act 1985.[45]

The effect of this proposal is that, in terms of the current thresholds contained in section 248, a company will only be able to take advantage of the exemptions specified in a particular accounting standard if it is neither a plc, nor has a plc as a subsidiary, and it meets two or more of the following criteria:

(a)   its turnover does not exceed £80m;

(b)   its balance sheet total does not exceed £39m;

(c)   the average number of persons employed in the year does not exceed 2,500.

Clearly, these criteria can hardly be regarded as relating to 'small companies', and it is apparent that they are designed to apply to companies other than very large ones. It is our view, however, that the ASC has introduced an unnecessary complication by including the size criteria in the exemption. It would have been more sensible if the ASC had merely distinguished between public and private companies in its exemption proposals.

To date, this exemption has been applied in relation to certain aspects of SSAP 13 (Revised) — *Accounting for research and development* — and has been incorporated in Exposure Draft 45, which deals with segmental reporting.

4.3   Is this the small company solution?

In arriving at their criteria for differentiation, the ASC stated that it recognised 'that there is a valid distinction to be drawn between larger and smaller companies as regards their financial reporting capabilities and user expectations'.[46] However, in formulating their solution to the problem, the ASC seems to have failed to consider the application of standards in the context of the objectives of small company financial reporting. Clearly, small companies do need standards; nor can it be disputed that the application of GAAP assists in the implementation of the Companies Act reporting requirements through, inter alia, the imposition of some form of accounting and reporting discipline. However, the discussion of whether or not small companies find accounting standards burdensome is spurious, since the findings of the ASC working party are largely immaterial to the real issue involved. This, of course, is whether existing standards provide small businessmen with a reporting framework which generates information which is useful, relevant and reliable for decision making purposes. The question, therefore, is not whether standards impose a burden on small companies, but whether they are of any value. In order to answer this, it is necessary first to establish a sensible definition of a small company for financial reporting purposes, in contrast to the ASC's definition based on arbitrary size criteria.

The criteria contained in section 248 of the Companies Act are clearly not suitable for the purposes of determining whether or not a company should be subject to alternative reporting requirements. To assume that, in the application of standards, small companies are merely simpler versions of large companies is to make the same mistake inherent in company law. Modern company law focuses on the large public company, and the Companies Act, with its 747 sections and 25 Schedules, is not appropriate to the small owner-managed company. Even if standards do not impose more burdens than the law, perhaps it is time to consider seriously the development of an alternative limited liability vehicle for the small proprietary company.

The fundamental criteria which distinguish a small company from others are the compositions of its membership and management. Companies with a limited number of members, all involved in the day to day operations, should be able to incorporate under a different and specially designed limited liability régime. It is within this structure that a more appropriate financial reporting framework can be developed.

If this structure is adopted, the question of small company compliance with existing standards will involve three distinct accounting issues — those of recognition, measurement and disclosure. The question, therefore, is not merely whether or not the application of existing standards should be relaxed, but whether alternative standards of recognition, measurement and/or disclosure would better achieve the objectives of financial reporting for such small companies.

General purpose financial statements are prepared on the assumption that there are no basic differences in the needs of those who will use them. However, as discussed in Chapter 2, the users of public companies' financial statements include existing and potential shareholders, loan creditors, financial analysts and advisers, the financial press, employees, etc. Small companies' financial statements, on the other hand, are prepared primarily for the benefit of owner-managers, their bankers and the Revenue authorities, who have little interest in the kind of information aimed at the broad spectrum of users of public companies' statements.

Furthermore, the owners of public companies are not generally involved in the management of the business. For this reason, a relationship of accountability is developed between owners and managers. Clearly, since a characteristic of a small proprietary company is that it is owner-managed, this accountability — together with the related reporting obligation — falls away, illustrating a major distinction between the objectives of financial reporting for the two types of company. The ASC's proposals for exemption do not, however, acknowledge this vital difference. It is therefore clear that the needs of users of financial statements should determine the objectives of financial reporting, leading ultimately to the form and content of financial statements. It is not until there is adequate research in this area that appropriate reporting practice for small companies can be developed.

5   THE DEARING REPORT

5.1   The need for a review of the standard-setting process

As the complexities of accounting issues and requirements for more sophisticated levels of financial reporting have mounted, the increased demands placed on the ASC have clearly indicated that it is unable to satisfactorily fulfil the standard setting role that it is expected to perform. The ASC has had to endure mounting criticism for being unable to either respond quickly to changing needs or deal adequately with fundamental issues such as inflation accounting, off-balance sheet transactions and goodwill. However, when one considers that the ASC essentially comprises a voluntary part-time committee, it has achieved a great deal. Nevertheless, as companies are required to report in a fast-moving and increasingly complex environment, the present standard-setting process is no longer appropriate.

Consequently, in November 1987 the CCAB appointed a Review Committee, under the chairmanship of Sir Ronald Dearing, to review and make recommendations on the standard-setting process, with the following terms of reference:

'1   To review the development of the standard-setting process in Great Britain and Ireland and in other major industrial countries during the past fifteen years, including the role of the International Accounting Standards Committee.

2   To have regard to the purpose of accounting standards in the future in the light of (a) major changes in the financial markets and in the approach by preparers of accounts to financial reporting and (b) the attitude of Government and the public towards the regulation of the corporate sector.

3   In the light of the above to consider:

- the most appropriate form which accounting standards should take;
- the status of standards in relation to company law;
- procedures for the monitoring of compliance with standards and the enforcement of standards;
- the identification of topics for consideration;
- the need for, and nature of, public consultation about draft standards;
- the funding of the cost of standard-setting; and
- the appropriate composition and powers of any body responsible for standard-setting and the manner in which appointment to that body should be made, taking into account the interests of the users, preparers and auditors of accounts in the standard-setting process.

4   To report and to make recommendations to the Consultative Committee of Accountancy Bodies (CCAB) in the course of 1988.'[47]

5.2   The Committee's recommendations

Probably not surprisingly, the Review Committee addressed many of the issues discussed in the Watts Report (see 1.3 above), and reached very similar conclusions. The principal recommendations, which were published in a report issued in November 1988 (the Dearing Report), are as follows:[48]

5.2.1   *The need for a conceptual framework*

The Committee concluded that the lack of a conceptual framework is a handicap to those setting accounting standards as well as to those applying them. It recommended that further work on a conceptual framework should be undertaken on a modest scale, building on the work already done by the FASB and IASC on their respective conceptual framework projects. However, the Committee further recommended that, whether or not a conceptual framework is successfully developed, when accounting standards are issued they should be accompanied by a statement of the principles underlying them and the reasons why alternatives were rejected. (See Chapter 2 for a detailed discussion of the need for a conceptual framework.)

5.2.2   *Quality of accounting standards vs quantity*

The report emphasised that the purpose of accounting standards is to provide authoritative but not mandatory guidance on the interpretation of what constitutes a true and fair view. Consequently, the Committee recommended that the revised standard-setting framework should concentrate on quality, timeliness, reducing the permitted options and promoting compliance — as opposed to attempting to produce a large volume of standards which attempt to cover every option.

5.2.3   *Application of standards to small companies*

The Committee was clearly influenced by the approach taken recently by the ASC in exempting small companies from the requirements of certain standards (see 4.2 above). Consequently, it has recommended that, on the basis of a cost/benefit test, it should be decided whether or not the accounting and/or disclosure requirements of a particular standard should apply to small companies.

5.2.4   *Public sector bodies*

The report discussed the application of standards to public sector bodies at some length. It concluded that there should be an underlying unity of approach to accounting standards across the public and private sectors, and that, therefore, public sector bodies should come within the framework of the proposals contained in the report, but with support for compliance with standards coming from the responsible Secretary of State.

5.2.5   *The role of the law*

The suggestion that accounting standards should be given legal effect is one which is mooted from time to time, and was considered by the Committee —

particularly in the light of developments in other countries where there has been a trend in giving accounting standards increased legal backing.

However, the Committee stated that it did not recommend the incorporation of standards into law 'because this inescapably requires a legalistic approach and a reduction in the ability of the financial community to respond quickly to new developments'.[49] Nevertheless, whilst attempting to avoid a legalistic approach, the Committee made the following recommendations in order to help provide a sound base for the development and implementation of standards:

(a)   in the case of all 'large companies', the directors should be required to state in the notes to the financial statements whether or not they have been prepared in accordance with applicable accounting standards, drawing attention to material departures and explaining the reasons for such departures;

(b)   there should be a statutory power for certain authorised bodies or the Secretary of State to apply to the courts for an order requiring the revision of accounts which do not give a true and fair view;

(c)   if there is a material departure from an accounting standard, then the onus of proof should be on the party who contends that the financial statements do give a true and fair view that this is the case. This should similarly apply in the case of auditors who give an unqualified opinion on financial statements which contain departures;

(d)   there should be a general presumption in any legal proceedings that all accounting standards will have the support of the courts — unless it can be demonstrated that, despite a material departure, the financial statements give a true and fair view.

5.2.6   A Financial Reporting Council

The Committee addressed the need for the involvement of a wide constituency of interests in the development of accounting standards. Consequently, it recommended that 'the institutional arrangements for developing accounting standards should reflect the need to involve the whole community of interests in financial reporting at the policy level, while providing for a separate professional capability to translate policy into accounting standards'.[50] Therefore, in order to achieve this, the Committee has recommended that a Financial Reporting Council should be created, covering at high level a wide constituency of interests. The Council's chairman would be appointed jointly by the Secretary of State for Trade and Industry and the Governor of the Bank of England, and the objectives of the Council would be to guide the standard-setting body on work programmes and issues of public concern; to see that the work on accounting standards is properly financed; and to act as a powerful proactive public influence for securing good accounting practice.[51]

It is recommended that the Council would meet three to four times a year, and have approximately 20 members which would include accountants in practice, as well as in industry, commerce and the public sector. There would be an equal

number of members drawn from all other relevant areas of interest, and the UK
and Irish Governments would be invited to nominate members or observers.[52]

5.2.7   An Accounting Standards Board

The Committee recommended that the ASC should be reconstituted into an
Accounting Standards Board (ASB) which would be able to issue accounting
standards on its own authority, instead of needing the approval of the Councils of
all the six accountancy bodies which make up the CCAB (see 1.1 above). The
ASB would have a full-time Chairman and Technical Director and its total
membership would not exceed nine. A majority of two-thirds would be required
for the approval of an accounting standard. Furthermore, in order to provide an
immediate and authoritative response to emerging issues the Committee
recommended that the ASB should establish a capability of publishing
authoritative, though non-mandatory, guidance on emerging issues.[53]

5.2.8   A Review Panel

The Committee addressed the difficult question of securing compliance with
accounting standards in support of the 'true and fair' requirement. It has therefore
been recommended that, with the objective of achieving 'good financial
reporting',[54] a Review Panel (possibly modelled on the Panel on Take-overs and
Mergers) should be established to examine any identified or alleged material
departures from accounting standards. The findings of the Review Panel should
spell out what revisions to the financial statements or what additional information
it considers should be made available to users to provide an acceptable set of
financial statements giving a true and fair view.[55]

5.2.9   Staffing and funding

To enable the bodies and procedures recommended by the report to operate
effectively, the Committee recommended that they should be well supported by an
adequate common secretariat involving approximately ten professional staff. The
Committee estimated that the total annual costs of implementing their proposals
would be approximately £1.5 million at current prices — compared with the
present ASC budget of £440,000. There are various suggestions as to how these
costs might be met, including the imposition of a nominal additional levy on
companies filing their annual returns; income from ASB publications; and a
contribution from The Stock Exchange from listing fees.[56]

6   CONCLUSION

UK GAAP incorporates the requirements of SSAPs, of the Companies Act and of
the Stock Exchange, together with other accounting practices which are generally
accepted by the accounting profession to be permissible. However, as
circumstances and environments change, accounting practices require
development and adaptation. GAAP, therefore, is a dynamic concept, which is
not restricted to the requirements of SSAPs and the law, and is continually
undergoing change as circumstances alter. Consequently, in order to obviate the
development of inappropriate and inconsistent practices, it is vital that emerging
issues are dealt with quickly and effectively on an authoritative basis.

In the time since it was set up nearly twenty years ago, the ASC has significantly improved the quality of financial reporting in the UK, which remains one of the leading countries in the world in this respect. Moreover, this has been achieved with minimal resources and has been wholly funded by the accounting profession, which deserves credit for its efforts to date. However, we believe that the ASC's authority and credibility have declined in recent years and this has impaired its ability to deal with difficult issues; also, it suffers from structural and constitutional weaknesses which seriously hamper its effectiveness. Accordingly, we believe the time is ripe to replace it with a newly constituted body which will be more able to deal with the challenges of the 1990s and beyond.

The recommendations of the Dearing Report represent a major step towards the achievement of this goal and the ultimate improvement of financial reporting practice. We see the establishment of an adequately funded and staffed independent standard-setting body as an essential ingredient for the development of UK GAAP. This can best be achieved through the medium of a body such as the ASB as recommended by the Dearing Report, together with the limited statutory backing which has been suggested. The Dearing Report is now under consideration by the CCAB, and it is therefore up to that body to put the implementation of the Report's recommendations into motion.

In the meantime, the DTI has issued a consultative document on the Dearing Report,[57] which calls for interested parties to submit comments on the Dearing Report as a whole and, more particularly, on those recommendations of the Report which would require legislative changes in order to be implemented. The reason for this is that the DTI sees the Companies Bill[58] as providing a suitable opportunity to make any agreed changes. Consequently, the areas on which the DTI has asked for specific comment to be submitted mainly involve the role of the law in the improvement in true and fair reporting, and does not, as such, deal with the standard-setting process. However, it is hoped that this consultative document, together with the necessary legislative changes, will provide a catalyst for the CCAB to implement the Report's recommendations.

References

1   The Institute of Chartered Accountants in England and Wales, Occasional Council and Other Pronouncements, *Statement of intent on accounting standards in the 1970s.*
2   *Ibid.*
3   At that stage, the Association of Certified Accountants and the Institute of Cost and Management Accountants respectively.
4   ICAEW, *Accounting Standards 1988/89*, p. 1.3.
5   *Ibid.*, p. 1.4.
6   Accounting Standards Committee, *Setting Accounting Standards: A consultative document.*
7   Accounting Standards Committee, *Setting Accounting Standards.*
8   CA 47, s 13(1), re-enacted as CA 48, s 149(1).

9   EC Fourth Directive, Article 2.
10 *Ibid.*, paras. 1—3.
11 *Ibid.*, paras. 4 and 5.
12 Statements of Standard Accounting Practice, *Explanatory foreword*, issued May 1975; revised August 1986, para. 1.
13 *Ibid.*, para. 2.
14 Leonard Hoffman QC and Mary H. Arden, The Accounting Standards Committee Joint Opinion, *Legal Opinion on 'True and Fair'*, reproduced in *Accountancy*, November 1983, pp. 154—156.
15 *Ibid.*, paras. 9 and 10.
16 *Lloyd Cheyham & Co Ltd v Littlejohn & Co* [1987] BCLC 303 at 313.
17 International Accounting Standards Committee, *Preface to Statements of International Accounting Standards*, para. 1.
18 *Ibid.*, para. 2.
19 Exposure Draft E32, *Comparability of Financial Statements*, IASC, January 1989.
20 APB Opinion No. 6, *Status of Accounting Research Bulletins*, Appendix A, paras. 1—3.
21 SEC, Accounting Series Release No. 150.
22 AICPA, *Code of Professional Conduct*, Rule 203—Accounting principles.
23 See Ross M. Skinner, *Accounting Standards in Evolution*, pp. 35—36.
24 CICA, *Handbook*, Volume 1, Section 1500.06.
25 *Ibid.*, Section 1000, paras. .48—.50, *passim*.
26 Commercial Code, Third Book, Second Section, *Supplementary Regulations for Companies*, § 264(2).
27 Jermyn Paul Brooks and Dietz Mertin, *Neues deutsches Bilanzrecht/New German Accounting Legislation*, Düsseldorf: IDW-Verlag GmbH, 1986.
28 CA 85, Sch. 4, para. 91.
29 CCAB, *TR 481: The determination of realised profits and disclosure of distributable profits in the context of the Companies Acts 1948 to 1981*, September 1982.
30 *Ibid.*, para. 4.
31 *Odeon Associated Theatres Ltd v Jones (Inspector of Taxes)* [1971] 1 WLR 442.
32 Leonard Hoffman QC and Mary H. Arden, *op. cit.*, paras. 9 and 10.
33 *Explanatory foreword*, para. 5.
34 *Ibid.*, para. 1.
35 See, for example: Department of Trade and Industry, *Accounting and Audit Requirements for Small Firms*, London: DTI, 1985; Department of Trade and Industry, *Burdens on Business, Report of a Scrutiny of Administrative and Legislative Requirements*, London: HMSO, March 1985; B. V. Carsberg et al., *Small Company Financial Reporting*, London: Prentice-Hall International, 1985; AICPA, Accounting Standards Division, Committee on Generally Accepted Accounting Principles for Smaller and/or Closely Held Businesses, *Report of the Committee on Generally Accepted Accounting Principles for Smaller and/or Closely Held Businesses*, New York: AICPA, August 1976; Institute of Chartered Accountants of British Columbia, *Task Force on Big GAAP/Little GAAP*, Report to Council, Submitted July 30, 1981.
36 Institute of Chartered Accountants of British Columbia, *op. cit.*, p. 3.
37 *Ibid.*, p. 4.
38 B. V. Carsberg et al., *op. cit.*, p. 83.
39 *Ibid.*, pp. 83—84.
40 *TR 690: Statement by the Accounting Standards Committee on the application of accounting standards to small companies*, February 1988.
41 *Ibid.*, para. 5.
42 *Ibid.*, para. 17.
43 *TR 706: Statement by the Accounting Standards Committee on the definition of 'small company' for the purpose of applying accounting standards*, July 1988, para. 1.1.
44 *Ibid.*, para. 5.1.
45 *Ibid.*, para. 5.2.

46 *Ibid.*, para. 2.1.
47 Report of the Review Committee under the chairmanship of Sir Ronald Dearing CB, *The Making of Accounting Standards*, September 1988, p. ix.
48 This summary of the recommendations has been extracted from the Dearing Report, *ibid.*, pp. 17—45, *passim*.
49 *Ibid.*, para. 10.2.
50 *Ibid.*, para. 11.1.
51 *Ibid.*, p. 44.
52 *Ibid.*, para. 11.3.
53 *Ibid.*, pp. 27—29.
54 *Ibid.*, p. 31.
55 *Ibid.*, p. 33.
56 *Ibid.*, paras. 19.1—19.6, *passim*.
57 *Report of the Review Committee under the Chairmanship of Sir Ronald Dearing CB on the Making of Accounting Standards: A Consultative Document from the Department of Trade and Industry*, DTI, January 1989.
58 Companies Bill, HL Bill 7, 21st December 1988.

Chapter 2

The quest for a conceptual framework for financial reporting

1   INTRODUCTION

The question of the desirability of developing an 'agreed conceptual framework' apparently first received serious consideration by the ASC in 1978 through the publication of its consultative document entitled 'Setting Accounting Standards'[1] (see Chapter 1 at 1.3). In that document, the ASC conceded that it had been frequently criticised for failing to develop a conceptual framework, but defended its position by claiming that 'while such a foundation would be a great advantage, it is unavailable at present.'[2] The reasons put forward for this view were based essentially on the premise that since the users of financial statements have different objectives, it would not be possible to develop an acceptable foundation which would be universally accepted.[3] Following this argument, the ASC went on to conclude that 'if an "agreed conceptual framework" is equated with a single undisputed "model", then this is a luxury which evades us at the moment.'[4] Nevertheless, as part of the consultative process, the ASC raised the following two questions on the subject:

1.   'Is it accepted that there is at present no single "model" or "agreed conceptual framework" which can be used as the touchstone for accounting standards?'[5]

2.   'Should the ASC encourage research into the possibility of finding an acceptable "model"?'[6]

Not surprisingly, the written submissions[7] on the consultative document indicated a unanimous 'Yes' in answer to the first question. However, what probably did surprise the ASC was that the second question also received an overwhelming 'Yes'; in fact, a significant number of respondents indicated that they saw the development of a conceptual framework as a matter of great urgency. For example, the Accounting Standards Review Committee of the ICAS stated in their submission that 'it is imperative that work should begin immediately on a conceptual framework rather than that the present practice of producing standards with no theoretical underpinning should continue.'[8]

The ASC's argument that a conceptual framework would not be attainable because the users of financial statements have different objectives was clearly regarded as spurious. This chapter will highlight the fact that different users should be furnished with different information appropriate to their various objectives, even if it means that in order to achieve this the conceptual framework should incorporate more than one accounting model. Consequently, there is no reason for ruling out an 'agreed conceptual model' by equating it with the unattainable 'single undisputed model'. As will be seen from the discussion below, different models might need to be developed to meet different purposes.

2   WHAT IS A CONCEPTUAL FRAMEWORK?

In general terms, a conceptual framework is a statement of generally accepted theoretical principles which form the frame of reference for a particular field of enquiry. In terms of financial reporting, these theoretical principles provide the basis for both the development of new reporting practices and the evaluation of existing ones. Since the financial reporting process is concerned with the provision of information that is useful in making business and economic decisions, a conceptual framework will form the theoretical basis for determining which events should be accounted for, how they should be measured and how they should be communicated to the user. Therefore, although it is theoretical in nature, a conceptual framework for financial reporting has a highly practical end in view.

3   WHY IS A CONCEPTUAL FRAMEWORK NECESSARY?

A conceptual framework for financial reporting is, therefore, inter alia a theory of accounting against which practical problems can be tested objectively. However, at present, the various standard-setting bodies around the world are attempting to resolve practical accounting and reporting problems through the development of accounting standards, without such an accepted theoretical frame of reference. The end result is that the standard-setters have determined the form and content of external financial reports, without resolving such fundamental issues as:

- What are the objectives of these reports?
- Who are the users of these reports?
- What are the informational needs of these users?
- What types of report will best satisfy their needs?

Consequently, as in the UK, for example, standards tend to be produced on a haphazard and 'fire-fighting' approach; evidence of this may be seen in the way in which the ASC has attempted to deal with issues such as off-balance sheet finance and the capitalisation of brand names. On the other hand, if an agreed framework existed, the role of the standard-setters would be changed from that of fireman to that of architect, by being able to design external financial reports on the basis of the needs of the user.

Furthermore, in the absence of an agreed conceptual framework, the same theoretical issues are re-visited on numerous occasions by different standard-setting working parties, sometimes resulting in the development of standards which are inconsistent with each other, or which are founded on incompatible concepts. For example, inconsistencies exist in UK accounting standards as a result of conflicts between substance vs. form; matching vs. prudence; and whether earnings should be determined through balance sheet measurements or by matching costs and revenue. Many of the present UK standards permit two or more methods of accounting for the same set of circumstances, whilst others permit certain accounting practices to be followed on an arbitrary and unspecified basis. This apparent ambiguity is perhaps indicative of the difficulty involved in determining what is 'true and fair'.

In the US, on the other hand, the FASB has produced a large number of highly detailed accounting rules. Clearly, the proliferation of accounting standards in the US stems from many factors; however, an agreed conceptual framework might reduce the need for such a large number of highly detailed standards, since more emphasis could be placed on general principles rather than specific rules.

However, it is not only the lack of a conceptual framework which is inhibiting standard-setters around the world; they must also contend with the politicisation of accounting caused by the conflicting interests of the various groups of users, preparers and auditors. Where proposed accounting standards are likely to affect the economic interests of a particular interested party, it is possible that the quality of the accounting standard will suffer. There are several instances where this is evident in the UK. For example, lobbying by the property industry led to the temporary exemption for investment properties from the requirements of SSAP 12; this temporary exemption was originally intended to last for one year, but was extended first for a further year and subsequently for a further 18 months before SSAP 19 became effective, and SSAP 12 was then amended to make the exemption for investment properties permanent.

The only defence that standard-setters can have against such political interference in the standard-setting process is to be able to demonstrate that a proposed accounting practice is derived from a sound theoretical foundation. Otherwise, how does one persuade, for example, an industry lobby that a particular accounting treatment which they perceive as adversely affecting their economic interests is better than one which does not?[9]

We are not suggesting that an agreed framework will be the panacea for all accounting problems. Nor will it obviate the need for judgement to be exercised in the process of resolving accounting issues. Nevertheless, what it can provide is a framework within which those judgements can be made.

4   A HISTORY OF THE QUEST FOR A CONCEPTUAL FRAMEWORK

4.1   Introduction

There have been numerous attempts over the years to define the purpose and nature of accounting. These are to be found in various writings on accounting theory, the authors of which have considered many of the conceptual issues which require resolution in the development of a conceptual framework for financial reporting. Perhaps not surprisingly, most of the earlier studies were carried out by either individual academics or academic committees in the US; for example, the writings in 1940 of Paton and Littleton[10] were intended to present a framework of accounting theory which would be regarded as a coherent and consistent foundation for the development of accounting standards, whilst the studies carried out over the years by various committees of the American Accounting Association have made a significant contribution to accounting theory.[11]

However, there was no corresponding interest in the UK in developing statements on accounting theory. This fact was explained by Solomons in a lecture given by him in 1980 as follows: 'The difference between the ferment in America over accounting principles and the relative apathy that has persisted in Britain until quite recently cannot be explained by any difference in the economic environment. It can only be explained by the difference in the scale of business education there and here, and in particular by the sheer weight of numbers of accounting academics. The American Accounting Association has about 6,000 academic members. In Britain, the Association of University Teachers of Accounting has about 175. Perhaps more importantly, most American practitioners have a university degree in accounting. They have met professors face to face and they do not think of them as troglodytes. Moreover, they know there is a subject called accounting theory; and they think of accounting academics as a distinct branch of the profession with their own contribution to make. It is more a question of quantity than quality. British accounting academics are simply not yet numerous enough to constitute a critical mass.'[12]

In addition to the research carried out by individuals and academic committees, professional accounting bodies around the world have also, from time to time, issued statements which deal with various aspects of accounting theory. These can be seen as the first attempts at developing some form of conceptual framework.

4.2   The Accounting Principles Board of the AICPA

4.2.1   Accounting Research Studies

The Accounting Principles Board (APB) of the AICPA was formed in 1959 to replace the former Committee on Accounting Procedure and the Committee on Terminology. During its existence, the Committee on Accounting Procedure had issued a series of Accounting Research Bulletins (ARBs); in 1953, the first 42 ARBs were revised and restated as a consolidated ARB No. 43 and, thereafter, a further eight ARBs were issued. The ARBs were supposedly aimed at the development of generally accepted accounting principles; however, the Committee met with considerable criticism over its failure to deal with contemporary accounting issues (such as leasing and business combinations), which could not be solved from precedents and required the development of accounting principles through pure accounting research.

As a direct response to this, the President of the AICPA set up the Special Committee on Research Program in 1957; in 1958 the Committee recommended the formation of the APB, and the appointment of a director of research with a permanent research staff. The Special Committee also recommended that 'an immediate project of the accounting research staff should be a study of the basic postulates underlying accounting principles generally, and the preparation of a brief statement thereof. There should be also a study of the broad principles of accounting. ... The results of these, as adopted by the [Accounting Principles] Board, should serve as the foundation for the entire body of future pronouncements by the Institute on accounting matters, to which each new release should be related.'[13]

This, therefore, was probably the first mandate given by a professional body for the development of a conceptual framework. The AICPA appointed Maurice Moonitz as its first Director of Accounting Research; Moonitz started work on the postulates study, and appointed Robert Sprouse to work with him on the study of broad accounting principles. The products of the research were contained in Accounting Research Study No. 1 — *The Basic Postulates of Accounting*[14] — and Accounting Research Study No. 3 — *A Tentative Set of Broad Accounting Principles for Business Enterprises* — which were published in 1961 and 1962 respectively.[15]

These studies, however, caused a storm of controversy. Instead of establishing a sound foundation of accounting theory through rigorous argument based on deductive reasoning, Moonitz and Sprouse attempted to persuade the accounting profession to accept a new system of financial reporting based on current values. Furthermore, the realisation principle was discarded on the basis of the assertion that 'profit is attributable to the whole process of business activity, not just to the moment of sale'.[16] This was reflected, for example, in the statement that 'inventories which are readily salable at known prices with negligible costs of disposal, or with known or readily predictable costs of disposal, should be measured at net realizable value'.[17]

However, the criticism which was levelled at these studies appeared to be based more on the fear of the unknown, rather that on any intellectual shortcomings. Consequently, they were viewed as being too radically different from contemporary generally accepted accounting practice to be accepted, and were rejected by the APB. This resulted in the commissioning of Grady's Accounting Research Study No. 7 — *Inventory of Generally Accepted Accounting Principles for Business Enterprises* — which was published in 1965 and which catalogued the various accounting methods which had been approved by ARBs, APB Opinions or some other precedent.

In all, 15 Accounting Research Studies were published during the life of the APB. However, following the rejection of ARS Nos. 1 and 3, the studies tended to be carried out on an ad hoc basis and without the support of a common foundation. Furthermore, the recommendations contained in the research studies appeared to have been largely ignored in the drafting of the 31 Opinions which the APB issued between 1962 and 1973. Consequently, generally accepted accounting principles in the US were continuing to be formulated without the benefit of research or the foundation of an agreed theoretical framework and, for all intents and purposes, the APB slowly resorted to the position of its predecessor, the Committee on Accounting Procedure.

In the meantime, some US corporations were taking full advantage of the accounting practices which were regarded as generally accepted. They were able to give the appearance of high rates of growth in assets and earnings by merely engaging in merger and acquisition activity, and adopting the permitted accounting practices which presented the most favourable result.

4.2.2   APB Statement No. 4

In 1965 the APB made a further attempt to provide a basis for guiding the future development of accounting by establishing a committee to carry out a study which could be used as a basis for understanding the broad fundamentals of accounting. In 1970, the APB approved Statement No. 4 — *Basic Concepts and Accounting Principles Underlying Financial Statements of Business Enterprises.*[18] The statement contained a description of (1) the environment of financial accounting, (2) the objectives of financial statements, (3) the basic features and basic elements of financial accounting and (4) a summary of existing generally accepted accounting principles.

It was, therefore, (on its own admission)[19] a descriptive statement, not prescriptive. For example, assets and liabilities were defined as economic resources and obligations 'that are recognised and measured in conformity with generally accepted accounting principles',[20] which meant that the definitions failed to provide a theoretical basis for the development of generally accepted principles. As a result APB No. 4 was deficient as a theory of accounting and did not respond to the problems which were facing the profession at the time and which had been brought about by the inconsistencies and inadequacies of financial reporting practice.

4.2.3   The Wheat and Trueblood Committees

In 1971, in response to continued criticism from both within the profession and from the SEC about its inability to establish sound accounting principles, the AICPA announced the formation of two study groups: the *Study Group on Establishment of Accounting Principles*, to be chaired by Francis Wheat, and the *Study Group on Objectives of Financial Statements*, to be chaired by Robert Trueblood. The Wheat Committee published its report in 1972, resulting in the establishment of the Financial Accounting Standards Board (FASB) in 1973 as the successor to the APB. This had the effect of taking the responsibility for setting accounting standards away from the accounting profession and placing it in the hands of an independent body in the private sector. The FASB comprises seven members appointed by the Financial Accounting Foundation (FAF), and is funded by the sale of publications and from contributions made to the FAF. The Board of Trustees of the FAF is appointed by its six sponsoring organisations, which includes, inter alia, the American Accounting Accounting Association and the AICPA.

The study carried out by the Trueblood Committee represents the next significant step in the attempt to develop a conceptual framework. In setting the terms of reference of the study group, the Board of Directors of the AICPA stated that the main purpose of the study was 'to refine the objectives of financial statements.'[21] They went on to suggest that APB Statement No. 4 would be a logical starting point for the study, whilst at the same time noting that APB 4 'contains objectives in terms of what is considered acceptable today rather than in terms of what is needed and what is attainable to meet these needs.'[22] The study group was asked to consider at least the following questions:

- Who needs financial statements?
- What information do they need?
- How much of the needed information can be provided by accounting?
- What framework is required to provide the needed information?[23]

The Trueblood Report[24] was published in October 1973 and developed twelve objectives of financial statements. The principal objective was stated in the following terms: 'the basic objective of financial statements is to provide information useful for making economic decisions.'[25] Having established its twelve objectives of financial statements, the report then discussed seven qualitative characteristics which information contained in financial statements should possess in order to satisfy the needs of users.[26] As will be seen below, the Trueblood Report's objectives of financial statements formed the basis for the development of the FASB's first concepts statement, whilst the qualitative characteristics identified were amongst those discussed in the second concepts statement.

4.3   The FASB Conceptual Framework Project

The Trueblood Committee was at work on its report when the FASB came into existence. Consequently, the Trueblood Report was effectively passed on to the FASB for consideration, thus signalling the beginnings of the FASB's Conceptual Framework Project. The FASB duly considered the report and in June 1974 published a Discussion Memorandum — *Conceptual Framework for Accounting and Reporting: Consideration of the Report of the Study Group on the Objectives of Financial Statements* — which asked for comments on the issues raised.[27] A public hearing was held during September 1974, and in December 1976 the FASB published its *Tentative Conclusions on Objectives of Financial Statements of Business Enterprises*. In December 1976 the FASB also published a paper — *Scope and Implications of the Conceptual Framework Project* — which summarised its aims for the project, the expected benefits to be derived and the main areas which were expected to be covered.[28]

Following the criticism and eventual replacement of first the Committee on Accounting Procedures, followed by the APB, the FASB was seen by many commentators to be the last opportunity of keeping accounting standard-setting in the private sector. The FASB was clearly aware that accounting standards had to regain the credibility of public opinion which had been lost as a result of the many perceived abuses of financial reporting during the 1960s. The FASB referred to this lack of public confidence, and the possible consequences thereof, as follows: 'skepticism about financial reporting has adverse effects on businesses, on business leaders, and on the public at large. One of these effects is the risk of imposition of government reporting and other regulatory requirements that are not justified — requirements that are not in the public interest because the perceived benefits do not exist or are more than offset by costly interference with the orderly operation of the economy. Skepticism creates adverse public opinion, which may be the antecedent of unjustified government regulation. Every company, every industry stands to suffer because of skepticism about financial reporting.'[29] The FASB, therefore, saw its conceptual framework project as the means of enhancing the credibility of financial statements in the eyes of the public.

The FASB's conceptual framework project has produced numerous discussion memoranda, exposure drafts and research reports. To date, these have resulted in the publication of six Statements of Financial Accounting Concepts, the contents of which are discussed at 5 below.

4.4   The Corporate Report

The first attempt by the accounting profession in the UK to develop a conceptual framework is to be found in a Discussion Paper which was issued in 1975 by the then styled Accounting Standards Steering Committee (now the ASC) and entitled *The Corporate Report.*[30]

The discussion paper deals with 'the fundamental aims of published financial reports and the means by which these aims can be achieved'[31] and uses the term 'corporate report' to mean 'the comprehensive package of information of all kinds which most completely describes an organisation's economic activity.'[32] It was suggested that this 'comprehensive package' should include more than the 'basic financial statements' (i.e., the balance sheet, profit and loss account and funds statement), and incorporates additional narrative and descriptive statements.[33] The discussion paper centres around three main elements: 'the types of organisation which should be expected to publish regular financial information; the main users of such information and their needs; and the form of report which will best meet those needs.'[34]

The discussion paper followed the basic approach that corporate reports should seek to satisfy, as far as possible, the information needs of users.[35] The committee argued that every economic entity of significant size has an implicit responsibility to report publicly, and concluded that general purpose reports designed for general purpose use are the primary means by which this public accountability is fulfilled. Users were defined 'as those having a reasonable right to information concerning the reporting entity',[36] a right which arises from the entity's public accountability.

The paper identifies seven user groups[37] as having a reasonable right to information, and discusses the basis of the rights of each group and their information needs. Not surprisingly, the committee identified a considerable overlap of interest between each of the user groups, including items such as 'evaluating the performance of the entity', 'estimating the future prospects of the entity', 'evaluating managerial performance', 'assessing the liquidity of the entity, its present or future requirements for additional fixed or working capital, and its ability to raise long and short term finance'.[38]

On this basis the committee concluded that 'the fundamental objective of corporate reports is to communicate economic measurements of and information about the resources and performance of the reporting entity useful to those having reasonable rights to such information.'[39] They went on to say that in order to fulfil this objective and be useful, corporate reports should be relevant, understandable, reliable, complete, objective, timely and comparable[40] (these qualitative characteristics identified were similar to those discussed in the Trueblood Report).

The discussion paper then reviewed the conventional thinking on the aim of published reports together with the then existing features of published financial statements of UK companies. The committee also conducted a survey of corporate objectives amongst the chairmen of 300 of the largest UK listed companies, and concluded that 'distributable profit can no longer be regarded as the sole or premier indicator of performance.'[41] Consequently, it was suggested that there was a need for additional indicators of performance in the corporate reports of all entities.[42]

Part II of the study considers the 'measurement and method' of achieving the above aims. This includes a discussion of the improvement of communication and publication methods of corporate report information, as well as consideration of the frequency and distribution of reports. Since the committee had concluded that current reporting practices did not fully satisfy the needs of users, it was suggested that the following additional statements should be published in the corporate report: a statement of value added, an employment report, a statement of money exchanges with government, a statement of transactions in foreign currency, a statement of future prospects and a statement of corporate objectives.[43] In addition, the committee recommended further study into methods of social accounting as well as the disaggregation of certain financial information.[44]

Finally, the committee discussed the concepts and measurements employed in the 'basic financial statements'. In considering the purpose of profit measurement, it concluded that income statements 'should be concerned with the measurement of performance although they may also be used in the measurement of capital maintenance and income distributability'.[45] It was, however, recognised that this dual purpose of income statements often gives rise to conflict in the application of accounting concepts — particularly the fundamental concepts of prudence and matching. Various measurement bases were then discussed in the context of the inadequacies of the historical cost system. The committee stated that 'the usefulness of financial statements in fulfilling user needs is restricted at the present time because of the defects of the basis of measurement generally used. Historical cost accounting fails, in times of rapidly changing prices and values, to ensure that sufficient provision is made for capital maintenance. When reported figures are not related to current values there may be over- or understatement of performance as measured by profits and return on assets.'[46]

The committee then briefly surveyed several bases of measurement, including historical cost, current purchasing power (CPP) and various current value bases such as replacement cost and net realisable value. The conclusion reached was that no one system of measurement is capable of the user needs identified in the study, and that, therefore, research should be undertaken into the feasibility of multi-column reporting, as well as into the development of a standardised system of current value accounting.[47]

The publication of the Corporate Report, however, closely coincided with the release of the Sandilands Report on inflation accounting,[48] resulting in the Corporate Report being very much overshadowed. This was probably to the relief of the business community who were concerned about the possibility of their reporting responsibility being extended beyond that of the existing requirements, through the development of the committee's concept of public accountability. In any event, the Corporate Report fell short of making a significant contribution towards the development of a conceptual framework by virtue of its failure to select the accounting models appropriate to the informational needs of the individual user groups which it had identified. It was quite clear from the conclusions reached by the committee that a single set of generalised external financial reports could not meet the informational needs of all the user groups identified in the report, and, in any event, financial information presented on the historical cost basis alone was clearly shown to be inadequate. The logical progression, therefore, would have been to suggest the presentation of specific supplementary information according to the measurement bases appropriate to meeting the needs of particular groups of users.

4.5   The Sandilands Report

The announcement of the membership and terms of reference of the government's Inflation Accounting Committee was made to the House of Commons by the Secretary of State for Trade and Industry on 21 January 1974. The Sandilands committee's principal term of reference was 'to consider whether, and if so how, company accounts should allow for changes (including relative changes) in costs and prices'.[49] The Sandilands Report followed a similar approach to that of the Corporate Report to the extent that it focused on the information needs of users. The report stated that 'the requirements of users of accounts should be the fundamental consideration in deciding the information to be disclosed in company accounts.'[50]

The report proposed that the development of accounting for inflation should be an evolutionary process towards a system of current cost accounting, the essential features of which are:

(a)   money is the unit of measurement (as opposed to the 'current purchasing power' basis of expressing financial information in terms of a unit of measurement of constant value when prices change);

(b)   assets and liabilities should be shown in the balance sheet at their 'value to the business'; and

(c)   operating profit (to be known as 'current cost profit') is calculated after charging the 'value to the business' of the assets consumed during the period, thereby excluding holding gains and showing them separately.[51]

4.5.1   *Current Purchasing Power accounting*

In formulating its system of current cost accounting, the committee examined three alternative accounting systems which had been developed in an attempt to overcome the deficiencies of historical cost accounting. The first of these systems studied was the 'current purchasing power' (CPP) method of inflation accounting recommended in the Provisional SSAP, PSSAP 7, which was published in May 1974.[52] Under PSSAP 7, companies were expected to supplement their conventional historical cost financial statements with a statement which illustrated the effects of changes in the purchasing power of money on these statements. The main features of PSSAP 7 were set out in the standard as follows:

'(a) companies will continue to keep their records and present their basic annual accounts in historical pounds, ie in terms of the value of the pound at the time of each transaction or revaluation;

(b) in addition, all listed companies should present to their shareholders a supplementary statement in terms of the value of the pound at the end of the period to which the accounts relate;

(c) the conversion of the figures in the basic accounts into the figures in the supplementary statement should be by means of a general index of the purchasing power of the pound;[53] and

(d) the standard requires the directors to provide in a note to the supplementary statement an explanation of the basis on which it has been prepared and it is desirable that directors should comment on the significance of the figures.'[54]

The committee concluded that the CPP method 'does not remedy the main deficiencies of historic cost accounting during a time of changing costs and prices and we do not recommend it as the best long-term solution to the problem of accounting for inflation.'[55] Numerous arguments were put forward to support this conclusion, for example:

- since, during a period of changing prices, historic cost figures expressed in terms of monetary units do not show the 'value to the business' of assets, a CPP supplementary statement will show the historic cost figures restated in units of current purchasing power, not the 'value to the business' of assets.[56] Thus, a major deficiency of historical cost accounts would not be overcome;

- since companies were required to express their CPP supplementary statements in terms of the current purchasing power of the pound at the closing balance sheet date, the unit of measurement in the supplementary statement would change from year to year. This was likely to cause confusion, compounded by the fact that companies which had different accounting dates would be preparing supplementary statements in terms of different units, resulting in a lack of comparability;[57]

- since a unit of measurement with an absolute value through time is unattainable, there is no advantage in preparing financial statements in CPP units rather than in units of money.[58]

4.5.2   Value accounting

The committee then examined three forms of 'value accounting' — a term used to describe a wide range of different accounting systems which measure net assets by reference to their 'value' rather than their cost. The three value accounting systems examined were replacement cost accounting, present value accounting and continuously contemporary accounting.

A   Replacement cost accounting based on current entry values

'Replacement cost' is the price which will have to be paid to replace an asset used or given up in exchange for another asset. Consequently, the basic principle underlying replacement cost accounting is that, since a business has to replace its assets over time in order to continue in operational existence, charges for the consumption or exchange of an asset should be based on the cost of replacing it. Consequently, assets are valued at the balance sheet date by reference to the price which would have to be paid at that date to purchase a similar asset in a similar condition — i.e. the replacement cost of the assets. This system, therefore, adopts a method of income determination which reflects changes in capital both at the point of realisation of assets and, before realisation, in the process of holding assets.

The pioneers of an income and value model based on replacement costs (entry values) were Edwards and Bell,[59] who attempted to interpret accounting concepts in terms of economic concepts. Their theory abandoned both the realisation principle and the idea of the 'unitary income statement' which does not separate operating profit from holding gains. They introduced a new concept of 'business profit', which was made up of current operating profit of the current period, realised holding gains of the same period and unrealised holding gains.

A major disadvantage of the replacement cost model is difficulty and subjectivity in assigning replacement costs; for example, are replacement costs based on identical or equivalent replacement, and how is technological obsolescence dealt with? However, this disadvantage is far outweighed by the usefulness of the information provided by the system in the form of meaningful balance sheet values and a segregated business profit figure. The Sandilands committee concluded that the replacement cost accounting system 'comes close to meeting the dominant requirements of users of accounts and the Committee's own proposals have many similarities with certain forms of this system of accounting.'[60]

B   Present value accounting

Present value accounting is based on the economic concept of income, and values an asset on the basis of the present value of the cash flows which are expected to be derived from that asset. In order to maintain the capital of the entity, an amount at least equal to the original investment should be reinvested, whilst the remaining cash flows are treated as realised. For example, if the discounted net present value of all expected future cash flows of an entity are £100,000 at the beginning of the year and £115,000 at the end of the year, and if the net cash flows arising during the year were £10,000, then the profit for the year will be £25,000, since this amount could be distributed whilst maintaining the original capital base of £100,000.

Whilst this approach might have some degree of theoretical soundness, it is totally impracticable. Issues such as risk, the determination of discount rates, changes in interest rates and the uncertainty of future cash flows present virtually insurmountable problems. The Sandilands committee rejected present value accounting on the grounds that use of economic value as the basis of valuation of an asset would not meet the needs of users, as it would only be in comparatively few cases that this would represent the value of an asset to a business.[61]

C   Continuously Contemporary Accounting (CoCoA)

The current value income model based on exit prices or realisable market values was first advocated by MacNeal in a book published by him in 1939 which dealt, inter alia, with the ethical issue of 'truth' in accounting.[62] MacNeal maintained that financial statements could only present the 'truth' if assets were stated at their current value and the profit and losses accruing from the changes in these values are included in income, and classified as either realised or unrealised. MacNeal did, however, concede that under certain circumstances the use of net realisable values was not appropriate, and that in such cases current replacement costs should be used.

The system known as continuously contemporary accounting (CoCoA) was formally introduced by Chambers in a book which he published in 1966,[63] and the case for exit value accounting was further developed by Sterling.[64] Chambers' theory is based on the premise that entities must be able to choose between alternative courses of action and, because resources are limited, they need to know what resources are available to enable them to engage in exchanges. Consequently, Chambers asserts that this capacity to engage in exchanges is measured by the opportunity cost of holding assets in their existing form, and that this opportunity cost is represented by the current cash equivalent of assets — which Chambers defines as being their current sales value. Initially, Chambers did not apply this principle rigorously and proposed that stocks should be valued at current replacement cost. However, he subsequently amended his view and now advocates that exit values should be applied to the valuation of all assets. A difference in the theories of Chambers and Sterling is, for example, that Chambers believes that net realisable values should be based on the assumption that assets are realised in an orderly manner based on sensible adaptations to changing circumstances; Sterling, on the other hand, believes that net realisable values should be based on immediate liquidation prices.

The capital maintenance concept adopted by CoCoA is based on the preservation of the purchasing power of shareholders' equity (using the monetary unit as the unit of measurement, and not the current purchasing power unit used in CPP accounting). Consequently, since all assets (both monetary and non-monetary) are measured at net realisable value, income is defined as the difference between opening and closing equity after maintaining the purchasing power or cash equivalent of such equity. Income for the year, therefore, will comprise (1) the net profit/loss on business operations, (2) the accrued profit/loss arising from the change in the current cash equivalent of assets and (3) the effect on the capital of the entity brought about by the change in the purchasing power of money.

However, despite the widespread publication of his theories, Chambers failed to gain any measure of support for CoCoA outside academic circles. Chambers believed that one of the reasons for this was the lack of empirical evidence that the users of financial statements needed financial information based on net realisable values. Consequently, he set about obtaining this evidence through an empirical survey which he published in 1980.[65] Through carefully designed (but somewhat simplistic) questions, Chambers was able to conclude that his empirical evidence justified the use of net realisable values as the primary basis of measurement.

Chambers' principal survey did, however, produce some anomalous and inconsistent answers, resulting in him having to conduct a supplementary survey of four questions. This highlighted several weaknesses in the formulation of his questions, and cast doubt about the validity of the survey as a whole. These doubts are expressed, for example, in an article by Edward Stamp[66] who stated that 'his questionnaire was inadequate and failed to include necessary questions on valuation, performance measures, and liabilities, that would not have been difficult to frame, even with the constraints imposed by Chambers.'[67] Consequently, these omissions and the style of his research undermine Chambers' claim that his empirical evidence demonstrates that CoCoA provides the best basis for financial reporting.

There is no doubt that there are some compelling theoretical arguments for the presentation of financial statements based on net realisable values; for example, they provide useful information in the assessment of liquidity and financial flexibility. However, net realisable value is unlikely to reflect an asset's 'value to the business', since, for example, an item of plant might have negligible net realisable value but substantial use value. Therefore, whilst the disclosure of net realisable values might provide useful supplementary information, the arguments in favour of CoCoA as the primary basis of accounting are unconvincing. CoCoA was rejected by the Sandilands committee on the basis that, as a whole, it did not satisfy the information needs of users which they had identified.[68] It is, however, noteworthy that in their recent discussion document — *Making Corporate Reports Valuable* — the Research Committee of the ICAS advocate a reporting system based on net realisable values[69] (see 6.2 below).

4.5.3   *Cash flow accounting*

The principal proponents of cash flow reporting are Lee[70] and Lawson,[71] although there are several other advocates of various approaches to cash flow reporting. Lee's system of cash flow reporting relies heavily on exit value theory and aims to report both actual and potential cash flows. Assets are classified according to their realisability, based on Chambers' principle of orderly liquidation. If a sale price does not exist, assets are to be accounted for as having a zero cash equivalent.[72] Lee has suggested the following four asset classifications for his statement of financial position:

1.   realised assets (e.g. bank balances);

2.   readily-realisable assets (i.e. assets which have a ready market and sale price, such as listed securities, debtors and stocks of finished goods);

3.   non-readily-realisable assets (i.e. assets which do have a market and sale price, but which would not be quickly realised because of the limited nature of the market, such as certain items of plant and work-in-progress);

4.   not-realisable assets (i.e. assets which have no known sales price and no market, and would therefore be ascribed a zero value, such as highly specialised or obsolete plant).[73]

Liabilities are classified according to payability, in line with conventional accounting practice.

Lee proposes that, in addition to a 'statement of financial position', the cash flow reporting system should present a 'statement of realised cash flow', a 'statement of realisable earnings' and a 'statement of changes in financial position'.[74] The statement of realised cash flow reports an entity's actual cash inflows and outflows during a particular period; it is noteworthy that the information contained in this statement would be broadly equivalent to that which would be presented in a statement of cash flows under SFAS 95 (see Chapter 15). The statement of realisable earnings reports periodic profit similar to that provided by a net realisable value accounting system, except that it is described in terms of realised and realisable cash flows. The statement provides an analysis of realised earnings (derived from the entity's operating cash flow), and unrealised earnings (which represent potential cash flows that have accrued during the period as a result of changes in the realisable values of assets, net of the changes in liabilities). The statement of changes in financial position is effectively a conventional funds statement presented on an exit value basis.

Although there are a number of practical accounting and disclosure problems in cash flow reporting, it does have considerable merit. Furthermore, a number of the problems are not unique to cash flow reporting, with equivalent issues remaining unsolved in historical cost accounting. However, one difficulty which does exist is caused by the artificial 12 month reporting period and the necessity to measure 'profitability' over that period and from one period to the next. The principal reason for the development of the accrual basis of accounting was that financial statements prepared on a cash basis (which was probably the oldest form of presentation) provided a distorted profit figures from one period to the next. Although the Sandilands committee stated that there was 'much of value in the cash flow accounting principle',[75] it was felt that cash flow accounting would rekindle all the 'old difficulties of assessing the profit or loss for the year when the accounting system does not match revenues against costs incurred in their generation.'[76] The committee therefore concluded that the abandonment of the existing concept of the profit and loss account in favour of a cash flow statement would result in the information needs of users not being met. Clearly, however, the committee had not considered the possibility of the presentation of a 'statement of realisable earnings' as advocated by Lee, which would provide a more stable basis for reporting profit than the statement of receipts and payments envisaged by the committee. Lee, however, recognised the problems created by the traditional 12 month reporting period, and suggested that a solution might be found in the use of multi-period aggregates for analysis purposes.

4.5.4   *Current cost accounting (CCA)*

The Sandilands committee recommended the development of a system of current cost accounting which used the monetary unit as the unit of measurement and dealt with the effects of specific price changes (as opposed to changes in the general purchasing power of money) on individual businesses. The committee recommended that the balance sheet should present the 'value to the business' of the company's assets, which was equated with the amount of the loss which would be suffered by an entity if the asset was to be lost or destroyed. Whilst it was stated that the 'value to the business' of an asset might, under certain circumstances, be its net realisable value or economic value, it would normally be based on its replacement cost. Because the committee recommended that financial statements be drawn up in terms of the monetary unit, no adjustment would be made for monetary items.[77] However, it is arguable that current cost accounting does not produce a balance sheet which seeks to be a statement of values of the resources of the company; it simply updates the costs at which they are recorded. This distinction can be illustrated by looking at the financial statements of an oil and gas exploration company. Even on a current cost basis, the carrying value of its principal assets is still based on the (backward-looking) cost of exploration expenditure incurred, not the (forward-looking) value of the oil and gas it has found.

Under the Sandilands system, an entity's 'current cost profit' for a period would be calculated by charging against income 'the value to the business' of assets consumed during the year. In simple terms, therefore, the current cost profit could be derived from the historical cost profit by means of an adjustment to depreciation and a cost of sales adjustment. The committee also recommended the presentation of a summary statement of total gains or losses for the period, which would present the entity's total gains/losses in terms of three classifications: operating gains/losses (i.e. current cost profit/loss), extraordinary gains/losses and holding gains/losses. An interesting observation regarding these two statements recommended by the committee is that they are each based on different capital maintenance concepts. The calculation of current cost profit was based on the concept of physical capital maintenance, whilst the summary statement of total gains was concerned with the maintenance of financial capital. However, because the calculation of current cost profit subsequently received greater prominence than the summary of total gains, it is generally thought that the Sandilands proposals were based on the concept of physical capital maintenance.[78]

The committee recommended that current cost accounting should replace historical cost accounting, and that its proposals should be incorporated in an accounting standard. Consequently, the ASC established the Inflation Accounting Steering Group, giving them the task of preparing a proposal for an exposure draft based on the Sandilands proposals, resulting in the publication in November 1976 of ED 18 — *Current cost accounting*. ED 18, however, met with little support, as did the Sandilands recommendations. The ASC attributed this to the fact that there was considerable objection to the replacement of historical cost accounting by a new untested system; the proposals were considered too complicated; and the profit figure was considered misleading without adjustment for monetary items.[79]

Nevertheless, the ASC perceived an urgent need for companies to disclose how their historical cost financial statements were affected by changing prices. Therefore, in order to find an immediate solution to this problem, the ASC published an interim recommendation in November 1977 which outlined a simplified version of current cost accounting (known as the 'Hyde Guidelines').[80] These guidelines recommended that the published financial statements of companies listed on The Stock Exchange should include a prominent separate statement which showed the profit/loss calculated on a current cost basis.[81] The

Hyde Guidelines recommended that three adjustments should be made to the historical cost results: in addition to the depreciation and cost of sales adjustments proposed by Sandilands, it was recommended that a 'gearing adjustment' be made as an interim solution to dealing with monetary items in inflation adjusted financial statements. Since no account of the existence of borrowings was taken in calculating current cost operating profit, the implication was that operating capability had to be maintained entirely out of the generation of revenues. However, the reality is clearly that this could be partly financed by borrowings; consequently, the gearing adjustment was designed to take account of the extent to which fixed assets and working capital were financed by borrowings.

According to the ASC, the response of the larger companies to the Hyde Guidelines was 'encouraging'.[82] However, the ASC stated that it was evident from comments made in annual reports and submitted directly to them, that many companies were reluctant to include price level information in their annual financial statements until an acceptable accounting method was proposed as a standard, and until more detailed guidance was available on problem areas.[83] Consequently, in April 1979 the ASC issued ED 24 — *Current Cost Accounting* — which was developed from the Hyde Guidelines, taking into account comments received on both the Guidelines and ED 18.

ED 24 followed the Hyde proposal that a separate statement be presented which disclosed the current cost adjustments made to the historical cost profit in respect of depreciation, cost of sales and gearing. However, the ED went further than the guidelines by:

(a)   introducing a further adjustment, called the 'monetary working capital adjustment', which effectively extended the cost of sales adjustment (which allowed for increases in the investment needed to maintain stocks when prices were increasing) to the other working capital items. Consequently, the monetary working capital adjustment represented an estimate of the extra investment in debtors, creditors and liquid resources required to maintain operations when prices were increasing;

(b)   proposing the presentation of a current cost balance sheet, in which fixed assets and stock would be measured on a current cost basis; and

(c)   proposing that listed companies disclose current cost earnings per share.[84]

ED 24 subsequently became SSAP 16,[85] which was issued in March 1980. SSAP 16 gave companies the choice as to how they could present their current cost information. They could either present historical cost accounts as their main accounts with supplementary current cost accounts, or they could present current cost accounts as the main accounts with supplementary historical cost accounts, or they could present current cost accounts as the only accounts 'accompanied by adequate historical cost information.'[86]

SSAP 16 perpetuated the concept of current cost operating profit based on the maintenance of physical capital, which had been extended to monetary working capital through the monetary working capital adjustment. The associated gearing adjustment probably arose as a result of the ASC's need to compromise with its critics in order to find an acceptable solution — as opposed to having any theoretically sound justification. On the other hand, in the US SFAS 33 — *Financial Reporting and Changing Prices* — which was issued in September 1979, required the disclosure of real holding gains and losses on net monetary items and physical assets (inventory and property, plant and equipment) after eliminating the effects of general inflation.[87] In December 1986, SFAS 33 was superseded by SFAS 89 — *Financial Reporting and Changing Prices* — which encourages (but does not require), the disclosure of supplementary information on the effects of changing prices, suggesting similar disclosures to those of SFAS 33 in respect of holding gains and losses.[88] Clearly, therefore, the FASB has adopted the concept of financial capital maintenance, and its commitment to this concept is borne out in Concepts Statement No. 5[89] (see 5.5 below). However, this is not to say that the FASB have found the solution to accounting for the effects of changing prices; SFAS 89 is, in several other respects, a somewhat nebulous and inconclusive standard.

At the time that SSAP 16 was issued, the ASC stated that it was their intention, as far as possible 'to make no change to SSAP 16 for three years so as to enable producers and users to gain experience in dealing with practical problems and interpreting the information.' However, this statement probably contributed to the eventual demise of the standard, because it was taken as an intention that it would inevitably be revised at the end of the three year period and allowed SSAP 16 to be characterised as 'experimental' or ' provisional'.[90] Over the next few years, there was a continuing decline in the level of compliance with the standard.

In July 1984, the ASC issued a further exposure draft ED 35 — *Accounting for the effects of changing prices*. This restricted the scope of the proposals to public companies which were neither value-based enterprises nor wholly-owned subsidiaries, but in respect of these it sought to make CCA a mandatory feature of the primary financial statements (rather than in supplementary statements), declaring that the inclusion of this information was essential to a true and fair view. However, it soon became clear that these proposals could not command general acceptance, and the exposure draft was withdrawn in early 1985.

Soon afterwards, in the face of increasing opposition to the standard, the CCAB bodies voted to make SSAP 16 non-mandatory, and it has since been completely withdrawn. The ASC persisted for some months to try to find a viable successor, seeking a more flexible approach and abandoning the proposition that it was essential to a true and fair view in the primary financial statements, but eventually gave up the search. Instead, it published *Accounting for the effects of changing prices: a Handbook*,[91] which was based on various of its earlier pronouncements on the subject together with some of its more recent, hitherto unpublished material. This remains its most recent publication on accounting for changing prices, and although it has never completely taken the topic off its agenda, there are no current moves to develop a fresh statement on the subject. Interest in the topic among companies in the private sector[92] also remains low; very few companies now offer any CCA information to readers of their financial statements.

4.6   The Macve Report

As a consequence of the written submissions received in response to its consultative document 'Setting Accounting Standards' (see 1 above), the ASC commissioned Professor Richard Macve to 'review critically current literature and opinion in the UK, US and elsewhere with a view to forming preliminary conclusions as to the possibilities of developing an agreed conceptual framework for setting accounting standards and the nature of such a framework; and to identify areas for further research.'[93]

Macve's report — *A Conceptual Framework for Financial Accounting and Reporting: the possibilities for an agreed structure* — was published in August 1981. As would be expected from his terms of reference, Macve concentrated his efforts on evaluating selected conceptual framework projects and studies, focusing in particular on the Corporate Report and the FASB's conceptual framework project. His discussions centred around the problems that arise in determining profit and net assets, and these he related to the difficulties involved in establishing what constitutes useful accounting information. He further highlighted the fact that the variety of user needs and conflicts of interest between different parties were likely to cause disagreement as to what information financial statements should provide.[94] On this issue, he came to the conclusion that 'recognition of the variety of user needs and of conflicts between different interests and different rights leads to the view that reaching agreement on the form and content of financial statements is as much a "political" process, a search for compromise between different parties, as it is a search for the methods which are "technically" best.'[95]

As far as the FASB's conceptual project was concerned, Macve concluded his review by saying that 'given the difficulties experienced in arriving at "useful" definitions of the elements of profit and loss accounts and balance sheets, it seems to me likely that the continuing attempts to develop "recognition criteria" and "measurement rules", that can both command general acceptance and have an impact on individual accounting disputes in relation to profit and net asset calculation, will be similarly unsuccessful.'[96] Bearing in mind that this comment was made prior to the FASB's publication in December 1984 of SFAC No. 5 — *Recognition and Measurement in Financial Statements of Business Enterprises* — his fears were later to be proved well founded. However, as discussed at 5 below, the FASB's failure to deal effectively with the recognition and measurement issues can be largely attributed to the fact that they were limited by the definitions of the elements of financial statements given in SFAC No. 3. On the other hand, SFAC No. 3 shows clear evidence of the compromise as a result of the 'political process' referred to by Macve.

Macve concluded his study by putting forward several suggestions for further research. As might have been expected, these centred around the need for further empirical study in various areas — such as the economic significance of accounting measures and the ways in which financial statements are used by the various classes of user — all of which might lead to a better understanding of the form and content of financial statements. However, what was probably the most practical suggestion was for the study of the process of introducing changes in accounting practice.[97] Clearly, no matter how theoretically sound proposed changes in reporting practice might be, standard-setting bodies will be faced with resistance not only from those groups who believe that their economic interests will be prejudiced by the changes, but also from those who resist change in whatever form it might take.

However, the ASC did not demonstrate any apparent inclination to pursue Macve's proposals for further research with any degree of fervour, and allowed his report to slowly fade into the background. It was not until the publication in January 1989 of the Solomons Report[98] that the ASC displayed any evidence that they were actively seeking conceptual guidelines to assist them in the standard-setting process (see 6.4 below).

4.7   The Stamp Report

In 1980, Professor Edward Stamp produced a research study for the Canadian Institute of Chartered Accountants which was 'intended to provide a Canadian solution to the problem of improving the quality of corporate financial reporting standards'.[99] Stamp adopted a similar approach to that of other studies (such as the Corporate Report and Trueblood) by looking at users, their needs, their rights to information and the qualitative characteristics of that information. Stamp identified a more detailed list of users (15 in all) than did, for example, the Corporate or Sandilands Reports. However, to a large extent his list merely broke down broad categories of users into smaller groups; for example, the Corporate Report identifies the 'business contact group' as a single user group (which includes suppliers, customers, competitors and business rivals),[100] whilst Stamp lists 'customers, suppliers, industry groups, and other companies' as individual groups.[101]

Stamp then developed a set of 20 qualitative criteria which could be used as yardsticks whereby standard-setters, as well as the preparers and users of published financial statements, can decide whether or not the financial statements are meeting the objectives of financial reporting and the needs of users. An interesting rider to this aspect of Stamp's study was that he subsequently used his list of qualitative criteria as the basis of an empirical study of the ASC members' assessment of the relative importance of each of the criteria.[102] Stamp supplied each member of the ASC with a copy of Chapter 7 of his CICA research study in which the significance and meaning of each of the 20 criteria were discussed. He also gave them each a questionnaire in which they were asked to rank the 20 criteria in order of importance.[103] Although the ranking revealed 'relevance' as the most important criterion and 'conservatism' as the least important this, in itself, was not the most significant aspect of Stamp's study; what was significant was the fact that he was able to demonstrate that it would be possible to establish rankings of characteristics of accounting information for each category of user. Such information, if combined with research into the objectives and information needs of the same groups of user, would provide a basis for determining whether or not differential standards of reporting should be developed for different categories of user.

In his CICA research study, Stamp also devoted a considerable amount of effort towards discussing certain fundamental conceptual issues; these included the problems of allocation, income measurement, capital maintenance, as well as the issue of the proprietary versus the entity theory and the question of which attribute accounting should measure.[104] On certain of the problems which he discussed, Stamp concluded by saying that they were 'irresolvable'; for example, the goodwill problem associated with using the balance sheet as a measure of the current worth of an enterprise. These issues are all fundamental to the development of a conceptual framework for financial reporting; however, as will be seen at 5 below, none was unequivocally resolved by the FASB in its framework project.

Stamp concluded his study by recommending that further research be carried out in various areas of user needs and decision-making processes, including (as did the Corporate Report) the investigation of and experimentation with multi-column reporting.[105]

5 THE FASB CONCEPTUAL FRAMEWORK

5.1 Introduction

As discussed at 4.3 above, the FASB has, since its inception, been engaged in the development of a series of Statements of Financial Accounting Concepts (SFACs) which are intended to establish the objectives and concepts that the FASB will use in developing standards of financial reporting. The FASB recognised that although there had been many attempts by individuals and organisations (such as the American Accounting Association) to develop a theory of accounting, none of these individual theories had become universally accepted or relied on in practice. The FASB, therefore, expressed a need for a '*constitution*, a coherent system of interrelated objectives and fundamentals that can lead to consistent standards and that prescribes the nature, function, and limits of financial accounting and financial statements.'[106] The conceptual framework was expected to:

(a) guide the body responsible for establishing standards;

(b) provide a frame of reference for resolving accounting questions in the absence of a specific promulgated standard;

(c) determine bounds for judgement in preparing financial statements;

(d) increase financial statement users' understanding of and confidence in financial statements; and

(e) enhance comparability.[107]

To date, the FASB has issued six concepts statements, of which one (SFAC No. 4) deals with the objectives of financial reporting by non-business organisations and is beyond the scope of this book, whilst another (SFAC No. 3) dealt with elements of financial statements by business enterprises, and was superseded by SFAC No. 6, which expanded the scope of SFAC No. 3 to encompass not-for-profit organisations.

The first phase of the FASB's conceptual framework project was to develop a statement of the objectives of financial reporting. Clearly, some pioneering work in this area had been done by the Trueblood Committee (see 4.2.3 above), and this formed the basis of the FASB's first concepts statement. Nevertheless, it was not until 1978 that the FASB finally published its first concepts statement.

5.2   The objectives of financial reporting

SFAC No. 1 — *Objectives of Financial Reporting by Business Enterprises* — starts off by making the point that financial reporting includes not only financial statements, but also incorporates other means of communicating financial and non-financial information; this may be achieved, for example, through the medium of stock exchange documents, news releases, management forecasts etc.[108] Having said this, the statement stresses that 'financial reporting is not an end in itself but is intended to provide information that is useful in making business and economic decisions.'[109] This, however, is no new revelation; it is the type of broad generalisation that has characterised numerous previous attempts at establishing a conceptual framework. On the other hand, what it does do is raise all the same issues which the Trueblood Committee had been asked to consider seven years previously, such as: For whom is this information intended? What types of 'business and economic decisions' do they make? What information do they need to enable them to make these decisions? What framework is required to provide this needed information?

The statement details an extensive list of potential users, distinguishing between those with a direct interest and those with an indirect interest in the information provided by financial reporting.[110] The groups of user which have a direct interest include owners, management, creditors and employees; whilst user groups such as financial analysts and advisers, journalists, regulatory authorities and trade unions are deemed to have an indirect interest, since they advise or represent those who have a direct interest. However, having identified this wide range of users, the statement focuses on the information needs of investors and creditors. These are encompassed in the first of three primary objectives identified in the statement: 'financial reporting should provide information that is useful to present and potential investors and creditors and other users in making rational investment, credit, and similar decisions.'[111]

This objective leads to the first of the two most significant and far-reaching conclusions in the statement, namely that 'financial reporting should provide information to help investors, creditors, and others assess the amounts, timing, and uncertainty of prospective net cash inflows to the related enterprise.'[112] In reaching this conclusion, the FASB was aware of the fact that it might precipitate an adverse reaction leading to the possible rejection of the statement through what might have been seen as an objective which would ultimately result in companies being required to present cash flow, management forecast or current value information. The FASB pre-empted this potential adverse reaction by stating that 'the objective focuses on the purpose for which information provided should be useful ... rather than the kinds of information that may be useful for that purpose. The objective neither requires nor prohibits "cash flow information," "current value information ," "management forecast information," or any other specific information. Conclusions about "current value information" and "management forecast information" are beyond the scope of this Statement. Paragraphs 42-44 [of SFAC No. 1] note that information about cash receipts and disbursements is not usually considered to be the most useful information for the purposes described in this objective.'[113]

However, in examining this objective, it is important to take cognisance of empirical research which has been conducted in this area. In 1979, Chang and Most investigated the views of individual investors, institutional investors and financial analysts in the the USA, UK and New Zealand as part of a study into the importance of financial statements for investment decisions.[114] Their study included an investigation into the investment objectives of individual and institutional investors, and reached the conclusion that 'the most important investment objective for both individual and institutional investors is long-term capital gains. This, and a combination of dividend income and capital gains, are considerably more important than short-term capital gains. It would appear that prediction of short-term cash flows would not be one of the more important investor uses of financial statements, and this calls in question the conventional assumption that a principal objective of financial statements is to assist users to predict future cash flows in terms of <u>timing</u>, as distinct from amount and relative uncertainty.'[115] On the other hand, it is, of course, possible that institutional investors are much more influenced by short-term expectations today than they were ten years ago; consequently, the findings of Chang and Most may no longer be valid.

The second fundamental conclusion reached in SFAC No. 1 which has far-reaching implications for the future development of accounting standards is concerned with the primary focus of financial reporting. During the early stages of the development of accounting rules in the first half of this century, the primary focus of financial statements was based on the principle of 'stewardship'. This arose from the fact that the management of an enterprise were primarily seen to be accountable to the owners for safeguarding the assets which had been entrusted to them, leading to a balance sheet emphasis in financial reporting. However, the focus has gradually shifted away from the notion of the balance sheet reporting on the custodianship of assets, to an earnings emphasis based on the principle that the income statement should present 'decision-useful' information. This is encapsulated in the statement in SFAC No. 1 that 'the primary focus of financial reporting is information about an enterprise's performance provided by measures of earnings and its components. Investors, creditors, and others who are concerned with assessing the prospects for enterprise net cash inflows are especially interested in that information.'[116]

SFAC No. 1 still recognises the fact that financial reporting should provide information about how the management of an enterprise has discharged its stewardship responsibility.[117] However, it goes on to say that 'earnings information is commonly the focus for assessing management's stewardship or accountability. Management, owners, and others emphasize enterprise performance or profitability in describing how management has discharged its stewardship accountability.'[118]

In other words, the statement is asserting that the measurement of earnings in the income statement should take precedence over the measurement of assets and liabilities in the balance sheet. This is an important principle which should have an important impact on the principles laid down in the development of future accounting standards. However, as will be seen below, the FASB's subsequent concepts statements have essentially avoided the issue of how to determine net income. Furthermore, recent statements issued by the FASB tend to suggest an uncertainty as to whether an earnings or balance sheet approach should be followed (for example, SFAS 96 — *Accounting for Income Taxes* — would appear to view the balance sheet as the primary statement).

In the UK, the recent publication of the Solomons Report[119] further highlights a lack of general acceptance of the principle laid down in SFAC No. 1 that the primary focus of financial reporting is information about an enterprise's performance provided by measures of earnings, since the main thrust of the Solomons Report focuses on the primacy of the balance sheet (see 6.4 below).

5.3   The qualitative characteristics of accounting information

The FASB's second Concepts Statement — *Qualitative Characteristics of Accounting Information* — examines the characteristics that make accounting information useful to the users of that information. The statement views these characteristics as 'a hierarchy of accounting qualities', which then form the basis for selecting and evaluating information for inclusion in financial reports. The hierarchy is represented in Figure 1 on the next page.[120]

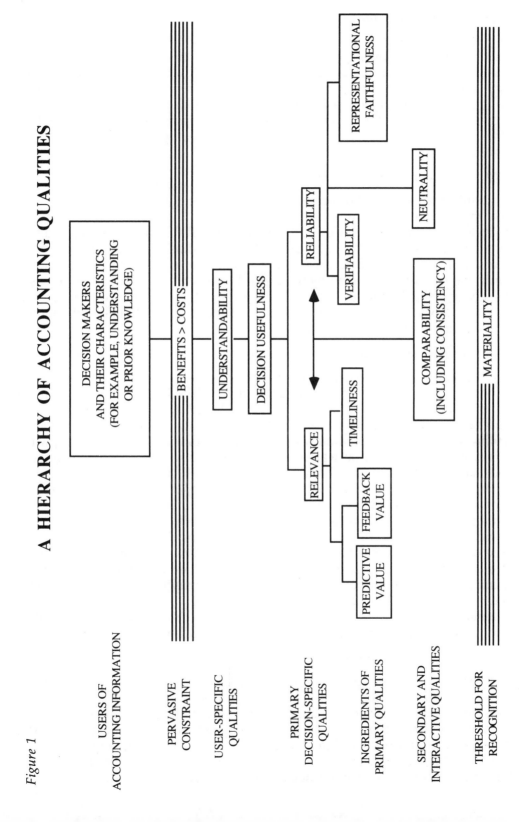

Figure 1

A HIERARCHY OF ACCOUNTING QUALITIES

5.3.1   The decision-makers

The decision-makers (users) appear at the top of the hierarchy against the background of their own specific characteristics. Whilst usefulness for decision-making is the most important quality that accounting information should possess, each decision-maker has to judge what information is useful to his specific decision. This judgement would be based on such factors as the nature of the decision to be made, the information already in his possession or available from other sources, the decision-making process that he employs and his capacity to process all the information that he obtains.

5.3.2   The cost/benefit constraint

Since information should be provided only if the benefits to be derived from that information outweigh the costs of providing it, the cost/benefit constraint pervades the hierarchy. However, the application of this constraint may cause a certain amount of difficulty, since the costs of providing financial information are normally borne by the enterprise (and ultimately passed on to its customers), whilst the benefits are reaped by the users. For this reason, the normal forces of demand and supply will not prevail in the market of financial information, since the external user will almost always view the benefits of additional information as outweighing the costs.

5.3.3   Understandability

The hierarchy depicts understandability as being the key quality for accounting information to achieve 'decision usefulness'. SFAC No. 1 stated that the information provided by financial reporting 'should be comprehensible to those who have a reasonable understanding of business and economic activities and are willing to study the information with reasonable diligence.'[121] Information, whilst it may be relevant, will be wasted if it is provided in a form which cannot be understood by the users for whom it was intended. SFAC No. 1 elaborated on the relationship between useful information and understandability as follows: 'financial information is a tool and, like most tools, cannot be of much direct help to those who are unable or unwilling to use it or who misuse it. Its use can be learned, however, and financial reporting should provide information that can be used by all—nonprofessionals as well as professionals—who are willing to learn to use it properly. Efforts may be needed to increase the understandability of financial information. Cost-benefit considerations may indicate that information understood or used by only a few should not be provided. Conversely, financial reporting should not exclude relevant information merely because it is difficult for some to understand or because some investors or creditors choose not to use it.'[122]

5.3.4   Relevance and reliability

The qualities that distinguish 'better' (more useful) information from 'inferior' (less useful) information are primarily the qualities of relevance and reliability, with some other characteristics that those qualities imply. SFAC No. 2 identifies relevance and reliability as 'the two primary qualities that make accounting information useful for decision making. Subject to constraints imposed by cost and materiality, increased relevance and increased reliability are the characteristics that make information a more desirable commodity — that is, one useful in making decisions.'[123] However, all this is not new — the qualitative characteristics of relevance and reliability have, been discussed in several preceding studies (such as the Trueblood and Corporate Reports). However, what is new (and probably the most significant aspect of SFAC No. 2), is the recognition of the fact that 'reliability and relevance often impinge on each other'.[124] Consequently, whenever accounting standards are set, decisions have to be made concerning the relative importance of these two characteristics, often resulting in trade-offs being made between them.

For example, one of the most common criticisms made about the various systems of value accounting which have been proposed over the years concerns the high degree of subjectivity involved in assigning values to assets and liabilities. Consequently, for any standard-setting body to propose that the historical cost system be replaced by an income and measurement system based on current values, a decision would have to be made as to the relative weights which should be attributed to presenting information which is both relevant and reliable. The perceived gain in the relevance of the information to the user would have to outweigh the uncertainties concerning the reliability of the current value information.

A   Relevance

The statement defines relevant accounting information as being information which is 'capable of making a difference in a decision by helping users to form predictions about the outcomes of past, present, and future events or to confirm or correct prior expectations.'[125] The statement further describes 'timeliness' as an 'ancillary aspect of relevance. If information is not available when it is needed or becomes available only so long after the reported events that it has no value for future action, it lacks relevance and is of little or no use.[126] Therefore, in the context of financial reporting, the characteristic of timeliness means that information must be made available to users before it loses its capacity to influence their decisions. However, timeliness alone cannot make information relevant, but a lack of timeliness can result in information losing a degree of relevance which it once had.[127] On the other hand, in many instances there also has to be a trade-off between timeliness and reliability, since generally the more timely the information the less reliable it is.

The hierarchy identifies 'predictive value' and 'feedback value' as the other components of relevance on the basis that 'information can make a difference to decisions by improving decision makers' capacities to predict or by confirming or correcting their earlier expectations.'[128] Predictive value is defined as 'the quality of information that helps users to increase the likelihood of correctly forecasting the outcome of past or present events',[129] whilst feedback value is defined as 'the quality of information that enables users to confirm or correct prior expectations.'[130] Clearly, however, in saying that accounting information has predictive value, it is not suggesting that it is itself a prediction.

B   Reliability

Reliability is the second of the primary qualities, and is ascribed three attributes in the hierarchy. The statement states that the 'reliability of a measure rests on the faithfulness with which it represents what it purports to represent, coupled with an assurance for the user, which comes through verification, that it has that representational quality.'[131] This definition gives rise to the three subsidiary qualities of 'representational faithfulness', 'verifiability', and 'neutrality'. Representational faithfulness is an unnecessary piece of jargon introduced into accounting terminology by SFAC No. 2; what it essentially means is that information included in financial reports should represent what it purports to represent. In other words, financial reporting should be truthful. For example, if a group's consolidated balance sheet discloses cash and bank balances, users would be justified in assuming that, in the absence of any statement to the contrary, the financial statements were truthful, and that these represented cash resources freely available to the group; however, if the reality of the situation was that the cash resources were situated in countries which had severe exchange control restrictions, and were, therefore, not available to the group, some might hold the view that the financial statements were not entirely 'representationally faithful'.

It should be noted, however, that there are degrees of representational faithfulness. Because the financial reporting process involves allocations, estimations and subjective judgments, it cannot produce an 'exact' result; consequently, the trade-off between relevance and reliability will often apply, resulting in the presentation of information which is assigned a high degree of relevance, but which sacrifices representational faithfulness. An example of where this might apply is in the context of fair value accounting, where fair values have to be assigned to the separable net assets acquired.

Reliable information should also be verifiable and neutral so that neither measurement nor measurer bias result in the information being presented in such a way that it influences the particular decision being made. Verifiability is a quality of representational faithfulness in that it excludes the possibility of measurement bias, whilst neutrality implies the provision of all relevant and reliable information — irrespective of the effects that the information will have on the entity or a particular user group.

5.3.5   Comparability

The hierarchy lists comparability as an additional quality that financial information should possess in order to achieve relevance and reliability. The quality of comparability includes the fundamental accounting concept of consistency, since the usefulness of information is greatly enhanced if it is prepared on a consistent basis from one period to the next, and can be compared with corresponding information of the same enterprise for some other period, or with similar information about some other enterprise.

5.3.6   Materiality

All the qualitative criteria discussed in SFAC No. 2 are subject to a materiality threshold, since only material information will have an impact on the decision-making process. However, the statement provides no quantitative guidelines for materiality, and it will be a matter of judgment for the providers of information to determine whether or not an item of information has crossed the materiality threshold for recognition. However, materiality is closely related to the characteristic of relevance, since both are defined in terms of what influences or makes a difference to an investor or other decision-maker. On the other hand, the two concepts can be distinguished; a decision by management not to disclose certain information may be made because users have no interest in that kind of information (i.e. it is not relevant to their specific needs), or because the amounts involved are too small to make a difference to the users' decisions (i.e. they are not material).

However, if the preparers of financial statements are to decide on what to include in their reporting package, they must have a clear understanding of the users of their reports and their specific information and decision-making needs. In so doing, they should be aware of the types of information likely to influence their decisions (i.e. relevance) as well as the associated magnitude of this information (i.e. materiality). Consequently, financial reporting will focus generally on information which is regarded as relevant, and specifically on that which is material. The principal difficulty with this, however, is that the materiality decisions of users vary from class to class and amongst individual users in the same class (see 7.4.2 below for further discussion of the concept of materiality).

5.3.7 *Conservatism*

SFAC No. 2 includes an interesting discussion on the convention of 'conservatism' (i.e. prudence).[132] In so doing, it draws a distinction between the 'deliberate, consistent understatement of net assets and profits',[133] and the practice of ensuring that 'uncertainties and risks inherent in business situations are adequately considered'.[134] The statement recognised the fact that, in the eyes of bankers and other lenders, deliberate understatement of assets was desirable, since it increased their margin of safety on assets pledged as security for debts. On the other hand, it was also recognised that consistent understatement was difficult to maintain over a period of any length, and that understated assets would clearly lead to overstated income in later periods when the assets were ultimately realised. Consequently, unwarranted and deliberate conservatism in financial reporting would lead to a contravention of certain of the qualitative characteristics, such as neutrality and representational faithfulness.

5.4 The elements of financial statements

SFAC No. 6 — *Elements of Financial Statements* — was issued in 1985 as a replacement to SFAC No. 3 — *Elements of Financial Statements of Business Enterprises* — having expanded its scope to encompass non-profit organisations. The statement defines ten 'elements' of financial statements that are directly related to the measurement of performance and financial status of an entity. However, the elements are very much interrelated, as six of them are arithmetically derived from the definitions of assets and liabilities.

5.4.1   Assets

Assets are defined as being 'probable future economic benefits obtained or controlled by a particular entity as a result of past transactions or events.'[135] However, the statement then goes on to say that the kinds of items that qualify as assets under this definition are also commonly called 'economic resources'. They are the scarce means that are useful for carrying out economic activities, such as consumption, production and exchange.[136] The common characteristic possessed by all assets is 'service potential' or 'future economic benefit' which eventually results in net cash inflows to the enterprise.[137]

Clearly, this definition will be adequate under most circumstances. However, in the context of historical cost accounting, a non-monetary asset is no more than a deferred cost; a cost which has been incurred before the balance sheet date and, in terms of the accruals concept, relates to future periods beyond the balance sheet date, thereby justifying it being carried forward as an asset. This applies to all non-monetary assets which are recognised in a historical cost balance sheet — whether they be tangible fixed assets, stock, prepayments or deferred development expenditure.

Consequently, there are certain occasions when items will be recognised as assets under the traditional historical cost system, but which will not fit the SFAC No. 6 definition of an asset. For example, if a company had to top up its pension fund to meet an experience deficiency but, in accordance with SSAP 24 (see Chapter 22), spreads the variation from regular pension cost forward, this will give rise to an asset in the balance sheet. Whilst this asset meets the 'deferred cost' criteria described above, it does not fall within the statement's definition, since it cannot be said to be an economic resource with future economic benefit; it is merely a cost awaiting recognition in the profit and loss account of future years. The same argument would apply to certain other deferred costs.

This difficulty highlights a deep-rooted problem with the FASB's conceptual framework project. Firstly, as far as SFAC No. 6 is concerned, since most of the elements defined in the statement are derived from the definition of an asset, doubts must exist as the validity of the definitions of certain of the other elements. Secondly, in defining the elements of financial statements before addressing the fundamental issues of how they are to be measured and on what concept of capital maintenance profit is to be determined, the FASB seriously limited their ability to address the issues of recognition and measurement properly. The result of this is that SFAC No. 5 — *Recognition and Measurement in Financial Statements of Business Enterprises* — has serious shortcomings (see 5.5 below).

5.4.2   Liabilities

Liabilities are defined as 'probable future sacrifices of economic benefits arising from present obligations of a particular entity to transfer assets or provide services to other entities in the future as a result of past transactions or events.[138] The statement goes on to say that a liability has three essential characteristics:

(a)   it embodies a present duty or responsibility to one or more other entities that entails settlement by probable future transfer or use of assets at a specified or determinable date, on occurrence of a specified event, or on demand;

(b)   the duty or responsibility obligates the entity, leaving it little or no discretion to avoid the future sacrifice; and

(c)   the transaction or other event obligating the entity has already happened.[139]

Thus, in terms of this definition, liabilities represent the amounts of obligations — giving rise to a problem similar to that outlined above in respect of the definition of assets. There are certain items which are currently recognised as liabilities, but which do not meet the statement's definition; the reason being that they are merely deferred credits awaiting recognition in the profit and loss account, rather than representing obligations to other entities. Examples of such items might include deferred government grants, and the deferred effects of favourable variations from regular pension cost.

5.4.3   Equity

Equity is defined as 'the residual interest in the assets of an entity that remains after deducting its liabilities.'[140] This is a somewhat tautological definition arising from the accounting equation that assets minus liabilities equals equity. Equity is, in fact, the sum of the equity investments made by the entity's owners, and the entity's earnings retained from its profit-making activities. Because of the way in which the definitions of the various elements are interrelated, it might appear to some that the FASB have taken the easy route in defining equity as net assets, rather than in terms of capital contributions plus retained earnings; a possible explanation for this might be that it enabled the FASB to define income in terms of changes in equity.

5.4.4   Investments by owners

Investments by owners are defined as being 'increases in equity of a particular business enterprise resulting from transfers to it from other entities of something valuable to obtain or increase ownership interests (or equity) in it.'[141] The statement goes on to say that although investments by owners are most commonly made in the form of assets, the investments can also be represented by services, or the settlement or conversion of liabilities of the enterprise.[142]

5.4.5   Distributions to owners

Distributions to owners are defined as 'decreases in equity of a particular business enterprise resulting from transferring assets, rendering services, or incurring liabilities by the enterprise to owners.'[143] Distributions to owners, therefore, incorporate all forms of capital distributions which result in a decrease in net assets.

5.4.6   Comprehensive income

Comprehensive income is defined as 'the change in equity of a business enterprise during a period from transactions and other events and circumstances from nonowner sources. It includes all changes in equity during a period except those resulting from investments by owners and distributions to owners.'[144] On its own, the term 'comprehensive income' is a somewhat meaningless term; for example, how did it tie in with the statement in SFAC No. 1[145] that 'the primary focus of financial reporting is information about an enterprise's performance provided by measures of earnings and its components'? Clearly, the FASB were keeping their options open by not defining earnings; in fact, they explained (in a footnote to SFAC No. 6) that whilst 'comprehensive income' is the term used in the statement for the concept that was called 'earnings' in SFAC No. 1, SFAC No. 5 had described earnings for a period as excluding certain cumulative accounting adjustments and other nonowner changes in equity that are included in comprehensive income for a period.[146]

5.4.7   *Revenues, expenses, gains and losses*

SFAC No. 6 identifies the remaining four elements as those which constitute the basic components of 'comprehensive income':

Revenues, which are 'inflows or other enhancements of assets of an entity or settlements of its liabilities (or a combination of both) from delivering or producing goods, rendering services, or other activities that constitute the entity's ongoing major central operations.'[147]

Expenses, which are 'outflows or other using up of assets or incurrences of liabilities (or a combination of both) from delivering or producing goods, rendering services, or carrying out other activities that constitute the entity's ongoing major or central operations.'[148]

Gains, which are 'increases in equity (net assets) from peripheral or incidental transactions of an entity and from all other transactions and other events and circumstances affecting the entity except those that result from revenues or investments by owners.'[149]

Losses, which are decreases in equity (net assets) from peripheral or incidental transactions of an entity and from all other transactions and other events and circumstances affecting the entity except those that result from expenses or distributions to owners.'[150]

Therefore, comprehensive income equals revenues minus expenses plus gains minus losses; however, although the statement states that revenues, expenses, gains and losses can be combined in various ways to obtain various measures of enterprise performance,[151] it fails to define net income.

The difficulty surrounding the FASB's definitions of the ten elements is that they are so interrelated, that in attempting to piece them together into a meaningful accounting framework, one gets caught up in a tautology of terms which all lead back to the definitions of assets and liabilities. However, if the primary focus of financial reporting is the measurement of earnings, then surely the starting point should be definitions of earnings and its components, with assets and liabilities being the residuals — rather than the other way around? Essentially what the FASB is saying is that assets minus liabilities equals equity and comprehensive income equals changes in equity (excluding transactions with owners), therefore comprehensive income equals the change in net assets. Consequently, the definition of comprehensive income would incorporate items such as capital contributions from non-owners, government grants for capital expenditure and unrealised holding gains. This is all very well, provided that the issues of measurement and capital maintenance have already been settled. However, this is clearly not the case, with the result that the FASB is either restricting itself in the future development of different accounting models for different purposes, or it might have to develop different definitions of the elements of financial statements as different models are developed.

5.5   Recognition and measurement

Throughout the framework project, the FASB had sometimes avoided dealing with certain fundamental issues on the basis that they were the 'subject of another project'.[152] The result was the publication in December 1984 of SFAC No. 5 — *Recognition and Measurement in Financial Statements of Business Enterprises* — which attempted to deal with all the previously unresolved issues. However, the statement was somewhat inconclusive — possibly as a consequence of both its self-imposed restrictions discussed above, and the need to reach compromises in order to complete this phase of the project. The statement tends to describe current practices, rather than indicate preferences or propose improvements; for example, in dealing with the issue of measurement attributes, the statement merely states that 'items currently reported in financial statements are measured by different attributes, depending on the nature of the item and the relevance and reliability of the attribute measured.'[153] Then, instead of either prescribing a particular measurement attribute, or discussing the circumstances under which particular attributes should apply, the statement discusses five different attributes which 'are used in present practice' — historical cost, current cost, current market value, net realisable value and present value of future cash flows — and concludes that 'the use of different attributes will continue'.[154] Furthermore, the statement fails to prescribe a particular concept of capital maintenance that should be adopted by an entity, although the FASB base their discussions on the concept of financial capital maintenance.[155]

The Statement defines recognition as 'the process of formally recording or incorporating an item into the financial statements of an entity as an asset, liability, revenue, expense, or the like'.[156] It goes on to discuss four 'fundamental recognition criteria' which any item should meet in order for it to be recognised in the financial statements of an entity. These criteria, which are subject to a cost-benefit constraint and a materiality threshold, are described as follows:

- *Definitions* — the item meets the definition of an element of financial statements.
- *Measurability* — the item has a relevant attribute measurable with sufficient reliability.
- *Relevance* — the information about the item is capable of making a difference in user decisions.
- *Reliability* — the information is representationally faithful, verifiable and neutral.[157]

Although it was probably worth setting out these criteria, they are no more than an encapsulation of certain criteria contained in Concepts Statements 2 and 6.

SFAC No. 5 does make some progress in distinguishing between comprehensive income, earnings and net income. It states that the concept of earnings is similar to net income in present practice, and that a statement of earnings will be much like a present income statement, although 'earnings' does not include the cumulative effect of certain accounting adjustments of earlier periods that are recognised in the current period.[158] However, the statement goes on to say that the FASB 'expects the concept of earnings to be subject to the process of gradual change or evolution that has characterised the development of net income.'[159] Whilst many would agree with the principle that gradual change is the best approach towards gaining general acceptance, one of the problems with SFAC No. 5 is that the FASB does not indicate what it considers to be the desirable direction for this gradual change to follow. Furthermore, the FASB seems to be saying that concepts will evolve as accounting standards are developed — instead of the other way around.

In an evaluation of the FASB's conceptual framework, Professor David Solomons (who, incidentally, was the principal author of SFAC No. 2) came to the following conclusion about SFAC No. 5: 'Under a rigorous grading system I would give Concepts Statement no. 5 an F and require the board to take the course over again—that is, to scrap the statement and start afresh.'[160]

5.6   Conclusion

In order to be able to assess the success or failure of the FASB's conceptual framework project, one must refer back to the originally perceived benefits of the project and evaluate whether or not any of them has been achieved (see 5.1 above). Perhaps the acid test may be found in analysing the extent to which the FASB have used the framework in the development of accounting standards. Possibly the best example of where the framework has been used as the basis for an accounting standard is in the development of SFAS 95 — *Statement of Cash Flows*; however, this is clearly the exception. An analysis of the Appendices headed 'Basis for Conclusions' in the more recently issued SFASs, reveals few references to the fact that the members of the FASB have used the concepts statements to guide their thinking — and where reference is made it is generally to broad objectives or qualitative characteristics. On the other hand, it might be argued that the concepts statements have guided the thinking of FASB members without it being expressly stated; however, if this were the case, why have the FASB not yet proposed the presentation of statements of earnings, comprehensive income and investments by and distributions to owners (as laid down in SFAC No. 5)?[161]

The weakness of the FASB's conceptual framework project may be attributed to a number of factors; however, the most significant reason will probably be shown to be the Board's failure to deal with the fundamental issues of recognition and measurement. To a certain extent, the FASB has fallen into the same trap as the AICPA did in APB Statement No. 4 — SFAC No. 5 is a descriptive rather than a prescriptive statement; a statement of accounting concepts should provide a frame of reference for the formulation of financial reporting practice, and not be a description of what current reporting practices are.

This is not to say that the FASB's project should be rejected out of hand; it contains some outstanding work, particularly in the area of qualitative characteristics. However, a way must be found to address the fundamental issues, without having to resort to compromise solutions; thereafter, a method of implementation will have to be developed which will make whatever transition is necessary acceptable to both the preparers and users of financial reports.

6   CONTEMPORARY CONCEPTUAL FRAMEWORK PROJECTS

6.1   Introduction

The last year or so has seen what might be viewed as a renewed vigour amongst various standard-setting bodies around the world towards seeking an acceptable framework for financial reporting. Each body might have its own reason for doing so, but it is clear that the accounting profession world-wide is coming under increasing pressure both as a result of the imprecision of existing accounting standards, and through not being able respond promptly and effectively to emerging issues, such as off-balance sheet finance and asset revaluations. However, as will be seen below, these recent attempts at developing a framework largely restate the same broad principles that have been repeated over the years, often comprising no more than a precis of previous studies, particularly those of the FASB; the only real breath of fresh air is the discussion document issued by the ICAS[162] (see 6.2 below).

6.2   The ICAS discussion document: 'Making Corporate Reports Valuable'

6.2.1   Background to the study

This discussion document, which was issued in 1988, is the product of a major research project undertaken by the Research Committee of the ICAS. However, it is vital that it is seen and evaluated taking into account the spirit in which it has been prepared; namely, that it has principally been prepared for the purpose of stimulating discussion and experimentation.[163] The reason why this paper is so refreshing revolves principally around the fact that the research committee started from the the basis of a 'clean sheet'. In other words, the members were able to ignore existing laws, accounting rules, terminology and all other constraints in order to try and achieve what they believed to be the best result. Clearly, this approach will have widespread practical implications for the ultimate implementation of any of its proposals; this fact is, however, recognised by the committee, and the document notes some of the implications of its suggestions.[164]

The committee starts off by explaining what motivated it to reconsider the nature of corporate reporting. The reasons given included the following basic conclusions:

- all financial reports ought to reflect economic reality;
- the information which investors need is the same in kind, but not in volume, as the information which managements need to run their entities;

- some of the information that management have but do not normally communicate comes out into the open when management want something — such as additional capital or to be able to defend a hostile takeover bid;
- present-day financial reports are deficient in that they are based on legal form rather than economic substance, on cost rather than value, on the past rather than the future, and on 'profit' rather than 'wealth';
- there is no consistent conceptual basis underlying the production of either the profit and loss account and the balance sheet, and some of the concepts used appear to defy normal understanding of financial affairs;
- corporate reports are not made public sufficiently speedily; and
- the audit report is insufficiently informative and often incomprehensible to non-auditors.[165]

6.2.2   Users and their needs

The committee then considered who are the users of financial reports and what are their informational needs. In so doing, they referred to the Corporate Report, concluding that corporate reporting should aim to communicate directly to only four of the groups identified in that report. These are:

(a)   the equity investor group;

(b)   the loan creditor group;

(c)   the employee group; and

(d)   the business contact group (which includes ordinary creditors).[166]

Having identified these four groups of users, the committee listed the following five fundamental information needs of these groups which external corporate reports should be able to contribute to meeting:

(a)   knowledge of the corporate objectives of the entity, and information which would enable users to evaluate the entity's performance against these objectives;

(b)   a comparison of the total wealth of the entity now as against what it was at the time of the last corporate report, together with an explanation of the reasons for change;

(c)   the ability to judge where the entity is going in the future and whether it has the necessary financial and other resources to do so;

(d)   adequate information about the economic environment within which the entity has been and will be operating; and

(e)   knowledge of the ownership and control of the entity and the experience and background of its directors and officials.[167]

As the committee pointed out, these proposals are a digest of the information needs of the equity investor group identified in the Corporate Report.[168] The committee suggested further that, in order to enable users to judge the reliability of management's planning based on past period performance, they should also be given information on:

(a) the entity's actual performance for the accounting period just past as compared with its previously published plan for that period;

(b) management's explanations of any significant variances between the two; and

(c) management's financial plan for the current and future accounting periods, together with explanations of the major assumptions used in preparing it.[169]

Clearly, these additional proposals are designed to provide information on how management of an entity has discharged its stewardship responsibility to owners and, as the committee suggests, this assessment should be based on earnings information and entity performance.

6.2.3 *Valuation of assets and liabilities*

The committee then discussed various bases for applying values to assets, focusing on historical cost, current replacement cost, current net realisable values and economic values. It is necessary to read the full text of the discussion document in order to properly appreciate the basis for the committee's conclusions; however, having discussed what they saw as the deficiencies of historical cost and economic value, the committee noted that current replacement cost and net realisable value both met its criteria of economic reality and 'additivity' (i.e. the total number in a statement should not mean something different in kind from its constituent numbers). However, the committee expressed a preference for net realisable value as the basis for applying values to assets, 'principally because it is value-based whereas replacement cost is cost-based',[170] and it was felt that 'value rather than cost is important in assessing financial wealth.'[171]

It is in this area that the paper is likely to attract the greatest amount of criticism and debate. For example, the committee dismisses replacement cost accounting by citing the problems associated with it, without giving equal consideration to the problems associated with net realisable value accounting. The problems attributed to the use of replacement costs were as follows:

'(a) there is an assumption that assets will be replaced, which is frequently not the case;

(b) there are significant practical problems in assessing replacement values if there have been improvements in technology; and

(c) arbitrary depreciation allocations are still required.'[172]

Whilst there can be no dispute that these are valid points, there are equally several practical and theoretical problems surrounding net realisable value accounting (see 4.5.2 above for a more detailed discussion of both models). For example, should net realisable values be based on the assumption that assets are realised in an orderly manner, or should they be based on immediate liquidation prices? Furthermore, there is the whole question of whether or not net realisable values do, in fact, necessarily measure the financial wealth of a going concern; for example, what about the case of plant which has negligible realisable value but significant use value? This also raises the further issue of how compatible are net realisable values with the qualitative characteristics of accounting information — particularly with respect to the primary quality of relevance?

In addition, it is noteworthy that the literature surveys[173] which were commissioned by the ICAS Research Committee in order to identify key issues for consideration in the production of the discussion paper reached the following conclusion on using net realisable values as the main basis for financial accounting: 'generally, the literature suggests that there is a strong case for the publication of NRV based figures as supplementary accounting information, as important information on liquidity, and on the adaptability of entities, is given which is not provided by the competing valuation bases. ... However, the arguments for the adoption of NRVs as the main valuation base of financial reports are uncompelling. The arguments against this, and in particular the lack of relevance of NRVs for many assets in most situations, are substantial. The income statement is likely to be misleading. One development which may be worthy of consideration is the publication of, possible supplementary, balance sheets based on net realisable values and income statements based on replacement costs or some other valuation base.'[174]

6.2.4   *The proposed new information package*

Despite the conclusions reached in the literature surveys, the committee proposed an entirely new information package, using net realisable values as the basis of valuation. In order to present the financial wealth of an entity, the committee proposed that the following four basic statements should replace the existing financial statements:

(a)   *Assets and Liabilities Statement*, which would present the assets and liabilities of the entity at the reporting date, each stated at its net realisable value. Net realisable values would normally be determined according to the principle of orderly disposal, unless the entity is in financial trouble, in which case 'a more appropriate method' (such as break-up values) should be used;[175]

(b)   *Operations Statement*, which calculates the financial wealth added to the entity by trading and by its operations generally. It differs from the present form profit and loss account in that:

(i)   there would be no depreciation charge,
(ii)   the stock would be accounted for at net realisable value, and
(iii)   the only exceptional or extraordinary items would be those arising out of unusual events of a revenue nature; exceptional or extraordinary gains or losses on fixed assets would be dealt with in the Statement of Changes in Financial Wealth outlined at (c) below;[176]

(c)   *Statement of Changes in Financial Wealth*, which shows the change in the worth of the business for the period under consideration, such change being split into its main components with an indication of how each of these arose. The committee proposes that the change in wealth would be measured in terms of year-end pounds, although 'in times of significant inflation it may be helpful if investors can be given an indication of the real change in financial wealth over the period concerned by applying the retail price index';[177] and

(d) *Distributions Statement*, which reflects the distributable change in financial wealth for the period plus any surpluses retained from previous periods, less dividends paid and proposed. In times of rising prices the 'real value' of capital should be maintained by an inflation adjustment which should be shown in the distributions statement and might be computed by applying the retail price index to the value of shareholders' contributed capital as at the start of the period. The paper goes on to say that entities wishing to maintain their operating capability in physical terms could make a further appropriation to maintain the asset portfolio or to provide for the replacement of the services which these assets have been supplying.[178]

6.2.5 Additional information

In addition to the four basic statements and the information relating to corporate objectives and future financial plans discussed under 6.2.2 above, the committee suggests the inclusion of the following additional information in the reporting package:

(a) a Cash Flow Statement showing the inflow and outflow of cash broken down into its main components, dealing with the current period and going three years forward.[179] This proposal is likely to prove highly controversial, particularly in the light of the recommendation that management should explain forecast variances (see 6.2.2 above);

(b) segmental information split by product, by manufacturing location, geographically and by currency;[180]

(c) information on related parties;

(d) information on accounting areas subject to uncertainty, for example management's view on the margin of error in accounting estimates;

(e) a statement on relative innovation which would illustrate the stance that the company is adopting in relation to innovation. In other words, the statement will show the proportion of production that is new and conceived internally or self-generated, and will compare this with that of its competitors;

(f) information on effectiveness and lead-time of research and development;

(g) information on the economic environment within which the entity operates, including an analysis of facts such as market share, market strength, market size, the activities of competitors etc.;

(h) comparative operational statistics 'culled from similar statements by its competitors or other entities in similar markets';[181]

(i) information on staff resources;

(j) information on ownership, management and their responsibilities.

The committee also makes the interesting suggestion that reports should be arranged on the basis of 'layering'.[182] In other words, each statement starts with the simplest possible presentation of the main factors, and as the user works through the information, it can be called down in layers of increasing complexity and detail.

6.2.6 Conclusion

This is one of the boldest, most innovative and refreshing discussion documents to be published by a professional body for a long time, exposing the several weaknesses of present day financial reporting practice. Of course it has flaws, and of course it can be criticised for either failing to address or inadequately addressing certain issues; however, it should be seen for what it is — a document designed to stimulate discussion, experimentation and further research. Nevertheless, there is always the danger that the document will be regarded as too revolutionary in its approach, and be dismissed as being an amusing intellectual exercise.

6.3   The IASC conceptual framework

In May 1988, the IASC issued an exposure draft — *Framework for the Preparation and Presentation of Financial Statements* — which sets out their understanding of 'the conceptual framework that underlies the preparation and presentation of financial statements.'[183] Although the ED is referred to as a 'proposed statement', it states clearly that it will not be issued as an International Accounting Standard; consequently, should the ED become a statement in the future, it will neither define standards for any particular measurement or disclosure issue, nor will it override any specific IAS.[184] Therefore, any statement which might eventually be issued will have much the same status as the FASB's concepts statements, although we believe that the IASC's draft will require a considerable amount of further development work before it can achieve credibility as a comprehensive theory of accounting. The reason for this is that whilst the ED commences with a useful and worthwhile discussion of the scope and objectives of financial statements, it is ultimately of limited use as a basis for deciding how financial reports could be better designed to meet these objectives.

On first reading the ED, one might be forgiven for thinking that it is merely an encapsulation of the FASB's six concepts statements; indeed, it is possible that the IASC, quite understandably, used the FASB project as a basis for their study. This might explain why it contains very much the same basic flaws as there are in the FASB's framework and which are discussed at 5 above. Furthermore, the impression that the ED creates is that the authors have attempted to justify the status quo; in other words, they appear to have tried to make the proposed framework consistent with current external financial reporting practice. This is evidenced, for example, by the statement in the introduction to the effect that financial statements normally include a balance sheet, a profit and loss statement, a statement of changes in financial position and notes;[185] the ED is then devoted to applying its 'framework' to this traditional financial reporting package, without, for example, following the ICAS approach of considering the possibility of an entirely new package.

The ED begins well, with a lucid exposition of the nature and purposes of financial statements and their qualitative characteristics. However, it then moves into describing the various elements of financial statements and the criteria for their recognition; although this is clearly a difficult area, it has not been dealt with convincingly. Thereafter, the ED loses its impetus altogether and deals with the measurement of these elements in a mere three paragraphs, only noting that a number of possibilities exist, including historical cost, current cost, realisable value and present value.[186]

However, the fundamental problem with this framework (as is the case with the FASB's framework) is that we do not believe that it is possible to develop general purpose rules on the recognition of elements of financial statements, whilst leaving open the questions of how they are to be measured and against what capital maintenance yardstick profit is to be determined. Furthermore, the ED has similar problems to SFAC No. 6 in its definitions of assets and liabilities, with the result that certain traditionally recognised assets and liabilities would be disqualified from appearing in the balance sheet. What the application of these definitions would mean is that there would be an attempt to 'get the balance sheet right' even at the expense of undermining the matching principle on which the profit and loss account is based; practical effects could include the immediate recognition in income of government grants as they are received, pension cost variations as soon as they are identified, and so on. The effect of this would be to change fundamentally the relationship between the profit and loss account and the balance sheet in a manner which could not be regarded as appropriate within the context of the historical cost convention. Therefore, until the measurement issue is resolved, it is futile to emphasise the balance sheet in a system where assets are measured at historical cost.

However, our purpose here is not to advocate one system as being superior to another; it is simply to explain that in our view it is not possible to fit all possible systems of accounting into one framework of rules on the elements of financial statements and their recognition. We believe that lack of clarity on this point has led to constant confusion on accounting concepts, where ideas which belong in discrete methodologies are used interchangeably and lead to a mish-mash which lacks any cohesion — an example is the practice of modifying historical cost accounting by revaluing assets in the balance sheet on a voluntary, arbitrary and unspecified basis, which thereby corrupts the measurement of profit in a way which the UK profession has been unable to rationalise. It should be the role of a conceptual framework study to unravel this tangle, but in this respect at least we believe that this document might simply compound the confusion by failing to distinguish the essential features which make different approaches mutually incompatible. We therefore hope that, in carrying their work forward, the authors of this ED find it possible to differentiate the features of alternative approaches which require the development of distinct rules on identification and recognition of the individual elements.

6.4   The Solomons Report

In May 1987, the Research Board of the ICAEW announced that it had decided to sponsor a project to address the need for guidelines for decisions in financial reporting; the project had been originally inspired by Professor Bryan Carsberg whilst he was the ICAEW's Director of Research, and Professor David Solomons, a recently retired academic, agreed to carry out the study. One of the reasons for the commissioning of the work was that in the written comments submitted to the ASC in response to various exposure drafts, reference had quite frequently been made to the fact that, until such time as an agreed conceptual framework was developed, it would be difficult to achieve either consistency in approach towards setting accounting standards, or resolution of certain of the fundamental accounting issues which were being encountered in practice. This was later borne out by the findings of the Dearing Committee, which concluded that 'the lack of a conceptual framework is a handicap to those involved in setting accounting standards as well as to those applying them.'[187]

Solomons followed what has become an almost traditional approach to a study of this nature; however, this is perhaps not surprising in view of the fact that he acted as consultant to the FASB on its conceptual framework project and was principal author of SFAC No. 2. He commenced by examining the purposes of financial reporting, the users of general purpose reports, their needs and how their needs are at present being met. His report then discusses the elements and sub-elements of financial statements and, in so doing, reaches a conclusion on the asset and liability vs the revenue and expense approach to financial accounting, thereby setting the scene for the rest of his study. This conclusion is that although 'there is no prospect of proving that one of these views is right and the other wrong, it is possible to find reasons for preferring one view to the other, and these Guidelines will be uncompromisingly based on the asset and liability view.'[188] Solomons' principal argument against the revenue and expense view of income determination is that it 'opens the door to all kinds of income smoothing';[189] he goes on to say that 'the revenue and expense view threatens the integrity of the balance sheet and its value as a useful financial statement. Its value is maximized if it can be seen as a statement of financial position; but it can only be that if all the items in it are truly assets, liabilities, and equity, and not other bits left over from the profit and loss account, and if all such items that are capable of being recognised are included in it.'[190]

It is noteworthy that Solomons' view of the primacy of the balance sheet is taken in the face of the findings of the empirical research conducted by Chang and Most referred to at 5.2 above. As part of their study, Chang and Most asked three user groups (individual investors, institutional investors and financial analysts) in three countries (the USA, UK and New Zealand) to rate the importance of selected parts of corporate annual reports for the purposes of making decisions about buying, holding and selling investments in equity. The results of their findings were that all three user groups in all three countries rated the income statement as the most important part of the corporate annual report.[191] It is, of course, possible that the views of users might change in the event of the balance sheet being presented on a basis of current values.

Having established the fact that he would be following an asset and liability approach, Solomons then sets about defining the elements of financial statements on much the same basis as was done in SFAC No. 6 (see 5.4 above). Assets are defined as 'resources or rights incontestably controlled by an entity at the accounting date that are expected to yield it future economic benefits',[192] whilst liabilities are defined as 'obligations of an entity at the accounting date to make future transfers of assets or services (sometimes uncertain as to timing and amount) to other entities.'[193] All the other elements are then derived from these basic definitions; for example, owners' equity comprises net assets and income is the change in net assets.[194]

Solomons then runs quickly through the qualitative characteristics of accounting information, giving what might be viewed as a summarised version of SFAC No. 2 (see 5.3 above). Thereafter he focuses his attention on the issues of recognition and measurement and the choice of an accounting model for use in preparing general purpose financial statements. In view of the fact that Solomons' guidelines are based on the recognition and measurement of assets and liabilities, it is not surprising that his recognition criteria focus on these two elements. Consequently, under Solomons' approach, an item should only be recognised in financial statements if:

'(a)   it conforms to the definition of an asset or liability or of one of the sub-elements derived therefrom; and

 (b)   its magnitude as specified by the accounting model being used can be measured and verified with reasonable certainty; and

 (c)   the magnitude so arrived at is material in amount.'[195]

Solomons then examined the present historical cost accounting model which is generally accepted in the UK, listing its deficiencies and pointing out that it is not a true historical cost model (as a result, for example, of asset revaluations and the translation of monetary assets and liabilities designated in foreign currencies at closing rates). Thereafter, he sets about devising an improved model for general purpose financial reporting, and lists the following five criteria that such an improved model should possess:

(a)   the balance sheet should be a true and fair statement of an entity's financial condition, showing all its assets and liabilities that satisfy the above recognition criteria and conform with the asset and liability definitions;

(b)   the entity's assets and liabilities should be carried in the balance sheet at their value to a going concern at the balance sheet date;

(c)   profits or losses should mean increases or decreases of real financial capital as compared with the amount at the beginning of the year;

(d)   the results shown by the financial statements should be measured consistently and should therefore be comparable from year to year, both in periods of fluctuating prices and stable prices;

(e)   all the information given by the financial statements should be verifiable and cost-effective.[196]

Solomons then sets out to prove that the model which satisfies these requirements better than any other rests on two concepts: value to the business (as espoused by the Corporate Report and Sandilands Committee) and the maintenance of real financial capital. Solomons sees an asset's value to the business as being the loss that the business would suffer if it were deprived of the asset; since, if deprived of an asset, the business would normally seek to replace it, replacement cost would determine value to the business. However, Solomons recognises that circumstances exist where an asset's value to the business might be be less than its replacement cost; for example, in the case of a plant asset which is technologically inferior to an equivalent new asset, the current cost of replacing the services rendered by the existing asset should be used. Furthermore, where an asset would not be replaced by a business if it were lost, its value to the business would be its recoverable amount, which is the higher of the assets present value and its net realisable value. Therefore, Solomons' final formula for value to the business is that it is equal to 'current cost or recoverable amount, if that is lower'.[197]

In the case of liabilities, the equivalent to an asset's deprival value is a liability's relief value. In other words, liabilities would be valued at the amount that the entity 'could currently raise by the issue of a precisely similar debt security or the cost of discharging the liability by the most economical means, whichever is the higher.'[198]

Solomons ends his discussion on 'value to the business' by referring to the ICAS Discussion Document — *Making Corporate Reports Valuable* — and explains why he believes net realisable values to be irrelevant, resulting in net realisable value accounting being unsuitable for general purpose financial statements.

As mentioned above, Solomons' model is based on the maintenance of real financial capital, with income being defined in terms of the change in net worth. However, because of the uncertainty surrounding the measurement and verification of intangible assets, the changes in such assets cannot be recognised in financial statements; consequently, income will only include changes in recognised tangible assets minus changes in recognised liabilities.[199] Solomons describes his income model as a 'current-cost-constant-purchasing-power model', differing in a number of respects from the SSAP 16 model. Firstly, it recognises both changes in the general level of prices and changes in specific prices and, secondly, it is based on the maintenance of real financial capital, not operating capacity.[200] It therefore does not require SSAP 16's unpopular gearing and monetary working capital adjustments.

The following pro forma profit and loss account illustrates how Solomons' version of real income is derived:[201]

		£
Sales revenue		xxx
Current cost (or lower recoverable amount) of goods sold		xxx
		xxx
Depreciation at current cost	xxx	
Other expenses	xxx	
		xxx
Current operating profit		xxx
Add:		
Holding gains less losses on non-monetary assets (net of inflation)	xxx	
Purchasing power gains on monetary liabilities less purchasing power losses on monetary assets	xxx	
		xxx
Real income		xxx

In an appendix to his report, Solomons discusses five specific accounting issues: deferred tax, pensions, financial commitments, goodwill and the recognition of the time value of money. Although it is beyond the scope of this chapter to discuss the contents of the appendix in detail, there are one or two interesting points worth noting. In the case of deferred tax, Solomons, builds up an argument against both the partial approach adopted by SSAP 15 and the non-recognition of deferred tax assets. Using accounts payable as an illustration of liabilities which are continually being paid off and replaced, he argues that non-replacement should not be the criterion for recognition of deferred tax liabilities. Similarly, in respect of deferred tax assets he asserts that, as is the case with accounts receivable and depreciable assets, deferred tax benefits, if expected to be recovered, with or without replacement, should be recognised as assets.[202]

As has been mentioned above, one of the consequences of the asset and liability approach proposed, for example, by both the IASC and Solomons results in a conflict with the generally accepted accounting practice of accounting for pensions under SSAP 24. It is therefore not surprising that this is one of the specific areas discussed by Solomons in the appendix to his report, in which he lays down a number of principles that deviate significantly from SSAP 24's approach. For example, if all or most of the assets of a pension plan can be freely moved back to the employer from the plan by a vote of the trustees, then the affairs of the plan should be consolidated with those of the employer. This approach is based on the view that a pension fund is, in effect, an off-balance sheet vehicle set up to meet a company's future obligations. Whilst this view might have considerable theoretical merit, the practical implications make Solomons' proposal completely unworkable; the reason being that each time the pension fund has an actuarial valuation, the slightest variation in the assumptions (which, by their nature, are highly volatile and imprecise) will have an unacceptable impact on the profit and loss account, which has no real bearing on operating performance or current wealth.

Furthermore, contrary to the requirements of both SSAP 24 and SFAS 87, Solomons maintains that past service cost resulting from a plan amendment during the year should be accounted for as a prior period adjustment to the extent that it applies to services rendered before the beginning of the current accounting period, and as an exceptional item in the profit and loss account of the current period to the extent that it applies to services rendered in the current period.[203]

On the subject of goodwill, Solomons states that non-purchased goodwill should not be recognised; his reason for this being that 'determining the value of goodwill where it is not the subject of a purchase and sale transaction and in the presence of a highly imperfect market is too subjective to yield a reliable measure for the purpose of recognition.'[204] What he is, in fact, saying is that since non-purchased goodwill does not have an historical cost, it is not possible to update an unknown cost in order to determine its current cost. The same argument applies to all internally generated intangibles, such as brand names.

Only time will tell what will ultimately become of Solomons' Guidelines. Their future will probably depend on what steps are taken to implement the Dearing report by forming a new body to take on the work of setting accounting standards in the UK. It may then be that the new Accounting Standards Board (or its equivalent) will use Solomons's Guidelines as the catalyst for a concerted effort towards finding an agreed conceptual framework.

6.5   The CICA financial statement concepts

In December 1988, the CICA *Handbook* Section 1000 — *Financial Statement Concepts* — was issued, describing the concepts underlying the development and use of accounting principles in the general purpose financial statements of profit oriented enterprises.[205] It is anticipated that the concepts will be used 'by preparers of financial statements and accounting practitioners in exercising their professional judgement as to the application of generally accepted accounting principles and in establishing accounting policies in areas in which accounting principles are developing.'[206] However, nothing in Section 1000 overrides any specific recommendation in any other Section of the CICA Handbook, or any other accounting principle considered to be generally accepted.

In fact, both the form and content of Section 1000 are very similar to the IASC's framework ED discussed at 6.3 above, dealing with the objective of financial statements, qualitative characteristics, elements of financial statements, recognition criteria and measurement in much the same way. The definitions of assets and liabilities are almost identical in the two pronouncements, and Section 1000 also does not establish standards for particular measurement or disclosure issues.

7 SSAP 2: DISCLOSURE OF ACCOUNTING POLICIES

Although SSAP 2,[207] which was issued in 1971, was not the first accounting standard to be published, it is probably the most fundamental since its principles pervade financial reporting practice in the UK. The overall objectives of SSAP 2 are to assist in user understanding and interpretation of financial statements by promoting the improvement in the quality of information disclosed. It seeks to achieve this by establishing as generally accepted accounting practice the disclosure in financial statements of clear explanations of the accounting policies followed in the preparation of the financial statements, in so far as these are significant for the purpose of giving a true and fair view.

SSAP 2 develops the standard accounting practice for the disclosure of accounting policies in three stages; firstly, it describes the four fundamental accounting concepts, it then relates these to the development of accounting bases, and finally it deals with the selection of accounting policies.

7.1 Fundamental accounting concepts

Fundamental accounting concepts are the broad basic assumptions which underlie the periodic financial statements of business entities. The use of the four concepts listed below is not generally stated in financial statements, but they have such general acceptance that they call for no explanation in published statements and their observance is presumed unless stated otherwise. They are practical rules rather than theoretical ideals and are capable of variation and evolution as accounting thought and practice develop.[208]

7.1.1 The going concern concept

This concept is applied on the basis that the reporting entity will continue in operational existence for the foreseeable future. This means in particular that the balance sheet and profit and loss account assume no intention or necessity to liquidate or curtail significantly the scale of business operations.[209]

7.1.2 The accruals (or matching) concept

In the presentation of the profit and loss account, revenue and profits recognised are matched with the associated costs and expenses incurred in earning them. In order to achieve this, revenues, profits, costs and expenses are accrued (i.e. recognised as they are earned or incurred, not as cash is received or paid), matched with one another in so far as their relationship can be established or justifiably assumed, and dealt with in the profit and loss account for the period to which they relate. However, where the accruals concept is inconsistent with the prudence concept (described at 7.1.4 below), the latter prevails.[210]

7.1.3   The consistency concept

In terms of the consistency concept, there should be consistency of accounting treatment of like items within each accounting period and from one period to the next.

7.1.4   The prudence concept

Under the prudence concept, revenue and profits are not anticipated but are recognised by inclusion in the profit and loss account only when realised in the form of cash or of other assets the ultimate cash realisation of which can be assessed with reasonable certainty. On the other hand, provision is made for all known liabilities whether the amount of these is known with certainty or is a best estimate in the light of the information available.

These four fundamental accounting concepts, together with a fifth concept, have broadly been adopted by the Companies Act 1985 as the accounting principles which should be used in the determination of all items shown in a company's financial statements, although the terms in which they are described are not identical.[211] The fifth principle introduced by the Companies Act is the principle of 'non-aggregation'. This principle states that 'in determining the aggregate amount of any item the amount of each individual asset or liability that falls to be taken into account shall be determined separately.'[212] For example, compensating inaccuracies in individual amounts should not be lost in one large total, and a group of assets should be valued on an individual asset basis, as opposed to a portfolio basis.

7.2   Accounting bases

Accounting bases are 'the methods developed for applying fundamental concepts to financial transactions and items, for the purpose of financial accounts, and in particular:

(a)   for determining the accounting periods in which revenue and costs should be recognised in the profit and loss account; and

(b)   for determining the amounts at which material items should be stated in the balance sheet.'[213]

Accounting bases, therefore, are accounting treatments which have evolved in response to the necessity of having to apply the fundamental concepts to areas of practice. However, because of the variety and complexity of types of business and business transactions, there may exist more than one legitimate accounting basis for dealing with a particular item; for example, there are several acceptable accounting bases for the depreciation of fixed assets, each of which is suited to particular types of assets and business circumstances.

7.3   Accounting policies

Having established that there exist several recognised accounting bases in respect of individual accounting issues, it is necessary for the management of an entity to select those bases which are most appropriate for their own particular circumstances; those bases selected then become the entity's accounting policies.

Consequently, accounting policies are defined as 'the specific accounting bases selected and consistently followed by a business enterprise as being, in the opinion of management, appropriate to its circumstances and best suited to present fairly its results and financial position.'[214] Thereafter, the accounting policies selected for dealing with items which are judged material in determining financial position and profit or loss for the year should be disclosed by way of note to the financial statements.[215]

This means, for example, that management should select those bases of depreciating fixed assets which are most appropriate to the types of assets and their use in the business so as to allocate depreciation as fairly as possible to the periods expected to benefit from the use of the assets, and these bases selected should be set out in an accounting policy note to the financial statements. However, this highlights an interesting conflict between SSAP 2 and SSAP 12 — *Accounting for depreciation.* Under SSAP 2, for example, the sum-of-digits and straight-line methods of depreciation are two acceptable accounting bases, each of which is appropriate to a particular pattern of asset use; in the event of management deciding that it would be more appropriate to depreciate an asset according to the sum-of-digits basis as opposed to the straight line basis, this would constitute a change in accounting basis, and therefore a change in accounting policy. SSAP 12, however, states that a change from one method of providing depreciation to another 'does not constitute a change of accounting policy';[216] furthermore, no explanation is given in SSAP 12 for this departure from the principles laid down in SSAP 2.

7.4 The missing accounting concepts: substance over form and materiality

It is possible to suggest several accounting concepts which might have been included in addition to the four listed in SSAP 2. However, there are two concepts which, arguably, are the most notable omissions from the standard, namely the concepts of 'substance over form' and 'materiality'.

7.4.1 Substance over form

Under this concept, transactions and other events are accounted for and presented in financial statements in accordance with their economic substance and financial reality and not merely with their legal form. This concept has been applied in the requirements relating to the capitalisation of finance leases in the financial statements of lessees under SSAP 21, and forms the basis of the approach adopted by the ASC in ED 42 in its attempt to deal with off-balance sheet finance (see Chapter 5). However, we believe that the adoption of substance over form as a fundamental accounting concept would go a long way towards ensuring that the spirit, as opposed to the letter, of the SSAPs is applied.

7.4.2 Materiality

SFAC No. 2 states that 'the essence of the materiality concept is clear. The omission or misstatement of an item in a financial report is material if, in the light of surrounding circumstances, the magnitude of the item is such that it is probable that the judgement of a reasonable person relying upon the report would have been changed or influenced by the inclusion or correction of the item.'[217] Materiality is mentioned both in the ASC's explanatory foreword to the SSAPs and in the Companies Act; the former says that 'accounting standards need not be applied to items whose effect is judged to be immaterial to an understanding of the financial statements',[218] while the latter says (in relation to Schedule 4) that 'amounts which in the particular context of any provision of this Schedule are not material may be disregarded for the purpose of that provision'.[219] In addition, there are several paragraphs in individual accounting standards and in company law which state that specific requirements should be overridden by materiality considerations. However, SSAP 2 does not give any general guidance on the meaning of the concept and how it should be applied, and this would be a useful addition in any future revision of the standard.

The concept should be seen, not as one which imposes financial reporting requirements of its own, but rather as one which can modify other requirements which have arisen in response to other concepts. For example, the concept of relevance might call for information of a certain kind to be shown, but if the information in question is immaterial then it ceases to be relevant and the requirement to disclose it falls away. The important question, however, is against which yardstick information should be judged to be material or immaterial.

Essentially, the frame of reference must be based on that information which the user of accounts would judge to be important in relation to decisions that he wishes to make on the basis of the financial statements. If the non-disclosure of certain information, or the alteration of a figure in the financial statements by a certain amount, would have no effect on the decisions of the user, then it can be disregarded as being immaterial.

The difficulty which then arises is that the many different users of the financial statements cannot be consulted by the preparer to discover what is material to them; the preparer must make that assessment on their behalf. Moreover, some users might have unreasonable expectations of the accuracy of financial statements, and it would not be possible to set materiality at a level which could accommodate their wishes; for example an adjustment of a single pound in the profit reported by the company will have a direct effect on the tax authorities' decision as to how much tax to assess, but it is clearly impossible to prepare accounts which measure results with this degree of accuracy. Accordingly materiality could be described more accurately as to be assessed in relation to the information which the preparer believes will be relevant to the decisions of those users of accounts who have legitimate expectations as to the accuracy of the information in the financial statements.

8   THE WAY AHEAD

The aims of this chapter have been twofold: firstly, we have attempted to provide an outline of the immense amount of energy that has been expended (both on the part of individuals and on the part of specifically constituted committees) in attempting to establish an agreed conceptual framework for financial reporting; secondly, in so doing, we have highlighted the irreconcilable differences that exist in the various accounting theories that have developed over the years. We see little prospect of general agreement ever being reached on issues such as entry values vs exit values or the primacy of the balance sheet vs the profit and loss account. The fact that these differences are irreconcilable is the very reason why it will not be possible to develop a single generally accepted general purpose accounting model.

However, this does not mean that the search should be abandoned; what it does mean is that an agreed conceptual framework might have to incorporate more than one accounting model so that different users can be furnished with different information appropriate to their various objectives and information needs. This would not necessarily involve supplying less financial information to individual user groups; rather it would mean making sure that each user group has all the information it needs for its investment and other decisions. Such a system might incorporate some form of multi-column reporting, or, alternatively, be arranged on the basis of 'layering' as proposed by the ICAS discussion document (see 6.2.5 above).

Even if the quest for a genuinely comprehensive framework can only be seen as a very long term ideal, a more limited goal might be attainable in the shorter term. Where equally meritorious choices of approach exist, such as whether to give primacy to the balance sheet or the profit and loss account, it must be better to adopt one approach consistently in all areas of accounting, rather than to apply different approaches whenever a fresh issue is addressed. It would therefore be helpful if the Accounting Standards Board (or whatever body takes on the task) were to examine these differences of approach and the arguments which lie behind them and, even if it is unable to decide between them on the merits of their intellectual appeal, resolve to apply whatever alternatives seem to be the most workable in practice.

References

1 ASC, *Setting Accounting Standards: A Consultative document.*
2 *Ibid.*, para. 7.2.
3 *Ibid.*
4 *Ibid.*, para. 7.7.
5 *Ibid.*, p. 47.
6 *Ibid.*
7 ASC, *Submissions on the Accounting Standards Committee's Consultative Document: Setting Accounting Standards*, in two volumes, ASC, 1979.
8 *Ibid.*, Volume I, p. 270.
9 For a full discussion on the politicisation of accounting see: David Solomons, 'The Politicization of Accounting', *Journal of Accountancy*, November 1978, p. 71.
10 W. A. Paton and A. C. Littleton, *An Introduction to Corporate Accounting Standards*, Monograph No. 3, American Accounting Association, 1940.
11 See, for example: American Accounting Association, Executive Committee, 'A Tentative Statement of Accounting Principles Affecting Corporate Reports', *Accounting Review*, June

1936, pp. 187—191; American Accounting Association, Executive Committee, 'Accounting Principles Underlying Corporate Financial Statements', *Accounting Review*, June 1941, pp. 133—139; American Accounting Association, Committee to Prepare a Statement of Basic Accounting Theory, *A Statement of Basic Accounting Theory*, 1966; American Accounting Association, Committee on Concepts and Standards for External Financial Reports, *Statement on Accounting Theory and Theory Acceptance*, 1977. The 1977 report concluded that closure on the debate was not feasible, which is perhaps indicative of the complexity of the problem.

12 David Solomons, 'The Political Implications of Accounting and Accounting Standard Setting', *Being the third Arthur Young Lecture delivered within the University of Glasgow on 22nd October, 1980*, p. 9.

13 Maurice Moonitz, *The Basic Postulates of Accounting*, Accounting Research Study No. 1, AICPA, 1961, Preface.

14 Maurice Moonitz, *op. cit.*

15 Robert T. Sprouse and Maurice Moonitz, *A Tentative Set of Broad Accounting Principles for Business Enterprises*, Accounting Research Study No. 3, AICPA, 1962.

16 *Ibid.*, p. 14.

17 *Ibid.*, p. 27.

18 APB Statement No. 4, *Basic Concepts and Accounting Principles Underlying Financial Statements of Business Enterprises*, AICPA, October 1970.

19 *Ibid.*, para. 3.

20 *Ibid.*, para. 132.

21 Report of the Study Group on the Objectives of Financial Statements, *Objectives of Financial Statements*, AICPA, October 1973, p. 65.

22 *Ibid.*

23 *Ibid.*

24 Report of the Study Group on the Objectives of Financial Statements, *Objectives of Financial Statements*, AICPA, October 1973.

25 *Ibid.*, p. 13.

26 *Ibid.*, pp. 57—60.

27 FASB Discussion Memorandum, *Conceptual Framework for Accounting and Reporting: Consideration of the Report of the Study Group on the Objectives of Financial Statements*, FASB, June 6, 1974.

28 FASB, *Scope and Implications of the Conceptual Framework Project*, FASB, December 2, 1976.

29 *Ibid.*, p. 5.

30 *The Corporate Report*, A discussion paper published for comment by the Accounting Standards Steering Committee, London, 1975.

31 *Ibid.*, para. 0.1.

32 *Ibid.*, para. 0.2.

33 The committee's recommended package of information which should be contained in the annual corporate reports of business enterprises is listed in Appendix 2 of the discussion paper.

34 *The Corporate Report*, para. 0.3.

35 *Ibid.*, para. 1.1.

36 *Ibid.*, para. 1.8.

37 *Ibid.*, para. 1.9. The seven user groups identified were: (a) the equity investor group, (b) the loan creditor group, (c) the employee group, (d) the analyst-adviser group, (e) the business contact group (f) the government and (g) the public.

38 *Ibid.*, paras. 2.1—2.40.

39 *Ibid.*, para. 3.2.

40 *Ibid.*, para. 3.3.

41 *Ibid.*, para. 4.30.

42 *Ibid.*, para. 4.40.

4 3 *Ibid.*, para. 6.56.

4 4 *Ibid.*, paras. 6.56 and 6.57.

4 5 *Ibid.*, para. 7.4.

4 6 *Ibid.*, para. 7.15.

4 7 *Ibid.*, paras. 7.40 and 7.43.

4 8 Report of the Inflation Accounting Committee, *Inflation Accounting*, Cmnd. 6225, London: HMSO 1975. (The Sandilands Report.)

4 9 *Ibid.*, p. iv.

5 0 *Ibid.*, para. 144.

5 1 *Ibid.*, Chapter 12.

5 2 SSAP 7 (Provisional), *Accounting for changes in the purchasing power of money*, May 1974.

5 3 SSAP 7 recommended that the RPI should be used for this purpose.

5 4 SSAP 7, para. 12.

5 5 The Sandilands Report, para. 20.

5 6 *Ibid.*, para. 422.

5 7 *Ibid.*, paras. 411 and 412.

5 8 *Ibid.*, para. 415.

5 9 Edwards and Bell have made significant contributions in the areas of income determination and value measurement — however, it is beyond the scope of this book to provide a detailed analysis of their theories. Their case for income and value measurement based on replacement costs may be found in their classic work: E. O. Edwards and P.W. Bell, *The Theory and Measurement of Business Income*, University of California Press, 1961.

6 0 The Sandilands Report, para. 453.

6 1 *Ibid.*, para. 499.

6 2 Kenneth MacNeal, *Truth in Accounting*, Philadelphia: University of Pennsylvania Press, 1939.

6 3 R. J. Chambers, *Accounting, Evaluation and Economic Behaviour*, Prentice-Hall, 1966.

6 4 R. R. Sterling, *Theory of the Measurement of Enterprise Income*, University of Kansas Press, 1970.

6 5 R. J. Chambers, *The Design of Accounting Standards*, University of Sydney Accounting Research Centre, Monograph No. 1, 1980.

6 6 Edward Stamp, 'Does the Chambers' Evidence Support the CoCoA System', *Accounting and Business Research*, Spring 1983, pp. 119—127.

6 7 *Ibid.*, p. 127.

6 8 The Sandilands Report, para. 510.

6 9 The Institute of Chartered Accountants of Scotland, *Making Corporate Reports Valuable*, London: Kogan Page, 1988, paras. 6.20—6.23.

7 0 Lee has published numerous papers on the subject of cash flow accounting, the ideas of which have been drawn together in his book: Tom Lee, *Cash Flow Accounting*, Wokingham, Van Nostrand Reinhold (UK), 1984.

7 1 Lawson has published widely on the subject of cash flow accounting — see, for example: G. H. Lawson, 'Cash-flow Accounting', *The Accountant*, October 28th, 1971, pp. 586-589; G. H. Lawson, 'The Measurement of Corporate Profitability on a Cash-flow Basis', *The International Journal of Accounting Education and Research*, Vol. 16, No. 1, pp. 11—46.

7 2 Tom Lee, *op. cit.*, p. 51.

7 3 *Ibid.*, pp. 51—52.

7 4 Lee presents a quantified example of his proposed cash flow reporting system, *op. cit.*, pp. 57—72.

7 5 The Sandilands Report, para. 518.

7 6 *Ibid.*, para. 517.

7 7 *Ibid.*, para. 537.

78 For a detailed discussion of the capital maintenance concepts which apply in the Sandilands proposals, see: H. C. Edey, 'Sandilands and the Logic of Current Cost', *Accounting and Business Research*, Volume 9, No. 35, Summer 1979, pp. 191—200.

79 ASC, *ED 24: Current cost accounting*, para. 6.

80 ASC, *Inflation accounting — an interim recommendation by the Accounting Standards Committee*, November 1977.

81 *Ibid*., para. 4.

82 ED 24, para. 8.

83 *Ibid*.

84 *Ibid*., para. 9.

85 SSAP 16, *Current cost accounting*, March 1980.

86 *Ibid*., para. 48.

87 SFAS No. 33, *Financial Reporting and Changing Prices*, paras. 47—56 *passim*.

88 SFAS No. 89, *Financial Reporting and Changing Prices*, paras. 34, 35 and 40—43 *passim*.

89 SFAC No. 5, *Recognition and Measurement in Financial Statements of Business Enterprises*, December 1984, paras. 45—48.

90 In January 1983, the Research Board of the ICAEW initiated a research project into the usefulness of current cost accounting. The research was divided into a number of studies designed to investigate the uses made by different interest groups, the benefits and the costs of current cost accounting; the whole project was undertaken under the control of the ICAEW's then Director of Research, Professor Bryan Carsberg. The project was completed in September 1983 and the results were made available to the ASC to assist with its review of SSAP 16. See: Bryan Carsberg and Michael Page (Joint Editors), *Current Cost Accounting: The Benefits and the Costs*, ICAEW, 1984.

91 Accounting Standards Committee, *Accounting for the effects of changing prices: a Handbook*, ASC, 1986.

92 It is still fairly widely used in the public sector, partly influenced by the Byatt Report — *Accounting for Economic Costs and Changing Prices* — published in 1986.

93 Richard Macve, *A Conceptual Framework for Financial Accounting and Reporting: the possibilities for an agreed structure*, A report prepared at the request of the Accounting Standards Committee, ICAEW, 1981, Preface, p. 3.

94 *Ibid*., Chapter 6, *passim*.

95 *Ibid*., p. 52.

96 *Ibid*., p. 64.

97 *Ibid*., p. 91.

98 David Solomons, *Guidelines for Financial Reporting Standards*, A Paper Prepared for The Research Board of the Institute of Chartered Accountants in England and Wales and addressed to the Accounting Standards Committee, ICAEW, 1989, (the Solomons Report).

99 Edward Stamp, *Corporate Reporting: Its Future Evolution*, a research study published by the Canadian Institute of Chartered Accountants, 1980, (the Stamp Report), Ch. 1, para. 3.

100 The Corporate Report, paras. 2.22—2.31.

101 Stamp's proposed user groups were as follows: shareholders, management, long and short-term creditors, analysts and advisers, employees, non-executive directors, customers, suppliers, industry groups, labour unions, government departments and ministers, the public, regulatory agencies, other companies, standard setters and academic researchers. See the Stamp Report, Table 1, p. 44.

102 Edward Stamp, 'First steps towards a British conceptual framework', *Accountancy*, March 1982, pp. 123—130.

103 Stamp's qualitative criteria were ranked (from most important to least important) by the ASC members as follows (*Ibid*., Figure 2, p. 126):
relevance, clarity, substance over form, timeliness, comparability, materiality, freedom from bias, objectivity, rationality, full disclosure, consistency, isomorphism, verifiability, cost/benefit effectiveness, non-arbitrariness, data availability, flexibility, uniformity, precision, conservatism.

104 The Stamp Report, Chapter 2.
105 *Ibid.*, Chapter 12.
106 FASB, *Scope and Implications of the Conceptual Framework Project*, p. 2.
107 *Ibid.*, pp. 5 and 6.
108 SFAC No. 1, *Objectives of Financial Reporting by Business Enterprises*, para. 7.
109 *Ibid.*, para. 9.
110 *Ibid.*, para. 24.
111 *Ibid.*, para. 34.
112 *Ibid.*, para. 37.
113 *Ibid.*, p. 18, footnote 6.
114 Lucia S. Chang and Kenneth S. Most, *Financial Statements and Investment Decisions*, Miami: Florida International University, 1979.
115 *Ibid.*, p. 33.
116 *Ibid.*, para. 43.
117 *Ibid.*, para. 50.
118 *Ibid.*, para. 51.
119 David Solomons, *Guidelines for Financial Reporting Standards*.
120 SFAC No. 2, *Qualitative Characteristics of Accounting Information*, p. 15.
121 SFAC No. 1, para. 34.
122 *Ibid.*, para 36.
123 SFAC No. 2, p. x.
124 *Ibid.*, para. 90.
125 *Ibid.*, p. xi.
126 *Ibid.*, para. 56.
127 *Ibid.*
128 *Ibid.*, para. 51.
129 *Ibid.*, p. xvi.
130 *Ibid.*
131 *Ibid.*, para. 59.
132 *Ibid.*, paras. 91—97.
133 *Ibid.*, para. 93.
134 *Ibid.*, para. 95.
135 SFAC No. 6, *Elements of Financial Statements*, para. 25.
136 *Ibid.*, para. 27.
137 *Ibid.*, para. 28.
138 *Ibid.*, para. 35
139 *Ibid.*, para. 36.
140 *Ibid.*, para. 49.
141 *Ibid.*, para. 66.
142 *Ibid.*
143 *Ibid.*, para. 67.
144 *Ibid.*, para. 70.
145 SFAC No. 1, para. 43.
146 SFAC No. 6, p. 1, footnote 1.
147 *Ibid.*, para. 78.
148 *Ibid.*, para. 80.
149 *Ibid.*, para. 82.
150 *Ibid.*, para. 83.
151 *Ibid.*, para. 77.
152 See, for example, SFAC No. 3, *Elements of Financial Statements of Business Enterprises*, para. 58.
153 SFAC No. 5, para. 66.
154 *Ibid.*, paras. 66—70.
155 *Ibid.*, paras. 45—48.

156 *Ibid.*, para. 58.
157 *Ibid.*, para. 63.
158 *Ibid.*, paras. 33 and 34.
159 *Ibid.*, para. 35.
160 David Solomons, 'The FASB's Conceptual Framework: An Evaluation', *Journal of Accountancy*, June 1986, pp. 114—124, at p. 124.
161 SFAC No. 5, para. 13.
162 The Institute of Chartered Accountants of Scotland, *Making Corporate Reports Valuable*, Kogan Page, 1988.
163 *Ibid.*, para. 0.2.
164 *Ibid.*, Chapter 8.
165 *Ibid.*, paras. 1.1—1.20, *passim.*
166 *Ibid.*, para. 3.6.
167 *Ibid.*, para. 3.11.
168 The Corporate Report, paras. 2.2—2.8.
169 ICAS, *Making Corporate Reports Valuable*, para. 3.12.
170 *Ibid.*, para. 6.36.
171 *Ibid.*
172 *Ibid.*, para. 6.24.
173 The Institute of Chartered Accountants of Scotland, *Making Corporate Reports Valuable — The Literature Surveys*, ICAS, 1988.
174 *Ibid.*, p. 301.
175 ICAS, *Making Corporate Reports Valuable*, paras. 7.12—7.20, *passim.*
176 *Ibid.*, para. 7.21.
177 *Ibid.*, paras. 7.23—7.26, *passim.*
178 *Ibid.*, paras. 7.27—7.32, *passim.*
179 *Ibid.*, para. 7.35.
180 *Ibid.*, 7.39.
181 *Ibid.*, para. 5.44.
182 *Ibid.*, para. 7.54.
183 IASC, *Framework for the Preparation and Presentation of Financial Statements*, IASC, May 1988.
184 *Ibid.*, para. 2.
185 *Ibid.*, para. 7.
186 *Ibid.*, paras. 97—99.
187 Report of the Review Committee under the chairmanship of Sir Ronald Dearing CB, *The Making of Accounting Standards*, September 1988, para. 7.2.
188 David Solomons, *Guidelines for Financial Reporting Standards*, p. 17.
189 *Ibid.*, p. 18.
190 *Ibid.*
191 Lucia S. Chang and Kenneth S. Most, *Financial Statements and Investment Decisions*, p. 61.
192 David Solomons, *Guidelines for Financial Reporting Standards*, p. 20.
193 *Ibid.*, p. 21.
194 *Ibid.*, pp. 23—28.
195 *Ibid.*, p. 43.
196 *Ibid.*, pp. 51—52.
197 *Ibid.*, p. 53.
198 *Ibid.*
199 *Ibid.*, p. 54.
200 *Ibid.*, p. 55.
201 *Ibid.*, p. 56.
202 *Ibid.*, p. 63.
203 *Ibid.*, p. 65.
204 *Ibid.*, p. 69.

205 CICA Handbook, General Accounting, Section 1000, *Financial Statement Concepts*, para. .01.
206 *Ibid.*, para. .02.
207 SSAP 2, *Disclosure of accounting policies*, November 1971.
208 *Ibid.*, para. 2.
209 *Ibid.*, para. 14.
210 *Ibid.*
211 CA 85, Sch. 4. paras. 9—13.
212 *Ibid.*, para. 14.
213 SSAP 2, para. 15.
214 *Ibid.*, para. 16.
215 *Ibid.*, para. 18.
216 SSAP 12, *Accounting for depreciation*, para. 21.
217 SFAC No. 2, para. 132.
218 Explanatory foreword to Statements of Standard Accounting Practice, para. 4.
219 CA 85, Sch. 4, para 86.

Chapter 3

Revenue recognition

1 THE NATURE OF REVENUE

Revenue is generally discussed in accounting literature in terms of inflows of assets to an enterprise which occur as a result of outflows of goods and services from the enterprise. For this reason, the concept of revenue has normally been associated with specific accounting procedures which were primarily directed towards determining the timing and measurement of revenue in the context of the historical cost double-entry system. For example, APB Statement No. 4 defined revenue as the 'gross increases in assets or gross decreases in liabilities recognized and measured in conformity with generally accepted accounting principles that result from those types of profit-directed activities of an enterprise that can change owners' equity'.[1] Consequently, the accounting principles which evolved focused on determining when transactions should be recognised in the financial statements, what amounts were involved in each transaction, how these amounts should be classified and how they should be allocated between accounting periods.

Historical cost accounting in its pure form avoids having to take a valuation approach to financial reporting by virtue of the fact that it is transactions based; in other words, it relies on transactions to determine the recognition and measurement of assets, liabilities, revenues and expenses. Over the life of an enterprise, its total income will be represented by net cash flows generated; however, because of the requirement to prepare periodic financial statements, it is necessary to break up the enterprise's operating cycle into artificial periods. The effect of this is that at each reporting date the enterprise will have entered into a number of transactions which are incomplete; for example, it might have delivered a product or service to a customer for which payment has not been received, or it might have received payment in respect of a product or service yet to be delivered. Alternatively, it might have expended cash on costs which relate to future exchange transactions, or it might have received goods and services which it has not yet paid for in cash. Consequently, the most important accounting questions which have to be answered revolve around how to allocate the effects of these incomplete transactions between periods for reporting purposes, as opposed to simply letting them fall into the periods in which cash is either received or paid. This allocation process is based on two, sometimes conflicting, fundamental accounting concepts: accruals (or matching), which attempts to move the costs associated with earning revenues to the periods in which the related revenues will be reported; and prudence, under which revenue and profits are not anticipated, whilst anticipated losses are provided for as soon as they are foreseen, with the result that costs are not deferred to the future if there is doubt as to their recoverability.

As a result, the pure historical cost balance sheet contains items of two types: cash (and similar monetary items), and debits and credits which arise as a result of shifting the effects of transactions between reporting periods by applying the accruals and prudence concepts; in other words, the balance sheet simply reflects the balances which result from the enterprise preparing an accruals based profit and loss account rather than a receipts and payments account. A non-monetary asset under the historical cost system is purely a deferred cost; a cost which has been incurred before the balance sheet date and, by applying the accruals concept, is expected (provided it passes the prudence test) to benefit periods beyond the balance sheet date, so as to justify its being carried forward. Similarly, the balance sheet incorporates credit balances which are awaiting recognition in the profit and loss account but, as a result of the application of the prudence concept, have been deferred to future reporting periods.

It is the aim of this chapter to suggest broad principles under the existing historical cost accounting system for the recognition of revenues earned from operations.

2   REALISED PROFITS

The term 'realised profits' was introduced into UK company legislation in the Companies Act 1980 as a result of the implementation of the 2nd EC Directive on company law. The 1980 Act restricted a company's profits available for distribution to its accumulated realised profits less accumulated realised losses. Although this provision reversed the principle which had been laid down in a number of legal cases which permitted companies to make distributions out of current profits without making good past losses, it did not define 'realised profits'. However, a definition was subsequently provided as a result of the implementation of the 4th EC Directive in the Companies Act 1981; this definition was later incorporated into Schedule 4 of the Companies Act 1985 as follows: '... references in this Schedule to realised profits, in relation to a company's accounts, are to such profits of the company as fall to be treated as realised profits for the purposes of those accounts in accordance with principles generally accepted with respect to the determination for accounting purposes of realised profits at the time when those accounts are prepared'.[2]

This definition, therefore, is not concerned with GAAP in its broad sense, but with generally accepted accounting principles for determining realised profits. However, it might be argued that such principles do not necessarily exist, since UK accounting principles are directed towards the recognition and disclosure of items in the financial statements of entities in order to present a true and fair view, and not towards the determination of realised profits. Nevertheless, in its technical release on the subject (TR 481), the CCAB indicated that the term 'principles generally accepted' incorporates the legal principles laid down in Schedule 4 of the Companies Act 1985 and the requirements of the SSAPs (particularly the fundamental accounting concepts of prudence and accruals as set out in

SSAP 2).[3] TR 481 concluded that 'a profit which is required by statements of standard accounting practice to be recognised in the profit and loss account should normally be treated as a realised profit, unless the SSAP specifically indicates that it should be treated as unrealised'.[4]

The difficulty that arises from this interpretation is that there are a number of areas of profit recognition which are not, as yet, dealt with in the SSAPs; furthermore, certain areas which are covered by SSAPs incorporate inconsistencies in approach. For this reason, it is necessary to establish broad principles for the purpose of determining 'realised profit'. Some might hold the view that SSAP 2's definition of the prudence concept does, in fact, provide a basis for recognising realised profits in that it states that 'revenue and profits are not anticipated, but are recognised by inclusion in the profit and loss account when realised in the form either of cash or of other assets the ultimate cash realisation of which can be assessed with reasonable certainty'.[5] However, this definition may be flawed, since the emphasis on 'cash' and 'ultimate cash realisation' would appear to rule out the recognition of barter transactions or even the accrual of investment income on a time basis.

In conclusion, therefore, we believe that it is unclear as to whether or not there exists at present a set of 'principles generally accepted with respect to the determination for accounting purposes of realised profits', as is suggested by the Companies Act 1985. It is, therefore, vital that the ASC (or its successor) should prepare a statement which defines realisation, rather than persevere with the unsatisfactory system of having to rely on ad hoc, obscure and sometimes conflicting interpretations which must be extracted from the SSAPs and other accounting literature.

3   THE TIMING OF REVENUE RECOGNITION

Under the historical cost system, revenues are the inflows of assets to an enterprise as a result of the transfer of products and services by the enterprise to its customers during a period of time, and are recorded at the cash amount received or expected to be received (or, in the case of non-monetary exchanges, at their cash equivalent) as the result of these exchange transactions. However, because of the system of periodic financial reporting, it is necessary to determine the point (or points) in time when revenue should be measured and reported. This is governed by what is known as the 'realisation principle', which acknowledges the fact that for revenue to be recognised it is not sufficient merely for a sale to have been made — there has to be a certain degree of performance by the vendor as well. In the US, this principle was formally codified in 1970 in APB Statement No. 4 as follows: 'revenue is generally recognised when both of the following conditions are met: (1) the earning process is complete or virtually complete, and (2) an exchange has taken place'.[6]

The accounting practice which had developed under this principle was essentially as follows:

(a)   revenue from the sale of goods was recognised at the date of delivery to customers;

(b)   revenue from services was recognised when the services had been performed and were billable;

(c)   revenue derived from permitting others to use enterprise resources (e.g. rental, interest and royalty income) was recognised either on a time basis or as the resources were used;

(d)   revenue from the sale of assets other than products of the enterprise was recognised at the date of sale.[7]

As stated above, revenue is recognised at the amount received or expected to be received as a consequence of the exchange transaction.

Although APB Statement No. 4 did acknowledge that were certain exceptions to the sales basis of revenue recognition established under the realisation principle (for example, in the case of long-term construction contracts and the mining of precious metals with assured sales prices),[8] many more exceptions have developed in recent years. As a result, no common basis of revenue recognition exists in contemporary financial accounting for all types of exchange transaction; different (and sometimes inconsistent) rules exist for different circumstances. Nevertheless, these rules have been derived from three broad approaches to the recognition of revenue, each of which is appropriate under particular circumstances.

3.1   The critical event approach

In general terms, the operating cycle of an enterprise involves the acquisition of merchandise or raw materials, the production of goods, the sale of goods or services to customers, the delivery of the goods or performance of the services and the ultimate collection of cash; in some cases it might even extend beyond the cash collection stage, for example, if there are on-going after-sales service obligations. The critical event approach is based on the belief that revenue is earned at the point in the operating cycle when the most critical decision is made or the most critical act is performed. It is therefore necessary to identify the event which is considered to be critical to the revenue earning process. In theory, the critical event could occur at various stages during the operating cycle; for example, at the completion of production, at the time of sale, at the time of delivery or at the time of cash collection.

Revenue recognition is subject to a number of uncertainties; these include the estimation of the production cost of the asset, the selling price, the additional selling costs and the ultimate cash collection. However, since these uncertainties fall away at various stages throughout the operating cycle, it is necessary to identify a point in the cycle at which the remaining uncertainties can be estimated with sufficient accuracy to enable revenue to be recognised. In other words, the critical event should not be judged to occur at a point when the prudence concept would preclude recognition by virtue of the uncertainties which still remain.

3.1.1 *The recognition of revenue at the completion of production*

Clearly, the uncertainty surrounding the cost of production is removed when the product is completed; it is therefore necessary to evaluate the remaining uncertainties in order to determine whether or not the completion of production can be used as the critical event for revenue recognition. Where the enterprise has entered into a firm contract for the production and delivery of a product, the sales price will have been determined and the selling costs will have already been incurred. Consequently, provided that both the delivery expenses and the bad debt risk can be satisfactorily assessed, it may be appropriate to report revenue on this basis. An application of this practice is the completed contract method of recognising revenue on construction contracts, in terms of which revenue is recognised only when the contract is completed or substantially completed.

It has also become accepted practice in certain industries to recognise revenue at the completion of production, even though a sales contract may not have been entered into. Normally, this practice would only be adopted in the case of the production of certain precious metals and agricultural commodities, provided that the following criteria are met:

(a)   there should be a ready market for the commodity;

(b)   the market price should be determinable;

(c)   the market price should be stable; and

(d)   selling should not be a major activity of the enterprise and there should be no substantial cost of marketing.

SFAC No. 5 refers to such assets as being 'readily realisable' (since they are saleable at readily determinable prices without significant effort), and acknowledges that revenue may be recognised on the completion of production of such assets, provided that they consist of interchangeable units and quoted prices are available in an active market that can rapidly absorb the quantity held by the enterprise without significantly affecting the price.[9] The accounting treatment for this basis would be to value closing stock at net realisable value (i.e. sales price less estimated selling costs), and write off the related production costs.

An extension of this approach is to be found in the generally accepted accounting practice adopted by many securities dealers and commodity traders of including commodities, futures and options in their financial statements at market value. (See Chapter 9 at 6.3.4 for further discussion of the principle of 'marking to market'.)

3.1.2 *The recognition of revenue at the time of sale*

The time of sale is probably the most widely used basis of recognising revenue from transactions involving the sale of goods. The reason is that, in most cases, the sale is the critical point in the earning process when most of the significant uncertainties are eliminated; the only uncertainties which are likely to remain are those of possible return of the goods (where the customer has the right to do so, thereby cancelling the sale), the failure to collect the sales price (in the case of a credit sale), and any future liabilities in terms of any express or implied customer warranties. However, under normal circumstances, these uncertainties will be both minimal and estimable to a reasonable degree of accuracy, based, inter alia, on past experience.

Nevertheless, the time of sale basis of revenue recognition is not always straightforward. In a large number of cases, a contract for the sale of goods would be entered into after the goods have been acquired or produced by the seller, and delivery takes place either at the same time as the contract, or soon thereafter. However, should revenues be recognised at the time of sale if the sale takes place before production, or if delivery only takes place at some significantly distant time in the future?

From a legal point of view, delivery does not necessarily have to have occurred for a sale to take place. Under the Sale of Goods Act 1979, 'a contract of sale of goods is a contract by which the seller transfers or agrees to transfer the property in goods to the buyer for a money consideration, called the price'.[10] Where, under a contract of sale, title to the goods is transferred from the seller to the buyer the contract is called a sale;[11] where the contract specifies that title to the goods will be transferred at some future date or transfer of title is subject to conditions to be fulfilled in the future, the contract is called an agreement to sell.[12] Consequently, the 'critical event' which determines whether a contract of sale is a 'sale' or whether it is an 'agreement to sell' is the passing of title.

Where the contract of sale contains no conditions as to the passing of title, and the goods are physically capable of immediate delivery to the purchaser, title will pass as soon as the contract is entered into (i.e. at the time of sale), regardless of the time fixed for payment or delivery.[13] However, where the seller is bound to do something to the goods before the purchaser is obliged to take delivery, title will pass as soon as that thing is done and the purchaser has been notified.[14] The passing of title, therefore, is a legal issue (and may be of crucial importance to the parties in certain circumstances, such as liquidation), which is governed by the terms of the contract and can occur at various stages along the earning process. As a result, for revenue recognition purposes, the time of sale is generally taken to be the point of delivery. This, in fact, would appear to be the principle implicit in the conditions for recognition set out in APB Statement No. 4 (see 3 above), where it is stated that revenue from the sales of products is recognised 'at the date of sale, usually interpreted to mean the date of delivery to customers'.[15]

This principle was reinforced by SFAC No. 5 as follows: 'Revenues are not recognized until earned. An entity's revenue-earning activities involve delivering or producing goods, rendering services, or other activities that constitute its ongoing major or central operations, and revenues are considered to have been earned when the entity has substantially accomplished what it must do to be entitled to the benefits represented by the revenues. ... If sale or cash receipt (or both) precedes production and delivery (for example, magazine subscriptions), revenues may be recognised as earned by production and delivery.'[16]

However, the use of the words 'substantially accomplished' in SFAC No. 5 suggest that delivery does not necessarily have to have taken place for revenue to be recognised. Where, for example, delivery is a relatively insignificant part of the earning process, the goods are on hand and available for delivery and there is every expectation that delivery will be made, it may be appropriate to recognise the sale as revenue before delivery takes place. (See 4.1.1 below for discussion of the principles laid down by IAS 18 for determining when to recognise revenue from a transaction involving the sale of goods.)

3.1.3 *The recognition of revenue subsequent to delivery*

Under certain circumstances, the uncertainties which exist after delivery are of such significance that recognition should be delayed beyond the normal recognition point. Where the principal uncertainty concerns collectibility, a possible approach would be to record the sale and defer recognition of the profit until cash is received; alternatively, it might be appropriate to defer recognition of the whole sale (and not just the profit) until collection is reasonably assured.

A further example of where it might be appropriate to defer the recognition of revenue beyond the date of delivery is where the enterprise sells its product but gives the customer the right to return the goods (for example, in the case of a mail order business where the customer is given an approval period of, say, 14 days). In such circumstances, revenue should only be recognised on delivery if future returns can be reasonably predicted; if this is not possible, then revenue should only be recognised on receipt of payment for the goods, or on customer acceptance of the goods and express or implied acknowledgement of the liability for payment, or after the 14 days have elapsed — whichever is considered to be the most appropriate under the circumstances.

This area of uncertainty is dealt with in the US under SFAS 48 — *Revenue Recognition When Right of Return Exists* — which states that if an enterprise sells its product but gives the buyer the right to return the product, revenue from the sales transaction shall be recognised at time of sale only if *all* of the following conditions are met:

(a)   the seller's price to the buyer is substantially fixed or determinable at the date of sale;

(b)   the buyer has paid the seller, or the buyer is obligated to pay the seller and the obligation is not contingent on resale of the product;

(c)   the buyer's obligation to the seller would not be changed in the event of theft or physical destruction or damage of the product;

(d) the buyer acquiring the product for resale has economic substance apart from that provided by the seller (i.e., the buyer does not merely exist 'on paper' with little or no physical facilities, having been established by the seller primarily for the purpose of recognising revenue);

(e) the seller does not have significant obligations for future performance to directly bring about resale of the product by the buyer; and

(f) the amount of future returns can be reasonably estimated.[17]

Revenue which was not recognised at the time of sale because the above conditions were not met, should be recognised either when the return privilege has 'substantially expired', or when all the above conditions are met, whichever occurs first.[18]

The ability to make a reasonable estimate of future returns depends on many factors and will vary from one case to the next. Furthermore, SFAS 48 lists the following factors as being those which might impair a seller's ability to make such an estimate:

(a) the susceptibility of the product to significant external factors, such as technological obsolescence or changes in demand;

(b) relatively long periods in which a particular product may be returned;

(c) absence of historical experience with similar types of sales of similar products, or inability to apply such experience because of changing circumstances; for example, changes in the selling enterprise's marketing policies or its relationships with its customers;

(d) absence of a large volume of relatively homogeneous transactions.[19]

These rules should be seen against the background of APB Statement No. 4's requirement that revenue should generally only be recognised when the 'earning process is complete or virtually complete'.[20] The right of return is, therefore, viewed as a significant uncertainty which would preclude recognition under certain circumstances.

3.2   The accretion approach

The accretion approach involves the recognition of revenue during the process of 'production', rather than at the end of a contract or when production is complete. There are three broad areas of enterprise activity where the application of the accretion approach might be appropriate.

3.2.1   *The use by others of enterprise resources*

The traditional accrual basis of accounting recognises revenue as enterprise resources are used by others; this approach is followed, for example, in the case of recognising rental, royalty or interest income. However, the question of uncertainty of collection should always be considered (for example, in the case of accrual of interest on third world debt), in which case it might be appropriate to delay recognition until cash is received or where ultimate collection is assured beyond all reasonable doubt.

3.2.2 Long-term contracts

The second accepted application of the accretion approach to revenue reporting may be found in the accounting practice for long-term construction contracts. Under certain circumstances, the amount of revenue to be recognised on construction contracts is determined according to the 'percentage-of-completion method', whereby revenue is estimated by reference to the stage of completion of the contract activity at the end of each accounting period. Normally, the main uncertainty which presents difficulty in the application of this approach is the estimation of the total costs, particularly in the early stages of the contract, or where factors such as excavation and the weather may cause added uncertainty. However, the selling price is sometimes uncertain as well, owing to contract modifications which give rise to revenue from 'extras'. (Accounting for long-term contacts is dealt with in detail in Chapter 9.)

3.2.3 Natural growth

Where an enterprise's activity involves production through natural growth or ageing, the accretion approach would suggest that revenue should be recognised at identifiable stages during this process. For example, in the case of growing timber or livestock, there would be market prices available at the various stages of growth; revenue could, therefore, be recognised throughout the production process by making comparative stock valuations and reporting the accretions at each accounting date. However, under the present historical cost accounting system, this approach would not be appropriate, since the earning process would be too incomplete, too many significant uncertainties would remain, and a profit could not be regarded as having been realised.

3.3 The revenue allocation approach

The revenue allocation approach is essentially a combination of the critical event and accretion approaches. One of the difficulties in adopting, for example, the time of sale as the critical event for revenue recognition, is the existence of the uncertainty surrounding after-sale costs (such as customer support service and warranty costs). One way of dealing with these costs could be to make a provision for the future costs to be incurred on the basis of best estimate; alternatively, an approach could be followed whereby revenue is apportioned on the basis of two or more critical events. Consequently, part of the sale price could be treated as revenue at the point of sale, and the balance could either be recognised on an accretion basis over a warranty period or on the expiration of the warranty. The recognition of profit by manufacturer/dealer lessors is an example of such an application (see Chapter 19 at 7.5).

4 FUNDAMENTAL RECOGNITION CRITERIA

It is a requirement of the Companies Act 1985 that 'only profits realised at the balance sheet date shall be included in the profit and loss account';[21] in establishing whether or not profits of a company should be treated as 'realised profits', reference should be made to 'principles generally accepted with respect to the determination for accounting purposes of realised profits'.[22] It is unclear as to whether or not generally accepted accounting principles exist for the purposes of determining realised profits for accounting purposes. The only direct reference to realisation is to be found in SSAP 2's definition of prudence; however, this definition would appear to be inadequate, as existing practice indicates that a wider interpretation is being placed on the concept of 'realisation' (see 2 above). For this reason, revenue recognition issues tend to be dealt with on an ad hoc basis, without either a clear definition of the concept of realisation or generally accepted recognition criteria.

Therefore, in order to establish general principles to be applied in practice for the recognition of revenue, it is helpful to examine the authoritative literature which exists internationally. Although this literature has no authority to dictate accounting practice in the UK, it may provide a basis for achieving some consistency in approach towards dealing with practical revenue recognition issues.

4.1   IAS 18

IAS 18 — *Revenue Recognition* — was issued in 1982 and defines revenue as the 'gross inflow of cash, receivables or other consideration arising in the course of the ordinary activities of an enterprise from the sale of goods, from the rendering of services, and from the use by others of enterprise resources yielding interest, royalties and dividends'.[23] The use of the phrase 'or other consideration' clearly indicates that (in contrast with SSAP 2's definition of prudence) revenue from barter and similar exchange transactions should be recognised in the profit and loss account. In this regard, IAS 18 states that where there is an exchange of non-monetary assets, 'the fair value of the assets or services exchanged is normally used to determine the amount of revenue involved'.[24] IAS 16 — *Accounting for Property, Plant and Equipment* — deals with the specific situation where an item of property, plant or equipment is acquired in exchange or part exchange for another asset. In such circumstances, IAS 16 requires that 'the cost of the asset acquired should be recorded either at fair value or at the net carrying amount of the asset given up, adjusted for any balancing payment or receipt of cash or other consideration'.[25] However, the IASC has recently issued an exposure draft, E32 — *Comparability of Financial Statements* — which seeks, inter alia, to remove this choice of measurement currently permitted by IAS 16. E32 proposes that the cost of an item of property, plant or equipment acquired in exchange for another *dissimilar* asset should be its fair value; however, when the item of property, plant or equipment is acquired in exchange for a *similar* asset that has a similar use in the same line of business and which has a similar fair value, it is proposed that the cost of the asset acquired should be measured at the net carrying amount of the asset given up, adjusted for any balancing payment or receipt of cash or other consideration.[26]

As will be seen below, IAS 18 broadly adopts the critical event approach for the recognition of revenues derived from the sale of goods and the rendering of services (in that it requires recognition to be delayed to a point in the earning process where no significant uncertainties remain), and an accretion approach in respect of revenues derived from the use by others of enterprise resources. One of the difficulties with the standard, however, is that it tends to be a codification of most existing revenue recognition practices, rather than a theory of recognition which would promote consistency in approach. For example, if revenue comprises the 'gross inflow of cash, receivables or other consideration', then cash or current cash equivalent should be the basis of measurement of a revenue transaction; if this principle were to be applied consistently, the measurement of the transaction would take the timing of the cash receipt into account. In other words, if the transaction only required payment at some future date, it should be measured at the current value equivalent of the cash consideration, and not the undiscounted face value of the cash consideration. Nevertheless, the standard ignores the timing of the inflow of cash in the measurement of revenue.

4.1.1 The sale of goods

IAS 18 states that a key factor in determining when to recognise revenue from a transaction involving the sale of goods is that the buyer has assumed from the seller the significant risks and rewards of ownership of the assets sold.[27] The standard cites the following three considerations as being relevant in deciding whether or not the significant risks and rewards of ownership have been transferred to the buyer:

(a) whether any significant acts of performance remain to be completed;

(b) whether the seller retains any continuing managerial involvement in, or effective control of, the goods transferred to a degree usually associated with ownership;

(c) whether the payment of the debt relating to the goods transferred is dependent on the derivation of revenue by the buyer from the goods.[28]

As a further condition for recognition, the standard requires that no significant uncertainty should exist in respect of:

(a) the consideration that will be derived from the sale of the goods;

(b) the associated costs to be incurred in producing or purchasing the goods;

(c) the extent to which goods may be returned.[29]

It is, therefore, necessary to establish at which point in the earning process both the significant risks and rewards of ownership are transferred from the seller to the buyer and any significant uncertainties (which would otherwise delay recognition) are removed. For example, the responsibilities of each party during the period between sale and delivery should be established, possibly by examination of the customer agreements. If the goods have merely to be uplifted by the buyer, and the seller has performed all his associated responsibilities, then the sale may be recognised immediately. However, if the substance of the sale is merely that an order has been placed, and the stock has still to be acquired by the seller, then the sale should not be recognised.

IAS 18 does, however, recognise that under certain circumstances goods are sold subject to reservation of title in order to protect the collectibility of the amount due; this is viewed as a 'non-significant risk of ownership' which should not normally preclude recognition of revenue[30] (this issue is discussed more fully at 5.2 below). Furthermore, the standard does acknowledge that in certain specific industries (such as the agricultural and mining industries), revenue may be recognised before sale where there exists a stable market for the product with assured selling prices; in other words, the completion of production would be deemed to be the critical event for recognition in these industries under appropriate circumstances (see 3.1.1 above).[31]

4.1.2   The rendering of services

In the case of a transaction involving the rendering of services, IAS 18 adopts the performance of the service as the critical event for revenue recognition. Performance should be measured either under the percentage-of-completion method or under the completed contract method, whichever relates the revenue to the work accomplished.[32] The percentage-of-completion method would be appropriate where performance consists of the execution of more than one act, and revenue is recognised proportionately by reference to the performance of each act. The completed contract method would be applied where performance consists of the execution of a single act, or where services are performed in more than a single act, and the services yet to be performed are so significant in relation to the transaction taken as a whole that performance cannot be deemed to have been completed until the execution of those acts.[33]

However, whichever method is adopted, performance should be regarded as having been achieved where no uncertainty exists regarding:

(a)   the consideration that will be derived from rendering the service; and

(b)   the associated costs incurred or to be incurred in rendering the service.[34]

At present, therefore, IAS 18 gives companies a reasonably free choice between adopting either the completed contract method or the percentage-of-completion method (subject to the proviso that the method chosen should relate revenue to the work accomplished). For this reason, the IASC exposure draft E32 seeks to remove the choice of using the completed contract method both in respect of the recognition of revenue on service contracts under IAS 18 and on construction contracts under IAS 11.[35]

4.1.3   The use by others of enterprise resources

IAS 18 states that revenues arising from the use by others of enterprise resources yielding interest, royalties and dividends should only be recognised when no significant uncertainty as to measurability or collectibility exists. These revenues are recognised on the following bases:

(a)   *Interest:* on a time proportion basis taking account of the principal outstanding and the rate applicable;

(b)   *Royalties:* on an accrual basis in accordance with the terms of the relevant royalty agreement;

(c)   *Dividends from investments not accounted for under the equity method of accounting:* when the shareholder's right to receive payment is established.[36]

The application of the accretion approach under these circumstances would not necessarily be in line with the principle of realised profits as contained in

SSAP 2's definition of prudence, since it would sometimes result in the recognition of revenue before it is either 'realised in the form of cash or of other assets the ultimate cash realisation of which can be assessed with reasonable certainty'; nevertheless, such an approach is generally accepted accounting practice in the UK.

4.2 The CICA

In September 1986, Section 3400, entitled 'Revenue', was added to the CICA *Handbook*. This Section is concerned with the recognition of revenue arising in the course of the ordinary activities of an enterprise from the sale of goods, the rendering of services and the use by others of enterprise resources yielding interest, royalties and dividends. It deals with the timing of the recognition of revenue and not the measurement of revenue, and is essentially a verbatim reproduction of IAS 18. Therefore, as is the case with IAS 18, Section 3400 would appear to be more like an accommodation of existing Canadian revenue recognition practices, rather than a theory of revenue recognition which could be used as the basis for the promotion of consistent revenue recognition and measurement practices.

In December 1988, the CICA published *Handbook* Section 1000 entitled 'Financial statement concepts'. The section deals, inter alia, with the criteria which should be applied for recognising an item in the financial statements of an entity. However, as far as the criteria for revenue recognition are concerned, the section merely states that 'revenues are generally recognized when performance is achieved and reasonable assurance regarding measurement and collectibility of the consideration exists. Gains are generally recognized when realized.'[37] Clearly, these criteria are of little practical help, since no explanation is given of the terms 'when performance is achieved' or 'realized'.

4.3 The US

4.3.1 'The general rule'

Chapter 1 of Accounting Research Bulletin No. 43 (issued in 1953) reprinted the six rules which had been adopted by the membership of the AICPA in 1934. The first of these rules stated that 'profit is deemed to be realized when a sale in the ordinary course of business is effected, unless the circumstances are such that the collection of the sale price is not reasonably assured'.[38] The rule then goes on to state that 'an exception to the general rule may be made in respect of inventories in industries (such as the packing-house industry) in which owing to the impossibility of determining costs it is a trade custom to take inventories at net selling prices, which may exceed cost'.[39] However, it is not entirely clear as to what the 'general rule' actually is. Does the term 'effected' mean that profit is realised when the sale takes place, when delivery takes place, or when title passes?

In addition, a number of further exceptions are created by other authoritative pronouncements. For example, Chapter 11 of ARB 43 (which deals with cost-plus-fixed-fee government contracts) states that 'delivery of goods sold under contract is normally regarded as the test of realization of profit or loss'.[40] Nevertheless, it then goes on to say that 'it is, however, a generally accepted accounting procedure to accrue revenues under certain types of contracts and thereby recognize profits, on the basis of partial performance, where the circumstances are such that total profit can be estimated with reasonable accuracy and ultimate realization is reasonably assured'.[41]

The percentage-of-completion method of recognising revenue on long-term construction contracts is another example of 'an exception to the general rule'. ARB 45 — *Long-Term Construction-Type Contracts* — recognises both the percentage-of-completion and completed contract methods of accounting for long-term contracts. The Bulletin states that 'in general when estimates of costs to complete and extent of progress toward completion of long-term contracts are reasonably dependable, the percentage-of-completion method is preferable. When lack of dependable estimates or inherent hazards cause forecasts to be doubtful, the completed-contract method is preferable'.[42] It would appear that the criteria to be applied in the selection of method are only broadly similar to those which should be applied in the case of cost-plus-fixed-fee contracts.

APB Statement No. 4 views these practices as exceptions to the realisation principle's exchange rule (see 3 above). However, as will be seen below, there exist a number of other variations to both the general rule laid down in ARB 43 and the realisation principle.

4.3.2   SFAC No. 5

As discussed in Chapter 2, the FASB's Concepts Statement No. 5 — *Recognition and Measurement in Financial Statements of Business Enterprises* — has primarily dealt with recognition issues from the angle of providing reliability of measurement. However, the broad principle for revenue recognition laid down by SFAC No. 5 is that revenues are not recognised until they are (a) realised or realisable and (b) earned.[43] According to the Statement, revenues are realised 'when products (goods or services), merchandise, or other assets are exchanged for cash or claims to cash', and are realisable 'when related assets received or held are readily convertible to known amounts of cash or claims to cash'.[44] The characteristics of 'readily convertible assets' are that they have '(i) interchangeable (fungible) units and (ii) quoted prices available in an active market that can rapidly absorb the quantity held by the entity without significantly affecting the price'.[45] Revenues are considered to have been 'earned' when the entity 'has substantially accomplished what it must do to be entitled to the benefits represented by the revenues'.[46]

The most significant difference between the recognition principles laid down in SFAC No. 5 as opposed to APB Statement No. 4 is that whilst the APB interpreted recognition and realisation as being broadly synonymous, SFAC No. 5 uses the terms 'realized' and 'realizability' to focus on conversion and convertibility of non-cash assets into cash or claims to cash. However, it is doubtful whether SFAC No. 5's revised interpretation of the realisation principle has made any significant progress towards providing a rigorous theory of recognition and measurement. This is highlighted by the fact that SFAC No. 5 provides guidance for applying its recognition criteria and, in so doing, goes on to condone certain existing revenue practices (for example, the percentage-of-completion method and the accrual of certain revenues on a time basis) which clearly are not in accordance with the basic principles laid down in the Statement, since an exchange for cash or claims to cash may not necessarily have occurred.

4.3.3 FASB statements

There exist a number of FASB Statements which deal with either the recognition of certain forms of revenue, or the recognition of revenue in certain specific industries. These are dealt with under 5 below.

4.4 Summary

The following table summarises the broad approaches to revenue reporting which would appear to have achieved general acceptance through existing reporting practice. The table indicates the circumstances under which it might be appropriate to apply each of the approaches; nevertheless, it is essential that each situation is considered on its individual merits, with particular attention being paid to the uncertainties which remain at each stage of the earning process:

The timing of recognition	Criteria	Examples of practical application
During production (accretion)	Revenues accrue over time, and no significant uncertainty exists as to measurability or collectibility. A contract of sale has been entered into and future costs can be estimated with reasonable accuracy.	The accrual of interest, royalty and dividend income. Accounting for long-term construction contracts using the percentage-of-completion method.
At the completion of production	The existence of a ready market for the commodity which could rapidly absorb the quantity held by the entity; the commodity should comprise interchangeable units; the market price should be determinable and stable; there should be insignificant marketing costs involved.	Certain precious metals and agricultural products.
At the time of sale (but before delivery)	Goods must have been acquired/manufactured; goods must be capable of immediate delivery to the customer; selling price has been established; all material related expenses (including delivery) have been ascertained; no significant uncertainties remain (e.g. ultimate cash collection, return of goods).	Certain sales of goods (e.g. 'bill and hold' sales). Property sales where there is an irrevocable contract.
On delivery	Criteria for recognition before delivery were not satisfied and no significant uncertainties remain.	Most sales of goods and services. Property sales where there is doubt that the sale will be completed.
Subsequent to delivery	Significant uncertainty regarding collectibility existed at time of delivery; at time of sale it was not possible to value consideration with sufficient accuracy.	Certain sales of goods and services (e.g. where the right of return exists). Goods shipped subject to conditions (e.g. installation and inspection/performance).
On an apportionment basis (the revenue allocation approach)	Where revenue represents the supply of initial and subsequent goods/services.	Franchise fees. Sale of goods with after sales service.

5 PROBLEM AREAS

Because of the lack of established generally accepted principles for revenue recognition, coupled with the fact that minimal guidance is given in the SSAPs as to the timing of revenue reporting, it is necessary to examine specific areas in practice which might be open to inconsistent, controversial or varied accounting practices. Many of the issues discussed below relate to specific industries which pose their own particular revenue recognition problems; in fact, much of the accounting literature on the subject has been developed (predominantly in the US) in the context of these industries.

5.1 Receipt of initial fees

The practice which has developed in certain industries of charging an initial fee at the inception of a service, followed by subsequent service fees, can present revenue allocation problems. The reason for this is that it is not always altogether clear what the initial fee represents; consequently, it is necessary to determine what proportion (if any) of the initial fee has been earned on receipt, and how much relates to the provision of future services. In some cases, large initial fees are paid for the provision of a service, whilst continuing fees are relatively small in relation to future services to be provided; if it is probable that the continuing fees will not cover the cost of the continuing services to be provided, then a portion of the initial fee should be deferred over the period of the service contract such that a reasonable profit is earned throughout the service period.

5.1.1 Franchise fees

The franchise agreements which form the basis of the relationships between franchisors and franchisees can vary widely both in their complexity and in the extent to which various rights, duties and obligations are dealt with in the agreements. For this reason, no standard form franchise agreement exists which would dictate standard accounting practice for the recognition of all franchise fee revenue. Consequently, only a full understanding of the franchise agreement will reveal the substance of a particular arrangement so that the most appropriate accounting treatment can be determined; nevertheless, the following are the more common areas which are likely to be addressed in any franchise agreement and which would be relevant to franchise fee revenue reporting:[47]

(a) *Rights transferred by the franchisor:* the agreement would give the franchisee the right to use the trade name, processes, know-how of the franchisor for a specified period of time or in perpetuity.

(b) *The amount and terms of payment of initial fees:* payment of initial fees (where applicable) may be fully or partially due in cash, and may be payable immediately, over a specified period or on the fulfilment of certain obligations by the franchisor.

(c) *Amount and terms of payment of continuing franchise fees:* the franchisee will normally be required to pay a continuing fee to the franchisor — usually on the basis of a percentage of gross revenues.

(d)   *Services to be provided by the franchisor initially and on a continuing basis:* the franchisor will usually agree to provide a variety of services and advice to the franchisee, such as:

- site selection;
- the procurement of fixed assets and equipment — these may be either purchased by the franchisee, leased from the franchisor or leased from a third party (possibly with the franchisor guaranteeing the lease payments);
- advertising;
- training of franchisee's personnel;
- inspecting, testing and other quality control programmes;
- bookkeeping services.

(e)   *Acquisition of equipment, stock, supplies etc.:* the franchisee may be required to purchase these items either from the franchisor or from designated suppliers. Some franchisors manufacture products for sale to their franchisees, whilst others act as wholesalers.

The Appendix to IAS 18 broadly discusses the receipt of franchise fees, stating that the allocation of franchise fee revenue 'is difficult and requires considerable judgement'.[48] However, the only guidance that it provides for the exercise of judgement is as follows:

(a)   the portion of the initial franchise fee that relates to tangible assets (if any) should be recognised when the items are delivered;

(b)   the portion that applies to future services (if any) should be deferred and recognised as revenue when the services are rendered;

(c)   if continuing fees receivable under the agreement are inadequate to cover the cost and a reasonable profit level for the continuing services, recognition of some or all of the initial franchise fee should be delayed.[49]

In the US, SFAS 45 — *Accounting for Franchise Fee Revenue* — states that franchise fee revenue should be recognised 'when all material services or conditions relating to the sale have been substantially performed or satisfied by the franchisor'.[50] Substantial performance for the franchisor means that:

(a)   the franchisor has no remaining obligation or intent (in terms of the franchise agreement, the law or trade practice) to refund any cash received or waive any debts receivable;

(b)   substantially all of the initial services of the franchisor required by the franchise agreement have been performed; and

(c)   no other material conditions or obligations related to the determination of substantial performance exist.[51]

SFAS 45 also deals with the issue of mixed revenue — i.e. where the initial franchise fee incorporates not only the consideration for the franchise rights and the initial services to be provided by the franchisor, but also tangible assets such as equipment, signs etc. In such cases, the portion of the initial fee which is 'applicable to the tangible assets shall be based on the fair value of the assets and may be recognized before or after recognizing the portion applicable to the initial services. For example, when the portion of the fee relating to the sale of specific tangible assets is objectively determinable, it would be appropriate to recognize that portion when their titles pass, even though the balance of the fee relating to services is recognized when the remaining services or conditions in the franchise agreement have been substantially performed or satisfied.'[52]

In summary, therefore, we suggest that the following basic principles may be applied for the recognition of initial franchise fees:

(a) firstly, it is necessary to break down the fee into its various components; for example, fee for franchise rights, fee for initial services to be performed by the franchisor, fair value of tangible assets sold etc. The reason for this is that the individual components may be recognised at different stages; the portion that relates to the franchise rights may be recognised in full immediately, or part of it may have to be deferred (see (b) below); the fee for initial services to be performed should only be recognised when the services have been 'substantially performed' (it is unlikely that substantial performance will have been completed before the franchisee opens for business); and the portion of the fee which relates to tangible assets may be recognised when title passes;

(b) next, it should be considered whether or not the continuing fee will cover the cost of continuing services to be provided by the franchisor. If not, then a portion of the initial fee should be deferred and amortised over the life of the franchise;

(c) if the collection period for the initial fees is extended and there is doubt as to the ultimate collectibility, revenue should be recognised on a cash received basis;

(d) in the event of the franchisor having the option to buy out the franchisee, and there is considered to be a significant probability that he will do so, initial franchise fee revenue should be deferred in full and credited against the cost of the investment when the buy-out occurs.

5.1.2 Advance royalty/licence receipts

Under normal circumstances, the accounting treatment of advance royalty/licence receipts is straightforward; under the accruals concept of SSAP 2, the advance should be treated as deferred income when received, and released to the profit and loss account when earned under the royalty/licence agreement. However, there are certain industries where the forms of agreement entered into are such that advance receipts comprise a number of components, each requiring different accounting treatments.

For example, in the record and music industry, a record company will normally enter into a contractual arrangement with either a recording artist or a production company to deliver finished recording masters over a specified period of time. The albums are then manufactured and shipped to retailers for ultimate sale to the customer. The recording artist will normally be compensated through participating in the record company's sales and licence fee income (i.e. a royalty), although he may receive a non-refundable fixed fee on delivery of the master to the record company.

Example 3.1   Revenue recognition for licensors in the record and music industry

For each recording master delivered by a pop group, Garth, the group (which operates through a service company) receives a payment of £1,000,000. This amount comprises a non-returnable, non-recoupable payment of £200,000, a non-returnable but recoupable advance of £600,000 and a returnable, recoupable advance of £200,000. The recoupable advances can be recouped against royalties on net sales earned both on the album concerned and on earlier and subsequent albums. This is achieved by computing the total royalties on net sales on all albums delivered under Garth's service company's agreement with its recording company, and applying against this total the advances and royalties previously paid on those albums.

It is clear that the non-recoupable advance should be recognised in income when received, since it is not related to any future performance; at the other end of the spectrum, recognition of the refundable advance should be deferred and recognised only when recouped. However, the question arises as to whether the non-refundable but recoupable advance on royalties should be recognised immediately or deferred. If one accepts that revenue may be recognised when it is absolutely assured, there is an argument to justify the immediate recognition of the recoupable advance, since it is non-refundable; furthermore, it might be argued that, as far as Garth is concerned, the earning process is complete, since the group does not have any further performance obligations. Conversely, some might argue that although the advance is non-refundable, it is not earned until it is recouped; furthermore, immediate recognition of royalty advances is likely to lead to a significant distortion of reported income, resulting in there being little correlation between reported income and album sales.

Clearly, therefore, there is no clear-cut answer, and it is our view that either approach is acceptable — i.e., the non-refundable but recoupable advance may be recognised in full as soon as the master is delivered to the recording company or, alternatively, it may be treated as deferred income when received and matched to subsequent album sales, being released to the profit and loss account in the period in which the sales are made. The most important point is that, whichever method is adopted, it is applied consistently.

It is, perhaps, noteworthy that the deferral approach is supported by the US accounting requirement contained in SFAS 50 — *Financial Reporting in the Record and Music Industry* — which states that where an amount is paid in advance by a licensee to a licensor for the right to sell or distribute records or music, 'the licensor shall report such a minimum guarantee as a liability initially and recognize the guarantee as revenue as the license fee is earned under the agreement. If the licensor cannot otherwise determine the amount of the license fee earned, the guarantee shall be recognized as revenue equally over the remaining performance period, which is generally the period covered by the license agreement.'[53]

Similar recognition principles should be applied in the case of advance fees paid on the sale of film/TV rights. Receipts which are non-refundable and non-recoupable should be recognised immediately, whilst any non-refundable but recoupable royalty advances may either be recognised immediately, or be deferred and recognised as earned; again, the accounting policy selected should be applied consistently.

5.1.3 Loan arrangement fees

The practice of recognising loan arrangement fees as income in the year that the loans are arranged was outlawed in the US through the publication of SFAS 91 — *Accounting for Nonrefundable Fees and Costs Associated with Originating or Acquiring Loans and Initial Direct Costs of Leases* — which requires loan origination fees to be deferred and recognised over the life of the related loan as an adjustment of interest income.[54] Similarly, direct loan origination costs should be deferred and recognised as a reduction in the yield of the loan.[55]

Since there is no corresponding requirement in the UK, the recognition of arrangement fees on receipt may be regarded as acceptable; however, our preferred approach is that the principles contained in SFAS 91 should equally be applied in the UK. Nevertheless, situations may exist where the lending institution is providing other financial services which are, in themselves, valuable to the borrower and which are covered by the arrangement fee. If this is the case, then it may be argued that the portion of the initial fee which relates to those services should be recognised as income immediately, provided that the interest rate to be charged on the loan is fair and reasonable in relation to the risk involved and that the arrangement fee is not merely an interest prepayment.

5.1.4 Commitment fees

Commitment fees are fees paid by potential borrowers for a commitment to originate or purchase a loan or group of loans within a particular period of time. According to the ICAEW Industry Accounting and Auditing Guide on banks, 'the fact that a commitment fee may be legally payable at the commencement of a facility should not be allowed to detract from the fact that the fee relates to the provision of a service over a future period of time. Consequently it should usually be accounted for on a time apportionment basis.'[56] This contrasts with the accounting treatment prescribed by SFAS 91, namely that the fee should be deferred until either the commitment is exercised or it expires. If the commitment is exercised, it should normally be recognised over the life of the loan as an adjustment to interest income, and if it expires unexercised it should be recognised in income on expiration.[57]

SFAS 91 does, however, allow the following two exceptions to this general rule:

(a) if the enterprise's experience with similar arrangements indicates that the likelihood that the commitment will be exercised is remote (i.e. the likelihood is slight that a loan commitment will be exercised prior to its expiration), the commitment fee should be recognised over the commitment period on a straight-line basis as service fee income. If the commitment is subsequently exercised during the commitment period, the remaining unamortised commitment fee at the time of exercise should be recognised over the life of the loan as an adjustment to interest income;[58]

(b) if the amount of the commitment fee is determined retrospectively as a percentage of the line of credit available but unused in a previous period, then the fee should be recognised as service fee income as of the determination date, provided that:

(i)   the percentage applied is nominal in relation to the stated interest rate on any related borrowing; and

(ii) the borrowing will bear a market interest rate at the date the loan is made.[59]

5.1.5   *Credit card fees*

There is an increasing trend in the UK for credit card companies to levy a charge, payable in advance, on its cardholders. Although such charges may be seen as commitment fees for the credit facilities offered by the card, they clearly cover the many other services available to cardholders as well. Accordingly, we would suggest that the fees which are periodically charged to cardholders should be deferred and recognised on a straight-line basis over the period the fee entitles the cardholder to use the card.[60]

5.2   Goods sold subject to reservation of title

The Romalpa case[61], which was decided in 1976, focused attention on the terms of a particular form of sale whereby the seller retains title to the goods sold and, in some cases, the right to other goods produced from them and the ultimate sale proceeds. The appropriate accounting treatment of such sales will depend on the commercial substance of the transaction, rather than its legal form. For example, it may be that the reservation of title is of no economic relevance to either party, except in the event of the insolvency of the purchaser; in other words, the goods are supplied and payment is due on an identical basis to other goods which are sold without reservation of title. In such circumstances, provided there is no significant uncertainty regarding the collectibility of the amount due, the sale should be recognised as revenue.

However, the circumstances surrounding the sale might be such that the parties view it as a consignment sale; for example, the purchaser may retain the right to return unsold goods to the seller, and the obligation to pay for the goods might be deferred until such time as the goods are sold to a third party. In such a case it would be inappropriate for the seller to recognise the sale until such time as the purchaser sells the goods and is liable for payment. (The accounting treatment of goods sold subject to reservation of title is discussed in a statement of guidance issued by the ICAEW in July 1976.)[62]

5.3   Subscriptions to publications

Publication subscriptions are generally paid in advance and are non-refundable. Nevertheless, since the publications will still have to be produced and delivered to the subscriber, the subscription revenue cannot be regarded as having been earned until production and delivery takes place. Consequently, we recommend that revenue should be deferred and recognised either on a straight-line basis over the subscription period or, where the publications vary in value, revenue should be based on the proportion of the sales value that each publication bears to the total sales value of all publications covered by the subscription.

5.4   Advertising revenue

As discussed at 4.1.2 above, IAS 18 adopts the performance of the service as the critical event for the recognition of revenue derived from the rendering of services. We concur with this broad approach; consequently, an appropriate application of this principle could be that advertising revenue should be deferred and recognised when the related advertisement or commercial appears before the public.

5.5   Software revenue recognition

There are a number of issues relating to the timing of revenue recognition in the software services industry. However, few of these issues have been addressed in the authoritative literature and, because of the nature of the products and services involved, applying the general revenue recognition principles to software transactions can sometimes be difficult. The issues which arise surround the question of when to recognise revenue from contracts to develop software, software licensing fees, customer support services and data services. Possible critical events for the recognition of revenue from the delivery of software products and related services include: date of signing of contract, deliverability of product or service, delivery, installation, acceptance, time of obligation to pay and payment.

5.5.1   *Granting the right to use, but not to own, software*

The most basic form of licensing arrangement is where a software company gives a customer the right to use a particular software product for a specific period of time. All that the software company has to do is either duplicate a delivery copy from the product master or load a copy of the product on to the customer's system. The question that arises is, assuming that the product is deliverable at the time of the signing of the contract, whether revenue should be recognised at the time of signing the contract or at the time of delivery of the product. The arguments in favour of recognition at the time of signing might suggest that since all costs to develop, produce and market the product have already been incurred, delivery is not a key event in the software company's earnings process. Alternatively, the view might be held that the licensing of a software product is similar to the sale of goods, and that the revenue from the sale of goods is generally recognised on delivery.

It could be argued that the granting of a software licence has no substance until the product is delivered and/or installed and available for use by the customer; consequently revenue should normally only be recognised on delivery. However, it is possible that the 'bill and hold' basis of recognition applicable to sale of goods could be applied to software products. Using this analogy, revenue could be recognised at the point when the product is deliverable, provided that a specific copy of the software product is prepared and assigned to the contract, the software company is obligated to deliver the product at any time which is suitable to the customer, the amount due for the product is billable and payment is not dependent on delivery.

5.5.2   *Products sold with significant vendor obligations*

Where companies are running well-established computer installations with systems and configurations which they do not wish to change, off-the-shelf software packages are generally not suitable for their purposes. For this reason, some software companies will enter into a customer contract whereby they agree to customise a generalised software product to meet the customer's specific processing needs. A simple form of customisation would be to modify the system's output reports so that they integrate with the customer's existing management reporting system. However, customisation will often entail more involved obligations; for example, having to translate the software so that it is able to run on the customer's specific hardware configuration, data conversion, system integration, installation and testing.

The question which arises, therefore, is on what basis should a software company be recognising revenue where it enters into this type of contract which involves significant contractual obligations? It is our view that the principles laid down in SSAP 9 — *Stocks and long-term contracts* — should be applied in this situation. SSAP 9 defines a long-term contract as 'a contract entered into for the design, manufacture or construction of a single substantial asset or the provision of a service (or of a combination of assets or services which together constitute a single product) where the time taken substantially to complete the contract is such that the contract activity falls into different accounting periods.'[63] The standard requires that 'long-term contracts should be assessed on a contract by contract basis and reflected in the profit and loss account by recording turnover and related costs as contract activity progresses. Turnover is ascertained in a manner appropriate to the stage of completion of the contract, the business and the industry in which it operates. Where it is considered that the outcome of a long-term contract can be assessed with reasonable certainty before its conclusion, the prudently calculated attributable profit should be recognised in the profit and loss account as the difference between the reported turnover and related costs for that contract.'[64]

Consequently, where the software company is able to make reliable estimates as to the extent of progress toward completion of a contract, related revenues and related costs, and where the outcome of the contract can be assessed with reasonable certainty, the percentage-of-completion method of profit recognition should be applied. However, where the uncertainties are such that prudence would preclude the accrual of profit, or where the contracts are of a relatively short duration, the completed contract method of accounting should be applied.

5.5.3   *Post-delivery customer support services*

Often, the software company will provide support services after the product has been delivered to the customer, installed and tested. These services may include a telephone help-line, further customisation, product enhancements, training of new staff etc., and are either included in the cost of the software product or sold separately through a support service contract (which, for example, might be renewable on an annual basis). Even if the contract does not specifically include free product enhancements, customers often enter into service contracts to obtain enhancements at favourable rates, or to ensure that they always have the latest version installed. On the other hand, software companies, to some extent, rely on service contracts as a source of funding of product enhancements; furthermore, the existence of a support service customer base makes it commercially attractive for a company to continue enhancing the product, since a ready market exists for the sale thereof.

It is quite clear that the matching concept would require that the revenue derived from customer support contracts should be deferred and recognised over the period of the contract. This is based on the premise that a liability to perform services is incurred at the inception of the contract, and is discharged over the life of the contract. It might be argued that revenues should be matched with actual costs incurred in rendering the support services; however, it would generally be impracticable to achieve this, and the costs of doing so would probably outweigh the benefits. Consequently, customer support revenue should normally be recognised on a straight-line basis over the term of the contract.

However, a further problem does exist where the fee for post-delivery customer support services is packaged together with the fee for the product, and is not, therefore, subject to a separate contract. It is our view that the revenue element which relates to the support services should be separated from the initial fee and recognised over time. This should present little difficulty where the price of similar support service contracts is readily available; however, if the software company does not normally sell support contracts separately, it will be necessary to make an allocation based on achieving a reasonable rate of return on the contracts in the light of the costs involved in providing the support service. The selling price of support service contracts is sometimes determined on the basis of a percentage of the selling price of the product which is being supported; under certain circumstances, therefore, this may be a practicable basis of separating the revenue elements where the product and support services are sold as a package.

5.5.4 Data services

Data services companies offer their customers various data processing services such as on-line access to data bases and applications programmes. Normally, the fees charged to customers are made up of three components:

- *subscription fees*, which are, effectively, log-on fees to the data services facilities, and either may or may not include a certain amount of 'free' processing time;
- *usage fees*, which are normally charged either on the basis of the volume of transactions or access time; contracts are often sold subject to a guaranteed minimum usage charge;
- *data storage fees*, which are charged for storing customer data on the data services company's computer facilities.

The first question which arises is whether non-refundable subscription fee revenue should be recognised immediately the contract is signed or recognised over the period of the contract. The argument in favour of immediate recognition is based on the premise that the subscription fees relate to costs already incurred at the commencement of the contract (e.g. marketing, the installation of data communications devices, data entry etc.), and that future costs are matched with usage fees. The argument against this is that the subscription fees are merely part of the revenue which the data services company receives over the period of the contract, and that (irrespective of the wording of the contract) the customer would, in law, be entitled to claim a refund of a portion of the subscription fees if the data services company failed to provide the processing facilities throughout the duration of the contract.

It is our view that the immediate recognition of the full subscription fee at the inception of the contract would generally not be appropriate, and that the fees should normally be recognised over the period of the contract. However, where there are significant incremental costs incurred at inception, a portion of subscription fee revenue may be recognised to the extent of costs incurred, and the revenues in excess of costs should be deferred and recognised over the term of the contract. In practice, this may be achieved by applying a formula based on a reasonable estimate of associated costs; for example, a policy might be established whereby 25% of subscription fee revenue is recognised at inception to cover associated incremental costs, with the balance of 75% being recognised on a straight-line basis over the term of the contract. However, where the subscription fee includes a portion of 'free' processing time, the fee should be recognised as this time is used up.

Where usage fees are charged on the basis of minimum usage, the question arises as to the basis on which such fees should be recognised. Should the fees be recognised on the basis of an absorption rate which is calculated according to the customer's expected usage during the period, or should they be recognised at the actual rate, with any unused portion being recognised at the expiration of the period? The following example illustrates these two bases:

Example 3.2   Recognition of usage fees for data services

A data services company enters into a 12 month contract to provide a customer with on-line access to a data base at the rate of £60 per hour, subject to a fixed minimum fee of £6,000 (i.e. 100 hours). Unused access time is forfeited at the end of the 12 month period. The company estimates that the customer will only utilise a maximum of 75 hours during the period. The two possible bases of recognising the revenue over the term of the contract are as follows:

- recognised on the basis of the customer's anticipated usage (i.e. revenue would be recognised at the rate of £80 per hour); or
- recognised at the actual rate of £60 per hour, with any unused portion being recognised on the expiration of the contract.

Because of the uncertainty involved in estimating the customer's usage, it is our view that the second of the two options is the preferable.

5.6   The disposal of land and buildings

Unlike the US, there are no laid down rules in the UK for the recognition of the proceeds on disposal of land and buildings. Consequently, the general principles of revenue recognition should be applied in order to determine the point in time at which property sales should be recognised in the profit and loss account. There are two significant points in the earning process which could, depending on the circumstances of the sale, be considered to be the critical event for recognition.

The first point is on exchange of contracts, at which time the vendor and purchaser are both bound by a legally enforceable contract of sale; whilst the second possible point of recognition is on completion of the contract. The following extracts illustrate the fact that both approaches are followed in practice:

Extract 3.1: Brixton Estate plc[65]

STATEMENT OF ACCOUNTING POLICIES [extract]

D. DEALING PROPERTIES [extract]
Profits on the disposal of dealing properties are taken when, in the opinion of the Directors, the developments are materially completed and the contracts are exchanged.

Extract 3.2: The Hammerson Property Investment and Development Corporation plc[66]

1   Accounting policies [extract]

(e)   Profits on sale of properties [extract]
      Profits on sale of properties are taken into account on the completion of contract and receipt of cash.

Although legal title and beneficial ownership do not pass until the contract is completed and the transfer is registered, it is likely that the earning process is sufficiently complete to permit recognition to take place on exchange of contracts. The reason for this is that the selling price would have been established, all material related expenses would have been ascertained and, usually, no significant uncertainties would remain. If, however, on exchange of contracts there exists doubt that the sale will be ultimately completed, recognition should take place on the receipt of sales proceeds at legal completion.

However, since both approaches appear to be widely used in practice, they should both be regarded as being acceptable accounting practice. Nevertheless, it is important to ensure that, whichever policy is adopted, it is applied consistently, although recognition should always be delayed until completion if significant uncertainties still exist on exchange of contracts. The income recognition policy of Crest Nicholson Plc is a good example of the application of this principle:

Extract 3.3: Crest Nicholson Plc[67]

1. ACCOUNTING POLICIES [extract]

iv Income recognition [extract]
Profit is recognised on houses when contracts are exchanged and building is substantially
complete. Profit is recognised on commercial property developments or units of development
which, at the year end, are substantially complete and subject to binding and unconditional
contracts of sale and where legal completion has occurred shortly thereafter. Where the sale
price is conditional upon letting, profit is restricted by reference to the space unlet at the year
end.

In the US, SFAS 66 — *Accounting for Sales of Real Estate* — lays down rigid
rules for the recognition of profit on real estate transactions, and distinguishes
between retail land sales (i.e., sales under a property development project) and
other sales of real estate. The statement contains extensive provisions which have
been developed to deal with complex transactions which are beyond the scope of
this book. However, the general requirements for recognising all of the profit on a
non-retail land sale are as follows:

Profit should not be recognised in full until all of the following criteria are met:

(a)   the sale is consummated;

(b)   the purchaser's initial and continuing investments are adequate to
       demonstrate a commitment to pay for the property;

(c)   the vendor's receivable is not subject to future subordination; and

(d)   the vendor has transferred to the purchaser the usual risks and rewards of
       ownership in a transaction that is in substance a sale and does not have a
       substantial continuing involvement with the property.[68]

A sale is not considered to be consummated until:

(a)   the parties are bound by the terms of the contract;

(b)   all consideration has been exchanged (i.e., either all monies have been
       received, or all necessary contractual arrangements have been entered into
       for the ultimate payment of monies — such as notes supported by
       irrevocable letters of credit from an independent lending institution);

(c)   any permanent financing for which the vendor is responsible has been
       arranged; and

(d)   all conditions precedent to closing the contract have been performed.[69]

SFAS 66 states that these four conditions are usually met 'at the time of closing
or after closing, not when an agreement to sell is signed or at a preclosing'.[70]

5.7   Film exhibition rights

Revenue received from the licensing of films for exhibition at cinemas and on television should be recognised in accordance with the general recognition principles discussed in this chapter. Contracts for the television broadcast rights of films normally allow for multiple showings within a specific period; these contracts usually expire either on the date of the last authorised telecast, or on a specified date, whichever occurs first. It is our view that the revenue from the sale of broadcast or exhibition rights may be recognised in full (irrespective of when the licence period begins), provided the following conditions are met:

(a)   a contract has been entered into;

(b)   the film is complete and available for delivery;

(c)   there are no outstanding performance obligations, other than having to make a copy of the film and deliver it to the licensee; and

(d)   collectibility is reasonably assured.

Rights for the exhibition of films at cinemas are generally sold either on the basis of a percentage of the box office receipts or for a flat fee. In the case of the percentage basis, revenue should be recognised as it accrues through the showing of the film. Where a non-refundable flat fee is received, we suggest that revenue be recognised on the same basis as described above for television broadcast rights.

In the US, under SFAS 53 — *Financial Reporting by Producers and Distributors of Motion Picture Films* — revenue from a television broadcast contract should only be recognised in full when the licence period begins, and all of the following conditions have been met:

(a)   the licence fee for each film is known;

(b)   the cost of each film is known or reasonably determinable;

(c)   collectibility of the full licence fee is reasonably assured;

(d)   the film has been accepted by the licensee in accordance with the conditions of the licence agreement; and

(e)   the film is available for its first telecast.[71]

The principle of only recognising revenue from television licence agreements when the film is available for its first telecast is applied by TVS ENTERTAINMENT PLC:

Extract 3.4: TVS ENTERTAINMENT PLC[72]

ACCOUNTING POLICIES [extract]

(c) TURNOVER [extract]
   Income from television licence agreements is recognised as each programme becomes available for transmission.

5.8   Sale and leaseback transactions

A sale and leaseback transaction takes place when an owner sells an asset and immediately re-acquires the right to use the asset by entering into a lease with the purchaser. The accounting treatment of any apparent profit arising on the sale of the asset will depend on whether the leaseback is an operating or finance lease. In general terms, if the leaseback is an operating lease, the seller-lessee has disposed of substantially all the risks and rewards of ownership of the asset, and so has realised a profit on disposal. Conversely, if the leaseback is a finance lease, the seller-lessee is, in effect, re-acquiring substantially all the risks and rewards of ownership of the asset; consequently, it would be inappropriate to recognise a profit on an asset which, in substance, was never disposed of.[73]

The accounting treatment of the profit arising on sale and leaseback transactions is discussed in Chapter 19 at 7.4.

6   CONCLUSION

The growing complexity and variety of business activity have given birth to a variety of forms of revenue-earning transactions which were never contemplated when the point of sale was established several decades ago as the general rule for revenue recognition. However, the gradual move away from strict adherence to the realisation concept has resulted in contemporary generally accepted practice for the recognition of revenue becoming haphazard, illogical and inconsistent. Whilst there appears to be a growing practice of recognising revenue during the course of productive activity, it is generally done on the basis of exception, rather than in terms of an established principle.

The fundamental problem lies with the fact that the meaning of realisation is not clearly defined; and until such time as the ASC prepares a statement which defines realisation and incorporates this definition into individual SSAPs, anomalous accounting practices will remain. Alternatively, if 'distributable profits' were to be adequately defined, a possible solution might be for the profit and loss account to be prepared on the basis of only reflecting legally distributable income, and for a statement of changes in financial wealth (for example, as proposed by the ICAS discussion document 'Making Corporate Reports Valuable') to be included as part of the financial reporting package.

References

1 APB Statement No. 4, *Basic Concepts and Accounting Principles Underlying Financial Statements of Business Enterprises*, AICPA, October 1970, para. 134.
2 CA 85, Sch. 4, para. 91.
3 CCAB, *The determination of realised profits and disclosure of distributable profits in the context of the Companies Acts 1948 to 1981 (TR 481)*, September 1982, paras. 4—6, *passim*.
4 *Ibid.*, para. 10.
5 SSAP 2, *Disclosure of accounting policies*, November 1971, para. 14.
6 APB Statement No. 4, para. 150.
7 *Ibid.*, para. 151.
8 *Ibid.*, para. 152.
9 SFAC No. 5, *Recognition and Measurement in Financial Statements of Business Enterprises*, FASB, December 1984, paras. 83 and 84.
10 Sale of Goods Act 1979, s 2(1).
11 *Ibid.*, s 2(4).
12 *Ibid.*, s 2(5).
13 *Ibid.*, s 18, Rule 1.
14 *Ibid.*, s 18, Rule 2.
15 APB Statement No. 4, para. 151.
16 SFAC No. 5, paras. 83 and 84.
17 SFAS 48, *Revenue Recognition When Right of Return Exists*, FASB, June 1981, para. 6.
18 *Ibid.*
19 *Ibid.*, para. 8.
20 APB Statement No. 4, para. 150.
21 CA 85, Sch. 4, para. 12(a).
22 *Ibid.*, para. 91.
23 IAS 18, *Revenue Recognition*, IASC, December 1982, para. 4.
24 *Ibid.*, para. 21.
25 IAS 16, *Accounting for Property, Plant and Equipment*, IASC, March 1982, para. 39.
26 E32, *Comparability of Financial Statements*, IASC, January 1989, paras. 59—63, *passim*.
27 IAS 18, para. 6.
28 *Ibid.*, para. 8.
29 *Ibid.*, para. 23.
30 *Ibid.*, para. 6.
31 *Ibid.*, para. 9.
32 *Ibid.*, para. 24.
33 *Ibid.*, para. 10.
34 *Ibid.*, para. 24.
35 Exposure Draft E32, paras. 48—53 and 82—84.
36 IAS 18, para. 25.
37 CICA *Handbook*, Section 1000, *Fundamental accounting concepts*, para. 41.
38 ARB 43, *Restatement and Revision of Accounting Research Bulletins*, AICPA, June 1953, Chapter 1, Section A, para. 1.
39 *Ibid.*
40 *Ibid.*, Chapter 11, Section A, para. 11.
41 *Ibid.*, para. 13.
42 ARB No. 45, *Long-Term Construction-Type Contracts*, AICPA, October 1955, para. 15.
43 SFAC No. 5, para. 83.
44 *Ibid.*
45 *Ibid.*
46 *Ibid.*
47 Based on the AICPA Industry Accounting Guide, *Accounting for Franchise Fee Revenue*, AICPA, 1973.

48 IAS 18, Appendix, Section B, para. 8.
49 *Ibid.*
50 SFAS 45, *Accounting for Franchise Fee Revenue*, FASB, March 1981, para. 5.
51 *Ibid.*
52 *Ibid.*, para 12.
53 SFAS 50, *Financial Reporting in the Record and Music Industry*, FASB, November 1981, para. 8.
54 SFAS 91, *Accounting for Nonrefundable Fees and Costs Associated with Originating or Acquiring Loans and Initial Direct Costs of Leases*, FASB, December 1986, para. 5.
55 *Ibid.*
56 C. I. Brown, D. J. Mallett and M. G. Taylor, *Banks: An Accounting and Auditing Guide*, Industry Accounting and Auditing Guide published by the ICAEW, 1983, para. 20.2.
57 SFAS 91, para. 8.
58 *Ibid.*, para. 8a.
59 *Ibid.*, para. 8b.
60 This is also the view taken in the US, see SFAS 91 at para. 10.
61 *Aluminium Industrie Vaassen B.V. v Romalpa Aluminium Limited* [1976] W.L.R. 676.
62 Accounting Recommendation 2.207, *Accounting for goods sold subject to reservation of title*, ICAEW, July 1976.
63 SSAP 9, *Stocks and long-term contracts*, Revised September 1988, para. 22.
64 *Ibid.*, paras 28 and 29.
65 Brixton Estate plc, Report and Accounts 1987, p. 24.
66 The Hammerson Property Investment and Development Corporation plc, Annual Report & Accounts 1987, p. 24.
67 Crest Nicholson Plc, Annual Report and Accounts 1988, p. 28.
68 SFAS 66, *Accounting for Sales of Real Estate*, FASB, October 1982, para. 5.
69 *Ibid.*, para. 6.
70 *Ibid.*
71 SFAS 53, *Financial Reporting by Producers and Distributors of Motion Picture Films*, FASB, December 1981, para. 6.
72 TVS ENTERTAINMENT PLC, Financial Statements 1988, p. 41.
73 ASC, *Guidance Notes on SSAP 21: Accounting for Leases and Hire Purchase Contracts*, August 1984, paras. 150—156, *passim.*

Chapter 4

Group financial statements

1   THE CONCEPT OF A GROUP

1.1   Introduction

Group financial statements are designed to extend the reporting entity to embrace other entities which are subject to its control or influence. They involve treating the net assets and activities of subsidiaries held by the holding company as if they were part of the holding company's own net assets and activities; the overall aim is to present the results and state of affairs of the group as if they were those of a single entity.

Although this is a widely accepted view of the objective of group financial statements, it is not described in quite these terms in the various authoritative requirements in force in the UK. The basic requirements for group accounts are presently to be found in the Companies Act 1985. These are that the group accounts should 'give a true and fair view of the state of affairs and profit or loss of the company and the subsidiaries dealt with by those accounts as a whole, so far as concerns members of the company',[1] and that they should comply with the requirements of Schedule 4 (so far as applicable) with respect to their form and content.[2] The accounting standard on group accounts (SSAP 14) goes on to say that 'in practice group accounts usually take the form of consolidated financial statements which present the information contained in the financial statements of the holding company and its subsidiaries as if they were the financial statements of a single entity'.[3] The Companies Act also makes it clear that consolidated financial statements are generally to be regarded as the appropriate form of group accounts.[4]

Various observations can be made about these requirements. First of all, the legal requirement contains the phrase 'so far as concerns members of the [holding] company', which makes it clear that the orientation of the group accounts is to that particular audience; it is not, for example, intended that the group accounts should be designed primarily to provide information for other user groups, such as minority shareholders in partly owned subsidiaries, or creditors of group companies. This is of relevance in deciding between certain accounting choices, as discussed further under 1.3 below. It might also be pointed out that this represents a rather narrower view of the objectives of financial reporting than has become accepted since these rules were introduced some forty years ago, as discussed more fully in Chapter 2. The equivalent pronouncement in the US is slightly broader; it says that the statements are 'primarily for the benefit of the shareholders and creditors of the parent company'.[5]

It is also worth noting that although both the Companies Act and SSAP 14 call for consolidated financial statements to be prepared, they recognise that in certain instances another form of group accounts might be chosen rather than consolidated financial statements.[6] However, both these pronouncements make it clear that this is to be the exception rather than the rule, and in practice it will rarely be the case that another form of group accounts (typically, holding company or partially consolidated financial statements with the financial statements of unconsolidated subsidiaries appended to them) can be regarded as a superior method of giving information about the group. For this reason, this option is not discussed further here, and group accounts are regarded for the purposes of this chapter as meaning consolidated financial statements. In the current Companies Bill, it is clear that consolidated financial statements are the required form of group accounts, so the alternative forms will not be permitted in the future.[7]

As well as consolidating the financial statements of subsidiaries, group accounts are also required to incorporate, in a more limited form, the underlying activities of associates by a process known as equity accounting. This is discussed more fully in 5 below.

1.2   What is a subsidiary?

The question of the definition of a subsidiary is fundamental to any discussion of group accounts because otherwise it is impossible to say what constitutes the entity which is the subject of the report. The question is also related to the subject of off-balance sheet financing, because frequently this hinges on whether the group balance sheet should embrace the financial statements of an entity which holds certain assets and liabilities which management may not wish to include in the group financial statements (see Chapter 5).

1.2.1   The legal definition

The basic definition is to be found in the Companies Act 1985, which states that 'a company is deemed to be a subsidiary of another if (but only if) —

(a)   that other either —

    (i)   is a member of it and controls the composition of its board of directors, or

    (ii)   holds more than half in nominal value of its equity share capital, or

(b)   the first-mentioned company is a subsidiary of any company which is that other's subsidiary'.[8]

For the purposes of this definition, equity share capital is defined, rather tortuously, as meaning, 'in relation to a company, its issued share capital excluding any part of that capital which, neither as respects dividends nor as respects capital, carries any right to participate beyond a specified amount in a distribution'.[9] In other words, only shares whose revenue and capital distribution rights are *both* limited to specified amounts do not fall within the definition of equity capital.

The definition of a subsidiary can produce some odd results. For example, it is possible for a company to be the subsidiary of two different holding companies, because one of them might own, say, 51% of the equity capital (thus satisfying part (a)(ii) above), while the other holds 49% but has the right to appoint a majority of the board (satisfying part (a)(i)).

It should also be noted that the definition requires a direct chain of control. The effective shareholding is not the relevant factor; it is whether or not such a chain of control exists. Thus it would be possible, as shown below, for one company to be the subsidiary of another where the holding company's effective share was only, say, 26% of another company, and also for a company *not* to be a subsidiary of another where the latter had an effective share in it of, say, 75%.

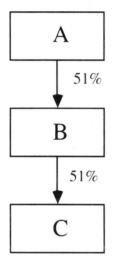

A's effective share of C is only 26% (0.51 x 0.51), yet C is a subsidiary of A.

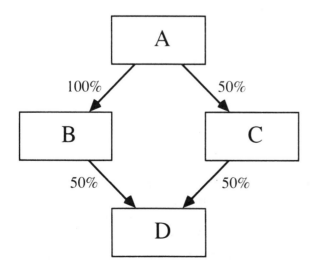

In this case, A's effective share of D is 75% ((1.0 x 0.5)+(0.5 x 0.5)), yet D is not a subsidiary of A (unless B controls the composition of the board of D).

1.2.2   The EC Seventh Directive

Although the above summarises the existing legal position in the UK, this will change in the near future when the EC Seventh Directive on Company Law is incorporated in the next UK Companies Act. These changes are expected to move the definition from one based strictly on the form of the shareholding relationship between the companies, nearer to one which reflects the substance of the commercial relationship and in particular who exercises de facto control. The main provisions of the Directive, and the manner in which they have been incorporated in the Companies Bill published on December 21, 1988, are summarised below.

Article 1 of the Directive sets out six sets of circumstances under which a parent/subsidiary relationship will be regarded as existing, so as to require the parent to present consolidated financial statements, and one further situation requiring consolidation even though such a relationship does not exist. The first four of these must be incorporated in UK law, while the remaining three are optional. The seven are as follows:

(a)   Majority of voting rights

The parent undertaking must consolidate the subsidiary if it holds a majority of its shareholders' or members' voting rights.[10] This is the main definition based on the power of one entity to control another through the exercise of shareholder voting control. Unlike the present definition of a subsidiary in the UK therefore, it concentrates on those shares which can exercise voting power rather than those which are defined in terms of their rights to participate beyond a specified amount in a distribution.

'Voting rights' is not defined by the Directive, but in August 1988 the Department of Trade and Industry announced that it is to be defined in UK law as rights conferred on shareholders in respect of their shares to vote in all (or substantially all) circumstances at general meetings of the company. Contingent voting rights (those which may only be exercised on the happening of an event not within the control of their holder) will not be taken into account unless the event has occurred at the date, or during the period, for which it is necessary to determine whether a parent/subsidiary relationship exists. For accounting purposes the contingent event will be treated as not having occurred unless the effect remains in existence at the end of the financial year in question.[11] The draft legislation in the Companies Bill follows these principles, but addresses many more detailed issues.[12]

(b)   Control of the board of directors

The parent must consolidate the subsidiary if it is a shareholder or member of it and has the right to appoint or remove a majority of the members of its administrative, management or supervisory body (i.e. the board of directors, in the context of the UK).[13] This is similar to the requirement in section 736 (1)(a)(i) of the Companies Act 1985. Essentially it is an anti-avoidance measure, which extends the control concept from control of the company in general meeting to control of the board, to cover situations where the latter exists but not the former.

The DTI announcement stated that when this provision is enacted in the UK, the right to control the composition of the board would be extended to include the right to appoint or remove members of the board entitled to a majority of the voting rights in all (or substantially all) circumstances at board meetings.[14] This is a further anti-avoidance measure, to cope with the situation where control of the board's decisions is achieved through the exercise of differential voting rights without having a majority in number of the membership of the board.

(c)   Control by contract

The parent must consolidate its subsidiary where it can exercise a dominant influence over it under a contract with it or under a provision in its memorandum or articles of association.[15] Such a contract, which is a feature of German business organisations, is not usually possible under general principles of UK company law, because it would conflict with the directors' fiduciary duty to conduct the affairs of the company in accordance with its own best interests, and is allowed only where the Memorandum and Articles specifically permit it. The Directive provides that this part of the definition applies only where it is consistent with the company law of the country concerned, and for this reason it will be enacted in the UK in a fairly restricted way; it will apply only in cases where the parent company has the right to give directions with respect to the operation and finances of the subsidiary which its directors are obliged to comply with whether or not they are for the benefit of the subsidiary, where the subsidiary's domestic law and its Memorandum and Articles permit a dominant influence to be exerted through such a contract, and where the contract in question is in writing.[16]

(d)   Control by agreement

The parent must consolidate its subsidiary if it is a shareholder or member of it and controls alone, under an agreement with other shareholders or members, a majority of the voting rights in the subsidiary.[17] This is a more stringent application of the concept of de facto control by a minority investor (see (e) below), requiring agreement with other shareholders rather than merely their tacit acceptance that control can be exercised. The Directive provides that the member states may introduce more particular requirements for the form and content of such agreements, and the Department of Trade and Industry announced that it intended to draft the legislation so that the agreement must be legally binding but need not be in writing, and that it should include agreements *not* to exercise voting rights as well as those to exercise them in a particular way.[18]

(e)   De facto control over appointment of the board

The parent shall consolidate its subsidiary if it is a shareholder or member of it and a majority of the members of the board who have held office throughout the year, the previous year, and up to the time of the issue of the consolidated accounts have *in fact* been appointed solely as a result of the exercise of the parent's voting rights.[19] This is to cater for the situation where, due to the fact that the majority of the shares are widely dispersed, a minority shareholder can exercise de facto control. The Directive provides that this criterion will not apply if the subsidiary is already the subsidiary of another body under one of the earlier definitions. It also allows member states not to implement this part of the definition, or to make it conditional on the holding of at least 20% of the voting rights; the UK government was opposed to this part of the definition at the time of the negotiation of the terms of the directive, and they appear to have decided to take advantage of the first of these exemptions, since the Companies Bill does not contain this provision.

(f)   Participating interest with dominant influence or unified management

The parent company must consolidate its subsidiary if it holds a participating interest in it and if either it exercises a dominant influence over it or the two entities are managed on a unified basis by the parent.[20] For this purpose, the definition of a 'participating interest' relies on the Fourth Directive, which in the UK means that this is equivalent to the definition of a related company (see 5.2.2 below). There is no further definition of the concept of either 'dominant influence' or 'managed on a unified basis'; both are concepts derived from German law. In practice this criterion is likely to be very similar to the one based on de facto control described at (e) above.

The Department of Trade and Industry's announcement said that it intended to exercise the member state option to introduce this definition into UK law in addition to the mandatory definitions set out in (a) to (d) above. The Department went on to say that they did not intend to elaborate on the definitions of either 'dominant influence' or 'managed on a unified basis', since they regarded this as an area to be more appropriately dealt with by means of accounting standards, although ultimately it is a matter of law to be interpreted by the courts. In the Companies Bill,[21] this part of the Directive has been introduced in a very broad form which is based on a wide definition of 'participating interest', with the clear intention of preventing artificial structures designed to achieve the purposes of off-balance sheet finance schemes.

(g)   Horizontal groups

Consolidated financial statements must be prepared for companies which have no shareholding relationship in either of two sets of circumstances. The first is if they are managed on a unified basis under the terms of a contract or provisions in their memorandum or articles of association; the second is if the same people form the majority of the members of the board of both companies during the year and for the period up to the preparation of the financial statements.[22] There are instances of major enterprises which are run under the first of these structures; one is Unilever, which comprises two separate parent companies, one British and one Dutch, which are run on a unified basis. In practice, Unilever does present financial statements on a combined basis as well as for the individual groups, but this is done voluntarily and does not need the intervention of a legal requirement to enable it to do so. Although the thinking behind the second set of circumstances is easy to understand, it would appear to result occasionally in the consolidation of separate enterprises which were associated with each other only by coincidence and whose combined financial statements would have neither meaning nor relevance to anyone. Neither of these provisions has been incorporated in the Companies Bill.

1.2.3 The approach used in other countries

There is no uniformity of practice as between other countries in deciding what constitutes a subsidiary. Some of the more prominent approaches are listed below:

IASC: The international accounting standard on consolidated financial statements simply defines a subsidiary as 'an enterprise which is controlled by another enterprise (known as the parent)'.[23]

US: A The basic statement which outlines the US approach to the consolidation of subsidiaries is ARB 51 — *Consolidated financial statements* — which was issued in 1959. The basic criterion on which the definition of a subsidiary rests is the holding of a controlling financial interest in it. Paragraph 2 of ARB 51 (as amended by SFAS 94) goes on: 'The usual condition for a controlling financial interest is ownership of a majority voting interest, and, therefore, as a general rule ownership by one company, directly or indirectly, of over fifty percent of the outstanding voting shares of another company is a condition pointing towards consolidation.'

A subsidiary is also described in APB 18 (which deals with equity accounting) as 'a corporation which is controlled, directly or indirectly, by another corporation. The usual condition for control is ownership of a majority (over 50%) of the outstanding voting stock. The power to control may also exist with a lesser degree of ownership, for example, by contract, lease, agreement with other stockholders or by court decree.'[24]

The SEC also has a relevant definition which is applicable to its registrants. A 'majority-owned subsidiary' is defined as 'a subsidiary more than 50% of whose outstanding voting shares is owned by its parent and/or the parent's other majority-owned subsidiaries'.[25]

Canada: The definition of a subsidiary is incorporated in the CICA *Handbook*, and says that 'a subsidiary is a company in which another company owns, directly and/or indirectly through other subsidiaries, a majority of shares carrying the right to elect at least a majority of the members of the board of directors'.[26]

Australia: The definition of a subsidiary contained in the Companies Code is modelled on that of the UK Companies Act, and says that a corporation shall be deemed to be the subsidiary of another corporation if —

(a)   that other corporation —

   (i)   controls the composition of the board of directors of the first-named corporation;

   (ii)   is in a position to cast, or control the casting of, more than one-half of the maximum number of votes that might be cast at a general meeting of the first-mentioned corporation; or

   (iii)   holds more than one-half of the issued share capital of the first-mentioned corporation (excluding any part of that issued share capital that carries no right to participate beyond a specified amount in a distribution of either profits or capital); or

(b)   the first-mentioned corporation is a subsidiary of any corporation that is that other corporation's subsidiary (including a corporation that is that other's subsidiary) by another application or other applications of this paragraph.[27]

However, an exposure draft in Australia has recently proposed an approach to the preparation of consolidated financial statements which embraces a wider range of companies. This is based on the view that the group accounts should include the financial statements of all those companies which form part of a single economic entity, based on the concept of control. Control is defined as 'the capacity of an entity to dominate decision-making, directly or indirectly, in relation to the financial and operating policies of another entity so as to enable that entity to operate with it as part of an economic unit in achieving the objectives of the controlling entity'.[28] Since this takes a significantly different approach from the law, some reconciliation between the two would appear to be necessary in order to allow it to be fully implemented.

New Zealand: The legal definition of a subsidiary is contained in the Companies Act 1955, and follows the UK Companies Act definition very closely. However, a New Zealand accounting standard, SSAP 8, has more recently introduced the concept of an 'in-substance subsidiary', which should also be consolidated unless the directors believe that the same or equivalent information would be presented by application of the equity method (with various additional disclosures).[29]

Under the standard, a company is deemed to be an in-substance subsidiary of another company if:

(a)   that other company controls directly, indirectly, or beneficially:

    (i)   the majority of the equity share capital or the rights thereto; or
    (ii)   the majority of the voting rights or the rights thereto; or
    (iii)   the majority of the voting rights of the Board of Directors or the rights to those voting rights; or
    (iv)   the rights to in excess of 50% of earnings or the rights thereto; or
    (v)   the rights to in excess of 50% of dividends or other distributions or the rights thereto on all equity other than equity redeemable in cash; or

(b)   that other company obtains under any other scheme, arrangement or device, in substance, the benefits or risks of majority ownership or control.[30]

1.3   Consolidating partly-owned subsidiaries

Various alternative ways of looking at a group become relevant when there are subsidiary companies which are not wholly-owned by the holding company; the particular matters which are affected are the elimination of the effects of inter-company transactions and the calculation of minority interests. There are two widely accepted concepts, referred to respectively as the entity concept and the proprietary concept, but the latter has a number of further variants. These are described in turn below.

1.3.1 The entity concept

The entity concept focuses on the existence of the group as an economic unit, rather than looking at it only through the eyes of the dominant shareholder group. It concentrates on the resources controlled by the entity, and regards the identity of owners with claims on these resources as being of secondary importance. It therefore makes no distinction between the treatment given to different classes of shareholders, whether majority or minority.

1.3.2 The proprietary concept

The proprietary concept might be regarded as the one which is closest to the traditional UK way of looking at a group, as it is defined in company law. It emphasises legal control, exercised by a controlling shareholding interest, and regards the purpose of the production of the consolidated financial statements as being primarily for the information of the shareholders of the holding company. Correspondingly, it makes no attempt to present financial statements which are relevant to the minority shareholders. This approach is sometimes referred to as the 'parent company' concept , and there is a variant of it known as the 'parent company extension' concept, which leans more towards the entity concept described above.

1.3.3 Comparison between the different concepts of a group

The distinction between the different methods in practice can best be illustrated by an example.

Example 4.1: Comparison between the different concepts of a group

Assume that company A buys 75% of company B for £1,200 when company B has total net assets with a fair value of £1,000 and a book value of £800. Under the three concepts shown above, the consolidated balance sheet of company A would incorporate the effects of the acquisition calculated as follows:

	Entity concept £	Proprietary concept £	Parent coy. extension concept £
Net assets of B	1,000	950	1,000
Goodwill	600	450	450
	1,600	1,400	1,450
Minority interest	400	200	250
Investor interest	1,200	1,200	1,200

Under the entity concept, both the tangible net assets and goodwill are reported in the balance sheet at the full amount of their fair value as determined by the transaction involving the majority shareholder. These amounts are then apportioned between the majority and minority shareholders. By way of contrast, the proprietary concept leaves the minority interest unaffected by the transaction of the majority shareholder; it is shown simply as their proportionate share of the book values of the assets of the company. This means that the goodwill is stated at a figure which represents the difference between the cost of the 75% investment (£1,200) and 75% of the fair value of the assets (£750). Perhaps more disturbingly, the assets are carried on a mixed basis which represents 75% of their fair value and 25% of their book value. This last feature is avoided in the parent company extension concept, which includes the assets at the whole amount of their fair value and apportions that between the majority and minority interests, but includes goodwill only as it relates to the majority investor.

The rules set out in the Companies Bill would not permit the use of the entity concept as set out above, because they require that goodwill be calculated by comparing the acquisition cost with the investor's proportionate share of the investee's net assets.[31] The entity method is also ruled out by the international standard on business combinations, IAS 22.[32] This permits either of the other two methods, without expressing a preference, but the recent exposure draft which seeks to reduce options within international accounting standards proposes that the proprietary concept should be the preferred approach, with the parent company extension method as a permitted alternative.[33]

All of these distinctions are eliminated if another possibility is adopted; that of proportional consolidation. Under this concept, the minority interest is disregarded altogether, being set against the assets and liabilities of the subsidiary on a line by line basis, so that only the majority investor's share of the subsidiary's assets are consolidated. In the above example, this would result in consolidation of assets of £750 and goodwill of £450, representing the total of the investment of £1,200.

The different concepts are also relevant to the calculation of the adjustments made to eliminate the effects of inter-company transactions. If company A in the above example sold an asset to company B for a profit of £100, and company B still held the asset in stock at the year end, it would be necessary to make an adjustment on consolidation to eliminate what was an unrealised profit from the group point of view. Under the proprietary concept, the minority shareholders are regarded as outsiders, and therefore there is a case for saying that 25% of the profit *has* been realised; this would be done by limiting the write-down of stock to £75, all of which is taken off the balance on the group profit and loss account. If the entity concept is followed, the adjustment would be effected by apportioning the whole write down of stock of £100 between the group profit and loss account and the minority interest in the ratio 75:25. Under the proportional consolidation method, only 75% of the stock would appear in the consolidated balance sheet in the first place, so the adjustment would simply be to deduct £75 from both the group profit and loss account and from the stock. In this case the Companies Bill permits inter-company profit eliminations to be made either at their gross amounts or in proportion to the investor's stake in the investee.[34]

A further practical situation where differences between the concepts emerge is when the partly owned subsidiary makes losses which put it into overall deficit. Under the entity concept, the consolidated financial statements would continue to account for these losses and apportion them between the majority and minority interests in proportion to their holdings, even if these created a debit balance for the minority interest in the balance sheet. A proprietary viewpoint would not normally permit the minority interest to be shown as a debit balance, because it could not usually be regarded as a recoverable asset from the point of view of the majority interest, which is the orientation of the financial statements under the proprietary concept. This is the position taken by SSAP 14, which says that 'debit balances should be recognised only if there is a binding obligation on minority shareholders to make good losses incurred which they are able to meet'.[35]

In reality therefore, it can be seen that UK practice in relation to group financial statements does not really follow any one concept consistently to the exclusion of the others. Although the proprietary concept would seem most consistent with the present view of a group as laid down in the legislation, it is likely that the parent company extension concept is most commonly applied in most practical situations. Proportionate consolidation is rarely applied except in relation to investments in certain types of joint ventures (the Companies Bill now contains proposed rules for when this method can be used).[36]

1.4   Principles of business combinations

The other major area where different conceptual views are taken is when new companies are brought into the group as subsidiaries. In reporting these transactions, the two common frameworks used are *acquisition* accounting and *merger* accounting. These are discussed in much more detail in 6 below.

2   HISTORICAL DEVELOPMENT OF RULES ON GROUP FINANCIAL STATEMENTS

2.1   Origins of group financial statements

The idea of using a holding company to own further investments in subsidiaries evolved in the US more than 150 years ago, but the preparation of consolidated financial statements to portray the results of the group did not become widely established until the early part of this century.

In the UK, groups of companies only became a significant form of business structure around the time of the First World War, and the first time that a company drew up a consolidated balance sheet for its members was when Nobel Industries Limited presented such a statement as at December 1920. At that time there was no reporting requirement for any profit and loss account (even unconsolidated) to be presented, and the first group profit and loss account was not published until 1933, when the Dunlop Rubber Co. Ltd included one in their annual accounts. The Stock Exchange made the publication of consolidated financial statements a requirement for new issuers in 1939, and the ICAEW published recommendations in 1944[37] which made such accounts best practice for all groups.

2.2   The UK legislative background

The first requirement for group financial statements was introduced into the law by the Companies Act 1947, which was consolidated soon thereafter into the Companies Act 1948. These basic requirements are those described in 1.1 above and they still apply, having been again consolidated into the Companies Act 1985.

The next legislative initiative will be the incorporation in UK law of the EC Seventh Directive on company law, which will be the principal purpose of the present Companies Bill. This Directive was issued by the Council of the European Communities in 1983, to establish a financial reporting framework for groups in all member states. Although this will represent a greater change for those countries where no group accounts requirement existed at all, there will nonetheless be certain changes in practice for the UK as well. The most significant ones will be the changes in the definition of a subsidiary, discussed at 1.2.2 above, and changes in the qualifying conditions for merger accounting, which are covered at 6.1.5 below.

2.3   Accounting Standards in the UK

The general accounting standard on group accounts in the UK is SSAP 14 —
Group accounts — issued in September 1978. This provides the broad
framework to support the basic legal requirements, and deals in particular with the
form which group accounts should take and the circumstances under which a
subsidiary should be excluded from consolidation. It also deals with various
miscellaneous matters in relation to the mechanics of the consolidation process.

More recently, further standards have been added to deal in more detail with
business combinations. SSAP 22 — *Accounting for goodwill* — was issued in
December 1984, and its companion, SSAP 23 — *Accounting for acquisitions and
mergers* — came out soon thereafter, in April 1985. The ASC has also now
issued a discussion paper for comment on the allocation of fair values following
an acquisition[38] and a further exposure draft proposing supplementary disclosures
concerning goodwill.[39] All of these matters are discussed in detail in 6 below.

The first accounting standard issued in this general area was, however, SSAP 1,
— *Accounting for associated companies*. This was originally published in
January 1971, and the most recent revision to it was made in April 1982. This is
covered in 5 below, which deals with equity accounting.

3   CONSOLIDATION OF SUBSIDIARIES

3.1   Basic principles

It is beyond the scope of this chapter to discuss the detailed mechanics of the
consolidation process; there are a number of basic texts which give a full
exposition of this subject. In fact there are no authoritative rules on the subject at a
detailed level: SSAP 14 merely states that 'the method of preparation of
consolidated financial statements on an item-by-item basis, eliminating intra-group
balances and transactions and unrealised intra-group profit, is well
understood ...'.[40] The most appropriate general objective to keep in mind is the
need to present the group as if it were a single entity, which necessarily involves
the aggregation of like items which appear in the financial statements of the
individual members of the group, and the elimination of the effects of transactions
which are internal to the group and would have received no recognition had the
group indeed been a single entity.

3.2   Uniform accounting policies

It is axiomatic that the figures being aggregated in the consolidation process must
have been compiled on a consistent basis and therefore that uniform accounting
policies should have been adopted by all the members of the group. Of course,
local reporting requirements for each subsidiary might dictate that different
policies must be used for domestic purposes; the only necessity where this occurs
is that appropriate adjustments are made in the course of the consolidation process
to eliminate the effects of such differences.

This is the basic requirement set out in SSAP 14. However, the standard goes on
to say that 'in exceptional cases where this is impracticable, different accounting

policies may be used provided they are generally acceptable and there is disclosure of:

(a)   the different accounting policies used;

(b)   an indication of the amounts of the assets and liabilities involved, and where practicable, an indication of the effect on results and net assets of the adoption of policies different from those of the group;

(c)   the reasons for the different treatment'.[41]

Notwithstanding this apparent loophole, the financial statements must still give a true and fair view of the group as a whole and it is difficult to imagine that this could be achieved by adding together figures which have been compiled using profoundly different policies unless the effect is not material. In practice, however, this relaxation in the standard does not seem to be relied on in many cases and groups generally do exert themselves to achieve consistency of policies unless the effect is insignificant.

The Companies Bill does not refer to accounting policies as such in this context, but says that 'where assets and liabilities ... have been valued by undertakings according to accounting rules differing from those used for the group accounts, the values shall be adjusted so as to accord with the rules used for the group accounts'.[42] However, this need not be done if there are special reasons for leaving them unchanged (in which case various disclosure requirements apply),[43] or if the effect is immaterial.[44]

3.3   Coterminous accounting periods

Since the group is seen as an extension of the parent company in UK law, it is necessary that the period covered by the group financial statements corresponds to the accounting reference period of the parent, both in terms of duration and balance sheet date. Once again, this requirement is implicit in the objective that the group financial statements should be prepared as if the group were a single entity.

Of course, there can again be reasons why the individual subsidiaries' own financial statements might be drawn up to a different date; for example, in certain countries their year end might be dictated by law, they might choose to adopt a particular accounting period for tax purposes or their trade may be seasonal and have a natural cycle which makes it appropriate to choose a particular reporting date. Another reason could be that they deliberately prepare their financial statements to a date shortly before that of the parent (as a materially accurate approximation to the period of the parent) so as to facilitate speedy reporting by the parent of the group results.

Where the period covered by the financial statements of an individual member of the group does not correspond to that of the parent, two solutions are possible. The first is for the subsidiary to prepare special financial statements solely for the purpose of the consolidation for a period which does match that of the parent, which may require certain legal permissions to be obtained. The legal rules when the financial year of the subsidiary does not match that of the parent are that the group accounts should consolidate the financial statements of the subsidiary for its year which ends last before the balance sheet date of the parent, unless the

Secretary of State directs otherwise as a result of an application from the parent company's directors.[45] In practice this means that, in order to be able to use special (rather than statutory) accounts of the subsidiary drawn up to the parent company's year end, it is necessary first to seek approval from the Department of Trade and Industry (which is generally obtained without any difficulty, although the company may be required to furnish a letter from its auditors confirming that the financial statements will not be qualified as a result).

The second solution is simply to evaluate how material the effect of using different periods is, and if the financial statements of the period actually used by the subsidiary are not materially different from those which would have been produced if they had used the parent company's accounting reference period, then it will be acceptable to use them as an appropriate surrogate. Where this course of action is adopted, it is necessary to be satisfied that there is no material distortion in either the balance sheet or the profit and loss account. The latter is frequently the more problematical of the two, and where the business of the subsidiary produces fluctuating results, so that the effect of using different periods can be significant, then it is likely that this will not be a possible option. Also, there can be problems in the year of acquisition of a company with a different year end from that of the parent, because the inclusion of profits up to its own year end would not portray the results for a period of the same duration as the post-acquisition period of ownership by the parent. (In these particular circumstances, an acceptable solution can sometimes be to 'top up' the results by the notional inclusion of an equivalent period of trading before the acquisition.)

SSAP 14 requires that, where coterminous year ends are *not* used in respect of any of the group's principal subsidiaries, there should be disclosure of the name of the subsidiaries involved, the year ends used (and duration of accounting periods, if different from that of the parent) and the reasons for the use of the different dates. It also requires that appropriate adjustments should be made to the consolidated financial statements for any abnormal transactions which have taken place between the respective balance sheet dates.[46] It is not entirely clear what this latter requirement is intended to cover, but it is obviously designed to mitigate any particular distortion which the use of different year ends might cause, such as the double counting of the same asset because it was transferred from one company to the other and appeared in the balance sheets of both at different dates.

It is clear from the above that both the law and the accounting standard do contemplate situations where non-coterminous periods are used and, in the case of SSAP 14, they seek to solve the problem by requiring disclosure. However, it remains the case that the group financial statements must still give a true and fair view of the group's state of affairs at the holding company's year end and of its results for the period ended on that date, so it is doubtful whether these provisions can be regarded as detracting from that requirement. To take an extreme example, if a non-trading holding company with a December year end had a single subsidiary with a March accounting reference date, it could scarcely be argued that consolidating the subsidiary's March financial statements without amendment would give a true and fair view of the state of affairs of the group nine months later and of the group results for the calendar year, unless they happened to be immaterially different from the figures that would have been shown in special financial statements drawn up to December. Accordingly, it would seem that the use of different year ends should be accepted only on grounds of materiality.

The Companies Bill contains provisions allowing the parent company to use either the accounts of the financial year of the subsidiary (but only if they are not more than three months out of date compared to the year end of the parent company) or else interim accounts made up to the parent company's year end.[47] In the latter case, no special permission need be obtained.

The use of the financial statements of foreign subsidiaries with non-coterminous year ends also raises the question of what exchange rate should be used for translation purposes. This point is covered in 3.4.1 of Chapter 18.

3.4 Elimination of unrealised profits on inter-company transactions

The reasons for making such an elimination are straightforward; 'no man can make a profit by trading with himself', and when a group is trying to present its results as if it were a single entity, it clearly must not regard internal transactions as giving rise to a realised profit.

The subject is not covered in SSAP 14 other than in the passing reference in the passage quoted in 3.1 above. However, in most cases the treatment is uncontentious and entails writing down the value of items of stock (if that is what is involved) held by one group company at the year end which have been purchased from another group company which has made a profit on the deal; the adjusting entry is simply to remove the profit element from the stock valuation and from the balance on the group profit and loss account (net of a deferred tax adjustment if appropriate; the elimination of this profit will give rise to a timing difference, because the group will still be taxed on the profit which is eliminated). Similar principles will apply to the transfer of fixed assets.

Complications can arise when either the selling or the purchasing company (or both) is not a wholly-owned subsidiary, or when one of the parties to the transaction is an associate rather than a subsidiary (SSAP 1 requires similar adjustments to be made in respect of associates).[48] There are essentially two questions: (a) what proportion of the profit in the stock is to be eliminated, and (b) whether, and if so how, to make the elimination against minority interests as well as group shareholders' funds. The second question has already been discussed to some extent in this chapter at 1.3 above, and the whole topic is dealt with in some detail in Wilkins' book on Group Accounts which illustrates the very wide range of differing views on the subject.[49] Our recommendation for the method to be used in practice is for the whole amount of the profit to be eliminated from stock, and then for the adjustment to be apportioned between the majority and minority interests in proportion to their holdings in the selling company.

Another question which sometimes arises is whether or not similar adjustments should be made following other intra-group transactions, such as the sale of an item manufactured by one company which becomes a fixed asset in the financial statements of another. In principle, the question is no different, but sometimes such transactions take place in circumstances where the relationship between the companies is almost incidental, which is rather different from the routine transfer of stock in a vertically integrated business, so it is sometimes questioned whether the same considerations automatically apply. The only general answer which can be given is that the financial statements should still seek to portray the group as if it were a single entity, and this would generally indicate that the fixed asset really represents an item manufactured for the entity's own use, and that accordingly profit should not normally be recognised on the transaction.

The foreign currency complications which can arise from inter-company transactions are dealt with in 3.7.2 of Chapter 18.

4   EXCLUSION OF SUBSIDIARIES FROM GROUP FINANCIAL STATEMENTS

As well as various rules on exclusion of particular subsidiaries, there are a number of provisions which exempt parent companies from having to present consolidated financial statements at all. Both SSAP 14[50] and the Companies Act[51] contain provisions that group accounts need not be produced if the reporting company is itself a wholly-owned subsidiary, although the Companies Act exemption applies only if it is owned by another British company. The present Companies Bill introduces more complicated rules which extend that exemption to companies owned by parents incorporated elsewhere in the EEC, and also does not require them to be wholly-owned, although in the latter case there are provisions which allow minority shareholders to demand the preparation of consolidated accounts. There are various further qualifying requirements.[52]

The Companies Bill also contains provisions to exempt parent companies from having to prepare consolidated financial statements if the group falls within certain size limits. A group will qualify for this exemption if it satisfies at least two of the following three tests:

(a)   its aggregate turnover is not more than £9.6 million;

(b)   its aggregate balance sheet total is not more than £4.7 million;

(c)   its aggregate number of employees is not more than 250.

Rather illogically, these figures are to be measured by adding up the relevant figures in the individual group companies' accounts *without* making any inter-company eliminations. The exemptions are also not available if any of the group companies is a public company (or equivalent), an authorised banking institution, an insurance company or an authorised person under the Financial Services Act 1986.[53]

4.1   Sources of rules on exclusion of particular subsidiaries

Where group accounts are required, there are various circumstances under which it is considered appropriate not to consolidate particular subsidiaries, but instead either to deal with them in some other manner or to exclude them from the group financial statements altogether. Both SSAP 14 and the Companies Act contain a list of such reasons, which partly overlap with each other.

Under SSAP 14, subsidiaries should be excluded from consolidation (but not from the group financial statements altogether) if:

(a)   their activities are dissimilar from those of the rest of the group;

(b)   they are not, in reality, controlled by the holding company;

(c)   they operate under severe restrictions which impair control;

(d)   control of them is intended to be temporary.[54]

The Companies Act states that group accounts (in any form) need not deal with a subsidiary if the holding company's directors believe that to include them would:

(a)   be impracticable;

(b)   be of no real value in view of the insignificant amounts involved;

(c)   involve disproportionate expense or delay;

(d)   be misleading;

(e)   be harmful;

or if the business of the subsidiary is so different from that of the holding company that they cannot reasonably be treated as a single undertaking.[55]

The circumstances under which these criteria might be applied are discussed in turn below.

4.2   Dissimilar activities

The specific rules on this in SSAP 14 are that 'a subsidiary should be excluded from consolidation if its activities are so dissimilar from those of other companies within the group that consolidated financial statements would be misleading and that information for the holding company's shareholders and other users of the statements would be better provided by presenting separate financial statements for such a subsidiary'.[56] The standard goes on to say that in these circumstances 'the group accounts should include separate financial statements for that subsidiary. They may be combined with the financial statements of other subsidiaries with similar operations, if appropriate. The separate financial statements should include the following information:

(a)   a note of the holding company's interest;

(b)   particulars of intra-group balances;

(c)   the nature of transactions with the rest of the group; and

(d)   a reconciliation with the amount included in the consolidated financial statements for the group's investment in the subsidiary which should be stated under the equity method of accounting.'[57]

On the face of it, the Companies Act provision that a subsidiary can be excluded from group accounts if 'the business of the holding company and that of the subsidiary are so different that they cannot reasonably be treated as a single undertaking'[58] appears similar to these rules. However, the rules in the standard are concerned with whether or not the subsidiary should be *consolidated*, not whether it should be excluded from the group financial statements altogether, which is what the legal provision deals with. The manner of presentation required under SSAP 14 is still a form of group financial statements, so the Companies Act exemption is not being used by companies which adopt this treatment. In practice it would be very rare to use the legal exemption and exclude the dissimilar subsidiary from the group financial statements altogether, and in any event this is only possible with the approval of the Secretary of State.[59]

These, then, are the rules; however, how should they be interpreted in practice and, in particular, when would activities be so dissimilar that to consolidate them would be misleading? It cannot have been the intention of the standard that the exclusion should allow diverse conglomerate groups to avoid the need for consolidation, and the mere fact that members of the group are engaged in different activities does not render their consolidation misleading. On the other hand, it could be misleading to consolidate financial statements which are prepared on entirely different bases of accounting; an obvious example would be a group which owned a subsidiary in the banking or insurance sector which applied substantially different accounting policies from the rest of the group. One such example is B.A.T Industries p.l.c., whose financial statements include the following policy note:

Extract 4.1: B.A.T Industries p.l.c.[60]

3   Financial Services [extract]
The group's investments in financial services consist of the following companies:

(i)   B.A.T Financial Services Ltd
(ii)   Allied Dunbar Assurance plc and its subsidiaries and
(iii)   Eagle Star Holdings PLC and its subsidiaries

They are included under the equity method of accounting applied to these companies' financial statements as prepared in accordance with their own accounting policies.

However, there are a number of companies which take a broader view than this, and exclude subsidiaries which they view as being in different businesses in less extreme circumstances than those mentioned above. The most common example would seem to be of those companies which have finance subsidiaries; one such example is Marks and Spencer p.l.c., which discloses the following policy:

Extract 4.2: Marks and Spencer p.l.c.[61]

Basis   of   consolidation
The Group financial statements incorporate the financial statements of:
a   The retailing activities of Marks and Spencer p.l.c. and its UK and overseas subsidiaries for the year to 31 March.
b   The financial activities of the group's wholly owned subsidiaries to 31 March. In order to reflect the different nature of the business of the financial activities and so present fairly the Group's state of affairs, the assets and liabilities of such activities are shown as a net investment in the Group balance sheet and are analysed separately in note 12 on pages 52 and 53.

It is not clear whether this kind of application of the exemption was intended by the ASC when they developed the standard. Although the balance sheets of finance subsidiaries may look different from those of the rest of the group, that by itself is not a reason for not consolidating them, and it does not seem an obvious conclusion that to consolidate them would be misleading, particularly when the business of the subsidiary is closely linked to the mainstream operations of the group. Nonetheless, the interpretation used by Marks and Spencer p.l.c. is reasonably widespread.

The question of dissimilar activities as a reason for non-consolidation has recently been addressed by the FASB in the US, as part of their wider project on consolidated financial statements. Under SFAS 94, issued in October 1987, it is no longer possible to avoid consolidation of a subsidiary because it has 'nonhomogeneous' operations. The statement explains its reasoning as follows:

'The managerial, operational and financial ties that bind an enterprise into a single economic unit are stronger than the differences between its lines of business ... differences between the varied operations of a group of affiliated corporations that constitutes an economic and financial whole do not preclude including them all in consolidated financial statements. Those differences also do not make the equity method a valid substitute for consolidation of majority owned subsidiaries.'[62]

A similar change has recently been agreed by the IASC. Formerly, under IAS 3,[63] it was possible to exclude from consolidation those subsidiaries which undertook dissimilar activities; this is no longer permitted under IAS 27.[64]

The Companies Bill still allows the concept of exclusion because of dissimilar activities, but the legislation has been drafted in a rather more restrictive way than in the previous Acts. It reads as follows:

'Where the activities of one or more subsidiary undertakings are so different from those of other undertakings to be included in the consolidation that their inclusion would be incompatible with the obligation to give a true and fair view, those undertakings shall be excluded from consolidation.

'This ... does not apply merely because some of the undertakings are industrial, some commercial and some provide services, or because they carry on industrial or commercial activities involving different products or provide different services.'[65]

It remains to be seen how these provisions will be interpreted after they have been enacted, and whether companies such as Marks and Spencer p.l.c. will in future consolidate their financial subsidiaries.

4.3 Lack of control

The wording in SSAP 14 is such that a subsidiary should be excluded from consolidation if 'the holding company, although owning directly or through other subsidiaries more than half the equity share capital of the subsidiary, either:

  (i)   does not own share capital carrying more than half the votes; or
  (ii) has contractual or other restrictions imposed on its ability to appoint the majority of the board of directors'.[66]

There is no direct equivalent in the Companies Act, but it would generally be regarded as an example of a case in which consolidation would be misleading.

Where a subsidiary is not consolidated because there are circumstances which bring it within the SSAP 14 criteria set out above, it should be dealt with either under the equity method of accounting (if it otherwise satisfies the SSAP 1 criteria) or carried in the group financial statements as a fixed asset investment (which would require it to be carried at cost or valuation less any provision needed to reflect permanent impairment in value).[67]

A prominent example of circumstances which meet this description is the investment by Trusthouse Forte PLC in The Savoy Hotel PLC, which at October 31, 1988 comprised 69% of the equity of the latter but gave entitlement to only 42.3% of its voting rights. The accounting policy in the financial statements of Trusthouse Forte PLC states that The Savoy Hotel PLC had not been consolidated because of the absence of voting control, but had instead been equity accounted because of the significance of the investment and its long term nature. The following note giving further information was included:

Extract 4.3: Trusthouse Forte PLC[68]

11 SUBSIDIARY NOT CONSOLIDATED
The consolidated profit and loss account of Savoy for the year ended 30th June, 1988 (see note (a)) and the Group's share of the results of Savoy for that period, which is included in the consolidated profit and loss account, are shown below.

	1988		1987	
		Group		Group
	Total	**share**	Total	share
	£m	**£m**	£m	£m
Total receipts	73		71	
Trading expenditure	(57)		(55)	
Depreciation	(3)		(3)	
Trading profit	13		13	
Investment income	—		—	
Profit before taxation	13	**8**	13	9
Taxation	(5)	**(3)**	(4)	(3)
Profit after taxation, attributable to shareholders	8	**5**	9	6

The consolidated net assets of Savoy at 31st December, restated on the basis set out in note (b) are as follows:

	1987 Total £m	1986 Total £m
Fixed assets — tangible assets		
Investment properties	2	2
Land and buildings	54	46
Revaluation surplus — note (b)	125	95
Plant and machinery	2	2
	186	145
Current assets — Stocks	6	5
— Debtors	7	7
— Cash	2	5
Creditors due within one year	(11)	(12)
Net current assets	4	5
Total assets less current liabilities	190	150
Creditors due after one year	(6)	(6)
Provision for liabilities and charges	(1)	(1)
	183	143

Notes
(a) The consolidated profit and loss account of Savoy comprises the results for the year ended 30th June, 1988 which are derived from the published audited accounts for the year ended 31st December, 1987 and the published unaudited half year statements for the half years ended 30th June, 1987 and 1988. The comparative amounts shown for the year ended 30th June, 1987 have been derived similarly. The Group has obtained a direction from the Secretary of State for Trade and Industry to account for Savoy on this basis.

(b) The consolidated net assets of Savoy set out above are published in the audited accounts for the year ended 31st December, 1987 which incorporate the most recent published balance sheet of Savoy, adjusted for the revaluation of properties disclosed in the Directors' Report of Savoy for that year. This Report states that the company's freehold and leasehold properties have, in the directors' opinion a value which exceeds the net book value at 31st December 1987 by more than £125 million. In the absence of any other information, this revaluation surplus has been added to Savoy fixed assets.

(c) With the exception of the accounting policy for property valuation which has been adjusted above, the directors are not aware of any other accounting policies adopted by Savoy which differ significantly from those set out on page 28.

The Group's share of the net assets of Savoy at 30th June, 1988 is calculated as follows	**1988** **£m**	1987 £m
Group's share of net assets at 31st December, 1987	**126**	99
Group's share of results for the half year ended 30th June, 1988	**2**	3
The Group's investment in Savoy	**128**	102
Comprising:		
Cost of investment	**42**	42
Share of post acquisition reserves		
Revaluation reserve	**54**	32
Profit and loss account	**24**	20
Goodwill on acquisition	**8**	8
	128	102

4.4   Operating under severe restrictions

The SSAP 14 rules for exclusion apply if 'the subsidiary operates under severe restrictions which significantly impair control by the holding company over the subsidiary's assets and operations for the foreseeable future'.[69] The Companies Act rule that subsidiaries should not be included in misleading circumstances would again seem to be the nearest equivalent. However, a more specific legislative requirement has now been proposed in the Companies Bill, which states that 'a subsidiary undertaking may be excluded from consolidation where ... severe long-term restrictions substantially hinder the exercise of the rights of the parent company over the assets or management of that undertaking.'[70]

The required accounting treatment in these circumstances is to 'freeze' the carrying value of the subsidiary at its equity amount at the time the restrictions came into force, and not to accrue for any trading results thereafter as long as the restrictions remain. However, a provision for permanent impairment in value of the investment may be needed. It is also necessary to disclose details of the subsidiary's net assets and results, together with amounts included in the profit and loss account in respect of dividends received from it or provisions made.[71] The most usual circumstances which require this rule to be invoked involve political unrest in the country in which the subsidiary is based.

An example of the disclosure relating to these circumstances is to be found in the financial statements of Booker plc. This is set out below:

Extract 4.4: Booker plc[72]

12 FIXED ASSET INVESTMENTS [extract]

	1987 **£ m**	1986 £m
Attributable net asset value of subsidiary companies not consolidated at 31 December 1987	**4.0**	3.2
Reduction required under stated accounting policy	**1.2**	.8
Balance sheet value 31 December 1987	**2.8**	2.4
Profit on ordinary activities before taxation attributable to parent company	**1.3**	.8
Attributable profit after extraordinary items	**1.0**	.4

CONSOLIDATION [extract]

Certain subsidiaries and associated companies operate in countries overseas where the amount of profit that may be remitted is restricted or where freedom of action may be limited. In the opinion of the directors, it would be misleading to consolidate these companies and the group share of their results is therefore included in profit only to the extent of remittances received. The group's total investment in these companies is shown as an asset at attributable asset value either at the date from which this accounting policy was adopted for such companies adjusted for capital subsequently invested or withdrawn, or attributable net asset value at the balance sheet date, whichever is the lower amount.

The reduction to net asset value at the balance sheet date is presumably to recognise a permanent impairment in value.

One thing which the standard does not make clear is what happens when the restrictions are removed; how should the trading results of the subsidiary which accrued during the period when the investment was carried at a frozen amount be accounted for subsequently? Our recommendation is that these should be dealt with as an exceptional item in the year in which the restrictions are lifted.

4.5   Control intended to be temporary

This ground for exclusion is stated, without elaboration, in SSAP 14[73] and again there is no direct equivalent in the Companies Act other than the 'misleading' one. Again, a specific ground for exclusion has now been proposed in the Companies Bill when 'the interest of the parent company was acquired and is held exclusively with a view to subsequent resale.'[74] SSAP 14 requires that the investment should be carried in the group balance sheet as a current asset, at the lower of cost and net realisable value.[75]

The question sometimes arises of whether this ground for exclusion refers to the intention only at the time of acquisition, or whether it applies whenever it is decided that the group no longer wants to retain the subsidiary in question. In our view, the former is the correct interpretation, and this appears to be consistent with the wording proposed in the Companies Bill as set out above. If the latter interpretation were applied, it would run contrary to the rules within SSAP 14 on the effective date of disposal of subsidiaries, which require the results of companies to continue to be consolidated until that time.[76] Accordingly, we believe that this reason for non-consolidation should be used only for those cases where a group acquires a majority holding in a subsidiary with the intention of selling it on soon thereafter.

Another question which can be significant in some circumstances is how to account for the interest cost of financing a temporary investment in a subsidiary; if no profits are consolidated during the period of ownership then the financing cost will result in the group reporting a loss. One way of dealing with this when part of a group which has been acquired is to be sold, is to value the segment to be disposed of at the net present value of the expected sale proceeds as part of the fair value exercise. An example of this can be seen in the 1987 financial statements of Unilever plc in relation to their acquisition of Chesebrough-Pond's Inc., which had occurred just before their 1986 year end.

Extract 4.5: Unilever plc[77]

Chesebrough-Pond's group of companies
Unilever's offer for Chesebrough-Pond's Inc. was declared unconditional on 30th December, 1986 and legal ownership of 95.4 per cent of the company's stock vested on that date, the company thus becoming a Unilever subsidiary.

In view of the temporary nature of Unilever's control over significant parts of the Chesebrough-Pond's group, and the imprecision with which the remaining parts could be valued in the time available, it was considered that the true and fair view in the Unilever 1986 Annual Accounts was better served by not consolidating Chesebrough-Pond's Inc. and its subsidiaries. Accordingly, the Unilever investment in Chesebrough-Pond's Inc. was included in the 1986 Unilever group accounts at cost.

In the 1987 Unilever group accounts Chesebrough-Pond's Inc. and those of its subsidiaries not identified for early disposal have been consolidated with effect from 1st January 1987. Unilever ownership of Chesebrough-Pond's Inc. was increased to 100 per cent on 10th February, 1987.

Those parts of the Chesebrough-Pond's group which were identified for early disposal, and which have now been sold, were valued on acquisition at the present value of the net proceeds of sale realised in 1987. Neither the 1987 results of those businesses nor interest on their acquisition values have been included in the Unilever results.

This does not offend the SSAP 14 requirement to carry such investments at cost, because in this case cost is derived from an allocation of the total purchase price on the basis of their fair value to the acquiring company.

4.6   Other Companies Act exclusions

The other grounds for exclusion from group financial statements which are contained in the Companies Act, but not yet covered in detail above, are where inclusion would be impracticable, of no real value in view of the insignificant amounts involved, would involve disproportionate expense or delay, or would be harmful. These are discussed briefly below.

Exclusion on the grounds of impracticability might apply if, for example, there was a state of war in the country in which the subsidiary was located as a result of which it was not possible to obtain any meaningful information; in other words, this reason should be used only in relatively extreme circumstances. It has been pointed out in this context that 'the word "impracticable" in the legal sense in which it is necessarily used in the Companies Acts has a meaning closely akin to "impossible". The word is not to be interpreted in the sense of "troublesome" or "inconvenient" in which it is sometimes used loosely in conversation.'[78] There is no equivalent of this ground for exclusion in the present Companies Bill.

To say that inclusion of the subsidiary in the group accounts would be of no real value to the members in view of the insignificant amounts involved, is in reality another way of saying that immaterial subsidiaries need not be included, which is in accordance with generally accepted notions of materiality. However, it is interesting to note that the Companies Act (written over forty years ago) bases this solely on whether the *members* would derive benefit from the information, whereas in most other circumstances we would now accept the general proposition that materiality should be assessed in relation to the informational value to a wider range of user groups. The present Companies Bill contains a more direct provision allowing exclusion on grounds of materiality, and does not specify any particular user group audience against whom materiality should be judged.[79]

Exclusion of the subsidiary because to include it would involve expense or delay out of proportion to the value to members can generally be thought to be another aspect of materiality, involving a cost/benefit test, and again the Companies Act addresses this solely from the perspective of the members. Again, this perspective is not continued in the present Companies Bill, which simply talks about 'disproportionate expense or undue delay', without saying from whose point of view these matters should be assessed.[80] Under the existing rules, where a cost/benefit test is involved, this exclusion might apply either because the cost is disproportionately high or because the benefit is disproportionately low, and the latter can sometimes be summoned as a reason even in cases when very substantial subsidiaries are involved. This has been the rationale used by some UK holding companies which are wholly-owned by a foreign parent, in order to escape the need to prepare UK group accounts; although, as a wholly-owned subsidiary they are exempted by SSAP 14 from producing group accounts,[81] the equivalent Companies Act exemption only applies where their holding company is also in the UK.[82] They are, however, often able to demonstrate that the preparation of UK group accounts would be of minimal value to their members (their foreign parent), so that the disproportionate expense exemption under existing legislation can be applied.

One question which is not entirely clear is whether the Companies Act exemptions are in effect overridden by SSAP 14, so that in the above situation it is necessary to find reasons for non-consolidation which satisfy both sets of rules. On the face of it, this is the situation, but it is sometimes argued that SSAP 14 does not strictly require group accounts to be presented, but only dictates the form of group accounts once the decision has been taken to present them; thus a company with only one subsidiary, whose exclusion from group accounts is permitted by the Companies Act, could argue that there is no requirement for it to present group accounts and therefore that SSAP 14 does not apply to it.

The ambiguity which leads to this difference of interpretation is found in the first sentence of part 3 of SSAP 14, which reads, 'A holding company should prepare group accounts in the form of a single set of consolidated financial statements covering the holding company and its subsidiary companies, at home and overseas.'[83] It is possible to read this as meaning either that 'a holding company should prepare group accounts ...' or that 'a holding company's group accounts should be in the form of a single set of consolidated financial statements ...'. Whatever the merits of this debate, we believe that the normal interpretation is that subsidiaries should be excluded from consolidation only if they satisfy the criteria of both SSAP 14 and the Companies Act.

The exemption which applies where inclusion would be harmful to the business of the group requires approval of the Secretary of State.[84] This is generally applied only in relation to companies carrying on foreign trade, and where public knowledge that trade was being conducted there could damage their trade in other countries. There is no equivalent in the present Companies Bill.

The decision on whether or not the consolidation of subsidiaries can be avoided on these various grounds under the Companies Act must be taken by the directors. Although this is obvious, in the sense that the directors have overall responsibility for the financial statements in any event, the law specifically makes these exemptions dependent on the directors forming the opinion that their situation falls within the relevant circumstances envisaged in the Act.[85] Most of the matters to be considered fall naturally within their direct knowledge, but where they are excluding a subsidiary on the grounds that to include it would involve disproportionate expense or delay compared to the value to the members, and where they are taking the view that the value to the members is low, rather than that the expense is high, they may be well advised to seek confirmation from the members that this is indeed their view.

5   EQUITY ACCOUNTING

5.1   Introduction

Traditionally, investments in companies which did not satisfy the criteria for classification as subsidiaries were carried at cost, and the revenue from them was recognised only on the basis of dividends received. However, in the 1960s it became increasingly recognised that there was a case for an intermediate form of accounting, since there was a growing tendency for groups to conduct part of their activities by taking substantial minority stakes in other companies and exercising a degree of influence over their business which fell short of complete control. Mere recognition of dividends was seen to be an inadequate measure of the results of this activity (and one which could be manipulated by the investor, where he could influence the investee's distribution policy). Moreover, since it was unlikely that the investee would fully distribute its earnings, the cost of the investment would give an increasingly unrealistic indication of its underlying value.

Equity accounting was first used by the Royal Dutch Shell group in 1964, and subsequently recognised in UK accounting literature by the issue of SSAP 1, *Accounting for associated companies*, in 1971. Although the standard has been revised twice since then, the basic rules are little changed. The essence of it is that it requires a modified form of consolidation of the results and assets of investees in the investor's financial statements when the investor is able to exercise 'significant influence', but not control, over the management of the investee. Rather than full scale consolidation on a line by line basis, equity accounting involves incorporation of the investor's share of results and assets of the investee in one line in the investor's profit and loss account and balance sheet.

Although the method is designed principally for associated companies, there are circumstances when it is used as a method of incorporating subsidiaries in group financial statements; the most common example of this is when the subsidiary is not consolidated because its activities are dissimilar from those of the rest of the group (see 4.2 above).

5.2 The definition of an associated company

5.2.1 SSAP 1

There are two alternative definitions of an associate in SSAP 1. The more commonly used one requires the investor to have a *long-term, substantial interest* in the investee which puts him in a position to exercise *significant influence* over the investee (which will depend on the disposition of the other shareholdings). The other definition requires the investor's interest to be 'effectively that of a partner in a *joint venture or consortium*' and similarly also to put him in a position to exercise *significant influence* over the investee. If either of these sets of criteria is met, the investee is an associated company within the terms of SSAP 1 and should be accounted for as such.[86] The various elements of the definitions shown above in italics are discussed further below.

'Long-term' is not defined in the standard, but can probably be taken to mean 'other than temporary'. There is a parallel to be drawn here with the circumstances in which a subsidiary is not consolidated because control of it is intended to be temporary, and as discussed in 4.5 above, this should be interpreted as relating to the intention at the time of acquisition, not subsequently. Thus, an investment does not cease to be an associate merely because the investor decides that he is no longer going to keep it for the long term but will dispose of it when a suitable opportunity arises; it should continue to be equity accounted for until the effective date of disposal.

'Substantial interest' is not defined, but the meaning of the term might have two aspects; the first is that insubstantial interests should be excluded, on grounds of materiality, but since this is a general proposition of accounting standards it is probably not the real point. The more important aspect is that only interests which are substantial are likely to confer the ability to exercise significant influence unless the associate is a vehicle for a joint venture or a consortium. The standard goes on to say that interests of 20% or more in the equity voting rights of the investee are likely to confer such influence over it, while those of a smaller amount are not; however, either of these presumptions is rebuttable (the latter requiring concurrence of the investee), because the real test is whether influence exists, not whether a particular percentage holding has been achieved.[87]

'Significant influence' is defined as involvement in the financial and operating policy decisions of the investee (including dividend policy), but not necessarily control of these policies. One indication of such participation is representation on the board, but this is not a conclusive test.[88] The ability to exercise influence through a minority stake obviously depends on the degree of influence or control exercised by the other shareholders; if they have the ability to act jointly or if there is a majority shareholder, then a minority investor could only exercise influence with their consent and could otherwise find his attempts to exercise influence frustrated by their controlling interest.

Where the investee is the vehicle for a joint venture, the implication is that there is a common purpose agreed by the participants for the conduct of the business without regard to the size of their respective holdings, and for this reason the size of the holding is not regarded by SSAP 1 as a persuasive indication of whether or not influence exists.

It should be noted that it is not necessary that significant influence is in fact exercised; the test is whether the investor has the ability to exercise it if he wants to. Thus, he may be entirely happy with the way that the investee is being managed and content to take no active part, but if he is in a position to intervene so as to inhibit the management from moving in a direction with which he disagrees, then the SSAP 1 test is met.

A 'joint venture or consortium' has no defined meaning, but can usually be regarded as describing the circumstances where a group of people get together to pursue a particular business opportunity — often a project with a limited life span, such as the construction of a property development or the exploitation of a natural resource asset. In these circumstances, they may contribute different amounts of capital to the venture, yet still have equal influence because there is agreement between them as to the general strategy of how the business is to be conducted. It may also be that they are individually contributing other resources to the venture apart from their capital investment.

5.2.2   The Companies Act 1985

The Companies Act contains requirements similar to SSAP 1, but these are not identical, and the first point of departure is that the term 'associated companies' is not used at all, the Act preferring instead 'related companies'. The essence of the definition is similar, but the words used are not the same. A related company under the Act is broadly one in which another company 'holds on a long-term basis a "qualifying capital interest" (equity shares with full voting rights) for the purpose of securing a contribution to that company's own activities by the exercise of any control or influence arising from that interest'. There is a rebuttable presumption that a holding of 20% or more is held on a long-term basis and for the purpose of securing such a contribution;[89] however, there is no opposite presumption (as in SSAP 1) that holdings of less than 20% are not held for such a purpose.

SSAP 1 comments that the definition of a related company is wider than that of an associated company, but does not elaborate on the differences.[90] The main difference is probably that the Companies Act definition does not specify the degree of influence required (indeed, strictly, it only says that the investment is to be for the purpose of achieving that influence, not that the influence has to be secured). However, the distinction is a fine one and in practice the two terms can usually be regarded as synonymous.

The present Companies Bill seeks to make some amendments to these rules in order to bring the requirements of Article 33 of the EC Seventh Directive into UK law. This will require an undertaking in which the group has a participating interest and over whose operating and financial policy it exercises a significant influence to be included on the equity basis if it is not consolidated. The Directive picks up the SSAP 1 presumption that a holding of 20% of the shareholders' or members' voting rights shall be presumed to confer significant influence (but not the contrary presumption). It also specifies the accounting process to be followed in some detail, including the transitional procedure to be adopted by those who are equity accounting for the first time. However, since the method is already generally accepted practice in the UK, this is unlikely to have any significant impact in this country.

5.2.3   IAS 28

The definition in the international accounting standard is in similar terms to that in SSAP 1. However, the IAS definition elaborates to a greater extent than the UK SSAP on ways in which significant influence might be exercisable; it says that this will usually be evidenced in one or more of the following ways:

(a)   representation on the board of directors or equivalent governing body of the investee;

(b)   participation in policy making processes;

(c)   material transactions between the investor and the investee;

(d)   interchange of managerial personnel; or

(e)   provision of essential technical information.[91]

This wording is based on the equivalent requirement in the US.[92]

5.3   The accounting treatment of associates

The basic approach of equity accounting involves adding the investor's share of post-acquisition profits to the cost of the investment and deducting dividends received so that the carrying value of the investment reflects the cost plus post-acquisition retained earnings of the investee. This approach was modified slightly in the 1982 revision of SSAP 1, which now requires the investment to be analysed into three components:

(a)   the investing group's share of the net assets other than goodwill of the associate stated, where possible, after attributing fair values to the net assets at the time of acquisition of the interest;

(b)   the investing group's share of any goodwill in the associated company's own financial statements; and

(c)   the premium paid (or discount) on the acquisition of the interests in the associated companies insofar as it has not already been written off or amortised.[93]

SSAP 1 does not specifically state how the goodwill is to be accounted for, but this is governed by SSAP 22, which applies the same rules to goodwill arising on the acquisition of associates as it does to goodwill emerging on the consolidation of subsidiaries. Consequently, such goodwill must be dealt with either by immediate elimination in reserves, or by amortisation in the profit and loss account.[94] The result of this change is that, assuming the former of these two options is adopted, the carrying value of the associate will represent the investor's share of its net assets (after attributing fair values at the date of acquisition).

The attribution of fair values can be problematical in practice because, again, the investor only has influence, not control, over the investee and cannot therefore insist on receiving the same degree of information that could be demanded from a subsidiary. It may therefore be that the exercise will have to be confined to the most significant items, such as the revaluation of major property assets, and this will often be acceptable on grounds of materiality. It should not be forgotten also that the subsequent share of the investee's profits recognised by the investor should also reflect any material adjustments based on this fair value allocation (such as adjustments to depreciation). This point is not specifically addressed in the standard, but it follows from the proposition that equity accounting is a modified form of consolidation and that the same general principles therefore apply. Similarly, adjustments should be made, where material, to bring the accounting policies of the associate into line with those of the investor.

The following example illustrates why such fair value adjustments are necessary:

Example 4.2:   Attributing fair values to the assets of associates

Company A buys a 40% stake in Company B for £2,000,000. Company B is an investment company and its only asset is a portfolio of investments with a book value of £3,000,000 but a fair value of £5,000,000.

If Company A did not apply fair value accounting to the analysis of its stake in Company B, it would record its share of the net assets of B at £1,200,000 and goodwill of £800,000, which, depending on its accounting policy for goodwill, would probably be written off to reserves. The proper treatment in this particular case would be to attribute all of its investment in B to the underlying portfolio of investments and to recognise no goodwill. (Tax effects have been ignored in this example for the sake of simplicity — see 6.4.3 F below.)

If one year later, Company B sells its portfolio for £6,000,000, it will report a pre-tax profit of £3,000,000, of which Company A's share will be £1,200,000. However, A must make an adjustment to this figure to eliminate the £800,000 fair value adjustment which reflected the pre-acquisition gain made by B, but not recorded in its own books at that time, and therefore record a profit of only £400,000.

The presentation of the figures relating to the associate in the investor's financial statements is relatively straightforward. In the profit and loss account, the share of the associate's pre-tax results are shown as one line, and the share of its tax charge similarly shown as an element of the investor's own tax charge. This contrasts with the treatment used in South Africa, where earnings are shown only at the post-tax level, the argument presumably being that it seems illogical to show the tax charge separately but not to show any of the other components of the associate's income. If the associate has extraordinary items, it will be necessary to consider whether these should also be regarded as extraordinary in the context of the investor's financial statements, but if they are, they should similarly be shown as an element of the investor's own extraordinary items; otherwise they should be reclassified as ordinary items (with corresponding adjustments to the tax related thereto).

In the balance sheet, the investment in the associate should again be shown as one line within fixed assets, (analysed between shares and any loans), and any material inter-company trading balances should be shown in current assets or liabilities. The investor's financial statements should also include their share of any reserve movements of the associate, such as a revaluation surplus (but obviously with regard to any fair value adjustment).

Where the associate is very material in relation to the investor, SSAP 1 suggests that the notes to the investor's financial statements should contain summarised profit and loss account and balance sheet information to indicate the scale and nature of the figures which underlie the 'one line' inclusion of the associate.[95] It is not particularly common to do this, but a number of groups have adopted the practice of showing the amount of their share of the turnover derived from the operations of associates. (See Extract 20.3 at 2.4.7 in Chapter 20 for an example.)

5.4   Other particular issues

5.4.1   Non-coterminous periods

The rules about the accounting period of the investee are somewhat confused. SSAP 1 contains the slightly odd requirement that the financial statements of the investee which are used as the source of figures to be equity accounted are to be either coterminous with the investor's accounting reference period or 'made up to a date which is either not more than six months before, or shortly after, the date of the financial statements of the investing group'.[96] It seems rather strange that the standard appears to tolerate a difference in year end of six months in one direction from the investor's year end, but a short but unspecified period in the other direction. If the overall objective is to give a true and fair view of the results for the investor's own financial year, any non-matching of the associate's year can presumably only be accepted on the grounds that the effect is not material, in which case the detail of the SSAP 1 rule seems of questionable relevance.

The standard goes on to say that where the associate's year end is before that of the investor, 'care should be taken to ensure that later information has not materially affected the view shown by the financial statements of the associated company'. It is not entirely clear what action is suggested where it is felt that subsequent events have materially changed this view; the same paragraph goes on to say that the financial statements should disclose the circumstances where the effect of using non-coterminous year ends is material, but a better solution would presumably be to use the updated information which showed that the effect was material to amend the figures incorporated in the financial statements. The international accounting standard deals with this problem by saying that 'adjustments are made for the effects of any significant events or transactions between the investor and the associate that occur between the date of the associate's financial statements and the date of the investor's financial statements'.[97]

Of course, it can be difficult to ensure that the associate provides up-to-date information when the investor has only a minority stake in it. A holding company is usually able to tell its subsidiary to change its year end to coincide with its own, but the various investors in an associate may all have different year ends, and none of them has the control which is needed in order to dictate when the associate's year end should be, nor can they necessarily demand the production of interim accounts for their own purposes (although this can sometimes give an indication of whether or not they do, in fact, exercise significant influence). There can, therefore, be very significant practical difficulties in obtaining information for a period which corresponds to that of the investor, and this can be compounded when the associate has a Stock Exchange listing, which means that only published information can be disclosed in the financial statements of the investor. Nevertheless the fundamental requirement to give a true and fair view of the results of the investor group for its own financial year remains, and cannot be satisfied by incorporating results for an entirely different period. Fortunately, however, the effect will rarely be material to the group.

5.4.2   Deficiency of assets

When an associate makes post-acquisition losses, to the extent that it has a deficiency of assets in its balance sheet, the question arises of whether the investor should continue to account for these results, and thus carry its investment at a negative amount. The position taken by SSAP 1 on the subject is that in these circumstances if the associate is still regarded as a long-term investment 'it will usually be supported by its shareholders (either by way of loans or by way of an agreement, either formal or informal, to support it)'. The standard goes on to say that 'in these circumstances, the investing group should reflect its share of the deficiency of net assets in its consolidated financial statements'.[98]

This approach is slightly different from that taken by the international accounting standard. This says that 'if, under the equity method, an investor's share of losses of an associate equals or exceeds the carrying amount of an investment, the investor ordinarily discontinues including its share of further losses. The investment is reported at nil value. Additional losses are provided for to the extent that the investor has incurred obligations or made payments on behalf of the associate to satisfy obligations of the associate that the investor has guaranteed or otherwise committed. If the associate subsequently reports profits, the investor resumes including its share of those profits only after its share of the profits equals the share of net losses not recognised.'[99]

This wording is substantially derived from the equivalent requirement in the US, but in that country the rule is complicated further by the additional requirement that the investor should 'provide for additional losses when the imminent return to profitable operations by an investee appears to be assured. For example, a material, non-recurring loss of an isolated nature may reduce an investment below zero even though the underlying profitable operating pattern of an investee is unimpaired.'[100] The effect of this is the apparently odd one that a US investor would provide for a loss of an investee which was going to be reversed, but not for one which was to be perpetuated, but presumably the distinction is simply that in the latter case the investor would be more likely simply to abandon the investment, and need not therefore provide for a loss which would never be suffered.

5.4.3   *Investor not preparing group financial statements*

A company which has no subsidiaries, but which has an investment in an associate has a particular problem because of the requirements of the Companies Act that only realised profits can be included in the profit and loss account.[101] Since it does not produce group financial statements, its profit and loss account will be a company profit and loss account, and the only income 'realised' from the associate in that context will be dividends received. For that reason, SSAP 1 suggests that it should equity account only by producing a supplementary pro forma profit and loss account in addition to the company profit and loss account or 'by adding the information in supplementary form to its own profit and loss account in such a way that its share of the profits of the associated companies is not treated as realised ...'.[102] An example of such a presentation is shown below:[103]

Example 4.3:   Unconsolidated profit and loss account incorporating associate's results

	£'000	£'000
Turnover		2,000
Cost of sales		1,400
Gross profit		600
Distribution costs	175	
Administrative expenses	125	
		300
Profit on ordinary activities before taxation		300
Tax on profit on ordinary activities		85
Profit on ordinary activities after taxation		215
Aggregate amount of dividends proposed		80
Amount set aside to reserves		135

Supplementary statement incorporating results of associated companies:

	£'000
Share of profits less losses of associated companies	50
Less tax	15
Share of profits less losses of associated companies	35
Profit on ordinary activities after taxation (as above)	215
Profit attributable to members of the investing company	250
Aggregate amount of dividends proposed	80
Net profit retained (£35,000 by associated companies)	170

Similar considerations apply in relation to the balance sheet. Where a group balance sheet is not presented, and as the company balance sheet will normally carry the investment at cost, SSAP 1 suggests either that a separate pro forma balance sheet should be given, presenting the associate on an equity accounting basis, or that the information should be added in supplementary form to the company balance sheet.[104] The situation arises only relatively seldom, because most companies who have equity stakes in associates also have subsidiary companies and have the obligation to present consolidated financial statements.

These difficulties do not exist in the US, and indeed the opposite position has been taken there, requiring the investor company to equity account for the investee in its own, entity accounts as well as in its group accounts.[105] The international standard permits associates either to be equity accounted or to be carried at cost.[106]

5.4.4   Unincorporated investees

Most of the discussion in SSAP 1 is in terms which describe the associate as a company; however, it is made clear that the same principles apply to investments in unincorporated bodies, such as partnerships. Frequently, such forms are used for the conduct of joint ventures. However, the nature of these vehicles gives rise to some further considerations.

The first is that the nature of the relationship with the investee might mean that there is some other, more appropriate form of presentation rather than one line equity accounting. For example, the investor may have a direct interest in certain assets which it has contributed to the venture, and the only other asset or liability to be recognised might be its entitlement or obligation to receive or pay sums under the profit sharing agreement and, in these circumstances, it may be appropriate to reflect these items directly in its balance sheet. Alternatively, it might be appropriate to reflect directly in its own financial statements its proportionate share of the assets and liabilities of the investee by a form of proportionate consolidation; such a treatment is frequently applied in such industries as oil and gas and construction.

Another consideration which should be borne in mind when there is an investment in an unincorporated investee is that the investor may well have joint and several liability for the liabilities of the investee, and this may need to be reflected in its financial statements, either as a contingent liability or even as a provision if it appears likely that it will be called on to meet this obligation without recovery from its fellow investors.

5.4.5 Loss of associate status

It is possible that the investee might cease to be an associate without any change having taken place in the investment held by the investor, either because the investor's stake has been diluted by the issue of shares by the investee to other parties or because the other shareholders now act together to prevent the investor from exercising influence over the investee. In the latter circumstance, the investment should not be restated to its original cost, but rather frozen at the amount of its equity value at the time when the influence was lost, and this figure should in effect be treated as equivalent to cost in the group financial statements. (The real cost should continue to be shown as such in the investor's own balance sheet.) The 'frozen' carrying value should be kept under review to see whether there has been any permanent impairment in value for which provision has to be made, and one reason for such a write-down might be the receipt of dividends paid out of profits which had been earned by the investee (and accounted for by the investor) during the period when significant influence was exercised.[107]

This is the treatment proposed by SSAP 1 whenever an investment ceases to be an associate. However, we believe that a different treatment might be required in the first of the two sets of circumstances outlined above, namely where the investor's stake has been diluted because the associate has issued shares to another party. In our view, in these circumstances the investor should adjust the carrying value of his investment and recognise a gain or loss depending on whether the shares were issued to the third party at a value which was higher or lower than the asset value of the associate as reflected in the financial statements of the investor. The remaining amount should then be 'frozen' and accounted for as above. This can be illustrated by the following example.

Example 4.4: Dilution in the holding of an investment in an associate

A company owns 200,000 £1 shares in an associated company which has a share capital of £1,000,000 and net assets of £2,500,000. The associate issues 600,000 shares to a third party for cash of £1,800,000.

The accounting will be as follows:

	£
Carrying value of associate	
before the transaction — 20% of £2,500,000	500,000
after the transaction — 12.5% of £4,300,000	537,500
Gain	37,500

If a company has ceased to be an associate because significant influence over it has been lost, SSAP 1 does not deal with the situation where circumstances again change so that the investor's ability to exercise influence is restored; in particular, how should the investor account for the share of the associate's results earned during the period when the investee was not regarded as an associate because of the absence of influence? Our recommendation is that these results should be accounted for as an exceptional item in the results for the year in which the investee again becomes an associate.

5.5   Disclosure requirements regarding associates

5.5.1   *Profit and loss account*

The following should be disclosed:

(a)   the investor's share of:

    (i)   pre-tax profits less losses;
    (ii)   tax relating thereto;
    (iii)   extraordinary items (if material and extraordinary in the context of the group;
    (iv)   net profits less losses retained;[108]

(b)   if they are of major significance in relation to the results of the investing group, these details of an individual associate's results:

    (i)   total turnover;
    (ii)   total depreciation charge;
    (iii)   total profits less losses before tax;
    (iv)   the amount of such profits attributable to the investing group;[109]

(c)   any amount written off goodwill relating to the investment in an associate.[110]

5.5.2   *Balance sheet*

The following should be disclosed:

(a)   the investor's share of net assets other than goodwill;

(b)   the individual or aggregate amount of;

    (i)   any premium or discount on acquisition;
    (ii)   the investor's share of any goodwill in the associate's own accounts;[111]

(c)   loans to or from the associate;[112]

(d)   debtors and creditors resulting from trading with the associate;[113]

(e)   the investor's share of post-acquisition reserves and movements therein, and any tax effect of distribution of these if they relate to overseas associates;[114]

(f)   if they are of major significance in relation to the financial position of the investing group, details of an individual associate's tangible and intangible assets and liabilities.[115]

5.5.3 Notes

It is necessary to disclose the following information about associates by way of note:

(a)   their names;

(b)   the proportion of the number of the issued shares of each class held by the investing group;

(c)   an indication of the nature of the associate's business;[116]

(d)   details concerning non-coterminous year ends, if material;[117]

(e)   details and reasons where the presumption that a 20% stake confers significant influence which justifies associate status, or the converse presumption, is rebutted.[118]

(f)   restrictions on ability of the associate to distribute profits.[119]

An example of a comprehensive note which shows disclosures relating to associated companies is to be found in the financial statements of J Sainsbury plc.

Extract 4.6: J Sainsbury plc[120]

4   Investment in associates [extract]

	Share of allotted capital	Share of Profit Before Tax 1988 £m	1987 £m
Savacentre Limited 16,180,050 "B"Ordinary shares of £1 each	50%	**10.0**	8.5
Haverhill Meat Products Limited 500,000 "B" Ordinary shares of £1 each	50%	**3.7**	3.2
Breckland Farms Limited 200,000 "B" Ordinary shares of £1 each) 141,532 1% Redeemable) Preference Shares of £1 each)	50%	**0.3**	0.3
Kings Reach Investments Limited 28,760 Ordinary shares of 1p each	28.76%	**1.0**	0.8
UK associates		**15.0**	12.8
Shaw's Supermarkets, Inc Share of profits until it became a subsidiary (28 weeks in 1988)		**3.2**	5.1
		18.2	17.9

	Group £m	Company £m
Investments		
Balance 21st March 1987	**28.4**	17.3
Adjustment in respect of Shaw's Supermarkets, Inc.	**(11.1)**	—
Balance 19th March 1988	**17.3**	17.3
Share of Post-Acquisition Reserves	**31.8**	—
Share of retained profits for the year	**10.6**	—
Share of revaluation surplus	**12.6**	—
Adjustment in respect of Shaw's Supermarkets, Inc.	**(7.2)**	—
Balance 19th March 1988	**47.8**	—
Long Term Capital Advances		
Balance 21st March 1987	**5.6**	**5.6**
Decrease	**(3.4)**	**(3.4)**
Balance 19th March 1988	**2.2**	**2.2**
Total investment 19th March 1988	**67.3**	**19.5**
21st March 1987	65.8	22.9

The proportion of the profits attributable to the Group and the reserves included in the Group balance sheet are taken from the audited accounts produced within three months of the balance sheet date, except Kings Reach Investments Limited where they are management accounts. The share of the results of Shaw's Supermarkets, Inc has been translated at the average rate of exchange for the relevant period.

> The reserves shown above are after deducting a dividend received by J Sainsbury plc of £1.0 million (1987 £1.1 million).
> All associates operate and are incorporated in the United Kingdom with the exception of Shaw's Supermarkets, Inc, which operates and is incorporated in the USA.
> The Long Term Capital Advances are interest free.

6   BUSINESS COMBINATIONS

6.1   Introduction

Business combinations is the generic term for the transactions which result in one company joining a group by becoming the subsidiary of another. In accounting terms there are two distinctly different forms of reporting the effects of such an event, referred to in the UK as acquisition accounting and merger accounting respectively (in the US, purchase accounting and pooling of interests).

There has been a great deal of debate in recent years over how to distinguish between the circumstances when each of these methods is appropriate, and although there is now an accounting standard in force in the UK on business combinations, the controversy continues and the ASC is considering possible revisions to the standard. In addition, the forthcoming Companies Act which will incorporate the requirements of the EC Seventh Directive in UK law will also have some consequences for the distinction. Accordingly, this is one of the fastest changing issues in UK accounting practice.

The two methods of accounting look at business combinations through quite different eyes. An acquisition is seen as the absorption of the target into the clutches of the predator; there is continuity only of the holding company, in the sense that only the post-acquisition results of the target are reported as earnings of the group, and the comparative figures remain those of the holding company (and any previously held subsidiaries). In contrast, a merger is seen as the uniting of the interests of two formerly distinct shareholder groups, and in order to present continuity of both entities there is retrospective restatement to show the group as if the companies had always been together, by combining the results of both companies pre- and post-combination and also by restatement of the comparatives. The difficulty for accountants, however, has been how to translate this difference in philosophy into criteria which permit particular transactions to be categorised as being of one type or the other.

6.1.1   ED 3

In the UK, the first pronouncement on the subject was ED 3, issued by the ASC in 1971. This defined a merger as occurring when all of the following conditions were met on the amalgamation of two or more companies:

(a)   the substance of the main businesses of the constituent companies continues in the amalgamated undertaking;

(b)   the equity voting rights of the amalgamated undertaking to be held by the shareholders of any one of the constituent companies is not more than three times the equity voting rights to be held by the shareholders of any of the other constituent companies;

(c)   the amalgamation results from an offer to equity voting shareholders and not less than 90% in value of the offer is in the form of equity voting capital with rights identical with the equity voting capital rights of the offeree company or companies already in issue; for this purpose convertible loan stock or equity voting capital which can be converted into cash through an underwriting agreement is not to be regarded as equity voting capital;

(d)   the offer is approved by the voting shareholders of the company making the offer and it is accepted by shareholders representing at least 90% of the total equity capital (voting and non-voting) of the company or companies receiving the offer.

As will be seen below, these conditions bear very little resemblance to the conditions which were eventually adopted in SSAP 23. In the event, ED 3 was never proceeded with, and was eventually withdrawn nearly ten years later. One of the reasons why the ASC did not persist with it was that there was a school of thought which held that merger accounting was in fact contrary to company law; this is because the mechanics of the method require the shares issued by the holding company as consideration for the shares of the subsidiary to be recorded at their nominal value rather than their fair value, and this was thought to be in possible contravention of the Companies Act rules on share premium account. This legal doubt was eventually confirmed in a tax case, *Shearer v Bercain,*[121] in 1980, and this prevented any further progress towards an accounting standard until the law was amended to facilitate merger accounting by introducing variations to the rules on share premium account (described as 'merger relief') inserted in the Companies Act 1981.

6.1.2 Merger relief

In order to be able to record shares issued at their nominal value, and the cost of an investment in a subsidiary acquired in exchange for these shares at the same amount, it is necessary to satisfy the requirements of what is now section 131 of the Companies Act 1985. This is the part in the Act which was originally introduced in the Companies Act 1981 to remove the obstacle to merger accounting which was revealed in the case of *Shearer v Bercain,* as discussed above.

The section broadly relieves companies from the basic requirement to set up a share premium account in respect of equity shares issued in exchange for shares in another company in the course of a transaction which results in the issuing company securing at least a 90% holding in the equity shares of the other company. (This paraphrases the words in the Act, and the precise wording should be referred to to ensure that any particular transaction falls within its terms). In addition there are further provisions with a similar purpose which apply to shares issued in the course of a group reconstruction.

The rules on merger relief and those on merger accounting are frequently confused with each other. However, not only are they based on the satisfaction of different criteria, they in fact have quite distinct purposes. Merger accounting is a form of financial reporting which applies to business combinations, but although the merger relief provisions were brought in to facilitate it, merger relief is purely a legal matter to do with the maintenance of capital for the protection of creditors and has very little to do with accounting per se. Moreover, merger relief may be available under transactions which are accounted for as acquisitions, rather than mergers, and the two are not interdependent in that sense.

The main differences between the qualifying conditions for merger accounting (which are described below, at 6.1.4) and those which attract merger relief are that the latter is available whenever the stake in a subsidiary crosses the 90% threshold, regardless of (a) the amount of any prior holding, and (b) the extent to which forms of consideration other than equity are given in exchange for the shares in the subsidiary. Thus, merger relief would be available in respect of shares issued to raise a stake in a subsidiary from 89% to 91% (but not from 91% to 100%, unless the shares were issued as part of the same arrangement). Also, merger relief would be available even if only a small part of the consideration given to acquire a subsidiary were in the form of shares, but of course it would only apply to these shares and therefore the effect of the relief would also be small.

There are some differences of legal opinion as to whether merger relief is in fact *compulsory* when the conditions of section 131 are met, or whether it is optional. The Act says that where the conditions are met, then section 130 does not apply to the premiums on the shares issued. Section 130 is the basic requirement to set up a share premium account where shares are issued at a premium and therefore some people argue that the effect of this relief is simply to make section 130 optional rather than mandatory, but others take the view that it makes it illegal to set up a share premium account. The most common treatment adopted by those who qualify for merger relief but account for the transaction as an acquisition is in fact to regard the issue as having taken place at fair value, but to record a 'merger reserve' rather than a share premium account, and to use this as a home for the write-off of goodwill emerging on the acquisition (see 6.5.2 C below).

6.1.3 ED 31

Once the legal obstacle was removed, the ASC was able to continue the development of an accounting standard to distinguish between the two types of business combination, and ED 31 — *Accounting for acquisitions and mergers* — was issued in October 1982. This proposed that the conditions which had to be satisfied in order to qualify for merger accounting were that:

(a) the business combination should result from an offer to the holders of all equity shares and the holders of all voting shares which are not already held by the offeror; the offer should be approved by the holders of the voting shares of the company making the offer; and

(b) the offer should be accepted by holders of at least 90% of all equity shares and of the shares carrying at least 90% of all votes of the offeree company; for this purpose, any convertible stock is not to be regarded as equity except to the extent that it is converted into equity as a result of the business combination; and

(c)   not less than 90% of the fair value of the total consideration given for the equity share capital (including that given for shares already held) should be in the form of equity capital; not less than 90% of the fair value of the consideration given for voting non-equity share capital (including that given for shares already held) should be in the form of equity and/or voting non-equity share capital.[122]

As this shows, two of the ED 3 criteria had been completely dropped and the other two retained in a varied form. The main casualty was the second of the ED 3 criteria, which was a comparative size test which was based on the view that there cannot be a genuine uniting of interests between a minnow and a whale — that if one company is more than three times the size of the other it cannot be a true merger. The other concept to be dropped was the rather nebulous one that 'the substance of the main businesses of the constituent companies continues in the amalgamated undertaking'. As a result, a merger as envisaged by ED 31 was to be defined very much by the form of the transaction which gave rise to the business combination, rather than by reference to qualitative factors.

The ED 31 conditions also introduced another requirement, albeit indirectly, that the holding company could not hold more than 10% of the shares in the subsidiary before making the offer. This is because the transaction had to involve an (i.e. one) offer which was accepted by holders of 90% of all equity and all voting shares, and therefore any prior holding of more than 10% would render these conditions impossible to fulfil.

The exposure draft put forward a new concept as the guiding principle as to what was a merger — that no material resources should leave the group.[123] This contrasted with the philosophy pursued by ED 3, which was based on a notion of 'continuing ownership in a continuing business'.[124]

6.1.4   SSAP 23

ED 31 was eventually transformed into a standard — SSAP 23 — issued by the ASC in April 1985. It continued to use the principle of 'no material resources leaving the group' as its central point of reference for defining a merger, but the detailed criteria for permitting a business combination to be treated as a merger were again changed slightly, to the following:

(a)   the business combination results from an offer to the holders of all equity shares and the holders of all voting shares which are not already held by the offeror; and

(b)   the offeror has secured, as a result of the offer, a holding of (i) at least 90% of all equity shares (taking each class of equity separately) and (ii) the shares carrying at least 90% of the votes of the offeree; and

(c)   immediately prior to the offer, the offeror does not hold (i) 20% or more of all equity shares of the offeree (taking each class of equity separately), or (ii) shares carrying 20% or more of the votes of the offeree; and

(d)   not less than 90% of the fair value of the total consideration given for the equity share capital (including that given for shares already held) is in the form of equity share capital; not less than 90% of the fair value of the total consideration given for voting non-equity share capital (including that given for shares already held) is in the form of equity and/or voting non-equity share capital.[125]

The main changes from the exposure draft which were made in the standard were the relaxation of the prior holding rule to 20% of the shares of the target (criterion (c)) above, and the dropping of the need to have the transaction approved by the offeror's own shareholders. More fundamentally, however, the standard made merger accounting *optional* when the criteria were met, whereas under ED 31, satisfaction of the criteria was expressed as leading to the *mandatory* use of merger accounting.

The SSAP 23 rules, therefore, still depend very much on the form of the transaction being undertaken, and many of its critics are concerned about the ease with which it is possible to vary the form in order to bring a transaction within these rules. For example, the '20% prior holding' rule can be circumvented by selling any holding in excess of that limit to a third party (such as a merchant bank) immediately before making the offer and then acquiring it again in the course of the general offer. Also, cash consideration could, in theory at least, be disguised as equity by issuing redeemable preference shares (which can be brought within the equity definition by giving them theoretical rights to participate beyond a specified amount in a distribution) as part of the consideration and then redeeming them a short time later, so that in substance the consideration is in cash. (In practice it is unlikely that this would be regarded as acceptable under SSAP 23, because in reality resources are leaving the group.)

A more widespread ploy has been the use of 'vendor rights' or 'vendor placings' as a means of coming within the merger criteria although still offering cash to the vendors. This involves offering shares to the vendor in exchange for his shares in the company being acquired, but with a side arrangement where, if the vendor would prefer to receive cash, the shares will be placed either with the acquirer's own shareholders (vendor rights) or with third parties (vendor placings) and the proceeds passed on to the vendors. Of course, whether or not this is seen as an abuse of the standard depends on what the accepted philosophy of a merger is; it does not involve the expenditure of the acquirer's own cash, so no material resources leave the group, and on that basis the spirit of the standard is not offended. However, it does go against the idea that a merger is the pooling of resources of two formerly independent groups of shareholders, with continuity of ownership by both groups. Also it produces a very different result from the accounting which would follow if the acquirer had a rights issue and then proceeded to make an acquisition for cash, although the essence of the transaction does not seem very different from that in substance.

6.1.5 EC Seventh Directive

The implementation of the EC Seventh Directive on Company Law in the forthcoming Companies Act will to some extent restrict the ability of UK companies to apply merger accounting. Article 20 of the Directive sets out the qualifying conditions for merger accounting, and this disqualifies transactions where the consideration includes a cash payment exceeding 10% of the nominal value of the shares issued to effect the business combination. Although this looks superficially similar to the rule in SSAP 23 that at least 90% of the fair value of the consideration must be in the form of equity share capital, there are two important differences.

The first is that the Seventh Directive refers to the *nominal* value of the shares issued, rather than their *fair* value in setting the 10% limit. Since shares cannot be issued at a discount, this limit will never be wider than the SSAP 23 equivalent, and will often be much narrower; the extent of this restriction will depend on how much higher is the fair value of the predator's shares compared with their nominal value.

The other difference is that the Seventh Directive rule is expressed in terms of the 10%, and refers to cash, whereas the SSAP 23 equivalent requires at least 90% to be in the form of equity. Other forms of consideration, such as loan stock, are not addressed directly by either rule and would be dealt with differently as a result. Thus it would be possible for a substantial part of the consideration to be in the form of loan stock without breaching the Seventh Directive limit, whereas this would breach the SSAP 23 rule if it exceeded 10% in value of the total consideration. However, in drafting the Companies Bill, the Department of Trade and Industry has extended the restriction on cash to cover any form of consideration other than equity, so that loan stock will not qualify.

The Bill proposes that the following conditions have to be met in order to apply merger accounting:

'(a)   that at least 70% of the relevant shares in the undertaking were acquired pursuant to an arrangement providing for the issue of equity shares by the parent company or one or more of its subsidiary undertakings,

 (b)   that as a result at least 90% of the relevant shares in the undertaking are held by or on behalf of the parent company and its subsidiary undertakings,

 (c)   that the fair value of any consideration other than the issue of equity shares given pursuant to the arrangement did not exceed 10% of the nominal value of the equity shares issued.'[126]

6.1.6   *IAS 22*

Under IAS 22, 'a business combination should be accounted for under the purchase method ... except in the rare circumstances when it is deemed to be a uniting of interests.'[127] The latter treatment is permitted only 'if the shareholders of the combining enterprises achieve a continuing mutual sharing in the risks and benefits attaching to the combined enterprise, and

(a)   the basis of the transaction is principally an exchange of voting common shares in the enterprises involved; and

(b)   the whole, or effectively the whole, of the net assets and operations of the combining enterprises are combined in one entity.'[128]

The recent exposure draft on the reduction of options in international standards seeks to define this more narrowly by adding a further condition; namely, that an acquirer cannot be identified. In addition, it seeks to make merger accounting mandatory, rather than optional, when the criteria are met.[129]

The concept of 'no acquirer can be identified' is a very restrictive test which is borrowed from Canadian accounting practice. In that country, the test is applied by reference to such aspects as whether the former owners of one of the combining companies hold more than half of the voting shares of the combined group, whether they dominate its board, actively manage it, and so on.[130] Only if no dominant party can be identified under any of these tests is merger accounting permitted. In practice it will be very seldom that any combination will qualify as a merger under these rules.

6.2 Acquisitions — basic principles

When company A acquires company B, it has to consolidate B's trading results from the effective date of acquisition onwards. Similarly, it thereafter includes B's assets and liabilities in its consolidated balance sheet, eliminating the share capital of B and its reserves at the acquisition date against the cost of A's investment in B's shares. In contrast to merger accounting, the pre-acquisition results and reserves of B are completely eliminated from the consolidated financial statements, rather than brought in retrospectively. The Companies Bill seeks to enshrine this principle in the law.[131]

The effective date of acquisition is defined as the earlier of these two dates:

(a)   the date when consideration passes; or

(b)   the date on which an offer becomes or is declared unconditional.[132]

In practice, the second of these is usually the relevant event, since consideration would not be likely to be paid in advance of a binding agreement being reached. As SSAP 14 notes, the effective date applies even if the purchase agreement purports to give the acquiring company the right to participate in profits of the subsidiary from an earlier date (such as the beginning of an accounting period). The reason for this is straightforward; under acquisition accounting, only post-acquisition profits can be accounted for and it should not be possible to circumvent this by, in effect, backdating the agreement.

The rule in the UK is not the same as that in the US, where the normal date of acquisition is the date on which assets are received and other assets are given or securities are issued — in other words, when consideration passes. In the US, the parties *are* allowed to designate the end of an accounting period as being the effective date, provided it is between the dates on which the business combination is initiated and consummated. However, where the effective date is before the date on which the consideration passes, US GAAP requires that the purchase price be adjusted for imputed interest on the amount of the consideration outstanding between these dates.[133] This is to prevent what would in effect be double counting during this period, because the acquiring company would be both recognising the profits from the new subsidiary and also continuing to enjoy the use of the funds which were to be paid to the vendors.

6.3   Acquisitions: measuring the fair value of the consideration

In order to account for the acquisition, the acquiring company must first measure the cost of what it is accounting for, which will normally represent both the cost of the investment in its own balance sheet and the amount to be allocated between the identifiable net assets of the subsidiary and goodwill in the consolidated financial statements. Where shares are issued as part of the consideration and merger relief under section 131 of the Companies act is available, it is possible for the cost of the investment in the acquiring company's balance sheet to be based on the nominal value of the shares issued, although SSAP 23 suggests that the normal treatment would be to use the fair value.[134] For acquisition accounting, SSAP 23 requires the cost to be based on the fair value of the consideration given, but does not elaborate on how this is to be determined.[135] However, in June, 1988 the ASC published a discussion paper on the subject of allocating fair values in the context of acquisition accounting, and this covers the subject in some detail; its main recommendations are discussed at 6.3.1 to 6.3.6 below:[136]

6.3.1   Securities

The fair value of ordinary shares (and other securities) given as part of the consideration should be based on the value at which they could have been issued for cash if there had been no knowledge of the intended acquisition. This value will usually be the average price in the period (ten working days is suggested) immediately prior to the announcement of the bid. However, if no suitable market exists, then the fair value will have to be based on estimates which take into account the price of shares with similar characteristics.[137]

In practice this can be the hardest part of the exercise, particularly when the securities being issued are not of a class already in issue and for which an appropriate value might be more readily apparent. The recommendation that a pre-bid price be used is one of the more controversial aspects of the discussion paper, because many British companies have been accustomed to using the price ruling at the date at which the offer became unconditional, rather than that in force before the offer was made. (One example is to be found in the financial statements of Travis & Arnold P.L.C., who explicitly say that this is their policy.)[138] There is relatively little authoritative guidance available elsewhere: IAS 22 is not specific on this point and in the US, APB 16 says, in terms which make the concept being pursued less than clear, that 'the market price for a reasonable period before and after the date the terms of the acquisition are agreed to and announced should be considered in determining the fair value of securities issued'.[139]

The view taken by the discussion paper can be supported by looking at the matter from a legal viewpoint. A lawyer would say that the purpose of the exercise is to value the shares issued by reference to the value of the consideration received (i.e. the value of the company being acquired) rather than the other way round; this view follows from the rules on share premium account, which make it clear that the directors must regard the consideration received as capital injected in the company and put a value on it for this purpose. Of course, the two amounts must be equal to each other, but the directors must first make an assessment of how much the target company is worth in deciding what to bid for it, and having done so they will have regard to their own present share price so as to decide how many of their own shares they will offer. Any subsequent movements in the share prices of the two companies during the bid period do not necessarily indicate that the value of the target has changed from this original evaluation, and therefore if the bid is successful, the correct course of action would be to stick to the original value in the absence of any evidence that the value of the target has in fact changed.

Sometimes, shares are issued by the acquirer which rank fully for dividends which are to be paid in respect of a period before the acquisition took place. In these circumstances, some companies apportion the subsequent dividend into two components when it is paid, with a 'pre-acquisition' element added to the cost of the investment in the subsidiary (and therefore increasing the goodwill) and leaving only the post-acquisition element to be taken out of the profit and loss account. One such example is to be found in the 1986 financial statements of Hanson Trust PLC, where a note describes the treatment in the following terms:

Extract 4.7: Hanson Trust PLC[140]

8 Dividends
£18m of the ordinary dividend for the year has been charged to the cost of the acquisition of Imperial Group plc. This represents the proportion of the dividends paid to shareholders of Imperial Group relating to the period before that company joined Hanson Trust.

6.3.2 Monetary items

'The fair value of cash or other monetary assets given, and monetary liabilities assumed, as part of the consideration should be based on the amount paid or payable', unless settlement is deferred.[141]

This recommendation is a straightforward one, and needs no further comment or explanation.

6.3.3 Non-monetary items

'The fair value of non-monetary assets given as part of the consideration will be their realisable value unless they are to be replaced, in which case it will be their [depreciated] replacement cost'.[142]

In this case the discussion paper is focusing on the value of the sacrifice made by the acquirer by giving up these assets, and invokes a concept similar to that of 'deprival value' which was used as the basis of valuations in current cost accounting. The loss suffered by the acquirer will be the alternative proceeds he could have received for the asset, unless he can make good his loss by replacing the asset, in which case it is the cost of such replacement.

6.3.4 Deferred consideration

'The fair value of deferred consideration will be based on the same principles as set out for other items above, subject to the need to discount the amounts involved'.[143] The discussion paper recommends that the discount rate be based on the company's weighted average cost of capital.

This is one of the relatively few occasions in UK accounting pronouncements when specific recognition is given to the time value of money, but the recommendation here is in line with the approach which would be taken in the US; incidentally, this would also deal with the issue discussed at 6.2 above, of adjusting the purchase consideration where the date of the offer becoming unconditional is significantly before the date on which consideration passes.

A number of responses to the discussion paper have criticised the recommendation that the weighted average cost of capital should be used as the appropriate discount rate; it is probably more appropriate to use the company's incremental borrowing rate.

6.3.5 *Contingent consideration*

'The fair value of contingent consideration will be based on its probable amount. When the actual amount is known, this should be recorded in the consolidated financial statements and an adjustment made to consolidated goodwill'.[144]

This is to cater for the frequent situation which arises where the eventual total amount of the purchase price is unknown because it has been made conditional, say, on the achievement of a certain level of future earnings. As well as providing the amount which will most probably be paid, the acquiring company should show any additional unprovided potential liability as a contingent liability.

In practice, most UK companies at present simply disclose their liabilities for contingent consideration rather than providing for the probable amount payable. The terms of the agreement may be such that it is impossible to say whether, and if so how much, additional consideration will be paid, and in that case companies will have no option but to deal with the matter by disclosure, rather than by provision. However, in some cases it will be clear that at least a certain amount is very likely to be payable, and in these circumstances it would seem appropriate to provide for that amount and note merely the remainder.

Since the corresponding adjustment is to goodwill (which is generally taken to reserves with no impact on earnings) the different treatments do not usually affect the profit and loss account although they do have an effect on the balance sheet. What that effect is will depend on whether the further consideration will be in the form of cash or shares. Where it is the former, the consideration will reduce both the net assets of the group and its equity; where it is the latter, the net assets and the total equity will be unaffected, but the classification of equity will change, reducing the group's reserves. (This is on the assumption that the obligation to issue shares to the vendors in the future is shown as a separate component of equity rather than as a liability; where there is uncertainty as to whether it will be paid in the form of cash or shares, because the vendor has the right to opt for one or the other, it would be more prudent to show it as a normal liability.)

An example of the common practice of merely disclosing (rather than providing) contingent consideration is shown below.

Extract 4.8: Saatchi & Saatchi Company PLC[145]

17. COMMITMENTS AND AUTHORISATIONS NOT PROVIDED [extract]
Additional capital payments may be made to the vendors of acquired companies in the years to 1993. Such payments are contingent on the future levels of profits achieved by the companies. The directors estimate that, at the rates of exchange ruling at 30th September 1987, the maximum payments that may be made are as follows:

	£ million
Within one year	**21.3**
From two to five years	**56.5**
Over five years	**29.9**
	107.7

The Group's cashflow projections for the same period indicate a net cash generation after taxation and dividends considerably in excess of these maximum contingent payments.

The balance sheet of the group at that time showed shareholders' funds of only £40.2 million, so if this contingent consideration had been fully provided and the resultant goodwill written off, it would have created an overall deficit. However, it is unlikely that the full amount of the potential liability would have been regarded as the probable amount payable, so the effect of making a provision would in practice have been somewhat less.

The financial statements of Ronald Martin Groome PLC show that they have made provision for further consideration which they expect to pay in respect of certain acquisitions, as disclosed below:

Extract 4.9: Ronald Martin Groome PLC[146]

14. PROVISION FOR LIABILITIES AND CHARGES [extract]

The movement on deferred purchase consideration during the year was as follows:

	Group and Company	
	1987	1986
	£'000	£'000
Beginning of the year	**1,200**	—
Arising on the acquisition of The Groome Group	**110**	1,200
Satisfaction of 1987 deferred consideration by share issue		
— Nominal value	**(30)**	—
— Premium on share issue	**(570)**	—
End of year	**710**	1,200

This illustrates a potential problem; where the further consideration is to be met in the form of shares, the number of shares to be issued, and the amount of merger reserve created, will not be known in advance. Accordingly the amount of the merger reserve which is available for the write-off of goodwill cannot be determined until all the consideration shares have been issued. The movement on Merger Reserve is shown as follows:

Extract 4.10: Ronald Martin Groome PLC[147]

18.   OTHER RESERVES [extract]

	Merger reserve £'000
Balance, beginning of year	(870)
Consolidated goodwill arising on the acquisition of subsidiaries	(590)
Premium arising on issue of shares to acquire subsidiaries	807
Other	(10)
	(663)

6.3.6   Acquisition costs

'Acquisition costs should be included in the cost of the investment unless they have been set against the share premium account'.[148]

Again, this recommendation is relatively uncontroversial. The reference to share premium account relates to the legal possibility of writing off share issue expenses and certain similar costs against this account.[149] Where the acquisition involves the issue of shares, it will be necessary to identify which costs can be regarded as eligible for such a write-off, which might in some cases involve apportionments of costs which had more than one purpose.

6.3.7   Pre-acquisition dividends

One other question which sometimes arises is how the acquiring company should account for dividends received from the subsidiary out of its pre-acquisition profits. The rules on this are less than clear. The traditional view was that this was, in effect, a return of the capital paid to acquire the company and was not in any sense a profit, and that accordingly it should be applied to reduce the cost of the investment in the acquiring company's balance sheet. This view was supported by some rather arcane wording that used to be in paragraph 15(5) of Schedule 8 to the Companies Act 1948, but this was changed in the Companies Act 1981.[150]

The more widely accepted view of the law is now that the question of whether or not pre-acquisition dividends have to be written off against the cost of the investment has to be subdivided into two sub-questions:

(a)   does the receipt of the dividend constitute a realised profit in the financial statements of the holding company? and

(b)   does provision for permanent impairment have to be made against the cost of the investment?

Of the two questions set out above, (a) is the more straightforward, provided it can be accepted that the receipt of the dividend can properly be described as a profit at all; the issue of whether it is realised is generally not in question. However, the one which really requires interpretation is (b). Because both the law and normal accounting practice require provision to be made only for *permanent* diminution in the value of a fixed asset, it is possible to advance the view that, provided the investment will eventually recover the value which has been removed from it by making the distribution (by earning further profits, say) then it is unnecessary to write it down and hence the dividend to the holding company can be passed on to its own shareholders.

Following this approach would allow an acquiring company to distribute immediately all the pre-acquisition profits shown in the subsidiary's balance sheet provided that it could foresee that the subsidiary would earn an equivalent amount of profits in the future. Even if this is good law, it is questionable whether it is good accounting. There is a strong argument that the receipt of a pre-acquisition dividend *is* a partial return of the purchase price and the true and fair way to account for it is to deduct it from the cost of the investment rather than to call it a profit, which is the conclusion favoured by Accountants Digest No. 189 on SSAP 23.[151]

It should of course be pointed out that the above discussion is based on the premise that the cost of the investment in the holding company's books does represent the fair value of the subsidiary. There may be circumstances where it does not, such as when merger relief has been taken or if the subsidiary was not purchased in an arm's-length transaction, and obviously this could require a different view to be taken. In such a case there would seem to be no reason to write down the value of the investment unless the effect of the dividend was to reduce the underlying value of the subsidiary below its carrying amount in the financial statements of the holding company.

6.4   Acquisitions: measuring the fair value of the net assets acquired

6.4.1   Basic principles

The central requirement to bring in the assets of the subsidiary in the group financial statements at their fair value rather than their book value in the subsidiary's own financial statements is contained in both SSAPs 14 and 23,[152] but again neither standard elaborates in much detail on how this should be done. The ASC discussion document on the subject referred to at 6.3 above, however, deals extensively with the subject.

The purpose of the fair value allocation is simply to establish a realistic starting point for the consolidation of the subsidiary's assets and results. The book values in the subsidiary's own financial statements are of no direct relevance for this purpose, because they do not stem from transactions of the reporting entity (the acquiring group), and in effect they are based on the original cost of what are second-hand assets from the group's point of view. The fair value exercise is an attempt to account fairly for the acquisition transaction by asking what the acquiring group has spent, and what it has got for its money.

It is therefore necessary to analyse the assets and liabilities acquired, to see what they are worth to the acquiring company. One way of focusing on this is to consider what the acquirer would have been prepared to pay for the individual item if it had been acquired directly, rather than as part of a package of assets and liabilities acquired as a going concern. An alternative way of looking at the same thing is to consider by how much the acquirer would have sought to adjust the purchase consideration had the relevant item not existed; this question can be easier to comprehend in relation to certain types of item, such as contingencies, tax losses and so on.

Of course, the purchase price for most acquisitions is not settled on the basis of an analysis of the individual assets and liabilities of the target company; it is based instead on factors such as the earnings and cash flows which can be brought to the acquiring group. In that sense the purchase allocation exercise is an artificial one rather than portraying the results of a real analysis which has formed part of a business decision. Nevertheless such an allocation has to take place if the group is to be able to present consolidated financial statements, and the hypothetical nature of the allocation does not render it invalid.

6.4.2   The use of hindsight

The fact that the process is, to that extent, an after-the-event rationalisation means that an accounting issue arises; how much hindsight can the acquirer impute into the values assigned, or must the allocation be based solely on the information which he had at the time when he was making his bid? There is a theoretical argument for the latter, which is that if he was unaware of a particular matter, such as the fact that there was a deficiency in the pension fund of the target, then it cannot have influenced the acquisition price and thus should not feature in any allocation of that price.

Whatever the merits of that view in theory, however, it cannot be used in practice. If the acquirer was only able to assign values to items that he knew about at the time of the acquisition, the exercise would in many cases be completely impossible, because, as noted above, most acquisitions are not primarily based on an assessment of the value of the assets and liabilities of the target company. It is therefore necessary to allow the acquirer a reasonable period of time in which to investigate the assets and liabilities which have been acquired and make a reasoned allocation of values to them. The remaining question is, how much time should be allowed?

The ASC discussion paper suggests that, as a practical matter, the date to be used as the limit of the hindsight period should in fact be the date on which the acquiring company has to present the first consolidated financial statements which incorporate the acquired subsidiary. Although this might seem to provide an uneven result, because some companies will have an extended time to contemplate their purchase while others will have very little time, it does recognise that to dictate any other time period would be arbitrary and also in practice ineffective, because the real date would then become the next reporting date after the hindsight period had theoretically lapsed. However, many commentators in responding to the discussion paper have said that they view this as an unrealistically tight deadline and it may be that any eventual standard will take a more relaxed view.

In the US, the rule is that an 'allocation period' is permitted for the management of the acquiring company to conduct an investigation of the assets and liabilities which have been acquired. The duration of this is not an absolute period of time, although it should usually not extend beyond one year from the acquisition date; the period in fact ends 'when the acquiring enterprise is no longer waiting for information which it has arranged to obtain and which is known to be available and obtainable'.[153]

Whatever period of hindsight is used, however, it is important that the allocation reflects conditions as they existed at the date of the acquisition, rather than being affected by subsequent events. There is a parallel to be drawn here with the accounting treatment of post-balance sheet events; only those events which provide further evidence of conditions as they existed at the acquisition date should be taken into account.

6.4.3 *Recommendations for individual assets and liabilities*

The ASC discussion paper contains the following recommendations for each class of asset or liability:

A   Non-monetary   items

The fair value of a non-monetary asset will usually be based on its replacement cost, unless the asset is to be disposed of or is not worth replacing, in which case the fair value will be its recoverable amount (i.e. the higher of net realisable value and value in use). The replacement cost will need to take into account the location and condition of the assets, and the grants which would normally have been available had they been acquired directly. Adjustments may also be necessary in arriving at the fair value of stock to take accrued profit into account.[154]

This relatively brief recommendation contains a large number of points, and the complete text of the discussion paper really needs to be read in order to be fully understood. Once again, the valuation concept has its origins in current cost accounting, and is based the idea of 'deprival value'.

Probably the most controversial aspect of this part of the discussion paper is the recommendation that stock should be valued to include profit earned to date, which will thus be pre-acquisition from the point of view of the acquiring group and hence will not appear in its results when the stock is subsequently sold. Although this practice is probably adopted by most companies in respect of long-term stocks, such as properties held for development or contract work in progress, it is probably not often applied in relation to stock of a manufacturing company with a shorter production cycle.

The discussion paper makes particular reference to intangible assets, such as patent rights, licences, brand names and publication titles, and solicits comments on whether such items should be regarded as separable assets or whether they should be dealt with as part of goodwill.[155] The recognition of such assets has recently become more frequent, and it is commonly the case that they are carried in the balance sheet without amortisation, subject only to write-down if they become permanently impaired. One such example is to be found in the financial statements of Reckitt & Colman plc, who disclose the following policy:

Extract 4.11: Reckitt & Colman plc[156]

INTANGIBLE ASSETS AND GOODWILL
On the acquisition of subsidiaries, businesses or related companies, the purchase
consideration is allocated over the underlying net tangible assets, significant intangible
assets and goodwill. Goodwill is deducted from reserves on acquisition. No annual provision
for depreciation is made in respect of intangible assets, which are wholly comprised of
Trademarks, as it is considered that their useful economic lives are not limited. Their carrying
value is reviewed annually by the directors to determine whether there should be a reduction to
reflect any permanent diminution in value.

Another example is that of Grand Metropolitan Public Limited Company who
recently changed their approach to accounting for intangible assets obtained as a
result of an acquisition, so as to attribute a significant amount of the value to
brand names (rather than to goodwill) relating to acquisitions made since 1985
(see Extract 4.20 below).

The distinction between such items and goodwill probably rests on whether or not
they can be regarded as separable assets, i.e. assets which can be identified and
sold without necessarily disposing of the business as a whole. There is no doubt
that such assets can be very valuable; the real test is whether the business would
remain if they were disposed of. This might depend on the facts of each individual
case, because in some cases the right to sell particular brands might be the very
essence of a business, while in others the ownership of such rights might be more
incidental to the main activities. This matter has been placed under review both in
the context of the fair value discussion paper and in relation to a review,
sponsored by the ASC in the latter part of 1988, of SSAPs 22 and 23. The
question of brands is discussed in more detail in Chapter 10.

B   Monetary items

The fair value of monetary items will be the amount of money involved, payable
or receivable. It may be appropriate to discount long-term payables and
receivables to present value.[157]

The only point about this which may prove contentious is the recommendation
that discounting should be applied to long-term items which are not at market rates
of interest. The theoretical basis for the recommendation is sound, but some may
see it as being inconsistent with usual accounting practice.

This recommendation is designed to deal with the situation, say, where the
acquired company has cheap borrowing, such as loan stock at a low coupon rate
of interest. The recommendation would require the group financial statements to
include that borrowing on a discounted basis, and for the interest charge in the
future to be a combination of the actual interest paid and the amortisation of the
discount, so that the combined finance charge would reflect borrowing rates
which were available at the time of the acquisition transaction.

C   Contingencies

Contingent liabilities should be treated as set out in SSAP 18, and contingent assets should be treated in the same way as SSAP 18 requires contingent liabilities to be treated.[158]

This is one of the most difficult areas in the discussion document and is bound to prove controversial, since it recommends that contingent assets which are only *probable* to be realised should be recognised in the balance sheet. Although this treatment seems imprudent at first sight, it is in fact designed to *exclude* from post-acquisition profits any windfall gains from transactions or events which took place before the acquisition was made. The reasoning which lies behind the recommendation is quite complex, and again the full text needs to be consulted for the arguments to be understood.

D   Provisions

There will be occasions where it is appropriate to provide for reorganisation costs and also losses arising in the process of running down a segment of the business. It is not appropriate to provide for future trading losses of a continuing business segment.[159]

In practice this is one of the areas of fair value accounting which has given rise to a great deal of controversy, and alleged abuse. The ability to provide for costs of reorganisation programmes without having to charge these costs in the profit and loss account is a very attractive opportunity, and one which understandably tempts some companies to be enthusiastic in their estimation of these provisions. The discussion paper has accepted the principle of making such provisions, but has sought to limit the scope for abuse by requiring that they can be made only if:

(a)   there is a clearly defined programme of reorganisation and those costs for which provisions are to be made have been specified in considerable detail; and

(b)   there was evidence that the costs were contemplated by the acquirer at the time of the acquisition.

The discussion paper also calls for proper disclosure relating to these provisions, asking that for each acquisition there should be disclosure of the broad details of the purposes to which the provisions are to be put, and subsequently that movements on the provisions should be shown, whether they have been used or released without being used. Requirements along these lines were subsequently proposed in ED 44 (see 6.8.2 below).

The question of whether or not provision should be made for future losses of the acquired subsidiary is a more difficult one. In practice this is frequently done, and it is argued that where a loss-making company is acquired, the acquiring company will allow for this in the price offered; the economics of the deal therefore regard the losses which will be sustained until the company can be turned round as part of the cost which the acquirer will pay in order to gain control of a company which is eventually expected to be profitable. In these terms it seems reasonable that provision for the losses should be permitted as part of the fair value allocation.

The discussion paper, however, adopts a contrary point of view. It acknowledges that the expectation of these losses will have been taken into account by the acquirer, but does not see the losses as an eligible item to be provided for, any more than an asset would be set up for expected profits of the subsidiary — the future trading results of the subsidiary do not represent one of its separable assets or liabilities, and they must be consolidated with those of the rest of the group from the effective date of acquisition as defined by SSAP 14. Thus, under the rules proposed by the discussion paper, the effect on the acquisition price of whatever future results were anticipated will fall to be dealt with as part of goodwill, positive or negative.

The discussion paper does, however, make one exception to this proposal. Where a segment of the acquired business is to be sold following the acquisition, the segment should be incorporated at its net realisable value, and this will include the effects of its trading results (which could be profits as well as losses) until the date of disposal.

One other question which sometimes arises is whether it is possible to provide for reorganisation costs or other similar expenses relating to the acquisition which are to be incurred by the acquiring company, rather than by the new subsidiary. For example, if as a result of the acquisition the group has excess capacity and has to close one of its factories, should it make any difference to the group financial statements whether the factory which is closed belonged to the acquiring company or the acquired company? Under US accounting rules,[160] it is necessary that such costs are attributable to the acquired company, otherwise they cannot be provided for in the course of the fair value exercise. However, there is no such rule in the UK, and the point is not dealt with in the discussion paper; some companies do appear to follow the rule which applies in the US as illustrated in the following extract:

Extract 4.12: APV plc[161]

ACCOUNTING FOR ACQUISITIONS The results of companies and businesses acquired or sold during the year are dealt with in the consolidated accounts from the date of acquisition or disposal. Goodwill arising on acquisitions is written off directly against reserves. The costs of integrating businesses acquired are reflected in the fair values ascribed to the net assets as at the date of acquisition. Costs incurred in the reorganisation of existing facilities which are consequent on acquisitions are treated as extraordinary. The effect of acquisitions made during the year is set out in note 20 to the accounts.

E   Pension schemes

The fair value of a pension scheme should be based on the acquirer's perspective and should be revalued based on the acquirer's methods and actuarial assumptions. No provision should be made for changes in benefits or number of employees following acquisition. An exception to this is where provision for redundancies has been made relating to a closure of a business segment, in which case account may be taken of the pension scheme implications of the redundancies.[162]

The recommendation has been designed to be consistent with the rules on accounting for pension costs (in SSAP 24) which are described in Chapter 22. Essentially the recommendation is based on the fact that a pension fund represents an off balance sheet resource (which may be positive or negative, depending on the solvency of the fund), and that post-acquisition results will be distorted unless recognition is given to the existence of this asset or liability at the time of the acquisition. The recommendation that the acquirer's viewpoint is to be used, including actuarial methods and assumptions, is consistent with the general philosophy of the fair value exercise that fair value is to be as perceived by the acquiring company.

It should, however, be noted that any post-acquisition amendments to the terms of the scheme itself should not be provided as part of the fair value allocation — these will properly represent post-acquisition costs, just as would the costs of harmonising pay rates or any other employment conditions, and should be accounted for as such.

F   Taxation

Provision should be made for deferred tax in the fair value exercise by reference to those tax implications viewed from an overall group perspective.[163]

This falls into two areas. First of all there will be existing timing differences within the acquired company which will give rise to a potential liability to deferred tax which will need to be considered. In addition, the adjustments made as a result of the fair value exercise may lead to quasi-timing differences which will also require provision for deferred tax. Account should be taken of the marginal effect of all such differences within the acquired company on the overall group tax position.

The difference between the fair values assigned and the tax base values of the assets and liabilities acquired are in fact not strictly timing differences within the SSAP 15 definition, but it is necessary to treat them as such in order to avoid distorting post-acquisition earnings. For example, if a provision for reorganisation costs is set up without a deferred tax adjustment, then the subsequent costs for which provision has been made will go to reduce the post-acquisition tax charge even though the costs themselves have not been reflected in post-tax earnings. The same equally applies to all the other fair value adjustments.

Existing practice in relation to this aspect is not easy to determine. Some companies (for example, Guinness PLC and P-E International plc, as shown in Extracts 4.16 and 4.17 below) have made specific reference to it in relation to reorganisation costs but not in relation to their other fair value adjustments. It is possible that existing practice is therefore quite varied.

6.4.4   Subsequent amendments to fair value

Where changes to fair values are made after the acquisition, the ASC discussion paper recommends that they should generally be treated as changes in estimate which should be dealt with in the profit and loss account of the period in which the change is made. The only circumstances in which a retrospective adjustment to the goodwill calculation could be regarded as appropriate would be if the original allocation was regarded as a fundamental error which required to be dealt with as a prior year adjustment under SSAP 6. However, this would probably be the case only if the original allocation was based on a complete misinterpretation of the facts which were available at the time; it would not apply simply because new information had come to light which changed the acquiring management's view of the value of the item in question.

It is not easy to determine whether this is the general practice which presently exists in the UK, but there are at least some examples of financial statements where post-acquisition adjustments of assigned values appear to have been made through reserves — effectively as adjustments to the goodwill figure previously assigned. One such example is to be found in the financial statements of Trafalgar House Public Limited Company, which acquired a subsidiary of British Shipbuilders, Scott Lithgow Limited, in 1984 for £12m, but made additional write-offs in reserves of £54.9m and £56.3m in its financial statements for the years to September 30, 1986 and 1987 respectively. These related to further provisions for losses made on a contract which was in progress at the time of the acquisition. The relevant note in the 1987 financial statements reads as follows:

Extract 4.13: Trafalgar House Public Limited Company[164]

23 Reserves [extract]
Scott Lithgow Limited
The accounts for the year ended 30 September 1986 reported that certain information had become available which demonstrated that the costs to complete on one contract were substantially greater than was indicated at the time of the acquisition. It has been necessary for the provisions for these costs to be further increased during the current year. It was also reported in the 1986 accounts that Trafalgar House had notified British Shipbuilders of its intention to submit a substantial claim for misrepresentation relating to the state of the contract in March 1984. The directors anticipate that a writ and statement of claim will be issued in the first half of 1988. The directors do not consider it prudent to take credit for any recoveries at this time, but in these circumstances consider that it is appropriate to treat the additional provision as an adjustment to cost of control which, under group accounting policies, is charged directly to reserves.

A further £17m was written off to cost of control in the following year, of which £13.4m was in respect of the anticipated costs of pursuing the claim against British Shipbuilders.[165]

Another example appeared in the financial statements of Tootal Group plc:

Extract 4.14: Tootal Group plc[166]

24 RESERVES [extract]

Goodwill on acquisition of subsidiaries
The calculation of goodwill relating to the acquisitions of Clover Leaf, Standard-Coosa-Thatcher and Sandhurst Marketing, as shown in the 1986/87 accounts, has now been reassessed in line with actual expenditure, pension funding requirements and remaining future costs. The effect of the reassessment is as follows:

	£'000
Reduction of provision made for the reorganisation and restructuring of American Thread Company and Standard-Coosa-Thatcher following merger and the reassessment of pension funding requirements	2,142
Reassessment of valuation of Sandhurst Marketing stocks at acquisition date	(582)
Reassessment of deferred consideration in relation to Clover Leaf acquisition and revaluation of Clover Leaf stock at acquisition date	(115)
Goodwill arising on other acquisitions	(1,045)
	400

A further example worth noting is that of Guinness PLC, who introduced a sentence into their accounting policy in their 1987 financial statements to deal with the possibility that certain of the provisions made in the course of a fair value allocation could prove to be excessive, and that to avoid falsely reporting the release of these as a profit, any such release would be dealt with as a recalculation of goodwill. However, it would appear that such adjustments only operate in that direction; there is no suggestion that a similar adjustment to goodwill would be made if the provisions proved to have been inadequate. The relevant policy reads as follows:

Extract 4.15: Guinness PLC[167]

Accounting for acquisitions and disposals [extract]
(c) Fair value adjustments and acquisition provisions
The net assets of companies acquired are incorporated in the consolidated accounts at their fair value to the Group and after adjustments to bring the accounting policies of companies acquired into alignment with those of the Group. Fair value adjustments include provision for reorganisation costs, anticipated future losses, and excess stocks. If the estimates on which these provisions are based prove to be in excess of actual expenditure or losses, the unutilised surplus provisions will not be taken to profit and loss, but will be credited to reserves as a recalculation of goodwill.

6.4.5 Disclosures of fair value adjustments

There is as yet no requirement to disclose what adjustments have been made in allocating fair values to the assets of an acquired subsidiary, although this has been proposed in an exposure draft;[168] the Companies Bill contains similar provisions.[169] The proposals contained in the exposure draft are discussed at 6.8.2 below. Recently, however, some companies have voluntarily included notes showing the main adjustments made, which is a welcome development and one to be emulated. Two such examples are shown below:

Extract 4.16: Guinness PLC[170]

14. Effect of acquisitions and disposals on the Consolidated Balance Sheet [extract]

(a)   Acquisitions
During the 12 months the Group has acquired Schenley and the Caldbeck group of companies. The following table sets out the effect of these acquisitions on the Consolidated Balance Sheet of the Group.

Net assets acquired	Unaudited consolidated accounts as of the date of acquisition £m	Fair value accounting adjustments £m	Total £m
Tangible assets	34	(10)	24
Investments in related companies	10	—	10
	44	(10)	34
Stocks	114	(11)	103
Debtors	89	—	89
Cash and Deposits	5	—	5
Creditors (amounts falling due within one year)	(93)	(34)	(127)
Net current assets	115	(45)	70
Long term debt	(7)	—	(7)
Provisions and other long term creditors	—	(44)	(44)
Deferred taxation	(2)	62	60
Minority interest	(6)	—	(6)
Total net assets acquired	144	(37)	107

Consideration paid	
Cash	261
Deferred consideration: payable within one year	22
payable after more than one year	61
	344
Goodwill arising on consolidation	237
Goodwill arising on the purchase of a minority interest	5
Total goodwill written off	242

Extract 4.17: P-E International plc[171]

11 Acquisitions [extract]

	Unaudited completion accounts of Inbucon Tenth June 1987 £000	Fair value accounting adjustments £000	Total £000
Consideration:			
Nominal value of Ordinary shares issued			425
Merger reserve arising on consolidation			8,075
			8,500
Expenses of issue			378
			8,878
Net assets acquired			
Fixed assets			
Tangible	180	(53)	127
Intangible	23	(23)	—
	203	(76)	127
Debtors	3,727	(18)	3,709
Cash at bank and in hand	188	—	188
Taxation	(132)	—	(132)
Other creditors	(938)	(1,150)	(2,088)
Net current assets	2,845	(1,168)	1,677
Deferred taxation	(4)	388	384
Total net assets acquired	3,044	(856)	2,188
Goodwill on consolidation written off to merger reserve			6,690

The principal fair value accounting adjustments are as follows:
(i) Certain tangible assets, representing furniture, fittings and equipment in premises which have been vacated following the group reorganisation, have been written off.
(ii) The intangible asset comprised purchased goodwill which has been written off in accordance with the group's accounting policy.
(iii) Reorganisation costs relating to the merger of the Inbucon business into the group's operating structure have been recognised.
(iv) Adjustments have been made to deferred taxation to reflect the effects of the above reorganisation costs

6.4.6 'Push-down accounting'

The term 'push-down accounting' relates to the practice of incorporating, or 'pushing-down', the fair value adjustments which have been made by the acquiring company into the financial statements of the acquired subsidiary. Such a practice is used in the US, where it has been required in certain situations by the

Securities and Exchange Commission.[172] It is argued that the acquisition, being an independently bargained transaction, provides better evidence of the values of the assets and liabilities of the subsidiary than those previously contained within its financial statements, and therefore represents an improved basis of accounting.

There are, however, contrary views, which hold that the transaction in question was one to which the reporting entity was not a party, and there is no reason why it should intrude into the entity's own accounting records. Also, the fair value allocation is conducted on the basis of the values perceived from the particular point of view of the acquiring company, and may be of little relevance to any other user of the subsidiary's financial statements.

Whatever the theoretical arguments, it is certainly true that push-down accounting can be an expedient practice, because it obviates the need to make extensive consolidation adjustments in each subsequent year, based on parallel accounting records. But in fact most of the adjustments which push-down accounting would entail would fall foul of the Companies Act valuation rules or of other accounting standards. It is possible, by using the alternative valuation rules, to revalue fixed assets directly in the subsidiary's financial statements, and where this constitutes a major part of the fair value adjustments then this can be a worthwhile move; however, most of the other adjustments discussed in 6.4.3 above could not be made directly in the subsidiary's financial statements. In practice, it would appear that push-down accounting is seldom applied in the UK in any form other than in relation to the revaluation of fixed assets.

6.5   Acquisitions: accounting for goodwill

6.5.1   Introduction

Once the fair values of both the consideration given and the net assets acquired have been measured, the difference between the two represents purchased goodwill which remains to be accounted for. How to account for it is a subject on which widely differing opinions are held, and this is evidenced both by the time which it took the ASC to develop a standard on the subject and by the fact that the eventual standard permitted a choice between two alternative methods: amortisation through the profit and loss account and immediate write-off direct to reserves.

The choice between these (and other) treatments depends to some extent on what goodwill is perceived to be in the first place. Some view it as an asset like any other, which has been acquired at a cost, and which needs to be accounted for in the same way as any other asset. The other main camp is occupied by those who do not regard goodwill as a real asset in the first place, but more in the nature of a consolidation difference which emerges as part of the accounting process and has to be dealt with in the least damaging manner possible. This divergence of view underlies much of the disagreement about the treatment of goodwill when it arises.

Those people who view goodwill as an asset say that it has been acquired at a cost, and, as would be done in the case of any other asset, this cost should be capitalised initially in the balance sheet, and charged to revenue over its economic life. At this point, the next divergence of view arises, because the fact that it is both intangible and not separately identifiable means that its economic life is very difficult if not impossible to determine.

Some people respond to this difficulty by taking the view that goodwill does not necessarily have a finite life at all and therefore should not be written off until there is evidence that its value has been impaired. They would maintain that any period of amortisation would be completely arbitrary. Others would take the view that such an approach would be impracticable because it is impossible to detect falls in value of the original goodwill other than in fairly extreme circumstances; they would therefore support the amortisation approach as the most practical way of eliminating the asset from the financial statements on a systematic basis, even if the choice of amortisation period is difficult to determine.

Those who do not regard goodwill as a real asset in the first place tend to favour eliminating goodwill directly against reserves in the year of acquisition. They would say that the financial statements should deal solely with identifiable items which arise from an acquisition; to try to deal with goodwill using normal accounting principles would be a futile attempt to account for the unaccountable. Goodwill in their eyes is simply a product of the accounting process and should be eliminated by an accounting entry, not reported as the consumption of an identifiable resource.

The ASC first considered this matter in a discussion paper published in 1980.[173] This adopted the view that goodwill was an asset, rather than simply a consolidation difference and should be accounted for as such. It recommended that it should be carried as a fixed asset in the balance sheet and subjected to annual amortisation, and written down to its recoverable amount to recognise any permanent impairment in value which became evident. It rejected the notion that it could be carried as a permanent asset, without amortisation. (This had already been ruled out by the EC Fourth Directive, and subsequently by the EC Seventh Directive).

Two years later, however, when the Committee issued an exposure draft (ED 30) on the subject, it had retreated from the attempt to mandate a single treatment; either amortisation through the profit and loss account or immediate elimination through reserves was to be permitted, provided the policy was applied consistently.[174] This choice was maintained in the eventual accounting standard, SSAP 22, which was issued at the end of 1984, but by now the direct write-off treatment had become the preferred one.[175]

As well as permitting two different treatments, which are based on different philosophical views on the nature of goodwill, SSAP 22 (unlike ED 30) even allows the same company to choose between the different methods to be applied in relation to different acquisitions. There have also been instances of companies who have started accounting for goodwill under one policy and changed to the alternative policy soon thereafter; most commonly this involves changing from amortisation to direct write-off (perhaps after adequate reserves have been built up to absorb the write-off), but there have been some instances of companies who have moved in the opposite direction, of which an example is British & Commonwealth Holdings PLC.[176]

This extreme form of flexibility of approach has led to substantial criticism of the standard, whose only real effect has therefore been to outlaw the practice of carrying goodwill as a permanent asset without amortisation, and some would say that even this consequence can be avoided by assigning value to some other form of intangible asset rather than goodwill, as discussed at 6.4.3 A above, and contending that it has an infinite life and need not be amortised.

The international standard also allows both treatments,[177] but it is proposed that the standard should be amended to require the amortisation approach to be used, and to outlaw the immediate write-off to reserves.[178] In the US, the amortisation approach must be applied.[179]

6.5.2   *Immediate write-off: which reserve?*

SSAP 22 does not specify which reserve should be the destination of goodwill write-offs, and a variety of practice has grown up, perhaps founded more on expediency than on any principle. The debate is complicated by the fact that, while the classification of reserves in a *company* balance sheet has particular legal significance because of the rules on distributions, this is not true in relation to the reserves in a *group* balance sheet; however, some of the arguments which have developed on the issue have not always recognised this fact. The more common possibilities are discussed below.

A   *Profit and loss account*

This is the most straightforward option, and has been quite widely used in practice. It can also be seen as the most conservative, since it has the greatest impact on the group's apparent ability or intention to make distributions, but as described above, this effect is more cosmetic than real because distributions are determined by the reserves of individual companies, not groups.

B   *Capital reserve*

There is no statutory requirement to maintain such a reserve (unlike 'capital redemption reserve', which is discussed at F below), but in fact this category is used voluntarily in a wide range of circumstances, not all of them either rational or systematically and consistently applied. Where such a reserve exists, however, it intuitively seems a natural home for charging goodwill which has arisen on what is perceived to be a 'capital' transaction.

Sometimes, the capital reserve will have arisen on other acquisition transactions in the form of 'negative goodwill' (which is discussed further at 6.5.5 below), and in this sense it will be consistent to take positive goodwill to the same place so that the balance on this reserve represents the total effect of charging and crediting goodwill directly to reserves. There is no prohibition in SSAP 22 in netting off these items in reserves. However, it should be noted that if the amount of positive goodwill exceeds that of the negative goodwill, a debit balance on the reserve will arise and it will take on the character of a 'goodwill write-off reserve', which is discussed further at G below.

C Merger reserve

Again, this term has no statutory meaning and there is no requirement to maintain such a classification. However, a practice has grown up of creating such a reserve in circumstances where share premium relief has been claimed on an issue of shares under section 131 of the Companies Act 1985, yet the shares issued have still been recorded at their fair value rather than their nominal value, generally because acquisition accounting is being used for the transaction in respect of which the shares were issued. In other words, it is a voluntarily created substitute for a share premium account where section 131 gives relief from the need to set up such an account, but unlike a share premium account it is not subject to statutory restrictions on its application or distribution. (This does not necessarily imply that it can be distributed, because it is arguable that the issue of shares at a premium does not give rise to a realised profit unless the consideration received on issue of the shares has been realised in a subsequent sale.) Even if the cost of the subsidiary is recorded in the acquiring company's balance sheet based on the nominal amount of the shares issued, it will still be necessary to create a merger reserve on consolidation; this is because SSAP 22 requires goodwill to be the difference between the fair value of the consideration given and the aggregate fair values of the net assets acquired.[180]

Since this reserve arises on an acquisition, it automatically becomes available as a possible home for writing off goodwill at exactly the same time as the goodwill itself emerges, and it has been widely used for this purpose. However, there is no exact relationship between the quantum of goodwill and the amount available on this reserve, although the amounts which arise under each category will tend to be higher or lower as the general level of share prices rises or falls. This means that the reserve may not be large enough to absorb the amount of goodwill, and the directors will have to decide whether to leave a net debit balance on this reserve or to absorb the excess elsewhere.

An example of the use of such a reserve category is to be found in the financial statements of Pineapple Group PLC:

Extract 4.18: Pineapple Group PLC[181]

23   Merger Reserve
In this Group, in accordance with Statement of Standard Accounting Practice No. 23, the difference between the nominal value of the shares issued in respect of mergers with Premium Pen PLC and Keymark Out and About Limited and the nominal value of the shares acquired has been treated as a reduction in reserves.
In the Company the premium on the shares issued as part of the consideration for these mergers has been credited to the merger reserve.
Goodwill arising on the consolidation in respect of acquisitions not treated as mergers has been eliminated from the accounts by write-off against the merger reserve. Goodwill arising where an acquisition has been stated in the books of the Company at the underlying net asset value has also been written off to the merger reserve.
In the case of Golden Key Promotions Limited, the premium on the shares issued has been credited to the merger reserve in accordance with the dispensation granted by sections 131 to 134 of the Companies Act 1985.

	Group 1987 £000	Group 1986 £000	Company 1987 £000	Company 1986 £000
Arising on merger of Premium Pen	(4,146)	(4,146)	3,391	—
Arising on merger of Keymark	(29)	(29)	69	—
Write-off of goodwill arising on other acquisitions during the year	(2,173)	—	(299)	—
Premium on shares issued in respect of Golden Key	572	—	572	—
	(5,776)	(4,175)	3,733	—

All amounts are stated net of expenses associated with the merger or acquisition.

Certain aspects of the above treatment are unusual, notably the decision to create a merger reserve in the financial statements of the company in circumstances where merger accounting is being applied in the group financial statements.

D   Revaluation reserve

Unlike the previous two categories, this is a statutory reserve and there are legal rules on how it may be reduced; these would appear to prohibit writing off goodwill to this reserve. However, at present these rules are framed only in terms of a single company rather than of a group, and it has not been beyond legal doubt that the same restrictions apply to the balance shown on revaluation reserve in a consolidated balance sheet. The DTI announced that this is a point which would be clarified in the Companies Bill; it would be made clear that the revaluation reserve is not available for this purpose, although it has been stated that the legislation will not have retrospective effect.[182] (This does not imply that any previous write-offs will thereby be ratified, because the DTI's view is simply that they are already illegal under existing legislation, so it is unnecessary to make the new rules explicitly retrospective.)

The Companies Bill intends to amend the rules contained in Schedule 4 of the Companies Act relating to revaluation reserves so that such reserves can only be reduced by way of capitalisation or 'to the extent that the amounts transferred to it are no longer necessary for the purposes of the valuation method used'.[183] The Bill effectively extends these provisions to consolidated financial statements by requiring that 'group accounts shall comply so far as practicable with the provisions of Schedule 4 as if the undertakings included in the consolidation ("the group") were a single company.'[184]

In the meantime there are some examples of companies which have written off goodwill against revaluation reserve; one of these is Grand Metropolitan Public Limited Company. Their 1987 financial statements contained the following note:

Extract 4.19: Grand Metropolitan Public Limited Company[185]

23 Reserves [extract]

Group	Share premium account £m	Revaluation reserve £m	Related companies' reserves £m	Profit and loss account £m	Total £m
At 30th September, 1986	419.8	(96.4)	10.7	1,272.4	1,606.5
Exchange adjustments	—	(5.5)	0.3	(17.2)	(22.4)
Retained profit for the year	—	—	3.2	354.7	357.9
Premiums on share issues, less expenses	6.0	—	—	—	6.0
Goodwill acquired during the year	—	(651.8)	—	—	(651.8)
Transfer of goodwill on disposal	—	120.9	—	(120.9)	—
Other transfers between reserves	—	(19.1)	—	19.1	—
At 30th September, 1987	425.8	(651.9)	14.2	1,508.1	1,296.2

Aggregate goodwill of £1,500.5m has been written off against the revaluation reserve. The goodwill written off in the year was mainly attributable to the acquisition of Heublein, Inc.

Subsequently, Grand Metropolitan Public Limited Company announced that they intended to change their approach to accounting for intangible assets obtained as a result of an acquisition, so as to attribute a significant amount of the value to brand names rather than to goodwill, and that this approach would be applied retrospectively to the acquisitions made since 1985. The reserves note in their 1988 financial statements accordingly showed the following:

Extract 4.20: Grand Metropolitan Public Limited Company[186]

23   Reserves [extract]

	Share premium account £m	Revaluation and special reserve £m	Related companies' reserves £m	Profit and loss account £m	Total £m
Group					
At 30th September, 1987					
as previously reported	425.8	(651.9)	14.2	1,508.1	1,296.2
Capitalisation of brands	—	630.0	—	(22.0)	608.0
As restated	425.8	(21.9)	14.2	1,486.1	1,904.2
Exchange adjustments	—	(5.8)	—	(13.3)	(19.1)
Retained profit for the year	—	—	2.2	570.4	572.6
Premiums on share issues, less expenses	7.1	—	—	—	7.1
Goodwill acquired during the year	—	(143.7)	—	—	(143.7)
Surplus on revaluation of property	—	643.1	—	—	643.1
Transfer of goodwill on disposal	—	62.0	—	(62.0)	—
Share premium transfer	(425.7)	425.7	—	—	—
Other transfers between reserves	—	(29.0)	—	29.0	—
At 30th September, 1988	7.2	930.4	16.4	2,010.2	2,964.2

Aggregate goodwill, net of disposals, of £952.2m has been written off against group revaluation and special reserves.

In accordance with the special resolution passed by shareholders on 10th March 1988 and confirmed by Court order registered on 26th July 1988, the share premium account has been reduced by £425.7m. This amount has been transferred to an undistributable special reserve in the company's balance sheet. In the group balance sheet the special reserve of £425.7m has been reduced by goodwill written off in the year of £143.7m.

From this it can be inferred that the balance on 'revaluation and special reserves' in fact comprises two balances — a balance of £282.0m on 'special reserve' (£425.7m less goodwill of £143.7m) and the remainder of £648.4m on revaluation reserve, which would have been £808.5m higher, at £1,456.9m, if the rest of the goodwill had not been written off against it. Accordingly, the change of policy in respect of acquired brands has only reduced the amount of goodwill set off against the revaluation reserve, not eliminated it altogether.

The transfer from the share premium account to create the special reserve is discussed further at E below.

E   *Share premium account*

Again, this is a statutory reserve, and it is clear that it may not be used as a home for goodwill being written off. Nevertheless a practice has grown up of using this reserve indirectly by applying to the court for release of the reserve under the provisions of the Companies Act which deal with the reduction of capital. The effect of this is that the court may agree that the share premium account can be cancelled and another reserve substituted for it; the court will normally impose restrictions on the distributability of that new reserve, but will permit it to be used to absorb the goodwill write-off. As with some other reserves, the subsequent write-off can sometimes exceed the amount of the reserve created by the cancellation of the share premium account, and the remaining debit balance then assumes the appearance of the 'goodwill write-off reserve' discussed at G below. One such example is to be found in the financial statements of Blue Arrow PLC:

Extract 4.21: Blue Arrow PLC[187]

17   Reserves [extract]

·The Group	Share premium account £000	Merger reserve £000	Capital reserve £000	Revaluation reserve £000	Profit and loss account £000
At 1 November 1986	28,669	—	—	830	5,315
Cancellation and reclassification	(28,669)	—	28,669	—	—
Premium on shares issued during the year	812,009	14,509	—	—	—
Expenses of issue	(33,042)	—	(8)	—	—
Retained profit for the year	—	—	—	—	13,480
Goodwill arising on consolidation written off	—	(14,509)	(856,256)	—	—
Currency exchange adjustments	—	—	—	(1,213)	—
At 31 October 1987	778,967	—	(827,595)	(383)	18,795

In accordance with the provisions of Section 131 of the Companies Act 1985, the Company has transferred to Merger Reserve the premium arising on the issue of shares as consideration for subsidiaries acquired during the year. The Group has applied this Merger Reserve to write down the goodwill arising on consolidation.

A Special Resolution was passed at an Extraordinary General Meeting of the Company held on 9 March 1987, whereby the whole amount then standing to the credit of the Company's Share Premium Account was cancelled and a capital reserve of an identical amount was created, against which goodwill arising on consolidation could be written off.

The confirmation of the Court was obtained in accordance with the Companies Act 1985 on 6 April 1987.

Total group reserves therefore show a negative figure of some £30m, which, when set against share capital of £35m, reduces shareholders' funds to £5m. Subsequent to the year end, the company once again applied to the court to have their new share premium account cancelled in order to allow most of the debit balance on capital reserve to be eliminated.

F   Capital redemption reserve

This, like share premium account, is a statutory reserve and is therefore subject to similar restrictions on its use; it may not be applied directly as a home for a goodwill write-off, although there seems no reason in principle why, as with share premium account, the company could not apply to the court to have its capital reduced and create a reserve against which goodwill could be offset by that means.

G   'Goodwill write-off reserve'

This term refers to a practice which some companies have applied, of simply setting up a new reserve category within shareholders' funds as the destination for goodwill write-offs, so that in effect the goodwill simply becomes a debit balance carried within equity. Some doubts have been expressed as to the propriety of such a move, but it does not in fact seem to offend any particular legal provision. It does, in fact, have the merit that it is evident from the disclosure how much goodwill has in fact been charged to reserves (assuming no other reserves have been used), whereas under some of the other treatments discussed it is difficult to trace this after the year in which the write-off has been made.

One example of a negative goodwill reserve is shown below:

Extract 4.22: Saatchi & Saatchi Company PLC[188]

15. RESERVES [extract]

GROUP	Special reserves £ million	Goodwill reserve £ million	Revaluation reserve £ million	Profit and loss account £ million
At beginning of year	—	(72.1)	0.5	52.2
Premium on Ordinary shares issued, less expenses, transferred to Special Reserves	60.5	—	—	—
Capitalisation of reserves	—	—	—	(3.7)
Goodwill arising in the year written off	—	(151.5)	—	—
Utilisation of Special Reserves	(60.5)	60.5	—	—
Exchange translation	—	—	—	(7.8)
Amortisation of goodwill reserve	—	2.8	—	(2.8)
Transfer from profit and loss account	—	—	—	47.0
At end of year	—	(160.3)	0.5	84.9

Total group reserves in this case are therefore a negative figure of £74.9m, and when set against the share capital of £115.1m, produce a net figure for shareholders' funds of only £40.2m.

H   Conclusion

In the present climate, therefore, there is a wide range of possible homes in which goodwill may be accommodated, and there appears to be no definite guiding principle which can be laid down which makes any one more appropriate than the others. Although the most straightforward treatment would be to use the profit and loss account balance, there is no particular reason why companies have to do so, and those who have large amounts of goodwill to dispose of may consider this to be an unattractive option.

6.5.3 *Effect on realised profits of writing off goodwill*

This subject is dealt with in Appendix 2 to SSAP 22, which starts by making it clear that the question is often irrelevant because the distribution rules in the Companies Act depend on profits realised in the financial statements of individual companies, not groups, whereas most goodwill is written off only on consolidation. Nevertheless, goodwill can also arise in the financial statements of a single company (for example, where it acquires an unincorporated business), so the question cannot be ignored.

The appendix acknowledges that the elimination of goodwill by the direct write-off approach leaves an unanswered question as to whether realised reserves have been diminished. There will be some circumstances when it is clear that the charge should be to realised reserves, such as when the value of the goodwill has been permanently impaired, but the appendix concludes that the mere decision to take goodwill to reserves does not imply that this has happened; the reason for taking it there is usually one of policy as to the exclusion of goodwill from the balance sheet, not to recognise that any loss has been suffered.

However, the appendix goes on to say that goodwill should not be regarded as having an infinite life, and that at some time its elimination must be regarded as having reflected a realised loss. It therefore suggests that, if the goodwill is originally written off against an unrealised reserve, it may be appropriate to make an annual transfer between that reserve and realised reserves to amortise the amount of the goodwill, thus simulating the effect on reserves which would have been achieved had the company followed a policy of amortisation in the profit and loss account.

Such a process necessarily involves taking a view on the economic life of the goodwill, and although this would have to have been taken anyway if a policy of amortisation in the profit and loss account had been followed, one of the reasons for using the reserve route in the first place is that such an estimate cannot readily be made. There is therefore a slight element of self-contradiction in the treatment.

An example of such a treatment can be found in the financial statements of Johnson Fry PLC, as shown in the extract reproduced below. As the extract shows, the transfer has been made only in respect of the goodwill (described as 'Purchased goodwill') carried in the holding company's accounts (presumably for the reason mentioned above, that the matter is of no relevance in the context of the group reserves).

Extract 4.23: Johnson Fry PLC[189]

20. Reserves [extract]
The movement on reserves during the year was as follows:

Group	Share premium £	Other reserves (arising on application of Section 131 Companies Act, 1985) £	Other reserves £	Retained profits £
Beginning of year	—	—	—	513,890
Retained earnings for the year	—	—	—	538,017
				1,051,907
Premium on allotments made:				
on placing	933,436	—	—	—
on acquisitions and investments	375,039	939,126	—	—
	1,308,475			
Costs of issue	(183,862)			
	1,124,613			
Applied on capitalisation:				
December 1986 (4:1)	(324,167)			
September 1987 (1:1)	(495,615)			
	(819,782)	—	—	—
Purchased goodwill:				
- written off	—	—	(230,000)	—
- amortisation	—	—	21,000	(21,000)
Goodwill eliminated on consolidation	—	(1,675,741)	—	—
End of year	£304,831	£(736,615)	£(209,000)	£1,030,907

Events may take place which mean that the amortisation period has to be varied, or the whole amount remaining in the unrealised reserve has to be transferred immediately. This would happen most obviously if the business to which the goodwill relates were to be sold, but it might also apply if it became clear that the value of the goodwill had been permanently impaired.

It should also be noted that in the case of a public company, writing off goodwill to reserves can have an impact on the company's distributable reserves even though it might have no impact on its realised reserves. This is because of the additional restriction on distributions for public companies which prevent their net assets from being reduced below the total of their share capital and non-distributable reserves.[190] The goodwill write-off will bring this restriction into consideration if it exceeds the company's distributable reserves.

6.5.4 Period of amortisation

Where goodwill is to be amortised, it will be necessary to make an estimate of the useful economic life which is to be the basis of the charge. This is a particularly problematical decision, because the asset to be amortised may be regarded as unidentifiable in the first place[191] and it may therefore be impossible to determine when its life can be thought to have ended.

A discussion paper published by the ASC in 1980 recommended that goodwill should be amortised in the profit and loss account over a period based on the P/E ratio of the company acquired.[192] In the subsequent exposure draft, this suggestion was dropped, and reference was instead made to 'the number of years during which the acquiring company may reasonably foresee super-profits resulting from the purchased goodwill which exists at the time of purchase'.[193] It went on to say that this would suggest a relatively short period, such as ten years or less, and recommended that in any event a maximum of twenty years should be imposed by the proposed standard. In fact, SSAP 22 does not lay down any definitive rule on the matter, although it does discuss the issue to some extent in Appendix 1 in rather nebulous terms.

The EC Fourth and Seventh Directives take a comparatively short period, five years, as their basic rule, but permit member states to extend this to the useful economic life of the asset if this is thought to be longer; the UK has embodied this in the Companies Act in implementing the Fourth Directive, and is likely also to do so in relation to the Seventh Directive.[194] At the other extreme, US GAAP imposes a maximum period for the amortisation of goodwill of 40 years,[195] and this has become widely adopted as the norm in practice in that country for most companies, although a shorter period is required in certain cases. The proposed maximum in the international exposure draft E32 is 20 years, and if the actual period used is more than 5 years it is suggested that the directors should be required to state their justification for this period in the notes to the financial statements.[196]

It is difficult to generalise about UK practice, because relatively few companies choose the amortisation approach in the first place, but those that do seem to gravitate towards a period somewhere between these two extremes, say from 10 to 20 years. There have been some instances of companies choosing to use 40 years, but in the main such a duration seems to be regarded as implausibly long. One recent example of a company which elected to use the amortisation route, having previously charged goodwill directly to reserves, is British & Commonwealth Holdings PLC, and the period of write-off which they chose was 25 years.[197]

6.5.5 Negative goodwill

Negative goodwill arises when the fair value of the net assets taken over in an acquisition transaction exceeds the fair value of the consideration given. On the face of it, the acquiring company has bought the business cheaply. This may have been the case for various reasons. The vendor may have been in a weak bargaining position relative to the acquirer; the assets may be of special value to the acquirer but this is not reflected in the acquisition price; or there may be an expectation of poor trading results which means that the business as a whole is at present worth less than is indicated by the values of the separable net assets.

There are a number of possible approaches which could be applied when accounting for negative goodwill. One is to say that, even if the separable net assets are worth more than the value of the business as a whole, they did not cost the acquirer that much, and that accordingly the negative goodwill should be applied to reduce the separable assets to their cost to the acquiring company. This is the approach followed in the US, where negative goodwill is eliminated by proportionately writing down the value of the fixed assets of the acquired company other than any marketable securities which it possesses; only when these have been written down to zero is it permissible to recognise negative goodwill, which is then classified as a deferred credit and amortised to the profit and loss account over the period expected to be benefited, with a maximum of forty years.[198] The effect of this is to recognise the negative goodwill in the profit and loss account, but this is done on a conservative basis by associating it with the cost of the items which have the longest lives.

Another approach is to try to identify why the negative goodwill arose, and to account for it based on that analysis. The ASC discussion paper on the subject issued in 1980 addressed the matter in these terms:

'... negative goodwill may arise as a consequence of the expectations of future losses (or reduced profits) or alternatively may just represent a bargain purchase by the acquiror. The logical treatment of negative goodwill which is related to future losses or reduced profits would be to amortise the capital reserve over the expected period of such losses or profits by crediting it to the profit and loss account (as the provision is progressively realised over this period). UK and Irish examples of this treatment in practice are rare but not unknown. Negative goodwill which arises due to a bargain purchase should, on the same basis, in principle be credited to the profit and loss account in the year in which the acquisition is made. However, because of the impracticability of defining the exact proportion of a transaction which represents a bargain purchase in all but exceptional circumstances, and because it would be imprudent so to treat negative goodwill which did not represent a bargain, the panel does not recommend this treatment.'[199]

The document went on to recommend 'that negative goodwill should generally be treated as the exact reverse of positive goodwill ..., viz. it should be passed through the profit and loss account, spread over the periods which are expected to benefit from the acquisition. Any such transfer should be separately disclosed. However, to ensure that only amounts which have been realised (as demonstrated by the use or realisation of the other assets concerned) are credited to the profit and loss account, the accumulated amount written off negative goodwill should never exceed the aggregate of:

(a)   the total depreciation charged for assets of that investee since acquisition by the group; together with

(b)   any element of the proceeds on disposal of assets by the investee which corresponds to a surplus at the date of acquisition of the fair value of those assets over their book value.'[200]

This was the foundation of the proposals on negative goodwill in the exposure draft which preceded SSAP 22, which contained the following requirements:

'Any excess of the fair value of the separable net assets over the fair value of the consideration given (negative goodwill) which arises as a result of a bargain purchase should be carried to reserves representing unrealised profits, from which it may be transferred to reserves of realised profits as the relevant assets are depreciated or sold. However, negative goodwill which represents an amount specifically set aside for future losses and/or costs taken into account in arriving at the purchase price should be set up as a provision in the balance sheet and released to the profit and loss account over the period in which the losses or costs are, or are expected to be, incurred, provided that at the time of the acquisition the directors of the acquiring company can foresee on reasonable evidence that losses or costs are likely to be incurred by the acquired company and that provision for those losses or costs is necessary in accordance with the prudence concept.'[201]

Under this approach, some forms of negative goodwill (if they were thought to represent provisions for costs or losses) would eventually be reported in earnings, and some would not, because they would simply be dealt with within reserves. This was in contrast to the discussion paper, which had recommended that both types of negative goodwill should be dealt with in the profit and loss account. This disparity of approach did not find favour with commentators on the exposure draft, and when SSAP 22 was published the required treatment had again changed. Provisions for costs or losses were to be treated as liabilities to be set up as part of the fair value exercise, rather than regarded as an element of negative goodwill.[202] The standard required that all negative goodwill be compulsorily taken to reserves. In contrast to the position for positive goodwill, there is no alternative which allows the option of amortisation into the profit and loss account, which is arguably a conceptually inconsistent approach.

The EC Seventh Directive in fact bears more than a passing resemblance to ED 30 (which was the ASC's current published thinking when the Directive was being finalised). It says that 'a negative consolidation difference may be transferred to the consolidated profit and loss account only:

(a)   where that difference corresponds to the expectation at the date of acquisition of unfavourable future results in that undertaking, or to the expectation of costs which that undertaking would incur, in so far as such an expectation materialises; or

(b)   in so far as such a difference corresponds to a realised gain'.[203]

However, this does not dictate that such a treatment must be applied, it simply restricts any transfers to the profit and loss account to those which fit these criteria. Indeed, the Companies Bill makes no reference as to how such a negative consolidation difference is to be accounted for.

The international standard on business combinations allows any of three treatments for negative goodwill. It may be taken to reserves immediately, treated as deferred income and released to the profit and loss account systematically, or proportionately applied to reduce the values assigned to individual depreciable non-monetary assets.[204] It has, however, recently been proposed that these choices should be restricted, and that the preferred treatment should be to apportion it against the individual non-monetary assets acquired (both depreciable and non-depreciable). An alternative, permitted treatment would be to treat it as deferred income over a period, but it is proposed to remove the option of taking it straight to reserves.[205]

6.6   Step-by-step acquisitions

6.6.1   Background

So far, this chapter has discussed acquisitions which result from a single purchase transaction, or at least a series of related transactions which occur over a relatively short period of time. However, in practice some subsidiaries are acquired in a series of steps which take place over an extended period, during which the underlying value of the subsidiary is likely to change, both because of the trading profits (or losses) which it retains and because of other movements in the fair values of its assets and liabilities. The accounting problems which this creates are therefore how to establish the fair values of the net assets acquired, and how to measure its pre-acquisition reserves.

6.6.2   Example

The problem can be illustrated by the following example, which is based on that in the ASC discussion paper on fair value accounting.[206]

Example 4.5:   Step-by-step acquisitions

Company A acquires an 80% holding in Company B as a result of four separate transactions over a number of years, as set out in the table below. At the time of these transactions, the fair values of the net assets of B were as shown, and for the purpose of this illustration, the consideration paid was exactly proportionate to the share of the net assets, at fair value, which was thereby being acquired.

Transaction Number	Holding acquired %	Total value of investee £m	Price paid £m	Cumulative holding %	Cumulative price paid £m
1	10	10	1.00	10	1.00
2	20	13	2.60	30	3.60
3	21	15	3.15	51	6.75
4	29	20	5.80	80	12.55
	80		12.55		

As the above table shows, Company B was merely an unconsolidated investment after transaction 1, became an associate as a result of transaction 2 and a subsidiary as a result of transaction 3, while transaction 4 resulted in the minority interest being reduced from 49% to 20%.

The accounting choices which are available are of two sorts; when to make the initial calculation of fair values for the purposes of determining goodwill, and whether to make a revised calculation when each successive change in the size of the holding takes place. As stated at 5.3 above, SSAP 1 requires that the investment in an associate should be analysed at the time of acquisition between the investor's share of the underlying separable net assets (at fair value, if possible) and goodwill, so the answer to the first question above is that this calculation should be made after transaction 2; however, if Company A is unable to get the information on fair values which is required for that exercise, it may be possible to carry it out only after transaction 3. The more significant question is whether each further purchase of shares thereafter should lead to a recalculation of the goodwill equation.

If the exercise were first carried out after transaction 2, and reperformed after each subsequent increase in the shareholding, the calculations would be as follows:

After transaction 2	£m
Cost of investment	3.60
Share of assets at fair value (30% of £13m)	3.90
Capital reserve on consolidation	0.30

Note that, in this particular example (because all purchases take place at the underlying asset value), the capital reserve in fact represents the increase in reserves attributable to the 10% stake held by Company A during the period when its value grew from £10m to £13m. However, it is beyond the scope of normal consolidation accounting entries to treat this as part of the group's post-acquisition reserves.

After transaction 3	£m
Cost of investment	6.75
Share of assets at fair value (51% of £15m)	7.65
	0.90
Less: post acquisition share of reserves of associate (30% of (£15m - £13m))	0.60
Capital reserve on consolidation	0.30

After transaction 4	£m	£m
Cost of investment		12.55
Share of assets at fair value (80% of £20m)		16.00
		3.45
Less: post acquisition share of reserves		
of associate (30% of (£15m — £13m))	0.60	
of subsidiary (51% of (£20m — £15m))	2.55	
		3.15
Capital reserve on consolidation		0.30

Although the accounting set out above may be appropriate in principle, it can give rise to difficulties in practice. One of these is that, once the shareholding crosses the 50% threshold, the assets of the investee will be consolidated on a line-by-line basis and it is thereafter difficult (and arguably inappropriate) to ascribe new fair values to them when further shares have been acquired, so as to reduce the size of the minority interest. If, in the above example, Company B owned a single investment property (and nothing else) which was appreciating in value throughout the period during which Company A's stake was changing, the accounting consequences would be as follows:

Example 4.6:   Step-by-step acquisitions: consolidating the assets concerned

After transaction 2	£m
Cost of investment as before	3.60

Represented by:

Share of associate's assets at fair value (30% of £13m)	3.90
Capital reserve on consolidation	(0.30)
	3.60

After transaction 3	£m
Cost of investment as before	6.75

Represented by:

Investment property	15.00
Minority interest (49% of £15m)	(7.35)
	7.65
Post acquisition reserves (as before)	(0.60)
Capital reserve on consolidation	(0.30)
	6.75

The post acquisition reserves would in fact represent Company A's 30% share of the revaluation reserve arising from the uplift in the value of the property from £13m to £15m.

After transaction 4	£m
Cost of investment as before	12.55

Represented by:

Investment property	20.00
Minority interest (20% of £20m)	(4.00)
	16.00
Post acquisition reserves (as before)	(3.15)
Capital reserve on consolidation	(0.30)
	12.55

In order to achieve this accounting, it is necessary to revalue the investment property in the consolidated accounts following transaction 4. (This also takes place implicitly following transaction 3, but is not obvious because an investment property appears in the consolidated balance sheet in substitution for an investment in an associate.) However, if the assets were not investment property, there is no compulsion for the group to revalue its assets in this way, and the ASC discussion paper on Fair Value mentions two other possibilities, which are discussed below:

The first of these is that they may retain the asset at £15m, in which case the consolidated financial statements after transaction 4 will show the following:

	£m
Cost of investment (as before)	12.55
Represented by:	
Property	15.00
Minority interest (20% of £15m)	(3.00)
	12.00
Post acquisition reserves (as after transaction 3)	(0.60)
Goodwill on consolidation*	1.15
	12.55

*This can be analysed as follows:

Cost of 29% acquired	5.80
Minority interest: 29% of £15m	(4.35)
	1.45
Capital reserve existing after transaction 3	(0.30)
	1.15

The defect with this treatment is that it overstates goodwill by attributing to it which is in reality attributable to the property. Conversely, the cost of the property to the group is understated and gains on any subsequent valuation or on disposal which are measured by reference to that cost will be overstated.

The discussion paper therefore offers a further alternative which involves accounting for the property on a 'mixed' basis which takes account of the cost of the different transactions. Applying this approach to transaction 4 would give the following result:

	£m
Cost of investment (as before)	12.55
Represented by:	
Property	16.45
Minority interest (20% of £15m)	(3.00)
	13.45
Post acquisition reserves (as after transaction 3)	(0.60)
Capital reserve on consolidation	(0.30)
	12.55

This is achieved by applying the cost of the transaction 4 investment of £5.8m to increase the asset by 29% of £5m (the increase in the stake of the uplift in value since the previous transaction) and applying the remainder to reduce the minority interest. Whatever the theoretical case for this treatment, it seems to produce figures which have little meaning or usefulness.

6.6.3   Conclusion

There is no ideal solution to this problem; each of the approaches shown in the above example would appear to have some defects. In theory, the best treatment (and the one recommended in the ASC discussion paper) would appear to be to recalculate fair values whenever there has been a significant change of stake as shown in the first of the treatments in the example. However, in practice companies seldom make any further adjustments to the fair values of the net assets of their subsidiaries after majority control has been secured, and we believe this is acceptable. The 'mixed' treatment shown above is also acceptable but is unlikely to be applied in practice.

Although the Companies Bill proposes certain detailed acquisition accounting rules which refer to fair values,[207] it does state that they apply 'where an undertaking becomes a subsidiary undertaking of the parent company',[208] they would, therefore, appear not to apply to acquisitions of shares in a company after it has become a subsidiary.

6.7   Mergers

6.7.1   Basic principles

In contrast to acquisition accounting, merger accounting involves retrospective restatement of the consolidated financial statements to show the reporting entity as if the combining companies had always been members of the group. This means that the effective date of the combination has no significance other than for the purposes of various disclosures; both pre- and post-combination results of the subsidiary are combined with those of the holding company in showing the results for the period of the combination, and it is therefore of little significance whether it took place at the beginning or the end of the year. Similarly, the comparative figures and any historical summaries should be restated to consolidate the results of the new subsidiary retrospectively, which will usually mean that the earnings trend will be significantly different from what it would have been had acquisition accounting been applied.

In the balance sheet, the assets and liabilities of both companies are combined on the basis of their book values, with adjustments made only to eliminate any differences in accounting policies between the two. Thus, there is no equivalent of the requirement under acquisition accounting to attribute fair values to the net assets of the subsidiary so as to reflect their cost to the group; merger accounting seeks to portray continuity of both of the combining entities, not that of the holding company, and therefore makes no amendment to the values at which the the assets of either are included.

As a variation on that treatment, there could be instances where fair values were attributed to the assets of *both* companies. This was referred to as the 'New Entity' method in the Appendix to ED 31, which in turn quoted the international exposure draft on Business Combinations, E22. In the event, the method was not dealt with in either of the eventual standards which were derived from these exposure drafts, and it does not appear to be used much in practice.

6.7.2 Equity eliminations

The cost of the investment will normally be carried at the nominal value of the shares of the holding company which have been issued to effect the combination, together with any other consideration given. (The ability to record these shares at nominal rather than fair values on issue depends on qualifying for merger relief under section 131 of the Companies Act 1985, which is discussed under 6.1.2 above.)

As well as combining the assets and liabilities of the companies concerned, it will be necessary to eliminate the share capital of the subsidiary against the cost of the investment as stated in the balance sheet of the holding company. This is in principle a straightforward exercise, but when the two amounts do not equate to each other, the question arises of what to do with the difference, positive or negative.

Where the cost of the investment is less than the nominal value of the share capital of the subsidiary, the elimination of these two amounts will leave a residual credit in shareholders' funds in the consolidated balance sheet; this is generally classified as a capital reserve.

Where the reverse situation applies, the net debit has to be eliminated against consolidated reserves in some way and choices have to be made as to the order in which the group's reserves should be applied for this purpose. There are no particular rules on the matter in any authoritative document, but the normal practice is to apply these first against the most restricted categories of reserves,[209] and subsequently if any excess remains, against the group's retained earnings. Where the reserves are in the subsidiary concerned then, in effect, this is equivalent to the partial capitalisation of the reserves of the subsidiary; if they had had a bonus issue out of their own reserves prior to the merger, to make their share capital equal to the consideration shares offered by the new holding company, no consolidation difference would have emerged.

Apart from the effects of dealing with any imbalance as discussed above, there is no other elimination of the reserves of the subsidiary, which are combined with those of the holding company, in contrast to the treatment under acquisition accounting. However, some of the subsidiary's reserves may need to be reclassified in order to make sense in the context of the group financial statements. One particular example is the share premium account, where to include such an amount relating to the subsidiary in the group balance sheet would have little meaning; probably the best way of dealing with this is to deal with it as part of the equity elimination, because in reality the distinction between share capital and share premium can be seen as somewhat arbitrary in this context. This is the treatment adopted by Belhaven plc as the following extract from their policy shows:

> *Extract 4.24: Belhaven plc*[210]
>
> BASIS OF CONSOLIDATION [extract]
> The acquisition of Garfunkels Restaurants plc is accounted for as a merger under the provisions
> of Statement of Standard Accounting Practice No 23 and the results are presented as if
> Garfunkels had been owned by Belhaven plc throughout the current and comparative accounting
> periods. The excess of the cost of acquisition of Garfunkels Restaurants plc over the nominal
> value of its share capital and its share premium account is included as Other Reserve.

As can be seen from that policy extract, Belhaven plc have elected to keep the
residual debit balance resulting from this elimination as a separate category
altogether and it appears as such in the group balance sheet.

6.7.3 Expenses of the merger

One other question which sometimes arises in this context is how to account for
the expenses of the merger. Some of these may properly be regarded as share
issue expenses and therefore qualify to be written off against the share premium
account of the holding company (if such an account exists). However, there will
almost certainly be further expenses which cannot be disposed of in this way. The
straightforward way of dealing with these would be to account for them in the
profit and loss account of the group in the period of the combination, possibly as
an extraordinary item if they otherwise fit the SSAP 6 criteria. However, an
argument exists for eliminating them through reserves, by adding them to the cost
of the investment in the subsidiary in the financial statements of the holding
company. This approach can also be supported by the fact that merger accounting
in effect treats the transaction as having happened retrospectively, rather than
currently, and that there is therefore an argument that the expenses of the
transaction should not be reflected in the financial statements of the current year.

6.7.4 Non-coterminous accounting periods

Particular practical problems in accounting for the merger can arise in the frequent
circumstances that the accounting periods of the combining companies do not
match each other. Although this can also create problems when acquisition
accounting is used, the requirement in merger accounting to restate the
consolidated financial statements retrospectively makes the difficulties particularly
severe.

Company law dictates that the financial statements of the group must give a true
and fair view in respect of the accounting period of the holding company, so this
will require the period used by the subsidiary to be made to conform to that of its
parent rather than the other way round. Naturally, the parent can change its own
accounting reference date, but this can only be done for the future, not
retrospectively. It will therefore be necessary to try to draw up financial
statements for the subsidiary at each of the relevant balance sheet dates of the
holding company.

The easiest part of the process will be to make sure that the subsidiary prepares a
balance sheet at the next balance sheet date of the holding company, to allow a
consolidated balance sheet at that date to be prepared. The difficult part will be to

recreate balance sheets at the dates previously used by the parent, which will be necessary not only for the purposes of comparative figures for the balance sheet but also in order to allow the profit and loss account and the funds statement of the current and comparative periods (together with any historical periods disclosed) to be drawn up.

Quite often it might prove impossible to draw up financial statements at these earlier dates with the same degree of accuracy which would be attainable in normal circumstances, because it is not possible after the event to institute normal year-end procedures such as stock counts and so on. It may therefore be necessary to make estimates of what such financial statements would have shown if they had been drawn up at that time, by relying on management information or by extrapolation between the reporting dates which were used (with allowance for seasonal or other relevant factors).

Another treatment which may be found appropriate would be to use non-coterminous years for the comparative figures, with the result that there will be the need to deal with the effects of either a 'gap' or an overlapping period as an adjustment to reserves. This was the solution chosen by Belhaven plc in relation to their acquisition of Garfunkels Restaurants plc; it was explained in these terms in the following extract, which is a continuation of the accounting policy disclosed in Extract 4.24 above.

Extract 4.25: Belhaven plc[211]

BASIS OF CONSOLIDATION [extract]
The accounting year end of Belhaven plc has been changed and the results are therefore presented for a nine-month period to December 31, 1987. The comparative figures combine the results of Belhaven plc for the year to March 31, 1987 and the audited results of Garfunkels Restaurants plc for the year to December 28, 1986, and the Balance Sheets of the two Groups as at these dates. The results for Garfunkels for the three months to March 31, 1987 are dealt with as a movement in reserves (Note 21).

A particular problem can arise when a company is incorporated specially for the purpose of acting as the new holding company of a merging group. Because, as noted above, the accounting reference period of the group must by law be that of the holding company, this may result in the inadvertent creation of an accounting period which is not the one which the group would have preferred. Moreover, unless the company has been in existence for two years, its statutory accounts will not be able to deal with the results of the group for the current and comparative periods, because strictly they can only go as far back as the date of incorporation of the holding company. One solution to this might be to present the information for the more relevant chosen period in supplementary pro forma form, but the problem can be avoided from the beginning by ensuring that the new holding company has an accounting reference date which suits that of the group, and has been in existence long enough to allow a full set of group accounts for the chosen period to be presented without having to resort to pro forma financial statements.

6.7.5   *Dividends of the subsidiary*

Since the profit and loss accounts of both the combining companies will be aggregated retrospectively, it will be necessary to consider how to deal with the dividends of the subsidiary paid before the date of the combination. Essentially, the pre-merger dividends of both the parent and the subsidiary will be combined and shown as distributions in the consolidated profit and loss account, although it would be helpful to distinguish them either on the face of the profit and loss account or in a note. However, after the date of the merger, the only dividends shown will be those of the parent (those of the subsidiary will by then be inter-company payments and will thus be eliminated on consolidation).

6.8   Disclosure requirements relating to business combinations

6.8.1   *General*

The following disclosure requirements apply to all business combinations, whether they be acquisitions or mergers:

(a)   the names of the combining companies;

(b)   the number and class of the securities issued in respect of the combination, and details of any other consideration given;

(c)   the accounting treatment adopted for the business combination (i.e. whether it has been accounted for as an acquisition or a merger);

(d)   the nature and amount of significant accounting adjustments by the combining companies to achieve consistency of accounting policies.[212]

6.8.2   *Acquisitions*

As well as the general requirements listed above, the following details must be disclosed for business combinations which are accounted for as acquisitions:

(a)   sufficient information about the results of the subsidiaries acquired to enable shareholders to appreciate the effect on the consolidated results;

(b)   the effective date of any major acquisitions;[213]

(c)   the accounting policy followed in respect of goodwill;[214]

(d)   the amount of goodwill recognised as a result of each separate acquisition made during the year (where material);[215]

(e)   where the amortisation treatment has been applied, the period selected for amortising the goodwill in question, and movements on the goodwill account during the year.[216]

In addition, the following disclosures have recently been proposed in an exposure draft issued by the ASC:

(a)   a table showing the book values, as recorded in the acquired company's books, and the fair values of each major category of asset and liability acquired;

(b)   an analysis of the adjustments made for consolidation purposes to the book values recorded in the acquired company's books, indicating the amounts attributable to:

    (i)   bringing accounting policies into line with those of the acquiring group;

    (ii)   revaluations;

    (iii)   provisions established in respect of the acquisition, with separate disclosure of provisions made in respect of future trading losses;

    (iv)   any other major item;

(c)   a brief explanation of the reasons for the adjustments set out in (b) above.[217]

The financial statements of Tesco PLC included the following information about their acquisition of Hillards plc:

Extract 4.26: Tesco PLC[218]

Basis of consolidation [extract]

Hillards plc, acquired on 15th May, 1987, has been consolidated by the means of acquisition accounting, adopting the merger relief provisions of the Companies Act 1985.

1 — Operating profit [extract]
Operating profit includes £13m in respect of the incremental contribution from the stores acquired with Hillards plc.

19 — Merger Reserve

	Hillards consolidated accounts at 2nd May 1987 £m	Acquisition accounting adjust- ments £m	Total £m
Net assets/(liabilities) acquired			
Goodwill on acquisition	—	193.9	193.9
Fixed assets	82.0	6.4	88.4
Stocks	16.2	(2.7)	13.5
Debtors	0.8	—	0.8
Cash at bank and in hand	14.6	—	14.6
Creditors falling due within one year	(41.6)	—	(41.6)
Net current liabilities	(10.0)	(2.7)	(12.7)
Creditors falling due after more than one year	(21.6)	—	(21.6)
Increase in consolidated reserves from 2nd May 1987 to 15th May 1987	—	0.3	0.3
Total net assets acquired	50.4	197.9	248.3
Reorganisation costs, net of taxation (a)	—	(10.3)	(10.3)
	50.4	187.6	238.0
Consideration paid			
Ordinary shares issued (b)			2.1
Cash			2.4
Merger reserve arising on consolidation			233.5
Less: Goodwill written off			193.9
			39.6

For presentation purposes, the audited Hillards' balance sheet at their 2nd May 1987 year-end has been used to illustrate the calculation of the merger reserve. The acquisition was made on 15th May, 1987, and the adjustment to reserves reflects this.

(a) Acquisition accounting adjustments

Adjustments have been made to the book values of the net assets acquired to reflect their fair value, to align the accounting policies of Hillards with those of the group and to provide for reorganisation costs subsequent to acquisition. The principal adjustments are as follows:

(i) Fixed Assets

Tangible assets have been included at fair value based principally on external professional property valuations and provisions against the disposal of fixtures and fittings arising from store conversions.

(ii) Stocks

Stocks have been adjusted mainly by writing down surplus stocks and providing for costs of realisation.

(iii) Reorganisation costs, net of taxation

The costs of reorganising Hillards' retailing, distribution, marketing and administration operations include principally head office and depot closure costs £3.6m, store conversion costs £4.2m and other items including alignment of accounting policies £2.5m.

(b) Ordinary shares issued

In accordance with Section 131 of the Companies Act 1985, the company has recorded the ordinary shares issued in respect of the acquisition at their nominal value excluding the share premium, and expenses of the share issue of £6.9m have been offset against the share premium account.

The number of shares issued was disclosed in the share capital note. As illustrated in 6.4.5 above, the financial statements of Guinness PLC and P-E International plc also contain most of the disclosures required by ED 44, even though they, and those of Tesco PLC, pre-dated the exposure draft.

The exposure draft also contains proposed requirements relating to disclosure of subsequent movements on provisions, goodwill on subsequent sales of business acquired, and earnings per share where the amortisation route has been chosen for disposing of goodwill.[219] The responses to the exposure draft have generally been favourable, and it is likely that a revised version of SSAP 22 will soon be introduced to incorporate most of its requirements; however the last-mentioned proposal, that earnings per share be disclosed before amortisation of goodwill, is unlikely to survive as a mandatory requirement, since many commentators have pointed out that any company wishing to give this information is at liberty to do so and a user of accounts could easily determine the figure unaided in any event.

6.8.3 Mergers

In addition to the requirements listed at 6.8.1, the following details must be disclosed for business combinations which are accounted for as mergers:

(a) the fair value of the consideration given by the issuing company;

(b) an analysis of the current year's attributable profit before extraordinary items between that of before and that of after the effective date of the merger;

(c)   an analysis of the attributable profit before extraordinary items of the current year up to the effective date of the merger and of the previous year between that of the issuing company and that of the subsidiary;

(d)   an analysis of extraordinary items so as to indicate whether each individual extraordinary item relates to pre- or post-merger events, and to which party to the merger the item relates.[220]

A good example of these disclosures is found in the financial statements of Belhaven plc:

Extract 4.27: Belhaven plc[221]

1. ACQUISITION OF GARFUNKELS RESTAURANTS PLC

On June 17, 1987, the offer made by Belhaven plc to acquire the whole issued share capital of Garfunkels Restaurants plc was declared unconditional, after which the remaining shares were acquired pursuant to Sections 428(2) and 429(2) of the Companies Act 1985.

The acquisition was effected by the issue of 134,326,056 ordinary shares of 25p in Belhaven plc, the fair value of which was £96,714,760 and the purchase of 2.3% of Garfunkels Restaurants plc shares for cash of £2,193,585. Other costs of acquisition amounted to £2,833,865.

The financial statements are presented following merger accounting principles and dealt with in the manner described in the Statement of Accounting Policies.

The analysis of the results for the nine month period before and after acquisition, was as follows:

	Belhaven plc £000	Garfunkels Restaurants plc £000	Total £000
Profit after taxation			
Pre-acquisition	303	860	1163
Post-acquisition			3,591
			4,754
Extraordinary costs			
Post-acquisition	44	—	44
Profit attributable to members			4,710

(The information required by (c) on the previous year is given in a separate note.)

6.8.4   *Transactions involving merger relief*

Where transactions involving merger relief under section 131 of the Companies Act 1985 have taken place, various additional statutory disclosures are required. It should be noted that these requirements do not simply arise when merger *accounting* has been adopted; they relate to any transaction where merger relief has been taken, regardless of the form of accounting used. In the description that follows, the parties are described as the acquiring company and the acquired company but these terms are not intended to signify that acquisition accounting is adopted, only that the acquired company becomes a subsidiary of the acquiring company as a result of a share exchange transaction. The requirements are:

(a) where merger relief has been taken on an issue of shares during the year, the acquiring company must disclose:

    (i)   the name of the company acquired;

    (ii)   the number, nominal values and classes of shares of both companies which were involved in the share exchange transaction;

    (iii)   the accounting treatment adopted by the acquiring company;

    (iv)   the effect (if any) on the group results for the year of the results of the acquired company in the period before the transaction.[222]

(b) where merger relief has been taken on an issue of shares during the last *three* years, the acquiring company must disclose the amount of any profit included in the group accounts which arises on the disposal of shares in the acquired company or of any fixed assets which belonged to the acquired company or its subsidiaries at the time of the merger. There is also a provision to deal with situations where there have been intercompany transfers of assets or shares in the intervening time which might otherwise frustrate the intention of the disclosure requirement.[223]

6.8.5 Companies Bill

Some of the above disclosure requirements, which are presently contained in accounting standards or exposure drafts, are also included in the Companies Bill[224] and, therefore, it is likely that they will be duplicated by similar statutory requirements in the forthcoming Companies Act.

In addition, the Companies Bill proposes that the following information is disclosed in respect of business combinations:

(a) the profit or loss of the subsidiary for the period up to the date of acquisition, and for the previous financial year.[225] This would appear to apply even where acquisition accounting has been used and such results are not included in the consolidated figures;

(b) the cumulative amount of goodwill resulting from acquisitions in that and earlier years which has been written off. This figure would be net of any goodwill attributable to subsidiaries or businesses which had been disposed of.[226]

The Bill intends that any information which will be required by the legislation need not be given in respect of an undertaking established under the law of a country outside the UK or an undertaking which carries on business outside the UK if the directors consider it would be prejudicial to the business of the undertaking or any other group member. However, this is subject to the agreement of the Secretary of State.[227]

7   DISPOSALS

7.1   Basic principles

The other possible change in the composition of a group involves the disposal of a group company. In principle the results of the company being disposed of should continue to be consolidated as part of the group results until the effective date of disposal, and the gain or loss on disposal should be determined by comparing the carrying value of the subsidiary's net assets at that date with the sales proceeds obtained. There are, however, a number of aspects which need to be considered, which are discussed more fully below.

7.2   Effective date of disposal

The date of disposal is defined in SSAP 14 in exactly the same terms as the effective date of acquisition, as the earlier of:

(a)   the date when consideration passes; or

(b)   the date on which an offer becomes or is declared unconditional.[228]

However, this is to some extent in conflict with the terms of SSAP 6 insofar as they relate to terminated activities. The latter requires that where a business segment is being discontinued, its trading results from the time of implementing the decision to discontinue it should be treated as part of the results of the termination (as an extraordinary item), rather than as part of the group's trading results from ordinary operations.[229]

There are a number of differences between these sets of requirements. First of all, SSAP 6 is discussing all types of termination of activities, which embraces closures as well as sales of businesses. Also, SSAP 6 is discussing discontinuance of business segments, and not all subsidiaries would fall into this category. However, in circumstances which do fall under both of the standards, it will be necessary to try to reconcile these requirements. The problems of interpreting the SSAP 6 requirements are discussed in more detail in 4.2 of Chapter 8.

One complication which can arise is when a decision has been taken before a year end to dispose of a subsidiary after the year end and a loss is expected to emerge. In these circumstances, provision should be made for the loss which is anticipated, and this should also take account of the trading results which are expected to arise up to the date of disposal, which will either be trading losses which increase the amount of the loss on disposal or trading profits which go to mitigate it. In these circumstances, the effective date of deconsolidation will be the balance sheet date, and the group financial statements for the following period will not include the results of the subsidiary being disposed of, except to the extent of any difference between the amount provided and the actual results until the date of disposal.

This treatment gives rise to questions of presentation of the deconsolidated subsidiary, both in the balance sheet and in the profit and loss account. In the balance sheet, the straightforward treatment would be to continue to consolidate the company on a line-by-line basis as normal, but an alternative treatment sometimes adopted is to show the net assets as one line in the balance sheet, possibly with a summarised balance sheet shown by way of note. In the profit and loss account, similarly, it is possible to continue to consolidate the results of the subsidiary in question as normal, but an alternative would be to segregate the results of the discontinued business from those of the continuing operations, in order to show the trend of results of those parts of the business which will be continued in the future.

Where a provision for losses up to the date of actual disposal has been made at the balance sheet date, the question arises of whether, and if so how, to show the actual results in the consolidated financial statements of the following year. A strict application of the rules on the effective date of disposal would require the results to continue to be consolidated until that date as normal, and to show an offsetting release of the provision made at the previous year end. However, frequently companies will show only the net effect of any over or under provision, and this treatment can be regarded as acceptable.

7.3   Partial disposals

When part of the investment in a subsidiary is sold, but a sufficient number of the shares are held for it to retain subsidiary or associate status, it is necessary to consider how to account for the disposal in the consolidated financial statements. When more than 50% of the shares are retained, all the assets[230] and liabilities remain consolidated on a line-by-line basis, so the accounting entries affect only the consolidated reserves and the minority interest. The calculation of the gain or loss on sale will be achieved by comparing the sale proceeds with the consolidated net asset value attributable to the shares sold at the date of the disposal, as in the following example:

Example 4.7:   Partial disposal of shares in a subsidiary

Company A has a 100% investment in Company B, based on an original investment of £4,000. Company B has subsequently earned profits of £6,000 which it has retained. The balance sheets of the companies and of the group show the following immediately before the sale:

	Company A £000	Company B £000	Consolidated £000
Investment in B	4		
Other net assets	20	10	30
	24	10	30
Share capital	10	4	10
Reserves	14	6	20
	24	10	30

Company A sells 40% of its shares in Company B to a third party for £7,000. It will compute its gain on this transaction (ignoring any taxation payable on the gain), in its own profit and loss account and in that of the group, thus:

	Own accounts £000	Group accounts £000
Sale proceeds	7.0	7.0
40% of investment/net assets	1.6	4.0
Gain on sale	5.4	3.0

The balance sheets will now show the following:

	Company A £000	Company B £000	Consolidated £000
Investment in B	2.4		
Other net assets	27.0	10.0	37.0
	29.4	10.0	37.0
Minority interest			4.0
Share capital	10.0	4.0	10.0
Reserves	19.4	6.0	23.0
	29.4	10.0	37.0

The same basic principles apply where only an associate holding is retained, the only difference being that the balance sheet will carry the underlying assets of Company B on one line. If Company A had sold 60% of its holding for £11,000, the effect on the profit and loss accounts and balance sheets (again ignoring the effects of any taxation payable) would have been as follows:

	Own accounts £000	Group accounts £000
Sale proceeds	11.0	11.0
60% of investment/net assets	2.4	6.0
Gain on sale	8.6	5.0

The balance sheets would now show the following:

	Company A £000	Company B £000	Consolidated £000
Investment in B	1.6		4.0
Other net assets	31.0	10.0	31.0
	32.6	10.0	35.0
Share capital	10.0	4.0	10.0
Reserves	22.6	6.0	25.0
	32.6	10.0	35.0

7.4   Goodwill of subsidiaries disposed of

Where a subsidiary has been acquired and then disposed of (particularly if the period of ownership was relatively short), it is appropriate to keep sight of what has happened to any goodwill, positive or negative, which arose on the acquisition. If it has been taken to reserves, then there is a danger that it will by-pass the profit and loss account altogether and result in a misstatement of the gain or loss on disposal because the goodwill has not been taken into account. The following example illustrates this point:

Example 4.8

A subsidiary is purchased in 19X1 for £5m and earns profits, which it retains, of £2m before being sold in 19X3 for £8m. On acquisition, the fair value of its net assets was £3.5m, and goodwill of £1.5m therefore arose and was written off against reserves.

The gain on sale could be calculated under either of these methods:

	£m	Option (a) £m	Option (b) £m
Carrying value of the subsidiary in the financial statements of the group:			
Fair value of assets acquired	3.5		
Retained profits	2.0		
		5.5	5.5
Sales proceeds		8.0	8.0
		2.5	2.5
Less: goodwill previously taken to reserves		—	1.5
Gain on sale reported		2.5	1.0

Under option (a), the carrying value of the net assets in the group balance sheet of £5.5m is compared with the sales proceeds of £8m to give a profit on sale of £2.5m. However, this calculation ignores the goodwill which has been written off to reserves, and it is clear that in fact the group has only made a total profit of £3m between the time of buying it and selling it (the difference between the acquisition and the sale prices), which represents trading profits of £2m and a gain on sale of a further £1m. Option (b) recognises this by bringing the £1.5m of goodwill into account to reduce the apparent gain on disposal of £2.5m to its true level of £1m.

Although this principle is a straightforward one, it can be difficult to apply in practice unless the subsidiary in question has been sold in exactly the same form as it was purchased. If the business of the subsidiary has been integrated with that of the rest of the group, or reorganised in any other way, then it is not necessarily the case that the sale of the company automatically means that the goodwill which was acquired with it has also been sold. There can also be practical difficulties in determining the relevant figures if the original acquisition took place some time ago and it is difficult to trace what happened to the goodwill.

Practice on this matter in the UK is not uniform; some companies do make a point of accounting for the goodwill on subsidiaries sold by channeling it through the profit and loss account on sale, but this is by no means universal practice.

However, the treatment could be thought to be governed by paragraph 31 of SSAP 14, which reads as follows:

'Where there is a material disposal, the consolidated profit and loss account should include ...

(b)   the gain or loss on the sale of the investment, being the difference at the time of the sale between:

  (i)   proceeds of the sale and
  (ii)   the holding company's share of its net assets together with any premium (less any amounts written off) or discount on acquisition.'

However, if this is intended to be a rule on the matter it is a most unsatisfactory one, because apart from favouring the treatment above which appears to give the less sensible answer (option (a)), it results in an inconsistent treatment between positive and negative goodwill. By applying the terms of this paragraph literally, companies would deal with negative goodwill as an augmentation of their gain on sale, but ignore positive goodwill as a reduction of it, unless the goodwill was carried in the balance sheet as an asset.

However, it is fair to say that the paragraph does not appear to be applied in practice, certainly not by all companies; it was drafted long before a standard was issued on the treatment of goodwill, and was probably not intended to have the effect which a literal reading of the words would suggest. Although we believe that option (a) is a permissible treatment, we do not prefer it to option (b), and we would not wish to interpret paragraph 31 of SSAP 14 as ruling out the latter.

Although not adjudicating between these alternatives, the ASC has proposed that where option (a) has been adopted in respect of the disposal of a business which was acquired within the previous three years, disclosure should be made of the amount of the goodwill which was previously written off to reserves and has therefore not been taken into account in measuring the gain or loss on sale.[231] The fact that they apparently condoned either of the two alternative treatments supports the view that the matter should not be regarded as determined by paragraph 31 of SSAP 14 as quoted above.

7.5   Companies Bill

The Companies Bill proposes that where there has been a disposal of a material subsidiary during the financial year, disclosure should be made of the results of the subsidiary up to the date of disposal.[232] However, a similar exemption to that in respect of business combinations indicated at 6.8.5 above applies.

8   GROUP REORGANISATIONS

8.1   Introduction

Group reorganisations involve the restructuring of the relationships between companies in a group by, for example, setting up a new holding company, changing the direct ownership of a subsidiary within the group, or transferring businesses from one company to another because of a process of divisionalisation. In principle, most of such changes should have no impact on the consolidated financial statements (provided there are no minority interests affected), because they are purely internal and cannot affect the group when it is being portrayed as a single entity. However, all such transactions can have a significant impact on the financial statements of the individual companies in the group, and this is described for each of the main types of transaction in the sections which follow. All the examples given assume that all the subsidiaries are owned 100% by the parent company.

8.2   Setting up a new top holding company

Reorganisations of this type may take place, for example, to introduce a public company over the top of an existing group as a vehicle for flotation, or to improve the co-ordination of diverse businesses. It involves H becoming the new holding company of A, as shown in the diagram below, and this may be achieved either by the shareholders subscribing for shares in H and then H paying cash for A or, more usually, by H issuing its own shares to the shareholders of A in exchange for the shares in A.

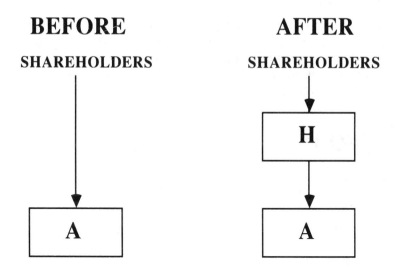

If H pays cash for A, it should (in theory at least) account for the transaction as an acquisition, which involves attributing fair values to A's assets, consolidating only the post-acquisition results of A and effectively freezing A's pre-acquisition reserves from being distributed to H's shareholders in the future. All these consequences are usually undesirable when the sole intention is to insert a new holding company at the top of the group, and it is relatively unlikely that this means of effecting the transaction will be chosen. However, some may take the view that transactions of this type are entirely different from the arm's length type of acquisition for which SSAP 23 was designed, and accordingly come to the view that the standard does not cater for this kind of group reorganisation, which means that the normal accounting rules need not necessarily be applied. (In the US, the basic rules on acquisition accounting do not apply to a transfer of assets or an exchange of shares between companies under common control.)[233] In any event, H could have difficulty in financing such a transaction, and A could not provide the necessary finance (e.g. by any kind of loan or guarantee) because UK company law does not permit a company to provide financial assistance for the purchase of its own shares.[234]

It is therefore more likely that the transaction will be effected by the exchange of shares. In this case the transaction will qualify as a merger in terms of SSAP 23 and hence the consolidated financial statements may continue to carry the assets and liabilities of A at their previous book values and all profits before and after the merger can continue to be consolidated (provided H has the same accounting period and has been in existence long enough — see 6.7.4 above). Also, the transaction will qualify for merger relief under section 131 of the Companies Act, so the investment in A can be recorded by H at the nominal value of the shares issued by H; the reserves of A will be 'frozen' as a result of the transaction only to the extent that the nominal value of H's shares exceeds that of A's shares.

8.3   Changing direct ownership of a company within a group

8.3.1   *Subsidiary moved 'up'*

This involves a 'grandson' subsidiary being moved up to become a 'son', as shown in the diagram below. Such a change might be made say, to allow B to be disposed of while C is retained, or because B and C are in different businesses and the group wishes to restructure itself so that the different businesses are conducted through directly owned subsidiaries.

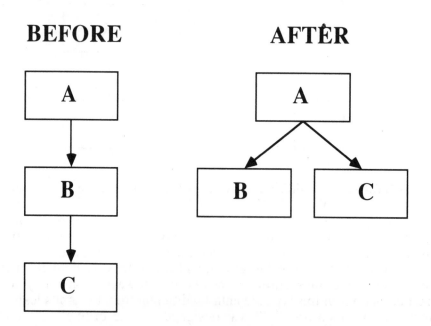

This result could be achieved either by B transferring its investment in C to A as a dividend in specie, or by A paying cash (or a cash equivalent) to B for the investment in C. It is not possible to effect this transaction by a share for share exchange, because an allotment by a holding company (A) to its subsidiary (B) is void.[235]

If the mechanism used is to be a dividend in specie then B must have sufficient distributable profits. If B has previously revalued its investment in C then the amount of that revaluation may be treated as a realised profit in deciding whether the dividend is legal and in accounting for the dividend; for example, if B's balance sheet is as follows:

	£
Investment in C (cost £100)	900
Other net assets	100
	1,000
Share capital	100
Revaluation reserve	800
Profit and loss account	100
	1,000

On the face of it, B cannot make a distribution of more than £100. However, if it makes a distribution in kind of its investment in C, the revaluation reserve can be treated as realised.[236]

Where the transaction is effected as a dividend in specie then the problem of how A accounts for it also arises. It will need to reflect its new investment in C at a value, but two questions then arise; what value to place on it, and whether the transaction gives rise to a realised profit. The legal position on both of these points is unclear. On the first question, a range of possible values would appear to be possible — the value might for example be agreed between the parties, it could be at current fair value, it could be the carrying value previously recorded in B's financial statements or it might even be nil. In practice, it might be convenient to use B's carrying value, but it cannot be said with certainty that this is the right answer. On the second issue, it may appear that A has realised a profit by being given a valuable asset (subject to the need to write down its investment in B), but it might be contended with some justification that this is not realised, since in substance nothing has changed — A still owns the same two subsidiaries as it did before. Where it is sufficiently significant (e.g. in relation to a proposed distribution), it may be advisable to seek legal advice on these points.

If A pays cash to B in exchange for its investment in C, the transaction is on the face of it straightforward. B will have to record a gain or loss on sale if the purchase price differs from the value at which it carried its investment in C, although frequently the transfer may be made on such terms that no gain or loss is recorded. However, there is a danger that a transfer at a price which does not fully reflect the true value of C (i.e. made at less than an arm's length price) will be regarded as having given rise to a distribution, and if the transaction is made to facilitate B's leaving the group, it could also be regarded as financial assistance which may be illegal — there are therefore various possible legal pitfalls which must be borne in mind.

Regardless of the value at which these transactions take place, there should be no effect on the group financial statements, because the group as a whole is in no different position from before; it has made neither an acquisition nor a disposal.

8.3.2   Subsidiary moved 'along'

This involves a 'grandson' subsidiary being moved along to become another 'grandson' but under a different 'son', as shown in the diagram below. It would be achieved by C paying cash or other assets to B rather than issuing shares, because otherwise the resulting holding of B in C would probably negate the desired effect of the transaction.

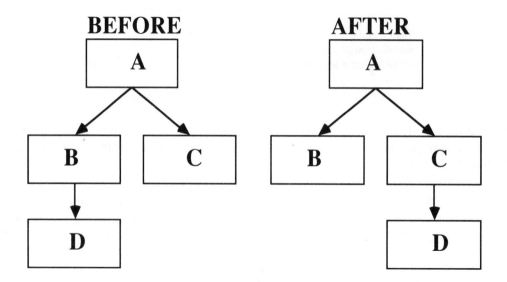

The accounting considerations are similar to those under 8.3.1 above, and once again there can be no effect on the group financial statements, because when the group is looked upon as a single entity there has been no change. The question of an effective distribution cannot arise because the purchaser is not the holding company. As above, if the transaction is a prelude to B leaving the group, or is intended to facilitate it, and C pays less than fair value then problems of financial assistance can arise.

8.3.3 Subsidiary moved 'down'

This involves a 'son' becoming a 'grandson' as shown in the diagram below. Such a change might be made, say, if A is a foreign holding company but B and C are UK companies who will form a UK tax group as a result of the reorganisation.

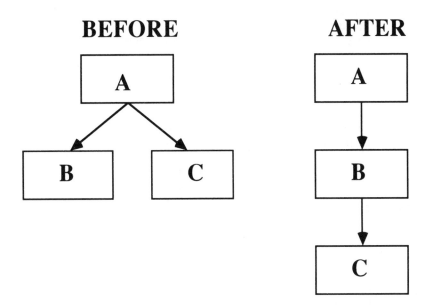

This reorganisation could be achieved either by B paying cash to A or by B issuing its shares to A in exchange for the shares in C. As in the previous two examples, there should be no effect on the group financial statements as a result of the reorganisation.

The accounting in the case of a cash transaction is relatively straightforward, following the principles described above in 8.3.1. However, if C is sold at an amount greater or smaller than its carrying value, the issue of whether A should recognise a gain or loss will again arise; as with the question discussed in 8.3.1 above, the law on this is unclear. The question of whether B has effectively made a distribution is again unlikely to arise; in the context of this transaction it could arise only if the transfer were made at a price which was in excess of the fair value of C, which is in practice unlikely.

In the case of a share for share exchange, the provisions of section 132 of the Companies Act 1985 become relevant. This section is designed to give partial relief from the requirement to set up a share premium account in the circumstances of a group reconstruction involving the issue of shares. It requires a share premium account of the 'minimum premium value' to be established; this is the amount by which the book value of the investment (or cost, if lower) exceeds the nominal value of the shares issued. The effect of this is to preserve the book value of the investment (any amount by which the investment had been revalued would effectively be reversed, but the investment could also be revalued again). The operation of the section is illustrated in the following example:

Example 4.9

The balance sheets of A and its direct subsidiaries B and C are as follows:

	A £	B £	C £	Group £
Investment in B	200			
Investment in C	100			
Other net assets	300	275	300	875
	600	275	300	875
Share capital	500	200	100	500
Profit and loss account	100	75	200	375
	600	275	300	875

B then issues 50 £1 shares to A in exchange for A's investment in C, which is shown in A's balance sheet at a cost of £100. The minimum premium value is therefore £50. The resultant balance sheets would be:

	A £	B £	C £	Group £
Investment in B	300			
Investment in C		100		
Other net assets	300	275	300	875
	600	375	300	875
Share capital	500	250	100	500
Share premium		50		
Profit and loss account	100	75	200	375
	600	375	300	875

Care must be taken in this situation to avoid issuing shares at a discount; this means that it must be possible to demonstrate that C is worth at least the nominal value of the shares issued by B.

8.4   Divisionalisation of an existing group

The term 'divisionalisation' in this context is used to signify the transfer of the assets and trades of a number of subsidiaries into one company so that the businesses are brought together. It is a means of rationalising and simplifying the group and can result in a saving of administration costs. Transactions of this type are usually effected for a cash consideration, which is often left outstanding on inter-company account as the shell company has no requirement for cash.

In principle the accounting treatment is straightforward. However, one complication which can arise is that there might be an apparent need to write down the investment in the shell company to reflect an impairment in its value, depending on the price at which the assets were transferred. This will typically arise where the shell company was originally purchased at a price which included goodwill, but the business is then transferred to another company at a price which reflects only the value of the net tangible assets; this will mean that, although the goodwill still exists, the business to which it relates is now in another company, and although the group as a whole is unaffected, the value of the investment in the shell company now falls short of its cost. This issue is discussed in Chapter 10 at 4.6.2.

8.5 Demergers

In this context, this refers to splitting up an existing group of companies into two or more separate groups of companies, in order to separate their different trades, possibly as a prelude, say, to floating off one of the businesses.

This could be achieved in a number of ways:

(a) company A transfers its shareholdings in a subsidiary, B, to its shareholders as a dividend in specie.

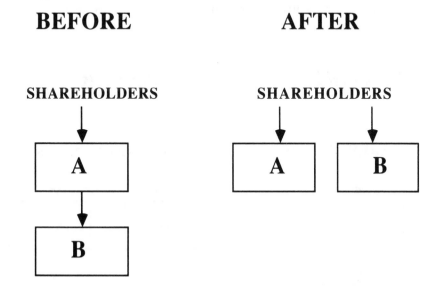

(b)   company A transfers a trade to another company C (usually formed for the purposes of the demerger) and in exchange C issues shares to the shareholders of A.

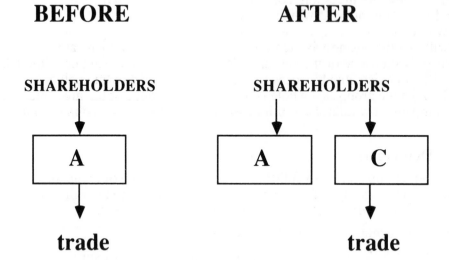

(c)   company A transfers its shareholding in a subsidiary, B, to another company, C; in return, shares in C are issued to some or all of the shareholders in A.

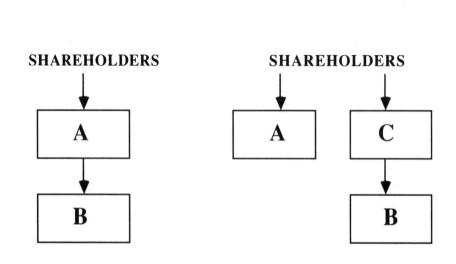

Whichever route is adopted, the transaction involves a distribution by A to its shareholders. This is less obvious in the second and third examples outlined above, but it is as though A had distributed the assets or shares in question to its own shareholders, which they then exchange for shares in C. Similar accounting issues arise in each case; for the purposes of illustration, an example is shown below of a transaction of type (c) above.

Example 4.10

B is a subsidiary of A and is to be demerged from the group. The form of the transaction is that a new company, C, is to be formed which will issue shares to the shareholders of A in exchange for A's investment in B. The balance sheets before the demerger are as follows:

	A	B	A group
	£	£	£
Investment in B	500		
Other net assets	1,200	800	2,000
	1,700	800	2,000
Share capital	1,000	500	1,000
Profit and loss account	700	300	1,000
	1,700	800	2,000

C is to issue 500 £1 ordinary shares to the shareholders of A in exchange for the shares in B held by A. In effect this amounts to a distribution of £500 by A to its shareholders so that, in the A group financial statements the company's net assets are reduced by £500 and the group's net assets by £800 (i.e. the net asset value of B). In the financial statements, the usual treatment is to disclose these amounts as movements on retained earnings, along the following lines:

Profit and loss account	Group	Company
	£	£
Balance at January 1, 19X1	1,000	700
Demerger of B	(800)	(500)
Profit for the year	350	350
Balance at December 31, 19X1	550	550

From C's point of view, the questions which arise are whether its shares are being issued at a premium and if so whether share premium relief should be taken. As this part of the transaction amounts to a merger of C with B, the answers to both questions are yes. However, if the demerger was of an unincorporated business, then merger relief would not be available, since it applies only to share exchanges and not to issues of shares in exchange for assets; this contrasts with group reconstruction relief, which is available for both — see 8.3.3 above. The same point applies to a transaction of type (b) above.

It also seems logical to use merger accounting for this kind of transaction, although in fact the SSAP 23 criteria are not fully satisfied in that they require that an 'offer' is made, which is not relevant to a demerger situation.

8.6   Capital contributions

One form of transaction which is sometimes made within a group is a 'capital contribution', where one company injects funds in another (usually its subsidiary) in the form of a non-returnable gift. This form of transaction may be preferred to the subscription of share capital because it can strengthen the recipient's balance sheet without incurring capital duty (unless it is associated with an issue of shares near to the date of the capital contribution), or to increase the distributable reserves of the recipient. Whenever capital contributions are made, complex tax considerations can arise and should be addressed.

Capital contributions have no real legal status in the UK — certainly the term is not used anywhere in the Companies Acts. This has led to uncertainty over the appropriate accounting treatment in the financial statements of both the giver and the receiver of the capital contribution, and various treatments are possible in theory; those which seem to have gained acceptance in practice are set out below.

8.6.1   *Treatment in the financial statements of the paying company*

In the most common situation, where the contribution is made by a company to one of its subsidiaries, the treatment is relatively straightforward; the amount of the contribution should be added to the cost of the investment in the subsidiary. However, it will not be possible to regard it as part of the purchase price of shares in the subsidiary, so it should be classified as a separate item when the cost of the investment is analysed. As with any fixed asset, it will be necessary to write down the investment whenever it is recognised that its value has been permanently impaired; this should be considered when subsequent dividends are received from the subsidiary which could be regarded as having been met out of the capital contribution and hence representing a return of it.

Where the contribution is made to a fellow-subsidiary, it will not be possible to regard it as an asset of any kind; it is neither an investment in the other company, nor can it be treated as a monetary receivable, since by definition there is no obligation on the part of the recipient to return it. Accordingly, the only available treatment to the paying company in these circumstances will be to write it off in the profit and loss account of the period in which the payment is made.

8.6.2   *Treatment in the financial statements of the receiving company*

The most common treatment adopted by the receiving company would appear to be to credit the amount received to a separate reserve with a suitable title, such as 'capital contribution', or 'capital reserve'. There is of course an argument that the contribution should be credited to the profit and loss account in the year of receipt, probably as an extraordinary item, in accordance with SSAP 6; however, this treatment is not widely adopted, presumably because the transaction is in substance a capital one between the company and its owners, and therefore does not form any part of its profits.

Notwithstanding this, it is generally considered that the contribution can be regarded for distribution purposes as a realised profit, and accordingly is available to be paid out by way of dividend. Where this is done, it may be regarded as appropriate to reclassify the reserve to which the contribution was originally taken as part of the profit and loss account balance.

There is no compelling reason why there need be symmetry of treatment between the accounting treatments used by the giving and receiving companies, although this will usually be the case; it would, for example, be theoretically possible for the giving company to add it to the cost of its investment, while the recipient credited the contribution to its profit and loss account. Whatever treatment is adopted, the whole effect of the transaction will be eliminated from the consolidated financial statements.

9 CONCLUSION

Almost all major companies in the UK operate through subsidiaries and/or associates and therefore require to present consolidated financial statements. The practices involved in the preparation of such statements are generally well established in this country, even if some of the underlying principles, such as the particular concept of a group being adopted, are sometimes hazy. However, the area of accounting rules where considerable room for improvement exists is that of business combinations.

The existing standards on business combinations allow a choice between acquisition and merger accounting on the basis of some rather mechanistic criteria which might bear little relation to the substance of the transaction. When the acquisition route is adopted, further choices remain, because there are as yet no detailed rules (other than in the ASC discussion paper) on the determination of fair values, which are necessary to allow the effect of the transaction to be appropriately measured, and the rules which do exist in relation to goodwill are extremely weak. These issues are under review, but until they are resolved, this part of the UK framework for consolidated financial statements will continue to be open to criticism.

References

1 CA 85, s 230(2).
2 *Ibid.*, s 230(1).
3 SSAP 14, *Group accounts*, September 1978, para. 1.
4 CA 85, s 229(5).
5 Accounting Research Bulletin No. 51, *Consolidated Financial Statements*, August 1959, para. 1.
6 CA 85, s 229(6) and SSAP 14 para. 22.
7 Companies Bill, Clause 5(1), s 227(2).
8 CA 85, s 736(1).
9 *Ibid.*, s 744.
10 EC Seventh Directive, Article 1(1)(a); Companies Bill, Clause 19, s 257(2)(a).
11 Announcement by the DTI on implementation of the EC Seventh Company Law Directive, August 16, 1988.

1 2 Companies Bill, Clause 19, s 258.
1 3 EC Seventh Directive, Article 1(1)(b); Companies Bill, Clause 19, s 257(2)(b).
1 4 Companies Bill, Clause 19, s 258(4).
1 5 EC Seventh Directive, Article 1(1)(c); Companies Bill, Clause 19, s 257(2)(c).
1 6 Companies Bill, Clause 19, s 258(5).
1 7 EC Seventh Directive, Article 1(1)(d)(bb); Companies Bill, Clause 19, s 257(2)(d).
1 8 Companies Bill, Clause 19, s 258(2).
1 9 EC Seventh Directive, Article 1(1)(d)(aa).
2 0 *Ibid.*, Article 1(2).
2 1 Companies Bill, Clause 19, ss 257(3) and 260.
2 2 EC Seventh Directive, Article 12.
2 3 IAS 27, *Consolidated Financial Statements and Accounting for Investments in Subsidiaries*, IASC, April 1989, para. 6.
2 4 APB 18, *The Equity Method of Accounting for Investments in Common Stock*, para. 3.
2 5 Rule 1-02(m) of Regulation S-X of the Securities and Exchange Commission.
2 6 CICA *Handbook*, Section 3050.03.
2 7 Australian Companies Code, section 7(1).
2 8 Australian ED 40, *Consolidated Financial Statements*, para. 5(b).
2 9 New Zealand SSAP 8, paras. 4.12 and 4.13.
3 0 *Ibid.*, para. 3.14.
3 1 Companies Bill, Schedule 2, para. 9(4).
3 2 IAS 22, *Accounting for Business Combinations*, IASC, November 1983, para. 45.
3 3 E32, *Comparability of Financial Statements*, IASC, January 1989, paras. 176—180.
3 4 Companies Bill, Schedule 2, para. 6.
3 5 SSAP 14, para. 34.
3 6 Companies Bill, Schedule 2, para. 18.
3 7 ICAEW, *Recommendation VII*.
3 8 ASC Discussion Paper, *Fair value in the context of acquisition accounting*, June 1988.
3 9 ED 44, *Accounting for goodwill — additional disclosures*, September 1988.
4 0 SSAP 14, para. 3.
4 1 *Ibid.*, para. 16.
4 2 Companies Bill, Schedule 2, para. 3(1).
4 3 *Ibid.*, para. 3(2).
4 4 *Ibid.*, para. 3(3).
4 5 CA 85, s 230(7).
4 6 SSAP 14, para. 18.
4 7 Companies Bill, Schedule 2, para. 2(2).
4 8 SSAP 1, *Accounting for associated companies*, Revised April 1982, para. 39.
4 9 R.M. Wilkins, *Group Accounts*, Second edition, London: ICAEW, 1979, pp. 165 — 173.
5 0 SSAP 14, para. 19.
5 1 CA 85, s 229(2).
5 2 Companies Bill, Clause 5, s 228.
5 3 *Ibid.*, Clause 12, s 248.
5 4 SSAP 14, para. 21.
5 5 CA 85, s 229(3).
5 6 SSAP 14, para. 21(a).
5 7 *Ibid.*, para. 23.
5 8 CA 85, s 229(3)(d).
5 9 *Ibid.*, s 229(4).
6 0 B.A.T Industries p.l.c., Annual Report and Accounts 1987, p. 28.
6 1 Marks and Spencer p.l.c., 1988 Annual Report and Financial Statements, p. 41.
6 2 SFAS 94, *Consolidation of All Majority-owned Subsidiaries*, FASB, October 1987, paras. 30 and 31.
6 3 IAS 3, *Consolidated Financial Statements*, IASC, June 1976, para. 37.
6 4 IAS 27, para. 12.

65 Companies Bill, Clause 5(3), s 229(4).
66 SSAP 14, para. 21(b).
67 *Ibid.*, para. 24.
68 Trusthouse Forte PLC, Report and Accounts 1988, pp. 33 and 34.
69 SSAP 14, para. 21(c).
70 Companies Bill, Clause 5(3), s 229(3)(a).
71 SSAP 14, para. 25 and 26.
72 Booker plc, Report and Accounts 1987, pp. 31 and 23.
73 SSAP 14, para. 21(d).
74 Companies Bill, Clause 5(3), s 229(3)(c).
75 SSAP 14, para. 27.
76 *Ibid.*, paras. 31 and 32.
77 Unilever plc, Accounts 1987, p. 5.
78 Sir T.B. Robson and S.M. Duncan, *Holding companies and their subsidiaries: consolidated and other group accounts; principles and procedures*, 4th edition, London: Gee, 1969, p. 22.
79 Companies Bill, Clause 5(3), s 229(2).
80 *Ibid.*, s 229(3)(b).
81 SSAP 14, para. 19.
82 CA 85, s 229(2).
83 SSAP 14, para. 15.
84 CA 85, s 229(4).
85 *Ibid.*, s 229(3).
86 SSAP 1, para. 13.
87 *Ibid.*, paras. 14 and 15.
88 *Ibid.*, para. 13.
89 CA 85, Sch. 4, para. 92.
90 SSAP 1, para. 53.
91 IAS 28, *Accounting for Investments in Associates*, IASC, April 1989, para. 5.
92 APB 18, para. 17.
93 SSAP 1, para. 26.
94 SSAP 22, *Accounting for goodwill*, paras. 3, 32 and 34.
95 SSAP 1, paras. 23 and 30.
96 *Ibid.*, para. 36.
97 IAS 28, para. 16.
98 SSAP 1, para. 33.
99 IAS 28, para. 19.
100 APB 18, para. 19(j).
101 CA 85, Sch. 4, para. 12(a).
102 SSAP 1, para. 24.
103 Example taken from Accountants Digest No. 126, *An Accountants Digest Guide to Accounting Standards — Accounting For Associated Companies*, p. 41.
104 SSAP 1, para. 35.
105 APB 18, para. 14. This paragraph has, in fact, been deleted by SFAS 94, but the principle has not been changed.
106 IAS 28, para. 12.
107 SSAP 1, para. 43.
108 *Ibid.*, paras. 19 — 22.
109 *Ibid.*, para. 23.
110 *Ibid.*, para. 32.
111 *Ibid.*, para. 26.
112 *Ibid.*, paras. 27 and 28.
113 *Ibid.*, para. 29.
114 *Ibid.*, para. 31.
115 *Ibid.*, para. 30.
116 *Ibid.*, para. 49.

117 *Ibid.*, para. 37.
118 *Ibid.*, para. 38.
119 *Ibid.*, para. 40.
120 J Sainsbury plc, 1988 Annual Report & Accounts, pp. 33 and 34.
121 Shearer (Inspector of Taxes) v. Bercain (Ltd.), (1980) 3 All E.R. 295.
122 ED 31, *Accounting for acquisitions and mergers*, October 1982, para. 17.
123 *Ibid.*, para. 3.
124 ED 3, *Accounting for acquisitions and mergers*, January 1971, para. 1.
125 SSAP 23, *Accounting for acquisitions and mergers*, April 1985, para. 17.
126 Companies Bill, Sch. 2, para. 10.
127 IAS 22, para 36.
128 *Ibid.*, para 37.
129 E32, paras.152—162.
130 CICA Handbook, paras. 1580.13—17.
131 Companies Bill, Sch. 2, para. 9 (2).
132 SSAP 14, para. 32.
133 APB 16, *Business Combinations*, AICPA, August 1970, para. 93.
134 SSAP 23, Appendix, para. 1.
135 *Ibid.*, para. 16.
136 ASC Discussion Paper, *Fair value in the context of acquisition accounting*.
137 *Ibid.*, paras. 5.40(a) — (c).
138 Travis & Arnold P.L.C., Report and Accounts 1987, p. 12.
139 APB 16, para. 74.
140 Hanson Trust PLC, Annual Report 1986, p. 47.
141 ASC Discussion Paper, *Fair value in the context of acquisition accounting*, para. 5.40 (d).
142 *Ibid.*, para. 5.40(e).
143 *Ibid.*, para. 5.40(f).
144 *Ibid.*, para. 5.40(g).
145 Saatchi & Saatchi Company PLC, Annual Report and Accounts, Year ended 30th September 1987, p. 49.
146 Ronald Martin Groome PLC, Annual Report and Accounts, Year Ended 31st December 1987, p. 22.
147 Ronald Martin Groome PLC, Annual Report and Accounts, Year Ended 31st December 1987, p. 23.
148 ASC Discussion Paper, *Fair value in the context of acquisition accounting*, para. 5.40 (h).
149 CA 85, s 130.
150 CA 81, s 40(3).
151 Accountants Digest No. 189, *A Guide to Accounting Standards — SSAP 23 Accounting for acquisitions and mergers*, Summer 1986.
152 SSAP 14, para. 29 and SSAP 23, para. 16.
153 SFAS 38, *Accounting for Preacquisition Contingencies of Purchased Enterprises*, para. 4 b.
154 ASC Discussion Paper, *Fair value in the context of acquisition accounting*, para. 6.46 (f).
155 *Ibid.*, para. 6.44.
156 Reckitt & Colman plc, Annual Report 1987, p. 33.
157 ASC Discussion Paper, *Fair value in the context of acquisition accounting*, para. 6.46 (g).
158 *Ibid.*, para. 7.14.
159 *Ibid.*, para. 8.16.
160 FASB Technical Bulletin 85-5.
161 APV plc, Report and Accounts 1987, p. 17.
162 ASC Discussion Paper, *Fair value in the context of acquisition accounting*, para. 9.15.
163 *Ibid.*, para. 10.19.
164 Trafalgar House Public Limited Company, Report and Accounts 1987, p. 43.
165 Trafalgar House Public Limited Company, Report and Accounts 1988, p. 45.
166 Tootal Group plc, Report and Accounts 1987/88, p. 46.
167 Guinness PLC, Report and Accounts 1987, p. 37.

168 ED 44, para. 2.
169 Companies Bill, Sch. 2, para. 12(5).
170 Guinness PLC, Report and Accounts 1987, p. 47.
171 P-E International plc, 53rd Annual Report and Accounts 1987, pp. 19 and 20.
172 Staff Accounting Bulletin No. 54, SEC, Washington, 1983.
173 ASC Discussion Paper, *Accounting for Goodwill*, 1980.
174 ED 30, *Accounting for Goodwill*, October 1982, para. 56.
175 SSAP 22, paras. 32 and 34.
176 British & Commonwealth Holdings PLC, Annual Report 1987, p. 37.
177 IAS 22, para. 40.
178 E32, paras. 164—168.
179 APB 17, *Intangible Assets*, AICPA, August 1970, para. 27.
180 SSAP 22, para. 29.
181 Pineapple Group PLC, Report and Accounts 1987, p. 19.
182 Announcement by the Department of Trade and Industry on July 5, 1988.
183 Companies Bill, Sch. 1, para 6.
184 *Ibid.*, Sch. 2, para. 1.
185 Grand Metropolitan Public Limited Company, Annual Report 1987, p. 49.
186 Grand Metropolitan Public Limited Company, Annual Report 1988, pp. 50 and 51.
187 Blue Arrow PLC, Report & Accounts 1987, pp. 41 and 42.
188 Saatchi & Saatchi Company PLC, Annual Report and Accounts, Year ended 30th September 1987, p. 48.
189 Johnson Fry PLC, Report and Accounts '87, p. 38.
190 CA 85, s 264.
191 SSAP 22, paras. 21 and 22.
192 ASC Discussion Paper, *Accounting for goodwill*, paras 8.1 — 8.7.
193 ED 30, para. 30.
194 The Companies Bill contains no specific rules on the treatment of consolidation goodwill. However, the application of Sch. 2, para. 1(1) of the Bill means that the present rules contained in the Companies Act will apply.
195 APB 17, para. 29.
196 E32, para. 168.
197 British & Commonwealth Holdings PLC, Annual Report 1987, p. 37.
198 APB 16, para. 91.
199 ASC Discussion Paper, *Accounting for goodwill*, paras 11.2 — 11.4.
200 *Ibid.*, para. 11.5.
201 ED 30, para. 58.
202 SSAP 22, para. 14.
203 EC Seventh Directive, Article 31.
204 IAS 22, paras, 40—42.
205 E32, paras. 169—175.
206 ASC Discussion Paper, *Fair value in the context of acquisition accounting*.
207 Companies Bill, Sch. 2, para. 9.
208 *Ibid.*, para. 7(1).
209 However, it is probably not permissible to use reserve categories which would not have been available as a destination for goodwill if acquisition accounting had been applied; see the discussion on this topic at 6.5.2.
210 Belhaven plc, Report and accounts 1988, p. 17.
211 Belhaven plc, Report and accounts 1988, p. 17.
212 SSAP 23, para. 21.
213 *Ibid.*, para. 22.
214 SSAP 22, para. 39.
215 *Ibid.*, para. 40.
216 *Ibid.*, para. 41.
217 ED 44, para. 2.

218 Tesco PLC, Annual Report and Accounts 1988, pp. 25, 29 and 39.
219 ED 44, paras. 3 — 5.
220 SSAP 23, para. 23.
221 Belhaven plc, Report and accounts 1988, p. 18.
222 CA 85, Sch 4, para 75(1).
223 CA 85, Sch 4, para 75(2) and (3).
224 Companies Bill, Sch. 2, para. 12.
225 *Ibid.*, para. 12(4).
226 *Ibid.*, para. 13.
227 *Ibid.*, para. 15.
228 SSAP 14, para. 32.
229 SSAP 6, *Extraordinary items and prior year adjustments*, para. 13.
230 If goodwill is carried as an asset, its value may change, depending on the concept of the group adopted (see 1.3.3 above).
231 ED 44, para. 4(b).
232 Companies Bill, Sch. 2, para. 14.
233 APB 16, para. 5 and AIN-APB 16, *Business Combinations: Accounting Interpretations of APB Opinion No. 16*, AICPA, March 1973, para. 39.
234 CA 85, s 151 *et seq.*
235 *Ibid.*, s 23.
236 *Ibid.*, s 276.

Chapter 5

Off-balance sheet transactions

1 INTRODUCTION

1.1 What are 'off-balance sheet transactions'?

'Off-balance sheet finance' has been defined as 'the funding or refinancing of a company's operations in such a way that, under legal requirements and existing accounting conventions, some or all of the finance may not be shown on its balance sheet'.[1] The term 'off-balance sheet transactions' is usually used to describe those transactions which meet such an objective. However, they can involve more than this; firstly, assets as well as liabilities are normally removed (or excluded) from a company's balance sheet and, secondly, an off-balance sheet transaction may also involve the removal (or exclusion) of profits or losses from the profit and loss account. In this chapter we have also considered transactions which use the legal requirements and existing accounting conventions to reflect borrowings under another heading, such as minority interest, on a group balance sheet to be off-balance sheet transactions. Other 'window dressing' transactions which are effectively transient in nature are discussed at 3.5 of Chapter 16.

1.2 Justifications for entering into off-balance sheet transactions

Some arguments put forward to justify the use of off-balance sheet transactions have included the following:

(a)   UK companies have historically had a relatively low level of gearing (compared to their counterparts in some other countries) and, therefore, need to use off-balance sheet transactions to maintain this. This may be due to perceptions of the views of brokers and others on permissible borrowing levels;

(b)   it has been argued that if a listed company has levels of borrowing which are thought by stock market analysts to be high, then a rights issue will be expected. This is then said to adversely affect the company's share price. Off-balance sheet transactions may then be used in order to lower the stated level of borrowing and the expectations of a rights issue;

(c)   during the development stage of assets there may be no income produced from them, although an income-producing stage will be reached once development is completed. It is argued that companies are worried by the possibility of the market taking a short-term view of their results and financial position. They therefore prefer to match any borrowings relating to the development of the assets with the non-income producing assets, and this is facilitated by an off-balance sheet transaction. Once the development stage is complete, the assets and related borrowings can then be brought 'on balance sheet'. This would leave the return on capital employed shown by the financial statements at a higher level than it otherwise would have been during the development stage;

(d)   a group of companies may be involved in a number of activities which are considered to be of a reasonably similar financial nature. However, certain areas of activity are said to have financial characteristics quite different from the others. Traditionally these have been leasing and financial service activities, which have, for example, a high gearing ratio. It is argued that such activities should be placed off-balance sheet (via an off-balance sheet transaction) in order that their different characteristics are kept separate.

All of these four possible justifications above essentially involve one rationale, which is that readers of financial statements cannot understand the reason for financial statistics being at particular levels; and that they must therefore be led to believe that the position is different from what it actually is.

1.3   Why the concern with off-balance sheet transactions?

The financial services industry is inventing a seemingly endless array of schemes involving off-balance sheet transactions. The result of this is that users of financial statements are not always able to appreciate fully the economic effect of such transactions on the state of affairs of companies which have entered into them. Disclosures required at present (by both SSAPs and the Companies Act 1985) do not address this problem, and the reader of the financial statements is unable to determine the impact of transactions from current disclosures in the financial statements which are generally very innocuous and brief.

There has been comment in the financial press which indicates that the current level of disclosure of off-balance sheet transactions in financial statements is thought to be insufficient. For example, off-balance sheet transactions have been described as 'the creative accounting trick which improves companies' balance sheets'.[2] A debate has developed within the accountancy profession as to how financial statements can be improved to overcome the perceived problems, possibly partly as a result of such press comments.

It is irrelevant whether an off-balance sheet transaction is entered into deliberately to give a desirable accounting treatment or if such a treatment is achieved unintentionally. In either case, if the financial statements and note disclosures do not allow a proper assessment of the company's results and state of affairs, then a problem can be said to exist.

One company which entered into off-balance sheet transactions was Burnett and Hallamshire Holdings plc. Their 1984 financial statements contained the following contingent liabilities note:

Extract 5.1: Burnett and Hallamshire Holdings plc[3]

24   Contingent   liabilities
(a)   The Company and relevant subsidiaries have given guarantees amounting to £41.25m (1983 — £6.3m) in respect of certain contracts and undertakings entered into in the ordinary course of business.
(b)   Legal claims amounting to £1.0m (1983 — £1.3m) have been instituted against a subsidiary. The Directors are of the opinion that no liability will arise from these claims in excess of the provisions already made in the accounts.
(c)   The Group may be required to purchase the 76% of the share capital of P.B.S. Coals Inc. not already owned in June, 1986 for the sum of US$7.6m. The Group has the option to purchase these shares on the same terms before that date. Borrowings of P.B.S. have been guaranteed up to US$25m.
(d)   At the 31st March, 1984 the following undertakings and obligations were in force in respect of related entities.
      (i)   A performance guarantee in respect of a hire purchase agreement with annual repayments of approximately £2.0m over 12 years.
      (ii)   An undertaking to a shareholder in a related company to find a purchaser at not less than cost for that holder's shares not later than April, 1985: the cost of the shares in question being approximately £6.8m.
      (iii) A guarantee of performance to a preference shareholder in a related company in respect of that company's payment of preference dividend and redemption of preference shares at the appointed time. The payments required total approximately £4.0m in the three years ending 31st March, 1988.
      (iv)   In certain circumstances, a subsidiary may be required to discharge a liability of approximately £7.3m in favour of a joint venture to which that subsidiary is a partner.

The Directors are of the opinion that no material loss would ensue should any of these contingencies arise.

The true nature of some of these contingent liabilities was revealed only when the company almost collapsed and a rescue package was put together. One commentator noted that the company's overall borrowings at March 31, 1984 were £154 million of which £83 million were off-balance sheet.[4] Some of these off-balance sheet borrowings related to a subsidiary, Rand London Coal Limited, which had entered into an onerous long-term shipping contract which it could not fulfil. Burnett and Hallamshire Holdings plc agreed to buy the ship, which had been built on the strength of the contract, under a hire purchase contract from Trinity Carriers Inc., the indirect beneficiaries of the contract. The purchase was made through a controlled non-subsidiary, Mincorp Shipping & Finance Limited (i.e. a company which was not a subsidiary of Burnett and Hallamshire Holdings plc as defined by company law but was effectively controlled by it). Burnett and Hallamshire Holdings plc guaranteed the performance of the hire purchase contract and was responsible for funding Mincorp Shipping & Finance Limited's cash requirements and losses. These assets and liabilities were significant and were disclosed in the 1985 financial statements as follows:

Extract 5.2: Burnett and Hallamshire Holdings plc[5]

16 Fixed assets — investments [extract]
(b) **Mincorp Shipping & Finance Limited**
Prior to the acquisition of the Group's interest in Rand London Corporation Limited in 1981
as part of the purchase of the Anglo International Mining Corporation PLC group, Rand
London Coal Limited, the principal operating subsidiary of Rand London Corporation Limited,
committed itself to an onerous long term take or pay freight contract.
On the strength of this contract Trinity Carriers Inc. ("Trinity"), the indirect beneficiary of
the arrangement, ordered the construction of a new bulk carrier now known as MV Hallam
Venture.
Rand London Coal Limited was unable to perform under the contract and was faced with losses
for breach of contract of a magnitude which Rand London Corporation Limited would have
been unable to sustain.
In order to protect its interests, the Group through Mincorp Shipping & Finance Limited
("M.S.F.") arranged to purchase the bulk carrier from Trinity on hire purchase for $27.4
million, plus interest, as a consequence of which the freight contract was cancelled. At the
same time M.S.F. acquired a 50% interest in Trinity for a nominal consideration and made a
loan to Trinity of $3.75 million to enable it to complete the original purchase.
Although the Group only had a 16.67% equity interest in M.S.F., the arrangements were such
that it receives substantial capital allowances. The Group guaranteed the performance of the
hire purchase contract and as a result of the severe depression in freight rates has in practice
had to fund all of M.S.F.'s cash requirements.
31 Adjusted Group Balance Sheet [extract]
As explained in the note below the Balance Sheets, the Directors have presented an Adjusted
Group Balance Sheet. The effect of this is to include in the Adjusted Group Balance Sheet total
assets of £56.7 million and liabilities of £48.6 million shown below:

	PBS Coals Inc. £'000	Mincorp Shipping & Finance Ltd £'000	Total £'000
Assets			
Tangible assets	28,656	10,772	39,428
Investments	—	3,050	3,050
Current assets	14,046	183	14,229
	42,702	14,005	56,707
Liabilities			
Borrowings	6,097	—	6,097
Other creditors	5,607	925	6,532
Creditors: amounts falling due after one year:			
Other creditors	8,433	21,725	30,158
Provisions	5,779	—	5,779
	25,916	22,650	48,566
Net assets (liabilities)	16,786	(8,645)	8,141

The total net asset figure is included in the Balance Sheet at 31st March, 1985 as:

	£'000
Investment in PBS Coals Inc.	16,786
Investment in Mincorp Shipping & Finance Limited	1,355
Provisions for liabilities and charges (Note 16(b))	(10,000)
	8,141

Another off-balance sheet scheme was revealed during the rescue operation, and related to the sale of development property in years prior to 1985 by Burnett and Hallamshire Holdings plc to a joint venture company in which they had a 50% interest. The profit on the sale of this property was recognised at the time of sale, even though the other party to the joint venture had the right to withdraw from the joint venture without any payment; that party then withdrew, the property became wholly-owned by the Group and the profit was found not to be realisable.[6]

When all of the off-balance sheet transactions of Burnett and Hallamshire Holdings plc were revealed, their 1985 financial statements reflected these by presenting an 'adjusted' group balance sheet. This was stated to be required by section 230(4) of the Companies Act 1985 which requires additional information if the requirements of the Act result in financial information which is not sufficient to give a true and fair view.

Extracts from the two 1985 balance sheets are shown below to highlight the significant differences which appear in certain items (in particular tangible assets and other creditors):

Extract 5.3: Burnett and Hallamshire Holdings plc[7]

Balance sheets [extract]

	Adjusted Group 1985 £'000	Group 1985 £'000
Fixed assets		
Intangible assets	718	718
Tangible assets	113,051	73,623
Investments	13,591	28,682
	127,360	103,023
Current assets		
Assets held for sale (net of borrowings)	3,997	3,997
Stocks and work-in-progress	32,754	27,497
Debtors	32,546	23,576
Cash at bank and in hand	2,267	2,265
	71,564	57,335
Creditors: amounts falling due within one year:		
Borrowings	(67,693)	(61,596)
Other creditors	(32,852)	(26,320)
Net current (liabilities) assets	(28,981)	(30,581)
Total assets less current liabilities	98,379	72,442
Creditors: amounts falling due after one year:		
Loans	(38,108)	(38,108)
Other creditors	(35,266)	(5,108)
Provisions for liabilities and charges	(25,832)	(30,053)
Accruals and deferred income	(3,411)	(3,411)
Net (liabilities) assets	(4,238)	(4,238)

The Burnett and Hallamshire Holdings plc example is certainly extreme in the sense that the off-balance sheet transactions were only revealed by the company's near collapse. However, it has highlighted the major problems which can be disguised when financial statements fail to reflect the full extent of off-balance sheet transactions. The level of disclosure and use of an 'adjusted' balance sheet in the 1985 financial statements emphasised the inadequacy of the 1984 financial statements which simply gave the required minimum disclosures of related companies and contingent liabilities and did not appear to deal with the substance of the transactions which had been carried out.

However, accounting for the substance of transactions rather than their form, particularly where controlled non-subsidiaries (which are further discussed in 2.1 below) were involved, was a problem for companies because of the DTI's statements subsequent to the *Argyll Foods* case.[8] This case involved the inclusion of a company in group financial statements on the grounds that the directors considered that they had effective control of the company even though it did not become a subsidiary until after the relevant accounting period end. The court judged that the directors were wrong to include the subsidiary. The DTI statement which was published following the case stated that it was 'axiomatic that any emphasis on substance over form must not be at the expense of compliance with the law'.[9] Attempts to include controlled non-subsidiaries in financial statements had to take account of this view that companies can only be consolidated within the terms of the Companies Act.[10]

1.4   How can a solution be reached?

The subject of off-balance sheet transactions involves consideration of the broad areas of:

(a)   a conceptual framework for financial reporting; and

(b)   the interaction of accounting concepts with the provisions of the Companies Act.

The former has been discussed in Chapter 2 where it was shown that little progress has been made in the UK towards the development of such a framework. (The only accounting standard which even impinges on this area is SSAP 2[11] which discusses fundamental concepts of accounting.) The lack of a conceptual framework can be said to have caused some difficulty in the area of off-balance sheet transactions (amongst others). However, factors discussed in that connection will be of importance to our analysis of possible solutions to the problem of reflecting off-balance sheet transactions in financial statements.

A debate has taken place between accountants and lawyers on the question of reconciling the provisions of the Companies Act with possible accounting treatments of off-balance sheet transactions. Two recent developments have fuelled this debate; the EC Seventh Directive on Company Law and the ASC's Exposure Draft 42 — *Accounting for Special Purpose Transactions*. The recent Companies Bill, which is to implement the requirements of the Seventh Directive, is proposing to change the definition of a subsidiary from that contained in the current Companies Act, whilst the proposed standard is an attempt to reflect all off-balance sheet transactions in financial statements. These are discussed further at 4.3 and 4.4 below.

Three possible ways of dealing with off-balance sheet transactions are as follows:

(a)   additional disclosure in the notes to the financial statements;

(b)   restatement of accounting treatment in the financial statements;

(c)   preparation of additional pro-forma financial statements.

These are considered at 6 below.

2   OFF-BALANCE SHEET TRANSACTIONS IN PRACTICE

2.1   Controlled non-subsidiaries

The most commonly used and well-known off-balance sheet transaction involves use of controlled non-subsidiaries. Essentially, these are companies which are effectively controlled by another but are not subsidiaries within the Companies Act definition.

2.1.1   *Companies Act definitions*

The definition of a subsidiary, at present, is given by section 736(1) of the Companies Act as follows:

'a company is deemed to be a subsidiary of another if (but only if) —

(a)   that other either:—

    (i)   is a member of it and controls the composition of its board of directors, or

    (ii)   holds more than half in nominal value of its equity share capital, or

(b)   the first mentioned company is a subsidiary of any company which is that other's subsidiary'.

This definition is fairly self-explanatory but makes use of the definition of equity in section 744: ' "equity share capital" means, in relation to a company, its issued share capital excluding any part of that capital which, neither as respects dividends nor as respects capital, carries any right to participate beyond a specified amount in a distribution'.

Equity shares are therefore those which are not limited to a known fixed monetary amount of either dividends or assets on a winding up. These amounts are treated as not being fixed if their calculation involves use of any unspecified figure e.g. dividends as a percentage of a level of profits over a predetermined (possibly large) level; assets on a winding up as a percentage of the share premium account at the time.

2.1.2   *Problems with the definition of subsidiary*

There are considered to be two main areas of difficulty with the existing Companies Act definition of subsidiary.

Firstly, the definition of subsidiary emphasises the level of equity holding rather than control of activities through the voting rights which attach to any shares held. This means that one company can hold all the ordinary shares of another company, yet that other company is not a subsidiary because other shares held by a third party qualify as equity capital and amount to 50% or more of the company's equity shares. Assuming the other party does not control the composition of the board, the company owning the ordinary shares may exert control because these shares have superior voting rights to the other classes of shares in issue and may effectively be entitled to virtually all of the profits of the 'subsidiary'. This problem stems from the definition of equity which make it very easy for a class of share to be structured such that it is equity within the Companies Act definition but has limited voting rights and dividend rights; i.e., in substance, the shares held by the third party are like preference shares. Indeed, the shares may be a type of preference share which has been structured to be 'equity' in terms of the Companies Act.

The second area of difficulty with the definition of subsidiary relates to the element which requires control of the composition of the board of the directors of the other company. This is not necessarily equivalent to control of the company's activities through the decisions of the board. Under the Companies Act a company is deemed to control the composition of a board of directors if it can appoint or remove the holders of all or a majority of the directorships.[12] In the scenario outlined above it is possible for the company owning the ordinary shares to be entitled to appoint or remove only half of the number of directors and, therefore, be unable to control the composition of the majority of a board, yet still achieve control of the business by ensuring that the directors it can appoint have more voting rights than the other directors.

2.1.3   Structuring controlled non-subsidiaries

Given the above problems existing in the current Companies Act definition of subsidiary, it follows that a controlled non-subsidiary, can be structured via some combination of the following:

(a)   the investor holds no more than 50% of the investee's equity share capital. The holding may be as low as zero. A 'friendly' third party may be used to hold the remaining, if not all, 'equity' shares in the investee. This may be, for example, the investor's bank or marketing company;

(b)   the investor cannot control the composition of the investee's board of directors. Whilst controlling the election of only up to one-half of the directors, it may actually control the investee's activities through the structure of the directors' voting rights;

(c)   the investor and/or the third party shareholder may have put or call options on shares held by each other;

(d)   the investor may receive the majority of the investee's profits through the structure of shareholder rights on distributions or management charges;

(e)   the investor may be committed to either fund the company's activities or guarantee any funds raised by the investee from third parties, for example, bank loans and overdrafts;

(f)   the investor may have indirect shareholdings which can be structured such that the investee is a member of the investor's group for tax purposes whilst not being a member of the group for Companies Act purposes.

Given the nature of controlled non-subsidiaries it is fairly difficult to establish from financial statements whether a company in which another has an investment, of up to 50% of equity share capital, falls into that category. The following extracts would appear to suggest the existence of controlled non-subsidiaries:

Extract 5.4: Cadbury Schweppes p.l.c.[13]

14 INVESTMENTS [extract]
Included above is an investment in Sodamate Inc. ("Sodamate"), a company formed in conjunction with Investors in Industry plc ("3i") to develop and market a range of in-home carbonated drink dispensers and related syrups in North America. The group currently holds a 15.25% equity interest together with convertible preference shares which, if converted, at the group's option and at no incremental cost, would give it an 88% equity interest.
Sodamate is being financed through a US$42 million facility from 3i. Loan repayments, which are due to be completed by April 1993, are expected to be financed by cash flows generated from the business. However, if Sodamate is unable to meet its commitments under the loan, the group is obligated to make good any shortfall in payments to 3i. The amount drawn down at 2 January 1988, and therefore the contingent liability of the Company, was US$6.9m and is projected to be US$9.6m at 31 December 1988.

Extract 5.5: Dixons Group plc[14]

31 Principal subsidiary and related companies [extract]
Related companies
Dixons Group plc owns 50 "A" ordinary shares (100%) and 900 preference shares (100%) of Timelark Limited. Dixons Group plc owns 50 "A" ordinary shares (100%) and nil "B" ordinary shares of Dovelamb Limited. Dovelamb Limited owns 50 "B" ordinary shares (100%) of Timelark Limited. Substantially all the economic benefit of both Timelark Limited and Dovelamb Limited is attributable to Dixons Group plc. Timelark Limited owns all the £1 ordinary share capital of Bill Donald Investments Limited, Easedram Limited and Jayhold Limited, which are all investment companies operating in the UK. Dixons Group plc owns all the preference share capital of Bill Donald Investments Limited amounting to £1.5m.

2.1.4   Why the concern?

Concerns with non-consolidated companies (both controlled non-subsidiaries and non-consolidated subsidiaries on the grounds of dissimilar activities per 2.2.3 below) stem from the view that consolidation is becoming optional to a very large extent. There would appear to be no limit to the scope for potential abuse, as a parent company can use these methods to exclude as many activities from its consolidated financial statements as it wishes. In this respect we note that the justification for introducing the requirement for group accounts in the Companies

Act 1948 was to allow readers of financial statements to gain an overall picture of the group's activities and affairs. If the current trend to use non-consolidated companies were to continue, this original objective of group accounts will be frustrated.

2.2 Off-balance sheet transactions involving controlled non-subsidiaries

The major areas where controlled non-subsidiaries have been used by companies in off-balance sheet transactions are considered below.

2.2.1 Sale of assets

Companies may sell assets to a controlled non-subsidiary for a number of reasons; it may be to transfer the assets and related borrowings which are presently shown on their balance sheet in order to reduce their gearing ratio shown in their financial statements; it may be done as an alternative to raising finance on the strength of the value of the assets, again in order that their gearing ratio shown by their financial statements is unaffected; or it may done so that the company can report profits on the transaction.

If a company sells an asset at more than its carrying value to a controlled non-subsidiary it will realise a profit on sale in the normal way. This profit will normally appear in the group financial statements of the company because, at most, the controlled non-subsidiary will be equity accounted as an associated company in those financial statements. However, SSAP 1 does require that where the effect is material, adjustments should be made in consolidated financial statements to eliminate unrealised profits on assets transferred to associated companies[15] (see 3.4 of Chapter 4).

The sale of the asset to a controlled non-subsidiary need not mean that the vendor company cannot then use it. This is because the asset can be rented to the vendor by the purchaser under an operating lease within the definition of SSAP 21. Such a lease would not be capitalised by the lessee/vendor and the sale and leaseback would therefore allow the vendor to account for the profit on sale as discussed above and not reflect the asset and the related lease obligation in its balance sheet.

One company which has entered into such transactions is The Burton Group plc. Their financial statements for the year ended August 30, 1986 included the following note:

Extract 5.6: The Burton Group plc[16]

25 Related companies [extract]
Hall & Sons Ltd: In August 1986, the Group entered into sale and leaseback arrangements with Hall & Sons Limited in respect of properties with a book and market value of £100m. At 30th August 1986 the assets of this company comprised properties at cost of £100 million and its liabilities comprised unsecured bank loans of £70 million and a subordinated amount due to The Burton Group plc of £30 million. The Group is entitled to and will account for the retained profits of Hall & Sons Ltd under the equity method, including profits arising on the sale of properties to third parties. No income arose from the Group's interest during the year.

There would not appear to be any profit effect of these transactions (as the market value equalled the book value at time of sale) but the borrowings of Hall & Sons Limited used to finance the properties are off-balance sheet for The Burton Group plc. It can be seen from Extracts 5.10 and 5.16 below that The Burton Group plc now give more information about this company.

As discussed at 1.3 above, Burnett and Hallamshire Holdings plc agreed to purchase an asset from a subsidiary (Rand London Coal Limited) through a controlled non-subsidiary such that a sale of the asset and the resulting profit was accounted for in the group accounts.

2.2.2 Acquisition of companies or assets

The acquisition of companies or assets can be made through a controlled non-subsidiary. This can involve the use of put and/or call options. The controlled non-subsidiary may have a put option to sell the acquired company or asset to the 'parent' and/or the 'parent' may have a call option to acquire it at a predetermined price.

One reason why a company may choose to acquire a company through a controlled non-subsidiary is if the acquiree is expected to make losses for a certain time after acquisition. If the acquiree were to have been acquired outright then these losses would probably have to be reported as post-acquisition losses as part of the group results of the acquiring company. (It may have been possible to make provision for such losses as part of the fair value exercise in acquisition accounting for the acquiree (see 6.4.3 D of Chapter 4).) By effectively postponing the date of acquisition by the group (through use of a controlled non-subsidiary to make the purchase) such losses will not be reported as part of the group's results and even if provision for such losses could have been made as part of the fair value exercise the need to estimate such losses of the acquiree as part of such an exercise is eliminated and no under/overprovision will affect the group results in the future.

One company which appears to have acquired a company in such a manner is Storehouse plc (formerly Habitat/Mothercare plc) in relation to its acquisition of Richard Shops Holdings Limited. They initially acquired 48% of the share capital of Richard Shops Holdings Limited on October 7, 1983 as indicated below:

Extract 5.7: Habitat Mothercare PLC[17]

8. Investments [extract]
On 7th October, 1983 the Company acquired 48% of the issued share capital of Richard Shops Holdings Limited for a total consideration (including expenses) of £233,000 in cash. The Company also made a medium-term unsecured loan of £15,000,000 to Richard Shops Holdings Limited to help finance the acquisition by that company of Richard Shops Limited. Under the terms of an agreement between the Company and Morgan Grenfell & Co. Limited, the Company has an option exercisable at any time to acquire a further 48% of the issued share capital of Richard Shops Holdings Limited for £126,000; Morgan Grenfell & Co. Limited also has an option exercisable on 30th January, 1988 to require the Company to purchase the shares for the same amount.

The shareholding was ultimately increased to 96% in September 1986, as indicated below:

Extract 5.8: Storehouse plc[18]

11. INVESTMENT IN RELATED COMPANIES [extract]
At 29 March 1986 the Group held 48% of the issued share capital of Richard Shops Holdings Limited ("Richards"). In September 1986, the Group exercised its option to acquire a further 48% of the issued share capital of Richards from Morgan Grenfell & Co Limited. The Group is currently exercising its option to purchase the remaining 4% of the issued share capital of Richards.
The turnover (excluding sales taxes) of Richards for the fifty-three weeks ended 4 April 1987 amounts to £61,785,000 (1986 — £43,755,000) and profit after tax amounts to £6,271,000 (1986 — £3,312,000 loss).
The Group has accounted for its 48% of the results of Richards for the twenty-four weeks to 13 September 1986. The results of Richards subsequent to that date have been included in the Consolidated Profit and Loss Account of the Group.

It would appear that the post-tax losses of Richard Shops Holdings Limited for the period, October 7, 1983 to September 13, 1986, were £4,506,000, of which Storehouse plc had accounted for £2,163,000.[19]

2.2.3   *Certain business activity conducted outside the group*

The exclusion of certain types of activity from consolidated financial statements can be achieved via either a controlled non-subsidiary or (more commonly) a non-consolidated subsidiary which is excluded due to dissimilar activities (see 4.2 of Chapter 4).

A company may want to exclude certain activities in this way because they are perceived as high risk or having a high debt to equity ratio. This is usually the case for leasing, insurance, property or financial service activities. Examples using non-consolidated subsidiaries are given in 4.2 of Chapter 4. Examples which seem to involve controlled non-subsidiaries are outlined below.

The Burton Group plc disclosed the following information about three related companies involved in financial services, which would appear to be controlled non-subsidiaries, in their financial statements for the year ended August 30, 1986:

Extract 5.9: The Burton Group plc[20]

25 Related companies [extract]
The principal related companies are:

	Country of Operation	Country of Registration	Activity	Equity Shareholding
BG Holdings Ltd	UK	England	Financial Services	42%
Burton Group Personal Account Ltd	UK	England	Financial Services	46%
Welbeck Finance plc	UK	England	Financial Services	10%

BG Holdings Ltd: The net assets attributable to the Group's investment are £7.0 million, represented mainly by debtors and other assets £27.2 million less bank loans and other creditors £20.2 million.

Burton Group Personal Accounts Ltd: The net assets attributable to the Group's investment are £26.1 million, represented mainly by debtors £162.5 million less bank loans and other creditors £136.4 million.

Welbeck Finance plc: A subsidiary owns the whole of the ordinary share capital of Welbeck Finance plc (which represents 10% of the equity share capital) and the whole of the restricted share capital. The remainder of the equity share capital is represented by deferred shares, none of which is held by the Group. The net assets attributed to the Group's investment are £52.7 million, represented mainly by debtors and other assets £324.1 million less bank loans and other creditors £271.4 million.

These companies have since been acquired by a new controlled non-subsidiary of The Burton Group plc, Burton Group Financial Services (Holdings) Limited, as indicated below:

Extract 5.10: The Burton Group plc[21]

25 Related companies [extract]
The principal related companies are:

	Country of Operation	Country of Registration	Shares in Issue	Group's Shareholding
Burton Group Financial Services (Holdings) Limited	UK	England	150 £1 "A" Ordinary	100%
			150 £1 "B" Ordinary	—
			2,000 £1 Preference	100%
High Street Property Investments Limited	UK	England	52 £1 "A" Ordinary	—
			52 £1 "B" Ordinary	100%
			19,948 £1 Preference	100%

Burton Group Financial Services (Holdings) Limited (BGFSH)
BGFSH holds the whole of the issued share capital of BG Holdings Limited, Burton Group Personal Accounts Limited, and Welbeck Finance plc, the principal companies who provide financial services for the Group.

High Street Property Investments (HSPI)
In August 1986 the Group entered into sale and leaseback arrangements with HSPI (formerly Hall and Sons Ltd), in respect of properties with a book value of £100.1 million. HSPI has granted ten year options to certain Group companies to repurchase the individual properties at market value and pre-emptive rights over the properties for a period of 20 years. The Group has no obligations to repurchase the properties or in respect of the repayment of loans made to HSPI by the lending banks. The Group is entitled to, and accounts for, the retained profits of HSPI under the equity method of accounting, including any profits which may arise on the sale of properties to third parties.

In addition to the above information it can be seen from Extract 5.16 in 3.2 below that The Burton Group plc now disclose far more information relating to their controlled non-subsidiaries.

Another company which appears to have controlled non-subsidiaries is S. & W. Berisford PLC. As can be seen from Extract 5.11 below, S. & W. Berisford PLC disclosed in their financial statements for the year ended September 30, 1987 that certain property interests were held via Torlap Limited which, because of its share structure, was dealt with as an associated company (although it was included within current asset investments under the category of 'property interests and loans'). Torlap Limited's share capital consisted of 97 'A', 2 'B' and 1 'C' £1 ordinary shares of which S. & W. Berisford PLC holds the 'A' and 'C' shares.[22] Presumably only the 'B' and 'C' shares are regarded as equity within the Companies Act definition as, otherwise, S. & W. Berisford PLC would own 98% of the equity shares and, therefore, Torlap Limited would be a subsidiary.

It can also be seen that Torlap Limited owns 100% of the issued share capital of Billingsgate City Securities PLC (BCS) which owns a property costing £79 million. It would appear that Torlap Limited are entitled to 69.56% of any increase in value of the property above £79 million.

Extract 5.11: S. & W. Berisford plc[23]

16. CURRENT ASSET INVESTMENTS [extract]

	UK Property Interests a) £000
Gross property assets	32,790
Interest in Billingsgate City Securities PLC ("BCS")	18,624
	51,414
Other assets (liabilities)	96
Group interest	51,510

a   UK Property interests

i)   The above UK property interests are held by Torlap Limited ("Torlap") which, as a result of the varying interests attaching to the various classes of shares, is an associated company. At 30 September, 1987 the interest of the Group in Torlap and its subsidiaries and BCS is represented by:

	1987 £000	1986 £000
Share Capital (Torlap — 100 ordinary shares of £1 each)	—	—
Loans	52,630	—
Share of profits (losses)	(1,120)	1,028
	51,510	1,028

At 30 September, 1986 Torlap and its subsidiaries borrowed £49m from third parties to repay loans from S. & W. Berisford PLC. On 1 October, 1986 these borrowings were repaid out of new monies lent by S. & W. Berisford PLC.

ii)   BCS owns the freehold interest in Montagu House. The summarised balance sheet of BCS at 30 September, 1987 is as follows:

	1987 £000	1986 £000
Property	79,000	79,000
Other net assets	1,599	1,297
£52,500,000 6⅛% Deep Discount Mortgage Bonds repayable 2006	(35,655)	(35,381)
Interests of Preferred Shareholders	(26,320)	(26,216)
Torlap Investment	18,624	18,700

Torlap owns 100% of the issued ordinary share capital of BCS but, as it does not control the Board of Directors, Torlap accounts for BCS as if it were an associated company.
The preferred Shareholders are entitled to dividends which, with the associated tax credit, amounts to 30.44% of the rental income of BCS, and, on liquidation, to repayment of the amount paid up on the shares (including premium) together with 30.44% of the increase in market value of Montagu House in excess of £79m. Torlap has an option to acquire the Preferred Shares in 2006 and at five-yearly intervals thereafter, at a price equal to that payable to the Preferred Shareholders on a liquidation of BCS at that time. This option is also exercisable in the event of the Preferred Shareholders passing a resolution, in 2001 or thereafter, to commence the liquidation of BCS.

Since September 30, 1987 it would appear that Torlap Limited (now called Berisford Properties Limited) has now sold the property interests, and a subsidiary of S. & W. Berisford PLC has acquired a majority of the Preferred Shares of BCS as indicated below:

Extract 5.12: S. & W. Berisford PLC[24]

16. Current Asset Investments [extract]

(£ millions)	UK Property Interests a)
Interest in Billingsgate City Securities PLC ("BCS")	60.9

a)   UK Property Interests
BCS owns the freehold interest in Montagu House. The summarised balance sheet of BCS at 15 March 1988 was as follows:

(£ millions)	1988	1987
Property	**110.0**	79.0
Other net assets	**1.7**	1.6
£52,500,000 6⅛% Deep Discount Mortgage Bonds repayable 2006	**(35.8)**	(35.7)
Interests of Preferred Shareholders	**(35.9)**	(26.3)
Interests of Ordinary Shareholders	**40.0**	18.6

Berisford Properties Limited (formerly Torlap Limited) owns 100% of the issued ordinary share capital of BCS but, as it does not control the Board of Directors, accounts for BCS as if it were an associated company.
As at 30 September 1988 Berisford (Switzerland) SA (formerly Erlanger Commercial Corporation SA) owned, or had received acceptances for, 59.2% of the Preferred Shares of BCS. Subsequent to that date a further 15.1% of the preferred shares have been acquired.
The Preferred Shareholders are entitled to dividends which, with the associated tax credit, amount to 30.44% of the rental income of BCS, and, on liquidation or sale of the property, to repayment of the amount paid up on the shares (including premium) together with 30.44% of the increase in market value of Montagu House in excess of £79m.
The Group's interest in BCS at 30 September 1988 can be summarised thus:

(£ millions)	1988	1987
Ordinary Shares	**40.0**	18.6
Preferred Shares	**20.9**	—
	60.9	18.6

2.2.4   *Example of typical off-balance sheet transactions involving a controlled non-subsidiary*

A   *Introduction*

The following example attempts to show how a transaction can be structured such that particular commercial objectives are achieved whilst a desired accounting treatment is also attained. It is a hypothetical case and takes no account of the tax implications of the transaction, but it highlights the differences in accounting treatment which can result. The accounting treatment that could be adopted at present is given before we examine a treatment which reflects the substance of the transactions.

It demonstrates two common uses of off-balance sheet transactions:

(a)   mortgaging a company's freehold property and crystallising the difference between original cost and its market value without increasing group borrowings or charging the profit and loss account with the full interest cost; and

(b)   investing in a loss making company and not accounting for its losses in the group profit and loss account until it becomes profitable.

B   *Example*

Example 5.1

(a) Group structure

Company A sets up Company B which has 100 ordinary shares of £1 each which are owned by Company A and 100 5% voting convertible preference shares of £1 each which are owned by a friendly third party. On a winding up the preference shares receive 10% of whatever is standing to the credit of Company B's share premium account together with the return of the amount originally subscribed. The conversion rights attributable to the preference shares give the holder the right to convert into 1,001 ordinary shares in six years' time. The friendly third party has a put option to Company A on Company B's preference shares (i.e. the right to sell the shares to Company A) exercisable in five years' time at a price of £1,000,000. Company A has a call option (i.e. the right to purchase the shares from the third party) exercisable at any time up to five years at a price of £100,000.

Company B then acquires Company C, a loss-making company, for £14,000,000 financed as shown below. The above events all take place in the first week of Company A's financial year. Company D is a long established wholly owned subsidiary of Company A. The group structure is, therefore, as follows:

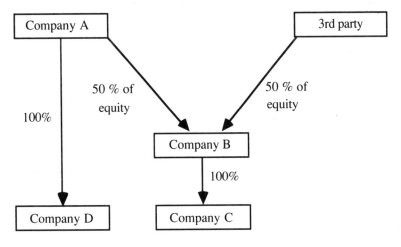

(b) Financing/mortgaging of freehold property

Company A sells freehold property to Company B for £15,000,000, a fair market value. The property was carried in the books of Company A at £13,000,000. The balance is kept on inter-company account. Company B then sells on the property to a bank for £15,000,000 and leases it back at an annual rental of £1,350,000 which is equivalent to interest at a rate of 0.5% below

LIBOR on the proceeds received. The bank has a put option to Company A on the property (i.e. the right to sell the property back to Company A) exercisable in five years' time and Company A has a call option (i.e. the right to purchase the property from the bank) exercisable at any time after three years. Both options are exercisable at £16,000,000. Company A continues to use the building without making any payment to Company B. A bank loan of £5,000,000 is also made to Company B which is repayable after five years and carries interest at 1% above LIBOR. The loan, interest payments and rental payments are guaranteed by Company A.

Note: LIBOR is at an average of 9.5% for this particular year.

(c) Loss making company

The end result of the above financing is that Company B has £20,000,000 in cash of which £14,000,000 is used to acquire the shares in Company C.

Company B lends Company C the remaining £6,000,000 interest free to provide working capital and Company A takes over management control of Company C as soon as the loan agreements are signed. Company A charges Company C a management charge of £500,000 p.a. Company B pays the interest and lease payments out of funds provided by Company A by way of a loan with an interest charge in the first year of £115,000.

On acquisition, Company C is expected to make £1,600,000 trading losses in the first two years and then move into profit in year 3. In year 1 the trading losses are £400,000 greater than expected.

(d) In year 1 the profit/(loss) before tax of each of the four companies is as follows:

	Company A £'000	Company B £'000	Company C £'000	Company D £'000
Trading profit/(loss)	5,000	—	(2,000)	1,000
Management charge	500	—	(500)	—
Profit on sale of property	2,000	—	—	—
Interest on £5m bank loan	—	(525)	—	—
Interest on inter-company loan	115	(115)	—	—
Operating lease rental	—	(1,350)	—	—
Profit/(loss) before tax	7,615	(1,990)	(2,500)	1,000

Two possible alternative treatments for the presentation of Company A's group results for year 1 are as follows:

	Method (i) £'000	Method (ii) £'000
Trading profit	6,000	4,000
Profit on sale of property	2,000	—
Management charge	500	—
Interest on inter-company loan	115	—
Interest on £5m bank loan	—	(525)
Notional interest on £15m bank loan	—	(1,550)
Share of associates' losses	(2,245)	—
	6,370	1,925

Method (i)

This treatment is based on the legal form of the transactions which have taken place.

Both the ordinary and preference shares of Company B meet the legal definition of equity since the preference shareholders can receive more than a specified amount on a winding up. Hence Company A only owns 50% of Company B's equity. This means that, under present law, Company B is not a subsidiary of Company A and therefore its financial statements need not be consolidated in the group financial statements of Company A. It is, however, an associated company and, therefore, is included in the financial statements using equity accounting.

Company A, therefore, only takes in 50% of the losses of the Company B group, i.e. £1,990,000 for Company B and £2,500,000 for Company C. In addition, the investment in net assets in the Company B group will be carried on one line of Company A's group balance sheet so that the debt in Company B will not be included as a liability in the Company A consolidated financial statements.

The disposal of the freehold property to Company B by Company A has given rise to a profit of £2,000,000. If Company B had retained the property then it could be argued that as Company A has a 50% stake in that company then an adjustment should be made in the group financial statements to eliminate that proportion of the profit. However, as a result of the sale and leaseback mentioned below, the property has then been sold on to a third party and, therefore, all of the profit can be said to be realised by the group and no elimination is necessary; accordingly, the profit of £2,000,000 is included in the group profit and loss account.

Company B has arranged a sale and leaseback with a bank at an annual rental of £1,350,000. Although the bank has a put option, this is with Company A, and, therefore, the leaseback is considered by B as an operating lease. Accordingly, the property is treated by Company B as having been sold and, therefore, is not included in Company B's balance sheet together with the related lease obligation.

As Company C is not a subsidiary of Company A, Company A's £500,000 management charge is therefore made outside the group, and because Company C is only 50% owned, Company A effectively takes half the fee to its consolidated profit and loss account (the full amount reflected in its own profit and loss account less its share of the charge reflected in Company C's financial statements).

Similarly, 50% of the interest charge of £115,000 made by Company A on Company B will effectively be included in the group profit and loss account. Although Company A has not received the interest, the debt that arises from it is considered to be recoverable in the long term because Company B's major 'asset' is the investment in Company C, which is expected to be a profitable company in the future.

As indicated above, the Company B group will be equity accounted in Company A's group financial statements. The Company A group balance sheet will, therefore, include the following amounts in respect of the Company B group:

	£'000
Investment in shares of Company B	—
Share of post-acquisition losses of Company B group	(2,245)
Loan to Company B (funding of loss for year)	1,990
Inter-company account (property proceeds)	15,000
	14,745

The group balance sheet excludes the £20m financing of the acquisition and the provision of working capital for Company C. The loans by Company A that fund the payments of interest and management charges are effectively netted against the share of losses of B Group, leaving the debt to A as a result of disposal of the property as an outstanding balance. The payment of this amount would be deferred until Company C was making enough profits to provide B with funds.

Consideration would, however, have to be given to the requirements of SSAP 1 in respect of disclosing information about the associated companies' results and assets and liabilities if they are considered to be sufficiently material in the context of the group financial statements.[25]

Method (ii)

This method adopts a substance over form approach to the situation.

The friendly third party holds a preference share stake in Company B with the prime intention of diluting the percentage of the equity of Company B held by Company A, so that Company B is legally not a subsidiary of Company A; the substance of the transaction, however, is that Company B (and therefore Company C) are under the control of Company A and should be treated as wholly owned subsidiaries of Company A. In addition, as a result of the put and call options on the preference shares it is highly probable that Company B will legally become a subsidiary in the foreseeable future.

Accordingly, the financial statements of Company B and Company C should be consolidated in the group financial statements of Company A. The group profit and loss account will reflect all of the trading losses of Companies B and C. (It may, however, be possible to make provision for the expected trading losses of Company C as part of the fair value exercise carried out on an acquisition (see 6.4.3 D of Chapter 4); however, as Company C has made greater losses than expected then the excess should be considered the responsibility of the new management and included as post-acquisition losses.)

As a result of Company B being considered to be part of the Company A group, the sale of property by Company B to the bank is not considered to give rise to a realised profit for the group. When Company B sells the property to the bank for £15,000,000 under the sale and leaseback agreement, the leaseback is a finance lease as far as the group is concerned in view of the put and call options on the property (it is very likely that Company A will buy back the property at £16,000,000 in five years' time, if not sooner). Under SSAP 21, the profit would be deferred and amortised over the life of the property. The property will also be depreciated over its useful life. (For the purposes of this example these have been ignored and the rental shown as the charge in the profit and loss account.) The lease obligation of £15,000,000 will be shown as a liability in the consolidated balance sheet. In addition, the extra £1 million would be regarded as additional interest under the lease to be spread over five years on an actuarial basis under SSAP 21 (for the purposes of this example, the interest has been amortised on a straight-line basis over the five years).

As Companies B and C are to be regarded as wholly owned subsidiaries of Company A, all of the inter-company charges will be eliminated on consolidation.

In the Company A group balance sheet the £20,000,000 financing should be included as part of group liabilities and goodwill calculated on the difference between the acquisition consideration and fair value of Company C's net assets.

C   Conclusion

It can be seen from the above example that depending on whether a 'legal' approach or a 'substance over form' approach is taken the financial statements could show markedly different results and financial position of the Company A group. Where method (i) is adopted, certain disclosures would have to be considered in the Company A group financial statements; in particular:

- Investment in Company B

This investment (and its subsidiary Company C) are associated companies of Company A and therefore the disclosure requirements of SSAP 1 will have to be complied with (see 5.5 of Chapter 4). As indicated above, consideration will have to be given to the requirements of SSAP 1 in respect of disclosing information about the associated companies' results and assets and liabilities if they are considered to be sufficiently material in the context of the group financial statements.

- Sale of property and financing

The existence of the put and call options on the property effectively mean that Company A is committed to buying back the property; accordingly, this should be disclosed as a capital commitment under the requirements of the Companies Act.[26]

The guarantees by Company A of the rental obligations of Company B and of the £5,000,000 loan and interest should be disclosed as contingent liabilities under the requirements of SSAP 18 and the Companies Act (see Chapter 17).

- Acquisition of Company B (and therefore Company C)

The existence of the put and call options on the preference shares of Company B effectively means that Company A is committed to buying these companies; accordingly, this should be disclosed as a financial commitment under the requirements of the Companies Act.[27]

As indicated at 1.4 above, the recent Companies Bill is proposing to change the definition of a subsidiary and this is likely to have an impact on schemes involving 'controlled non-subsidiaries' (see 4.4 below).

2.3   Other off-balance sheet transactions

2.3.1   *Sale of assets with option to repurchase*

The vendor of an asset may have an option to repurchase the asset at a later date. This may, of course, be a normal transaction of the company but certain characteristics can result in it justifiably being described as an off-balance sheet transaction. The repurchase price, for example, may be lower than market value and calculated as being the original selling price plus notional interest. In such a case the sale and repurchase of the asset can be seen to be, in substance, a loan secured on the asset. However, if the repurchase price is to be market value at that time then the transaction would not appear to be off-balance sheet in nature. This is because the risks and rewards of ownership (as regards fluctuations in market value) do not lie with the vendor throughout the period, which distinguishes it from an off-balance sheet transaction.

S. & W. Berisford plc disclosed the following information in a note to their financial statements for the year ended September 30, 1986:

Extract 5.13: S. & W. Berisford plc[28]

25. FINANCING [extract]
In addition to the finance included in the Balance Sheet, the Group accounts reflect the
following financing transactions:

(i) The Group in the ordinary course of its business from time to time finances part of its
commodity stocks by selling such stocks for immediate delivery with a reciprocal agreement
to repurchase for delivery at a future date. At the year end commodity stocks financed in this
manner for maturity prior to 31st December 1986, and therefore not shown in the Group
balance sheet, totalled £20 million (1985 £64 million).

It is interesting to note that S. & W. Berisford plc apparently closed these
transactions by the following year end as their financial statements for the year
ended September 30, 1987 do not contain any reference to it.

ED 42, which discusses these types of transactions, states that 'an agreement to
sell commodity stocks at the current spot price and to buy them back at the spot
price applicable three months hence should be accounted for as a sale and
repurchase, since control over the amount of the net future cash flows available
from the commodities would have been relinquished. By contrast, a sale and
repurchase agreement in which the repurchase price was predetermined and
covered primarily interest and holding costs should be treated as a financing
arrangement.'[29]

It continues: 'similar considerations would apply to a transaction involving the
sale of properties used in an enterprise's business on terms that continued to make
them available to the enterprise. A reasonable accounting analogy for such a
transaction would often be a sale and leaseback, in which case the principles of
SSAP 21 — *Accounting for Leases* — would be applied, whether or not a formal
lease was involved. The terms of any rent payable, the duration of the
arrangement and the ability of the enterprise to benefit from holding gains or
development profits from the properties would be relevant considerations in
assessing whether control over future economic benefits represented by the
properties had been transferred.'[30]

2.3.2 Consignment stocks

Stocks held on a consignment basis are common in certain trades; largely in motor
vehicle dealerships. Basically, this usually involves the manufacturer retaining
title to stock despatched to customers. The stock is only paid for by the customer
when it is sold or used by him, at which time title will pass. Whether such stocks
can be described as an off-balance sheet transaction will depend on the terms of
the relevant agreement.

Terms indicating that the consignment stock agreement is simply a method of
raising finance would be where:

(a)   an obligation to purchase the stock arises after a certain period of time even
       if the customer has not sold or used it; and/or

(b)   the purchase price of the stock increases throughout the holding period to reflect the manufacturer's cost of financing the stockholding.

ED 42 states 'the accounting treatment of consignment stock, where goods are supplied by a manufacturer to a dealer on a sale or return basis, depends very much on the provisions of the agreement. If the dealer can return the stock without incurring a significant penalty, it does not carry the inherent risk of stockholding and would not normally include the stock on its balance sheet. The absence of risk in this case is generally more important than the possible future benefit represented by the stock, since the latter could only be realised by a sale. On the other hand where the dealer is obliged ultimately to purchase the stock or where the price structure is such that holding gains or losses on the stock accrue to the dealer, inclusion of the stock in the dealer's balance sheet under the appropriate description would be necessary.'[31]

2.3.3   Selling debts

A   Debt factoring

If a company factors its debts such that there is no recourse to it if any of the constituent debts are later found to be uncollectible, there would appear to be no off-balance sheet transaction implications. The debts have quite simply been sold, with the proceeds reducing the level of debt due and any remaining book value of the debt being written off as the cost of factoring.

The main problem arises where a company has factored its debts and there is recourse to it if any of the debts later become irrecoverable.

There is an argument that this constitutes an off-balance sheet transaction, as a loan has effectively been raised using these debts as security. Such a loan can be taken as bearing interest equal to the cost of the factoring; i.e. the book value of the debts which are not recovered from the factoring company.

It can be argued, however, that the possibility of recourse to the original debt holder should be taken account of in the normal way; i.e. a provision should be made for any element of the factored debts which he expects are reasonably likely to become uncollectible (based on past experience). This is the approach taken by ED 42 which states 'debt factoring includes a wide range of arrangements, some of which are closer to sales and some to financing arrangements. In origin, debt factoring exemplifies the disposal of an asset. The future benefit embodied in trade debtors is the cash receivable on settlement. Once cash has been received through the sale of debts to the factor, no further benefit remains for the balance sheet to display. The benefit of debtors is subject to the risk of default — a risk which is left with the reporting enterprise if debts are factored with recourse. However, provision for such risk should be made whether or not debts are factored. The extent of any remaining risk would be indicated by disclosing in the notes the amount of factored debts outstanding.'[32]

The exposure draft does, however, go on to say 'by contrast, arrangements that require the seller of trade debts effectively to finance debts that remain unpaid beyond a certain time would not constitute disposal of an asset, since they would not remove the inherent risk and cost of slow paying debtors. Such debts and a liability for the amount due to the factor should be shown on the balance sheet until they are settled or written off.'[33]

B   *Securitisation*

At present, securitisation is mainly associated with the mortgage market and involves a company which has originated mortgages (the originator), packaging a group of the mortgages and transferring them to another company, which will finance the purchase by issuing loan notes (the issuer). The originator of the mortgages will generally hold an equity investment in the issuer (it may, in fact, constitute a controlled non-subsidiary of the originator) and will conduct administrative matters such as setting the mortgage rate and credit control.

As the mortgages are generally transferred to the issuer without recourse to the originator in the event of default by the mortgagees, an off-balance sheet treatment would appear to be valid. ED 42 seems to support this view as long as the possible risks and rewards retained by the original mortgagor are not significant. (This may not be the case if the issuer is a controlled non-subsidiary.) The exposure draft identifies five categories of risk which have to be considered:[34]

(a)   bad debt risk;

(b)   delays in collecting repayments;

(c)   interest risk;

(d)   reinvestment risk; and

(e)   administration risk.

The exposure draft then states 'if the combined effect of the above represents a significant risk of benefit to the originator the mortgages should be retained in its balance sheet with a corresponding liability for the amount due to the issuer. Presentation of the full debtor and liability amounts in the balance sheet would in such circumstances be the most appropriate way of displaying the continued exposure of the originator to the effects of small movements in the servicing cost and income of two large and potentially independently moving numbers.'[35]

One company which has carried out such transactions with a controlled non-subsidiary is The National Home Loans Corporation plc as indicated in the following extract:

Extract 5.14: The National Home Loans Corporation plc[36]

10. Associated Companies

	Shares in Associated Companies £000	Loans to Associated Companies £000	Total £000
Valuation			
At 1st October, 1987	2	—	2
Investments during the year	—	39,477	39,477
Revaluation during the year	499	—	499
At 30th September, 1988	501	39,477	39,978

Finance for Home Loans Holdings Limited ("Holdings") is an associated company operating in England. The Company holds 50% of the issued equity share capital of Holdings as shown below:—

Issued Equity Share Capital		Proportion Held
Number	Class	
100	Ordinary Shares of £1 each	100%
400	Preferred Ordinary Shares of £1 each	100%
500	5% Preference Shares of £1 each	Nil

Holdings is not a subsidiary company as defined by Section 736 of the Companies Act 1985 and accordingly its accounts are not consolidated with the accounts of the Company. The Board of Holdings consists of four Directors of whom one is a Director and one is an Employee of the Company. These latter Directors both have "A" Director status which confers greater powers. Any profits distributed by Holdings will first be applied to paying the dividend on the 5% Preference Shares of £1 each and then to the Company by virtue of its holding of Preferred Ordinary Shares and Ordinary Shares.

Holdings has a number of wholly owned subsidiaries. Each has an independent board of four Directors of whom one is an employee of the Company. Any dividend proposed by the boards of these subsidiaries and approved by Holdings as shareholder would be payable to Holdings.

The consolidated profit and loss account for Holdings recorded a net profit of £764,000 after taxation for the year ended 30th September, 1988 (1987: loss of £265,000). As a result of the increase in the consolidated retained profits of Holdings, the Company's investment has been revalued by £499,000.

Five subsidiaries of Holdings have acquired portfolios of mortgages from The National Home Loans Corporation plc. They have issued securities or entered into loan agreements, secured on the mortgages concerned, to finance the purchase of those mortgages as overleaf:

	Date of Acquisition of Portfolio	Portfolio Size	Financed by
NHL First Funding Corporation PLC	5th March, 1987	£50 million	£50,000,000 Mortgage Backed Floating Rate Notes 2013
NHL Second Funding Corporation PLC	8th October, 1987	£110.7 million	£100,000,000 Series A and £11,000,000 Series B Mortgage Backed Floating Rate Notes 2014
NHL Third Funding Corporation PLC	30th November, 1987	£110.4 million	£100,000,000 Series A and £10,500,000 Series B Mortgage Backed Floating Rate Notes 2014
NHL First Finance Limited	1st February, 1988	£50 million	A loan facility of £50,000,000
Blue Chip Mortgage Passthrough (No 1) Limited	30th June, 1988	£128.3 million	A loan facility of £128,300,000

The Series B Notes issued by NHL Second Funding Corporation PLC and NHL Third Funding Corporation PLC are subordinated to the Series A Notes and were acquired by The National Home Loans Corporation plc. The loan agreement entered into by Blue Chip Mortgage Passthrough (No 1) Limited includes a subordinated participation of £12,800,000 by the Company.

The Company has entered into agreements with these companies under which it administers and manages the mortgages purchased by them. Other than its responsibilities with regard to these arrangements, the Company has no commitment to repurchase these mortgages and has no liability in respect thereof, other than the warranties given in the mortgage sale agreements.

At 30th September, 1988 the mortgages administered by The National Home Loans Corporation plc on behalf of itself and for its associated companies, and the relevant borrowings were as follows:

	The Company £000	Holdings £000	Total £000
Mortgage Loans	1,353,312	371,497	1,724,809
$8\frac{1}{4}$% Convertible Unsecured Loan Stock 2005	7,953	—	7,953
Loan notes due 1992 and 1993	110,178	—	110,178
Mortgage Backed Floating Rate Notes issued by associates	—	219,301	219,301
Loans Agreements entered into by associated companies	—	164,771	164,771
Other Loans	1,168,766	—	1,168,766
	1,286,897	384,072	1,670,969

It can be seen that even though The National Home Loans Corporation plc effectively control Finance for Home Loans Holdings Limited and administer and manage the mortgages, because there is no recourse to The National Home Loans

Corporation plc in the event of default by the mortgagee, the mortgages and the related finance are kept off the balance sheet.

2.3.4   *Preference shares issued by a subsidiary*

If a subsidiary within a group issues preference shares other than to its parent company then these will normally be disclosed in the group financial statements as part of minority interest rather than as share capital or borrowings. This may be seen as an off-balance sheet transaction by structuring the preference shares such that they are both redeemable and also have a dividend level dependent on prevailing interest rates (although some would argue that this is a form of 'window dressing'). In such a case the preference shares can, in substance, be argued to be borrowings of the group.

The preference shares are normally still shown as part of minority interest even where the obligation to redeem is current (i.e. will take place within the following year). Another possible advantage of this minority interest treatment is that any dividends will be charged to profit and loss account after the tax line (as part of the minority interest share of profits). In the earnings per share calculation, however, this possible advantage will be lost as the minority interest deduction from profit for the year is made when calculating the profit figure used in the earnings per share calculation.

One company which includes such preference shares in minority interest is Ultramar plc; however, it can be seen from the following extract that they give full disclosure about the shares:

Extract 5.15: Ultramar PLC[37]

11 Minority   interest
During 1985, a wholly owned Canadian subsidiary company issued two series of Cumulative Redeemable Retractable Preferred Shares of Can$125 million each. The First Series of Canadian Preferred Shares carries a dividend of $8^{1}/_{4}$% p.a., is retractable by shareholders on 30th June 1990 and redeemable by the subsidiary company on or after that same date. The Second Series carries a dividend equal to 65% of the average of five Canadian banks' prime interest rates and has been retractable and redeemable since 1st December 1986. During 1987, Can$23.6 million of Series II Shares were retracted and repaid. In addition, at 31st December 1987, Can$27.0 million of shares retracted were held by another Canadian subsidiary with a view to reissue at a later date. Therefore, at 31st December 1987, Can$74.4 million of these shares were repayable at call. Subsequent to 31st December 1987, a further Can$16.4 million has been bought from shareholders exercising retraction rights. Ultramar PLC has entered into a support agreement in connection with both of these issues . . .
During 1986, a wholly owned US subsidiary company issued US$150 million of Preferred Auction Rate Shares. The Preferred Auction Rate Shares carry dividends which are set every 49 days through an auction process. The average dividend rate during 1987 was $5^{1}/_{2}$%. The shares are redeemable by the subsidiary company at any time. Subsequent to 31st December 1987, a further US$50 million of shares with similar rights have been issued.
  Both issues are shown as minority interest in the Group balance sheet and the dividends paid and payable are shown similarly in the profit and loss account.

---

3   CURRENT TREATMENT OF OFF-BALANCE SHEET TRANSACTIONS IN FINANCIAL STATEMENTS

3.1   General

Current practice is to give a level of disclosure of off-balance sheet transactions which is usually the minimum required by current UK standards and legislation. Full details of the many aspects of an off-balance sheet transaction are therefore not often given in financial reports. This is despite the ability to use the true and fair override of the Companies Act[38] to permit accounting treatments different from those specified. In turn, this may reflect an uncertainty concerning the applicability of the override. This is discussed at 4.2 below in the context of controlled non-subsidiaries. In other situations it would appear to be the case that current practice is against use of the override in order to reflect the substance of transactions where this is different from their legal nature. ED 42 represents an attempt to alter this approach.

It is currently very difficult to determine whether disclosures which are given in financial statements relate to an off-balance sheet transaction. This is simply because, by their very nature, off-balance sheet transactions will result in few disclosures of what is actually taking place. Because of this, the examples used in this chapter can normally only be assumed to be off-balance sheet transactions; the reader is not aware of either all reasons for a transaction being structured in the way it was, nor all details of a particular transaction.

Disputes regarding the interpretation of events as off-balance sheet transactions can therefore arise. A survey of financial statements published by the ICAEW used B.A.T Industries plc as an example in its off-balance sheet financing chapter. The example was of financing through a company in which the investor has less than a majority owned interest. B.A.T Industries plc took exception to their use as such an example as, they argued, the implication was that their associates were part of off-balance sheet transactions and this was argued by them not to be the case.

3.2   Current disclosure requirements affecting off-balance sheet transactions

The main areas of current disclosure requirements under existing standards and legislation which are likely to impact on disclosures required about off-balance sheet transactions are as follows:

(a)   significant investments

Where a company holds either more than 10% of any class of equity share capital of another company or more than 10% of the total allotted share capital of another company, the Companies Act requires certain information to be given in respect of that investment.[39] Additional information is required if more than 20% of the total allotted share capital is held.[40] Information is also required about investments having a book value in excess of 10% of the investing company's own assets.[41]

Where a 20% holding in equity voting shares is held then the investment is likely to come within the definition of an associated company under SSAP 1 (and of a related company under the Companies Act). The disclosure requirements of SSAP 1 are outlined in 5.5 of Chapter 4. Particular consideration should be given to the requirement to disclose 'more detailed information about the associated companies' tangible and intangible assets and liabilities if the interests in the associated companies are so material that more detailed information about them would assist in giving a true and fair view'.[42] More detailed disclosures about the results of such associated companies are also required.[43]

The above disclosure requirements will be relevant in those off-balance sheet transactions involving controlled non-subsidiaries (see 2.1 and 2.2 above).

One company which now gives much more information about such companies is The Burton Group plc, which discloses the following information about their investments in Burton Group Financial Services (Holdings) Limited (BGFSH) and High Street Property Investments Limited (HSPI) (see also Extract 5.10 in 2.2.3 above):

Extract 5.16: The Burton Group plc[44]

25 Related companies [extract]
The Group's interests in the net assets of BGFSH and HSPI as at 3rd September 1988 are set out below.

		1988 BGFSH £'m	1988 HSPI £'m	1987 BGFSH £'m	1987 HSPI £'m
notes	**Fixed assets**				
	Freehold and long leasehold properties at cost	—	100.3	—	100.1
	Other tangible assets	7.3	—	6.2	—
	Investments	—	—	0.6	—
	Other assets	6.1	—	3.5	—
		13.4	100.3	10.3	100.1
	Current assets				
(a)	Receivables	541.4	0.1	501.9	—
	Cash and bank balances	2.2	2.5	10.9	1.5
		543.6	2.6	512.8	1.5
	Total assets	557.0	102.9	523.1	101.6
	Liabilities				
(b)	Bank and other borrowings	398.7	70.0	378.1	70.0
(c)	Loans from The Burton Group plc — interest free	21.0	30.1	29.1	30.1
(d)	Creditors	49.8	0.9	36.2	0.6
	Deferred taxation	2.4	—	1.5	—
		471.9	101.0	444.9	100.7
	Net assets	85.1	1.9	78.2	0.9

---

notes

(a) Receivables

Accounts receivable within one year	**383.3**	**—**	391.6	—
Accounts receivable after more than one year	**116.4**	**—**	69.1	—
Other debtors	**9.0**	**0.1**	4.0	—
Prepayments	**5.9**	**—**	9.4	—
Finance leases and HP contracts receivable within one year	**9.1**	**—**	11.4	—
Finance leases and HP contracts receivable after one year	**10.7**	**—**	16.4	—
Advance corporation tax	**7.0**	**—**	—	—
	541.4	**0.1**	501.9	—

(b) Bank and other borrowings

Acceptance credits and loan facilities	**390.2**	**—**	366.1	—
Bank loans and overdrafts:				
due within one year	**4.3**	**2.0**	5.0	—
due between one and two years	**—**	**—**	—	2.0
due between two and five years	**—**	**3.5**	—	2.5
over five years	**—**	**64.5**	—	65.5
Obligations under finance leases:				
under one year	**2.4**	**—**	2.9	—
between two and five years	**1.8**	**—**	4.1	—
	398.7	**70.0**	378.1	70.0

(c) Loans from The Burton Group plc, include subordinated amounts due:

	—	**30.1**	29.0	30.1

(d) Creditors

Trade creditors	**2.4**	**—**	0.4	—
Other creditors and accruals	**22.0**	**0.3**	21.8	—
Taxation	**25.4**	**0.6**	14.0	0.6
	49.8	**0.9**	36.2	0.6

Disclosures such as these allow the reader of financial statements to prepare a pro-forma group balance sheet which includes such controlled non-subsidiaries.

(b)   contingencies

The Companies Act and SSAP 18 require certain disclosures to be made about contingent liabilities (see Chapter 17).

These will be relevant where:

(i)   a company has guaranteed the borrowings or obligations of a controlled non-subsidiary (for example, see Extract 5.4 in 2.1.3 above);

(ii)   a company has factored its debts and there is still recourse to the company in the event of non-payment by the debtors in question;

(iii)   a company has guaranteed the dividends and/or capital repayments in respect of preference shares issued by a subsidiary company. This is illustrated in the following extract:

Extract 5.17: Ultramar PLC[45]

28   **Contingent items** [extract]
b)   Ultramar PLC has entered into a support agreement as to dividends and the repayments of capital in respect of Can$199.4 million Cumulative Redeemable Retractable Preferred Shares issued by a subsidiary company (Note 11).

(Note 11 is reproduced in Extract 5.15 in 2.3.4 above.)

(c)   commitments

The Companies Act requires disclosure of capital commitments[46] and of other financial commitments.[47]

These will be relevant where:

(i)   a company has sold assets and is committed to repurchase them (see Extract 5.13 in 2.3.1 above);
(ii)   a company has sold assets and as a result of put and call options is effectively committed to repurchasing them;
(iii)   a company as a result of put and call options is effectively committed to purchasing the remaining equity shares of a controlled non-subsidiary (see Extracts 5.7 and 5.8 in 2.2.2 above);
(iv)   a company is committed to financing a controlled non-subsidiary's cash requirements (see Extract 5.2 in 1.3 above);
(v)   a company has consignment stock, which is not reflected on the balance sheet, and which the company is effectively committed to purchasing.

In addition to the above disclosure requirements, there may be other requirements of accounting standards and the Companies Act which impinge on the particular type of off-balance sheet transaction, e.g. extraordinary and exceptional items, segmental reporting.

4   PROPOSALS FOR THE FUTURE

4.1   ICAEW Technical Release

The ICAEW issued Technical Release 603 in December 1985 as a preliminary document for discussion.

It detailed certain points to be considered by preparers of financial statements in examining off-balance sheet transactions:

'(1)   In financial statements which are intended to give a true and fair view the economic substance of such transactions should be considered rather than their mere legal form when determining their true nature and thus the appropriate accounting treatment. Where items are included in the accounts on the basis of the substance of the transactions concerned and this is different from their legal form, the notes to the accounts should disclose the legal form of those transactions and the amounts of the items involved.

(2)   In the rare circumstances where accounting for a material transaction on the basis of its substance rather than its legal form would not comply with the requirements of the Companies Act, adequate disclosure should be made in order to provide a true and fair view, possibly by presenting separate pro-forma accounts prepared on the basis of the economic substance of the transactions.'[48]

4.2   The Law Society's response to TR 603

The Law Society stated that whilst agreeing with TR 603's basic objectives, they disagreed with its proposed method of solution. It was argued that a major purpose of financial statements is to provide comparability and consistency and this is best achieved by keeping subjectivity to a minimum. Further the desired level of objectivity was said to be best achieved by reflecting the legal position relating to assets and liabilities in a set of financial statements.

Whether this is a valid purpose of financial statements again brings us to a discussion of a conceptual framework (see 1.4 above). Further, the use of substance over form was said by the Law Society to contradict section 228 of the Companies Act which (in part) states:

'(2)   The balance sheet shall give a true and fair view of the state of affairs of the company as at the end of the financial year; and the profit and loss account shall give a true and fair view of the profit or loss of the company for the financial year.'

'(4)   If the balance sheet or profit and loss account drawn up in accordance with those requirements would not provide sufficient information to comply with subsection (2), any necessary additional information must be provided in the balance sheet or profit and loss account, or in a note to the financial statements.

(5)   If, owing to special circumstances in the case of any company, compliance with any such requirement in relation to the balance sheet or profit and loss account would prevent compliance with subsection (2) (even if additional information were provided in accordance with subsection (4)), the directors shall depart from that requirement in preparing the balance sheet or profit and loss account (so far as necessary in order to comply with subsection (2)).'

Similar requirements exist for group accounts at section 230 of the Companies Act.

It was argued by the Law Society that substance over form should only be used if disclosure of the details of a transaction would not be sufficient to satisfactorily inform the readers of the financial statements. This seems to equate the substance over form approach with the use of the true and fair override of section 228(5). Such an argument implies that the accounting profession cannot include substance over form as an accounting concept without specific legal permission.

It can be argued that the Law Society's approach placed undue emphasis on the 'true' element of the true and fair requirement of the Companies Act. Fairness of financial statements can be said to be achieved by reflecting the substance of transactions where appropriate (with note disclosures being given to allow assessment of the form of the transactions).

4.3   ED 42

The ASC issued ED 42 — *Accounting for special purpose transactions* — in April 1988 which seeks to deal with the issue of off-balance sheet transactions. The exposure draft differs from many produced by the ASC in that it addresses the issue from a conceptual angle rather than laying down a set of detailed rules. The essence of the argument it sets out is as follows:

The concept of 'true and fair' demands that transactions should be accounted for in accordance with their substance rather than their legal form; this should be determined by examining all the aspects and implications of a transaction (or series of transactions, if they are linked), and concentrating on those which are likely to have commercial effect in practice.[49]

The substance should be determined by identifying whether the transaction has increased or decreased the assets or liabilities which should be recognised in the financial statements of the enterprise.[50] Existing rules for the recognition and measurement of assets and liabilities should continue to be applied.[51] (The characteristics of assets and liabilities are discussed further below.)

When it has been determined that assets and liabilities should be recognised in the financial statements, they should be accounted for individually, rather than offset against each other: a right of set-off alters this principle only if the items are of the same type as each other.[52] This would also mean that where a lender has only limited recourse to the assets of the company as security for his loan, this is not a justification to take the loan and the related assets off the balance sheet.

A *special purpose transaction* is defined as one 'which combines or divides up the benefits and obligations flowing from it in such a way that they fall to be accounted for differently or in different periods depending on whether the elements are taken step by step or whether the transaction is viewed as a whole'.[53] Where such transactions give rise to the recognition of assets and liabilities in the financial statements, there should be disclosure of how they have done so, and even where they are not fully recognised, there may nonetheless be a need for disclosure of the nature and effects of such transactions in order that the financial statements should give a true and fair view.[54]

There are specific rules to deal with controlled non-subsidiaries. A *controlled non-subsidiary* is defined in the exposure draft as 'a company, trust or other vehicle which, though not fulfilling the Companies Act definition of a subsidiary, is directly or indirectly controlled by and a source of benefits and risks for the reporting enterprise or its subsidiaries that are in substance no different from those that would arise were the vehicle a subsidiary'.[55] The exposure draft asserts that such a vehicle should be consolidated as if it were a subsidiary,[56] and supports this line by quoting legal advice on the matter obtained from leading counsel.[57] It says that such a treatment is generally a justifiable use of the 'true and fair override', so that the vehicle should be included directly in the consolidated financial statements (with certain disclosures), but even where this argument is not invoked then it calls for the vehicle to be consolidated in supplementary pro-forma financial statements which are published with equal prominence to the statutory financial statements.[58]

Finally, it is stated that disclosure is not an adequate substitute for proper accounting as required by the terms of the exposure draft.[59]

Much of the argument within the proposed standard rests on whether or not the transaction in question is regarded as giving rise to an asset or liability. These are described in the exposure draft in the following terms:

Assets are described as 'probable future benefits controlled by and accruing to a particular enterprise as a result of past transactions and events'.[60] The various elements of that description are discussed further in detail in the exposure draft, particularly features which frequently arise in relation to linked transactions.[61] For example, as a general rule, an asset would not be recognised until ownership had passed to the enterprise, and the mere existence of an option to purchase it would not result in recognition of the asset; the only thing which the enterprise owns at that stage is the option.[62] However, some off-balance sheet transactions involve the sale of an item with an option to repurchase it on such terms that it is clear from the outset that the option will be exercised. In these circumstances the exposure draft suggests that it would be inappropriate to regard the exercise of the option as the critical event giving rise to the ownership of the asset, but rather to look at the substance of the series of transactions as a whole, which might indicate that the risks and rewards of ownership had never been disposed of in the first place.[63]

Liabilities are described as 'present obligations of the enterprise entailing probable future sacrifices of economic benefits by transferring assets or providing service to other entities in the future'.[64] Again, these individual elements are discussed in more detail in the exposure draft.[65]

The explanatory note of the exposure draft examines the application of the principles of the proposed standard to a number of familiar transactions and arrangements (most of these have been considered in 2.3 above).[66]

4.4   Companies Bill

The EC Seventh Company Law Directive is expected to be effective for accounting periods beginning on or after January 1, 1990 and a Companies Bill has recently been issued to implement the provisions of the Directive.

As indicated at 2.1 above, there are problems with the current definition of a subsidiary contained in the Companies Act such that it is possible to structure enterprises which, although controlled by the parent company, fail to meet the definition of a subsidiary.

The Companies Bill intends to change the definition of a subsidiary which is to be included in the consolidated financial statements from one based strictly on the form of the shareholding relationship between the companies, nearer to one which reflects the substance of the commercial relationship and in particular who exercises de facto control. It is also extending the enterprises which may be regarded as subsidiaries to include partnerships and unincorporated associations carrying on a trade or business, with or without a view to profit.[67] The circumstances under which a parent/subsidiary relationship will be regarded as existing are discussed at 1.2.2 of Chapter 4.

It is likely that the definition of a 'subsidiary undertaking' contained in the Companies Bill, if enacted in its present form, will limit the situations under which it is possible to structure 'controlled non-subsidiaries'. However, it remains to be seen whether new schemes will be devised to circumvent the new definition when enacted so that enterprises do not have to be regarded as 'subsidiary undertakings' which have to be included in the group financial statements.

5 COMPARISON WITH US AND IASC PRONOUNCEMENTS

5.1 US

5.1.1 *General*

Unlike the UK, the concept of 'substance over form' is well established in the US. APB Statement No. 4 — *Basic Concepts and Accounting Principles* — which was issued in 1970, states 'financial accounting emphasizes the economic substance of events even though the legal form may differ from the economic substance and suggest different treatment'.[68] Since then the FASB have issued a number of Statements of Financial Accounting Concepts ('SFACs'). The concept of 'substance over form' is not explicitly included within SFAC No. 2 — *Qualitative Characteristics of Accounting Information*, the reason being 'substance over form is an idea that also has its proponents, but it is not included because it would be redundant. The quality of reliability and, in particular, of representational faithfulness leaves no room for accounting representations that subordinate substance to form.'[69]

Another concept statement is SFAC No. 6 — *Elements of Financial Statements*. This statement describes, *inter alia*, the characteristics of assets and liabilities[70] which have essentially been used in ED 42 in the UK.

Despite such a conceptual background, accounting for off-balance sheet transactions has been a problem in the US as it has in the UK. For this reason, in addition to the above statements, there are a number of other pronouncements in the US which deal with many of the issues relating to off-balance sheet transactions.

5.1.2 *Controlled non-subsidiaries*

The general US approach to the consolidation of subsidiaries is summarised in 1.2.3 of Chapter 4. The SEC, through the application of Article 3(a) of Regulation S-X, applies a definition of subsidiaries based on substance.

As indicated in 4.2 of Chapter 4 the question of dissimilar activities as a reason for non-consolidation of subsidiaries has recently been addressed by the issue of SFAS 94 — *Consolidation of All Majority-Owned Subsidiaries* — which makes it no longer possible to avoid consolidation of a subsidiary because it has 'nonhomogeneous' operations. As stated in paragraph 22 'this statement is a major step in resolving the growing problem of off-balance sheet financing'.

5.1.3   Sale of assets

In the area of sale of assets, SFAS 49 — *Accounting for Product Financing Arrangements* — is of interest. A product financing arrangement is a transaction in which an enterprise sells a product to another entity and in a related transaction agrees to repurchase the product (or a substantially identical product).[71] Where the arrangement is such that the product will be repurchased at a predetermined price, which is not subject to change except for fluctuations due to finance and holding costs,[72] then the original sale will not be treated as such but, rather, as a liability.[73] Such a treatment also applies where the enterprise has an option to repurchase the product and will be subject to a significant penalty if it fails to exercise the option or where the other party has an option whereby it can require the enterprise to purchase the product.[74]

5.1.4   Project financing

In March 1981, the FASB issued SFAS 47 — *Disclosure of Long-Term Obligations* — in response to requests to consider accounting for project financing arrangements. These are arrangements relating to the financing of a major capital project in which the lender looks principally to the cash flows and earnings of the project as the source of funds for repayment and to the assets of the project as collateral for the loan.[75] As stated in paragraph 12 'the particular requests related to whether the unconditional purchase obligations and indirect guarantees of indebtedness of others typical of project financing arrangements result in participants acquiring ownership interests and obligations to make future cash payments that should be recognised as assets and liabilities on their balance sheets. The Board concluded . . . that the accounting questions could be answered better after further progress is made on the conceptual framework for financial accounting and reporting.' The statement is, therefore, an interim measure and only requires disclosures to be made about the obligations under such arrangements. Although SFAC No. 6 was issued in December 1985, SFAS 47 has not yet been superseded.

5.1.5   Transfers of receivables with recourse

In December 1983 SFAS 77 — *Reporting by Transferors for Transfers of Receivables with Recourse* — was issued. This requires that a transfer of receivables with recourse should be treated as a sale and no longer reflected in the balance sheet if all of the following conditions are met:

(a)   the transferor surrenders control of the future economic benefits embodied in the receivables;

(b)   the transferor's obligation under the recourse provisions can be reasonably estimated;

(c)   the transferee cannot require the transferor to repurchase the receivables except pursuant to the recourse provisions.[76]

The difference between the sales proceeds and the receivables transferred should be recorded as a gain or loss on the sale of the receivables.[77]

If any of the above conditions are not met, then no sale should be recognised and the amount of the proceeds from the transfer should be shown as a liability.[78]

5.1.6   *Financial instruments*

In May 1986 the FASB added a project on financial instruments and off-balance sheet financing to its agenda. The first document issued for comment as part of that project is the exposure draft — *Disclosures about Financial Instruments* — issued in November 1987. As stated in the introduction to the exposure draft 'issues to be addressed include whether assets or liabilities should be recognized or derecognized as a result of certain transactions involving financial instruments; how to account for financial instruments that seek to transfer market and credit risks and for the underlying assets and liabilities to which the risk-transferring items are related; how financial instruments should be measured; how issuers should account for financial instruments with both debt and equity characteristics; and how best to disclose the potential favorable or unfavorable effects of instruments whether recognized or unrecognized as assets or liabilities'.[79]

In view of the complexity of the issues, statements covering such issues will only be developed after 'extensive Board deliberations and after issuance of initial discussion documents, exposure drafts, and public hearings. As an interim measure, pending completion of the recognition and measurement phases of the financial instruments project, the Board decided that improved disclosures about recognized and unrecognized financial instruments are necessary to provide better information about financial instruments.'[80] The exposure draft proposes that disclosure should be made of information about credit risks, future cash receipts and payments, interest rates, and market values.[81]

The comment period on the proposed statement ended on April 30, 1988 and in the light of comments received, the FASB are considering the next phase of the development of a statement in this area.

5.2   IASC

The IASC has not issued any specific pronouncements dealing with off-balance sheet transactions. However, IAS 1 — *Disclosure of Accounting Policies* — states that three considerations should govern the selection and application of appropriate accounting policies. These are prudence, materiality and substance over form. The last of these is expressed as 'transactions and other events should be accounted for and presented in accordance with their substance and financial reality and not merely with their legal form'.[82]

The IASC has also recently issued an exposure draft — *Framework for the Preparation and Presentation of Financial Statements* — which deals with conceptual issues relating to financial reporting (see 6.3 of Chapter 2).

6   CONCLUSION

6.1   Introduction

As indicated in 1.4 above, there would appear to be three possible methods of dealing with off-balance sheet transactions. These are:

(a)   additional disclosure in the notes to the financial statements;

(b)   restatement of accounting treatment in the financial statements;

(c)   preparation of additional pro-forma financial statements.

6.2   Disclosure as a solution?

This is the approach preferred by the Law Society as detailed both in their response to TR 603 (see 4.2 above) and in their comments during the development of ED 42.

Proponents of this solution argue that disclosure is sufficient to give a true and fair view within the terms of section 228 of the Companies Act. This would mean that there is no need for a restatement of the financial statements.

The problem with such an approach is that narrative type disclosure can be drafted to conceal certain aspects of off-balance sheet transactions. It is relatively easy to use a wording which does not specifically detail the exact nature of an off-balance sheet transaction.

It can also be argued that readers of the financial statements will concentrate on the balance sheet and profit and loss account only and will not generally examine the notes in great detail. A persuasive case can be put for the view that disclosure should explain what is in the financial statements rather than add to that information. As indicated in 4.3 above the ASC have taken the view (in developing ED 42) that disclosure cannot compensate for an inappropriate accounting treatment.

6.3   Restatement of accounting treatment in the financial statements as a solution?

As discussed in 4.3 above this is the approach which the ASC has adopted in ED 42. It is intended that such an approach will improve comparability between financial statements by treating transactions similarly which are, in substance, of a similar economic effect. As we will now examine, the problem with such an approach is that the level of subjectivity is increased.

Restatement of the accounting treatment in the financial statements involves the preparer in 'as-if' type accounting whereby he must attempt to account for the off-balance sheet transaction using a 'reasonable accounting analogy' of a more conventional transaction. An argument could be made that this is a strange approach because the treatment adopted depends on whichever type of analogous transaction existed prior to the off-balance sheet transaction concerned. If we had always used off-balance sheet transactions in certain areas would we now be treating currently conventional transactions as if they were off-balance sheet?

A possibly more important problem is deciding what the economic substance of an off-balance sheet transaction really is. It is only after this has been decided that we can use the analogy approach noted in the previous paragraph. There is obviously great scope for argument between interested parties in trying to decide what the economic substance of any transaction is. The interested parties are likely to include the company's directors, auditors and solicitors, and the debate between them may be fairly lengthy due to the subjective nature of the decision. It is unlikely that a company's directors will want to openly admit that a transaction is, even partly, of an off-balance sheet nature. Further, their solicitors will presumably not be amenable to reflecting the substance of the transaction to the possible contradiction of its form. The auditor is therefore likely to have a difficult task in achieving what he perceives as the desired accounting treatment.

Despite the many practical problems that a restatement would involve, the ASC is currently arguing that this is the most appropriate treatment of off-balance sheet transactions. As we have already stated, this stems from their views of both an appropriate conceptual framework for financial reporting and the interpretation of section 228.

6.4   Additional pro-forma financial statements as a solution?

This approach can be seen to lessen the problems of the restatement approach at 6.3 above. The subjectivity introduced by that approach could be argued to be of less importance when it affects financial statements which are additional to those required by the Companies Act. ED 42 requires the use of pro-forma consolidated financial statements to incorporate controlled non-subsidiaries where, in 'rare cases' the true and fair override of the Companies Act cannot be used.

An example of the use of pro-forma financial statements to reflect the effects of off-balance sheet transactions was given by Burnett and Hallamshire Holdings plc. This is detailed at 1.3 above and concerned a situation where the company had just been rescued and the extent of its off-balance sheet transactions had been revealed.

There would appear to be two possible problems in the pro-forma approach. Firstly, the use of substance over form is already achieved by SSAP 21 as it relates to finance leases. What is currently being proposed by the ASC's preferred route of restating the financial statements is merely an extension of this approach. If we can accept the SSAP 21 treatment why is this extension invalid?

The second possible problem with a pro-forma approach is that we must consider if the reader of the financial statements will understand the different basis of preparation of the two sets of financial statements. Once again, this depends on our view of the conceptual framework and, in particular, who is assumed to read the financial statements and their assumed level of understanding.

References

1 ICAEW, TR 603, *Off-balance sheet finance and window dressing*, para. 5(i).
2 *The Guardian*, December 22, 1987.
3 Burnett and Hallamshire Holdings plc, Report and Accounts 1984, p. 35.
4 *The Financial Times*, January 24, 1986.
5 Burnett and Hallamshire Holdings plc, Report and Accounts 1985, pp. 27 and 37.
6 Burnett and Hallamshire Holdings plc, Report and Accounts 1985, p. 20.
7 Burnett and Hallamshire Holdings plc, Report and Accounts 1985, p. 14.
8 For a report on the case see 'Unfair accounts — Argyll directors summoned', *Accountancy*, August 1981, p. 19.
9 *Accountancy*, February 1982, p. 11.
10 CA 85, ss 229 and 230.
11 SSAP 2, *Disclosure of accounting policies*, November 1971.
12 CA 85, s 736(2).
13 Cadbury Schweppes p.l.c., Annual Report 1987, p. 48.
14 Dixons Group plc, Annual Report 1987 — 88, p. 45.
15 SSAP 1, *Accounting for associated companies*, Revised April 1982, para. 39.
16 The Burton Group plc, Annual Report 1986, p. 79.
17 Habitat Mothercare PLC, Report and Accounts for the year ended 25th March 1984, p. 18.
18 Storehouse plc, Report & Accounts 1987, p. 46.
19 See Storehouse plc, Report & Accounts 1987, p. 46. This discloses that £2,163,000 was transferred out of investment in related companies as a result of Richard Shops Holdings Limited becoming a subsidiary; as this figure relates to a 48% interest then 100% would be £4,506,000.
20 The Burton Group plc, Annual Report 1986, p. 78.
21 The Burton Group plc, Annual Report 1988, p. 54.
22 S. & W. Berisford, Report & Accounts 1987, p. 55.
23 S. & W. Berisford, Report & Accounts 1987, pp. 45 and 46.
24 S. & W. Berisford, Report & Accounts 1988, pp. 49 and 50.
25 SSAP 1, paras. 23 and 30.
26 CA 85, Sch. 4, para. 50(3)(b).
27 *Ibid.*, para. 50(5).
28 S. & W. Berisford plc, Report & Accounts 1986, p. 37.
29 ED 42, *Accounting for special purpose transactions*, March 1988, para. 39.
30 *Ibid.*, para. 40.
31 *Ibid.*, para. 41.
32 *Ibid.*, para. 37.
33 *Ibid.*, para. 38.
34 *Ibid.*, para. 44.
35 *Ibid.*, para. 45.
36 The National Home Loans Corporation plc, Report & Accounts 1988, pp. 23 and 24.
37 Ultramar PLC, Annual Report 1987, pp. 36 and 37.
38 CA 85, ss 228 and 230.
39 *Ibid.*, Sch. 5, paras. 7 and 8.
40 *Ibid.*, paras. 15 and 16.
41 *Ibid.*, para. 9.
42 SSAP 1, para. 30.
43 *Ibid.*, para. 23.
44 The Burton Group plc, Annual Report 1988, p. 55.
45 Ultramar PLC, Annual Report 1987, p. 44.
46 CA 85, Sch. 4, para. 50(3).
47 *Ibid.*, para. 50(5).
48 TR 603, para. 17.

49 ED 42, para. 57.
50 *Ibid.*, para. 58.
51 *Ibid.*, para. 61.
52 *Ibid.*, para. 62.
53 *Ibid.*, para. 56.
54 *Ibid.*, paras. 63 and 64.
55 *Ibid.*, para. 54.
56 *Ibid.*, para. 65.
57 *Ibid.*, Preface, para. 1.21.
58 *Ibid.*, para. 65.
59 *Ibid.*, para. 68.
60 *Ibid.*, para. 14.
61 *Ibid.*, paras. 15 — 21.
62 *Ibid.*, para. 19.
63 *Ibid.*, para. 20.
64 *Ibid.*, para. 22.
65 *Ibid.*, paras. 23 — 27.
66 *Ibid.*, paras. 36 — 47.
67 Companies Bill, Clause 20, s 259(1).
68 APB Statement No. 4, *Basic Concepts and Accounting Principles Underlying Financial Statements of Business Enterprises*, AICPA, October 1970, para. 127 F-12.
69 SFAC No. 2, *Qualitative Characteristics of Accounting Information*, FASB, May 1980, para. 160.
70 SFAC No. 6, *Elements of Financial Statements*, FASB, December 1985, paras. 25 — 43.
71 SFAS 49, *Accounting for Product Financing Arrangements*, FASB, June 1981, para. 3.
72 *Ibid.*, para. 5.
73 *Ibid.*, para. 8.
74 *Ibid.*, para. 5.
75 SFAS 47, *Disclosure of Long-Term Obligations*, FASB, March 1981, para. 23(a).
76 SFAS 77, *Reporting by Transferors for Transfers of Receivables with Recourse*, FASB, December 1983, para. 5.
77 *Ibid.*, para. 6.
78 *Ibid.*, para. 8.
79 Financial Accounting Series No. 054, *Disclosures about Financial Instruments*, FASB, November 1987, para. 1.
80 *Ibid.*, para. 2.
81 *Ibid.*, paras. 7 — 23.
82 IAS 1, *Disclosure of Accounting Policies*, IASC, January 1975, para. 9(b).

Chapter 6

Earnings per share

1   INTRODUCTION

Earnings per share (EPS) is one of the most widely quoted statistics in financial analysis. It came into great prominence in the US during the late 1950s and early 1960s due to the widespread use of the price earnings ratio (PE) as a yardstick for investment decisions. By the late 1960s, its popularity had switched across the Atlantic and for the purposes of consistency and comparability, it became important that an agreed method of computed EPS was established.

In March 1971, the Accounting Standards Steering Committee issued an exposure draft, ED 4 — *Earnings per share*. The exposure draft represented a departure by UK accounting bodies into the area of financial ratios and financial analysis. ED 4 was, in general, favourably received and in February 1972, SSAP 3 — *Earnings per share* — was issued with the objective of providing a minimum standard for disclosure of EPS in financial statements and the basis of its calculation.

Reported and forecast EPS can, through the PE ratio, significantly affect a company's share price. This is evident whenever events occur that alter market expectations of future EPS. For example, on June 25, 1987, there was a significant decline in share prices in the stores sector. The following day, the Financial Times explained the drop as follows:

'The widespread decline was triggered by the Argyll group's decision to treat the £90m cost of reorganising its Presto stores as an "exceptional" item rather than an "extraordinary" one. The move, following the company's £681m acquisition of Safeway in January will reduce the company's pre-tax profits and earnings per share over the next four years. Worries that acquisitive companies would have to reduce their profits in a similar way affected the sector overall.'[1]

Given such market sensitivity to EPS and shareholders' natural concern about share price performance (since this ultimately affects their wealth), EPS has also served as a means of assessing the stewardship and management role performed by company directors and managers. By linking remuneration packages to EPS growth performance, some companies deliberately increase the pressure on management to improve EPS. Not surprisingly, such powerful factors and incentives have all contributed to the growth of attempts to distort EPS including the tendency to treat losses as extraordinary in the profit and loss account and over providing for future reorganisation costs when acquisition accounting.

2   SCOPE OF SSAP 3

SSAP 3 applies to all companies with an equity listing on The International Stock Exchange (except certain insurance, shipping and banking companies, if they prepare special category accounts). Companies whose shares are traded on the Unlisted Securities Market are expected by The Stock Exchange to comply with SSAP 3. Although there are no specific requirements regarding the disclosure and computation of EPS by companies whose shares are traded on the Third Market, compliance with SSAP 3 is strongly recommended.

3   THE BASIC EPS

3.1   Definition

Earnings per share is defined in SSAP 3 as:

'The profit in pence attributable to each equity share based on the consolidated profit of the period after tax and after deducting minority interests and preference dividends but before taking into account extraordinary items divided by the number of equity shares in issue and ranking for dividend in respect of the period.'[2]

Expressed as an equation:

$$EPS = \frac{E}{N} \text{ where}$$

E is the profit after tax but before extraordinary items attributable to equity shareholders; and

N is the number of equity shares in issue and ranking for dividend in respect of the period.

The phrase 'to each equity share' used in the definition of EPS should be interpreted in the light of the definition of 'equity share capital' in the Companies Act 1985. Equity share capital is defined therein as 'the issued share capital of a company excluding any part of the capital which, neither as respects dividends nor as respects capital, carries any right to participate beyond a *specified amount* (emphasis added) in a distribution'.[3] Hence, preference shares which participate to an unspecified amount either in profits or on liquidation would be classed as equity shares.

3.2   Disclosure

SSAP 3 requires disclosure of the basic EPS on the face of the profit and loss account for both the period under review and for the corresponding previous period.[4] The basis of the calculation should be explained either in the profit and loss account or in a note to the financial statements. Such disclosure should include the amount of the earnings and the number of equity shares used in the calculation.[5]

Extract 6.1: Vickers P.L.C.[6]

CONSOLIDATED PROFIT AND LOSS ACCOUNT [extract]

	Notes	**1987**	1986
EARNINGS PER 50p ORDINARY SHARE	9	**17.4p**	16.3p

9 EARNINGS PER SHARE
The calculation of earnings per 50p Ordinary Share is based on the profit after taxation and before extraordinary items of £44.8m (1986: £39.0m) less the preference dividends of £0.4m (1986: £0.4m) and the average number of Ordinary Shares ranking for dividend of 254,664,862 (1986: 237,063,773).

Where a company has more than one class of equity shares (for example, ordinary shares and participating preference shares), Appendix 1 to SSAP 3 states that separate EPS calculations to be performed for each class.[7] The calculation of EPS for each separate class should be based on the number of shares in that particular class which were in issue during the period. The apportionment of earnings between each separate class of equity is dealt with in 5.5 below.

The calculation of the basic EPS is often simple but a number of problems can arise. The problems arising can be considered under two headings:

(a)   changes in equity share capital;

(b)   matters affecting the earnings figures.

4   CHANGES IN EQUITY SHARE CAPITAL

Changes in equity share capital can occur under a variety of circumstances, the most common of which are dealt with below. Whenever such a change occurs during the accounting period, an adjustment is required to the number of shares in the EPS calculation for that period; furthermore, in certain situations the EPS for previous periods will also have to be recalculated.

4.1   Issue for cash at full market price

If new equity shares have been issued for cash at full market price the earnings should be apportioned over the average number of shares ranking for dividend during the period weighted on a time basis.

Example 6.1:   Weighted average calculation

At January 1, 3,000,000 ordinary shares were in issue ranking for dividend. On September 30, 1,000,000 further shares were issued for cash at full market price to rank for dividend for the year to December 31.

The number of shares to be used in the calculation of EPS will be:

	m
For 9/12 (of the year) x 3m (shares in issue)	2.25
For 3/12 (of the year) x 4m (shares in issue)	1.00
Number of shares to be used in the calculation	3.25

The use of a weighted average number of shares is necessary because the increase in the share capital would have affected earnings only for that portion of the year during which the issue proceeds were available to management for use in the business.

4.2   Bonus issue

A bonus issue has the effect of increasing the number of shares in issue without any inflow of funds to the company. Consequently, no additional earnings will accrue as a result of the issue. Assuming the bonus shares rank for dividend, they should be treated as being in issue for the whole year and also included in the previous year's EPS calculation to give a comparable result. The EPS for the earlier period should therefore be adjusted by the following fraction:

$$\frac{\text{Number of shares before the bonus issue}}{\text{Number of shares after the bonus issue}}$$

Similar considerations apply where equity shares are split into shares of smaller nominal value. Financial ratios for earlier periods, which are based on the number of equity shares ranking for dividend at a year end (e.g. dividend per share) should also be adjusted by the above factor.

The notes to the financial statements will have to be adapted in order to refer to the adjustments made, along the following lines:

Extract 6.2: Blue Circle Industries PLC[8]

GROUP PROFIT AND LOSS ACCOUNT [extract]

	Notes	1987	1986
Earnings per £1 Ordinary Share	10	47.7p	38.3p

9 Dividends [extract]

		1987	1986
		£m	£m
Ordinary Shares: Interim of 5.0p per £1 share		12.9	7.7
(1986 3.0p — adjusted for capitalisation issue)			
Final of 10.0p per £1 share		25.9	21.9
(1986 8.5p — adjusted for capitalisation issue)			
		38.8	**29.6**

10 Earnings per £1 Ordinary Share

The earnings per £1 Ordinary share for each year are calculated by dividing the profit, after charging tax and before extraordinary items, attributable to ordinary shareholders (£123.0m) (1986 £98.6m) by the average number of Ordinary Shares in issue during the year (258.1m) (1986 257.2m — adjusted for capitalisation issue). Earnings per share calculated on earnings after charging depreciation only on original cost would be approximately 50.7p (1986 41.7p — adjusted for capitalisation issue).

4.3 Rights issue

A rights issue is a popular method through which public companies are able to tap the stock market for further capital. Under the terms of such an issue, existing shareholders are given the opportunity to acquire further shares in the company on a pro-rata basis to their existing shareholdings. The stock market's reaction to the call for new cash is largely governed by the same factors that always concern shareholders, namely: how profitable is the company, what are its immediate trading prospects, what is the current state of its finances?

The 'rights' shares will usually be offered either at the current market price or at a price below that. In the former case, the treatment of the issue for EPS purposes is as discussed in 4.1 above. However, where the rights price is at a discount to market it is not quite as straightforward, since the issue is equivalent to a bonus issue combined with an issue at full market price. In such cases, Appendix 1 to SSAP 3 states that it is necessary to adjust the number of shares in issue before the rights issue to reflect the bonus element inherent in the issue.[9]

The bonus element of the rights issue is given by the following fraction, sometimes referred to as the bonus fraction:

$$\frac{\text{Actual cum-rights price on last day of quotation cum-rights}}{\text{Theoretical ex-rights price}}$$

The 'cum-rights price' is the *actual* price at which the shares are quoted inclusive of the right to take up the future shares under the rights issue.

The 'ex-rights price' is the *theoretical* price at which the shares would be quoted, other stock market factors apart, after the rights issue shares have been issued.

Example 6.2:   Illustration of calculation of EPS following a rights issue at less than full market price

Capital structure

Issued share capital at December 31, 19X2
24m Ordinary shares of 50p each, fully paid.

Trading results

	19X2	19X1
	£	£
Profit on ordinary activities after taxation	1.2m	1.0m

A rights issue took place on August 31, 19X2 on a 1 for 4 basis at 80p. The actual cum-rights price on the last day of quotation cum-rights was £1 per share.

The calculation of EPS can be tackled in the following manner:

A   *What is the theoretical ex-rights price?*

The theoretical ex-rights price is calculated as follows:

	No		p
Initial holding of	4	shares, market value	400
Rights taken up	1	share, at a cost of	80
New holding	5	shares, theoretical value	480

$$\text{Theoretical ex-rights price} = \frac{480}{5} = 96 \text{ pence}$$

which is the average price per share of the final holding.

B   *What is the bonus element inherent in this issue?*

The *bonus element* of the rights issue is given by the fraction:

$$\frac{\text{Actual cum-rights price}}{\text{Theoretical ex-rights price}} = \frac{100}{96} = \frac{25}{24}$$

This corresponds to a bonus issue of 1 for 24. Circumstances may arise where the actual cum-rights price on the last day of quotation cum-rights is less than the theoretical ex-rights price giving a bonus fraction of less than 1, in which case the rights issue should be treated as an issue for cash at full market price for EPS purposes (see 4.1). This may be the case where, for example, the market has suffered a significant downturn during the rights period which was not anticipated when the rights issue was announced.

Hence, the rights issue can be split into a bonus issue of 1 for 24, which will reduce the theoretical price per share to 96 pence, combined with an issue of the residue of the shares at the new theoretical price per share of 96 pence. This can be illustrated by considering the position of a shareholder who holds 360 shares before the rights issue takes place.

	No		£
Initial holding of	360	shares, valued at	360
Bonus issue (1 for 24)	15	shares,	—
	375	shares, (theoretical price per share : 96p)	360
Issue at full market	75	shares, at a cost of	72
New holding	450	shares, cost	432

The shareholder is indifferent as to whether he is offered a 1 for 4 rights issue at 80 pence a share *or* a combination of a 1 for 24 bonus issue (bringing the market price down from £1 to 96p) and a 1 for 5 rights issue at full market price (i.e. 96p). Consequently, it is appropriate to treat the rights issue as a combination of a bonus issue and a rights issue at full market price.

C   Weighted average share capital

In order to calculate the earnings per share for the year in which a rights issue is made, it will be necessary to calculate the weighted average share capital for the year after adjusting the capital in issue before the rights issue for that part which represents the bonus element. The number of shares in issue before the rights issue, adjusted for the bonus element would be:

$$24m \times \frac{25}{24} = 25m$$

The number of shares after the rights issue would be:

$$24m \times \frac{5}{4} = 30m$$

The share issue may be summarised as follows:

		m
1.1.X2	Opening number of shares	24
31.8.X2	Bonus issue (1 for 24)	1
Adjusted opening number of shares		25
31.8.X2	Full market price issue (1 for 5)	5
31.12.X2	Closing number of shares	30

Therefore the weighted average number of shares during the year will be:

For 8/12 (of the year) x 25m	16,666,667
For 4/12 (of the year) x 30m	10,000,000
Weighted average number of shares	26,666,667

D EPS calculation

To make the previous year's EPS comparable, the number of shares used in the recalculation has to increase to take into account the bonus element. This can be done by adjusting the earnings per share figure by the reciprocal of the bonus element fraction (i.e. 24/25ths). Thus:

Current year's EPS   Previous year's EPS

$$\frac{£1.2m}{26,666,667} = 4.50p \qquad \overset{was}{\frac{£1m}{24,000,000}} = 4.17p \qquad 4.17p \times \overset{now\ is}{\frac{24}{25}} = 4.00p$$

A suitable description of the calculation of the EPS following a rights issue is illustrated in the following extract:

Extract 6.3: S. G. Warburg Group plc[10]

CONSOLIDATED PROFIT AND LOSS ACCOUNT [extract]

	Note	1988	*1987*
Earnings per Ordinary Share before extraordinary items	5		
Actual		**37.4p**	*41.3p*
Diluted		**33.2p**	*36.8p*

5 EARNINGS PER SHARE BEFORE EXTRAORDINARY ITEMS
Actual earnings per Ordinary Share are calculated on the earnings attributable to Ordinary shareholders before extraordinary items of £64,505,000 *(1987 £62,452,000)*, and on 172,581,140 Ordinary Shares being the average number of shares in issue during the year ended 31st March, 1988 *(1987 151,017,100 after adjustment to reflect the bonus element of the rights issue)*.
Diluted earnings per Ordinary Share are calculated on adjusted profits of £70,737,000 *(1987 £67,392,000)* and on 213,329,179 Ordinary Shares *(1987 182,836,822 after adjustment)*.

4.4 Issue for cash at less than full market price

Shares allotted as a result of open offers, placings and other offerings of equity shares not made to existing shareholders should be regarded as being at a fair market price even if they are offered at a discount to the market price. They should be dealt with on a weighted average basis without calculating any bonus element when computing the EPS for the period concerned.

4.5 Purchase and redemption of own shares

A company may, if it is authorised to do so by its articles and it complies with the related provisions of the Companies Act, purchase/redeem its own shares. In such circumstances the earnings should be apportioned over the weighted average share capital in issue for the year.

4.6 Post-balance sheet changes in capital

The EPS shown in the profit and loss account should not normally reflect a change in the capital structure occurring after the accounting date, but before the preliminary announcement of the results of the period, because any proceeds received from the issue were not available for use during the period. However, it is desirable that the effect on the basic EPS of any bonus issue, share split or bonus element inherent in a rights issue which occurs shortly after the balance sheet date should be disclosed.[11]

It is worth noting that in Canada the CICA requires disclosure of pro-forma EPS figures (for both basic and fully diluted EPS) where, shortly after the balance sheet date, ordinary shares are issued:

(a) to redeem debt or preference shares;

(b) as a result of conversion;

(c) in a reorganisation.[12]

The pro-forma EPS figures are calculated as if the share issue had occurred at the beginning of the period. The objective behind this is to enable users of financial statements to obtain a better assessment of probable EPS for the future. Similar disclosures are also required to be included in financial statements prepared in accordance with US GAAP.[13]

4.7 Issue to acquire another business

As a result of a share issue to acquire another business, funds or other assets will flow into the business and extra profits will be generated. When calculating EPS, it should be assumed that the shares were issued on the first day that profits of the newly acquired business are recognised in the profit and loss account (even if the actual date of issue is later). Under SSAP 14, this will be the 'effective date of acquisition' which is defined as the earlier of:

(a) the date on which consideration passes; and

(b) the date on which an offer becomes or is declared unconditional.[14]

If the business combination is accounted for as an acquisition, this means that when calculating EPS, the period for which earnings of the acquired company are consolidated should be the same as the period for which the shares are weighted, thus achieving comparability within the EPS calculation.

In contrast, where a business combination has been accounted for as a merger in accordance with SSAP 23, the number of shares taken as being in issue for both the current and preceding years should include those issued as purchase consideration as though they had been in issue throughout the whole of both years. This treatment reflects the fact that earnings are combined for both years and is appropriate even where not all of the consideration given for the equity share capital in the 'offeree' company is in the form of equity share capital.

At present, SSAP 23 does not require the continuance of share ownership in a business combination for merger accounting to be used. As a result, merger accounting may be used where vendor placings, vendor rights issues or vendor placings with clawback[15] take place. Hence, for EPS purposes, the treatment suggested in the preceding paragraph will apply in all of these situations.

4.8   Group reconstructions

In the case where a new holding company is established by means of a share for share exchange and merger accounting principles have been adopted, the number of shares taken as being in issue for both the current and preceding periods should be the number of shares issued by the new holding company in the reconstruction. However, EPS calculations for previous periods in the new holding company's financial statements would have to reflect any issues for cash by the former holding company that may have occurred in those periods as illustrated in the example below.

Example 6.3:   Calculation of EPS where a new holding company is established

Company A has acquired Company B in a one for one share exchange on June 30, 19X1. At that date, Company B has 1,000,000 £1 ordinary shares in issue. Previously, on June 30, 19X0 Company B had issued 200,000 £1 ordinary shares for cash at full market price. Both companies have a December 31 year end and the trading results of Company B are as follows:

	19X1 £	19X0 £
Profit for equity shareholders after taxation	500,000	300,000

The earnings per share calculation of Company A is shown below:

	19X1		19X0
Number of equity shares		$800,000 \times \dfrac{6}{12}$ = 400,000	
		$1,000,000 \times \dfrac{6}{12}$ = 500,000	
	1,000,000		900,000

EPS	$\dfrac{500,000}{1,000,000}$ = 50p	$\dfrac{300,000}{900,000}$ = 33.33p

If, in the above example, the share exchange did not take place on a one for one basis, but Company A issued three shares for every one share held in Company B, then the number of shares issued by Company B in 19X0 would have to be apportioned accordingly before carrying out the weighted average calculation. The earnings per share calculation would, therefore, have been as follows:

	19X1	19X0
Number of equity shares	$2,400,000 \times \dfrac{6}{12}$	$=1,200,000$
	$3,000,000 \times \dfrac{6}{12}$	$=1,500,000$
	$3,000,000$	$2,700,000$
EPS	$\dfrac{500,000}{3,000,000} = 16.67\text{p}$	$\dfrac{300,000}{2,700,000} = 11.11\text{p}$

4.9 Adjustments to EPS in five year summaries

In order to ensure comparability of EPS figures quoted in a five year summary, the previously published EPS figures should be adjusted for subsequent bonus issues and rights issues at less than market value in the manner described in 4.2 and 4.3 above; they should also be adjusted for merger accounting, to the extent that the results of the merged companies have been combined. The resultant figures should be described as the adjusted EPS and should be disclosed separately from other financial data which is not so adjusted.[16] Where there is more than one capitalisation and/or rights issue, these factors will operate cumulatively.

5 MATTERS AFFECTING THE EARNINGS FIGURES

5.1 Earnings for equity

The earnings figure should normally comprise the consolidated profit of the year after tax, minority interests and preference dividends but before extraordinary items net of taxation and minority interests; attributable earnings of associated companies should also be included.

5.2 Preference dividends

If a company has cumulative preference shares, the full preference dividend for the year should be deducted (the net amount) in arriving at earnings for EPS purposes, whether or not it has been earned or declared. However, if the preference shares are non-cumulative, then the amount to be deducted in arriving at the earnings figure is the actual preference dividend paid or proposed (the net amount).[17]

5.3 Losses

Where a loss is incurred or the amount earned for equity is a negative figure, EPS should be determined in the normal manner and shown as a loss per share.[18]

Where the tax charge for a year is reduced by losses brought forward, the actual tax charge in the profit and loss account should still be used in the EPS calculation. However, the effect of loss relief on EPS for the years affected should still be disclosed by way of a note to the financial statements.[19]

5.4 Prior year adjustments

Where comparative figures have been restated (e.g. to correct a fundamental error or as a result of a change in accounting policy), earnings per share for the corresponding previous period should also be restated.

5.5 Different classes of equity shares

If there is more than one class of equity shares or where some of the shares are not fully paid, earnings should be apportioned over the different classes of shares in accordance with their dividend rights or other rights to participate in profits.[20]

Example 6.4: *Partly paid shares*

Capital structure

Issued share capital at December 31, 19X2:

540,000 Ordinary shares of £1 each, fully paid (19X1 — fully paid)
756,000 Ordinary shares of £1 each, 71p paid (19X1 — 26p paid)

On June 30, 19X2, a 45p call was made on the partly paid shares.

Trading results

	19X2 £
Profit on ordinary activities before taxation	400,000
Tax on profit on ordinary activities	110,000
Profit on ordinary activities after taxation	290,000

Dividend rights

Partly paid shareholders are to receive such proportion of the dividend entitlement due to fully paid shareholders so as to reflect the extent and period that the shares are partly paid.

Calculation of EPS

		Fully paid shares	Partly paid shares
Number of ordinary shares		540,000	756,000
Earnings for equity:	£	£	£
Pre-call	145,000	106,305	38,695*
Post-call	145,000	72,718	72,282
	290,000	179,023	110,977

$$* \text{ being} \quad \frac{756,000 \times 26\%}{(756,000 \times 26\%) + 540,000} \quad \times \quad £145,000$$

Therefore EPS
$$\frac{179,023}{540,000} = 33.15\text{p} \qquad \frac{110,977}{756,000} = 14.68\text{p}$$

'New' shares of the same class as existing equity shares, which are separately quoted for a time only because they are transferable in a different form or because they rank for a later (e.g. final) but not for an earlier (e.g. interim) dividend in respect of the period under review, should not be treated as a separate class of shares.

In the case where a company has both ordinary and participating preference shares (another form of equity share capital — see 3.1 above) in issue the apportionment of earnings may be achieved by first establishing the amounts attributable to the participating preference shares, namely:

(a)   the fixed part of the dividend on the participating preference shares; and, either

(b)   if the participating element is limited (say subject to a maximum), the entire participating preference share dividend; or

(c)   if the participating element is unlimited, the appropriate proportion of the earnings for the period.

These amounts should be deducted from the total earnings in arriving at the earnings attributable to the ordinary shares for EPS purposes.

5.6   'Net' and 'nil' bases

The tax charge in the profit and loss account will often include:

(a)   some elements which do not vary with the proportion of the profit distributed by way of dividend; for example, corporation tax on profits, tax attributable to dividends received, unrelieved overseas tax arising because the rate of overseas tax exceeds the rate of UK corporation tax;

(b)   some elements which do vary according to the amount of profit distributed and would be absent if no distributions were made, for example, irrecoverable ACT on ordinary dividends.

The *net basis* of computing EPS takes account of all the elements of the tax charge (i.e. the tax charge as stated in the financial statements) when arriving at the earnings figure to be used in the calculation of EPS.

The *nil basis* recognises only those components of the tax charge which are unaffected by the level of equity distribution. It is called the nil basis because it seeks to arrive at what the earnings would be if the distributions to the equity shareholders were nil.

5.6.1   Net or nil ?

The question of what is the most appropriate basis for calculating EPS has given rise to considerable controversy in the past. Those favouring the 'nil' basis argue that 'it produces a figure of earnings which is not dependent on the level of distribution, and so provides an indicator of one company's performance more closely comparable with that of the other'.[21]

The counter arguments against this are; firstly, the fact that comparison of earnings of different companies is fraught with difficulty, in view of diversity of accounting practice within certain areas of accounting, even before tax implications are considered, appears to be totally ignored; and, secondly, it ignores the fact that irrecoverable ACT reduces the company's cash flow and its ability to reinvest in stocks and plant and machinery. Such a cash drain will affect future profitability and assuming the directors' present/future likely dividend policy will continue, the future earnings stream is likely to fall even further. Hence, the EPS calculation using the nil basis does not reflect the consequences of a company not being able to fully offset against corporation tax the ACT on its dividend payments.

Changes in tax law during the last few years have meant that companies are now less likely to incur the 'variable' elements of the tax charge than before. For example, the Finance Act 1984 removed 100% first year allowances thereby putting more companies into a tax paying position or requiring them to provide for deferred taxation. This change has increased the chances of recovering all the ACT which is paid to the Inland Revenue when companies pay dividends. Also, the Finance Act 1986 eliminated restrictions on the double tax credit (DTR) available for overseas tax suffered on foreign income remitted to the UK. In the past, it was considered that ACT set-off was given priority and, in certain cases, this resulted in loss of the full DTR entitlement that could have otherwise been claimed. Under the new rules, the DTR credit ought to be claimed in priority to ACT set-off thereby maximising the utilisation of the DTR credit available (this treatment is beneficial because unlike surplus ACT, unused DTR entitlements cannot be carried forward). Hence, the debate about which of the net or nil basis is preferable has lost significance since calculations using either basis will, in most cases, produce the same outcome.

SSAP 3 prefers the 'net' basis because it 'takes account of all the relevant facts, including the additional tax liabilities inherent in the dividend policy pursued by the company'.[22] However, the standard does emphasise the desirability of disclosing the EPS on the nil basis whenever it is 'materially' different from that calculated on the net basis.[23] 'Material' is not defined for this purpose but is taken to be 5% or more elsewhere in the standard.[24]

5.6.2 Calculation of nil basis EPS

The example below illustrates the calculation of the nil basis EPS. SSAP 3 states that the variable element of the tax charge referred to above should be adjusted for in calculating EPS on a 'nil' basis.[25] The objective is to arrive at what the earnings would be assuming that the company had *always* pursued a 'nil' distribution policy.

Example 6.5:   Calculation of nil basis EPS

Capital structure

Issued share capital:

45,000,000 Ordinary shares of £1 each
10,000,000 5% Preference shares of £1 each

Trading results

	£'000
Profit on ordinary activities before taxation	6,519
Tax on profit on ordinary activities (Note 1)	916
Profit on ordinary activities after taxation	5,603
Minority interests	72
Profit after taxation and before extraordinary items	5,531
Extraordinary items	(581)
Profit for the financial year attributable to the members of the holding company	4,950
Preference dividends	(500)
Ordinary dividends	(2,301)
Retained profit for the year	2,149

Note 1	
Tax on profit on ordinary activities	
Corporation tax	2,459
Deferred tax	(685)
Overseas taxation	195
Advance corporation tax written back	(983)
Prior year adjustments	(70)
	916

The abnormal tax charge has resulted due to a large ACT write-back in view of changes introduced by a Finance Act.

Included within the ACT write-back is £134,000 relating to preference dividends.

Calculation of EPS

On a net basis:

	£
Profit after taxation and before extraordinary items	5,531,000
Preference dividends	(500,000)
Earnings for equity on a net basis	5,031,000
Number of ordinary shares:	45,000,000

$$\text{Therefore EPS} = \frac{5,031,000}{45,000,000} = 11.18\text{p}$$

On a nil basis:

	£
Earnings for equity on a net basis	5,031,000
Less: ACT written back relating to ordinary dividends	(849,000)
Earnings for equity on a nil basis	4,182,000

$$\text{Therefore EPS} = \frac{4,182,000}{45,000,000} = 9.29\text{p}$$

As this is materially different (16.9%) from the figure for EPS on a net basis, it would be desirable to disclose this figure in the financial statements. It must be emphasised that where EPS is calculated on a nil basis that it is only the ACT written off or written back which relates to the equity shares for which adjustment is made.

One company which discloses EPS on both a net and a nil basis is Carless, Capel & Leonard PLC as shown below:

Extract 6.4: Carless, Capel & Leonard PLC[26]

CONSOLIDATED PROFIT & LOSS ACCOUNT [extract]

	Note	**1988**	1987
Earnings per ordinary share	12		
Earnings after taxation before extraordinary items			
- Net basis		**2.3p**	1.1p
- Nil distribution basis		**2.9p**	1.9p

NOTES ON THE ACCOUNTS [extracts]
All figures are stated in thousands
of pounds except where indicated
8. Tax on profit on ordinary activities

	1988	1987

The tax charge is based on the profit for the year and comprises:

	1988	1987
ACT written-off	**937**	880
Corporation tax (at 35%)	—	43
Overseas tax charge	**7**	—
Deferred PRT charge	**159**	—
Adjustment of corporation tax in respect of prior years	—	(3)
	1,103	920

No corporation tax charge arises due to the availability of tax losses
in group companies

12. Earnings per ordinary share

Earnings per share have been calculated using the following:

	1988	1987
Earnings - net basis	**3,904**	1,298
- nil distribution basis	**4,841**	2,178

The weighted average number of shares in issue during the year was
167.2 million (1987: 115.4 million).

5.7   Other bases

In practice, most companies tend to confine their EPS disclosure to the minimum disclosure requirements prescribed within SSAP 3. However, in view of diversity in accounting practice within certain areas of accounting, some companies give additional EPS disclosures to facilitate fair comparison. For example:

Extract 6.5: British & Commonwealth PLC[27]

Group Profit and Loss Account [extract]

		Notes	1987 £m	1986 £m
EARNINGS per ordinary stock unit		10		
a) **Before goodwill amortisation** -	basic		**22.5p**	**14.8p**
-	fully diluted		**21.2p**	**N/A**
b) After goodwill amortisation -	basic		18.1p	14.8p
-	fully diluted		17.9p	N/A

10. EARNINGS PER ORDINARY STOCK UNIT of 10p

Earnings per ordinary stock unit are calculated on profits before extraordinary items and before amortisation of goodwill and after taxation, minority interests and preference dividends amounting to £73.1 million (1986 - £30.4 million).

Earnings per ordinary stock unit are also calculated in accordance with SSAP 3 on profits before extraordinary items and after amortisation of goodwill, taxation, minority interests and preference dividends amounting to £58.7 million (1986 - £30.4 million).

The weighted average number of ordinary stock units in issue during 1987 was 325,408,452 (1986 - 204,914,455).

Fully diluted earnings per ordinary stock unit are based on adjusted earnings of £91.7 million before goodwill amortisation and £77.3 million after goodwill amortisation and a weighted average number of ordinary stock units of 432,606,286.

Some companies also give disclosure of EPS computed on a different basis than that required by SSAP 3. In most of these cases, an attempt is made to identify earnings attributable to continuing operations, excluding exceptional and extraordinary items, as illustrated in the following extract:

Extract 6.6: Williams Holdings PLC[28]

CONSOLIDATED PROFIT AND LOSS ACCOUNT [extract]

	Notes	1987 £000	1986 £000
Earnings per share excluding exceptional items:	11		
Basic		20.8p	16.5p
Fully diluted		20.4p	15.0p

11. EARNINGS PER SHARE

The directors are of the opinion that it is more meaningful for earnings per share to be calculated before both exceptional and extraordinary items and accordingly it is on this basis that earnings per share are shown on the consolidated profit and loss account. Basic earnings per share are therefore calculated on an adjusted profit of £40,002,000 (1986 £15,407,000) and a weighted average number of ordinary shares in issue during the year of 192,687,000 (1986 93,405,000). Fully diluted earnings per share are calculated on adjusted profits of £41,731,000 (1986 £16,490,000) and a weighted average number of shares of 204,493,000 (1986 109,926,000).

Earnings per share in accordance with SSAP 3, calculated on profits after exceptional items are 21.1p (1986 18.2p). Fully diluted earnings per share on this basis are 20.8p (1986 16.5p). Comparative figures have been adjusted to reflect the capitalisation issue in September 1987.

Although Williams Holdings PLC disclose the EPS required by SSAP 3 in a note to the financial statements, it could be argued that such a treatment is technically not in accordance with the standard as the EPS required by SSAP 3 is not disclosed on the face of the profit and loss account.

We consider that where companies wish to disclose an EPS computed on a different basis from that required by SSAP 3, it is preferable to give equal, if not more, prominence to the EPS required by the standard (see Extract 6.2 above).

For some companies, the conventional method of assessing performance by reference to reported earnings is not an entirely satisfactory basis of assessment. For example, property companies consider the 'net assets per ordinary share' to be a very important and more appropriate performance indicator. In such circumstances, in addition to the requirements of SSAP 3, we believe that it is more meaningful to give disclosure of other performance statistics that are appropriate to assessing the company's performance including an adequate explanation of the basis of calculation.

6   FULLY DILUTED EARNINGS PER SHARE

6.1   The need for fully diluted EPS

As discussed earlier, the basic EPS takes into account only those equity shares in issue that have ranked for dividend in respect of the period. However, a company may have entered into obligations that could dilute the EPS in the future. For example, the company may have in issue at the balance sheet date:

(a)   a separate class of equity shares which do not rank for any dividend in the period under review but which will do so in the future; or

(b)   debentures, loan stock or preference shares convertible into equity shares of the company; or

(c)   outstanding options or warrants to subscribe for equity shares of the company.

A company may also have entered into deferred consideration agreements under which it may be required to issue additional shares at a future date (see 6.3.5 below).

Since investors are concerned not only with past performance but more importantly with forecasting future earnings per share, it is important to disclose the effect of any future dilution. This can be achieved by adjusting the basic EPS for the effects of all such dilutive effects to give a fully diluted EPS.

The need for fully diluted EPS arises because companies can use convertible securities to achieve illusory growth in basic EPS. Consider a company that has used convertible loan stock or convertible preference shares to finance an acquisition or expansion. These securities usually carry a low fixed interest or dividend coupon rate due to the presence of a compensatory factor, the conversion privilege. It is therefore possible to boost basic EPS so long as the incremental post-tax finance cost is covered and current performance is sustained. However, examination of the underlying trend in the fully diluted EPS figures will reveal a more 'real' growth in earnings so far as concerns existing equity shareholders since an attempt is made to reflect the ultimate 'cost' of using convertible securities to finance growth in earnings.

6.2   Disclosure of fully diluted EPS

In each of the circumstances noted above SSAP 3 requires that the fully diluted EPS should be calculated and disclosure of both the fully diluted EPS and the basic EPS on the face of the profit and loss account is required unless:

(a)   the dilution is less than 5% of the basic EPS;[29] or

(b)   the fully diluted EPS is greater than the basic EPS;[30] or

(c)   the basic EPS is negative.[31]

Whenever the fully diluted EPS is shown, the basis of the calculation should also be disclosed. Furthermore, the fully diluted EPS should be disclosed as prominently as the basic EPS.[32] One company which gives particularly good disclosure of their fully diluted EPS (even though the dilution does not meet the criteria referred to in (a) above and, therefore, need not have been disclosed) is Wm Morrison Supermarkets plc as illustrated below:

Extract 6.7: Wm Morrison Supermarkets plc[33]

Consolidated profit and loss account [extract]

	Notes	1988	1987
Earnings per share	11	17.16p	14.37p
Fully diluted	12	17.12p	14.27p

11. Earnings per share

The calculation of earnings per share is based on the profit after taxation (but before extraordinary items) less the preference dividend, £16,011,000 (1987 £13,353,000) and a weighted average of 93,285,000 (1987 92,894,000) shares in issue throughout the year.

12. Fully diluted earnings per share

The calculation of fully diluted earnings per share is based on the profit on ordinary activities after taxation, and after adjusting for the proceeds from the exercise of options being invested in $2\frac{1}{2}\%$ consolidated stock, of £16,969,000 (1987 £13,519,000), and the following number of ordinary shares.

	1988 000's	1987 000's
Weighted average of ordinary shares in issue throughout the year	93,285	92,894
Weighted average of convertible preference shares presuming full conversion at the rate of 28 ordinary shares for each 100 convertible preference shares	3,901	—
Number of ordinary shares on option at the beginning of the financial period and also at the end	1,387	1,166
Weighted average of options granted during the year	569	660
	99,142	94,720

The standard states that the fully diluted EPS for the corresponding period should not be shown unless the assumptions on which it was based still apply.[34] Unfortunately, the standard does not give examples of such 'assumptions' but typically, these include the terms of the conversion rights of convertible stockholders, conditions determining the number of equity shares to be issued at a future date pursuant to a deferred consideration agreement etc. The justification provided for this position is that investors are primarily concerned with future dilution based on current facts and comparatives for corresponding periods become meaningless unless the assumptions inherent in the fully diluted calculation remain unchanged. However, a strict literal interpretation of the recommendation conflicts with the purpose of including comparatives in financial statements. It is our view that disclosure of comparative fully diluted EPS figures should be made notwithstanding changes in assumptions inherent in its calculation in subsequent years.

6.3   Calculation of fully diluted EPS

Fully diluted EPS should be calculated on the assumption that the conversion rights or options to subscribe had been exercised in full on the first day of the accounting period[35] or the date of issue of the securities giving rise to the rights or options if later, in which case a weighted average calculation should be performed.

6.3.1   *Equity shares with future dividend entitlement*

If there is a class of equity capital not yet ranking for dividend but which will do so in the future, the number of shares used in the basic EPS calculation will be increased at some future date. However, since there will be no inflow of funds to the company accompanying the change in dividend rights, aggregate earnings would not be affected. Fully diluted EPS is therefore calculated using the same earnings figure but on the assumption that the shares ranked for dividend from the beginning of the period or date of their issue if later.[36]

Example 6.6:   Simple fully diluted EPS calculation

Capital structure

Issued share capital as at December 31, 19X1:
£200,000 'A' ordinary shares of 50 pence each.

On July 1, 19X2 the company issued 80,000 'B' ordinary shares which will not rank for dividend until 19X5 whence they will have the same dividend rights as the 'A' ordinary shares.

Trading results

Profit for equity shareholders after taxation:

	£
Year ending December 31, 19X1	55,000
Year ending December 31, 19X2	74,000

Calculation of basic EPS

	19X2	19X1
Earnings	74,000	55,000
Number of equity shares ranking for dividend	400,000	400,000
Basic EPS =	18.5p	13.75p

Calculation of fully diluted EPS

Number of shares	19X2	19X1
'A' ordinary	400,000	400,000
New issue 80,000 'B' ordinary x 6/12	40,000	—
	440,000	400,000

Fully diluted EPS	74,000	Same as
	440,000	basic EPS

$$= \quad 16.82p$$

The fully diluted EPS indicates a dilution of 9.08% of the basic EPS which would be 'material'. No comparative would be required in this case because the company did not have any obligations which would have diluted the EPS.

6.3.2 Convertible securities

In order to permit a lower rate of interest, companies sometimes attach benefits to loan stock or debentures in the form of conversion rights. These permit the stockholder to convert his holdings in whole or part into equity capital. The right is normally exercisable between specified dates. The ultimate conversion of the loan stock will have the following effects:

(a) there will be an increase in earnings by the amount of the loan stock interest no longer payable. Because this interest is allowable for corporation tax purposes, the effect on earnings will be net of corporation tax relief;

(b) the number of shares ranking for dividend will increase. The fully diluted EPS should be calculated assuming that the loan stock is converted into the maximum possible number of shares.

Example 6.7:   Treatment of convertible loan stock in fully diluted EPS calculations

Assuming no conversion occurs during the year:

Capital structure

Issued share capital at December 31, 19X1:
1,000,000 ordinary shares of £1 each

Since January 1, 19X0, there has been £200,000 of 10% convertible loan stock in issue. The terms of conversion are, for every 100 nominal value of loan stock:

On	March 31, 19X1	115 ordinary shares
	March 31, 19X2	120 ordinary shares
	March 31, 19X3	125 ordinary shares
	March 31, 19X4	130 ordinary shares

Trading results

	19X1	19X0
Profit for equity shareholders after taxation	250,000	175,000

Corporation tax for both periods is 35%
Income tax is 25%.

The company has surplus ACT carried forward as at December 31, 19X1 which has been written off as irrecoverable.

Calculation of basic EPS

		19X1	19X0
Earnings		250,000	175,000
Number of equity shares ranking for dividend		1,000,000	1,000,000
Basic EPS	=	25p	17.5p

Calculation of fully diluted EPS

Impact on earnings:

	19X1	19X0
	£	£
Profit for basic EPS	250,000	175,000
Add: Interest saved	20,000	20,000
Less: Corporation tax relief*	(2,000)	(2,000)
Adjusted earnings for equity	268,000	193,000

* Corporation tax relief is after writing back irrecoverable ACT. Just as a reminder, the maximum set-off of ACT against corporation tax for any year is the amount of ACT that would have been payable in respect of a dividend equal to the taxable profits for that year.

Number of equity shares if loan stock was converted:

	19X1	19X0
Number of equity shares for basic EPS	1,000,000	1,000,000
On conversion 200,000 x $\frac{120}{100}$	240,000	230,000*
Adjusted capital	1,240,000	1,230,000

* At December 31, 19X0 the conversion terms were 115 shares for every £100 of loan stock.

It should be noted that even though it is assumed that the shares have been in issue throughout the year any conversion terms during the year are not relevant if the stockholders did not take advantage of the opportunity to convert. The maximum number of shares that could be issued in the future as determined at the balance sheet date should be used in the fully diluted EPS calculation irrespective of whether, by the time the financial statements are finalised, the amount of loan stock actually converted at the next conversion date is known.

Fully diluted EPS		268,000	193,000
		1,240,000	1,230,000
	=	21.61p	15.69p

Note that the fully diluted EPS comparative has been disclosed even though the assumptions (namely the conversion terms) on which last year's computation was based no longer apply.

Partial conversion during the year:

Where part of the loan stock is converted during the current accounting period, provided the new shares rank for dividend, the weighted average of shares in issue during the year should be used in the calculation of the basic EPS.

When calculating the fully diluted EPS, the maximum number of shares in issue and issuable at the end of the accounting period must take into account the stock still to be converted.

Final conversion during the year:

Similar considerations to those outlined above for a partial conversion will apply on final conversion. However, unless the conversion takes place on the first day of the current year in which case the shares issued would therefore have ranked for dividend for *the full year*, the fully diluted EPS should be shown for the current year, if material.[37]

This recommendation is consistent with the objective of the fully diluted EPS calculation, namely to disclose any material dilution in future earnings per share. The fully diluted EPS figure calculated in this instance will give an indication of next year's basic EPS, assuming no earnings growth and no changes in equity share capital.

The rules for convertible preference shares are very similar to those detailed above in the case of loan stock, i.e. the dividend is added back to earnings and the maximum number of ordinary shares that could be issued on conversion should be used in the calculation. Irrecoverable ACT which has been written off as part of the tax charge for the year and relates to preference share dividends would have to be added back to earnings when calculating the fully diluted EPS.

One company which discloses fully diluted EPS as a result of, *inter alia*, convertible loan stock is Pentos plc as indicated below:

Extract 6.8: Pentos plc[38]

CONSOLIDATED PROFIT AND LOSS ACCOUNT [extract]

NOTES		**1987**	1986
9	Earnings per ordinary share of 10p	**9.20p**	7.67p
9	Fully diluted earnings per ordinary share of 10p	**7.20p**	5.73p

NOTES TO THE ACCOUNTS

9   EARNINGS PER ORDINARY SHARE

The calculation of basic earnings per ordinary share is based on profit before extraordinary items, after deducting preference dividends, of £6,388,000 (1986 — £4,432,000) and on 69,401,414 (1986 — 57,840,573) ordinary shares, the weighted average number of ordinary shares in issue and ranking for dividend during the year. The fully diluted earnings per ordinary share is based on 95,147,765 (1986 — 83,020,012) ordinary shares and adjusted earnings of £6,858,000(1986 — £4,758,000) on the following assumptions:

(a)   The options referred to in note 19 had been exercised on 1 January 1987 and the proceeds had been invested in 2.5% Consols.

(b)   One deferred share equals two ordinary shares (see note 19).

(c)   The convertible unsecured loan stock had been converted on 1 January 1987 on the basis disclosed in note 17 to the accounts with a consequent saving on interest payments.

17   CREDITORS [extract]

(a)   Holders of both series of the 13½% Convertible Unsecured Loan Stock 1990 have an option to convert their stock into fully paid ordinary shares of the company during a specified period of one month in any of the years 1988 to 1990 inclusive at the rate of 50p nominal of ordinary share capital for every 300p nominal of stock converted in respect of £1,000,000 of the stock and 40p nominal of ordinary share capital for every 300p nominal of stock converted in respect of the £516,011 Series A stock.

The company may, subject to certain conditions and provided that not less than 75% of the stock has already been converted, convert the whole of the outstanding stock on the basis outlined above. On the company giving notice of such an intention any stockholder may elect, in lieu of conversion, to have his stock repaid at par.

All stock not previously purchased by the company or converted will be redeemed at par on 31 December 1990.

19   SHARE CAPITAL [extract]

ALLOTMENTS DURING YEAR

On 30 June 1987, the annual conversion date of the 13½% Convertible Unsecured Loan Stock 1990 (Series A), conversion notices had been received from holders of £21,345 of the loan stock. On 1 July 1987 28,460 ordinary shares of 10p each were issued in respect of the conversion and the loan stock was cancelled.

On 9 June 1987 3,190,662 ordinary shares of 10p each were placed by Kitkat & Aitken & Co with their investment clients at a price of 128.5p per share, the ruling market price at the time being 134p per share. The shares were placed in order to finance the purchase by the group of a freehold property in Oxford.

During the year executives exercised their options to subscribe for shares under the share option schemes approved by shareholders in 1975 and 1985, as adjusted for the rights issue in 1986. 165,791 ordinary shares of 10p each and 92,893 deferred ordinary shares of 20p each were issued for cash. A further 576 ordinary shares of 10p each were issued following the exercise of options under the savings related share option scheme approved by shareholders in 1986.

Wm Morrison Supermarkets plc is an example of a company which discloses fully diluted EPS as a result of, *inter alia*, convertible preference shares (see Extract 6.7 in 6.2 above).

6.3.3 *Options or warrants to subscribe for equity shares*

Companies may grant options to directors and senior executives or issue warrants which give holders (not usually employees) the right to subscribe for shares at fixed prices on specified future dates. If the options or warrants are exercised then:

(a) the shares ranking for dividend will be increased; and

(b) funds will flow into the company and these will produce income.

As it is not possible to estimate the earnings which these proceeds will generate, SSAP 3 requires that it is to be assumed that the new funds are invested on the first day of the accounting period in $2\frac{1}{2}$% Consolidated Stock.[39] This notional income (net of corporation tax) is then used to compute adjusted earnings for the fully diluted EPS calculation. The price of $2\frac{1}{2}$% Consolidated Stock can be found in the Financial Times. If the price is £25, this indicates a yield of 10%.

As in the case of convertible stocks, it should be assumed that the maximum number of new shares had been issued under the terms of the options or warrants and that these had been exercised on the first day of the period or the date of issue if later.[40] Similar considerations to those described in 6.3.2 above apply on final subscriptions in the case of options or warrants to subscribe.

Example 6.8:   Treatment of share options in fully diluted EPS calculations

Capital structure

Issued share capital for both years ending December 31, 19X1 and 19X2:
100,000 ordinary shares of 25p each.

Options have been granted to the directors and certain senior executives giving them the right to subscribe for ordinary shares between 19X6 and 19X8 at 90 pence per share.

Options outstanding at	December 31, 19X1	40,000
	December 31, 19X2	50,000
The price of $2\frac{1}{2}$% Consols	December 31, 19X0	£25.00
	December 31, 19X1	£20.83

Trading results

Profit for equity shareholders after taxation:

Year ending December 31, 19X1	£60,000
Year ending December 31, 19X2	£70,000

Assume corporation tax at 35%.

Calculation of basic EPS

		19X2	19X1
Earnings		70,000	60,000
Number of equity shares ranking for dividend	=	400,000	400,000
	=	17.5p	15p

Calculation of fully diluted EPS

Impact of conversion on earnings:

	19X2 £	19X1 £
Profit for basic EPS	70,000	60,000
Notional income on proceeds of options issuable		
(50,000 @ 90p) x 12%*	5,400	—
(40,000 @ 90p) x 10%	—	3,600
Less taxation thereon (35%)	(1,890)	(1,260)
Adjusted earnings for equity	73,510	62,340

$$* \text{ The market yield on the } 2\tfrac{1}{2}\% \text{ Consols} = \frac{2.5}{20.83} \times 100 = 12\%$$

Number of equity shares after exercise of options:

	19X2 No	19X1 No
Number of equity shares for basic EPS	400,000	400,000
Maximum issuable	50,000	40,000
Adjusted capital	450,000	440,000

		19X2	19X1
Fully diluted EPS	=	73,510	62,340
		450,000	440,000
	=	16.34p	14.17p

In the above example, the dilution in 19X2 is sufficiently material (6.63%) to require disclosure of fully diluted EPS. In our view the comparative figure of 14.17p should also be disclosed even though the assumptions on which it was based no longer apply (i.e. the yield on the $2\tfrac{1}{2}\%$ consols is no longer 10%).

6.3.4 *Fully diluted EPS calculations involving more than one type of potentially dilutive security*

Companies may have more than one type of convertible debenture or loan stock (or preference shares) in issue with differing conversion rights, or may also have issued shares to rank for dividend in a future period or have granted warrants or options to subscribe. In these situations, the fully diluted EPS should take into account only those 'convertibles' or shares or options or warrants which would have a diluting effect on the basic earnings per share and disregard those which do not have a diluting effect.[41] Hence, when performing the fully diluted EPS calculation in such cases, the effect of each potentially dilutive security on the basic EPS should be considered first so as to establish whether inclusion in the 'cumulative' fully diluted EPS calculation is warranted.

6.3.5 Deferred consideration agreements

Some agreements drawn up for the sale and purchase of businesses call for additional consideration to be paid in the future in the event that certain conditions are fulfilled. The agreement may require that the additional consideration should be satisfied by the issue of further equity. Such arrangements could lead to future dilution in EPS.

SSAP 3 does not specifically address the implications of deferred consideration clauses on EPS calculations and disclosure in financial statements. The guidance given below is based on guidelines contained in the US standard on earnings per share.[42] Since these guidelines are consistent with the objective of disclosing fully diluted EPS, we recommend their use in the UK.

Not surprisingly, the conditions that determine the amounts of 'additional consideration' payable differ from agreement to agreement. However, in general, they involve either:

(a)   future levels of earnings: or

(b)   the share price of the issuing company at future dates; or

(c)   mixture of both future earnings and future prices of the shares.

A   Earnings conditions

In general, earnings conditions that determine the additional number of shares to be issued require either:

(a)   the *maintenance* of current or a higher level of earnings over a certain period (the 'earn-out' period); or

(b)   the *attainment* of progressively higher levels of earnings over the earn-out period.

The conditions may apply either to each year individually within that period or on a cumulative or average basis. Some agreements specify a minimum and/or a maximum number of shares to be issued (regardless of earnings) and could specify whether equity shares (to be issued in satisfaction of the additional consideration due) are issued each year or in total, at the end of the earn-out period.

If such deferred consideration agreements have been outstanding during the year, the effect of additional equity shares that may have to be issued in the future should be taken into account when calculating fully diluted EPS but only if it has a diluting effect. This will mean that if the earnings condition requires the maintenance or attainment of a higher level of earnings, earnings should be adjusted to reflect the increase required by the particular condition. In the case where different levels of earnings are specified, the level that would result in the largest potential dilution should be used. Naturally, where the agreement has specified a minimum and/or maximum number of shares to be issued, the number of additional shares to be issued computed in accordance with the earnings conditions would have to lie within the specified range.

Where additional consideration is satisfied in the form of equity shares issued after the period end, such shares should be considered in the basic EPS calculation for that period (since the profits which triggered the issue relate to that period) if they rank for any dividend in respect of that period. Previously reported fully diluted EPS data should not be restated to give retrospective effect to shares actually issued as a result of attainment of specified increased earnings levels or other earnings conditions. However, if shares previously considered outstanding become unissuable (because of a decline of earnings or because the higher earnings levels are not attained), previously reported fully diluted EPS should be restated once the earn-out period has elapsed and no additional consideration is found to be necessary.

B   Share price conditions

In some agreements, the acquiring company (the issuing company) will give future share price guarantees. For example, the company may guarantee that its share price will increase to some stated amount or, alternatively, will not decrease below some stated amount within some time period. To the extent that the share price moves contrary to the guarantee, the issuer would have to issue additional shares or pay cash at a future date to make up the difference.

Where the additional consideration has to be satisfied by an issue of additional shares, the fully diluted EPS should reflect the number of shares potentially issuable based on the share price at the year end. The comparative fully diluted EPS figures should be restated if the number of shares issued or contingently issuable subsequently changes because of changes in the share price.

C   Conditions involving both future earnings and future share prices

Under the terms of some agreements, the number of shares contingently issuable (additional consideration) may depend on both future earnings and future prices of the shares. In such cases, the number of shares which would be issuable in the future should be estimated and included in the fully diluted EPS calculation (if the arrangement has a diluting effect on EPS). The estimated number of shares should be based on both conditions, i.e. the share price at the year end and earnings to date as of the end of each period reported on. If the number of shares issued or contingently issuable subsequently changes from the number of shares previously included in past fully diluted EPS calculations, the comparative fully diluted EPS data should be restated.

Financial reporting practice in this whole area is in general quite poor. We recommend full disclosure of the potential impact on EPS of any outstanding deferred consideration agreements. For example:

Extract 6.9: Lanca PLC[43]

Consolidated Profit and Loss Account [extract]

	Note	**1987** £	1986 £
Earnings per ordinary share	10		
Basic		**5.65p**	3.01p
Fully diluted		**4.85p**	2.66p

Notes to the Financial statements

10. Earnings per share
Basic
The calculation of earnings per share is based on earnings on £605,922 (1986 - £323,331) divided by the weighted average number of shares in issue during the year of 10,731,661 (1986 - 10,728,572)
Fully diluted
The fully diluted earnings per share assumes that:
(i)   the maximum deferred consideration as defined in note 18 will be payable on the acquisition of Frankel and Roth (International) Limited and that, including any shares to be issued way of vendor placing, 1,719,047 additional shares will be issued, determined by reference to an average mid-market price of 70p per share.
(ii)   The options relating to 440,000 shares referred to in note 18 are fully taken up.
(iii)   The shares referred to in (i) and (ii) above have been in issue during the whole of 1987 and the previous year, giving a theoretical weighted average number of shares of 12,890,708 (1986 - 12,887,619).

18. Called up share capital [extract]
Deferred consideration:
Under the terms of the agreement for the acquisition of Frankel and Roth (International) Limited, further consideration of up to a maximum of £1,140,000 (based on the profits for the two years to 31st December 1988) may be payable to the vendors.
Any deferred consideration due under that agreement will be payable in two stages on 31st May 1988 and 31st May 1989 or, if later, within 21 days of the relevant pre-tax profits for the respective financial years being determined and will be settled as to half in cash (to be satisfied by a vendor placing of the company's shares) and as to the remainder in shares. The number of shares to be issued, if any (excluding any shares issued by way of vendor placing) will be determined by reference to 90% of the average mid-market price of the company's shares as quoted in the Daily Official List of the Stock Exchange in London during the three months prior to the relevant payment date.

In the above illustration, it appears that the only adjustment that has been made to the earnings figure used in the fully diluted EPS calculation relates to the income on the proceeds from the exercise of the options.

7   COMPARISON WITH US PRONOUNCEMENTS

The American Institute of Certified Public Accountants (AICPA) have issued several statements on earnings per share. The principal statement, APB Opinion No. 15 — *Earnings per Share* — was published in May 1969 and requires the calculation of two earnings per share figures, the primary EPS and the fully diluted EPS.

7.1   The primary EPS

The calculation of primary EPS is similar to that of the basic EPS except that it is based upon not only outstanding shares of common stock (i.e. ordinary shares) but also other securities which are in substance 'common stock equivalents' and have a dilutive effect on the basic EPS.

APB 15 describes a 'common stock equivalent' as 'a security which is not, in form, a common stock but which usually contains provisions to enable its holder to become a common stockholder and which, because of its terms and the circumstances under which it was issued, is in substance equivalent to a common stock'.[44] The key test of equivalency is whether the security or right gives the holder an expectation of sharing in increases in the value of the common stock. Hence, options and warrants are always common stock equivalents. Tests have been devised for identifying other securities that should be regarded as common stock equivalents. These tests have to be carried out at the time the security is issued and based on conditions at the time of issuance. For instance, a convertible security should be considered to be a common stock equivalent if, at the time of issuance, it has an effective yield of less than $66^2/_3\%$ of the then current average Aa corporate bond yield[45] (i.e. average yields on bonds of equal quality to these rated Aa by Moody's or Standard & Poor's) or where the convertible security is sold/issued outside the US, the most comparable long-term yield in the country of issue. The classification of a security as a common stock equivalent remains unchanged as long as that security is outstanding.

Because of the 'quasi-equity' nature of common stock equivalents and the greater likelihood that holders of such securities will exercise their rights to convert, the US standard states that it would be misleading to calculate a basic EPS figure leaving them out. However, common stock equivalents that, in aggregate, dilute basic EPS by less than 3% need not be taken into consideration.[46]

Except in certain cases (see paragraph 37 and 38 of APB 15), where the conversion of the common stock equivalent causes an inflow of resources into the company (e.g. on the exercise of an option), APB 15 requires the use of the 'treasury stock' method when calculating the primary EPS.[47] Under this method, the exercise of the option is assumed to occur at the beginning of the period or at the time of issue if later. Shares of common stock are assumed to be issued and the proceeds received on the exercise of the option are assumed to be used to purchase the company's own shares at the 'exercise' date using an average price for the period. The difference between the number of shares of common stock assumed to be issued on exercise of the option and those which are assumed to be purchased back by the company is added to the number of shares in issue to get the denominator for the primary EPS calculation. Note that unlike SSAP 3, there is no adjustment to the earnings figure using this method.

7.2   Fully diluted EPS

The purpose of the fully diluted EPS is to show the maximum potential dilution of the basic EPS. Hence, it will include the dilutive effects of convertibles which were not classified as current stock equivalents in the calculation of primary EPS. The method of calculation is similar to that used in calculating the primary EPS except that the treasury stock calculations are based upon share prices ruling at the end of the period.

7.3 Disclosure

EPS data should be disclosed prominently on the face of the profit and loss account. Such data should be presented for:

- income from continuing operations;[48]
- income before extraordinary items;[49]
- the cumulative effect of a change in accounting principle;[50] and
- net income.[51]

The bases on which primary and fully diluted EPS have been calculated should be disclosed in a footnote to the financial statements. This disclosure should include, inter alia, the identification of common stock equivalents and all the assumptions used.[52] The following illustrates the disclosure of primary earnings per share data required by APB 15 (to be presented at the bottom of the income statement). A similar level of disclosure will also be appropriate for fully diluted EPS.

	19X2	19X1
Earnings per common share and common equivalent share, primary (Note 8):		
Income (loss) from continuing operations	$4.18	$3.01
Income (loss) from discontinued operation	(.19)	2.27
Extraordinary item — bond redemption	—	(.13)
(Loss) from cumulative prior years' effect of change in accounting for income taxes	(.31)	—
Net income per common share of stock	$3.68	$5.15

Notes to consolidated financial statements

Note 8   Earnings per common share

Primary earnings per common share are based on the weighted average number of shares outstanding during the period plus common stock equivalents consisting of shares subject to stock options. The primary weighted average number of common shares outstanding was 31.8 million and 36.6 million for the years ending March 31, 19X1 and March 31, 19X2 respectively. Primary earnings per common share are also adjusted for dividend requirements on preferred stocks.

References

1   D. Waller, 'Shares in stores sector hit by accounting move', *Financial Times*, June 25, 1987.
2   SSAP 3, *Earnings per share*, Revised August 1974, para. 10.
3   CA 85, s 744.
4   SSAP 3, para. 14.
5   *Ibid.*, para. 5.
6   Vickers P.L.C., Report and Accounts 1987, pp. 26 and 32.
7   SSAP 3, Appendix 1, para. 10.
8   Blue Circle Industries PLC, Report & Accounts 1987, pp. 12 and 17.
9   *Ibid.*, Appendix 1, para. 18.
10 S. G. Warburg Group plc, Annual Report 31st March 1988, pp. 39 and 47.
11 Ibid., Appendix 1, para. 11.
12 CICA *Handbook*, Section 3500, para. 38—40.
13 APB 15, *Earnings per Share*, AICPA, May 1969, para. 22.
14 SSAP 14, *Group accounts*, September 1978, para. 32.
15 A 'vendor placing with clawback' is where the existing shareholders of the offeror company
    are given the opportunity to acquire the new shares on a pro-rata basis to their current holding
    but, unlike vendor rights, the shareholders do not receive renouncable allotment letters which
    can be sold in the market.
16 SSAP 3, Appendix 2, para. 1.
17 *Ibid.*, Appendix 1, para. 4.
18 *Ibid.*, Appendix 1, para. 6.
19 *Ibid.*, Appendix 1, para. 7.
20 *Ibid.*, Appendix 1, para. 10.
21 *Ibid.*, para. 8.
22 *Ibid.*
23 *Ibid.*, para. 9.
24 *Ibid.*, para. 16.
25 *Ibid.*, para. 12.
26 Carless, Capel & Leonard PLC, Report and Accounts 1988, pp. 26, 34 and 35.
27 British & Commonwealth PLC, Annual Report 1987, pp. 33 and 44.
28 Williams Holdings PLC, Annual Report 1987, pp. 30 and 36.
29 SSAP 3, para. 16.
30 *Ibid.*, Appendix 1, para. 27.
31 *Ibid.*, Appendix 1, para. 24.
32 *Ibid.*, para. 16.
33 Wm Morrison Supermarkets plc, Report and Financial Statements 1988, pp. 8 and 13.
34 SSAP 3, para. 16.
35 *Ibid.*, Appendix 1, para. 22.
36 *Ibid.*, Appendix 1, para. 29.
37 *Ibid.*, Appendix 1, para. 33.
38 Pentos plc, Annual Report and Accounts 1987, pp. 24, 31, 36 and 37.
39 SSAP 3, Appendix 1, para. 31.
40 *Ibid.*
41 *Ibid.*, Appendix 1, para. 27.
42 APB 15, Appendix A, paras. 61—65 and AIN-APB 15, *Computing Earnings per Share:
    Accounting Interpretations of APB Opinion No. 15*, AICPA, July 1970, paras. 88—91.
43 Lanca PLC, Annual report 1987, pp. 12, 18 and 21.
44 APB 15, para. 25.
45 SFAS 85, *Yield Test for Determining whether a Convertible Security is a Common Stock
    Equivalent*, FASB, March 1985, para. 3.
46 APB 15, para. 14.
47 *Ibid.*, para. 36.

48 APB 30, *Reporting the Results of Operations—Reporting the Effects of Disposal of a Segment of a Business, and Extraordinary, Unusual and Infrequently Occurring Events and Transactions,* AICPA, June 1973, para. 9.

49 APB 15, para. 13.

50 APB 20, *Accounting Changes,* AICPA, July 1971, para. 20.

51 APB 30, para. 12.

52 APB 15, paras. 20—21.

Chapter 7

Taxation

1 GENERAL PRINCIPLES

1.1 The nature of taxation

A discussion of how to deal with taxation in financial statements must begin with some consideration of what it is that is to be accounted for. Although it might be supposed that this is a simple question, and that taxation is a business expense to be dealt with in the same manner as any other cost, it has certain characteristics which set it apart from other costs and which might justify a different treatment. These characteristics include the fact that tax payments are not made in exchange for any goods or services and the fact that the business has no say in whether or not the payments are to be made. It is held by some that these elements mean that taxation is more in the nature of a distribution than an expense; in essence that the government is a stakeholder in the success of the business and participates in its results (generally in priority to other stakeholders).

The validity of this suggestion rather depends on what view is taken as to the purpose of financial statements and the nature of the reporting entity. It is consistent with a perspective which is sometimes adopted that business entities have an existence which is independent from that of their shareholders, and should account not simply to their legal owners but to all those with an economic interest in their activities.

Adoption of the 'distribution' view of taxation would render irrelevant most of the accounting questions which follow; these are generally to do with how to allocate taxation expense to accounting periods. If taxation were regarded as a distribution, however, the question of allocation would not arise, since distributions are generally not allocated to accounting periods in the same way as is done for items of expense.

It is fair to say, however, that the 'distribution' view of taxation is not generally adopted in practice, although some of the accounting approaches that are still proposed to deal with certain issues have their roots within it. For all practical purposes, taxation is dealt with as an expense of the business, and the accounting rules which have been developed are based on that premise.

1.2   Allocation between periods

1.2.1   Background

The most significant accounting question which arises in relation to taxation is how to allocate the tax expense between accounting periods. The recognition of trading transactions in the financial statements relating to a particular year is governed primarily by the application of generally accepted accounting principles, and to a certain extent by the impact of company law. However, the timing of recognition of transactions for the purposes of measuring the taxable profit is governed by the application of tax law, which in some cases follows different rules from those under which the financial statements are drawn up. It is necessary to seek some reconciliation between these different sets of rules in order to apply a matching approach to the allocation of tax expense to accounting periods, and this is where the concept of deferred taxation is brought into use.

The differences between the profit as calculated for accounting and for taxation purposes can be analysed into two categories, 'permanent differences' and 'timing differences'. The former comprises those items of income which are not taxable, or items of expense which are not deductible, and which therefore do not appear in the tax computation of any period; the latter represent items of income or expenditure which *are* either taxable or deductible against tax, but in periods different from those in which they are dealt with in the financial statements. Timing differences therefore arise when items of income and expenditure enter into the measurement of profit for both accounting and taxation purposes, but in different accounting periods. They are said to 'originate' in the first of these periods and 'reverse' in one or more subsequent periods; examples of these are given in 1.2.3 below. Deferred taxation is the taxation which relates to timing differences.

1.2.2   Permanent differences

A permanent difference can arise in two main ways under the UK tax system:

(a)   where non-taxable income is included in the accounting profit, for example if certain government grant income is received; and

(b)   where certain types of expenditure are charged against accounting profit but not allowed as an expense against taxable profit, for example if charitable donations are made, or if depreciation is charged against fixed assets for which there is no corresponding tax deduction.

It is generally accepted that there is no need to adjust the financial statements for permanent differences. The transaction giving rise to the permanent difference is accounted for in accordance with generally accepted principles and has no tax effect. Although the tax charge for the year in which the item is reported in the financial statements will deviate from the charge which would have been expected if the normal tax rate had been applied to the reported profits, this is not a distortion of the charge, which requires to be corrected in any way; indeed, any 'correction' would introduce such a distortion.

1.2.3 Timing differences

A timing difference can arise in a number of ways:

(a) income is included in the financial statements but recognised in taxable profit in later years, for example bank interest receivable would be accrued in the financial statements but only taxed in the period in which it was actually received;

(b) income may be included in taxable profit in a year earlier than it is recognised in the financial statements, for example interest might be received in advance and therefore be taxed before it was treated as earned in the financial statements;

(c) expenditure or losses in the financial statements might not be deductible in arriving at taxable profit until a later period, for example a general bad debt provision could be charged in the financial statements, but a tax deduction given only when the specific bad debt charge was known;

(d) expenditure or losses might be deducted from taxable income prior to their being charged against accounting profit, for example research and development expenditure might be allowed as an immediate deduction against tax, but capitalised in the financial statements and amortised over its useful life.

The common characteristic of all timing differences is the fact that the period in which the accounting effect of the transaction is recognised is different to the period in which the transaction falls to be taxed or deducted against taxable profit. The tax benefit or cost associated with such differences always reverses in future periods.

Timing differences are sometimes split into two categories, short-term and other. A short-term timing difference is one which arises because an item is treated on a cash basis for tax purposes whereas the accruals concept is used in the financial statements; it usually reverses within a year of its origination (hence the name), although each reversal is often followed by replacement by a new, originating difference. A typical example of a short-term timing difference is interest payable, where a timing difference will originate in respect of a year end accrual for interest due but unpaid. This gives rise to a timing difference because, although the financial statements have reported the charge against profits, the tax computation allows a deduction for interest paid, but no deduction for interest accrued.

The most common form of 'other' (i.e. other than 'short-term') timing difference is created by the effect of capital allowances and the charge for depreciation. Capital allowances are the amounts by which fixed assets may be written down to arrive at taxable profit, and are therefore the tax equivalent of the charge for depreciation in the financial statements. Since they are deducted from profit to arrive at the taxable profit, the amount charged in the financial statements for depreciation is always disallowed in the tax computation. Usually, because capital allowances might be given to provide some economic incentive for businesses to invest, the tax allowance will be given at a faster rate than the rate at which depreciation is charged in the financial statements, and the timing differences created are thus sometimes referred to as '*accelerated* capital allowances'.

A timing difference arises since both the charge for depreciation and the capital allowance (after an adjustment for a balancing charge or allowance) will reduce the cost of the asset to its recoverable amount at the end of its useful life, but the sums charged against accounting profit and against taxable profit, although the same in total, are likely to differ in each year. An example will illustrate the impact:

Example 7.1:   Illustration of timing differences

An item of plant and machinery is purchased in 1987 for £48,000 and is estimated to have a seven year useful life, at the end of which it is estimated that it will be sold for £6,000. The depreciation charge will therefore be £6,000 p.a. (£48,000 — £6,000 over seven years).

The rate of capital allowance for plant and machinery is 25% p.a. on a reducing balance basis.

The timing differences will arise as follows (all figures in £'000):

	1987	1988	1989	1990	1991	1992	1993
Financial statements							
Carrying value of asset	48	42	36	30	24	18	12
Depreciation charge	6	6	6	6	6	6	6
Written down value	42	36	30	24	18	12	6
Tax computation							
Carrying value of asset	48	36	27	20	15	11	8
Capital allowance	12	9	7	5	4	3	2
Tax written down value	36	27	20	15	11	8	6
Timing difference arising							
Charge in accounts	6	6	6	6	6	6	6
Allowed in tax computation	12	9	7	5	4	3	2
Originating/(reversing)	6	3	1	(1)	(2)	(3)	(4)

The table shows that there is an originating difference of £6,000 p.a. in the first year, but this progressively diminishes and eventually reverses in subsequent years. For each of the first three years of the asset's life, the tax currently assessed (and hence the amount provided in the financial statements as the current year tax charge for those years) is lower than the tax that will eventually fall to be paid on the profit reported in the financial statements. The difference reverses from year four onwards, when the tax allowances have fallen below the level of the depreciation charge. The tax assessed (and hence the amount provided in the financial statements as the current year tax charge for those years) will be higher than the sum due on the profit reported in the financial statements.

The timing differences may be looked at either in terms of the profit and loss account or the balance sheet, and correspondingly computed in either of two ways. The timing difference arising in any year may be determined by comparing the depreciation provided in the financial statements with the capital allowance given in the tax computation:

Computation of the timing difference	1987 £'000	1988 £'000
Depreciation per financial statements	6	6
Capital allowances	12	9
Originating timing difference	6	3

Or the cumulative timing difference may be computed by comparing the written down value of the asset in the financial statements with its written down value in the capital allowance computation:

Computation of the cumulative timing difference	1987 £'000	1988 £'000
Written down value per financial statements	42	36
Written down value per tax computation	36	27
Cumulative timing difference	6	9

The computation of the total timing differences in existence at any point in time is essentially a mathematical exercise. It is after this point that the picture becomes less clear, and different points of view arise as to:

(a)   what rate of tax the timing difference should be provided at; and

(b)   whether a company should account for deferred tax that it does not expect to pay, because it can foresee that timing differences will not reverse in the future.

These questions lead us initially into the consideration of various methods of providing for deferred tax, and then into the area of the 'partial provision' approach to deferred tax.

1.2.4   The deferral method

The deferral method is an approach which places emphasis on the profit and loss account, and seeks to quantify the extent to which it has been affected by tax deferrals arising through the incidence of timing differences. On reversal of the timing difference, the deferral method is based on the view that it is the former tax deferral which has become payable, and accordingly the deferred tax account is maintained in terms of the rates of tax which were in force when the various timing differences originated. On reversal, the amount taken out of the deferred tax account will be the amount that was accrued there when the timing difference was provided for. The profit and loss account is therefore charged with a reversal which is unaffected by changes in the rates of tax in the years between origination and reversal.

By contrast, the method does not seek, as its primary purpose, to generate deferred tax figures in the balance sheet which represent accurate measurements of assets and liabilities. Where tax rates change, the balance on the deferred tax account will no longer be the amount that the company will pay or receive in future years when the timing differences reverse, because the reversal will be taxed at the rate ruling at the time of the reversal, and the rate ruling at the time that the difference originated will be of no relevance to the amount of tax paid.

Deferred tax balances under this method might be more properly thought of as deferred income and deferred expenditure, which could be said to represent the tax benefit or cost derived from the effect of timing differences quantified by reference to the rate of tax ruling at the date that the timing difference originated. This is seen as the deferral of a cost which otherwise would have arisen that year and accordingly the rate of tax applicable to that year is the one most appropriate to use in quantifying the benefit derived. On reversal the cost arising is seen as merely the amount of the earlier benefit which has now been withdrawn.

1.2.5   The liability method (with full provision/comprehensive allocation)

In contrast to the deferral method, the liability method places emphasis on the balance sheet rather than the profit and loss account, and focuses on the future rather than on the past. It treats the tax effects of timing differences as liabilities for taxes payable in the future (or as assets recoverable in the future), and the practical effect of this is that it responds to changes of tax rate by recalculating the asset or liability in the balance sheet on the basis of the new rate. This means that the charge for deferred tax in the profit and loss account will include the effects of any such change in rate which is applied to the opening balance of cumulative timing differences.

The principal objective of the liability method is to quantify the amount of tax that will become payable or receivable in the future. It follows, therefore, that the deferred tax balance is maintained at the current rate of tax since this rate is the best estimate of the rate that is likely to apply in the future when the timing differences reverse. Of course if the future rates of tax are already set, then it is necessary to examine the periods in which the timing differences will reverse, and then provide the amount of tax that is foreseen to arise as each year's reversal occurs.

The difference between the deferral method and the liability method can be illustrated as follows:

Example 7.2:   Illustration of the difference between the two methods

A company invests £48,000 in a fixed asset at the beginning of 19X1, and depreciates it at £6,000 p.a. The asset attracts capital allowances of £12,000 in 19X1 and £9,000 in 19X2. In 19X1, the tax rate is 50% and in 19X2 it falls to 30%.

Under the deferral method, the calculation would be made by reference to the timing differences arising in each year in the profit and loss account, thus:

Computation of the timing difference	19X1 £	19X2 £
Depreciation per financial statements	6,000	6,000
Capital allowances	12,000	9,000
Originating timing difference	6,000	3,000
Deferred tax provided, at 50%/30%	3,000	900
Deferred tax balance carried forward	3,000	3,900

(Under the deferral method, it is a matter of no concern that the balance carried forward, of £3,900, has no meaning in terms of the cumulative timing difference of £9,000 and the present tax rate of 30%.)

Under the liability method, the deferred tax account would be calculated by reference to the cumulative timing difference (computed by comparing the net book value of the asset in the financial statements with its written down value in the capital allowance computation, thus):

Computation of the cumulative timing difference	19X1 £	19X2 £
Net book value per financial statements	42,000	36,000
Written down value per tax computation	36,000	27,000
Cumulative timing difference	6,000	9,000
Deferred tax balance, at 50%/30%	3,000	2,700
Deferred tax provided/(released)	3,000	(300)

The amount of deferred tax in the profit and loss account is simply the movement between the two balance sheet figures. In this example the £300 release in 19X2 is reconciled thus:

	£
Originating timing difference in 19X2 — £3,000 @ 30%	900
Effect of change in rate on opening balance of cumulative timing differences — £6,000 x (50% — 30%)	(1,200)
	(300)

Where the whole amount of the cumulative timing difference is reflected in the amount provided in the balance sheet, the approach can be described as 'full provision', or 'comprehensive allocation'. This is to distinguish the method from a variant of the liability approach, 'partial provision', which is described below.

1.2.6   The liability method (with partial provision)

Partial provision is an approach to deferred tax in which the full amount of the deferred tax liability is first calculated, but only a portion of that full liability is actually provided in the financial statements. The amount provided is based on an estimate of the liability that is expected to arise in the future, based on a projection of the extent, in net terms, to which the cumulative timing differences are expected to reverse. A proportion of the timing differences can be viewed as non-reversing and therefore equivalent to permanent differences (on which deferred tax is not provided).

Individual timing differences (by definition) will always reverse. However, the partial provision approach permits these reversals to be offset by such new originating timing differences as can be predicted with sufficient certainty to arise in the future. This can be illustrated by an example:

Example 7.3:   Illustration of partial provision

Consider a company which commenced trade in 19X1 by purchasing fixed assets for £1,000,000. It has an annual capital expenditure budget for the next four years of £400,000, £500,000, £600,000 and £700,000 respectively. Assets are depreciated over their useful lives of ten years and are expected to have a nil recoverable amount at that time. Capital allowances are 25% p.a. on a reducing balance basis, and tax is charged at a rate of 35%.

Fixed assets in financial statements	19X1	19X2	19X3	19X4	19X5
	£'000	£'000	£'000	£'000	£'000
Opening balance	—	900	1,160	1,470	1,820
Additions	1,000	400	500	600	700
Depreciation	(100)	(140)	(190)	(250)	(320)
Closing balance	900	1,160	1,470	1,820	2,200

Tax computation	19X1	19X2	19X3	19X4	19X5
	£'000	£'000	£'000	£'000	£'000
Opening balance	—	750	862	1,022	1,216
Additions	1,000	400	500	600	700
Writing down allowance	(250)	(288)	(340)	(406)	(479)
Closing balance	750	862	1,022	1,216	1,437
Timing difference	150	298	448	604	763
Increase therein		148	150	156	159

This can be shown in the form of a graph, thus:

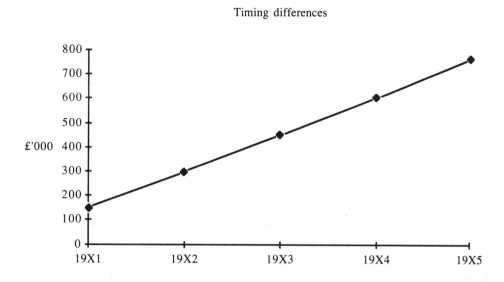

Timing differences

Under the full provision approach, the company would provide deferred tax at the end of 19X1 of £52,500, being 35% of the timing difference of £150,000 at that time. However, the partial provision approach would consider whether any net reversal of the timing difference could be foreseen to arise in the future, and since the cumulative amount of timing differences is expected to rise, would make no provision at all in this case.

If timing differences were in fact expected to decline below the present level in the future, then provision would be made for the extent to which the timing differences were expected to reverse. Thus if the figures were the same as those above, except that the cumulative timing differences at the end of 19X1 amounted to £400,000 rather than £150,000, then provision would be made for the net reversal which could be foreseen to arise when they fell to £298,000. The amount provided would be £35,700 ((£400,000 — £298,000) @ 35%). This pattern is shown in the following graph:

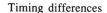

Timing differences

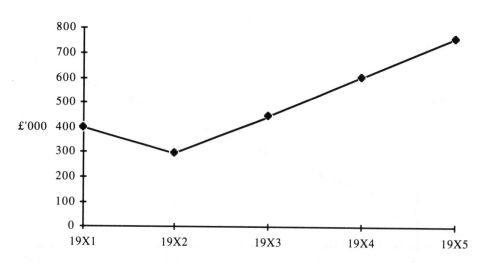

It should be noted that provision has to be made for this reversal, even though the reversal itself is expected to be temporary (in the sense that the timing differences expected to arise beyond 19X2 will again lift the cumulative level above the present level). The basic rule is that provision should be made for tax on the excess of the present level of timing differences over the lowest level to which it is expected to fall at any year end in the future.

Where a converse pattern is foreseen (as shown in the next graph), the same basic rule still applies; in the following example, therefore, no provision would be needed because, although net reversals can be foreseen at the end of years 19X4 and 19X5, they do not bring the cumulative level at the end of the period below its present level. However, if it were expected that this declining pattern would continue beyond 19X5, it would be necessary to see to what level the timing differences could be expected to fall in the longer term, and if at any time it was expected that they would be less than the present level of £400,000, then provision would have to be made for the effect of that net reversal.

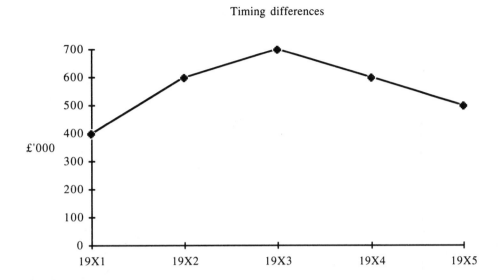

Timing differences

Because timing differences can be either positive or negative (representing the deferment or acceleration of tax), it is possible that the projection of future timing differences will show that they will cross the zero axis, as shown on the graph below. In these circumstances, the whole amount of the potential liability would be provided (£175,000 in the example — £500,000 @ 35%), but no provision would be made for the further effect of the future timing differences which went beyond the axis. The partial provision basis does not involve accounting for timing differences based on their future level; it simply seeks to identify whether a 'hard core' of timing differences exists, and if so, to avoid making provision for that amount because in substance it represents a permanent deferment of tax.

Timing differences

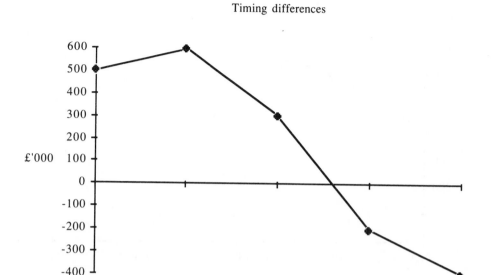

The partial provision approach arouses strong passions, both from those who support it and from those who condemn it. Most of the arguments in favour are in fact criticisms of the full provision approach on the grounds that it can lead to the provision of large sums for deferred tax which have only a remote likelihood of becoming payable. To provide for deferred tax on timing differences which are unlikely on reversal to give rise to a tax liability is said by advocates of the partial provision method to be pursuing form rather than substance and to mislead the users of financial statements through the understatement of profit and capital employed. It can thereby portray companies as being more highly geared than they are in reality and give a false impression of poor creditworthiness. Further it could affect a company's borrowing powers if they were computed by reference to reserves, because those reserves were understated because of a provision for deferred tax which might be regarded as unnecessary.

Those people who criticise the partial provision approach generally say that the failure to provide for an expected reversal on the grounds that replacement will take place wrongly anticipates a future event (such as that a certain level of capital expenditure will take place). This is thought to be inappropriate partly because it may be at variance with the prudence concept, but partly also because it departs from normal accounting rules which account for the effects of individual transactions in isolation, rather than in combination with the effects of transactions which have not yet occurred. It is also argued that the method brings volatility and distortion into the profit and loss account, because earnings are affected by the incidence of transactions unrelated to trading performance, such as the acquisition of fixed assets which attract allowances for which no deferred tax provision is made.

1.2.7 The hybrid method

This method seeks to combine features of the two principal methods of accounting for deferred tax, (i.e. the deferral method and the liability method), by selecting the most appropriate method for the particular type of timing difference which has arisen, such that the deferred tax balance consists of elements derived under the deferral method and other elements derived under the liability method.

As discussed at 1.2.3 above, there are four basic classes of timing differences:

(a)   income can be recognised in the financial statements before being taxed;

(b)   income can be taxed before being recognised in the financial statements;

(c)   expenditure can be recognised in the financial statements before being allowed for tax;

(d)   expenditure can be allowed for tax before being recognised in the financial statements.

The hybrid method draws a distinction between those ((a) and (c) above) where the first leg of the timing difference passes through the financial statements and those where it passes through the tax computation ((b) and (d) above).

When items of income or expenditure have been recognised in the financial statements but not recognised for tax purposes, the deferred tax liability cannot be quantified with absolute certainty. It is not possible to determine the tax consequences of these transactions as they will only be apparent in the future, and the ultimate liability will be determined by the rate of tax in effect at the time of the reversal. Accordingly the best estimate of the future liability is made and tax is provided at the latest known rate. Thus deferred tax on these types of timing differences is provided using the liability method.

However, when items of income or expenditure pass through the tax computation before they are recognised in the financial statements, the tax effect of those transactions are known, and the tax expense or benefit is fixed. The benefit or expense which has arisen is determined by the rate of tax presently in effect and so the deferred tax impact of these transactions on the current year's results is known. Accordingly, deferred tax on these types of timing differences is provided using the deferral method.

If the hybrid method is used the effect of a change in the rate of tax will affect only that part of the balance computed using the principles of the liability method. That part of the deferred tax balance computed using the deferral method is not adjusted since the tax effects of these timing differences is already known.

Although there is a degree of theoretical merit in this approach, it is not adopted as standard accounting practice in any of the major developed countries of the world. This may be because it is more complicated to apply, rather than being a reflection of any lack of theoretical soundness to the approach. It is not considered further in this chapter.

1.2.8 Discounting the liability

Another suggestion which is sometimes made is that deferred tax should be provided on a discounted basis. This has obvious theoretical merit, because by definition deferred tax involves the postponement of the tax liability, and it is possible therefore to regard the deferred liability as equivalent to an interest-free loan from the tax authorities. An appropriate way to reflect the benefit of this postponement could be to discount the liability by reference to the period of the deferment, and accordingly to record a lower tax charge by reason of that discount. The discount would then be amortised over the period of the deferment.

Such an approach has been advocated by some respondents to ASC exposure drafts on deferred tax, and it is not specifically precluded by SSAP 15, but it has seldom been adopted in practice in the UK. It raises questions about how to account for the time value of money, which are relevant to a number of accounting issues; but UK practice in this regard could be described as relatively unsophisticated other than in relation to a few specific issues, such as leasing contracts and certain financial instruments.

1.2.9 The net of tax method

The net of tax approach is not a discrete method of measuring the tax effects of timing differences, but is concerned with the manner of its presentation in the financial statements. The method recognises the tax effects of timing differences as an integral part of the asset or liability that caused the timing difference to arise. Before applying the net of tax approach the deferred tax liability is computed via the deferral method or the liability method (or conceivably the hybrid method), but then included in the carrying value of the item to which the difference relates. Thus, a deferred tax liability arising from accelerated capital allowances would be deducted from the balance sheet carrying value of the asset concerned, or the amount of a disallowable provision (such as a general bad debt provision) would be stated net of the tax effect which would arise when the provision was utilised and became tax deductible.

This method has seldom been used in practice, although there are occasions, particularly in relation to net-of-tax provisions as described above, where it has been applied. SSAP 15 dismisses it by saying that 'it fails to distinguish between a transaction and its tax consequences and therefore should not be used in financial statements'.[1]

1.3 Allocation within periods

As well as allocating tax to particular accounting periods, it is also sometimes necessary to allocate it within an accounting period for presentation purposes. Normally, it will be shown in the profit and loss account under the caption of tax on profit on ordinary activities, but it may have to be allocated to other movements in shareholders' equity, such as extraordinary items, results of discontinued activities, prior year adjustments or revaluation reserve.

Where there is an extraordinary item which has an effect on the tax charge, it is necessary to state the extraordinary item net of the tax effect. To calculate the amount to be allocated to the extraordinary item, SSAP 6 requires the 'with-and-without' method to be applied.[2] This means that the tax charge should be calculated as if the extraordinary item had not existed, then recalculated with the inclusion of the extraordinary item; the difference between the two calculations should be attributed to the extraordinary item. A similar approach should be applied where there is any other modification of the profit and loss account presentation which shows components of the profit in different places (such as the results of discontinued activities), and it is desired to show the tax related to these activities separately.

Where deferred tax is provided in respect of the revaluation of an asset, the tax effect should follow the revaluation surplus by being taken to revaluation reserve. Similarly, where a prior year adjustment is made and involves an adjustment to the opening balance on shareholders' funds, any tax effect attributable to the adjustment should be dealt with in the same way.

2 THE DEVELOPMENT OF ACCOUNTING FOR TAXATION IN THE UK

2.1 Accounting for tax payable

2.1.1 ED 12

The introduction of the imputation system of taxation in the Finance Act, 1972, which took effect from April 1973, meant that the earlier guidance on the treatment of tax in the financial statements of companies, contained in the ICAEW statement N27 needed amendment. An exposure draft [3] was issued by the ASC in May 1973, entitled 'The treatment of taxation under the imputation system in the financial statements of companies'. Its principal requirements were as follows:

(a) the particulars in the profit and loss account of the charge for corporation tax should show, where material, the relief for recoverable ACT and the amount of any irrecoverable ACT;

(b) appropriations for dividends payable should not include either the related ACT or the attributable tax credit;

(c) proposed dividends should be included in current liabilities without the addition of attributable ACT: the ACT on proposed dividends, whether or not recoverable, should be included as a current tax liability. Recoverable ACT on proposed dividends should be deducted from the deferred tax account if available, or otherwise shown as a deferred asset; and

(d) dividends receivable from UK resident companies could be shown either inclusive or exclusive of the related tax credit (so long as the policy was applied consistently).

2.1.2 SSAP 8

The exposure draft was converted into a Statement of Standard Accounting Practice in the following year, with comparatively little change; however, it removed the option mentioned at 2.1.1 (d) above, by requiring that dividends receivable should be included at an amount which included the associated tax credit. The requirements of SSAP 8 are dealt with in 3.1 below.

2.2   Accounting for deferred tax

2.2.1   ED 11

The first exposure draft on deferred tax in the UK was published in May 1973.[4] Until that time, most companies had accounted for deferred tax, but it was not mandatory to do so and a variety of practices were followed. The exposure draft was controversial in that it proposed that the deferral method should be used, whereas most UK companies had up to that time been using the liability method. It also specified that revaluations of assets should be regarded as giving rise to timing differences, for which deferred tax should therefore be provided; not all companies had been taking that view.

2.2.2   SSAP 11

The exposure draft was converted into an accounting standard in 1975, to be effective for periods beginning on or after January 1, 1976.[5] However, the standard was different from the exposure draft in one fundamental respect. The requirement to use the deferral method had been relaxed, and companies were now offered the option of using the liability method as an alternative.

SSAP 11 was short lived. In many ways it was issued at precisely the wrong time. The UK was in its highest period of inflation for very many years. Capital allowances were at their most accelerated, and there was a system of 'stock appreciation relief' in force which gave businesses a tax deduction for the increase in the balance sheet value of stocks held by them. The net result was that, even though there were comparatively high nominal rates of tax in force (50 — 52%), a large number of companies were paying no corporation tax at all, other than ACT.

As a result of these factors many companies began to build up large deferred tax provisions in their balance sheets, when in reality they could not see that the liability was ever likely to be paid. A campaign began to gather momentum to have the subject re-examined. In the meantime, the ASC was formulating a statement on current cost accounting, which dealt with a wide range of accounting issues, and the exposure draft which was published on this subject contained the radical proposal that deferred tax should be calculated on the basis of only those timing differences which were expected to reverse without being replaced — the partial provision approach.[6] In the light of this, in October 1976 the Committee suspended indefinitely the implementation date of SSAP 11 (effectively before it came into force).

2.2.3   ED 19

A further exposure draft was issued in 1977 which was based on the approach which had been set out in ED 18.[7] This proposed that deferred tax should be provided in full, using the liability method, unless it could be demonstrated with reasonable probability that the tax reduction would continue for the foreseeable future. It also proposed that disclosure should be required of the full potential liability to deferred tax by way of note, analysed into categories of timing difference and showing how much had been provided in respect of each category.

The exposure draft differentiated short-term timing differences from others, saying that it was generally accepted that provision should be made in full for short-term differences, but that the remaining timing differences should be considered jointly to see whether it could be established that some part of the potential liability need not be provided. The reason for this distinction was not more fully explained.

2.2.4 SSAP 15

In October 1978, the ASC finally withdraw SSAP 11 and issued SSAP 15, which was based on ED 19.[8] However, there were a number of significant changes from the exposure draft, as summarised below:

(a) the liability method was no longer mandated, and indeed the standard did not make any mention of either the liability method or the deferral method. Implicitly, therefore, the deferral method was allowed even though it did not fit naturally with the forward-looking orientation of the partial provision approach;

(b) more specific criteria were laid down which had to be satisfied in order to justify the non-provision of deferred tax. These were that the company had to be a going concern, and that the directors had to be able to foresee, on reasonable evidence, that no liability was likely to arise as a result of reversal of timing differences for some considerable period (at least three years) ahead, and that there was no indication after that period that the situation was likely to change so as to crystallise the liabilities;

(c) it was even more clearly stipulated that full provision was required on short-term timing differences;

(d) a disclosure requirement was added in relation to the effect of unprovided deferred tax on the tax charge in the profit and loss account; and

(e) the standard changed the approach to deferred tax in relation to revalued fixed assets, by stating that provision need be made in respect of a timing difference arising from a revaluation only if it had been decided in principle to dispose of the asset in question and if no rollover relief was available.

The standard took effect for accounting periods commencing on or after January 1, 1979.

2.2.5 ED 33

The ASC set up a working party to review SSAP 15 in 1982, for two principal reasons:

(a) to incorporate the new legal requirements of the Companies Act 1981 into the standard; and

(b) to take account of the change in the basis of stock relief in the Finance Act 1981.

The revision was also intended to take into account comments arising out of the experience gained from applying SSAP 15 in practice. On the basis of this review, a further exposure draft was issued in 1983.[9] This proposed the following main changes:

(a)　the exposure draft described the liability method as the appropriate approach to use, because the deferral method was not compatible with the partial provision concept. However, this was not stated explicitly as a requirement;

(b)　the previous requirement to set up deferred tax unless it could be demonstrated that it would not be required was expressed more neutrally, by saying that deferred tax should be provided to the extent that it was probable that a liability would crystallise and not set up to the extent that it would not;

(c)　there was no longer a specific reference to a period (mentioned in SSAP 15 as at least three years) for which positive evidence should be sought as to the likelihood of the liability crystallising;

(d)　the distinction between short-term and other timing differences was discontinued; all timing differences were to be considered jointly when considering the need to make provision for deferred tax;

(e)　more guidance was added on the criteria to be considered in deciding whether debit balances in respect of deferred tax could be regarded as recoverable. It was stated that they could be carried forward only where their recovery without replacement by equivalent debit balances was assured beyond reasonable doubt;

(f)　the requirement to show the deferred tax which was provided analysed into its principal categories was to be replaced by one which required disclosure of the period or periods of time in which the liability was expected to crystallise;

(g)　the requirement to show the full potential liability to deferred tax, analysed into its components, was replaced by a requirement to show a similar analysis of only the unprovided amount; and

(h)　a requirement was proposed that, where deferred tax was not provided in respect of overseas earnings of a subsidiary on the grounds that there was no intention to remit them to the UK, that the intention not to remit them should be disclosed.

2.2.6　*SSAP 15 (Revised)*

A revised version of SSAP 15[10] was issued in 1985, which was very similar to ED 33, but which included the following further changes:

(a)　it was now explicitly stated that the liability method was the required method of provision for deferred tax;

(b)　the proposal to require disclosure of the period or periods of time in which the liability was expected to crystallise was dropped; and

(c)　the proposed requirement to state that overseas earnings were not planned to be remitted to the UK (where applicable) was replaced with one to state simply that no deferred tax had been provided in respect of these earnings.

The requirements of SSAP 15 (Revised) are set out in more detail in 3.2 below. For the remainder of this chapter, all references to SSAP 15 are to this revised version.

2.3 Other ASC pronouncements

As well as dealing with the accounting treatment of tax on profits as described above, the ASC has addressed the treatment of certain other taxes. The pronouncements which deal with these are described below, but are not otherwise discussed further in this chapter.

2.3.1 SSAP 5

The ASC published a statement on accounting for value added tax in 1974,[11] based on an exposure draft which had been published in the previous year.[12] The statement is a very brief one, simply requiring that:

(a)   turnover should be shown net of VAT on taxable outputs (or shown as a deduction if the gross amount is also shown);[13] and

(b)   irrecoverable VAT should be included in the cost of fixed assets and any other disclosed items in the financial statements to which it relates, where it is practicable to do so and material.[14]

2.3.2 ED 28

In 1981, The ASC issued an exposure draft of a statement on Accounting for Petroleum Revenue Tax.[15] The subject was not proceeded with and the exposure draft was subsequently withdrawn. However, the topic is now being studied by the Oil Industry Accounting Committee, who are seeking to produce a franked SORP on this issue. The tax is a highly complex one which presents difficult accounting problems, but its specialised nature places it beyond the scope of this chapter.

3   THE REQUIREMENTS OF THE RELEVANT ACCOUNTING STANDARDS AND COMPANY LAW

3.1   SSAP 8

3.1.1   Outgoing dividends and the related ACT

The standard considers whether ACT on outgoing dividends should be treated as part of the cost of the dividend or whether it should be treated as part of the tax on the company's profits. The amount declared as a dividend (as a sum payable per share or as a percentage) is the amount that will be received by the members. The fact that the dividend will carry a tax credit is considered to be a matter which affects the member as a recipient, rather than a matter which affects the company and the way in which it should be accounted for. It is therefore considered appropriate that outgoing dividends should be shown in the profit and loss account at the amount paid or payable to the shareholders.[16]

In the UK, outgoing dividends are accounted for in the period to which they relate, which contrasts with the treatment in the United States where they are accounted for in the period in which they are declared. Accordingly, if the final dividend is expected to be declared after the year end then, even though it is subject to shareholder approval, it should be provided for in the financial statements for the year just completed.

The ACT payable in respect of dividends proposed but not paid at the year end will fall due for payment to the Inland Revenue within a period of approximately three months after the dividend has been paid. The ACT due on the dividend will therefore in most cases be a current liability. It will generally rank for set off against mainstream corporation tax payable (a minimum of) 21 months after the year end, because ACT paid may only be set off against the mainstream liability of the period in which the ACT is paid. ACT on proposed dividends therefore cannot normally be offset against the tax due on profits for the year to which the dividend relates.

3.1.2   Recoverable ACT

Recoverable ACT is defined in SSAP 8 as that amount of the ACT paid or payable on outgoing dividends paid and proposed which can be:

(a)   set off against a corporation tax liability on the profits of the period under review or of previous periods; or

(b)   properly set off against a credit balance on deferred tax account; or

(c)   expected to be recoverable taking into account expected profits and dividends — normally those of the next accounting period only.

Irrecoverable ACT is defined as ACT paid or payable on outgoing dividends paid and proposed other than recoverable ACT.[17]

The amount of ACT available under (a) above is therefore the ACT paid in the accounting period together with any ACT previously paid and not yet set off.

Under (b), the ACT is set against deferred tax because it would be available to relieve the expected reversal of timing differences at some point in the future. This is considered more fully in 4.5 below.

The amount of ACT to be carried forward under (c) is ostensibly restricted by the standard to that amount which is likely to be relieved out of the taxable profits of the next accounting period, although the inclusion of the word 'normally' leaves some apparent room for manoeuvre. In certain cases, there may be a reasonable argument for carrying the ACT forward if the company foresees with reasonable certainty that its expected profits and planned dividends will allow the ACT to be relieved outside the strict one year timescale laid down by the standard. The question of carrying forward ACT as an asset is also dealt with in SSAP 15, as discussed in 3.2.3 below.

ACT which is carried forward on the grounds that it will be recovered against future taxable profit, when not shown as a reduction of the deferred tax account, should be shown as a deferred asset, and would be generally shown under the caption of 'prepayments and accrued income'.

The availability for set off of ACT is perhaps best illustrated by an example.

Example 7.4: Set off of ACT

A company has a financial year end of March 31, 1988, in which it made a taxable profit of £500,000. An interim dividend of £50,000 was paid on June 26, 1987 and the directors recommend a final dividend of £100,000, to be paid on May 15, 1988. Last year's final dividend was £350,000, and was paid on May 15, 1987.

The corporation tax provided on the taxable profits for the year would be £175,000 (35% of £500,000). The company will have submitted a return of franked payments for the quarter ended June 30, 1987, because of the interim dividend paid on June 26, together with the final dividend paid on May 15. The ACT paid amounted to 27/73rds of £400,000, or £147,945. The sum due would have been paid by July 14, 1987 (14 days after the end of the quarter).

When the final dividend is paid on May 15, 1988, the company will make a second return of franked payments in respect of the quarter ending June 30, 1988. The ACT payable will depend on the basic rate of income tax ruling at that time, and a current liability of 25/75ths of £100,000, or £33,333 is therefore provided. Both the dividend and the ACT are included in the financial statements for the year ended March 31, 1988. The ACT due on the final dividend will be paid by July 14, 1988.

Assuming that the company has a 'short' payment date for its mainstream tax liability, this will be due nine months after the year end, i.e. on December 31, 1988. The mainstream liability arising in respect of the accounting period to March 31, 1988 can be reduced only by the amount of ACT paid in that accounting period.

Firstly, the maximum amount of ACT which can be offset is calculated: this is the amount of ACT which together with the related dividend absorbs the whole of the company's taxable income for the accounting period. The taxable income for the year is £500,000, so the maximum ACT which may be set off is 27/73rds of this, or £184,932.

Then the amount of ACT paid in the year is calculated:

Dividend paid on May 15, 1987	£129,452	(27/73rds of £350,000)
Dividend paid on June 26, 1987	18,493	(27/73rds of £50,000)
	£147,945	

This is within the maximum set off allowed. Accordingly the ACT paid in respect of the interim dividend can be offset against the mainstream liability. The ACT on the final dividend cannot be offset (because it is not paid until July 14, 1988, which is after the end of the accounting period). The mainstream liability is therefore £175,000 — £147,945, or £27,055 which is a current liability at the March 1988 year end.

The ACT relating to the final dividend is carried forward (since it cannot be netted off against the liability) either as a deduction from the deferred tax account (subject to certain limitations), or if this account is insufficient, as a deferred asset. The earliest date that it may be used is December 31, 1989, being the date that a mainstream liability would be due if taxable profits are made in the year ending March 31, 1989.

3.1.3 Incoming dividends

SSAP 8 discusses two possible ways of dealing with franked investment income in the financial statements:

(a)   to bring into the profit and loss account the cash received or receivable; or

(b)   to bring in the full amount of the franked investment income, i.e. including the tax credit, with an equivalent amount then being treated as part of the tax charge.[18]

The standard requires the second option to be adopted on the basis that it allows recognition of the income at both the pre-tax and the post-tax stage in a way which is consistent with every other item of income and expenditure. Accordingly, incoming dividends from United Kingdom resident companies are to be included in the profit and loss account at the amount of cash received plus the related tax credit.[19]

3.1.4   *Disclosure of the tax charge in the profit and loss account*

SSAP 8 requires that the following items be included in the tax charge in the profit and loss account and, where material, should be separately disclosed:

(a)   the amount of the United Kingdom corporation tax specifying:

   (i)   the charge for corporation tax on the income of the year (where such corporation tax includes transfers between the deferred tax account and the profit and loss account these should also be separately disclosed where material),
   (ii)   tax attributable to franked investment income,
   (iii)   irrecoverable ACT,
   (iv)   the relief for overseas taxation;

(b)   the total overseas taxation, relieved and unrelieved, specifying that part of the unrelieved overseas taxation which arises from the payment or proposed payment of dividends.[20]

As general guidance, Appendix 1 to the standard gives one method of showing (by way of note) the required information, whilst acknowledging that in simple cases the information may be given entirely within the profit and loss account.

Appendix 1 is as follows:

	£'000
Corporation tax on income at x per cent	
(including £b transferred to/from deferred taxation account)	a
Less relief for overseas taxation	c
	d
Overseas taxation*	e
Tax credit on UK dividends received	f
Irrecoverable advance corporation tax	g
	H

* Including £J arising from the payment of dividends

In practice, most companies show corporation tax and deferred tax as separate items rather than in the above format. See, for example, Extract 7.1 at 3.2.4 below.

A   Tax rate

If the rate of corporation tax is not known for the whole or part of the period covered by the accounts, the latest known rate should be used and disclosed.[21]

If the company's accounting period is other than a year ending March 31, in a period of changing rates of corporation tax, the rate applied to the profits will need to be apportioned and the effective rate of tax disclosed. For example, if a company's accounting period was December 31, 1986, the first three months of the company's profit fell to be taxed at 40%, being the rate applicable up to March 31, 1986, and the remainder at the rate of 35% which was in force for the following year. The following calculation gives the effective rate of tax to be disclosed in the financial statements:

		%
The period January 1, 1986 to March 31, 1986	3/12 @ 40% =	10.00
The period April 1, 1986 to December 31, 1986	9/12 @ 35% =	26.25
Effective rate of corporation tax		36.25

B   Irrecoverable ACT

As noted above, the standard requires that the amount of irrecoverable ACT should be separately disclosed if material. This is required because although the most appropriate treatment is to regard the irrecoverable amount as a charge to tax on the company's profits, (the alternative view being that it is part of an appropriation), some readers or analysts may wish to regard ACT 'in some other manner',[22] and separate disclosure enables them to make any adjustment they deem necessary.

C   Unrelieved overseas tax

Appendix 2 to the standard considers the case of unrelieved overseas tax. If the rate of overseas tax on the company's overseas income exceeds the rate of UK tax, then the excess element of the overseas tax will be unrelieved.

If the company pays all or part of a dividend out of its overseas income, i.e. where the dividend and related ACT is substantially in excess of the taxable UK income, then the ACT on the dividend paid out of overseas income will not be available for the purpose of calculating double tax relief. Thus the payment of a dividend in these circumstances may give rise to unrelieved tax, depending on the rate of overseas tax. Unlike the irrecoverable ACT, however, this unrelieved tax is not available for carry forward. The standard suggests that the same accounting treatment should be applied to unrelieved overseas tax as is applied to unrelieved ACT. Accordingly, it should be treated as part of the tax charge, and separately disclosed if material.

3.2   SSAP 15

3.2.1   General approach

The standard indicates that it is concerned with accounting for tax on profits and surpluses which are recognised in the financial statements in one period but assessed in another. It thus relates primarily to deferred corporation tax and income tax in the United Kingdom and in the Republic of Ireland and, insofar as the principles are similar, to overseas taxes on profits payable by UK and Irish enterprises or their subsidiaries.[23]

Interestingly, the standard considers other taxes also, by providing that 'a number of other taxes, including value added tax, petroleum revenue tax and some overseas taxes, are not assessed directly on profits for an accounting period and are therefore not addressed specifically in this statement. For such taxes, enterprises should generally follow the principle underlying this statement, that deferred tax should be provided to the extent that it is probable that a liability or asset will crystallise but not to the extent that it is probable that a liability or asset will not crystallise.'[24]

The standard chooses the partial provision method as its general approach, and summarises it as follows:

'deferred tax should be accounted for in respect of the net amount by which it is probable that any payment of tax will be temporarily deferred or accelerated by the operation of timing differences which will reverse in the foreseeable future without being replaced. Partial provision recognises that, if an enterprise is not expected to reduce the scale of its operations significantly, it will often have what amounts to a hard core of timing differences so that the payment of some tax will be permanently deferred. On this basis, deferred tax has to be provided only where it is probable that tax will become payable as a result of the reversal of timing differences.'[25]

The standard considers that there are two main methods of computation, the liability method and the deferral method. It then points out that the liability method is the method consistent with the aim of partial provision, which is to provide the deferred tax which it is probable will be payable or recoverable.[26]

3.2.2   Definitions

Part 2 of the standard contains the definitions of the terms that are used throughout its text.

Deferred tax is the tax attributable to timing differences.[27]

Timing differences are differences between profits or losses as computed for tax purposes and results as stated in financial statements, which arise from the inclusion of items of income and expenditure in tax computations in periods different from those in which they are included in financial statements. Timing differences originate in one period and are capable of reversal in one or more subsequent periods.[28]

The following definitions are given for specific timing differences:

(a) a loss for tax purposes which is available to relieve future profits from tax constitutes a timing difference;[29]

(b) the revaluation of an asset (including an investment in an associated or subsidiary company) will create a timing difference when it is incorporated into the balance sheet, insofar as the profit or loss that would result from realisation at the revalued amount is taxable, unless disposal of the revalued asset and of any subsequent replacement assets would not result in a tax liability, after taking account of any expected rollover relief;[30]

(c) the retention of earnings overseas will create a timing difference only if:

(i) there is an intention or obligation to remit them; and
(ii) remittance would result in a tax liability after taking account of any related double tax relief.[31]

The *liability method* is a method of computing deferred tax whereby it is calculated at the rate of tax that it is estimated will be applicable when the timing differences reverse. Under the liability method deferred tax not provided is calculated at the expected long-term tax rate.[32]

3.2.3 *Detailed accounting requirements*

A *Method of computation*

Deferred tax should be computed under the liability method. Tax deferred or accelerated by the effect of timing differences should be accounted for to the extent that it is probable that a liability or asset will crystallise. Tax deferred or accelerated by the effect of timing differences should not be accounted for to the extent that it is probable that a liability or asset will not crystallise.[33] For this purpose, the combined effect of all timing differences should be considered rather than looking at individual categories in isolation.[34]

B *Future projections*

The assessment of whether deferred tax liabilities or assets will or will not crystallise should be based upon reasonable assumptions. The assumptions should take into account all relevant information available up to the date on which the financial statements are approved by the board of directors, and also the intentions of management. Ideally this information will include financial plans or projections covering a period of years sufficient to enable an assessment to be made of the likely pattern of future tax liabilities. A prudent view should be taken in the assessment of whether a tax liability will crystallise, particularly where the financial plans or projections are susceptible to a high degree of uncertainty or are not fully developed for the appropriate period.[35]

Under the original SSAP 15, it was possible for an enterprise to ignore the partial provision approach and to remain fully provided, simply by failing to produce, or pleading an inability to produce, future plans or projections. Under the revised requirements, it is now not permissible to do this, as there are two separate requirements, to provide for the tax that is expected to crystallise, and not to provide for tax that is not expected to crystallise.

There is no longer a minimum time period which should be covered by the projections, which is a change from SSAP 15 in its original form, where 'normally three years' was quoted, although the Appendix to the standard now mentions a period of three to five years as an example of a relatively short period which might be appropriate where the pattern of timing differences is expected to be regular.[36] In practice the projection will obviously become less reliable the further into the future it goes, and the period which may be forecast with a reasonable degree of accuracy is perhaps no more than two years. Much depends on whether a pattern of originating or reversing timing differences can be discerned, which will depend on such factors as whether expansion is envisaged, and whether capital expenditure has a cyclical nature.

Each year the pattern of expected timing differences should be compared against the reversal of timing differences experienced in the past. Plans and projections require regular review; they can be influenced by many indirectly related factors, for example the reassessment of asset lives, a decision to close part of the business which renders certain assets no longer needed, or the provision of a sum in respect of the permanent diminution of an asset.

It is important that the plans and projections are based on reasonable and realistic assumptions. In particular, a planned expansion programme may allow timing differences to be projected as continuing to originate well into the future, but the working capital resources to finance the expansion need to be available to the enterprise for that expansion programme to take place.

C   Debit balances

(a)   General

The provision for deferred tax liabilities should be reduced by any deferred tax debit balances arising from separate categories of timing differences and any advance corporation tax which is available for offset against those liabilities.[37] This provides for the situation where there is advance corporation tax recoverable (in excess of the mainstream tax liability), which will effectively rank as a payment on account for the tax due on the future reversal of any timing differences. Further, it allows unrelieved tax losses to be netted off against deferred tax liabilities.

Deferred tax net debit balances should not be carried forward as assets, except to the extent that they are expected to be recoverable without replacement by equivalent debit balances.[38] This is simply the obverse of the same rule for liabilities. Under SSAP 15, a liability is not provided where there is a 'hard core' of timing differences which represent a postponement of tax; correspondingly, a hard core of timing differences which represents a permanent acceleration of the tax liability should not be regarded as an asset.

(b)   Tax losses

Particular guidance is given in the Appendix to the standard on when it is permitted to regard tax losses as recoverable assets (which is distinguishable from when they may be set off against deferred tax liabilities). The conditions to be satisfied are as follows:

(i)   the loss has resulted from an identifiable and non-recurring cause; and

(ii)   the enterprise, or predecessor enterprise, has been consistently profitable over a considerable period, with any past losses being more than offset by income in subsequent periods; and

(iii)   it is assured beyond reasonable doubt that future taxable profits will be sufficient to offset the current loss during the carry-forward period prescribed by tax legislation.[39]

There are corresponding rules relating to capital losses, which prescribe the following conditions:

(i)   a potential chargeable gain not expected to be covered by rollover relief is present in assets which have not been revalued in the financial statements to reflect that gain and which are not essential to the future operations of the enterprise; and

(ii)   the enterprise has decided to dispose of these assets and thus realise the potential chargeable gain; and

(iii)   the unrealised chargeable gain (after allowing for any possible loss in value before disposal) is sufficient to offset the loss in question, such that it is assured beyond reasonable doubt that a tax liability on the relevant portion of the chargeable gain will not crystallise.[40]

(c)   ACT

Debit balances arising in respect of advance corporation tax on dividends payable or proposed at the balance sheet date should be carried forward to the extent that it is foreseen that sufficient corporation tax will be assessed on the profits or income of the succeeding accounting period, against which the advance corporation tax is available for offset.[41] The advance corporation tax on an unpaid dividend cannot be offset against the mainstream liability for the period, since this can only be reduced by ACT actually paid in the period. Accordingly, ACT on a proposed dividend is normally recorded as a current liability (representing the payment that will be made to the Inland Revenue when the dividend is remitted to shareholders), and as a deferred asset or a deduction from a deferred tax liability (representing the recoverability of the amount paid to the Inland Revenue against a future mainstream tax liability).

The standard requires that debit balances arising in respect of ACT other than on dividends payable or proposed at the balance sheet date should be written off unless their recovery is assured beyond reasonable doubt. It further provides that such recovery will normally be assured only where the debit balances are recoverable out of corporation tax arising on profits or income of the succeeding accounting period, without replacement by equivalent debit balances.[42]

3.2.4   *Disclosure*

The standard requires disclosure of the following:

(a)   The amount of deferred tax charged or credited in the profit and loss account for the period, split between that relating to ordinary activities and that relating to any extraordinary items.[43]

A good example of this split is given in the financial statements of THORN EMI plc:

Extract 7.1: THORN EMI plc[44]

5.   TAXATION

	1988 £ m	1987 £m
Taxation on profit on ordinary activities		
United Kingdom:		
corporation tax at 35% (1987 35%)	**(35.5)**	(37.0)
double taxation relief	**1.0**	1.5
	(34.5)	(35.5)
Overseas taxation	**(32.1)**	(26.0)
Deferred taxation		
United Kingdom	**(10.7)**	12.2
overseas	**0.1**	(4.1)
Prior year adjustments	**6.8**	3.9
Tax on share of profits less losses of related companies:		
United Kingdom	**(4.0)**	(2.8)
overseas	**(4.6)**	(4.7)
	(79.0)	(57.0)

The charge for taxation has been reduced by £2.7m (1987 nil) being UK taxation likely to be deferred for the foreseeable future in respect of timing differences.

6.   EXTRAORDINARY ITEMS LESS TAXATION

	1988 £ m	1987 £m
Disposals and closures of businesses	**(16.7)**	(37.5)
Profit on flotation of Thames Television plc	**—**	10.8
Net extraordinary loss before taxation	**(16.7)**	(26.7)
United Kingdom taxation:		
current	**3.0**	(1.4)
deferred	**(1.3)**	3.3
Overseas taxation:		
current	**0.5**	—
deferred	**0.3**	0.1
	(14.2)	(24.7)

There is also a requirement within SSAP 6 to disclose the amount of taxation (i.e. not just deferred taxation) attributable to extraordinary items.[45]

(b)   The amount of any unprovided deferred tax in respect of the period, analysed into its major components.[46]

A good example of this disclosure, which is one which sometimes seems to be overlooked in practice, is shown in the financial statements of Glaxo Holdings p.l.c.:

Extract 7.2: Glaxo Holdings p.l.c.[47]

7   TAXATION

	1988	1987
	£m	£m
On profits of the year	125	106
UK corporation tax at 35%	37	21
	88	85
Overseas taxes	149	137
Deferred taxation	19	23
	256	245
Attributable to:		
Holding company and subsidiaries	237	226
Associated companies	19	19

Taxation has been significantly affected by reliefs in certain overseas companies. It also has been reduced by £22m (1987 — £14m) because of accelerated capital allowances for which no deferred taxation has been provided. In accordance with SSAP 15 no deferred tax has been provided in respect of profit on inter-company stocks. If deferred tax had been provided the taxation charge would have been reduced by £10m (1987 — increased by £7m).

An alternative, but less common way of conveying this information can be found in the financial statements of Halma p.l.c.

Extract 7.3: Halma p.l.c.[48]

		£000
6 Tax on Profit on		
ordinary activities	**1988**	**1987**
Corporation tax at 35%	3,030	2,139
Overseas taxation	220	168
	3,250	2,307
Relief for timing differences not provided: Fixed assets	(20)	(19)
	3,230	2,288
Prior year adjustments	7	(13)
	3,237	2,275
Comprising:		
Current taxation	3,284	2,301
Deferred taxation	(47)	(26)
	3,237	2,275

(c) Any adjustments to deferred tax passing through the profit and loss account which relate to changes in tax rates or in tax allowances. If the change in the tax system is regarded as sufficiently fundamental, this may be treated as an extraordinary item if the effect is sufficiently material.[49]

(d) The deferred tax balance, analysed into its major components, and the amount of unprovided deferred tax, similarly analysed.[50] Where no information on unprovided deferred tax in respect of a revalued asset is given on the grounds that it is argued not to be a timing difference (because it will never crystallise), the fact that the potential liability has not been quantified should be stated.[51]

Examples of the analysis of the deferred tax balance can be found in the financial statements of Pilkington plc and Associated Newspapers Holdings plc:

Extract 7.4: Pilkington plc[52]

Note 21 [extract]

Deferred taxation	1988 £m	1987 £m
The balances included in provisions relate to:		
Capital Allowances in excess of related depreciation	10.2	18.6
Other timing differences:		
provisions and accruals	6.6	(.1)
future benefit of tax losses	—	(.7)
recoverable United Kingdom advance corporation tax	(2.0)	(3.6)
	14.8	14.2
Deferred taxation which has not been provided amounted to:		
Capital Allowances in excess of related depreciation	167.1	121.4
Revaluation of fixed assets and capital gains	72.0	87.2
Other timing differences	(33.2)	(11.8)
	205.9	196.8

Extract 7.5: Associated Newspapers Holdings p.l.c.[53]

23 Deferred Taxation [extract]	**Group** £m	£m	**Company** £m	£m
Accelerated capital allowances	**16.8**	22.2	—	—
Other timing differences	**0.6**	(1.1)	**1.4**	1.0
	17.4	21.1	**1.4**	1.0
Less Advance corporation tax payable in respect of dividends proposed	**(2.7)**	(2.6)	**(1.4)**	(1.0)
	14.7	18.5	—	—
If provision had been made for all timing differences, further deferred taxation as follows would have been included in the balance sheet:				
Accelerated capital allowances	**7.6**	6.9	—	—
Other timing differences	**(1.4)**	(1.1)	—	—
	6.2	5.8	—	—

This excluded the liability which in certain circumstances might arise in the event of the Group's properties and investments being sold at valuation. These are set out Notes 13(v), 16(i), and 17(ii).

Rather than analysing the *unprovided* amount as required by the standard, a number of companies continue to follow the requirement of the original SSAP 15 (before it was amended in 1985), which involved showing the full potential liability and the amount which has been provided, analysed by category.[54] Of course, this information allows the reader to derive the analysis of the unprovided amount, by a simple process of subtraction. An example of this form of disclosure is to be found in the financial statements of Sears PLC:

Extract 7.6: Sears PLC[55]

17. PROVISIONS FOR LIABILITIES AND CHARGES [extract]
Details of the potential liability for deferred taxation and the extent to which provision has been made in these financial statements are set out below:

	1987/88		1986/87	
	Potential liability £m	Provision made £m	Potential liability £m	Provision made £m
Capital allowances	48.3	10.1	55.7	8.6
Investment property surpluses	6.4	6.4	4.8	4.8
Short-term and other timing differences	(13.2)	(13.2)	(3.0)	(3.0)
	41.5	3.3	57.5	10.4

Where appropriate, deferred taxation has been provided at 35% in respect of excess capital allowances.
Provision has been made for deferred taxation on both revaluation and realised surpluses arising on the investment properties of Galliford Sears Estates Limited. The potential liability on capital gains which might arise on a disposal of properties at amounts at which they are stated in the balance sheet, or which have been deferred by virtue of roll-over relief, has not been quantified because the probability of any material tax liability arising is remote, since it is not intended to make any substantial disposals.

It is in fact arguable that the analysis of the full potential liability gives more meaningful information than can be obtained by analysing the amount which has been provided or the amount which has not been provided. Since SSAP 15 specifies that all categories of timing difference are to be considered in aggregate rather than individually for the purposes of deciding the overall net reversal which is to be provided for, it often makes little sense to try to say which particular category has been included in the provision and which has not.

(e)   Transfers to and from the deferred tax balance.[56]

(f)   Movements in reserves which relate to deferred tax.[57]

(g)   Where the value of an asset is disclosed by way of note and differs from its book value, the tax effect of disposing of it at that value.[58]

An example of this is contained in the financial statements of Associated Newspapers Holdings plc:

Extract 7.7: Associated Newspapers Holdings p.l.c.[59]

13 Fixed tangible assets [extract]

(v) The liability for taxation, had the revalued properties been sold at the balance sheet date for their net book values, would be:-

	1987 **£m**	1986 £m
Freehold properties	**4.2**	4.3
Leasehold properties — long	**2.1**	2.0
— short	**0.4**	0.4
	6.7	6.7

No allowance has been made in calculating the above figures for "roll-over" relief, for which most of the Group's properties would be eligible as they are occupied for trading purposes.

(h) Any assumptions regarding the availability of group relief and the payment therefor which are relevant to an understanding of the company's deferred tax position.[60]

(i) The fact (if applicable) that provision has not been made for tax which would become payable if retained earnings of foreign subsidiaries were remitted to the UK.[61]

THORN EMI plc include the following footnote in their financial statements to explain this point:

Extract 7.8: THORN EMI plc[62]

17. DEFERRED TAXATION [extract]

No provision has been made for further taxes which could arise if subsidiary or related companies are disposed of at or above their present net asset value or if overseas companies were to remit reserves to the UK in excess of that anticipated in these accounts: it is considered impracticable to estimate the amount of such taxes.

3.3   Companies Act 1985

The Companies Act also imposes various disclosure requirements in relation to taxation. These can be summarised as follows:

(a) the basis on which the tax charge has been computed;[63]

(b) any special circumstances affecting the liability to tax on profits, income or capital gains for the current or future years;[64]

(c)   the amount of the tax charge on ordinary activities and on extraordinary items, respectively analysed into:

    (i)   UK corporation tax, and the amount by which it has been reduced by the application of double tax relief,

    (ii) UK income tax,

    (iii) overseas tax;[65]

(d)   the amount of the taxation creditor balance.[66] Where there is an amount receivable in respect of tax, the Schedule 4 formats do not specify that it should be shown separately, although it is likely that it will be disclosed if material as a separate item within debtors;

(e)   movements during the year on any provision in respect of tax;[67]

(f)   the amount of any provision for taxation other than deferred taxation.[68]

As can be seen from the above, there is substantial overlap between the disclosure requirements of accounting standards and those of the Companies Act. Illustrations of most of these disclosures have already been given; see for example THORN EMI plc, shown at Extract 7.1 above.

4   PROBLEM AREAS

4.1   Combining different categories of timing difference

SSAP 15 requires timing differences to be looked at in aggregate for the purposes of determining what net reversal need be provided for, rather than individually.[69] This is illustrated by the following example:

Example 7.5:   Combination of timing differences

Assume that a company has the following projected cumulative timing differences for the next five years, and it is preparing financial statements at the end of 19X1:

	19X1 £'000	19X2 £'000	19X3 £'000	19X4 £'000	19X5 £'000
Accelerated capital allowances	500	600	450	800	900
Other timing differences	(300)	(350)	(400)	(450)	(500)
Net position	200	250	50	350	400

This position could be represented in graphical form as follows:

Cumulative timing differences

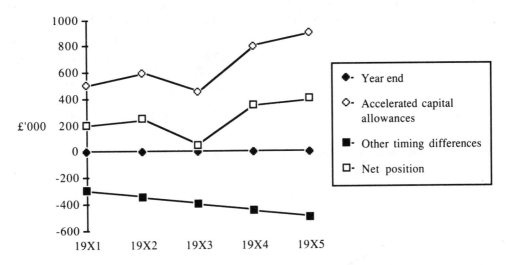

The important line to focus on is the one which shows the net position, rather than either of the two which represent its components. Accordingly, the amount to be provided is determined by the extent to which the net deferral of £200,000 will fall — it can be seen that there will be a fall to £50,000 at the end of 19X3, and accordingly the amount to be provided, at 35%, is £52,500.

Although the terms of the standard clearly state that the timing differences are to be looked at in aggregate rather than individually, it is sometimes argued that those timing differences which would give rise to debit balances may not be used to offset other timing differences if they are expected to be perpetuated. Accountants Digest No. 174 contains the following passage:

'It is important to note that, just as deferred tax liabilities should not be created unless it is probable that a liability will crystallise, so deferred tax liabilities should not be reduced by deferred tax debit balances which will not crystallise because recovery of the tax is continually deferred. For example, deferred tax liabilities should not be reduced by deferred tax debit balances arising from timing differences on recurring general bad debt provisions.'[70]

It can be argued that this approach produces anomalous results, as demonstrated by the following example:

Example 7.6:   Combination of timing differences involving continuing debit balances

Assume that the same company had different expectations as to the accelerated capital allowance element of its projected cumulative timing differences, so as to give rise to the following figures for the next five years. It is still preparing financial statements at the end of 19X1:

	19X1 £'000	19X2 £'000	19X3 £'000	19X4 £'000	19X5 £'000
Accelerated capital allowances	300	200	100	100	100
Other timing differences	(300)	(350)	(400)	(450)	(500)
Net position	—	(150)	(300)	(350)	(400)

This position could again be represented in graphical form as follows:

Cumulative timing differences

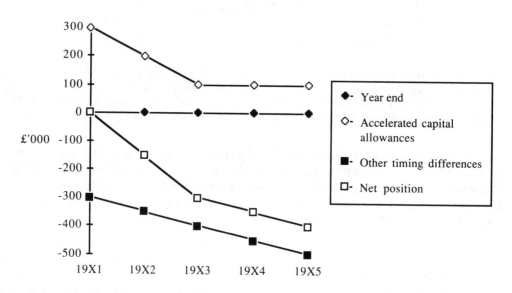

Under the approach suggested in the Accountants Digest, the company would provide £70,000 (£200,000 @ 35%) for deferred tax in 19X1, even though the incidence of timing differences experienced by it has been completely neutral in its effect, resulting in neither a postponement nor an acceleration of tax suffered. The provision would be, in effect, a provision for the effects of the acceleration of tax which was expected to occur in the future but had not yet taken place. This does not seem to produce a sensible result; it would be more appropriate to look at the effect of the timing differences in aggregate rather than individually, than to anticipate effects that will be experienced in 19X2 and beyond.

4.2   Tax losses and deferred tax

4.2.1   *Tax losses which have been incurred*

The accounting treatment for tax losses which have been incurred is relatively straightforward, and the treatment depends upon the particular way in which the loss is to be relieved.

If the loss is to give rise to a refund of tax previously paid, then the amount of the refund is recorded in the balance sheet as a debtor (if appropriate this may be a long-term debtor).

Alternatively, the loss may be carried forward to be utilised against taxable profits which arise in the future. In such circumstances the tax loss can only be recognised in the financial statements if there is sufficient taxable profit likely to emerge in the future. It is probable that a taxable profit will emerge in the future if the company has a balance on its deferred tax account, since under the rules of partial provision, the company will have provided for deferred tax only if there is the probability of a tax liability crystallising. As the timing differences which have been identified (and provided for) reverse in future accounting periods, they will automatically give rise to taxable income against which the tax losses can be set.

Accordingly, the deferred tax account is the first point of set off for tax losses which are carried forward. An example is to be found in the financial statements of Associated British Engineering plc:

Extract 7.9: Associated British Engineering plc[71]

16. Deferred taxation	Provided		Potential	
	1988	1987	1988	1987
	£000s	£000s	£000s	£000s
The Group liability for future taxation at 35% is:				
Taxation deferred by capital allowances	153	216	153	217
Relief for losses and other timing differences	(141)	(204)	(141)	(204)
Chargeable gains at 35%	—	—	—	78
	12	12	12	91

The amount of deferred tax provided in the financial statements should be reduced to the extent of the tax effect of the available losses. However, particular care is needed if the enterprise carries on a number of different trades, because the offset of a credit balance arising from one trade may not be capable of offset against a debit balance of another trade, or if the loss arises in a company which is in a different tax jurisdiction from the profitable companies, so that again no offset would be possible in practice. It will only be legitimate to make the kind of offset shown above if the loss could in fact be applied to prevent the payment of tax having to be made if the timing differences reversed so as to crystallise a liability.

The more difficult practical problems arise when the amount of the loss is so great that the set off against deferred tax is such that the loss would be carried as an asset. This is permissible only in certain circumstances. As explained in 3.2.3 above, the tax effect of a current trading loss should only be treated as a recoverable asset when:

(a)   the loss results from an identifiable and non-recurring cause; and

(b)   the enterprise, or predecessor enterprise, has been consistently profitable with any past losses being more than offset by income in subsequent periods; and

(c)   it is assured beyond reasonable doubt that future taxable profits will be sufficient to offset the current loss during the carry forward period prescribed by tax legislation.[72]

These rules are framed in an attempt to ensure that an asset is only recognised when its recoverability is assured with a very high degree of certainty and, in practice, these conditions can seldom be met.

4.2.2   Tax losses which have yet to be incurred

This is an area which causes a great deal of debate. A fundamental question emerges when looking at the foreseeable future for the purposes of assessing the deferred tax provision — if a trading loss is foreseen in the future, may it be taken into account when assessing the level of deferred tax to be provided? Take the following example:

Example 7.7:   Future tax losses

A company is preparing its financial statements for the year ended December 31, 19X1, during which it earned a taxable profit of £100,000, on which tax of £35,000 is payable.

In considering the deferred tax provision that should be set up in its 19X1 financial statements, the company foresees a reversal of timing differences amounting to £150,000 in 19X2, but has identified a trend from 19X3 onwards of a level of capital expenditure that should give rise to originating timing differences when compared to the amount of depreciation which will be charged in the profit and loss account.

However, the company forecasts that a trading loss of £100,000 will be made in 19X2 and therefore expects that the tax effect of these losses will at least partly mitigate the timing difference reversal.

The amount on which the company should base its provision is either £150,000 or £50,000, but which?

Those in favour of reducing the deferred tax liability would argue that the loss when incurred will reduce the amount of tax payable, and under the partial provision rules (which require that tax should be accounted for to the extent that it is probable that a liability will crystallise, and should not be accounted for to the extent that it is probable that a liability will not crystallise) would say that, since tax on only £50,000 will be payable, then that is all that should be provided.

The counter argument to this is that the deferred tax account cannot be reduced by a trading loss which has not yet been incurred and which has not been accounted for. The proponents of this argument would maintain that it is only correct to recognise the tax consequences of an event when the accounting consequences have been recognised, and not before. There is no suggestion that the deferred tax provision would be *increased* if a trading *profit* were foreseen in the following year (so that in effect the originating timing differences would not offset the reversals arising in that year). It is not the function of deferred tax to anticipate the effects of future trading results, only to account for the impact of timing differences which have affected trading results reported to date.

Supporters of this view would argue that it is only possible to take account of future timing differences in assessing the deferred tax liability which is to be provided This explains why it is considered to be legitimate to anticipate the effects of future capital expenditure but not to anticipate future trading results. Part of the confusion in this area is related to the question of whether trading losses do in fact give rise to timing differences. As mentioned at 3.2.2 above, SSAP 15 states that a loss for tax purposes which is available to relieve future profits from tax constitutes a timing difference. This is true in respect of current and past trading losses; they have been dealt with in the financial statements, but not yet in arriving at the liability to tax as assessed in the tax computation. However, it is not true in respect of future trading losses, which so far have been dealt with in *neither* statement. Indeed, to recognise the tax effects of future losses, but not otherwise to provide for them in the financial statements would have the effect of *creating* a timing difference where none had previously existed.

We prefer the second of these two arguments, and accordingly believe that the forecast loss should not figure in the assessment of the reversing timing differences and the deferred tax provision should be based on timing differences of £150,000 in this example. In general terms the effects of a tax loss may only be recognised if the loss has been incurred and accounted for in the financial statements. Anticipated tax losses may not be used to reduce, or to avoid, a provision for deferred taxation.

4.3   Tax losses and group relief

4.3.1   Background

Where a member of a group has tax losses it may surrender them to another group member to be set off against their taxable profits of the same period, subject to a number of detailed provisions of the tax legislation. Such a transfer may be made with or without payment by the company receiving the group relief; this is a matter of policy for the group to decide. Where payment is made it is usually at the applicable tax rate in force, so that the profitable company is in effect paying as group relief what it would otherwise have paid in tax, and the loss-making company is having its losses relieved at the same rate.

4.3.2   The financial statements of the profitable company

Group relief gives rise to no significant accounting implications so far as the profitable company is concerned, so long as it is being paid for at the effective rate of tax as described above; whether it pays tax to the revenue or a payment for group relief to another company, the financial impact on it will be the same. The only difference will be that it will disclose the payments made as 'group relief' within its note analysing the tax charge, rather than as corporation tax payable.

However, where it is receiving relief without payment, different considerations apply. Where the incidence of the relief gives rise to an unusually low tax charge, it will generally be appropriate to disclose the reason for this because it is a 'special circumstance affecting the liability to tax on profits for the current year'.[73] The more significant effect, however, may be on deferred tax, because the company may be told by the holding company that there is no need to provide for the tax arising on the expected reversal of timing differences because it will be relieved without cost by losses made available to it by other group companies.

The availability of group relief without charge might strictly be thought to represent a permanent difference, because it features in the company's tax computation, and not in its financial statements. In general, we believe that it is inappropriate to anticipate the effect of future permanent differences as a reason for not providing for an expected reversal of timing differences. However, even if this is true as a general rule, it is specifically contradicted in relation to group relief by SSAP 15, which states that, 'where a company is a member of a group, it should, in accounting for deferred tax, take account of any group relief which, on reasonable evidence, is expected to be available and any charge which will be made for such relief'.[74]

The standard does not explain the reasoning behind this ruling. However, it could be justified on the view that the profitable company *is* in fact providing for deferred tax, but at the rate at which it will pay for the group relief rather than at the tax rate in force. Where the group relief rate has been set at 0%, therefore, the amount of the provision will properly be calculated as being nil.

This has no overall effect on the amount of deferred tax provided by the group as a whole, because the position of the group has to be looked at as a separate exercise in any event (see 4.4 below).

4.3.3 *The financial statements of the loss-making company*

From the point of view of the loss-making company, any losses surrendered without payment to other group companies clearly have no value to it. However, where the losses are being surrendered for consideration, the effect will be to allow the company to recoup some value from these losses sooner, and with greater certainty, than it otherwise might. In most cases, credit will be taken in the year in which the taxable loss arises, as the holding company will generally have determined the group relief situation within the group. Nevertheless, in some situations, on grounds of prudence, it may be appropriate to take no credit for this until it is certain that it will be received, which may not be until the group election has been made. Where a credit for these losses appears within the tax charge note it should be described as 'group relief receivable'.

4.4   Tax in the financial statements of a group

The financial statements of the group are prepared as if it were a single entity, and the question of how to portray the tax affairs of the whole group has to be considered in that light; it will not simply be a matter of aggregating the financial statements of all the group companies, who have to consider their own tax position in isolation, but rather one of reassessing the position of the group as a whole. However, individual group companies may operate in different tax jurisdictions, or be subject to other constraints which keep their tax affairs separate, so it will be necessary to have regard to these factors in deciding what can be netted off for the purposes of the group accounts.

Where one company expects to have reversals of timing differences in the future, and another expects to have originating timing differences, these may in principle be looked at in aggregate to see whether any overall reversal need be provided for, subject to certain caveats. Even if one company ends up paying more tax because of the reversal, the other will pay less because of its originating differences, and the overall effect on the group will therefore be as if the timing differences had been in one company. However, this approach will have to be modified if the companies are paying tax at different rates, or if the company with originating timing differences is put into a tax loss situation which cannot be relieved, so that the group suffers a net cash outflow: in these circumstances it will be necessary to provide for the effects of that inability to treat the companies as one for tax purposes. An example will illustrate these points.

Example 7.8: Assessing the deferred tax position in a group

Company S is a wholly owned subsidiary of company H. At the end of 19X1, the companies assess that their future patterns of cumulative timing differences will be as follows:

	19X1 £'000	19X2 £'000	19X3 £'000	19X4 £'000	19X5 £'000
Company H	400	500	600	650	700
Company S	500	300	250	200	200
Aggregate	900	800	850	850	900

It is expected that no reversal of timing differences will take place beyond 19X5 in either company.

Taking the companies in isolation, company H would make no provision for deferred tax because it foresaw no reversal of timing differences; however, it would not be permitted to anticipate the benefit of future originating timing differences, so its balance sheet would carry neither a deferred tax asset nor a liability. Company S, on the other hand, would have to provide for tax on its anticipated reversals of £300,000 (£500,000 — £200,000).

When the group is considered as a whole, it can be seen that net reversals of only £100,000 are expected to occur (£900,000 — £800,000) so in the normal course of events, the group's deferred tax liability need be calculated only on that figure; that is the amount which would have been the basis of the provision if all the timing differences had been in a single company, and that will represent the effect of timing differences on the group as a whole.

Complications arise, however, if the companies are situated in different tax jurisdictions. If, for example, company S is in a country where tax is payable at a rate of 50%, while company H is paying tax at 35%, it is necessary to recompute the above calculation to take account of the tax rates involved. This results in the following picture:

	19X1 £'000	19X2 £'000	19X3 £'000	19X4 £'000	19X5 £'000
Company H — tax effects at 35%	140	175	210	227	245
Company S — tax effects at 50%	250	150	125	100	100
Aggregate	390	325	335	327	345

On this basis it can be seen that deferred tax of £65,000 should be provided (£390,000 — £325,000) in respect of the reversal of gross aggregate timing differences of £100,000. This is simply because the reversal in company S is taxed at a higher rate than the relief obtained in company H from its originating timing differences.

A further complication may arise if the originating timing differences anticipated by company H are likely to result in taxable losses in that company. If the two companies were in the UK, that would not make any difference, because the effect of these losses could then be transferred to S in the form of group relief. However, where the countries are in different jurisdictions, this will not be possible and the group will experience the adverse effects of company S's reversal without the benefit of any tax saving in respect of company H. In these circumstances, provision should be made in the group financial statements for the deferred tax liability which relates to company S.

The implications of the above are that it is necessary to assess the deferred tax position of the group carefully to see what will be the real result, in tax terms, of future movements in timing differences. As a practical matter, it may be helpful to approach this by examining the overall position for all the group companies in each tax jurisdiction as an interim stage in the process. In general terms, the deferred tax effects of companies in different jurisdictions should not be netted off where there is a significant possibility that increased tax charges in one country might not be offset by tax savings in others.

4.5   ACT

4.5.1   *ACT carried forward as an asset*

The rules regarding the carry-forward of ACT are somewhat confused. As described in 3.1.2 above, SSAP 8 says that ACT can be carried forward as an asset if it is 'expected to be recoverable taking into account expected profits and dividends — normally those of the next accounting period only'.[75] However, SSAP 15 has slightly different rules, which deal separately with ACT on dividends which are payable and proposed at the balance sheet date and ACT relating to dividends from earlier periods. The former 'should be carried forward to the extent that it is foreseen that sufficient corporation tax will be assessed on the profits or income of the succeeding accounting period, against which the advance corporation tax is available for offset'.[76] The latter 'should be written off unless their recovery is assured beyond reasonable doubt', and 'such recovery will normally be assured only where the debit balances are recoverable out of corporation tax arising on profits or income of the succeeding accounting period, *without replacement by equivalent debit balances*'[77] (emphasis added).

The application of the final part of the last rule treats ACT as if it were a timing difference, subject to the normal rules of deferred tax set out in SSAP 15, rather than a prepayment of tax, which is what it actually is. However, it is difficult to see whether this rule overrides the one set out in SSAP 8, and even if it does, whether the word 'normally' provides some latitude in its interpretation on this point. In our view, a sensible construction to be placed on these rules in combination should permit ACT to be carried forward as an asset provided it meets the basic SSAP 8 test that it is expected to be recoverable, and we do not believe that replacement by an asset of a similar amount in respect of ACT paid subsequently should inhibit this.

4.5.2   *ACT set against the deferred tax liability*

As stated above, ACT is a prepayment of tax, not a timing difference, but it is appropriate to deal with it as a deduction from deferred tax insofar as it would be available to offset the deferred tax liability if it became payable. There is a limit within the tax legislation on the offset of ACT against mainstream tax liabilities, and this is referred to in both SSAP 8 and SSAP 15 in terms which seek to restrict the proportion of the deferred tax account which may be offset in this way. SSAP 8 states that 'only a proportion of the balance on the account. . . can be used for this purpose'.[78] SSAP 15 seems more doubtful however; 'It *may* be incorrect to carry forward an amount of ACT to offset an equal credit amount of deferred tax'[79] (emphasis added).

In practice a variety of treatments appear to be applied. Some companies apply these paragraphs literally, setting ACT against their deferred tax balances to the extent of 25/35ths (the proportion applicable for 1988/89), and dealing with the remainder as an asset; some offset it against deferred tax without regard for the limit (such as Imperial Chemical Industries PLC); and some treat it all as an asset and ignore the deferred tax liability altogether (such as Sears plc). Provided the ACT can be regarded as recoverable, these are simply matters of classification in the balance sheet, and any of these three treatments is probably, therefore, acceptable.

Extract 7.10: Imperial Chemical Industries PLC[80]

7 *TAX ON PROFIT ON ORDINARY ACTIVITIES* [extract]

	GROUP		COMPANY	
	1987	1986	1987	1986
	£m	£m	£m	£m
DEFERRED TAXATION				
The amounts of deferred taxation accounted for and the potential amounts of deferred taxation are:				
ACCOUNTED FOR AT BALANCE SHEET DATE				
Timing differences on UK capital allowances and depreciation	51	66	41	48
Miscellaneous timing differences	(8)	(3)	(6)	(4)
Advance corporation tax recoverable	(63)	(60)	(63)	(60)
	(20)	3	(28)	(16)
Corporation tax effect of deferred petroleum revenue tax provision		(21)		
	(20)	(18)	(28)	(16)
NOT ACCOUNTED FOR AT BALANCE SHEET DATE				
UK capital allowances utilised in excess of depreciation charged	333	364	327	325
Miscellaneous timing differences	(21)	(16)	14	(5)
	312	348	341	320
FULL POTENTIAL DEFERRED TAXATION	292	330	313	304

Extract 7.11: Sears plc[81]

12. DEBTORS

	Group		Company	
	1987/88	1986/87	**1987/88**	1986/87
	£m	£m	**£m**	£m
Due within one year:				
Trade debtors	**208.7**	70.2	—	—
Group companies			**145.8**	215.2
Taxation recoverable	**2.1**	3.8	—	—
Other debtors	**39.3**	19.9	—	—
Prepayments and accrued income	**39.7**	24.9	—	—
	289.8	118.8	**145.8**	215.2
Due after one year:				
Trade debtors	**8.5**	—	—	—
Other debtors	**3.7**	1.8	—	—
Advance corporation tax	**16.3**	16.6	**16.3**	16.6
	318.3	137.2	**162.1**	231.8

As can be seen from Extract 7.6 above, the balance on Sears plc's deferred tax account was only £3.3 million.

SSAP 8 also states that 'to the extent to which the deferred taxation account represents deferred chargeable gains, it is not available for [offsetting ACT]'.[82] This is no longer the case; as a result of recent changes in the tax legislation, it is now possible to offset ACT against tax payable in respect of chargeable gains.

Where the holding company has no trade of its own to give rise to a deferred tax liability, it will generally recover its ACT by surrendering it to its subsidiaries to be offset against their tax or deferred tax liabilities. In these circumstances, it will be appropriate for it to carry forward such ACT as it expects to recover as an asset in its own balance sheet.

4.6 Deferred tax and government grants

Government grants can generally be classified as falling into two types, either capital based, or revenue based, although in practice the dividing line between the two can become blurred, as discussed in Chapter 14. Capital grants are recognised in the profit and loss account over the estimated useful life of the asset, either by crediting the amount received to the fixed asset account and charging depreciation on the net sum, or by crediting the grant received to a separate deferred credit account and releasing a portion of the balance based on the useful life of the asset.

Some capital grants are totally free of tax: the grant itself is not taxed as income and the asset which it subsidises still attracts capital allowances on the gross cost. In such circumstances the amount of the grant constitutes a permanent difference. It is important that the choice of method of accounting for the grant described above does not interfere with the calculation of the deferred tax liability, as illustrated in the following example:

Example 7.9:   Alternative calculations of deferred tax on grant-aided assets

An asset costs £10,000 and is depreciated over ten years on a straight line basis. A grant of £1,500 is received in respect of it, and it also qualifies for writing down allowances of 25% p.a. for tax purposes on the full cost of £10,000. The tax rate is 35%.

The deferred tax might be calculated in either of two ways:

	Option (a) £	Option (b) £
Cost	10,000	10,000
Less grant	1,500	—
	8,500	10,000
Less depreciation	850	1,000
Net book value at end of 19X1	7,650	9,000
Cost for tax purposes	10,000	10,000
Less writing down allowance	2,500	2,500
Tax written down value at end of 19X1	7,500	7,500
Timing difference	150	1,500
Tax effect at 35%	52	525

In calculating the amount of the timing difference, option (a) uses the carrying value of the asset net of the government grant, whereas option (b) makes the same calculation on a gross basis. This may be an inadvertent side-effect of the treatment used for accounting for the grant itself, under the two optional presentations offered by SSAP 4 and described in Chapter 14.

The effect of using option (a) would be to take the whole effect of the permanent difference to the profit and loss account in the first year, whereas that of using option (b) spreads it over the life of the asset. We would regard option (b) as the correct treatment, because the tax effect of permanent differences should be recognised in the period in which the item giving rise to the difference is dealt with in the financial statements; the grant is spread over the life of the asset, and the tax benefit of the grant should be dealt with in the same way. Where the 'net' approach of accounting for the grant is used, therefore, the asset should be grossed up for the purpose of computing the timing differences on which the deferred tax calculation is based.

Where grants are not free of tax, because capital allowances are available only on the net cost of the asset after deduction of the amount of the grant received, there is no permanent difference. Where the 'net' treatment is used for accounting for the grant, the timing difference is calculated as normal by taking the difference between the carrying value of the asset in the financial statements (i.e. the cost of the asset, net of the grant, less accumulated depreciation) and the tax written down value of the asset. Where the grant is taken instead to a deferred credit account, it will be necessary to net that off against the carrying value of the asset for the purposes of computing the timing difference.

Revenue based grants are normally accounted for and taxed in the same accounting period and generally, therefore, are unlikely to have any deferred tax implications. Revenue grants may be held as deferred credits if they are received but not recognised in the profit and loss account (because of the matching principle), and if the grant is taxed on receipt then the timing difference will represent a deferred tax asset.

4.7   Changes in tax rates and allowances

4.7.1   *Changes in the rates of tax*

A   *Corporation tax*

In providing for the amount of current corporation tax that should be accrued in the financial statements the best estimate of the amount payable is made. This involves a number of estimates, including the extent of disallowable expenditure (for items such as entertaining, legal fees, etc.), the amount of expenditure that will qualify for capital allowances (particularly expenditure on certain types of plant and machinery), and the standard rate of corporation tax that will apply to the taxable profits. Companies which qualify for the small companies rate or for marginal relief should make the provision in their financial statements on the basis of these concessions if they estimate that the taxable profits are at the appropriate level.

In the past, the standard rate of corporation tax was always set retrospectively, but this practice has tended to change recently, so that rates are set in advance — for example, the standard rate of corporation tax for the year to March 31, 1989 was set at 35% in the March 1988 budget. There is, of course, a possibility that the budget proposals, in the form of the Finance Bill, are not successful in their passage through Parliament, and the rate suffered may therefore eventually be different to the 35% used by companies in the preparation of their financial statements. If this is so, then the under or over accrual flows through the company's profit and loss account as (a separately disclosed) part of the following year's tax charge. (Similarly if companies provided tax in their financial statements using the small companies rate or marginal relief concessions, and the final agreed profits fell to be taxed at the standard rate, then a charge will arise in the following year's profit and loss account representing the under accrual.)

B   *Deferred tax*

At each year end a company will provide for the appropriate level of deferred tax and will use the best estimate of the rate that will be payable on the taxable profits when the timing differences reverse. This is the fundamental approach of the liability method.

Timing differences by their very nature will reverse over many years and the rate of tax will not normally be known in advance for any of these years. Of course, if rates were set some years in advance then those rates would be applied to the element of timing differences expected to reverse in each of the future years, and the liability computed accordingly. This was the situation following the 1984 Finance Act when rates were set some three years into the future.

Generally, the best estimate of the rate of tax that will be applied to reversing differences is the standard rate of tax currently in force, and accordingly deferred tax provisions are made on this basis. Any under or over accrual arising from a rate change will pass through the company's profit and loss account as (a separately disclosed) part of the deferred tax charge for the year, in the year in which the rate changes, or the change is announced, whichever is the earlier. Indeed, if the change of rate is announced after the year end but before the financial statements are prepared, the effect will be reflected in the year which has already ended; this is given in the Appendix to SSAP 17 as an example of an adjusting event.[83] This is computed by taking the net timing differences on which deferred tax was provided in the preceding year's balance sheet and applying the difference between the old rate and the new rate.

There are exceptions to the above for those companies which qualify for the small companies rate or for marginal relief. Those companies which suffer tax at the small companies rate should generally provide for deferred tax at that rate unless they foresee that the taxable profits in the forthcoming years will rise above the small company threshold. Such taxable profits are not just the timing differences that are expected to reverse in a particular year, but must include an estimate of the taxable trading profit that will arise, since this will form part of the total taxable profits of the company. A similar estimate should be made to determine if the marginal relief provisions will apply to any of the forthcoming years, but this can be even more difficult to assess. It may in certain circumstances be impossible to determine if the marginal reliefs will apply, and in such cases the prudent view should prevail and the standard rate of tax should be used to calculate the provision.

4.7.2   Changes in tax allowances

The problem posed by the way in which to account for changes in tax allowances was brought to a head following the provisions of the 1984 Finance Act, which sought to simplify the corporation tax system. In outline, the Finance Act 1984 provided that first year capital allowances would be phased out over three years (from 100% for certain types of assets), and at the same time the rate of corporation tax would be reduced in steps, from 50% to 35%, over the same period.

The good news was that any deferred tax on timing differences which was provided (on the basis that they were to reverse in the next few years), had been provided at too high a rate of tax. The bad news, however, was much more serious and often outweighed the beneficial effect of the rate change. Many companies had not provided any deferred tax in respect of fixed asset timing differences because they believed that the generous system of first year allowances would continue, thus preventing the net reversal of timing differences. With the abolition of first year allowances most of the assumptions made by companies about the level of future timing differences that would be generated were completely invalid, and companies were faced with large underprovisions for deferred tax.

The question of whether such underprovisions were part of the current year's tax charge, an extraordinary item or indeed gave rise to a prior year adjustment were uppermost, and different presentations were adopted.

ED 33 had been issued in June 1983; accordingly it was possible to advance the argument that standard accounting practice was suspended, or at least in a state of flux, because paragraph 28 of the exposure draft provided that 'adjustment to the deferred tax balance arising solely from changes in tax rates or in rates of relief should be accounted for in the same manner as that adopted when the relevant part of the deferred tax balance first arose and should be separately disclosed where material. Significant adjustments to the deferred tax balance arising from changes in the basis of taxation should be treated as extraordinary items.'

In an attempt to clarify the position, the ASC issued a statement in April 1984 summarising their view that the original SSAP 15 remained in force, and together with SSAP 6 on extraordinary items and prior year adjustments, any deferred tax provision calculated in the light of the tax changes proposed by the Finance Bill would have to comply with the requirements of these two standards. Considerable press comment was passed following this statement; much of it was critical, because of the conclusion that could be drawn, condoning a relatively novel presentation whereby the additional charge was shown on the face of the profit and loss account as a deduction from retained earnings brought forward, rather than as a charge against the current year's net of tax profits.

A majority of companies reported the increased provisions as extraordinary items, and the present position is almost unchanged from ED 33, since paragraph 36 of the revised version of SSAP 15 requires that 'adjustments to deferred tax arising from changes in tax rates and tax allowances should normally be disclosed separately as part of the tax charge for the period. However the effect of a change in the basis of taxation, or of a significant change in Government fiscal policy should be treated as an extraordinary item where material'. However, this does not really settle the question conclusively, because it is difficult to discern exactly when changes in the tax rules are of such magnitude that they fall within the extraordinary category; consequently, each case will have to be judged on its merits.

4.8 Revaluations of fixed assets

SSAP 15 discusses the revaluation of fixed assets in relation to the tax consequences which would arise if they were disposed of at their revalued amounts. However, it contains no discussion of the effects of revaluation on the calculation of deferred tax relating to timing differences between the amounts of depreciation charged in the financial statements and of capital allowances in the tax computation. Furthermore, the standard does not contain a clear statement of the concept on which it is based, from which it might be possible to infer what the treatment should be. The rules on this issue are therefore obscure; the two main possibilities are described below.

For the purposes of this discussion, it is assumed that the assets in question are depreciated and attract capital allowances, so that they will be written off over a period for both accounting and tax purposes. For certain assets this will not be so;

they might not be depreciated (as is the case with some assets, which are thought to maintain their value) or they might not qualify for capital allowances, because, for example, they are commercial buildings. In either of these cases, a timing difference will not arise.

The first way of looking at the revaluation of a depreciable asset is that it creates a further timing difference, because in effect it is an adjustment of depreciation, which is itself an element of a timing difference. Where, for example, an asset is purchased for £10,000, subsequently depreciated to £6,000 and then revalued to £9,000, the £3,000 revaluation surplus could be regarded as reinstating the depreciation which was previously charged, and therefore reversing the deferred tax effect of charging that depreciation. On this basis, the £9,000 would be compared with the tax written down value of the asset in order to determine the amount of the timing difference which gives a potential liability to deferred tax. This is the view taken by the Accountants Digest on SSAP 15.[84]

The alternative viewpoint sees the revaluation as giving rise to a permanent difference. This is on the basis that the revaluation, and its subsequent reversal through depreciation, has no equivalent within the tax computation and hence does not give rise to a timing difference. The revaluation is not a reversal of previous depreciation, which properly reflected the consumption of part of the asset based on its then carrying value; it simply means that the remaining part of the asset has a different value and its consumption will be measured at a different amount. The future depreciation charge will have two components; the original charge based on cost, and the further amount based on the revaluation surplus. That further amount has no tax equivalent and it would be wrong to make any tax adjustment in respect of it.

We believe that both of these arguments are coherent, and in the absence of more definitive guidance from the standard itself, we consider that they are both acceptable, so long as the approach taken is consistently applied.

Where the revaluation takes the value of the asset above its original cost, it takes the matter out of the realm of accelerated capital allowances and into that of chargeable gains. As mentioned above, SSAP 15 does deal with this issue and says that a timing difference will be created 'insofar as the profit or loss that would result from realisation at the revalued amount is taxable, unless disposal of the revalued asset and of any subsequent replacement assets would not result in a tax liability, after taking account of any expected rollover relief'.[85] Provision for this should then be considered if it is intended to dispose of the asset, unless the tax effect would be mitigated by the effects of other originating timing differences.

4.9   Overseas earnings

When a UK group incorporates the earnings of a foreign subsidiary or associate in its consolidated financial statements, a timing difference will arise if the earnings are to be remitted to the UK in a later period and will give rise to incremental tax payments when they are remitted. SSAP 15 requires that these timing differences should be taken into account in the calculation of deferred tax unless it is intended to retain the earnings in the foreign country indefinitely so that no further tax liability will arise.

In practice it can be extremely difficult to determine how much to provide, since this will be subject to many uncertainties; the amount of any liability will depend on factors such as the relative tax rates of the UK and the foreign country concerned, the provisions of any tax treaty between the countries, and the level of UK taxable profits at the time of the remittance. Nonetheless it is necessary that companies which expect that a liability will emerge should make the best estimate that they can in the circumstances.

As indicated in 3.2.4 above, it is necessary to disclose the fact that no provision has been made, where this is the case.[86] However, the reasoning behind this is perhaps somewhat confused. This requirement was added in substitution for the proposed requirement in ED 33 to state that there were no plans to remit overseas earnings, where this applied,[87] but the two cannot be regarded as equivalent to one another. Even where earnings *will* be remitted, and where tax *will* become payable as a result, it might be concluded that no provision is needed because other originating timing differences are forecast to arise in the year of remittance. Accordingly, it is not really possible to read very much into this disclosure when it is made.

5   COMPARISON WITH US AND IASC PRONOUNCEMENTS

5.1   IASC

International Accounting Standard No. 12 — *Accounting for Taxes on Income* — was published in 1979. In general terms the requirements of IAS 12 are sufficiently similar to those of the revised version of SSAP 15 to ensure that compliance with SSAP 15 gives automatic compliance with the international standard.

At present, the international standard allows either the deferral method or the liability method to be used, and permits both comprehensive allocation and partial provision. However, in January 1989 the IASC published a new exposure draft[88] which proposed that only the liability method should be permitted, and that comprehensive allocation should be the preferred method, although partial provision would remain a permitted alternative. It remains to be seen whether these proposals are adopted.

5.2   US

5.2.1   APB 11

Until recently, accounting for taxation in the USA was governed by an Opinion of the Accounting Principles Board issued in 1967 — APB 11.[89] This required full provision for deferred tax using the deferral method. Its objective was to match initial tax effects of timing differences with related income and expense recognised in pre-tax profits. Such an approach focused on obtaining matching in the profit and loss account, thereby largely disregarding the composition of the deferred tax debits and credits that accumulated in the balance sheet.

The computation of deferred tax on originating timing differences was conducted using the 'with-and-without' approach (i.e. with and without the inclusion of the transaction representing the timing difference). Reversals of timing differences were calculated using either the 'net change' method (i.e. at current tax rates) or the 'gross change' method (i.e the rates at which the originating timing difference was recorded).

The tax benefit of losses carried forward could be recognised as an asset if its realisation were assured beyond reasonable doubt. In the year of realisation (if later than the year of the loss) the benefit of the loss on the tax charge would be reported as an extraordinary item.

The deferred tax account was analysed and disclosed as either current or non-current in the balance sheet, depending on the classification of the asset to which it related.

5.2.2   SFAS 96

In 1987, the FASB issued SFAS 96 — *Accounting for Income Taxes*.[90] This Statement becomes effective for accounting periods beginning on or after December 15, 1989, and supersedes APB 11 and other related pronouncements. Its main features are set out below. There were a number of reasons for what was a fundamental change of approach to the whole subject of accounting for taxation, but one of the most significant was that the balance sheet figures created by the deferral approach which APB 11 required were increasingly regarded as having very little meaning. In particular, they did not conform to the definitions of assets and liabilities which the FASB had adopted in their conceptual framework study.[91]

In contrast to APB 11, SFAS 96 requires a liability approach, focusing on the balance sheet amounts in order to allocate tax between different accounting periods. Under this approach, deferred tax represents tax payable or refundable in future years as a result of existing differences between the book and tax bases of the company's assets and liabilities. These differences are described in SFAS 96 as 'temporary differences' and include differences between the assigned fair values and the tax bases of assets and liabilities recognised in an acquisition.

The annual computation of the deferred tax liability or asset involves:

(a)   scheduling the temporary differences at the balance sheet date over the years when they are expected to result in taxable or tax deductible amounts; and

(b)   carrying out pro-forma tax computations for each future year assuming no other taxable or tax deductible amounts will occur in those years.

Separate scheduling is necessary for each different tax (e.g. in the UK context, corporation tax, petroleum revenue tax, etc.) and also for items which are subject to the same tax but assessed under different headings (e.g. income assessed under Schedule D Case I and capital gains and losses).

When calculating the tax payable for each future year, enacted tax rates and tax law as at the balance sheet date should be used, which means, for example, that no account can be taken of changes announced in a Budget but not incorporated in the related Finance Act by the year-end. The aggregate amount of tax computed for each future year should be recognised as a deferred tax liability or asset (see below) and the difference between this amount and the opening balance is the deferred tax charge or credit for the year.

Under SFAS 96, a deferred tax asset can be recognised generally in circumstances where tax paid in the current or a prior year is refundable. Thus, an asset should be recognised in respect of the tax benefits associated with net deductible amounts expected to reverse in a future year only to the extent that they can be carried back either to reduce the current deferred tax liability, or to result in a refund of taxes paid in the current or prior years.

Unlike APB 11, no asset is recognised for any unused 'net deductible amounts' or in respect of any unused tax losses carried forward, regardless of the probability that they will be realised in the future.

Deferred tax balances are classified as current or non-current, depending on when the temporary difference is expected to result in a taxable or deductible amount.

5.2.3 *Main differences between US and UK requirements*

The shift from the deferral method required by APB 11 to the liability method eliminates a major difference between the UK and US approach to accounting for deferred taxes. However, there are still a number of important differences.

A   *Timing versus temporary differences*

SSAP 15 is concerned solely with accounting for taxes that have been deferred or accelerated due to differences in the timing of recognition of revenues and expenses for accounting and tax purposes. Under SFAS 96, there are more differences than just those between accounting and taxable profits for which deferred taxes must be provided; for example, temporary differences arising due to the fair value exercise on an acquisition.

The discussion paper published by the Accounting Standards Committee (see 6.4.3 F of Chapter 4) in the UK on accounting for fair values following an acquisition suggests that fair value adjustments should lead to timing differences which will require provision for deferred tax. The discussion paper states that account should be taken of the marginal effect of such timing differences within the acquired company on the overall group tax position.

B   *Basis of provision*

SSAP 15 requires the partial provision method of deferred tax accounting. Under this method, deferred tax should be provided in respect of the tax effects of all timing differences, based on forecasts of whether a liability or asset will crystallise. When making such forecasts, timing differences are looked at on a combined basis taking into account future levels of capital expenditure and other financial plans or projections.

SFAS 96 does not allow any assumptions to be made concerning future events, other than the recovery of net assets at their recorded amounts. However, it permits the effect of tax planning strategies to be taken into account. A full provision method of accounting for deferred tax is required, which involves scheduling all temporary differences and carrying out pro-forma tax computations for each future year scheduled, assuming no other taxable or tax deductible amounts arise in those years.

C   Deferred tax assets

Both standards permit recognition of the benefits associated with tax losses carried forward through offset against the deferred tax liability resulting from the reversal of temporary/timing differences. Also, surplus ACT carried forward at the balance sheet date can be offset against the aggregate deferred tax liability subject to constraints imposed by tax law.

Under SSAP 15, net deferred tax debit balances (arising due to tax losses or the effect of timing differences) should not be carried forward as a deferred tax asset unless recovery without replacement by equivalent debit balances is assured beyond reasonable doubt. Proper forecasts would normally be prepared in order to justify carry-forward as a deferred tax asset.

Recognition of deferred tax assets under SFAS 96 is limited to cases where net tax deductible amounts scheduled to occur in future years could be carried back from the period of reversal and offset taxable income of the current or prior year, thereby giving rise to a theoretical refund of taxes paid or provided in the balance sheet.

D   Tax rates

SSAP 15 requires deferred tax provisions to be calculated at the rate at which tax is likely to be paid. Usually, the current tax rate is used as the best estimate. However, if changes in tax rates are known in advance, they may be used even though they have not been enacted. Under SFAS 96, enacted tax rates and tax law should be used when computing deferred taxes. Both standards require adjustment to deferred tax balances in the event of future changes in tax rates and tax law.

E   General

In general, SSAP 15 offers much more flexibility when calculating provision for deferred tax. Whilst the SSAP does emphasise the need to adopt a prudent view when assessing whether a tax liability will crystallise or when recognising deferred tax assets, deferred tax provisions established using SSAP 15 principles would tend to be lower than if the more prescriptive SFAS 96 method were used.

6   CONCLUSION

The most significant issue in accounting for taxation in the UK remains the application of the partial provision approach to deferred tax. The interpretation of some of the rules provides various alternatives, the estimation on which liabilities need be provided for leaves room for significant judgement, and the method itself remains controversial in an international context. However, the steady decline in recent years in the rates of taxation and in the allowances available to companies in calculating their taxable profit, have made these issues of less significance than they originally were when SSAP 15 was first introduced.

References

1 SSAP 15, *Accounting for deferred tax*, Revised May 1985, para. 16.
2 SSAP 6, *Extraordinary items and prior year adjustments*, Revised August 1986, para. 38.
3 ED 12, *The treatment of taxation under the imputation system in the accounts of companies*, May 1973.
4 ED 11, *Accounting for deferred taxation*, May 1973.
5 SSAP 11, *Accounting for deferred taxation*, August 1975.
6 ED 18, *Current cost accounting*, November 1986, paras. 244 — 257.
7 ED 19, *Accounting for deferred taxation*, May 1977.
8 Original SSAP 15, *Accounting for deferred taxation*, October 1978.
9 ED 33, *Accounting for deferred tax*, June 1983.
10 SSAP 15, *Accounting for deferred tax*, Revised May 1985.
11 SSAP 5, *Accounting for value added tax*, April 1974.
12 ED 10, *Accounting for Value Added Tax*, May 1973.
13 SSAP 5, para. 8.
14 *Ibid.*, para. 9.
15 ED 28, *Accounting for Petroleum Revenue Tax*, March 1981.
16 SSAP 8, *The treatment of taxation under the imputation system in the accounts of companies*, August 1974, para. 24.
17 *Ibid.*, para. 20.
18 *Ibid.*, para. 13.
19 *Ibid.*, para. 25.
20 *Ibid.*, para. 22.
21 *Ibid.*, para. 23.
22 *Ibid.*, para. 9.
23 SSAP 15, para. 1.
24 *Ibid.*, para. 2.
25 *Ibid.*, para. 12.
26 *Ibid.*, para. 14.
27 *Ibid.*, para. 17.
28 *Ibid.*, para. 18.
29 *Ibid.*, para. 19.
30 *Ibid.*, para. 20.
31 *Ibid.*, para. 21.
32 *Ibid.*, para. 23.
33 *Ibid.*, paras. 24 — 26.
34 *Ibid.*, Appendix, para. 4.
35 *Ibid.*, paras. 27 and 28.
36 *Ibid.*, Appendix, para. 4.
37 *Ibid.*, para. 29.
38 *Ibid.*, para. 30.
39 *Ibid.*, Appendix, para. 14.
40 *Ibid.*, Appendix, para. 15.
41 *Ibid.*, para. 31.
42 *Ibid.*, para. 32.
43 *Ibid.*, paras. 33 and 34.
44 THORN EMI plc, Annual Report 1988, pp. 51 and 52.
45 SSAP 6, para. 37.
46 SSAP 15, para. 35.
47 Glaxo Holdings p.l.c., Annual Report and Accounts 1988, p. 40.
48 Halma p.l.c., Annual report and accounts 1988, p. 27.
49 SSAP 15, para. 36.
50 *Ibid.*, paras. 37 and 40.

51 *Ibid.*, para. 41.
52 Pilkington plc, Annual Report for the year ended 31st March 1988, p. 48.
53 Associated Newspapers Holdings p.l.c., Report and Accounts 1987, p. 25.
54 Original SSAP 15, para. 33.
55 Sears PLC, Annual Report 1987/88, p. 42.
56 SSAP 15, para. 38.
57 *Ibid.*, para. 39.
58 *Ibid.*, para. 42.
59 Associated Newspapers Holdings p.l.c., Report and Accounts 1987, p. 25.
60 SSAP 15, para. 43.
61 *Ibid.*, para. 44.
62 THORN EMI plc, Annual Report 1988, p. 60.
63 CA 85, Sch. 4, para. 54(1).
64 *Ibid.*, para. 54(2).
65 *Ibid.*, para. 8 Profit and loss account formats and para. 54(3).
66 *Ibid.*, para. 8 Balance sheet formats.
67 *Ibid.*, para. 46.
68 *Ibid.*, para. 47.
69 SSAP 15, Appendix, para. 4.
70 Accountants Digest No. 174, ICAEW, *A Guide to Accounting Standards — Deferred Tax*, Summer 1985.
71 Associated British Engineering plc, Annual Report 1988, p.17.
72 SSAP 15, Appendix, para. 14.
73 CA 85, Sch. 4, para. 54 (2).
74 SSAP 15, para. 43.
75 SSAP 8, para. 20(c).
76 SSAP 15, para. 31.
77 *Ibid.*, para. 32.
78 SSAP 8, para. 7.
79 SSAP 15, Appendix, para. 17.
80 Imperial Chemical Industries PLC, Annual Report 1987, p. 39.
81 Sears PLC, Annual Report 1987/88, p. 39.
82 SSAP 8, para. 7.
83 SSAP 17, *Accounting for post balance sheet events*, August 1980, Appendix, item (g) of examples of adjusting events.
84 Accountants Digest No. 174, p. 12.
85 SSAP 15, para. 20.
86 *Ibid.*, para. 44.
87 ED 33, para. 35.
88 E33, *Accounting for Taxes on Income*, IASC, January 1989.
89 APB 11, *Accounting for Income Taxes*, AICPA, December 1967.
90 SFAS 96, *Accounting for Income Taxes*, FASB, December, 1987.
91 SFAC No. 6, *Elements of Financial Statements*, FASB, December 1985, paras. 25 and 35.

Chapter 8

Extraordinary items and prior year adjustments

1 THE NEED FOR A STANDARD

1.1 Income measurement

Chapter 2 discusses the concept of income and outlines the emphasis placed on the transactions approach to income measurement in the development of historical cost accounting theory. In other words, financial accounting under the historical cost system essentially involves allocating the effects of transactions between reporting periods, with the result that the balance sheet consists of the residuals of the income measurement process. Despite the conflict between the asset and liability vs. the revenue and expense viewpoints discussed in Chapter 2, the importance attributed to income measurement is highlighted by the FASB's Concepts Statement No. 1, which states that 'the primary focus of financial reporting is information about an enterprise's performance provided by measures of earnings and its components. Investors, creditors, and others who are concerned with assessing the prospects for enterprise net cash inflows are especially interested in that information'.[1] In addition, the emphasis that analysts place on companies' reported earnings as a measurement of performance further illustrates the importance of income measurement.

Although the term 'income' is used to describe a concept, rather than something which is specific or precise, specific rules and procedures have been developed by accountants to measure income. These rules have been based on the concept of financial capital maintenance, which has been subscribed to by the FASB in SFAC No. 6 in terms of 'comprehensive income'. Comprehensive income is defined as 'the change in equity of a business enterprise during a period from transactions and other events and circumstances from nonowner sources'.[2] Therefore, the comprehensive income of a business enterprise over its entire lifetime will be the net of its cash receipts and cash outlays.[3]

However, the need to measure income over shorter periods for financial reporting purposes highlighted two major accounting issues. Firstly, there was the issue of how to allocate the effects of transactions between accounting periods for reporting purposes, instead of merely allowing them to fall in the periods in which the transactions took place. This issue is dealt with through the development of allocation rules based on the fundamental accounting concepts of matching and prudence. The second issue which arose was whether or not all recorded transactions should be included in the calculation of the figure for 'net profit/loss for the period'. Some accountants have held the view that net profit/loss should reflect the effects of all recorded transactions, whilst others have contended that net profit/loss should not be distorted by abnormal, unusual and non-recurring events and transactions. These differing viewpoints have led to two basic concepts of income: the all inclusive concept and the current operating performance concept.[4]

1.1.1   The all inclusive concept

Under this concept, net profit/loss would include all transactions (except dividends and capital transactions) which affect the net change in equity. Proponents of the all inclusive concept put forward the following arguments in favour of this basis of income measurement:

(a)   the annual reported net profits/losses, when aggregated over the life of the business enterprise, should be equal to the comprehensive income of the enterprise. Therefore, since charges and credits arising from extraordinary events and from corrections of prior periods are part of an enterprise's earnings history, the omission of such items from periodic income statements will result in the misstatement of the net profit/loss for a series of years;

(b)   the omission of certain charges and credits from the computation of the net profit/loss for a period, opens the door to possible manipulation or smoothing of results over a period;

(c)   a profit and loss account which includes the effects of all transactions is more easily understood and less subject to variations resulting from the application of subjective judgements;

(d)   full disclosure in the profit and loss account of the nature of all transactions will enable users to make their own assessments of the importance of the items and derive an appropriate measurement of income based on their own specific needs.

1.1.2   The current operating performance concept

Under this concept, the emphasis is on the ordinary, normal, recurring operations of the enterprise during the accounting period. If extraordinary or prior period transactions have occurred, their inclusion in the current period's profit and loss account 'might impair the significance of net income to such an extent that misleading inferences might be drawn from the amount so designated'.[5] Advocates of the current operating performance concept put forward the following arguments in its favour:[6]

(a)   users attach a particular business significance to the profit and loss account and the net profit/loss reported therein. While some users are able to analyse a profit and loss account and to eliminate from it those extraordinary and prior period transactions which may tend to impair its usefulness for their purposes, many users are not trained to do this. They believe that management (subject to the attestation of the independent auditors) is in a better position to do this and eliminate the effect of such items from the amount designated as net profit/loss for the period;

(b)   extraordinary and prior period transactions should be disclosed as direct adjustments of retained earnings, since this eliminates any distortive effect on reported earnings for the period, resulting in a more meaningful figure for inter-period and inter-firm comparison.

1.1.3   Which concept?

The fundamental difference in the two concepts of income discussed above lies in the perceived objectives of reporting net operating income for a particular period. SFAC No. 1 states that 'financial reporting should provide information about an enterprise's financial performance during a period. Investors and creditors often use information about the past to help in assessing the prospects of an enterprise. Thus, although investment and credit decisions reflect investors' and creditors' expectations about future enterprise performance, those expectations are commonly based at least partly on evaluations of past enterprise performance.'[7] Since the current operating net income for a period emphasises an enterprise's current financial performance for each period, predictions concerning future enterprise performance might be facilitated through the elimination of non-recurring and prior period transactions. Nevertheless, because of the artificial nature of the accounting period and the subjectivity necessary in the application of the current operating performance concept, the assessment of future performance can best be achieved if it is based on the *entire* historical performance of the enterprise over a series of several years.

Notwithstanding the various arguments concerning the respective merits and demerits of the two basic concepts of income, there was clearly a need for the standardisation of accounting practice in this area of reporting. Reserve accounting was prevalent through companies excluding capital and non-recurring items from the profit and loss account. In the UK, the ASC has come very close to adopting the all inclusive concept of income in SSAP 6.[8] There are, however, certain refinements such as the distinction between ordinary and extraordinary activities and some specified exceptions, which include prior year adjustments and items directly accounted for in reserves such as goodwill and certain foreign exchange differences.

1.2   The development of UK standards

Prior to SSAP 6, unusual or non-recurring transactions were frequently excluded from the profit and loss account for the year and accounted for as a movement in reserves so that the trend in reported results was not distorted by such transactions. However, the subjectivity inherent in determining whether an event was unusual or non-recurring would result in similar items in different companies receiving different treatments, thus rendering comparisons of the reported results of different companies relatively meaningless.

The first official guidance was given in 1958, in the form of an Accounting Recommendation issued by the ICAEW,[9] and in fact supported the distinction between capital and revenue as a means of determining what items should be included in the profit and loss account. However, the recommendation was insubstantial as it effectively permitted capital items to be accounted for either through the profit and loss account or through reserves — depending on which treatment would facilitate the presentation of a true and fair view.

1.2.1   The original SSAP 6

Consequently, the principal objects of ED 5[10] (issued in 1971), ED 7[11] (issued in 1972), and the first version of SSAP 6 (issued in 1974), were to ensure that all extraordinary or prior year items, with certain specified exceptions, should be accounted for through the profit and loss account for the period and not through reserves. In order to achieve this without losing information on the performance of the ongoing operations, SSAP 6 required the separate disclosure of profits and losses on extraordinary items after the profit or loss on ordinary activities, defining which items could be regarded as extraordinary. The standard also prescribed the only two instances where items could be retrospectively adjusted through reserves by means of a prior year adjustment.

Although SSAP 6 reduced the extent of reserve accounting, it inadvertently caused the development of a multiplicity of items classified as 'extraordinary', which would consequently be excluded from profit or loss on ordinary activities after taxation, and earnings per share. There was evidence of significant inconsistencies between the way different companies disclosed the effect of apparently similar events in their profit and loss accounts.

1.2.2   The revision of SSAP 6

The new accounts formats introduced in the Companies Act 1981[12] required separate disclosure in the profit and loss account of extraordinary items and the associated tax thereon after the profit or loss on ordinary activities, and thus standardised and gave statutory backing to the disclosure requirements of SSAP 6. This added impetus to the growing disquiet as to the effectiveness of the standard and in 1983 the ASC issued a discussion paper,[13] which identified some of the problems that had arisen since the introduction of SSAP 6 and proposed some solutions. In 1985, as a result of responses to this discussion paper, the ASC issued ED 36[14] (the exposure draft of the revision to SSAP 6), which embodied some of the solutions originally proposed in the 1983 discussion paper.

ED 36 attempted to reduce the problem of inconsistency in classification of items as extraordinary in three ways:

(a)   extending a list of examples given in the original SSAP 6 of events which are likely to be classified as extraordinary and contrasting this with a list of exceptional items;[15]

(b)   discussing the effects of terminating parts of operations and introducing a definition of a business segment to clarify when the discontinuance of part of a business could be treated as extraordinary;[16]

(c)   defining 'ordinary activities' and 'exceptional items' in order to clarify how extraordinary items could be distinguished.[17]

There were also a number of other new ideas introduced both in the body of the exposure draft and in the preface. These included:

(a) separate disclosure of profit before exceptional items and exceptional items on the face of the profit and loss account if necessary to show a true and fair view;[18]

(b) disclosure of a statement of movements on reserves, or a reference to where the statement is disclosed in the notes, on the face of the profit and loss account;[19]

(c) standardisation of the method of calculation of the tax charge or credit on extraordinary items;[20]

(d) inclusion of extraordinary and exceptional items in the preliminary and half-yearly announcements of listed companies;[21]

(e) restatement of historical summaries retroactively in the event of a prior year adjustment;[22]

(f) disclosure of earnings per share both pre- and post-extraordinary items.[23]

The first five of these points were all included in the revised standard when it was finally issued, however, the recommendation to disclose earnings per share both pre- and post-extraordinary items was in fact dropped as it was believed that a change in disclosure requirements for earnings per share fell outside the scope of this standard.

The exposure draft also dealt with a number of issues in relation to the revaluation of fixed assets which were not subsequently included in the revised standard as it was decided to deal with the issues as a separate project. These are discussed in greater detail in 5 of Chapter 10.

2   THE REQUIREMENTS OF SSAP 6 (REVISED)

2.1   Identification of extraordinary and exceptional items

The standard gives guidance as how to identify exceptional and extraordinary items and attempts to clarify the distinction by defining each of the terms and giving lists of examples of items which might fall into each category.

2.1.1   *Definitions*[24]

The definitions of extraordinary and exceptional items were not changed in substance from the original SSAP 6, although the term 'exceptional' had not previously been defined.

Extraordinary items are material items which derive from events or transactions that fall outside the ordinary activities of the company and which are therefore expected not to recur frequently or regularly.

Exceptional items are material items which derive from events or transactions that fall within the ordinary activities of the company, and which need to be disclosed separately by virtue of their size or incidence if the financial statements are to give a true and fair view.

Ordinary activities, which were not previously defined, are any activities which are usually, frequently or regularly undertaken by the company and any related activities in which the company engages in furtherance of, incidental to, or arising from those activities. They include, but are not confined to, the trading activities of the company.

The key factors to be considered when attempting to classify an item are therefore:

(a)   identification of the event; it is the event that results in the profit or loss that must be classified, rather than the transaction itself. Consequently, individual items derived from a single extraordinary event should be aggregated to arrive at a net extraordinary profit or loss;

(b)   materiality; the item must be material, and therefore for a company that is a member of a group the item could be material in the context of the company's financial statements but not in the context of the group's financial statements;

(c)   ordinary activities; for the item to be classified as extraordinary the event must be outside the ordinary activities of the entity. Therefore items which are extraordinary in one company may not be in another, due to differences in their ordinary activities. As in (b) above, events which are extraordinary in relation to a company which is a member of a group may not necessarily be regarded as extraordinary in the context of the group;

(d)   frequency of recurrence; for the item to be classified as extraordinary the event or transaction should not be expected to recur frequently or regularly.

2.1.2 Examples

Examples of items which might be treated as exceptional or extraordinary which are given by the standard are set out below and have been contrasted where applicable.

	Exceptional[25]	Extraordinary[26]
Rationalisation, reorganisation and redundancy costs	costs relating to continuing business segments	costs arising from the discontinuance of a business segment, either through termination or disposal
Fixed assets	profits/losses on disposals arising from an exceptional event	profits/losses on disposals arising from an extraordinary event
	write off of previously capitalised intangible assets	provisions for a permanent diminution in value of fixed assets, (including investments), because of an extraordinary event
		profits/losses arising from expropriation of assets
		profits/losses arising from the sale of an investment not held for resale
Other	costs of employee share schemes	
	abnormal bad debt charges	
	abnormal write offs of stock or work in progress or losses on long-term contracts	
	surpluses or receipts arising from insurance claims	
		effect of changes in the basis of taxation or fiscal policy

Although the standard lists these examples, it also emphasises that the classification of items will depend on the particular circumstances and that items which are classified as extraordinary in one company will not necessarily be extraordinary in another because of differences in their ordinary activities.[27] It is therefore essential that the primary method of classification of items is by reference to the definitions and that the examples are only used as a guide.

2.2   Terminated activities

The discontinuance of a business segment is one of the examples given by the standard of an extraordinary event.[28] The standard requires a provision to be made for the effect of all decisions made to discontinue entire business segments prior to the balance sheet date.[29]

The standard also makes the point that due to the long-term nature of a programme for discontinuing a business segment, provisions may be required in successive accounting periods for the consequence of one event, but this does not preclude them being treated as extraordinary items in each period.[30] Furthermore if a company discontinues further business segments in future years, the fact that such an event has recurred does not preclude all such events from being regarded as extraordinary.

2.2.1   Identification of a business segment

The standard attempts to distinguish between:

(a)   the discontinuance of a distinct business segment which should be classified as extraordinary; and

(b)   programmes of reorganisation which do not result in the discontinuance of a business segment which should be classified as exceptional.[31]

This distinction therefore hinges on the definition of a *business segment*: a material and separately identifiable component of the business operations of a company whose activities, assets and results can be clearly distinguished from the remainder of the company's activities. A business segment will normally have its own separate product lines or markets.[32]

2.2.2   Items to be taken into account in evaluating the effect of discontinuing a business segment

When a decision has been taken to discontinue a business segment, provision will be required for the costs of all the consequences of the decision. The standard includes a list of the likely costs, the aggregate of which should be treated as an extraordinary item:[33]

(a)   net redundancy costs and pension costs;

(b)   labour and overhead costs employed in the running off period;

(c)   profits or losses arising from the disposal of assets;

(d)   debts not recovered as a result of a closure;

(e)   trading results after implementation of a closure programme;

(f)   losses due to penalty clauses in contracts.

2.2.3   *Decision date and implementation date*

The standard distinguishes two key dates for a closure programme:

(a)   the *decision date*—the date at which the decision is made to discontinue a business segment;

(b)   the *implementation date*—the date at which the implementation of the scheme commences.[34]

Once the decision has been made, a provision should be made for the net costs relating to the closure including trading losses expected to arise after the implementation date.

Trading results for the period before the implementation date are part of the trading results for the year and are not to be included in the extraordinary item. However, they may require separate disclosure to enable the results of the continuing operations to be ascertained.[35] This raises questions as to what profit and loss information should be separately disclosed and whether it is the results of the segment since the decision date, or the results since the beginning of the accounting period that should be identified. If the latter, then there is a further question as to whether the results of the segment during the prior year should also be disclosed to provide full comparatives. Although the standard gives no further guidance on these questions, it is our view that, where it has been decided to show discontinued activities separately then, as a minimum, the turnover and operating profit of the segment for the current and prior period should be disclosed. However, if the segment is a major part of the total operations of the company then it might be helpful to disclose full profit and loss account information for the segment by way of note.

One company which has disclosed information relating to its discontinued activities is Beecham Group p.l.c. as illustrated below:

Extract 8.1: Beecham Group p.l.c.[36]

Segment information [extract]

Discontinued operations

The analysis of sales and trading profit by business sector and geographical area of the businesses sold during 1987/88 and 1986/87, or in course of disposal at each year end, is as follows:

	Sales		Trading profit	
	1987/88	1986/87	**1987/88**	1986/87
	£ m	£m	**£ m**	£m
Business sector:				
Pharmaceutical products	**0.7**	6.9	—	—
Consumer products	**101.5**	531.8	**6.1**	13.5
Total	**102.2**	538.7	**6.1**	13.5
Geographical area:				
United Kingdom	**0.7**	248.2	—	8.9
Rest of Europe	—	52.6	—	1.6
The Americas	**101.5**	228.1	**6.1**	2.8
Rest of the World	—	11.5	—	0.2
Intra–group sales	—	(1.7)	—	—
Total	**102.2**	538.7	**6.1**	13.5

In addition to the information given in the above extract, Beecham Group p.l.c. segregate the total sales and profits relating to the discontinued activities in disclosing the analysis of the total sales and trading profit of the group by business sector and by geographical area, and segregate the total sales relating to the discontinued operations in the analysis of sales by geographical location of customer; accordingly, the segmental information relating to their continuing operations is apparent.

Once a scheme for discontinuing a business segment has been implemented, all trading results relating to the discontinued activities should be included within the extraordinary item. However, there still remains the obligation to satisfy the statutory profit and loss disclosure which includes all items in the profit and loss format adopted by the company and the various additional disclosures such as staff costs, depreciation etc. In our view sufficient detail should be given of the amounts included within the extraordinary item to enable statutory disclosure requirements to be met; however, there is very little evidence of such disclosures being made in practice.

2.3   Tax attributable to extraordinary items

The standard requires the tax on the extraordinary item, whether it be a profit or a loss, to be disclosed.[37] The disclosure requirements of the Companies Act 1985 are slightly more detailed in that it is specified that the tax on the net total of extraordinary gains and losses should be disclosed separately and the proportions relating to UK corporation tax, double tax relief, UK income tax and overseas taxation be specified. Deferred tax on the extraordinary items should also be disclosed separately to comply with the requirements of SSAP 15.[38]

A method of calculating the tax attributable to extraordinary items is also given. The tax charge should be determined by computing the total tax charge with and without the extraordinary item, the difference being the tax charge or credit which should be disclosed as extraordinary.[39]

It is frequently not a straightforward matter to identify the tax relating to extraordinary items as the following example illustrates:

Example 8.1

A company has no corporation tax liability for an accounting period as it has net taxable losses for the period of £200,000. Profits on ordinary activities are £450,000 after deduction of net disallowable expenditure of £350,000. Extraordinary losses (which are fully tax allowable) amount to £1m. (Assume no provision is required for deferred taxation.) The relevant corporation tax rate for the period is 35%.

Although the company has no overall tax liability, by following the method recommended in the standard it is necessary to disclose a tax charge on the profit on ordinary activities and a tax credit relating to the extraordinary item as shown below:

	£'000	£'000
Profit on ordinary activities before taxation		450
Taxation charge		280
Profit on ordinary activities after taxation		170
Extraordinary loss	(1,000)	
Tax credit on extraordinary loss	280	
		(720)
Loss for the period		(550)

Note:
The tax credit on the extraordinary item is calculated as follows:

Tax charge on taxable profits excluding the extraordinary losses—£800,000 @ 35%	280
Actual tax charge/credit for period	—
Tax credit relating to extraordinary item is, therefore,	(280)

The extraordinary tax credit must equal the tax charge to result in an overall nil charge and therefore will not, as might have been expected, be 35% of the extraordinary losses, i.e. £350,000. This is because £200,000 of the extraordinary item has only given rise to tax losses carried forward for which no credit is taken in the financial statements.

2.4   Statement of movements on reserves

As discussed in 1.1.3 above the standard is based on the 'all inclusive concept'. However, as indicated in 2.5 and 2.7 below, there are instances when changes in shareholders' equity during an accounting period are not taken through the profit and loss account for the period. It is considered that the change in total reserves and how they are made up are among the most important pieces of information in financial statements, and ought therefore to be shown prominently.[40] There is therefore a specific requirement for financial statements to include a statement of all movements on reserves, i.e. not just the profit and loss account reserve, either on, or in a note referred to on, the face of the profit and loss account.[41]

This requirement is interpreted in practice in a number of ways. Our preferred interpretation is to disclose within a note, referred to on the face of the profit and loss account, a table reconciling the movements on each category of reserve to the opening and closing balances on those reserves. An example of such a disclosure is shown in Extract 8.6 in 3.5 below.

2.5   Prior year adjustments

2.5.1   Definition

Prior year adjustments are those material adjustments applicable to prior years arising from changes in accounting policies or from the correction of fundamental errors. They do not include normal recurring corrections or adjustments of accounting estimates made in prior years.[42]

2.5.2   Identification of prior year adjustments

The standard emphasises that 'the majority of items relating to prior years arise mainly from the corrections and adjustments which are the natural result of estimates inherent in accounting and more particularly in the periodic preparation of financial statements. They are therefore dealt with in the profit and loss account of the year in which they are identified and their effect stated where material.'[43] Prior year items of the type discussed in 2.5.3 and 2.5.4 below, which are to be accounted for as prior year adjustments, are considered to be rare.

The standard goes on to say 'estimating future events and their effects requires the exercise of judgement and will require reappraisal as new events occur, as more experience is acquired or as additional information is obtained. Since a change in estimate arises from new information or developments, it should not be given retrospective effect by a restatement of prior years. Sometimes a change in estimate may have the appearance of a change in accounting policy and care is necessary in order to avoid confusing the two.'[44]

2.5.3   Changes in accounting policy

An accounting policy should only be changed if the new policy is preferable to the policy it replaces because it will give a fairer presentation of the results and of the financial position of the business. A characteristic of a change in policy is that it is the result of a change between two accounting bases. An example of such a change which has occurred recently, is the capitalisation of finance leases on adoption of SSAP 21.

As indicated in 2.5.2 above, a change in estimate may have the appearance of a change in accounting policy and care is necessary in order to avoid confusing the two; for example, a company may change the level of its general bad debt provision from 3% to 5%. Such a change is probably not a change in accounting policy but a change in estimate of the recoverable amount of debtors and, therefore, the effect of such a change should be reflected in the profit and loss account for the current year.

2.5.4   Correction of fundamental error

The standard stresses that a fundamental error is only likely to occur in exceptional circumstances. The term 'fundamental' is implicitly defined as being of such significance as to destroy the presentation of a true and fair view and hence the validity of those financial statements and furthermore would have led to withdrawal of those financial statements had the errors been recognised at the time.[45]

It is tempting to think of any adjustment which relates to an event or circumstance which arose in a prior year as a prior year item; however, if the adjustment derives from new information about that event, then it simply represents a change in the estimate of the effect of that event and is therefore a current period item. For example, if a company has to write off a debt which it previously considered to be recoverable, then the charge should be reflected in the current year's profit or loss and not accounted for by way of prior year adjustment. It is therefore appropriate to consider whether the information which indicates that a fundamental error has arisen was actually available at the time that the financial statements for the prior period were approved.

2.5.5   Accounting treatment

In both examples quoted within the definition, the standard states that it is not appropriate to include the adjustments required in the current period profit and loss account and therefore they should be accounted for by restating prior years with the result that the opening balance of retained profits will be adjusted accordingly.[46] The following example illustrates the mechanics of such a process:

Example 8.2

Up until December 31, 19X5, a company has adopted a policy of writing off its development expenditure in the year in which it was incurred. The company's financial statements for the year ended December 31, 19X5 disclosed the following:

Profit and loss account

	19X5	19X4
	£'000	£'000
Profit on ordinary activities before taxation	4,200	3,800
Taxation	(1,575)	(1,400)
Profit on ordinary activities after taxation	2,625	2,400
Dividends	(600)	(500)
Retained profit for year	2,025	1,900

Balance sheet

	19X5	19X4
Tangible fixed assets	8,000	7,100
Net current assets	2,025	800
	10,025	7,900
Deferred taxation	(1,000)	(900)
	9,025	7,000
Share capital	1,000	1,000
Profit and loss account	8,025	6,000
	9,025	7,000

In preparing its financial statements for the year ended December 31, 19X6 it considers that a policy of capitalising the development expenditure and amortising it over a period of four years from the date of commencing production would give a fairer presentation of the results and financial position of the company. Accordingly, it will be necessary to restate the figures for 19X5 on the basis of the new policy. This initially involves computing:

(i)   the net book value of the development expenditure at December 31, 19X5;

(ii)   the amortisation charge for the year ended December 31, 19X5; and

(iii)   the net book value of the development expenditure at December 31, 19X4.

The development expenditure incurred in each of the five years ended December 31, 19X5 and the calculation of the above figures are as follows (for the purposes of this example the date of commencing production is taken to be January 1 following the year in which the development expenditure was incurred):

Year	Development expenditure incurred £'000	(i) £'000	(ii) £'000	(iii) £'000
19X1	260	—	65	65
19X2	100	25	25	50
19X3	240	120	60	180
19X4	400	300	100	400
19X5	40	40	—	—
		485	250	695

The adjustment to the pre-tax profit for 19X5 will, therefore, be a reduction of £210,000 being the amortisation of £250,000 less the development expenditure of £40,000 previously charged to the profit and loss account.

Having computed these figures it is then necessary to ascertain whether any other figures in the financial statements will be affected by the change in policy; in particular, deferred taxation and stocks. For the purposes of this example the only other figures, apart from retained profits, affected by the change in policy are those relating to deferred taxation. Assuming that the development expenditure has been fully allowed as a deductible expense in arriving at the corporation tax payable in respect of the year in which it was incurred, then the new policy will give rise to timing differences for which deferred tax may have to be provided. The company considers that full provision has to be made for deferred tax and accordingly the provision at December 31, 19X5, the charge for the year then ended, and the provision at December 31, 19X4 have to be adjusted as follows:

	Gross timing difference £'000	Provision at 35% £'000
December 31, 19X5	485	170
December 31, 19X4	695	243
Tax charge for year		(73)

As a result of these calculations the financial statements for the year ended December 31, 19X6 will therefore show the following figures in the profit and loss account and balance sheet (the 19X6 figures having been prepared on the basis of the new accounting policy):

Profit and loss account

	19X6	Restated 19X5
	£'000	£'000
Profit on ordinary activities before taxation	5,000	3,990
Taxation	(1,820)	(1,502)
Profit on ordinary activities after taxation	3,180	2,488
Dividends	(700)	(600)
Retained profit for year	2,480	1,888

Statement of retained profits

	19X6	19X5
Retained profits at beginning of year		
— as previously reported	8,025	6,000
Prior year adjustment	315	452
— as restated	8,340	6,452
Retained profit for year	2,480	1,888
Retained profits at end of year	10,820	8,340

Balance sheet

	19X6	Restated 19X7
Fixed assets		
Intangible	1,090	485
Tangible fixed assets	10,000	8,000
	11,090	8,485
Net current assets	2,212	2,025
	13,302	10,510
Deferred taxation	(1,482)	(1,170)
	11,820	9,340
Share capital	1,000	1,000
Profit and loss account	10,820	8,340
	11,820	9,340

The comparative figures for the statement of retained profits would not normally be shown as the statement of movements in reserves should cover all categories of reserves and only the movements in the current years' profits/reserves would be included in the statement. However, where the only category of reserves is 'retained profits' then we believe that it is preferable if they are shown in the manner above.

It must be emphasised that where prior year figures are restated it will be necessary (unless the effect would be immaterial) to restate the balance sheet, profit and loss account *and* statement of source and application of funds for the previous year; this last requirement will generally involve restating the balance sheet at the *beginning* of the previous year. Care should also be taken to ensure that all figures affected by the change in policy are adjusted, in particular, deferred taxation.

An example of the disclosure of a change in accounting policy is included in Extract 8.5 in 3.4 below.

2.6 Historical summaries, half-yearly reports and preliminary profit statements

The Stock Exchange requires listed companies and companies with shares dealt on the Unlisted Securities Market (USM) to separately disclose extraordinary and exceptional items in historical summaries produced for the purpose of listing particulars, circulars or prospectuses. Furthermore, The Stock Exchange requires that extraordinary items should be disclosed in all half-yearly reports and preliminary profits statements of listed companies.[47]

On the basis that omission of such information might lead to misunderstanding as to the profit trend, the standard also tries to close two gaps in The Stock Exchange's requirements by encouraging disclosure of:[48]

(a)   both extraordinary and exceptional items in the historical summaries, included in listed and USM companies' annual reports;[49]

(b)   exceptional items in half-yearly reports and preliminary profit statements.

Historical summaries should normally also be restated retrospectively for prior year adjustments, but if this is not practical, the part of the summary which has not been restated should be identified and the reason for not restating it explained.[50]

2.7 Exceptions from the standard

The standard requires all profits and losses, with the exception of items accounted for as prior year adjustments and certain exceptions permitted or required by law or other accounting standards to be accounted for as reserve movements, to be included in computing the profit or loss for the period.

2.7.1 *Reserve movements permitted or required by other accounting standards*

There are three instances referred to in the standard where changes in shareholders' equity during an accounting period are required or permitted by other accounting standards to be accounted for as a direct adjustment to reserves. This treatment is justified because these adjustments do not constitute profits or losses and, accordingly, should not be included in the determination of profit or loss for the year. The three instances are as follows:

(a)   changes in the value of investment properties during an accounting period are required to be accounted for as adjustments to a separate investment valuation reserve under SSAP 19 — *Accounting for investment properties* (see Chapter 11);[51]

(b)   certain exchange differences which are required to be accounted for as an adjustment to reserves under SSAP 20 — *Foreign currency translation* (see Chapter 18);[52]

(c)   the immediate write-off of goodwill against reserves under SSAP 22 — *Accounting for Goodwill* (see Chapter 4).[53]

These instances could be added to if ED 43 — *The accounting treatment of government grants* — becomes a standard; this proposes that where government grants are given on the condition that all or a proportion of the grant is treated as share capital, then the amount involved should be credited direct to non-distributable reserves.[54]

2.7.2   *Reserve movements permitted or required by law*

A   Permitted adjustments to the share premium account

Certain specific items of expenditure are permitted by law to be accounted for by write-off directly against the share premium account:

(a)   the preliminary expenses of a company;[55]

(b)   the expenses of, or the commission paid on, any issue of shares or debentures;[56]

(c)   the discount allowed on any issue of debentures and the premium payable on a redemption of debentures;[57]

(d)   the premium payable on redemption of, or purchase of, own shares subject to certain conditions.[58]

It could be argued that such items should be accounted for in the profit and loss account with a corresponding transfer made between share premium account and the profit and loss account to reflect the fact that the Companies Act allows such items to be written off against share premium account. However, this is seldom done in practice.

B   Revaluation adjustments taken to the revaluation reserve

Where assets are valued under the alternative accounting rules,[59] the amount of any profit or loss must be credited or debited to a separate reserve, the revaluation reserve (see 5 of Chapter 10).[60]

2.7.3   *Value based companies*

The Articles of Association of many property and investment holding companies require these companies to take the profits on sale of their properties or investments to capital reserve or other non-distributable reserve. However, the standard comments that, even if this is the case, the profit should be dealt with through the profit and loss account for the year and then a transfer be made between the profit and loss account reserve and the capital reserve to comply with the company's articles.

Investment trust companies are identified as a special case and in this instance the standard accepts that it may be appropriate to exclude gains or losses on disposal of investments from the profit and loss account and account for them in a separate reserve. If this is the case the separate reserve should be disclosed prominently either in the balance sheet or in a note to the accounts.[61]

3   DISCLOSURE REQUIREMENTS

Disclosure of extraordinary and exceptional items and prior year adjustments is governed in part by the requirements of SSAP 6 and also by the requirements of Schedule 4 to the Companies Act 1985.

3.1   Profit and loss account format

The relevant disclosure requirements are as follows:

(a)   the profit and loss account should show separately and in order:[62]

    (i)   profit or loss on ordinary activities;
    (ii)   extraordinary profit or loss;
    (iii)   profit or loss for the financial year; and
    (iv)   dividends and other appropriations;

(b)   the profit or loss on ordinary activities before taxation should be shown on the face of the profit and loss account.[63]

An example showing all these points is as follows:

Extract 8.2: Asda Group plc[64]

Consolidated profit and loss account [extract]

52 weeks ended 30 April 1988	1988	52 weeks ended 2 May 1987
	£m	£m
Profit before tax and profit sharing	218.3	195.5
Profit sharing	3.0	3.5
Profit on ordinary activities before taxation	215.3	192.0
Taxation	69.9	62.3
Profit on ordinary activities after taxation	145.4	129.7
Extraordinary profits after taxation	288.7	—
Profit for the financial year	434.1	129.7
Dividends	47.6	40.2
Retained profit	386.5	89.5

3.2   Extraordinary items

The relevant disclosure requirements are as follows:

(a)   the following items shall be disclosed separately, if material, after the profit or loss on ordinary activities after taxation:[65]

  (i)   extraordinary income;
  (ii)   extraordinary charges;
  (iii)   taxation on extraordinary profit or loss;

(b)   particulars shall be given of any extraordinary income or charges arising in the financial year;[66]

(c)   the amount of each extraordinary item shall be shown individually and an adequate description shall be given of each item to enable its nature to be understood;[67]

(d)   amounts in respect of items representing income may not be set off against amounts in respect of items representing expenditure;[68]

(e)   the tax on the net extraordinary profit or loss and the extraordinary profit or loss attributable to minority shareholders shall be shown;[69]

(f)   taxation on extraordinary items should be split between United Kingdom corporation tax, income tax, overseas tax and double tax relief;[70]

(g)   deferred tax relating to extraordinary items should be shown as a separate part of the tax charge on extraordinary items;[71]

(h)   the investing group's share of aggregate extraordinary items dealt with in the associated company's financial statements should be included with the group's extraordinary item provided that it still falls within the definition of extraordinary in the context of the group. If material, it should be disclosed separately from the extraordinary items of group companies.[72]

An example which illustrates most of the above requirements is as follows:

Extract 8.3: United Newspapers plc[73]

7 EXTRAORDINARY ITEMS [extract]

	1987 £'000	1986 £'000
Extraordinary income:		
Profit on sale of subsidiaries and businesses	**23,926**	20,252
Profit on sale of investments	**672**	30,140
Profit on sale of properties	**1,060**	9,094
	25,658	59,486
Extraordinary charges:		
National newspaper restructuring	**(69,007)**	—
Provision for loss on sale of investments and subsidiaries	**(1,758)**	(864)
Share of extraordinary items of related companies	**(95)**	—
Closure and reorganisation costs	**—**	(10,561)
Other	**(521)**	(68)
	(71,381)	(11,493)
Extraordinary items before taxation:	**(45,723)**	47,993
Tax on extraordinary items:		
Corporation tax	**18,270**	(17,872)
Deferred tax	**4,426**	186
	(23,027)	30,307

3.3   Exceptional items

The relevant disclosure requirements are as follows:

(a)   exceptional items should be disclosed separately either by way of note, or on the face of the profit and loss account if necessary to give a true and fair view. Whether shown on the face of the profit or loss account or by way of note, the items should be distinguishable as exceptional items by describing them as such. If disclosed on the face of the profit and loss account, the profit before exceptional items should also be disclosed separately. Whichever means is used to disclose the exceptional items, a description of the nature of each item should be given;[74]

(b)   the effect of any transactions that are exceptional by virtue of size or incidence should be disclosed even though they fall within the ordinary activities of the company.[75]

An example of exceptional items disclosed on the face of the profit and loss account is as follows:

Extract 8.4: STC PLC[76]

CONSOLIDATED PROFIT AND LOSS ACCOUNT [extract]

	Note	1987	1986
		£m	£m
Operating profit (before exceptional items)		196.2	163.0
Exceptional items	3	6.1	15.0
Operating profit		190.1	148.0
Investment income		7.7	7.7
Interest payable		9.8	21.5
Profit on ordinary activities before taxation		188.0	134.2

NOTES TO THE ACCOUNTS [extract]

3 Exceptional items	1987	1986
	£m	£m
Redundancies and related costs	6.0	6.1
Asset write downs, plant reorganisation and closure costs	0.1	(2.3)
Out-of-period contract adjustments	—	11.2
	6.1	15.0

Many companies in disclosing exceptional items on the face of the profit and loss account do not describe them as such but only describe the nature of the item; for example, 'Profit on disposal of properties' or 'Profit sharing'. Such an approach is also taken by a number of companies disclosing such items only by way of note.

3.4   Prior year adjustments

The relevant disclosure requirements are as follows:

(a)   where the corresponding amount of an item for the preceding year is not comparable with the amount to be shown for the item in question in respect of the financial year to which the financial statements relate, the comparative amount should be adjusted and particulars of the adjustment and the reasons for it should be disclosed in a note to the accounts;[77]

(b) the effect on the preceding year's profit and loss account result should be disclosed where practicable;[78]

A good example of the disclosures in respect of a prior year adjustment arising from a change in accounting policy is illustrated in the following extract:

Extract 8.5: The BOC Group plc[79]

ACCOUNTING POLICIES [extract]

(a) Change in accounting policy
As indicated in the 1986 report and accounts, with effect from 1st October 1986 the group has changed its accounting policy in respect of fixed assets to restrict revaluations to land and buildings. Comparative financial data for 1986 and earlier years has been restated appropriately including reversals of earlier revaluations. The effects of the change for 1986 is to increase profit before tax by £21.3 million and to reduce capital employed by £107.6 million.

NOTES ON FINANCIAL STATEMENTS [extract]

Fixed assets—tangible assets	Land & buildings £ million	Plant machinery & vehicles £ million	Cylinders £ million	Construction in progress £ million	Total £ million
Gross book value					
At 1st October 1986	360.2	1,680.6	421.6	97.8	2,560.2
Accounting policy change	—	(321.3)	(179.3)	—	(500.6)
Amounts restated	360.2	1,359.3	242.3	97.8	2,059.6
Depreciation					
At 1st October 1986	84.1	909.4	217.3	—	1,210.8
Accounting policy change	—	(262.0)	(131.0)	—	(393.0)
Amounts restated	84.1	647.4	86.3	—	817.8

	Share Premium Account £ million	Revaluation Reserve £ million	Profit & Loss Account £ million	Related Companies Reserve £ million
Reserves				
At 1st October 1986	184.4	153.4	516.1	62.1
Change in accounting policy	—	(94.0)	—	—
Amounts restated	184.4	59.4	516.1	62.1

In addition to the above disclosures, The BOC Group plc also stated at the top of their consolidated profit and loss account and consolidated balance sheet that 'Comparative figures have been restated for change of accounting policy—see page 25'.[80] (An alternative treatment would have been to have 'Restated' at the top of the columns for the comparative figures.) They also indicated in their five year record that the figures for prior years had been restated for the change in policy.[81]

3.5 Statement of movement in reserves

The relevant disclosure requirements are as follows:

(a) the financial statements should include a statement of movements on reserves either immediately following the profit and loss account or in a note referred to on the face of the profit and loss account;[82]

(b) any amount set aside or proposed to be set aside, or withdrawn, or proposed to be withdrawn from reserves must be separately disclosed;[83]

(c) where any amount is transferred to or from reserves, the amounts of the reserve at the beginning and end of the financial year, the amounts transferred to or from the reserves and the sources and application of these amounts must be disclosed.[84]

An example of a statement meeting the above requirements is as follows:

Extract 8.6: Imperial Chemical Industries PLC[85]

RESERVES [extract]

	Share premium account	Revalu-ation	Other	Profit and loss account	Related com-panies	1987 Total	1986 Total
GROUP RESERVES ATTRIBUTABLE TO PARENT COMPANY							
At beginning of year	115	84	368	2,476	(35)	3,008	2,838
Profit retained for year				427	56	483	319
Amounts taken direct to reserves							
Share premiums	111					111	41
Goodwill				(577)		(577)	(220)
Exchange adjustments		(10)	(38)	(213)	5	(256)	29
Other movements		5	2	(18)	11		1
	111	(5)	(36)	(808)	16	(722)	(149)
Other movements between reserves	10	(1)	(16)	(131)	138		
At end of year	236	78	316	1,964	175	2,769	3,008

In addition to the above note to their financial statements, Imperial Chemical Industries PLC also include the following statement of reserves at the foot of their group profit and loss account:

Extract 8.7: Imperial Chemical Industries PLC[86]

GROUP RESERVES ATTRIBUTABLE TO PARENT COMPANY

	Note	1987 £m	1986 £m
At beginning of year		**3,008**	2,838
Profit retained for year: Company		389	137
Subsidiaries		38	182
Related companies		56	—
		483	319
Amounts taken direct to reserves		(722)	(149)
At end of year	11	**2,769**	3,008

Although this gives prominence to the movements in reserves, since only one figure is given for amounts taken direct to reserves it is still necessary for users of the financial statements to refer to the note shown in Extract 8.6 above to find out what such movements are. As it is the movements in the individual reserves which are going to provide the most useful information to the users of the financial statements, many companies dispense with giving a statement such as that contained in Extract 8.7 above, and just include a reference on the face of the profit and loss account to the note where the statement of movements on reserves can be found. This is generally done either by cross-referring the retained profit for the year to the appropriate note or by including a note along the following lines at the foot of the profit and loss account:

Extract 8.8: Beecham Group p.l.c.[87]

A statement of the movement on reserves is shown in note 22 on page 50.

4   PROBLEM AREAS

4.1   Definition of extraordinary items

The definition of an extraordinary item, and the key factors in classifying an item as extraordinary, were indicated in 2.1.1 above. The important issues in the definition are that the event or transaction must be *outside the ordinary activities* of the company and therefore *not expected to recur frequently or regularly*. Although *ordinary activities* are defined in the standard (see 2.1.1 above) no indication is given as to what recurring frequently or regularly means. It could be argued that where an event has occurred in the past then this provides evidence in assessing whether such an event is likely to recur. For example, if a company has sold a subsidiary in the past, has subsequently sold another one and it still has subsidiaries which it might sell in the future, then it would seem that such items should not be classified as extraordinary. These considerations would also apply to other items such as closure costs and disposal of fixed assets, including properties. However, it would appear that in practice companies are not interpreting the definition of extraordinary items in such a way, since companies often disclose extraordinary items of the same type in successive accounting periods. This may be due to the fact that companies are referring to the list of *possible* examples of extraordinary items contained in paragraph 4 of the standard (see 2.1.2 above) and applying it rigidly. In the case of terminated activities, paragraph 12 of the standard also appears to undermine the 'not expected to recur frequently or regularly' test by stating that provisions in respect of terminated activities 'are not prevented from being extraordinary items merely because they occur and are recognised over a number of accounting periods where this is either the ongoing result of a single decision or *because of a number of separate decisions* (emphasis added)'.

4.2   Terminated activities

4.2.1   *Definition of business segment*

In carrying out the review of the original SSAP 6 the working party noted that expenditure incurred on termination and reorganisation was an area which frequently caused problems of classification between exceptional and extraordinary.

The review proposed that the key criterion to be applied in deciding whether a scheme of reorganisation was extraordinary is whether the scheme involved the termination of a significant and identifiable part of the business, i.e. a distinct business segment. Costs and credits arising from the termination of a business segment do not relate to the continuing businesses and therefore should be treated as extraordinary. However, where a scheme does not involve the closure of a business segment but is intended to keep the existing business running or increase its efficiency, the associated costs and credits should be treated as part of the ordinary activities of the business. For example, Lucas Industries plc makes this distinction between termination and reorganisation of continuing businesses, where only terminations are treated as extraordinary items:

Extract 8.9: Lucas Industries plc[88]

Reorganisation costs

When a decision to reorganise a business has been made the anticipated costs are provided. Costs relating to the reorganisation of continuing businesses are charged in arriving at the profit before taxation and those relating to withdrawal from business segments are charged as extraordinary items. The operating results of business segments from which the group is withdrawing are excluded from the date the decision is taken and are shown separately in the notes to the accounts.

ED 36 and subsequently the revised SSAP 6 therefore sought to clarify the distinction through defining a business segment. However, the definition of a business segment given in SSAP 6[89] can in fact be interpreted quite widely. Most large companies should have records of sufficient detail to enable them to analyse their assets and results into a large number of discrete units, whether it be by product line, market or geographical location. Consequently a segment, as defined in SSAP 6, can be interpreted as meaning as small a subsection of the business as the management consider appropriate, and therefore the associated closure costs are usually treated as extraordinary.

Consider the example of a company which manufactures both synthetic and woollen suits. Applying the SSAP 6 definition of a business segment, which suggests that separate markets and product lines are appropriate criteria for determining whether an activity constitutes a business segment, the following activities could probably be regarded as distinct segments:

(a)   the manufacture of woollen suits;

(b)   the manufacture of synthetic suits;

(c)   the manufacture of suits for a specific country, as styles will usually be modified for different markets;

(d)   the manufacture of 'extra large' suits;

(e)   the manufacture of suits for one of the entity's major suppliers.

As long as the company keeps records so that the assets and results relating to these activities are distinguishable then these could be argued to meet the definition of a business segment within SSAP 6.

It is interesting to note that there is rarely any consistency between the way a business segment is interpreted for this standard and how it is interpreted for the segmental reporting required by the Companies Act[90] and discussed in Chapter 20. In many cases those activities which are regarded as business segments for the purposes of this standard will only form part of a larger segment for segmental reporting purposes.

4.2.2   *Identification of decision date and implementation date*

The standard requires that where a decision has been made to discontinue a business segment during a period, a provision is necessary at the balance sheet date for the consequences of that decision, even if it is not immediately due for implementation. The provision will include all the estimated costs of executing the decision and any trading losses that are expected to occur after the commencement of implementation.

It is, therefore, important to accurately identify the decision date in order to ensure that appropriate provisions have been made for all decisions where the period between decision date and implementation date spans the year end. Furthermore, it may be appropriate to disclose the trading results of these operations separately. However, no guidance is given in the standard as to how to identify the decision date.

In the US, APB 30 defines the measurement date (equivalent to the decision date in SSAP 6) as the date on which the management having authority to approve the action commits itself to a formal plan to dispose of a segment of the business, whether by sale or abandonment. The plan of disposal should include, as a minimum:

(a)   identification of the major assets to be disposed of;

(b)   the expected method of disposal;

(c)   an active programme to find a buyer if disposal is to be by sale;

(d)   the estimated results of operations of the segment from the measurement date to the disposal date; and

(e)   the estimated proceeds or salvage to be realised by disposal.[91]

In the absence of any guidance in SSAP 6 as to what the 'decision date' is, we recommend that companies should consider the above criteria in determining the relevant date.

Similarly, no guidance is given in SSAP 6 as to how to identify the implementation date. The importance of this date is that the standard implies that all trading results which arise after that date, relating to the business segment which is to be discontinued, should be accounted for as part of the extraordinary item; the trading results prior to that date being included as part of the trading results for the year. By applying the criteria referred to above then the implementation date and the decision date will effectively be the same.

The standard does not require separate disclosure of any trading results included as part of the extraordinary item and it only suggests that separate disclosure of the trading results prior to the implementation date may be required. It is, therefore, rare to find, either within an accounting policy, an extraordinary item note, or elsewhere in the financial statements, sufficient description to clarify or give any indication as to whether companies are distinguishing between the decision and implementation dates.

As shown in Extract 8.1 in 2.2.3 above, Beecham Group plc distinguish the trading results of discontinued businesses, which include the results of businesses in the course of disposal at the year end, within the segmental information. By implication this would indicate that they have identified a date at which the decision to dispose of these businesses was taken, but as implementation has not yet commenced, the results thereafter are not regarded as extraordinary. This would appear to be consistent with the spirit of the standard.[92]

As illustrated in Extract 8.9 above, Lucas Industries plc treat the trading results of discontinuing business segments for periods after the decision date as extraordinary. Detailed disclosure is given in their financial statements of the business segments to which the current year's extraordinary charge relates, as well as a summary of the losses charged against the provision during the year.

Extract 8.10: Lucas Industries plc[93]

Note 7: Extraordinary items [extract

	1988 £ million	1987 £ million
Cost of withdrawing from the following business segments:		
Aerostructures, aerospace engine fabrications and combustion technology	**24.0**	—
Automotive starters and alternators	**6.5**	13.4
Automotive electro-mechanical instrumentation	—	9.9
Automotive lighting	—	5.7
Diesel fuel injection equipment — In-line pumps	—	8.3
Other	**.2**	6.5
	30.7	43.8

Note 18: Provision for liabilities and charges [extract]

	Discontinuing business segments £ million
Group:	
At 1 August 1987	**72.3**
Utilised/paid in the year	**(52.5)**
Charged in the year	**30.7**
At 31 July 1988	**50.5**

The losses before tax of the discontinuing business segments for the periods from the dates the decisions were taken are summarised as follows:

		1988 £ million
Turnover (including £18.8 million intra-group)		93.9
Raw materials, consumables and stock decrease	45.3	
Staff costs	41.3	
Depreciation	2.5	
Other operating charges	57.3	146.4
		(52.5)

It is noteworthy that Lucas Industries plc make no reference to the implementation date; consequently it is not clear whether they regard the decision date as coincidental with the implementation date, or whether the trading results for the period between the decision date and the implementation date are treated as extraordinary. The latter situation would conflict with the view expressed in the standard that such results are still part of the ordinary activities of the entity.

4.3   Disclosure requirements relating to exceptional and extraordinary items

In requiring disclosure of exceptional and extraordinary items SSAP 6 only requires an adequate description of each item to be given to enable its nature to be understood. In respect of costs relating to discontinuance of business segments, companies generally use such phrases as 'closure costs' or, in the case of disposals, 'profit/(loss) on sale of subsidiaries'. In addition, amounts relating to the disposal of different business segments are frequently aggregated. Although such descriptions probably comply with the standard, we believe that they are insufficient to enable users of the financial statements to identify the effect of each 'extraordinary event'. In our view it would be preferable if companies, in respect of such items, disclosed the following information:

(a)   the closure costs or the profit/loss on disposal in respect of each segment;

(b)   the name of the segment involved;

(c)   the major components of the closure costs; in particular, those items referred to in paragraph 11 of the standard.

4.4   Historical summaries, half-yearly reports and preliminary profits statements

The standard encourages compliance with its recommended disclosures in all historical summaries, half-yearly reports and preliminary profits statements issued under the rules or recommendations of The Stock Exchange for the continuing obligations of listed companies. As there is no absolute requirement, there are a number of listed companies which do not comply with the recommendations of the standard and therefore the value of such statements for properly assessing the results or profit trend of such companies must be questioned.

5   SUGGESTED CHANGES TO SSAP 6

As SSAP 6 was only recently revised, in August 1986, it is unlikely that the Accounting Standards Committee in its present form would envisage any further revisions in the foreseeable future.

However, it is our view that the recent revision has not achieved its objective of narrowing the areas of difference and variety in accounting practice and that the only way to achieve consistency of treatment of items in the profit and loss account is to impose much stricter criteria in defining an extraordinary item and to require extra disclosure, particularly in relation to terminated activities. Possible solutions would be as follows:

(a)   items should only be classified as extraordinary if the events from which they arise are outside the control of the directors (or their equivalent in the case of unincorporated entities). This would mean, for instance, that activities which are terminated as a result of one of many strategic decisions taken by the directors/management of the entity would not be categorised as extraordinary;

(b)   an alternative solution to (a) above would be to clarify further the definitions used in the standard. The detailed interpretation and examples found in US GAAP illustrate one way that this could be effectively achieved (see 6.1.1 below);

(c)   greater disclosure should be required about terminated activities. Our preference is that the profit or loss before taxation arising from terminated activities should be disclosed separately from the profit or loss before taxation arising from continuing activities but included within the profit on ordinary activities before taxation. This figure would then be supplemented with note disclosure of turnover, cost of sales, etc., relating to the terminated activities. A similar treatment in the balance sheet should be adopted for the net assets or liabilities of the discontinued activities.

6   COMPARISON WITH US AND IASC PRONOUNCEMENTS

6.1   US

There are a number of US pronouncements which have been issued relating to this area of accounting. The main ones which are still relevant today are as follows: APB Opinion No. 20 — *Accounting Changes*; APB Opinion No. 30 — *Reporting the Results of Operations–Reporting the Effects of Disposal of a Segment of a Business, and Extraordinary, Unusual and Infrequently Occurring Events and Transactions*; AIN–APB 30 — *Reporting the Results of Operations: Accounting Interpretations of APB Opinion No. 30*; and SFAS 16 — *Prior Period Adjustments*. The major differences between these pronouncements and SSAP 6 are dealt with below. It must be emphasised, however, that US GAAP interprets the 'all inclusive concept' much more strictly than SSAP 6; consequently significantly fewer items can be classified as extraordinary or prior period adjustments.

6.1.1   Extraordinary items

The US position on extraordinary items is primarily contained within APB 30. The key issues addressed are very similar to those addressed in SSAP 6; i.e. the definition of an extraordinary item; the treatment of the results of discontinued activities; and the definition of a business segment. However, the effect of the opinion (together with the related interpretation, AIN—APB 30) is that very few of the items which are presently being disclosed as extraordinary in financial statements in the UK would remain so under US GAAP.

The definition of extraordinary[94] is broadly similar to that used in SSAP 6, in that it incorporates the two key elements that the event must be of an unusual nature and that the event would not reasonably be expected to recur in the foreseeable future. However, differences in interpretation arise for two principal reasons; firstly, APB 30 gives a detailed interpretation of the definition of extraordinary by discussing the two key terms 'unusual nature' and 'infrequency of occurrence'.[95] Secondly, it lists a number of items which should not be reported as extraordinary;[96] this is complemented by AIN—APB 30 which gives specific examples of items which would be regarded as extraordinary and those which would not.[97]

The detailed discussion of the definition of extraordinary and the terms used in the definition results in a very narrow interpretation of the term. For example, APB 30 comments that an unusual event should possess a high degree of abnormality and be of a type clearly unrelated to the ordinary and typical activities of the company.[98] Furthermore, in discussing 'infrequency of occurrence' APB 30 comments that the event or transaction should be of such a type that would not be expected to occur again in the foreseeable future.[99] In contrast the definition in SSAP 6 includes the phrase 'expected not to recur frequently or regularly'.[100] This appears to allow scope for the event to occur again in the foreseeable future, although not often.

The examples of items listed in APB 30 which should not be reported as extraordinary items because they are usual in nature or may be expected to recur as a consequence of customary and continuing business activities include, *inter alia*, write-down or write-off of assets, e.g. debtors and stocks, and gains or losses from sale or abandonment of property, plant and equipment. Such items are frequently treated as extraordinary in the financial statements of UK companies. APB 30 recognises that there may be occasions when such items can be properly treated as extraordinary items, but emphasises that these will be rare; for example, as result of an earthquake or expropriation.[101] It also specifically states that gains or losses on disposal of a segment of a business should not be treated as an extraordinary item (see 6.1.2 below).

One of the examples given in AIN—APB 30 which illustrates the differences in interpretation is that of a disposal of an investment in another company held for investment purposes. If the company has never owned another investment, then clearly the disposal is of an unusual nature and could not in current circumstances ever recur and therefore the gain or loss can be regarded as extraordinary. However, if the company holds a portfolio of investments, even if their disposal is infrequent, the disposal cannot be regarded either as unusual or unlikely to recur.[102]

One other particular requirement which is worthy of note is provided by SFAS 4,[103] which expressly requires the disclosure of gains or losses arising from early extinguishment of debt to be disclosed as extraordinary.

6.1.2   *Terminated activities (discontinued operations)*

APB 30 also deals with terminated activities and uses the term 'business segment' in order to determine whether the effect of certain activities being discontinued merits separate accounting treatment.

Although the definitions of a business segment contained in APB 30 and SSAP 6 are broadly the same, the examples contained within AIN—APB 30 assist in preventing too wide an interpretation of the definition, as is currently possible under SSAP 6, particularly with regard to the interpretation of what comprises a separate major line of business as distinct from a product line.

For example, the interpretation discusses the case of a suit manufacturer who manufactures suits from both wool and synthetic raw materials, but decides to close down its operations dedicated to wool. This situation is an example of the disposal of a product line but not a major line of business and therefore would not be treated as discontinued operations.[104] There are further examples to illustrate the points that geographical location of operations or markets and corporate structure are not by themselves criteria for determining separate segments.

However, companies in the UK which apply a wide interpretation of business segment probably do so in order that any gain or loss on termination of the segment may be treated as an extraordinary item. As indicated in 6.1.1 above APB 30 does not allow such a treatment.[105]

APB 30 requires that the income statement be completely reclassified so that the results of discontinued operations up to the measurement date (decision date) are disclosed separately after the results of continuing operations. Any gain or loss on disposal of these activities would also be disclosed with these results,[106] although any gain would not be recognised until it is realised.[107] Disclosure is also required about the identity of the segment; the expected disposal date; the expected manner of disposal; description of the remaining assets and liabilities of the segment at the balance sheet date; and the profit or loss from operations and any proceeds from disposal during the period from the measurement date to the balance sheet date.[108] On the other hand, SSAP 6 only suggests that disclosure of the results prior to the commencement of implementation of termination may be required.[109] If the disclosure requirements of APB 30 were required in the UK, then many companies might change their attitude to interpreting a 'business segment' as widely as they do at present.

In addition, as already discussed in 4.2.2 above, APB 30 gives criteria for determining the measurement date.

6.1.3 Prior year adjustments

US accounting practice on changes in accounting policy and prior year adjustments is prescribed by APB 20 and SFAS 16 respectively.

The major difference between US GAAP and SSAP 6 relates to the accounting treatment of a change in accounting policy or principle. Under US GAAP, the general rule is that where a company voluntarily changes an accounting policy, the cumulative effect of the change, i.e. the difference between retained profits at the beginning of the year as previously reported and the figure that would have been reported if the new policy had been applied retroactively for all prior periods, should be disclosed in the profit and loss account, albeit after the profit or loss on extraordinary items.[110] Consequently, comparative figures are not restated although pro forma comparatives should be disclosed for the profit or loss before extraordinary items and the net profit or loss for the year.[111] Comparatives are not adjusted as a strict interpretation of the 'all inclusive concept' results in the conclusion that the effect of the changes should be included in computing the net profit or loss for the period. APB 20 also comments that there could potentially be a dilution of public confidence in financial statements if prior periods were restated.[112]

However, there are certain specific exceptions, where the effect of a change in accounting policy must be accounted for retroactively as a prior period adjustment. The principal exceptions are as follows:[113]

(a)   a change from the LIFO method of stock valuation;

(b)   a change in the method of accounting for long-term construction-type contracts;

(c)   a change from the 'full cost' method in the oil and gas and similar extractive industries.

In addition, prior period adjustments are also required for correction of an error in prior periods.[114]

6.2   IASC

The international position is set out in IAS 8 — *Unusual and Prior Period Items and Changes in Accounting Policies*. The standard is, however, much less detailed than either SSAP 6 or US GAAP and allows sufficient alternatives to be consistent with both. It does not address terminated activities. Consequently, compliance with SSAP 6 will ensure compliance with IAS 8.

The IASC has recently issued an exposure draft, E32 — *Comparability of Financial Statements* — which proposes to amend, *inter alia*, the requirements of IAS 8. The main change proposed is that the preferred treatment for prior period items (i.e. adjustments for fundamental errors) and changes in accounting policies will be that opening retained earnings should be adjusted and comparative figures restated. The alternative treatment of including such items in current income for the period will still be allowed, although comparative information should be presented on a pro forma basis.[115]

References

1   SFAC No. 1, *Objectives of Financial Reporting by Business Enterprises*, FASB, November 1978, para. 43.
2   SFAC No. 6, *Elements of Financial Statements*, FASB, December 1985, para. 70.
3   *Ibid.*, para. 73.
4   For a full discussion of these two concepts of income, see ARB No. 43, *Restatement and Revision of Accounting Research Bulletins*, AICPA, June 1953, Chapter 8, or APB 9, *Reporting the Results of Operations*, AICPA, December 1966, paras. 9 — 14.
5   APB 9, para. 10.
6   APB 9, para. 11.
7   SFAC No. 1, para. 42.
8   SSAP 6, *Extraordinary items and prior year adjustments*, Revised August 1986.
9   ICAEW, Accounting Recommendation N18, *Presentation of balance sheet and profit and loss account*, October 1958.
10 ED 5, *Extraordinary items and prior year adjustments*, August 1971.

1 1 ED 7, *Accounting for extraordinary items*, July 1972.
1 2 CA 81, Sch. 1, Pt. 1, Section B; now CA 85, Sch. 4, Pt. 1, Section B.
1 3 ASC discussion paper, *A review of SSAP 6*, 1983.
1 4 ED 36, *Extraordinary items and prior year adjustments*, January 1985.
1 5 *Ibid.*, paras. 6 and 8.
1 6 *Ibid.*, paras. 14, 15 and 32.
1 7 *Ibid.*, paras. 29 and 31.
1 8 *Ibid.*, para. 37.
1 9 *Ibid.*, para. 36.
2 0 *Ibid.*, para. 39.
2 1 *Ibid.*, para. 27.
2 2 *Ibid.*, para. 18.
2 3 *Ibid.*, preface para. 1.21.
2 4 SSAP 6, paras. 28—30.
2 5 *Ibid.*, para. 2.
2 6 *Ibid.*, para. 4.
2 7 *Ibid.*
2 8 *Ibid.*
2 9 *Ibid.*, para. 11.
3 0 *Ibid.*, para. 12.
3 1 *Ibid.*, para. 14.
3 2 *Ibid.*, para. 32.
3 3 *Ibid.*, para. 11.
3 4 *Ibid.*, paras. 11 and 13.
3 5 *Ibid.*, para. 13.
3 6 Beecham Group p.l.c., Annual Report 1988, pp. 37 and 38.
3 7 SSAP 6, para. 37.
3 8 SSAP 15, *Accounting for deferred tax*, Revised May 1985, para. 34.
3 9 SSAP 6, para. 38.
4 0 *Ibid.*, para. 25.
4 1 *Ibid.*, para. 35.
4 2 *Ibid.*, para. 31.
4 3 *Ibid.*, para. 16.
4 4 *Ibid.*, para. 17.
4 5 *Ibid.*, para. 19.
4 6 *Ibid.*, paras. 18, 19 and 39.
4 7 The Council of the Stock Exchange, *Admission of securities to listing*, Section 5, Chapter 2, para. 25(b)(vi).
4 8 SSAP 6, para. 26.
4 9 The production of historical summaries in listed companies' annual reports is not a requirement contained in *Admission of securities to listing*, but has been recommended by The Stock Exchange since 1964.
5 0 SSAP 6, para. 18.
5 1 SSAP 19, *Accounting for investment properties*, November 1981, para. 13.
5 2 SSAP 20, *Foreign currency translation*, April 1983, paras. 51, 53, 57 and 58.
5 3 SSAP 22, *Accounting for goodwill*, December 1984, para. 32.
5 4 ED 43, *The accounting treatment of government grants*, June 1983, para. 32.
5 5 CA 85, s 130.
5 6 *Ibid.*
5 7 *Ibid.*
5 8 *Ibid.*, ss 159—162.
5 9 *Ibid.*, Sch. 4, para. 31.
6 0 *Ibid.*, para. 34.
6 1 SSAP 6, para. 24.

6 2 *Ibid.*, para. 34.
6 3 CA 85, Sch. 4, para. 3(6).
6 4 Asda Group plc, Annual Report and Accounts 1988, p. 26.
6 5 CA 85, Sch. 4, para. 1(b).
6 6 *Ibid.*, para. 57(2).
6 7 SSAP 6, para. 37.
6 8 CA 85, Sch. 4, para. 5.
6 9 SSAP 6, para. 37.
7 0 CA 85, Sch. 4, para. 54(3).
7 1 SSAP 15, para. 34.
7 2 SSAP 1, *Accounting for associated companies*, Revised April 1982, para. 21.
7 3 United Newspapers plc, Annual report and accounts 1987, p. 37.
7 4 SSAP 6, paras. 3 and 36.
7 5 CA 85, Sch. 4, para. 57(3).
7 6 STC PLC, Annual Report 1987, pp. 26 and 32.
7 7 CA 85, Sch. 4, paras. 4(2) and 58(2).
7 8 SSAP 6, para. 39.
7 9 The BOC Group plc, Report & Accounts 1987, pp. 25, 35 and 41.
8 0 The BOC Group plc, Report & Accounts 1987, pp. 20 and 21.
8 1 The BOC Group plc, Report & Accounts 1987, p. 46.
8 2 SSAP 6, para. 35.
8 3 CA 85, Sch. 4, para. 3(7).
8 4 *Ibid.*, para. 46.
8 5 Imperial Chemical Industries PLC, Annual Report 1987, p. 40.
8 6 Imperial Chemical Industries PLC, Annual Report 1987, p. 32.
8 7 Beecham Group p.l.c., Annual Report 1988, p. 32.
8 8 Lucas Industries plc, 1988 Report to Shareholders, p. 29.
8 9 SSAP 6, para. 32.
9 0 CA 85, Sch. 4, para. 55(1).
9 1 APB 30, *Reporting the Results of Operations–Reporting the Effects of Disposal of a Segment of a Business, and Extraordinary, Unusual and Infrequently Occurring Events and Transactions*; AICPA, June 1973, para. 14.
9 2 Beecham Group p.l.c., Annual Report 1988, pp. 37 and 38.
9 3 Lucas Industries plc, 1988 Report to Shareholders, pp. 32 and 36.
9 4 APB 30, para. 20.
9 5 *Ibid.*, paras. 21 and 22.
9 6 *Ibid.*, para. 23.
9 7 AIN—APB 30, *Reporting the Results of Operations: Accounting Interpretations of APB Opinion No. 30*; AICPA, November 1973, Examples 10—17.
9 8 APB 30, para. 20.
9 9 *Ibid.*
100 SSAP 6, para. 30.
101 APB 30, para. 23.
102 AIN—APB 30, Examples 12 and 16.
103 SFAS 4, *Reporting Gains and Losses from Extinguishment of Debt*, an amendment of APB Opinion No. 30, FASB, March 1975.
104 AIN—APB 30, Example 7.
105 APB 30, para. 8.
106 *Ibid.*
107 *Ibid.*, para. 15.
108 *Ibid.*, para. 18.
109 SSAP 6, para. 13.
110 APB 20, *Accounting Changes*, AICPA, July 1971, para. 20.
111 *Ibid.*, para. 21.

112 *Ibid.*, para. 18.
113 *Ibid.*, para. 27.
114 SFAS 16, *Prior Period Adjustments*, FASB, June 1977, para. 11.
115 E32, *Comparability of Financial Statements*, IASC, January 1989, para. 40.

Chapter 9

Stocks and long-term contracts

1 INTRODUCTION

1.1 The importance of stocks and long-term contracts within financial statements

Accounting for stock involves the determination of both the cost of goods sold during the period and the amount that should be carried forward as stock to be matched against future revenues. Some of the thorniest conceptual and practical problems arise as a result of these measurement issues, many of which have yet to be settled. For example, there is the question of which cost flow assumption should be used in the determination of cost of sales and, secondly, there is the 'direct costing' vs. 'full absorption costing' debate surrounding the costing of the stock asset.

1.2 What are stocks and long-term contracts?

SSAP 9 uses the following definitions:[1]

'*Stocks* comprise the following categories:

(a)   goods or other assets purchased for resale;

(b)   consumable stores;

(c)   raw materials and components purchased for incorporation into products for sale;

(d)   products and services in intermediate stages of completion;

(e)   long-term contract balances; and

(f)   finished goods.'

'*Long-term contract:* a contract entered into for the design, manufacture or construction of a single substantial asset or the provision of a service (or of a combination of assets or services which together constitute a single project) where the time taken substantially to complete the contract is such that the contract activity falls into different accounting periods. A contract that is required to be accounted for as long-term by this accounting standard will usually extend for a period exceeding one year. However, a duration exceeding one year is not an essential feature of a long-term contract. Some contracts with a shorter duration than one year should be accounted for as long-term contracts if they are sufficiently material to the activity of the period that not to record turnover and attributable profit would lead to a distortion of the period's turnover and results such that the financial statements would not give a true and fair view, provided that the policy is applied consistently within the reporting entity and from year to year.'

The US and IASC definitions of stock (or 'inventory'), which are almost identical to each other, appear more restrictive than the UK definition in that they require stock to be 'tangible'. This seems an unnecessary refinement, since a strict interpretation of this might, for example, preclude a service company from including any unbilled work in its financial statements.

It is noteworthy that when SSAP 9 was revised it was considered necessary to go into such detail in defining long-term contracts, while, in contrast, both the US and international standards merely give a general description of them. The reason for this detailed definition in SSAP 9 is that it is attempting to meet objections raised to the arbitrariness of the definition in the original SSAP 9, in terms of which duration was the key criterion for deciding whether or not a contract was long-term. Arguably, however, whilst solving this issue, the revised definition will create further problems.

Long-term contracts are effectively a special category of stocks and all the rules and principles relating to stocks also apply to long-term contracts. Consequently, this chapter looks at these subjects separately, but on the basis that all matters relating to stocks apply equally to long-term contracts. However, there are additional factors stemming from the time taken to complete long-term contracts, which require separate consideration; these are discussed at 7 below.

1.3   Objectives of stock measurement

It is generally accepted that, within the historical cost accounting system, the principal objective of stock measurement is the proper determination of income through the process of matching costs with related revenues.[2] In order to match costs and revenue, 'costs' of stocks should comprise that expenditure which has been incurred in the normal course of business in bringing the product or service to its present location and condition.[3] The result of this is that all costs incurred in respect of stocks should be charged as period costs, except for those which relate to those unconsumed stocks[4] which are expected to be of future benefit to the entity. These should be carried forward to be matched with the revenues that they will generate in the future. Therefore, in the income measurement process, stocks have characteristics similar to those of prepaid expenses or fixed assets such as plant and equipment.

If, however, there is expected to be no future benefit, or if the future benefit is expected to be less than the associated costs, then the prudence concept is applied, and the carrying value of those stocks must be reduced to the value of their future benefit. This gives rise to the basic rule for the balance sheet valuation of stocks, i.e. that they should be stated at the lower of cost and net realisable value.[5] Clearly, however, the application of this rule can result in stocks being reported at amounts which neither reflect the historical costs which have been incurred in bringing them to their present location or condition, nor the replacement cost of such stocks.

A second objective of stock measurement is to present a value of stock for the purpose of presentation in the balance sheet. The value at which stocks are reported in the balance sheet is governed by the interpretation that is intended to be placed on such valuation; for example, realisable value is the cash amount that the entity could receive on the sale of its stock in the ordinary course of business, whilst current replacement cost is the amount of cash that would be required if the entity did not hold the goods, but had to acquire them. However, because of the present emphasis on matching historical costs with revenues, the balance sheet 'lower of cost and net realisable value' of stock has little interpretation value. Furthermore, it should be stressed that under the historical cost framework, the amount reflected in the balance sheet represents no more than deferred costs which are yet to be matched.

A third objective is to present users with information which will assist them in predicting the firm's future cash flows. Clearly, in the context of the historical cost framework, this objective is not easily attainable, since stock stated at the lower of cost and net realisable value will neither assist in the prediction of cash inflows from future sales, nor assist in the prediction of cash outflows required for the replacement of the stock to be sold in the next accounting period.

2 DETERMINING THE COST OF STOCK

As stated above, SSAP 9 defines cost in relation to stock as 'that expenditure which has been incurred in the normal course of business in bringing the product or service to its present location and condition'.[6] There should be included in the expenditure both cost of purchase and such costs of conversion 'as are appropriate to that location and condition'.[7] Cost of purchase comprises 'purchase price including import duties, transport and handling costs and any other directly attributable costs, less trade discounts, rebates and subsidies';[8] whilst cost of conversion comprises:

'(a) costs which are specifically attributable to units of production, eg, direct labour, direct expenses and sub-contracted work;

(b) production overheads (as defined in paragraph 20 [of SSAP 9]);

(c) other overheads, if any, attributable in the particular circumstances of the business to bringing the product or service to its present location and condition'.[9]

In the past, before production processes became complex, it was common for manufactured stocks to be costed at 'prime cost' — i.e. only the cost of materials and direct labour were included. At that time, this was a justifiable basis of determining cost, since prime costs constituted a high percentage of total costs. However, as manufacturing systems became more mechanised with the advent of assembly lines, overheads grew in relative proportion to total costs until it became clear that to continue valuing stock only at prime cost resulted in a figure which did not reflect the full costs involved in manufacture. Consequently, businesses developed costing systems in order to facilitate the allocation of production overheads to the cost of stock — primarily as an aid to making product pricing decisions.

2.1 Direct costing vs. full absorption costing

Although it was inevitable that individual firms would develop their own unique costing systems, the methods adopted could be classified between two broad approaches; namely, 'full absorption' and 'direct' costing. These systems differed in only one fundamental conceptual respect: the treatment of fixed overheads. Under direct costing, fixed overheads are expensed on a time basis and are therefore excluded from the cost of manufactured products, whilst under absorption costing fixed overheads are applied to the cost of the product, to be subsequently released to expense as part of cost of sales. Over the years, numerous arguments have been put forward both for and against each of the approaches. In essence, advocates of direct costing argue that fixed production overheads (e.g. rent) are more closely related to the *capacity* to produce, rather than to the production of individual products, and should therefore be expensed in the period in which they are incurred. Conversely, advocates of absorption costing maintain that fixed costs should be included in the cost of stock, since they are costs necessarily incurred to produce the goods.

A further complication arises through the conflict in the objectives of internal vs. external financial reporting. Because of the importance of contribution analysis in managerial accounting and performance measurement, many businesses adopt the direct costing approach for internal reporting purposes. On the other hand, the accounting standard setting bodies advocate at least some degree of absorption costing for external financial reporting purposes. For example, SSAP 9 states that the costs of stock 'will include all related production overheads'[10] and the definition of cost of conversion as stated above implies that at least direct fixed overheads should be allocated to the cost of stock. IAS 2 requires that 'the historical cost of manufactured inventories should include a systematic allocation of those production overhead costs that relate to putting the inventories in the present location and condition';[11] whilst in the US, ARB 43 states that 'cost means in principle the sum of the applicable expenditures and charges directly or indirectly incurred in bringing an article to its existing condition and location'.[12] Consequently, under SSAP 9, IAS 2 and ARB 43, fixed production overheads should only be excluded from the valuation of manufactured stocks in cases where they do not relate to 'bringing the stocks to their present location and condition'.

3 DETERMINING THE COST OF SALES

As discussed above, in the historical cost framework the principal objective of accounting for stock is the matching of costs with related revenues. However, since costs are continually changing over time, this objective is difficult to achieve in practice. Consequently, accountants have found it necessary to develop systematic bases for the recognition of the cost of sales, founded on certain cost flow assumptions. Some cost flow assumptions are based on the premise that the cost of sales should be identified with the physical flow of goods; whilst others disregard the physical flow of goods and attempt to achieve a more accurate matching of current costs with current revenues.

3.1   Cost flow assumptions based on the physical flow of goods

The explanatory note to SSAP 9 states that 'the methods used in allocating costs to stocks need to be selected with a view to providing the fairest possible approximation to the expenditure actually incurred in bringing the product to its present location and condition'.[13] Consequently, SSAP 9 sees the allocation of actual costs on the basis of the physical flow of goods as the ideal.

3.1.1   Specific identification/actual cost

Where it is both possible and practicable to attach a specific cost to each item of stock, the costs of goods sold are specifically identified and matched with the goods physically sold. In practice this is a relatively unusual method of valuation as the clerical effort required does not make it feasible unless there are relatively few high value items being bought or produced. Consequently, it would normally be used where the stock comprised items such as antiques, jewellery and cars in the hands of dealers. In spite of this, however, News International plc is an example of a company which states that it values its stock on the basis of actual cost:

Extract 9.1: News International plc[14]

Stocks and Work-in-Progress

Stocks and work-in-progress are valued at the lower of cost and net realisable value.
In general, cost represents actual cost of the stock concerned and, in respect of manufactured items, includes an appropriate proportion of production overheads.

3.1.2   FIFO (first-in, first-out)

In the vast majority of business situations it will not be practicable to keep track of stock cost on an individual unit basis; nevertheless, the objective of stock measurement is still to match costs and revenues. The FIFO method probably gives the closest approximation to actual cost flows, since it is assumed that when stocks are sold or used in a production process, the oldest are sold or used first and that, therefore, the balance of stock on hand at any point represents the most recent purchases or production. This can best be illustrated in the context of a business which deals in perishable goods, since clearly such a business will dispose of the earliest goods received before fresher goods. Therefore, by allocating the earliest costs incurred against revenue, actual cost flows are being matched with the physical flow of goods with reasonable accuracy. In any event, even in the case of businesses which do not deal in perishable goods, this would reflect what would probably be a sound management policy. Consequently, in practice where it is not possible to value stock on an actual cost basis, the FIFO method is generally used since it is most likely to approximate the physical flow of goods sold, resulting in the most accurate measurement of cost flows. Era Group Plc disclose a comprehensive FIFO stock policy:

Extract 9.2: Era Group Plc[15]

Stocks and work in progress
Stocks and work in progress are stated at the lower of cost and net realisable value. In general, cost is determined on a first in first out basis and includes transport and handling costs; in the case of manufactured products cost includes all direct expenditure and production overheads based on the normal level of activity. Net realisable value is the price at which stocks can be sold in the normal course of business after allowing for the costs of realisation and, where appropriate, the cost of conversion from their existing state to a finished condition. Provision is made where necessary for obsolete, slow moving and defective stocks.

3.2 Cost flow assumptions which disregard the physical flow of goods

3.2.1 Weighted average

This method, which is suitable where stock units are identical or near identical, involves the computation of an average unit cost by dividing the total cost of units by the number of units. The average unit cost then has to be revised with every receipt of stock, or alternatively at the end of predetermined periods. The justification for this approach is that 'it is illogical to distinguish between similar stock items merely because different levels of cost existed at the time they were purchased or produced'.[16] In practice, weighted average would appear to be less widely used than FIFO as it involves more clerical effort, and its results are not very different from FIFO in times of relatively low inflation, or where stock turnover is relatively quick.

3.2.2 LIFO (last-in, first-out)

This method is, as its name suggests, the opposite to FIFO and assumes that the most recent purchases or production are disposed of first; in certain cases this could represent the physical flow of stock (e.g. if a store is filled and emptied from the top). This is in an attempt to match current costs with current revenues so that the profit and loss account excludes the effects of holding gains. Essentially, therefore, LIFO is an attempt to achieve something closer to replacement cost accounting for the profit and loss account, whilst disregarding the balance sheet. Consequently, the period end balance of stock on hand represents the earliest purchases of the item, resulting in stocks being stated in the balance sheet at amounts which usually bear little relationship to recent cost levels. For this reason, LIFO is ordinarily not permitted to be used under SSAP 9[17] despite the fact that it is specifically allowed under the legislation.[18] However, since the balance sheet value of stock merely represents a deferred cost, and bears no relationship to the stock's worth to the firm, we do not see any conceptual difficulty in using LIFO in an historical cost accounting framework which is profit and loss oriented. The difficulty which does arise is that LIFO distorts the calculation of working capital ratios and makes inter-firm comparisons difficult. The simple solution to this would be to report current stock valuations as supplementary information (in any event, the Companies Act requires a company to disclose the difference between the replacement cost of stocks and their book value, where this difference is material).[19]

LIFO has not been widely used in the UK, principally because the Inland Revenue have never permitted its use for tax purposes. The position is different in the US, where the Internal Revenue Codes of 1938 and 1939 officially recognised LIFO as an acceptable method for the computation of tax, provided that it was used consistently for tax and financial reporting purposes. Therefore, if LIFO is used by individual companies in a group for tax purposes, it must also be used for reporting purposes in the financial statements of those companies as well as in the group financial statements.

Some companies have used LIFO as a method of attempting to solve the problem of accounting for changes in price levels, even to the extent of viewing it as a substitute for the cost of sales adjustment under SSAP 16.[20] Although this does achieve a measure of success in that the profit and loss account reflects current costs of sales, it does not fully adjust income for general price changes (although neither did the SSAP 16 cost of sales adjustment); in addition, there is the danger that the profit and loss account can be seriously distorted if stock quantities fall and cause very old costs to be included in cost of sales.

3.2.3 Base stock

This is another valuation method which is permitted by the legislation[21] but not approved by SSAP 9 (using the same reasoning as for LIFO).[22] Under this method a fixed quantity of stock is stated at a fixed price and any amount over the fixed quantity is valued using more usual methods, such as FIFO. The philosophy behind this method is that any on-going business must hold a certain minimum quantity of stock at all times; this base level of stock is then viewed as being more in the nature of a fixed asset, rather than stock to be sold or consumed. The fixed quantity is taken to be that level of stock which must always be held to maintain normal operating levels. The base stock method is not permitted for tax purposes in either the UK or US, and is rarely seen in practice. It is important to note that the use of the base stock method would only be permitted by the Companies Act 1985 in the case of 'assets of a kind which are constantly being replaced where—

(a)   their overall value is not material to assessing the company's state of affairs; and

(b)   their quantity, value and composition are not subject to material variation'.[23]

Although IAS 2 currently allows the use of the base stock method of valuation, E32 — *Comparability of Financial Statements* — proposes that the base stock formula should be removed as a permitted option.[24]

The following two extracts illustrate instances of where the base stock method is used — which is generally in respect of commodities:

Extract 9.3: Tate & Lyle PLC[25]

Molasses Trading

Stocks of blackstrap molasses up to a fixed maximum tonnage are valued at a base price. Such base stock is the amount currently regarded as the normal operating quantity necessary for trading and distribution. The maintenance of this tonnage is necessary for the continuance of the business and it is not normally available for disposal. The consistent use of the base stock method ensures that fluctuations in prices are eliminated from stock values. The base stock price of molasses is denominated in US$. Values and volumes are amended from time to time to give effect to changes which are regarded as permanent.

Any excess of the stock of blackstrap molasses over the base tonnage is valued at the lower of cost and net realisable value. Beet molasses and other molasses related stocks are also valued on this basis.

Extract 9.4: BICC plc[26]

8 Stocks [extract]

Manufacturing work in progress and all stocks are valued at the lower of cost and net realisable value, except for the UK base stock of copper which is valued at a fixed price below net realisable value. Cost comprises raw material and conversion costs including depreciation and production overheads.

16 Stocks

	BICC Group		BICC plc	
	1987 £m	1986 £m	1987 £m	1986 £m
Contracting work-in-progress	1,782.3	1,680.1	4.9	4.9
Progress applications	(1,649.8)	(1,571.9)	(4.4)	(4.6)
	132.5	108.2	.5	.3
Manufacturing work-in-progress	69.8	56.6	22.7	21.4
Raw materials and consumables	62.5	68.6	23.5	23.7
Finished goods and goods for resale	98.7	89.5	27.1	24.0
	363.5	322.9	73.8	69.4

Contracting work in progress includes development and housing land and work in progress of £57.1m (1986: £22.2m).
Raw materials in the Group include UK copper stocks valued on base stock principles at £3.2m (1986: £3.2m). Had this been valued at net realisable value, the value would have been £6.4m (1986: £5.0m) and profit before interest would have increased by £1.4m (1986: decreased by £0.3m).

It is noteworthy that Tate & Lyle PLC state that the use of the base stock method is a departure from SSAP 9,[27] and include their base stocks within tangible fixed assets; whilst BICC plc make no mention of any departure (presumably because the amounts involved are relatively immaterial), and include their base stocks within the total of stocks.

3.3   Example

The following example illustrates the practical effect of various cost flow assumptions:

Example 9.1:   Illustration of the effect of different cost flow assumptions

Company A's stock transactions for the three months ended 31 March 19X1 were as follows:

	Units	Unit cost	Unit selling price
		£	£
Stock on hand: 1 January 19X1	60	30	
January purchases	90	45	
January sales	(40)		60
February purchases	55	60	
February sales	(45)		100
March purchases	60	75	
March sales	(75)		130
Stock on hand: 31 March 19X1	105		

The company maintains its stock records on the perpetual system, and all purchases are made on the first day of the month.

The value of cost of sales for the three months ended 31 March 19X1 and closing stock at that date under various costing methods are as follows:

	FIFO	Weighted average	LIFO
	£	£	£
Sales	16,650	16,650	16,650
Cost of sales	(6,450)	(7,805)	(9,825)
Gross profit	10,200	8,845	6,825
Stock at 31 March 19X1	7,200	5,845	3,825

The above example illustrates that, under the historical cost framework, accounting for stock is merely a cost allocation process, and that stock disclosed in the balance sheet is no more than a deferred cost. Therefore, it is necessary to decide how much of the cost of goods available for sale during the period should be written off, and how much should be deferred. In this example, the total costs of £13,650 are allocated/deferred according to the three costing methods illustrated.

Clearly, the extent of the divergence in results under the three methods illustrated above is a function of the rate of price changes. In times of rising prices, FIFO tends to overstate profit because earlier and lower unit costs are matched with current prices, whilst valuing period-end stocks at the most recent costs which are the more realistic measures of current cost. Conversely, LIFO more realistically reflects profit by matching the most recent unit costs with current selling price, whilst valuing period-end stocks at the oldest and, therefore, less realistic unit costs.

4   THE DEVELOPMENT OF SSAP 9 (REVISED)

4.1   The original SSAP 9

SSAP 9 was originally issued in 1975 because, as the preamble to the standard stated, 'no area of accounting has produced wider differences in practice than the computation of the amount at which stocks and work in progress are stated in financial accounts'.[28] The standard commenced by stating the basic requirement that stocks and work in progress should normally be stated at the lower of cost and net realisable value.[29] It made it clear that production overheads must be included in stock by requiring that 'such costs [of stocks and work in progress] will include all related production overheads, even though these may accrue on a time basis'.[30] Furthermore, it emphasised that the approach previously taken by some companies of excluding certain overheads from stocks on the grounds of prudence was unacceptable, by stating that 'in so far as the circumstances of the business require an element of prudence in determining the amount at which stocks and work in progress are stated, this needs to be taken into account in the determination of net realisable value and not by the exclusion from cost of selected overheads'.[31]

In relation to contracting work in progress SSAP 9 required a different treatment only in respect of those contracts which extend for more than one year.[32] (Any work in progress in respect of contracts lasting less than one year had to be accounted for on the normal basis, i.e. at the lower of cost and net realisable value. This immediately gave rise to a conceptual problem in that activities which are identical in nature were required to be accounted for in different ways because of an artificial distinction based on an arbitrary duration.) The difference in treatment arose from the requirement to include 'attributable profit'[33] within the balance sheet figure for long-term contract work in progress. In arriving at this balance sheet figure one also had to deduct any foreseeable losses and progress payments received and receivable.[34] This latter rule ensured that for the most part long-term contract work in progress was stated at the lower of: (i) cost plus attributable profit and (ii) net realisable value.

The reason why a different treatment is required for long-term contracts is that if the basic rule of accounting for stocks was applied to them this would result in an annual profit and loss account reflecting the outcome only of contracts completed during the year, which, in a contracting company, might bear no relation to the company's actual level of activity for the year. Obviously, if a company operated at the same level of activity over the years on contracts of similar size and duration there would be no real difference in the results reported each year under the percentage of completion and the completed contracts methods. However, in practice this is not the way things happen in any contracting industry and therefore attributable profit has to be accrued on uncompleted contracts in order to present a consistent view of the results of the company's activities during the period.

4.2   The need for revision

One of the accounting rules introduced by the Companies Act 1981 in its implementation of the EC Fourth Directive was that current assets are to be stated at the lower of their cost and net realisable value. This principle has been carried through to the Companies Act 1985 via paragraphs 22 and 23 of Schedule 4, which state that 'the amount to be included in respect of any current asset shall be its purchase price or production cost. If the net realisable value of any current asset is lower than its purchase price or production cost, the amount to be included in respect of that asset shall be the net realisable value.' This immediately resulted in a conflict with SSAP 9, which required long-term work in progress in the balance sheet to include attributable profit. The legislation was not outlawing the inclusion of the attributable profit in the profit and loss account, merely the inclusion of it within the value of a current asset. However, there was scope within the legislation to depart from the detailed accounting rules if this was necessary to give a true and fair view and if full details of the departure, including its effect, were given in a note to the accounts (the 'true and fair override').[35] Prior to the implementation of SSAP 9 (Revised), this has been used as the justification for including profit in long-term work in progress and thereby complying with SSAP 9.

There have essentially been two approaches taken to the requirement to disclose the details and the effect of the departure from the statutory valuation rules:

Extract 9.5: The Plessey Company plc[36]

16 Stocks [extract]
In accordance with the provisions of SSAP 9, attributable profit amounting to £36.6m (1987 — £35.0m) has been included in the value of long term contract work-in-progress. The directors are of the opinion that this departure from statutory valuation rules is necessary to enable the accounts to give a true and fair view.

> *Extract 9.6: The Peninsular and Oriental Steam Navigation Company*[37]
>
> **18 Stocks** [extract]
> To enable the accounts to give a true and fair view, attributable profit is included in long term work in progress. This is a departure from the statutory valuation rules but is required by section 228 of the Companies Act 1985. Work in progress is stated net of progress payments of £1,366.2m (1986 £1,090.8m) which cannot be allocated between the related cost and profit.

Representatives of the Department of Trade and Industry (DTI) had made it clear that they were unhappy with the use of the true and fair override in such a general way as it was intended that it only be used in very rare circumstances.

4.3   SSAP 9 (Revised)

As a result of the DTI's objections, a working party was set up by the ASC to review SSAP 9. This resulted in ED 40 being published in November 1986, and ultimately in the release of SSAP 9 (Revised) in September 1988. Its provisions are to be regarded as standard in respect of financial statements relating to accounting periods beginning on or after July 1, 1988. There are effectively no changes to the accounting and disclosure requirements contained in the original standard in respect of stocks and work in progress. The changes made, therefore, are only in respect of long-term contracts and are principally two-fold: one concerns the presentation of long-term contract balances within the balance sheet and is designed to meet the DTI's objections, while the other is a revision to the definition of a long-term contract and is intended to remove the problems associated with the arbitrariness of the 12 month rule within the definition in the original standard.

The requirements of SSAP 9 (Revised) in respect of stocks and work in progress are dealt with in 6 below; long-term contracts are dealt with in 7 below.

5   THE REQUIREMENTS OF THE COMPANIES ACT 1985

The legal requirements of accounting for and disclosure of stocks within a company's financial statements are included along with most other legal accounting requirements in Schedule 4 to the Companies Act 1985. There is no specific mention made in the legislation of long-term contracts. This is because the legislation treats all current assets in the same way and is the principal reason why SSAP 9 was revised.

5.1   Lower of cost and net realisable value

Paragraphs 22 and 23, which apply to all current assets and not just stocks, are very similar to paragraph 26 of SSAP 9 and provide that current assets should be stated at the lower of their cost and net realisable value.

5.2   Stock included at a fixed amount

As discussed at 3.2.3 above in the context of the base stock method of costing stock, paragraph 25 provides that stocks of raw materials and consumables which are constantly being replaced may be included at a fixed quantity and value provided that the overall value of such stocks is not material to the company's balance sheet and that their quantity, value and composition are not subject to material variation.

5.3   Determination of purchase price or production cost

Paragraph 26 states the rules that apply in arriving at the cost of an asset:

(a)   the purchase price of an asset should include any expenses incidental to the acquisition of that asset, e.g. customs duties;

(b)   the production cost of an asset should include, in addition to the cost of the raw materials and consumables, any other directly attributable production costs, e.g. direct labour costs;

(c)   costs of distribution by the company may not be included in production costs;

(d)   in addition to the costs at (b) above there may be included some costs 'which are only indirectly attributable to the production of that asset'. Most commonly these would be costs that vary with time rather than production, e.g. rent, rates and insurance;

(e)   'Interest on capital borrowed to finance the production' may also be included in stock. Capitalisation of interest is discussed in Chapter 12.

Any costs that fall to be included under (d) and (e) above can only be included to the extent that they accrue during the period of production, and the amount of any interest included must be separately disclosed.

5.4   Costing method

Paragraph 27 provides that stocks may be stated using FIFO, LIFO, weighted average or any other method similar to any of those, but whichever method is chosen, it must be appropriate to the circumstances of the company. However, where any item of stock is valued by one of these methods rather than at actual cost the difference between the amount at which it is included in the financial statements and its replacement cost or most recent actual purchase price or production cost is required to be disclosed if that difference is material. A strict interpretation of the paragraph could require some meaningless disclosures to be given. If a category of stock is valued at a combination of actual cost and one of the methods permitted by paragraph 27 then it is only the difference between the replacement cost of the stock that is not carried at actual cost and its carrying amount that is required to be disclosed.[38] Not surprisingly, such information is rarely given. In practice, if an amount is disclosed it is either the difference between the total replacement cost and the total carrying value, or the total replacement cost of stocks is also disclosed.

Extract 9.7: The British Petroleum Company p.l.c.[39]

19   Stocks

	1987 £m	1986 £m
Petroleum	1,765	1,851
Chemicals	259	232
Minerals	111	142
Nutrition	143	142
Other	160	158
	2,438	2,525
Stores	278	374
	2,716	2,899
Replacement cost	2,694	3,015

However, more often than not a statement is included to the effect that the difference between the replacement cost and the carrying value is not material.

Extract 9.8: Lucas Industries plc[40]

Note 12: Stocks [extract]

The current replacement cost of stock is not materially different from the above.

It should be noted that paragraph 27(5) of Schedule 4 permits the use of the most recent actual purchase price or production cost rather than replacement cost if the former appears more appropriate to the directors of the company. The Laird Group PLC is an example of a company where the directors make use of this provision:

Extract 9.9: The Laird Group PLC[41]

13 Stocks [extract]
The value of stock and work in progress is not materially different to its production cost or recent actual purchase price as appropriate.

However, a large number of companies are silent on the matter of replacement cost. Without inside knowledge, one can only guess at the possible reasons for this. These might be that:

- stocks are valued at actual cost;
- the difference to be disclosed is not material; or
- the cost of computing and disclosing the amount outweighs the benefits to be derived from it.

5.5 Current cost

Paragraph 31 allows stocks to be included at their current cost. This provision is not often seen in practice, however, as almost all companies prepare their statutory financial statements under the historical cost convention.

6 STOCKS

6.1 The accounting and disclosure requirements of SSAP 9 (Revised)

6.1.1 Suitable analysis of stocks

Stocks should be stated in financial statements at 'the total of the lower of cost and net realisable value of the separate items of stock or of groups of similar items'.[42] Stocks should be sub-classified on the face of the balance sheet or in the notes thereto, so as to indicate the amounts held in each of the main categories in the standard balance sheet formats contained in Schedule 4 to the Companies Act 1985.[43] These sub-headings are as follows:

- raw materials and consumables
- work in progress
- finished goods and goods for resale
- payments on account.[44]

In practice, most companies follow these classifications and present stock as a note to the financial statements as follows:

Extract 9.10: Lucas Industries plc[45]

Note 12: Stocks	1988 £ million	1987 £ million
Raw materials and consumables	53.7	50.8
Work in progress	183.4	170.9
Finished goods	141.3	136.3
Payments on account	(22.5)	(25.6)
	355.9	332.4

The application of these classifications should, however, be done in conjunction with the requirements of Schedule 4, paragraph 3(3), which states that 'in preparing a company's balance sheet or profit and loss account the directors of the company shall adapt the arrangement and headings and sub-headings ... in any case where the special nature of the company's business requires such adaptation'.[46]

It is therefore the responsibility of the directors to ensure that the classifications used are appropriate to the nature of the company's business. Although adaptations are rarely found in practice, B.A.T Industries p.l.c. is an example of a company where the directors do take the particular circumstances of the company into account:

Extract 9.11: B.A.T Industries p.l.c.[47]

16 Stocks	Raw materials and components		Consumable stores		Finished goods and work in progress		Goods purchased for resale		Total stocks	
	1987	1986	1987	1986	1987	1986	1987	1986	1987	1986
	£ millions									
Tobacco	674	871	41	50	229	266	25	27	969	1214
Retailing			4	3			533	582	537	585
Paper	60	71	21	26	98	90	28	29	207	216
Other trading activities	38	38	4	9	53	82	2	2	97	131
	772	980	70	88	380	438	588	640	1,810	2,146

6.1.2 Accounting policies

The original version of SSAP 9 required that 'the accounting policies which have been used in calculating cost, net realisable value, attributable profit and foreseeable losses (as appropriate) should be stated'.[48] In the light of this requirement, one might have expected to see some fairly detailed policies describing, for instance, assumptions about the flow of stocks and therefore costs, which costs are included in stock and the basis for allocating indirect costs to stocks. In practice, however, the disclosures which have been made vary widely in the amount of detail that they give:

Extract 9.12: Beecham Group p.l.c.[49]

Stocks
Stocks are stated at the lower of cost and net realisable value generally using the first in, first out method of valuation. The cost of finished goods and work in progress comprises raw materials, direct labour and expenses, and related production overheads.

Extract 9.13: GKN plc[50]

13 Stocks [extract]
Stocks have been consistently valued at the lower of cost and estimated net realisable value, due allowance being made for obsolete or slow-moving items. Cost includes the relevant proportion of works overheads assuming normal levels of activity.

Extract 9.14: Blue Circle Industries PLC[51]

8 Stocks
The basis of valuation is the lower of cost and net realisable value. Cost includes direct costs and appropriate overheads.

Extract 9.15: Tarmac PLC[52]

Stocks
Stocks are valued at the lower of cost and net realisable value. Cost includes appropriate overheads.

Extract 9.16: Trusthouse Forte PLC[53]

Stocks: Stocks are stated at the lower of cost and net realisable value.

None of the above extracts is ideal, even though some are more detailed than others. For example, Extract 9.12 leaves the reader to guess as to the basis on which overheads are applied, while Extract 9.13 is silent on the assumption(s) made about the flow of costs. However, the above extracts are a fair representation of the policies which have been stated in the past under the requirements of the original SSAP 9.

The revision of SSAP 9, however, does not appear to have improved the situation. The revised requirement merely states that the accounting policy that has been applied to stocks should be stated and applied consistently within the business and from year to year.[54] We therefore do not foresee any likely improvement in disclosure in this area.

Our recommendation, however, is that the accounting policy for stock should at least provide as much information as was required under the original SSAP 9, for example:

Stocks

Stocks are stated at the lower of cost and net realisable value as follows:

Cost incurred in bringing each product to its present location and condition:

Raw materials and goods for resale   —   purchase cost on a first-in, first-out basis.

Work in progress and finished goods   —   cost of direct materials and labour plus attributable overheads based on normal level of activity.

Net realisable value is based on estimated selling price less further costs expected to be incurred to completion and disposal.

6.2   Comparison with US and IASC pronouncements

6.2.1   *US*

In the US, accounting for stocks is governed by Chapter 4 of Accounting Research Bulletin No. 43.[55] As with SSAP 9, ARB 43 recognises that the matching concept is the main principle underlying the accounting for stocks. The underlying principles of the bulletin are as follows:

(a)   stocks should normally be stated at the lower of cost or market ('market' as used here follows a formula reflecting net realisable value).

Depending on the character of the stock, in certain circumstances the rule of lower of cost or market may be applied to the total of stock (see 6.3.2 below);

(b)   the basis of stating stocks and the cost flow assumption used should be disclosed and should be consistently applied. The assumption made on the flow of costs should be that which most clearly reflects periodic income. As discussed at 3.2.2 above, the LIFO method of costing is permitted.

In certain circumstances, principally where there is an organised and liquid market at fixed prices (e.g. precious metals) with little or no selling costs, stocks may be stated at market value, even where this is greater than cost.

6.2.2   *IASC*

IAS 2 — *Valuation and Presentation of Inventories in the Context of the Historical Cost System* — has similar requirements to both SSAP 9 and ARB 43, Chapter 4. The principal rule is that 'inventories should be valued at the lower of historical cost and net realisable value'.[56]

The stated preference in IAS 2 is for using either FIFO or weighted average as the assumption on cost flows.[57] Nevertheless, both the LIFO and base stock methods of costing are permitted, provided that there is disclosure of the difference between the amount of the stocks as disclosed in the balance sheet and either (a) the lower of the amount arrived at in accordance with either the FIFO or weighted average methods and net realisable value, or (b) the lower of current cost at the balance sheet date and net realisable value.[58]

The remainder of the standard states how to arrive at historical cost and net realisable value as well as the disclosure to be made in financial statements, and follows the principles contained in SSAP 9.

The IASC has recently issued an exposure draft, E32 — *Comparability of Financial Statements* — which proposes, inter alia, to amend the requirements of IAS 2. The main change proposed is that IAS 2 should not permit the use of the base stock method.[59]

6.3 Problem areas

6.3.1 Constituents of cost

For the most part there are few problems over the inclusion of direct costs in stocks. Problems tend to arise, however, over certain overheads and with regard to the question of how overheads are to be incorporated into stock valuation.

A Distribution costs

By law distribution costs may not be included in the cost of stocks (see 5.3 above). However, SSAP 9 defines cost as 'that expenditure which has been incurred in the normal course of business in bringing the product or service to its present location and condition'.[60] As a result, a company which includes in stock the cost of transporting goods from its factory to its warehouse in accordance with the standard may not be complying with the law. In practice, however, the costs of such transport are not likely to be material and the company can take advantage of paragraph 86 of Schedule 4 to the Companies Act 1985 which provides that immaterial amounts may be disregarded for the purposes of any provision of Schedule 4. Where such costs are material it may be necessary for the company to invoke the 'true and fair override'.[61] However, an alternative and more reasonable view might be that the 'distribution costs' referred to in paragraph 26 of Schedule 4 to the Companies Act 1985 are costs of distribution to customers, and that therefore the costs of transporting goods to a warehouse would not fall within the meaning of the prohibition.

B Selling costs

SSAP 9 states that normally only purchase and production costs should be included in the cost of stocks. However, in certain specific circumstances the standard recognises that it might be appropriate to include other types of cost in stock:

'Where firm sales contracts have been entered into for the provision of goods or services to customer's specification, overheads relating to design, and marketing and selling costs incurred before manufacture may be included in arriving at cost.'[62]

Ordinarily such costs should be expensed in the period in which they are incurred. The matching concept requires, however, that in the above circumstances the costs should be deferred and matched against their related revenues.

Extract 9.17: Westland Group plc[63]

9 Stocks [extract]
(b) Cost of manufactured parts and work-in-progress against customers' contracts comprises prime cost plus full overheads (including administration, distribution and selling expenses).

C Storage costs

Storage costs are not costs which would normally be incurred in bringing a product to its present location and condition. However, where it is necessary to store raw materials or work in progress prior to a further processing or manufacturing stage, the costs of such storage should be included in production overheads. In addition, the costs of storing maturing stocks, such as whisky, should be included in the cost of production.

D   General/administrative overheads

SSAP 9 makes it clear that the costs of general, as opposed to functional, management are not normally costs of production and should therefore be excluded from the value of stock.[64] However, the standard recognises that in smaller organisations there may not be a clear distinction of management functions and that 'in such organisations the cost of management may fairly be allocated on suitable bases to the functions of production, marketing, selling and administration'.[65] Overheads relating to service departments, such as accounts and personnel departments, should be allocated to the main functions of production, marketing, selling and administration on a basis which reflects the amount of support supplied by the service department to the particular main function. SSAP 9 states that 'problems may also arise in allocating the costs of central service departments, the allocation of which should depend on the function or functions that the department is serving. For example, the accounts department will normally support the following functions:

(a)   production — by paying direct and indirect production wages and salaries, by controlling purchases and by preparing periodic financial statements for the production units;

(b)   marketing and distribution — by analysing sales and by controlling the sales ledger;

(c)   general administration — by preparing management accounts and annual financial statements and budgets, by controlling cash resources and by planning investments.

Only those costs of the accounts department that can be allocated to the production function fall to be included in the cost of conversion.'[66]

E   Allocation of overheads

SSAP 9 makes it clear that the overheads to be included in stock must be allocated on the basis of a company's normal level of activity.[67] Unfortunately 'normal' is not defined although the standard does give some guidance as to the factors to be considered:

'(a)   the volume of production which the production facilities are intended by their designers and by management to produce under the working conditions (e.g. single or double shift) prevailing during the year;

(b)   the budgeted level of activity for the year under review and for the ensuing year;

(c)   the level of activity achieved both in the year under review and in previous years'.[68]

In practice, a normal level of activity is established by reference to the budgeted or expected level of activity over several years; however, during a start-up period, and until normal operating conditions are reached, the actual level of activity will generally be taken as normal. The reason for this is that it would arguably be unfair to expense to the profit and loss account start-up costs which are expected to result in future revenues. It has been suggested that the overhead recovery rate in a start-up period 'should be based on the level of activity which obtains when the plant is working at normal production capacity';[69] but this is unlikely to be done in practice as the first year's results will be depressed through the recognition of non-recurring costs involved in the start-up.

No matter how overheads are being allocated to stock, it is necessary to ensure that only 'normal' costs are being included and that 'abnormal' costs, e.g. excess scrap and the cost of excess facilities, are being expensed as period costs. This occurs automatically as a result of using standard costing, assuming that the standards are regularly reviewed and variances are properly analysed and appropriately dealt with. However, where a standard costing system is not in place, it is necessary for an exercise to be carried out to ensure that no such abnormal costs have been included in closing stock. It is important to bear in mind that this exercise should be carried out on all cost categories, including direct costs.

The overheads to be included based on the normal level of activity should be applied by reference to the most significant direct cost. Thus if a process is particularly capital intensive the overheads should be applied to stock by an overhead recovery rate based on direct machine hours, while if labour costs are more significant the recovery rate should be based on direct labour hours. In practice a recovery rate based on direct labour hours has often been used because, historically speaking, labour has been regarded as the key limiting factor on the level of production.

In computing the costs to be allocated via the overhead recovery rate, costs such as distribution and selling must be excluded, together with cost of storing raw materials and work in progress, unless it is necessary that these latter costs be incurred prior to further processing.

6.3.2 Net realisable value

As already mentioned, it is the basic rule of accounting for stocks that they are stated at the lower of their cost and net realisable value. SSAP 9 defines net realisable value as follows:

'*Net realisable value:* the actual or estimated selling price (net of trade but before settlement discounts) less:

(a)   all further costs to completion; and

(b)   all costs to be incurred in marketing, selling and distributing.'[70]

Appendix 1 to SSAP 9 identifies the following situations where net realisable value might be less than cost:

'(a) an increase in costs or a fall in selling price;

(b) physical deterioration of stocks;

(c) obsolescence of products;

(d) a decision as part of a company's marketing strategy to manufacture and sell products at a loss;

(e) errors in production or purchasing'.[71]

In addition it points out that when a company has excess stocks on hand the risk of situations (a) to (c) above occurring increases and must be considered in assessing net realisable value. A provision will also be required for losses on commitments made for both the future purchases and sales of stocks.

SSAP 9 requires that the comparison of cost and net realisable value should be done on an item by item basis or by groups of similar items.[72] In the US, ARB 43 states that 'depending on the character and composition of the inventory, the rule of *cost or market, whichever is lower* may properly be applied either directly to each item or to the total of the inventory (or, in some cases, to the total of the components of each major category). The method should be that which most clearly reflects periodic income.'[73] The reasoning behind allowing the comparison to be done on an overall basis in certain circumstances, is that 'the reduction of individual items to *market* may not always lead to the most useful result if the utility of the total inventory to the business is not below its cost. This might be the case if selling prices are not affected by temporary or small fluctuations in current costs of purchase or manufacture. Similarly, where more than one major product or operational category exists, the application of the *cost or market, whichever is lower* rule to the total of the items included in such major categories may result in the most useful determination of income'.[74]

This highlights an important difference in approach between the UK and US. Net realisable value, as it would be applied in the UK, depends on the ultimate selling price of a completed product. Thus, a whisky distiller, for example, would not write down his stock of grain because of a fall in the grain price, so long as he expected still to sell the whisky at a profit. However, the US definition of market is partly based on *replacement cost*, so a different result might follow unless stocks are looked at in aggregate.

The following example illustrates the different effects that can be achieved by applying the 'lower of cost and net realisable value' rule to individual items, groups of items and to the total stock:

Example 9.2:   *Alternative methods of applying the lower of cost and net realisable value rule*

	Value of stock at:		Application of rule to:		
	Cost	Net realisable value	Individual items	Major groups	Total stock
	£	£	£	£	£
Group 1					
Item A	2,000	3,000	2,000		
Item B	4,000	2,500	2,500		
Item C	5,000	3,000	3,000		
TOTAL	11,000	8,500	7,500	8,500	
Group 2					
Item D	1,000	1,500	1,000		
Item E	8,000	16,000	8,000		
Item F	10,000	6,000	6,000		
TOTAL	19,000	23,500	15,000	19,000	
TOTAL STOCK	30,000	32,000	22,500	27,500	30,000

The valuation of £30,000 which arises from the application of the rule to the total of stock is not acceptable in the UK, as it results in what are regarded as realised losses being offset against what are regarded as unrealised gains. The valuation of £27,500 which results from the application of the rule to groups of similar items is acceptable, provided the individual items within the groups are sold together — because the stock is effectively being regarded as consisting of two major lines. The valuation of £22,500 is, of course, acceptable as it is the result of the strictest application of the rule.

The comparison of cost and net realisable value of finished goods is normally straightforward where there are established selling prices for the finished goods. Where a provision is required in respect of finished goods, the carrying value of any related raw materials, work in progress and spares must also be reviewed to see if any further provision is required.

Where the selling price of finished goods varies with the price of raw materials and there has been a fall in the price of the raw materials then some provision may be required in respect of any stock of the finished goods (as well as possibly being required in respect of stocks of the raw materials and any forward purchase contracts).

Often raw materials are bought in order to make different product lines. In these cases it is normally not possible to arrive at a particular net realisable value for each item of raw material based on selling price. Therefore, current replacement cost might be the best guide to net realisable value in such circumstances. If current replacement cost is less than historical cost, however, a provision is only required to be made if the finished goods into which they will be made are expected to be sold at a loss. No provision should be made just because the anticipated profit will be less than normal.

6.3.3 *The valuation of high volumes of similar items of stock*

Practical problems in the valuation of stock arise in the case of businesses which have high volumes of various line items of stock. This situation occurs almost exclusively in the retail trade where similar mark-ups are applied to all stock items or groups of items, and the selling price is marked on each individual item of stock (e.g. in the case of a supermarket). In such a situation, it may be time-consuming to determine the cost of the period-end stock on a more conventional basis; consequently, the most practical method of determining period-end stock may be to record stock on hand at selling prices and then convert it to cost by removing the normal mark-up. Not surprisingly, this method of stock valuation is known as the 'retail method'.

However, a complication in applying the retail method is in determining the margin to be applied to the stock at selling price to convert it back to cost. Since different lines and different departments may have widely different margins, it is normally necessary to subdivide stock and apply the appropriate margins to each subdivision. Furthermore, where stocks have been marked down to below original selling price, adjustments have to be made to eliminate the effect of these markdowns so as to prevent any item of stock being valued at less than both its cost and its net realisable value. In practice, however, companies which use the retail method, tend to apply a gross profit margin computed on an average basis, rather than apply specific mark-up percentages.

Marks and Spencer p.l.c. is an example of a company which applies the retail method:

Extract 9.18: Marks and Spencer p.l.c.[75]

Stocks [extract]
Retail stocks consist of goods for resale which are valued at the lower of cost and net realisable value. Cost is computed by deducting the gross profit margin from the selling value of stock. When computing net realisable value an allowance is made for future markdowns.

It is noteworthy that Appendix 1 to SSAP 9 states that this method 'is acceptable only if it can be demonstrated that the method gives a reasonable approximation to the actual cost'.[76]

6.3.4 *Commodity dealers*

The practice has developed, principally among commodity dealing companies, of stating stock at market value and also taking into account profits and losses arising on the valuation of forward contracts ('marking to market'). This represents a departure from the statutory valuation rules in that stocks are being stated at more than cost, but this is generally justified as being necessary in order to show a true and fair view. SSAP 9 does not specifically deal with this issue; in fact it is difficult to come to any conclusion other than that the requirement in the standard that stocks should be included at the lower of cost and net realisable value has, in this instance, been dispensed with. Advocates of marking to market would argue, however, that this is a specialised development to which the generality of SSAP 9 should not apply and which was not envisaged when SSAP 9 was being originally developed. Unfortunately the problem of marking stock at market value was not addressed when SSAP 9 was revised. However, as discussed at 6.2.1 above, there is support for this practice under US GAAP.

It is our opinion that, despite the departure from the standard, marking to market is acceptable in certain circumstances. We would suggest that appropriate criteria might be that:

(a) the company's principal activity is the trading of commodities and/or marketable securities;

(b) the nature of the business is such that the commodities traded do not alter significantly in character between purchase and sale;

(c) the commodities are or can be traded on an organised terminal or futures market; and

(d) the market is sufficiently liquid to allow the company to realise its stock and forward contracts at prices close to those used in their valuation.

Kleinwort Benson Lonsdale plc is an example of a company which has adopted a policy of marking to market:

Extract 9.19: Kleinwort Benson Lonsdale plc[77]

ACCOUNTING POLICIES [extract]

(d) Gold, Silver and Other Precious Metals
Bullion liabilities, stock and loans are valued at year end spot prices, except those matched with forward contracts which are carried at cost adjusted for accrued forward premium or discount. Bullion and other metal held for customers on an allocated basis is not included in these accounts.

(e) Dealing and Investment Securities
The Group distinguishes between securities held for dealing and longer term investment purposes.

(i) Dealing positions
Marketable obligations and dealing positions held by the securities companies are stated at market value, and all revaluation differences are dealt with in the profit and loss account. Certificates of deposit, bills discounted and other short term marketable obligations are stated at cost plus accrued income.

(ii) Investment positions
Listed investments held by Kleinwort Benson Investment Trust Limited are carried at 6th April 1965 valuation or subsequent cost to the Group.
Listed investments with no fixed maturity date held by other companies in the Group are carried at the lower of cost and market value. Other investments are carried at cost adjusted to amortise any premium or discount on purchase over the period to maturity.
Unlisted investments are carried at the lower of cost or Directors' valuation.
Amounts written off and profits and losses on disposals of investments are dealt with in the profit and loss account.

---

7   LONG-TERM CONTRACTS

7.1   The accounting and disclosure requirements of SSAP 9 (Revised)

As has been discussed in 4.2 above, the need for the revision of SSAP 9 arose principally as a result of the conflict which existed between the original statement and the Companies Act regarding the balance sheet measurement of long-term contract balances. At the same time it was decided to redefine 'long-term contract' so as to remove the problems associated with the arbitrariness of the 12 month rule within the definition in the original standard.

7.1.1   *Definition*

The original SSAP 9 defined a long-term contract as 'a contract entered into for manufacture or building of a single substantial entity or the provision of a service where the time taken to manufacture, build or provide is such that a substantial proportion of all such contract work will extend for a period exceeding one year'.[78] This definition had an illogical practical result in that two contracts which were identical in all respects except for duration had to be accounted for differently: a 51-week contract had to be treated as short-term, whilst a 53-week contract had to be treated as long-term. A possible solution to this anomalous situation might have been that if a company was substantially engaged in long-term contracts, then *all* contracts should be accounted for as long-term on the percentage of completion basis — even if there were some which lasted for less than a year. Conversely, if a company was substantially engaged in short-term contracts, then *all* contracts should be accounted for as short-term on the completed contracts basis — even if some contracts extended for more than a year. However, such an approach would not have been in compliance with the original SSAP 9, and would probably only have been acceptable on grounds of materiality.

SSAP 9 (Revised) has removed the arbitrary nature of this one-year rule whilst, at the same time, retaining one year as one criterion which might distinguish a long-term contract. The revised definition is as follows: a *long-term contract* is 'a contract entered into for the design, manufacture or construction of a single substantial asset or the provision of a service (or of a combination of assets or services which together constitute a single project) where the time taken substantially to complete the contract is such that the contract activity falls into different accounting periods. A contract that is required to be accounted for as long-term by this accounting standard will usually extend for a period exceeding one year. However, a duration exceeding one year is not an essential feature of a long-term contract. Some contracts with a shorter duration than one year should be accounted for as long-term contracts if they are sufficiently material to the activity of the period that not to record turnover and attributable profit would lead to a distortion of the period's turnover and results such that the financial statements would not give a true and fair view, provided that the policy is applied consistently within the reporting entity and from year to year.'[79]

The practical impact of this revised definition is that short-term contracting businesses will probably be able to account for all their contracts as short-term (even if some contracts extend for more than a year), and long-term contracting businesses will be able to account for all their contracts as long-term (even if some are for less than a year). However, if a business is clearly in both the short-term and long-term contracting businesses, criteria must be established for distinguishing between such contracts, and appropriate accounting policies must be established and applied consistently.

However, it should be noted that whilst the revised definition of a long-term contract does eliminate the rigid one-year rule, it does create a new area of potential controversy with regard to the accrual of profit on short-term contracts. This is discussed at 7.3.4 below.

7.1.2 Turnover, related costs and attributable profit

Long-term contracts should be:

(a)   assessed on a contract by contract basis; and

(b)   reflected in the profit and loss account by recording turnover and related costs as contract activity progresses.[80]

The standard fails to lay down a method for determining turnover and merely states that 'turnover is ascertained in a manner appropriate to the stage of completion of the contract, the business and the industry in which it operates'.[81] SSAP 9 then states that 'where it is considered that the outcome of a long-term contract can be assessed with reasonable certainty before its conclusion, the prudently calculated attributable profit should be recognised in the profit and loss account as the difference between the reported turnover and related costs for that contract'.[82] Based on this requirement, it would appear that the attributable profit is merely the balancing figure once 'turnover' and 'related costs' have been determined. One would therefore have expected SSAP 9 to define 'related costs' and require companies to disclose an accounting policy for the determination of 'related costs'. However, instead it defines 'attributable profit' and requires an accounting policy which sets out how it has been ascertained. As a result, either turnover or related costs will be the balancing figure.

'Attributable profit' is defined as 'that part of the total profit currently estimated to arise over the duration of the contract, after allowing for estimated remedial and maintenance costs and increases in costs so far as not recoverable under the terms of the contract, that fairly reflects the profit attributable to that part of the work performed at the accounting date. (There can be no attributable profit until the profitable outcome of the contract can be assessed with reasonable certainty.)'[83]

7.1.3   *Accounting policies*

SSAP 9 requires that companies must disclose their accounting policies in respect of long-term contracts, in particular the method of ascertaining both turnover and attributable profit. These policies must be applied consistently within the business and from year to year.[84]

The following are examples of appropriate accounting policies:

Turnover

Turnover, which is stated net of value added tax, represents amounts invoiced to third parties, except in respect of long–term contracts where turnover represents the sales value of work done in the year, including estimates in respect of amounts not invoiced.

Long-term contracts

Profit on long–term contracts is taken as the work is carried out if the final outcome can be assessed with reasonable certainty. The profit included is calculated on a prudent basis to reflect the proportion of the work carried out at the year end, by recording turnover and related costs [as defined in stocks policy] as contract activity progresses. Turnover is calculated as that proportion of total contract value which costs incurred to date bear to total expected costs for that contract. Revenues derived from variations on contracts are recognised only when they have been accepted by the customer. Full provision is made for losses on all contracts in the year in which they are first foreseen.

Current reporting practice reflects a wide variety in the amount of detail given by companies in their accounting policies for turnover and profit recognition. Some companies which have long-term contracts merely state that turnover represents, for example, the invoiced value of sales, making no mention of contracting activity. This may mean that the attributable profit included in long-term work in progress has been brought into the profit and loss account by adjusting cost of sales. On the other hand some companies state that attributable profit is included by adjusting turnover.

However, BICC plc is an example of a company which does give detailed disclosure of its turnover and profit recognition policies:

Extract 9.20: BICC plc[85]

4   Turnover

Turnover represents amounts invoiced to outside customers, except in respect of contracting activities where turnover represents the value of work carried out during the year including amounts not invoiced. Turnover includes the Group's share of sales by related companies and joint ventures and excludes value added tax. Export turnover includes work carried out abroad relating to materials supplied by, and engineering services rendered by, UK group companies and includes intra-group sales.

5   Profit   recognition   on   contracts

Profit on contracting activities is taken as work progresses. Unless a more conservative approach is necessary, the percentage margin on each individual contract is the lower of margin earned to date and that forecast at completion, taking account of agreed claims. Profit is recognised on property developments when they are subject to a substantially unconditional contract for sale and on housebuilding on completion of the sale of individual houses. Full provision is made for all known or expected losses at completion immediately such losses are forecast on each contract. Profit is not taken on contracts in certain overseas territories where it is considered that restrictions on repatriation may arise. Profit for the year includes settlement of claims arising on contracts completed in prior years.

It should be emphasised, however, that under the revised SSAP 9, the accounting policies must state the *method* that has been applied in ascertaining turnover and attributable profit. In other words, it is not sufficient to merely state what turnover and attributable profit represent; the bases on which they have been calculated should be given.

7.1.4   *The financial statement presentation of long-term contracts*

In order to solve the conflict between the original SSAP 9 and the Companies Act, the revised standard requires that long-term contracts should be disclosed in the financial statements as follows:

'(a)   the amount by which recorded turnover is in excess of payments on account should be classified as 'amounts recoverable on contracts' and separately disclosed within debtors;

(b)   the balance of payments on account (in excess of amounts (i) matched with turnover; and (ii) offset against long-term contract balances) should be classified as payments on account and separately disclosed within creditors;

(c) the amount of long-term contracts, at costs incurred, net of amounts transferred to cost of sales, after deducting foreseeable losses and payments on account not matched with turnover, should be classified as 'long-term contract balances' and separately disclosed within the balance sheet heading 'Stocks'. The balance sheet note should disclose separately the balances of:

    (i)   net cost less foreseeable losses; and

    (ii)   applicable payments on account;

(d) the amount by which the provision or accrual for foreseeable losses exceeds the costs incurred (after transfers to cost of sales) should be included within either provisions for liabilities and charges or creditors as appropriate.'[86]

Naturally, consequent upon applying the above requirements, comparative figures will have to be restated.

The 'amounts recoverable on contracts' represent the excess of the value of work carried out to the balance sheet date (which has been recorded as turnover) over cumulative payments on account. 'The amount and realisability of the balance therefore depend on the value of work carried out being ascertained appropriately. The balance arises as a derivative of this process of contract revenue recognition and is directly linked to turnover. In substance, it represents accrued revenue receivable and has the attributes of a debtor.'[87]

7.1.5   *Illustrative examples of the disclosure of long-term contracts*

The following example is based on Appendix 3 to SSAP 9, and serves to illustrate the financial statement disclosure requirements of SSAP 9 as they apply to the various circumstances which might arise in respect of long-term contracts.

Example 9.3: *Application of the principles of SSAP 9 to long-term contracts*

The following assumptions apply to each of the contracts, and in each case the company's summarised profit and loss account for the year ended October 31, 19X9 and a balance sheet as at that date is illustrated:

(1)   This is the first year of the contract.

(2)   The company has only one contract.

(3)   All payments on account have actually been received in the form of cash.

(4)   All costs incurred have been paid in cash.

(5)   All the information is as at the balance sheet date, October 31, 19X9.

(6)   Share capital is minimal and is ignored.

(7)   Any necessary finance is provided by bank overdraft.

Contract 1

	£'000
Turnover	145
Cost of sales	110
Payments on account	100
Costs incurred	110

Financial statement presentation of Contract 1 (SSAP 9, para. 30):

SUMMARISED PROFIT AND LOSS ACCOUNT
for the year ended October 31, 19X9

	£'000
Turnover	145
Cost of sales	110
Gross profit on long-term contracts	35

SUMMARISED BALANCE SHEET
as at October 31, 19X9

	£'000
Current assets	
Debtors	
Amounts recoverable on contracts [145 - 100]	45
Current liabilities	
Overdraft	10
Net current assets	35
Profit and loss account	35

Contract 2

	£'000
Turnover	520
Cost of sales	450
Payments on account	600
Costs incurred	510

Financial statement presentation of Contract 2 (SSAP 9, para. 30):

SUMMARISED PROFIT AND LOSS ACCOUNT
for the year ended October 31, 19X9

	£'000
Turnover	520
Cost of sales	450
Gross profit on long-term contracts	70

SUMMARISED BALANCE SHEET
as at October 31, 19X9

Current assets	
Stocks (Note 1)	—
Cash	90
	90
Current liabilities	
Payments on account [600 - 520 - 60]	20
Net current assets	70
Profit and loss account	70

Note 1
Long-term contract balances

Net cost [510 - 450]	60
less: payments on account	(60)
	—

Contract 3

	£'000
Turnover	380
Cost of sales	350
Payments on account	400
Costs incurred	450

Financial statement presentation of Contract 3 (SSAP 9, para. 30):

SUMMARISED PROFIT AND LOSS ACCOUNT
for the year ended October 31, 19X9

	£'000
Turnover	380
Cost of sales	350
Gross profit on long-term contracts	30

SUMMARISED BALANCE SHEET
as at October 31, 19X9

	£'000
Current assets	
Stocks	
Long-term contract balances (Note 1)	80
Current liabilities	
Overdraft	50
	30
Profit and loss account	30

Note 1
Long-term contract balances

	£'000
Net cost [450 - 350]	100
less: payments on account [400 - 380]	20
	80

Contract 4

	£'000
Turnover	200
Cost of sales	250
Payments on account	150
Costs incurred	250
Provision for foreseeable losses (not included in cost of sales above)	40

Financial statement presentation of Contract 4 (SSAP 9, para. 30):

SUMMARISED PROFIT AND LOSS ACCOUNT
for the year ended October 31, 19X9

	£'000
Turnover	200
Cost of sales [250 + 40]	290
	───
Gross (loss) on long-term contracts	(90)
	═══

SUMMARISED BALANCE SHEET
as at October 31, 19X9

Current assets	
Debtors	
Amounts recoverable on contracts [200 - 150]	50
Current liabilities	
Overdraft	100
Provision for foreseeable losses	40
	───
	140
	───
Net current (liabilities)	(90)
	═══
Profit and loss account	(90)
	═══

(Note that the provision for foreseeable losses of 40 is not offset against the debit balance of 50 included in debtors.)

Contract 5

	£'000
Turnover	55
Cost of sales	55
Payments on account	80
Costs incurred	100
Provision for foreseeable losses (not included in cost of sales above)	30

Financial statement presentation of Contract 5 (SSAP 9, para. 30):

SUMMARISED PROFIT AND LOSS ACCOUNT
for the year ended October 31, 19X9

	£'000
Turnover	55
Cost of sales [55 + 30]	85
Gross (loss) on long-term contracts	(30)

SUMMARISED BALANCE SHEET
as at October 31, 19X9

	£'000
Current assets	
Stocks	
Long-term contract balances (Note 1)	—
Current liabilities	
Overdraft	20
Payments on account [80 - 55 - 15]	10
Net current (liabilities)	(30)
Profit and loss account	(30)

Note 1	
Long-term contract balances	
Net cost (after deducting foreseeable losses) [100 - 55 - 30]	15
less: payments on account	(15)
	—

7.2   Comparison with US and IASC pronouncements

7.2.1   *US*

In the US, accounting for contracting activity is governed by Accounting Research Bulletin No. 45 — *Long-Term Construction-Type Contracts* — issued in 1955. ARB 45 allows both the percentage of completion and the completed contract methods of accounting for long-term contracts, although it expresses a preference for the former 'when estimates of costs to complete and extent of progress toward completion of long-term contracts are reasonably dependable'.[88] It is emphasised under both methods that full provision must be made for anticipated losses.

7.2.2   *IASC*

IAS 11 — *Accounting for Construction Contracts* — is very similar to ARB 45 and also permits both methods of accounting to be used, although use of the percentage of completion method is restricted to those cases where 'the outcome of the contract can be reliably estimated'.[89] There are conditions laid down in IAS 11 for different types of contract (fixed price and cost plus), which, if satisfied, would indicate that the appropriate degree of reliability had been provided.[90] In the case of fixed price contracts, this degree of reliability would be provided only if all the following conditions are satisfied:

'(a)   total contract revenues to be received can be reliably estimated, and

(b)   both the costs to complete the contract and the stage of contract performance completed at the reporting date can be reliably estimated, and

(c)   the costs attributable to the contract can be clearly identified so that actual experience can be compared with prior estimates'.[91]

In the case of cost plus contracts the required degree of reliability would be provided only if both the following conditions are satisfied:

'(a)   the costs attributable to the contract can be clearly identified, and

(b)   costs other than those that will be specifically reimbursable under the contract can be reliably estimated'.[92]

The statement points out that the specific duration of the contract performance is not used as a distinguishing feature of a construction contract; the distinguishing feature is in fact that the dates of commencement and completion fall in separate accounting periods.[93]

We see the principal shortcoming of IAS 11 as being that, having set conditions to be met before the percentage of completion method can be used, it allows the completed contract method to be used even where those conditions have been met. However, it does specify that 'when a contractor uses a method for a particular contract, then all other contracts that meet similar criteria should be accounted for by the same method'.[94]

This is an area which has been addressed by the IASC in its exposure draft, E32 — *Comparability of Financial Statements*. E32 recognises that the completed contract method is inconsistent with the recognition criteria contained in the IASC's proposed conceptual framework (see Chapter 2 at 6.3), and that it results in the understatement of revenue. For these reasons, E32 proposes that the choice of using the completed contract method should be removed.[95]

7.3 Problem areas

7.3.1 How much profit?

Although SSAP 9 requires the accrual of attributable profit into long-term contract balances, it does not give adequate guidance on how the amount is actually to be computed. The following example illustrates difficulties which may arise under certain circumstances:

Example 9.4: Calculation of attributable profit

Halfway through its 19X1 financial year a company commences work on a contract that will last for 24 months. The total sales value is £1,200 and this is to be invoiced in total on completion of the contract. The total expected costs are £600 and these will be incurred evenly throughout the contract. Everything goes according to plan for the rest of the financial year. During the following financial year, 19X2, the company runs into problems on this contract and incurs additional costs of £100 which will not be recovered from the customer. At the end of that year the company is reasonably certain that costs to complete will still be the planned £150. Future experience bears this out.

What profit should be attributed to each period?

Using the definition of attributable profit in paragraph 23 of SSAP 9, the profit taken could be calculated as follows:

	19X1 £	19X2 £	19X3 £
Total expected profit on contract	600	500	500
Percentage of contract completed	25%	75%	100%
∴ total profit to be attributed	150	375	500
Less: profit already taken	—	150	375
Attributable profit for the period	150	225	125

Some might hold the view that the above does not reflect the results of 19X2 and 19X3 fairly, however, as it effectively defers inefficiencies of 19X2 into 19X3. The additional costs in 19X2 are an unfortunate incident occurring in that year which, while impacting on the overall profitability of the contract, do not affect the costs to complete at the end of that year and should consequently be expensed in 19X2. A fairer allocation of profits might be as follows:

	19X1 £	19X2 £	19X3 £
Turnover (being sales value of work done)	300	600	300
Cost of sales	150	*400	150
Attributable profit	150	200	150

* Comprises anticipated cost of sales of £300 and the additional costs of £100.

Paragraph 9 of SSAP 9 states that 'any known inequalities of profitability in the various stages of a contract' should be taken into account in calculating the attributable profit. It then goes on to confirm the latter treatment illustrated in the above example, by detailing the procedures which should be followed in order to take the inequalities into account. The procedures are 'to include an appropriate proportion of total contract value as turnover in the profit and loss account as the contract activity progresses. The costs incurred in reaching that stage of completion are matched with this turnover, resulting in the reporting of results that can be attributed to the proportion of work completed.'[96] As the above example shows, it is in fact desirable that such inequalities be taken into account, as otherwise there may not be a proper matching of costs and revenues.

In the above example the inequality was an inefficiency which had to be taken into account by being written off as a period expense. Some inequalities have to be taken into account in a different way, however. For example, where a contract is split into various stages with each stage having a separate price established, it may be necessary to allocate the total contract price over all the stages to as to reflect the 'real' profit on each stage. Obviously, where each stage's price reflects the relative value of that particular stage, this is not a problem and no adjustment is required; however, where there has been a payment in advance (or 'front-end loading') some adjustment will be necessary or profit will be taken in advance and not over the duration of the contract as it is earned.

7.3.2 How much turnover?

SSAP 9 states that it deliberately does not define turnover because of the different methods used in practice to determine it.[97] It does require, however, that the means by which turnover is ascertained be disclosed. Although there are a wide variety of methods used, whichever is selected the amount should represent an appropriate proportion of total contract value.[98] The following example illustrates some of the more common methods of computing turnover:

Example 9.5: Determination of turnover

A company is engaged in a long-term contract with an expected sales value of £10,000. It is the end of the accounting period during which the company commenced work on this contract and they require to compute the amount of turnover to be reflected in the profit and loss account for this contract.

Scenario (i)   An independent surveyor has certified that at the period-end the contract is 55% complete and that the company is entitled to apply for cumulative progress payments of £5,225 (after a 5% retention). In this case the company would record turnover of £5,500 being the sales value of the work done. (If it is anticipated that rectification work will have to be carried out to secure the release of the retention money then this should be taken into account in computing the attributable profit — it should have no bearing on the amount of turnover to be recorded.)

Scenario (ii) No valuation has been done by an independent surveyor as it is not required under the terms of the contract. The company's best estimate is that the contract is 60% complete. There is no real difference here from the first scenario. The value of the work done and, therefore, the turnover to be recognised is £6,000.

Scenario (iii) The company has incurred and applied costs of £4,000. £3,000 is the best estimate of costs to complete. The company should therefore recognise turnover of £5,714, being the appropriate proportion of total contract value, and computed thus:

$$\frac{4{,}000}{7{,}000} \times 10{,}000 = 5{,}714$$

If the costs incurred to date included, say, £500 in respect of unapplied raw materials, then the turnover to be recognised falls to £5,000 being

$$\frac{\text{costs incurred and applied}}{\text{total costs}} \quad \frac{(4{,}000\text{-}500)}{7{,}000} \times 10{,}000 = 5{,}000$$

There are, however, other ways than cost of measuring work done, e.g. labour hours. The use of cost will tend to lead to an overstatement of progress (because materials are usually acquired upfront), and the use of labour hours might lead to a more realistic basis for computing turnover.

Note that in each of the above scenarios the computation of the amount of turnover is quite independent of the question of how much (if any) profit should be taken. This is as it should be, because even if a contract is loss-making the sales price will be earned and this should be reflected by recording turnover. In the final analysis, any loss arises because costs are greater than revenue, and costs should be reflected through cost of sales. In view of the different results that can arise from the use of different methods, the importance of disclosing the particular method used is highlighted.

The above example applies only to fixed-price contracts. Where a contract is on a cost-plus basis, it is necessary to examine the costs incurred to ensure they are of the type and size envisaged in the terms of the contract. Only once this is done and the recoverable costs identified can the figure be grossed up to arrive at the appropriate turnover figure.

7.3.3   Approved variations and claims

Appendix 1 to SSAP 9 states that 'where approved variations have been made to a contract in the course of it and the amount to be received in respect of these variations has not yet been settled and is likely to be a material factor in the outcome, it is necessary to make a conservative estimate of the amount likely to be received and this is then treated as part of the total sales value. On the other hand, allowance needs to be made for foreseen claims or penalties payable arising out of delays in completion or from other causes.'[99]

Due to the extended periods over which contracts are carried out and sometimes to the circumstances prevailing when the work is being done or due to be done, it is quite normal for a contractor to submit claims for additional sums to a customer. Such claims arise 'from circumstances not envisaged in the contract' or 'as an indirect consequence of approved variations'[100] and their outcome can be crucial in determining whether the related contract will be profitable. Because their settlement is by negotiation (which can in practice be very protracted), they are subject to a very high level of uncertainty; consequently, no credit should be taken for them until they have been agreed at least in principle. In the absence of an agreed sum, the amount to be accrued should be prudently assessed.

7.3.4   Should profits be accrued on short-term contracts?

In discussing the revised definition of a long-term contract at 7.1.1 above, it was mentioned that the new definition creates a new area of potential controversy with regard to the accrual of profit on short-term contracts. This arises as a result of the last sentence of the definition, which states that 'some contracts with a shorter duration than one year should be accounted for as long-term contracts if they are sufficiently material to the activity of the period that not to record turnover and attributable profit would lead to a distortion of the period's turnover and results such that the financial statements would not give a true and fair view, provided that the policy is applied consistently within the reporting entity and from year to year'.[101]

The implication of this requirement is that even if a company is purely involved in short-term contracting work and has adopted the completed contract method, if it has a material amount of uncompleted short-term contracts at the year-end, they should be accounted for as long-term contracts — i.e. turnover should be recorded and profit accrued. Since many contracting companies are likely to be in this position, it seems that, on the face of it, most short-term contracts will have to be accounted for as long-term — irrespective of the accounting policy adopted. Our view, however, is that this could hardly have been the standard's intention. Consequently, we believe that the crucial factor in applying this definition is to ensure that whatever policy is applied, it is used on a consistent basis. If contracts with a shorter duration than one year are accounted for as long-term contracts, this should be a stated accounting policy, and not applied only when it is expedient to do so.

7.3.5 *Inclusion of interest*

Paragraph 26(3)(b) of Schedule 4 to the Companies Act 1985 states that 'there may be included in the production cost of an asset—interest on capital borrowed to finance the production of that asset, to the extent that it accrues in respect of the period of production'.[102] Appendix 1 to SSAP 9 deals with this issue in the context of long-term contracts, and states that 'in ascertaining costs of long-term contracts it is not normally appropriate to include interest payable on borrowed money. However, in circumstances where sums borrowed can be identified as financing specific long-term contracts, it may be appropriate to include such related interest in cost, in which circumstances the inclusion of interest and the amount of interest so included should be disclosed in a note to the financial statements.'[103]

It is our view that, provided that all the criteria for capitalisation of interest costs are met (e.g. qualifying assets, period of production, etc.), it is perfectly acceptable to do so. (See Chapter 12 for a detailed discussion of the circumstances under which interest may be capitalised.)

References

1 SSAP 9, *Stocks and long-term contracts*, Revised September 1988, paras. 16—25.
2 See, for example, SSAP 9, para. 1; Accounting Research Bulletin No. 43, AICPA, June 1953, Chapter 4, *Inventory Pricing*, Statement 2; and Eldon S. Hendriksen, *Accounting Theory*, p. 299.
3 SSAP 9, para. 3.
4 The term 'stocks' as used in this chapter, includes 'manufacturing work-in-progress'.
5 This basic rule is entrenched in the UK, US and IASC pronouncements on stock: SSAP 9, para. 27; ARB 43, Chapter 4, Statement 5; IAS 2, *Valuation and Presentation of Inventories in the Context of the Historical Cost System*, IASC, October 1975, para. 20.
6 SSAP 9, para. 17.
7 *Ibid.*
8 *Ibid.*, para. 18.
9 *Ibid.*, para. 19.
10 *Ibid.*, para. 3.
11 IAS 2, para. 21.
12 ARB 43, Chapter 4, Statement 3.
13 SSAP 9, para. 4.
14 News International plc, 1988 Annual Report, p. 8.
15 Era Group Plc, Annual Report & Accounts 1987, p. 18.
16 Accountants Digest No. 158, *A Guide to Accounting Standards — Valuation of Stocks and Work in Progress*, Summer 1984, p. 7.
17 SSAP 9, Appendix 1, para. 12.
18 CA 85, Sch. 4, para. 27.
19 *Ibid.* This requirement does not apply if stocks are valued at actual cost.
20 SSAP 16, *Current cost accounting*. This statement was withdrawn in April 1988.
21 CA 85, Sch. 4, para. 25.
22 SSAP 9, *loc. cit.*

2 3 CA 85, *loc. cit.*
2 4 E32, *Comparability of Financial Statements*, IASC, January 1989, para. 29.
2 5 Tate & Lyle PLC, Annual Report 1988, p. 37.
2 6 BICC plc, Annual report 1987, pp. 25 and 29.
2 7 Tate & Lyle PLC, Annual Report 1988, p. 37.
2 8 SSAP 9 (Original), *Stocks and work in progress*, May 1975.
2 9 *Ibid.*, para 1.
3 0 *Ibid.*, para. 3.
3 1 *Ibid.*, Appendix 1, para. 10.
3 2 *Ibid.*, para. 22.
3 3 *Ibid.*, para. 27.
3 4 *Ibid.*
3 5 CA 85, Sch. 4, para. 15.
3 6 The Plessey Company plc, Report and Accounts 1988, p. 36.
3 7 The Peninsular and Oriental Steam Navigation Company, Annual Report and Accounts 1987; p. 33.
3 8 For example, Courtaulds plc state in the notes to their financial statements that 'the replacement cost of standing timber held as raw materials exceeds the balance sheet value by £24.2m (1987 £9.9m).' See Courtaulds plc, Report & Accounts 1987 — 1988, p. 41.
3 9 The British Petroleum Company p.l.c., Annual Report and Accounts 1987, p. 44.
4 0 Lucas Industries plc, 1988 Report to Shareholders, p. 34.
4 1 The Laird Group PLC, Report & Accounts 1987, p. 39.
4 2 SSAP 9, para. 26.
4 3 *Ibid.*, para. 27.
4 4 CA 85, Sch. 4, para. 7.
4 5 Lucas Industries plc, 1988 Report to Shareholders, p. 34.
4 6 CA 85, Sch. 4, para. 3(3).
4 7 B.A.T Industries p.l.c., Annual Report and Accounts 1987, p. 40.
4 8 SSAP 9 (Original), para. 28.
4 9 Beecham Group p.l.c., Annual Report 1988, p. 36.
5 0 GKN plc, Report & Accounts 1987, p. 39.
5 1 Blue Circle Industries PLC, Report & Accounts 1987, p. 11.
5 2 Tarmac PLC, Annual Report 1987, p. 11.
5 3 Trusthouse Forte PLC, Report and Accounts 1988, p. 28.
5 4 SSAP 9, para. 32.
5 5 ARB 43, Chapter 4, *Inventory Pricing*.
5 6 IAS 2, para. 20.
5 7 *Ibid.*, para. 24.
5 8 *Ibid.*, para. 26.
5 9 E32, para. 29.
6 0 SSAP 9, para. 17.
6 1 See CA 85, Sch. 4, para. 15. The company's directors will have to explain in the financial statements that their policy represents a departure from the statutory valuation rules, but has been applied in order to comply with SSAP 9 and is necessary to give a true and fair view. The full particulars and effects of the departure will also have to given.
6 2 SSAP 9, Appendix 1, para. 2.
6 3 Westland Group plc, Annual Report 1988, p. 33.
6 4 SSAP 9, Appendix 1, para. 5.
6 5 *Ibid.*, para. 6.
6 6 *Ibid.*, para. 7.
6 7 *Ibid.*, para. 8.
6 8 *Ibid.*
6 9 Accountants Digest No. 158, p. 12.
7 0 SSAP 9, para. 21.

7 1 *Ibid.*, Appendix 1, para. 20.

7 2 *Ibid.*, para. 26.

7 3 ARB 43, Chapter 4, Statement 7.

7 4 *Ibid.*, para. 11.

7 5 Marks and Spencer p.l.c., 1988 Annual Report and Financial Statements, p. 42.

7 6 SSAP 9, Appendix 1, para. 14.

7 7 Kleinwort Benson Lonsdale plc, Report and Accounts 1987, p. 33.

7 8 SSAP 9 (Original), para. 22.

7 9 SSAP 9, para. 22.

8 0 *Ibid.*, para. 28.

8 1 *Ibid.*

8 2 *Ibid.*, para. 29.

8 3 *Ibid.*, para. 23.

8 4 *Ibid.*, para. 32.

8 5 BICC plc, Annual report 1987, p. 25.

8 6 SSAP 9, para. 30.

8 7 *Ibid.*, Appendix 3, para. 5.

8 8 Accounting Research Bulletin No. 45, *Long-Term Construction-Type Contracts*, AICPA, October 1955, para. 15.

8 9 IAS 11, *Accounting for Construction Contracts*, IASC, March 1979, para. 43.

9 0 *Ibid.*

9 1 *Ibid.*

9 2 *Ibid.*

9 3 *Ibid.*, para. 3.

9 4 *Ibid.*, para 45.

9 5 E32, para. 53.

9 6 SSAP 9, para. 9.

9 7 *Ibid.*, Appendix 1, para. 23.

9 8 *Ibid.*, para. 9.

9 9 *Ibid.*, Appendix 1, para. 26.

100 *Ibid.*, Appendix 1, para. 27.

101 *Ibid.*, para. 22.

102 CA 85, Sch. 4, para. 26(3)(b).

103 SSAP 9, Appendix 1, para. 21.

Chapter 10

Fixed assets and depreciation

1   INTRODUCTION

1.1   Background

The UK does not yet have an accounting standard that deals with the general principles of accounting for fixed assets. The subject is dealt with by a number of accounting standards in a piecemeal fashion; there are accounting standards dealing with depreciation (SSAP 12 — *Accounting for depreciation*), some revaluations (SSAP 19 — *Accounting for investment properties*), and some intangibles (SSAP 13 — *Accounting for research and development* and SSAP 22 — *Accounting for goodwill*). There are no accounting standards which cover the cost or carrying value of an asset or revaluations in general, except that the depreciation of revalued assets is covered by SSAP 12.

This position may be changing in that the ASC has now established a working party to develop an accounting standard on fixed assets.

Since the implementation of the EC Fourth Directive into UK legislation in the Companies Act 1981, however, company law deals with certain accounting practices and valuation rules as they relate to fixed assets. These are included in what is now Schedule 4 to the Companies Act 1985. Fixed assets are defined as assets intended for use on a continuing basis in the companies' activities and any assets not intended for such use are taken to be current assets. The balance sheet formats give further information as to what is intended as a fixed asset: intangible assets including development costs and goodwill, tangible fixed assets and investments held for the long term.[1] Investments include shares in subsidiary and associated companies.[2] The full balance sheet formats for fixed assets are given in 6.1.2 below. The statutory requirements also cover depreciation, permanent and temporary diminutions in value, the components of the cost of an asset, whether purchased or self-constructed, and the bases of valuation of fixed assets.

1.2   The meaning of fixed assets

As described above, there are no accounting standards that deal with the cost of fixed assets; there is no definition of what actually constitutes a fixed asset. Even the Companies Act 'definition', which differentiates between fixed as against current assets is not entirely clear, since fixed assets are defined in terms of 'use', yet the balance sheet formats permitted under the Act include intangibles and fixed asset investments as well as tangible fixed assets. To what extent and in what sense is an investment intended for 'use' in a business? There are problems caused by 'assets' such as development costs, which are further described in Chapter 13 on research and development. Are these fixed assets, which will then require to be amortised over their useful life, or are they deferred expenditure, a variety of prepayment, that would then be matched to the revenue to which it related?

Developments in fair value accounting have focused attention on intangible assets and the introduction of intangibles such as brand names into balance sheets has caused controversy. Initially, companies were only attributing values to brand names of companies which had been acquired. They were recognising the fact that the brand names were part of the separable net assets which had been bought and therefore part of the cost of the acquisition had to be allocated to them as part of the fair value exercise. No recognition was being given in the balance sheet to the companies' own brands. However, Ranks Hovis McDougall PLC has recently incorporated a valuation of all its brand names as indicated below:

Extract 10.1: Ranks Hovis McDougall PLC[3]

Intangible assets   Until the end of the current financial year intangible assets (including brands) have been written off to reserves. With effect from 3 September 1988 brands, both acquired and created within the Group, are included at their 'current cost'. Such cost, which will not be subject to amortisation, will be reviewed each year.

The accounting treatment of goodwill is considered, as previously, on an individual basis and elimination against reserves has been selected as appropriate for the current year.

The prior year figures, including reserves, have not been restated because of the impracticality of establishing a meaningful cost of all brands previously acquired; the Group results of the previous year are unaffected. An amount has been transferred from revaluation reserve in respect of the estimated cost of brands acquired in the last six years.

1 2 INTANGIBLES

	The Group 1988 £ m	The Company 1988 £ m
Brands		
At 5 September 1987	—	—
Valuation at 3 September 1988	678.0	—
At 3 September 1988	678.0	—

The Group has valued its brands at their 'current use value to the Group' at 3 September 1988 in conjunction with Interbrand Group plc, branding consultants.

This basis of valuation ignores any possible alternative use of a brand, any possible extension to the range of products currently marketed under a brand, any element of hope value and any possible increase of value of a brand due to either a special investment or a financial transaction (e.g. licensing) which would leave the Group with a different interest from the one being valued.

There are both positive and negative aspects for a company which capitalises its brand names. The principal advantages from the company's viewpoint are that to do so strengthens the general presentation of its balance sheet, enhancing the company's net asset per share and gearing ratio. A further benefit of the improvement to total shareholders' funds might be to increase the company's borrowings allowed by its articles of association or loan covenants. The principal negative effect of capitalisation is that any fixed asset which has a limited useful life must be depreciated; the effect of this might be that the resultant impact on earnings could outweigh the advantages of strengthening the balance sheet. However, as can be seen from Extract 10.1 above, some companies which capitalise their intangible assets take the view that such assets do not have a finite life, and therefore need not be depreciated. Although this might be valid in the case of some intangible assets (e.g. publishing titles), it is questionable as to whether or not it is possible to be sufficiently certain that a brand name has an infinite life.

In January 1989, the ASC issued a statement of its thinking on the question of accounting for intangible assets of this sort.[4] This said that they had formed the following provisional views.

'(a)   In considering accounting for intangibles, the ASC has kept in mind that the balance sheet does not purport to be a statement of corporate value, and the amounts at which assets are stated in the balance sheet do not in themselves determine a company's market value.

(b)   Generally, the ASC encourages companies to disclose information useful to users about significant intangibles, including brands, in the notes to the accounts.

(c)   As required by paragraph 30 of SSAP 22 "Accounting for goodwill", where acquired brands or other intangibles are separately identifiable and their share of the acquisition cost can be identified with reasonable certainty, they should be recognised on a company's balance sheet.

(d)   There may be limited circumstances in which the cost of specific intangibles can be capitalised under the provisions of SSAP 13 "Accounting for research and development".

(e)   Where brands or similar intangibles which have a limited useful economic life are included in the balance sheet, an appropriate policy for provision for depreciation and/or diminution in value should be adopted and disclosed. The ASC believes there is a rebuttable presumption that intangibles, including brands, have a limited useful economic life.

(f)   At the present time, the ASC discourages companies from incorporating revaluations of intangibles such as brands in the balance sheet. In arriving at this view, the ASC has taken account of the absence of a generally accepted method of calculation, and current uncertainties as to the basis and reliability of the resulting figures.

(g)   Where intangibles have been included in the balance sheet, revaluations should comply with the alternative accounting rules of the Companies Act 1985, and should only be incorporated in the balance sheet as part of a consistent policy of revaluation of intangibles.

The statement concluded by saying that work was proceeding on the development of an exposure draft on accounting for fixed assets, and that in the meantime the

ASC urged companies not to change their existing practice for accounting for intangibles. In our view, the ASC's statement is broadly sensible, but it remains to be seen whether companies will wish to conform with it.

Investments are fixed assets under the Companies Act, but other items, such as loans to subsidiary and associated companies, can also be so treated: see the formats in 6.1.2 below. Investments are not excluded from the depreciation rules of the Act (although they are excluded from the provisions of SSAP 12), but these do not usually apply because they do not generally have a finite life. For this reason, questions of impairment of value and whether they are permanent or temporary tend to assume a greater importance. This is particularly true if investments are held at market value; it will often be a matter of judgement as to whether a particular investment will recover lost value or whether it was purchased at what was, for the foreseeable future, the top of the market. The general issues of permanent impairments are dealt with in 4 below.

The specific problems and circumstances of investment trusts and investment companies are outside the scope of this chapter.

1.3   Comparison with US and IASC

1.3.1   US

As in the UK, there is no general accounting standard in the US that covers all aspects of accounting for fixed assets; ARBs 43 and 44 (revised) cover some aspects of depreciation.[5] An important item in the cost of assets constructed for a business's own use or resale, the capitalisation of interest, is covered by SFAS 34.[6] There are also industry-specific standards such as SFAS 67[7] which deals with the costs of constructing buildings for real estate developers.

1.3.2   IASC

Here the picture is different as IAS 16 — *Accounting for property, plant and equipment*, covers cost, carrying value (including improvements and repairs, recoverable amount and revaluations), disposals and disclosure. IAS 16 is the only authoritative guidance on the issues raised by improvements and repairs which are discussed in further detail in 2.7 below. IAS 25[8] deals with accounting for investments, including fixed asset investments, while depreciation is covered by IAS 4.[9]

2   COST

2.1   Introduction

As noted in 1.1 above, the cost of fixed assets is not covered by UK accounting standards, but is dealt with and defined by statute in the accounting rules in the Act. The Act requires that, subject to any provision for depreciation or diminution in value, the amount to be included in respect of any fixed asset shall be its purchase price or production cost.[10]

2.2 Purchase price

According to the Act, 'the purchase price of an asset shall be determined by adding to the actual price paid any expenses incidental to its acquisition'.[11]

'Purchase price' is itself further defined as to include any consideration, whether in cash or otherwise, given by the company in respect of that asset.[12]

The phrase 'actual price paid' has been interpreted by some as not to permit the deduction from the cost of capital grants received, one of the treatments permitted by SSAP 4,[13] on the accounting treatment of government grants (see Chapter 14). It is argued that the deduction may be a breach of the statutory rules against the setting off of assets and liabilities. For this reason the proposed revision to the SSAP, ED 43,[14] permits grants to be treated only as deferred credits and released to the profit and loss account in line with depreciation.[15] Notwithstanding this, there is an alternative interpretation which could permit the deduction of grants, namely that the 'actual price' is that borne by the purchaser after taking account of such receipts as well as trade or other discounts. In addition, the grant would not normally represent a liability if it is recognised in the financial statements in accordance with general principles.[16]

'Expenses incidental to its acquisition' are those costs which have been incurred as a direct consequence of the purchase of the asset and are necessary in order to make it available for use. For example, in the case of an item of plant or equipment, these costs could include site preparation, delivery and handling charges, installation costs and professional fees. In purchasing an investment (and this could include a subsidiary company), costs could include stamp duty and legal fees. These costs can include expenses incurred prior to the purchase of the asset itself (see 2.5 below).

Many problems in defining incidental expenditure arise when one asset is being replaced by another, for example, when a company replaces an item of machinery or moves into new premises. The extent to which any costs incurred should be treated as part of the profit or loss on disposal of the old asset or should be capitalised as part of the cost of the new one is an issue which will require judgement and depend on the circumstances of individual cases. The asset may have been purchased with the intention of redevelopment, in which case all costs, including those of purchasing the asset itself, are properly part of the cost of the new asset. In other cases the removal costs of an asset which has been in use in the business should form part of the calculation of profit or loss on disposal, but there may be expenses for which the answer is not clear; for example, it may not be possible in practice to distinguish between site preparation and asset removal costs.

2.3 Production cost

The definition in the Act of the production cost of any asset, fixed or current, is that it :

'shall be determined by adding to the purchase price of the raw materials and consumables used the amount of the costs incurred by the company which are directly attributable to the production of that asset.

In addition there may be included in the production cost of an asset—

(a) a reasonable proportion of the costs incurred by the company which are only indirectly attributable to the production of that asset, but only to the extent that they relate to the period of production; and

(b) interest on capital borrowed to finance the production of that asset, to the extent that it accrues in respect of the period of production.'[17]

There are a number of problems that arise from this legal definition of production cost. These include the meanings of 'directly' and 'indirectly' attributable costs and 'period of production'. These are discussed below in further detail. Capitalisation of interest is dealt with in Chapter 12.

2.4   Directly and indirectly attributable costs

Directly attributable costs will include, in addition to the costs of raw materials and consumables referred to in the definition, direct labour, direct expenses and sub-contracted work. There is no further indication as to what is meant by indirectly attributable costs, but these will generally be regarded to be overheads.

As noted in 2.3 above, the definition of production cost applies to both fixed and current assets. SSAP 9 requires the cost of a current asset to include the costs of conversion and these include production overheads and any other overheads attributable in the particular circumstances of the business to bringing the product or service to its present location and condition.[18] The practical problems of identifying production overheads as part of the costs of conversion of current assets, stock and work-in-progress, are discussed in Appendix 1 to SSAP 9. This describes how overheads should be classified by function rather than whether the overhead varies with time or volume and goes into detail as to how, for example, the costs of central service departments, such as the accounts department, should be allocated between the functions of production, marketing, selling and administration and how only those that relate to the production function should be included in the costs of conversion and hence in work in progress.[19] In principle these overheads can also be allocated to the function of producing assets for the enterprise's own use. However, because of the likely scale of production of fixed assets relative to total operations, few enterprises will be able to allocate any part of such central costs to the construction of their own assets. Exceptions could include major manufacturing or construction concerns where some items of plant and machinery or buildings are self-constructed; companies, often part of a group, that build properties for own use or for investment; and industries where there are many outlets, such as multiple retailers; restaurant or hotel chains where there may be significant administration costs associated with acquiring, building and refurbishing property. The organisations may employ suitably qualified professional personnel, for example architects, surveyors and lawyers. These costs may, in part at least, be incurred before there has been any development work on the asset itself, and the circumstances in which they may be capitalised are described in 2.5 below.

Companies' financial statements rarely reveal their policies with regard to the capitalisation of overheads. For example, eleven of the companies in the FT 30

Index as at October 1987 disclose capital assets in the course of construction as part of their fixed asset disclosures; only one, British Telecommunications plc, has a policy that includes the capitalisation of overheads as part of the cost of self constructed assets, and even here it is not clear what costs are covered by the policy. This makes it difficult to determine which costs, if any, companies are actually capitalising.

Extract 10.2: British Telecommunications plc [20]

Tangible fixed assets [extract]
(a) Cost
Cost in the case of network services comprises expenditure up to and including the last distribution point before customers' premises and includes contractors' charges and payments on account, materials, direct labour and related overheads.

2.5   The period of production

As indicated in 2.3 above indirectly attributable costs and interest can only be included in production cost to the extent that they relate to the period of production. ('Period of production' in the specific context of capitalised borrowing costs is discussed in further detail in 3.2 of Chapter 12.)

There is no guidance in the Act to help determine when the period of production actually commences. However, whatever the asset being constructed, activities that are necessary to get the asset ready for its intended use must be in progress for the period of production to have begun.

Occasionally costs may be incurred before the asset has been acquired or before there has been any development work on the asset itself. The Act would appear to only allow such costs to be capitalised if they are *directly* attributable to the acquisition or production of the asset.[21] Although not specifically applicable to assets held for own use, guidance in this area can be sought from SFAS 67 in the US. Following the principles laid down in this standard in respect of preacquisition costs,[22] then such costs can be capitalised if:

(a)   the costs are directly identifiable with the specific asset;

(b)   the costs would be capitalised if the asset were already acquired; and

(c)   acquisition of the asset is probable when the costs are incurred.

If such costs are only *indirectly* attributable to the production of the asset then it would appear that under the Act they can only be capitalised if it can be argued that the period of production has commenced.[23]

Capitalisation of overheads and interest must cease at the end of the period of production. This is usually straightforward in the case of plant and machinery or buildings constructed for the enterprise's own use; capitalisation should cease when the asset becomes available for use, whether or not it is actually brought into use at that time. It may be much harder to determine the end of the period in the case of development of investment properties and the issues are discussed in 3.2.2 of Chapter 12.

'Period of production' need not refer exclusively to the period of construction; another example of a period of production during which overhead costs and interest may be capitalised is the refitting and refurbishment of retail outlets or hotels. Trusthouse Forte PLC's accounting policy covers capitalisation, as part of the cost of the asset, of interest and other costs incurred in the period before trading commences.

Extract 10.3: Trusthouse Forte PLC[24]

Interest, internal professional fees and pre-opening expenses: Interest on capital employed on land awaiting development and on the construction and major redevelopment of hotels and restaurants and also internal professional costs incurred until these enterprises start to trade are capitalised as part of the costs of construction. In addition, pre-opening and development expenses incurred up to the commencement of full trading are deferred and written off over five years.

In this case, the accounting policy appears to cover two separate assets with two 'periods of production'. The first of these is for the purpose of capitalising costs as part of the fabric of the building, which continues until the asset is available for use. The other, for the capitalisation of pre-opening and development expenditure, is by reference to the income-producing potential of the hotel or restaurant and this continues until the (undefined) commencement of full trading. Five years is presumably the period expected to benefit from this expenditure; it would be possible to base it on, for example, the average period between refurbishments.

2.6   Abnormal costs and cost inefficiencies

It has been argued, for example in IAS 16, that abnormal costs or cost inefficiencies should be excluded from capitalisation. The IAS states that 'cost inefficiencies in the production of self-constructed assets, whether due to temporarily idle capacity, industrial disputes or other causes, are normally not considered to be suitable for capitalisation. It is normally appropriate to have regard to a comparison with the cost of equivalent purchased assets...'.[25] This is similar to the position taken by SSAP 9,[26] where costs that would not be incurred under 'normal operating conditions' are excluded from the costs of conversion of stock.

The argument behind the IAS's position is that such costs certainly do not add anything to the value of the asset. However, 'value' is not immediately relevant when it comes to determining which costs should initially be capitalised in the balance sheet. It is our view that the total cost to the enterprise of the asset should be established. Once this has been done it becomes possible to assess whether there has been a permanent impairment in value (see 4 below) and, if there has been, the carrying value of the asset should be reduced to its recoverable amount This appears to be a more logical approach as well as one that complies with the requirements of the Companies Act; see the definition of 'production cost' in 2.3 above.

2.7   Improvements and repairs

It is often very difficult to decide whether expenditure on improvements and repairs is capital or revenue in nature and whether such expenditure should be capitalised as part of the original asset or as a separate category of fixed asset.

IAS 16 addresses this problem, and defines expenditure that can be capitalised and added to the gross carrying amount of the asset as that which increases the future benefits from the asset beyond its previously assessed standard of performance.[27] Examples of such benefits given by the IAS in its explanation include:[28]

(a)   an extension in the asset's estimated useful life;

(b)   an increase in capacity; or

(c)   a substantial improvement in the quality of output or a reduction in previously assessed operating costs.

The definition and examples are helpful in assessing whether expenditure is capital, but there are a number of points to be made.

Firstly, the IAS definition refers to the 'previously assessed standard of performance' and by this appears to mean the standard assessed when the asset was originally brought into use. This would imply, for example, that no repairs to a building should be capitalised unless they actually extend its originally assessed life or capacity. This seems unnecessarily restrictive, so there is an alternative interpretation which is that it refers to an assessment made at the time the repair is undertaken.

Secondly, the IAS definition refers only to expenditure which can be included in the gross carrying amount, but it is not clear as to whether the 'gross carrying amount' refers to total assets or just to the asset on which money is being spent. It is reasonable to assume that it means the former, as otherwise it would exclude capitalisation of items that have a different life to the one being repaired.

There are many types of improvement expenditure that have a different, usually shorter, life than the original asset. For example a new roof might undoubtedly increase the asset's estimated useful life; equally it may not have the same life as the fabric of the remainder of the building. This also applies to other forms of building repairs and improvements, such as rewiring or refitting. The fact that such improvements may not extend the asset's life beyond that originally assessed and may have a shorter life than the asset should not preclude their being capitalised. They should be capitalised separately from the original asset and depreciated over the period until they are due for replacement.

There are two other points to be made. Firstly, there is always a danger of duplication when repairs and improvements are capitalised. If the roof or other improvement has to be replaced before it has been fully depreciated then the net book value of the original item must be written off immediately.

Secondly, care will always have to be taken in assessing the recoverable amount of the asset, to ensure that the new carrying value is not more than the amount recoverable from further use (see 4.4 below for a discussion of recoverable amount).

3   DEPRECIATION

3.1   Introduction

This section deals with the general principles of depreciation and depreciation as it applies to assets carried at historical cost. The specific problems of depreciation of assets carried at valuation are dealt with in 5.11 below.

3.2   The meaning of depreciation

Why must companies charge depreciation in the first place? It is because they have long-life assets that may be used in the company's activities, that may ultimately, and for a variety of reasons, cease to have any function to the business and because they must periodically draw up financial statements that in some way measure the results of those activities. Depreciation must be charged in order to get a 'fairer' measure of profit as at a company's period end, although this date will probably be arbitrary in terms of the company's activities.

It is defined in SSAP 12 as follows:

'Depreciation is the measure of the wearing out, consumption, or other reduction in the useful life of a fixed asset whether arising from use, effluxion of time or obsolescence through technological or market changes.'[29]

Therefore, depreciation is a measure of consumption, not a measure of value and, in this respect the UK and US approaches are the same. In historical cost terms this may result in depreciation being treated as an allocation of cost, with assets being seen as costs that will be consumed over the period expected to benefit from their use by being matched to the appropriate revenues. This corresponds to the treatments of depreciation following from ARB 43 (see 3.16.1 below), SSAP 12 (Revised) and IAS 4. Depreciation as consumption also underlies the concept of depreciation in current cost accounting, i.e. in SSAP 16 and the Handbook that has replaced it. This latter states that, in order to maintain the element of operating capital that is made up of fixed assets it is necessary to charge against revenue the current cost of the fixed assets consumed in earning the revenue.[30]

However, depreciation has often been seen as a measure of loss of value, not least by the management of many companies unwilling to provide depreciation on certain assets. Under this viewpoint depreciation would only be charged if the value of an asset at the end of an accounting period was less than the carrying value at the beginning of the accounting period. The original SSAP 12 defined depreciation as, amongst other things, a measure of loss of value and this was always a cause of confusion as to the nature of depreciation.[31]

The purpose of depreciation has also been seen by some as being to provide a replacement provision. The use of depreciation for such a purpose was specifically considered and rejected in the US.[32]

3.3   The development of an accounting standard in the UK

The current SSAP 12, revised in 1987, has a long history to it. The standard was originally published in 1977 (following ED 15, which was published in January 1975) and for the first time UK companies were required to provide depreciation on all fixed assets with a finite life. The standard's requirements were controversial from the start as many companies were reluctant to depreciate freehold properties. This was especially so with respect to property held for its investment potential. This position was exacerbated by the Companies Act 1981, which introduced a statutory requirement to depreciate assets.

Some of the problems of the property industry, which had received a temporary exemption from implementing the original SSAP, were resolved by the introduction of SSAP 19 on accounting for investment properties in November 1981; investment properties are to be carried at their market value as at the year end and are not generally to be depreciated (see Chapter 11). In the light of the above, in 1982 the ASC issued a discussion paper on SSAP 12. A number of the issues raised by this paper concerned the effect of revaluations on depreciation; others included supplementary depreciation and the estimation of useful lives.[33] This was followed by ED 37 in April 1985 and finally by SSAP 12 (Revised) in January 1987.

The main changes to the standard over this process have been the incorporation of many definitions — the original standard only defined depreciation itself — and the clarification of issues. There have been no real changes in the underlying principles of the standard .

3.4   The requirements of the Companies Act

The Companies Act requires any fixed asset that has a limited useful economic life to be depreciated over that life, on a systematic basis, down to its residual value (if any).[34] Depreciation is to be based on the carrying value; on the purchase price or production cost under the historical cost rules,[35] and on the revalued amount if the alternative accounting rules are being followed.[36] Depreciation of revalued assets is dealt with in 5.11 below.

3.5   The requirements of SSAP 12

The following are the main requirements of the standard:

3.5.1   Scope

The standard covers all fixed assets except for the following:

(a)   investment properties, which are dealt with by SSAP 19 — *Accounting for investment properties* (see Chapter 11);

(b)   goodwill, which is dealt with by SSAP 22 — *Accounting for goodwill* (see 6.5 of Chapter 4);

(c)   development costs, which are dealt with by SSAP 13 — *Accounting for research and development* (see Chapter 13);

(d)   investments, which are not covered by any UK accounting standard.

3.5.2   *Definitions*

The following are the definitions in paragraphs 10 to 13 of SSAP 12 (Revised):

Depreciation is the measure of the wearing out, consumption, or other reduction in the useful life of a fixed asset whether arising from use, effluxion of time or obsolescence through technological or market changes.

The *useful economic life* of an asset is the period over which the present owner will derive economic benefits from its use.

Residual value is the realisable value of the asset at the end of its useful economic life, based on prices prevailing at the date of acquisition or revaluation, if this has taken place, and after taking account of realisation costs.

Recoverable amount is the greater of the net realisable value of an asset and, where appropriate, the amount recoverable from its further use.

3.5.3   *Accounting treatment*

Provision for depreciation is the allocation of the cost or revalued amount of an asset, less its residual value, as fairly as possible over the periods expected to benefit from its use, i.e. over its useful economic life.[37]

There is to be consistency of treatment between the profit and loss account and the balance sheet, so that if an asset is carried at a revalued amount the depreciation must be based on this. Split depreciation is not permitted; the whole of the depreciation charge must go through the profit and loss account. Supplementary depreciation in excess of that based on the carrying value of the asset is not allowed.[38]

3.5.4   *Asset lives*

Asset lives must be realistically assessed and the same life must be used in historical cost and current cost financial statements. They should be regularly reviewed.[39]

The standard goes on to point out that if asset lives are regularly reviewed, no material distortions to future results or financial position should arise when they are revised; the net book amount should be written off prospectively over the remaining useful life of the asset. However, if future results would be materially distorted then the adjustment to accumulated depreciation should be made through the profit and loss account for the current year. It should be treated as an exceptional or extraordinary item in accordance with the requirements of SSAP 6 — *Extraordinary items and prior year adjustments* (see Chapter 8).[40]

3.5.5   *Permanent diminutions*

Immediate provision should be made for permanent diminutions in value. The carrying value should be written down to the estimated recoverable amount, which should then be written off over the remaining useful life of the asset. The provision should be made through the profit and loss account for the period. If the reasons for making the provision cease to apply, the provision should be written back to the extent that it is no longer necessary.

Two reasons for a permanent diminution are suggested: obsolescence or a fall in demand for a product.[41]

3.5.6   *Change in method*

A change from one method of providing depreciation to another is only permitted if the new method will more fairly present the enterprise's results and financial position. A change of method is not a change in accounting policy.[42]

3.5.7   *Depreciation on revalued assets*

Depreciation is to be based on the revalued amounts and the remaining life of the asset at the time of the valuation. It is not permitted to write back to the profit and loss account any depreciation charged prior to the revaluation, except to the extent that it represents a provision for diminution in value now no longer necessary.[43]

3.5.8   *Depreciation on land and buildings*

Freehold land does not normally require to be depreciated unless it is subject to depletion, although its value may be adversely affected by changes in its surroundings which may require a provision for diminution in value.

Buildings are assets with a finite life and therefore should be subject to depreciation in the same way as other assets.[44]

3.6   Useful economic life

The useful economic life of an asset must be assessed before its residual value and depreciation can be calculated.

It should be noted that the useful economic life is the period over which the present owner will benefit and not the total potential life of the asset; the two will not always be the same. For example, a company may have a policy of replacing all of its cars after three years, so this will be their estimated useful life.

Secondly, the standard requires that asset lives be estimated on a realistic basis and reviewed regularly. Regular review will mean that the initial estimate of the life, which is often performed without actual experience of the asset in question, can be reassessed in the light of experience.

It would appear that many companies do not undertake such an exercise. Asset lives are somewhat arbitrary and based on perceived norms and, as a result, very many companies are using fully depreciated assets. This is so commonplace that ED 37 introduced a requirement that fully depreciated assets be reinstated if it was considered necessary in order for the financial statements to give a true and fair view.[45] It was not clear what kind of circumstances were envisaged and the requirement was dropped from the revised standard.

An example of a company that explicitly states that it regularly reviews asset lives is Imperial Chemical Industries PLC. As a result the accounting policy note cannot give the period over which the assets are depreciated, except as global averages, as illustrated below:

> *Extract 10.4: Imperial Chemical Industries PLC*[46]
>
> DEPRECIATION [extract]
> The Group's policy is to write off the book value of each tangible fixed asset evenly over
> its estimated remaining life. Reviews are made periodically of the estimated remaining lives
> of individual productive assets, taking account of commercial and technological
> obsolescence as well as normal wear and tear. Under this policy it becomes impracticable
> to calculate average asset lives exactly; however, the total lives approximate to 23 years
> for buildings and 14 years for plant and equipment.

3.7   Residual values

Both the standard and the Act require residual values to be taken into account
when calculating depreciation on an asset. The importance of residual values has
increased during the period since the original standard was introduced. The
original SSAP 12 stated in its explanatory note that where residual value was
likely to be small in relation to cost it was convenient to regard it as nil.[47] This was
partly a recognition of the problems in determining the residual values — as the
explanatory note to the original standard said, the precise assessment of residual
value is normally a difficult matter.[48]

The revised standard contains a definition of residual value, given in 3.5.2 above.
When assets are being carried at historical cost the residual value must be based
on prices prevailing at the time of purchase. For example, if an asset has an
estimated useful life of six years, the company should look at the net realisable
value of a six year old equivalent asset as at the date of purchase and not consider
how much the asset will be worth in six years' time. Other factors to be taken into
account will include location (in the case of property), the risk of obsolescence
and anticipated maintenance expenditure. This obviously makes a realistic
assessment of residual value difficult.

Basing residual values on prices prevailing at the time of purchase means that it is
not permitted to anticipate inflationary holding gains and this has always been
contentious. During periods of price increases, and other things being equal, a
company that has calculated the residual value in accordance with the requirements
of the standard will provide more depreciation than is necessary to reduce the
carrying value to the actual residual value and will realise a profit on disposal of
the asset.

This has caused most difficulty in the case of property, as many companies can
demonstrate that, historically, their buildings have often been disposed of for an
amount that exceeds historical cost. Consequently, they have argued against
providing depreciation on their buildings (see 3.13 below).

3.8   Depreciation methods

Depreciation methods are not prescribed in SSAP 12 , which merely states that the
depreciable amount of the asset should be allocated 'as fairly as possible to the
periods expected to benefit from their use. The depreciation methods used should
be the ones which are the most appropriate having regard to the types of asset and
their use in the business.'[49]

Paragraph 8 in the explanatory note section of SSAP 12 states:

'There is a range of acceptable depreciation methods. Management should select the method regarded as most appropriate to the type of asset and its use in the business so as to allocate depreciation as fairly as possible to the periods expected to benefit from the asset's use. Although the straight line method is the simplest to apply, it may not always be the most appropriate.'

This is not altogether helpful, as no further guidance is given as to what 'fair' means in this context, nor as to the circumstances in which the straight line method is not appropriate. Nevertheless, the straight line method is overwhelmingly the most popular among large companies. All of the companies in the FT 30 Index [50] use it for most of their assets; only three companies use any other method to a sufficient extent to disclose it in the policy note.

The other methods most commonly found in practice are reducing balance, sum of digits, annuity and unit of production. In the following examples, for simplicity, the residual value of the asset is assumed to be nil.

3.8.1 Straight line method

The asset is written off in equal instalments over its estimated useful life. The method is the easiest to apply, and the one in which it is easiest to make revisions to estimates.

3.8.2 Reducing balance method

The same percentage of the asset's net book value is written off annually.

Example 10.1

An asset costs £8,000. Depreciation is to be provided at 25% on the reducing balance.

		£
Year 1	cost	8,000
	depreciation at 25% of £8,000	2,000
	net book value	6,000
Year 2	depreciation at 25% of £6,000	1,500
	net book value	4,500
Year 3	depreciation at 25% of £4,500	1,125
	net book value	3,375

Under this method, the carrying value of the asset is never completely written off.

It is argued in favour of this method that it allies the depreciation charge to the costs of maintaining and running the asset. In the early years these costs are low and the depreciation charge is high, while in later years this is reversed.

The method may correspond to tax allowances on the asset, for example, in the case of motor vehicles where allowances of 25% on the reducing balance are available. However, it is not appropriate within SSAP 12 for depreciation to be determined by the rates of capital allowances as these have no relevance in determining a fair allocation of the cost of the asset to the periods expected to benefit, although it might be convenient as there could be no timing differences and hence no deferred tax implications (see Chapter 7).

3.8.3   Other reducing balance methods

A   Double declining balance

This method is sometimes applied in the US, where it has corresponded to tax allowances on assets. The method involves determining the asset's depreciation on a straight line basis over its useful life. This annual amount is multiplied by an appropriate factor (it does not have to be doubled) to give the first year's charge and depreciation at the same percentage rate is charged on the reducing balance in subsequent years.

Example 10.2

An asset costs £6,000 and has a life of ten years, which means that, calculated on the straight line basis, the annual depreciation charge would be £600. On the double declining balance method (assuming an appropriate factor of two), the depreciation charge for the first year would be £1,200 and depreciation would continue to be charged at 20% on the reducing balance thereafter.

B   Sum of digits

This is another form of reducing balance method, but one that is based on the estimated life of the asset and which can therefore easily be applied if the asset has a residual value. If an asset has an estimated useful life of four years then the digits 1, 2, 3, and 4 are added together, giving a total of 10. Depreciation of four-tenths, three-tenths and so on, of the cost of the asset will be charged in the respective years.

3.8.4   Annuity method

This is a method where account is taken of the cost of capital notionally invested in the asset. Notional interest and depreciation combined will give an approximately constant charge to revenue: depreciation is therefore low in the early years when the capital invested is high.

The BOC Group plc apply this method to certain of their production plants as illustrated below:

Extract 10.5: The BOC Group plc[51]

4 Tangible fixed assets [extract]
(a) No depreciation is charged on freehold land or construction in progress. Depreciation is charged on all other fixed assets on the straight line basis over the effective lives except for certain tonnage plants where depreciation is calculated on an annuity basis over the life of the contract.

These 'tonnage plants' are built to supply specific long-term fixed contract customers.

3.8.5 Unit of production method

Under this method, the asset is written off in line with its estimated total output. By relating depreciation to productive capacity it reflects the fact that the useful economic life of certain assets, principally machinery, is more closely linked to its usage and output than to time.

This method is also normally used in extractive industries, for example, to amortise the costs of development of productive oil and gas facilities[52] as shown in the following extract:

Extract 10.6: The British Petroleum Company p.l.c.[53]

Depreciation [extract]
Oil, minerals and coal production assets are depreciated using a unit-of-production method based upon estimated proved reserves.

3.9 Choice of depreciation method

Each of the various methods of calculating depreciation has its adherents who believe that conceptually it gives the 'best' answer in a given accounting context. In most circumstances using historical cost accounting, the straight line method will give perfectly acceptable results. For certain assets where economic life is more linked to usage than to time, the unit of production method is preferable. As well as the extractive industries mentioned above, this could also apply to vehicles and aircraft. However, a complicating factor here, particularly in the case of aircraft, is that there may be many component parts, each of which has a separate life which may be measured by mileage or hours of service.

3.10 Changes in method of providing depreciation

As noted in 3.5.6 above, a change from one method of providing depreciation to another is only permitted if this will give a fairer presentation of an enterprise's results and financial position. The standard does not permit such a change to be dealt with as a prior year adjustment but requires it to be dealt with prospectively through the financial statements as it states that 'such a change does not, however, constitute a change of accounting policy; the net book value of the asset should be written off over the remaining life, commencing with the period in which the change is made'.[54] This accounting treatment, which can also be necessitated by a change in estimated life, is described in 3.11 below.

In our view there is a possible conflict between the above treatment required by SSAP 12 and the treatment which would be suggested by SSAP 2 — *Disclosure of accounting policies* and SSAP 6. According to SSAP 2, 'depreciation of fixed assets' is an accounting base[55] and this presumably means charging or not charging depreciation. If this is the case, a particular method of depreciation would appear to be an *accounting policy* in terms of SSAP 2. Accounting policies are defined in SSAP 2 as 'the specific accounting bases selected and consistently followed by a business enterprise as being, in the opinion of the management, appropriate to its circumstances and best suited to present fairly its results and financial position'.[56] But for the specific requirement of SSAP 12, a change from one method of charging depreciation to another could, therefore, be a change in accounting policy which under SSAP 6 would require an enterprise to make a prior year adjustment.[57]

3.11   Changes in estimated life

The position under the original standard was unambiguous. When there was a revision of life of an asset, the unamortised cost was to be charged to revenue over the remaining life of the asset. There have always been those, however, who argued that this was an incorrect approach as it meant that future depreciation charges would always be wrong; future accounting periods would, in effect, be 'penalised' (if the revised life was shorter) for the past errors in estimation.

The revised standard requires a similar treatment, but now permits, in certain circumstances, the adjustment to accumulated depreciation to be made through the profit and loss account for the year. This means that such revisions are neither to be dealt with as changes in accounting policy, nor as fundamental errors, either of which would require a prior year adjustment.

Example 10.3

A company purchases an asset costing £1,200. The original estimate of its useful life is ten years. At the beginning of year 4 the remaining life is assessed as being three years and therefore the total life is revised to six years. Depreciation is being provided on a straight line basis.

Year	1	2	3	4	5	6
A. Prospective write off						
Depreciation charge	120	120	120	280	280	280
B. Cumulative catch up						
Depreciation charge	120	120	120	440	200	200
Difference in effect on profit and loss account charge	—	—	—	160	(80)	(80)

The cumulative adjustment is only permitted through the current year's results if future results would be materially distorted. It is important to note that the adjustment could be a debit or a credit, i.e. could result from the lengthening as well as shortening of asset lives.

Extract 10.7: Bridport-Gundry plc[58]

The expected useful lives of netting machines were re-assessed during the year and changed from 10 to 15 years. It is considered that a material distortion would affect future results if this change was effected by writing down the present balances over the remaining useful lives. Therefore, under the provisions of SSAP 12, depreciation has been recalculated from the dates of acquisition of the machines and the total change credited to the profit and loss account as an exceptional item.

The usual treatment, however, should be the prospective write off over the remaining life of the asset (an example of this treatment, from the financial statements of Rolls Royce plc, is illustrated in Extract 10.33 in 6.1.4 below); it must be pointed out that changing the life of an individual asset will only in unusual circumstances have a material effect on the financial statements. If the class of asset continues to be replaced with equivalent assets (which have the new, revised life), then the annual depreciation charge will soon be the same whether or not there was an adjustment to accumulated depreciation in the year of review, although the cumulative catch up may well lead to a material adjustment in that year's results.

There is in principle no reason why the life of an asset should not be reassessed in exactly the same way when it has been fully depreciated or written down to a nominal amount, although regular review of asset lives will prevent this happening. This is notwithstanding the fact that the requirement to reinstate fully depreciated assets was not included in SSAP 12 (Revised); this is described in 3.6 above.

3.12 Treatment of minor items

Some types of business may have a very large number of minor fixed assets such as tools, cutlery, containers or sheets and towels. There are practical problems in recording them on an asset by asset basis in an asset register; they are difficult to control and frequently lost. The main consequence is that it becomes very difficult to provide depreciation on them.

There are a number of ways in which companies attempt to deal with the problems of depreciating minor assets. The items may be written off to the profit and loss account (the company will probably have a minimum value for capitalising assets), they may be capitalised at a fixed amount, a treatment which is permitted in the Act, or the company may have some other form of policy that avoids the problem of identifying them individually and depreciating them.

Marks and Spencer p.l.c. include a policy in their financial statements which describes the write off to revenue of minor items:

Extract 10.8: Marks and Spencer p.l.c.[59]

Repairs and renewals
Expenditure on repairs, renewals and minor items of equipment is written off in the year in which it is incurred.

Some other companies capitalise their minor items at a fixed amount, for example, when they are originally provided, as a form of capital 'base stock'; additions are not capitalised and depreciation is not charged.

This is permitted under the accounting rules in the Companies Act, which state that tangible fixed assets may be included at a fixed amount provided that their overall value is not material to assessing the company's state of affairs and their quantity, value and composition are not subject to material variation.[60]

Although this is a common accounting practice, it does not conform to the requirement of SSAP 12 that all assets be depreciated, and companies that do apply such a policy do so on the basis that the constant loss and replacement of stock items does lead to a materially fixed valuation. It is only acceptable as an accounting policy on the grounds of materiality. In periods of inflation the difference between the carrying value of these assets and their actual cost could quickly become very marked so care will have to be taken.

An example of the third type of approach is given by Cadbury Schweppes p.l.c., who capitalise additions to returnable container stocks, but regard losses and breakages as the equivalent of depreciation.

Extract 10.9: Cadbury Schweppes p.l.c.[61]

(k) Tangible fixed assets [extract]
Returnable containers, including those in customers' hands, are valued at average cost with due provision for obsolescence where required. The measure of depreciation is the breakage or loss of containers calculated at average cost, charged to profit and loss account as the loss arises. The quantity, value and composition of returnable containers are not subject to material variation in relation to cost of sales.

The amounts in question are not insignificant as the notes to the financial statements make clear.

Extract 10.10: Cadbury Schweppes p.l.c.[62]

13 TANGIBLE FIXED ASSETS [extract]
Plant and equipment also includes returnable containers of £54.0m (1986—£45.4m) whose value at most recent purchase price would be £60.0m (1986—£63.3m).

3.13   Non-depreciation of property

3.13.1   *Reasons for not depreciating buildings*

The need to depreciate buildings has always been disputed in the UK and this is manifested by the number of companies that avoid charging it on at least some of their properties. Non-depreciation of freehold and long leasehold properties is covered in the ICAEW's annual survey of UK published accounts. In the 1987—1988 survey, of the total of 300 companies, 54 did not depreciate part or all of their properties. This applied to 16% of the sample of large and medium sized listed companies (32 out of 200) and 22% of the large unlisted companies (22 out of 100).[63] Of these, 42 do not provide depreciation because it is not material, because the residual value exceeds cost or because of the level of maintenance expenditure. In fact there is considerable overlap within these categories and the distinction between the categories is more blurred than is suggested by the survey table, as is demonstrated by the following extract:

> *Extract 10.11: Grand Metropolitan Public Limited Company*[64]
>
> **Fixed assets and depreciation** [extract]
> No depreciation is provided on freehold land or on freehold and long leasehold public
> houses and hotels. . . It is the group's policy to maintain all its public houses and hotels
> to a high standard in order to protect their trade. Because of this, such properties
> maintain residual disposal values in the aggregate at least equal to their book values
> and accordingly no provision for depreciation is made.

3.13.2 *High standards of maintenance as a reason for not providing depreciation*

As soon as SSAP 12 was published, two groups made their objections known. One of these was the property industry whose ultimate success has already been described; SSAP 19, which was published in 1981, requires investment properties to be carried at the current market valuation without provision for depreciation, except in the case of leasehold properties where the lease has fewer than 20 years remaining.

The other group comprised brewers. In 1978 the finance directors of some of the major breweries arranged a meeting with members of the ASC in order to present their case that licensed premises did not have to be depreciated.

Their argument rested on a number of points, of which the most important was that brewers have to maintain their premises to high standards in order to attract and retain custom. Every year a proportion of the premises would be refurbished and the costs charged to revenue. While it was not easy to demonstrate the residual values of individual premises as there was no meaningful open market value in existing use for them (few are sold on the open market), experience had demonstrated that when they were sold for other purposes they realised at least their historical cost.

However, the brewers did not succeed in their aim of exempting their companies from the requirements of SSAP 12. Instead, it was acknowledged that the combination of very long life and high residual value meant that there was not a significant amount of depreciation to be charged. An example of the resulting policy has already been given; see Extract 10.11 above. Another is that given by Allied-Lyons PLC as illustrated below:

> *Extract 10.12: Allied-Lyons PLC* [65]
>
> **DEPRECIATION** [extract]
> No depreciation is provided on land or on licensed and other properties which are freehold
> or held on lease for a term of or exceeding 100 years unexpired. . . It is the group's policy
> to maintain properties comprising the licensed estate in such condition that the value of
> the estate, taken as a whole, is not impaired by the passage of time. Such expenditure
> is charged to profits in the year in which it is committed. As a consequence, any element
> of depreciation would, in the opinion of the directors, be immaterial and no provision
> for depreciation has been made.

This argument had become so well established that it was incorporated into ED 37:[66] It was not included in the revised standard because, as the ASC statement that accompanied the publication of SSAP 12 (Revised) stated,[67] 'a significant number of commentators expressed concern that the proposal could be open to misinterpretation or misuse. It was believed that it might represent a loophole in the standard, permitting non-depreciation of many types of property, in addition to freehold land and investment properties'. The statement went on to point out that the general principle of SSAP 12 should be applied in all cases but that there may be circumstances where it would not be appropriate to charge depreciation.

Notwithstanding this, the practice has spread to multiple retailers (for example, The Burton Group plc[68]) and to the financial sector, notably banks. National Westminster Bank PLC changed their policy in 1985, describing the change thus:

Extract 10.13: National Westminster Bank PLC [69]

(viii) Depreciation [extract]
Land is not depreciated. It is the Group's policy to maintain its properties in a state of good repair. In the case of freehold and long leasehold properties, the directors have reassessed the lives of these properties and consider that residual values are such that depreciation is not significant; consequently, from 1 January 1985 these properties are no longer depreciated. Previously freehold and long leasehold properties were depreciated over 50 years, the charge for 1984 being £12m.

There is a danger that maintenance expenditure alone may be used by companies as a reason to avoid charging depreciation, without demonstrating that it does apply in the company's specific circumstances and without taking into account other factors that affect residual values (see 3.7 above).

If a company wishes to use the 'length of life' argument it must be aware of its one major drawback. Although depreciation may not be material in the context of a single year's results, it will ultimately become so in cumulative terms. A company that has such a policy must frequently reassess it to ensure that the point has not been reached where depreciation ought to be charged.

3.14   Non-depreciation of other fixed assets

It is sometimes argued that assets not in use, for example ships that have been laid up, do not need to be depreciated. This argument is based on a view of depreciation as part of the cost of using an asset, to be matched against the revenue earned by it. However, depreciation is an allocation of the cost of an asset over its useful life so it should normally continue to be charged while the asset is not used. The lack of use may affect the asset's estimated useful life or be symptomatic of circumstances that affect its residual value (for example, it may be caused by a major slump in the world shipping markets), either of which may affect the amount of depreciation being charged. It may be argued that where an asset has not been used in a particular year its useful economic life has effectively been extended; in which case depreciation will still need to be charged, albeit at a reduced rate.

If the asset is being depreciated using the unit of production method, then it might seem appropriate not to depreciate it when it is not in use. However, the unit of production method is sometimes applied with an assumed minimum amount of production, which means that a charge is still made in periods of no activity. Once again this may be a sign that there is a problem with the recoverable amount of the asset; there may, for example, be a decline in demand for the product. (see 4.4 below).

As discussed in 1.2 above, many companies do not depreciate intangible assets, on the grounds of the assets not having a finite life.

3.15 Comparison with US and IASC pronouncements

3.15.1 US

There is no single standard covering depreciation in the US.

Depreciation is defined in ARB 43 as follows:

'A system of accounting which aims to distribute the cost or other basic value of tangible capital assets, less salvage (if any), over the estimated useful life of the unit (which may be a group of assets) in a systematic and rational manner. It is a process of allocation, not of valuation.'[70]

There are a number of standards that deal with detailed aspects of depreciation.[71] Disclosure is dealt with by paragraphs 4 and 5 of APB 12.

3.15.2 IASC

IAS 4 on accounting for depreciation requires that all assets with a limited useful life be written down to their residual value over that life. Its requirements are relatively brief, and none of them are in conflict with SSAP 12.

4 PERMANENT DIMINUTIONS

4.1 Introduction

Few areas of accounting for fixed assets have caused more controversy or led to more inconsistency of treatment than the issue of permanent diminutions in value, particularly as it relates to revalued assets. It is not an area covered in depth by UK accounting standards. SSAP 12 (Revised) refers to the treatment of permanent diminutions in the case of assets carried at cost, but specifically excludes revalued assets when covering the profit and loss account treatment of provisions.[72] The statutory accounting rules in Schedule 4 require provisions for diminution in value to be made in appropriate circumstances as well as requiring certain disclosures.

This section covers permanent diminutions both in general and as they apply to assets carried at historical cost. The specific problems relating to assets carried at valuation are dealt with in 5.10 below.

4.2 Companies Act requirements

The Act requires provisions for diminution in value to be made in respect of any fixed asset if the reduction in value is expected to be permanent.

The provisions are to be made through the profit and loss account.[73] Provisions no longer required are to be written back, again through the profit and loss account.[74] In either case, amounts not shown in the profit and loss account must be disclosed in the notes to the accounts.[75] Although provision must be made for all permanent diminutions, the Act states that provisions *may* be made for any diminution in value in the case of fixed asset investments.[76] It must be noted that, except in the circumstances of a revaluation of all assets (see 5.14 below), the Act requires any provision to be treated as a realised loss for distribution purposes whether it is considered to be permanent or temporary.

4.3 SSAP 12 and permanent diminutions

The requirement to provide for permanent diminutions in value was included in the original SSAP 12. SSAP 12 (Revised) requires provisions to be made, if at any time there is a permanent diminution in value, to write the net book amount of the asset down to its estimated recoverable amount. This should then be written off over the remaining useful life of the asset. If the reasons for making the provision cease to apply it should be written back to the profit and loss account.[77]

Provisions for permanent diminutions in value of assets (and any reversals) should be charged (credited) in the profit and loss account for the period.[78]

4.4 The estimation of recoverable amount

SSAP 12 (Revised) is clear as to when a permanent diminution has occurred: it is when the net book value of the asset will not be recoverable in full. Recoverable amount is the greater of the net realisable value of an asset and the amount recoverable from its further use.[79]

There are a number of indicators that the asset has suffered an impairment in value; for example, a decision may have been made to dispose of it, it may be underutilised or idle, there may have been a decline in demand for the product or the company may have made losses on that particular product.

Usually a company will only consider the net realisable value of an asset if it is to be sold or scrapped. In such cases the recoverable amount should be simple to calculate as it will be the net realisable value after taking account of realisation expenses.

It is a different matter when it comes to the recoverable amount of an asset that will continue in use. There are usually great practical difficulties in estimating the amount that will be recoverable from further use. As a result the exercise is not often undertaken and when it is, the results seem often to be ignored.[80]

In principle, the recoverable amount should be measured by reference to future revenues to be generated by the asset. However, it may be impossible to assign future revenue streams to individual assets: they may be interchangeable or revenues may be jointly earned. It is also difficult to predict future economic conditions.

There is no guidance as to whether the recoverable amount should be based on cash flows or on the profit and loss generated by the asset; nor on the level at which either should be measured, e.g whether it should be gross or net profit, or whether it should be before or after interest costs.

In both cases, direct costs or expenses that would not have to be incurred were the asset disposed of should be taken into the calculation. It would seem to be reasonable therefore to take either the net direct cash flow or gross profit less other direct costs, but excluding overheads that will continue to be borne by the enterprise, as the recoverable amount. While in principle it would give a better answer to discount the future cash flows or revenue streams, this is not the usual accounting practice in the UK.

There are only a few circumstances where it will be possible to calculate a residual value for individual assets, for example in the case of ships or aircraft or highly specialised individual machines with a discrete product. However, there is one industry sector, oil and gas, where guidance has been issued on residual values. This is in connection with the annual ceiling test carried out on the carrying value of the enterprise's interest in that pool or field. The ceiling test should determine whether the carrying value (whether determined under full cost or successful efforts methods), less any provisions for abandonment costs and deferred production or revenue-related taxes, is covered by the anticipated future net revenue attributable to the company's interests.[81] The rules laid down in the SORP for the purposes of the calculation, which correspond to the suggestions given above, are as follows:

(a) future net revenues are the estimated revenues from production of commercial reserves less operating costs, production or revenue-related taxes (including UK petroleum revenue tax), insurance and royalties, future development costs and abandonment costs. General financing costs and taxation on profits (including UK corporation tax) should not be deducted in the calculation of future net revenues;

(b) prices and cost levels used should be those ruling at the date as of which the ceiling test is applied; and

(c) estimates of future net revenues and costs should not be discounted.[82]

Note that while 'operating costs' will include overheads, in the context of the industry these are likely to be specific to the pool or the field being assessed.

When assessing the recoverable amount, there may be temporary shortfalls, i.e. periods when net income is less than depreciation. Usually it will be possible to ignore a single year in which this is the case; it will be only one of the factors about the future taken into account. With a longer period of shortfall it may be necessary to take a prudent view of the carrying value of the asset, especially when it is borne in mind that future estimates are necessarily less certain.

4.5   Diminutions in value of individual assets or portfolio of assets

Provisions for permanent diminutions in value of assets should normally be done on an asset by asset basis. Accordingly, in calculating the provision necessary in respect of an asset, no account should be taken of any potential profits, either through sale or use, of other fixed assets. However, there may be instances where it might be appropriate to take account of such profits in considering provisions for diminution in value of assets. Such instances might be:

(a)   where a decision has been taken to dispose of a number of assets and it is intended that they are sold as a group of assets, for example, as part of the termination of a business segment. This would be consistent with SSAP 6 which states that *profits* or losses arising from the disposal of assets will usually be included in any provision necessary where a decision has been made to discontinue a business segment;[83]

(b)   where assets of a particular type are considered to be inter-changeable. For example, container ships of the same class, where the future trading results of the fleet may be more meaningful than those of individual vessels, any one of which may receive a future charter or, alternatively, be laid up. This approach is only relevant where the assets will continue in use. Where a decision has been taken to dispose of any of the assets within the class then any provision for diminution in value in respect of those assets should be calculated on an asset by asset basis;

(c)   where they form a set that can be considered a single asset. In practice, a company may wish to consider its investments in two or more of its subsidiaries as constituting a single asset; the specific problems raised here are dealt with in 4.6 below.

4.6   The special problems of the carrying values of investments in subsidiaries

It has already been noted that investments in subsidiaries are fixed assets and therefore subject to the statutory rules governing the carrying values. There are a number of circumstances when the possibility of an impairment in value must be considered. These include:

(a)   losses made by the subsidiary;

(b)   the payment of dividends out of pre-acquisition profits;

(c)   group reconstructions leaving shell companies.

The situation where pre-acquisition dividends are paid up is discussed in 6.3.7 of Chapter 4.

4.6.1   Loss-making subsidiaries

If a subsidiary company makes losses then its net asset value may fall below the amount at which the investment is stated in the company's balance sheet. A provision must be made if there has been a permanent reduction in profitability which has resulted in a real reduction in value and there is no prospect of an improvement in fortunes in the future.

As described in 5.6.1 below, it is quite common for holding companies to carry investments in subsidiaries at net asset value with the result that temporary diminutions are taken to revaluation reserve. However, where the diminution is expected to be permanent then it should be charged to the profit and loss account.

4.6.2 Shell companies

A common form of group reconstruction involves the transfer to another group company of the tangible assets and trade of a subsidiary. As a result of the original purchase price including an element of goodwill the remaining shell may have a carrying value in the parent company's balance sheet in excess of its net worth. It could be argued that as the subsidiary is now a shell company a provision should be made against the carrying value to reduce it to its net worth. However, in such a reorganisation there has been no loss either to the holding company or to the group. Foster, in the Butterworths Company Law Guide, makes this point and goes on to state, 'the goodwill inherent in the original purchase is still present on a group basis. Consequently no permanent impairment has arisen. However in this situation the directors would have to acknowledge that the shell company is an integral part of the business for which it was acquired and that it will not be disposed of whilst this business is being carried on by the group.'[84]

However, the impairment in carrying value should always be recognised if the assets and/or the trade transferred are themselves sold. It is only possible not to recognise the loss as long as the matching gain elsewhere in the group has not been realised or otherwise impaired in value.

4.7 Comparison with US and IASC pronouncements

4.7.1 US

The US statements that deal with depreciation do not directly address permanent diminutions in value. However, basic US accounting concepts would suggest the recognition of impairments in value. APB Statement No. 4 states:

'In unusual circumstances persuasive evidence may exist of impairment of the utility of productive facilities indicative of an inability to recover cost although the facilities have not become worthless. The amount at which those facilities are carried is sometimes reduced to recoverable cost and a loss recorded prior to disposition or expiration of the useful life of the facilities.'[85]

In 1980 an issues paper was produced by an AICPA task force entitled 'Accounting for the Inability to Fully Recover the Carrying Amounts of Long Lived Assets'. The main conclusions of the paper were:[86]

(a) the inability to fully recover the carrying amounts of long lived assets should be reported in financial statements;

(b) the concept of permanent decline is unsatisfactory and an alternative concept should be sought;

(c)   the probability test in SFAS 5 (see 3.1 of Chapter 17) is a workable alternative to the concept of permanent decline;

(d)   judgment is necessary in selecting the asset measurement that best predicts future economic benefits as it is difficult to select one measurement that would be appropriate in all circumstances;

(e)   if the ability to fully recover the carrying amounts of long lived assets is recorded in the financial statements, future upward adjustments (not to exceed carrying amounts before the writedowns) should be permitted if evidence indicates a recovery.

In more recent years the FASB Emerging Issues Task Force has discussed the issue of what generally accepted accounting principles should be used for determining whether a write-down should be recorded, but was unable to reach a consensus. They did make the following observations:

(a)   current practice indicates that write-downs as a result of economic impairment are permissible;

(b)   practice is not to write down assets below a break-even point, based on future cash flows measured either on a gross basis or on a discounted basis;

(c)   once written down, the assets are not subsequently written back up.[87]

4.7.2   IASC

IAS 16 covers diminutions in value of property, plant and equipment carried at historical cost and at valuation. Impairments in the carrying value of investments are dealt with by IAS 25. The requirements where assets are carried at revalued amount are dealt with in 5.15.2 below.

IAS 16 states that, if there is a permanent impairment to an item or a group of items of property, plant and equipment and the recoverable amount falls below the net carrying amount, the net carrying amount should be reduced to the recoverable amount and the difference charged to income immediately.[88]

There are two points to make: firstly, this applies only to assets carried at historical cost (see 5.15.2 below for the accounting treatment of assets carried at valuation); secondly, what is meant by a 'group' of assets is not made clear in the standard. It may therefore be possible to adopt a portfolio approach in situations other than those discussed in 4.5 above.

5   REVALUATIONS

5.1   Introduction

5.1.1   *Background*

The incorporation of revalued assets into historical cost financial statements was widespread during the early 1970s when the country was suffering from unprecedented levels of inflation. There has more recently been a movement away from the inclusion of revalued assets in companies' financial statements. This has been commented on by the ICAEW in their surveys of published accounts, for the first time in 1985—1986's survey. Here it was observed that there was a discernable trend away from revaluations especially amongst companies other than the large listed ones,[89] and the same point was repeated in the survey for 1987—1988.[90] There seem to be a number of reasons for this new trend. The general level of inflation is now much lower, although property prices in certain sectors have continued to boom. Certain companies have come to feel that the practice of incorporating revaluations puts them at a disadvantage when their performance is compared with that of companies that do not revalue their assets. This argument was put forward by English China Clays P.L.C. in their financial statements for the year ended September 30, 1987 and the decision was made to discontinue revaluations (previously carried out every five years) although earlier revaluations were not reversed. Land, buildings and mineral rights are now included at the amount of the revaluation as at October 1, 1982. The directors' report stated the following:

Extract 10.14: English China Clays P.L.C.[91]

FREEHOLD AND LEASEHOLD PROPERTIES [extract]
After careful review, the directors have decided that the practice of incorporating the results of property revaluations in the accounts places the group at a disadvantage when its performance is compared with that of other United Kingdom companies which do not adopt a similar practice. The Group Statistical record on page 37 draws attention to the effect of this practice on the Group's performance, but the directors believe that its impact may not be fully recognised and that the interests of the shareholders may be better served by not continuing with it.

This company has joined a list that includes The BOC Group plc, which, with effect from the year ended September 30, 1987, has ceased to carry plant and machinery at valuation,[92] and Pilkington plc, which has reverted to historical cost for most of its assets from April 1, 1986.[93]

SSAP 12 (Revised) requires the profit and loss account charge for depreciation on revalued assets to be based on carrying amount, so a company that revalues its depreciable assets will show a lower earnings per share as a result. (This point may also be connected with the spreading practice of not providing depreciation on properties: see 3.13 above.) Revaluations may also destroy the comparability of balance sheet ratios such as the return on capital. However, most major companies include some of their fixed assets at revalued amounts. For example, 22 of the companies in the FT 30 Index as at October 1987 included at least some of their assets at valuation.

The ASC encourages revaluations of tangible fixed assets on the grounds that they give 'useful and relevant information to users of accounts', and this paragraph goes on to state, 'This statement does not prescribe how frequently assets should be revalued but, where a policy of revaluing assets is adopted, the valuations should be kept up to date.'[94] In spite of this statement (which, however, is in the explanatory notes and so does not form part of the standard itself), the valuations of property in major companies' financial statements may be undertaken at infrequent intervals and be some years out of date. Valuations are permitted on an asset-by-asset basis; they do not have to cover all of the assets in a particular class and in practice rarely do so. Companies usually do not disclose a policy on revaluations and the current situation of ad hoc valuations may mean that in fact they do not have one; they need give no reasons as to why certain assets have been revalued and others excluded. Finally, it is rarely clear as to exactly which basis of valuation has been used. The Companies Act is vague; 'market value 'and 'current cost', the two permitted bases for the valuation of tangible fixed assets, would permit a number of different interpretations (see 5.4 and 5.5 below).

There is no consistency of treatment within the same sector. Three supermarket groups offer an interesting contrast. J Sainsbury plc include only a few properties at valuation in their 1988 financial statements, £40.0 million out of a total, at cost or valuation, of £1,329.1 million, and the revaluation was in 1973.[95] The Dee Corporation PLC carry just under one-third of their properties at valuation: £241.0 million out of £791.6 million. Most of these valuations were reasonably current; approximately two-thirds had been performed in 1986.[96] Finally, Tesco PLC's financial statements include no revaluations at all.[97]

5.1.2   *The responses of the accountancy profession*

The present situation is one where many financial statements include valuations of some assets, almost always land and buildings, but there is no overall rationale for the inclusion of revalued assets in the first place. This has made it very difficult to develop a systematic and consistent approach to the accounting problems which result from their inclusion: permanent and temporary diminutions in value, depreciation and disposals. In particular the accounting profession has not found it possible to decide whether the treatment in the profit and loss account should be consistently based on the balance sheet carrying value.

SSAP 6 — *Extraordinary items and prior year adjustments* , when it was originally issued in 1974, required that unrealised surpluses on revaluation of fixed assets should be credited direct to reserves. This was then followed by ED 16 which, *inter alia*, expanded on this basic requirement and proposed that:

(a)   unrealised deficits should be taken to the profit and loss account to the extent that they exceeded any previous revaluation surpluses relating to the same assets which were in reserves;

(b)   profits or losses on the disposal of fixed assets were to be based on their book value and any unrealised revaluation surplus which became realised was not to be included as part of the profit or loss for the year.[98]

This approach was later recommended in the ASC's discussion paper on the review of SSAP 6 which was issued in 1983.[99] However, it also stated that such a treatment for the disposal of revalued fixed assets would conflict with the general aim of consistency underlying the discussion paper for the following reasons:

(a)   a company's results may be materially affected by the fact that it has previously revalued a property which it has now disposed of or by the timing of any such revaluation;

(b)   the proposed treatment will result in an element of profit becoming realised but never recognised in the profit and loss account.[100]

Following comments on the discussion paper the ASC then reversed their approach and ED 36 proposed that the profit or loss on disposal of revalued fixed assets was to be based on depreciated original cost.[101] However, following further comments on the exposure draft, which confirmed the deep division of views on this matter, all references to it were dropped from the revised SSAP 6. In practice companies adopt a variety of approaches to disposals.

As a result of this, the only accounting standard (apart from SSAP 19 which deals with investment properties—see Chapter 11) which addresses any aspect of this issue is SSAP 12 which only deals with depreciation of revalued assets and requires that the depreciation charge in the profit and loss account be based on the carrying value of the asset (see 5.11 below).

Ad hoc valuations and a variety of accounting treatments have led, therefore, to a situation where the bases of the amounts included for fixed assets in some companies' financial statements are arbitrary, if not almost meaningless, where there is very little comparability between companies, and where there is as yet little sign of order being imposed.

5.2   Bases of valuation

The main influence on accounting for revaluations is the Companies Act 1985; the Alternative Accounting Rules in Part C of Schedule 4 of the Act give the statutory bases and rules regarding revaluations. These are considered below.

In addition to historical cost, the Act recognises the following bases of valuation for the various classes of fixed asset:

(a)   tangible fixed assets may be included at market value or current cost;[102]

(b)   intangibles, except goodwill, may be included at current cost;[103]

(c)   investments may be included at market value or at directors' valuation.[104]

In each case 'market value' is at the date of the asset's last valuation.

5.3   Open market value of land and buildings

'Market value' is not defined further in the Act. SSAP 19 requires investment properties to be included on the basis of open market values[105] and the Handbook on accounting for the effects of changing prices has the same requirement for the current cost of non-specialised land and buildings.[106] Neither is more specific, although open market value can have a number of different meanings; these are described below.

In February 1974 a joint working party of members of the Institute of Chartered Accountants in England and Wales (ICAEW) and the Royal Institution of Chartered Surveyors (RICS) was set up; this resulted in the issuance by the RICS of guidance notes on the valuation of properties for the purposes of companies' financial statements. At this time the ICAEW issued an accounting recommendation[107] which stated that these notes contained the acceptable bases for valuation and the circumstances in which they should be used.

The RICS guidance notes have been regularly updated, most recently in 1986, but the ICAEW has never revised its original statement. The new guidance notes state that valuations of land and buildings will normally be on the basis of open market values and will have regard to evidence of open market transactions in similar properties.[108] 'Open market value' is defined as the best price that might be obtained for an interest in a property at the date of valuation assuming:

(a)   a willing seller or lessor;

(b)   a reasonable period in which to negotiate the sale or letting taking into account the nature of the property and the state of the market;

(c)   that values will remain static during the period;

(d)   that the property will be freely exposed to the open market; and

(e)   that no account will be taken of any higher price or rent that might be paid by a purchaser or lessee with a special interest.[109]

However, as the guidance notes state:

'such valuations may reflect either:

(a)   the use of the property for the same or similar purposes as hitherto (Open Market Value for Existing Use). This includes properties normally sold as fully operational business units and valued with regard to trading potential, such as hotels, public houses, cinemas and many other properties;

(b)   the prospective use of the property for other purposes (Open Market Value for Alternative Use).'[110]

Therefore, in a property valuation report by a chartered surveyor, the expression 'open market value' without reference to either existing or alternative use will have regard to both, to the extent to which they are reflected in the price obtainable on the open market.[111]

5.3.1   *Existing use value*

Existing use value is an open market value with the added condition that the property will continue to be owner-occupied in its existing use. These conditions are not as restrictive as they may at first appear as the definition is not referring to the existing user, and existing use does not necessarily mean the continuance of the specific trade currently being undertaken on the property. The RICS background paper explains this as follows:

'Many buildings are general purpose structures suitable for a wide variety of different trades. Similar industrial buildings will probably have the same values irrespective of the different trades that are carried on, and this will also apply to shops. A factory is valued as a factory, not as a particular type of factory, and a shop as a shop, not as a particular type of shop (unless the market differentiates between the two).'[112]

Many companies' accounting policies include a general statement that properties
are held at valuation, but do not indicate the basis of valuation (although this will
generally be given in the fixed asset note in the year the valuation is incorporated
in the financial statements). Sears plc do disclose, as part of the fixed asset note,
that properties occupied by group companies are valued on the basis of open
market values for existing use while others have an open market value without
this restriction. The validity of the use of values that may reflect alternative uses is
described in 5.3.3 below.

Extract 10.15: Sears plc[113]

9. FIXED TANGIBLE ASSETS [extract]
The majority of the group's properties were professionally valued by Healey & Baker
and Edward Erdman at 31st January 1988. The basis of valuation was open market value
and for those properties occupied by the group, open market value for existing use.

5.3.2   *Valuations that include trading potential*

This is another form of 'existing use' valuation that takes account of the purpose
to which a property is adapted and for which it is currently being used.

There are certain types of property that are valued on a basis that has regard to the
trading potential which attaches to the property. Such properties, which can
include hotels, public houses, cinemas, theatres, petrol stations, betting shops or
specialised leisure and sporting facilities, are sold on the open market as fully
operational business units at prices based directly on trading potential. The
valuation will therefore include all of the assets of the business as a going
concern, including fixtures and fittings and the value of the trading potential. The
report may not distinguish between the various elements that make up the
valuation.

The problem for the valuer is in distinguishing between the value of the trading
potential which runs with the property and the value of goodwill which has been
created in the business by the present owner and which may be transferable on
sale. The RICS Guidelines state that only the former should be included in the
valuation.[114]

The capitalised trading potential is not 'goodwill' as defined by SSAP 22.
Paragraph 15 of the standard states the following: 'This treatment is not dealt with
in Part 3 of the standard as it concerns the treatment of other assets, not of
goodwill.' If it has arisen on the acquisition of a property it may be appropriate to
capitalise it as part of the cost of the asset; SSAP 22 recommends further
additional disclosures.[115]

Trading potential valuations can also cause problems in respect of fixtures and
fittings. The trading potential valuation will include those so-called tenant's
fixtures and fittings that are necessary for the business to function. For example, a
hotel's valuation would have to include beds, bed linen and other necessary
furnishings. A valuation may also be performed on the hotel in its current
condition, i.e. including fixtures and fittings that have been added by the existing
owner over and above this basic level. However, part or all of either category of

fixtures and fittings may have been purchased by the current owner and included in the financial statements, probably at cost, as a separate category of fixed asset.

There is an obvious danger of double counting if the cost of the hotel is revalued without excluding the elements that relate to other assets. This problem is recognised by the RICS, who in the background paper state 'Where the Valuer is required to provide a figure for the land and buildings for balance sheet purposes, this will normally include the landlord's fixtures and fittings and the items of plant and machinery referred to in GN 25.[116] Obviously for this purpose the valuation should exclude, if necessary by apportionment from a global figure, the value of furniture, tenant's fixtures and fittings, stock and goodwill which has been created in the business of the present owner as opposed to such value which is reflected in the trading potential which runs with the property. Separate figures may be required by the Directors for these latter items for balance sheet purposes.'[117]

Some enterprises avoid the problem by having a single class of asset comprising the properties and their fittings. An example is Bass PLC, which in incorporating a valuation of its properties in its financial statements for 1987 changed to this basis for its landlord's fixtures and fittings as illustrated below:

Extract 10.16: Bass PLC [118]

c) Fixed assets and depreciation [extract]
ii) Tangible assets
On 1st October 1986, landlord's fixtures and fittings were reclassified as properties, as shown in note 11.

11 TANGIBLE FIXED ASSETS [extract]

Movements during the year	Licensed and unlicensed properties £ m	Fixtures, fittings, tools and equipment £ m
Cost or valuation		
At 30th September 1986	845.7	678.1
Reclassification of landlord's fittings	280.6	(280.6)
Revaluation transferred to reserves	699.4	—
Depreciation		
At 30th September 1986	46.2	227.9
Reclassification of landlord's fittings	69.1	(69.1)
Revaluation transferred to reserves	(109.3)	—

A professional valuation of all properties (other than holiday centres) at 1st October 1986 was carried out by the Group's own professionally qualified staff in conjunction with Chesterton, Surveyors and Valuers.
. . . In respect of the portfolio of licensed public houses, hotels, off-licensed properties, betting shops, bingo halls and depots together with non-trading properties, the basis was open market value for the existing use in the business of the Group.

Such an approach will have avoided any possibility of double counting for such fixtures and fittings in incorporating the valuation of the properties. It is unclear, however, whether Bass PLC no longer depreciate such items now that they are included with the properties in line with their depreciation policy for hotels and public houses.

Finally, it should be noted that the valuation of property held for its rental potential may also include an element that is based on capitalised estimated rental values, so the basis of valuation is, in this sense, not unusual.[119]

5.3.3 *Alternative use*

An alternative use basis is not normally considered appropriate for assets in use in a business as financial statements are usually prepared on the assumption that the business is a going concern.[120] Land and buildings that are surplus to requirements or that have been purchased with the intention of redevelopment may, however, be valued on a basis that takes account of any alternative use.[121]

5.4 Current cost

There are specialised buildings that do not have a readily obtainable market value because they are rarely, if ever, sold on the open market except as part of the whole business; it will, therefore, be necessary for these to be incorporated on the basis of current cost under the Act.

There is no definition of 'current cost' in the Act. It is taken to have the same meaning as in current cost accounting;[122] the Handbook states that the current cost (or value to the business) of an asset is the lower of its net current replacement cost and its recoverable amount, which is the higher of its net realisable value and the amount recoverable from its future use.[123]

It will, therefore, generally be acceptable for companies to incorporate valuations for such properties on the basis of depreciated replacement cost. Examples of the type of property to which this treatment applies are oil refineries, power stations, breweries or buildings so specific to their owner's requirements that a valuer cannot arrive at a conclusion based on open market transactions. Another group of properties are those in a particular geographical area or of such a size or otherwise so modified to the occupier's requirements that the valuer cannot arrive at a conclusion on the basis of open market transactions.[124]

The depreciated replacement cost of a building includes the open market value of the land in its existing use together with an estimate of the gross replacement cost of the buildings. This is then reduced to allow for age, condition and functional obsolescence, in order to arrive at the value to the business at the valuation date.[125]

Guinness PLC values its breweries and distilleries using depreciated replacement cost as illustrated below:

Extract 10.17: Guinness PLC [126]

Tangible assets and depreciation [extract]
In the case of distilleries, breweries and related specialised properties, valuations are principally on a depreciated replacement cost basis.

Depreciated replacement cost must always be used with care as a basis for the valuation of property, as it is often likely to give a higher valuation than one done on an open market basis (see the example quoted in 5.7 below). For this reason, it is necessary to ensure that the property really is so specialised that an open market value cannot be obtained.

5.5   Other bases of valuation

There are a number of other bases of valuation that may be encountered in a company's financial statements. The bases described below include net asset value for investments, and forced sale values.

5.5.1   *Net asset value*

Many companies carry their investments in subsidiary companies in their own balance sheets at net asset value; this is an example of a directors' valuation.

Extract 10.18: Royal Insurance Public Limited Company[127]

SUBSIDIARIES & ASSOCIATED COMPANIES [extract]
Subsidiary companies are valued in the Parent Company Balance Sheet at the Company's shareholding proportion of their net assets (including investments at market value) plus the net indebtedness of the subsidiaries to the Company in respect of any loans and current balances.

The problems that may arise with regard to carrying value in the parent company balance sheet if the subsidiaries are loss making are dealt with in 4.6.1 above.

5.5.2   *Forced sale values*

This is an open market value with the added condition that there is a time limit which cannot be considered a reasonable period in which to negotiate the sale: see 5.3 above. This is the appropriate basis of valuation when a company's financial statements are being prepared on the break up basis because it is no longer a going concern.

5.6   Valuations of other assets

Few companies carry any assets other than property at valuation. One fairly common exception is the carrying of investments in subsidiaries at net asset value, which is described in 5.5.1 above. Most remaining cases fall into one of three groups: a few companies carrying all, or almost all, of their assets on a basis that accords with the principles of current cost accounting, those that hold marketable securities as long-term investments but carry them at market value and those that have commenced carrying their intangible assets at valuation.

Maxwell Communication Corporation plc continues to carry its plant and machinery at depreciated current replacement cost based on expert opinion, a method advocated by the Handbook on changing prices,[128] as illustrated below:

Extract 10.19: Maxwell Communication Corporation plc[129]

12 TANGIBLE ASSETS [extract]
(a) Valuation of property and plant and machinery
The Group's plant and machinery was revalued as at 31st December 1983 at each Group
company by Colebrook, Evans & McKenzie, Auctioneers and Valuers, on an existing use
value, which was determined by reference to the depreciated current replacement cost. The
directors adopted the existing use valuation for the majority of assets, but in certain cases
decided, in view of future plans, to value assets at amounts lower than their existing use
valuation supplied by the valuers.

Royal Insurance Public Limited Company is an example where investments held
for the long term are valued at market price:

Extract 10.20: Royal Insurance Public Limited Company[130]

INVESTMENTS [extract]
Investments are shown at market value, for which purpose unlisted investments are included
at directors' valuation and properties at professional valuation.

Bass PLC carries some intangibles, betting and bingo licences, at 'current value to
the business' as indicated below:

Extract 10.21: Bass PLC[131]

FIXED ASSETS AND DEPRECIATION [extract]
i) Intangible assets
a) These comprise betting and bingo licences, relating to properties in which the Group has
an interest, and are valued annually by the Group's professional staff at their current value to
the business. Surpluses arising from such valuations are taken direct to revaluation reserve.

'Current value to the business' is used in the Handbook as a synonym for current
cost.[132]

Another example of the valuation of intangibles at current cost is Ranks Hovis
McDougall PLC (see Extract 10.1 at 1.2 above). It should be emphasised that
under the Companies Act 1985, intangibles can only be included at current cost
and not market value (see 5.2 above).

5.7   The comparability of valuations

Although the valuation bases described above are the ones most commonly found
in practice and should be the only ones that are incorporated into company
financial statements, there are yet others that may be encountered such as fire
insurance values or valuations for bank security purposes. It is always of the
utmost importance to establish the basis and purpose of any valuation as the
different methods may come up with widely different values.

Westwick, in his book on property valuations, quotes a series of valuations and
these clearly demonstrate the dangers of using the values prepared for one

purpose for any other purpose. These were performed by Richard Ellis on a very substantial food preparation factory. This particular building was a border-line case; arguments could have been put forward for valuing it on an open market value or by depreciated replacement cost. The former value came to £3.5 million, the latter to £6.5 million. The fire insurance value, the gross replacement cost of the building, was highest; this amounted to £8.4 million. The lowest, which was the forced sale value, amounted to £3 million.[133]

5.8   Accounting for revaluations

When an asset is revalued the Companies Act states that the 'profit or loss' on revaluation must go to a separate reserve, the revaluation reserve.[134]

The revaluation reserve shall be reduced if amounts standing to its credit are, in the opinion of the directors, 'no longer necessary for the purpose of the accounting policies adopted by the company'.[135] Amounts may be released to the profit and loss account only if they were previously charged to the account or if they represent realised profits.[136] This permits transfers from revaluation reserve for the depreciation which has been charged through the profit and loss account on the revaluation surplus and for the surplus realised on the sale of a revalued asset. It also allows a company to change its policy from one where assets are revalued and to write back the reduction in the carrying value against the surplus.

5.8.1 Accounting for revaluation surpluses

There are four ways in principle that a surplus arising on the revaluation of a depreciated asset might be accounted for, as illustrated in the following example:

Example 10.4

On January 1, 19X1 a company acquires an asset for £1,000. The asset has an economic life of ten years and is depreciated on a straight line basis. The residual value is assumed to be £nil. At December 31, 19X4 the asset is valued at £1,200. The four possible methods are as follows:

	(i)	(ii)	(iii)	(iv)
Fixed assets	£	£	£	£
Cost or valuation				
At January 1, 19X4	1,000	1,000	1,000	1,000
Surplus on revaluation	200	200	200	600
At December 31 19X4	1,200	1,200	1,200	1,600
Depreciation				
At January 1, 19X4	300	300	300	300
Provided during the year	100	100	100	100
Surplus on revaluation	(400)	(400)	(400)	—
At December 31, 19X4	—	—	—	400
Net book value				
At December 31, 19X4	1,200	1,200	1,200	1,200
At December 31, 19X3	700	700	700	700
Revaluation surplus				
Revaluation reserve	600	200	200	600
Retained profits	—	400	—	—
Profit or loss for year	—	—	400	—
	600	600	600	600

(i) This method is based on the view that the revaluation establishes a new base of a *used* asset and, accordingly, the surplus to be taken to the revaluation reserve is the difference between the valuation and the net book value at the date of the valuation. In addition, no depreciation should be added back to retained profits, or the profit and loss account, as it was correct to charge depreciation in previous years. This is supported by paragraph 22 of SSAP 12. It is also considered that this treatment is that required by the Companies Act which states that the amount of the profit to be credited to the revaluation reserve is to be 'after allowing, where appropriate, for any provisions for depreciation or diminution in value made otherwise than by reference to the value so determined'.

(ii)This method is based on the view that the depreciation charged to date was unnecessary and that retained profits should reflect the position which would have existed had no such depreciation been charged. However, we believe that as depreciation is effectively a measure of consumption of an asset then this argument is inappropriate. It is unclear whether this treatment is prohibited by paragraph 22 of SSAP 12 as it could be interpreted as only prohibiting crediting the accumulated depreciation to the profit and loss account for the year.

Another reason for adopting such a method is that it is argued that the write-back of the depreciation is a realised profit. This issue was raised but not resolved by the CCAB in the guidance statement on realised profits TR No. 482, *The determination of distributable profits in the context of the Companies Acts 1948 to 1981*, para. 18:

'...there is at present no unanimity of opinion as to whether such a surplus, to the extent that it represents the writing back of a realised loss, particularly where the realised loss arises from past depreciation, constitutes a realised profit. In view of the division of opinion on this matter, and in the absence of any statutory rule or clearly decisive precedent in case law, it is considered inappropriate to offer guidance on the question in this statement. Where reliance is placed on such a profit being realised in order to make a distribution, it may be appropriate for the directors of the company to seek legal advice'.

Although the 1981 Act has been superseded by the 1985 Act, this still remains the current position.

In view of these uncertainties we believe that companies should not adopt this treatment.

(iii) This is a variant of method (ii) above. Such an approach has been used in the past but it can no longer be used because of the prohibition contained in paragraph 22 of SSAP 12.

(iv) This method is based on the view that as depreciation has been charged on the asset in the past, and the revaluation does not alter that fact, then it should be retained. However, it suffers from the deficiency that the valuation is now stated to be £1,600, which is not the case—it treats the valuation in net book value terms. The Companies Act requires the valuations to be regarded as gross[137] and, therefore, such a treatment is unacceptable, unless the company adopts current cost accounting for the asset, which requires an annual reappraisal of cost and depreciation.

For the reasons mentioned above, we consider that method (i) is the appropriate treatment for accounting for revaluations.

5.8.2 The treatment of downward valuations

There are three ways in principle in which a downward valuation of an asset could be implemented in a company's financial statements; these are shown in the following example which, for simplicity, ignores depreciation:

Example 10.5

On January 1, 19X1 a company acquires an asset for £1,000. At December 31, 19X2 it is valued at £1,200 giving rise to a revaluation reserve of £200. At December 31, 19X4 it is revalued at £900. The three possible methods are as follows:

	(i) £	(ii) £	(iii) £
Valuation			
At January 1, 19X4	1,200	1,200	1,200
Deficit on valuation	(300)	(300)	(300)
At December 31, 19X4	900	900	900
Revaluation reserve			
At January 1, 19X4	200	200	200
Deficit on valuation	(300)	(200)	—
Transfer to realised reserves	—	—	(200)
At December 31, 19X4	(100)	—	—
Charge to profit and loss account	—	100	300

(i) Under this method the whole deficit is charged to the revaluation reserve. This treatment is based on the fact that under the alternative accounting rules contained in the Companies Act surpluses and *deficits* arising on the revaluation of an asset can be dealt with through the revaluation reserve.[138] It is clearly permissible for temporary diminutions in value to be charged to the reserve and there appears to be no statutory bar to an overall debit balance arising on the revaluation reserve. This treatment is also consistent with SSAP 19 except that the standard requires (somewhat illogically) that an overall deficit must be charged to revenue reserves.[139]

(ii) Under this method the downward movement is split, with previous valuations being reversed while the deficit below depreciated historical cost is charged to the profit and loss account. This means that only the element that represents a diminution in historical cost terms is reflected in the profit and loss account. This is the approach proposed by ED 16. It is also that suggested by the ASC Discussion Paper on depreciation which stated 'It appears that an overall deficit on a revaluation of a fixed asset may be debited to the revaluation reserve and that the reserve itself may be, in aggregate, in debit; however, the prudence concept would normally require a provision to be made in the profit and loss account in such a circumstance.' If this method is adopted then there is no need to consider whether the revaluation deficit is temporary or permanent in nature as the treatment will be the same in either case.

(iii) Under this method the whole deficit is charged to the profit and loss account; any previous revaluation above cost is dealt with as a reserve movement. This method is based on the view that the £1,200 valuation became the new substitute for cost when it was incorporated in the financial statements in 19X2 and that the original cost is now irrelevant so far as future accounting for the asset is concerned. It also assumes that the fall in value to £900 is expected to be permanent. However, it is usually argued that it is inappropriate to take the 'good news'—the upward valuation—to an unrealised reserve, while having to take all of a downward movement to the profit and loss account.

In our view, method (i) is appropriate only in cases where the diminution in value is expected to be temporary. Where the diminution is expected to be permanent, or is considered to be indicative of a permanent impairment in value of the asset, such a treatment is inconsistent with the accounting concept of prudence not to provide for at least that part below depreciated historical cost in the profit and loss account (see 5.9 below). Accordingly, it will be necessary for companies to consider whether this is the case.

In our view, methods (ii) and (iii) are both acceptable methods of dealing with deficits on valuation, although (iii) is not often met with in practice.

5.9   Downward valuations and permanent diminutions

One particular accounting problem with revalued assets is how to deal with permanent diminutions in value. Although the requirement in SSAP 12 to provide for such diminutions in value (by writing down the net book value immediately to the estimated recoverable amount) is equally valid for assets carried at valuation, the standard does not discuss the treatment of such provisions.[140]

Again, there are three ways in principle in which such permanent diminutions can be accounted for and these are illustrated in Example 10.5 above and are considered in turn below.

Method (i), i.e. charging the whole deficit to revaluation reserve. The Alternative Accounting Rules in Section C of Schedule 4 to the Act contain no reference to permanent diminutions in value, which are dealt with in Section B (historical cost accounting rules). Some have therefore argued that permanent diminutions do not arise in the context of revalued assets; instead there are revaluation deficits, whether temporary or permanent, that may be charged to the revaluation reserve even if this results in an overall deficit on that reserve. It is not clear whether this interpretation is supported by the wording of the Act. This requires that the 'profit or loss' arising from the valuation 'after allowing, where appropriate, for any provisions for depreciation or diminution in value made otherwise than by reference to the value so determined and any adjustments of any such provisions made in the light of that determination' be credited or debited to the revaluation reserve.[141] The Act is not explicit as to the treatment of the diminutions but their exclusion from the surpluses or deficits on revaluation does suggest that they should be accounted for as are other permanent diminutions on fixed assets— through the profit and loss account. In our view this treatment is only acceptable if there is a revaluation reserve relating to the same asset sufficient to cover all of the deficit. If it is insufficient then in our view it is inappropriate as it is not consistent with the accounting concept of prudence not to provide for at least that part below depreciated historical cost in the profit and loss account.

Method (ii), i.e. the downward movement is split, with previous valuations being reversed while the deficit below depreciated historical cost is charged to the profit and loss account. The proponents of this approach argue that the amount charged in the profit and loss account for the permanent diminution should be the same as if the asset had never been revalued previously. As indicated in Example 10.5 above if this method is adopted for revaluation deficits then there is no need to consider whether the deficit is temporary or permanent in nature—the treatment is the same.

Method (iii), i.e. the whole deficit is charged to the profit and loss account; any previous revaluation above cost is dealt with as a reserve movement. The proponents of this approach argue that the provision for such a diminution in value is effectively an acceleration of depreciation and, therefore, should be accounted for in the same way as depreciation on a revalued asset (see 5.10 below). This was the approach proposed in ED 37 but was dropped from the final version of the standard.

We consider that either method (ii) or (iii) is acceptable but whichever method is adopted should be consistent with the accounting policy adopted for the disposal of revalued assets (see 5.11 below).

5.10 Depreciation of revalued assets

As indicated in 3.5.7 above depreciation is to be based on the revalued amount and the remaining life of the asset at the time of the valuation. The estimated residual value to be taken into account should be based on prices prevailing at the date of the valuation.[142]

SSAP 12 then requires the whole of the depreciation charge to be passed through the profit and loss account.[143] This represents an amendment to the original SSAP in order to outlaw the practice of 'split depreciation', whereby depreciation in the balance sheet was based on the asset's carrying amount but only the portion that related to depreciation on historical cost was passed through the profit and loss account; the balance being charged directly to the revaluation reserve.

This practice of split depreciation may be argued to be permitted by the Companies Act (whether by accident or design) as the depreciation rules require that the provision be based on the carrying amount but does not specify that the whole charge must pass through the profit and loss account.[144]

Nobes states that the arguments in favour of split depreciation are:

(a) a consistent charge for depreciation can be maintained over the life of an asset, irrespective of ad hoc revaluations;

(b) connected to this, the depreciation charge is more objective than if it can be drastically altered at the whim of management;

(c) the total charge against profit over the life of an asset is its cost, whereas with revalued depreciation the charge exceeds cost.[145]

Split depreciation is also consistent with the usual treatment of diminutions in value of revalued assets, where only that part of the diminution below depreciated historical cost is passed through the profit and loss account.

Although the standard prohibits the practice of split depreciation, it does not make any reference to the accounting treatment of the revaluation reserve relating to the asset which is being depreciated. The possible treatments are considered in the following example:

Example 10.6

On January 1, 19X1 a company acquires an asset for £1,000. The asset has an economic life of ten years and is depreciated on a straight line basis. The residual value is assumed to be £nil. At December 31, 19X4 the asset is valued at £1,200. The company accounts for the revaluation using method (i) illustrated in Example 10.4 above. Accordingly, £600 is credited to the revaluation reserve. At December 31, 19X4 the economic life of the asset is considered to be the remainder of its original life, i.e. six years, and its residual value is still considered to be £nil. In the year ended December 31, 19X5 and later years depreciation charged to the profit and loss account is £200 p.a. The possible treatments for the revaluation reserve are as follows:

(i) retain at £600.
This will result in a revaluation reserve being maintained indefinitely even after the asset ceases to exist, which does not seem sensible, unless the objective of revaluing assets is regarded as a means of retaining funds for the replacement, in which case, this should be accomplished in a systematic way, not by an occasional and voluntary programme of revaluations. As indicated in 3.2 above retention of funds for replacement is not the objective of depreciation. This treatment should only be used if the financial statements are being prepared under the current cost convention.

(ii) transfer £100 p.a. from the revaluation reserve to the profit and loss account in arriving at the pre-tax profit or loss.
This treatment is based on para. 34(4) of Sch. 4 of the Companies Act which allows amounts to be transferred to the profit and loss account if the amount has previously been charged there or is a realised profit. A transfer is possible because the amount of £100 is a realised profit in terms of s 275(2) of the Companies Act. However, this treatment has a similar effect to 'split depreciation' although no part of the depreciation charge is being set *directly* against reserves. We believe that such a treatment offends the spirit of SSAP 12 and is not to be recommended.

(iii) transfer £100 p.a. from the revaluation reserve to the profit and loss account after arriving at the profit or loss for the financial year.
This is a variant of method (ii) above. It does not, however, offend the spirit of SSAP 12 because the profit or loss for the financial year is arrived at after deducting a depreciation charge based on the carrying amount of the asset.

(iv) transfer £100 p.a. from the revaluation reserve to retained profits within the reserves note.
This is very similar to method (iii), the only difference being where the transfer is shown. It could be argued that such a treatment is not in accordance with the Companies Act since the profit and loss account is required to show any amount withdrawn or proposed to be withdrawn from reserves.[146] However, it would appear that in practice many companies do adopt such an approach.[147]

For the reasons mentioned above we recommend that companies adopt either method (iii) or method (iv).

5.11   Disposal of revalued assets

When a revalued asset is disposed of, the profit or loss recorded in the profit and loss account can be based either on the carrying amount in the balance sheet, with the revaluation surplus on that asset transferred as a reserve movement to realised reserves, or on the depreciated historical cost, in which case the revaluation surplus is treated as part of the calculation of profit on disposal.

The following example illustrates these alternative treatments:

Example 10.7

The asset which was revalued at £1,200 in Example 10.6 above is sold for £1,300 on December 31, 19X6. The annual depreciation charge for 19X5 and 19X6 is £200 and the company has made an annual transfer from revaluation reserve to realised reserves of £100, which represents the annual depreciation on the revaluation surplus. The disposal is treated as part of the ordinary activities of the company and for the purposes of this example taxation has been ignored. The carrying value and the depreciated historical cost of the asset at the date of sale are as follows:

	Carrying value £	Historical cost £
Cost or valuation		
At December 31, 19X6	1,200	1,000
Depreciation		
At January 1, 19X6	200	500
Charge for year	200	100
At December 31, 19X6	400	600
Net book value at December 31, 19X6	800	400

The profit on disposal based on the balance sheet carrying value is £500; based on depreciated original cost it is £900.

	(i) £	(ii) £
Profit on trading activities	1,000	1,000
Profit on sale of revalued asset	500	900
Retained profit for the financial year	1,500	1,900
Retained profits		
Opening balance	6,000	6,000
Retained profit for the financial year	1,500	1,900
Transfer from revaluation reserve—realised on sale	400	—
Transfer from revaluation reserve—depreciation	100	100
Closing balance	8,000	8,000

Revaluation reserve

Opening balance	500	500
Transfer to profit and loss account—realised on sale	—	(400)
Transfer to retained profits—realised on sale	(400)	—
Transfer to retained profits—depreciation	(100)	(100)
Closing balance	—	—

(i) based on carrying value.

This is the approach suggested by ED 16[148] and the ASC's discussion papers on 'extraordinary items and prior year adjustments'[149] and 'depreciation'.[150] It can be seen that this method in accounting for the gain or loss on sale of the asset is consistent with those methods which are recommended and normally used by companies in dealing with any excess depreciation resulting from the revaluation of assets in that the amount included in the profit and loss account is based on the carrying amount.

(ii) based on depreciated historical cost.

This is based on the contention that there is no reason why two companies which undertake the same transactions should report different profits and earnings per share simply because one of them has revalued its assets between the dates the assets are purchased and sold. This is the approach suggested by ED 36 (see 5.1.2 above).

As noted in 5.1.2 above, the approach suggested by ED 36, i.e. that the profit or loss on disposal be calculated by reference to depreciated original cost, was not repeated in the revised SSAP 6 nor has it been included in any subsequent exposure draft or accounting standard. As a result, both of the above methods are acceptable treatments and this is, therefore, another area of accounting where there is no consistency between companies.

However, there does appear to be a move by companies towards adopting method (ii) above, i.e. basing the gain or loss on disposal on the depreciated historical cost of the asset. This is exemplified by Sears PLC, who have recently switched to this method, treating it as a change in policy giving rise to a prior year adjustment as indicated below:

Extract 10.22: Sears PLC [151]

Fixed assets and depreciation [extract]
(a) Tangible assets
The surplus or deficit arising on a disposal of property represents the difference between the depreciated original cost and the net proceeds and is dealt with through the profit and loss account. This represents a change in accounting policy; prior year figures have been amended to the same basis and profits before taxation in 1985/86 have been increased by £1.6 million.

5.12　Other uses of the revaluation reserve

We have seen in 5.8.2, 5.9, 5.10 and 5.11 above that there are occasions when revaluation surpluses taken to the revaluation reserve may be reduced. These all related to accounting for revalued assets generally. Are there any other situations in which the revaluation reserve may be reduced? As indicated in 5.13 below amounts credited to revaluation reserve represent unrealised profits and, as such, are unavailable for distribution. However, the revaluation reserve may be used to pay up bonus shares as long as this is not forbidden by the company's articles.

It would appear from the legislation that the revaluation reserve should not be reduced in any other circumstance. It is widely considered that it may not be used to write off goodwill, either goodwill that has arisen in the single company or on consolidation. This was the view taken by the Department of Trade and Industry (DTI) when examination of the issue was necessitated by the implementation of SSAP 22. The requirement in SSAP 22 that goodwill arising on consolidation be written off or amortised led some companies to seek to use the revaluation reserve for this purpose. In the DTI's consultative paper issued in April 1986, it was stated that the revaluation reserve should only be reduced by amounts that are no longer necessary for the valuation accounting policies of the company, not any accounting policy of the company.[152] The DTI's argument is based on the relevant Article in the Fourth Directive, from which the Schedule 4 rules are derived and where the position is much more clear. Article 33(2)(c) notes that 'the revaluation reserve must be reduced to the extent that the amounts transferred thereto are no longer necessary for the implementation of the valuation method used and the achievement of its purpose', i.e. the revaluation reserve can only be used in connection with accounting policies that relate to revaluations.[153]

However, although the intention of the legislators was clear, the resulting legislation is ambiguous and the issue has never been resolved by the courts. This uncertainty has meant that some companies have used the revaluation reserve to write off consolidation goodwill (see Extract 4.19 in Chapter 4 for an example of a company adopting such a treatment). This issue is likely to be resolved as the recent Companies Bill intends to amend the provisions so that the revaluation reserve can only be reduced 'to the extent that the amounts transferred to it are no longer necessary for the purposes of the valuation method used' or on capitalisation.[154]

Where the revaluation reserve has been used for another purpose such as writing off goodwill or making a bonus issue then consideration has to be given as to what effect this has on the accounting issues dealt with in 5.8.2, 5.9, 5.10 and 5.11 above.

In the former situation we see no reason why companies should not continue to adopt such treatments as they would have adopted if the goodwill had not been written off against the revaluation reserve; effectively treating the reserve in gross terms as being a revaluation surplus net of cumulative goodwill write-offs. This may result in the reserve becoming a debit balance and assuming the appearance of a 'goodwill write-off reserve'. This would appear to be the approach adopted by Grand Metropolitan Public Limited Company (see Extracts 4.19 and 4.20 of Chapter 4).

Where, however, the reserve has been reduced by making a bonus issue further problems arise. To the extent that the revaluation reserve no longer exists, it could be argued that such amount can no longer be used for making any transfers which a company normally makes between revaluation reserve and retained profits (or to profit and loss account in respect of disposals, if this is the case) or for writing off that part of a permanent diminution in the value of an asset which the company could have charged to revaluation reserve. If all of the revaluation reserve has been capitalised then no such transfers or write-offs could be made. In most situations only some of the reserve will have been capitalised and, therefore, under this approach it will be necessary either to:

(a)   decide that specific revaluation surpluses have been capitalised and, therefore, no transfers or write-offs can be made in respect of the assets to which the surpluses related. However, transfers and write-offs in respect of other assets can continue;

(b)   decide that a proportion of each revaluation surplus has been capitalised and, therefore, a proportion still remains. Accordingly, a proportion of the amount of the transfers or write-offs which would have been made can be made;

(c)   continue to make the transfers or write-offs until the remaining surplus has been extinguished.

All three methods are probably acceptable.

Another approach altogether is to regard the fact that part of the revaluation reserve has been capitalised as being irrelevant and continue to make the transfers or write-offs as normal. This was effectively the approach suggested by ED 36 in accounting for the disposal of previously revalued assets. Paragraph 26 of the exposure draft stated 'The standard requires that, on the disposal of a previously revalued asset, any previously unrealised surplus on the revaluation of the asset should be included in the profit and loss account for the year. Where the revaluation reserve is insufficient to make this transfer to profit for the year, because it has previously been capitalised to make a bonus issue of shares, to achieve this it will be necessary to make an appropriation or transfer from other available reserves to revaluation reserve to make up the shortfall.' Such an approach may be appropriate where a company adopts method (ii) in Example 10.7 at 5.11 above, i.e. basing the gain or loss on disposal on the depreciated historical cost of the asset. However, it does not seem a sensible approach if a company generally transfers amounts from revaluation reserve to retained profits because they would probably just be transferring amounts from retained profits to revaluation reserve with a view to transferring them back again.

5.13   Distributable profits and revaluations of fixed assets

A revaluation surplus is not a realised profit and may only be transferred to the profit and loss account on realisation.[155] It is not available for distribution.[156]

In order to determine a company's profits available for distribution all provisions of the type mentioned in paragraphs 88 and 89 of Schedule 4 to the Companies Act, i.e. provisions for depreciation or diminution in value of assets and provisions for liabilities, are normally to be treated as realised losses.[157] This means that even where a temporary diminution in value of a fixed asset has been taken to revaluation reserve then as the loss is defined by reference to the provision against the asset, not the reserve to which it has been written off, such a loss will normally be regarded as a realised loss. However, an exception is made for a provision in respect of a diminution in value of a fixed asset appearing on a revaluation of *all* of the fixed assets other than goodwill of the company.[158]

The directors are not required to formally revalue all fixed assets and incorporate these revaluations into the financial statements in order to take advantage of the exception; the value only has to be 'considered', and this does not imply that the book amount of the asset has to be altered.[159] The Act states that fixed assets that have not actually been revalued are to be treated as if they had, if the directors are satisfied that the aggregate value of all fixed assets is not less than the amount at which they are currently stated in the company's accounts.[160] Thus a downward valuation of a fixed asset need not be treated as a realised loss if the directors are satisfied that the company's fixed assets are worth, in total, not less than their net book value.

This exception can only be taken if the following note disclosure is made:[161]

(a)   that the directors have considered the value of some of the fixed assets of the company, without actually revaluing those assets;

(b)   that they are satisfied that the aggregate value of those assets at the time in question is or was not less than the aggregate amount at which they are being stated in the company's accounts; and

(c)   that the relevant items are accordingly stated in the relevant accounts on the basis that a revaluation of all of the company's fixed assets which was deemed to have taken place included the assets that have suffered a diminution in value.

It is emphasised that the note must be repeated in subsequent financial statements for as long as advantage is to be taken of the exemption as these may become 'relevant accounts', i.e. those on which a distribution is to be based.[162]

One company which has given such disclosure is Edinburgh Financial Trust plc as shown in the following extract:

Extract 10.23: EFT Group plc[163]

11. Investments, Subsidiaries and Related Companies [extract]
The company's investment holding portfolio was valued at 31 December 1988 at market value in the case of listed investments and at directors' valuation in the case of unlisted investments. The remaining fixed assets of the company, its investments in subsidiary and related companies, have not been revalued in the accounts, but the directors consider that their aggregate value at 31 December 1988 was not less than the net book value shown in the accounts.

5.14   Comparison with US and IASC pronouncements

5.14.1 US

Under usual conditions, revaluations of fixed assets are not permitted in US financial statements. In APB 6 it is stated: 'Property, plant and equipment should not be written up by an entity to reflect appraisal, market or current values which are above cost to the entity.'[164]

5.14.2   IASC

A   General

IAS 16 covers property, plant and equipment carried at revalued amounts. Revaluations of fixed asset investments are dealt with in IAS 25.

Both of these standards differ from UK requirements in that they require a more systematic approach to revaluations. IAS 16 requires that an entire class of assets be selected for revaluation, or the selection of assets for revaluation be made on a systematic basis. This basis should be disclosed.[165] The requirements of IAS 16 in respect of diminutions in value are considered below.

In the case of investments, there must be a policy for the frequency of revaluations, which should be disclosed, and an entire category of long-term investments should be revalued at the same time.[166]

B   Diminutions in value

IAS 16 requires that a decrease in the net carrying amount of property, plant and equipment arising from a revaluation of assets should be charged directly to income except to the extent that such a decrease is related to an increase which was previously recorded as a credit to revaluation surplus and which has not been subsequently reversed or utilised, it should be charged directly to that account.[167]

It is not clear whether the related increase against which deficits may be taken must be on the same asset or on, for example, the same class of asset (the SSAP 19 approach—see 2.3 of Chapter 11).The situation with regard to investments is different in that IAS 25 on accounting for investments is unambiguous: deficits may be only charged against surpluses previously credited on the same investment (see 4.2 (c) of Chapter 11).

If a revalued item of property, plant and equipment suffers a permanent impairment in value, IAS 16 requires its net carrying amount to be reduced to recoverable amount.[168] The standard does not clearly prescribe the accounting treatment; the two alternatives that would appear to comply involve taking the whole deficit through the profit and loss account or following the accounting treatment for downward valuations outlined above.

IAS 25 requires that a provision for temporary diminution in value of an investment be debited to the profit and loss account unless the investment was previously carried at valuation. Therefore, a treatment permitted under UK law and accounting practice, to offset temporary diminutions in the revaluation reserve against surpluses on other revalued items, conflicts with the requirements of the international standard.

C   IAS E32

The IASC has recently issued an exposure draft, E32 — *Comparability of Financial Statements* — which proposes to amend, inter alia, the requirements of IAS 16 and IAS 25. The main change to IAS 16 is that the preferred treatment for property, plant and equipment is that they should be carried at amounts based on historical cost, although revaluations will still be allowed as an alternative treatment, provided that certain additional information is disclosed.[169] The only change to the provisions dealing with the accounting for revaluations of such assets is that revaluation surpluses which relate to assets where a revaluation deficit has previously been charged to income must now be credited to income (and not to revaluation reserve as presently allowed).[170]

The exposure draft also proposes to change IAS 25 such that the preferred treatment for long-term investments and investment properties is that they should be carried at amounts based on historical cost, although revaluations will still be allowed as an alternative treatment, provided additional information is given.[171] The only change to the provisions dealing with the accounting for revaluations of such assets is that on disposal of a revalued asset any revaluation surplus remaining in the revaluation reserves relating to the disposed asset should be transferred to retained earnings (and not to income as presently allowed).[172]

6 DISCLOSURE

6.1 Introduction

The disclosure requirements are contained in the Companies Act and in accounting standards. In discussing these requirements, they are dealt with in the order in which they are usually encountered in a company's annual report: directors' report, balance sheet and profit and loss account, accounting policies and notes to the accounts. The additional disclosure requirements for revalued amounts are dealt with in 6.1.5 below.

6.1.1 Directors' report

If any significant changes to the fixed assets of the company or any subsidiary have occurred during the year, particulars of the change are to be given in the directors' report.[173] As the term 'fixed assets' also includes intangibles and investments (see 6.1.2 below) then particulars of changes in these items are required; it is not just changes in *tangible* fixed assets that have to be covered.

It is common and acceptable for this to take the form of a cross reference to the notes to the financial statements as illustrated below:

Extract 10.24: Blue Circle Industries PLC[174]

FIXED ASSETS
 The Directors consider that the market value of the Group's property interests significantly exceeds the value included in the Balance Sheet.
 Movements in tangible fixed assets are shown in Note 11 to the Accounts and Investments in Note 12.

Such an approach will normally only disclose the nature of the assets which have changed because of the categorisation of the fixed assets within the notes. Some companies will, therefore, expand on the statement to give an explanation of the movements along the lines of the following extract:

Extract 10.25: Ladbroke Group PLC[175]

FIXED ASSETS
Changes in fixed assets during the year are shown in notes 10 to 13 on pages 42 to 45 and
include the purchases of Hilton International Co. and a strategically important chain of
off-track betting units in London. Also included are the sales of the group's holiday centres,
its retail catering businesses, two of its publishing businesses, its 20% shareholding in
Central Independent Television PLC, a number of UK hotels, and Rodeway Inns, the North
American hotel franchise company. Since the year end the group has purchased the remaining
75% interest in 3 of its UK hotels and has disposed of its health and leisure operation in
Scotland and its remaining publishing business.

The market value of 'interests in land' (taken to mean land and buildings)[176]
should also be disclosed if it differs substantially from the amount at which the
assets are carried in the balance sheet and if, in the directors' opinion, the
difference is of such significance that it should be brought to the attention of the
members or debenture holders. The difference should be quantified 'with such
degree of precision as is practicable'.[177]

In some cases, companies do not quantify the difference (see, for example,
Extract 10.24 above); in others, they explain that they cannot quantify the
difference, as shown in the following extract:

Extract 10.26: Sears PLC [178]

Properties
In the opinion of the directors the current market values of the group's properties exceed
the amounts at which they are stated in the balance sheet. In the absence of a full
valuation the excess cannot at present be quantified and the directors have commissioned
a professional valuation of the properties as at January 1988.

However, in the following year Sears PLC did quantify the difference:

Extract 10.27: Sears PLC [179]

Properties
The majority of the group's properties were professionally valued as at 31st January
1988. Freehold properties, and leaseholds having unexpired terms exceeding 25 years,
have been included in the balance sheet at their revalued amounts and the net
surplus amounting to £312.4 million has been added to reserves. A surplus of £83 million
on leaseholds expiring within 25 years has not been taken up in these accounts.

It can be seen that in addition to disclosing the difference in value, information
regarding the surpluses incorporated into the accounts was also given, although
this is not strictly required by the Act.

6.1.2 *Balance sheet and profit and loss account*

There are various statutory disclosures with regard to the balance sheet and profit and loss account.

The statutory formats require that fixed assets be disclosed under the following headings:[180]

I	Intangible assets
	1. Development costs
	2. Concessions, patents, licences, trademarks, and similar rights and assets
	3. Goodwill
	4. Payments on account

II	Tangible assets
	1. Land and buildings
	2. Plant and machinery
	3. Fixtures, fittings, tools and equipment
	4. Payments on account and assets in course of construction

III	Investments
	1. Shares in group companies
	2. Loans to group companies
	3. Shares in related companies
	4. Loans to related companies
	5. Other investments other than loans
	6. Other loans
	7. Own shares

Companies' financial statements usually include only the net book amounts of intangible and tangible assets and investments on the face of the balance sheet, with the information required by the Arabic numerals relegated to the notes.

As is permitted by the Act, the format categories with Arabic numerals are frequently modified to suit the circumstances of the business. Allied-Lyons PLC, for example, have two main categories of 'industrial properties and production facilities' and 'licensed and other properties'. The former is analysed between 'properties', 'plant and machinery' and 'vehicles, casks and sundry equipment'; the latter between 'properties' and 'furniture, fittings and equipment'.[181]

If profit and loss account Formats 2 or 4 are chosen, then 'depreciation and other amounts written off tangible and intangible fixed assets' must be shown, either on the face of the profit and loss account or in the notes.[182]

If Formats 1 or 3 are chosen, the equivalent information must be given in the notes to the accounts.[183]

If a provision for permanent diminution in value of any fixed asset has been made then it must be disclosed in the notes to the accounts if it is not shown in the profit and loss account.[184]

6.1.3 *Accounting policies*

SSAP 12 requires that disclosure be made, for each major class of depreciable asset, of the depreciation method used and the useful economic lives or the depreciation rates used.[185] This information is usually given in the accounting policies.

Certain categories of asset, for example plant and machinery, will probably include items depreciated at a variety of rates. It is usual to disclose a range of lives and/or rates in order to satisfy the disclosure requirements.

Extract 10.28: Bass PLC [186]

FIXED ASSETS AND DEPRECIATION

i) Intangible assets
a) These comprise betting and bingo licences, relating to properties in which the Group has an interest, and are valued annually by the Group's professional staff at their current value to the business. Surpluses arising from such valuations are taken direct to revaluation reserve.
b) These licences are not depreciated.
c) No value is attributed to trademarks, concessions, patents and similar rights and assets, including hotel franchises and management contracts, whether purchased or created by the Group.

ii) Tangible assets
a) Expenditure on additions and improvements to tangible fixed assets is capitalised for major projects on the basis of measured work completed, for other property projects on the basis of orders placed, and for all other expenditure as incurred.
b) Surpluses arising from time to time from professional valuations of properties are taken direct to revaluation reserve. Valuation surpluses realised on sale are transferred from revaluation reserve to profit.
c) Freehold land is not depreciated.
d) Freehold properties comprising hotels and United Kingdom public houses are maintained, as a matter of company policy, by a programme of repair and refurbishment such that the residual values of these properties taken as a whole are at least equal to their book values. Having regard to this, it is the opinion of the directors that depreciation of any such property as required by the Companies Act 1985 and standard accounting practice would not be material.
e) Other freehold properties are written off over 50 years, except breweries and maltings which are written off over 25 years, from the later of the date of acquisition or latest valuation.
f) Leasehold hotels and United Kingdom public houses are amortised over the unexpired term of the lease when less than 100 years.
g) Other leasehold properties are written off either over the periods as in (e) above or the term of the lease, whichever is the shorter.
h) Cost of plant, machinery, fixtures, fittings, tools and equipment (owned or leased) is spread, by equal annual instalments, over the estimated useful lives of the relevant assets, namely:

	Years
Plant and machinery	4-20
Equipment in retail outlets	3-10
Vehicles	3-10
Aircraft	16-20

The life of moveable plant and machinery is pro-rated for double-shift working.

iii) Investments
Fixed asset investments are stated at cost less any provision for diminution in value.

6.1.4 Notes to the financial statements

The note disclosures with regard to cost and depreciation of fixed assets are based on the requirements of the Companies Act and SSAP 12. The requirements of the Act cover all fixed assets; SSAP 12 excludes investments and some intangibles (see 3.5.1 above). For each of the categories of fixed asset shown in the statutory formats (see 6.1.2 above) the Companies Act requires the following to be disclosed:

(a)   the appropriate amounts at the beginning of the financial year and as at the balance sheet date, based either on historical cost (purchase price or production cost) or alternative accounting rules;[187]

(b)   all movements during the year, including revaluation surpluses and deficits, acquisitions, disposals and transfers.[188]

       Other movements that might also be reflected in the carrying value of the asset, such as exchange differences, will also be disclosed in the note;

(c)   the cumulative amount of depreciation as at the beginning and end of the financial year on the appropriate basis of cost or valuation, the depreciation charge for the period and adjustments in respect of disposals or for other reasons.[189]

In addition to the information noted in 6.1.3 above, SSAP 12 requires that, for each major class of depreciable asset, the following is disclosed:

(a)   total depreciation charged for the period;[190]

(b)   the gross amount of depreciable assets and the related accumulated depreciation.[191]

Companies will generally comply with these requirements by including separate notes for each major category of fixed asset; i.e. intangible fixed assets, tangible fixed assets and investments. An example of such a note for tangible fixed assets is illustrated below:

Extract 10.29: Bass PLC[192]

11 TANGIBLE FIXED ASSETS [extract]

	Breweries and other industrial properties	Licensed and un- licensed properties	Plant and machinery	Fixtures fittings, tools and equipment	Group total	Com- pany total
a)Movements during the year £m	**£m**	**£m**	**£m**	**£m**	**£m**	**£m**
Cost or valuation						
At 30th September 1987	197.6	1,958.7	401.5	503.0	3,060.8	16.6
Exchange and other adjustments	(.2)	(10.6)	(1.0)	(2.5)	(14.3)	—
Revaluation of investment properties	—	1.1	—	—	1.1	—
Expenditure	11.0	303.1	57.9	156.9	528.9	5.9
Disposals	(4.4)	(55.3)	(135.6)	(60.2)	(255.5)	(3.5)
At 30th September 1988	204.0	2,197.0	322.8	597.2	3,321.0	19.0
Depreciation						
At 30th September 1987	7.0	12.7	161.4	184.7	365.8	5.9
Exchange and other adjustments	(.2)	(.5)	(.2)	(.6)	(1.5)	—
Of subsidiaries acquired	—	.1	.2	5.2	5.5	—
Provided for the year	4.7	9.7	32.7	67.9	115.0	2.9
On disposals	(.2)	(.6)	(35.9)	(36.9)	(73.6)	(.5)
At 30th September 1988	11.3	21.4	158.2	220.3	411.2	8.3
Net book value at 30th September 1988	192.7	2,175.6	164.6	376.9	2,909.8	10.7
at 30th September 1987	190.6	1,946.0	240.1	318.3	2,695.0	10.7
DEPRECIABLE ASSETS At 30th September 1988 the cost or valuation of depreciable assets included above is	173.3	423.3	322.8	597.2	1,517.0	19.0

It can be seen from the above extract that Bass PLC has given separate disclosure of the gross amount of depreciable assets as required by SSAP 12 (the related accumulated depreciation is effectively given in the table). In many cases, such information will not be presented directly but can be inferred from the disclosures of the totals of assets and the cost of revalued assets as most items will be depreciable. Where this latter approach is taken it will be necessary to disclose the amount of freehold land included in land and buildings so that the depreciable amount, i.e. that relating to the buildings, can be deduced as illustrated below:

Extract 10.30: Argyll Group PLC[193]

11.0 Tangible Fixed Assets [extract]
Of the total amount of land and buildings, £104,675,000 represents land not subject to depreciation (1987 — £72,170,000).

As indicated earlier the disclosures required by the Companies Act also have to be given for investments; this can become quite complicated particularly where a company has associated (or related) companies. One approach is that of The Plessey Company plc as shown below:

Extract 10.31: The Plessey Company plc[194]

13 Investments—Other [extract]	Related companies £m	Group Other invest- ments £m	Total £m	Sub- sidiaries £m	Company Other invest- ments £m	Total £m
Shares at cost						
At beginning of year	23.1	3.3	26.4	194.3	0.1	194.4
Currency translation	2.2	0.5	2.7	19.9	—	19.9
Additions	0.7	—	0.7	73.8	0.8	74.6
Disposals	—	—	—	46.9	—	46.9
At end of year	21.6	2.8	24.4	201.3	0.9	202.2
Loans						
At beginning of year	—	0.3	0.3	260.0	0.3	260.3
Currency translation	—	—	—	1.7	—	1.7
Advanced during year	6.5	—	6.5	0.7	—	0.7
Repaid during year	0.2	0.3	0.5	123.1	0.3	123.4
At end of year	6.3	—	6.3	135.9	—	135.9
Amounts written off						
At beginning of year	21.2	0.1	21.3	0.4	0.1	0.5
Currency translation	2.1	—	2.1	—	—	—
Written off during year	4.9	—	4.9	—	—	—
At end of year	24.0	0.1	24.1	0.4	0.1	0.5
Post acquisition reserves						
At beginning of year	8.7		8.7			
Currency translation	1.5		1.5			
Retained for year	4.2		4.2			
At end of year	11.4		11.4			
Net book values						
At beginning of year	10.6	3.5	14.1	453.9	0.3	454.2
At end of year	15.3	2.7	18.0	336.8	0.8	337.6

It can be seen from the above extract that provisions (i.e. amounts written off) have been deducted from the total of shares and loans of each category of investment. A strict interpretation of the Companies Act would require provisions to be deducted separately from shares and loans. However, in practice, where a company has shares in, and loans to, the same company it will generally regard these as one investment; any provision which is necessary will be made against the total investment. One company which has made an allocation of the provision is Courtaulds plc as illustrated in the following extract:

Extract 10.32: Courtaulds plc[195]

14 INVESTMENTS HELD AS FIXED ASSETS [extract]

GROUP	Related Companies Shares £m	Loans £m	Other Shares £m	Total £m
Cost or amount under equity method of accounting				
At 31 March 1987	29.8	2.3	2.6	34.7
Exchange adjustments	(3.3)	(0.1)	(0.1)	(3.5)
Additions	0.2	0.1	1.6	1.9
Disposals	—	(1.3)	(0.1)	(1.4)
Retained profits of related companies	6.5	—	—	6.5
At 31 March 1988	33.2	1.0	4.0	38.2
Provisions				
At 31 March 1987	3.4	0.3	1.8	5.5
Movement in year	0.8	—	(0.1)	0.7
At 31 March 1988	4.2	0.3	1.7	6.2
Net book amount				
At 31 March 1988	29.0	0.7	2.3	32.0
At 31 March 1987	26.4	2.0	0.8	29.2

Shares in related companies include £21.1m in respect of the Group's share of post acquisition retained profits of those companies. The Group's share of net tangible assets amounts to £29.0m.

COMPANY	Group Shares £m	Companies Loans £m	Related Companies Shares £m	Other Shares £m	Total £m
Cost					
At 31 March 1987	238.1	228.9	0.4	0.9	468.3
Additions	149.6	13.2	—	1.3	164.1
Disposals	(0.8)	—	—	—	(0.8)
At 31 March 1988	386.9	242.1	0.4	2.2	631.6
Provisions					
At 31 March 1988 and 31 March 1987	—	—	—	0.7	0.7
Net book amount					
At 31 March 1988	386.9	242.1	0.4	1.5	630.9
At 31 March 1987	238.1	228.9	0.4	0.2	467.6

SSAP 12 also requires that where there has been a change in the depreciation method used, the effect, if material, should be disclosed in the year of change.

The reasons for the change should also be disclosed.[196] An example of such disclosure is shown below:

Extract 10.33: Rolls-Royce plc[197]

Depreciation [extract]
Depreciation is provided on the original cost of plant and equipment and is calculated on the straight line basis over the estimated lives in the range 5 to 25 years (1986 5 to 14 years).

Book values of plant and equipment at December 31, 1986, including those for assets which were fully depreciated at that date, have not been restated; these values are being written off over the revised remaining lives of the assets concerned.

The effect of implementing the 1987 revision of Statement of Standard Accounting Practice No. 12 has been to increase profit before taxation by £10m.

The Companies Act also requires the carrying amount of 'land and buildings' to be analysed between that held under freehold and long and short leaseholds.[198] Long leases are those with more than 50 years unexpired as at the balance sheet date.[199] This is normally achieved either by splitting the 'land and buildings' category in the fixed asset note into the three sub-categories or by making separate note disclosure as illustrated in the following extract:

Extract 10.34: Cadbury Schweppes p.l.c.[200]

13 TANGIBLE FIXED ASSETS [extract]

	GROUP		COMPANY	
	1987	1986	**1987**	1986
Land and buildings	**£ m**	£m	**£ m**	£m
Freehold	**148.3**	142.4	**28.2**	28.4
Long leasehold	**19.8**	17.8	**11.6**	11.4
Short leasehold	**5.2**	5.4	**0.4**	0.4
Net book value	**173.3**	165.6	**40.2**	40.2

6.1.5 Additional disclosures for items carried at valuation

The Companies Act requires that where assets have been included in the accounts at amounts based on a valuation then the items affected and the basis of valuation adopted should be disclosed in a note to the accounts.[201] In the case of each balance sheet item affected disclosure should be made of either:

(a) the comparable amounts based on historical costs; or

(b) the differences between the amounts in (a) above and the amounts actually included in the balance sheet.[202]

The comparable amounts are the gross amounts and cumulative provisions for depreciation or diminution in values and should relate to *all* of the assets covered by the balance sheet item.[203]

Most major companies would appear to adopt the former method of disclosure. A good example of disclosure is that of Blue Circle Industries PLC as illustrated below:

Extract 10.35: Blue Circle Industries PLC[204]

11 Tangible fixed assets [extract]

	Land and buildings			Plant and mach-inery £m	Assets under constr-uction £m	Total £m
	Freehold £m	Long lease £m	Short lease £m			
Group						
Net book value at 31 December 1987	260.4	7.8	5.6	521.5	33.8	829.1
Net book value at 31 December 1986	271.9	7.2	8.6	571.0	25.9	884.6
Historical cost at 31 December 1987	272.1	6.9	5.9	700.1	33.8	1018.8
Accumulated historical depreciation	46.8	1.1	2.1	230.2	—	280.2
Net historical cost at 31 December 1987	225.3	5.8	3.8	469.9	33.8	738.6

It can be seen from the above extract that almost all of the categories of tangible fixed assets have been affected by valuations and Blue Circle Industries PLC have, therefore, included the disclosure as part of their fixed asset table; in most situations, it will only be land and buildings which are affected by valuations and disclosure will generally be given by way of note.

Although the Act requires the amounts to be disclosed to be in respect of all the assets included in the balance sheet item affected by valuations some companies disclose the comparable historical cost information for only the assets which have been revalued. Where such an approach is taken then it is necessary to disclose the gross amount and accumulated depreciation for the revalued assets which are included in the balance sheet so that the total figures, in historical cost terms, can be deduced. This is shown in the following extract:

Extract 10.36: Imperial Chemical Industries PLC[205]

12 *TANGIBLE FIXED ASSETS* [extract]

| | GROUP | | | | COMPANY | | | |
| | Land and buildings | | Plant and equipment | | Land and buildings | | Plant and equipment | |
	1987 £m	1986 £m	1987 £m	1986 £m	1987 £m	1986 £m	1987 £m	1986 £m
Revalued assets included in tangible fixed assets:								
Revalued amount	187	219	232	233	45	46	78	81
Depreciation	64	64	169	177	39	40	72	74
Net book value	123	155	63	56	6	6	6	7
If the amount of these revalued assets had been determined according to historical cost accounting rules they would have been included at:								
Cost	86	92	201	208	30	32	49	51
Depreciation	43	47	165	184	27	28	46	47
Net book value	43	45	36	24	3	4	3	4

For all items (other than listed investments) that are carried at valuation, the Companies Act also requires the years in which the assets were valued and the amounts at which they were valued to be disclosed.[206] An example of this disclosure is given by the following extract from the notes to the financial statements of Blue Circle Industries PLC.

Extract 10.37: Blue Circle Industries PLC[207]

11 Tangible fixed assets [extract]

	Land and buildings			Plant and mach-inery £m	Assets under constr-uction £m	Total £m
	Freehold £m	Long lease £m	Short lease £m			
Analysis of gross book value at 31 December 1987						
Company: Valuation at 1 January 1979	116.8	0.5	5.3	156.1	—	278.7
At cost	73.3	1.1	1.0	300.9	15.9	392.2
	190.1	1.6	6.3	457.0	15.9	670.9
Subsidiaries:						
At valuation						
1974	0.4	—	—	—	—	0.4
1979	—	1.5	—	0.2	—	1.7
1980	2.7	—	0.1	10.3	—	13.1
1981	0.1	2.1	—	—	—	2.2
1984	—	—	0.2	—	—	0.2
1985	9.2	—	—	—	—	9.2
1987	3.5	—	—	34.2	—	37.7
At cost	107.9	3.6	2.1	268.4	17.9	399.9
	313.9	8.8	8.7	770.1	33.8	1135.3

The information shown in the above extract is generally the only information given by companies in respect of past valuations, notwithstanding the fact that, as mentioned earlier, the Companies Act also requires the basis of valuation to be disclosed. However, some companies do give more information than the statutory minimum, for example, by disclosing the names and professional qualifications of valuers in respect of valuations that took place in previous years, as illustrated in the following extract:

Extract 10.38: Sears PLC[208]

9. FIXED TANGIBLE ASSETS [extract]
The majority of the group's properties were professionally valued by Healey & Baker at 31st December 1982 or 31st January 1983, as appropriate in relation to the financial year end of subsidiary companies. The basis of valuation was open market value assuming vacant possession of those parts of the properties then occupied by the group. Completed overseas development properties held for investment were valued by Richard Ellis on the basis of open market value. Freeholds, and leaseholds neither expiring nor containing a rent review clause operative within twenty-five years of the date of valuation, are included at 1982/1983 valuations amounting to £451.8 million. The other leaseholds have been included at cost; the 1982/1983 valuations exceeded the book amount of those properties at 31st January 1983 by approximately £68 million. The remaining properties, mainly those of William Hill Organisation plc and Butler Shoe Corporation, were not revalued in 1982/83 and are included at cost.

Where fixed assets (other than investments) have been revalued during the year, then the Companies Act also requires disclosure of the names or qualifications of the persons making the valuation and the bases used by them.[209] An example of such disclosure is as follows:

Extract 10.39: The Peninsular and Oriental Steam Navigation Company[210]

13 Properties [extract]
The valuation of properties at 31 December 1987 were made on an open market value basis by Healey & Baker, totalling £484.4m, and by the group chief surveyor R A Knight FRICS, totalling £189.1m.

In addition, SSAP 12 requires, in the year of valuation, disclosure of the effect of the revaluation on the depreciation charge, if material.[211] Such disclosure is very rarely seen in practice. This could be due to the fact that most revaluations relate to property and, therefore, any effect is immaterial due to the long lives of the properties (if indeed depreciation is being charged at all on the properties).

The revaluation reserve itself should be included as a separate sub-heading in the position shown in the formats, but need not be so-called.[212] The treatment for tax purposes of amounts credited or debited to the revaluation reserve must be disclosed in a note to the accounts.[213]

References

1 CA 85, Sch. 4, para. 77.
2 The Companies Act uses the term 'related company'. For a definition of this expression, which is nearly synonymous with associated company, see CA 85, Sch. 4, para. 92. See also 5.2.2 of Chapter 4.
3 Ranks Hovis McDougall PLC, Annual Report and Accounts 1988, pp. 23 and 29.
4 TR 738: The ASC's provisional views on accounting for Intangible assets with particular reference to brands.
5 ARB No. 43, *Restatement and Revision of Accounting Research Bulletins*, Chapter 9 and ARB No. 44 (Revised), *Declining-balance Depreciation*.
6 SFAS 34, *Capitalization of Interest Cost.*
7 SFAS 67, *Accounting for Costs and Initial Rental Operations of Real Estate Projects.*
8 IAS 25, *Accounting for Investments.*
9 IAS 4, *Depreciation Accounting.*
10 CA 85, Sch. 4, para. 17.
11 *Ibid.*, para. 26(1).
12 *Ibid.*, para. 90.
13 SSAP 4, *The accounting treatment of government grants*, para. 9.
14 ED 43,
15 CA 85, Sch. 4, para. 5.
16 See M Renshall and K Walmsley (Ed.), *Butterworths Company Law Guide*, p. 293, para. 9.59.
17 CA 85, Sch. 4, paras. 26(2) and 26(3).
18 SSAP 9, *Stocks and long-term contracts*, para. 19.

19 *Ibid.*, Appendix 1, paras 4—7.
20 British Telecommunications plc, Report and accounts 1988, p. 30.
21 CA 85, Sch. 4, paras. 26(1) and (2).
22 These are the criteria given in SFAS 67, *Accounting for Costs and Initial Rental Operations of Real Estate Projects*, para. 4. While this standard is intended only to apply to the development of property for resale, these conditions are of general application.
23 CA 85, Sch. 4, para. 26(3).
24 Trusthouse Forte PLC, Report and Accounts 1988, p. 28.
25 IAS 16, *Accounting for Property, Plant and Equipment*, paras. 16 and 3.
26 SSAP 9, Appendix 1, para. 1.
27 IAS 16, para. 19.
28 *Ibid.*, para. 16.
29 SSAP 12, para. 10.
30 ASC, *Accounting for the effects of changing prices: a Handbook*, para. 3.8.
31 The definition ran (in part): ' depreciation is the measure of the wearing out, consumption *or other loss of value* of a fixed asset. . . ' Original SSAP 12, para. 15.
32 ARB 43, para. 7. Note that this consolidates the earlier ARB 33 that dates from 1947, but has not been superseded.
33 ASC, *A review of SSAP 12 — Accounting for depreciation*, paras. 3.1—3.4, 6.1—6.2 and 4.1—4.6.
34 CA 85, Sch. 4, para. 18.
35 *Ibid.*
36 *Ibid.*, para. 32.
37 SSAP 12, para. 15.
38 *Ibid.*, para. 16.
39 *Ibid.*, para. 17.
40 *Ibid.*, para. 18.
41 *Ibid.*, paras. 19 and 20.
42 *Ibid.*, para. 21.
43 *Ibid.*, para. 22.
44 *Ibid.*, paras. 23 and 24.
45 ED 37, *Accounting for depreciation*, para. 20.
46 Imperial Chemical Industries PLC, Annual Report 1987, p. 35.
47 Original SSAP 12, para. 4.
48 *Ibid.*
49 SSAP 12, para. 15.
50 Based on the accounts of the companies that were in the October, 1987, index.
51 The BOC Group plc, Report & Accounts 1988, p. 45.
52 See the SORP on accounting for oil and gas exploration and development activities, paras. 62—65 and 84—87.
53 The British Petroleum Company p.l.c., Annual Report and Accounts 1987, p. 32.
54 SSAP 12, para. 21.
55 SSAP 2, *Disclosure of accounting policies*, para. 13.
56 *Ibid.*, para. 16.
57 SSAP 6, paras. 31 and 39.
58 Bridport-Gundry plc, Report & Accounts 1986/7, p. 18.
59 Marks and Spencer p.l.c., 1988 Annual Report and Financial Statements, p. 42.
60 CA 85, Sch. 4, para. 25.
61 Cadbury Schweppes p.l.c., Annual Report 1987, p. 40.
62 Cadbury Schweppes p.l.c., Annual Report 1987, p. 46.

63 L.C.L. Skerratt and D.J.Tonkin (eds.), ICAEW, Financial Reporting 1987—1988, A Survey of UK Published Accounts, p. 183.

	large listed	medium listed	large unlisted	total
Number of companies	100	100	100	300
	%	%	%	%
Reason given for not depreciating:				
Depreciation not material	5	5	4	5
Frequently revalued	0	1	0	0
MV exceeds NBV	7	4	6	5
Maintenance standards high	2	5	4	4
No reason given	2	2	8	3
	16	16	22	17
Buildings depreciated	84	83	74	82
Buildings not material	0	1	4	1
	100	100	100	100

Notes:
1. This table includes companies for which only a specified part of their freehold or leasehold property is not depreciated.
2. Investment properties are not included within the scope of this table.

64 Grand Metropolitan Public Limited Company, Annual Report 1988, p. 34.

65 Allied-Lyons PLC, Report & Accounts 1988, p. 37.

66 ED 37, para. 25, stated, 'In certain very restricted instances it may not be appropriate to charge depreciation in respect of what would normally be a depreciable asset. This would arise only where the asset is maintained to such a standard that:
a) the estimated residual value is equal to or greater than its net book amount, or
b) its estimated useful economic life is either infinite or such that any depreciation charge would be insignificant.'

67 Technical Release 648, *Statement on the publication of SSAP 12 (Revised) Accounting for depreciation*, para. 10.

68 The Burton Group plc, Annual Report 1988, p. 44.

69 National Westminster Bank PLC, Annual Report and Accounts 1985, p. 38.

70 ARB 43, Chapter 9, para. 5.

71 These include ARB 43, Chapter 9A which discusses whether assets should be depreciated more quickly to compensate for inflation and rejects the idea, and a number of statements that deal with depreciation methods approved by the Internal Revenue and the timing differences that may result, including ARB 44 (Revised), APB 1 and paragraph 20 of APB 6.

72 SSAP 12, para. 20.

73 CA 85, Sch. 4, para. 19(2).

74 *Ibid.*, para. 19(3).

75 *Ibid.*, paras. 19(1) and (2). The use of the word 'shown' makes the wording ambiguous, but it is generally considered to mean that the provisions must be made through the profit and loss account and either disclosed on the face of the profit and loss account or in the notes to the accounts.

76 *Ibid.*, para. 19(1).

77 SSAP 12, para. 19.

78 *Ibid.*, para. 20.

79 *Ibid.*, para. 13.

80 See, for example, D. Egginton, *'When is a fixed asset overvalued?'*, Accountancy, September 1986, pp. 101 and 102. A small sample of nine public companies' accounts was examined.

These were submitted by their auditors because of problems of recoverable amount. In only two cases was a write down actually taken in the historical cost accounts. One company had written the assets in question down to zero for CCA purposes, yet apparently the issue of a historical cost impairment was not even discussed.

8 1 SORP on accounting for oil and gas exploration and development activities, para. 66.
8 2 *Ibid.*, para. 67.
8 3 SSAP 6, *Extraordinary items and prior year adjustments*, para. 11.
8 4 D. Foster, *Accounting Requirements — Law and Practice*, Butterworths Company Law Guide, p. 307, para. 9.97.
8 5 APB Statement No. 4, *Basic Concepts and Accounting Principles* para. 183 M-5C.
8 6 AICPA Accounting Standards Division's Task Force on Impairment of Value, *Accounting for the Inability to Fully Recover the Carrying Amounts of Long Lived Assets*, para. 42.
8 7 EITF Abstract Issue No. 84—28, *Impairment of Long-Lived Assets.*
8 8 IAS 16, para. 41.
8 9 L.C.L. Skerratt and D.J.Tonkin (eds.), ICAEW, Financial Reporting 1985—1986, A Survey of UK Published Accounts, p. 148.
9 0 L.C.L. Skerratt and D.J.Tonkin (eds.), ICAEW, Financial Reporting 1987—1988, A Survey of UK Published Accounts, p. 182.
9 1 English China Clays P.L.C., Annual Report & Accounts 1987, p. 19.
9 2 The BOC Group plc, Report & Accounts 1987, p. 25.
9 3 Pilkington plc, Annual Report for the year ended 31st March 1987, p. 38.
9 4 SSAP 12, para. 5.
9 5 J Sainsbury plc, Annual Report & Accounts 1988, p. 32.
9 6 The Dee Corporation PLC, Report and Accounts 1988, p. 53.
9 7 Tesco PLC, Annual Report and Accounts 1988.
9 8 ED 16, *Supplement to 'Extraordinary items and Prior Year Adjustments'*, paras. 13 and 14.
9 9 ASC Discussion Paper, *A review of SSAP 6 — Extraordinary items and prior year adjustments*, para. 2.11.
100 *Ibid.*, para. 2.12.
101 ED 36, *Extraordinary items and prior year adjustments*, para. 26.
102 CA 85, Sch. 4, para. 31(2).
103 *Ibid.*, para. 31(1).
104 *Ibid.*, para. 31(3).
105 SSAP 19, para. 11.
106 *Accounting for the effects of changing prices: a Handbook*, para. A1.35.
107 (S20) 2.205, *Valuation of company property assets and their disclosure in directors' reports or accounts of companies.*
108 RICS, Guidance Notes No. GN 1, para. 2.1.1.
109 *Ibid.*, No. GN 4, para 1.
110 *Ibid.*, No. GN 1, para. 2.1.2.
111 *Ibid.*, No. GN 1, para. 2.1.3.
112 *Ibid.*, Background Paper No BP 1.
113 Sears plc, Annual Report 1987/1988, p. 38.
114 See RICS, Guidance Notes Background Paper No. BP 7 for a discussion of valuations having regard to trading potential.
115 SSAP 22 recommends that the assets concerned should be disclosed separately and that the notes to the accounts make it clear that the practice has been followed and that the amount at which the assets are stated does not exceed their open market value. SSAP 22, para. 15.
116 These are items normally considered part of the building, e.g. wiring, gas mains, boilers and central heating systems, air conditioning, etc. See RICS, Guidance Notes 25, *passim.*
117 RICS, Guidance Notes Background Paper No. BP 7, para. 5.
118 Bass PLC, Annual Review 1987, pp. 34, 42 and 43.
119 See, for example, C. A. Westwick, *Property Valuations and Accounts*, p. 47.
120 R.I.C.S. Guidance Notes Background Paper No. BP 2, para. 2.

121 This is the basis of valuation suggested in *Accounting for the effects of changing prices: a Handbook*, para. A1.43. Other non-specific land and buildings should be valued taking account of the existing use, but the straightforward open market value, i.e. taking account of any alternative use, is appropriate for such assets.

122 Butterworths Company Law Guide, p. 314, para. 9.106.

123 *Accounting for the effects of changing prices: a Handbook*, paras. A1.3 and A1.4.

124 See *Accounting for the effects of changing prices: a Handbook*, paras. A1.37 and A1.38 and RICS, Guidance Notes Background Paper No BP 3 for a further discussion of depreciated replacement cost.

125 RICS, Guidance Notes Background Paper No. BP 3, para. 2.

126 Guinness PLC, Report & Accounts 1987, p. 38

127 Royal Insurance Public Limited Company, Annual Report & Accounts 1987, p. 23.

128 *Accounting for the effects of changing prices: a Handbook*, para. A1.24.

129 Maxwell Communication Corporation plc, 1987 Report and Accounts, p. 46.

130 Royal Insurance Public Limited Company, Annual Report & Accounts 1987, p. 23.

131 Bass PLC, Annual Review for the year ended 30th September 1988, p. 37.

132 *Accounting for the effects of changing prices: a Handbook*, para. A1.3.

133 C.A. Westwick, *Property Valuation and Accounts*, pp. 57 — 58.

134 CA 85, Sch. 4, para. 34(1).

135 *Ibid.*, para. 34(3).

136 *Ibid.*, paras. 34(3)(a) and (b).

137 *Ibid.*, paras. 32(1) and 42(2).

138 *Ibid.*, para. 34(1).

139 SSAP 19, para. 13.

140 SSAP 12, paras. 19 and 20.

141 CA 85, Sch. 4, para. 34(3).

142 SSAP 12, para. 13.

143 *Ibid.*, para. 16.

144 CA 85, Sch. 4, paras. 32(1) and (3).

145 C. Nobes, *Depreciation Problems in the Context of Historic Cost Accounting*, p. 26.

146 CA 85, Sch. 4, para. 3(7)(a).

147 See, for example, Bass PLC, Annual review for the year ended 30th September 1988, pp. 53 and 49 and BTR plc, Annual Report & Accounts 1987, p. 46.

148 ED 16, para. 14.

149 ASC Discussion Paper, *A review of SSAP 6 — Extraordinary items and prior year adjustments*, para. 2.11.

150 ASC Discussion Paper, *A review of SSAP 12 — Accounting for depreciation*, paras. 7.2 and 7.3.

151 Sears PLC, Annual Report 1986/1987, p. 32.

152 Department of Trade and Industry, *The rules relating to depreciation charged on revalued assets and the use of the revaluation reserve — a consultative note.*

153 The Fourth Directive and the accounting rules in Sch. 4 only apply to single entity accounts and not to consolidated ones. The DTI concludes that the same restrictions apply to the revaluation reserve in consolidated accounts, and bases this on paras. 61 and 62 to Sch. 4. These require that the consolidated accounts shall comply as far as practicable with the requirements of the Schedule and of the Act as if they were the accounts of an actual company.

154 Companies Bill, Sch. 1, para. 6.

155 CA 85, Sch. 4, para. 34(3).

156 *Ibid.*, s 263(3).

157 *Ibid.*, s 275(1).

158 *Ibid.*, s 275(1).

159 See D. Foster, *Accounting Requirements — Law and Practice*, Butterworths Company Law Guide, p. 306, para. 9.88, where this interpretation is given.

160 CA 85, s 275(5).
161 *Ibid.*, s 275(6).
162 'Relevant accounts' are defined in *ibid.*, ss 270—273.
163 EFT Group plc, Report and Accounts For Year Ended 31 December 1988, p. 25.
164 APB 6, para. 17. This continues: 'This section is not intended to change accounting practices followed in connection with quasi-reorganisations or reorganisations. This section may not apply to foreign operations under unusual conditions such as serious inflation or currency devaluation. However, when the accounts of an enterprise with foreign operations are translated into US currency for consolidation, such write-ups normally are eliminated. Whenever appreciation has been recorded in the books, income shall be charged with depreciation computed on the written-up amounts.'
165 IAS 16, para. 44.
166 IAS 25, para. 47.
167 IAS 16, para. 47.
168 *Ibid.*, para. 48.
169 E32, *Comparability of Financial Statements*, para. 58.
170 *Ibid.*, para. 68.
171 *Ibid.*, paras. 195 and 203.
172 *Ibid.*, para. 220.
173 CA 85, Sch. 7, para. 1(1).
174 Blue Circle Industries PLC, Report & Accounts 1987, p. 9.
175 Ladbroke Group PLC, Annual Report and Accounts 1987, p. 28.
176 Interpretation Act 1978, Sch. 1.
177 CA 85, Sch. 7, para. 1(2).
178 Sears PLC, Annual Report 1986/1987, p. 26.
179 Sears PLC, Annual Report 1987/1988, p. 28.
180 CA 85, Sch. 4, para. 8, balance sheet formats.
181 Allied-Lyons PLC, Report & Accounts 1988, pp. 46 and 47.
182 CA 85, Sch. 4, para. 8, profit and loss account formats.
183 *Ibid.*, note (17) on the profit and loss account formats.
184 *Ibid.*, paras. 19(1) and 19(2).
185 SSAP 12, paras 25(a) and (b).
186 Bass PLC, Annual Review for the year ended 30th September 1988, pp. 37 and 38.
187 CA 85, Sch. 4, paras. 42(1)(a) and 42(2)
188 *Ibid.*, para. 42(1)(b).
189 *Ibid.*, para. 42(3).
190 SSAP 12, para. 25(c).
191 *Ibid.*, para. 25(d).
192 Bass PLC, Annual Review for the year ended 30th September 1987, p. 46.
193 Argyll Group PLC, Report & Accounts 1988, p. 40.
194 The Plessey Company plc, Report and Accounts 1988, p. 35.
195 Courtaulds plc, Report & Accounts 1987—1988, p. 40.
196 SSAP 12, para. 26.
197 Rolls-Royce plc, Annual Report 1987, p. 20.
198 CA 85, Sch. 4, para. 44.
199 *Ibid.*, para. 83(1).
200 Cadbury Schweppes p.l.c., Annual Report 1987, p. 46.
201 CA 85, Sch. 4, paras. 33(1) and (2).
202 *Ibid.*, para. 33(3).
203 *Ibid.*, para. 33(4).
204 Blue Circle Industries PLC, Report & Accounts 1987, p. 18.
205 Imperial Chemical Industries PLC, Annual Report 1987, p. 42.
206 CA 85, Sch. 4, para. 43(a).
207 Blue Circle Industries PLC, Report & Accounts 1987, p. 18.

208 Sears PLC, Annual Report 1986/1987, p. 36.
209 Para. 43(b), Sch. 4.
210 The Peninsular and Oriental Steam Navigation Company, Annual Report and Accounts 1987, p. 30.
211 SSAP 12, para. 26.
212 CA 85, Sch. 4, para. 34(2).
213 *Ibid.*, para. 34(4).

Chapter 11

Investment properties

1 THE DEVELOPMENT OF AN ACCOUNTING STANDARD IN THE UK

In recent years, depreciation has been the most controversial issue relating to accounting for completed investment properties. The property industry has consistently argued that it is inappropriate to depreciate investment properties, as it is the current value of such properties which is of prime importance as a measure of performance. Lobbying by the property industry and others led to temporary exemption for investment properties when SSAP 12[1] was published in December 1977, requiring all assets with finite useful lives to be depreciated. The temporary exemption was originally intended to last for one year, but was extended first for a further year and subsequently for a further 18 months before SSAP 19[2] became effective, and SSAP 12 was then amended to make the exemption for investment properties permanent.

Whilst the position of the property industry was being considered, it was necessary also to consider the EC Fourth Directive, enacted in the UK in 1981, which made depreciation a legal requirement. A compromise was eventually reached based on the proposition that to depreciate investment properties would lead to the financial statements not giving a true and fair view, and it was therefore necessary to invoke the 'true and fair override'.[3] Whilst this proposition may well be debatable, it was politically expedient at the time since it provided a means of reconciling the views of all those involved in the controversy, thus enabling SSAP 19 to be published in November 1981.

The ASC issued ED 26[4] in September 1980, with the objective that it should form the basis of an additional section to SSAP 12, dealing specifically with the accounting for investment properties; in fact, ED 26 led ultimately to the publication of SSAP 19. The ASC published a statement together with ED 26, wherein the members of the committee set out their reasoning for permitting current value accounting in the case of investment properties. The ASC justified their position as follows:

'It is, however, persuasively argued that a different treatment is required for a fixed asset which is not held for "consumption" in the business operations of an enterprise but is held as a disposable investment. In such a case the current value of the investment, and changes in that current value, are of prime importance rather than a calculation of systematic annual depreciation.

'The argument therefore proceeds:

(a)   the financial statements of enterprises holding investments are more helpful to users of financial statements if the investments are accounted for at current values rather than on the basis of a cost or valuation established some time in the past; and

(b)   depreciation is only one element which enters into the annual change in the value of a property and as the use of a current value places the prime emphasis on the values of the assets, it is not generally useful to attempt to distinguish, estimate and account separately for the element of depreciation; and

(c)   depreciation, although not separately identified, will be taken into account in dealing with changes in current values.'[5]

SSAP 19 relates to investment properties generally, and therefore applies to any company owning such properties, and not just to property companies. In fact, a significant minority of those responding to ED 26 favoured an approach applying only to property or other investment based companies rather than to all companies.

Apart from the debate over depreciation, there are a number of other issues relating to accounting for investment properties. These, however, are specific to property companies and are discussed at 5 below.

Investment properties under development give rise to a number of interesting problems. Most of these relate to the capitalisation of net property outgoings, including interest, during development. These problems are not dealt with in this chapter but the principles involved are discussed in Chapter 12.

2   THE REQUIREMENTS OF SSAP 19

2.1   Definition of investment property

An investment property is defined as an interest in land and/or buildings:

(a)   in respect of which construction work and development have been completed; and

(b)   which is held for its investment potential, any rental income being negotiated at arm's length.[6]

Excluded from this definition are properties owned and occupied by a company for its own purposes and properties let to and occupied by other companies in the same group.[7]

As already mentioned in 1 above, it should be noted that this definition does not confine itself to properties held by property companies. Charities are, however, exempted from SSAP 19.[8]

2.2   Balance sheet valuation

Investment properties should be included in the balance sheet at their open market value. They should not be depreciated except for leasehold property which should be depreciated at least over the last twenty years of the lease period.[9]

SSAP 19 does not require the valuations to be carried out by qualified or independent valuers, but recommends that 'where investment properties represent a substantial proportion of the total assets of a major enterprise (e.g. a listed company) the valuation thereof would normally be carried out :

a)   annually by persons holding a recognised professional qualification and having recent post-qualification experience in the location and category of the properties concerned; and

b)   at least every five years by an external valuer'.[10]

2.3   Revaluation reserve

Changes in the value of investment properties should be disclosed as a movement on an investment revaluation reserve. If the total on the revaluation reserve is insufficient to cover a deficit, the excess of the deficit over the reserve should be charged in the profit and loss account.[11]

2.4   Disclosure

The carrying value of investment properties and the investment revaluation reserve should be shown prominently in the financial statements.[12] The following details concerning the valuation should also be given:

(a)   the basis of the valuation;

(b)   the names or qualifications of the valuers; and

(c)   if the valuation was made by an officer or employee of the company or group owning the property, the financial statements should disclose this fact.[13]

3   ISSUES ARISING FROM SSAP 19

3.1   Relevant Companies Act requirements

3.1.1   *Disclosure on use of 'true and fair override'*

The company law requirement to depart from the usual legal rules if to follow them would lead to the financial statements not showing a true and fair view (the 'true and fair override') was referred to in 1 above, as was the reliance of this requirement as a basis for SSAP 19. When the 'true and fair override' is used, the Companies Act requires disclosure of 'particulars of the departure, the reasons for it and its effect' in a note to the financial statements.[14] This disclosure is usually included in the accounting policies as is the case with the extract shown below:

> *Extract 11.1: Peachey Property Corporation plc*[15]
>
> *(d) Depreciation and amortisation* [extract]
> In accordance with standard accounting practice investment properties are revalued annually
> and the aggregate surplus or deficit is transferred to the revaluation reserve. No depreciation
> or amortisation is provided in respect of freehold investment properties and leasehold
> investment properties with over twenty years to run. The Directors believe that this
> accounting policy is necessary for the accounts to give a true and fair view. Depreciation or
> amortisation is only one of the factors reflected in the annual valuation, and the amount
> attributable to this factor cannot be separately identified or quantified.

The above follows closely the wording recommended by the British Property
Federation when SSAP 19 was first introduced.

3.1.2 *Diminutions in value*

SSAP 19 effectively adopts a portfolio approach and requires only overall deficits
on revaluation to be charged to profit and loss account as opposed to deficits on
individual properties. The Companies Act, on the other hand, requires permanent
deficits below historical cost on individual properties to be charged to profit and
loss account but permits temporary valuation deficits to be included in revaluation
reserve even if this results in a negative reserve.[16] SSAP 19 makes no reference to
the distinction between temporary and permanent deficits.

Since SSAP 19 was introduced, the property market has generally been buoyant
so the conflict between SSAP 19 and the Companies Act has probably not had
any significant impact on financial statements. Many property companies do not
state in their accounting policies how valuation deficits are treated, but, of those
which do, a majority follow SSAP 19. A notable exception is The Hammerson
Property Investment and Development Corporation plc whose accounting policy
is shown below:

> *Extract 11.2: The Hammerson Property Investment and Development
> Corporation plc*[17]
>
> **(g) Valuation of properties** [extract]
> Any surplus or deficit arising from revaluation is transferred to a revaluation reserve except
> that shortfalls against the original cost, together with any subsequent adjustments, are
> included as extraordinary items in the profit and loss account.

This policy is certainly prudent and, in fact, follows the treatment required by
IAS 25, which is to charge any reduction below original cost (whether temporary
or permanent) on an individual investment to profit and loss account (see 4.2(c)
below).[18]

Thus SSAP 19, the Companies Act 1985 and IAS 25 are at variance with each
other in respect of the accounting for revaluation deficits. In our view, whilst
permanent diminutions in value of individual properties *must* be taken to profit
and loss account, temporary diminutions should be taken to revaluation reserve.

3.1.3 Revaluation reserve

SSAP 19 refers to an 'investment revaluation reserve'[19] but in practice this term is not used in financial statements. Most companies prefer just 'revaluation reserve' although some take advantage of the freedom allowed by the Companies Act to change this particular heading[20] with headings such as 'property revaluation reserve' and 'unrealised capital account'.

SSAP 19 requires that the carrying value of investment properties and the investment revaluation reserve be 'displayed prominently in the financial statements'.[21] This means that if assets other than investment properties are revalued, the revaluation reserve should be split to show the amount relating to investment properties as opposed to other revalued assets. In practice, such splits are seldom seen, but an example is shown below:

Extract 11.3: Aberdeen Construction Group plc[22]

25   Reserves

	Group £000	Company £000
Investment property revaluation reserve:		
At 1st January 1986	18,954	18,241
Revaluation adjustment	(11,042)	(11,042)
At 31st December 1986	7,912	7,199
Other property revaluation reserve:		
At 1st January 1986	2,325	—
Transfer to profit and loss account reserves	(109)	—
Amortisation of revaluation reserve	(36)	—
At 31st December 1986	2,180	—
Total revaluation reserves at 31st December 1986	10,092	7,199

3.1.4 Balance sheet classification

The Companies Act balance sheet formats require the following split to be given for tangible fixed assets:

'1.   Land and buildings

2.   Plant and machinery

3.   Fixtures, fittings, tools and equipment

4.   Payments on account and assets in course of construction.'[23]

Headings to which Arabic numbers are assigned in the Companies Act formats may be adapted to suit the nature of a company's business[24] and many companies with investment properties do adapt these headings, often by splitting tangible fixed assets into two headings, one for investment properties and one for other tangible fixed assets.[25] Where appropriate, the former figure should be analysed between completed investment properties and properties under development to give information equivalent to that required by the fourth heading above. Some companies give this analysis on the face of the balance sheet, others in the notes to the financial statements.[26] The latter figure is usually analysed in the notes to the financial statements between the headings shown above, although this is not strictly necessary where the total of other tangible fixed assets is immaterial.[27]

3.2   Frequency of independent valuation

A number of property companies have no stated policy on the frequency of independent valuations; however, most have regular valuations. Examples of companies having a stated policy on the subject are shown below:

Extract 11.4: Capital & Counties plc[28]

(c) Completed investment properties
Completed investment properties are professionally valued on an open market basis by independent firms of valuers at the end of each financial year. The valuations are adopted in the accounts and surpluses and deficiencies arising are reflected in the unrealised capital account.

Extract 11.5: McKay Securities plc[29]

Properties [extract]
Properties other than short leaseholds and those in the course of development are revalued annually in accordance with Statement of Standard Practice No 19. The valuation is carried out every three years by independent external valuers and in the intervening years by the Directors. An external valuation was carried out as at 31st March, 1987.

Extract 11.6: Laing Properties plc[30]

Investment properties [extract]
1 It is the directors' intention that properties under this heading will be valued externally every three years. Investment properties will not be valued in the intervening two years, and in this respect the Company's accounting policies do not comply fully with SSAP 19.

These all comply with the guidance included in SSAP 19 as to frequency of independent valuations (see 2.2 above), but the policy shown in Extract 11.6 does not comply with SSAP 19, in that no internal valuation takes place in the years between external valuations. Investment properties should be included in the balance sheet at their open market value at the balance sheet date. The financial statements of Laing Properties plc attracted a qualified audit report in 1987 (and in

1985), but not in 1986 when a valuation took place. However, they have subsequently decided to revalue their properties at the end of 1988, and thereafter to incorporate annual revaluations in their financial statements.[31]

4 COMPARISON WITH US AND IASC PRONOUNCEMENTS

4.1 US

The US position on accounting for investment properties contrasts starkly with that in the UK. No special treatment is allowed for investment properties and revaluations are not permitted.[32] Real estate companies tend to have unclassified balance sheets with all properties shown under the same heading. Some give supplementary current value information.

4.2 IASC

IAS 25 on accounting for investments permits investment properties to be classified either as property or as long-term investments.[33] If classified as property, they must be depreciated in accordance with IAS 4.[34] If classified as long-term investments they may be either revalued or retained at cost.[35]

Other requirements of IAS 25 which are relevant to investment properties are:

(a) if revaluations are used, a policy for the frequency of revaluations should be adopted and an entire category of long-term investments should be revalued at the same time;[36]

(b) provision must be made for permanent diminutions in the value of long-term investments. This must be done for each investment individually;[37]

(c) increases in value on a revaluation should be credited to revaluation reserve. Any reduction below cost on an individual investment should be charged to profit and loss account. A subsequent reversal of such a decrease should be credited to profit and loss account;[38]

(d) if short-term investments are carried at the lower of cost and market value, revaluations should be reversed on a reclassification from long-term to short-term;[39]

(e) the financial statements should disclose:

(i) the accounting policies for determining the carrying amount of investments and the treatment of revaluation surpluses on the disposal of revalued investments;

(ii) the fair value of investment properties if treated as long-term investments and not revalued;

(iii) for long-term investments carried at valuation:

- the policy for the frequency of revaluations;
- the date of the latest revaluation; and
- the basis of revaluation stating whether an external valuer was used;

(iv) movements on revaluation surplus and the nature of such movements; and

(v) for enterprises whose main business is the holding of investments, an analysis of the portfolio of investments.[40]

The IASC has recently issued an exposure draft, E32 — *Comparability of Financial Statements* — which proposes to amend, *inter alia*, the requirements of IAS 25. The main change proposed is that the preferred treatment for investment properties is that they should be measured at cost and depreciated in accordance with IAS 4. However, the alternative treatment of dealing with such assets as long-term investments carried at valuation will still be allowed, provided additional information is given.[41] The only change to the provisions dealing with the accounting for revaluations of such assets is that on disposal of a revalued asset any revaluation surplus remaining in the revaluation reserves relating to the disposed asset should be transferred to retained earnings (and not to income as presently allowed).[42]

5   ISSUES SPECIFIC TO PROPERTY COMPANIES

5.1   Profit and loss account presentation

Investment status used to be very important because a gain on disposal of an investment property is taxed as a capital gain as opposed to a trading receipt and the tax rate on such gains used to be considerably lower than the usual corporation tax rate. Property groups, therefore, went to great lengths to emphasise the distinction between their trading activities, where properties were acquired primarily with the intention of realising a profit on disposal in the short or medium term, and their investment activities where properties were acquired primarily for their rental return and long-term capital appreciation. Some adopted articles prohibiting the distribution of capital profits, carried out trading and investment in separate companies and distanced gains on disposal of investment properties from trading profits in their financial statements. Under current tax rates, the distinction has become far less important.

The two main methods used to separate trading and capital profits were:

(a) completely separate trading and capital profit and loss accounts; and

(b) gains on disposal of investment properties treated as extraordinary items.

Both of these can still be seen in practice, although the former is difficult to reconcile with the Companies Act requirements to disclose the 'profit or loss on ordinary activities before taxation'.[43] Strictly, to comply with the Companies Act, it is necessary to disclose a total of the two separate pre-tax profit figures. Many companies ignore this as a technicality. Furthermore, the separate capital profit and loss account does not fit well with SSAP 6, which envisages a single profit and loss account but does not specifically preclude the account being split into two. Despite these difficulties, we consider separate trading and capital profit and loss accounts to be the clearest presentation for a property company's profit and loss account.

It is also difficult to reconcile the extraordinary item treatment with the definition of extraordinary items in SSAP 6; since it is part of the business of a property investment company to reassess its investment portfolio, it follows that disposals are regular occurrences.[44] Inclusion in pre-tax profits is, therefore, to be preferred when a single profit and loss account is being presented. Given that tax status is now of lesser importance and that such inclusion will generally improve earnings per share, it is hardly surprising that, in recent years, there has been a trend towards this treatment. Examples of the three different treatments are shown below:

Extract 11.7: Peachey Property Corporation plc[45]

Consolidated Profit and Loss Account for the year ended 24th June 1988

REVENUE	1988 £'000		1987 £'000
Net rents	**16,243**		12,980
Interest receivable	**726**		75
Other income	**—**		123
		16,969	13,178
Administrative expenses	**2,523**		1,950
Interest payable	**6,558**		4,361
		9,081	6,311
Net property investment income		**7,888**	6,867
Profit on trading properties		**6,541**	4,783
Profit on ordinary activities before taxation		**14,429**	11,650
Taxation on profit on ordinary activities		**5,046**	3,657
Profit attributable to shareholders		**9,383**	7,993
Dividends		**1,974**	3,575
Retained for the year		**7,409**	4,418
Earnings per share		**23.4p**	22.3p

REALISED CAPITAL
Sales of investment properties:

	1988	1987
Proceeds less book value (after tax of £154,000, 1985 - £587,000)	**994**	298
Previous valuation surpluses/(deficits) transferred from revaluation reserve (after tax of Nil, 1987 - £24,000)	**1,899**	1,654
Retained for the year	**2,893**	1,952

Extract 11.8: The Hammerson Property Investment and Development Corporation plc[46]

(e) Profits on sale of properties
Profits on sale of properties are taken into account on the completion of contract and receipt of cash. Profits arising from the sale of properties acquired with a view to resale are included in the profit and loss account as part of the ordinary activities of the group. Profits arising from the sale of properties acquired for investment and development are treated as extraordinary items.

Extract 11.9: Daejan Holdings PLC[47]

(j) Sales of Investment Properties
It is Group policy to sell, as individual units, flats in residential blocks which have been held as investments but which are now considered uneconomic to retain. Occasionally there are sales of residential and commercial investment blocks. Since such sales of all types of investment property are expected to continue, the resulting surplus based on the excess of sales proceeds over original cost, plus subsequent additions, is included within the Group profit. Taxation on the gains arising on these sales is shown as part of the taxation charge.

5.2 Reclassifications from investment property to trading property

Occasionally, property companies will transfer properties from their investment portfolio to their trading portfolio. The question then arises as to what should happen to the revaluation surplus/deficit which had previously been recognised when the property was regarded as an investment property. A few companies reflect these reclassifications in their group financial statements as if they were transactions with third parties, and treat them as having become realised.

There may be an argument for saying that the property has realised its investment potential on becoming a trading property. Also, such transfers are usually between two distinct companies (i.e. an investment and a trading company) so the profit is realised in the transferor company. However, it is difficult to reconcile a treatment as realised in the group financial statements, as opposed to an individual company's financial statements, with the notion that consolidation is intended to represent the group as a single economic entity. Nevertheless, in the case of a company having a separate capital profit and loss account, such profits at least do not distort the revenue profit since they are capital in nature. For example:

Extract 11.10: Capital & Counties plc[48]

(g) Reclassification of properties
No inter-company profit is recognised on the transfer of trading properties to the investment portfolio. Transfers from the investment portfolio to trading stock are recorded at book value and any valuation surpluses or deficiencies are reflected in the realised capital account.

An alternative treatment is to leave the property at its valuation on transfer but not to treat the accumulated valuation surplus as realised. If this treatment is adopted, interest capitalised on any subsequent development should be based on cost (see 3.3.6 of Chapter 12).

Another approach is to reverse any revaluation surplus/deficit relating to a property transferred and include it in trading property at the lower of cost and net realisable value; this will ensure consistency in the accounting treatment of all trading properties. For example:

Extract 11.11: Daejan Holdings PLC[49]

(g) Properties [extract]
(ii) Trading and Development Properties
These properties are stated at the lower of cost and net realisable value. In the case of properties acquired from other Group companies any profit in the transferor company is eliminated on consolidation until realised by the Group.

5.3   Reclassifications from trading property to investment property

On a reclassification from trading property to investment property, the basis of valuation in the financial statements will change from the lower of cost and net realisable value to open market value. As discussed in 5.2 above, such transfers are usually between two separate companies, but any intra-group profit should be eliminated on consolidation. To fail to do so would distort the revenue profit, as is recognised by Capital & Counties plc who do not eliminate capital profits on transfers from the investment portfolio to trading properties, but do eliminate revenue profits on transfers from trading properties to the investment portfolio (see Extract 11.10 in 5.2 above).

5.4   Turnover definition

Definitions of turnover vary considerably between property investment companies. Rental income is invariably included but variations encountered in practice include:

(a)   service charges may be either included or excluded;

(b)   some companies include proceeds on sale of investment and/or trading properties;

(c)   some companies define turnover as being net rental income (i.e. after property outgoings) rather than gross; and

(d)   some companies do not define any figure as turnover but give equivalent information to those which do.[50]

Of the various possibilities, gross rental income, including service charges, and proceeds of sale of trading properties seems to be most closely in line with the Companies Act definition of turnover as '... amounts derived from the provision of goods and services falling within the company's ordinary activities ...'.[51] This is illustrated by the following extract :

Extract 11.12: Slough Estates plc[52]

1 Turnover and operating income [extract]
Turnover comprises: rent and recharges charged to tenants; the net realised value of trading properties and the value of work, including attributable profit, carried out during the year on presold trading property developments; and the amounts invoiced to utilities and merchandise customers.

There is an argument for saying that service charges should be excluded because the provision of electricity, for example, does not fall within the ordinary activities of a property investment company. However, the properties could not be let without the appropriate services, so service charges to cover their cost are really an integral part of rental income.

Whichever definition is adopted, net rental income must be shown to comply with the Companies Act 1985.[53] Aggregate rents receivable must also be disclosed to comply with SSAP 21 and this disclosure should apparently be net of service charges.[54]

Although property companies adopt different definitions of turnover (and may not include certain items within turnover), they generally disclose sufficient information on investment and trading property sales, rental income and property outgoings so that a comparison can be made. Usually, it is only the effect of different treatments of service charges which is not apparent, as the amount of these is not required to be disclosed. However, in most cases these charges will not be material.

5.5   Revenue recognition

Some companies recognise sales of investment properties on exchange of contracts, others on completion. See 5.6 of Chapter 3 for a fuller discussion of this subject.

5.6   Lessee accounting

SSAP 21 requires the following disclosures to be made by lessees in respect of operating leases:

'... the lessee should disclose the payments which he is committed to make during the next year, analysed between those in which the commitment expires within that year, in the second to fifth years inclusive and over five years from the balance sheet date, showing separately the commitments in respect of leases of land and buildings and other operating leases'.[55]

This applies to ground rent payable on leasehold investment properties,[56] but the disclosure is rarely given by property companies. Most companies make no comment on the matter but MEPC plc is an exception. The company includes the note shown below in its financial statements:

Extract 11.13: MEPC plc[57]

27   Commitments [extract]
In the opinion of the directors, the disclosure requirements of SSAP 21 to show leasing commitments in respect of ground rents are not relevant to a property investment company.

It is not clear why the disclosure is regarded as irrelevant. If the commitment is a significant one, disclosure can help give an appreciation of the financial position of the reporting company or group. Often it may not be significant as ground rents on long leasehold properties tend to be minimal, and this may explain the lack of disclosure by property companies.

6   CONCLUSION

Undoubtedly, SSAP 19 has helped to standardise the balance sheet valuation of investment properties. However, it might have been preferable to develop a standard for property and other investment based companies, rather than one which applies to investment properties per se. This would have had the advantage of ensuring that the accounting treatment prescribed for property and other types of investment would have been the same, which would be more logical than the present position which requires investment properties to be revalued annually but permits other types of investment to be retained at cost.

The difficulty is that this would involve changes to the law, firstly, to extend the definition of an investment company[58] to include property investment companies and, secondly, to prescribe a special layout for the financial statements of such companies, as Member States may opt to do under the EC Fourth Directive.[59] It seems unlikely that Parliamentary time would be found merely to render a workable but illogical system more logical. However, turning from the basic approach to the detail of the standard, the conflict with the Companies Act 1985 in respect of diminutions in value of individual properties is a matter which ought to be corrected in the standard.

Clearly, there are a number of different accounting treatments for investment properties, and many of these are quite specific to the property industry. The industry, therefore, appears to be a suitable candidate for an industry specific SORP to reduce these areas of difference. Until such time as this can be achieved, more disclosure by property companies on the treatments adopted by them in these areas would be of assistance. This would include giving accounting policies on:

- treatment of valuation deficits;

- frequency of external valuations;

- accounting treatment of transfers between investment and trading properties and vice versa;

- 'turnover' definition; and

- revenue recognition.

References

1 SSAP 12, *Accounting for depreciation*, December 1977, para. 22.
2 SSAP 19, *Accounting for investment properties*, November 1981.
3 CA 85, s 228(5).
4 ED 26, *Accounting for investment properties — an addition to SSAP 12 'Accounting for depreciation'*, September 1980.
5 *Statement by the Accounting Standards Committee on the publication of ED 26 'Accounting for investment properties'*, paras. 7 and 8.
6 SSAP 19, para. 7.
7 *Ibid.*, para. 8.
8 *Ibid.*, para. 9.
9 *Ibid.*, paras. 10 and 11.
10 *Ibid.*, para. 6.
11 *Ibid.*, para. 13.
12 *Ibid.*, para. 15.
13 *Ibid.*, para. 12.
14 CA 85, s 228(6).
15 Peachey Property Corporation plc, Accounts 24th June 1988, p. 11.
16 CA 85, Sch. 4, paras. 19 and 34.
17 The Hammerson Property Investment and Development Corporation plc, 1987 Annual Report, p. 24.
18 IAS 25, *Accounting for Investments*, March 1986, para. 48.
19 SSAP 19, para. 13.
20 CA 85, Sch. 4, para. 34(2).
21 SSAP 19, para. 15.
22 Aberdeen Construction Group plc, Report and Accounts 1986, p. 25.
23 CA 85, Sch. 4, para. 8.
24 *Ibid.*, Sch. 4, para. 3(3).
25 See, e.g., Capital & Counties plc, 1987 Annual Report, p. 27.

26 Capital & Counties give the information in their balance sheet (1987 Annual Report, p. 27), whilst MEPC plc give it in the notes (Report and Financial Statements 1988, p. 27).
27 CA 85, Sch. 4, para. 3(4).
28 Capital & Counties plc, 1987 Annual Report, p. 29.
29 McKay Securities plc, 1988 Annual Report, p. 12.
30 Laing Properties plc, 1987 Annual Report, p. 12.
31 Laing Properties plc, Interim Report at June 1988.
32 APB Opinion No. 6, *Status of Accounting Research Bulletins*, October 1965, para. 17.
33 IAS 25, para. 45.
34 *Ibid.*
35 *Ibid.*, para. 47.
36 *Ibid.*
37 *Ibid.*
38 *Ibid.*, para. 48.
39 *Ibid.*, para. 51(a).
40 *Ibid.*, para. 55.
41 E32, *Comparability of Financial Statements*, January 1989, para. 203.
42 *Ibid.*, para. 220.
43 CA 85, Sch. 4, para. 3(6).
44 See SSAP 6, para. 30 for the definition of 'extraordinary items'. In terms of this definition, extraordinary items are 'expected not to recur frequently or regularly'.
45 Peachey Property Corporation plc, Accounts 24th June 1988, p. 8.
46 The Hammerson Property Investment and Development Corporation plc, 1987 Annual Report, p. 24.
47 Daejan Holdings PLC, Annual Report 1988, p. 11.
48 Capital & Counties plc, 1987 Annual Report, p. 29.
49 Daejan Holdings PLC, Annual Report 1988, p. 11.
50 See Daejan Holdings PLC, Annual Report 1988, p. 12 for an example of a company including service charges in turnover. Great Portland Estates PLC excludes service charges from its equivalent of turnover. It is also an example of a company not defining any figure as turnover — see their 1988 Annual Report, p. 17. Daejan Holdings PLC is an example of a company including proceeds on sale of investment properties in turnover.
51 CA 85, Sch. 4, para. 95.
52 Slough Estates plc, Annual Report 1987, p. 20.
53 *Ibid.*, para. 53(5).
54 SSAP 21 does not categorically state that the disclosure should be net of service charges but this is implicit from paras. 43 and 60. The disclosure should be split between finance and operating leases but most property leases will be operating leases as they do not transfer substantially all the risks and rewards of ownership.
55 SSAP 21, para. 56.
56 Osborn's Concise Law Dictionary describes ground rent as follows: 'When land is leased to a person on condition that he erects certain buildings on it, the rent reserved (which is small in comparison with the rent of the land when built on) is called the ground-rent.' (p. 286). Given that ground rent relates to the site itself which to all intents and purposes has an infinite life, this particular lease will not usually transfer substantially all the risks and rewards of ownership and will, therefore, be an operating lease. See SSAP 21, paras. 15 — 17.
57 MEPC plc, Report and Financial Statements 1988, p. 39.
58 CA 85, s 266.
59 EC Fourth Directive, Article 5(1).

Chapter 12

Capitalisation of borrowing costs

1   INTRODUCTION

1.1   The development of the practice of capitalisation

The accounting treatment of the costs incurred on borrowings obtained to finance asset acquisitions achieved prominence in the UK through the growth of the large property companies in the 1950s and 1960s. However, as a result of the House of Lords decision in the *Chancery Lane* case[1] in 1966, the accounting treatment of property company development interest was frequently governed by the achievement of a particular tax result, rather than being based on sound accounting principles.

In *Chancery Lane*, the company had borrowed money on mortgage to finance the rebuilding of its premises and the erection of new buildings. On the advice of its auditors, and in order to increase the amount available for dividends, the company capitalised a proportion of the interest in its financial statements. It was held, however, that since the company's decision to attribute part of the interest to capital had a practical effect on the distributable fund represented by the balance on the profit and loss account, the company could not make an inconsistent attribution for tax purposes. Thus the principle was established whereby interest paid by a company and charged directly to capital was not tax deductible.

As a result, property groups used one of two methods to achieve the effect of capitalisation without losing tax relief. The first of these involved writing off the borrowing costs in the financial statements of individual companies within a group, and capitalising only in the consolidated financial statements. The second method was to charge the interest in the profit and loss account, but subsequently to remove it as a reserves transfer. The latter method, however, was regarded as questionable, especially following the decision of the House of Lords in the *Fitzleet* case[2] in 1977. In this case, the company's appeal came to the House of Lords on the basis that, although *Chancery Lane* applied, it had been wrongly decided. The company's appeal was, however, dismissed on the grounds that the *Chancery Lane* decision was a correct application of the Revenue law, and that it was, therefore, up to the Revenue to review their position. Consequently, the appeal was probably instrumental in persuading the Revenue to reconsider this seemingly anomalous situation whereby varied accounting treatments of similar transactions resulted in different tax results. This may be summed up in the following extract from Lord Wilberforce's judgment:

'My Lords, it may be—I do not know—that a result which causes property companies which, as advised by their accountants, capitalise interest on investments or development, to suffer fiscally as compared with those who charge their interest payments to revenue, or, perhaps more accurately, do not decide to capitalise them, is unjust or economically unsound. But the remedy for this does not lie here. It is for the Revenue not merely to rest upon its victory, but to consider the broad merits or otherwise of the result, after such representations as the affected taxpayers may make.'[3]

Nevertheless, the practice of capitalising interest on consolidation appeared unaffected by the case law; so the tax treatment depended not on whether interest was capitalised, but on how the capitalisation was presented in the financial statements. An inquiry was eventually set up by the Inland Revenue, leading to the 1981 Finance Act amendment[4] which permitted capitalised interest to be charged to income for tax purposes. Also in 1981, the capitalisation of interest was referred to in company law for the first time, with the Companies Act 1981, which made it clear that interest could be included in the production cost of an asset.[5] Since 1981, the practice of capitalising borrowing costs has become increasingly common in the UK in other industries which have major fixed asset developments, such as supermarkets and hotels. However, there is still no UK accounting standard on the subject, so capitalisation remains optional, and accounting treatments varied and inconsistent.

In the US, the capitalisation of borrowing costs received renewed attention in the early 1970s, following the increased use of borrowed funds to finance business operations, coupled with a sharp rise in interest rates. Prior to that, it was predominantly the public utility companies which capitalised borrowing costs, with most other companies accounting for interest cost as a current period expense. In 1971, the Accounting Principles Board set up a committee to consider the subject; however, although the committee prepared a comprehensive working paper setting out the principal issues to be considered, its activities were terminated before a pronouncement could be issued. In 1974, the SEC became concerned about the growing popularity of interest capitalisation, when it noted an increase in the number of non-utility registrants that were adopting a policy of capitalising interest as part of the cost of certain assets. This was causing inconsistency between those companies whose earnings were boosted by capitalisation and others which expensed interest costs as incurred. In 1974, the SEC imposed a moratorium[6] on companies adopting or extending a policy of interest capitalisation (public utilities[7] and registrants covered by AICPA Guides *Accounting for Retail Land Sales* and *Audits of Savings and Loan Associations* were excluded from the moratorium). Shortly thereafter, the FASB agreed to consider the subject, and added the project to its technical agenda. This ultimately led to the publication of SFAS 34[8] in 1979, which made capitalisation of interest compulsory for certain assets requiring a period of time to get them ready for their intended use.[9]

In March 1984, the IASC published IAS 23,[10] which provides a more flexible approach to the issue than does SFAS 34. Under IAS 23, capitalisation is optional, but certain rules are laid down if a policy of capitalisation is adopted.

There is thus a major difference in approach between the UK, US and IAS 23. In the UK, capitalisation is permitted under the Companies Act, but there are no rules laid down as to how it should be applied; in the US, capitalisation is mandatory under certain prescribed conditions, subject to certain exemptions; whilst IAS 23 allows flexibility within a framework of rules.

1.2 Arguments for and against capitalisation

The arguments for and against capitalisation are evenly balanced, and this was clearly evidenced by the fact that SFAS 34 was only adopted by a margin of four votes to three.[11] However, in general terms, proponents of the view that borrowing costs should be capitalised under prescribed conditions, usually advance the following arguments:[12]

(a) borrowing costs incurred as a consequence of a decision to acquire an asset are not intrinsically different from other costs that are commonly capitalised. If an asset requires a period of time to bring it to the condition and location necessary for its intended use, the borrowing costs incurred during that period as a result of expenditures on the asset are a part of the cost of acquiring the asset;

(b) a better matching of income and expenditure is achieved, in that interest incurred with a view to future benefit is carried forward to be expensed in the period or periods expected to benefit. Consequently, the failure to capitalise the borrowing costs associated with the acquisition of assets will reduce current earnings as a consequence of the acquisition of assets;

(c) this method results in greater comparability between companies constructing assets and other companies buying similar completed assets, as well as between the costs of those assets paid for in stages and those paid for on completion within an individual company. This is because the purchase price of completed assets acquired will normally include interest, as the vendor needs to take into account all his costs, including interest, in pricing the asset.

On the other hand, proponents of the view that borrowing costs should always be charged to income, regardless of how the borrowings are applied, generally advance the following arguments to support their view:[13]

(a) borrowing costs are incurred in support of the whole of the activities of the enterprise. Any attempt to associate borrowing costs with a particular asset is necessarily arbitrary;

(b) capitalisation of borrowing costs results in the same type of asset having a different carrying amount, depending on the method of financing adopted by the enterprise;

(c) treating borrowing costs as a charge against income results in financial statements giving more comparable results from period to period, thus providing a better indication of the future cash flows of an enterprise. Interest costs fluctuate with the borrowing levels and rates which give rise to them, not with asset acquisition.

1.3   The accounting alternatives

There are essentially three possible methods of accounting for borrowing costs; these are as follows:[14]

(a)   account for interest on debt as an expense of the period in which it is incurred;

(b)   capitalise interest on debt as part of the cost of an asset when prescribed conditions are met; and

(c)   capitalise interest on debt and imputed interest on shareholders' equity as part of the cost of an asset when prescribed conditions are met.

In drafting SFAS 34, the FASB considered these three methods and concluded that alternative (b) should be adopted. In arriving at its conclusions, reference was also made to the possibility of capitalising interest, not just as a cost of acquiring assets, but also as a cost of holding assets. However, this idea was rejected on the grounds that under the present accounting model, costs are not added to assets subsequent to their readiness for use; therefore, consideration of such a proposal would require a comprehensive re-examination of this fundamental principle.[15]

1.3.1   *Account for interest on debt as an expense of the period in which it is incurred*

This was the approach favoured by the three dissenting FASB members, who held the view that 'interest cost, like dividends, is more directly associable with the period during which the capital giving rise to it is outstanding than the material, labor, and other resources into which capital is converted.'[16] It was therefore being suggested that interest should not be allocated to assets in the way that other costs are; the reasoning being that the financing structure of an enterprise is used to finance all its activities, and any allocation of particular sources of finance to particular assets is arbitrary. A decision to discontinue a particular project will not usually result in immediate repayment of any borrowings allocated as financing it, since the borrowings will normally continue to finance the remaining activities. As a cost of obtaining finance, interest should be expensed as incurred over the period of availability of the finance. The dissenting FASB members also held the view that capitalisation misstated the calculation of the return on a company's total capital employed — a computation often made by users of financial statements.

Conversely, the majority members of the FASB argued that an enterprise which is funded wholly by equity capital is not the same as one which has borrowed funds; and, similarly, an enterprise that is making substantial expenditures for asset construction differs from one which is not. They therefore maintained that 'those who assert that comparability among enterprises would be greater if all interest cost were expensed would create an illusion of comparability that may disguise the differences in facts.'[17]

1.3.2   Capitalise interest on debt as part of the cost of an asset when prescribed conditions are met

This alternative was both adopted by SFAS 34 and sanctioned by IAS 23. The FASB experienced some difficulty in reconciling capitalisation based on cost of capital (see 1.3.3 below) with the historical cost convention, and it was this that led to their conclusion that the capitalisation rate should be based on rates of interest on outstanding borrowings. In arriving at this conclusion, the FASB put forward the following argument:

'In the present accounting framework, the cost of a resource is generally measured by the historical exchange price paid to acquire it. However, funds are an unusual kind of resource in that, although an enterprise obtains funds from various sources, only borrowed funds give rise to a cost that can be described as a historical exchange price. Although a historical exchange transaction may occur when equity securities are issued, that transaction is not the basis generally advocated for measuring the cost of equity capital. It is generally agreed that the use of equity capital entails an economic cost, but in the absence of a historical exchange price, the cost of equity capital is not reliably determinable. The Board concluded, therefore, that the cost of financing expenditures for a qualifying asset should be measured by assigning to the asset an appropriate proportion of the interest cost incurred on borrowings during the period of its acquisition.'[18]

It then remained to be determined exactly which borrowings should be used as a basis for the capitalisation rate. The FASB adopted the concept of borrowings which could have been avoided in the absence of expenditure on the asset as being most consistent with the arguments quoted above. It also concluded that interest capitalised should not exceed interest incurred for similar reasons.

1.3.3   Capitalise interest on debt and imputed interest on owners' equity in respect of qualifying assets during their production period

This method is based on the premise that an asset must be financed during its production period and that finance has an associated cost. The FASB developed the argument as follows:

'Financing has a cost. The cost may take the form of explicit interest on borrowed funds, or it may take the form of a return foregone on an alternative use of funds, but regardless of the form it takes, a financing cost is necessarily incurred. On the premise that the historical cost of acquiring an asset should include all costs necessarily incurred to bring it to the condition and location necessary for its intended use, the Board concluded that, in principle, the cost incurred in financing expenditures for an asset during a required construction or development period is itself a part of the asset's historical acquisition cost.'[19]

Some FASB members were of the opinion, therefore, that there is a valid conceptual argument for measuring the cost of financing the acquisition of certain assets on the basis of the enterprise's cost of capital, which would include imputed interest on equity capital, as well as interest on borrowed capital. Nevertheless, in view of the fact that, in the present accounting framework, the cost of a resource is generally measured by the historical exchange price paid to acquire it, all the FASB members agreed that recognition of the cost of equity capital does not conform to this framework.[20] Fortunately, this obviated the necessity of having to resolve the issue of how to account for the credit corresponding to the imputed interest.

2   A COMPARISON BETWEEN THE UK, US AND IASC

2.1   The current UK position

As already mentioned, there is no UK accounting standard on capitalisation of interest, which remains optional but is an increasingly common practice. Interest is referred to in Appendix 1 to SSAP 9 in the following terms, which would appear to discourage rather than encourage capitalisation in the case of long-term contracts:

'In ascertaining costs of long-term contracts it is not normally appropriate to include interest payable on borrowed money. However, in circumstances where sums borrowed can be identified as financing specific long-term contracts, it may be appropriate to include such related interest in cost, in which circumstances the inclusion of interest and the amount of interest so included should be disclosed in a note to the financial statements.'[21] (See 7.3.5 of Chapter 9.)

The Companies Act 1985 permits the inclusion in the production cost of an asset of:

'(a)   a reasonable proportion of the costs incurred by the company which are only indirectly attributable to the production of that asset; and

(b)   interest on capital borrowed to finance the production of that asset, to the extent that it accrues in respect of the period of production;

provided, however, in a case within paragraph (b) above, that the inclusion of the interest in determining the cost of that asset and the amount of the interest so included is disclosed in a note to the accounts'.[22]

The wording of (b) above raises the question as to whether or not capitalisation can only take place where there have been specific borrowings made for the financing of a specific asset. For example, if a company has held a vacant piece of land for several years, and now begins to develop it using internally generated financial resources without incurring any additional borrowings, can it, nevertheless, capitalise other unrelated borrowing costs despite the absence of 'capital borrowed to finance the production of that asset'? The answer appears to be that in practice companies apply a more liberal interpretation to this provision, and capitalise interest costs irrespective of whether or not they relate to incremental or specific borrowings (this issue is discussed further in 3.3.1 below).[23]

However, the words 'interest on capital borrowed ...' in (b) above clearly indicate that actual borrowings must have been incurred before capitalisation can take place. This would, therefore, appear to rule out the capitalisation of 'notional interest' (see 3.3.2 below).

Companies listed on The Stock Exchange[24] and USM companies[25] must also disclose the amount of interest capitalised during the year and give an indication of the amount and treatment of any related tax relief.

2.2 US

SFAS 34 makes capitalisation of interest compulsory for certain assets requiring a period of time to get them ready for their intended use. These are referred to as 'qualifying assets'. Since its introduction, SFAS 34 has been amended by two subsequent standards: SFAS 58[26] and SFAS 62.[27]

2.2.1 Qualifying and non-qualifying assets

Qualifying assets are defined as follows:

(a) assets that are constructed or otherwise produced for an enterprise's own use (including assets constructed or produced for the enterprise by others for which deposits or progress payments have been made);[28]

(b) assets intended for sale or lease that are constructed or otherwise produced as discrete projects (e.g. ships or real estate developments);[29]

(c) investments accounted for by the equity method 'while the investee has activities in progress necessary to commence its planned principal operations provided that the investee's activities include the use of funds to acquire qualifying assets for its operations.'[30]

The following are non-qualifying assets:

(a) inventories that are 'routinely manufactured or otherwise produced in large quantities on a repetitive basis';[31]

(b) assets that are in use or ready for their intended use;[32]

(c) assets not in use which are not being prepared for use;[33]

(d) assets that are not included in the consolidated balance sheet of the parent company and consolidated subsidiaries;[34]

(e) investments accounted for by the equity method after the planned principal operations of the investee begin.[35]

Land that is not undergoing activities necessary to get it ready for its intended use is not a qualifying asset. If activities are undertaken for the purpose of developing land for a particular use, the expenditures to acquire the land qualify for interest capitalisation while those activities are in progress.[36]

2.2.2 Capitalisation rate

The amount to be capitalised is the interest cost which could theoretically have been avoided if the expenditure on the qualifying asset were not made. This is determined by applying an interest rate (the 'capitalisation rate') to the average amount of accumulated expenditure for the asset during the financial year. The capitalisation rate must be based on borrowings outstanding during the year. The borrowings used may be specific borrowings used to finance the qualifying asset.

Alternatively, a weighted average rate of interest on other borrowings may be used, provided that the borrowings are selected with the objective in mind of capitalising that part of the interest cost which could theoretically have been avoided in the absence of expenditure on the qualifying asset. Also, with this objective in mind, it follows that interest capitalised must not exceed the interest cost incurred by the enterprise.[37] In consolidated financial statements, this limitation would be based on the total borrowing costs incurred by the parent company and its consolidated subsidiaries.[38]

The expenditure to which the capitalisation rate is applied is not necessarily the same as the amount capitalised for the asset in question. If a significant part of the amount capitalised relates to costs which have effectively been financed interest-free by third parties (e.g. retention money) that part must be excluded from the expenditure on which interest is capitalised.[39]

2.2.3   Capitalisation period

Generally, the period during which interest should be capitalised is defined in terms of the following three conditions:

(a)   expenditures for the asset must have been made;

(b)   activities that are necessary to get the asset ready for its intended use are in progress; and

(c)   interest cost is being incurred (including the imputation of interest on certain types of payables in accordance with APB Opinion No. 21 — *Interest on Receivables and Payables*).

The capitalisation period begins when all three conditions are present and continues as long as they remain present. The capitalisation period ends when the asset is substantially complete and ready for its intended use.[40]

If an asset is completed in parts and each part is capable of being used independently while work continues on the other parts, then capitalisation should cease on each part when it is substantially complete and ready for use.[41]

Interest capitalisation is not discontinued merely because it is necessary to write the asset down to a value below cost. In that case, the provision is increased to take account of the capitalised interest.[42]

2.2.4   Disclosure

The financial statements must disclose the total interest cost incurred and the amount capitalised during the financial year.[43]

2.3   IASC

In common with many other international standards, IAS 23 allows a choice of treatments. In this case, the choice is between adopting a policy of capitalising or of not capitalising borrowing costs in respect of 'assets that take a substantial period of time to get them ready for their intended use or sale'.[44] For those enterprises adopting a policy of capitalisation, the standard is broadly similar to the US position discussed in 2.2 above. The amount of borrowing costs that have been capitalised during the financial year must be disclosed.[45]

For companies capitalising interest, the main difference between the US requirements and IAS 23 is that the latter is less specific. In particular:

(a) qualifying assets are not defined in IAS 23. The reference to 'assets that take a substantial period of time to get them ready for their intended use or sale' mentioned in the preceding paragraph is supplemented only by references that make it clear that:

    (i) property, plant, equipment and inventory come within the scope of the standard;[46]

    (ii) the standard follows the line taken in the US on investments (as outlined in 2.2.1 above), except that it is not confined to investments accounted for using the equity method;[47] and

    (iii) 'borrowing costs are not usually capitalised for inventories that are routinely manufactured or otherwise produced in large quantities on a repetitive basis';[48]

(b) the wording used in describing the appropriate capitalisation rate is less prescriptive in IAS 23 than in SFAS 34. Nevertheless, IAS 23 establishes the same basic principle of only capitalising 'that part of the total borrowing costs that would have been avoided if expenditure for an asset had not been made'.[49] However, IAS 23 does not entirely rule out methods other than a specific or weighted average rate but it does make it clear that:

    (i) borrowing costs capitalised must not exceed actual borrowing costs, and in consolidated financial statements this limitation must be based on the consolidated borrowing costs;[50] and

    (ii) if borrowings specific to a project are temporarily invested until needed then the capitalisation rate for that project should take into account the related investment income;[51]

(c) there is no reference in IAS 23 equivalent to that appearing in SFAS 34 on the subject of costs not financed by borrowings (see 2.2.2 above);

(d) if an asset is completed in parts and each part is capable of being used whilst work continues on the other parts then 'it is usual to cease capitalisation of borrowing costs for each part as it is completed'.[52]

The IASC has recently issued an exposure draft, E32 — *Comparability of Financial Statements* — which proposes to amend, inter alia, the requirements of IAS 23. The main change proposed is that the preferred treatment for borrowing costs is that they should be recognised as an expense when incurred, although the alternative treatment of capitalising such costs will still be allowed, provided certain information is given.[53]

2.4 The balance of opinion

The conclusion of the majority members of the FASB was that the approach laid down in SFAS 34 'is preferable to the alternatives of (a) excluding interest from asset acquisition cost in all circumstances or (b) imputing interest on equity capital'.[54]

In view of the merits of both sides of the capitalisation argument, we agree that SFAS 34 is a reasonable compromise, but recommend IAS 23 as a model for UK companies choosing to capitalise borrowing costs. This is because, although SFAS 34 and IAS 23 are similar in approach, the former precludes certain treatments which we believe should be regarded as acceptable (see 3.1 and 3.2.2 below).

Nevertheless, SFAS 34 is far more detailed than IAS 23, and thus is a useful source of guidance on specific matters not addressed by the international standard.

3   ISSUES ARISING IN PRACTICE

3.1   Qualifying assets

In the UK, the range of assets on which companies have capitalised interest includes both fixed assets and stock. Specific examples of the types of assets included are property developments, ships, aircraft, maturing whisky stocks and tobacco. The Companies Act is sufficiently widely drawn to permit interest to be included in the production cost of any fixed or current asset,[55] but in practice capitalisation only takes place where the production period is sufficiently long for borrowing costs to be significant in relation to the total production cost.

However, as described in 2.2.1 above, the US definition of qualifying assets is narrower than this. In particular, capitalisation of interest on stocks which are routinely manufactured or otherwise produced in large quantities on a repetitive basis is not permitted in the US. The reason given by the FASB for this was that they considered that 'the informational benefit does not justify the cost of so doing.'[56] This principle could also be applied to maturing whisky or tobacco stocks, on the basis that, although an individual batch of whisky or tobacco may be held in stock for a significant period, there is a constant flow of product into and out of stock; hence, the effect on earnings of capitalising interest on such items usually would not be significant in the long run. In addition, some commentators argued that the aging of such stocks is not part of the production process.[57] However, interpretational difficulties of the phrase 'routinely manufactured or otherwise produced in large quantities on a repetitive basis'[58] may lead companies to capitalise interest in these situations. IAS 23, on the other hand, does not altogether rule out interest capitalisation in such circumstances. It merely takes the line that it is not usual (see 2.3 above). Given the length of the maturation period for whisky stocks, interest incurred in financing them is likely to be significant, and it seems reasonable to regard it as a cost of bringing the stocks to their final location and condition.[59] It can therefore be argued that the circumstances are sufficiently unusual to justify capitalisation under IAS 23. A similar argument could be applied to tobacco.

3.2   Period of production

Problems are frequently encountered in defining the capitalisation period — when it should start and when to stop capitalising. Many companies give no indication of their interpretation of the capitalisation period despite the fact that difficulties can arise at virtually every stage in the production period.

3.2.1 Commencement of capitalisation period

Property developments provide a good illustration of the sort of difficulties which can arise in defining the commencement of the capitalisation period. There are a number of possible stages in the development which might be relevant to such a definition:

- the decision to develop a site;

- earliest purchase of part of the development site;

- completion of purchase of the entire development site;

- vacant possession of the entire site;

- when planning permission has been obtained;

- entering into a building contract; and

- commencement of building work (or of demolition).

In deciding which of these factors is most appropriate, the particular circumstances of the individual development need to be carefully considered. The US principles described in 2.2.3 above are also a good guide. For example, the first factor listed above (decision to develop) would not usually be appropriate because it would generally occur before expenditures had been made on the development. However, there are circumstances where the decision date could be appropriate. For example, where the company decides to purchase a property adjacent to an existing investment property and redevelop both sites together, it could be appropriate to start capitalising interest from the date of the decision provided the decision was acted upon promptly.

Land awaiting development often causes difficulties. Given that there must be a period of production, the mere holding of a land bank is not a sufficient justification for capitalisation.

Companies tend not to define the beginning of their capitalisation period in their financial statements. In the case of property developments, this may well be because the basis for selecting a commencement date depends very much on the individual development.

The important thing to bear in mind when selecting the appropriate commencement date is that the Companies Act only permits capitalisation of interest during a period of production,[60] and therefore it is necessary that the company has embarked on the production of a specific asset.

3.2.2 End of capitalisation period

As with commencement of capitalisation, many companies do not explain how the end of their capitalisation period is defined. The following are examples of companies which have an accounting policy on the subject:

Extract 12.1: The Peninsular and Oriental Steam Navigation Company[61]

Ships and other non-property fixed assets [extract]
Interest incurred in respect of payments on account of vessels under construction up to
the date of delivery is capitalised to the cost of the vessel concerned.

Extract 12.2: Capital & Counties plc[62]

(d) Investment properties under development [extract]
A property is regarded as completed when its rental income equates to 80% of that
anticipated when the building is fully let or when the rental income exceeds the interest
and property outgoings, whichever occurs first. If this policy would result in a property
being treated as under development for a period exceeding one year from the date of
practical completion, the continuance of this status is subject to specific review
and confirmation by the Board.

Extract 12.2 above is fairly typical of the accounting policies of property
companies with developments. The development is not regarded as ready for its
intended use until a reasonable period of time has been allowed to find tenants,
i.e. until it is (or ought to be) income-producing. The US standard would not
allow this treatment, as capitalisation would have to cease on each part of the
development as it became substantially complete and ready for use.[63] IAS 23
effectively states that it would be usual to follow the US treatment[64] but does not
rule out other treatments. In cases such as this, we believe that the SFAS 34
approach is unrealistic because it treats as several different assets something
which ought to be regarded as one: the financing of the development would never
be considered on such a piecemeal basis.

3.2.3   Interruptions and delays during development

It is sometimes argued that capitalisation of interest should be suspended when
interruptions or delays occur during development. The basis for this is that
interest incurred during an interruption or delay does not add to the value of the
development. Whilst this is true, it is also true that delays and interruptions add to
the cost of a development. It therefore seems more appropriate to continue to
capitalise interest even though a write down may be necessary. If the development
is abandoned completely, then the interest costs should be written off together
with other abortive expenditure incurred on the development.

3.3   Determination of amount to be capitalised

3.3.1   Borrowings and capitalisation rate

Few companies give any indication of their method of calculating interest to be
capitalised. However, it seems likely that there is a wide divergence in methods
used, as literature[65] on the subject discusses a variety of possible methods of
calculation including:

(a)   rate of interest on borrowings specifically taken out to finance the development;

(b)   weighted average rate of interest. This could be based on:

    (i)   all borrowings; or
    (ii) selected borrowings, e.g. as in SFAS 34 and IAS 23 where the borrowings are selected as representing avoidable interest costs (see 2.2.2 and 2.3 above);

(c)   highest rate of interest;

(d)   rate of interest on most recent borrowings;

(e)   market capitalisation rate. This is a measure of the rate of return investors could earn elsewhere and could be either a general rate or specific to a particular industry; and

(f)   total interest charge as a percentage of total funds available, including shareholders' funds. This method assumes that finance has been provided pro rata by shareholders and lenders so, in effect, interest is capitalised only on that part of the asset presumed to have been financed out of borrowings.

Of the above, we prefer methods (a) or (b)(ii) using a selection of borrowings intended to represent those which would have been avoided in the absence of expenditure on the qualifying asset. Note that these methods assume that the asset is financed entirely by borrowings. Method (f), on the other hand, assumes that the asset is financed by a combination of borrowings and shareholders' funds, but only accounts for the cost of borrowings. We do not believe that any strong arguments can be advanced in favour of methods (c) to (e) although these methods might fit the circumstances of a particular case at a given point in time.

The Companies Act wording quoted in 2.1 above appears only to permit method (a) in that it refers to capital borrowed to finance the production of *that* asset. It could be argued that capitalisation can only take place where specific borrowings can be identified with specific assets. However, it is not reasonable or practicable to take such a strict line. This would mean, for example, that a company which chose not to repay a particular borrowing because it was needed to finance a development would not be able to capitalise the interest on that borrowing. In practice, therefore, a more liberal interpretation is applied.

The following example illustrates the application of the preferred methods (contrasted with method (f)):

Example 12.1: Calculation of capitalisation rate

On April 1, 19X1 a company engages in the development of a property which is expected to take five years to complete, at a cost of £6,000,000. The balance sheets at December 31, 19X0 and December 31, 19X1, prior to capitalisation of interest, are as follows:

	December 31,19X0 £	December 31,19X1 £
Development property	—	1,200,000
Other assets	6,000,000	6,800,000
	6,000,000	8,000,000
Loans		
8% debenture stock	2,500,000	2,500,000
Bank loan at 10% p.a.	—	2,000,000
Bank loan at 12% p.a.	1,000,000	1,000,000
	3,500,000	5,500,000
Shareholders' equity	2,500,000	2,500,000

The bank loan at 10% was taken out on March 31, 19X1 and the total interest charge for the year ended December 31, 19X1 was as follows:

	£
£2,500,000 x 8%	200,000
£2,000,000 x 10% x 9/12	150,000
. £1,000,000 x 12%	120,000
	470,000

Expenditure was incurred on the development as follows:

	£
April 1, 19X1	600,000
July 1, 19X1	400,000
October 1, 19X1	200,000
	1,200,000

(a) If the bank loan at 10% p.a. is a new borrowing taken out specifically to finance the development, then the amount of interest to be capitalised is:

	£
£600,000 x 10% x 9/12	45,000
£400,000 x 10% x 6/12	20,000
£200,000 x 10% x 3/12	5,000
	70,000

(b) If all the borrowings would have been avoided but for the development then the amount of interest to be capitalised is:

$$\frac{\text{Total interest expense for period}}{\text{Weighted average total borrowings}} \times \text{Development expenditure}$$

i.e. $\dfrac{470{,}000}{3{,}500{,}000 + (2{,}000{,}000 \times 9/12)} = 9.4\%$

	£
£600,000 x 9.4% x 9/12	42,300
£400,000 x 9.4% x 6/12	18,800
£200,000 x 9.4% x 3/12	4,700
	__65,800__

If the 8% debenture stock was irredeemable then as the borrowings could not have been avoided the above calculation would be done using the figures for the bank loans and their related interest costs only.

If method (f) is used then the interest rate to be applied would be:

$$\frac{\text{Total interest expense for period}}{\text{Weighted average total borrowings} + \text{weighted average shareholders' equity}}$$

i.e. $\dfrac{470{,}000}{5{,}000{,}000 + 2{,}500{,}000} = 6.27\%$

Accordingly, a lower amount of interest would be capitalised reflecting the fact that part of the development is financed by shareholders' equity.

As mentioned above, few companies give any indication of their method of calculating interest to be capitalised. Two exceptions are BICC plc and MEPC plc, as illustrated below:

Extract 12.3: BICC plc[66]

8 Stocks [extract]
Contracting work in progress is valued at estimated sales value except for land, property developments not subject to a substantially unconditional contract for sale and housebuilding which are valued at the lower of cost (including interest on external borrowings directly related to specific development projects) and estimated sales value.

Extract 12.4: MEPC plc[67]

Properties [extract]
An amount equivalent to interest and other outgoings less rental income attributable to properties in course of development is transferred to the cost of properties. For this purpose the interest rate applied to funds provided for property development is arrived at by reference, where appropriate, to the actual rate payable on borrowings for development purposes and, in regard to that part of the development cost financed out of general funds, to the average rate paid on funding the assets employed by the Group.

3.3.2 Limitation on interest capitalised

We have seen in 2.2.3 and 2.3 that it is generally considered that the maximum amount which should be capitalised in any one period is the actual interest incurred in the period. If a company has received interest income during the period the question then arises — is the maximum amount which can be capitalised the net interest incurred after deducting such interest or is it the gross interest incurred?

In the US, interest earned is not offset against interest cost in determining either capitalisation rates or limitations on the amount of interest cost to be capitalised, except in situations involving the acquisition of qualifying assets financed by the proceeds of tax-exempt borrowings if those funds are externally restricted to finance the acquisition of specified qualifying assets or to service the related debt.[68] The provisions in SFAS 34 for determining the amount of interest cost to be capitalised deal solely with the interest cost incurred and the rates applicable to borrowings outstanding. Temporary or short-term investment decisions are not related to the determination of the acquisition cost of the asset or to the allocation of that cost against revenues of the periods benefited by the asset.

This is in stark contrast with IAS 23, which states that if borrowings specific to a project are temporarily invested until needed, then the capitalisation rate for that project should take into account the related investment income.[69] This is because it is this amount which could theoretically have been avoided in the absence of expenditure on the qualifying asset.[70] It could, therefore, be argued that the net figure should be used as it is a more objective measure of the interest cost which could have been avoided, because otherwise the maximum amount to be capitalised is dependent on the level of surplus funds and borrowings which the company chooses to have.

As shown below, Wm Morrison PLC do, in fact, capitalise interest in excess of gross interest incurred. They are thereby effectively capitalising notional interest.

Extract 12.5: Wm Morrison Supermarkets PLC[71]

Capitalisation of interest

The cost of financing property developments prior to the opening date is included in the cost of the project and capitalised net of tax relief. Due to the nature of the business there are occasions when amounts paid on developments under construction exceed loans outstanding. In order to give a true and fair view of the total cost of all property the company does, in such circumstances, capitalise interest foregone net of tax.

5 Net interest receivable	1988 £000's	1987 £000's
Interest receivable on short term deposits	1,128	86
Interest payable		
On loans not repayable within 5 years	(22)	(22)
On short term loans and bank overdrafts	(2,931)	(575)
On finance lease	(21)	(2)
	(1,846)	(513)
Interest capitalised/foregone	3,267	1,153
Net interest receivable	1,421	640

The wording used in the Companies Act appears to permit capitalisation only of interest actually incurred (see 2.1 above). Although the Companies Act provision is interpreted liberally in other respects (see 3.3.1 above and 3.5.4 below), we believe that the capitalisation of interest should be limited to the amount of interest incurred.

3.3.3   Gross or net of tax relief

Some companies capitalise interest net of the related tax relief whilst others capitalise gross. The argument usually advanced in favour of capitalising net is that the tax relief should follow the accounting charge which gives rise to it.[72] Against this, it can be argued that it is not usual to account for assets net of tax effects. Where capital allowances are received in respect of the costs of fixed assets then the tax benefit is reflected in the tax charge in the profit and loss account. Provision is made under SSAP 15 for the reversal of this timing difference only if it is likely that it will reverse in the foreseeable future. If no provision is necessary, then the full benefit is reflected in the profit and loss account. Capitalisation of interest also creates a timing difference which should be accounted for in accordance with SSAP 15. Of the two treatments, we consider the arguments in favour of capitalisation gross to be the stronger.

Capitalisation net of tax relief used to be the more common treatment but in recent years, there has been a trend towards capitalising gross so that now companies are probably fairly evenly divided between those who capitalise net and those who capitalise gross. Unfortunately, not all companies explain which treatment they have adopted, in spite of The Stock Exchange requirement to give 'an indication of the amount and treatment of any related tax relief.'[73] The Hammerson Property and Development Corporation plc is an example of a company who changed from capitalisation net to capitalisation gross and in this case not only is interest capitalised but other development outgoings are also capitalised.[74]

3.3.4   Compounding

Another question which frequently arises in practice is whether interest should be capitalised on a compound basis. On the face of it, the basis should be compound because the cost of the asset is the amount being funded, and capitalised interest is part of the cost. However, where it is only interest on specific borrowings which is being capitalised, regard should be had as to whether interest is actually suffered on a compound basis under the terms of the borrowings, which may not be the case where interest is paid as it falls due.

Example 12.2: Capitalising interest on a compound basis

The facts are as in Example 12.1 above (see 3.3.1 above) with the 10% bank loan representing a loan specifically financing the development. In addition to the £1,200,000 expended on the development in 19X1, a further £800,000 is incurred on January 1, 19X2. All interest falls due on June 30 and December 31 each year and is paid on the due dates. Interest incurred on the bank loan in 19X2 is, therefore, £200,000.

If interest is capitalised on a compound basis, amounts capitalised in 19X1 and 19X2 will be as follows:

19X1: (as before) £70,000
19X2: (£1,200,000 + £70,000 + £800,000) x 10% = £207,000

The interest capitalised in 19X2 therefore exceeds the interest incurred on the specific borrowing. This results purely from capitalising interest on a compound basis when it is not actually suffered on a compound basis. In cases such as this, interest should not be capitalised on a compound basis.

If the interest was not paid half-yearly but was rolled-up and payable when the loan was to be repaid then it would be likely that interest would be required to be compounded. If it were to be compounded on an annual basis then the charge for 19X2 would have been £215,000 and therefore the interest could be capitalised on a compound basis.

Where the borrowings taken into account in determining the capitalisation rate include bank overdrafts then it would be appropriate to capitalise interest on a compound basis. Any interest paid is likely to be financed out of the bank overdrafts and therefore interest will be incurred on a compound basis.

3.3.5   Accrued costs

In principle, costs of a qualifying asset which have only been accrued but have not yet been paid in cash should be excluded from the amount on which interest is capitalised. It should be noted that the effect of applying this principle is often merely to delay the capitalisation of interest since the costs will be included once they have been paid in cash. In most cases it is unlikely that the effect will be material as the time between accrual and payment of the cost will not be that great. However, the effect is potentially material where a significant part of the amount capitalised relates to costs which have been financed interest-free by third parties for a long period. An example of this is retention money which is not generally payable until the asset is completed.

3.3.6 *Asset not previously held at cost*

An asset may appear in the financial statements prior to the capitalisation period on a basis other than cost, i.e. it may have been written down below cost or revalued above cost. The question then arises as to whether the calculation of interest to be capitalised should be based on cost or book value. In these circumstances, cost should be used as this is the amount that the company or group has had to finance. In the case of an asset previously written down, the circumstances giving rise to the provision may still be present (see 3.5.1 below).

3.4 Group financial statements

3.4.1 *Borrowings in one company and development in another*

A question which often arises in practice is whether it is appropriate to capitalise interest in the group financial statements on borrowings where the borrowings appear in the financial statements of a different group company from that carrying out the development. Based on the preference already stated, capitalisation in such circumstances would only be appropriate if the amount capitalised fairly reflected the interest cost of the group on borrowings from third parties which could theoretically have been avoided if the expenditure on the qualifying asset were not made.

Although it may be appropriate to capitalise interest in the group financial statements, the company carrying out the development should not capitalise any interest in its own financial statements as it has no borrowings (see 3.3.2 above). If, however, the company has intra-group borrowings then interest on such borrowings can be capitalised.

3.4.2 *Qualifying assets held by investments accounted for using the equity method*

The circumstances in which capitalisation would be permitted in the US for such assets are described in 2.2.1 above. In the UK, property developments are often carried out as joint ventures, frequently through the medium of associated companies. In such cases, the joint venture may be financed principally by equity and the joint venture partners may have financed their equity investment by borrowings. It is not appropriate to capitalise interest in the associate on the borrowings of the partners as the interest charge is not a cost of the associate. Neither would it be appropriate to capitalise interest in the individual (as opposed to group) financial statements of the investing companies because the qualifying asset does not belong to them. The asset which the investing companies have is an equity investment which is not in the course of production. However, the question does arise as to whether an adjustment may be made in the investor's group financial statements to capitalise interest on the borrowings financing the equity investment when the associate is equity accounted.

Example 12.3

A company has a 50% investment in an associate whose balance sheet at December 31, 19X1 is as follows:

	£'000	£'000
Share capital		100
Share premium		900
		1,000
Borrowings: 10% loan		1,000
		2,000
Expenditure on development	1,600	
Capitalised interest	100 *	
		1,700
Cash		300
		2,000

     * £1,600,000 x 10% restricted to actual interest incurred of £100,000.

The cost of the investment was £500,000 which was financed by a borrowing at 9% p.a. The investing company could, therefore, capitalise additional interest of £27,000 (being £600,000 x 50% x 9%) in its group financial statements (recognising that only 50% of the development expenditure not funded by borrowings is funded by the investing company).

Capitalisation in these circumstances appears to be justified on the basis that the borrowings are effectively financing the company's share of the development. It would have been possible for a similar result to be shown if the investing companies had decided to finance the associate with borrowings and only a nominal amount of equity.

Where the qualifying assets are held by an investment which is not effectively an interest in a joint venture or consortium it is unlikely that an adjustment should be made in the group financial statements. This is because the interest in the investing company would probably not have been avoided if the investee had not incurred the costs on the qualifying asset.

3.5 Other issues

3.5.1 Provisions for diminution in value

Care is needed to ensure that interest capitalisation does not result in assets being carried at too high a value. In this context, the following circumstances are worth noting:

(a) assets which had been written down prior to the capitalisation period (see 3.3.6 above for a discussion of the basis for the amount to be capitalised in these circumstances);

(b) delays and interruptions during development may increase interest costs to the extent that a provision becomes necessary.

It is worth reiterating that interest capitalisation should not cease merely because a provision becomes necessary (see 3.2.3 above for the rationale for this). In determining the amount of the provision, all future costs, *including interest*, to be incurred to completion should be taken into account.

3.5.2 Change of policy to capitalise interest

When interest is capitalised for the first time, SSAP 6 requires that a prior year adjustment be made as this is a change of accounting policy. In theory, the adjustment should be made in respect of all assets still held which would, during their period of production, have satisfied the criteria adopted for capitalisation. This can create considerable difficulty in the case of fixed assets which were produced many years ago. Accordingly, some compromises may have to be made in calculating the prior year adjustment but it should be possible to produce a materially accurate figure.

3.5.3 Exchange differences as a borrowing cost

Borrowings in one currency may have been used to finance a development the costs of which are incurred primarily in another currency, e.g. a US dollar loan financing a sterling development. This may have been done on the basis that, over the period of the development, the interest cost, after allowing for exchange differences, was expected to be less than the interest cost of an equivalent sterling loan. In these circumstances, there is a good argument for capitalising the interest cost and the exchange difference. This is discussed further in 3.1.5 A of Chapter 18.

3.5.4 Assets produced by others

According to the Companies Act 1985, the production cost of an asset 'shall be determined by adding to the purchase price of the raw materials and consumables used the amount of the costs incurred by the company which are directly attributable to the production of that asset'.[75] Interest may be included in production cost as described in 2.1 above. This could be interpreted as meaning that interest may only be capitalised on assets produced by the company itself rather than assets produced by others for the company, because if the assets are produced entirely by others the production costs are not incurred by the company.

This would rule out capitalisation on most development and construction projects which hardly seems logical given that the rationale for capitalising interest is strongly dependent on the view that it is an integral part of cost. Not surprisingly, therefore, a wider interpretation of the Companies Act is used in practice. SFAS 34 makes it clear that qualifying assets include 'assets constructed or produced for the enterprise by others for which deposits or progress payments have been made',[76] but IAS 23 is silent on this point.

3.5.5   Depreciation

It is sometimes argued that capitalised interest should be written off faster than the depreciation rate of other costs of a development on the basis that it is less tangible. Certainly this is a conservative approach, but it is not a rational one. The basis for capitalising interest in the first place depends strongly on the view that it is an integral part of cost so there is no reason to treat it separately for depreciation purposes.

4   DISCLOSURE

4.1   Balance sheet and related notes

If interest is included in the production cost of an asset, the Companies Act 1985 requires disclosure of 'the amount of the interest so included'.[77] This presumably means the cumulative amount of capitalised interest as opposed to the amount capitalised during the year. If the asset in question is a fixed asset, then it would seem that the disclosure ought to continue beyond the production period and presumably the amount disclosed should be net of any depreciation or provision for diminution in value. Such disclosure would be useful because it would show the cumulative effect on the financial statements of the decision to capitalise interest. However, this information is not available in practice as the Companies Act requirement is generally being interpreted as requiring disclosure only during the production period. No information is therefore available on the interest content of completed stock or fixed assets.

Where interest is being capitalised on a tangible fixed asset it is likely that the asset to which it relates will have to be disclosed separately from other tangible fixed assets as the balance sheet formats require 'payments on account and assets in course of construction' to be disclosed.[78]

4.2   Profit and loss account and related notes

The Companies Act requires the interest on certain categories of borrowing to be disclosed.[79] This information is normally given in a note to the financial statements. Interest capitalised is usually shown as a deduction from interest incurred within this note. For companies capitalising net of tax relief, a similar presentation is often used for the tax note. For example:

Interest payable	19X2 £'000	19X1 £'000
On bank loans and overdrafts and other loans repayable within five years	1,000	750
On other loans	700	900
	1,700	1,650
Interest capitalised on development properties	(800)	(600)
	900	1,050

Tax on profit on ordinary activities	19X2 £'000	19X1 £'000
Corporation tax at 35%	2,500	2,000
Deferred tax	500	250
Tax relief attributable to capitalised interest	280	210
	3,280	2,460

Companies capitalising gross generally disclose the tax relief on capitalised interest in narrative form, for example:

Interest payable	19X2 £'000	19X1 £'000
On bank loans and overdrafts and other loans repayable within five years	1,000	750
On other loans	700	900
	1,700	1,650
Interest capitalised on development properties	(800)	(600)
	900	1,050

Tax on profit on ordinary activities	19X2 £'000	19X1 £'000
Corporation tax at 35%	2,500	2,000
Deferred tax	500	250
	3,000	2,250

The above charge is net of tax relief attributable to capitalised interest of £280,000 (19X1: £210,000).

4.3   Accounting policy

The following information should be clear from the accounting policy of a company capitalising interest (some of the information is already required, as indicated in the footnotes):

(a)   the classes of assets on which interest is capitalised;[80]

(b)   the method of calculation, e.g. whether specific borrowings are used and, if not, the basis of selection of the borrowings used in the calculation;

(c)   whether capitalisation is gross or net of tax relief;[81] and

(d)   how the capitalisation period is defined.

Nevertheless, many companies capitalising interest give rather less information than the above. However, MEPC plc's policy, reproduced below, is fairly comprehensive.

Extract 12.6: MEPC plc[82]

Properties [extract]
An amount equivalent to interest and other outgoings less rental income attributable to properties in course of development is transferred to the cost of properties. For this purpose the interest rate applied to funds provided for property development is arrived at by reference, where appropriate, to the actual rate payable on borrowings for development purposes and, in regard to that part of the development cost financed out of general funds, to the average rate paid on funding the assets employed by the Group.
A property ceases to be treated as being in course of development at the earliest of:
(1) the date when the development becomes fully let and income producing
(2) the date when income exceeds outgoings
(3) a date up to three years after completion to allow for letting.
Any liability to development taxation is added to the cost of the properties.

Taxation [extract]
Where a transfer of an amount equivalent to interest and other outgoings attributable to properties in course of development is made and tax relief is receivable for the cost of such interest and other outgoings, the tax relief so claimed is treated as a reduction of development cost.

5   CONCLUSION

As mentioned in 1.2 above, the arguments for and against capitalising interest are evenly balanced. We therefore believe that disclosure of the effects of capitalising interest is important. However, as observed in 4.1 above, financial statements do not at present fully explain the cumulative effect of the decision to capitalise interest. In fact, neither is the overall effect on the profit for the year clear from present disclosures, as the interest content of the charge for depreciation or amortisation is not disclosed. Neither IAS 23 nor SFAS 34 require such disclosure so the UK is not alone in not requiring this information.

In the absence of an accounting standard on the subject in the UK, a wide variety of methods of capitalisation are being used. Greater consistency would be achieved if companies adopting a policy of capitalisation were to use IAS 23 as a model.

References

1   *Chancery Lane Safe Deposit and Offices Co. Ltd. v. I.R.C.* [1966] A.C. 85.
2   *Fitzleet Estates Ltd. and Others v. Cherry (H.M. Inspector of Taxes)* [1977] 51 T.C., 708.
3   *Ibid.,* at 718.
4   Taxes Act 1970, ss 248(5)(a), 269 as amended by Finance Act 1981, s 38 (now Taxes Act 1988, s 338(3)).
5   CA 85, Sch. 4, para. 26(3)(b).
6   The moratorium was imposed on November 14, 1974 by Accounting Series Release No. 163, *Capitalization of Interest by Companies Other Than Public Utilities.* Washington D.C.: Securities and Exchange Commission, 1974.
7   'Public utilities' was defined to include electric, gas, water, and telephone utilities.
8   SFAS 34, *Capitalisation of Interest Cost*, FASB, October 1979.
9   For a more detailed discussion of the background to SFAS 34, see Appendix A to the statement.
10 IAS 23, *Capitalisation of Borrowing Costs*, IASC, March 1984.
11 For a full understanding of the reasons for the dissenting vote, see SFAS 34 for the text of the statement issued by the dissenting members of the FASB.
12 IAS 23, para. 6.
13 *Ibid.,* para. 7.
14 SFAS 34, para. 36.
15 *Ibid.,* para. 38.
16 SFAS 34, text of the statement issued by the dissenting members of the FASB.
17 *Ibid.,* para. 54.
18 *Ibid.,* para. 49.
19 *Ibid.,* para. 40.
20 *Ibid.,* Appendix B, para 49.
21 SSAP 9, *Stocks and long-term contracts*, May 1975, Appendix 1, para. 21.
22 CA 85, Sch. 4, para. 26(3).
23 It is noteworthy that J Sainsbury plc have adopted the accounting policy whereby 'interest incurred on borrowings to finance specific property developments is capitalised', thereby

applying a strict interpretation of CA 85, Sch. 4, para. 26(3)(b). See J Sainsbury plc, 1988 Annual Report and Accounts, p. 31.

24 The Council of The Stock Exchange, *Admission of Securities to Listing*, Section 5, Chapter 2, para. 21(g).

25 The Council of The Stock Exchange, *The Stock Exchange Unlisted Securities Market*, General Undertaking, para. 10(g).

26 SFAS 58, *Capitalization of Interest Cost in Financial Statements That Include Investments Accounted for by the Equity Method*, FASB, April 1982.

27 SFAS 62, *Capitalization of Interest Cost in Situations Involving Certain Tax-Exempt Borrowings and Certain Gifts and Grants*, FASB, June 1982.

28 SFAS 34, para. 9.

29 *Ibid.*

30 SFAS 58, para. 5.

31 SFAS 34, para. 10.

32 *Ibid.*

33 *Ibid.*

34 SFAS 58, para. 6.

35 *Ibid.*

36 SFAS 34, para. 11.

37 *Ibid.*, paras. 12—15.

38 *Ibid.*, para. 15.

39 *Ibid.*, para. 16.

40 *Ibid.*, paras. 17 and 18.

41 *Ibid.*, para. 18.

42 *Ibid.*, para. 19.

43 *Ibid.*, para. 21.

44 IAS 23, para. 21.

45 *Ibid.*, para. 28.

46 *Ibid.*, para. 10.

47 *Ibid.*, para. 24.

48 *Ibid.*, para. 11.

49 *Ibid.*, para. 15.

50 *Ibid.*, para. 27.

51 *Ibid.*, para. 16.

52 *Ibid.*, para. 12

53 E32, *Comparability of Financial Statements*, January 1989, para. 188.

54 SFAS 34, para. 54.

55 CA 85, Sch. 4, paras. 17, 22 and 26(3).

56 SFAS 34, para. 10.

57 *Ibid.*, paras. 10, 45 and 46.

58 *Ibid.*, para. 10.

59 SSAP 9, para. 19(c).

60 CA 85, Sch. 4, para. 26(3)(b).

61 The Peninsular and Oriental Steam Navigation Company, Annual Report and Accounts 1987, p. 23.

62 Capital & Counties plc, Annual Report and Accounts 1987, p. 29.

63 SFAS 34, para. 18.

64 IAS 23, para. 12.

65 See for example Rickwood, *Accounting treatment of capitalised interest*, pp. 20—22 and G.A. Milnes and D.R. Tillett, *Property Company Accounts*, pp. 25—30.

66 BICC plc, 1987 Annual Report, p. 25.

67 MEPC plc, Report and Financial Statements 1988, p. 23.

68 SFAS 62, para. 3.

69 IAS 23, para. 16.

70 SFAS 34, para. 12.
71 Wm Morrison Supermarkets PLC, Report and Financial Statements 1988, pp. 7 and 12.
72 G.A. Milnes and D.R. Tillett, *op. cit.*, p. 31.
73 *Admission of Securities to Listing*, Section 5, Chapter 2, para. 21(g).
74 The Hammerson Property and Development Corporation plc, 1985 Annual Report, p. 22.
75 CA 85, Sch. 4, para. 26(2).
76 SFAS 34, para. 9(a).
77 CA 85, Sch. 4, para. 26(3).
78 *Ibid.*, para. 8.
79 *Ibid.*, para. 53(2).
80 *Ibid.*, para. 26(3).
81 *Admission of Securities to Listing*, Section 5, Chapter 2, para. 21(g).
82 MEPC plc, Report and Financial Statements 1988, p. 23.

Chapter 13

Research and development

1   INTRODUCTION

1.1   Possible accounting treatments of research and development expenditure

There are essentially four possible methods of accounting for research and development expenditure. These are as follows:

(a)   charge all costs to expense when incurred; or

(b)   capitalise all costs when incurred; or

(c)   capitalise costs when incurred providing specified conditions are fulfilled and charge all others to expense; or

(d)   accumulate all costs in a special category distinct from assets and expenses until the existence of future benefits can be determined.

Each of the above may be considered in turn.

1.1.1   Charge all costs to expense when incurred

This is the required treatment in the US (see 5.1 below). The five factors offered by the FASB as support for its requirements to expense all expenditure immediately were as follows:[1]

(a)   uncertainty of future benefits.

The primary reason offered by the FASB for expensing research and development costs was the uncertainty associated with such costs. It was argued that research and development projects have considerable risk, i.e. a large probability of failure and consequently all such costs should be expensed. In support, the FASB cited one study of a number of industries that found an average of less than 2% of new product ideas and less than 15% of product development projects were commercially successful.

(b)   lack of causal relationship between expenditure and benefits.

The FASB cited in its statement three research studies that generally failed to find a significant connection between research and development expenditure and increased future benefits by subsequent sales, earnings or share of industry sales. However, the fact that the three studies cited failed to find a causal relationship between expenditure and benefits does not mean that such a relationship does not exist. If this was the case companies would be much more reluctant to incur such expenditure.

(c)   research and development does not meet the accounting concept of an asset.

The FASB argued that to be an asset the expenditure would need to be subject to reasonable measurement. They stated that 'the criterion of measurability would require that a resource not be recognised as an asset for accounting purposes unless at the time it is acquired or developed its future economic benefits can be identified and objectively measured'.[2] However, this could be argued in relation to practically any asset at the time it is acquired.

(d)   matching of revenues and expenses.

The FASB argued that because of the uncertainty of future benefits of research and development expenditure there was an insufficient cause and effect relationship to justify the carrying forward of research and development expenditure to future periods.

(e)   relevance of resulting information for investment and credit decisions.

The FASB stated that APB Statement No. 4 indicates that certain costs are immediately recognised as expenses because allocating them to several accounting periods is considered to serve no useful purpose. The FASB went on to state that 'the relationship between current research and development costs and the amount of resultant future benefits to an enterprise is so uncertain that capitalisation of any research and development costs is not useful in assessing the earnings potential of the enterprise.[3]

1.1.2   Capitalise all costs when incurred

Enterprises undertake research and development expenditure in the hope of future benefits. Hence, it could be argued that if future benefits were unlikely then the expenditure would not be incurred. Whilst this may be the case for some projects, it is undoubtedly not so for all such expenditure. One could, however, perhaps argue that since future benefits will be gained from some of the expenditure, then an enterprise should capitalise all such costs and match the total costs to the future benefits derived from some of them.

However, a meaningful method of amortisation would be impossible to achieve since the expenditure would be carried out at different points in time and also the period of benefit would be extremely difficult to determine.

1.1.3   Capitalise costs when incurred if certain conditions are met

A prerequisite of this treatment is the establishment of conditions that must be fulfilled before research and development costs may be capitalised. Furthermore, such conditions once established must be capable of being applied by all enterprises. If the specified conditions are not met, then costs are to be expensed.

1.1.4 Accumulation of costs in a special category

At a future date such costs could then be either transferred to assets if future benefits could reasonably be established or written off if it were reasonably established that no significant future benefits would arise.

This treatment would draw attention to the uncertainty surrounding the expenditure and would also delay the decision of whether to capitalise or expense. However, such accumulated costs would arguably serve little purpose insofar as analysts and others are concerned.

1.1.5 Which treatment should be adopted?

The choice of an appropriate accounting treatment for research and development centres on the application of fundamental accounting concepts 'including the "accruals" concept by which revenue and costs are accrued, matched and dealt with in the period to which they relate and the "prudence" concept by which revenue and profits are not anticipated but are recognised only when realised in the form either of cash or of other assets the ultimate cash realisation of which can be established with reasonable certainty. It is a corollary of the prudence concept that expenditure should be written off in the period in which it arises unless its relationship to the revenue of a future period can be assessed with reasonable certainty.'[4]

1.2 Development of accounting standards in the UK

1.2.1 ED 14

As a result of the different possible accounting treatments that were being adopted, the ASC issued ED 14 — *Accounting for Research and Development* — in January 1975. Although the exposure draft made a distinction between pure and applied research and development expenditure, it proposed that all research and development expenditure should be written off as incurred to the profit and loss account, with very minor exceptions. The ED received widespread criticism, particularly from the aerospace industry. The bulk of such criticism was concerned with the treatment of development expenditure. It was pointed out that the design and development stage of a new aircraft took at least five years prior to the delivery of the first production aircraft to a customer, and that sales of a successful aircraft then continued for at least ten years with delivery of spares continuing well beyond that point.[5]

1.2.2 ED 17

Due to the criticism received ED 14 was withdrawn and replaced by ED 17 — *Accounting for research and development—revised* — which was issued in April 1976. Whilst still proposing that pure and applied research expenditure be expensed in the year in which it was incurred, it recognised that some development expenditure could be clearly matched to future benefits which were reasonably certain. Consequently, the exposure draft concluded that such expenditure should be capitalised provided certain criteria were met. This ED was more favourably received. However, a number of commentators made the point that 'where companies wished to write off development expenditure, even though the projects fulfilled the conditions in ED 17 which would justify carrying forward the expenditure, they should be permitted to do so provided the treatment was disclosed in notes to the accounts'.[6]

1.2.3   SSAP 13

Consequently, when SSAP 13 was issued in December 1977, although the standard contained essentially the same requirements as those of ED 17, it did not *require* companies to defer development expenditure but, where certain criteria were fulfilled, *allowed them the choice* between immediate write off or capitalisation.[7]

1.2.4   ED 41

Since the issue of SSAP 13, the Fourth EC Company Law Directive was enacted in UK company law, following which the ASC embarked on a policy of reviewing its existing accounting standards. (The relevant requirements of the Companies Act which relate to research and development expenditure are discussed at 3 below.) As a result ED 41 — *Accounting for research and development* — was issued in June 1987. The principal change to SSAP 13 proposed by ED 41 related to the disclosure of the amount of research and development costs charged to the profit and loss account in the current period. The exposure draft also proposed to categorise research and development expenditure as an intangible fixed asset rather than deferred expenditure, as it was classified under SSAP 13.[8] The exposure draft also intended to continue the requirement of SSAP 13 that development expenditure once written off should not be reinstated even though the uncertainties which led to its being written off no longer apply.[9] However, such a treatment conflicts with the Companies Act requirements relating to fixed assets. Paragraph 19(3) of Schedule 4 to the Companies Act requires any provisions against the value of a fixed asset to be released when the reasons for its creation cease to apply.

1.2.5   SSAP 13 (Revised)

In January 1989, SSAP 13 (Revised) — *Accounting for research and development* — was issued, and it essentially followed the line taken by ED 41. The main changes between the standard and the exposure draft are as follows:

(a)   although the standard requires the amount of research and development costs charged to the profit and loss account to be disclosed, certain enterprises are to be exempt from this disclosure;

(b)   the proposal that development expenditure once written off should not be reinstated even though the uncertainties which led to its being written off no longer apply has not been included in the standard, presumably in view of the conflict with the Companies Act referred to at 1.2.4 above.

The revised standard is mandatory for accounting periods beginning on or after January 1, 1989, although earlier application is recommended.[10]

2   REQUIREMENTS OF SSAP 13 (REVISED)

2.1   Definitions

Research and development expenditure is defined in SSAP 13 as 'expenditure falling into one or more of the following broad categories (except to the extent that it relates to locating or exploiting oil, gas or mineral deposits or is reimbursable by third parties either directly or under the terms of a firm contract to develop and manufacture at an agreed price calculated to reimburse both elements of expenditure):

(a)   pure (or basic) research: experimental or theoretical work undertaken primarily to acquire new scientific or technical knowledge for its own sake rather than directed towards any specific aim or application;

(b)   applied research: original or critical investigation undertaken in order to gain new scientific or technical knowledge and directed towards a specific practical aim or objective;

(c)   development: use of scientific or technical knowledge in order to produce new or substantially improved materials, devices, products or services, to install new processes or systems prior to the commencement of commercial production or commercial applications, or to improving substantially those already produced or installed'.[11]

The definitions of the different types of research and development used in the standard are based on those used by the Organisation for Economic Co-operation and Development (OECD).[12]

However, as paragraph 4 of the standard states 'the dividing line between these categories is often indistinct and particular expenditure may have characteristics of more than one category. This is especially so when new products or services are developed through research and development to production, when the activities may have characteristics of both development and production.' For example, a project may start out as basic research, the results of which may lead to the development of new products or systems, particularly in, say, the pharmaceutical industry.

It can be seen that the standard specifically excludes from the definition:

(a)   expenditure incurred in locating and exploiting oil, gas and mineral deposits. However, development of new surveying methods and techniques as an integral part of research on geographical phenomena should be included in research and development;[13]

(b)   research and development expenditure which is reimbursed by a third party. Any such expenditure which has not been reimbursed at the balance sheet date should be dealt with as contract work in progress.[14]

2.2   Accounting

The accounting treatment prescribed by SSAP 13 is as follows:

2.2.1   *Fixed assets*

The cost of fixed assets acquired or constructed in order to provide facilities for research and development activities over a number of accounting periods should be capitalised and written off over their useful life through the profit and loss account.[15] The depreciation so written off should be included as part of the expenditure on research and development.[16] Where an asset is used in the course of the development activities, however, the depreciation thereon can be regarded as part of the overhead costs to be included as part of development costs, if such costs are to be deferred (see 2.2.3 below).

2.2.2   *Pure and applied research*

Expenditure on pure and applied research (other than the cost of fixed assets used for the purpose of research activities) should be written off in the year of expenditure through the profit and loss account.[17] This is because such expenditure 'can be regarded as part of a continuing operation required to maintain a company's business and its competitive position. In general, no one particular period rather than any other will be expected to benefit and therefore it is appropriate that these costs should be written off as they are incurred.'[18] In addition, the Companies Act does not allow pure or applied research to be treated as an asset (see 3.1 below).

2.2.3   *Development expenditure*

The standard proposes a different treatment for development expenditure. This is because 'the development of new products or services is, however, distinguishable from pure and applied research. Expenditure on such development is normally undertaken with a reasonable expectation of specific commercial success and of future benefits arising from the work, either from increased revenue and related profits or from reduced costs. On these grounds it may be argued that such expenditure, to the extent that it is recoverable, should be deferred to be matched against the future revenue.'[19] Consequently, the standard allows such expenditure to be deferred, but only if certain conditions are met.

The standard requires that 'development expenditure should be written off in the year of expenditure except in the following circumstances when it *may* be deferred to future periods:

(a)   there is a clearly defined project, and

(b)   the related expenditure is separately identifiable, and

(c)   the outcome of such a project has been assessed with reasonable certainty as to:

    (i)   its technical feasibility, and

    (ii)   its ultimate commercial viability considered in the light of factors such as likely market conditions (including competing products), public opinion, consumer and environmental legislation, and

(d)   the aggregate of the deferred development costs, any further development costs, and related production, selling and administration costs is reasonably expected to be exceeded by related future sales or other revenues, and

(e)   adequate resources exist, or are reasonably expected to be available, to enable the project to be completed and to provide any consequential increases in working capital'.[20]

The above conditions fall into two basic categories:

(a)   that an asset, and its cost, can be identified (conditions (a) and (b) above). It will only be practicable to evaluate the potential future benefits if this is the case;[21]

(b)   that the asset can be shown to be recoverable with sufficient certainty (conditions (c) — (e) above). The standard emphasises that the elements of uncertainty inherent in such a consideration are considerable.[22]

Although the standard allows a choice as to whether development expenditure which meets the conditions is to be deferred or not, it does require that where a policy of deferral is adopted, such a policy is to be applied to *all* development projects that meet the conditions laid down.[23]

A   Policy of deferral

Where a policy of deferral is adopted, then the expenditure should be deferred to the extent that its recovery can reasonably be assured.[24]

The development costs should be amortised and the amortisation 'should commence with the commercial production or application of the product, service, process or system and should be allocated on a systematic basis to each accounting period, by reference to either the sale or use of the product, service, process or system or the period over which these are expected to be sold or used'.[25]

The deferred development expenditure should be reviewed at the end of each accounting period and, where the circumstances that justified the deferral no longer apply, or are considered doubtful, the expenditure, to the extent that it is considered irrecoverable, should be written off immediately. This should be done on a project by project basis.[26]

2.3   Disclosure

The disclosure requirements of SSAP 13 are as follows:

(a)   the accounting policy on research and development expenditure should be stated and explained;[27]

(b)   the total amount of research and development expenditure charged in the profit and loss account should be disclosed, analysed between the current year's expenditure and amounts amortised from deferred expenditure.[28] It is emphasised that the amounts disclosed should include any amortisation of fixed assets used in the research and development activity.

(c)   movements on deferred development expenditure and the amount carried forward at the beginning and the end of the period should be disclosed. The expenditure should be disclosed under intangible fixed assets in the balance sheet.[29]

However, the information contained in (b) above need only be given by:[30]

(a)   public companies (as defined in section 1 of the Companies Act 1985) or holding companies that have one or more public companies as a subsidiary;

(b)   special category companies (as defined in section 257 of the Companies Act 1985) or holding companies that have one or more special category companies as a subsidiary;

(c)   private companies (and other enterprises) which do not satisfy the criteria, multiplied in each case by ten, for defining a medium-sized company under the Companies Act.

At present, this means that enterprises with any two of the following will have to give the extra information:

(i)   turnover exceeding £80m,
(ii)   total assets exceeding £39m,
(iii)   average number of employees exceeding 2,500.

2.4   Current reporting practice

Most major companies which incur research and development costs adopt a policy of writing off the expenditure as it is incurred.[31] One company which adopts such a policy is Beecham Group p.l.c. as illustrated below:

Extract 13.1: Beecham Group p.l.c.[32]

Research and development expenditure
Expenditure on laboratory buildings and equipment is capitalised and written off in accordance with the Group's depreciation policy. Other research and development expenditure is written off in the year in which it is incurred.

It can be seen that Beecham Group p.l.c. treat their fixed assets which are used in research and development activities in the same way as any other fixed asset which is what SSAP 13 requires. Another company which adopts a similar policy is Reckitt & Colman plc:

Extract 13.2: Reckitt & Colman plc[33]

RESEARCH AND DEVELOPMENT
This expenditure is written off in the year in which it is incurred, except for expenditure on related fixed assets which is written off over the expected useful life of these assets.

One company which adopts the policy of deferring certain development costs is United Scientific Holdings Plc as illustrated below:

Extract 13.3: United Scientific Holdings Plc[34]

7 . RESEARCH AND DEVELOPMENT
    (a) Research and general development expenditure not recoverable under contract is written off in the year in which it is incurred. Expenditure recoverable under design and development contracts is included in work in progress.
    (b) Expenditure on the development of specific products is carried forward when its recoverability can be foreseen with reasonable assurance and is amortised in line with the future life of the product.

It is unclear whether United Scientific Holdings Plc has actually incurred any development expenditure which meets the criteria of category (b) of their policy so that it is deferred as no 'intangible assets' or 'deferred expenditure' appear in their balance sheet or notes thereon.

Another company which adopts a policy of deferring development expenditure is The Laird Group PLC; such expenditure is included as intangible assets as shown below:

Extract 13.4: The Laird Group PLC[35]

Accounting policies [extract]
Research and development
Research costs are written off in the year in which they are incurred.
Development expenditure is written off as incurred except where it is material and is separately identifiable with a project on which the revenues will be earned in future accounting periods. In such cases, the expenditure is deferred and amortised having regard to production levels achieved and to the ultimate commercial viability of the project.

Notes on the accounts [extract]
1 0 Intangible assets
Intangible assets relate to deferred development expenditure less accumulated amortisation.

	1987 £'000	1986 £'000
Gross expenditure	3,659	1,750
Accumulated depreciation	(283)	—
Net book value	3,376	1,750

The note to the accounts in the above extract does not show the movements in the deferred development expenditure which is required by SSAP 13 and the Companies Act; however, this may be due to the fact that this is the first year that any amount has been amortised and the movement in the gross amount can be deduced.

Although the revision to SSAP 13 requiring the amount of research and development costs charged in the profit and loss account to be disclosed is not yet mandatory and there was no similar requirement in the original SSAP 13, some companies presently disclose the amount of research and expenditure charged in the profit and loss account.[36]

3   REQUIREMENTS OF THE COMPANIES ACT 1985

3.1   Accounting

The accounting treatment for research and development costs required by SSAP 13 is in effect backed up by the requirements of the Companies Act 1985. The Act permits a company's balance sheet or profit and loss account to include an item representing or covering the amount of any asset or liability, income or expenditure not otherwise covered by any of the items listed in the formats set out in Schedule 4 to the Act, but prohibits the treatment of costs of research as an asset.[37] Paragraph 20(1) of Schedule 4, however, states that 'development costs' which are included under the heading of 'fixed assets' in the balance sheet can only be included in 'special circumstances'. There is no definition in the Act of 'special circumstances', but it is reasonable to assume that the circumstances under which development expenditure is deferred in accordance with SSAP 13 satisfy the term 'special circumstances' as ED 41 stated that the DTI had confirmed that the recommended practice concerning deferral of development expenditure.satisfied the term.[38]

As deferred development costs are to be treated as fixed assets, then all of the Companies Act requirements relating to fixed assets apply to such costs (see Chapter 10).

3.2   Disclosure

3.2.1   Financial statements

Where an amount is included in a company's balance sheet in respect of development costs the following information must be given in a note to the accounts:

(a)   the period over which the amount of those costs originally capitalised is being written off; and

(b)   the reasons for capitalising the development costs in question.[39]

The disclosure requirements relating to fixed assets generally will also apply (see Chapter 10).

3.2.2   Directors' report

The directors' report should contain an indication of the activities (if any) of the company and its subsidiaries in the field of research and development.[40] However, in practice this frequently results in a fairly minimal statement on the subject being given.

A good example of disclosure is that of Glaxo Holdings p.l.c., who devote over three pages of their annual report to meeting the requirement.[41] However, this is only to be expected from a company which states that it 'is an integrated research based group of companies whose corporate purpose is the discovery, development, manufacture and marketing of safe, effective medicines of the highest quality'.[42]

3.3 Distributable profits

The Companies Act only allows distributions to be made out of a company's net realised profits.[43] In determining such net realised profits, any amount shown in respect of development costs, which is included as an asset in the balance sheet, is to be treated as a realised loss. However, this will not apply if:

(a) there are special circumstances in the company's case justifying the directors in deciding that the amount shown in respect of development costs is not to be treated as a realised loss; and

(b) the note to the accounts required by paragraph 20 of Schedule 4 to the Companies Act (see 3.2.1 (b) above) states that the amount is not to be so treated and explains the circumstances relied upon to justify the decision of the directors to that effect.[44]

4 PROBLEM AREAS

4.1 What activities should be included within research and development?

Although the definition of research and development is very broad, there are difficulties in determining what types of activity constitute 'research and development'. SSAP 13 states that 'research and development activity is distinguished from non-research based activity by the presence or absence of an element of innovation. If the activity departs from routine and breaks new ground it should normally be included; if it follows an established pattern it should normally be excluded.'[45]

Examples of activities that would normally be included in research and development are as follows:[46]

(a) experimental, theoretical or other work aimed at the discovery of new knowledge, or the advancement of existing knowledge;

(b) searching for applications of that knowledge;

(c) formulation and design of possible applications for such work;

(d) testing in search for, or evaluation of, product, service or process alternatives;

(e) design, construction and testing of pre-production prototypes and models and development batches;

(f) design of products, services, processes or systems involving new technology or substantially improving those already produced or installed;

(g) construction and operation of pilot plants.

Examples of activities which should not be included are as follows:[47]

(a) testing and analysis either of equipment or product for purposes of quality or quantity control;

(b)   periodic alterations to existing products, services or processes even though these may represent some improvement;

(c)   operational research not tied to a specific research and development activity;

(d)   cost of corrective action in connection with break-downs during commercial production;

(e)   legal and administrative work in connection with patent applications, records and litigation and the sale or licensing of patents;

(f)   activity, including design and construction engineering, relating to the construction, relocation, rearrangement or start-up of facilities or equipment other than facilities or equipment whose sole use is for a particular research and development project;

(g)   market research.

Although the above items are not normally to be included within 'research and development' and accounted for as such under SSAP 13, this does not mean that all costs of such activities will invariably be charged to the profit and loss account as incurred. This may be appropriate for certain of the costs (such as (a) or (b) above), but for some of the other costs it may be possible to regard them as part of the cost of a fixed asset (such as (f) above).

4.2   What costs should be included within the category of research and development?

Having decided which activities are to be included as research and development it is then necessary to determine what costs are to be included as the cost of those activities. SSAP 13 does not give guidance on the types of costs which can be included. However, guidance can be sought from both SFAS 2 in the US and IAS 9 as these identify the elements of costs which should be included (see 5.1 and 5.2 below). It must be remembered, however, that where development expenditure is to be deferred as an intangible asset, the accounting rules for fixed assets under Schedule 4 to the Companies Act must be taken into account (see 2 of Chapter 10).

4.3   Availability of choice between immediate write off and capitalisation of development expenditure

As indicated at 2.2.3 above, it is possible for a company to choose a policy of either writing off, or deferring and amortising, development expenditure which fulfils all the conditions laid down in paragraph 25 of SSAP 13. In view of this choice, is it possible for a company to change from a policy of writing off such expenditure to one of deferring and amortising or vice versa? We believe that a change of policy will normally be acceptable, but it will be necessary to restate comparative figures to reflect the new policy in accordance with SSAP 6 (see 2.5 of Chapter 8). However, where a change from a policy of writing off such expenditure to one of deferring and amortising is contemplated, care should be taken to ensure that all the conditions which require to be fulfilled were applicable at the time the expenditure was incurred. If the conditions were not met at that time, then the costs should not be capitalised under the new policy but should remain written off; this is because such costs would not have been capitalised if the new policy had been in force at the time the expenditure was incurred.

4.4 Elimination of uncertainty in respect of development expenditure

4.4.1 *Expenditure previously not capitalised*

The last three conditions laid down in paragraph 25 of SSAP 13 effectively mean that development expenditure should only be deferred if it can be shown to be recoverable with sufficient certainty (see 2.2.3 above). What happens if a company has not capitalised development expenditure because the conditions were not met, but at a later date the uncertainties which led to its write-off no longer apply?

The original SSAP 13 (and ED 41) made it clear that such expenditure could not be reinstated as an asset; however, SSAP 13 as revised is silent on the matter. Nevertheless, we believe that in such circumstances the expenditure should not be reinstated as an asset.

4.4.2 *Deferred expenditure previously capitalised and subsequently written down*

Paragraph 29 of SSAP 13 requires deferred development expenditure to be reviewed annually and to be written down to its recoverable amount (see 2.2.3 A above). What happens if at a later date the uncertainties which gave rise to that write-down no longer apply?

Again, SSAP 13 is silent on this issue; however, consideration in this instance has to be given to the requirements of the Companies Act relating to provisions for diminutions in value of fixed assets. These require that where the reasons for which any provision was made have ceased to apply to any extent, then the provision shall be written back to the extent that it is no longer necessary.[48] These requirements of the Companies Act do not apply to the situation discussed at 4.4.1 above as no asset was recorded in the first instance.

5 COMPARISON WITH US AND IASC PRONOUNCEMENTS

5.1 US

The principal standard in the US which deals with this issue is SFAS 2 — *Accounting for Research and Development Costs* —which was issued in October 1974.[49] The statement defines 'research' and 'development' as follows:

'*Research* is planned search or critical investigation aimed at discovery of new knowledge with the hope that such knowledge will be useful in developing a new product or service (hereinafter "product") or a new process or technique (hereinafter "process") or in bringing about a significant improvement to an existing product or process.'

'*Development* is the translation of research findings or other knowledge into a plan or design for a new product or process or for a significant improvement to an existing product or process whether intended for sale or use. It includes the conceptual formulation, design, and testing of product alternatives, construction of prototypes and operation of pilot plants. It does not include routine or periodic alterations to existing products, production lines, manufacturing process, and other on-going operations even though those alterations may represent improvements and it does not include market research or market testing activities.'[50]

It can be seen that no distinction is made between 'pure' and 'applied' research as is done in SSAP 13, and that a more detailed definition of 'development' is given.

Like SSAP 13, SFAS 2 provides examples of those activities that would normally be included in research and development and those that would not.[51] In addition, however, SFAS 2 identifies elements of costs which shall be identified with the research and development activities; these are as follows:

(a)   materials, equipment and facilities;

(b)   personnel;

(c)   intangibles purchased from others;

(d)   contract services;

(e)   indirect costs.[52]

The main difference between SSAP 13 and SFAS 2 is that SFAS 2 requires that all research and development costs encompassed by the statement should be charged to expense when incurred, for the reasons discussed at 1.1.1 above. SFAS 2 requires all enterprises to disclose the amount expensed whereas SSAP 13 exempts certain enterprises from disclosing such information (see 2.3 above).

It should be noted that SFAS 2 encompasses research and development costs incurred in the process of creating a software product. SFAS 86 — *Accounting for the Costs of Computer Software to be Sold, Leased, or Otherwise Marketed* — specifically states that 'all costs incurred to establish the technological feasibility of a computer software product to be sold, leased or otherwise marketed are research and development costs'. Those costs shall be charged to expense when incurred as required by SFAS 2.[53] Technical feasibility is established upon completion of a detail program design or, in its absence, completion of a working model.[54]

5.2   IASC

The relevant international standard is IAS 9 — *Accounting for Research and Development Activities* — which was issued in July 1978. The requirements of this standard are basically similar to those of SSAP 13 with one exception; under IAS 9 'development costs once written off should not be reinstated even though the uncertainties which had led to their being written off no longer exist'.[55] Although the original SSAP 13 had a similar requirement, the revision of SSAP

13 has dropped this requirement in view of the conflict with the Companies Act (see 1.2.5 above).

The definitions of 'research' and 'development' contained in IAS 9 are as follows:

'*Research* is original and planned investigation undertaken with the hope of gaining new scientific or technical knowledge and understanding.'

'*Development* is the translation of research findings or other knowledge into a plan or design for the production of new or substantially improved material, devices, products, processes, systems or services prior to the commencement of commercial production.'

Like SFAS 2, no distinction is made between 'pure' and 'applied' research.

IAS 9 also identifies the costs which should be included within research and development costs as follows:

(a) the salaries, wages and other related costs of personnel engaged in research and development activities;

(b) the costs of material and services consumed in such activities;

(c) the depreciation of equipment and facilities to the extent that they are used for such activities;

(d) a reasonable allocation of overhead costs related to such activities;

(e) other costs, such as the amortisation of patents and licences.[56]

The standard provides that the amount of research and development costs, of the type stated above, should be charged as an expense of the period in which they are incurred except to the extent that they represent development costs; in which case they may be deferred, provided similar conditions to those laid out in SSAP 13 are satisfied, and accounted for in the same manner as required by SSAP 13. [57]

Like SFAS 2, IAS 9 requires all enterprises to disclose the amount of research and development expenditure charged as an expense to be disclosed, whereas SSAP 13 exempts certain enterprises from disclosing such information (see 2.3 above).

The IASC has recently issued an exposure draft, E32 — *Comparability of Financial Statements* — which proposes to amend, *inter alia*, the requirements of IAS 9. The main change proposed is that the preferred treatment for research and development costs is that they should all be charged as an expense when incurred, although the alternative treatment of recognising development costs which meet the laid down criteria as an asset will still be allowed, provided certain information is given.[58]

References

1 SFAS 2, *Accounting for Research and Development Costs*, FASB, October 1974, paras. 39 — 50.
2 *Ibid.*, para. 44.
3 *Ibid.*, para. 50.
4 SSAP 13, *Accounting for research and development*, December 1977, para. 1.
5 Letter dated 15 August 1975 from The Society of British Aerospace Companies Ltd to the Technical Director of ICAEW.
6 Technical Release 264, *Statement by the Accounting Standards Committee on the publication of SSAP 13 Accounting for research and development.*
7 Original SSAP 13, para. 21.
8 ED 41, *Accounting for Research and Development*, June 1987, para. 33; Original SSAP 13, para. 28.
9 ED 41, para. 29.
10 SSAP 13, para. 33.
11 *Ibid.*, para. 21.
12 *Ibid.*, para. 2.
13 *Ibid.*, para. 18.
14 *Ibid.*, para. 17.
15 *Ibid.*, para. 23.
16 *Ibid.*, para. 16.
17 *Ibid.*, para. 24.
18 *Ibid.*, para. 8.
19 *Ibid.*, para. 9.
20 *Ibid.*, para. 25.
21 *Ibid.*, para. 10.
22 *Ibid.*, para. 13.
23 *Ibid.*, para. 27.
24 *Ibid.*, para. 26.
25 *Ibid.*, para. 28.
26 *Ibid.*, para. 29.
27 *Ibid.*, para. 30.
28 *Ibid.*, para. 31.
29 *Ibid.*, para. 32.
30 *Ibid.*, para. 22.
31 L.C.L. Skeratt and D.J. Tonkin (eds), *Financial Reporting 1987 — 88: A Survey of UK Reporting Practice*, p. 213.
32 Beecham Group p.l.c., Annual report 1988, p. 35.
33 Reckitt & Colman plc, Annual report 1987, p. 33.
34 United Scientific Holdings Plc, Annual report 1988, p. 21.
35 The Laird Group PLC, Report & Accounts 1987, pp. 32 and 36.
36 For example, see Beecham Group p.l.c., Annual Report 1988, p. 32; Glaxo Holdings p.l.c., Annual report and Accounts 1988, p. 38; Imperial Chemical Industries PLC, Annual report 1987, p. 38.
37 CA 85, Sch. 4, para. 3(2).
38 ED 41, Preface para. 1.5.
39 CA 85, Sch. 4, para. 20(2).
40 *Ibid.*, Sch. 7, para. 6(c).
41 Glaxo Holdings p.l.c., Annual report and accounts 1988, pp. 19 — 22.
42 Glaxo Holdings p.l.c., Annual report and accounts 1988, p. 1.
43 CA 85, s 263.
44 *Ibid.*, s 269.
45 SSAP 13, para. 5.

46 *Ibid.*, para. 6.
47 *Ibid.*, para. 7.
48 CA 85, Sch. 4, para. 19(3).
49 See also, for example, SFAS 7, *Accounting and Reporting by Development Stage Enterprises*, FASB, June 1975 and SFAS 68, *Research and Development Arrangements*, FASB, October 1982.
50 SFAS 2, para. 8.
51 *Ibid.*, paras. 9 and 10.
52 *Ibid.*, para. 11.
53 SFAS 86, *Accounting for the Costs of Computer Software to be Sold, Leased, or Otherwise Marketed*, para. 3.
54 *Ibid.*, summary.
55 IAS 9, *Accounting for Research and Development Activities* , IASC, July 1978, para. 22.
56 Ibid., paras. 6 and 15.
57 Ibid., paras. 16 — 21.
58 E32, *Comparability of Financial Statements*, January 1989, para. 47.

Government grants

1   INTRODUCTION

Government grants are defined in ED 43, the latest ASC pronouncement on the subject, as 'assistance by government in the form of cash or transfers of assets to an enterprise in return for past or future compliance with certain conditions relating to the operating activities of the enterprise'.[1] Such assistance has been available to commercial enterprises for many years, although its form and its extent have undergone many changes in parallel with the shifting economic philosophies of the government of the day.

The accounting issue which arises as a result of the various forms of government assistance which are currently being given, is how to deal with the income which the grant represents. Before any accounting standard on the subject was developed, the treatment adopted by different companies was diverse. At that time, the grants which were available were generally of a capital nature, intended to subsidise the purchase of fixed assets. Some companies adopted the policy of crediting the grant directly to income when received; some spread it over the life of the assets involved; some took it directly to reserves as a capital receipt so that it never featured in the profit and loss account at all. SSAP 4 — *The accounting treatment of government grants* — issued in 1974, elected for the second of these three options, adopting a matching approach as its guiding principle. This matching approach is still evident in ED 43, the exposure draft which seeks to revise SSAP 4, but ED 43 now offers more guidance on how to apply the principle to the many different kinds of government assistance which now exist.

2   THE DEVELOPMENT OF SSAP 4 AND ED 43

2.1   SSAP 4

SSAP 4 was preceded by ED 9 — *The Accounting Treatment of Grants under the Industry Act 1972* — which was published in March 1973. As the title of the exposure draft suggests, it was introduced to deal with a very specific matter — the treatment of the Regional Development Grants introduced by that Act to provide a subsidy for capital expenditure.

SSAP 4 itself was issued in April 1974 and, although it has a less specific title, it is still relatively narrow in its scope. It extends to a mere ten paragraphs, eight of which comprise the explanatory note, and of the remaining two which state the standard accounting practice to be adopted, the second merely gives the date from which the standard was to be applied. It concentrates solely on capital grants, stating that revenue grants 'do not produce accounting problems as they clearly should be credited to revenue in the same period in which the revenue expenditure to which they relate is charged'.[2]

2.2   ED 43

Although the general principle underlying SSAP 4 of matching the grant with the expenditure to which it relates has never been seriously in question since its issue, it has become increasingly evident over the years that the standard does not give adequate guidance on the widely varying forms of government assistance which have become available. Furthermore, the terms on which certain grants are currently being made do not precisely identify the expenditure to which they relate; as a result, accountants are often faced with the problem of how to ascribe grants to specific expenditure.[3] In addition, the ASC noted that the requirements of IAS 20 — *Accounting for Government Grants and Disclosure of Government Assistance* — which was issued in 1983 are not reflected in SSAP 4, and that this should therefore be considered in a revision of SSAP 4.

Consequently, the ASC issued a proposed revision to the standard, ED 43, in June 1988. A significant difference between the exposure draft and the existing standard is the depth in which the subject is discussed; it follows the same basic approach, but runs to 45 paragraphs rather than SSAP 4's 10, and also has an Appendix illustrating the application of the rules to the particular forms of assistance available.

3   REQUIREMENTS OF SSAP 4 AND PROPOSALS OF ED 43

3.1   Accounting

3.1.1   *Treatment of capital grants*

The single rule set out in SSAP 4 is that grants which relate to fixed assets should be credited to revenue over the expected useful life of the asset concerned.[4] This may be accomplished either:

(a)   by setting the grant directly against the cost of the asset in the balance sheet, so that depreciation is charged on the net figure; or

(b)   by carrying the grant in the balance sheet as a deferred credit, and releasing it to income over the life of the related asset to offset the depreciation charge.[5]

ED 43 follows the same matching principle as SSAP 4, namely that grants of all kinds (both capital and revenue) should be recognised in income at the same time as the expenditure which they subsidise.[6] In respect of grants on fixed assets, however, the exposure draft seeks to eliminate option (a) above, requiring instead that the deferred credit approach be adopted. It advances three reasons for this proposed change:

(a)   the netting approach might be in conflict with the Companies Act rules that fixed assets should be carried at their purchase price or production cost,[7] or that amounts representing assets should not be set off against amounts representing liabilities;[8]

(b)   the deferred credit approach allows the amount of grant credited to income to be disclosed (which is a separate proposed new disclosure requirement, see 3.2 below), whereas the netting approach loses this amount within the depreciation charge;

(c)   if grants become repayable, and the netting approach has been adopted, then there may need to be retrospective adjustments to the cost and depreciation of the asset concerned, which may be confusing to the user of the financial statements.

However, a number of commentators have questioned the need for this change, stressing that the netting approach is a convenient practical method, and expressing doubt that a conflict with company law necessarily exists. It therefore remains to be seen whether the revised standard continues to allow both methods.

The exposure draft makes a number of further proposals for accounting for grants which have no equivalent in the existing SSAP 4. These are set out below.

3.1.2   Accounting for receipt and repayment of grants

ED 43 proposes a rule that grants should not be recognised in the financial statements until the earlier of

(a)   their receipt; or

(b)   the satisfaction of all the conditions for their receipt (and there is reasonable assurance that they will be received).[9]

This does not address the question of when they should be recognised in income, but simply whether it is possible to recognise a grant as receivable in advance of it being received in cash.

Grants are frequently received on terms which could result in their repayment if certain conditions are not met throughout a subsequent qualifying period. The exposure draft says that provision should be made for such repayment only if it is probable to occur.[10] Again, the existence of these conditions does not directly enter into the question of when the grants should be recognised in income.

Where a grant does become repayable, the exposure draft proposes that the repayment should be accounted for by setting it off against any unamortised deferred credit relating to the grant, with any excess being charged to the profit and loss account.[11] This has the effect of minimising the impact on the profit and loss account; it means that any part of the grant which has not been retained will have been matched against depreciation of the earlier years of the asset's life (if a capital grant). An alternative approach would have been to recompute the release of grant to income as if the amount repaid had never been received, with the result that the reduced amount of the grant (if any) would be spread over the whole life of the asset involved, rather than allocated to the earlier years.

3.1.3   Treatment of revenue-based grants

The general rule of ED 43, that grants should be recognised in the profit and loss account so as to match them with the expenditure towards which they are intended to contribute, applies equally to revenue-based grants as it does to capital grants. In some situations, the revenue costs towards which a grant is given may already have been incurred, in which case the grant would be included in the profit and loss account immediately when it is capable of being recognised. However, where a grant has been received, but not all of the revenue costs have been incurred, it will be necessary to defer a proportion of the grant so as to match it with those costs.

One of the difficulties which face companies is that grants are given to provide assistance for projects which involve both revenue and capital costs; the question then arises as to which costs the grant should be matched. The ED proposes that 'in the absence of persuasive evidence to the contrary, government grants should be assumed to contribute towards the expenditure which is the basis for their payment'.[12] Another difficulty is where grants are based on criteria such as the creation of jobs; in this case it is proposed that such grants are 'matched as closely as possible with the costs involved in meeting the specified criteria'.[13] These problems are considered further at 4 below.

3.1.4   Grants taken directly to reserves

The exposure draft introduces an exceptional treatment for a particular class of grant which is offered on the condition that all or part of the grant is treated as share capital. Where this applies, the proposed treatment is to credit the amount involved directly to undistributable reserves for subsequent capitalisation. By extension of this principle, the exposure draft proposes a general rule that the normal principles of the standard can be overridden if particular conditions attach to the grant which make these principles inappropriate, or if a particular accounting treatment is demanded.[14] Although no specific abuses of this can presently be foreseen, there is a danger that this could lead to some unwarranted departures from the philosophy of the standard if grants with unusual terms and conditions are developed in the future.

3.2   Disclosure

SSAP 4 contains only one explicit disclosure requirement: the amount of any deferred credit in respect of grants should be shown separately if it is material, and should not be included in shareholders' funds.[15] In terms of the Companies Act formats, this amount will normally be shown under the heading of 'Accruals and deferred income' in one of two optional positions in the balance sheet.[16]

Imperial Chemical Industries PLC is an example of a company which treats government grants in respect of fixed assets as a deferred credit, giving the following disclosure in their financial statements:

Extract 14.1: Imperial Chemical Industries PLC[17]

ACCOUNTING POLICIES [extract]

GOVERNMENT GRANTS
Grants related to expenditure on tangible fixed assets are credited to profit over a period approximating to the lives of qualifying assets. The grants shown in the balance sheets consist of the total grants receivable to date less the amounts so far credited to profit.

BALANCE SHEETS
at 31 December 1987 [extract]

	GROUP		COMPANY	
	1987 £m	1986 £m	1987 £m	1986 £m
CREDITORS DUE AFTER MORE THAN ONE YEAR				
Loans	1,511	1,538	578	478
Other creditors	70	83	549	733
	1,581	1,621	1,127	1,211
PROVISIONS FOR LIABILITIES AND CHARGES	295	276	12	25
DEFERRED INCOME: Grants not yet credited to profit	139	183	97	114

ED 43 retains this disclosure requirement of SSAP 4 by stating that 'deferred credits in respect of grants received should be included in the balance sheet under the heading "Accruals and deferred income" and identified separately in a note to the balance sheet'.[18] However, ED 43 then goes on to introduce the following additional disclosures:

(a) the accounting policy adopted for government grants should be disclosed[19] (this is already required in general terms by SSAP 2);

(b) the total amount credited to the profit and loss account for the year in respect of grants should be disclosed in a note;[20]

(c) any potential liability to repay grants in specified circumstances should, if necessary, be disclosed in accordance with paragraph 16 of SSAP 18[21] (which means that no disclosure is necessary if the possibility is remote, although consideration would have to be given to the requirements of the Companies Act).[22] Once again, this disclosure is clearly already required in terms of SSAP 18 (and the Companies Act).

In the explanatory note section of the exposure draft, a further disclosure requirement is proposed. This is that the period or periods over which grants are released to the profit and loss account should be given;[23] however, this requirement does not explicitly appear in the standard section of the exposure draft, so its status is unclear.

As discussed at 3.1.1 above, ED 43 seeks to remove the alternative permitted under SSAP 4 of setting-off grants in respect of fixed assets directly against the cost of the asset. However, this accounting treatment is currently widely used in practice, an example of which can be seen in the financial statements of Edbro plc:

Extract 14.2: Edbro plc[24]

Notes on accounts [extract]

1 Accounting policies [extract]

Government grants
Government grants on capital expenditure are deducted from the cost of the related assets. Other grants are released to revenue over the life of the related project.

1 2 Tangible fixed assets [extract]

	Land and buildings		Plant and	
	Freehold	Long leasehold	equipment	Total
Consolidated	£000	£000	£000	£000
Cost at start of year as previously reported	749	3,713	9,479	13,941
Finance leases capitalised	—	—	1,061	1,061
Cost at start of year (a)	749	3,713	10,540	15,002
Exchange differences	(14)	(3)	(63)	(80)
Additions at cost less government grants	—	714	2,092	2,806
Disposals at cost	—	(4)	(263)	(267)
Cost at end of year	735	4,420	12,306	17,461
Depreciation at start of year as previously reported	197	1,185	5,610	6,992
Depreciation on finance leases capitalised	—	—	219	219
Depreciation at start of year (a)	197	1,185	5,829	7,211
Exchange differences	(2)	(2)	(37)	(41)
Charge for the year	19	127	1,034	1,180
Eliminated on disposals	—	(1)	(237)	(238)
Depreciation at end of year	214	1,309	6,589	8,112
Net book value:				
at end of year	521	3,111	5,717	9,349
at start of year (a)	552	2,528	4,711	7,791

(a) restated in accordance with the accounting policy change set out in note 1.

As illustrated in the above extract, Edbro plc charge depreciation on fixed assets net of government grants, thereby releasing the grant to income over the lives of the related assets in the form of a reduced depreciation charge.

Not all companies who adopt the deferred credit approach disclose the balance of the amount deferred under the 'Accruals and deferred income' heading. For example, Bass PLC disclose the deferred credit under the heading 'Provisions for liabilities and charges';[25] Howden Group PLC disclose the deferred credit as a separate heading in the balance sheet immediately below 'Minority Interests'.[26]

4 PROBLEM AREAS

4.1 Achieving the most appropriate matching

It is possible to characterise all the common problems which emerge in relation to accounting for grants as falling into a single category: namely, that of interpreting the requirement to match the grant against the expenditure towards which they are expected to contribute. This apparently simple principle can be extremely difficult to apply, because it is sometimes far from clear what the essence of the grant was, and in practice grants are sometimes given for a particular kind of expenditure which forms an element of a larger project, making the allocation a highly subjective matter. For example, government assistance which is in the form of a training grant might be:

(a)   matched against direct training costs; or

(b)   taken over a finite period of time against the salary costs of the employees being trained, e.g. over the estimated duration of the project; or

(c)   taken over the estimated period for which the company or the employees are expected to benefit from the training; or

(d)   not distinguished from other project grants received and matched against total project costs; or

(e)   taken to income systematically over the life of the project, e.g., the total grant receivable may be allocated to revenue on a straight-line basis; or

(f)   as in (d) or (e) above, but using, instead of project life, the period over which the grant is paid; or

(g)   taken to income when received in cash.

Depending on the circumstances, any of these approaches might produce an acceptable result. However, we would comment on them individually as follows:

Under method (a), the grant could be recognised as income considerably in advance of its receipt, since often the major part of the direct training costs will be incurred at the beginning of a project and payment is usually made retrospectively. As the total grant receivable may be subject to adjustment, this may not be prudent or may lead to mismatching.

Methods (b) to (e) all rely on different interpretations of the expenditure to which the grant is expected to contribute, and could all represent an appropriate form of matching.

Method (f) has less to commend it, but the period of payment of the grant might in fact give an indication (in the absence of better evidence) of the duration of the project for which the expenditure is to be subsidised.

Similarly, method (g) is unlikely to be the most appropriate method per se, but may approximate to one of the other methods, or may, in the absence of any conclusive indication as to the expenditure intended to be subsidised by the grant, be the only practicable method which can be adopted.

4.2   Grants paid on the creation of new jobs

ED 43 states that 'certain grants are based not on the incurring of specific expenditure but on other criteria such as the creating of jobs. Such grants should be recognised in the profit and loss account so as to match them as closely as possible with the costs involved in meeting the specified criteria, for example in providing the jobs.'[27] Therefore, where grants are paid on the creation of additional jobs, the broad principle still applies of matching the grant with the costs of creating and maintaining these jobs. For example, a company's ability to create new jobs might necessitate the acquisition of plant, the building or expansion of training facilities etc.; in such cases, it may be possible to match the grants received with the additional costs incurred.

However, in practice it is often difficult to separately identify those costs which specifically relate to the creation of new jobs; for example, the job creation scheme might merely be utilising previously under-utilised training and plant facilities, with the result that the identifiable marginal costs incurred might bear no relation to the grants received. In such cases, therefore, it is necessary to first attempt to identify the expenditure (capital or revenue) which has been incurred in the creation and maintenance of the new jobs created, and second, to match the grants received with this expenditure on the basis of the firm's accounting policy for capital and revenue grants. Thereafter, where grants are unmatched or expenditure is unidentifiable, the grants may be taken to income when received in cash.

4.3   Taxation of grants

Many grants are taxed as income on receipt; consequently, this is often the argument advanced for taking grants to income when received in cash. However, ED 43 specifically states that 'the manner in which a grant is taxed should not influence its accounting treatment'.[28] Consequently, the recognition of a grant in the profit and loss account in a period different to that when it is taxed gives rise to a timing difference, and should be accounted for in accordance with SSAP 15 — *Accounting for deferred tax.*

4.4   Guidelines

In the face of the problems (described above) of attributing a grant to related expenditure, it is difficult to offer definitive guidance; companies will have to make their own judgments as to how the matching principle is to be applied. The only overriding considerations are that the method should be systematically and consistently applied, and that the policy adopted (in respect of both capital and revenue grants, if material) should be adequately disclosed. However, it is possible to offer the following points for consideration:

4.4.1 Should the grant be split into its elements?

The grant received may be part of a package, the elements of which have different costs/conditions. It may be appropriate to treat these different elements on different bases rather than accounting for the entire grant in one way.

4.4.2 What was the purpose of the grant?

ED 43 states that 'in the absence of persuasive evidence to the contrary, government grants should be assumed to contribute towards the expenditure which is the basis for their payment'.[29] However, the method by which the amount of grant receivable is calculated does not conclusively determine the accounting treatment. For example, the amount of the grant may be based on capital expenditure but it may be intended to contribute towards working capital or other expenditure as well. It will be necessary to examine the full circumstances of the grant in order to determine its purpose.

4.4.3 What is the period to be benefited by the grant?

The qualifying conditions which have to be satisfied are not necessarily conclusive evidence of the period to be benefited by the grant. For example, certain grants may become repayable if assets cease to be used for a qualifying purpose within a certain period; notwithstanding this condition, the grant should be recognised over the whole life of the asset, not over the qualifying period. The same may apply to the period during which new jobs have to be maintained (although the contrary suggestion is made in the explanatory note to ED 43).[30]

4.4.4 Is a grant capital or revenue?

In general, we recommend that grants should be regarded as linked to capital expenditure where this is a possible interpretation and there is no clear indication to the contrary. However, we believe that the most important consideration where there are significant questions over how the grant is to be recognised, and where the effect is material, is that the financial statements should explicitly state what treatment has been chosen and what is the financial effect of adopting that treatment.

5   COMPARISON WITH THE IASC PRONOUNCEMENT

IAS 20 — *Accounting for Government Grants and Disclosure of Government Assistance* — was issued in April 1983. It follows the same basic approach that is adopted in the UK, although there are some additional matters covered in the international standard. Inevitably, because of the international context in which it is written, it does not address specific questions which relate to particular types of grant which are available in individual countries.

The standard sets conditions under which grants may be immediately taken to income. These are that the grant must be receivable as compensation for expenses or losses already incurred, or that it is for the purpose of giving immediate financial support to the enterprise with no further related costs to be incurred.[31] There is no direct equivalent of these rules within SSAP 4 or ED 43.

The standard allows either of the two balance sheet presentations of capital grants presently permitted by SSAP 4 (see 3.1.1 above).

References

1   ED 43, *The accounting treatment of government grants*, June 1988, para. 25.
2   SSAP 4, *The accounting treatment of government grants*, April 1974, para. 2.
3   ED 43, Preface para. 1.2.
4   SSAP 4, para. 9.
5   *Ibid.*
6   ED 43, para. 27.
7   CA 85, Sch. 4, para. 17.
8   *Ibid.*, para. 5.
9   ED 43, para. 26.
10 *Ibid.*, para. 31.
11 *Ibid.*
12 *Ibid.*, para. 28.
13 *Ibid.*, para. 29.
14 *Ibid.*, para. 32.
15 SSAP 4, para. 9.
16 CA 85, Sch. 4, para. 8.
17 Imperial Chemical Industries PLC, Annual Report 1987, pp. 33 and 35.
18 ED 43, para. 35.
19 *Ibid.*, para. 34.
20 *Ibid.*, para. 36.
21 *Ibid.*, para. 37.
22 CA 85, Sch. 4, para. 50(2).
23 ED 43, para. 19.
24 Edbro plc, 1988 Report and Accounts, pp. 9 and 12.
25 Bass PLC, Annual Review 1988, p. 52.
26 Howden Group PLC, Annual Report and Accounts 1988, p. 15.
27 ED 43, para. 29.
28 *Ibid.*, para. 33.
29 *Ibid.*, para. 28.
30 *Ibid.*, para. 12.
31 IAS 20, *Accounting for Government Grants and Disclosure of Government Assistance*, IASC, April 1983, para. 40.

Chapter 15

Statements of cash and funds flow

1 INTRODUCTION

1.1 What is a funds statement?

There are only two types of financial statement: a statement which reports stocks of resources and claims against them at a single point in time (e.g. a balance sheet); and a statement which reports flows of resources (e.g. a profit and loss account). The gradual shift in emphasis in external financial reporting from the balance sheet to the profit and loss account highlighted the fact that the profit and loss account was not able to reflect the full resource flow activities of a business enterprise. Because it is only concerned with resource flows that are part of the earnings activity, the profit and loss account fails to distinguish between the different types of resources consumed in the earnings activity; nor does it report changes in resources resulting from the business's investing or financing activities.[1]

Therefore, in order to provide users with a more complete picture of their resource flows over an accounting period, companies started including a statement of source and application of funds in their annual reports.[2] This was evidenced in the 1950s by widespread experimentation by US companies with the inclusion of various forms of 'funds statement'[3] in annual reports.[4]

However, this experimentation caused concern for the AICPA, who were prompted into commissioning a research study on cash flow analysis and the funds statement.[5] It is clear from the director's preface to this study that the AICPA saw 'the increased use of the statement of source and application of funds and the recent emergence of an amorphous concept known as "cash flow" ' as a threat to the perfection of the accrual basis of accounting.[6]

In 1963, following the publication of the study, the Accounting Principles Board issued its Opinion No. 3 — *The Statement of Source and Application of Funds* — which encouraged (but did not require) the presentation of a funds statement. This was the first official pronouncement on funds statements to be issued by a major accounting body, and it received wide support from the principal stock exchanges and the business community in the US. This resulted in a significant increase in the inclusion of such statements in US company annual reports, and in 1970 the SEC made the funds statement an obligatory element of financial statement filing.

In 1971 APB Opinion No. 3 was superseded by APB Opinion No. 19,[7] which required that when financial statements purporting to present both financial position and results of operations are issued, a 'statement summarizing changes in financial position should also be presented as a basic financial statement for each period for which an income statement is presented'.[8]

In contrast to the US, there was a much slower acceptance in the UK of the view that the funds statement should be presented as a complementary statement to the balance sheet and profit and loss account. Prior to the 1970s, there was relatively little evidence of British companies publishing funds statements; and whilst in the US and Canada the emphasis was on achieving the most useful form and content of the funds statement, UK companies were still trying to answer the question as to whether or not a funds statement should be included in their annual reports. It was not until ED 13[9] was issued in April 1974 that the ASSC offered any guidance on the subject. ED 13 led ultimately to the publication in July 1975 of SSAP 10,[10] which had the objective of establishing 'the practice of providing source and application of funds statements as a part of audited accounts and to lay down a minimum standard of disclosure in such statements'.[11]

1.2   The form and content of the funds statement

The form and content of the funds statement are directly governed by two principal factors: the objectives of the statement and the interpretation of the concept of 'funds'. In the UK, there appears to be widespread dissatisfaction with the funds statement in its present form. This seems to be largely due to the fact that SSAP 10 fails to either establish the objectives of a funds statement or define 'funds' adequately; furthermore, it does not prescribe a specific format which would produce a statement which provides useful and meaningful information for the user in a consistent manner between companies. A common criticism of the funds statement is that it is merely a rearrangement of figures already appearing in the financial statements, and that it is therefore repetitive and unnecessary. In fact, the following extract from SSAP 10 bears out this charge, and confirms that it sees the funds statement as being merely a rearrangement of the balance sheet, profit and loss account and notes, providing little new information for the user:

'The funds statement will provide a link between the balance sheet at the beginning of the period, the profit and loss account for the period and the balance sheet at the end of the period. ... The figures from which a funds statement is constructed should generally be identifiable in the profit and loss account, balance sheet and related notes.'[12]

This contrasts significantly with the purpose of the funds statement which is set out in a study on the subject by the Accountants International Study Group as follows:

'The objective of the funds statement is to provide information as to how the activities of the enterprise have been financed and how its financial resources have been used during the period covered by the statement. It is not intended to, nor can it, supplant the balance sheet, income statement and retained earnings statement; neither is it a supporting schedule to these statements. The funds statement is, rather, a complementary statement which is important in its own right and which is designed to present information that the other financial statements either do not provide or provide only indirectly.'[13]

However, US companies were also encountering difficulties with the form and content of the funds statement presented under APB Opinion No. 19. The FASB had identified certain practical problems, 'including the ambiguity of terms such as *funds*, lack of comparability arising from diversity in the focus of the statement (cash, cash and short-term investments, quick assets, or working capital) and the resulting differences in definitions of funds flows from operating activities (cash or working capital), differences in the format of the statement (sources and uses format or activity format), variations in classifications of specific items in an activity format, and the reporting of net changes in amounts of assets and liabilities rather than gross inflows and outflows'.[14] This diversity in reporting practice was seen to be caused mainly by the lack of clear objectives for the funds statement.[15]

1.3   The objectives of the funds statement

1.3.1   The funds statement and cash flows

There has been an increasing acknowledgement in recent years of the critical role played by cash in the operation of any economic entity. Hendriksen states that 'in the final analysis, cash flows into and out of a business enterprise are the most fundamental events upon which accounting measurements are based and upon which investors and creditors are assumed to base their decisions'.[16]

The importance of providing cash flow information has been reinforced by the FASB through its concepts statements. SFAC No. 1 states that 'financial reporting should provide information to help present and potential investors and creditors and other users in assessing the amounts, timing, and uncertainty of prospective cash receipts from dividends or interest and the proceeds from the sale, redemption, or maturity of securities or loans. The prospects for those cash receipts are affected by an enterprise's ability to generate enough cash to meet its obligations when due and its other cash operating needs, to reinvest in operations, and to pay cash dividends ... Thus, financial reporting should provide information to help investors, creditors, and others assess the amounts, timing, and uncertainty of prospective net inflows to the related enterprise.'[17]

Further recognition of the need for business enterprises to provide cash flow information in their external reporting was given more recently by SFAC No. 5, which states that 'a full set of financial statements for a period should show: ... cash flows during the period'.[18] It then goes on to say that 'a statement of cash flows directly or indirectly reflects an entity's cash receipts classified by major sources and its cash payments classified by major uses during a period. It provides useful information about an entity's activities in generating cash through operations to repay debt, distribute dividends, or reinvest to maintain or expand operating capacity; about its financing activities, both debt and equity; and about its investing or spending of cash. Important uses of information about an entity's current cash receipts and payments include helping to assess factors such as the entity's liquidity, financial flexibility, profitability, and risk.'[19]

Liquidity reflects an asset's or liability's nearness to cash; whilst financial flexibility is the ability of an entity to raise cash at short notice so that it can meet unforeseen contingencies or take advantage of favourable opportunities that may arise. Although the balance sheet includes information that is often used in assessing an entity's liquidity and financial flexibility, it only provides an incomplete picture of these factors, unless it is used in conjunction with at least a cash flow statement.[20]

As a result of this increasing recognition of the significance of cash flow information, coupled with the diversity in the formats caused by the lack of objectives for the funds statement, the FASB issued SFAS 95 — *Statement of Cash Flows*. SFAS 95 supersedes APB Opinion No. 19 and requires that 'a business enterprise that provides a set of financial statements that reports both financial position and results of operations shall also provide a statement of cash flows for each period for which results of operations are provided'.[21]

This requirement to present a statement of cash flows reflects a worldwide trend in financial reporting, where several standard-setting bodies have recently re-examined the nature and objectives of the funds statement, and have concluded that the statement should focus on flows of cash rather than flows of working capital, or some other concept of funds.[22]

1.3.2 SSAP 10 and the objectives of the funds statement

It is indeed difficult to determine precisely what the drafters of SSAP 10 saw as the objectives of the funds statement. The following extracts from the standard illustrate conflicting views:[23]

'The objective of such a statement is to show the manner in which the operations of a company have been financed and in which its *financial resources* have been used and the format selected should be designed to achieve this objective.'[24]

'... it is necessary also to identify the movements in net assets, liabilities and capital which have taken place during the year and the resultant effect on *net liquid funds*'.[25]

'It should show clearly the funds generated or absorbed by the operations of the business and the manner in which any resulting surplus of *liquid assets* has been applied or any deficiency of such assets has been financed, distinguishing the long term from the short term.'[26]

'The statement should distinguish the use of funds for the purchase of new fixed assets from funds used in increasing the *working capital* of the company.'[27]

It is not surprising that a financial statement which purports to accommodate all of the above objectives and requirements will be largely meaningless, and certainly the standard has not promoted uniformity in reporting practice. This is clearly illustrated by the varying ways in which SSAP 10 has been interpreted by companies in practice (see 3 below). The principal shortcoming of the above requirements is that the focus of interest is on balance sheet classifications rather than the activities of the business. In other words, the statement analyses the sources and applications of funds (however defined) in terms of movements within individual categories and groupings of assets and equities, rather than in terms of how the various activities of the business have either generated or absorbed funds. This accounts for the fact that a funds statement prepared in terms of SSAP 10 will largely be a reconciliation of balance sheet changes, rather than provide additional information useful to the user.

2   THE REQUIREMENTS OF SSAP 10

Since there is no statutory requirement for companies to present a funds statement in their annual financial statements, SSAP 10 has entrenched the funds statement in generally accepted accounting practice by stating that it applies 'to all financial accounts intended to give a true and fair view of financial position and profit or loss other than those of enterprises with turnover or gross income of less than £25,000 per annum'.[28] It goes on to say that, subject to this exemption, audited financial statements should include a funds statement for both the current and previous financial periods.[29] The detailed requirements of SSAP 10 are brief and are limited to specifying the following minimum information which must be disclosed in the funds statement:[30]

(a)   the profit or loss for the period together with the adjustments required for items which did not use (or provide) funds in the period;

(b)   dividends paid;

(c)   acquisitions and disposals of fixed and other non-current assets;

(d)   funds raised by increasing, or expended in repaying or redeeming, medium or long-term loans or the issued capital of the company;

(e)   the increase or decrease in working capital sub-divided into its components, and movements in net liquid funds.

'Net liquid funds' is defined in SSAP 10 as 'cash at bank and in hand and cash equivalents (e.g. investments held as current assets) less bank overdrafts and other borrowings repayable within one year of the accounting date'.[31] In our view, this should include the current portion of long-term debt, which should, therefore, be included in the disclosure of 'movements in net liquid funds' in the funds statement.

The explanatory note to SSAP 10 contains the following additional guidance:

(a)   so as not to mask the significance of individually important figures, a minimum of 'netting off' should take place;[32]

(b)   the figures from which a funds statement is constructed should generally be identifiable in the profit and loss account, balance sheet and related notes. If adjustments to those published figures are necessary, 'details should be given to enable the related figures to be rapidly located';[33]

(c)   where group accounts are being prepared, the funds statement should be based on these accounts. Where there have been acquisitions or disposals of subsidiaries during the year, these should be disclosed either as separate items in the body of the statement, or by reflecting the effects on the separate assets and liabilities dealt with in the statement. In either case, a note summarising the effects of acquisitions or disposals should be given, showing the total acquisition or disposal price and, in the case of an acquisition, how much of the purchase price has been discharged in cash and how much by the issue of shares.[34]

Clearly, the above requirements provide the preparers of funds statements with little assistance with the form that the statement should take. Consequently, this opens the door to an almost limitless variety of funds statement presentations. These, however, may be grouped into the following three broad categories:

(a)   Balanced

Sources and applications of funds are shown separately but with equal totals. This format is becoming less evident in practice, and is generally only used when the 'all in' approach is followed of merely analysing the changes in each balance sheet line item as either a source or an application, without attempting to focus on any particular aspect of the balance sheet (see, for example Extract 15.5 below).

(b)   Remainder

Applications are deducted from sources, leaving a residual amount. Generally, the residual amount indicates the company's interpretation of 'funds', and usually represents the change in net borrowings, working capital, or net liquid funds (see 3 below). The examples given in the Appendix to SSAP 10 are prepared according to this format, using the increase/decrease in working capital as the remainder (see, for example, Extracts 15.1 and 15.2 below).

(c)   Reconciling

A funds statement prepared in this form analyses the increase/decrease in funds for the period in terms of sources and applications, and then reconciles this difference with the company's opening and closing fund balances (see, for example, Extract 15.3 below).

3   THE MEANING OF 'FUNDS'

The second principal factor which governs the form and content of the funds statement is the interpretation placed on the concept of 'funds'. SSAP 10 provides little assistance in explaining what is meant by 'funds', and in fact the only term defined in the standard is that of *net liquid funds* (see 2 above).

Numerous interpretations have been placed on 'funds', and in fact the Accountants International Study Group suggested nine possible definitions.[35] In practice in the UK, however, the following are the most commonly used interpretations:

(a)   net liquid funds;

(b)   working capital;

(c)   net borrowings;

(d)   total external financing.

The principal difficulty with the preparation of a funds statement under SSAP 10 is that one is tied down to the 'all financial resources' concept in the presentation of the statement. This concept originated from APB Opinion No. 3, and intended to include in the funds statement all additions to, distributions of, and changes in composition of the financial resources of the entity. This concept has been carried through into SSAP 10, and although the examples given in the Appendix to the standard seem to emphasise a 'working capital' interpretation of funds, the funds statement nevertheless should include all movements in financial resources. For example, therefore, paper transactions such as the issue of shares for non-cash consideration or the conversion of loans to share capital should still be included in the funds statement, even if they do not affect working capital. Thus, irrespective of the interpretation that a company places on 'funds', its funds statement will still reflect all movements that have occurred between its opening and closing balance sheets.

The ICAEW's 1987—88 survey of published accounts revealed the following spread of definitions of funds used in practice:[36]

Funds statements: Definition of funds used

	Large listed		Medium listed		Large unlisted		Total	
Number of companies	100	(100)	150	(150)	50	(50)	300	(300)
	%	(%)	%	(%)	%	(%)	%	(%)
Net liquid funds	33	(31)	29	(33)	26	(36)	30	(33)
Working capital	10	(13)	36	(33)	50	(48)	30	(29)
Net borrowing	38	(42)	21	(19)	14	(8)	26	(25)
External financing	7	(2)	3	(3)	0	(0)	4	(2)
All in: Sources = Applications	12	(12)	11	(11)	10	(8)	11	(11)
	100	(100)	100	(100)	100	(100)	100	(100)

Note: Comparative figures from the 1986—87 survey are shown in parentheses.

The above table indicates that unlisted companies tend to follow the SSAP 10 working capital format, whilst the large listed companies tend to prefer the net liquid funds and net borrowings interpretation. The following extracts from published financial statements illustrate the practical application of each of these interpretations.

3.1   Net liquid funds

As indicated in the above table, this interpretation is widely used in practice — probably as a result of the fact that it is the only term defined in SSAP 10. The following is an example of a 'remainder' statement using the net liquid funds definition:

Extract 15.1: Glaxo Holdings p.l.c.[37]

Consolidated Source and Application of Funds
for the year ended 30th June 1988

	1988 £m	1988 £m	£m	1987 £m
SOURCES				
Profit on ordinary activities before taxation		832		746
Depreciation	73		55	
Increase in pension and other provisions	1		8	
Investment and development grants credited to profit	(1)		(1)	
Share of profits of associated companies	(31)		(30)	
		42		32
		874		778
Profit on disposal of businesses		13		14
Exchange translation adjustments		(44)		(8)
Dividends from associated companies		9		9
Shares issued under share option scheme		—		1
		852		794
APPLICATIONS				
Purchase of tangible fixed assets	275		193	
Disposals	(11)		(25)	
		264		168
Purchase of goodwill		6		—
Investments in associated companies		(4)		3
Dividends paid to minority interests		—		1
Increase/(decrease) in working capital:				
Stocks	22		12	
Debtors	62		73	
Creditors	(54)		(57)	
		30		28
Tax paid		217		234
Dividends paid to ordinary shareholders		156		111
		669		545
INCREASE IN NET LIQUID FUNDS (Note 21)		183		249

3.2 Working capital

Dunhill Holdings Plc uses the working capital interpretation of funds, and prepares its funds statement according to the format given in the Appendix to SSAP 10.

Extract 15.2: Dunhill Holdings Plc[38]

CONSOLIDATED STATEMENT OF SOURCE AND APPLICATION OF FUNDS
for the year ended 31st March 1988

	1988	1988	1987	1987
	£'000	£'000	£'000	£'000
SOURCE OF FUNDS				
Profit on ordinary activities before taxation		**35,222**		24,751
Extraordinary profit before tax		**10,887**		1,505
Items not involving the movement of funds:				
Depreciation and amounts written off tangible fixed assets, adjusted for profits/losses on sales	**3,080**		2,958	
Exchange rate adjustments	**(2,959)**		194	
Provisions for liabilities and charges excluding deferred tax	**(491)**		1,121	
		(370)		4,273
(Decrease) in bank loans, other loans and other creditors falling due after more than one year		**(1,317)**		(9,409)
Proceeds from sale of tangible fixed assets		**56**		66
Disposal of net assets of subsidiary		**9,290**		—
		53,768		21,186
APPLICATION OF FUNDS				
Tax paid		**8,233**		14,118
Expenditure on tangible fixed assets (less grants received)		**8,015**		4,138
Parent company dividends paid		**3,427**		2,545
Purchase of goodwill on acquisition of subsidiary		**—**		451
		19,675		21,252
CHANGE IN WORKING CAPITAL		**34,093**		(66)

REPRESENTING			
Increase in stocks	**3,427**		3,108
Increase in debtors	**6,176**		2,943
(Increase) in creditors: amounts falling due within one year, excluding taxation, proposed dividend, bank loans, other loans and overdrafts	**(9,863)**		(1,405)
Movement in net liquid funds:			
Increase in bank balances, and investments held as current assets	**29,118**	9,626	
Decrease/(increase) in bank loans, other loans and overdrafts	**5,235**	(14,338)	
	34,353		(4,712)
	34,093		(66)

This format, in order to comply with the specific requirements of SSAP 10, necessarily applies a modified form of the working capital definition. The reason for this is that SSAP 10 specifically requires the separate disclosure of dividends paid,[39] thereby necessitating the movement in proposed dividends to be excluded from creditors. Further, although not a requirement of SSAP 10, it has become common practice to disclose taxation paid in a similar manner.

It is noteworthy that when the working capital definition is applied, the movements in net liquid funds should, in order to comply with SSAP 10,[40] be disclosed as a sub-section to the analysis of changes in working capital.

3.3   Net borrowings

Woolworth Holdings PLC adopts the net borrowings interpretation of funds, and includes in its funds statement a reconciliation between its opening and closing net borrowing positions.

Extract 15.3: Woolworth Holdings PLC[41]

CONSOLIDATED STATEMENT OF SOURCE AND APPLICATION OF FUNDS
For the financial year ended 30 January 1988

	1988 £m	1987 £m
SOURCE OF FUNDS		
Arising from trading		
Profit on ordinary activities before taxation	177.0	115.3
Property realisation profits	(6.4)	(6.2)
Profit on sale and leaseback of properties	(35.2)	
Depreciation	41.3	28.3
	176.7	137.4
Funds from other sources		
Disposal of tangible assets	102.0	44.2
Shares issued	253.4	3.7
Other		1.1
Total source of funds	532.1	186.4
APPLICATION OF FUNDS		
Increase in working capital		
Stock	37.9	48.8
Debtors	23.2	13.1
Creditors	(12.9)	(41.8)
	48.2	20.1
Other applications		
Purchase of subsidiaries	282.7	6.2
Purchase of tangible assets	196.2	175.9
Extraordinary items		18.0
Tax paid	18.9	20.3
Dividends paid	32.9	21.6
Total application of funds	578.9	262.1
INCREASE IN BORROWINGS	46.8	75.7
MOVEMENT IN BORROWINGS		
At beginning	(328.8)	(258.0)
Subsidiaries at acquisition	(25.5)	4.9
At end:		
current instalments due on loan notes		1.0
bank overdrafts	176.3	123.8
loan stock	146.3	146.7
bank loans	140.0	100.0
cash at bank and in hand	(61.5)	(42.7)
	46.8	75.7

3.4   Total external financing

Total external financing comprises net liquid funds, medium and long-term borrowings and share capital. Imperial Chemical Industries PLC have adopted this definition, and present their funds statement as follows:

Extract 15.4: Imperial Chemical Industries PLC[42]

STATEMENT OF SOURCES AND APPLICATIONS OF GROUP FUNDS

For the year ended 31 December 1987

	Notes	1987 £m	1986 £m
SOURCES			
FUNDS GENERATED FROM OPERATIONS			
Trading profit		1,297	1,049
Depreciation		464	491
Petroleum revenue tax paid, less provided			(42)
Government grants credited to profit, less received		(19)	(9)
Dividends from related companies		65	56
Miscellaneous items, including exchange		(9)	(60)
		1,798	1,485
LESS: INTEREST AND TAXATION PAID DURING YEAR			
Interest (net)		**(141)**	(125)
Taxation		**(349)**	(298)
SOURCES NET OF INTEREST AND TAXATION		**1,308**	1,062

APPLICATIONS
DIVIDENDS PAID DURING YEAR

Parent company		254	222
Subsidiaries to minority shareholders		29	27
		283	249

FIXED ASSETS

Tangible assets		708	643
Disposals of tangible assets		(26)	(35)
Acquisitions of new investments	24	544	578
Disposals of subsidiaries and related company investments	24	(114)	(30)
		1,112	1,156

WORKING CAPITAL CHANGES

Stocks increase (1986 decrease)		169	(115)
Debtors increase (1986 decrease)		68	(45)
Creditors and provisions increase (excluding dividends and taxation) (1986 decrease)		(50)	66
		187	(94)

TOTAL APPLICATIONS		**1,582**	1,311
DEFICIT		**(274)**	(249)

FINANCED BY

Issues of ICI Ordinary Stock		140	50
Repayment of ICI Preference Stock			(7)
Other external finance		(6)	(7)
Net repayment of loans (1986 net of new borrowings)		(24)	178
Increase in short-term borrowings (1986 decrease)		118	(70)
Decrease in cash and short-term investments		46	105
		274	249

NOTES RELATING TO THE ACCOUNTS

24 *ACQUISITIONS AND NEW INVESTMENTS*

	GROUP	
	1987	1986
Acquisitions of new investments comprised:	£m	£m
Fixed assets	167	245
Goodwill	550	252
Related companies	26	108
Net current assets	91	85
Employee benefit provisions	(60)	—
Rationalisation and other provisions	(95)	(21)
Minorities	—	(7)
	679	662
Financed by:		
Cash	544	578
Loans assumed	135	84
	679	662

The purchase consideration for the companies acquired during the year was met from the Group's cash resources.

Disposals in 1987 comprised businesses and subsidiaries £70m (1986 £1m) and related and other companies £44m (£29m).

Goodwill includes £456m in respect of the acquisition of the Stauffer companies, and £83m in respect of Société Européenne de Semences S.A.. The Stauffer assets and liabilities included above exclude the basic and speciality chemicals businesses which were sold during the year.

3.5   Other formats

Although the above extracts illustrate the four principal interpretations of funds to be found in practice, there are numerous variations on these themes. For example, some companies reconcile their funds statement to an amount representing 'net funds', 'total group funds' or 'net assets'. However, as discussed above, there is still the overriding requirement of SSAP 10 for the funds statement to include all movements in financial resources. For this reason, a number of companies still present a 'balanced' funds statement, which merely presents all financial resource movements as either sources or applications, without focusing on any particular aspect of the balance sheet. The following is a good example of this form of presentation:

Extract 15.5: BPB Industries plc[43]

Group Source and Use of Funds

Year to 31st March 1988		1988 £m		1987 £m
Source of funds				
Profit before tax		**182.3**		144.7
Depreciation		**39.0**		33.6
Other non-cash items		**(6.8)**		(1.1)
Share of profit retained in related companies		**(3.7)**		(2.5)
Total generated from operations		**210.8**		174.7
Shares issued		**72.6**		0.9
Government grants		**1.2**		1.0
Sales of tangible fixed assets		**5.2**		1.4
Currency adjustments		**(7.0)**		0.8
		282.8		178.8
Use of funds				
Additions to tangible fixed assets		**70.9**		48.3
Subsidiaries acquired — *Note 21*		**76.5**		37.5
Investments		**8.3**		1.5
Net decrease in loans		**2.7**		2.7
Tax paid		**55.0**		40.1
Dividends paid to:				
Shareholders of BPB Industries plc		**28.5**		19.1
Minority shareholders of subsidiaries		**0.1**		0.2
Increase in working capital:				
Stocks	**(1.9)**		4.5	
Debtors	**1.4**		26.4	
Creditors	**(3.2)**		(11.8)	
Net liquid funds	**44.5**		10.3	
		40.8		29.4
		282.8		178.8

4   PROBLEM AREAS

In view of the fact that SSAP 10 is limited to specifying certain minimum disclosure requirements, there are a number of issues which directly affect the presentation of the funds statement and, therefore, need to be addressed.

4.1   The starting point — before or after taxation?

SSAP 10 is silent on the issue of the disclosure of taxation in the funds statement; consequently, there are a number of alternative options available, all of which depend largely on what is selected as the starting point of the statement. This can be profit on ordinary activities either before or after taxation. If the 'after tax' method is adopted, the charge or credit for deferred tax in the profit and loss account is adjusted as a non-fund item, and the movement in the corporation tax liability is included as one of the components of the increase/decrease in working capital. However, where the deferred tax movements include ACT transfers, these will not be treated as non-fund items but, instead, should be shown as sources or applications as appropriate.

If the 'before tax' method is adopted, there is a choice of disclosing either *tax paid* or *tax expense* (as per the profit and loss account) as an application of funds. If *tax paid* is disclosed, then the movement in the taxation liability will not appear in the funds statement; whilst if *tax expense* is disclosed, then the movement in the taxation liability will be included in the components of the increase/decrease in working capital, and the movement in deferred tax would be shown either as a source or application.

Example 15.1: Comparison of the after tax and before tax methods in the funds statement

The following information relates to company A for the year ended 31 December 19X2:

	19X2 £'000	19X1 £'000
Profit on ordinary activities before taxation	**200**	90
Tax on profit on ordinary activities (Note 1)	76	34
Profit on ordinary activities after taxation	**124**	56
Extraordinary item after taxation (Note 2)	25	—
Profit for the financial year	**99**	56
Note 1: Tax on profit on ordinary activities		
Corporation tax	66	32
Deferred taxation (Note 3)	10	2
	76	34
Note 2: Extraordinary item		
Extraordinary loss on discontinuance of a business segment	39	—
Corporation tax relief thereon	(14)	—
	25	—

	19X2 £'000	19X1 £'000
Note 3: Deferred taxation provided		
Capital allowances in advance of depreciation	26	15
Other short-term timing differences	3	4
	29	19
Less: Advance corporation tax	(10)	(6)
	19	13
Note 4: Creditors: amounts falling due within one year		
Corporation tax	62	38

Company A has the following options for the disclosure of taxation in its funds statement (for the purposes of this illustration, no corresponding figures are given for 19X1):

After tax method:

	£'000
Sources of funds	
Profit on ordinary activities after taxation	124
Adjustments for items not involving the flow of funds:	
Deferred tax provision [29 - 19]	10
Total generated from operations	134
Increase in creditors	24
Applications of funds	
Advance corporation tax	4
Extraordinary item (after taxation)	25

Before tax method:

	£'000
Source of funds	
Profit on ordinary activities before taxation	200
Total generated from operations	200

Applications of funds	
Tax paid [6 + (32 - 6)]	32
Extraordinary item (before tax)	39

Although both of the above methods give the same net result (i.e. a net source of funds of 129), they present somewhat different pictures of the generation of funds from operations. Both methods are compatible with SSAP 10 and are therefore acceptable; however, our preference lies with the before tax method which, as illustrated in Extracts 15.1 to 15.5 above, would appear to be consistent with generally accepted accounting practice.

4.2   Funds absorbed by operations

Where the company has suffered a loss on ordinary activities, the question arises as to whether this should be shown as an application or a negative source. Again, either approach is acceptable. However, our preference lies with disclosing the loss as an application, thereby representing funds used by the entity's operating activities. Nevertheless, where a company has a loss on ordinary activities but, because of adjustments, has generated funds, it should be shown as a source, for example:

		£'000
Source of funds		
Loss on ordinary activities before taxation		(100)
Adjustments for items not involving the flow of funds:		
Depreciation	80	
Loss on sale of fixed assets	30	
		110
Total generated from operations		10

Conversely, where a profit on ordinary activities is turned into 'funds absorbed', it should be shown as an application, for example:

	£'000
Application of funds	
Profit on ordinary activities before taxation	100
Adjustments for items not involving the flow of funds:	
Depreciation	40
Profit on sale of fixed assets	(160)
Total absorbed by operations	(20)

Where a company has generated funds in one year, but absorbed funds in the other, a suitable means of presenting this situation in the funds statement would be as follows:

	19X1 £'000	19X0 £'000
Source of funds		
Total generated from operations*	10	—
Application of funds		
Total absorbed by operations*	—	(20)
*Total generated from/(absorbed by) operations:		
(Loss)/profit on ordinary activities before taxation	(100)	100
Adjustments for items not involving the flow of funds:		
Depreciation	80	40
Loss/(profit) on sale of fixed assets	30	(160)
	10	(20)

4.3   Extraordinary items

The disclosure of extraordinary items in the funds statement depends on whether or not they involve the flow of funds. Furthermore, the item will be adjusted for tax and/or deferred tax, depending upon whether the before or after tax method is followed (see 4.1 above). Example 15.1 above illustrates the treatment of an extraordinary item which did involve the flow of funds; however, where the extraordinary item represents, for example, a profit or loss on disposal of an asset, this amount would not be shown separately, but the proceeds would be disclosed as a source of funds.

The Appendix to SSAP 10 suggests that extraordinary items should be dealt with as an adjustment to profit/loss on ordinary activities in arriving at total funds generated from/absorbed by operations, and this is clearly an acceptable treatment; however, it is our view that fund flows arising outside the ordinary activities of the entity should be disclosed separately from funds flowing from normal operating activities.

4.4   Netting off of transactions

The explanatory note to SSAP 10 states that 'a minimum of "netting off" should take place as this may mask the significance of individually important figures'.[44] We concur with this recommendation and believe that all material fund flows should be disclosed. Specific examples of where netting off should be avoided are as follows:

(a)   the acquisition and disposal of fixed assets;

(b)   loans raised and repaid;

(c)   capital-based government grants received should be shown gross as a source of funds, rather than netted off against the funds applied for the acquisition of the corresponding capital assets.

4.5   Prior year adjustments

Prior year adjustments arise either from a change in accounting policy or the correction of a fundamental error. In both cases, the funds statement should be prepared on the basis of the restated comparative figures included in the financial statements.

In compiling the comparative figures for the funds statement, the figures previously reported would need to be adjusted to take the prior year adjustment into account.

4.6   Foreign currency differences

The treatment of foreign currency differences in funds statements is not specifically dealt with in either SSAP 10 or SSAP 20; the method of presentation, therefore, is entirely at the discretion of the preparers. Nevertheless, we consider that the overriding principle of eliminating from the funds statement those items which do not involve the flow of funds applies equally to exchange differences.

4.6.1   *Exchange differences in individual companies*

Under SSAP 20, most exchange differences arise on monetary items and will be taken to the profit and loss account; the rationale for this treatment is that the exchange differences will have been already reflected in cash flows, in the case of settled transactions, or will be in the future in the case of unsettled transactions. The treatment of such differences in the funds statement will depend on whether they relate to items which the company regards as funds for the purposes of the funds statement. Clearly, where a company has, or has had, net liquid funds denominated in foreign currency, such as bank deposits or overdrafts, then any exchange difference arising on such items will have increased or decreased such funds; accordingly, no adjustment should be made to eliminate the effect of the exchange difference. A similar treatment should be adopted where a company has, or has had, working capital items denominated in foreign currency, such as debtors or creditors, and they adopt a 'working capital' definition of funds. This will normally also be the case where a company does not adopt such a definition; this is probably due to the fact that most companies like the movements in working capital items to be reconcilable to the balance sheet figures (and also the fact that in many cases it would be extremely impracticable to eliminate the effects of exchange differences on the individual categories).

Adjustments will usually be made, however, to eliminate the effect of exchange differences in the funds statement where a company has any long-term monetary items denominated in foreign currency. For example, where a company has taken out a long-term loan denominated in a foreign currency during the year, then the receipt of such a loan should be treated as a source of funds. The amount to be shown as the source should be the amount of foreign currency received translated at the rate ruling at the date of the receipt; accordingly, it will be necessary to treat any exchange difference on the borrowing since that date up to the balance sheet date as an adjustment not involving the flow of funds, and adjusted against profit in arriving at the total funds generated from operations. A similar treatment should be adopted in later years for any further exchange differences relating to the borrowing.

4.6.2   Exchange differences on consolidation

Where a company uses the closing rate method for translating the financial statements of foreign subsidiaries, then all exchange differences relating to the retranslation of the net assets of the subsidiaries will have been taken directly to reserves. As such differences do not represent or measure changes in actual or prospective cash flows, it could be argued that the effects of such exchange differences should be eliminated entirely from the funds statement.

This treatment, however, produces a conflict between the objectives of the funds statement on the one hand, and the requirements of SSAP 10 that the figures from which the funds statement is constructed should be identifiable in the financial statements on the other. If the exchange differences are not eliminated, the funds statement will not reflect true funds flows and will merely present the arithmetical differences shown by the balance sheet (it will be necessary to include in the funds statement the exchange difference taken to reserves); while if they are eliminated, there will be unexplained differences between the opening and closing figures for some assets and liabilities. One approach, which appears to be followed by a large proportion of companies in practice, is to include a note similar to the following on the face of the funds statement:

> *Extract 15.6: Hawker Siddeley Group PLC*[45]
>
> The movements do not correspond to the changes shown on the face of the balance sheet due to the effects of eliminating exchange rate differences.

Another way of dealing with this conflict would be to present the funds statement in a columnar format, in which the effects of the exchange differences are shown separately on a line-by-line basis. However, this approach is seldom seen in practice and, although it could be argued that it is necessary in order to comply with all the objectives of SSAP 10, in our view, it adds little to the quality of information in the funds statement in terms of fulfilling the objectives of such a statement.

A further approach adopted by companies is not to eliminate all the effects of the translation differences; but only to eliminate those that relate to non-fund items, such as fixed assets and long-term borrowings, of the subsidiaries. As a result, sources and application of funds relating to such items will generally be included in the funds statement at the equivalent of the foreign currency amount translated at the closing rate of exchange (where companies translate the results of foreign subsidiaries at an average rate, they may wish to include such items at an appropriate average rate). The effects of the exchange differences on working capital items will not be eliminated and, therefore, the movements in such items shown in the funds statement will, generally, be reconcilable to the balance sheet figures. By adopting such an approach, it will be necessary to include in the funds statement the remaining exchange difference which has been taken to reserves (effectively, that relating to working capital items). This can be done by either including such amount as:

(a)   an adjustment not involving the movement of funds in arriving at funds generated from operations; or

(b)   another source or application of funds; or

(c)   a separate amount in the analysis of the movements in working capital.

In our view, method (a) should not be adopted, as the amount is different in nature to the other items normally included in that part of the funds statement; such other items have been charged or credited in arriving at the profit used as the starting point for the funds statement and the adjustment is being made to eliminate their effect on the funds generated from the operations. Method (c) is effectively the same as eliminating all translation differences, except that it avoids having to calculate the effect of exchange differences on individual categories of working capital.

Where a company translates the results of foreign subsidiaries at average rates, then part of the exchange difference taken to reserves will relate to the difference between the results as translated and the results translated at closing rates. It will be necessary for such an amount to be included in the funds statement; this can be done by adopting either of method (a) or method (b) above. Although such an exchange difference has not been charged or credited in arriving at the profit used as the starting point of the funds statement, it could be argued that the use of method (a) has some logic in that the exchange difference relates to the profit and loss account.

Where a company uses the temporal method to translate the financial statements of a foreign subsidiary, then as the exchange difference taken to the profit and loss account relates to the monetary assets/liabilities of the subsidiary, a similar treatment to that explained at 4.6.1 above for exchange differences in individual companies should be adopted.

4.6.3 Cover method

If the 'cover' method under SSAP 20 is being used, the gains/losses on the borrowings are offset, as a reserve movement, against the exchange differences arising on the investment; any differences on the borrowings which cannot be offset are written off to the profit and loss account. As far as the funds statement is concerned, the same principles as outlined at 4.6.1 above will apply.

Where the borrowings concerned are long-term borrowings then to the extent that the exchange differences are taken to reserves, they can be ignored for the purposes of the funds statement. To the extent that they have been taken to the profit and loss account, they should be treated as an adjustment not involving the movement of funds.

Where the borrowings concerned are short-term borrowings, then it will be necessary for the exchange differences, to the extent that they are taken to reserves, to be included in the funds statement. Again, the alternative treatments are those outlined at 4.6.2 above for exchange differences relating to working capital items. To the extent that the exchange difference has been taken to the profit and loss account, no adjustment will be necessary in respect of the exchange difference.

4.7 Group financial statements

SSAP 10's guidance in respect of group financial statements is limited to specifying that the funds statement should be prepared so as to reflect the operations of the group.[46] The explanatory note to SSAP 10 includes a discussion on the disclosure of purchases and disposals of subsidiary companies,[47] and the examples contained in the Appendix to the standard illustrate the recommended alternative options available for such disclosure. However, there are several other important issues relating to the preparation of a consolidated funds statement which need to be addressed.

4.7.1 Minority interests

As discussed at 1.3 of Chapter 4, there are three alternative approaches which can be followed in the preparation of consolidated financial statements; these are based on the entity theory, the proprietary (or parent company) theory and a hybrid of the two known as the parent company extension theory. These theories affect two aspects of consolidated financial statements whenever a minority interest exists in a subsidiary, namely:

(a)   the amounts attributed to the minority interests in subsidiaries; and

(b)   the valuation at which the assets and liabilities of subsidiaries are included in
       the group financial statements.

Examples 2 and 3 of the Appendix to SSAP 10 apply the proprietary theory in the
disclosure of minority interests in the funds statement. The examples start with
'Profit before tax and extraordinary items, less minority interests', and then add
back the 'Minority interests in the retained profits of the year' as a non-fund
adjustment.

The alternative approach under the entity theory would be to start with 'Profit on
ordinary activities before taxation', and to make no further adjustment for the
minorities, unless dividends have been paid to them — in which case these should
be separately disclosed as an application of funds. Glaxo Holdings p.l.c. provide
a good illustration of the application of this approach (see Extract 15.1 above),
and this would appear to be the more common approach followed in practice.

We have no preference as to which approach should be followed, although,
clearly, it is desirable that the funds statement presentation of minority interests
should be consistent with the overall approach followed in the preparation of the
group financial statements.

4.7.2   *Investments in associated companies*

There are two principal alternative treatments of income from associated
companies:

(a)   firstly, the investing group's share of earnings of the associated companies
       may be included in full as part of the funds generated from operations, with
       an application of funds for the reinvestment of the unremitted part of those
       earnings. The rationale for this approach is that the investing group, by
       virtue of its ability to exercise a significant influence over the associates, is
       able to dictate the timing of the conversion of those earnings into cash.
       Therefore, the full earnings should be treated as a source of funds, and the
       unremitted portion thereof should be shown as an application of funds to
       increase the book value of the investment.

(b)   secondly, the earnings of the associates may be included only to the extent
       that dividends are received or receivable. This approach assumes earnings
       from associates are not a source until dividends are received or receivable
       and is based on the view that the unremitted earnings of the associates do
       not represent current resources available to the investing group.

If the 'all financial resources' interpretation of funds is properly applied (as
SSAP 10 purports to do), then the alternative under (a) above should be
followed. However, the examples in the Appendix to SSAP 10 add back 'Profits
retained in associated companies' as a non-fund adjustment, thereby only
recognising dividends receivable as a source. Although either approach is
acceptable under SSAP 10, our preferred approach (and also that proposed by
IAS 7, the relevant International Accounting Standard on the subject)[48] is that
only dividends received or currently receivable should be included as a source of
funds.

In any event, alternative (a) is rarely seen in practice; however, where alternative (b) is followed, companies tend to follow a number of different methods of disclosure. For example Glaxo Holdings p.l.c. (see Extract 15.1 above) includes the dividends as 'another source', rather than as part of funds generated from operations; on the other hand, both Imperial Chemical Industries PLC and BPB Industries plc (see Extracts 15.4 and 15.5 above, respectively) include dividends receivable from associated companies as part of funds generated from operations, although they employ different methods of disclosure to achieve this.

Nevertheless, where a true cash flow statement is being prepared (as discussed at 5.1 below) only dividends received in cash would be included.

4.7.3 Acquisitions and disposals of subsidiaries

The presentation of acquisitions and disposals of subsidiaries in the funds statement is a further example of the conflict between the 'all financial resources' concept of funds which permeates SSAP 10, and the emphasis given to 'working capital' in the Appendix to the standard. Where, for example, the acquisition of a subsidiary is made partly in exchange for shares, the issue of shares in exchange for fixed assets would not, from the 'working capital' viewpoint, need to be shown in the funds statement; however, it would clearly be confusing if only that part of the transaction which affects working capital were to be shown. For this reason, SSAP 10 adopts a broad view of funds for the disclosure of acquisitions and disposals of subsidiaries in the funds statement, irrespective of the overall emphasis placed on funds in the statement.

Although it is not a requirement of the standard, SSAP 10 suggests the following two ways in which the acquisition or disposal of a subsidiary may be presented:

(a)   either as separate items (for example, by showing 'shares issued in consideration of the acquisition of subsidiaries' as a source, and 'acquisition of subsidiaries' as an application); or

(b)   'by reflecting the effects on the separate assets and liabilities dealt with in the statement, so that the acquisition of a subsidiary company would be dealt with as an application of funds in acquiring the fixed assets (including goodwill) of that subsidiary and as a change in working capital'.[49]

In either case, SSAP 10 recommends that, in the interests of clarity, the effects of acquisitions and disposals should be summarised in a footnote which indicates, in the case of an acquisition, how much of the purchase price has been discharged in cash and how much by the issue of shares[50] (see Extract 15.4 for an illustration of the disclosure of an acquisition).

An alternative method of presenting this information, which is sometimes used in practice, is to analyse the sources and applications of funds, between operations and acquisitions and disposals, in the body of the funds statement. B.A.T Industries p.l.c. is an example of a company which has adopted this form of presentation:

Extract 15.6: B.A.T Industries p.l.c.[51]

GROUP FUNDS STATEMENT
funds provided and applied for the year ended 31 December

			Acquisitions and disposals included in total movements	
	Total movements			
	1987	1986	1987	1986
Funds provided	£ millions			
Net profit attributable to B.A.T Industries' shareholders before extraordinary items	787	793		
Dividends (paid £216 million 1986 £180 million)	(248)	(209)		
	539	584		
Extraordinary items	(36)	75	(4)	(47)
Increase in share capital	2	3		
Reserve movements	(733)	(148)	(6)	(220)
Net (decrease)/increase in B.A.T Industries' shareholders' interests	(228)	514	(10)	(267)
Net (decreases)/increases in				
Interest of minority shareholders	(66)	66	(12)	4
Provisions for unfunded pensions	(7)	50	(16)	(8)
Deferred taxation	(13)	121		
Borrowings — due beyond one year	(167)	(115)	(7)	21
	(481)	636	(45)	(250)
Funds applied				
Tangible fixed assets				
Expenditure	361	499	4	92
Disposals and exchange differences	(467)	(191)	(109)	(262)
Depreciation of the year	(240)	(266)		
Net tangible fixed assets	(346)	42	(105)	(170)
Financial services	20	348		72
Other fixed assets	(100)	(131)	(3)	(222)
	(426)	259	(108)	(320)
Working capital				
Stocks	(336)	(92)	(55)	(175)
Debtors	(453)	(141)	(44)	(288)
Current investments, deposits and cash	354	524	97	421
	(435)	291	(2)	(42)
Borrowings — due within one year	251	26	11	49
Other provisions and creditors	129	60	54	63
Net (decrease)/increase in working capital	(55)	377	63	70
(Decrease)/increase in net assets	(481)	636	(45)	(250)

Where method (b) above is adopted for the acquisition of a subsidiary, then where the subsidiary which is being acquired is not wholly-owned, the minority interest at the time of the acquisition will have to be disclosed as a source of funds (see 4.7.1 above); any subsequent change in the holding company's interest in the subsidiary would also have to be reflected in the funds statement. Where any of the outstanding minority interest is acquired, the underlying net assets will have already been incorporated in the group financial statements, and their movements will, therefore, be automatically dealt with in the funds statement; under method (b) above, the only item necessary in the funds statement will, therefore, be any goodwill arising on the acquisition of the minority interest

Where the increased investment in an associated company, previously accounted for on the equity method, results in its consolidation as a subsidiary for the first time, the most straightforward treatment is to disclose the acquisition as an application of funds in one line, with an analysis of the net assets being consolidated being shown in a footnote. However, where method (b) above is adopted, the carrying value of the associated company at the date of becoming a subsidiary would normally be shown as a source of funds.

5   COMPARISON WITH US AND IASC REQUIREMENTS

5.1   US

5.1.1   *Introduction*

In 1980, as part of its conceptual framework project, the FASB issued a Discussion Memorandum — *Reporting Funds Flows, Liquidity, and Financial Flexibility* — which discussed funds flow reporting issues. The major issues which were raised in the Discussion Memorandum relating to funds flow reporting included (a) the concept of funds that should be adopted as the focus of the funds flow statement, (b) the reporting of transactions that have no direct impact on funds, (c) the approaches for presenting information about funds flows, (d) the presentation of information about funds flows from operations, and (e) the separation of funds flow information about investing activities into outflows for maintenance of operating capacity, expansion of operating capacity, or non-operating purposes.

Although this Discussion Memorandum was followed by an Exposure Draft of a proposed concepts statement — *Reporting Income, Cash Flows, and Financial Position of Business Enterprises* — which suggested that funds flow reporting should focus on cash rather than working capital, the FASB decided not to issue a final statement on the subject. Instead, the FASB chose to consider the subject in connection with its study of recognition and measurement concepts. As discussed at 1.3.1 above, the outcome was that Concepts Statement No. 5 — *Recognition and Measurement in Financial Statements of Business Enterprises* — concluded that a full set of financial statements should include a statement of cash flows. This led to the FASB setting up a Task Force on Cash Flow Reporting, and ultimately to the publication in November 1987 of SFAS 95 — *Statement of Cash Flows*. In February 1989, SFAS 102 — *Statement of Cash Flows — Exemption of Certain Enterprises and Classification of Cash Flows from Certain*

Securities Acquired for Resale — was issued as an amendment to SFAS 95; these amendments have been incorporated in the discussion of SFAS 95 below.

5.1.2   Focus of SFAS 95

SFAS 95 concluded that the primary purpose of a statement of cash flows is to provide relevant information about the cash receipts and cash payments of an enterprise during a period.[52] The information provided by the statement, if used in conjunction with related disclosures in the other financial statements, should assist users to:

(a)   assess the enterprise's ability to generate positive future net cash flows;

(b)   assess the enterprise's ability to meet its obligations, pay dividends and meet its needs for external financing;

(c)   assess the reasons for differences between net income and related cash receipts and payments;

(d)   assess the effects on the enterprise's financial position of both cash and non-cash investing and financing transactions during the period.[53]

In order to achieve these objectives, the statement focuses on the change during the period in *cash* and *cash equivalents*, rather than working capital; ambiguous terms such as 'funds' are not to be used. The total amounts of cash and cash equivalents at the beginning and end of the period shown in the statement of cash flows will be the same amounts as presented in the balance sheets as of those dates. A statement of cash flows is not required for defined benefit pension plans and certain other employee benefit plans or for certain investment companies.[54]

5.1.3   Cash equivalents

SFAS 95 defines cash equivalents as short-term, highly liquid investments that are both:

(a)   readily convertible to known amounts of cash; and

(b)   so near their maturity that they present insignificant risk of changes in value because of changes in interest rates.[55]

Generally, only an investment with original maturity (i.e. original maturity to the entity holding the investment) of three months or less qualify under the above definition.[56]

It is noteworthy that not all investments that qualify are required to be treated as cash equivalents; for example an enterprise may classify short-term, highly liquid investments as investments rather than cash equivalents. However, a company must disclose its policy for determining cash equivalents, and any change to that policy is considered to be a change in accounting principle, requiring restatement of comparative financial statements.

5.1.4   Form and content of the statement of cash flows

SFAS 95 states that a statement of cash flows must classify cash receipts and cash payments as resulting from investing, financing or operating activities.[57]

Each cash receipt or payment is to be classified according to its nature without regard to whether it stems from an item intended as a hedge of another item. For example, the proceeds of a borrowing are a financing cash inflow whether or not the debt is intended as a hedge of an investment, and the purchase or sale of a futures contract is an investing activity without regard to whether the contract is intended as a hedge of a firm commitment to purchase inventory.

5.1.5 *Investing activities*

Investing activities include:

(a)   making and collecting loans;

(b)   acquiring and disposing of

      (i)   securities that are not cash equivalents;
      (ii)   property, plant and equipment;
      (iii)   other productive assets, other than inventory materials.[58]

Investing activities exclude acquiring and disposing of certain loans or other debt or equity instruments that are acquired specifically for resale.[59]

Cash inflows from investing activities are:

(a)   receipts from collections or sales of loans made by the enterprise and of other entities' debt instruments (other than cash equivalents and certain debt instruments that are acquired specifically for resale) that were purchased by the enterprise;

(b)   receipts from sales of equity instruments of other enterprises (other than certain equity instruments carried in a trading account), and from returns of investments in those instruments;

(c)   receipts from sales of property, plant and equipment and other productive assets (including interest capitalised as part of the cost of those assets).[60]

Cash outflows for investing activities are:

(a)   disbursements for loans made by the enterprise, and payments made to acquire debt instruments of other entities (other than cash equivalents and certain debt instruments that are acquired specifically for resale);

(b)   payments to acquire equity instruments of other enterprises (other than certain equity instruments carried in a trading account);

(c)   payments to acquire property, plant and equipment and other productive assets (including interest capitalised as part of the cost of those assets).[61]

5.1.6 *Financing activities*

Financing activities include obtaining resources from owners and providing them with a return on, and a return of, their investment; borrowing money and repaying amounts borrowed, or otherwise settling the obligation; and obtaining and paying for other resources obtained from creditors on long-term credit.[62]

Cash inflows from financing activities are:

(a)   proceeds from issuance of equity securities;

(b)   proceeds from issuing bonds, mortgages, notes and from other short- or long-term borrowing.[63]

Cash outflows for financing activities are:

(a)   payments of dividends to owners;

(b)   cash outlays to repurchase the enterprise's shares;

(c)   repayments of amounts borrowed;

(d)   other principal payments to creditors who have extended long-term credit.[64]

5.1.7   *Operating activities*

Operating activities include:

(a)   all transactions and other events not defined as investing or financing activities;

(b)   delivering or producing goods for sale and providing services;

(c)   generally, the cash effects of transactions and other events that enter into the determination of income.[65]

Cash inflows from operating activities are:

(a)   cash receipts from sales of goods or services (the term 'goods' includes certain loans and other debt and equity instruments of other enterprises that are acquired specifically for resale);

(b)   cash receipts from returns on loans (interest) and on equity securities (dividends);

(c)   all other cash receipts that do not stem from transactions defined as investing or financing activities (e.g. amounts received in settlement of lawsuits).[66]

Cash outflows for operating activities are:

(a)   cash payments to acquire materials for manufacture or goods for resale (the term 'goods' includes certain loans and other debt and equity instruments of other enterprises that are acquired specifically for resale);

(b)   cash payments to other suppliers and employees for other goods or services;

(c)   cash payments to governments for taxes, duties, fines etc.;

(d)   cash payments to lenders and other creditors for interest;

(e)   all other cash payments that do not stem from transactions defined as investing or financing activities.[67]

5.1.8 *Receipts and payments are presented gross*

In general, a greater and more meaningful assessment of cash flows can be derived from reporting gross, rather than net, cash receipts and cash payments. Items whose turnover is quick, the amounts are large and whose maturities are short-term may be reported net (i.e. investments — other than cash equivalents — loans receivable and debt, provided that the original maturity of the asset or liability is three months or less). Items with these characteristics may be reported net, since knowledge of gross cash receipts and payments related to them is not necessary to understand the enterprise's operating, investing and financing activities.

5.1.9 *Non-cash activities are disclosed separately*

Information about all investing and financing activities of an enterprise during a period that affect recognised assets or liabilities, but that do not result in cash receipts or cash payments in the period shall be reported in related disclosures. Disclosure may be narrative or summarised in a schedule; examples include converting debt to equity, acquiring assets by assuming directly related liabilities (e.g. purchasing a building by incurring a mortgage to the seller), obtaining an asset by entering into a capital lease.[68]

5.1.10 *Choice of using the direct or indirect methods*

Two presentation options are available for reporting net cash flow from operating activities: the *direct method* and the *indirect method*. However, regardless of which of the two methods is used, SFAS 95 requires that a reconciliation of net income to net cash flow from operating activities be presented, and that interest and income tax payments be presented.[69]

A *The direct method*

The direct method reports as its principal components operating cash receipts and payments (i.e. cash received from customers and cash paid to suppliers and employees). The difference between these components is the net cash flow from operating activities.[70] If the direct method is used, the reconciliation of net income to net cash flow from operating activities should be presented in a separate schedule.[71]

B *The indirect method*

The indirect method begins with net income and adjusts it for revenue and expense items that are not the result of operating cash transactions in the current period to reconcile it to net cash flow from operating activities; consequently, it does not disclose operating cash receipts and payments.

It is noteworthy that although SFAS 95 recommends that the direct method be used to report the net cash flow from operating activities, the AICPA's 1988 survey of accounting practices revealed that of the 110 survey companies presenting a statement of cash flows, only five used the direct method.[72]

5.1.11 Illustrative examples

Appendix C to SFAS 95 contains several illustrative examples for the preparation of statements of cash flows, using both the direct and indirect methods. The following extracts from the Appendix illustrate the alternative methods of presenting a statement of cash flows for a US corporation engaged principally in manufacturing activities:[73]

A   The direct method

COMPANY M
CONSOLIDATED STATEMENT OF CASH FLOWS
FOR THE YEAR ENDED DECEMBER 31, 19X1
Increase (Decrease) in Cash and Cash Equivalents

CASH FLOWS FROM OPERATING ACTIVITIES:

Cash received from customers	$13,850	
Cash paid to suppliers and employees	(12,000)	
Dividend received from affiliate	20	
Interest received	55	
Interest paid (net of amount capitalized)	(220)	
Income taxes paid	(325)	
Insurance proceeds received	15	
Cash paid to settle lawsuit for patent infringement	(30)	
Net cash provided by operating activities		$1,365

CASH FLOWS FROM INVESTING ACTIVITIES:

Proceeds from sale of facility	600	
Payment received on note for sale of plant	150	
Capital expenditures	(1,000)	
Payment for purchase of Company S, net of cash acquired	(925)	
Net cash used in investing activities		(1,175)

CASH FLOWS FROM FINANCING ACTIVITIES:

Net borrowings under line-of-credit agreement	300	
Principal payments under capital lease obligation	(125)	
Proceeds from issuance of long-term debt	400	
Proceeds from issuance of common stock	500	
Dividends paid	(200)	
Net cash provided by financing activities		875
Net increase in cash and cash equivalents		1,065
Cash and cash equivalents at beginning of year		600
Cash and cash equivalents at end of year		$1,665

Reconciliation of net income to net cash provided by operating activities:

Net income		$ 760
Adjustments to reconcile net income to net cast provided		
by operating activities:		
Depreciation and amortization	$ 445	
Provision for losses on accounts receivable	200	
Gain on sale of facility	(80)	
Undistributed earnings of affiliate	(25)	
Payment received on installment note receivable for		
sale of inventory	100	
Change in assets and liabilities net of effects from		
purchase of Company S:		
Increase in accounts receivable	(215)	
Decrease in inventory	205	
Increase in prepaid expenses	(25)	
Decrease in accounts payable and accrued expenses	(250)	
Increase in interest and income taxes payable	50	
Increase in deferred taxes	150	
Increases in other liabilities	50	
Total adjustments		605
Net cash provided by operating activities		$1,365

Supplemental schedule of noncash investing and financing activities:

The Company purchased all of the capital stock of Company S for $950. In conjunction with the acquisition, liabilities were assumed as follows:

Fair value of assets acquired	$1,580
Cash paid for the capital stock	(950)
Liabilities assumed	$ 630

A capital lease obligation of $850 was incurred when the Company entered into a lease for new equipment.

Additional common stock was issued upon the conversion of $500 of long-term debt.

Disclosure of accounting policy:

For the purposes of the statement of cash flows, the Company considered all highly liquid debt instruments purchased with a maturity of three months or less to be cash equivalents.

B   *The indirect method*

COMPANY M
CONSOLIDATED STATEMENT OF CASH FLOWS
FOR THE YEAR ENDED DECEMBER 31, 19X1
Increase (Decrease) in Cash and Cash Equivalents

CASH FLOWS FROM OPERATING ACTIVITIES:

Net income		$ 760
Adjustments to reconcile net income to net cash provided by operating activities:		
Depreciation and amortization	$ 445	
Provision for losses on accounts receivable	200	
Gain on sale of facility	(80)	
Undistributed earnings of affiliate	(25)	
Payment received on installment note receivable for sale of inventory	100	
Change in assets and liabilities net of effects from purchase of Company S:		
Increase in accounts receivable	(215)	
Decrease in inventory	205	
Increase in prepaid expenses	(25)	
Decrease in accounts payable and accrued expenses	(250)	
Increase in interest and income taxes payable	50	
Increase in deferred taxes	150	
Increase in other liabilities	50	
Total adjustments		605
Net cash provided by operating activities		1,365
CASH FLOWS FROM INVESTING ACTIVITIES:		
Proceeds from sale of facility	600	
Payment received on note for sale of plant	150	
Capital expenditures	(1,000)	
Payment for purchase of Company S, net of cash acquired	(925)	
Net cash used in investing activities		(1,175)
CASH FLOWS FROM FINANCING ACTIVITIES:		
Net borrowings under line-of-credit agreement	300	
Principal payments under capital lease obligation	(125)	
Proceeds from issuance of long-term debt	400	
Proceeds from issuance of common stock	500	
Dividends paid	(200)	
Net cash provided by financing activities		875
Net increase in cash and cash equivalents		1,065
Cash and cash equivalents at beginning of year		600
Cash and cash equivalents at end of year		$1,665

Supplemental disclosures of cash flow information:

Cash paid during the year for:	
Interest (net of amount capitalized)	$ 220
Income taxes	325

Supplemental schedule of noncash investing and financing activities:

The Company purchased all of the capital stock of Company S for $950. In conjunction with the acquisition, liabilities were assumed as follows:

Fair value of assets acquired	$1,580
Cash paid for the capital stock	(950)
Liabilities assumed	$ 630

A capital lease obligation of $850 was incurred when the Company entered into a lease for new equipment.

Additional common stock was issued upon the conversion of $500 of long-term debt.

Disclosure of accounting policy:

For the purposes of the statement of cash flows, the Company considered all highly liquid debt instruments purchased with a maturity of three months or less to be cash equivalents.

The major criticism of SFAS 95 is that it permits the indirect method of reporting net cash flow from operating activities. Some hold the view that, in so doing, the FASB has foregone the opportunity to make a significant contribution to the quality of financial reporting and to enhanced user understanding of cash flows from operating activities. As stated above, practice to date indicates that the indirect method will be followed almost exclusively. The reasons for this are probably that the indirect method will be a lot less onerous and expensive to apply, together with the fact that the direct method provides users with information which companies may not wish to disclose.

5.2　IASC

The IASC issued IAS 7 — *Statement of Changes in Financial Position* — in October 1977. However, the standard is even less prescriptive than SSAP 10, and contains virtually no requirement as to the form or content of the funds statement; in fact, the only specific requirements are that:

(a)　a statement of changes in financial position must be presented for each period for which an income statement is presented;

(b)　funds provided from or used in the operations of an enterprise should be presented separately from other sources of funds; and

(c)　unusual items which are not part of the ordinary activities of the enterprise should be separately disclosed in the statement.[74]

The standard goes on to state that 'each enterprise or group of enterprises should adopt the form of presentation for the statement of changes in financial position which is most informative in the circumstances'.[75] This means that companies can place whatever interpretation they like on 'funds', although the explanation section of the standard states that 'the term "funds" generally refers to cash, to cash and cash equivalents, or to working capital'.[76]

6   CONCLUSION

There is a trend amongst certain countries to require the presentation of a statement of cash flows similar to that laid down in SFAS 95. In the UK, on the other hand, there is nothing to prevent companies presenting a funds statement in the style of SFAS 95, whilst at the same time remaining within the framework of SSAP 10. However, SSAP 10 (in its present form) is clearly inadequate as a means of encouraging improved financial reporting practice in this area. Consequently, whilst there are some companies which are experimenting with the presentation of some cash flow information in their funds statements,[77] there is unlikely to be a widespread move in this direction without a corresponding change in the accounting standard, which we believe is urgently required. It is noteworthy that the ICAS discussion document *Making Corporate Reports Valuable* suggests the inclusion of a SFAS 95-type cash flow statement in the financial reporting package of companies.[78]

References

1   See Ross M. Skinner, *Accounting Standards in Evolution*, Canada: Holt, Rinehart and Winston of Canada, Limited, 1987, p. 397.

2   There is evidence of companies publishing funds statements as far back as 1862 in the UK and 1863 in the US — see L.S. Rosen and Don T DeCoster, ' "Funds" Statements: A Historical Perspective'. *The Accounting Review*, January 1969, pp. 124—136. However, it was not until the 1950s (in the US) and the early 1970s (in the UK) that the funds statement was commonly presented in annual reports in one form or another.

3   The term 'funds statement' has been used throughout this chapter in preference to the alternatives of 'statement of source and application of funds' or 'statement of changes in financial position'. As described at section 3 of this chapter, the format and presentation of the funds statement is dependent on the interpretation placed on the concept of 'funds'.

4   A review of the 1959 annual reports of the 600 US industrial companies included in the AICPA's publication *Accounting Trends and Techniques* revealed that in 190 cases some form of funds statement was presented.

5   AICPA Accounting Research Study No. 2, *"Cash Flow" Analysis and The Funds Statement*, New York: AICPA, 1963.

6   *Ibid.*, p. xi.

7   APB 19, *Reporting Changes in Financial Position*, AICPA, 1971.

8   *Ibid.*, para. 7.

9   ED 13, *Statements of Source and Application of Funds*, April 1974.

10 SSAP 10, *Statements of source and application of funds*, July 1975.

11 See the foreword to SSAP 10.

12 SSAP 10, para. 4.

13 Accountants International Study Group, *The Funds Statement: Current Practices in Canada, the United Kingdom and the United States*, 1973, para. 8.

14 SFAS 95, *Statement of Cash Flows*, FASB, November 1987, para. 1.

15 *Ibid.*

16 Eldon S. Hendriksen, *Accounting Theory*, Fourth Edition, Illinois: Richard D. Irwin, Inc., 1982, p. 236.

17 SFAC No. 1, *Objectives of Financial Reporting by Business Enterprises*, FASB, November 1978, para. 37.

18 SFAC No. 5, *Recognition and Measurement in Financial Statements of Business Enterprises*, FASB, December 1984, para. 13.

19 *Ibid.*, para. 52.

20 See SFAC No. 5, at para. 24.

21 SFAS 95, *Statement of Cash Flows*, FASB, November 1987, para. 3.

22 For example, the US, Canada, New Zealand and South Africa.

23 The emphases have been added in all the extracts.

24 SSAP 10, para. 2.

25 *Ibid.*, para. 1.

26 *Ibid.*, para. 3.

27 *Ibid.*

28 *Ibid.*, para. 9.

29 *Ibid.*, para. 10.

30 *Ibid.*, para. 11.

31 *Ibid.*, para. 8.

32 *Ibid.*, para. 4.

33 *Ibid.*

34 *Ibid.*, para. 5.

35 See Accountants International Study Group, *op. cit.* at paras. 33 to 37. The nine interpretations are: (1) working capital, (2) quick assets less current liabilities, (3) cash and marketable securities less current liabilities, (4) cash and marketable securities less short-term credit, (5) cash and marketable securities, (6) cash, (7) total funds employed in the business, (8) total shareholders' funds, and (9) equity interests.

36 L. C. L. Skerratt and D. J. Tonkin (eds.), *Financial Reporting 1987 — 88: A Survey of UK Reporting Practice*, London: ICAEW, 1988, p. 189.

37 Glaxo Holdings p.l.c., Annual Report and Accounts 1988, p. 34.

38 Dunhill Holdings Plc, Report and Accounts 1987/88, p. 24.

39 SSAP 10, para. 11.

40 *Ibid.*

41 Woolworth Holdings PLC, Report and Accounts 1987/1988, p. 32.

42 Imperial Chemical Industries PLC, Annual Report 1987, pp. 34 and 48.

43 BPB Industries plc, Report and Accounts 1988, p. 18.

44 SSAP 10, para. 4.

45 Hawker Siddeley Group PLC, 1987 Annual Report & Accounts, p. 32.

46 SSAP 10, para. 12.

47 *Ibid.*, para. 5.

48 IAS 7, *Statement of Changes in Financial Position*, IASC, 1977, paras. 13—15.

49 SSAP 10, para 5.

50 *Ibid.*

51 B.A.T Industries p.l.c., Annual Report and Accounts 1987, p. 33.

52 SFAS 95, para. 4.

53 *Ibid.*, para. 5.

54 *Ibid.*, para. 3.

55 *Ibid.*, para. 8.

56 *Ibid.*
57 *Ibid.*, para. 14.
58 *Ibid.*, para. 15.
59 *Ibid.*
60 *Ibid.*, para. 16.
61 *Ibid.*, para. 17.
62 *Ibid.*, para. 18.
63 *Ibid.*, para. 19.
64 *Ibid.*, para. 20.
65 *Ibid.*, para. 21.
66 *Ibid.*, para. 22.
67 *Ibid.*, para. 23.
68 *Ibid.*, para. 32.
69 *Ibid.*, para. 29.
70 *Ibid.*, para. 27.
71 *Ibid.*, para. 30.
72 AICPA, *Accounting Trends & Techniques: Annual Survey of Accounting Practices Followed in 600 Stockholders' Reports*, 1988, p. 354.
73 Extracted from SFAS 95, Appendix C, Example 1.
74 IAS 7, paras. 20 and 21.
75 *Ibid.*, para. 22.
76 *Ibid.*, para. 4.
77 See, for example, the annual report of Cadbury Schweppes p.l.c.
78 The Institute of Chartered Accountants of Scotland, *Making Corporate Reports Valuable*, London: Kogan Page, 1988, paras. 7.35—7.38.

Post balance sheet events

1 THE DEVELOPMENT OF ACCOUNTING FOR POST BALANCE SHEET EVENTS

1.1 Introduction

A 'post balance sheet event' is defined by SSAP 17 — *Accounting for post balance sheet events* — as 'those events, both favourable and unfavourable, which occur between the balance sheet date and the date on which the financial statements are approved by the board of directors'.[1] This definition, therefore, incorporates all events occurring between those dates — irrespective of whether or not they relate to conditions which existed at the balance sheet date. Consequently, the principal issue to be resolved is which post balance sheet events should be reflected in the financial statements?

Since the financial statements of an entity purport to present, inter alia, its financial position at the balance sheet date, it is clear that the statements should be adjusted for all post balance sheet events which offer greater clarity of conditions that existed at the balance sheet date. However, the application of the prudence concept might take this further and suggest that *all* post balance sheet events which adversely affect the value of assets and liabilities should be reflected in financial statements — even if they relate to conditions which arise subsequent to the balance sheet date. Indeed, this argument could be taken even further to suggest that provisions may be required to take account of events which could not have been foreseen at the balance sheet date.

It is as a result of the conflict between matching and prudence and the variation of positions taken by different businesses, that the accounting treatment of post balance sheet events and their presentation in financial statements, has varied considerably.

In addition to the above, there has sometimes been a practice of manipulating the balance sheet in order to display 'in such a way as to give a falsely favourable impression of the facts, the arrangement of a balance sheet so as to suggest that the business concerned is more prosperous than it is,'[2] by going outside the normal trading pattern of the business on a short-term basis. This has been done by either delaying or bringing forward specific transactions or by entering into transactions, which are reversed shortly after the balance sheet date. The term used to cover such practices is 'Window Dressing'.

1.2   Companies Act 1948

Prior to the enactment of the Companies Act 1948, it was not uncommon for companies to manipulate their results and eliminate significant fluctuations by the use of secret reserves. This would involve the creation of excessive provisions against assets and for liabilities. Thus if any event occurred after the balance sheet date but before approval by the board of directors, there would normally be adequate cover within the reserves to meet any adjustments considered necessary.

The Companies Act 1948, introduced additional disclosures which effectively stopped the use of secret reserves.[3] This was done by requiring separate disclosure of each material reserve and provision, and any movements thereon. As a result of this the treatment of post balance sheet events gained in importance as their effect could no longer be hidden.

1.3   ICAEW Recommendation N17

In October 1957, the ICAEW issued Recommendation N17 'Events occurring after the balance sheet date'. This discussed the treatment of post balance sheet events and gave examples of how specific items should be treated.

N17[4] stated that events which are known to have occurred after the balance sheet date should not be reflected in the financial statements unless either:

(a)   they assist in forming an opinion as to the amount properly attributable, in the conditions on the balance sheet date, to any item the amount of which was subject to uncertainty on that date; or

(b)   they arise from legislation affecting items in the accounts, for example changes in taxation, or are required by law to be shown in the accounts, for example appropriations and proposed appropriations of profit.

The Recommendation[5] discussed the realisation of certain assets and liabilities subsequent to the balance sheet and how consideration should be given to additional evidence received upon realisation of those assets and liabilities.

It also stated that there may be events occurring after the balance sheet date which should be excluded from the financial statements but may be of such importance to shareholders that they would need to be disclosed in some other way. Examples given of such events were the disposal of a significant part of a business or a profit or loss, either capital or revenue, which would have a considerable influence on 'the financial resources of the business'.[6]

1.4   ED 22

Despite the recommendations in N17, a variety of disclosures continued to be adopted by businesses and some confusion remained as to what represented events that required disclosure to shareholders and how events that had a significant effect on a business's continuing existence should be reflected. This led to the ASC issuing ED 22 — *Accounting for post balance sheet events* — in February 1978.

ED 22 differentiated between 'adjusting events' and 'non-adjusting events' and gave examples of each.[7] It explained that no separate disclosure was required for adjusting events as they merely gave additional evidence in support of items in financial statements but non-adjusting events needed to be disclosed where their materiality would mean that not to do so would result in the financial statements presenting a misleading financial position. ED 22 stated that disclosure should be made of non-adjusting events which:

'(a) do not affect the condition of assets or liabilities at the balance sheet date, but do represent abnormal changes to them since that date; or

(b) do not relate to the financial position at the balance sheet date, but are of such importance that their non-disclosure would affect the ability of the users of the financial statements to make proper evaluations'.[8]

ED 22 clarified the date up to which post balance sheet events should be taken into account for inclusion in the financial statements.[9]

1.5 SSAP 17

In general the contents of ED 22 were supported by those who commented on it. However, concern was expressed that no guidance was given on what to do when the going concern concept was questioned by a post balance sheet event, which was defined as a non-adjusting event in the ED. In addition, the ASC was forced to react to increasing adverse opinion about the practice of window dressing, including pressure from the Government of the day.

These problems were therefore dealt with when SSAP 17 — *Accounting for post balance sheet events* — was issued in August 1980. The detailed provisions of the standard are discussed at 2 below.

2 REQUIREMENTS OF SSAP 17

2.1 Definitions

As stated in 1.1 above, SSAP 17 defines post balance sheet events as 'those events, both favourable and unfavourable, which occur between the balance sheet date and the date on which the financial statements are approved by the board of directors'.[10]

This therefore includes events that provide additional evidence as to conditions which existed at the balance sheet date and those that do not.

Adjusting events are 'post balance sheet events which provide additional evidence of conditions existing at the balance sheet date. They include events which because of statutory or conventional requirements are reflected in the financial statements.'[11]

Examples given of events normally classified as adjusting are as follows:[12]

(a) the subsequent determination of the purchase price or the sales proceeds of fixed assets purchased or sold before the year end;

(b)   a valuation of property which indicates a permanent diminution in value of the asset at the balance sheet date;

(c)   the receipt of information, such as financial statements of an unlisted company, which provides evidence of a permanent diminution in value of a long-term investment;

(d)   the sale of stock after the balance sheet date showing that the estimate of net realisable value was incorrect;

(e)   the discovery of evidence showing that estimates of accrued profit on a long-term contract were inaccurate;

(f)   a trade debtor going into liquidation or receivership;

(g)   the declaration of dividends by subsidiaries and associated companies for periods prior to the balance sheet date;

(h)   a change in taxation rates applicable to periods before the balance sheet date;

(i)   the receipt of insurance claims which were in the process of negotiation at the balance sheet date;

(j)   the discovery of significant errors or frauds which show that the financial statements were misstated.

The standard states that non-adjusting events are 'post balance sheet events which concern conditions which did not exist at the balance sheet date'.[13]

The appendix to the standard gives examples of items which would usually be classified as non-adjusting events.[14] These include:

(a)   mergers and acquisitions;

(b)   reconstructions and proposed reconstructions;

(c)   the issue of shares and debentures;

(d)   the purchase or disposal of fixed assets and investments;

(e)   the loss of fixed assets or stocks due to a catastrophe such as a fire or a flood;

(f)   the opening of new trading activities or extension of existing trading activities;

(g)   the closing of a significant part of trading activities if this was not foreseen at the balance sheet date;

(h)   a decrease in the value of property and investments held as fixed assets, if it can be shown that the decline took place subsequent to the balance sheet date;

(i)   changes in foreign currency exchange rates;

(j)   government action, such as nationalisation;

(k)   strikes and other labour disputes;

(l)   the augmentation of pension benefits.

2.2   Events requiring adjustment

SSAP 17 requires that the financial statements be adjusted by:

(a)   an adjusting event; or

(b)   a post balance sheet event which indicates that the application of the going concern concept to the whole or a material part of the company is no longer appropriate.[15] This could include a deterioration of trading results and the financial position, or the refusal of the bank to continue overdraft facilities.

2.3   Events not requiring adjustment but requiring disclosure

The standard states that an event of this type should be disclosed where:

'(a)   it is a non-adjusting event of such materiality that its non-disclosure would affect the ability of the users of financial statements to reach a proper understanding of the financial position; or

(b)   it is the reversal or maturity after the year end of a transaction entered into before the year end, the substance of which was primarily to alter the appearance of the company's balance sheet.'[16] Such alterations include those commonly known as 'window dressing' (see 3.5 below).

The ambiguity which renders SSAP 17 relatively meaningless in the case of (a) above is the *date* at which the financial position is to be understood by the users. If it is the balance sheet date (which is what the law requires), then non-adjusting events need never be disclosed, since it is difficult to see how the financial statements could ever fail to give a true and fair view of the year end position because of the absence of such disclosure. What the standard's requirements in this area boil down to, therefore, is to highlight those major non-adjusting post balance sheet events which have resulted in the financial position at the date of approval being significantly different from that portrayed by the balance sheet.

The non-adjusting events which appear most regularly in financial statements are possibly the acquisition of a fixed asset, normally an investment, or a merger subsequent to the balance sheet date. We consider the following extracts to be good examples of disclosure in such situations:

Extract 16.1: Cadbury Schweppes p.l.c.[17]

26 POST BALANCE SHEET EVENT

In December 1987 agreement was reached in London with Midial S.A. for the purchase of Chocolat Poulain S.A., the consideration being FFr.950m payable in cash at completion. Following approval from the French Ministry of Finance and fulfilment of other conditions, the purchase was completed on 22 February 1988. The purchase has been financed out of the Group's existing borrowings facilities.

Chocolat Poulain is a leading French manufacturer of branded chocolate products, based at Blois, some 200km south-west of Paris, and employing approximately 700 people. France is the second largest confectionery market in Continental Europe. In 1986 Chocolat Poulain had a 17% share of the moulded sector, 23% of the cocoa-based beverages sector and smaller shares in the assortments, sugar confectionery and chocolate spread sectors. Its principal brands are Noir Extra, Tres Tendre, Super Rocher, Super Poulain, Grand Arome and Poulain Leger.

On the basis of the local audited accounts the 1987 results show sales turnover of FFr.841m and net earnings of FFr.59m. The earnings have been adjusted to conform with group accounting policies and to eliminate certain overheads which will not apply under Cadbury Schweppes ownership, the principal item being royalties for trademarks which were transferred into Chocolat Poulain prior to completion.

On the basis of the local audited accounts at 31 December 1987 the adjusted assets and liabilities were as follows:

	FFr.m
Fixed assets	94.6
Stock	74.9
Debtors	216.3
Creditors	(233.8)
Cash (net of borrowings)	1.5
	153.5

The following table sets out the net indebtedness of Cadbury Schweppes p.l.c. and its subsidiaries at the close of business on 26 February 1988.

	£ m
Secured	
First mortgage debenture stocks	6.6
Bank overdrafts and other loans	7.6
Unsecured	
8% Convertible bonds 2000 (US$8.2m)	4.6
Commercial paper (US$66.4m)	37.5
Bank loans	220.6
Other loans	2.3
Obligations under finance leases	66.5
Gross indebtedness	345.7
Cash, short term loans and deposits	(76.6)
Net indebtedness	269.1

At 26 February 1988 contingent liabilities in respect of guarantees to third parties amounted to £59.5m. Save as disclosed above and apart from intra-Group indebtedness and bank guarantees, neither Cadbury Schweppes p.l.c. nor any of its subsidiaries had outstanding at the close of business on 19 February 1988 any borrowings, loan capital created but unissued, term loans or other indebtedness in the nature of borrowing, including bank overdrafts and liabilities under acceptances (other than normal trade bills) or acceptance credits, mortgages, charges, hire purchase or leasing commitments or guarantees (except product guarantees) or other material contingent liabilities.

At 26 February 1988 the net borrowings of Chocolat Poulain S.A. included above amounted to FFr.25.9m.

Extract 16.2: Scottish Television plc[18]

21 POST BALANCE SHEET EVENT

On 31 March 1988 the Company acquired the whole of the issued share capital of Pauline Hyde & Associates Limited.

The total consideration is not expected to exceed approximately £6.5 million and will be satisfied as follows:

— an initial payment of £2.6 million satisfied as to £850,000 in cash and by the allotment of 439,033 Scottish Television Ordinary Shares, which rank for the final dividend for 1987.

— additional consideration payable based on the achievement of defined profit targets in respect of the financial years ending 31 December 1988, 1989 and 1990 leading to maximum further payments totalling £3.9 million satisfied approximately 25% in cash and the balance in the Company's Ordinary Shares.

Extract 16.3: Hanson PLC[19]

23 Subsequent events

On August 16, 1988, it was announced that Kidde Inc and Hanson Kidde International Holdings Ltd, had agreed to sell most of the Walter Kidde Worldwide Fire Protection operations to Pilgrim House Group PLC for a total consideration of $265.8 million. The transaction was completed on November 30, 1988.

On October 3, 1988 Hanson PLC sold the majority of its interest in Westland PLC to GKN PLC.

On October 31, 1988 Hanson Industries signed a conditional agreement to sell its Durkee industrial foods and food service assets and related rights to Unilever United States Inc for a total consideration of $185 million. The transaction was completed on December 6, 1988.

On November 8, 1988 Hanson Industries sold its Allied/Egry and Walton Printing Company business forms operations to Allied Acquisitions, a private investor group, for a total consideration of $56 million.

On November 15, 1988 Hanson Industries agreed to sell Kidde Credit Corporation's US and Canadian operations for approximately $71.4 million which includes $10.0 million of debt assumed by the buyers.

2.4   Disclosure requirements

As SSAP 17 requires consideration to be given to events which occur up to the date on which the financial statements are approved by the board of directors, then the standard requires that date to be disclosed.[20] This is normally done by dating the signature of the directors signing the balance sheet.

SSAP 17 states that for each post balance sheet event for which disclosure is required as per 2.3 above, the nature of the event and an estimate of its financial effect should be stated by way of note in financial statements. Where it is not practicable to estimate the financial effect, then a statement should be made explaining this fact.[21]

In addition, the Companies Act 1985 states that the directors' report must include 'particulars of any important events affecting the company or any of its subsidiaries which have occurred since the end of the financial year'.[22] This would seem to imply that both adjusting and non-adjusting events should be disclosed; however, in practice, only non-adjusting events will normally be included.

There is considerable diversity in the financial statement disclosure of post balance sheet events. Some companies disclose these events in both the directors' report and notes to the financial statements, whilst others provide disclosure in either the directors' report or notes.

The following extracts are examples of companies which have discussed post balance sheet events in the directors' report, but not in the notes to the financial statements:

Extract 16.4: Trusthouse Forte PLC[23]

REPORT OF THE DIRECTORS [extract]

Post Balance Sheet Events
In December 1987, the Group acquired the Skylight Inns chain of 13 modern economy hotels in the United States, for a consideration of $49 million.

Extract 16.5: Sketchley PLC[24]

REPORT OF THE DIRECTORS [extract]

Post Balance Sheet Event
Subject to contract, the Company has entered into an agreement under which it will acquire Jeeves of Belgravia Limited and Lilliman & Cox Limited. The two companies form a high quality dry cleaning chain, operating from nine outlets in Central London. The consideration amounts to some £4.8 mn, to be satisfied by the issue of 910,000 ordinary shares in the Company.

It would appear that these companies have taken the view that SSAP 17 does not require disclosure of these events as 'non-adjusting events', but that the

Companies Act does. This highlights an important difference between a non-adjusting post balance sheet event under SSAP 17 (requiring disclosure in the notes), and a post balance sheet event under the Companies Act (requiring disclosure in the directors' report). Whilst SSAP 17 requires disclosure of non-adjusting events which are of such materiality that their non-disclosure 'would affect the ability of the users of financial statements to reach a proper understanding of the financial position'[25] of the company, the Companies Act has the much wider requirement for disclosure of 'any important events affecting the company or any of its subsidiaries which have occurred since the end of the financial year'.[26]

Where it is considered that a post balance sheet event requires disclosure under both SSAP 17 and the Companies Act, then theoretically disclosure should be made both in the notes to the financial statements and in the directors' report. However, in our view it would suffice if disclosure is made in either the notes or the directors' report, with an appropriate cross reference in the other.

3   PROBLEM AREAS

3.1   Reclassification of a non-adjusting event as adjusting in exceptional circumstances

The general guidance given in the Appendix to SSAP 17, states that 'in exceptional circumstances, to accord with the prudence concept, an adverse event which would normally be classified as non-adjusting may need to be reclassified as adjusting. In such circumstances, full disclosure of the adjustment would be required.'[27]

Whilst this may appear to be a concession by the ASC, following the comments raised during the exposure period of ED 22 that the definition of adjusting events was too narrow, it should be emphasised that the issue has been dealt with in the Appendix to SSAP 17, rather than in the main body of the standard. Consequently, three issues arise in the application of this provision: firstly, it has limited status, and therefore may result in inconsistency in its application; secondly, its application will negate the fundamental distinction between an adjusting and non-adjusting event; and, thirdly, what is meant by the phrase 'in exceptional circumstances', as the Appendix fails to provide any guidance as to the circumstances under which the provision should be applied?

The argument always exists that if full details of the non-adjusting event are disclosed in the directors' report and/or notes to the financial statements, users will be able to make their own adjustments and evaluate the impact of the event for themselves. However, it is our view that this application of the prudence override should only be used when the loss due to the post balance sheet event is of such magnitude that its exclusion from the financial statements would render them completely misleading.

In the US, it has been long established practice that events which provide evidence with respect to conditions that did not exist at the balance sheet date, but arose subsequent to that date, should not result in adjustment of the financial statements. This is referred to in the above terms in SAS 1 — *Codification of Auditing Standards and Procedures.*[28] However, SAS 1 goes on to say that some of these events 'may be of such a nature that disclosure of them is required to keep the financial statements from being misleading. Occasionally such an event may be so significant that disclosure can best be made by supplementing the historical financial statements with pro forma financial data giving effect to the event as if it had occurred on the date of the balance sheet. It may be desirable to present pro forma statements, usually a balance sheet only, in columnar form on the face of the historical statements.'[29]

In the UK, companies may prefer to follow the US approach of presenting pro forma financial statements, rather than adopt the more drastic step of reflecting the non-adjusting event in the financial statements.

3.2   The valuation of stock realised after the balance sheet date

The sale of stock after the balance sheet date is normally a good indicator of the realisable value at that date. However, there will be circumstances where there is evidence which suggests that a fall in realisable value took place because of conditions which did not exist at the balance sheet date.

The problem, therefore, is determining when the fall in realisable value occurred; did the fall in value occur as a result of circumstances which existed at the balance sheet date, or did it occur as a result of circumstances which arose subsequently? A decrease in price is merely a response to changing conditions, and so it is important that the reasons behind these changes are fully assessed.

This can be seen by reviewing some examples of changing conditions.

(a)   Price reductions due to a sudden increase in cheap imports

Whilst it could be argued that the 'dumping' of cheap imports after the balance sheet date is a condition that has arisen subsequent to that date, it is more likely to be the case that this will be a reaction to a condition which already existed, such as overproduction in other parts of the world. Thus, it might be appropriate in such a situation to be prudent and adjust the value of stock to its subsequent net realisable value.

(b)   Price reductions due to increased competition

It is common for companies to adjust the valuation of stocks when their fall in value is due to price reductions of competitors. This is because the reasons for price reductions will not have arisen overnight, but will normally have occurred over a period of time. For example, a competitor may have built up a comparative advantage because of investment in more efficient machinery in the past. Thus, it is usually appropriate for a company to adjust their valuation in stocks, as their past investment in technology will have been inferior to their competitors, and will not have arisen subsequent to the balance sheet date.

(c)   Price reductions due to the introduction of an improved competitive product

As an improved product introduced by competitors is unlikely to have been developed overnight it is correct to adjust the valuation of stock to its net realisable value following that introduction. This is because it reflects the company's failure to maintain its position in relation to technological improvements.

It can be seen in these cases that when a company is forced to reduce its prices after the balance sheet date, the fall provides additional evidence of conditions which existed at the balance sheet date. The reason for this is that, in general, the post balance sheet reduction in the realisable value of stock represents the culmination of conditions which existed over a relatively long period of time, with the result that the effects thereof would normally require adjustment in the financial statements. However, there will be certain types of stock for which there is clear evidence of a higher price available at the year end, when it would be inappropriate to write down the stock to reflect a subsequent decline. An example of this would be stocks for which there was a price on the international commodities market.

3.3 Long-term contracts

It is not uncommon for events to take place after the balance sheet date which provide further evidence as to the profitability of long-term work in progress. It is our view that *all* further evidence of eventual profit should be taken into account in determining the valuation of long-term contract balances.

3.4 Acquisitions and disposals of fixed assets

If at the balance sheet date there are fixed assets in the process of being bought or sold, where there has been a contract signed before the year end, but there is uncertainty as to the amounts involved, the subsequent realisation of those amounts should be treated as an adjusting event.

An example of such a treatment can be seen in the following extract:

Extract 16.6: Sears PLC[30]

13. ACQUISITIONS AND DISPOSALS [extract]
(b) Assets in course of disposal
Assets in course of disposal at 31 January 1988 are stated at the amounts subsequently realised as follows:

	1987/88 £m
Lewis's store business	72.7
The Butler Group Inc.	22.6
	95.3

The net losses arising from these disposals have been fully provided for as Extraordinary Items (note 6).

Clearly, it is appropriate to make provision for known losses on the disposal of fixed assets which were in the process of being sold at the year end; and this applies whether or not a contract had been signed before the balance sheet date. However, a difficulty arises in the case where the assets are sold at a profit. Should the gain on disposal be recognised in the profit and loss account as an adjusting event? The answer lies in determining whether or not the sale had been completed at the year end. It is unlikely that a sale would be complete if the sale price had yet to be determined; however, if this were the case then the sale should be recognised in the financial statements.

Disposals of fixed assets after the balance sheet date are generally non-adjusting events. However, if a large loss results it may suggest that the depreciation that had been charged in the past was inadequate, and so an adjustment to the net book value may be appropriate.

An asset that is not in use should be valued at its net realisable value, therefore any sale after the balance sheet date will affect the valuation at that date.

The following extract is a good example of a disposal of a fixed asset disclosed as a non-adjusting post-balance sheet event:

Extract 16.7: Rush & Tompkins Group PLC[31]

23. Subsequent events
On 28 April, 1988 the group informed shareholders that they had completed the sale of the freehold interest at Marlowe House, Sidcup, Kent to Marlowe House Nominees Limited a subsidiary company of Dunbest Holdings Limited. Marlowe House comprises 174,000 sq. ft. of office accommodation on 16 floors.

The gross consideration passing is £12,250,000 which is payable as to £4.5 million on completion of the sale, £4 million on 31 March, 1989 and £3.75 million on 29 March, 1991. The deferred payments have been secured by Promissory Notes.

The contract is subject to the purchase of certain underleases, the repayment of a mortgage and the completion of refurbishment works, amounting in total to approximately £4.75 million. The net sale proceeds of approximately £7.5 million will be utilised to reduce borrowings and towards the group's development programme.

The net rental income from Marlowe House was £616k for the year to 31 March 1988 and the net book value was £10 million as at 31 March 1988. There will be no impact on the current year's shareholders' funds.

3.5   Window dressing

SSAP 17 requires the disclosure of the reversal or maturity after the year end of transactions entered into before the year end, the substance of which was primarily to alter the appearance of the company's balance sheet.[32] Such alterations include those commonly referred to as 'window dressing'.

The difficulty that arises is that there is no clear view of what 'window dressing' is; this fact was conceded by the ASC in their Technical Release issued on the publication of SSAP 17.[33] The term can encompass both:

(a)   the fraudulent falsification of accounts to make things look better than they really are; and

(b)   the lawful arrangement of affairs over the year end to make things look different from the way they usually are.[34]

Nevertheless, the ASC indicated that as the 'fraudulent falsification of accounts is clearly unacceptable and unlawful and is not a subject for an accounting standard',[35] the term 'window dressing' as used in SSAP 17 is confined to the meaning in (b) above.[36] However, this interpretation raises the question as to whether or not it is the function of the balance sheet to reflect the company's typical financial position throughout the year. For example, should the balance sheet illustrate the typical gearing throughout the year, or only at the year end? Companies quite legitimately select the year end as being the time when stocks are lowest, their monthly creditors have been paid etc. Therefore, in order to develop any rule which requires disclosure or restatement of disclosure from the norm, we need to understand what the norm actually is. Furthermore, if what are regarded as artificial transactions are discovered, should they not be restated, rather than merely disclosed?

The end result is that the SSAP 17 definition of these so called window dressing transactions is inadequate. Consequently, SSAP 17 is inevitably ineffectual in this regard, and this is possibly supported by the fact that there is no significant evidence of such disclosure in practice.

3.6   Valuations of property

If an asset is revalued after the balance sheet date and a significant fall in the value of that asset is revealed, there are two matters which need to be considered.

The first is whether or not the fall in value indicates a permanent diminution in value. If it is considered that it does, then either the deficit below depreciated historical cost should be charged to the profit and loss account (with the balance charged against any existing revaluation reserve in respect of the asset) or the full loss charged to the profit and loss account (any balance on the revaluation reserve being transferred as a reserve movement).

The second matter to be considered is the determination of the period in which the deficit should be charged. In general, a valuation would indicate that the decline in value took place prior to the balance sheet date and so the financial statements should be adjusted. If, however, there is sufficient evidence to show that the asset had fallen in value after the year end, then no adjustment should be made but full disclosure should be made of the subsequent fall in value.

3.7   Insolvency of a debtor

The insolvency of a debtor and his inability to pay his debts usually builds over a period of time which would commence long before the balance sheet date.

Consequently, if a debtor has an amount outstanding at the year end, and this amount has to be written off due to information received subsequent to the period end, it is normal to classify the event as adjusting. If, however, there is evidence to suggest that the solvency of the debtor has been determined solely by an event occurring after the balance sheet date, then the event should be treated as non-adjusting.

4   COMPARISON WITH US AND IASC PRONOUNCEMENTS

4.1   US

The accounting treatment and disclosure of post balance events in financial statements is referred to in SAS 1 — *Codification of Auditing Standards and Procedures* — issued in November 1972. However, guidance on accounting for subsequent events appears in several accounting standards, including SFAS 12, SFAS 52 and SFAS 96.

SAS 1 follows a similar line to that of SSAP 17, in that it recognises two categories of 'subsequent events' which require consideration by management. The first category consists of those events which provide additional evidence with respect to conditions that existed at the balance sheet date and affect the estimates inherent in the process of preparing financial statements. The statement requires that all information that becomes available prior to the issuance of the financial statements should be used by management in its evaluation of the conditions on which the estimates were based, and the financial statements should be adjusted for any changes in estimates resulting from the use of such evidence.[37]

The second category of subsequent event consists of those events which provide evidence with respect to conditions that did not exist at the date of the balance sheet, but arose subsequent to that date. SAS 1 states that these events should not result in adjustment of the financial statements.[38] However, provision is made for the presentation of additional pro forma information where 'such an event may be so significant that disclosure can best be made by supplementing the historical financial statements'[39] (see 3.1 above).

4.2   IASC

IAS 10 — *Contingencies and Events Occurring After the Balance Sheet Date* — was issued in October 1978. Although it does not specifically use the terminology of 'adjusting' and 'non-adjusting' events, IAS 10's accounting and disclosure requirements in respect of post balance sheet events are essentially the same as those of SSAP 17.

However, in respect of non-adjusting events, IAS 10 states that 'assets and liabilities should not be adjusted for, but disclosure should be made of, those events occurring after the balance sheet date that do not affect the condition of assets or liabilities at the balance sheet date, but are of such importance that non-disclosure would affect the ability of the users of the financial statements to make proper evaluations and decisions.'[40] This would imply that the provision made in the Appendix to SSAP 17 for the reclassification of a non-adjusting event as adjusting in exceptional circumstances (see 3.1 above) is not permitted under

IAS 10. Instead it would appear that the US approach of providing pro forma financial information would be more appropriate (see 4.1 above).

IAS 10 also deals specifically with the accounting treatment of dividends, and provides that 'dividends stated to be in respect of the period covered by the financial statements that are proposed or declared after the balance sheet date but before approval of the financial statements should be either adjusted or disclosed.'[41] This provision is presumably intended to allow flexibility as between, for example, the US and UK, since dividends are accounted for in the US when they are declared, whereas in the UK they are accounted for in the period to which they relate.

5   CONCLUSION

SSAP 17 essentially deals with three principal issues: adjusting events (including the appropriateness of the continued application of the going concern concept), non-adjusting events and window dressing. The standard is generally useful in respect of adjusting events, and it is normally clear as to which events should be adjusted in financial statements. In the case of non-adjusting events, a preferable requirement might be that companies should be required to present supplementary pro forma financial statements (made up to the date on which the financial statements are approved by the board of directors) which reflect these events.

In the case of window dressing, not only is it unclear as to what the term actually means, but it appears strange that the statement calls for the disclosure, rather than restatement, of what are regarded as artificial transactions. In any event, SSAP 17 does not seem to deal adequately with those artificial transactions which it suggests should be disclosed.

References

1 SSAP 17, *Accounting for post balance sheet events*, August 1980, para. 18.
2 C. Brown, 'Window-dressing — not just a problem for the auditor', *Accountancy*, April 1980, pp. 59-60.
3 CA 48, Sch 8, para. 7.
4 N17, *Events occurring after the balance sheet date*, October 1957, para. 16.
5 *Ibid.*, paras. 3 — 12.
6 *Ibid.*, para. 13.
7 ED 22, *Accounting for post balance sheet events*, February 1978, para. 6.
8 *Ibid.*, para. 18.
9 *Ibid.*, para. 14.
10 SSAP 17, para. 18.
11 *Ibid.*, para. 19.
12 *Ibid.*, Appendix.
13 *Ibid.*, para. 20.
14 *Ibid.*, Appendix.

15 *Ibid.*, para. 22.
16 *Ibid.*, para. 23.
17 Cadbury Schweppes p.l.c., Annual Report 1987, p. 60.
18 Scottish Television plc, Annual Report 1987, p. 41.
19 Hanson PLC, Annual Report 1988, p. 51.
20 SSAP 17, para. 26.
21 *Ibid.*, para. 24.
22 CA 85, Sch. 7, para. 6(a).
23 Trusthouse Forte PLC, Report and Accounts 1987, p. 22.
24 Sketchley PLC, Annual Report & Accounts 1987, p. 24.
25 SSAP 17, para. 23(a).
26 CA 85, Sch. 7, para. 6(a).
27 SSAP 17, Appendix.
28 AICPA, *Codification of Statements on Auditing Standards*, AU § 560.05.
29 *Ibid.*
30 Sears PLC, Annual Report 1987/88, p. 40.
31 Rush & Tompkins Group PLC, Report and Accounts 1988, p. 23.
32 SSAP 17, para. 23(b).
33 TR 398, *Statement by the Accounting Standards Committee on the publication of SSAP 17 accounting for post balance sheet events*, para. 14.
34 *Ibid.*
35 *Ibid.*
36 *Ibid.*
37 AICPA, *Codification of Statements on Auditing Standards*, AU § 560.03.
38 *Ibid.*, AU § 560.05.
39 *Ibid.*
40 IAS 10, *Contingencies and Events Occurring After the Balance Sheet Date*, October 1978 para. 32.
41 *Ibid.*, para. 31.

Chapter 17

Contingencies

1 THE DEVELOPMENT OF ACCOUNTING FOR CONTINGENCIES

1.1 Introduction

A contingency is defined in SSAP 18 as 'a condition which exists at the balance sheet date, where the outcome will be confirmed only on the occurrence or non-occurrence of one or more uncertain future events. A contingent gain or loss is a gain or loss dependent on a contingency.'[1]

Disclosure of contingencies can involve conflicting interests. There has often been a need for management to provide details of contingencies in order to make the financial statements more meaningful; however this may not have been done fully, due to a reluctance to divulge confidential and sensitive information. Thus, details of the amounts involved and the likelihood of an event occurring have not always been sufficiently disclosed to enable the reader to assess the most likely financial effect on a company.

1.2 The historical background

The Companies Act 1948 required that the general nature of any contingent liabilities which had not been provided for, together with the aggregate amount or estimated amount not provided, where practicable, should be disclosed.[2] In addition, it required disclosure of any charge on the assets of a company to secure the liabilities of any other person, including, where practicable, the amount secured.[3] These were subsequently restated in the Companies Act 1967.[4]

Prior to 1980 there was little to extend the statutory requirements. Recommendations N17 and N18 of the ICAEW issued in 1957 and 1958 respectively, did provide some additional guidance. N17 stated that contingent liabilities could not be ignored merely because the amounts were unknown or uncertain,[5] whilst N18 stated that 'where some contingent liabilities are not suitable for aggregation with others the amount or estimated amount of each contingent liability or group of contingent liabilities should be shown if practicable'.[6] Both of these statements were later withdrawn following the publication of SSAP 18.

Following the issue of IAS 10 — *Contingencies and events occurring after the balance sheet date* — in October 1978, the ASC issued ED 23 — *Accounting for contingencies* — in November 1978. This incorporated the Companies Act 1967 requirements and extended them. The proposals set out in ED 23 were closely followed in SSAP 18 which was published in August 1980, with certain amendments made to take account of comments raised in the exposure period.

The requirements of SSAP 18 are discussed further in 2 below.

The Companies Act 1981, which was later consolidated in the Companies Act 1985, extended the provisions of the 1967 Act by requiring disclosure of the details of any valuable security provided by the company in respect of contingent liabilities not provided for.[7]

2   REQUIREMENTS OF SSAP 18

2.1   Definition of contingency

As stated in 1.1 above, SSAP 18 defines a contingency as a 'condition which exists at the balance sheet date, where the outcome will be confirmed only on the occurrence or non-occurrence of one or more uncertain future events'.[8]

It is not intended that normal uncertainties connected with accounting estimates should fall within the scope of the standard. For example:

(a)   the lives of fixed assets;

(b)   the amount of bad debts;

(c)   the net realisable value of stocks and work in progress;

(d)   the expected outcome of long-term contracts;

(e)   the valuation of properties;

(f)   the valuation of foreign currency balances.

Contingencies can result in both gains and losses, the treatment of which is determined by the likelihood of their expected outcome.

2.2   Contingent gains

A contingent gain is defined by SSAP 18 as a gain dependent on a contingency.[9] However, contingent gains should not be credited to income, since to do so would mean the recognition of income prior to realisation. Consequently, SSAP 18 does not permit such gains to be accrued, and only allows their disclosure if realisation is probable.[10] This means that contingent gains should not be disclosed if it is only possible or there is only a remote chance that they will be realised. The standard, therefore, restricts the amount of disclosure in a company's financial statements in this respect, as it would be considered misleading to disclose the existence of future gains where the likelihood of realisation is less than probable. However, when the realisation of the gain becomes 'reasonably certain', then the gain is not a contingency and accrual should be made.[11]

An example of a contingent gain might be the expected compensation to be received from the expropriation of property, and which is subject to arbitration. However, when a contingent gain is disclosed in financial statements, it is essential that care is taken to avoid making misleading statements as to the likelihood or amount of realisation.

2.3 Contingent losses

SSAP 18 defines a contingent loss as a loss dependent on a contingency.[12] It explains that the treatment and disclosure of contingent losses varies depending on how probable it is that the loss will crystallise.[13]

Where it is probable that a loss will be confirmed by an event or events in the future and, at the date the board of directors approve the financial statements, that loss can be estimated with reasonable accuracy, then it should be accrued in the financial statements. If it is not possible, with reasonable accuracy, to estimate the probable loss then it should not be accrued but it is necessary to disclose information about the loss by way of note, in order that the financial statements are not misleading.

If it is not probable that a loss will occur then it should not be accrued but the circumstances should be disclosed by way of note, unless the chances of a loss being confirmed are remote; in which case no disclosure is required by the standard.

An example of a contingent loss would be litigation involving a claim outstanding against the company at the year end where the outcome will not be settled until a date in the future.

The following matrix summarises the above accounting and disclosure requirements of SSAP 18:

Likelihood of outcome	Accounting treatment: contingent loss	Accounting treatment: contingent gain
Reasonably certain	Not a contingency, therefore accrue	Not a contingency, therefore accrue
Probable	Accrue if amount can be estimated with reasonable accuracy, otherwise disclose	Disclose
Possible but not probable	Disclose	No disclosure permitted
Remote	No disclosure required under SSAP 18, but consider disclosure under CA 85, Sch. 4, para. 50	No disclosure permitted

2.4   Offsets

The explanatory note to SSAP 18 discusses the situation where a contingency is matched by a related counter claim or a claim by or against a third party; for example, where a contingent loss arising from the supply of defective goods is matched by a contingent gain arising from a claim against the supplier of materials causing the defect in the goods. In such a situation, the amount accrued or the amount disclosed by way of a note in the financial statements should be reduced by taking into account the probable outcome of the claim. However, in calculating any net gain or loss, a separate assessment must be made of the probability of each and where appropriate this should be separately disclosed.[14] In general, separate disclosure would be required unless it is highly likely that the claim against the third party would also succeed if the claim against the company succeeds.

2.5   Groupings

SSAP 18 states that where both the nature of, and the uncertainties which affect, a contingency are common to a large number of transactions, the financial effect of these contingencies may be based on the group of transactions. For example, where a company has several claims against it for the supply of faulty products it would be possible to treat these as a single claim.[15]

2.6 Disclosure requirements

SSAP 18 requires that for all contingent gains or losses requiring disclosure in the financial statements, the following details should be given by way of note:

(a) the nature of the contingency;

(b) the uncertainties that are expected to affect the ultimate outcome;

(c) a prudent estimate of the financial effect as at the date the board of directors approve the financial statements or a statement that it is not practicable to make such an estimate.[16]

Where the contingency is a loss, it should be reduced by any amounts that have been accrued and any element of the contingency which is considered remote.[17]

Any estimate given should be before taking account of taxation but where necessary for a proper understanding of the financial statements, the taxation implications of the contingency occurring should be given.[18]

Examples of disclosure in practice are illustrated throughout 3 below.

3 PROBLEM AREAS

3.1 Probable, possible or remote

As discussed in 2.3 above, in order to determine the appropriate accounting treatment and disclosure of a contingent gain or loss, a decision must be made as to whether the likelihood of the event occurring is reasonably certain, probable, possible (but not probable) or remote.

SSAP 18 does not define these terms, and fails to provide any detailed guidance as to the criteria which should be applied in determining the level of probability of an event occurring. However, SFAS 5 defines similar terms to the last three as follows:

Probable	— the future event or events are likely to occur.
Reasonably possible	— the chance of the future event or events occurring is more than remote but less than likely.
Remote	— the chance of the future event or events occurring is slight.[19]

Whilst these definitions may be helpful in determining the appropriate treatment for contingencies under SSAP 18, they still do not solve the problem of converting these verbal perceptions of likelihood into numerical probabilities. For example, a company financial director and his auditor might both agree that the probability of a particular loss occurring is 60%; however, they might disagree as to whether this probability is 'probable' or 'possible' for SSAP 18 purposes.

This problem was highlighted by a study carried out in Canada aimed at determining how accountants and lawyers perceived the terms 'likely', 'unlikely' and 'possible' in percentage terms, the results of which indicated that there were significant differences in how levels of probability were understood by these two groups.[20]

Bearing in mind that there are clearly different perceptions of what percentage levels of probability should be applied to the terminology used in the standard, we believe that the following ranges of percentage levels could provide a guide to the terminology used in determining the treatment of a contingency:

Likelihood of outcome	*Level of probability*
Reasonably certain	95% — 100%
Probable	50% — 95%
Possible	5% — 50%
Remote	0% — 5%

Clearly, since each set of circumstances must be considered on its merits, the above guide cannot be regarded as a definitive interpretation. It is essential that all known relevant information is considered up to the date the financial statements are approved by the board of directors.

It is therefore often difficult to decide the status of a contingency having taken account of the above factors and indeed there is a great deal of subjectivity involved. It is preferable therefore to err on the side of prudence when arriving at the appropriate treatment and disclosure.

3.2   Estimating the amount of a contingency

SSAP 18 requires that where a contingent loss is to be accrued the loss must be capable of being estimated with reasonable accuracy.[21] This estimate should be made by the directors having taken into account all events occurring after the balance sheet date. Obviously such an assessment should be the company's best estimate of the loss.

In many cases companies should be able to arrive at such an estimate. However one particular difficulty with estimating a loss is where the loss could be within a range of possible outcomes. The standard gives no guidance on what should be done in such a case.

FASB Interpretation No. 14 has addressed this problem. It states that where a contingent loss could fall within a range of amounts then if there is a best estimate within the range this should be accrued with the remainder noted as a contingent liability. However, if there is no best estimate then the lowest figure within the range should be accrued, with the remainder up to the maximum potential loss noted as a contingent liability.[22] Accrual of such a contingent loss should not be delayed until a single amount can be reasonably estimated. Similar guidance is given in IAS 10.[23]

The approach adopted by these pronouncements can be illustrated by the following example:

Example 17.1

Company X is involved in litigation at its year end. After taking legal advice, they consider that it is probable that they will lose the court case and that the amount of damages that they are likely to have to pay will be at least £1m and could be as high as £4m. How should this contingent loss be treated in their financial statements?

If it were considered that £2m were a better estimate of the amount of damages than any other amount then that amount should be accrued and the remaining £2m disclosed.

If no single amount within the range is a better estimate than any other amount, then £1m should be accrued and the exposure to the remaining £3m should be disclosed.

An alternative view is sometimes held that if the provision cannot be estimated with reasonable certainty, then no provision should be made and only disclosure should be given of the amount claimed against the company.

We believe, however, that it is preferable that companies in the UK should adopt the approach shown in Example 17.1 above in making provision for contingent losses and that not to provide for at least the minimum amount of the loss would be inconsistent with the prudence concept contained in SSAP 2.[24]

There is a school of thought which argues that the amount provided in respect of a contingent loss should be based on the percentage probability of the loss arising. For example, if a company is being sued for £100,000 and it is estimated that there is a 40% probability of the claim succeeding, some might argue that a contingent liability of £40,000 should be provided. It is our view that this approach should not be followed.

3.3   Disclosure of the financial effect of a contingency

SSAP 18 requires in respect of each contingency disclosed 'a prudent estimate of the financial effect, made at the date on which the financial statements are approved by the board of directors; or a statement that it is not practicable to make such an estimate'.[25] It is unclear exactly what is meant by 'financial effect'. Is it the *potential* amount of the loss or is it the *expected* amount of the loss?

In our view the former would be preferable, and this is supported by the FASB Interpretation referred to above as was seen in Example 17.1. If in that example the company had assessed the risk of loss as only being possible then no amount should be accrued and disclosure of the range of the loss should be given.

However, it would appear that in practice, companies tend not to disclose the potential amounts involved but comment that once resolved there is unlikely to be any significant effect where claims have been made against them or they are involved in litigation, as illustrated in the following extract:

Extract 17.1: The British Petroleum Company p.l.c.[26]

28   Contingent liabilities [extract]
BP Petroleum Development Limited is the operator of the Ninian Pipeline System and one of the participants in the Sullom Voe Oil Terminal. The Shetland Islands Council has commenced court action against BP Petroleum Development Limited and others claiming, *inter alia*, ownership of the Terminal and arrears of rent. The defendants dispute the basis of this action, which is being actively defended.
Standard Oil, a subsidiary of BP America, is engaged in judicial and administrative proceedings in which the State of Alaska is challenging the valuation of crude oil reported by Standard Oil since 1977 for royalty and 1978 for tax purposes. Standard Oil believes it has complied with applicable legislation and provisions for royalties contained in its Prudhoe Bay leases, and is disputing the State's claims. While the amounts claimed and subject to claim are substantial, it is believed that the ultimate resolution of these disputes will not have a significant effect on the financial position of the group.

3.4   Litigation and disclosure of potentially prejudicial information

One of the reasons why companies adopt such an approach may be that they consider that disclosing the full potential liability under such claims could prejudice their position in settling the claims.

The arrival of SSAP 18 was not welcomed in many quarters because it did not grant exemption from the disclosure of sensitive information which could prejudice a company's position. This was particularly important in the area of litigation where it was believed that an assessment of the estimated likely outcome of a pending legal claim could compromise the amount of any settlement.

Possibly the most difficult sort of contingency to assess is litigation. This is due to the inherent uncertainty in the judicial process itself and to the occasional reluctance of the legal profession to express an opinion on the potential outcome of litigation.

Appendix A to SFAS 5 lists the following three factors which should be considered in determining whether accrual and/or disclosure is required with respect to pending or threatened litigation:

(a)   the period in which the underlying cause for action of the pending or threatened litigation occurred;

(b)   the degree of probability of an unfavourable outcome; and

(c)   the ability to make a reasonable estimate of the amount of loss.[27]

However, the overriding consideration is that it is desirable that a company should disclose all relevant information necessary for the users of the financial statements to gain a proper understanding of that company's financial position.

Other areas where a company may be unwilling or unable to give quantified disclosure are as follows:

(a) Inland Revenue investigations and additional claims over and above the company's tax computation;

(b) breach of copyright or infringement of patent rights, where to disclose the contingency would advertise the breach.

3.5   Disclosure of remote contingencies

SSAP 18 states that where the possibility of a contingent loss being confirmed is remote disclosure is not required.[28] The Accountants Digest which deals with accounting for contingencies states that 'the application of this concession is, however, limited by the over-riding requirements of the 1948 and 1967 Companies Acts which require disclosure of the "general nature of any contingent liabilities not provided for and, where practicable, the aggregate amount or estimated amount of those liabilities, if it is material".'[29]

Since the publication of the Accountants Digest, the Companies Act provisions have been amended to require disclosure of the following information in respect of any material contingent liability not provided for:

(a) the amount or estimated amount of the liability;

(b) its legal nature; and

(c) whether any valuable security has been provided by the company in connection with that liability and if so, what.[30]

Consequently, because of this apparent overriding Companies Act requirement to disclose *all* material contingent liabilities not provided for, it would appear that in practice companies sometimes include information in their financial statements on contingencies which could be considered to be remote. Examples of such disclosures often given are as follows:

(a) guarantees of subsidiary company liabilities;

(b) bills discounted with recourse;

(c) membership of VAT groups;

(d) performance bonds.

The following extract illustrates the disclosure of contingencies which might be considered to be remote, but are presumably disclosed in compliance with the Companies Act requirement:

Extract 17.2: Beecham Group p.l.c.[31]

24 Contingent liabilities

Contingent liabilities existed at 31st March 1988 in connection with guarantees given by the parent company on behalf of its subsidiaries and other guarantees and contingencies arising in the ordinary course of business. These are not expected to give rise to any material financial loss. In addition, there existed litigation and other potential issues, including U.S. environmental matters, which in so far as they are not provided in the accounts, are not considered material to the Group or parent company.

		1988 £m	1987 £m
(i)	Amount outstanding against guarantees given by the parent company on behalf of its subsidiaries in respect of their loans	134.5	288.2

		Group		Company	
		1988 £m	1987 £m	1988 £m	1987 £m
(ii)	Other contingent liabilities, mainly in respect of short term warranties in connection with asset disposals and bank guarantees, for which no provision is considered necessary	20.3	14.2	3.2	3.2

A number of questions often arise as to what should be disclosed in respect of the situations listed above and these are considered in 3.6 below.

3.6   Other problem areas

3.6.1   *Guarantees — year-end or maximum liability*

Where companies are disclosing the fact that they have guaranteed the liabilities of another party, consideration has to be given as to what amount should be disclosed in respect of the guarantee. The disclosure often given is merely the year-end liability guaranteed, whilst in other cases it is not stated whether the amount given is the year-end liability or the maximum liability guaranteed. It could be argued that both amounts require disclosure as the maximum amount is part of the 'nature' of the guarantee and the year-end amount is the 'estimate' of the financial effect. We therefore believe that best practice is to disclose both the year-end liability and the maximum amount guaranteed, as shown in the following extract:

Extract 17.3: Ultramar PLC[32]

28 Contingent items [extract]
a) Ultramar PLC has guaranteed the following obligations of subsidiary and associated companies:
  i)   Bank and other loan facilities amounting to a maximum of £509.8 million (1986, £820.3 million), of which £220.7 million was utilised at 31st December 1987 (1986, £262.0 million).
  iv) Trading and other obligations with a maximum liability of £131.4 million (1986, £208.5 million), of which £30.0 million was outstanding at 31st December 1987 (1986, £32.3 million).

Where the amount of the liability at the year end varies significantly with the amount at the date on which the financial statements are approved by the board of directors, consideration should be given to disclosing both amounts.

One interesting form of disclosure is that of George Wimpey PLC. It can be seen that they have deducted the amount secured on assets (presumably those of the subsidiaries), thereby effectively reducing the 'potential liability' under the guarantees:

Extract 17.4: George Wimpey PLC[33]

24 CONTINGENT LIABILITIES

	GROUP		PARENT	
	1987	1986	1987	1986
	£m	£m	£m	£m
AMOUNTS OUTSTANDING IN RESPECT OF BORROWINGS UNDER GUARANTEES GIVEN ON BEHALF OF:				
Subsidiary companies	—	—	11.6	44.0
Less secured on assets	—	—	(9.6)	(7.0)
	—	—	2.0	37.0
Associated companies and joint ventures	21.9	39.0	17.2	34.0
Less secured on assets	—	(6.0)	—	—
	21.9	33.0	17.2	34.0

There are contingent liabilities in respect of guarantees relating to building and other agreements entered into in the normal course of business.

3.6.2 *Discounted bills of exchange*

Clearly, where a company discounts bills without recourse in the event of the bills being dishonoured on maturity, no contingent liability exists and, therefore, no disclosure is required.

However, where bills are discounted with recourse, the question arises as to what amount should be disclosed in the financial statements as the contingent liability. Is it the amount which relates to all bills discounted at the balance sheet date, or is it the amount which relates to those bills which have yet to mature at the date of approval of the financial statements? It could be argued that it is the latter and, therefore, if all the bills have matured by that date no disclosure is required. However, if the company is continually discounting bills of exchange then at the date of approval the company will have a contingent liability in respect of bills discounted since the year end. Consequently, we believe that in order to provide information relevant to the financial position of the company, the amount of bills outstanding at the balance sheet date should be disclosed.

3.6.3   VAT groups

Companies may be part of a VAT group and as such have a joint and several liability for the whole of the group VAT liability. Again, similar considerations as to the amount to be disclosed as were discussed at 3.6.2 above in relation to discounted bills apply to such a contingent liability. Consequently, we believe that the amount of this contingent liability at the balance sheet date should be disclosed in each group member's financial statements. For example:

Extract 17.5: Allied-Lyons PLC[34]

2 5 CONTINGENT LIABILITIES [extract]

	1988 £m	1987 £m
Parent company		
Uncalled liability in respect of partly paid shares.	6.4	6.3
Value added tax of certain subsidiary companies under group registration scheme.	19.4	25.3
Guarantees of stocks, bonds and notes of subsidiary companies.	254.2	283.9
No security has been given in respect of any contingent liability.		

3.6.4   Performance bonds

It is common practice in many industries for companies to guarantee to customers that goods will be delivered to a specific standard. The question then arises as to whether the existence of such a performance bond means that the company has a contingent liability which has to be disclosed. The granting of the performance bond does not normally impose any greater liability on the company than does the contract itself. If a company regularly produces goods either on time or up to the required standard and there is nothing to suggest that there are any unusual circumstances which might affect this, then there is justification in deciding that there is no contingency which needs to be disclosed.

In addition to performance bonds, companies may also give tender bonds (i.e. a guarantee against the company withdrawing from the contract after having submitted a tender for the contract which has been accepted) and advance payment bonds (i.e. a guarantee to reimburse advance payments made by the customer if the company cannot fulfil the contract).

In most cases the above bonds or guarantees will be given by the company's bankers and the company will indemnify the bank. Again, this does not normally impose any greater liability on the company than that under the contract with the customer.

Although it could be argued that in most cases above no contingent liability arises and therefore no disclosure is necessary, it would appear that many companies do give some disclosure in respect of such bonds. In practice, many companies merely note the existence of such bonds, for example:

> *Extract 17.6: BICC plc*[35]
>
> **29   Contingent liabilities** [extract]
> BICC plc and certain subsidiary companies have, in the ordinary course of business, entered into counter indemnities in respect of bonds relating to the Group's own contracts.

Other companies do, however, quantify the amount of the bonds or guarantees, for example:

> *Extract 17.7: NSM plc*[36]
>
> **26   Contingent liabilities** [extract]
> The Company and relevant subsidiaries have guaranteed in the ordinary course of business, bonds issued by third parties to a value of £15.2 million (1987–£16.1 million) securing the performance by Group companies of certain contracts and undertakings from which no liabilities are expected to arise other than those provided for in these Accounts.

In our view, given the fact that the company in most cases will incur no extra liability as a result of the performance bond, it is sufficient just to disclose the existence of the bonds without quantification. Where, however, a parent company or other group company guarantees or counter-indemnifies a bank for the performance of another group company then it would be preferable if the amount were quantified as this would be consistent with the approach generally taken in respect of guarantees of group borrowings.

4   COMPARISON WITH US AND IASC PRONOUNCEMENTS

4.1   US

In March 1975, the FASB published SFAS 5 — *Accounting for Contingencies* — which superseded ARB No. 50 — *Contingencies*. The requirements within the statement are broadly similar to those adopted by SSAP 18, although the level of disclosure is more extensive.

A contingency is defined in SFAS 5 as 'an existing condition, situation, or set of circumstances involving uncertainty as to possible gain ... or loss ... to an enterprise that will ultimately be resolved when one or more future events occur or fail to occur.'[37] The statement requires that the estimated loss from a loss contingency should be accrued if both the following conditions are met:

'a.   Information available prior to issuance of the financial statements indicates that it is probable that an asset had been impaired or a liability had been incurred at the date of the financial statements. It is implicit in this condition that it must be probable that one or more future events will occur confirming the fact of the loss.

b.   The amount of loss can be reasonably estimated.'[38]

The principal difference is that SFAS 5 requires disclosure of certain loss contingencies even though the possibility of loss may be remote. The standard states that the common characteristic of such a contingency is a 'guarantee'. Examples given include:

(a)   guarantees of indebtedness to others;

(b)   guarantees to repurchase receivables that have been sold in certain situations;

(c)   obligations of banks under 'standby letters of credit'.[39]

However, it should be noted that although SSAP 18 does not require the disclosure of a contingency where the possibility of loss is remote, disclosure would probably be required in the UK in terms of the requirements of the Companies Act 1985 (see 3.5 above).

In September 1976, the FASB published FASB Interpretation No. 14 — *Reasonable Estimation of the Amount of a Loss* — to give guidance on the treatment to be adopted where a loss is probable, and the amount lay within a range of figures (see 3.2 above).

4.2   IASC

IAS 10 — *Contingencies and Events Occurring After the Balance Sheet Date* — includes requirements which are in essence the same as those of SSAP 18. IAS 10's disclosure requirements in respect of the estimated financial effect of a contingent loss are less detailed that those of SSAP 18, in that IAS 10 does not require disclosure of the taxation implications of a contingency crystallising.[40] Consequently, by complying with SSAP 18, compliance with IAS 10 is assured.

References

 1 SSAP 18, *Accounting for contingencies*, August 1980, para. 14.
 2 CA 48, Sch. 8, para. 11(5).
 3 *Ibid.*, para. 11(4).
 4 CA 67, Sch. 2, paras. 11(4) and (5).
 5 N17, *Events occurring after the balance sheet date*, October 1957, para. 3.
 6 N18, *Presentation of balance sheet and profit and loss account*, October 1958, para. 25.
 7 CA 85, Sch. 4, para. 50(2).
 8 SSAP 18, para. 14.
 9 *Ibid.*
10 *Ibid.*, para. 17.
11 *Ibid.*, para. 4.
12 *Ibid.*, para. 14.
13 *Ibid.*, para. 15.
14 *Ibid.*, para. 6.
15 *Ibid.*, para. 21.
16 *Ibid.*, para. 18.
17 *Ibid.*, para. 19.
18 *Ibid.*, para. 20.
19 SFAS 5, *Accounting for Contingencies*, FASB, March 1975, para. 3.

20 G.R. Chesney and H.A. Weir, 'The challenge of contingencies: Adding precision to probability', *CA Magazine*, April 1985, pp. 38 — 41.

21 SSAP 18, para. 15.

22 FASB Interpretation No. 14, *Reasonable Estimation of the Amount of a Loss*, FASB, September 1976, para. 3.

23 IAS 10, *Contingencies and Events Occurring After the Balance Sheet Date*, IASC, October 1978, para. 9.

24 SSAP 2, para. 14.

25 *Ibid.*, para. 18.

26 The British Petroleum Company p.l.c., Annual Report and Accounts 1987, p. 46.

27 SFAS 5, Appendix A, para. 33.

28 SSAP 18, para. 16.

29 Accountants Digest No. 113, *Accountants Digest Guide to Accounting Standards — Accounting for Contingencies*, Winter 1981/82, p. 5.

30 CA 85, Sch. 4, para. 50(2).

31 Beecham Group p.l.c., Annual Report 1988, p. 51.

32 Ultramar PLC, Annual Report 1987, p. 44.

33 George Wimpey PLC, Annual Report 1987, p. 48.

34 Allied-Lyons PLC, Report & Accounts 1988, p. 51.

35 BICC plc, Annual Report 1987, p. 33.

36 NSM plc, Report and Accounts 1988, p. 31.

37 SFAS 5, para. 1.

38 *Ibid.*, para. 8.

39 *Ibid.*, para. 12.

40 SSAP 18, para. 20.

Chapter 18

Foreign currencies

1   THE DEVELOPMENT OF AN ACCOUNTING STANDARD IN THE UK

1.1   Background

A company can engage in foreign currency operations in two ways. It may enter directly into transactions which are denominated in foreign currencies, the results of which need to be translated into the currency in which the company reports. Alternatively, it may conduct foreign operations through a foreign enterprise, normally a subsidiary or associated company, which keeps its accounting records in a foreign currency and, in order to prepare consolidated financial statements, will need to translate the financial statements of the foreign enterprise into its own reporting currency.[1] Accounting for these translation processes has been one of the most significant problem areas in financial reporting in recent years.

Essentially, there were four distinct methods which could be used in the translation process:

(a) *current rate method* — all assets and liabilities are translated at the current rate of exchange, i.e. the exchange rate at the balance sheet date;

(b) *temporal method* — assets and liabilities carried at current prices are translated at the current rate of exchange, e.g. cash, debtors, creditors, investments at market value. Assets and liabilities carried at past prices, e.g. property, investments at cost, prepayments, are translated at the rate of exchange in effect at the dates to which the prices pertain;

(c) *current/non-current method* — all current assets and current liabilities are translated at the current rate of exchange. Non-current assets and liabilities are translated at historical rates, i.e. the exchange rate in effect at the time the asset was acquired or the liability incurred;

(d) *monetary/non-monetary method* — monetary assets and liabilities, i.e. items which represent the right to receive or the obligation to pay a fixed amount of money, are translated at the current rate of exchange. Non-monetary assets and liabilities are translated at the historical rate.

There was no consensus either in the UK or internationally on the best theoretical approach to adopt. In essence, the arguments surround the choice of exchange rates to be used in the translation process and the subsequent treatment of the exchange differences which arise. The fact that foreign exchange rates have become increasingly more volatile has only magnified the effects of using different approaches. As a result of these problems, the subject of foreign currency translation had been on the agenda of the ASC since the early 1970's.

1.2   SSAP 6

When SSAP 6[2] was issued in April 1974, although dealing mainly with extraordinary items and prior year adjustments, it gave recognition to the problem by stating 'At a time of frequent movement of foreign currency exchange rates, the accounting treatment of foreign currency transactions and conversions and the distinguishing of items that are extraordinary present many problems. These problems are currently under study with a view to the issue of a separate accounting standard. In the meantime, the accounting policies adopted should be disclosed and explained in accordance with Statement of Standard Accounting Practice No. 2 Disclosure of accounting policies.'[3]

1.3   ED 16

The first pronouncement by the ASC on the treatment of the problems was in ED 16[4] issued in September 1975. This did not require any particular method of translation to be adopted other than to require foreign currency borrowings to be translated at closing rates of exchange.[5] It mainly set out how exchange differences were to be dealt with; namely, in the profit and loss account as part of the ordinary activities of the business except:

(a)   differences arising from extraordinary items, which were themselves to be treated as extraordinary items;

(b)   differences arising on translation of fixed assets, which were to be treated as if they were revaluations of fixed assets, i.e. taken direct to reserves unless they represented losses not covered by gains on the same items held in reserves or gains on items where losses had previously been taken to profit and loss account;

(c)   exchange losses arising on the translation of foreign currency net borrowings, which could be taken to reserves to offset gains arising in (b) above which had also been taken to reserves.[6]

The ASC acknowledged that this was just a temporary measure by stating 'The subject is one in which conflicting opinions are strongly held and it must be expected that some time will elapse before a standard is issued which will describe the method or methods of accounting to be applied.'[7]

1.4   ED 21

The next step by the ASC was to issue ED 21[8] in September 1977. This limited the options of accounting methods by permitting the use of either the closing rate or temporal methods.[9]

If the closing rate method were to be used, exchange differences would be treated in the same way as required by ED 16, except that the differences which were to be dealt with in the profit and loss account as part of the ordinary activities of the business were now to be treated as a quasi-extraordinary item, i.e. as a separate item after the profit for the year from ordinary operations.[10]

If the temporal method were to be used then all exchange differences would be reported as part of the profit from ordinary operations unless they arose from items which would themselves be treated as extraordinary.[11]

The main comments received on ED 21 were that:[12]

(a)   there was a lack of clarity in the distinction between the treatment of exchange differences in individual companies and differences arising on consolidation;

(b)   two methods of translation should not be allowed when the closing rate was so widely adopted in the UK;

(c)   the occasions when the cover concept could be applied were not clear;

(d)   the different treatment given to current assets as opposed to fixed assets was not supported;

(e)   support for the use of the closing rate and the average rate for translating the profit and loss account was evenly divided;

(f)   the net investment concept in ED 21 was inadequately developed;

(g)   there was strong support for keeping exchange differences out of operating profit but little support for displaying them as quasi-extraordinary items;

(h)   the global concept for offsetting gains and losses on exchange was thought to be imprudent.

1.5   ED 27

The reason why ED 16 and ED 21 permitted the use of either the closing rate or the temporal method was that the latter method was the only method which could be used in the USA. Following the implementation of SFAS 8 in the USA it gradually became evident that when consolidated accounts are drawn up in a relatively weak currency , such a method produces results which do not seem to make commercial and economic sense. As a result the FASB decided to review its existing standard, SFAS 8.[13] In Canada, the Canadian Institute of Chartered Accountants (CICA) which had published its standard on foreign currencies in 1978,[14] advocating the use of the temporal method, suspended it in 1979 pending further study. Conscious of the need for international harmonisation in this field, there then followed a long period of consultation between the ASC, the FASB and the CICA.

So it was that the ASC issued ED 27 in October 1980. This was based on the closing rate/net investment concept and proposed an approach to translation which is related to the cash flow consequences of exchange movements. Exchange differences which give rise to cash flows, i.e. those resulting from business transactions, are reported as part of the profit or loss for the period. Other exchange differences which do not give rise to cash flows, because they result from retranslations of the holding company's long-term investment in the foreign subsidiary, are reported as reserve movements. ED 27 also introduced another version of the cover concept where a foreign currency loan has been used to finance the purchase of an investment in a foreign subsidiary.

1.6   SSAP 20

The majority of commentators supported the principles set out in ED 27 and so it eventually formed the basis of SSAP 20. However, since the exposure draft was issued the Companies Act 1981 had been enacted. The accounting rules contained in the Act had certain ramifications on the treatment of exchange differences and these had to be resolved. It was not, therefore, until April 1983 that SSAP 20 was finally issued.

2   REQUIREMENTS OF SSAP 20

2.1   Objectives of translation

SSAP 20 states that 'the translation of foreign currency transactions and financial statements should produce results which are generally compatible with the effects of rate changes on a company's cash flows and its equity and should ensure that the financial statements present a true and fair view of the results of management actions. Consolidated statements should reflect the financial results and relationships as measured in the foreign currency financial statements prior to translation.'[15] It will be seen when looking at the requirements of the standard that in certain situations these objectives conflict.

2.2   Definitions of terms

The main definitions of terms which are contained in SSAP 20 are as follows:[16]

A *foreign enterprise* is a subsidiary, associated company or branch whose operations are based in a country other than that of the investing company or whose assets and liabilities are denominated mainly in a foreign currency.

A *foreign branch* is either a legally constituted enterprise located overseas or a group of assets and liabilities which are accounted for in foreign currencies.

Translation is the process whereby financial data denominated in one currency are expressed in terms of another currency. It includes both the expression of individual transactions in terms of another currency and the expression of a complete set of financial statements prepared in one currency in terms of another currency.

A company's *local currency* is the currency of the primary economic environment in which it operates net cash flows.

An *exchange rate* is a rate at which two currencies may be exchanged for each other at a particular point in time; different rates apply for spot and forward transactions.

The *closing rate* is the exchange rate for spot transactions ruling at the balance sheet date and is the mean of the buying and selling rates at the close of business on the day for which the rate is to be ascertained.

A *forward contract* is an agreement to exchange different currencies at a specified rate. The difference between the specified rate and the spot rate ruling on the date the contract was entered into is the discount or premium on the forward contract.

The *net investment* which a company has in a foreign enterprise is its effective equity stake and comprises its proportion of such foreign enterprise's net assets; in appropriate circumstances, intra-group loans and other deferred balances may be regarded as part of the effective equity stake.

Monetary items are money held and amounts to be received or paid in money and, where a company is not an exempt company, should be categorised as either short-term or long-term. Short-term monetary items are those which fall due within one year of the balance sheet date. (An exempt company is essentially a bank or an insurance company.)

2.3 Individual companies

As indicated in 1.1 above a company can either enter directly into foreign currency transactions or it may conduct foreign operations through a foreign enterprise. The standard therefore requires that the procedures to be adopted when accounting for foreign operations should be considered in two stages, namely the preparation of the financial statements of the individual company and the preparation of the consolidated financial statements.

The first stage to be considered is the preparation of the financial statements of an individual company. The procedures to be followed should be applied to each company within a group prior to the preparation of the consolidated accounts. The general requirements of SSAP 20 are as follows.

2.3.1 *Recording of transactions*

Generally, all foreign currency transactions entered into by a company should be translated into its local currency at the exchange rate ruling on the date the transaction occurs. An average rate for a period is acceptable if rates do not fluctuate significantly during the relevant period. Where the transaction is to be settled at a contracted rate then that rate should be used.[17]

2.3.2 *Retranslation of monetary/non-monetary assets and liabilities at balance sheet date*

At the balance sheet date, monetary assets and liabilities denominated in foreign currencies resulting from unsettled transactions should be translated using the closing rate. Again, where the transaction is to be settled at a contracted rate then that rate should be used.[18]

Non-monetary assets should not be retranslated but should remain translated at the rate ruling when they were originally recorded.[19]

2.3.3   Treatment of exchange differences

Exchange differences will arise when transactions are settled at exchange rates which are different from those used when the transactions were previously recorded. They will also arise on any unsettled transactions at the balance sheet date if the closing rate differs from those used previously.[20] All exchange differences should be included as part of the profit or loss for the period from ordinary activities, unless they arise as a result of events which themselves are treated as extraordinary, in which case they should be included as part of such items. This treatment should be adopted for all monetary items irrespective of whether they are short-term or long-term and irrespective of whether the exchange differences are gains or losses.[21]

The rationale for the above treatment is that the exchange differences have already been reflected in cash flows, in the case of settled transactions, or will be in the future in the case of unsettled transactions.[22] This is consistent with the accruals concept; it results in reporting the effect of a rate change that will have cash flow effects when the event causing the effect takes place. As paragraph 10 of SSAP 20 explains, 'exchange gains on unsettled transactions can be determined at the balance sheet date no less objectively than exchange losses; deferring the gains whilst recognising the losses would not only be illogical by denying in effect that any favourable movement had occurred but would also inhibit fair measurement of the performance of the enterprise in the year. In particular, this symmetry of treatment recognises that there will probably be some interaction between currency movements and interest rates and reflects more accurately in the profit and loss account the true results of currency involvement'.

2.3.4   Worked examples

The above general requirements can be illustrated in the following examples:

Example 18.1

A UK company purchases plant and machinery on credit from a US company for US$350,000 in November 19X1 when the exchange rate is £1=US$1.75. The company records the asset at a cost of £200,000. At the UK company's year end at December 31, 19X1 the account has not yet been settled. The closing rate is £1=US$1.88. The creditor would be retranslated at £186,170 in the balance sheet and an exchange gain of £13,830 would be reported as part of the profit or loss for the period from ordinary operations. The cost of the asset would remain as £200,000.

Example 18.2

A UK company sells goods to a German company for DM174,000 on June 30, 19X1 when the exchange rate is £1=DM2.90. It receives payment on September 30, 19X1 when the exchange rate is £1=DM3.00. On June 30 the company will record a sale and corresponding debtor of £60,000. When payment is received on September 30 the actual amount received is only £58,000. The loss on exchange of £2,000 would be reported as part of the profit or loss for the period from ordinary operations.

2.3.5 Examples of accounting policies

> *Extract 18.1: United Biscuits (Holdings) PLC[23]*
>
> *Foreign currency translations* [extract]
> *Company*
> Monetary assets and liabilities denominated in foreign currencies are translated at the rate of exchange ruling at the balance sheet date. Transactions in foreign currencies are recorded at the rate ruling at the date of the transaction, all differences being taken to the profit and loss account.

> *Extract 18.2: Argyll Group PLC[24]*
>
> **Foreign Currency** [extract]
> Transactions in foreign currencies are translated into sterling at the rates of exchange current at the dates of the transactions. Foreign currency monetary assets and liabilities in the balance sheet are translated into sterling at the rates of exchange ruling at the end of the year. Resulting exchange gains and losses are taken to the profit and loss account.

2.3.6 Exchange gains where there are doubts as to convertibility or marketability

As indicated in 2.3.3 above SSAP 20 requires both exchange gains and losses on long-term monetary items to be recognised in the profit and loss account. However, paragraphs 11 and 50 of the standard indicate that where there are doubts as to the convertibility or marketability of the currency in question then it may be necessary to consider on the grounds of prudence whether the amount of any exchange gain, or the amount by which exchange gains exceed past exchange losses on the same items, to be recognised in the profit and loss account should be restricted.

2.3.7 Foreign equity investments financed by borrowings

One exception to the rule that non-monetary items are not retranslated is where foreign equity investments have been financed by foreign currency borrowings or where the borrowings have been taken out to hedge the exchange risks associated with existing equity investments. Application of the procedures set out in 2.3.1 to 2.3.3 above would cause exchange differences on loans to pass through the profit and loss account while no exchange differences would arise on the equity investments. The standard recognises that in such situations a company may be covered in economic terms against any movement in exchange rates and states that it would be inappropriate in such cases to record an accounting profit or loss when exchange rates change.[25]

Paragraph 51 of the standard therefore allows companies in such situations, subject to the conditions set out below, to treat the cost of the investments as being denominated in the appropriate foreign currencies and retranslating them at the closing rates each year. Where this is done the resulting exchange differences should be taken to reserves. The exchange differences arising on the related foreign currency borrowings should also be taken to reserves and should not be reported as part of the profit or loss for the period.

The conditions to be fulfilled are:

(a)   exchange gains or losses arising on the borrowings may be offset only to the extent of exchange differences arising on the equity investments in that particular period;

(b)   the foreign currency borrowings should not exceed the total amount of cash that the investments are expected to generate, whether from profits or otherwise; and

(c)   the accounting treatment should be applied consistently from period to period.

Example 18.3

A UK company purchases equity shares in a Swiss company for SFr1,200,000 on September 30, 19X1 when the exchange rate is £1=SFr2.50. It partially finances the investment by borrowing SFr1,000,000 on the same date. The investment would therefore be recorded as £480,000 and the loan as £400,000. At the UK company's year end of December 31, 19X1 the closing rate is £1=SFr2.40. The loan would be retranslated as £416,667 resulting in an exchange loss of £16,667. The investment would be translated as £500,000 resulting in an exchange gain of £20,000. Both the exchange gain and the exchange loss would be taken to reserves.

If the UK company did not wish to adopt the treatment contained in paragraph 51 of the standard then the exchange loss of £16,667 would have to be reported as part of the profit or loss for the period and the investment would have been retained at its original cost of £480,000 with no exchange gain being recognised.

Examples of accounting policies of companies which have adopted such a treatment are illustrated below:

Extract 18.3: Ladbroke Group PLC[26]

Foreign currencies [extract]
Gains or losses arising on the translation of the net assets of overseas subsidiaries and related companies are taken to reserves, net of exchange differences arising on related foreign currency borrowings, as are differences arising on equity investments denominated in foreign currencies in the holding company's accounts.

Extract 18.4: Imperial Chemical Industries PLC[27]

FOREIGN CURRENCIES [extract]
In the Group accounts exchange differences arising on consolidation of the net investments in overseas subsidiary and related companies are taken to reserves, as are differences arising on equity investments denominated in foreign currencies in the Company accounts. Differences on foreign currency loans are taken to reserves and offset against the differences on net investments.

2.3.8 *Forward contracts*

The standard recognises that where a company has covered a foreign currency transaction by entering into a related or matching forward contract it may not be appropriate to record the transaction using the spot rate ruling at the date of the transaction or to retranslate the monetary asset or liability at the closing rate. Accordingly, paragraphs 46 and 48 allow companies to use the rate of exchange specified in the related or matching forward contract instead.

Example 18.4

A UK company sells goods to a German company for DM100,000 on October 31, 19X1 at which date the exchange rate is £1=DM2.98. As payment is not due until January 31, 19X2, the company decides to hedge its exposure to exchange risk by entering into a forward contract to sell DM100,000 in three months time at a rate of £1=DM2.945. As a result the company has fixed the amount of sterling it will realise from the sale at £33,956. The standard allows the company to record the sale and corresponding debtor at that amount and not at £33,557 using the rate ruling at the date of the transaction. If at its year end of December 31, 19X1 the exchange rate is £1=DM3.05 there is no need for the company to retranslate the debtor at £32,787 and record a loss on exchange, but it retains it at £33,956. This treatment recognises the fact that as a result of entering into the forward contract the company is no longer susceptible to exchange rate movements and therefore there should be no effect on its profit or loss if exchange rates do change.

An example of an accounting policy of a company which adopts such a treatment is illustrated below:

Extract 18.5: Reckitt & Colman plc[28]

FOREIGN CURRENCY TRANSLATION [extract]

Transactions denominated in foreign currencies are translated at the rate of exchange on the day the transaction occurs or the contracted rate if the transaction is covered by a forward exchange contract.

Assets and liabilities denominated in a foreign currency are translated at the balance sheet date at the exchange rate ruling on that day or if appropriate at the forward contract rate.

2.4 Consolidated accounts

The second stage to be considered is the preparation of consolidated financial statements.

2.4.1 *Scope*

The procedures to be adopted apply not only to the inclusion of subsidiaries but also to the incorporation of the results of associated companies. They also apply when the results of a foreign branch are to be incorporated into the accounts of an individual company.[29]

2.4.2 *Choice of method*

The standard requires that the method to be used for translating the financial statements of a foreign enterprise should reflect the financial and other operational relationship which exists between the holding company and its foreign enterprise.[30] It recognises that in most cases this means that the consolidated accounts will be prepared using the closing rate/net investment method as described in 2.4.3 below. However, as explained in 2.4.4 below in certain circumstances the standard requires the temporal method to be used.

The method used for translating the financial statements of a foreign enterprise should only be changed when the financial and other operational relationship changes and renders the method used inappropriate.[31]

2.4.3 *Closing rate/net investment method*

For most investing companies in the UK where foreign operations are carried out by foreign enterprises it is normally the case that the foreign enterprises operate as separate or quasi-independent entities.[32] The day to day operations of the foreign enterprise will be based in its local currency, are likely to be financed wholly or partly in its own currency, and will not be dependent on the reporting currency of the holding company. The foreign enterprise will be managed so as to maximise the local currency profits attributable to the holding company. Consequently, the financial statements of the foreign enterprise expressed in its local currency will be the best available indicator of its performance and value to the group. In order to preserve the inherent relationships included in these local currency financial statements it is therefore necessary to use a single rate of exchange when translating the financial statements when preparing the consolidated financial statements.[33]

A   *Balance sheet*

The standard therefore requires that under the closing rate/net investment method the balance sheet of the foreign enterprise should be translated into the reporting currency of the investing company using the rate of exchange at the balance sheet date, i.e. the closing rate.[34]

B   *Profit and loss account*

The profit and loss account of the foreign enterprise under this method should be translated at the closing rate or at an average rate for the period.[35] In our view the use of the closing rate is preferable as this will achieve the objective of translation of reflecting the financial results and relationships as measured in the foreign currency financial statements prior to translation.[36] The use of an average rate is justified by SSAP 20 on the grounds that it reflects more fairly the profits or losses and cash flows as they arise to the group throughout an accounting period.[37] Although the standard allows a choice as to which rate is used it does require that the one selected is applied consistently from period to period.[38]

C   *Treatment of exchange differences*

Exchange differences will arise under the closing rate/net investment method if the exchange rate used for translating the balance sheet differs from that ruling at the previous balance sheet date or at the date of any subsequent capital injection or reduction.[39] Exchange differences will also arise where an average rate is used for translating the profit and loss account and this differs from the closing rate.[40] The standard requires that both such exchange differences should be recorded as a movement on reserves.[41] As paragraph 19 of SSAP 20 explains 'If exchange differences arising from the retranslation of a company's net investment in its foreign enterprise were introduced into the profit and loss account, the results from trading operations, as shown in the local currency financial statements would be distorted. Such differences may result from many factors unrelated to the trading performance or financing operations of the foreign enterprise; in particular, they do not represent or measure changes in actual or prospective cash flows. It is therefore inappropriate to regard them as profits or losses and they should be dealt with as adjustments to reserves'.

Example 18.5

A UK company owns 100% of the share capital of a German company which was set up ten years ago in 19W1 when the exchange rate was £1=DM4. It uses the closing rate method for incorporating the accounts of the subsidiary in its consolidated accounts for the year ended December 31, 19X1. The exchange rate at the year end is £1=DM2 (19X0: £1=DM3). The profit and loss account of the subsidiary for that year and its balance sheet at the beginning and end of the year in local currency and translated into sterling are as follows:

Profit and loss account

	DM	£
Sales	35,000	17,500
Cost of sales	(33,190)	(16,595)
Depreciation	(500)	(250)
Interest	(350)	(175)
Profit before taxation	960	480
Taxation	(460)	(230)
Profit after taxation	500	250

Balance sheets	19X0 DM	19X1 DM	19X0 £	19X1 £
Fixed assets	6,000	5,500	2,000	2,750
Current assets				
Stocks	2,700	3,000	900	1,500
Debtors	4,800	4,000	1,600	2,000
Cash	200	600	67	300
	7,700	7,600	2,567	3,800
Current liabilities				
Creditors	4,530	3,840	1,510	1,920
Taxation	870	460	290	230
	5,400	4,300	1,800	2,150
Net current assets	2,300	3,300	767	1,650
	8,300	8,800	2,767	4,400
Long-term loans	3,600	3,600	1,200	1,800
	4,700	5,200	1,567	2,600
Share capital	1,000	1,000	250	250
Retained profits	3,700	4,200	1,317	2,350
	4,700	5,200	1,567	2,600

The movement in retained profits is as follows:

	£
Balance brought forward	1,317
Profit for year	250
Exchange difference	783
	2,350

The exchange difference of £783 is the exchange difference on the opening net investment in the subsidiary and is calculated as follows:

Opening net assets at opening rate	— DM4,700 at DM3=£1	=	£1,567
Opening net assets at closing rate	— DM4,700 at DM2=£1	=	£2,350
Exchange gain on net investment			£ 783

This exchange gain should be shown as a movement on reserves and should not be reflected in the profit and loss account.

If the company were to have adopted a policy of translating the profit and loss account at an average rate of exchange and the appropriate weighted average rate was DM2.5=£1 then the profit and loss account would have been as follows:

	DM	£
Sales	35,000	14,000
Cost of sales	(33,190)	(13,276)
Depreciation	(500)	(200)
Interest	(350)	(140)
Profit before taxation	960	384
Taxation	(460)	(184)
Profit after taxation	500	200

The difference between the profit and loss account translated at an average rate, i.e. £200, and at the closing rate, i.e. £250, would be recorded as a movement in reserves.

Examples of accounting policies of companies using this method of translation are illustrated below:

Extract 18.6: Guinness PLC[42]

Foreign currencies [extract]

The profit and loss accounts and balance sheets of overseas subsidiary and related companies are translated into sterling at closing rates of exchange.

Exchange adjustments arising from the translation to sterling of the opening balance sheets of subsidiary and related companies at the closing rate of exchange are taken to reserves.

Extract 18.7: The British Petroleum Company p.l.c.[43]

Foreign currencies [extract]

On consolidation, assets and liabilities of subsidiary companies are translated into sterling at closing rates of exchange. Income and source and application of funds statements are translated at average rates of exchange.

Exchange differences resulting from the translation at closing rates of net investments in subsidiary and related companies, together with differences between income statements translated at average rates and at closing rates, are dealt with in reserves.

2.4.4 Temporal method

As already indicated in 2.4.2 above the standard recognises that in certain circumstances it would be inappropriate to use the closing rate/net investment method for translating the financial statements of a foreign enterprise and requires the temporal method to be used.

Such a method is to be used where the trade of the foreign enterprise is more dependent on the economic environment of the investing company's currency than that of its own reporting currency. By using the temporal method the consolidated accounts reflect the transactions of the foreign enterprise as if they had been carried out by the investing company itself.[44]

A　　Determination of dominant currency

It is impossible to specify any one factor which would indicate when the temporal method should be used. The standard indicates that the following factors should be taken into account:[45]

(a)　'the extent to which the cash flows of the enterprise have a direct impact upon those of the investing company' (e.g. whether there is a regular and frequent movement of cash between the holding company and the foreign enterprise or whether there are only occasional remittances of, for example, dividends);

(b)　'the extent to which the functioning of the enterprise is dependent directly upon the investing company' (e.g. whether management is based locally or at head office and whether pricing decisions are based on local competition and costs or are part of a worldwide decision process);

(c)　'the currency in which the majority of the trading transactions are denominated' (e.g. whether the foreign currency is used for both invoicing goods and paying expenses, or whether the majority of such items are denominated in the currency of the investing company);

(d)　'the major currency to which the operation is exposed in its financing structure' (e.g. whether the company is dependent on local financing or whether the majority of the financing is in the currency of the investing company and possibly obtained through, or guaranteed by, that company).[46]

B　　Example of situations

Situations where the temporal method may be appropriate are where the foreign enterprise:

(a)　'acts as a selling agency receiving stocks of goods from the investing company and remitting the proceeds back to the company';

(b)　'produces a raw material or manufactures parts or sub-assemblies which are then shipped to the investing company for inclusion in its own products';

(c)　'is located overseas for tax, exchange control or similar reasons to act as a means of raising finance for other companies in the group'.[47]

C　　Method

The mechanics of the temporal method are essentially the same as those procedures used in preparing the accounts of an individual company[48] discussed in 2.3 above. In theory, this means translating each transaction of the foreign enterprise at the rates ruling at the date of each transaction. In order to simplify the translation process, however, average rates may be used as an approximation.

Example 18.6

Using the same basic facts as Example 18.5 above, i.e. a UK company owns 100% of the share capital of a German company which was set up ten years ago in 19W1 when the exchange rate was £1=DM4. It uses the temporal method for incorporating the accounts of the subsidiary in its consolidated accounts for the year ended December 31, 19X1. The exchange rate at the year end is £1=DM2 (19X0: £1=DM3) and the average exchange rate for the year is £1=DM2.5.

Details of fixed assets are as follows:

Date of acquisition	January 1, 19W7	July 1, 19W8
	DM	DM
Cost	2,500	5,000
Aggregate depreciation — 31/12/X0	668	832
Depreciation charge for year	167	333
Aggregate depreciation — 31/12/X1	835	1,165
Net book value — 31/12/X0	1,832	4,168
Net book value — 31/12/X1	1,665	3,835

The relevant exchange rates at the dates of acquisition are £1=DM3.8 and £1=DM3.4 respectively. The average rates of exchange relating to opening and closing stocks are £1=DM3.3 and £1=DM2.4.

The profit and loss account of the subsidiary for that year and its balance sheet at the beginning and end of the year in local currency and translated into sterling using the temporal method are as follows:

Profit and loss account

	DM	Exchange rate	£
Sales	35,000	Average — DM2.5	14,000
Opening stock	2,700	Historical — DM3.3	818
Purchases	33,490	Average — DM2.5	13,396
Closing stock	(3,000)	Historical — DM2.4	(1,250)
Cost of sales	(33,190)		(12,964)
Gross profit	1,810		1,036
Depreciation	(500)	Historical — DM3.8/3.4	(142)
Interest	(350)	Average — DM2.5	(140)
Translation loss		Balance	(596)
Profit before taxation	960		158
Taxation	(460)	Average — DM2.5	(185)
Profit after taxation	500		(27)

Balance sheets	19X0 DM	Exchange rate	19X0 £	19X1 DM	Exchange rate	19X1 £
Fixed assets	6,000	DM3.8/3.4	1,708	5,500	DM3.8/3.4	1,566
Current assets						
Stocks	2,700	DM3.3	818	3,000	DM2.4	1,250
Debtors	4,800	DM3	1,600	4,000	DM2	2,000
Cash	200	DM3	67	600	DM2	300
	7,700		2,485	7,600		3,550
Current liabilities						
Creditors	4,530	DM3	1,510	3,840	DM2	1,920
Taxation	870	DM3	290	460	DM2	230
	5,400		1,800	4,300		2,150
Net current assets	2,300		685	3,300		1,400
	8,300		2,393	8,800		2,966
Long-term loans	3,600	DM3	1,200	3,600	DM2	1,800
	4,700		1,193	5,200		1,166
Share capital	1,000	DM4	250	1,000	DM4	250
Retained profits	3,700	Balance	943	4,200	Balance	916
	4,700		1,193	5,200		1,166

The translation loss of £596 which is shown in the profit and loss account represents the exchange loss on monetary items during the year and is calculated as follows:

	Opening monetary items DM	Closing monetary items DM
Debtors	4,800	4,000
Cash	200	600
Creditors	(4,530)	(3,840)
Taxation	(870)	(460)
Long-term loans	(3,600)	(3,600)
	(4,000)	(3,300)

			£	£
Opening monetary items at opening rate	— DM(4,000) at DM3	=	(1,334)	
Opening monetary items at closing rate	— DM(4,000) at DM2	=	(2,000)	
				(666)
Change in monetary items at average rate	— DM700 at DM2.5	=	280	
Change in monetary items at closing rate	— DM700 at DM2	=	350	
				70
Total exchange loss				(596)

2.4.5 *Foreign equity investments financed by borrowings*

We have already seen in 2.3.7 above that where a company has used foreign currency borrowings to finance, or provide a hedge against, its foreign equity investments the standard allows the exchange differences on the borrowings to be taken to reserves rather than profit and loss account.

A similar provision for consolidated accounts is contained in paragraph 57 of the standard. This is because under the closing rate method exchange differences on the net investment in foreign enterprises are taken to reserves and not reflected in the profit for the year. It would therefore be inappropriate for exchange differences on group borrowings which have been used to finance the investments or provide a hedge against the exchange risk associated with the investments to be taken to profit and loss account. As the group is covered in economic terms against any movement in exchange rates then the exchange differences on the borrowings should be taken to reserves to offset the exchange differences on the net investments in the foreign enterprises.[49]

Where foreign currency borrowings of the group, therefore, have been used to finance, or provide a hedge against group equity investments then, subject to the conditions set out below, the exchange differences arising on the related foreign currency borrowings may be offset against the exchange differences arising on the retranslation of the net investments as a movement on reserves so that they are not reported as part of the profit or loss for the period.[50]

The conditions to be fulfilled are:

(a)   the relationships between the investing company and the foreign enterprises concerned justify the use of the closing rate method for consolidation purposes;

(b)   exchange gains or losses arising on foreign currency borrowings are offset only to the extent of the exchange differences arising on the net investments in foreign enterprises in that particular period;

(c)   the foreign currency borrowings should not exceed the total amount of cash that the net investments are expected to generate, whether from profits or otherwise; and

(d)   the accounting treatment should be applied consistently from period to period.[51]

The last three conditions are similar to those contained in paragraph 51 of the standard relating to the offset procedures for individual companies. The first condition is necessary as it is only when the closing rate method is used that the financial statements would not otherwise reflect the fact that the group is covered in economic terms against movements in exchange differences. Where a foreign enterprise is consolidated using the temporal method then, as all exchange differences are taken to the profit and loss account, any exchange differences on related borrowings should also be taken to the profit and loss account.

Although the general principles of paragraph 57 of the standard are the same as those used in the offset procedures for individual companies there are a number of differences in detail. These will normally require the calculations used in the individual companies' financial statements to be reversed on consolidation and the amount recalculated for the purposes of the consolidated financial statements:

(a)   in the individual companies' financial statements *all* equity investments are included in the calculation, whereas for the consolidated financial statements investments which are consolidated using the temporal method are excluded;

(b)   in the individual companies' financial statements it is the exchange difference on the carrying value of the investment which is included in the calculation, whereas for the consolidated financial statements it is the exchange difference on the underlying net assets which is included; and

(c)   in the individual companies' financial statements only borrowings of the company can be included in the calculation, whereas in the consolidated financial statements borrowings of any group company can be included.

The only situation in which there will be no need to recalculate the amount of the offset is where the provisions of paragraph 51 of the standard have been applied in the investing company's financial statements to a foreign equity investment which is neither a subsidiary nor an associated company. This is because paragraph 58 of the standard allows the amount of the offset in the individual company's financial statements to be carried forward to the consolidated financial statements, since the exchange risk is hedged in both the company and the group. It should be borne in mind, however, that this does not mean that all such equity investments throughout the group can be retranslated at closing rates and the resulting exchange differences used in the offset process.

Example 18.7

A UK company is preparing its financial statements for the year ended December 31, 19X1. It has two wholly owned subsidiaries :

(i) A Japanese company which it acquired a number of years ago at a cost of ¥500m. It incorporates the financial statements of the subsidiary in its consolidated financial statements using the closing rate method. During 19X0 the company borrowed ¥1,000m repayable in ten years' time in 19Y0, to provide a hedge against the investment, which was then considered to be worth in excess of ¥1,500m. The net assets of the subsidiary at December 31, 19X0 were ¥1,200m.

(ii) A French company which it set up on February 1, 19X1 at a cost of FFr10m. It is going to incorporate this subsidiary in its consolidated financial statements using the temporal method. The exchange loss for the period is £41,081. It partially financed the acquisition of the shares by borrowing FFr8m repayable in 19X6.

In addition, the UK company has a 10% investment in a US company which it acquired in 19X0 at a cost of US$2m, financed by means of a US dollar loan of the same amount. At December 31, 19X1 none of the loan has been repaid.

The relevant exchange rates are:

	£1=¥	£1=FFr	£1=US$
31/12/X0	235		1.48
1/2/X1		9.25	
31/12/X1	225	10.00	1.88

Using the provisions of paragraphs 51, 57 and 58 of the standard the treatment in the company and consolidated financial statements would be as follows:

Company financial statements	Profit/loss for year £	Reserves £
Investment in Japanese company		
31/12/X0 — ¥500m @ 235 = £2,127,660		
31/12/X1 — ¥500m @ 225 = £2,222,222		
Exchange gain £ 94,562		94,562
¥1,000m Loan		
31/12/X0 — ¥1,000m @ 235 = £4,255,319		
31/12/X1 — ¥1,000m @ 225 = £4,444,444		
Exchange loss £ (189,125)	(94,563)	(94,562)
Investment in French company		
1/2/X1 — FFr10m @ 9.25 = £1,081,081		
31/12/X1 — FFr10m @ 10.00 = £1,000,000		
Exchange loss £ (81,081)		(81,081)
FFr8m Loan		
1/2/X1 — FFr8m @ 9.25 = £864,865		
31/12/X1 — FFr8m @ 10.00 = £800,000		
Exchange gain £ 64,865		64,865
Investment in US company		
31/12/X0 — US$2m @ 1.48 = £1,351,351		
31/12/X1 — US$2m @ 1.88 = £1,063,830		
Exchange loss £ (287,521)		(287,521)
US$2m Loan		
31/12/X0 — US$2m @ 1.48 = £1,351,351		
31/12/X1 — US$2m @ 1.88 = £1,063,830		
Exchange gain £ 287,521		287,521
Net exchange loss	(94,563)	(16,216)

The exchange loss on the ¥1,000m loan taken to reserves has had to be restricted as a result of condition (a) of paragraph 51 of the standard.

It can be seen that where an exchange gain arises on a foreign loan and it is taken to reserves under paragraph 51 then it is possible to have a net exchange loss being taken to reserves as the exchange loss on the investment can exceed the exchange gain on the related loan.

Consolidated financial statements			Profit/loss for year £	Reserves £
Net investment in Japanese company				
31/12/X0 — ¥1,200m @ 235	=	£5,106,383		
31/12/X1 — ¥1,200m @ 225	=	£5,333,333		
Exchange gain		£ 226,950		226,950
¥1,000m Loan				
31/12/X0 — ¥1,000m @ 235	=	£4,255,319		
31/12/X1 — ¥1,000m @ 225	=	£4,444,444		
Exchange loss		£ (189,125)		(189,125)
Investment in French company				
Exchange loss (as given)			(41,081)	
FFr8m Loan				
1/2/X1 — FFr8m @ 9.25	=	£864,865		
31/12/X1 — FFr8m @ 10.00	=	£800,000		
Exchange gain		£ 64,865	64,865	
Investment in US company				
31/12/X0 — US$2m @ 1.48	=	£1,351,351		
31/12/X1 — US$2m @ 1.88	=	£1,063,830		
Exchange loss		£ (287,521)		(287,521)
US$2m Loan				
31/12/X0 — US$2m @ 1.48	=	£1,351,351		
31/12/X1 — US$2m @ 1.88	=	£1,063,830		
Exchange gain		£ 287,521		287,521
Net exchange gain			23,784	37,825

In the consolidated financial statements all of the exchange loss on the ¥1,000m loan can be taken to reserves as it is less than the exchange gain on the net investment in the Japanese subsidiary. The exchange gain on the FFr8m loan has to be taken to the profit/loss for the year as the temporal method is used and therefore condition (a) of paragraph 57 of the standard is not met. It can be seen that the same treatment is adopted for the US$ investment and loan as in the company financial statements as a result of paragraph 58.

2.4.6 Associated companies

As indicated in 2.4.1 above, the provisions of the standard relating to consolidated financial statements apply to the incorporation of the results of all foreign enterprises, including associated companies. The definition of associated companies and the required accounting treatment are dealt with in SSAP 1[52] and are discussed in Chapter 4.

When incorporating the results of foreign associated companies, therefore, the closing rate/net investment method should normally be used. In view of the fact that the investing company only has significant influence over the associated company and does not control it, it is unlikely that the affairs of the associated company are so closely linked with those of the investing company that the use of the temporal method will be appropriate. The requirements of the closing rate/net investment method have been explained in 2.4.3 above.

2.4.7 Foreign branches

The provisions of the standard relating to consolidated financial statements also apply to the incorporation of the results of foreign branches, not only in the consolidated financial statements but also in the financial statements of an individual company.[53] The definition of a foreign branch contained in the standard is such that it includes not just a legally constituted enterprise located overseas but also a group of assets and liabilities which are accounted for in foreign currencies.[54]

The reason for this wide definition was to cater for the situation where a company had international assets such as ships or aircraft which earn revenues in a foreign currency, normally US dollars, financed by borrowings in the same currency and to allow the use of the closing rate/net investment method. If this had not been done, then under the provisions of the standard it would have been necessary for such assets to be translated at historical rates, the borrowings to be translated at closing rates and any exchange difference thereon taken to the profit or loss for the year. The cover method contained in paragraphs 51 and 57 of the standard would not have applied as these provisions only deal with borrowings which finance equity investments and not other types of non-monetary assets.

A   Possible situations

In addition to the situation referred to above, the statement issued by the ASC on the publication of the standard also quoted the following as being examples of situations where a group of assets and liabilities should be accounted for under the closing rate/net investment method:

(a)   a hotel in France financed by borrowings in French francs;

(b)   a foreign currency insurance operation where the liabilities are substantially covered by the holding of foreign currency assets.[55]

B   Treatment

The results of a foreign branch should be incorporated in the financial statements in the same way as foreign subsidiaries are included in the consolidated financial statements, i.e. the closing rate/net investment method should normally be used.[56] The use of this method is explained in 2.4.3 above.

However, in many cases the operations of a branch are a direct extension of the trade of the investing company and its cash flows have a direct impact upon those of the investing company in which case the temporal method is required to be used. It should not automatically be assumed, therefore, that the closing rate/net investment method is the correct method to use and careful consideration should be given to the factors referred to in 2.4.4 above.

Clyde Petroleum plc adopts such a treatment in respect of their foreign currency assets and liabilities in both subsidiaries and branches, as is illustrated in their accounting policy below:

Extract 18.8: Clyde Petroleum plc[57]

(h) Foreign currencies
Transactions in foreign currencies during the year are recorded in sterling at the rates of exchange ruling at the date of the transaction. The results for the year are translated into sterling at an average rate. Assets and liabilities in foreign currencies are translated into sterling at the rates ruling at the balance sheet date.
Exchange differences resulting from the translation of assets and liabilities of foreign currency denominated subsidiaries and branches into sterling at year-end rates of exchange, together with those differences resulting from the restatement of profits and losses from average to year-end rates, are taken directly to reserves. All other exchange differences are taken to the profit and loss account.

2.5   Disclosures

2.5.1   *Requirements of SSAP 20*

The standard requires the following disclosures to be made in the financial statements:

(a)   the methods used in the translation of the financial statements of foreign enterprises, i.e. closing rate method or temporal method. Where the closing rate method is used it should also be stated whether the closing rate or an average rate has been used to translate the profit and loss account;[58]

(b)   the net amount of exchange gains and losses on foreign currency borrowings less deposits charged or credited to the profit and loss account.[59] It should be noted that exchange differences on deposits have to be taken into account; it is not just the exchange differences on borrowings;

(c)   the net amount of exchange gains and losses on foreign currency borrowings less deposits offset in reserves under the provisions of paragraphs 51, 57 and 58 of the standard;[60]

(d)   the net movement on reserves arising from exchange differences.[61] This will normally be the exchange differences on the net investments of those subsidiaries translated using the closing rate method.

There is no requirement for exchange differences taken to profit and loss account, other than those referred to in (b) above, to be disclosed. This is because the ASC considered 'that such disclosure is not necessarily helpful since it is influenced by the extent to which the company's trade is conducted in foreign currencies and the extent to which the company covers its exchange risk by entering into forward exchange contracts. Moreover, an agreement to settle a transaction in a foreign currency reflects only one aspect of the pricing or purchasing decision involved in normal trading. In any case a small difference may disguise a significant gain and significant loss and disclosure of the net figure will not indicate the risks inherent in trading in foreign currencies.'[62]

2.5.2 *Examples of disclosures*

Examples of disclosures of the methods used have been illustrated earlier in the chapter in giving extracts of accounting policies used. A good example of an accounting policy for foreign currencies which covers most of the various aspects is that of Reckitt & Colman plc.

Extract 18.9: Reckitt & Colman plc[63]

FOREIGN CURRENCY TRANSLATION

Transactions denominated in foreign currencies are translated at the rate of exchange on the day the transaction occurs or the contracted rate if the transaction is covered by a forward exchange contract. Assets and liabilities denominated in a foreign currency are translated at the balance sheet date at the exchange rate ruling on that day or if appropriate at the forward contract rate.

Exchange differences arising in the accounts of individual companies are included in the profit and loss account except that where foreign currency borrowings have been used to finance equity investments in foreign currencies, exchange differences arising on the borrowings are dealt with through reserves to the extent that they are covered by exchange differences arising on the net assets represented by the equity investments.

The accounts of overseas subsidiaries and related companies are translated into sterling on the following basis:

Assets and liabilities at the rate of exchange ruling at the year-end date of Reckitt & Colman plc except for fixed assets of companies operating in countries where hyper-inflation exists which are translated at historical rates of exchange.

Profit and loss account items at the average rate of exchange ruling during the financial year. An inflation adjustment is charged in arriving at local currency profits operating in hyper-inflation countries before they are translated to reflect the impact on the companies' working capital requirements.

Exchange differences arising on the translation of accounts into sterling are recorded as movements on reserves on the group balance sheet.

(The particular problem of hyper-inflation is discussed in 3.4.9 below.)

The requirements to disclose those exchange differences taken to reserves are usually met in one of two ways:

(a)   Show both types of exchange difference separately.

Extract 18.10: Reckitt & Colman plc[64]

10. OTHER RESERVES [extract]

	Group	Subsidiaries and related companies	Parent
	£m	£m	£m
Net exchange profit on foreign currency borrowing*	9.73	—	9.73
Exchange differences arising on translation of net investments in overseas subsidiaries and related companies	(48.01)	(29.00)	(19.01)

* Net exchange profits of £0.85m (1986, £1.11m) have been dealt with in arriving at trading profit.

(b)   Show a net figure but disclose that relating to borrowings by way of a note.

Extract 18.11: Imperial Chemical Industries PLC[65]

11 RESERVES [extract]

	Revaluation £m	Other £m	Profit and loss account £m	Related companies £m	1987 Total £m
Exchange adjustments	(10)	(38)	(213)	5	(256)

In the group accounts, £108m of net exchange gains on foreign currency loans in 1987 have been offset in reserves against exchange losses on the net investment in overseas subsidiary and related companies.

In our view the former treatment is better in that it would show the category of reserves to which the exchange differences on the borrowings have been taken.

It can be seen from Extract 18.10 above that Reckitt & Colman plc has disclosed the exchange difference on borrowings less deposits which have been taken to the profit and loss account in their reserves note. They have also given the same information in their 'Profit is stated after charging/(crediting)' note.[66]

An alternative way of disclosing this information is to include the amount as a separate item in the interest payable/receivable note as done by Imperial Chemical Industries PLC.

Extract 18.12: Imperial Chemical Industries PLC[67]

6 NET INTEREST PAYABLE [extract]

	1987 £m	1986 £m
EXCHANGE GAINS ON SHORT-TERM CURRENCY BORROWINGS AND DEPOSITS	(9)	(5)

3   PROBLEM AREAS

3.1   Individual companies

3.1.1   *Date of transaction*

The basic requirement of paragraph 46 of SSAP 20 is that transactions should be recorded at the rate ruling at the date the transaction occurred. No guidance is given in the standard as to what that date should be. SFAS 52 gives some help by defining the transaction date as being the date at which a transaction is recorded in accounting records in conformity with generally accepted accounting principles.[68] The following example illustrates the difficulty in determining the transaction date.

Example 18.8: Establishing the transaction date

A UK company buys an item of stock from a German company. The dates relating to the transaction, and the relevant exchange rates, are as follows:

Date	Event	£1=DM
February 24, 1988	Goods are ordered	2.99
March 4, 1988	Goods are shipped from Germany and invoice dated that day	3.00
March 7, 1988	Invoice is received	3.05
March 8, 1988	Goods are received	3.07
March 17, 1988	Invoice is recorded	3.10
March 31, 1988	Invoice is paid	3.12

In our view the date of the transaction should be when the company should recognise an asset and liability as a result of the transaction. This will normally be when the risks and rewards of ownership of the goods have passed to the UK company.

It is unlikely at the date the goods are ordered that all the risks and rewards of ownership of the goods have passed to the UK company and therefore this date should not be used as the date of the transaction.

If the goods are shipped free on board (f.o.b.) then as the risks and rewards of ownership pass on shipment then this date should be used.

If, however, the goods are not shipped f.o.b. then the risks and rewards of ownership normally pass on delivery and therefore the date the goods are received should be treated as the date of the transaction.

The dates on which the invoice is received and is recorded are irrelevant to when the risks and rewards of ownership pass and therefore should not be considered to be the date of the transaction. In practice, it may be acceptable that as a matter of administrative convenience that the exchange rate at the date the invoice is recorded is used, particularly if there is no undue delay in processing the invoice. If this is done then care should be taken to ensure that the exchange rate used is not significantly different from that ruling on the 'true' date of the transaction.

It is clear from SSAP 20 that the date the invoice is paid is not the date of the transaction because if it were then no exchange differences would arise on unsettled transactions.

Most companies do not indicate in their accounting policies what is meant by the date of transaction. One company which does is Racal Electronics Plc.

Extract 18.13: Racal Electronics Plc[69]

4 Foreign currencies [extract]
United Kingdom exports in foreign currencies are converted at the rates relative to the period
of shipment.

3.1.2   *Use of average rate*

As indicated in 2.3.1 above, rather than using the actual rate ruling at the date of
the transaction 'if the rates do not fluctuate significantly, an average rate for the
period may be used as an approximation'.[70] For companies which engage in a
large number of foreign currency transactions it will be more convenient for them
to use an average rate rather than using the exact rate for each transaction. If an
average rate is to be used, what guidance can be given in choosing and using such
a rate?

(a)   Length of period
       As an average rate should only be used as an approximation of actual rates
       then care has to be taken that significant fluctuations in the day to day
       exchange rates do not arise in the period selected. For this reason the period
       chosen should not be too long. We believe that the maximum length of
       period should be one month and where there is volatility of exchange rates it
       will be better to set rates on a more frequent basis, say, a weekly basis,
       especially where the value of transactions is significant.

(b)   Estimate of average rate
       The estimation of the appropriate average rate will depend on whether the
       rate is to be applied to transactions which have already occurred or to
       transactions which will occur after setting the rate. Obviously, if the
       transactions have already occurred then the average rate used should relate to
       the period during which those transactions occurred; e.g. purchase
       transactions for the previous week should be translated using the average
       rate for that week, not an average rate for the week the invoices are being
       recorded.
       If there is no time delay between the date of the transaction and the date of
       recording and the rate is therefore being set for the following period then the
       rate selected should be a reasonable estimate of the expected exchange rate
       during that period. This could be done by using the closing rate at the end of
       the previous period or by using the actual average rate for the previous
       period. We would suggest that the former be used. Although a forward rate
       could be used, it should be remembered that forward rates are *not* estimates
       of future exchange rates but are a function of the spot rate adjusted by
       reference to interest differentials (see 3.3.1 A below). Whatever means is
       used to estimate the average rate, the actual rates during the period should be
       monitored and if there is a significant move in the exchange rate away from
       the average rate then the rate being applied should be revised.

(c) Application of average rate
We believe that average rates should only be used as a matter of convenience where there are a large number of transactions. Even where an average rate is used we would recommend that for large one-off transactions the actual rate should be used; e.g. purchase of a fixed asset or an overseas investment or taking out a foreign loan. Where the number of foreign currency transactions are small it will probably not be worthwhile setting and monitoring average rates and therefore actual rates should be used.

3.1.3 Dual rates or suspension of rates

One practical difficulty in translating foreign currency amounts is where there is more than one exchange rate for that particular currency depending on the nature of the transaction. In some cases the difference between the exchange rates can be small, such as in the case of the Belgian franc. At December 31, 1988 the closing rate for the commercial franc was £1=BF67.40 and for the financial franc was £1=BF67.55. In these circumstances it probably does not matter which rate is actually used. However, in other cases, such as the South African rand, the difference can be quite significant. At December 31, 1988 the closing rate for the commercial rand was £1=R4.30 whereas for the financial rand the rate was £1=R6.96. In these circumstances, what rate should be used? SSAP 20 is silent on this matter, but some guidance can be found in SFAS 52. It states 'the applicable rate at which a particular transaction could be settled at the transaction date shall be used to translate and record the transaction. At a subsequent balance sheet date, the current rate (closing rate) is that rate at which the related receivable or payable could be settled at that date'.[71] Companies should therefore look at the nature of the transaction and apply the appropriate exchange rate. If there are doubts as to whether funds will be receivable at the more favourable rate then it may be necessary on the grounds of prudence to use the less favourable rate.

Another practical difficulty which could arise is where for some reason exchangeability between two currencies is temporarily lacking at the transaction date or at the subsequent balance sheet date. Again SSAP 20 makes no comment on this matter but SFAS 52 requires that the first subsequent rate at which exchanges could be made shall be used.[72]

3.1.4 Monetary or non-monetary

As discussed in 2.3.2 above, SSAP 20 generally requires that monetary items denominated in foreign currencies be retranslated using closing rates at each balance sheet date and non-monetary items should not be retranslated. Monetary items are defined as 'money held and amounts to be received or paid in money'.[73] The only examples of such items given in the standard are the obvious ones such as 'cash and bank balances, loans and amounts receivable and payable'.[74] Examples of non-monetary items given are equally obvious; 'plant, machinery and equity investments'.[75] Further examples of non-monetary items are those items listed in SFAS 52 as accounts to be remeasured using historical exchange rates when the temporal method is being applied.[76] Even with this guidance there are a number of particular items where the distinction may not be that clear.

A   *Deposits or progress payments paid against fixed assets or stocks*

Companies may be required to pay deposits or progress payments when acquiring fixed assets or stocks from overseas. The question then arises as to whether such payments should be retranslated as monetary items or not.

Example 18.9

A UK company contracts to purchase an item of plant and machinery for US$10,000 on the following terms:

Payable on signing contract (December 1, 19X1)   — 10%
Payable on delivery (December 22, 19X1)   — 40%
Payable on installation (January 11, 19X2)   — 50%

At December 31, 19X1 the company has paid the first two amounts on the due dates when the respective exchange rates were £1=US$1.82 and £1=US$1.83. The closing rate at its balance sheet date, December 31, 19X1, is £1=US$1.88.

	(i) £	(ii) £
First payment — US$1,000	549	532
Second payment — US$4,000	2,186	2,128
	2,735	2,660

(i) If the payments made are regarded as progress payments then the amounts should be treated as non-monetary items and included in the balance sheet at £2,735. This would appear to be consistent with SFAS 52 which in defining 'transaction date' states 'A long-term commitment may have more than one transaction date (for example, the due date of each progress payment under a construction contract is an anticipated transaction date)'.[77]

(ii) If the payments made are regarded as deposits, and are refundable, then the amounts should probably be treated as monetary items and included in the balance sheet at £2,660 and an exchange loss of £75 recorded in the profit and loss account.

In practice, it will often be necessary to consider the terms of the contract to ascertain the nature of the payments made in order to determine the appropriate accounting treatment.

B   *Long-term contracts*

Companies carrying out long-term contracts, which are accounted for under SSAP 9 by including an appropriate proportion of profit[78] (see Chapter 9) may enter into a contract where the contract price is expressed in a foreign currency. At present most balances relating to such contracts are included in the balance sheets under the category of 'stock and work in progress'. It should be borne in mind that any amounts under this category which represent amounts due under the contract should be included at closing rates of exchange as they are effectively monetary items. This is consistent with the treatment required for such balances by the recent revision to SSAP 9.[79]

C   Debt securities held as investments

Companies may acquire or invest in overseas debt securities which have a fixed term of redemption, e.g. a US treasury bond or loan stock of an American company.

Example 18.10

A UK company invests in US$1m 8% Treasury bonds at a cost of US$950,000 on June 30, 19X1 when the exchange rate was £1=US$1.75. The bonds are redeemable at par on June 30, 19X6. At the company's year end, December 31, 19X1, the closing rate of exchange is US$1.88.

In our view whether the investment is a monetary item or not depends on the company's intention for realising the investment.

(i) If the company intends holding the investment to the redemption date and is amortising the difference between cost and redemption value over the period to redemption we believe that the carrying amount is in the nature of a monetary item and therefore should be retranslated at the closing rate:

Cost	$950,000		
Amortisation — $50,000 ÷ 10	5,000		
	$955,000	@ £1=US$1.88	= £507,979

If the company does not adopt a policy of amortising the difference between cost and redemption value over the period to redemption then we believe the investment should not be retranslated as it is not being accounted for as if it were a monetary item.

(ii) If the company does not intend to hold the investment until the redemption date but intends to sell it beforehand then the investment should be regarded as a non-monetary item and recorded at a cost of £542,857 and no exchange difference taken to profit and loss account. If the investment is written down because the market value at the year end is lower than cost or is revalued upwards because the market value is greater than cost then the investment should be translated using the rate of £1=US$1.88 as this is the rate relevant to the measurement date of the item.

D   Foreign currency loans convertible into equity shares

Some companies in the UK in recent years have issued bonds (or debentures), expressed in a foreign currency (usually US dollars), which are convertible into a fixed number of ordinary shares of the UK company at the holder's option. The terms of the bonds normally require the company to redeem the bonds at a fixed amount (expressed in the foreign currency) at the end of their term. The holders and/or the company may also have the option of redeeming the bonds at an agreed amount (expressed in the foreign currency). The question then arises — do the bonds represent a monetary liability to be translated at closing rates or, because they may never be repaid in cash if they are converted for shares, do they represent a non-monetary item which should not be retranslated at closing rates?

Example 18.11

A UK company issues US$100m 6% convertible bonds on June 30, 19X0 when the exchange rate was £1=US$1.53. The share price at that date was £3.00 per share and the conversion terms are based on a share price of £3.27. The bonds are expressed as being convertible into shares at a share price of £3.27 per share and at a fixed exchange rate of £1=US$1.53. Assuming full conversion, therefore, the maximum number of shares which would be issued would be 19,987,607. (The conversion terms could have been expressed as 'convertible into shares at a fixed price of US$5.00' or as 'convertible into 1,000 shares for each US$5,000 of bonds held'; the number of shares to be issued would effectively be the same.) The bonds are only redeemable in 20 years' time on June 30, 19Z0.

How should the company account for these bonds in its accounts for the year ended December 31, 19X0 and the year ended December 31, 19X1? The exchange rates at the balance sheet dates are £1=US$1.48 and £1=US$1.88 respectively. No bonds have been converted by December 31, 19X1.

	Option 1 £m	Option 2 £m	Option 3 £m	Option 4 £m
Accounts for December 31, 19X0				
Issue price	65.4	65.4	65.4	65.4
Exchange loss taken to p/l account	2.2	—	2.2	2.2
Balance sheet liability	67.6	65.4	67.6	67.6
Accounts for December 31, 19X1				
Exchange gain taken to p/l account	(14.4)	—	(2.2)	(2.2)
Exchange gain deferred	—	—	—	(12.2)
Balance sheet liability	53.2	65.4	65.4	53.2

Option 1

It could be argued that until such time as the bonds have been converted they are monetary liabilities of the company and therefore should be retranslated at the closing rate of exchange at each year end. The fact that the company may never actually pay any cash if all the bondholders exercise their right of conversion is irrelevant. At the time of conversion the bondholder will assess whether it is beneficial to convert his holding into shares with regard to the then sterling amount of the bond using the exchange rate at that time. It is therefore this value which the company should treat as having received in return for the issue of shares.

Option 2

It could be argued that as the terms are likely to be set so that it is probable that conversion will take place during the term of the bond then as no cash will actually be paid by the company the bonds should not be treated as a monetary liability. They should, therefore, not be retranslated at closing rates of exchange at each balance sheet date but should be translated at the historical rate of US$1.53. The company should treat the amount received on the issue of the bonds as being the amount received on the issue of the shares.

Option 3

This is a variation of option 2 above. The difference is that until conversion has taken place some recognition should be given to the fact that the bonds may be redeemed and if the bonds translated at closing rate gives a greater liability than that using the historical rate then, on the grounds of prudence, a loss should be recognised. Gains would only be recognised to the extent that they matched losses previously taken to profit and loss account.

Option 4
This is a variation of option 1 above. The difference is that as the bonds may be converted into shares and not repaid in cash it is considered that they may not ultimately be a monetary item and therefore some recognition of this fact should be given. This is done by not recognising any gains in the profit and loss account except to the extent that they offset previously recognised losses. On the grounds of prudence any excess gains would be treated as a deferred credit as they may not ultimately be realised if the bonds are converted.

Although we would prefer option 4, in our view there are good arguments for all of the above options and therefore probably all of them are acceptable.

It would appear that such bonds are commonly treated as monetary items as they are retranslated at closing rates of exchange. However, frequently the cover method (see 2.3.7 and 2.4.5 above) is applied and the exchange differences on the bonds are taken to reserves and not reflected in the profit or loss for the year.[80] London & Scottish Marine Oil PLC in fact used to translate their convertible bonds at the fixed rate of exchange but changed their accounting policy in 1987.

Extract 18.14: London & Scottish Marine Oil PLC[81]

1   Restatement of prior years
In the past, the liability under the 9 1/4 per cent Convertible Bonds Due 1999 (which are denominated in US dollars, and are convertible into ordinary shares at the option of the bond holders) was translated into sterling at the fixed exchange rate contained in the conditions of the Bonds. To reflect more accurately the liability prior to conversion, the liability has been translated at the exchange rate current at the balance sheet date. Prior years have been restated to reflect the above.

3.1.5   Treatment of exchange differences

The general rule of SSAP 20 is that all exchange differences on monetary items should be recognised as part of the profit or loss for the year.[82] Apart from the possible treatment of gains on long-term monetary items (see 2.3.6 above) and the treatment of exchange differences on borrowings financing, or hedging against, foreign equity investments (see 2.3.7 above) are there any other circumstances where it is possible for exchange differences not to be taken as part of the profit or loss for the year?

A   Capitalisation of exchange differences

On many occasions where a UK company is acquiring an asset (other than an equity investment) from overseas it finances the acquisition by means of a foreign loan. The general rules of SSAP 20 require the asset to be translated at historical rates and for the loan to be translated at closing rates.[83] Consequently, exchange differences on the loan are taken to profit and loss account with no offsetting exchange difference on the asset. One means of avoiding this situation is if the asset and liability can be regarded as a foreign branch as discussed in 2.4.7 above. However, it will not always be possible to regard them as such and therefore consideration has to be given to any other way in which the exchange differences on the loan need not be taken to the profit or loss for the year.

In our view the only other possible circumstance is where the asset is still in the course of production. The Companies Act 1985 requires assets to be included at their purchase price or production cost.[84] Production cost can include indirect overheads attributable to the production of the asset to the extent that they relate to the period of production[85] (see 2 of Chapter 10 for a fuller discussion of these requirements). One of the overheads that the Companies Act 1985 specifically allows to be included is interest on borrowings.[86] It is often argued that exchange differences on foreign borrowings are really part of the interest cost of the foreign borrowing. A UK company may take out a borrowing in a 'hard' currency, e.g. Swiss franc, rather than in sterling so as to benefit from the low interest rate. However, as this lower interest charge is likely to be offset by exchange losses on the borrowing then these losses should be treated as part of the interest cost of the borrowing. Indeed, paragraph 68 of the standard suggests that exchange differences on borrowings should be disclosed as part of 'other interest receivable/payable and similar income/expense' in the profit and loss account. As a result we believe that exchange differences on foreign currency loans should be capitalised as part of the cost of the asset when interest costs on the same borrowings are being capitalised. Capitalisation of borrowing costs is discussed more fully in Chapter 12. Where such a treatment is being adopted then similar disclosure to that of the interest costs shown in 4.2 of that chapter should be given for the exchange differences on the borrowings. However, as it is possible to adopt a policy of not capitalising borrowing costs, then even if the interest costs are not being capitalised we believe it is acceptable to capitalise the exchange differences on the borrowings which arise during the period of production.

B   Hedging transactions — deferment of exchange differences

The only specific reference which SSAP 20 makes to hedging is in respect of foreign currency borrowings providing a hedge against its foreign currency equity investments.[87] It also allows transactions to be recorded at the rate specified in a related forward contract,[88] which is another way of hedging. A further method by which companies may hedge against a foreign currency exposure is by matching foreign currency debtors in one currency with creditors in the same currency. By requiring the exchange differences on both these items to be taken to profit and loss account then SSAP 20 recognises this matching. However, what happens if one of the items is only a commitment (e.g. an agreement to purchase a fixed asset) and is still to be recognised in the accounts?

Example 18.12

A UK company has a debtor of US$1m resulting from a sale on March 1, 19X1 and expects to receive payment on March 31, 19X1. On March 15, 19X1 the company signs a contract for the purchase of a fixed asset for US$1m from a US company. The asset is due to be delivered on April 15, 19X1 with payment due on May 31, 19X1. Rather than entering into a forward contract for the purchase of the US$1m to fix the sterling cost of the asset the company decides on March 15, 19X1 that it will retain the US$1m once it is received from the debtor in a US$ bank account as a hedge against the cost of the fixed asset. Is it possible for the company to freeze the debtor at the rate ruling on March 15, 19X1 and record the asset at the same amount? If not, can the exchange differences on the debtor and the bank balance be deferred and included in recording the cost of the asset?

It would appear that under SSAP 20 the answer to both questions is no. The debtor and bank balance are monetary items requiring to be translated at closing rates and the exchange differences on the settlement of the debtor and the bank balance taken to profit and loss account. The fixed asset should be recorded at the rate ruling at the date of the transaction. i.e. the date of delivery. It could be argued that this is illogical as the company could have entered into two forward contracts on March 15, 19X1, one to buy US$1m to fix the cost of the fixed asset and one to sell US$1m to fix the amount to be received, and therefore have achieved what it wished.

SFAS 52 recognises this illogicality by requiring not only exchange gains and losses on a forward contract that is intended to hedge an identifiable foreign currency commitment to be deferred and included in the cost of the related foreign currency transaction but also those which arise on other foreign currency transactions, e.g. cash balances, which are intended to hedge an identifiable foreign currency commitment.[89] This is because the accounting for the transaction should reflect the economic hedge of the foreign currency commitment.[90] Losses should not be deferred, however, if it is estimated that deferral would lead to recognising losses in later periods.[91] The requirements of SFAS 52 relating to forward contracts are more fully discussed in 3.3 below.

One company which does adopt such a policy and retains deposits held to meet commitments for capital expenditure at historical rates of exchange is Cable and Wireless plc.

Extract 18.15: Cable and Wireless plc[92]

C Foreign currencies [extract]
Foreign currency deposits held to meet known commitments for capital expenditure are translated at rates of exchange at the date of purchase of such deposits.

3.2 Exchange gains on long-term monetary items

Paragraphs 11 and 50 of SSAP 20 indicate that where there are doubts as to the convertibility or marketability of the currency in question then it may be necessary to consider on the grounds of prudence whether the amount of any exchange gain, or the amount by which exchange gains exceed past exchange losses on the same items, to be recognised in the profit and loss account should be restricted.

3.2.1 In what circumstances do 'doubts as to convertibility or marketability' arise?

Such circumstances do not include normal currency fluctuations after the year end or even devaluations of a foreign currency after the year end.[93] It is thought that such circumstances will be rare and would only arise when there is political upheaval or very stringent exchange control regulations in the country whose currency is being considered.[94]

Such events will probably only arise in those countries whose currencies are weakest and therefore UK companies are unlikely to have liabilities expressed in the foreign currency on which exchange gains would arise. Even if a UK company did have a liability expressed in such a currency why should it not recognise the gain? It is unlikely that the UK company would have to pay more than the foreign currency amount at the closing rate and if anything is likely to pay less as the foreign currency will probably continue to weaken.

It is more likely that UK companies will have amounts receivable in these foreign currencies and therefore exchange losses are likely to arise. If for some reason such a currency were to strengthen against sterling so that exchange gains did arise on the amounts receivable the restriction of exchange gains suggested by SSAP 20 is irrelevant in these circumstances. If these circumstances did apply then it will probably be necessary for a UK company to make provision against all amounts receivable in that currency, whether short-term or long-term, to reduce them to their expected recoverable amounts.

If it is considered that the restriction of exchange gains contained in SSAP 20 is sufficient to deal with the situation, there are a number of problem areas relating to the accounting for the restriction.

3.2.2   Past exchange losses

Paragraph 50 of the standard states that 'the amount of the gain, or the amount by which exchange gains exceed past exchange losses on the same items to be recognised in the profit and loss account should be restricted'. It is unclear whether this means that where there have been past exchange losses on the same item a company has the option of restricting either the whole amount of the gain arising in the year or only the excess over the past losses. In our view the proper interpretation of this paragraph is that past losses are to be taken into account in determining the amount to be restricted.

3.2.3   Settled or unsettled transactions

The part of paragraph 50 quoted above refers to past exchange losses on the 'same items'. This is clearly meant to stop companies taking into account past exchange losses on unrelated items. However, what if part of a transaction has been settled and only part of it remains unsettled? If a realised loss arose on the part that was settled can this be taken into account in determining the amount of the gain on the unsettled portion to be restricted? In our view as the gain only relates to the unsettled portion then only past exchange losses on that portion should be taken into account in determining the amount to be restricted.

3.2.4   Current portion of long-term item

Paragraph 50 of the standard only relates to long-term items. What happens, therefore, where a company has an amount receivable part of which is due within one year of the balance sheet date and part which does not? It could be argued that all of the item should be regarded as a long-term item and therefore all of the exchange gain is to be restricted. However, this would mean that the current portion would be treated differently from any other amount receivable in that same currency within one year. It could therefore be argued that the current portion should be excluded and it is only the non-current portion which is the long-term item. It is only the exchange gain on that part which is restricted and the exchange gain on the current portion has to be taken to the profit or loss for the year. In our view it is illogical to treat the gains differently and if it is necessary in the circumstances envisaged by the standard for exchange gains on long-term items expressed in one currency to be excluded from the profit and loss account on the grounds of prudence then a similar treatment should be adopted for short-term items in the same currency.

3.2.5   *Restriction of gain*

It is not clear from the standard how gains in these circumstances should be restricted. Three possible treatments would be:

(a)   subtract the gain from the monetary item, i.e. effectively translate it at the historical rate; or

(b)   credit the gain to a deferral account; or

(c)   credit the gain directly to reserves.

In our opinion, treatment (b) is to be preferred as it treats the item as a monetary amount and excludes the gain from the net equity of the company. However, we consider that the other treatments are acceptable as they achieve the objective of paragraph 50 of the standard by excluding gains which ultimately may not be realised from the profit or loss for the year.

3.3   Forward contracts, currency swaps and currency options

In view of the volatility of exchange rates nowadays many companies are entering into such transactions to protect themselves from the potentially adverse effects of foreign currency rate movements. As indicated in 2.3.8 above, SSAP 20 only mentions forward contracts very briefly and does not say anything about currency swaps or currency options. How should companies therefore account for them?

3.3.1   *Forward contracts*

A   *What are forward contracts?*

A forward contract is an agreement to exchange different currencies at a specified future date and at a specified rate.[95] A contract will normally be for a fixed period; e.g. one month, three months, six months, from the date of entering the contract. The rate under the contract is not an estimate of what the exchange rate will be at the end of the contract but is essentially a function of:

(a)   the spot rate at the date the contract is taken out; and

(b)   the interest rate differential between the two countries.

This is illustrated in the following example:

Example 18.13

On March 31, 19X1 a UK company wishes to enter into a forward contract to buy US$1m in six months' time. Ignoring any profit which the bank would take on the transaction the rate under contract would be calculated as if the bank had on March 31, 19X1 :

    (i)   sold the company an amount of US dollars at the spot rate on that date, which would yield a total of US$1m in six months' time;

    (ii)   placed the amount of US dollars in (i) above on deposit for the company; and

    (iii)   lent the company the amount of sterling in (i) above repayable, with interest, in six months' time.

At March 31, 19X1 the spot rate is £1=US$1.888 and the US dollar and sterling interest rates are 7%p.a. and 8.75%p.a. respectively.

The amount of US dollars which the bank would 'sell' to the company would be US$966,184. Interest on the 'deposit' at 7%p.a. for six months would be US$33,816 which would mean that the company would be entitled to US$1m in six months' time.

The amount of sterling 'lent' to the company would be £511,750. Interest on this loan at 8.75%p.a. for the six months would be £22,389 and therefore the company would have to pay £534,139 at the end of the six months.

This cost of £534,139 for the US$1m gives an exchange rate of £1.872.

Normally, forward contract rates are not quoted as single figures in the UK but are quoted as being either at a discount or premium on the spot rate. To arrive at the contract rate a discount is *added* to the spot rate and a premium is *deducted* from the spot rate.

B   *Reasons for companies taking out forward contracts*

In most situations companies enter into a forward contract to protect themselves from the risks of exchange rate variations. This will normally be done to hedge:

(a)   a future commitment or transaction which will require the purchase or sale of foreign currency; or

(b)   an existing foreign currency monetary asset or liability; or

(c)   an investment in a foreign enterprise, such as an overseas subsidiary; or

(d)   the results of a foreign enterprise.

In the first two situations a company is hedging the transaction to fix the amount of cash in sterling terms which will be required, whereas in the other two situations a company is hedging to offset the effect of translating the investment or results of the foreign enterprise.

In addition, companies may also enter into a forward contract by way of speculation in the hope that they can make a profit out of doing so.

In our view the accounting for forward contracts should be based on the economic rationale for the company entering into the contract in the first place and therefore will be different in each of these situations. We will now look at how this can be done by considering examples of each of these situations.

C   *Forward contracts taken out to hedge future commitments or transactions*

Example 18.14

On September 30, 19X0 a UK company contracts to buy an item of plant and machinery from a US company for US$500,000, with delivery on January 31, 19X1 and payment due on March 31, 19X1. In order to hedge against the movements in exchange rates it enters into a forward contract on September 30, 19X0 to buy US$500,000 in six months' time. The premium on such a contract is US$0.02 and based on the spot rate of £1=US$1.63 gives a contracted rate of £1=US$1.61.

The relevant spot rates are:

	£1=US$
December 31, 19X0	1.88
January 31, 19X1	1.77
March 31, 19X1	1.89

How should the company account for these transactions in its financial statements for the years ended December 31, 19X0 and December 31, 19X1?

There are two basic methods:

(i) Record the asset and the liability at January 31, 19X1 at £310,559 being US$500,000 translated at the contracted rate of £1=US$1.61. No exchange loss would be recognised on the forward contract in either year and no exchange gain on the liability to the supplier would be recognised in the year ended December 31, 19X1. This treatment is straightforward and reflects the fact that the company has eliminated all currency risks by entering into the forward contract.

It could however be argued that such a treatment is not allowed by SSAP 20. Paragraph 46 of the standard only refers to *trading* transactions being translated at rates specified in related forward contracts. Trading transactions are not defined in SSAP 20 and a narrow interpretation would preclude capital transactions, such as the purchase of fixed assets, from being so treated. However, it would appear that some companies adopt a wider interpretation as indicated in 3.3.1 D below. We concur with such an interpretation.

(ii) The forward contract and the acquisition of the asset are accounted for as two separate transactions. The asset and the liability to the supplier are initially recorded at January 31, 19X1 at £282,486 (US$500,000 @ 1.77). An exchange gain on the amount due to the supplier up to the date of payment of £17,936, being £264,550 (US$500,000 @ 1.89) less £282,486, is recognised in the profit and loss account for the year ended December 31, 19X1.

The exchange difference on the forward contract up to the transaction date is not recognised in the profit and loss account but is deferred and included in the recorded amount of the asset. Thereafter, any exchange difference on the contract is matched against the exchange difference on the liability to the supplier. Accordingly, although there is an exchange loss on the contract at December 31, 19X0 of £40,792, being £306,749 (US$500,000 @ 1.63) less £265,957 (US$500,000 @ 1.88) this is not recognised in the profit and loss account but is deferred. In 19X1 there is an exchange gain on the contract up to the date of the transaction on January 31, 19X1 of £16,529, being £282,486 (US$500,000 @ 1.77) less £265,957. Again, this is not recognised in the profit and loss account. This gain together with the loss previously deferred is included in recording the asset. Accordingly, the asset is recorded at £306,749 (£282,486 + £40,792 − £16,529). This is equivalent to the asset being recorded at the spot rate ruling when the forward contract was entered into.

Following the transaction date there is an exchange loss on the forward contract of £17,936 which should be taken to the profit and loss account. It can be seen that this will offset the exchange gain on the amount due to the supplier in the same period and therefore reflects the fact that the company had hedged its exposure to exchange differences.

In addition to the exchange difference on the forward contract, recognition has to be given to the premium on the contract, i.e. the difference between the contracted amount translated at the contracted rate and translated at the spot rate when the contract was taken out. In this case the premium is £3,810 being £310,559 (US$500,000 @ 1.61) less £306,749 (US$500,000 @ 1.63). As this premium essentially represents an interest cost (see Example 18.13 above) over the period of the contract then this should be amortised over that period as a finance charge. Accordingly, £1,905 would be charged to the profit and loss account in the year ended December 31, 19X0 and £1,905 in the following year. This second method is that suggested by SFAS 52.[96]

We believe that both of these methods are acceptable but would recommend that companies adopt the approach suggested in SFAS 52 as outlined in (ii) above. However, it should be borne in mind that where an exchange loss on the forward contract arises it should not be deferred if it would lead to recognising losses in later periods.[97] An alternative treatment allowed by SFAS 52 for the premium or discount on a contract which hedges a future commitment or transaction is to include that proportion of the premium or discount which relates to the commitment period, i.e. up to the date of the transaction, as part of the transaction.[98]

It should be noted that the treatment discussed in the second method in the above example is only allowed by SFAS 52 if the contract is designated as a hedge and the foreign currency commitment is firm.[99] Accordingly, if in the above example the company had not contracted for the plant and machinery at September 30, 19X0 but it was only their intention at that date to enter into such contract then the US standard would not have allowed deferral of any of the exchange differences on the forward contract prior to contracting for the plant. We believe that in the UK it is unnecessary for such a stringent test to be applied and the treatment can be applied where a company has a reasonable expectation of entering into the transaction.

D   *Forward contracts taken out to hedge an existing foreign currency monetary asset or liability*

Example 18.15

Suppose the UK company in the previous example enters into the same forward contract. However, this time it does so because it has an existing loan of US$500,000 which is due for repayment on March 31, 19X1 and wishes to hedge against any further exchange risk.

How should the forward contract and the loan be treated in the financial statements for the years ended December 31, 19X0 and December 31, 19X1?

There are three basic methods:

(i) Translate the loan at the contracted rate of £1=US$1.61, i.e. £310,559. The difference between this amount and the recorded amount at September 30, 19X0 based on the spot rate at that date, i.e. £306,749, is written off in the profit and loss account for the year ended December 31, 19X0 along with the previous exchange differences on the loan. No amounts are recorded in the profit and loss account for the year ended December 31, 19X1.

(ii) Again, translate the loan at the contracted rate. However, as the difference of £3,810 (£310,559 less £306,749) represents the premium on the contract then it is deferred and amortised over the period of the contract. Accordingly, £1,905 is charged in the profit and loss account for the year ended December 31, 19X0 and £1,905 in the following year.

It has been suggested that the treatment of the loans in each of these methods is not allowed by SSAP 20 as loans are not trading transactions.[100] However, we believe this to be a narrow interpretation of the standard and it would appear that companies do translate loans at rates specified in forward contracts. (see Extracts 18.16 and 18.17 below)

(iii) Treat the loan and the forward contract as two separate transactions. The loan is translated at the closing rate at December 31, 19X0 and the exchange difference thereon is taken to profit and loss account. This exchange difference will include an exchange gain of £40,792 for the period from September 30, 19X0 to December 31, 19X0, being £306,749 (US$500,000 @ 1.63) less £265,957 (US$500,000 @ 1.88). The forward contract should also be regarded as a foreign currency transaction on which an exchange difference arises. SSAP 20 does not make this clear. However, it is clear from SFAS 52 that a forward contract is a foreign currency transaction.[101] Accordingly, an exchange loss of £40,792 on the contract should be recognised in the profit and loss account for the year ended December 31, 19X0. This will offset the gain on the loan and therefore the results will not be affected by exchange differences from September 30, 19X0, which was the purpose of taking out the contract. In the profit and loss account for the year ended December 31, 19X1 a further exchange gain of £1,407, being £265,957 less £264,550 (US$500,000 @ 1.89) will be recognised on the loan offset by an equivalent exchange loss on the forward contract. As in method (ii) the premium on the contract would be amortised over the period of the contract. This method is that required by SFAS 52.[102]

We believe that all three methods are acceptable but would recommend that companies adopt method (iii). However, it would appear that at least some companies are translating loans at contracted rates as the following extract shows:

Extract 18.16: British Airways Plc[103]

FOREIGN CURRENCY BALANCES [extract]
Foreign currency balances are translated into sterling at the rates ruling at the balance sheet date except for certain loan repayment instalments which, at the balance sheet date, have been covered forward and are translated at the forward contract rates.

E   Forward contracts taken out to hedge a foreign currency investment

Example 18.16

A UK company has a US subsidiary which had net assets of US$1m at December 31, 19X0. On that date the UK company enters into a forward contract to sell US$400,000 in six months' time as a means of partially hedging against the investment in the subsidiary. The premium on such a contract is US$0.04 and based on the spot rate of £1=US$1.48 gives a contracted rate of £1=US$1.44. On maturity of the contract the company buys US$400,000 at the spot rate in order to fulfil the contract. At that time it decides not to enter into another forward contract.

The relevant spot rates are:

	£1=US$
June 30, 19X1	1.61
December 31, 19X1	1.88

The exchange difference on the net investment in the subsidiary taken to reserves in the consolidated financial statements for the year ended December 31, 19X1 will be a loss of £143,762, being £675,677 (US$1m @ 1.48) less £531,915 (US$1m @ 1.88), of which £54,559 relates to the six months to June 30, 19X1.

The overall gain which the company has made on the contract is £29,331 being £277,778 (US$400,000 @ 1.44) less £248,447 (US$400,000 @ 1.61). This gain represents the exchange gain on the contract of £21,823, being £270,270 (US$400,000 @ 1.48) less £248,447, and the premium of £7,508 (£277,778 less £270,270).

How should the forward contract be accounted for in the consolidated financial statements for the year ended December 31, 19X1?

(i) It could be argued that all of the gain of £29,331 should be reflected in the profit and loss account. This is based on the fact that SSAP 20 only refers to forward contracts in the context of recording related transactions or monetary items. In this case there is no corresponding transaction or monetary item. However, this fails to recognise the rationale for entering into the contract which was to hedge against exchange rate movements on the investment in the subsidiary.

(ii) In order to recognise the rationale for entering into the contract, the exchange gain of £21,823 should be taken to reserves to be offset against the exchange loss on the investment. This will reflect the fact that the exchange loss on the investment for the six months to June 30, 19X1 of £54,559 was hedged to the extent of 40%. The premium of £7,508 should be reflected in the profit and loss account.

The effect of such a treatment is similar to that which would have arisen if the company had decided to hedge the investment by borrowing US$400,000 for six months and investing the proceeds in a sterling deposit for the same period.

This second method is essentially that required by SFAS 52.[104] An alternative treatment for the premium would be to take it to reserves in addition to the exchange gain on the contract which is an option allowed by SFAS 52.[105]

In the absence of specific requirements in SSAP 20, we believe that both methods are acceptable although we would recommend that companies adopt the second method as it more fairly recognises the rationale for entering into the contract.

F   *Forward contracts taken out to hedge the results of a foreign currency*
       investment

Example 18.17

Suppose in the previous example the company took out the forward contract not as a hedge
against the net investment in the subsidiary but against the expected profits of the subsidiary for
the year ended December 31, 19X1. The company normally translates the results of the
subsidiary at closing rates. The actual profits of the subsidiary were US$500,000, all of which
were retained by the subsidiary.

How should the company account for the results of the subsidiary and the forward contract?

(i) The profits of the subsidiary should be translated at the closing rate and, therefore, included as
£265,957 (US$500,000 @ 1.88). The total gain on the contract of £29,331 should also be
included in the profit and loss account. This will, therefore, reflect the fact that the company
hedged against the effects of movements in the exchange rate up to June 30, 19X1 on the results
but not for exchange rate movements after that date.

(ii) That part of the profits covered by the forward contract should be translated at the contracted
rate and the balance translated at the closing rate. This would mean that the profits included
would be as follows:

	£
US$400,000 @ 1.44 =	277,778
US$100,000 @ 1.88 =	53,191
	330,969

It can be seen that this is greater than the total profits arrived at under (i) above by £35,681. It
will therefore be necessary to charge losses of a similar amount as a movement in reserves. This
amount represents the loss on exchange on the US$400,000, which has been translated at the
contracted rate, as a result of retaining those profits in the subsidiary from June 30, 19X1 until
December 31, 19X1, being £248,447 (US$400,000 @ 1.61) less £212,766 (US$400,000 @
1.88).

It could be argued that this method is not allowed by SSAP 20 as it is only *transactions* of
individual companies which can be translated at rates specified in forward contracts and the
translation of the results of subsidiaries for the purposes of consolidation is not a transaction.
Another argument against this method is that it is effectively translating some of the results at
an 'average' rate and some at the closing rate.

For these reasons we believe method (i) to be more appropriate, particularly
where companies normally translate results of foreign subsidiaries at closing rates
and the forward contract only covers part of the period.

Where companies translate the results of subsidiaries at an average rate or the
contract covers the full period of the results then using method (ii) will be
acceptable. If in the above example the contract had been for the full year then the
overall gain on the contract would have been £65,012, being £277,778 less
£212,766 (US$400,000 @ 1.88). Accordingly, both methods would have
yielded the same overall profit of £330,969.

Where a forward contract is taken out towards a year end with the intention of
hedging the remainder of a subsidiary's results for the current year and its

expected results for the following year then that part of the exchange difference on the contract which relates to the current year's results should be taken to the profit and loss account and the remainder deferred until the following year. The premium should preferably be amortised over the period of the contract.

It can be seen from Examples 18.16 and 18.17 above that different treatments for the contract arise depending on what the contract is supposed to be hedging; the net investment or the results of the investment. For this reason it is particularly important that the company recognises at the time of taking out the contract the reason for doing so.

One company which appears to translate the results of subsidiaries at contracted rates is Smith & Nephew Associated Companies plc as the following extract from their accounting policy indicates:

Extract 18.17: Smith & Nephew Associated Companies plc[106]

Foreign currencies [extract]
Profits and losses of overseas subsidiaries and related companies are translated at the average rates for the year, except where profits and losses are matched with forward currency transactions.

G   Speculative forward contracts

Example 18.18

A UK company enters into a forward contract on September 30, 19X0 to sell US$500,000 in six months' time in the hope that it will make a profit out of doing so. It has no monetary liabilities in US dollars and is not planning to enter into any transaction which requires US dollars.

The relevant spot rates are:

	£1=US$
September 30, 19X0	1.63
December 31, 19X0	1.88

The premium on the contract is US$0.02, giving a contracted rate of £1=US$1.61. At December 31, 19X0 the company still has the contract. The premium on three month contracts at that date is US$0.01 giving a contract rate of £=US$1.87.

How should the company account for the contract in its financial statements for the year ended December 31, 19X0?

There are three possible methods:

(i) Record an exchange gain of £40,792, being £306,749 (US$500,000 @ 1.63) less £265,957 (US$500,000 @ 1.88). In addition, recognise the proportion of the premium of £3,810, being £310,559 (US$500,000 @ 1.61) less £306,749 which relates to the period up to December,19X0, i.e. £1,905. This is the same treatment which has been recommended if the contract had been taken out to hedge an amount of US$500,000 receivable on March 30, 19X1. However, as in this case the reason for taking out the contract was speculative then it is likely that a company will 'close' such a contract at such time either when it considers that it has made the maximum profit it will make or to cut its losses. Rather than deferring the premium to a period where the contract may be closed out, an alternative approach is not to give any separate recognition to the premium but to recognise the gain or loss on the contract based on its 'realisable value'.

(ii) One method of doing this would be to record a gain of £44,602, being £310,559 (US$500,000 @1.61) less £265,957. This represents the difference between the sterling amount receivable under the contract and the dollar amount translated at the spot rate. This effectively assumes that the company could buy the required amount of foreign currency at the spot rate on the balance sheet date and therefore fix the gain at that amount. However, this ignores the cost of holding the currency until the contract matures.

(iii) The method which overcomes the deficiencies in the other two methods is to record a gain of £43,179, being £310,559 less £267,380 (US$500,000 @ 1.87). This effectively represents the difference between the sterling amount receivable under the contract less the amount it would cost to take out an equal and opposite forward contract to buy US$500,000 on the date the existing contract matures. This method is that required by SFAS 52.[107]

In the absence of detailed requirements in SSAP 20 we believe that all three methods are acceptable although we would recommend that companies adopt method (iii) above.

H   Conclusion

It can be seen from the above examples that different treatments of a forward contract are possible depending on the reason for entering into the contract in the first place. It is therefore important that companies should establish the reason for so doing prior to or at the same time as entering into the contract.

The methods recommended, and the other suggested possibilities, in each of the above examples follow the general principle in SSAP 20 that there should be symmetry of treatment of exchange gains and losses and should meet the objectives of translation contained in the standard. However, as there are no specific requirements relating to forward contracts in the standard then it may be possible that other treatments such as recognising losses but not profits on such contracts or treating them as 'commitments' are acceptable. Where such alternative treatments are adopted then the policy adopted should be disclosed and details of the financial commitments under the contracts will probably be required to meet the requirements of the Companies Act.[108]

3.3.2   Currency swaps

Another way in which companies can hedge against the risk of exchange rate movements is by entering into currency swaps. SSAP 20 makes no reference to such agreements and therefore the question arises as to how these should be accounted for. As currency swaps are essentially similar in nature to forward contracts then we believe that they should be accounted for in the same way as we have suggested for forward contracts above. Indeed, SFAS 52 states that 'agreements that are , in substance, essentially the same as forward contracts, for example, currency swaps, shall be accounted for in a manner similar to the accounting for forward contracts'.[109]

Most companies who have entered into currency swaps appear to do so to hedge against foreign currency borrowings and translate their borrowings at the swap rate. For example:

Extract 18.18: The British Petroleum Company p.l.c.[110]

22 Finance debt [extract]
Borrowings which are swapped into currencies other than the original currencies of denomination are recorded as liabilities in the currencies under the swap contracts.

One company which has entered into currency swaps to hedge against the results of its foreign subsidiaries is Booker plc:

Extract 18.19: Booker plc[111]

TRANSLATION OF FOREIGN CURRENCIES [extract]
The group's 1987 net US$ earnings were hedged under currency swap transactions. The effective rate at which the trading results of US companies were translated was $1.54=£1.

Normally, the results of the subsidiaries would have been translated at the closing rate which was $1.88=£1.

3.3.3 Currency options

Where companies use forward contracts and currency swaps to hedge against exchange risks they eliminate not only the risk of exchange losses but also the possibility of exchange gains. One way that companies can eliminate the 'downside' of exchange losses but still participate in the 'upside' of exchange gains is to enter into currency options. As the name suggests these give companies the *right* to buy or sell foreign currency on or by a certain date in the future at a specified rate, but they are not *obliged* to do so. A company which purchases an option will have to pay a premium at the outset. The amount of the premium will depend on:

(a) the current spot rate;

(b) the specified rate (generally referred to as the strike price);

(c) the period to the expiry of the option; and

(d) the volatility of the exchange rate.

How should companies account for currency options?

SSAP 20 makes no reference to currency options at all. Due to the nature of currency options it is not really possible to translate transactions or monetary items in foreign currencies at the rates ruling under related currency options as they may never be exercised. Accordingly, it will be necessary to account for the currency option and any related transaction, asset or liability separately.

In accounting for the currency option it must be remembered that the maximum loss that the company can make is the cost of the premium.There are essentially two ways of calculating the gain or loss on a currency option:

(i) The premium paid for the option should initially be recorded as an asset. At a subsequent balance sheet date this should be revalued to the current premium for the currency option, known as 'marking to market'. If the exchange rate has moved such that it is likely that the currency option will be exercised then the premium will have increased. This increase will represent the gain that the company can make by closing out the option. If the exchange rate has moved such that it is unlikely that the currency option will be exercised then the premium will have decreased. If the time remaining to the expiry date is short then the premium is likely to be a nominal sum. This decrease will represent the loss on the option.

(ii) Again the premium is initially recorded as an asset. At a subsequent balance sheet date the currency amount under the option is translated at the current rate. If this shows an exchange gain when compared to the rate under the option then this gain is recognised. However, it will then be necessary to offset against this gain the cost of the option. If the comparison with the spot rate shows a loss exceeding the amount of the premium then the premium paid should be written off. If the loss is less than the premium paid then the premium should be written off to the extent of the loss.

These methods can be illustrated in the following example:

Example 18.19

On February 17, 19X1 a UK company records a debtor of US$2,250,000 which it is due to receive on April 30, 19X1. The exchange rate at February 17, 19X1 is £1=US$1.75 and the debtor is recorded at £1,285,714. The company decides to take out some April call option contracts at a strike price of US$1.80 in order to provide a hedge against the debtor. Accordingly, it takes out 100 contracts of £12,500 on the London Stock Exchange at a premium of US$0.0145 per £1. The total premium paid is £10,357 (being 100 x £12,500 x US$0.0145 =US$18,125 @ £1=US$1.75).

At March 31, 19X1, the company's balance sheet date, the debtor is translated at the exchange rate ruling on that date of £1=US$1.89 at £1,190,476, thereby recording an exchange loss of £95,238.

At March 31, 19X1 the premium on April call option contracts is now US$ 0.095 per £1. Accordingly, under method (i) above, the gain on the option contracts is as follows:

Premium at March 31, 19X1 — 100 x £12,500 x US$0.095 = US$118,750 @ 1.89 = £62,831

Less premium paid	10,357
Gain on option contracts	£52,474

Under method (ii) above the gain is as follows:

Currency amount of contracts = 100 x £12,500 x US$1.80 =   US$ 2,250,000

Amount receivable at option rate —	US$2,250,000 @ 1.80 = £1,250,000	
Amount receivable at current rate —	US$2,250,000 @ 1.89 = £1,190,476	
Exchange gain on option contracts		£ 59,524
Less premium paid		10,357
Gain on option contracts		£ 49,167

In the absence of detailed guidance in SSAP 20, we believe either method of calculation is acceptable, although we would recommend that the first method be adopted if possible as the gain or loss recognises the 'time value' contained in the premium.

The accounting for such gains or losses on the currency options should essentially follow the same principles as those outlined for forward contracts in 3.3.1 above and will again depend on the reason for taking out the currency option.

3.4   Consolidated accounts — closing rate/net investment method

3.4.1   Subsidiary with non-coterminous year end

It is sometimes the case that UK companies consolidate the financial statements of foreign subsidiaries made up to a date which is not coterminous with the year end of the parent company. Where the results of the subsidiary are consolidated using the closing rate/net investment method the question then arises — which closing rate is to be used? The rate applying to the subsidiary's balance sheet date or the one applying to the parent company's balance sheet date?

SSAP 20 makes no reference to which one it should be. However, guidance can be drawn from SFAS 52 which states that the rate to be used is the one in effect at the date of the subsidiary's balance sheet.[112] The reason for this is that this presents the functional currency performance of the subsidiary during the subsidiary's financial year and its position at the end of that period in terms of the parent company's reporting currency.[113] The subsidiary may have entered into transactions in other currencies, including sterling, and monetary items in these currencies will have been translated using rates ruling at the subsidiary's balance sheet date. The profit and loss account of the subsidiary will reflect the economic consequences of carrying out these transactions during the period ended on that date. In order that the effects of these transactions in the subsidiary's financial statements are not distorted, the financial statements should be translated using the closing rate at the subsidiary's balance sheet date.

An alternative argument can be advanced for using the closing rate ruling at the parent company's balance sheet date. All subsidiaries within a group should normally prepare financial statements up to the same date as the parent company so that the parent company can prepare consolidated accounts which show a true and fair view of the state of affairs of the group at the parent company's balance sheet date and of the results of the group for the period then ended. The use of financial statements of a subsidiary made up to a date earlier than that of the parent is only an administrative convenience and must be recognised as being a surrogate for financial statements made up to the proper date. In view of this the closing rate which should be used is that which would have been used if the financial statements were made up to the proper date, i.e. that ruling at the date of the balance sheet date of the parent company. Another reason for using this rate is that there may be subsidiaries who have the same functional currency who make up their financial statements to the same date as the parent company and therefore in order to be consistent it is necessary for the same rate to be used.

We believe that both treatments are acceptable. In many cases where companies have such subsidiaries it is unclear from their accounting policies which treatment is adopted as they just refer to the financial statements being translated at the 'closing rate'. However, it would appear that where companies do make it clear which treatment is adopted the use of the rate ruling at the parent company's balance sheet date is favoured. Two companies which have subsidiaries with non-coterminous year ends and would appear to use such a rate are Blue Circle Industries PLC and Imperial Chemical Industries PLC. Extracts from their accounting polices are illustrated below:

Extract 18.20: Blue Circle Industries PLC[114]

4 Foreign currency [extract]
Profit and loss accounts in foreign currencies are translated into sterling at average rates for the year.
Assets and liabilities in foreign currencies are translated into sterling at the rates of exchange ruling at 31 December.

Extract 18.21: Imperial Chemical Industries PLC[115]

FOREIGN CURRENCIES [extract]
Profit and loss accounts in foreign currencies are translated into sterling at average rates for the relevant accounting period. Assets and liabilities are translated at exchange rates ruling at the date of the Group balance sheet.

3.4.2 *Dual rates or suspension of rates*

The problems of dual rates and suspension of rates in relation to the accounts of an individual company have already been discussed in 3.1.3 above and many of the points made in that section apply equally to the consolidated accounts.

SSAP 20 makes no reference to what should happen when applying the closing rate/net investment method when there is more than one exchange rate for a particular currency. Again, guidance can be sought from SFAS 52 which states that the rate to be used to translate foreign statements should be, in the absence of unusual circumstances, the rate applicable to dividend remittances.[116] The reason for this is that the use of that rate is more meaningful than any other rate because cash flows to the parent company from the foreign enterprise can be converted only at that rate, and realisation of a net investment in the foreign enterprise will ultimately be in the form of cash flows from that enterprise.[117]

As mentioned in 3.1.3 above one currency where there are dual rates is the South African rand. One company with subsidiaries in South Africa is Consolidated Gold Fields PLC. They use the commercial rand, which is applicable to dividend remittances, for translating the financial statements of their South African subsidiaries as indicated by the relevant rates of exchange disclosed in their accounting policy as illustrated below:

Extract 18.22: Consolidated Gold Fields PLC[118]

Foreign currencies [extract]

Rates used include:	1988		1987	
	average	30 June	average	30 June
Australia	$2.418	$2.161	$2.300	$2.237
South Africa	R3.666	R3.962	R3.330	R3.302
United States	$1.761	$1.708	$1.529	$1.613

Another company which appears to use the commercial rand in translating the financial statements of their South African subsidiaries is The Rio Tinto-Zinc Corporation PLC.[119]

3.4.3   *Calculation of average rate*

Paragraph 54 of SSAP 20 allows the profit and loss account of foreign enterprises to be translated at an average rate for the period. No definitive method of calculating the average rate has been prescribed and all the standard says is that 'the average rate used should be calculated by the method considered most appropriate for the circumstances of the foreign enterprise'. It does, however, give some guidance on the factors to be taken into account in determining what is most appropriate — 'Factors that will need to be considered include the company's internal accounting procedures and the extent of seasonal trade variations; the use of a weighting procedure will in most cases be desirable.'[120] What methods are, therefore, available to companies to use? Possible methods might be:

(a)   mid-year rate;

(b)   average of opening and closing rates;

(c)   average of month end/quarter end rates;

(d)   average of monthly average rates;

(e)   monthly/quarterly results at month end/quarterly end rates; or

(f)   monthly/quarterly results at monthly/quarterly averages.

Example 18.20

A UK company has a US subsidiary and is preparing its consolidated accounts for the year ended June 30, 19X1. It intends to use an average rate for translating the results of the subsidiary. The relevant exchange rates for £1=US$ (rounded to two decimal places) are as follows:

Month	Month end	Average for month	Average for quarter	Average for year
June 19X0	1.53			
July 19X0	1.49	1.51		
August 19X0	1.49	1.49		
September 19X0	1.45	1.47	1.49	
October 19X0	1.41	1.43		
November 19X0	1.43	1.43		
December 19X0	1.48	1.44	1.43	
January 19X1	1.51	1.51		
February 19X1	1.55	1.53		
March 19X1	1.61	1.59	1.54	
April 19X1	1.66	1.63		
May 19X1	1.63	1.67		
June 19X1	1.61	1.63	1.64	1.53

Average of month end rates — 1.53
Average of quarter end rates — 1.54

The results of the subsidiary for each of the 12 months to June 30, 19X1 and the translation thereof under each of the above methods (using monthly figures where appropriate) are shown below:

Month	US$	(e) quarterly £	(e) monthly £	(f) quarterly £	(f) monthly £
July 19X0	1,000		671		662
August 19X0	1,100		738		738
September 19X0	1,200	2,276	828	2,215	816
October 19X0	2,000		1,418		1,399
November 19X0	4,000		2,797		2,797
December 19X0	10,000	10,811	6,757	11,189	6,944
January 19X1	5,000		3,311		3,311
February 19X1	1,300		839		850
March 19X1	1,350	4,752	839	4,968	849
April 19X1	1,300		783		798
May 19X1	1,400		859		838
June 19X1	1,400	2,547	870	2,500	859
Total	31,050	20,386	20,710	20,872	20,861

Method (a)	US$31,050 @ 1.48= £20,980
Method (b)	US$31,050 @ 1.57= £19,777
Method (c) — monthly	US$31,050 @ 1.53= £20,294
Method (c) — quarterly	US$31,050 @ 1.54= £20,162
Method (d)	US$31,050 @ 1.53= £20,294

It can be seen that by far the simplest methods to use are the methods (a) — (d).

In our view methods (a) and (b) should not be used as it is unlikely in these times of volatile exchange rates that they give appropriate weighting to the exchange rates which have been in existence throughout the period in question. They are only going to give an acceptable answer if the exchange rate has been static or steadily increasing or decreasing throughout the period.

Method (c) based on quarter end rates has similar drawbacks and therefore should not normally be used.

Method (c) based on month end rates and method (d) are better than the previous methods as they do take into account more exchange rates which have applied throughout the year with method (d) being preferable as this will have taken account of daily exchange rates. Average monthly rates for most major currencies are likely to be given in publications issued by the government, banks and other sources and therefore it is unnecessary for companies to calculate their own. The work involved in calculating an average for the year, therefore, is not very onerous. Method (d) will normally give reasonable and acceptable results when there are no seasonal variations in items of income and expenditure.

Where there are seasonal variations in items of income and expenditure then this will not be the case. It can be seen from the above example that because more than 60% of the results arise in the Winter months when the US dollar has been stronger in relation to sterling compared to during the whole of the period, method (d) has deflated the results shown by method (f), which is more accurate. In these situations appropriate exchange rates should be applied to the appropriate items. This can be done by using either of methods (e) or (f) preferably using figures and rates for each month. Where such a method is being used care should be taken to ensure that the periodic accounts are accurate and that cut-off procedures have been adequate, otherwise significant items may be translated at the wrong average rate.

Where there are significant one-off transactions then it is likely that actual rates at the date of the transaction should be used to give a more accurate weighting. Indeed, SFAS 52 requires that for revenues, expenses, gains, and losses the exchange rate at the date on which these elements are recognised should be used or an appropriately weighted average.[121]

Most companies do not indicate how they have applied an average rate, but merely state that the results are translated at average rates or weighted average rates. Two companies which are more specific in their accounting policies on the use of average rates are Allied-Lyons PLC and The Boots Company PLC as illustrated below:

Extract 18.23: Allied-Lyons PLC[122]

FOREIGN CURRENCIES [extract]
The profits of overseas subsidiary companies are translated at the weighted average of month-end rates and the difference in relation to closing rates are dealt with through reserves.

Extract 18.24: The Boots Company PLC[123]

Foreign currencies [extract]
The results of overseas companies are translated into sterling on an average exchange rate basis, weighted by the actual results of each month.

3.4.4 *Change from closing rate to average rate or vice versa*

By allowing companies the choice of either using the closing rate or an average rate for the period in translating the results of foreign enterprises, the question then arises — can a company change the method used by switching from closing rate to an average rate or vice versa?

Paragraph 17 of the standard states that the use of either method is permitted 'provided that the one selected is applied consistently from period to period'. It could be argued that this means that once a company has chosen a particular method no change should be made on the grounds of consistency. However, in view of the arguments expressed in paragraph 17 about the use of each of the methods it would seem possible that a company could justify changing from one method to the other on the grounds that it was adopting a better method.

If a change is made, it could be argued either that it is a change in accounting policy needing a prior year adjustment under SSAP 6[124] and therefore the previous year's profit and loss account changed to the new basis or that it is only a refinement of the existing policy which would not require a prior year adjustment. A refinement of an accounting policy is normally one that seeks to give a more accurate estimation in pursuit of the same basis of measurement; for example, a provision for stock obsolescence. This is not the case here, and in view of the conceptual differences of each method discussed in paragraph 17 of SSAP 20 we believe that this suggests a change in accounting policy. This would also appear to be required by paragraph 17 when it says that the method should be applied consistently from period to period.

A number of companies did change from the closing rate method to the average rate method in 1985/86. This was probably due to the dramatic weakening of the US dollar from January/February 1985 to the Autumn of that year. In particular, the exchange rate moved from £1=US\$1.08 at the end of February to £1=US\$1.24 at the end of March. Companies were finding that, in addition to depressing their reported results, they were having to reassess their expected results due to the change in the exchange rate. They were also finding that figures previously reported in their interim announcements could be remarkably different when the annual figures were being translated at the closing rate. This particular problem is discussed in 3.4.11 below.

One company which changed their accounting policy at that time and restated their comparative figures was Redland PLC. Their accounting policy stated:

Extract 18.25: Redland PLC[125]

c) Foreign currencies [extract]

Assets and liabilities denominated in foreign currencies are translated into £ sterling at the exchange rates ruling at the year end. Profits and losses of overseas companies are translated into £ sterling at average rates of exchange. The latter represents a change in accounting policy from previous years and, therefore, comparative figures for 1983/84 have been restated, where applicable. The more important rates of exchange are:

	1984/85		1983/84	
Rate to the £:	30.3.85	Average Rate	31.3.84	Average Rate
$ Australia	1.77	1.51	1.54	1.66
$ United States of America	1.24	1.26	1.44	1.49
Deutschemark	3.81	3.73	3.74	3.92

The effect of such a change in policy was also explained as follows:

Extract 18.26: Redland PLC[126]

As already announced, the Redland Board has changed its accounting policy for the translation of overseas profits from using year-end exchange rates to using average rates. The very sharp movements that occur with increasing regularity in a number of the major currencies relevant to Redland's results mean that the use of year-end exchange rates makes it difficult for management confidently to forecast the final result prior to the year-end. For instance, the movements in exchange rates between the end of December 1984 and the end of March 1985 would, if profit had been translated at the rates ruling on those dates, have shown profit being higher at the December rates by £6 million. The average rates that have been used for translating the profit produce a result that was £3.2 million higher than if the 30 March 1985 rates had been used but was £2.8 million lower than if the 31 December rates had been applied.

The previous year's results have been re-stated by using average rates for that year which caused a £2.1 million decrease in profit from that previously reported.

Other companies which changed to using average rates at that time included The Boots Company PLC and Blue Circle Industries PLC. However, they did not restate the comparative figures as the effect would not have been material.[127]

Since then more companies have changed to using average rates. A survey of financial statements included in the 1987—88 edition of Financial Reporting published by the ICAEW shows that 51 out of 100 large listed companies use the average rate method.[128] The corresponding survey in the 1984—85 edition showed that only 25% of 96 large listed companies used the average rate method.[129]

One company which has recently changed its policy and restated its comparative figures is Beecham Group p.l.c.[130] The company, in fact, forewarned its shareholders of such a change in its Annual Report for 1987 as follows:

Extract 18.27: Beecham Group p.l.c.[131]

The translation of overseas companies' sales and pre-tax profit at 31st March 1987 rates of exchange, compared with the rates at 31st March 1986, has had the effect of increasing sales and pre-tax profit by £9.4m and £2.4m respectively. The Group has now decided, in order to mitigate the effects of the continuing volatility of exchange rates, to translate the results in future at average rates of exchange.

If average rates had been used for translating the 1986/87 results the reported sales would have been £2,769.5m and the pre-tax profit £352.3m.

3.4.5 Which reserve should exchange differences be taken to?

SSAP 20 requires that exchange differences arising from the retranslation of the net investment at the closing rate should be recorded as a movement on reserves; however, it does not specify the category of reserves to which they should be taken. A number of companies take them to retained profits.[132] Many companies in addition to showing such exchange differences as movements on retained profits also show them as movements on other reserves such as revaluation reserves and capital reserves.[133] However, this is likely to be as a result of items dealt with in 3.4.6 below.

Some companies, on the other hand, do take the exchange differences to another category of reserve; Allied-Lyons PLC to a capital reserve (although they also show currency translation adjustments on retained profits, revaluation reserve and the capital reserve);[134] Jaguar plc to 'other reserves';[135] and BTR plc to revaluation reserves.[136] Argyll Group PLC took them to a currency translation reserve.[137]

The treatment adopted by Argyll Group PLC is effectively that which is required by SFAS 52, i.e. to be taken to and accumulated in a separate component of shareholders' equity.[138] For the reasons indicated in 4.3 it may be preferable for companies in the UK to adopt a similar approach.

3.4.6 Post-acquisition capital or revaluation reserves

As indicated above, SSAP 20 does not specify the reserve to which the exchange difference arising from the retranslation of the net investment at the closing rate should be taken. Normally, they should be taken to only one category of reserve. However, the foreign enterprise may have a non-distributable capital reserve which arose after the company was acquired by the investing company. Alternatively, it may have revalued some assets since it was acquired and therefore has a revaluation reserve. As these reserves will not be reported as part of retained profits in the consolidated financial statements the question then arises — if exchange differences are normally taken to retained profits, should part of the exchange difference be taken to these other categories of reserves so that they are effectively translated at the closing rate?

Example 18.21

A UK company has a German subsidiary which was set up on January 1, 19X0 with a share capital of DM500,000. In the year to December 31, 19X0 the subsidiary made a post-tax profit of DM100,000 and at its year end transferred 5% thereof to a non-distributable legal reserve. In the following year the subsidiary made no profit or loss and therefore made no further transfer to the legal reserve. In the consolidated financial statements at December 31, 19X0 the legal reserve was treated as a capital reserve and the exchange difference on the net investment was taken to retained profits. How should the capital reserve and the current year's exchange difference be treated in the consolidated financial statements at December 31, 19X1?

The relevant exchange rates are:

	£1=DM
January 1, 19X0	3.54
December 31, 19X0	2.86
December 31, 19X1	2.97

	31 December 19X1 DM	31 December 19X0 £	(i) 31 December 19X1 £	(ii) 31 December 19X1 £
Net assets	600,000	209,790	202,020	202,020
Share capital	500,000	141,243	141,243	141,243
Opening retained profits	90,000	—	65,051	65,051
Profit for year	—	34,965	—	—
Transfer to capital reserve	—	(3,496)	—	—
Exchange difference	—	33,582	(7,770)	(7,641)
Closing retained profits	90,000	65,051	57,281	57,410
Opening capital reserve	10,000	—	3,496	3,496
Transfer from retained profits	—	3,496	—	—
Exchange difference	—	—	—	(129)
Closing capital reserve	10,000	3,496	3,496	3,367
	600,000	209,790	202,020	202,020

(i) This method has continued to take the exchange difference on the opening net investment to retained profits. The capital reserve has been retained at the rate ruling at which the reserve was created.

(ii) This method has taken that part of the exchange difference which relates to the net investment which is not distributable to the capital reserve so that the reserve represents the amount which is non-distributable at the closing rate. It should be borne in mind, however, that the split of consolidated reserves between distributable and non-distributable amounts are really irrelevant as it is the parent company's reserves which are important in determining whether a company can legally make a distribution. In any case, the figure for retained profits does not represent the amount that the subsidiary could distribute translated at the closing rate.

In our view either of these treatments is acceptable, although it should be noted that SFAS 52 would not allow either of them as all differences have to be taken to a separate component of shareholders' equity.[139]

Example 18.22

A UK company has a French subsidiary which was set up on July 1, 19X0 with a share capital of FFr1m. The main asset of the subsidiary is an investment property which it acquired on the same day that the company was set up at a cost of FFr800,000. The subsidiary made a profit after tax of FFr50,000 for the six months to December 31, 19X0 and a profit after tax of FFr100,000 in the following year. The property was revalued at December 31, 19X0 at FFr950,000 which was incorporated in its financial statements. The valuation was updated at December 31, 19X1 to FFr1.2m. The exchange difference on the net investment was taken to a separate exchange reserve in the 19X0 financial statements. How should the revaluation reserve and the current year's exchange difference be treated in the consolidated financial statements at December 31, 19X1?

The relevant exchange rates are:

	£1=FFr
July 1,19X0	10.76
December 31, 19X0	9.45
December 31, 19X1	10.04

	31/12/X0 FFr	31/12/X0 £	31/12/X1 FFr	(i) 31/12/X1 £	(ii) 31/12/X1 £
Investment property	950,000	100,529	1,200,000	119,522	119,522
Other assets	250,000	26,455	350,000	34,860	34,860
	1,200,000	126,984	1,550,000	154,382	154,382
Share capital	1,000,000	92,937	1,000,000	92,937	92,937
Opening retained profits			50,000	5,291	5,291
Profit for year	50,000	5,291	100,000	9,960	9,960
Closing retained profits	50,000	5,291	150,000	15,251	15,251
Opening revaluation reserve			150,000	15,873	15,873
Surplus for year	150,000	15,873	250,000	24,900	24,900
Exchange difference					(932)
Closing revaluation reserve	150,000	15,873	400,000	40,773	39,841
Opening exchange reserve				12,883	12,883
Exchange difference		12,883		(7,462)	(6,530)
Closing exchange reserve		12,883		5,421	6,353
Total capital and reserves	1,200,000	126,984	1,550,000	154,382	154,382

(i) This method has continued to take the exchange difference on the opening net investment to the separate exchange reserve. Surpluses credited to the revaluation reserve are retained at the rates ruling at the date the surpluses arise.

(ii) This method has taken that part of the exchange difference on the opening net investment which arises only because of the fact that the investment property has been revalued to the revaluation reserve. If the property had been retained at cost then that exchange difference would not have arisen in the consolidated financial statements. This treatment means that the revaluation reserve in the consolidated financial statements represents the revaluation reserve expressed in the foreign currency translated at the closing rate. It also represents the difference between the carrying amount of the asset in the consolidated financial statements and the historical cost of the asset translated at the closing rate which should be included in the historical cost information required by the Companies Act 1985 in respect of assets affected by revaluations.[140] (see 6.1.5 of Chapter 10) i.e.

	£
Carrying value at December 31, 19X1	119,522
Historical cost at December 31, 19X1	
FFr800,000 @ £1=FFr10.04 =	79,681
	39,841

Although we believe both methods to be acceptable, in our view method (ii) is preferable for the reasons stated above. It would appear that this is the method adopted by a number of companies as indicated in 3.4.5 above.

3.4.7   Treatment of exchange differences on disposal of subsidiary

The issues relating to the calculation of the gain/loss on disposal of subsidiaries are discussed in Chapter 4. In relation to foreign subsidiaries there is one further issue — what should happen to the cumulative exchange differences on the net investment in a foreign subsidiary when all or part of it is sold?

SSAP 20 does not specifically deal with this. In the statement issued by the ASC when the standard was published the reason given was that 'ASC considers that the treatment of this exchange element should be consistent with the treatment of the revaluation surplus on the disposal of an asset which has been previously revalued. Comments were specifically requested on the latter point in two ASC Discussion Papers: 'A review of SSAP 6 — Extraordinary items and prior year adjustments' and 'A review of SSAP 12 — Accounting for depreciation'. The matter will therefore not be resolved until the review of these two standards is complete'.[141]

Since then both of these standards have been revised and in view of comments received neither of them dealt with the problem of such revaluation surpluses so there is still no authoritative guidance in the UK on that particular issue, (see Chapter 10 for a discussion of this topic), so we are no further forward in dealing with the problem of cumulative exchange differences when a subsidiary is sold.

Example 18.23

A UK company has a US subsidiary which was set up on January 1, 19X0 with a share capital of US$200,000 when the exchange rate was £1=US$1.16. The subsidiary is included at its original cost of £172,414. The profits of the subsidiary, all of which have been retained by the subsidiary, for each of the three years ended December 31, 19X2 were US$40,000, US$50,000 and US$60,000 respectively. In the consolidated financial statements the results of the subsidiary have been translated at the respective closing rates of £1=US$1.45, £1=US$1.48 and £1=US$1.88. All exchange differences have been taken to a separate exchange reserve. The consolidated reserves have therefore included the following amounts in respect of the subsidiary:

	Retained profit £	Exchange reserve £
January 1, 19X0	—	—
Movement during 19X0	27,586	(34,483)
December 31, 19X0	27,586	(34,483)
Movement during 19X1	33,784	(3,355)
December 31, 19X1	61,370	(37,838)
Movement during 19X2	31,915	(41,691)
December 31, 19X2	93,285	(79,529)

The net assets at December 31, 19X2 of US$350,000 are included in the consolidated financial statements at £186,170.

On January 1, 19X3 the subsidiary is sold for US$400,000 (£212,766), thus resulting in a gain on sale in the parent company's books of £40,352, i.e. £212,766 less £172,414. On consolidation the gain on sale is reduced to £26,596, being the difference between the proceeds of £212,766 and net asset value of £186,170. How should the cumulative exchange difference of £(79,529) be treated in the consolidated financial statements for 19X3?

Option (i) — Leave it as a negative exchange reserve.
In our view this is illogical as the consolidated financial statements will include in retained profits a different amount in respect of the subsidiary than has actually been realised by the parent company and included in its own retained profits. In addition, a consolidation entry will be required forever more in respect of the former subsidiary.

Option (ii) — Transfer it to retained profits as a reserve movement.

This is based on the view that the consolidated retained profits should reflect the same amount of retained profits that the parent company has realised and recorded in its own financial statements. This treatment, therefore, overcomes the criticism made above in respect of the previous option. It also means that the retained profits position is now the same as it would have been if the company had adopted the policy of taking the exchange differences to retained profits as they arose rather than taking them to a separate reserve.

Option (iii) — Transfer it to the profit and loss account for the year and treat it in a similar way as the gain on sale.

This is based on the view that one of the objectives of SSAP 20 is to produce results which are compatible with the effects of rate changes on a company's cash flow; that is why exchange differences on monetary items are normally recognised as part of the profit or loss for the year. Exchange rate changes in this instance have ultimately caused the company to receive less cash and therefore should be reflected at some time in arriving at the profit or loss for the year. It could also be argued in this particular case that not to do so would mean that the company has reported more profits in the consolidated profit and loss account than has actually been realised, contrary to the requirements of the Companies Act 1985.[142]

The treatment suggested in option (iii) above is that which is required by SFAS 52 upon the sale or upon complete or substantially complete liquidation of an investment in a foreign entity.[143] Indeed, under US GAAP if a partial sale takes place then the relevant proportion of the accumulated exchange difference should be included in the gain/loss on sale.[144] In the above example if 25% of the shares in the subsidiary had been sold then £(19,882) would have been included in the calculation of the gain/loss on sale.

In our view all three treatments are acceptable although we would prefer companies to adopt option (iii). In any event, we believe that companies should adopt a similar treatment to that adopted for disposals of revalued assets.

It would appear that in practice most companies do not include the cumulative exchange differences in the profit and loss account in the year of disposal, and no transfer between reserves is generally required as the exchange differences are already in retained profits. For those companies which we indicated as taking exchange differences to a category of reserves other than retained profits (see 3.4.5 above) it is not always possible to determine exactly what is done on disposal of the subsidiaries. It would appear that Argyll Group PLC made a transfer between reserves as indicated below:

Extract 18.28: Argyll Group PLC[145]

GROUP PROFIT AND LOSS ACCOUNT [extract]

	1987 £'000	1986 £'000
Retained Profit/(Deficit) for the year	20,355	(4,742)
Retained Profit, beginning of year	50,962	55,883
Transfer from currency translation reserve	247	—
Goodwill written off	(19,561)	(179)
Retained Profit, end of year	52,003	50,962

20.0 Other Reserves [extract]
The movement on currency translation reserve during the year was:

	1987 £'000	1986 £'000
Beginning of year	852	2,300
Restatement of opening net assets	(1,825)	(4,190)
Translation of profits at weighted average compared with closing rate	(285)	(240)
Related foreign currency borrowings	1,505	2,982
Transfer to profit and loss account	(247)	—
End of year	—	852

No indication is given as to why the transfer has been made but it presumably was as a result of selling their overseas drinks division.

On the other hand, it would appear that BTR plc take the cumulative exchange differences to the profit and loss account for the year when the subsidiaries are sold as the extract from their reserves note indicates below:

Extract 18.29: BTR plc[146]

24 Reserves [extract]
£ millions

	Share premium account	Revaluation reserves	Capital reserve	Related companies reserve	Profit and loss account
Consolidated					
Beginning of year	252.1	43.6	2.3	2.1	529.0
Currency fluctuations					
– net assets		(153.0)		(5.8)	
– long term borrowings		50.4			
Premium on shares issued	1.8				
Goodwill			(2.3)	(4.1)	(84.7)
Property and plant revaluations		1.1		1.9	
Depreciation transfer		(2.4)			2.4
Disposals		(82.7)		(7.0)	7.0
Retained profit				9.0	305.8
End of year	253.9	(143.0)		(3.9)	759.5

Consolidated revaluation reserves include £23.7 million surplus (£30.8 million) arising on fixed tangible assets. The balance represents accumulated currency fluctuations.

Although some of the figure of £82.7 million shown for disposals will relate to revalued assets which have been disposed of, most of it would appear to relate to cumulative exchange differences and as there is no corresponding amount in the profit and loss account column it is presumed that this has been taken into account in arriving at the retained profit for the year of £305.8 million.

One company which explicitly states that it takes such exchange differences to the profit and loss account in the year of disposal is Consolidated Gold Fields PLC, as illustrated below:

Extract 18.30: Consolidated Gold Fields PLC[147]

Foreign currencies [extract]
On the disposal of an overseas entity related exchange adjustments arising on the net
investment in that entity, which have previously been taken directly to Group reserves, are
released to the Group profit and loss account.

6 Extraordinary charge [extract]
The estimated loss incurred on the disposal of the North American industrial interests,
managed by Gold Fields American Industries Inc, has been fully offset by a release of £82.0m
from Group reserves of the cumulative exchange adjustments relating to these businesses
which have been built up over the years as a result of the strengthening of the US dollar
against sterling since these investments were purchased.

3.4.8 Change from closing rate/net investment method to temporal method or vice versa

As indicated in 2.4.2 above, the method used for translating the financial
statements of a foreign enterprise should normally only be changed when the
financial and other operational relationship changes and renders the method used
inappropriate. Where this is the case, therefore, it must be remembered that, as it
is a change in the circumstances which has given rise to the change in method,
this is not a change in accounting policy and therefore a prior year adjustment
under SSAP 6 is inappropriate. How should the change, therefore, be accounted
for?

SSAP 20 does not deal with this situation, however, guidance can be sought from
SFAS 52.

A   Change from closing rate/net investment method to temporal method

SFAS 52 states that the translated amounts of non-monetary assets at the end of
the period prior to the change should become the accounting basis for those assets
for the current and future periods.[148] There is therefore no need to translate these
assets at the historical rates that applied when the assets were acquired. The
cumulative exchange differences that have been taken to reserves in prior periods
should not be taken to the profit and loss account in the year of change but should
remain in reserves. SFAS 52 actually requires these exchange differences to
remain in equity.[149]

B   Change from temporal method to closing rate/net investment method

SFAS 52 states that the adjustment attributable to restating non-monetary assets,
previously translated at historical rates, at closing rates should be reported in the
cumulative translation adjustments component of equity.[150] This adjustment
should, therefore, be treated as a reserve movement.

3.4.9   Hyperinflation

One particular problem with the use of the closing rate/net investment method is when it is applied to a foreign enterprise which operates in a country where a very high rate of inflation exists. Consider the following example:

Example 18.24

On June 30, 19X0 a UK company sets up a subsidiary in Brazil. On that date the subsidiary acquires property for 10,000 Cruzados. Ignoring depreciation on the property, this asset would be included in the group financial statements at June 30, 19X0 and June 30, 19X6 as follows:

	Cruzados	Exchange rate	£
June 30, 19X0	10,000	£1=0.123Cr	81,301
June 30, 19X6	10,000	£1=21.18Cr	472

This example illustrates the 'disappearing assets' problem and it is for this reason that SSAP 20 says that in these circumstances 'it may not be possible to present fairly in historical cost accounts the financial position of a foreign enterprise simply by a translation process'.[151] It suggests, therefore, that the local currency financial statements should be adjusted where possible to reflect current price levels before the translation process is undertaken. No indication is given as to whether this restatement should be done based on specific price changes (current cost principles) or general price changes (current purchasing power principles), so either would appear to be acceptable.

SSAP 20 does not define what 'a very high rate of inflation' is. SFAS 52, on the other hand, states that a highly inflationary economy is one that has cumulative inflation of approximately 100% or more over a three year period.[152] Although this sounds high, this is equivalent to an annual inflation rate of 26% compounded over that period.

Countries which have recently had three-year cumulative inflation of 100% or more, include:[153]

Argentina	Mexico	Sudan	Yugoslavia
Bolivia	Nicaragua	Syria	Zaire
Brazil	Peru	Tanzania	Zambia
Ecuador	Poland	Turkey	
Gambia	Sierra Leone	Uganda	
Ghana	Somalia	Uruguay	

Information on inflation rates in various countries is available in *International Financial Statistics*, published monthly by the International Monetary Fund.

Where it is not practical to adjust the local currency financial statements to reflect current price levels an alternative solution may be to translate the financial statements using the temporal method. This is the treatment required by SFAS 52 which effectively regards the reporting currency of the investing company as if it were the functional currency of the foreign enterprise.[154] Although this may result in a fairer presentation of the balance sheet of the foreign enterprise, as SSAP 20 only allows the temporal method to be used where the foreign enterprise *is* more dependent on the economic environment of the investing company[155] care should be taken to ensure that the profit and loss account is not misstated by including exchange differences on monetary items which would otherwise have been taken to reserves.

We can see the effect of using the methods suggested by SSAP 20 and SFAS 52 on the 'disappearing assets' problem illustrated above in the following example:

Example 18.25

(a)   SSAP 20

The relevant consumer price indices at June 30, 19X0 and June 30, 19X6 are 100 and 23,436 respectively. The asset would therefore be included in the group financial statements at June 30, 19X6 as follows:

10,000 Cruzados X 23,436/100 = 2,343,600 Cruzados @ £1=21.18Cr = £110,652.

(b)   SFAS 52

The asset would be translated at the historical rate of exchange and therefore would be included at £81,301 (10,000 Cruzados @ £1=0.123Cr).

One company which has an accounting policy on this matter is Reckitt & Colman plc:

Extract 18.31: Reckitt & Colman plc[156]

FOREIGN CURRENCY TRANSLATION [extract]
The accounts of overseas subsidiaries and related companies are translated into sterling on the following basis:
Assets and liabilities at the rate of exchange ruling at the year-end date of Reckitt & Colman plc except for fixed assets of companies operating in countries where hyper-inflation exists which are translated at historical rates of exchange.
Profit and loss account items at the average rate of exchange ruling during the financial year. An inflation adjustment is charged in arriving at local currency profits operating in hyper-inflation countries before they are translated to reflect the impact on the companies' working capital requirements.

It would appear that Reckitt & Colman plc adopts a mixture of the guidance contained in both standards.

Another company which makes reference to taking account of inflation in its accounting policy is Marley plc in relation to its related companies in South America:

> *Extract 18.32: Marley plc*[157]
>
> FOREIGN CURRENCIES [extract]
> Earnings of overseas companies are translated at the average rates of exchange except for
> those of the related companies in South America where, after making appropriate adjustments
> for local inflation, closing rates at 31st December are used.

It is not clear from their accounting policies whether similar inflation adjustments
are made in reflecting the share of net assets of these South American companies
in the balance sheet.

3.4.10 *Goodwill on consolidation*

One of the options allowed by SSAP 22 — *Accounting for goodwill* — is to treat
goodwill as an intangible asset and amortise it through the profit and loss account
on a systematic basis over its useful economic life.[158] Where such a treatment is
adopted in respect of goodwill arising on the purchase of a foreign enterprise, the
question then arises as to whether or not such goodwill should be retranslated at
closing rates.

Example 18.26

A UK company acquires all of the share capital of a German company on September 30, 19X1 at
a cost of DM3m. The fair value of the net assets of the German company at that date was
DM2.1m. In the consolidated financial statements at December 31, 19X1 it is intended that any
goodwill is treated as an intangible asset and amortised over its useful economic life. (For the
purposes of this example, amortisation for the three months to December 31, 19X1 is ignored.)
The relevant exchange rates at September 30, 19X1 and December 31, 19X1 are £1=DM3.00 and
£1=DM2.96 respectively. At what amount should the goodwill on consolidation be included in
the balance sheet?

	DM	(i) £	(ii) £
Goodwill	900,000	300,000	304,054

(i) This method regards goodwill as being the excess of (a) the sterling price paid over (b) the fair
value of the net assets of the subsidiary expressed in the foreign currency translated into sterling
at the date of acquisition. i.e. a sterling asset which does not fluctuate with changes in the
exchange rate. Although not specifically covered by SSAP 20 this would appear to be the
method adopted by the standard.

Paragraph 53 of the standard only refers to the exchange difference on the net investment being
taken to reserves and the definition of the net investment contained in the standard refers to the
net assets of the foreign enterprise.[159] As the goodwill only arises on consolidation and is not
included in the balance sheet of the foreign enterprise then it could be argued that the goodwill is
not part of the net assets of the foreign enterprise. This view is supported by the statement
issued by the ASC on the publication of SSAP 20 which indicated that any goodwill element
contained in the carrying amount of the investment in the investing company's financial
statements would not be available for offset on consolidation when applying the cover method
provisions of paragraph 57 of the standard.[160]

(ii) This method regards goodwill as being the excess of (a) the foreign currency price paid or the
sterling price paid translated into the foreign currency at the date of acquisition over (b) the fair

value of the net assets of the subsidiary expressed in the foreign currency, i.e. a currency asset which is retranslated at closing rates.

This treatment is required by SFAS 52[161] and is, in our view, more logical as the value of the foreign company as a whole is likely to be based on the expected future earnings stream expressed in the foreign currency and the goodwill relates to a business which operates in the economic environment of that currency.

For these reasons we believe method (ii) to be preferable.

3.4.11 Inter-period comparisons

As indicated in 2.4.3 above the use of the closing rate/net investment method is intended to reflect in the consolidated financial statements the financial results and relationships as measured in the foreign currency financial statements of the foreign enterprise prior to translation. This is likely to be the case for amounts within the profit and loss account for the year; amounts within the balance sheet; and the relationship of the profit or loss for the year to the balance sheet, particularly where the closing rate is used for translating the results of the foreign enterprise. However, this will not be the case when a comparison is made between figures for the current year and figures for the previous year or, alternatively, figures for the first half of the year and figures for the second half. This is normally more important when looking at a comparison of the results for the respective periods.

Example 18.27

A UK company has a wholly-owned US subsidiary. In preparing its consolidated financial statements the company translates the results of the subsidiary using the closing rate. The profits of the subsidiary for the four six-month periods ended December 31, 19X1 and the rate of exchange at the end of each period are as follows:

Six-month period ended	US$	£1=US$
June 30, 19X0	100,000	1.53
December 31, 19X0	110,000	1.48
June 30, 19X1	121,000	1.61
December 31, 19X1	133,100	1.88

The two interim financial statements ended 30 June and the two annual financial statements ended 31 December for the group therefore include the profits of the subsidiary as follows:

	US$	£1=US$	£
Six months ended June 30, 19X0	100,000	1.53	65,359
Six months ended December 31, 19X0	110,000	Balance	76,533
Year ended December 31, 19X0	210,000	1.48	141,892
Six months ended June 30, 19X1	121,000	1.61	75,155
Six months ended December 31, 19X1	133,100	Balance	60,005
Year ended 31 December 19X1	254,100	1.88	135,160

It can be seen from the above that the reported sterling figures do not show the 10% increase each period that the US dollar figures show. In fact, in 19X1, the annual profit shows a decrease of approximately 5% compared to the 19X0 profit whereas in US dollar terms the profit has increased by 21% and the second half results appear to show a decrease of approximately 20% compared to the results of the first half instead of the 10% increase. This latter effect is caused by the second half results effectively including the exchange adjustment resulting from restating the first half's results at the year-end exchange rate. The results of the first half translated at the year-end rate are £64,362 and therefore a loss of £10,793 is effectively included in the second half's results. This restatement of previously reported figures is one of the reasons why some companies have changed to using average rates when translating profit and loss accounts. Even where this is done this problem will still arise if each period's results are not translated at the average rate for that period, i.e. if the annual results are translated at an average rate for the year, although the effect is unlikely to be particularly significant.

If average rates had been used in the above example the figures would have been as follows:

Example 18.28

	US$	Method (i) £1=US$	£	Method (ii) £1=US$	£
Six months ended June 30, 19X0	100,000	1.48	67,568	1.48	67,568
Six months ended December 31, 19X0	110,000	Balance	75,289	1.46	75,342
Year ended December 31, 19X0	210,000	1.47	142,857	Balance	142,910
Six months ended June 30, 19X1	121,000	1.59	76,101	1.59	76,101
Six months ended December 31, 19X1	133,100	Balance	78,838	1.69	78,757
Year ended December 31, 19X1	254,100	1.64	154,939	Balance	154,858

Method (i) translates the results for the year at the average rate for the year and method (ii) translates each six-month period at the average rate for the respective period. It can be seen that using average rates the reported sterling figures for 19X1 show an annual increase of approximately 8.5% compared to 19X0 and the second half profits show an increase of approximately 3.5% compared to the first half profits. These still do not show the same relationships as shown by the US dollar figures but at least the difference is not quite as marked.

In order to try to overcome this, some companies have disclosed the effect of using different exchange rates. For example:

Extract 18.33: Guinness PLC[162]

2. Geographical analysis of turnover and profit [extract]
The results for the 12 months ended 31 December 1987 for overseas subsidiary and related companies have been translated at 31 December 1987 exchange rates. If these had been translated at 31 December 1986 exchange rates, turnover would have been £149m higher at £2,967m and profit before taxation would have been £12m higher at £420m.

An alternative treatment is to express the comparative figures at current year end exchange rates. For example:

Extract 18.34: BTR plc[163]

CONSOLIDATED PROFIT AND LOSS ACCOUNT [extract]

£ millions	1987	1986 1987 year end rates	1986 1986 year end rates
Sales turnover	4149.2	3718.3	4019.2
Profit on ordinary activities before taxation	590.3	461.7	504.8
Earnings for the year	398.4	322.5	352.4
Earnings per ordinary share	23.6p	19.4p	21.2p

These were the only comparative figures which were stated at 1987 year end rates.

Although this extra disclosure can only help a user of financial statements it must be remembered that this mathematical effect of different exchange rates ignores the economic effect of the changes in the exchange rates on the actual trading results of the foreign enterprises. SFAS 52 states that the Financial Accounting Standards Board when preparing the standard 'considered a proposal for financial statement disclosure that would describe and possibly quantify the effects of rate changes on reported revenue and earnings. This type of disclosure might have included the mathematical effect of translating revenue and expenses at rates that are different from those used in a preceding period as well as the economic effects of rate changes, such as the effects on selling prices, sales volume, and cost structures'. The Board rejected requiring such disclosures 'primarily because of the wide variety of potential effects, the perceived difficulties of developing the information, and the impracticality of providing meaningful guidelines'. However, the Board encouraged management to give extra disclosure of 'an analysis and discussion of the effects of rate changes on the reported results of operations. The purpose is to assist financial report users in understanding the broader economic implications of rate changes and to compare recent results with those of prior periods.'[164]

3.4.12 Branches

We have discussed previously the application of the provisions of SSAP 20 in relation to branches and we have seen that the definition of a foreign branch is a very wide one in that it includes a group of assets and liabilities which are accounted for in foreign currencies. This was mainly to cater for international assets which are financed by foreign borrowings, since the cover method could not be used as it is only applicable to equity investments. In many cases, therefore, the reason for regarding assets and liabilities as a foreign branch will be to allow exchange differences on the related borrowing to be taken to reserves rather than to the profit and loss account.

Once a company has decided that a particular category of assets and liabilities should be regarded as a foreign branch consideration should be given as to which assets and liabilities should be included. In our view the minimum which can be included is the international asset itself, e.g. aircraft, ship or oil and gas interest, and the related borrowing. However, we recommend that, in addition, any trading balances, e.g. debtors and creditors, should also be included. In particular, as the branch should not be an integral part of the company's business and its cash flows should not have an impact upon those of the rest of the company in order to justify the use of the closing rate/net investment method, the bank account through which most of the cash flows of the branch will flow should be considered to be part of the branch assets and liabilities.

It should be borne in mind that the exchange difference which is taken to reserves is on the net investment in the branch. As such this amount can be a net exchange gain or loss and the exchange difference on the borrowings included in the branch can exceed the corresponding exchange difference on the branch assets. There is, therefore, no restriction on the exchange differences on the borrowings taken to reserves as there would be if the provisions of the cover method applied.

3.5   Cover method

We have looked at the basic requirements of the cover method in 2.3.7 above and 2.4.5 above as it is applied in individual companies' financial statements and consolidated financial statements respectively. There are, however, a number of problem areas resulting from the provisions of the standard which we believe have to be addressed. Many of these problem areas are relevant to both sets of financial statements.

3.5.1   What are 'foreign currency borrowings'?

By adopting the cover method companies can take some, if not all, of the exchange differences arising on the foreign currency borrowings to reserves. Borrowings are not defined in the standard, so what should be regarded as borrowings?

The statement issued by the ASC on the publication of the standard in commenting on these provisions referred to 'loans'[165] but even then we do not believe that this term should be interpreted too literally.

The Stock Exchange, in requiring disclosure of indebtedness in listing particulars of listed companies, includes within this category loan capital, term loans, bank overdrafts, liabilities under acceptances (other than normal trade bills), acceptance credits and hire purchase commitments.[166] In our view all of these items can be regarded as borrowings for the purpose of the standard although it is unlikely that liabilities under hire purchase contracts, or finance leases, will have been taken out with a view to providing a hedge against foreign equity investments. Normal trade creditors and trade bills should not be regarded as borrowings, although it has been suggested that extended credit from a supplier could be included as the economic effects are the same as for a straightforward loan.[167]

3.5.2   Borrowings taken out before or after the investment

The provisions of the standard apply to borrowings which have been used to finance, or provide a hedge against, its foreign equity investments. Accordingly, the provisions not only apply to borrowings taken out at the same time as the investment is made but also to borrowings which have been taken out before the investment is made and to borrowings which are taken out after the investment is made. How should the provisions be applied, therefore, in the first accounting period when the investment holding period has been different from the period for which the borrowing has been in place?

A   Borrowings taken out before the investment

Example 18.29

A UK company is intending to invest in a US company so on May 1, 19X1 it borrows US$500,000, repayable in five years' time, which it places in a US$ deposit account in the meantime. On May 31, 19X1 it purchases all of the shares of the US company at a cost of US$800,000 using the US$500,000 in the deposit account and the balance paid out of its sterling bank account. How should the company apply the cover method in its financial statements for the period to December 31, 19X1?

The relevant exchange rates are:

	£1=US$
May 1, 19X1	1.66
May 31, 19X1	1.63
December 31, 19X1	1.88

		Option (i) P/L account £	Option (i) Reserves £	Option (ii) P/L account £	Option (ii) Reserves £
Exchange differences					
Investment					
US$800,000	@ 1.63 = £490,798				
	@ 1.88 = £425,532				
			(65,266)		(65,266)
Deposit					
US$500,000	@ 1.66 = £301,205				
	@ 1.63 = £306,748				
		5,543		5,543	
Borrowing					
US$500,000	@ 1.66 = £301,205				
	@ 1.63 = £306,748				
			(5,543)	(5,543)	
	@ 1.88 = £265,957		40,791		40,791
		5,543	(30,018)	nil	(24,475)

Option (i) is based on the view that as the borrowings were used to finance the purchase of the investment all of the exchange difference on the borrowings can be offset against the exchange differences as long as the criteria of the standard are met. However, in our view this ignores the fact that for the period prior to purchasing the investment the borrowing was effectively matched against the deposit and therefore our preference would be for the exchange difference on the borrowing for the period up to purchasing the investment to be taken to profit and loss to offset the exchange difference on the deposit as shown in option (ii).

We also believe that such a treatment should be adopted if the proceeds of the borrowings had been placed in a sterling deposit account as the company would have been uncovered during that period. The effect of exchange differences would have impacted on the cash flow of the company as it would have been required to pay an extra £5,543 out of its sterling bank account to purchase the investment. Accordingly, the exchange difference should be taken to profit and loss account.

Problems also arise when borrowings are taken out as a hedge against existing foreign investments.

B   Borrowings taken out after the investment

Example 18.30

A UK company has an equity investment in a German company which it acquired in 19W1 at a cost of DM500,000 when the exchange rate was £1=DM5.00. Up until 19X1 the UK company has had no foreign borrowings so the investment has been carried in the company's financial statements at its historical sterling cost of £100,000. On April 30, 19X1 the company considered the investment to be worth DM1,000,000 and in order to provide a hedge against the investment borrowed DM1,000,000, repayable in three years' time, and used the proceeds to reduce its sterling overdraft. How should the company apply the cover method in its financial statements for the year ended December 31, 19X1?

The relevant exchange rates are:

	£1=DM
December 31, 19X0	2.86
April 30, 19X1	2.98
December 31, 19X1	2.96

	P/L £	Reserves £
Option (i)		
Exchange differences		
Investment — DM500,000 @ 5.00 = £100,000		
@ 2.96 = £168,919		
		68,919
Borrowing — DM1,000,000 @ 2.98 = £335,570		
@ 2.96 = £337,838		
		(2,268)
		66,651

	P/L £	Reserves £

Option (ii)

Exchange differences

Investment — DM500,000 @ 5.00 = £100,000
@ 2.86 = £174,825

		74,825

@ 2.96 = £168,919 ... (5,906)

Borrowing — DM1,000,000 @ 2.98 = £335,570
@ 2.96 = £337,838

	(2,268)	
	(2,268)	68,919

Option (iii)

Exchange differences

Investment — DM500,000 @ 5.00 = £100,000
@ 2.98 = £167,785

		67,785

@ 2.96 = £168,919 ... 1,134

Borrowing — DM1,000,000 @ 2.98 = £335,570
@ 2.96 = £337,838

	(1,134)	(1,134)
	(1,134)	67,785

Option (i) regards all of the exchange gain on the investment which is recognised in this accounting period as being available for offset against the exchange loss on the total borrowing. This would appear to meet the conditions laid down in paragraphs 51 and 57 of the standard.

Option (ii) regards only the exchange difference arising on the investment during the year as being available for offset. As this is a loss, and a loss has also arisen on the borrowing, then under the conditions of the above paragraphs the exchange loss on the borrowings must be taken to profit and loss for the year.

Neither of these options, although acceptable under the standard, reflect the rationale for taking out the borrowings in the first place which was to hedge the exchange risk on the investment from the date it was decided to do so, i.e. April 30, 19X1. To achieve this, the exchange differences on the investment available for offset should be those which arise during the same period as the borrowing has been in existence.

Option (iii) is done on this basis and it can be seen that only half of the exchange loss on the borrowings can be offset against the exchange difference on the investment. This is due to the fact that the investment is recorded at original cost of DM500,000 whereas the borrowing is twice that amount. In order for the company to reflect fully the rationale behind their decision they should incorporate the investment at its valuation of DM1,000,000. If this were done, then all of the exchange loss on the borrowing could be taken to reserves.

3.5.3   *Repayment of borrowings*

Similar problems also arise when a company repays a foreign currency borrowing which has provided a hedge against a foreign equity investment.

A   *Treatment of exchange differences*

Example 18.31

A UK company has an equity investment in a Swiss company which it acquired for a cost of SFr3m when the exchange rate was £1=SFr3.00. It financed the acquisition by borrowing SFr3m. In the financial statements up to April 30, 19X1 the cover method has been applied. On March 31, 19X2 the company took advantage of the strong pound and decided to repay the borrowings in full. The company has no other foreign borrowings. How should the company apply the cover method in its financial statements for the year ended April 30, 19X2?

The relevant exchange rates are:

	£1=SFr
April 30, 19X1	2.46
March 31, 19X2	2.58
April 30, 19X2	2.61

		Option (i)		Option (ii)	
		P/L £	Reserves £	P/L £	Reserves £
Exchange differences					
Investment					
SFr3,000,000	@ 2.46 = £1,219,512				
	@ 2.58 = £1,162,791				
			(56,721)		(56,721)
Borrowing					
SFr3,000,000	@ 2.46 = £1,219,512				
	@ 2.58 = £1,162,791				
		56,721			56,721
		56,721	(56,721)	nil	nil

Option (i) is based on the view that as there are no borrowings at the year end then the cover method does not apply and the matching should be considered as having ceased at the beginning of the accounting period. As the exchange gain on the loan has arisen on a settled transaction it should be reported as part of the profit or loss for the year. However, it could be argued that this does not comply with condition (c) of paragraph 51 of the standard which requires the accounting treatment adopted to be applied consistently. Again, such a treatment does not reflect the fact that the company had hedged its investment up to March 31, 19X2 and it is only after that date that it has not been covered. Accordingly, we believe that option (ii) should be followed.

Another problem which arises when such borrowings are repaid is — how should the related investment which is no longer hedged subsequently be accounted for in the financial statements of the investing company?

B   Subsequent treatment of investment

Example 18.32

In the above example, how should the investment be included in the balance sheet at April 30, 19X2 and at subsequent year ends?

Option (i) — The investment should be retained at the exchange rate ruling at the final date of repaying the loan, i.e. £1,162,791 (£1=SFr2.58). No further retranslation should take place until another borrowing is taken out to provide a hedge. This method regards the investment as being a currency asset only during the period there are related currency borrowings. This would appear to be the method suggested by other commentators.[168] It does mean, however, that the figure for the investment in future periods is rather meaningless as it represents neither the historical cost in sterling terms nor the currency amount at closing rates. It does not even necessarily represent the actual sterling cost of the investment, as not all of the investment may have been financed by borrowings and the borrowings may have been repaid at different dates.

Option (ii) — The investment is translated at the closing rate of £1=SFr2.61 and included at £1,149,425 and is retranslated each year at closing rates. This is based on the view that the company *has* used foreign currency borrowings to finance the investment and therefore the provisions of paragraph 51 can still be applied. It also means that the accounting treatment for this investment is being applied consistently from period to period. Even if it were considered that such a policy was not in accordance with the standard then it would be possible for the company to adopt such a treatment by retaining a nominal borrowing in the foreign currency!

Option (iii) — The investment is retained at the rate ruling at the beginning of the period, i.e. £1,219,512 (£1=SFr2.46). This is based on the same premise as option (i) in the previous example.

Option (iv) — The investment should be restated at the historical rate ruling at the date of purchase, i.e. £1,000,000 (£1=SFr3.00). This is based on the view that the company no longer has a hedge against its investment and should account for it as if this had always been the case. The financial statements will, therefore, reflect the effect on net equity of choosing to finance the investment for the period it was so financed only by including the net exchange difference on the borrowing in reserves.

In our view all of the above options are acceptable, but the one chosen should be consistently applied.

Cadbury Schweppes p.l.c. is an example of a company which adopts option (i) as indicated in their accounting policy:

Extract 18.35: Cadbury Schweppes p.l.c.[169]

(e) Foreign currencies [extract]
Where overseas investments are financed by borrowings in foreign currencies the cost of these investments in the Company's balance sheet is adjusted to reflect exchange rate movements up to the date of repayment.

3.5.4   *Goodwill on consolidation*

We have already discussed in 3.4.10 above the question of whether or not goodwill on consolidation, which arises on the acquisition of a foreign enterprise and is capitalised and amortised, is a currency asset. We indicated that our preference was to treat it as a currency asset. Where the investment is financed by foreign currency borrowings the question then arises, can the exchange differences arising on the goodwill be used in the offset process under the provisions of paragraph 57 of the standard? Indeed, if the company has chosen to write off goodwill on consolidation immediately to reserves can any of the exchange differences on the related borrowing be taken to reserves in the consolidated financial statements?

Example 18.33

A UK company acquired all the equity share capital of a German company for DM3m on September 30, 19X1. The acquisition was financed by taking out a loan of DM3m which is repayable over ten years commencing March 31, 19X2. As the net assets of the German company are negligible, all of the purchase price is represented by goodwill. The company has applied the cover method in its own financial statements for the period ended December 31, 19X1. The relevant exchange rates at September 30, 19X1 and December 31, 19X1 are £1=DM3.00 and £1=DM2.96 respectively.

Accordingly, the investment and the loan are both included in the company's financial statements at £1,013,514 and an exchange gain on the investment of £13,514 and a corresponding exchange loss on the loan are taken to reserves.

If the company chooses to capitalise the goodwill on consolidation and treat it as a currency asset and translate it at closing rate then, ignoring any amortisation of the goodwill for the three months to December 31, 19X1, an exchange gain of £13,514 on the goodwill will arise and be taken to reserves in the consolidated financial statements. Can the company apply the cover method under paragraph 57 of the standard and take the exchange loss on the loan to reserves?

It would appear that the answer to this question is no.

Paragraph 57 of the standard only allows the exchange difference on the borrowing to be taken to reserves to the extent that it is offset by the exchange difference on the net investment which is taken to reserves and the definition of the net investment contained in the standard refers to the net assets of the foreign enterprise.[170] As the goodwill only arises on consolidation and is not included in the balance sheet of the foreign enterprise then it could be argued that the goodwill is not part of the net assets of the foreign enterprise. This view is supported by the statement issued by the ASC on the publication of SSAP 20 which indicated that any goodwill element contained in the carrying amount of the investment in the investing company's financial statements would not be available for offset on consolidation when applying the cover method provisions of paragraph 57 of the standard.[171]

However, we believe that in such circumstances the company should be able to apply the cover method provided that condition(c) of paragraph 57 is met.

The goodwill is being regarded as a currency asset which is retranslated at closing rates. This treatment is required by SFAS 52[172] and, in our view, more logical as the value of the foreign company as a whole is likely to be based on the expected future earnings stream expressed in the foreign currency and the goodwill relates to a business which operates in the economic environment of that currency. Not to take into account the exchange differences arising on the goodwill in applying the cover method ignores the economic reality that the group is covered against movements in exchange rates.

What if the company had chosen to write off the goodwill to reserves immediately?

Again, it could be argued that the cover method cannot be applied. No asset is being recognised in the financial statements and therefore there can be no exchange differences arising thereon against which the exchange difference on the loan can be offset. However, most companies who choose a policy of writing off goodwill immediately do so as a matter of policy, not because of the fact that the goodwill has suddenly become worthless and it could be argued that the treatment of exchange differences on borrowings should not be affected by the choice of accounting policy for goodwill. We believe, therefore, there is a case to say that such goodwill, which would have been included in the consolidated balance sheet had a policy of capitalisation and amortisation been followed, can be taken into account when applying the cover method.

3.5.5 All investments/borrowings?

Companies may have more than one foreign currency investment which have been financed, or are hedged by, more than one foreign currency borrowing. The question may then arise, can a company apply the cover method for some investments/borrowings and not apply it for others?

Example 18.34

On September 30, 19X1 a UK company acquires all the equity share capital of two foreign companies as follows:

(i)   A German company at a cost of DM3m financed by a loan of DM3m repayable in five years' time.

(ii) A US company at a cost of US$1,630,000 financed by a loan of US$1,630,000 repayable in five years' time.

The company wishes to apply the cover method to the German investment and related loan but not to apply it to the US investment and related loan in its financial statements for the year ended December 31, 19X1. Is such a treatment possible under SSAP 20?

The relevant exchange rates are:

	£1=DM	£1=US$
September 30, 19X1	3.00	1.63
December 31, 19X1	2.96	1.88

The effect of such a treatment is as follows:

		P/L account £	Reserves £
Exchange differences			
Investments			
— DM 3,000,000	@ DM3.00 = £1,000,000		
	@ DM2.96 = £1,013,514		
			13,514
— US$1,630,000	@ US$1.63 = £1,000,000		
	@ US$1.63 = £1,000,000		
			—
Loans			
— DM 3,000,000	@ DM3.00 = £1,000,000		
	@ DM2.96 = £1,013,514		
			(13,514)
— US$1,630,000	@ US$1.63 = £1,000,000		
	@ US$1.88 = £ 867,021		
		132,979	—
		132,979	—

It can be seen that by applying the cover method to the German investment/loan only the exchange gain on the US$ loan has been taken to profit and loss account whereas the exchange loss on the DM loan has been taken to reserves offset by a corresponding exchange gain on the net investment. It would appear that this is allowed by SSAP 20, as paragraph 51 states that the equity investments *may* be denominated in foreign currencies. It must be emphasised, however, that where exchange losses on the investments are arising but are not being recognised consideration has to be given as to whether a provision for permanent diminution in value is necessary. Paragraph 57 in dealing with the consolidated financial statements is equally permissive as it states that the exchange differences on the borrowings *may* be offset as reserve movements. If in the above example the net assets of the US company at the date of acquisition were equivalent to the price paid then although an exchange loss of £132,979 would be taken to group reserves, the company could continue to take the exchange gain on the loan to the profit and loss account.

It has been suggested that the final condition of paragraphs 51 and 57 requires companies to apply the cover method to all matched investments.[173] The final condition requires companies to apply the same accounting policy from *period to period* and therefore this suggestion seems to be a rather broad interpretation of the provisions. Nevertheless, we believe it is preferable for companies to adopt the same policy for all matched investments.

3.5.6   Must currencies be the same?

All of the previous examples which we have considered have been based on situations where the investment and the related borrowing have been expressed in the same foreign currency. The provisions of the standard actually make no reference to the currencies of the borrowings or the investments, and consequently it is not necessary for this to be the case. ED 27 included such a restriction but this was removed 'since a number of commentators considered it to be unacceptably rigid, particularly having regard to the wide variety of loan arrangements available and to the multi-currency nature of many of them. Since the alternative of a complete offset of currencies would allow too much freedom and carry the risk of imprudent accounting, a compromise solution has been adopted. The offset is now permitted only to the extent that the underlying foreign currency borrowings do not exceed the amount of cash expected to be generated by the net investments, either from profits or otherwise. ASC considers that this restriction should ensure that offset is permitted only when there is genuine cover for the related exchange gains and losses, whilst at the same time recognising the realities of treasury management'.[174] Specific problems relating to this compromise solution are addressed at 3.5.8 and 3.5.9 below.

An illustration of the cover method provisions where the currencies are not the same can be seen in the following example:

Example 18.35

On January 1, 19X1 a UK company acquires an equity investment in a Dutch company at a cost of DFl 4,700,000 and finances the acquisition by borrowing 73,400,000 Belgian francs repayable in seven years' time. Based on the exchange rates at that date both amounts are equivalent to £1,000,000. By applying the cover method in SSAP 20 the amounts of the investment and the borrowing in the financial statements for each of the years ended December 31 up until 19X6 would be as follows:

	Investment		Borrowing	
	£1=DFl	£	£1=BF	£
December 31, 19X1	4.25	1,105,882	75.6	970,899
December 31, 19X2	4.45	1,056,180	80.8	908,416
December 31, 19X3	4.13	1,138,015	73.4	1,000,000
December 31, 19X4	3.99	1,177,945	72.4	1,013,812
December 31, 19X5	3.25	1,446,154	59.5	1,233,613
December 31, 19X6	3.34	1,407,186	62.0	1,183,871

The treatment of exchange differences under the cover method would be as follows:

	Investment	Borrowing	
	Reserves	Reserves	P/L account
	£	£	£
December 31, 19X1	105,882	—	29,101
December 31, 19X2	(49,702)	49,702	12,781
December 31, 19X3	81,835	(81,835)	(9,749)
December 31, 19X4	39,930	(13,812)	—
December 31, 19X5	268,209	(219,801)	—
December 31, 19X6	(38,968)	38,968	10,774
	407,186	(226,778)	42,907

In 19X1 as both the investment and the borrowing are showing exchange gains then none of the exchange gain in the borrowing can be offset in reserves and therefore all of the gain must be taken to profit and loss account.

In 19X2 although there is a total exchange gain on the borrowing of £62,483, only £49,702 can be offset in reserves as that is the extent of the exchange loss on the investment. The balance of £12,781 has to be taken to profit and loss account.

Similarly, in 19X3 the exchange loss which is capable of being offset is limited. No account can be taken of the previous exchange gains on the investment which are sitting in reserves. It is only the exchange difference arising in the year which can be used in the offset process. It can be seen from the figures for 19X2 and 19X3 that this applies whether or not the exchange difference on the borrowing is a gain or a loss.

In 19X4 and 19X5 all of the exchange loss on the borrowing can be offset in reserves. In 19X6 the exchange gain on the borrowing is restricted as it was in 19X2.

It can be seen from the above example that when the cover method contained in SSAP 20 is used in circumstances where the investment and borrowings are in different currencies it can lead to inconsistent treatment of the exchange differences on the borrowing. In the above example in three of the years part of the exchange difference is taken to reserves and part to profit and loss account. In two of the years all of the difference is taken to reserves and in the other year all of the difference is taken to profit and loss account. In our view this makes a nonsense of the consistency concept.

Another weakness of the cover method when different currencies are involved can be illustrated by the following example:

Example 18.36

A UK company has a Spanish subsidiary. At December 31, 19X0 the net assets of the subsidiary are Ptas222m. On January 1, 19X1 the company decides to double its investment in the Spanish company by investing a further Ptas222m and borrows 2,980,000 Swiss francs repayable in five years' time.

The relevant exchange rates are as follows:

	£1=Ptas	£1=SFr
December 31, 19X0		
and January 1, 19X1	222	2.98
December 31, 19X1	196	2.40

Using the cover method, the financial statements would reflect the following treatment for the resulting exchange differences:

Exchange gain on investment

Ptas444m	@ 222 = £2,000,000	
	@ 196 = £2,265,306	
	———————————	£265,306

Exchange loss on borrowing

SFr2,980,000	@ 2.98 = £1,000,000	
	@ 2.40 = £1,241,666	
	———————————	(241,666)

| Net gain taken to reserves | | £ 23,640 |

The cover method allows all of the exchange difference on the investment to be used in the offset process. However, the result of the decision to finance the extra investment by the Swiss loan has been:

Gain on increased investment of Ptas222m	£132,653
Loss on Swiss loan	(241,666)
	£(109,013)

Although a net loss has arisen as a result of the decision no loss is reflected in the profit and loss account.

The above examples demonstrate that the cover method of SSAP 20 does not produce sensible results which reflect the economic substance of the transactions when different currencies are involved.

In our view proper cover can only exist if the risk of exposure to currency movements is removed. This can only happen if the borrowings, which are providing the hedge, are in the same currency as the investment. One of the arguments put forward by the ASC for removing the restriction of having the same currency was that it was too rigid 'particularly having regard to the wide variety of loan arrangements available and to the multi-currency nature of many of them'.[175] We consider the fact that companies can borrow in most of the major foreign currencies means that having a requirement for the same currency would not be too rigid because they can arrange to have the borrowings in the currency they want in order to provide effective cover against their investments.

Another criticism of the cover method in SSAP 20 is that 'the position taken by the ASC is that if there is a gain on a net investment and a loss on borrowings, then ex-post facto there has been cover; if there has been a gain on both or a loss on both, then there has been no cover. The basic flaw here is that cover by its very nature — to remove the risk — is a matter of premeditated intent. Evidence of this intent is a key feature of SFAS 52's approach to cover.'[176]

SFAS 52 requires that exchange gains and losses on transactions that are designated as, and are effective as, economic hedges of a net investment in a foreign entity shall not be included in the profit and loss account but shall be reported in the same manner as the translation adjustments relating to the net investment.[177] Ordinarily, a transaction that hedges a net investment should be denominated in the same currency as the net investment. SFAS 52 recognises that it may not be practical or feasible for this to be the case and, therefore, in these situations allows the hedging transaction to be in a currency which generally moves in tandem with the currency of the net investment.[178]

3.5.7 Pooled basis?

Where companies have a number of investments financed by a number of borrowings, how should the cover method be applied? Should it be applied on a pooled basis, i.e. by aggregating all the investments and all the borrowings and comparing the net exchange difference on each; or should it be done on an individual basis if specific borrowings can be identified or on a currency by currency basis?

Depending on how it is done different treatments are likely to arise. We can see
this from the following example.

Example 18.37

A UK company has two wholly owned foreign subsidiaries, a Canadian company and a Japanese
company. The net investment in these subsidiaries at December 31, 19X0 are C$4.5m and
¥300m respectively. The original investments in these companies were financed by borrowings
of C$3m and ¥400m respectively. How should the company apply the cover method in its
consolidated financial statements for the year ended December 31, 19X1?

The relevant exchange rates are:

	£1=C$	£1=¥
December 31, 19X0	2.05	235
December 31, 19X1	2.45	229

		(i) P/L account £	Reserves £	(ii) Reserves £
Exchange difference on investments				
Canadian company				
— C$4.5m	@ 2.05 = £2,195,122			
	@ 2.45 = £1,836,735			
			(358,387)	(358,387)
Japanese company				
— ¥300m	@ 235 = £1,276,596			
	@ 229 = £1,310,044			
			33,448	33,448
				(324,939)
Exchange difference on borrowings				
Canadian dollar loan				
— C$3m	@ 2.05 = £1,463,415			
	@ 2.45 = £1,224,490			
			238,925	238,925
Japanese yen loan				
— ¥400m	@ 235 = £1,702,128			
	@ 229 = £1,746,725			
		(11,149)	(33,448)	(44,597)
				194,328
		(11,149)	(119,462)	(130,611)

Method (i) has applied the cover method by regarding the investments/borrowings as being in
two separate pools of currencies. As a result, that part of the loss on the yen loan which has not
been covered by exchange gains on the yen investments has been taken to profit and loss
account.

Method (ii) has taken a global approach and as there are sufficient net losses on the investments to offset the net gains on the borrowings then all of the exchange differences can be offset to reserves.

It has been suggested that SSAP 20 requires an aggregate basis as illustrated in method (ii). The reason being that companies usually manage their treasuries on a pool basis and finance groups of investments with the basket of loans, often in different currencies.[179] In our view companies are permitted to apply the cover method on an individual basis or a currency by currency pool basis as illustrated in method (i) above. We believe that such a basis is preferable as it is only when the currencies are the same that proper cover exists.

The global approach will have the same effect where all the investments in each particular currency exceed the amount of the borrowings in each particular currency. However, where there may be a shortfall of investments in any particular currency when compared to borrowings in the same currency, the global approach has the effect of regarding the excess borrowings as providing a hedge against investments in different currencies.

Whichever method is used it should be applied consistently from period to period.

Most companies do not indicate whether they are applying the cover method on a pooled basis or not. One company which does give some indication as to their approach is Lonrho Plc as indicated below:

Extract 18.36: Lonrho Plc[180]

23 Reserves [extract]
Exchange adjustments to matched net borrowings amounting to a surplus of £.8m for the Group and £2.7m for the Company (1987 – £7.9m for the Group and £11.7m for the Company) relate to foreign currency loans in U.S. Dollars, Deutsche Marks and Swiss Francs which are matched against equity investments designated in these currencies.

3.5.8 *What is meant by condition (b) of paragraph 51 and condition (c) of paragraph 57?*

These conditions require that the foreign currency borrowings used in the offset process should not exceed the total amount of cash that the investments are expected to be able to generate, whether from profits or otherwise. As explained in 3.5.6 above the reason for this condition was to allow the cover method to be used when different currencies were involved. No guidance is given in the standard as to how such amount of cash should be determined. How should these conditions therefore be applied?

Example 18.38

A UK company acquires an equity investment in a Dutch company at a cost of DFl 4m on January 1, 19X1. During 19X0 the company had taken out a loan of 13 million French francs repayable in five years' time with a view to investing in a French company. However, this investment was never made and the company was left with the loan. In preparing its financial statements for the year ended December 31, 19X1 the company wishes to regard the French franc loan as providing a hedge against the Dutch investment and apply the cover method. How should this be done?

The relevant exchange rates are:

	£1=DFl	£1=FFr
December 31, 19X0		10.85
January 1, 19X1	3.99	
December 31, 19X1	3.25	9.46

Exchange differences

Investment — DFl 4m	@ 3.99 = £1,002,506	
	@ 3.25 = £1,230,769	
Exchange gain	———————	£228,263
Loan — FFr13m	@ 10.85 = £1,198,157	
	@ 9.46 = £1,374,207	
Exchange loss	———————	£(176,050)

By just applying condition (a) of paragraph 51 of the standard it would seem that all of the exchange loss on the loan can be taken to reserves as there are sufficient exchange gains on the investment available for offset.

However, what about condition (b)? How should the amount of cash which the investment is expected to generate be determined?

(i) It could be argued that it should be calculated as being the amount that would be raised if the investment were sold immediately.

If this is equivalent to its book value at the year end, i.e. £1,230,769, then as the loan exceeds this amount it could be argued that the cover method cannot be applied and therefore all of the exchange loss on the loan of £176,050 should be taken to profit and loss account and the investment should be recorded at the historical rate. i.e. £1,002,506. Alternatively, it could be argued that a proportion of the loan can be used in the offset process to the extent that it is covered by the value of the investment.This means that FFr11,643,074 (£1,230,769 @ £1=FFr9.46) can be used in the process. The exchange loss on this amount is £157,675 and it is this amount which can be taken to reserves. The remainder of the exchange loss on the loan of £18,375 would be taken to profit and loss account. We believe the latter approach is the more appropriate treatment.

What if the amount at which the investment could be sold is in excess of its book value? It may be that the investment is now worth DFl 4.5m which is equivalent to £1,384,615. It would appear that in these circumstances all of the exchange loss on the borrowing can be offset in reserves, even although the financial statements do not reflect the fact that the borrowings are covered. On the grounds of prudence, we believe it would be preferable to use the carrying value of the investment.

(ii) It could be argued that it is not necessary to consider an immediate sale of the investment, particularly as it is unlikely that such a course of action is the intention of the investing company, but that regard should be given to future profits which will result in further dividends being received or an increase in the amount ultimately received when the investment is sold. No guidance is given at all in the standard as to the period over which profits are to be taken into account. In view of the impracticalities of forecasting future dividend streams and ultimate sale proceeds, we believe that companies in applying these provisions should consider the cash proceeds which would be received from the immediate sale of the investment as in (i) above. If a future sale and future dividends have to be taken into account then consideration should also be given to the future interest expense which will be incurred on the borrowing.

Where the currencies are the same, in most situations condition (b) of paragraph 51 and condition (c) of paragraph 57 are irrelevant. This is because of the requirement that exchange differences on the borrowings can only be offset in reserves to the extent that there are corresponding exchange differences on the related investment. This ensures that full cover will only arise if the carrying value of the investment is at least equivalent to the amount of the borrowings. If the investment will not generate cash equivalent to the amount of the borrowings then provision should be made against the carrying value of the investment. This means that the amount of exchange differences on the net investment will correspondingly be less and therefore the exchange differences on the borrowings which exceed that amount will have to be taken to profit and loss account.

However, even where the currencies are the same, problems can arise in the year the conditions are not met.

3.5.9 What should happen in the year of change of the above conditions not being met?

A   Investment making losses

Example 18.39

A UK company has a wholly owned Japanese subsidiary which it set up several years ago at a cost of ¥1,000m. Up until 19X0 the subsidiary was profitable and on January 1, 19X1 the company borrowed ¥1,000m repayable in four years' time to provide a hedge against its investment. During 19X1 the subsidiary began to make losses such that at December 31, 19X1 the net assets of the subsidiary had been reduced to ¥1,000m. In its financial statements for the year ended December 31, 19X1 the company applied the cover method and exchange losses of £1,234,043 were offset in reserves. At that date, exchange gains on the investment included in the company and consolidated reserves were £1,875,000 and £2,500,000 respectively. In the year to December 31, 19X2 the subsidiary has made further losses of ¥400m but it is now considered that the losses have been stemmed and that the subsidiary will break even in the next three years. The results of the subsidiary are translated using closing rates. Assuming that the net asset value at December 31, 19X2 is considered to be the cash expected to be generated by the investment, how should the cover method be applied in the financial statements for the year ended December 31, 19X2?

The relevant exchange rates are:

	£1=¥
December 31, 19X1	235
December 31, 19X2	229

Exchange differences

Investment — ¥1,000m	@ 235 = £4,255,319	
	@ 229 = £4,366,812	
	————	£111,493
Loan — ¥1,000m	@ 235 = £4,255,319	
	@ 229 = £4,366,812	
	————	£(111,493)

As the exchange loss on the loan is matched by the exchange gain on the investment it would appear that none of the exchange loss on the loan need be taken to profit and loss account. However, as the cash expected to be generated from the investment is only ¥600m then this condition has to be considered. The possible effects of this on the cover method are as follows:

(a) Abandon the cover method with retrospective effect.

It could be argued that as the amount of the loan exceeds the cash expected to be generated then the cover method cannot be applied and therefore all of the losses on the loan, including the £1,234,043 in respect of 19X1, should be reflected in the profit and loss account for the year and in the company financial statements the investment translated at historical rates and the exchange gains of £1,875,000 on the investment reversed. This reflects the position which would have been shown if the cover method had not been applied, except for the fact that the loss for the previous year is included in the current year. A prior year adjustment is inappropriate as it is a change in circumstances which has given rise to the cover method not being used.

(b) Abandon the cover method for the current year and thereafter.

It could be argued that as it is only this year that the company has not met all the conditions for applying the cover method it is only this year's exchange loss on the loan which should be reflected in the profit and loss account. Last year the company was hedged and therefore the financial statements should still reflect that fact. In the company's financial statements the investment would not be retranslated using the closing rate but a provision of £1,635,232 would be made against the investment to reduce it to ¥600m @ £1=229, i.e. £2,620,087.

(c) Apply the cover method for the current year but abandon it thereafter.

The calculation of exchange differences is based on opening figures for the investment and the loan. At that time the cash expected from the investment was sufficient to meet the loan, and accordingly the cover method can still be applied and therefore all of the exchange loss on the loan can be taken to reserves. However, provision would have to made in the company's financial statements to reduce the retranslated cost of investment of £4,366,812 to its recoverable amount of £2,620,087.

(d) Apply the cover method to the amount recoverable.

This treatment considers that in applying the cash restriction the loan is effectively split into two parts; (i) an amount equivalent to the cash expected to be generated and (ii) the excess over this amount. The first part is still considered to hedge the investment and the cover method can still be applied to that part. The second part is no longer providing a hedge against any investment and therefore any exchange differences relating to this part must be taken to profit and loss account. In this example, therefore, the treatment would be as follows:

Exchange gain on investment (as above)		£111,493
Exchange loss on restricted loan		
¥600m	@ 235 = £2,553,191	
	@ 229 = £2,620,087	
	———————	
		(66,896)
		———————
Net exchange gain taken to reserves		£ 44,597
		———————

The exchange loss on the remainder of the loan, of £44,597, would be taken to the profit and loss account. In the company's financial statements a provision of £1,746,725 would be made to reduce the retranslated cost of investment to its recoverable amount as in (c) above.

In our view all of these treatments are acceptable under the standard but we believe that method (d) is preferable as this recognises that the company is still hedged to a certain extent.

B   Respective currency movements

We indicated earlier that the reason for condition (b) of paragraph 51 and condition (c) of paragraph 57 of the standard was to allow the cover method to be used when different currencies were involved. Although companies may decide to invest in one currency and borrow in another with the expectation or hope that they will generally move in tandem in relation to sterling this will not always be the case. In any period some currencies will strengthen in relation to sterling and others will weaken and of those that move in the same direction the extent to which they strengthen or weaken can be markedly different. As a result, the cash restriction conditions may become relevant where they have not been before.

Example 18.40

On January 1, 19X0 a UK company invests in a German company at a cost of DM3,540,000. How should the company apply the cover method in its financial statements for the year ended December 31, 19X0 if it financed the investment with (a) a loan of 3,990,000 Dutch guilders or (b) a loan of 290 million Japanese yen ?

The relevant exchange rates are:

	£1=DM	£1=DFl	£1=¥
January 1, 19X0	3.54	3.99	290
December 31, 19X0	2.86	3.25	235

		(a) £	(b) £
Exchange gain on investment			
DM3,540,000 @ 3.54 = £1,000,000 @ 2.86 = £1,237,762		237,762	237,762
Exchange loss on loan			
(a)DFl 3,990,000 @ 3.99 = £1,000,000 @ 3.25 = £1,227,692		(227,692)	
(b)¥290m @ 290 = £1,000,000 @ 235 = £1,234,043			(234,043)
		10,070	3,719

It can be seen that in both cases that the hedging has been successful and the cover method can be applied.

We now look at the position in the financial statements for the following year,19X1. The relevant exchange rates at the year end are £1=DM2.97=DFl 3.33=¥229.

	(a)	(b)
	£	£
Exchange loss on investment		
DM3,540,000 @ 2.86 = £1,237,762		
@ 2.97 = £1,191,919		
	(45,843)	(45,843)
Exchange difference on loan		
(a)DFl 3,990,000 @ 3.25 = £1,227,692		
@ 3.33 = £1,198,198		
	29,494	
(b)¥290m @ 235 = £1,234,043		
@ 229 = £1,266,376		
		(32,333)

It can be seen that in the case of the DFl loan condition (a) of paragraph 51 of the standard is met and therefore it would appear that the cover method can be applied. However, if the book value of the investment is considered to be the recoverable amount of the investment then condition (b) has to be considered as the book value of £1,191,919 is less than the amount of the loan which is £1,198,198.

This is due to the fact that although both currencies have weakened in relation to sterling the DM has weakened more than the DFl.

In the case of the yen loan the cover method cannot be applied as there are exchange losses on both the investment and the loan. This is because the currencies have moved in opposite directions in relation to sterling with the yen continuing to strengthen. Again, consideration has to be given to the effect of condition (b) as this loan is even more clearly not covered by the amount of the investment.

The possible treatments of condition (b) are those which were considered in the previous example. In the case of the DFl loan in this example, adopting either of methods (b) or (c) will have the curious effect of actually improving the results shown in the profit and loss account as all or part of the exchange gain on the loan will be reflected therein.

3.6   Intra-group long-term loans and deferred trading balances

3.6.1   General requirement

SSAP 20 requires that all monetary items are translated at closing rates[181] and the resulting exchange differences are taken to profit and loss account.[182] This requirement is equally valid for amounts due to or from other companies within the group.[183] Any exchange differences on these inter-company accounts would be reflected, initially, in the profit and loss account of the group company which was exposed to the currency risk. On consolidation, such exchange differences would normally remain in the profit and loss account in the same way as exchange differences on monetary items resulting from transactions with third parties.

In certain circumstances, however, a holding company may decide to finance a subsidiary with loan capital rather than equity share capital with the intention of providing long-term capital for the subsidiary. This may be done for a variety of reasons; there may be tax advantages of so doing; the subsidiary may be restricted in paying dividends but not interest payments; or it may be easier to recover loans rather than equity in the event of nationalisation of the subsidiary.

Whatever the reason, the substance of the transaction is to provide long-term finance for the subsidiary and therefore the question arises of why the financial statements should show a different result by including exchange differences on the loan in the profit and loss account when exchange differences relating to the equity finance would be taken to reserves.

3.6.2 *Paragraphs 20 and 43*

Paragraph 20 of SSAP 20 recognises this and the fact that companies may finance subsidiaries by deferring trading balances as follows:'Although equity investments in foreign enterprises will normally be made by the purchase of shares, investments may also be made by means of long-term loans and inter-company deferred trading balances. Where financing by such means is intended to be, for all practical purposes, as permanent as equity, such loans and inter-company balances should be treated as part of the investing company's net investment in the foreign enterprise; hence exchange differences arising on such loans and inter-company balances should be dealt with as adjustments to reserves.'

The definition of 'net investment' in paragraph 43 of the standard states that 'in appropriate circumstances, intra-group loans and other deferred balances may be regarded as part of the effective equity stake'.

3.6.3 *How permanent is permanent?*

It can be seen from the above that this treatment for the exchange differences should be applied where such inter-company accounts are intended to be, for all practical purposes, as permanent as equity. How should this be interpreted?

It could be argued that if it is planned or intended to repay the inter-company amount at any time while the company is a subsidiary then it is not as permanent as equity and the exchange differences should be taken to profit and loss account. The amount should only be considered as permanent as equity if it will be repaid only when the holding company disinvests entirely from the subsidiary. This would mean that even if a company had financed a subsidiary by providing it with a loan which was due to be repaid in twenty or thirty years time and the intention was that this would be repaid at that time then the exchange differences on the loan during that period should be recorded in the profit and loss account. This is because the exchange differences will ultimately be reflected in cash flows.

However, it is recognised that in such circumstances this would be unrealistic and therefore a shorter timespan should be considered. It has been suggested by other writers that if there is no intention to repay the amount within the foreseeable future then the inter-company account can be regarded as permanent as equity.[184]

The term 'foreseeable future' is used in paragraph 12 of SSAP 15 — *Accounting for deferred taxation* — and, although not defined, is often taken to mean a period of approximately three to five years.[185] It has been suggested that this same criterion is used in considering whether an inter-company account is as permanent as equity.[186]

It is probably easier to regard a long-term loan which is not repayable until twenty or thirty years as being as permanent as equity. What if the loan is a short-term one which is continually rolled over? In our view, if the intention is that the loan will continue to be rolled over so that it is effectively a long-term one which is not repayable in the foreseeable future, then the loan can be regarded as permanent as equity. However, we believe that if the intention is that the loan will only be rolled over until such time as the subsidiary can repay the loan, then the loan should not be regarded as permanent as equity.

The standard also allows deferred trading balances to be regarded as permanent as equity.[187] As well as including balances arising from purchase and sale of goods and services these could also include interest payments and dividend payments which have not been paid for in cash but are accumulated in the inter-company account.

In our view, such balances should only be regarded as permanent if cash settlement is not made or planned to be made in the foreseeable future. If a subsidiary makes payment for purchases from its parent company, but is continually indebted to the parent company as a result of new purchases, then in these circumstances, as individual transactions are settled, no part of the inter-company balance should be regarded as permanent. Accordingly, such exchange differences should be taken to profit and loss account.

3.6.4   What happens in year of change?

It may happen that a company will decide that its subsidiary requires to be refinanced and instead of investing more equity capital in the subsidiary decides that an existing inter-company account, which has previously been regarded as a normal monetary item, should become a long-term deferred trading balance and no repayment of such amount will be requested within the foreseeable future. How should the company treat the exchange differences relating to the inter-company account in the consolidated financial statements in the year it was so designated?

Example 18.41

· A UK company has a wholly owned US subsidiary whose net assets at December 31, 19X0 were US$2,000,000. These net assets were arrived at after taking account of a liability to the UK parent of £500,000. Using the closing exchange rate of £1=US$1.48 this liability was included in the US company's balance sheet at that date at US$740,000. On June 30, 19X1 the company decided that in order to refinance the US subsidiary that it would regard the liability of £500,000 as a long-term liability which would not be called for repayment in the foreseeable future. Consequently, the company thereafter regarded such loan as being part of its net investment in the subsidiary. In the year ended December 31, 19X1 the US company made no profit or loss other than any exchange difference to be recognised on its liability to its parent company. The relevant exchange rate at that date was £1=US$1.88.

The financial statements of the subsidiary in US$ and translated using the closing rate are as follows:

Balance sheet	December 31, 19X1		December 31, 19X0	
	US$	£	US$	£
Assets	2,740,000	1,457,447	2,740,000	1,851,351
Amount due to parent	940,000	500,000	740,000	500,000
Net assets	1,800,000	957,447	2,000,000	1,351,351

Profit and loss account		
Exchange difference	(200,000)	

The normal treatment would be for this exchange loss to be translated at the closing rate and included in the consolidated profit and loss account as £106,383. As the net investment was US$2,000,000 then there would have been an exchange loss taken to reserves of £287,521, i.e. £1,351,351 less £1,063,830 (US$2,000,000 @ £1=1.88).

However, as the company now regards the amount due as being as permanent as equity it has to be included in the net investment. The question then arises as to when this should be regarded as having happened and how the exchange difference on it should be calculated. The only guidance given in SSAP 20 is in paragraph 16 which states that when applying the closing rate/net investment method, exchange differences arise if the rate ruling at the balance sheet date differs from the rate ruling at the date of subsequent capital injection. In this case there has been no capital injection as such, merely a 'redesignation' of a previous inter-company balance.

One treatment would be to regard the 'capital injection' as having taken place at the beginning of the accounting period and, therefore, the net investment increased at that date to US$2,740,000. The exchange loss on this amount is £393,904, i.e. £1,851,351 less £1,457,447, and this amount should be taken to reserves. Accordingly, all of the exchange loss included in the subsidiary's profit and loss account would be taken to reserves on consolidation. This has the merit of treating all of the exchange loss for this year consistently in the same way and it could be argued that this treatment is necessary as none of the exchange loss has any impact on the prospective cash flows of the group.

An alternative treatment would be to regard the 'capital injection' as having occurred when it was decided to redesignate the inter-company account and to take the exchange difference arising on the account up to that date to the profit and loss account. Only the exchange difference arising thereafter would be taken to reserves. At June 30, 19X1 the subsidiary would have translated the inter-company account as US$805,000 (£500,000 @£1=1.61) and therefore the exchange loss up to that date was US$65,000. Translated at the closing rate this amount would be included in the consolidated profit and loss account as £34,574. Accordingly, £71,809 (£106,383 less £34,574) would be taken to reserves.

This amount represents the exchange loss on the 'capital injection' of US$805,000. Translated at the closing rate this amounts to £428,191 which is £71,809 less than the original £500,000. This treatment has the merit of treating the inter-company account up to the date of redesignation consistently with previous years and taking the same exchange difference to reserves which would have been taken if a capital injection had taken place at June 30, 19X1. For these reasons we believe that this treatment is preferable to the former treatment although both treatments are acceptable.

Suppose, instead of the inter-company account being £500,000, it was denominated in dollars at US$740,000. In this case the parent company would be exposed to the exchange risk; what would be the position?

The subsidiary's net assets at both December 31, 19X0 and 19X1 would be:

Assets	US$2,740,000
Amount due to parent company	740,000
Net assets	US$2,000,000

As the inter-company account is expressed in US dollars, there will be no exchange difference thereon in the subsidiary's profit and loss account.

There will, however, be an exchange loss in the parent company as follows:

US$740,000   @ 1.48 = £500,000
             @ 1.88 = £393,617
                      £106,383

Again, in the consolidated financial statements as the inter-company account is now regarded as part of the equity investment some or all of this amount can be taken to reserves. If the treatment of regarding this as happening at the beginning of the period is adopted then all of the exchange loss would be taken to reserves. This gives the same result as when the account was expressed in sterling.

If the alternative treatment is adopted then the position would be:

$740,000   @ 1.48 = £500,000
            @ 1.61 = £459,627
            ————   £40,373

            @ 1.61 = £459,627
            @ 1.88 = £393,617
            ————   £66,010

The exchange loss up to June 30, 19X1 of £40,373 would be taken to profit and loss account and the exchange loss thereafter of £66,010 would be taken to reserves. This is different from when the account was expressed in sterling because the 'capital injection' in this case is US$740,000 whereas before it was effectively US$805,000.

3.6.5   Is such a treatment allowed in the company financial statements?

We saw in the above example that when the inter-company account was expressed in US dollars an exchange difference arose in the parent company and how this would be treated in the consolidated financial statements. What about the parent company financial statements? Is a similar approach allowed?

Some people take the view that SSAP 20 does not permit exchange differences on loans and deferred trading balances which are considered to be as permanent as equity to be taken to reserves in the parent company's own financial statements.[188] This is because the standard only refers to such treatment when discussing the closing rate/net investment method and in defining the net investment in the foreign enterprise.[189] As a result, it is only relevant to consolidated financial statements. No allowance is made in the provisions of SSAP 20 dealing with the financial statements of individual companies for such a treatment. These provisions require all exchange differences on monetary items to be taken to profit and loss account (except in circumstances which are not relevant here).[190] The parent company's financial statements should therefore reflect in the results the effect of the parent company being exposed to exchange risk on its inter-company account as it is a monetary item.

Another view is that the parent company's financial statements should reflect the fact that in substance the inter-company account is not a monetary item.[191] If the account is intended to be as permanent as equity then the financial statements of the parent company should effectively show the same results and financial position as if it were an equity investment. One of the objectives of SSAP 20 is to produce results which are compatible with the effects of exchange rate changes on a company's cash flows.[192] As there is no intention for the inter-company account to be repaid until disinvestment or at least in the foreseeable future then there will be no effect on the company's cash flows as no repayments are being made. Accordingly, no exchange differences relating to the inter-company account should be reflected in the profit and loss account. We believe that this is the approach which companies should be adopting.

3.6.6   *If so, how should loans be translated?*

Example 18.42

Suppose in the previous example the inter-company account of US$740,000 initially arose when the exchange rate was £1=US$1.25. The possible treatments would be:

(a) Translate at closing rate

The reason for this treatment is to reflect the fact that the inter-company account is a monetary item and as such should be retranslated at closing rate. However, as the exchange differences will not impact on cash flows they should not all be taken to the profit and loss account for the year but some or all of them should be taken to reserves as explained in 3.6.4 above. It could be argued that as paragraph 20 of the standard refers to exchange differences being taken to reserves that this is the treatment required by the standard.

(b) Translate at historical rate ruling when account originally arose

As the account is considered to be as permanent as equity then it should be translated as such. Equity investments should be included at the historical rate of exchange (unless they have been financed or hedged by foreign borrowings). The account would therefore be included in the parent company balance sheet at £592,000, i.e. US$740,000 @ £1=US$1.25. The difference between this and the previously recorded amount of £500,000, or the amount when it was regarded as permanent, of £459,627, should be treated as a reserve movement.

(c) Retain at the rate ruling when the account was considered to be permanent

The reason for this treatment is that the decision during the year is a change in circumstance. Accordingly, the nature of the account only changed on June 30, 19X1 and it is this date which is relevant for determining the historical rate of exchange. The account would therefore be translated as £459,627 and no further exchange difference would be recorded. (If the former treatment referred to in 3.6.4 above is adopted on consolidation then a consistent treatment in the parent company's financial statements would be to retain the account at the amount included in the previous balance sheet, i.e. £500,000.)

All previous exchange differences relating to the account should not be reversed as they arose when the inter-company account was considered to be a monetary amount.

In our view method (c) is preferable as this would be the amount included if it were an equity investment; however, all three methods are probably acceptable.

3.6.7   *U.K subsidiary with loan from overseas parent company*

The previous sections have dealt with a UK parent considering that an amount due by a foreign subsidiary is as permanent as equity. What about the opposite situation where an amount is owed by a UK company to its overseas parent company, expressed in the foreign currency? Can similar treatments be adopted where the overseas parent company considers the amount due by the UK company as permanent as equity so that exchange differences on the inter-company account do not need to be reflected in the UK company's profit or loss for the year in its own financial statements?

SSAP 20 does not deal with this specific point. It could be argued that if there is no intention that such an amount will be repaid then any exchange differences will have no effect on the cash flows of the UK company and, therefore, they should not be reflected in the profit and loss account. To adopt similar treatments to those referred to above would reflect the substance of the transaction.

We believe, however, that the UK company has to translate the inter-company account at closing rate and take the exchange differences arising thereon to the profit and loss account. This is because the amount will be shown as a liability in the balance sheet and cannot be shown as equity until such time as shares are issued to the parent company or the parent company writes off the inter-company account as a capital contribution.

3.7   Other intra-group transactions

As indicated in 3.6.1 above, exchange differences on intra-group transactions should normally be treated in the same way as if they arose on transactions with third parties. However, there are two further problem areas which arise when preparing the consolidated financial statements.

3.7.1   *Dividends*

The first area relates to dividends payable by a foreign subsidiary to its UK parent company.

If a subsidiary pays a dividend to the parent company during the year the UK company should record the dividend at the rate ruling when the dividend was declared. An exchange difference will arise in the parent company's own financial statements if the exchange rate moves between the declaration date and the date the dividend is actually received. This exchange difference requires to be taken to profit and loss account and will remain there on consolidation. However, on consolidation another exchange difference is likely to arise as the dividend paid by the subsidiary will be translated at closing rate (or average rate) and this is likely to be different from the dividend received recorded by the parent company.

Example 18.43

A UK company has a wholly owned US subsidiary. On June 30, 19X1 the subsidiary declares a dividend of US$0.10 per share and is due to pay a dividend of US$100,000 to the UK parent company. In preparing the consolidated financial statements for the year ended December 31, 19X1 the UK company uses the closing rate/net investment method and translates the results of the US subsidiary at the closing rate. The relevant exchange rates at June 30, 19X1 and December 31, 19X1 are £1=US$1.61 and £1=US$1.88 respectively. Accordingly, the dividend received is recorded at £62,112 and the dividend paid in the translated profit and loss account is £53,191. What should happen to the difference of £8,921 when the inter-company dividends are eliminated on consolidation?

One treatment would be to take it to the profit and loss account as an adjustment of the subsidiary's profit or loss as suggested by Westwick.[193] This has the effect of including in the consolidated profit and loss account the profits of the subsidiary which were distributed at the sterling amount received and the profits retained by the subsidiary translated at the closing rate.

An alternative treatment would be to treat it as a movement on reserves as the consolidated profit and loss account should reflect the profits of the subsidiary translated at the closing rate. This method will therefore retain the same financial relationships shown in the subsidiary's own financial statements in the consolidated financial statements. Consequently, we consider this treatment to be preferable.

We believe that such a treatment should also be adopted even if the dividend was unpaid at the year end. In the above example, if this had been the case, by the year end the parent company would have recorded an exchange loss of £8,921 on the dividend receivable in its own profit and loss account. We consider that this loss should remain in the profit and loss account and the difference on consolidation taken to reserves even although it is a gain of the same amount.

Another situation concerning intra-group dividends is when a dividend is proposed by the subsidiary company and this is recorded at the year end in both companies' financial statements. There is no problem in that year as both the intercompany accounts and the dividends will eliminate on consolidation with no exchange differences arising. However, as the dividend will not be received until the following year an exchange difference will arise in the parent company's financial statements in that year.

Example 18.44

A UK company has a wholly owned French subsidiary. When preparing the financial statements for the year ended December 31, 19X0 it was decided that the French company would propose a dividend of FFr0.20 per share for the year then ended payable on June 30, 19X1, resulting in a dividend due to the parent company of FFr200,000. The parent company, therefore, recorded in its financial statements for the year ended 31 December 19X0 a dividend receivable of FFr200,000, which translated at the exchange rate ruling on that date of £1=FFr9.46, amounted to £21,142. As the subsidiary was consolidated using the closing rate/net investment method then the dividend receivable and the dividend payable cancelled each other out on consolidation. On June 30, 19X1 the dividend was paid and as the exchange rate was then £1=FFr9.83 the amount actually received was £20,346 and, therefore, the parent company recorded an exchange loss of £796. How should this exchange difference be dealt with in the consolidated financial statements for the year ended December 31, 19X1?

This exchange difference should remain in the profit and loss account as it is no different from any other exchange difference arising on inter-company accounts resulting from other types of inter-company transactions. It should not be taken to reserves.

It may seem odd that the consolidated results can be affected by exchange differences on inter-company dividends. In order to minimise the effect of exchange rate movements companies should, therefore, arrange for inter-company dividends to be paid on the same day the dividend is declared, or as soon after the dividend is declared as possible. In addition, they should consider not booking proposed dividends in the year to which they relate but when they are actually declared unless there are commercial reasons for doing so, e.g. in order to maximise the distributable profits of the parent company shown in the year end financial statements.

3.7.2   Unrealised profits

The other problem area is the elimination of unrealised profits resulting from inter-company transactions when one of the parties to the transaction is a foreign subsidiary whose results are incorporated into the consolidated financial statements using the closing rate/net investment method.

Example 18.45

A UK company has a wholly owned US subsidiary. On October 31, 19X1 the subsidiary sold goods to the parent company for US$1,000. The cost of the goods to the subsidiary was US$700. The goods were recorded by the parent company at £581 based on the exchange rate ruling on October 31, 19X1 of £1=US$1.72. All of the goods are unsold by the year end, December 31, 19X1. The exchange rate at that date was £1=US$1.88. How should the inter-company profit be eliminated?

SSAP 20 contains no guidance on this matter and it has been suggested that it would be logical to use the rate ruling at the date of the transaction.[194]

The profit shown by the subsidiary is US$300 which translated at the rate ruling on the transaction of £1=US$1.72 equals £174. Consequently, the goods will be included in the balance sheet at:

Per parent company balance sheet	£581
Less unrealised profit eliminated	174
	£407

It can be seen that the resulting figure for stock is equivalent to the original dollar cost translated at the rate ruling on the date of the transaction. This is the treatment required by SFAS 52.[195] However, it should be remembered that SFAS 52 requires the results of foreign enterprises to be translated using actual or weighted average rates[196] and, therefore, is to be recommended when a weighted average is being used. Where the closing rate is being used then such an approach does not eliminate the profit from the profit and loss account. In this example, the profit of the subsidiary includes $300 which translated at US$1.88 equals £160 and the amount eliminated is £174. We believe it is the former amount which should be eliminated even though this will not result in a balance sheet figure for the goods equivalent to the original cost of the goods to the group.

Consequently, where the closing rate is used to translate the results of foreign subsidiaries then we would recommend that any adjustment made to eliminate any of those profits which are unrealised as far as the group is concerned should be calculated using that closing rate. If a weighted average rate is used then the rate ruling on the date of the transaction should be used.

If in the above example the goods had been sold by the UK company to the US subsidiary then we believe the amount to be eliminated is the amount of profit shown in the UK company's financial statements. Again, this will not necessarily result in the goods being carried in the consolidated financial statements at their original cost to the group.

4   MAIN CRITICISMS OF SSAP 20 AND SUGGESTED SOLUTIONS

We believe that SSAP 20 has improved the reporting of foreign currency transactions in financial statements. However, in our view a number of criticisms can be made against the standard and further improvements could be made to ensure greater comparability between companies both within the UK and internationally.

4.1   Forward contracts and similar hedging contracts

4.1.1   Criticisms

We have looked at the many problem areas which arise in accounting for these types of transactions in 3.3 above. In our view there are two main criticisms of the approach taken by SSAP 20 in relation to forward contracts and other similar hedging contracts, such as options and currency swaps.

A   Insufficient guidance

Firstly, there is insufficient guidance on the accounting for such contracts. Forward contracts are only mentioned by stating that the contract rate may be used to record transactions and monetary assets and liabilities.[197] Although reference is made to the discount or premium on the forward contract when defining what a forward contract is,[198] no further guidance is given as to how to account for the discount or premium. As indicated in 3.3.1 above, a forward contract can be taken out as a hedge against an investment in a foreign enterprise, the results of a foreign enterprise, an existing monetary asset or liability position, or a future commitment, or it may be taken out as a speculative transaction. In each case the accounting for the contract is not necessarily the same.

No mention is made of currency swaps and other agreements which are essentially the same as forward contracts or of currency options.

B   Use of forward rates is optional

Secondly, by stating that the rates included in forward contracts *may* be used to record transactions or translate monetary assets or liabilities has meant that the accounting for the forward contracts has become optional. Companies can choose to ignore a related forward contract if they wish. As a result consistency of treatment between different companies is unlikely to be achieved.

4.1.2   Solution

We believe that SSAP 20 should be amended to deal with the topic of forward contracts and similar agreements, such as currency swaps, in a similar way to SFAS 52 as suggested in 3.3 above, except that companies should be able to account for forward contracts which are designated as a hedge against anticipated future transactions rather than just those which are the subject of a firm commitment.

4.2   Cover method

4.2.1   Criticisms

We have looked at a number of problem areas relating to the use of the cover method in 3.5 above. In our view there are three main criticisms which can be made against the provisions of SSAP 20 in respect of borrowings which have been used to finance, or provide a hedge against, equity investments.

A   Use is optional

Firstly, by stating that the equity investments *may* be denominated in foreign currencies [199] the standard allows companies to choose whether or not they wish to apply the cover method provisions. As a result comparability between different companies is unlikely to be achieved. This also applies to the provisions relating to consolidated financial statements as exchange differences *may* be offset as reserve movements.[200]

B   Cover may not exist when borrowings are in different currencies

Secondly, the absence of a requirement that borrowings be in the same currency as the investment means that cover may not exist. Different currencies may move in different directions in relation to sterling or to a different extent in the same direction in relation to sterling. Accordingly, companies cannot be assured that they will always be covered. In order to eliminate the exchange risk completely it is necessary for the borrowings to be in the same currency as the investment.

C   It can lead to inconsistent treatment from period to period

Thirdly, by allowing borrowings to be in different currencies from the investments then the exchange differences on the borrowings will not necessarily be treated the same way each year. In those periods in which the criteria contained in SSAP 20 are met exchange differences will be taken to reserves, and in periods in which they are not met exchange differences will either all be taken to profit and loss account or some will be taken to reserves and the rest to profit and loss account.

4.2.2   Solution

We believe that SSAP 20 should be amended along similar lines to that contained in SFAS 52.[201]

A   Designation requirement

Exchange differences on transactions (including borrowings) that are designated, and are effective, as economic hedges of an equity investment or the net investment in a foreign enterprise should be taken to reserves and should not be taken to profit and loss account, commencing from the designation date. Such treatment will ensure that the accounting for the exchange differences reflect the economic rationale of the decision taken by the company.

B   *Same currency requirement with exception for use of tandem currency*

The transaction which hedges the equity investment or the net investment in the foreign enterprise should be denominated in the same currency as the investment. Where it is not practical or feasible for the currency to be the same then the hedging transaction may be in a currency which generally moves in tandem with the currency of the hedged investment. Such a requirement will recognise that an effective hedge can only arise where the currencies are the same.

4.3   Reserve accounting

4.3.1   *Criticism*

A   *Exchange differences on investments, and borrowings which are a hedge, never pass through the profit and loss account*

SSAP 20 requires that exchange differences on the net investments in foreign enterprises be taken to reserves and not to profit and loss account.[202] The rationale for this treatment is that they do not represent or measure changes in actual cash flows.[203] Although we agree with this basic treatment, in our view exchange differences will ultimately be reflected in cash flows when dividends are received from the investments or when the investments are ultimately sold. No provisions are contained in SSAP 20 as to what should happen to the cumulative exchange differences which have arisen on the investments when the investments are sold or dividends are received. As a result, the exchange differences are usually not reflected in the profit and loss account at any time, even when the investment is sold.

Similarly, exchange differences on borrowings which have financed or provided a hedge against equity investments are normally taken to reserves even although they will have an impact on the cash flows of the company. It is therefore possible for the borrowings to have been completely repaid and none of the exchange differences thereon taken through the profit and loss account.

In our view such a treatment is akin to reserve accounting and is inconsistent with the general approach taken in SSAP 6. We believe that such exchange differences should at some stage pass through the profit and loss account as they will ultimately have an effect on the cash flows of the company.

4.3.2   *Solution*

In our view, SSAP 20 should be amended so that exchange differences which are taken to reserves are eventually taken to profit and loss account when they are realised and have an impact on cash flows. Exchange differences arising on the retranslation of the net investment in a foreign enterprise should be taken to a separate reserve within shareholders' interests. Exchange differences on hedging transactions should be taken to the same reserve. This will enable users of the financial statements to identify the exchange differences which have still to be reflected in the profit and loss account.

The cumulative exchange differences relating to a particular net investment should be taken to profit and loss account when the investment is sold as part of the gain or loss on sale of the investment. Where a partial disposal is made then a proportion of the cumulative exchange difference should be taken to profit and loss account. This is similar to the approach taken in the US.[204] We believe that this realisation principle should be extended so that a proportion of the cumulative exchange differences is also taken to profit and loss account when dividends out of previously reported profits are received from the foreign enterprise in the UK or when inter-company accounts which were considered to be as permanent as equity are repaid.

Exchange differences on hedging transactions should also be taken to profit and loss account when they have an impact on cash flows; e.g. where a loan is repayable by instalments then the cumulative exchange differences relating to each instalment should be taken to profit and loss account as the instalment is paid.

4.4   Conclusion

We believe that the reporting of foreign currency transactions would be significantly improved if SSAP 20 were amended as suggested above and greater comparability of results between companies within the UK and internationally would be achieved. As all of the suggestions are compatible with the existing provisions of SSAP 20 we would recommend that companies adopt such treatments presently.

5   RELATED COMPANIES ACT 1985 REQUIREMENTS

There are a number of requirements of the Companies Act 1985 which have to be considered when accounting for foreign exchange transactions. The main implications are considered below.

5.1   Realised profits

Most companies in the UK when preparing their financial statements have to comply with the accounting requirements of Schedule 4 of the Companies Act 1985.

5.1.1   *Schedule 4, paragraph 12*

Paragraph 12 of Schedule 4 requires that items in a company's financial statements shall be determined on a prudent basis and only profits which are realised at the balance sheet date can be included in the profit and loss account. However, what is meant by realised profits?

5.1.2   *Schedule 4, paragraph 91*

Paragraph 91 of Schedule 4 states that realised profits should be interpreted as 'such profits of the company as fall to be treated as realised profits for the purposes of those accounts in accordance with principles generally accepted with respect to the determination for accounting purposes of realised profits at the time when those accounts are prepared'.

The main reference to realised profits by the accountancy profession in the UK is in SSAP 2 when defining the concept of prudence. This states 'revenue and profits are not anticipated, but are recognised by inclusion in the profit and loss account only when realised in the form either of cash or of other assets the ultimate cash realisation of which can be assessed with reasonable certainty'.[205]

The normal requirement for exchange differences in the financial statements of a company is that they are taken to profit and loss account. As a result the ASC in considering this treatment for exchange differences had to give some guidance as to whether exchange gains were to be regarded as realised or not and whether the treatment of such gains required by the standard was consistent with the provisions of paragraph 12.

SSAP 20 identifies three categories of exchange gains which have to be considered.

5.1.3   Settled transactions

Firstly, those arising on settled transactions. As such exchange gains have already impacted on the cash flows of the company then they are clearly realised in cash terms and, therefore, their inclusion in the profit and loss account does not conflict with paragraph 12.

5.1.4   Short-term monetary items

Secondly, those arising on short-term monetary items. A short-term monetary item is defined in SSAP 20 as one which falls due within one year of the balance sheet date.[206] The statement issued by the ASC at the time the standard was issued said that such exchange gains could be regarded as realised in accordance with the prudence concept contained in SSAP 2, as their ultimate cash realisation can normally be assessed with reasonable certainty. Accordingly, their inclusion in the profit and loss account is not considered to be in conflict with paragraph 12.[207]

5.1.5   Long-term monetary items

Thirdly, those arising on long-term monetary items. It is generally considered that such gains are probably unrealised. The ASC recognised this potential conflict with paragraph 12 but still decided that exchange gains on such items should be taken to the profit and loss account. They considered that a symmetrical treatment of exchange gains and losses was necessary to show a true and fair view of the results of a company involved in foreign currency operations. This treatment acknowledges that exchange gains can be determined no less objectively than exchange losses and it would be illogical to deny that favourable movements in exchange rates had occurred whilst accounting for adverse movements. As there will probably be some interaction between currency movements and interest rates then the profit and loss account will reflect the full impact of the currency involvement.[208] So how was the conflict resolved?

One way would have been to invoke the true and fair view override allowed by what is now section 228 of the Companies Act 1985. However, as the problem was with one of the accounting principles contained in Schedule 4 it was decided to invoke paragraph 15 of that schedule.[209]

This paragraph specifically permits a departure from the accounting principles where there are special reasons and it is considered that the need for a symmetrical treatment constitutes a special reason. As a result, companies who have taken exchange gains on long-term monetary items need to disclose the particulars of the departure, the reasons for it and its effect in a note to the financial statements. An example of such disclosure is as follows:

The profit and loss account includes gains on translation of long-term monetary items. The inclusion of these gains represents a departure from the statutory requirement that only realised profit may be included in the profit and loss account. The directors consider that this accounting treatment, which is in accordance with SSAP 20, is necessary in order to give a true and fair view. The unrealised gains included for the year amounted to £10,000 (19X1–£5,000) and the cumulative amount included at December 31, 19X2 is £15,000.

A   *Problem areas*

In 3.2 above we considered a number of problem areas in relation to exchange gains on long-term monetary items which will also be relevant in deciding whether it is necessary to invoke paragraph 15 and give the necessary disclosures, in particular the amount of the exchange gains which are involved.

(a)   Past exchange losses

      It could be argued that past exchange losses on a long-term monetary item should be ignored and that all of the exchange gain in the current year is unrealised and therefore disclosure is required of the full amount. This would appear to be an ultra cautious view.[210]

      Our view is that past exchange losses should be taken into account and that disclosure is only required to the extent that the exchange gain exceeds the net losses previously recognised. Any exchange gain up to the amount of the past losses is effectively a reversal of a provision for losses no longer required. This would appear to be the approach taken by other writers.[211]

      Accordingly, if the exchange gain is less than the past exchange losses no disclosure is required under paragraph 15.

(b)   Settled or unsettled transactions

      As the exchange gain in question relates to an unsettled long-term monetary item then in considering the effect of past exchange losses we believe that it is only the past exchange losses which relate to the proportion which is still outstanding which should be taken into account. Past exchange losses and any current year's exchange losses which relate to amounts which have already been settled should be ignored.

(c)   Current portion of long-term monetary items

      As any current portion at the end of the financial year will be reflected in cash flows within one year then any exchange gains relating thereto should be regarded as realised. Accordingly, if a long-term item at the end of the previous period has all become due within one year at the end of the current period then no disclosure is required under paragraph 15.

In view of these problem areas we would recommend that companies keep a detailed record of the exchange differences which have arisen on all long-term monetary items since origination.

5.2   Distributable profits

5.2.1   *Section 263(3)*

Under section 263(3) of the Companies Act 1985, dividends can only be paid by a company out of cumulative realised profits less realised losses and, therefore, the question of whether exchange gains are realised or not, or indeed whether exchange losses are realised or not, has an important bearing on the distributable profits of a company. The distributable profits of a public company are further restricted to the extent that unrealised losses exceed unrealised profits.[212]

The statement issued by the ASC at the time the standard was published made it clear that the statement only set out the standard accounting practice for foreign currency translation and was not intended to deal with the determination of distributable profits. It emphasised that the question of distributability depends upon the interpretation of company legislation and should be resolved by individual companies, with legal advice where necessary.[213] It did, however, comment on two possible problem areas.

5.2.2   *Long-term monetary items*

The first area was in relation to exchange gains on long-term monetary items. In the previous section we considered whether such gains were realised or not. Where the exchange gains are unrealised, then even although they can be taken to the profit and loss account, they cannot be included in arriving at the distributable profits of a company.[214] This makes it even more important for companies to keep a detailed record of exchange differences on such items.

5.2.3   *Section 275 and Schedule 4, paragraph 89*

So much for exchange gains, what about exchange losses?

Section 275 of the Companies Act 1985 requires that for the purposes of determining distributable profits a provision of any kind mentioned in paragraph 89 of Schedule 4 is to be treated as a realised loss.

Paragraph 89 states that 'references to provisions for liabilities or charges are to any amount retained as reasonably necessary for the purpose of providing for any liability or loss which is either likely to be incurred, or certain to be incurred but uncertain as to amount or as to the date on which it will arise'.

It is generally recognised that exchange losses on settled transactions and on unsettled short-term monetary items should be regarded as realised losses. It is also considered, on the grounds of prudence, that exchange losses on long-term monetary items should also be regarded as realised. However, this brings us to the second possible problem area — the cover method.

5.2.4   *Cover method*

As the cover method can be applied in individual companies' financial statements this will result in exchange gains and losses on borrowings being taken to reserves to be offset against exchange differences on related equity investments. If exchange losses have arisen on the borrowings should these be regarded as realised?

A   TR 504 — paragraph 33(b)

It could be argued that any exchange loss on a borrowing should be regarded as a provision under paragraph 89 of Schedule 4 and therefore a realised loss which would have to be deducted before arriving at distributable profits, whereas the compensating exchange gain on the investment would be unrealised and not available for distribution. However, as stated by the ASC 'this does not reflect the economic realities of hedging which is designed to avoid the creation of any loss and it can therefore be argued that the exchange 'loss' on the borrowing is not a provision (nor a realised loss) 'either likely to be incurred, or certain to be incurred but uncertain as to amount or as to the date on which it will arise'.

B   Problem of timing — income required before payment of loan

We believe that one possible approach to this problem is to consider the timing of the cash flows relating to the investment and the borrowings. The statement by the ASC makes no reference to the fact that some of the exchange losses which have been offset in reserves may relate to borrowings which have already been repaid. We believe that such losses should be regarded as realised as they have been reflected in the cash flows of the company. If the company has regarded the borrowing as a hedge against its investment it is likely to have received dividends from the investment to enable it to repay the borrowings. As the dividends will be recorded at the rate ruling when the dividends were due these will reflect an element of exchange difference since the investment was made. The inherent exchange gain will offset the realised exchange loss on the borrowings which have been repaid.

In considering whether any exchange losses on the borrowings which are still outstanding should be regarded as realised or not, regard should be had to the timing of the income to be received from the investment. If sufficient dividends will be received from the investment prior to each instalment on the borrowings being repaid then it could be argued that there will be no loss on the borrowings. Although any exchange loss will become realised at the time the instalment is paid this will be offset by the inherent exchange gain in the dividend. Accordingly, any exchange losses on the borrowings do not represent a provision for a loss and therefore do not have to be regarded as a realised loss under section 275. We believe that this approach recognises the economic reality that the company is hedged.

If insufficient dividends will be received prior to an instalment of the borrowing being repaid then to the extent that the borrowing is uncovered the exchange loss relating to that portion should be regarded as a realised loss.

Although we believe such an approach to be a sensible one it is unclear as to whether the courts would take a similar view. Accordingly it is important to emphasise the advice given by the ASC in its statement that where the existence of an economic hedge would have to be taken into account in order to make a distribution, it may be appropriate for the directors of the company to seek legal advice.[215]

5.2.5 *Branch accounting*

Another area, which the ASC did not deal with in its statement, is where an individual company has a foreign branch. As we have already seen the definition of a foreign branch is a wide one and can include a group of assets and liabilities which are accounted for in foreign currencies.[216] The standard requires the exchange difference on the net investment in the foreign branch to be taken to reserves.[217] The question then arises, is this one net exchange difference which has to be regarded as a realised or unrealised item, or is it an amalgamation of a number of exchange differences some of which may be realised and some of which may be not?

It could be argued that the former treatment is the more correct, particularly as the closing rate/net investment method should only be used if there is no cash flow impact on the rest of the company. If all of the net cash flows of the branch are retained in the foreign currency and not converted into sterling then why should any of the exchange difference be regarded as realised?

In our view it is likely that this former treatment can only be applied where the branch is a legally constituted branch overseas. Where the branch is a group of assets and liabilities then it is likely that the latter approach will have to be applied as the legal entity is the company. This, therefore, gives rise to a couple of problems.

A   *Similar to cover method*

Firstly, the main asset is likely to be a non-monetary item and the main liability is likely to be a long-term monetary item. This gives rise to a similar problem as that discussed in relation to the cover method above in that the exchange differences on the asset will be unrealised and the exchange differences on the borrowing could be regarded as realised. We believe, however, that it would be sensible to adopt a similar approach to that suggested in relation to borrowings under the cover method above.

B   *Short-term monetary items*

Secondly, it is likely that part of the branch will be represented by trading balances i.e. debtors, creditors, and bank balances. As these are all short-term monetary items then any exchange gains or losses should be regarded as realised.

As a result of the above it is recommended that detailed records are kept of the breakdown of exchange differences on the net investment in the foreign branch. The cumulative exchange difference at each year end should be split into:

(a)   the cumulative exchange difference on the non-monetary assets.

   This will be the difference between the net book value in currency terms translated at closing rate and translated at historical rates applying at the date of purchase. This difference should be regarded as an unrealised difference;

(b)   the cumulative exchange difference on the borrowings.

   This will be the difference between the amount outstanding in currency terms translated at closing rate and translated at historical rate when the

borrowing originated. This difference should then be determined to be
realised or unrealised as recommended above, i.e. consider whether
sufficient net income will be received from the asset prior to paying each
instalment of the borrowing;

(c)   the remainder.

This should represent the exchange differences on assets which have been
depreciated or sold, borrowings which have been repaid, and on the
monetary trading balances. All of this amount should be regarded as
realised.

We would emphasise that although we believe such an approach to be a sensible
one the courts may take a different view and therefore if it is necessary in order to
make a distribution to regard some of the exchange differences on the borrowings
as unrealised because they are covered by foreign currency assets then it may be
appropriate for the directors of the company to seek legal advice.

5.3   Disclosure

There are a number of provisions of the Companies Act which have to be
considered in relation to disclosure within a company's financial statements.

5.3.1   *Basis of translation*

A   Schedule 4, paragraph 58(1)

Paragraph 58(1) of Schedule 4 requires that 'where sums originally denominated
in foreign currencies have been brought into account under any items shown in
the balance sheet or profit or loss account, the basis on which those sums have
been translated into sterling shall be stated'.

B   SSAP 20, paragraph 59

This effectively extends the requirement of paragraph 59 of the standard so that
disclosure of the method of translating monetary and non-monetary items by
individual companies is given. Paragraph 59 only requires the method used in
translating the financial statements of foreign enterprises to be disclosed.

5.3.2   *Treatment of exchange differences in profit and loss account*

A   Formats

The profit and loss formats contained in Schedule 4 set out the headings of
income and expenditure which a company should use in preparing its profit and
loss account. It will therefore be necessary for companies to consider under which
heading exchange differences reported as part of the profit or loss for the year
should be included. Distinction is effectively made in the formats between
operating income and expenditure and other income and expenditure.
Accordingly, the nature of each exchange difference will have to be considered.

B   SSAP 20, paragraph 68

Guidance is given in paragraph 68 of the standard. Gains or losses arising from
trading transactions should normally be shown as 'other operating income or
expense' while those arising from arrangements which may be considered as

financing should be disclosed separately as part of 'other interest receivable/payable and similar income/expense'. The amounts included do not have to be separately disclosed; however, it should be borne in mind that the standard requires the net exchange difference on foreign currency borrowings less deposits to be disclosed.

5.3.3 Reserve movements

A   Schedule 4, paragraph 46

Paragraph 46 of Schedule 4 requires the following information to be disclosed about movements on any reserve:

(a)   the amount of the reserve at the date of the beginning of the financial year and as at the balance sheet date respectively;

(b)   any amounts transferred to or from the reserve during that year; and

(c)   the source and application respectively of any amounts so transferred.

B   SSAP 20, paragraph 60

These requirements are unlikely to have any major impact as paragraph 60 of the standard requires the net movement on reserves arising from exchange differences to be disclosed.

5.3.4 Movements on provisions for liabilities and charges

A   Schedule 4, paragraph 46

The requirements referred to above in respect of reserve movements apply equally to movements on provisions for liabilities and charges, e.g. a provision for deferred tax. Accordingly, it will be necessary to disclose separately the net movement on the provision which arises from exchange differences.

5.3.5 Movements on fixed assets

A   Schedule 4, paragraph 42

Paragraph 42 of Schedule 4 requires, inter alia, disclosure of movements on fixed assets resulting from:

(a)   acquisitions of any assets during the year;

(b)   disposals of any assets during the year; and

(c)   any transfer of assets of the company to and from another category of asset during the year.

Similarly, movements on provisions for depreciation or diminution in value have to be shown.

As a result of these requirements, where fixed assets are translated at closing rates it will be necessary to disclose separately the net movements arising on the cost or valuation of the fixed assets and on any related provision resulting from exchange differences.

5.4 Alternative accounting rules

5.4.1 *Schedule 4, Part II, section C*

Section C of Part II of Schedule 4 allows companies to include assets in the balance sheet at amounts based on valuations or current costs rather than being included at amounts based on historical costs. Where this is done there are a number of requirements which have to be followed, e.g. disclosure of comparable figures based on historical costs.

The question then arises — does the process of translating assets at closing rates constitute a departure from the normal historical cost rules and the requirements of Section C apply?

It could be argued, particularly where the cover method is being used and investments are translated at closing rates or where a tangible asset is regarded as part of a branch and translated at closing rates, that items do have a sterling historical cost and if they are included at an amount other than that cost then it must be a departure.

5.4.2 *SSAP 20, paragraph 66*

Paragraph 66 of SSAP 20, however, makes it clear that this is not the view taken by the standard. The translation process by itself merely translates the historical cost expressed in foreign currency at a closing rate of exchange. It does not result in a valuation of the asset or express it at its current cost. Accordingly, if it is thought that the provisions of SSAP 20 do result in a departure from the historical cost rules then it would appear that the provisions of the Companies Act are being breached. This is because the alternative accounting rules only allow assets to be included at a valuation, normally a market value, or at current cost.

6 COMPARISON WITH US AND IASC PRONOUNCEMENTS

6.1 US

6.1.1 *General comment*

The equivalent standard in the US is SFAS 52 — *Foreign Currency Translation*. Prior to the issue of the respective exposure drafts of both SSAP 20 and SFAS 52 there was a long period of consultation between the standard setting bodies of the two countries, together with that of Canada.

Accordingly, the requirements of SSAP 20 and SFAS 52 are both based on the same conceptual theory in that they both advocate the use of the closing rate/net investment method when dealing with the financial statements of foreign enterprises whose functional currency is different from that of the reporting currency of the holding company. Nevertheless, there are a number of differences between the two standards, of which the main ones are outlined below.

6.1.2 Main differences

A Results of foreign enterprises

Where the closing rate/net investment method is being used, SFAS 52 requires the revenues, expenses, gains, and losses of foreign enterprises to be translated at the exchange rates ruling when those elements are recognised or at an appropriate weighted average rate for the period.[218]

SSAP 20, on the other hand, allows a choice of translating the results of the foreign enterprise either at the closing rate of exchange or at an average rate for the period.[219]

B Cover method

The cover method in SFAS 52 can only be applied where the investment which is being hedged is consolidated or equity accounted.[220] However, the hedging transaction is not restricted to being a foreign currency borrowing but can be any foreign currency transaction which provides a hedge.[221] SFAS 52 requires such a transaction to be designated as, and effective as, an economic hedge of the net investment in the foreign enterprise. If a transaction is designated a hedge then all exchange differences until such time it is no longer designated must be taken to reserves.[222] In order that the hedge is effective the transaction has to be in the same foreign currency as the investment or, if this is impossible to arrange, in a foreign currency which moves in tandem with that of the investment.[223]

The cover method in SSAP 20 can be applied in individual companies' financial statements to investments which are carried at cost. However, the cover method only applies to foreign currency borrowings. The method may or may not be applied to such borrowings which provide a hedge as long as the treatment is applied consistently from period to period. The borrowings need not be in the same foreign currency as the investment but the exchange difference taken to reserves is restricted to the offsetting exchange difference on the investment.[224]

C Forward exchange contracts

SFAS 52 contains detailed requirements in respect of forward exchange contracts, including agreements that are essentially the same as forward exchange contracts.[225] The accounting for such contracts depends on whether they are taken out as a hedge against a foreign currency exposure or are merely speculative. Where the contract is a hedge then any exchange gain or loss on the contract is accounted for separately from the discount or premium on the contract. The accounting for these amounts will depend on whether the contract is a hedge against:

(a)   a net investment in a foreign enterprise; or

(b)   a foreign currency commitment; or

(c)   other foreign currency exposures.

Where the forward contract is speculative then no separate accounting recognition is given to the discount or premium on the contract.

The requirements of SFAS 52 in respect of such contracts are dealt with in 3.3.1 above.

SSAP 20 contains very little guidance on accounting for forward exchange contracts. It allows, but does not require, companies to record transactions and monetary assets and liabilities using the forward rate specified in any related or matching forward contract.[226]

D   Hyperinflation

SFAS 52 defines a highly inflationary economy as one that has cumulative inflation of approximately 100% or more over a three year period. Where a company has an investment in a foreign enterprise in a highly inflationary economy then the financial statements of the enterprise have to be remeasured as if its functional currency were the reporting currency, i.e. effectively translated using the temporal method.[227]

SSAP 20 gives no guidance as to what it means by ' a very high rate of inflation'. Where a company has an investment in a foreign enterprise which operates in a country with a high rate of inflation then the financial statements should be adjusted where possible to reflect current price levels before the translation process takes place.[228]

E   Disclosure

SFAS 52 requires the net exchange gain or loss included in net profit to be disclosed.[229] It also requires the translation adjustments which result from translating the foreign enterprise's financial statements to be taken to a separate component of equity. Accordingly, the cumulative exchange differences will be disclosed.[230]

SSAP 20 does not require the net exchange gain or loss included in net profit to be disclosed. It does, however, require the net exchange gain or loss on borrowings less deposits included in net profit to be disclosed.[231]

SSAP 20 only requires the translation adjustments which result from translating the foreign enterprise's financial statements to be taken to reserves and for the movement in reserves during the period to be disclosed.[232] They do not have to be taken to a separate reserve and therefore the cumulative exchange differences will not be apparent from the financial statements.

F   Disposal of investment

SFAS 52 and FASB Interpretation 37 requires that where all or part of an investment in a foreign enterprise is sold, or it is substantially liquidated, then the cumulative exchange differences included in the separate component of equity relating to the part which is sold or liquidated shall be included in the net profit for the period as part of the gain or loss on sale or liquidation.[233]

SSAP 20 contains no provisions as to what should happen to the cumulative exchange differences when the investment is sold or liquidated.

6.2 IASC

The relevant International standard which deals with this topic is IAS 21, *Accounting for the Effects of Changes in Foreign Exchange Rates*, which was issued in 1983. The standard follows the same general approach as SSAP 20 and SFAS 52 and is flexible enough in most areas so that compliance with either of these standards will normally ensure compliance with IAS 21. It also allows exchange differences on long-term monetary items to be deferred and recognised in the profit and loss account on a systematic basis.[234]

The main areas where compliance with SSAP 20 will not necessarily comply with IAS 21 are as follows.

6.2.1 Cover method

IAS 21 adopts a similar approach to that taken by SFAS 52 as discussed in 6.1.2 B above in that the loans or transactions are to be designated and effective as a hedge.[235]

6.2.2 Forward exchange contracts

IAS 21 requires that when a forward exchange contract is entered into to establish the amounts of the reporting currency required or available at the settlement date of foreign currency transactions, the difference between the forward rate and the spot rate at the inception of the contract should be recognised in income over the life of the contract. For short-term transactions, the forward rates specified in the related foreign exchange contracts may be used as the basis for measuring and reporting the transactions.[236]

As indicated earlier in 6.1.2 C above SSAP 20 contains little guidance in this area and allows companies to use the forward rate in recording transactions and translating monetary items, including long-term items.

6.2.3 Disclosure

IAS 21 requires the net exchange difference taken to profit and loss account as a result of using the temporal method of translation to be disclosed.[237] SSAP 20 only requires the net exchange gain or loss on borrowings less deposits included in net profit to be disclosed.

6.2.4 IAS E32

The IASC has recently issued an exposure draft, E32 — *Comparability of Financial Statements* — which proposes to amend, inter alia, the requirements of IAS 21. The main changes proposed which will mean that the requirements in the UK differ from the international standard are as follows:

(a) income statement items of foreign enterprises are to be translated at the rates ruling at the dates of the transactions (or at an average rate that approximates the actual rate);[238] the option of using the closing rate no longer being available;

(b) exchange differences on long-term liabilities are to be deferred where a hedge exists between the liability and a foreign currency non-monetary asset. A hedge will be deemed to exist where the liability and the asset are identified as a hedge for one another and:

(i)   there is reasonable assurance that they are, and will continue to be, effective as a hedge for one another, and

(ii) the liability will be settled and the exchange differences from the sale of the asset will be realised at or around the same time.[239]

Under SSAP 20, the exchange differences on such liabilities would have to be taken to the profit and loss account unless such an asset and liability could be regarded as being a 'foreign branch' which could be translated using the closing rate method (see 2.4.7 and 3.4.12 above).

(c)   financial statements of an enterprise that reports in the currency of a hyper-inflationary economy are to be restated, in accordance with the proposed international standard on financial reporting in hyper-inflationary economies, before the translation process is undertaken.[240] SSAP 20 only recommends that a similar approach is adopted 'where possible'.

The other main changes proposed by the exposure draft are as follows:

(a)   exchange differences on long-term monetary items will no longer be able to be deferred and recognised on a systematic basis;[241]

(b)   the preferred treatment for exchange differences arising from severe devaluation on assets invoiced in foreign currency will be that they should be recognised in income, although the alternative treatment of including the exchange differences in the carrying amount of the related asset will still be allowed, provided certain information is given.[242]

References

1   SSAP 20, *Foreign currency translation*, April 1983, para. 1.
2   SSAP 6, *Extraordinary items and prior year adjustments*, April 1984.
3   *Ibid.*, para. 6.
4   ED 16, *Supplement to extraordinary items and prior year adjustments*, September 1975.
5   *Ibid.*, para. 17.
6   *Ibid.*, paras. 15 — 16.
7   *Ibid.*, para. 5.
8   ED 21, *Accounting for foreign currency transactions*, September 1977.
9   *Ibid.*, para. 30.
10 *Ibid.*, paras. 32 — 34.
11 *Ibid.*, para. 35.
12 ED 27, *Accounting for foreign currency translations*, October 1980, para. 92.
13 SFAS 8, *Accounting for the translation of foreign currency transactions and foreign currency financial statements*, FASB, October 1975.
14 CICA Handbook, Section 1650, *Translation of foreign currency transactions and foreign currency financial statements*.

15 SSAP 20, para. 2.
16 *Ibid.*, paras. 36 — 44.
17 *Ibid.*, para. 46.
18 *Ibid.*, para. 48.
19 *Ibid.*, para. 47.
20 *Ibid.*, para. 7.
21 *Ibid.*, paras. 49 and 50.
22 *Ibid.*, para. 8.
23 United Biscuits (Holdings) PLC, Annual Report 1987, p. 36.
24 Argyll Group PLC, Report & Accounts 1988, p. 31.
25 SSAP 20, para. 28.
26 Ladbroke Group PLC, Annual Report and Accounts 1987, p. 36.
27 Imperial Chemical Industries PLC, Annual Report 1987, p. 35.
28 Reckitt & Colman plc, Annual Report 1987, p. 32.
29 SSAP 20, para. 52.
30 *Ibid.*, para. 13.
31 *Ibid.*, para. 14.
32 *Ibid.*, para. 21.
33 ED 27, para. 98.
34 SSAP 20, para. 16.
35 *Ibid.*, para. 54.
36 *Ibid.*, para. 2.
37 *Ibid.*, para. 17
38 *Ibid.*
39 *Ibid.*, para. 16.
40 *Ibid.*, para. 54.
41 *Ibid.*, paras. 53 — 54.
42 Guinness PLC, Report and Accounts 1987, p. 37.
43 The British Petroleum Company p.l.c., Annual Report and Accounts 1987, p. 34.
44 SSAP 20, para. 22.
45 *Ibid.*, para. 23.
46 Accountants Digest No. 150, *A guide to accounting standards — foreign currency translation*, Winter 1983/84, p. 9.
47 SSAP 20, para. 24.
48 *Ibid.*, para. 22.
49 *Ibid.*, para. 30.
50 *Ibid.*, para. 51.
51 *Ibid.*
52 SSAP 1, *Accounting for associated companies*, Revised April 1982.
53 SSAP 20, para. 52.
54 *Ibid.*, para. 37.
55 Technical Release 504, *Statement by the Accounting Standards Committee on the publication of SSAP 20: Foreign currency translation*, April 1983, para. 24.
56 SSAP 20, para. 52.
57 Clyde Petroleum plc, Report & Accounts 1987, p. 24.
58 SSAP 20, para. 59.
59 *Ibid.*, para. 60.
60 *Ibid.*
61 *Ibid.*
62 TR 504, para. 28.
63 Reckitt & Colman plc, Annual Report 1987, p. 32.
64 Reckitt & Colman plc, Annual Report 1987, p. 40.
65 Imperial Chemical Industries PLC, Annual Report 1987, p. 40.
66 Reckitt & Colman plc, Annual Report 1987, p. 38.

67   Imperial Chemical Industries PLC, Annual Report 1987, p. 38.
68   SFAS 52, *Foreign currency translation*, FASB, December 1981, para. 162.
69   Racal Electronics Plc, 1988 Annual report & accounts, p. 18.
70   SSAP 20, para. 46.
71   SFAS 52, para. 27.
72   *Ibid.*, para. 26.
73   SSAP 20, para. 44.
74   *Ibid.*, para. 6.
75   *Ibid.*, para. 5.
76   SFAS 52, para. 48.
77   *Ibid.*, para. 162.
78   SSAP 9, para. 29.
79   *Ibid.*, para. 30(a).
80   Cadbury Schweppes p.l.c., Annual report 1987;   Fisons plc, Annual report and accounts 1987; London & Scottish Marine Oil PLC, Annual report and accounts 1987;   Lonrho Plc, Annual Report 1988; Pearson plc, Annual report 1987.
81   London & Scottish Marine Oil PLC, Annual report and accounts 1987, p. 33.
82   SSAP 20, para. 49.
83   *Ibid.*, paras. 46 and 47.
84   CA 85, Sch. 4, paras. 17 and 22.
85   *Ibid.*, para. 26(3).
86   *Ibid.*
87   SSAP 20, para. 51.
88   *Ibid.*, para. 46.
89   SFAS 52, paras. 21 and 132.
90   *Ibid.*, para. 133.
91   *Ibid.*, para. 21.
92   Cable and Wireless plc, Report and accounts 1988, p. 37.
93   Accountants Digest No. 150, p. 6.
94   C.A. Westwick, *Accounting for Overseas Operations*, p. 18.
95   SSAP 20, para. 43.
96   SFAS 52, paras. 17,18 and 21.
97   *Ibid.*, para. 21.
98   *Ibid.*, para. 18.
99   *Ibid.*, para. 21.
100 Accountants Digest No. 150, p. 5.
101 SFAS 52, para. 17.
102 *Ibid.*, paras. 17 and 18.
103 British Airways Plc, Report and Accounts 1987—88, p. 33.
104 SFAS 52, paras. 18 and 20.
105 *Ibid.*, para. 20.
106 Smith & Nephew Associated Companies plc, Report and Accounts 1987, p. 24.
107 SFAS 52, para. 19.
108 CA 85, Sch. 4, para. 50(5).
109 SFAS 52, para. 17.
110 The British Petroleum Company p.l.c., Annual Report and Accounts 1987, p. 45.
111 Booker plc, Report and Accounts 1987, p. 23.
112 SFAS 52, para. 28.
113 *Ibid.*, para. 139.
114 Blue Circle Industries PLC, Report and accounts 1987, p. 11.
115 Imperial Chemical Industries PLC, Annual Report 1987, p. 35.
116 SFAS 52, para. 27.
117 *Ibid.*, para. 138.
118 Consolidated Gold Fields PLC, Annual Accounts 1988, p. 21.

119   The Rio Tinto-Zinc Corporation PLC, Annual Report and Accounts 1987, p. 26.
120   SSAP 20, para. 18.
121   SFAS 52, para. 12.
122   Allied-Lyons PLC, Report & Accounts 1988, p. 37.
123   The Boots Company PLC, Report & Accounts 1988, p. 21.
124   SSAP 6, paras. 31 and 39.
125   Redland PLC, Report and Accounts 1985, p. 36.
126   Redland PLC, Report and Accounts 1985, pp. 11 and 12.
127   The Boots Company PLC, Report and Accounts 1985, p. 13 and Blue Circle Industries PLC, Report & Accounts 1985, p. 31.
128   L.C.L. Skeratt and D. J. Tonkin (eds.), *Financial Reporting 1987—88: A Survey of UK Reporting Practice*, London: ICAEW, 1988, p. 187.
129   D.J. Tonkin and L.C.L. Skeratt (eds.), *Financial Reporting 1984—85: A Survey of UK Published Accounts*, London: ICAEW, 1984, p. 127.
130   Beecham Group p.l.c., Annual Report 1988, p. 35.
131   Beecham Group p.l.c., Annual Report 1987, p. 25.
132   See, for example, The Boots Company PLC, Report & Accounts 1988, p. 32 and The General Electric Company, p.l.c., Report & Accounts 1988, p. 26.
133   See, for example, The BOC Group plc, Report & Accounts 1988, p. 41, Guinness PLC, Report and Accounts 1987, p. 54, and The Plessey Company plc, Report and Accounts 1988, p. 41.
134   Allied-Lyons PLC, Report & Accounts 1988, pp. 38 and 54.
135   Jaguar plc, Annual Report 1987, p. 38.
136   BTR plc, Report & Accounts 1987, p. 46.
137   Argyll Group PLC, Report & Accounts 1987, p. 52.
138   SFAS 52, para. 12.
139   *Ibid.*
140   CA 85, Sch. 4, para. 33.
141   TR 504, para. 34(g).
142   CA 85, Sch. 4, para. 12.
143   SFAS 52, para. 14.
144   FASB Interpretation No. 37, *Accounting for Translation Adjustments upon Sale of Part of an Investment in a Foreign Entity*, FASB, July 1983, para. 2.
145   Argyll Group PLC, Report & Accounts 1987, pp. 36 and 52.
146   BTR plc, Report & Accounts 1987, p. 46.
147   Consolidated Gold Fields PLC, Annual Accounts 1986, pp. 31 and 37.
148   SFAS 52, para. 46.
149   *Ibid.*
150   *Ibid.*
151   SSAP 20, para. 26.
152   SFAS 52, para. 11.
153   International Monetary Fund, *International Financial Statistics*.
154   SFAS 52, para. 11.
155   SSAP 20, para. 55.
156   Reckitt & Colman plc, Annual Report 1987, p. 32
157   Marley plc, Annual Report 1987, p. 30.
158   SSAP 22, *Accounting for Goodwill*, December 1984, para. 34.
159   SSAP 20, para. 43.
160   TR 504, para. 21.
161   SFAS 52, para. 101.
162   Guinness PLC, Report and Accounts 1987, p. 40.
163   BTR plc, Report & Accounts 1987, p. 34.
164   SFAS 52, para. 144.
165   TR 504, paras. 18 and 19.

166   The Council of The Stock Exchange, *Admission of Securities to Listing*, Section 3,
       Chapter 2, para. 5.16(b).
167   Westwick, *op. cit.*, p. 22.
168   Touche Ross & Co., *Manual of Financial Reporting & Accounting*, Second Edition, London:
       Butterworths, 1985, p. 196, and N. Spinney, *The Accountant's Magazine*, May 1983,
       p. 178.
169   Cadbury Schweppes p.l.c., Annual report 1987, p. 39.
170   SSAP 20, para. 43.
171   TR 504, para. 21.
172   SFAS 52, para. 101.
173   Accountants Digest No. 150, p. 7.
174   TR 504, para. 18.
175   *Ibid.*
176   D. Hegarty, *Accountancy*, November 1983, p. 147.
177   SFAS 52, para. 20.
178   *Ibid.*, para. 130.
179   Accountants Digest No. 150, p. 7.
180   Lonrho Plc, Annual Report 1988, p. 92.
181   SSAP 20, para. 48.
182   *Ibid.*, para. 49.
183   *Ibid.*, para. 12.
184   See Westwick, *op. cit.*, p. 99 and J. Carty, *Foreign Currency Accounting — A practical
       guide for 1982 financial statements*, pp. 21 and 22.
185   SSAP 15, appendix, para. 4.
186   Carty, *op. cit.*, pp. 21 and 22.
187   SSAP 20, para. 20.
188   See Accountants Digest No. 150, p. 16 and Westwick, *op. cit.*, p. 99.
189   SSAP 20, paras. 20 and 43.
190   *Ibid.*, paras. 46 — 51.
191   Touche Ross, *op. cit.*, p. 192.
192   *Ibid.*, para. 2.
193   Westwick, *op. cit.*, p. 101.
194   Accountants Digest No. 150, p. 15.
195   SFAS 52, para. 25.
196   *Ibid.*, para. 12.
197   SSAP 20, paras. 46 and 48.
198   *Ibid.*, para. 42.
199   *Ibid.*, para. 51.
200   *Ibid.*, para. 57.
201   SFAS 52, paras. 20, 128 and 130.
202   SSAP 20, para. 53.
203   *Ibid.*, para. 19.
204   See SFAS 52, para. 14 and FASB Interpretation No. 37, para. 2.
205   SSAP 2, para. 14(d).
206   SSAP 20, para. 44.
207   TR 504, para. 10.
208   *Ibid.*, para. 11.
209   *Ibid.*, para. 12.
210   Westwick, *op. cit.*, p. 77.
211   *Ibid.* and Accountants Digest No. 150, p. 32.
212   CA 85, s 264.
213   TR 504, para. 32.
214   *Ibid.*, para. 33(a).
215   TR 504, para. 32.

216   SSAP 20, para. 36.
217   *Ibid.*, para. 53.
218   SFAS 52, para. 12.
219   SSAP 20, para. 54.
220   This is due to the definition of 'foreign entity' in SFAS 52, para. 162.
221   SFAS 52, para. 20(a).
222   *Ibid.*
223   *Ibid.*, para. 130.
224   SSAP 20, paras. 51 and 58.
225   SFAS 52, paras. 17 — 20.
226   SSAP 20, paras. 46 and 48.
227   SFAS 52, para. 11.
228   SSAP 20, para. 26.
229   SFAS 52, para. 30.
230   *Ibid.*, paras. 13 and 31.
231   SSAP 20, para. 60(a).
232   *Ibid.*, paras. 54 and 60(b).
233   SFAS 52, para. 14 and FASB Interpretation No. 37, para. 2.
234   IAS 21, para. 28.
235   *Ibid.*, para. 30.
236   *Ibid.*, para. 26.
237   *Ibid.*, para. 37.
238   E32, *Comparability of Financial Statements*, IASC, January 1989, para. 146.
239   *Ibid.*, para. 132.
240   *Ibid.*, para. 148.
241   *Ibid.*, paras. 117 — 125 *passim.*
242   *Ibid.*, para. 137.

Chapter 19

Leases and hire purchase contracts

1   INTRODUCTION

1.1   Historical development

The level of leasing activity in the UK has increased rapidly since the early 1970s. The Equipment Leasing Association's members account for 80% to 90% of all lessors in the UK and the cost of assets they acquired for leasing rose from £288m in 1973 to £6,024m in 1987.[1] The combination of high tax rates, high first-year allowances and high interest rates is thought to have been largely responsible for this. Although recent changes in the UK tax environment have removed most of these justifications, it is widely thought that leasing will continue to provide one of the major sources of asset funding.

1.2   What are leases and hire purchase contracts?

'A *lease* is a contract between a lessor and a lessee for the hire of a specific asset. The lessor retains ownership of the asset but conveys the right to the use of the asset to the lessee for an agreed period of time in return for the payment of specified rentals.'[2] The term 'lease' is also used to refer to any arrangement with a similar result.

'A *hire purchase contract* is a contract for the hire of an asset which contains a provision giving the hirer an option to acquire legal title to the asset upon the fulfilment of certain conditions stated in the contract';[3] usually, this merely involves the payment of a specified final rental.

1.3   The tax position

The position for both lessees and lessors can be briefly outlined as follows:

(a)   *lessees* — the total rentals payable are an allowable expense (with a restriction for cars costing more than £8,000) whilst no capital allowances are received;

(b)   *lessors* — the total rentals receivable are taxable income and capital allowances are given on the cost of the leased assets.

For hire purchase contracts, however, any capital allowances are receivable by the hirer not the owner. As a result, the hirer can only claim the interest element of rentals payable as a tax deductible expense.

The tax treatment of leases is of interest for two major reasons. Firstly, it affects the methods of income recognition used by lessors and, secondly, the tax treatment of a lease is irrelevant for the purpose of classifying a lease (see 2 below).

1.4   SSAP 21

SSAP 21 — *Accounting for leases and hire purchase contracts* — was issued in August 1984 after a fairly lengthy and active exposure/discussion period. ED 29,[4] which led to SSAP 21, was issued in October 1981 after approximately five years of debate. It was argued that comparability between companies would require capitalisation of finance leases by lessees; in particular, the effects of non-capitalisation on companies' gearing and rates of return on assets were said to seriously affect comparability. It was further argued that readers of financial statements could not determine the economic substance of asset financing transactions from the financial statements. One case highlighting this was that of Court Line Limited, a public company which collapsed in 1974. The group used leased aircraft to operate a package holiday business, and at 30th September 1973 had undisclosed leasing obligations relating to assets costing £40m.[5] The shareholders' funds shown in the group balance sheet at that date amounted to approximately £18m.[6] As the Inspectors stated, 'the amounts involved were material and should have been disclosed'.[7] Although this suggested that full disclosure might suffice (rather than new accounting treatments), it certainly highlighted the need for changes in financial statement presentation in order that readers could fully appreciate the financial position of a company involved in leasing.

At the time that it was issued, SSAP 21 was one of the most controversial accounting standards, as it effectively invoked a substance over form approach to give an accounting treatment possibly different from the legal ownership position. As discussed below, this is not done explicitly, however, as the lessee is required to capitalise the present value of minimum lease payments under a finance lease, not the leased asset itself. In practice, the fair value of the asset will approximate to the present value of minimum lease payments, and the inclusion of the latter as an asset achieves the accounting result of substance over form.

SSAP 21 essentially involves a decision as to whether or not a lease meets the given definition of a finance lease; if not, then an operating lease exists. Such decisions will be made independently by both the lessee and lessor to determine the appropriate accounting treatment and disclosures. Broad guidelines and requirements are given in SSAP 21, but many areas are not specifically covered or are discussed only in the Guidance Notes issued with it.[8]

Under SSAP 21, hire purchase contracts which are of a financing nature should be treated similarly to finance leases, whilst the others should be treated similarly to operating leases. The vast majority will be of a financing nature and were already, in fact, being accounted for similarly to the finance lease treatment required by SSAP 21. This is because it is usually intended that the hirer will obtain title to the asset concerned at the end of the hire period. All references in this chapter to leases include hire purchase contracts of the appropriate type, unless the context requires otherwise.

SSAP 21 'does not apply to lease contracts concerning the rights to explore for or to exploit natural resources such as oil, gas, timber, metals and other minerals. Nor does it apply to licensing agreements for items such as motion picture films, video recordings, plays, manuscripts, patents and copyrights'.[9] This, however, does not preclude SSAP 21 from being referred to for general guidance where it is considered appropriate.

1.5 Accounting requirements of SSAP 21

Lessees should capitalise finance leases and recognise a corresponding obligation in creditors. The capitalised asset should then be depreciated over the shorter of the leased asset's useful life or the lease term (see 2.1.5 below); capitalised hire purchase contracts should be depreciated over the hired asset's useful life. The obligation will be reduced by the element of rental payments which is calculated to relate to such a repayment. Lessee accounting is discussed in detail at 3 below.

Lessors should treat finance leases to their customers as amounts receivable included in debtors, i.e. the assets which are so leased will not be included as fixed assets. The amount receivable will be reduced by the element of rental receipts which is calculated to relate to such a reduction. Lessor accounting is discussed in detail at 5 below.

As discussed at 1.3 above, the tax treatment of finance leases differs from the accounting treatment per SSAP 21 for both lessors and lessees, giving rise to timing differences in the calculation of any deferred taxation provision.

SSAP 21 involves no amendment to the accounting treatment of operating leases unless the rentals are payable/receivable by the lessee/lessor other than on a straight-line basis. In such a case the rentals should be taken to profit and loss account on a straight-line basis unless a more systematic basis is more appropriate. This is discussed at 3.6 and 5.2 below for lessees and lessors respectively.

SSAP 21 specifies certain disclosures to be made by lessees and lessors in addition to the adoption of the required accounting treatments above. The disclosures are outlined and examples given at 4 (lessee) and 6 (lessor) below.

2 DETERMINING THE LEASE TYPE

2.1 The 90% test

A finance lease is defined as 'a lease that transfers substantially all the risks and rewards of ownership of an asset to the lessee',[10] whilst an operating lease 'is a lease other than a finance lease'.[11]

SSAP 21 gives guidelines for deciding whether 'substantially all the risks and rewards' have passed to a lessee. It is stated that 'it should be presumed that such a transfer of risks and rewards occurs if at the inception of a lease the present value of the minimum lease payments, including any initial payment, amounts to substantially all (normally 90 per cent or more) of the fair value of the leased asset. The present value should be calculated by using the interest rate implicit in the lease ... . Notwithstanding the fact that a lease meets [these] conditions ... , the presumption that it should be classified as a finance lease may in exceptional circumstances be rebutted if it can be clearly demonstrated that the lease in question does not transfer substantially all the risks and rewards of ownership (other than legal title) to the lessee. Correspondingly, the presumption that a lease which fails to meet [these] conditions ... is not a finance lease may in exceptional circumstances be rebutted'.[12]

The more important terms used in performing the 90% test in SSAP 21 are explained below:

2.1.1   *The fair value*

This 'is the price at which an asset could be exchanged in an arm's length transaction less, where applicable, any grants receivable towards the purchase or use of the asset'.[13] If this fair value cannot be determined for the purposes of the 90% test, then an estimate thereof should be used. This will not usually be required for lessors, but may be for lessees who are unaware of the cost of the leased asset.

2.1.2   *The implicit interest rate*

This 'is the discount rate that at the inception of a lease, when applied to the amounts which the lessor expects to receive and retain, produces an amount (the present value) equal to the fair value of the leased asset'.[14]

The amounts the lessor expects to receive and retain comprise the following:

(a)   the minimum lease payments to the lessor (all elements (a) to (c) at 2.1.3 below); plus

(b)   any unguaranteed residual value; less

(c)   any part of (a) and (b) above for which the lessor will be accountable to the lessee.

If the implicit interest rate cannot be calculated due to inadequate information then an estimate may be used. This will not usually apply to the lessor as he is likely to have all relevant information available. However, a lessee may not have access to this information and may be unable to make estimates thereof. If the interest rate implicit in the lease is not determinable, it should be estimated by reference to the rate which a lessee would be expected to pay on a similar lease.

2.1.3   *The minimum lease payments*[15]

There are three possible elements to this:

(a)   the minimum payments over the remaining part of the lease term;

(b)   any residual amount guaranteed by the lessee or a party related to him; and

(c)   any residual amounts guaranteed by any other party.

The elements to be included depend on the intended use of the minimum lease payments calculation as follows:

(i)   all elements are used in the calculation of the implicit interest rate (for use in the 90% test), (see 2.1.2 above);

(ii)   all elements are used in the 90% test performed by the lessor. The total of these elements plus any unguaranteed residual value will represent the lessor's gross investment in the lease (see 5.3 below);

(iii)   elements (a) and (b) are used in the 90% test performed by the lessee. The present value of this minimum lease payments figure will represent both the capitalised fixed asset and the initial finance lease obligation for the lessee (see 3.2 and 3.3 below respectively).

The minimum lease payments should not include any contingent rentals, e.g. those dependent on the level of use of the equipment. However if, for example, the lessee guaranteed to use the equipment to a certain level, then that level of rentals would be included. Another example of contingent rentals are those which will be adjusted to take account of inflation (e.g. via the Retail Prices Index). SFAS 29 in the US states that such rentals should be included in the minimum lease payments by assuming that the inflation rate at the lease inception date will continue.[16] Any movements from that rate are contingent and will not be included in minimum lease payments but, rather, will be expensed when payable. We believe that it would be best practice in the UK to follow this treatment.

2.1.4   *An unguaranteed residual value*

This is 'that portion of the residual value of the leased asset (estimated at the inception of the lease), the realisation of which by the lessor is not assured or is guaranteed solely by a party related to the lessor'.[17]

2.1.5   *The lease term*

This is 'the period for which the lessee has contracted to lease the asset and any further terms for which the lessee has the option to continue to lease the asset, with or without further payment, which option it is reasonably certain at the inception of the lease that the lessee will exercise'.[18] Usually a lease can be easily divided into the primary term during which the lessee is committed to make certain rental payments (with a termination rental payable upon termination before the end of the primary term) and a secondary term for which the lessee can extend the lease if desired. It is general practice that any secondary term is only included in the lease term for 90% test calculations if it is highly probable that the term will be so extended, i.e. the 'reasonably certain'[19] criterion is generally strictly interpreted. If a peppercorn (nominal) rental is payable in the secondary lease term period, the lease term should normally include the secondary term although the rentals can probably be ignored on materiality grounds in performing the 90% test.

2.2   90% test example

The following example illustrates the application of the 90% test:

Example 19.1

Details of a non-cancellable lease are as follows:

(i)   Fair value (per 2.1.1 above) = £10,000
(ii)   Five annual rentals payable in advance of £2,000
(iii)   Total estimated residual value at end of five years = £3,000 of which £2,000 is guaranteed
        by the lessee.

The implicit interest rate in the lease (per 2.1.2 above) is that which gives a present value of
£10,000 for the five rentals plus the total estimated residual value at the end of year 5. This rate
can be calculated as 10.93%.

This rate is then used to calculate the present value of the minimum lease payments. As
explained in 2.1.3 above, this example gives rise to identical minimum lease payments from
both the lessee's and lessor's points of view. This is because there is no guarantee of any part of
the residual by a party other than the lessee and the minimum lease payments will be the five
annual rentals plus the residual guaranteed by the lessee of £2,000. The present value of these
minimum lease payments is calculated as £9,405.

This present value figure is 94.05% of the asset's fair value and a finance lease is therefore
indicated.

All of the above information will be known to the lessor as he will have used it in his pricing
decision for the lease. However, the lessee may not know either the fair value or the
unguaranteed residual value and, therefore, the implicit interest rate. If either of the first two of
these is not known, the lessee is permitted by SSAP 21 to estimate what they are and so
calculate the implicit interest rate. Alternatively, he may feel that such an estimation is better
made of the implicit interest rate directly, rather than of a parameter which will then allow that
rate to be calculated.

It is important to note that the 90% test can result in different answers being given
for the lessor and lessee, e.g. it may indicate a finance lease from the lessor but an
operating lease to the lessee. There are two possible reasons for this. Firstly, and
most commonly, the lessor may receive a guarantee of the estimated (significant)
residual of the leased asset by a party other than the lessee and accordingly, using
the 90% test, an operating lease may be indicated for the lessee whereas a finance
lease is indicated for the lessor. Secondly, as shown above, the lessee may not
have the full information available to the lessor and his estimates of fair value or
residual value may be so different from the correct figures (known to the lessor)
that his classification of the lease is incorrect.

2.3   Determining the lease type — other factors

Although the 90% test outlined above is important, there are a number of other
factors which may influence the decision on whether substantially all the risks and
rewards of ownership have passed. Affirmative answers to the following
questions would tend to indicate that a finance lease exists:

(a)   If the lessee can cancel the lease, will he bear any losses in residual value
      associated with the cancellation?

(b)   Will the lessee gain from any fluctuations in the market value of the residual? (For example, he may receive a rental rebate equalling most of the sales proceeds at the end of the lease.)

(c)   Does the lessee have the ability to continue the lease for a secondary period at a nominal rental?

(d)   Does the lessee continue to pay rentals for the assets whilst they are idle due to production problems or obsolescence?

(e)   Is the expected lease term equal to substantially all of the asset's expected useful life?

(f)   Is the lessee responsible for insurance, maintenance etc. of the leased asset?

(g)   Are the leased assets of a specialised nature such that only the lessee (or a limited number of other parties) can use them without major modifications being made?

In evaluating the risks and rewards, one should consider which factors are most likely to have an economic effect on the parties to the lease. The various factors are interdependent to some extent, e.g. if the lease term is for substantially all of the asset's expected useful economic life, or the asset is of a specialised nature, then the residual value is likely to be very low.

3   ACCOUNTING BY LESSEES

3.1   Introduction

When it is determined that material finance leases exist for a lessee on the basis of 2 above, there are two elements of the accounting entries which must be considered — the capitalised fixed asset and the related rental obligations. Each of these is dealt with in turn below.

3.2   Capitalised fixed asset

A finance lease should be capitalised at the present value of the minimum lease payments (MLP). The MLP have already been discussed at 2.1.3 above. The elements of MLP to be included for this purpose are:

(a)   the minimum payments over the remaining part of the lease term; and

(b)   any residual amounts guaranteed by the lessee or a party related to him.

This present value will be calculated using the implicit interest rate in the lease (the calculation of which is detailed at 2.1.2 above). In most cases the fair value of the leased asset at the inception of the lease will approximate to this amount. This is because we are calculating a present value of the relevant MLP using all MLP elements also used in the calculation of implicit interest rate, other than:

(a)   any residual amounts guaranteed by a party other than the lessee (or parties related to him); and

(b)   any part of either the total MLP to the lessor or unguaranteed residual value
        for which the lessor will be accountable to the lessee.

In most cases, these items will be insignificant, and the fair value of leased assets
will, therefore, usually approximate to the present value of the relevant MLP.
Example 19.1 at 2.2 above involved a situation where the present value of
minimum lease payments was 94% of the fair value. This is lower than 100%
because a part of the total estimated residual value is unguaranteed, i.e. the
present value of the unguaranteed residual value (of £1,000) is 6% of the fair
value of the asset. In such a situation a lessee would probably be entitled to take
the fair value (of £10,000) as an approximation of the present value of MLP (of
£9,405).

The capitalised fixed asset is then depreciated on a similar basis to owned assets
(i.e. over the asset's useful economic life). For finance leases (but not hire
purchase contracts) the depreciation should be calculated over the lease term, if
this is shorter than the asset's useful economic life. The lease term should include
any secondary periods over which it is reasonably certain that the lessee will
exercise his extension option.

3.3   Finance lease obligation

Accounting for this can be split into three stages as follows:

(a)   the allocation of total rental payments over the lease term between finance
        charges and repayment of lease obligation;

(b)   the allocation of the total finance charges to accounting periods; and

(c)   the reduction of the obligation by the element of total rentals payable not
        allocated at (b).

In allocating total rental payments between finance charges and the repayment of
lease obligation the total finance charge is calculated as the difference between the
undiscounted total of MLP per 3.2 above, (i.e. including any residual amount
guaranteed by the lessee), and the amount at which the lessee records the asset at
the inception of the lease. This latter amount will, of course, be the discounted
value of the relevant MLP (with the fair value of the leased asset usually being a
close approximation to this). The discount element will, therefore, equal the total
finance charges over the lease term.

The obligation under finance leases will be set up at an amount equal to the
present value of relevant MLP with the other side of this accounting entry being
the capitalised fixed asset described above.

3.4   Methods of allocating finance charges to accounting periods

In allocating the total finance charges over the lease term to accounting periods,
SSAP 21 requires that this is done 'so as to produce a constant periodic rate of
charge on the remaining balance of the obligation for each accounting period, or a
reasonable approximation thereto'.[20]

The guidance notes to SSAP 21 detail three methods — actuarial, 'sum of the digits' ('rule of 78') or straight-line.[21] These are progressively easier to apply but also give progressively less accurate answers. There is, therefore, a trade-off to be made between the costs versus benefits of achieving complete accuracy. In making this trade-off, the question of materiality is important because differences between allocated finance charges under the three methods may be immaterial, such that the simpler methods may be used for convenience. The following example illustrates the actuarial and sum of the digits methods of allocating finance charges to accounting periods.

Example 19.2

A five year lease of an asset commences on 1 January 19X1. The rental is £2,600 p.a. payable in advance. The fair value of the asset at lease inception is £10,000 and it is expected to have a residual at the end of the lease of £2,372 (being its tax written down value at that time) which will be passed to the lessee as a refund of rentals. In addition, the lessee is responsible for all maintenance and insurance costs.

The minimum lease payments are 5 x £2,600 = £13,000 which gives finance charges of £13,000 — 10,000 = £3,000. The actuarial method attempts to calculate the finance charge in each period to give a constant periodic rate of charge on the remaining balance of the obligation for each period. This is done as follows:

Year	Capital sum at start of period £	Rental paid £	Capital sum during period £	Finance charge (15.15% per annum) £	Capital sum at end of period £
19X1	10,000	2,600	7,400	1,121	8,521
19X2	8,521	2,600	5,921	897	6,818
19X3	6,818	2,600	4,218	639	4,857
19X4	4,857	2,600	2,257	343	2,600
19X5	2,600	2,600	—	—	—
		13,000		3,000	

The finance charge of 15.15% is that which results in a capital sum at the end of 19X5 of zero and can be found by trial and error, using a financial calculator, computer program, mathematical formula or present value tables.

This lease involves fairly straightforward figures but it is still not easy to calculate manually. It is, therefore, possible to use the sum of the digits method to give an allocation of finance charge which is a close approximation to that given by the actuarial method.

The sum of the digits method calculations, for example, are as follows:

Year	number of rentals not yet due		x	total finance charge ──────────────── sum of number of rentals	=	Finance charge per annum £
19X1	4	}				1,200
19X2	3	}				900
19X3	2	}	x	£3,000 ÷ 10	=	600
19X4	1	}				300
19X5	—	}				—
	10	}				3,000

We can now compare the finance charges in each of the five years under the actuarial and sum of the digits methods:

Year	Finance charge as % of total		Finance charge	
	Actuarial %	Sum of the digits %	Actuarial £	Sum of the digits £
19X1	37	40	1,121	1,200
19X2	30	30	897	900
19X3	21	20	639	600
19X4	12	10	343	300
19X5	—	—	—	—
	100	100	3,000	3,000

In situations where the lease term is not very long (typically not more than seven years) and interest rates are not very high, the sum of the digits method gives an allocation of finance charges which is close enough to that under the actuarial method to allow the simpler approach to be used.[22]

It should be noted that the expected residual of £2,372 (which will be paid to the lessee) does not affect any of the above calculations. This expected residual will merely influence the depreciation policy of the lessee as regards the capitalised asset. He will depreciate to an expected residual of £2,372 and any difference between this net book value figure and the amount received by the lessee will give rise to a gain or loss on disposal of the asset.

3.5   Carrying values

At any point during the lease term the depreciated book value of a capitalised leased fixed asset and the remaining finance lease obligation under that lease will not usually be equal. Normally, this is because the method of depreciation bears no relation to that for allocating finance charges to accounting periods, as can be seen in the following example:

Example 19.3

If the lessee in the previous example depreciates the asset to its residual value of £2,372 on a straight-line basis over its life of five years, then the net book value compared with the outstanding lease obligation (using the actuarial method) at the end of each year will be as follows:

Year	Net book value £	Outstanding lease obligation £
19X1	8,474	8,521
19X2	6,948	6,818
19X3	5,422	4,857
19X4	3,897	2,600
19X5	2,372	—

3.6 Operating leases

SSAP 21 requires that operating lease rentals are charged to profit and loss account on a straight-line basis over the lease term irrespective of when payments are due.[23] This is logical as, for example, a large upfront payment should be allocated to the period over which a benefit is gained. Alternatively, leases of land and buildings sometimes have a rent free period in the early part of the lease, followed by a relatively higher rental over the remainder. In such a case, the rentals should again be charged to profit and loss account on a straight-line basis. If, however, a more systematic and rational basis is more appropriate, then that basis may be used; e.g. if the level of the use of the asset determines the level of rentals, then it would be appropriate to charge rentals when incurred.

4 DISCLOSURE BY LESSEES

4.1 SSAP 21 requirements

The following lessee disclosures are required by SSAP 21:

(a) policies adopted in accounting for operating and finance leases;[24]

(b) total operating lease rentals charged, analysed between those payable in respect of hire of plant and machinery and other operating leases.[25] All hire charges should be treated as operating lease rentals including very short-term rentals and rental of property;

(c) aggregate finance charges allocated for the period in respect of finance leases;[26]

(d) aggregate depreciation charged in the period on assets held under finance leases and hire purchase contracts;[27]

(e) totals of gross amount and accumulated depreciation for each major class of asset held under finance leases and hire purchase contracts. If this information is combined with owned assets then the net amount included in the overall total should be disclosed;[28]

(f)   net obligations under finance leases and hire purchase contracts split between amounts payable in the next year, in two to five years inclusive and after five years. Alternatively, this may be shown as gross obligations with future finance charges being deducted from the total. The net obligations analysis may be combined with other obligations and liabilities;[29]

(g)   payments committed to be made *in the next year* under operating leases for (1) leases of land and buildings, and (2) other leases; both amounts split between those expiring:

(i)   within one year;
(ii)   in the second to fifth years inclusive;
(iii) in over five years.[30]

This is a rather unusual requirement as it is not the *total* amount payable under such leases which is to be disclosed and split by time periods (as is required for finance leases). As a result, a number of companies seem to have given incorrect disclosure of this item (see 4.3 below);

(h)   commitments in respect of finance leases and hire purchase contracts existing at the balance sheet date when at that date neither has the asset been brought into use nor have rentals started to accrue.[31]

4.2   Related Companies Act requirements

The main disclosure requirements of the Companies Act which affect lessees are as follows:

(a)   amount charged to revenue in respect of sums payable for the hire of plant and machinery.[32] This will be met if the disclosures required in (b) to (d) in 4.1 above are given;

(b)   the balance sheet formats require creditors falling due within one year to be shown separately from creditors falling due after more than one year.[33] The net obligations under finance leases and hire purchase contracts will have to be split accordingly;

(c)   particulars of financial commitments which:

(i)   have not been provided for; and
(ii)   are relevant to assessing the company's state of affairs.[34]

Since finance leases are capitalised and the obligations are provided, this will normally only be relevant for operating leases. Usually, the disclosures required in (g) in 4.1 above will meet this requirement. Where, however, there are contingent rentals which have not been provided for, extra disclosure may be required.

There are a number of other disclosures required by the Companies Act which may affect lessees and these should also be considered; e.g. details of movements in fixed assets[35] and details in relation to creditors.[36]

4.3   Disclosure in practice

The following are examples of disclosures given in practice by lessees:

Extract 19.1: British Telecommunications plc[37]

Accounting Policies [extract]

VIII   Leased Assets
Equipment acquired under finance leases, which transfer to the lessee substantially all benefits and risks of ownership, and the capital element of the related rental obligations are included in the balance sheet. The interest element of rental obligations is charged against profit in proportion to the reducing capital element outstanding. The equipment is depreciated over the shorter of the lease term and the estimated useful life of the asset.
Rentals applicable to operating leases, under which substantially all the benefits and risks of ownership remain with the lessor, are charged to the profit and loss account as incurred.

Notes to the accounts

3 Operating costs [extract]

	1987
	£m	£m
Operating costs included the following: Rental costs relating to operating leases, including plant and equipment hire £23m (1987- £29m)	121	129

9 Tangible fixed assets [extract]

	Group 1987		Company 1987	
	£m	£m	£m	£m
Details of leased items included within plant and equipment were as follows:				
Depreciation charge for year	53	48	45	45
Net book value at 31 March	134	176	84	136

13 Loans and other borrowings [extract]

Lease finance *(f)*	92	133	60	102

(f) Lease finance
The obligations under finance leases represent the total present value of future minimum lease payments discounted at the interest rates inherent in each lease.

Future minimum finance lease payments at 31 March were as follows:

	Group	1987	Company	1987
	£m	£m	£m	£m
Payable within:				
One year	29	44	28	41
Two years	15	34	10	28
Three years	12	15	7	11
Four years	11	12	6	8
Five years	11	13	6	7
Thereafter	35	43	12	23
Minimum lease payments	113	161	69	118
Amounts representing interest	(21)	(28)	(9)	(16)
	92	133	60	102

19 Financial commitments [extract]

Future minimum operating lease payments at 31 March were as follows:

	Group	1987	Company	1987
	£m	£m	£m	£m
Payable within:				
One year	93	82	83	75
Two years	87	78	79	70
Three years	82	74	75	68
Four years	76	71	70	66
Five years	72	68	68	63
Thereafter	1,030	1,224	1,003	1,214
	1,440	1,597	1,378	1,556

Operating lease commitments were mainly in respect of leases of land and buildings.

It can be seen that British Telecommunications plc have actually given more information in respect of their finance lease obligations by disclosing the amounts due in *each* of the second to fifth years. One disclosure item required by SSAP 21 which is not given (presumably on the grounds of materiality) is the finance charge in respect of finance leases.

As noted at 4.1 (g) above, the disclosure requirement which is sometimes given incorrectly is that for payments committed to be made in the next year under non-cancellable operating leases. Indeed, the relevant disclosure given by British Telecommunications plc above would appear to be incorrect as it relates to total operating lease payments according to when they fall payable. The following extract illustrates the correct disclosure:

Extract 19.2: Cadbury Schweppes p.l.c.[38]

23 LEASING COMMITMENTS
The minimum lease payments to which the group was committed under non-cancellable operating leases during the year following 2 January 1988 were as follows:

	Property		**Plant & Machinery**	
	1987	1986	**1987**	1986
	£m	£m	**£m**	£m
On leases expiring:				
Within one year	**0.6**	1.0	**1.9**	2.7
Between two and five years	**5.1**	2.6	**13.5**	7.3
After five years	**5.2**	5.0	**1.1**	1.5
	10.9	8.6	**16.5**	11.5

SSAP 21 should apply to leases of land and buildings as for any other assets. However, as discussed in Chapter 11, where property companies act as lessees of long leasehold investment properties, the commitments for ground rents under these operating leases are not usually shown. MEPC plc state that this is because these SSAP 21 requirements are 'not relevant to a property investment company'.[39] The reason for this view is unclear.

As noted at 4.1 (e) and (f) above, there are alternative methods of disclosure of finance lease fixed assets and obligations. Rather than including the finance leases within fixed assets and disclosing net book values and depreciation charged for each category as British Telecommunications plc do, as illustrated in Extract 19.1 above, Walter Lawrence P.L.C. disclose leased assets separately in the fixed asset note as illustrated below:

Extract 19.3: Walter Lawrence P.L.C.[40]

8. Tangible fixed assets [extract]

	Land & Buildings £'000	Plant & Machinery Owned £'000	Plant & Machinery Leased £'000	Motor Vehicles Owned £'000	Motor Vehicles Leased £'000	Fixtures & Fittings Owned £'000	Fixtures & Fittings Leased £'000	Total £'000
Cost								
1 January 1987	6,332	5,707	1,569	978	1,646	1,322	387	17,941
Additions	1,240	600	269	309	636	431	2	3,487
Transfers to work in progress	(1,486)	–	–	–	–	–	–	(1,486)
Disposals	(2,467)	(3,170)	(1,131)	(239)	(436)	(413)	(91)	(7,947)
31 December 1987	3,619	3,137	707	1,048	1,846	1,340	298	11,995
Amortisation and Depreciation								
1 January 1897	242	4,079	431	509	730	860	152	7,003
Charge for the year	35	410	159	211	368	248	71	1,502
Disposals	(6)	(2,052)	(254)	(163)	(280)	(252)	(58)	(3,065)
31 December 1987	271	2,437	336	557	818	856	165	5,440
Net Book Value								
1987	**3,348**	**700**	**371**	**491**	**1,028**	**484**	**133**	**6,555**
1986	6,090	1,628	1,138	469	916	462	235	10,938

For obligations under finance leases, British Telecommunications plc deduct future interest payments separately, as shown in Extract 19.1 above. The alternative is to split the obligations by date of payment net of such payments. Coats Viyella Plc adopt this form of disclosure as illustrated below:

Extract 19.4: Coats Viyella Plc[41]

19 Creditors (amounts falling due after more than one year) [extract]

	1987 £m	1986 £m
Finance lease obligations are repayable as follows:		
Within one year	**6.6**	3.8
Between 2 and 5 years inclusive	**16.7**	12.0
Over 5 years	**7.6**	4.5
	30.9	20.3

5 ACCOUNTING BY LESSORS

5.1 Introduction

Essentially, a lessor is required to show amounts due from lessees under finance leases as amounts receivable in debtors, and assets leased out under operating leases as tangible fixed assets. The mechanics of lessor accounting for finance leases is more complex than that for a lessee. The criteria which determine the classification of leases as either finance or operating are outlined at 2 above.

5.2 Operating leases

Rentals receivable under an operating lease should be recognised on a straight-line basis (irrespective of when rentals are actually receivable) unless another systematic and rational basis is more representative of the time pattern in which the benefit from the leased asset is receivable.[42] This requirement of SSAP 21 is an attempt to ensure a proper matching of revenues with associated costs. A non-straight-line basis may be appropriate where, for example, operating lease rentals are dependent on the level of use of the leased asset. In this case, rentals should be recognised in the periods they become receivable.

Examples of situations where a lessor should recognise operating lease rentals on a straight-line basis, even if they are not so received, are where there is a rent free period at the beginning of a lease of land or buildings, or where a balloon payment is to be made at the beginning or end of the lease period.

5.3 Finance leases

Broadly, there are two stages in accounting for finance lease receivables; firstly, the calculation of the gross earnings (finance lease income) element of total lease rentals receivable and, secondly, the allocation of gross earnings to accounting periods over the lease term. Gross earnings represent:[43]

(a)   the lessor's gross investment in the lease which is the total of the minimum lease payments and any unguaranteed residual value estimated as accruing to the lessor; less

(b)   the cost of the leased asset less any grants receivable towards purchase or use of the asset.

Gross earnings should then be allocated to accounting periods to give a constant periodic rate of return on the lessor's net cash investment.[44] The net cash investment is the amount of funds invested in a lease by the lessor and comprises the cost of the asset plus or minus certain related payments or receipts.[45]

The allocation of gross earnings to accounting periods is detailed at 5.5 (finance leases) and 5.6 (hire purchase contracts) below.

Having calculated the allocation of gross earnings to accounting periods, the lessor must then consider the amount at which the receivable should be shown in his balance sheet. The finance lease receivable should equal the lessor's net investment in the lease. This net investment will initially equal the cost of the asset less any grants receivable (i.e. the fair value) and will then be reduced by a portion of total rentals received. This portion will be the element of rentals receivable in a period which is not taken as gross earnings in the calculations described above.

5.4   Choice and disclosure of methods

As will be seen at 5.5 and 5.6 below, there are a number of possible alternative treatments available in the allocation of gross earnings to accounting periods over the lease term. One would, therefore, expect a reasonable level of disclosure by lessors of treatments adopted. In this respect, the ICAEW's survey of published financial statements for 1987/88 indicated that, despite a marginal increase in disclosure of income recognition policy, 15 of the 51 companies with evidence of lessor activity did not disclose their policies.[46] The reason for this may, however, have been that the leasing activity was thought to be immaterial in relation to the companies' other activities.

5.5   Allocation of gross earnings — finance leases

5.5.1   Introduction

Due to differences in tax treatments (see 1.3 above), different methods are used to allocate gross earnings to accounting periods under finance leases and hire purchase contracts. The latter is dealt with at 5.6 below, and the justification for the different treatments of finance leases and hire purchase contracts is considered at 5.5.5 below.

For finance leases, the gross earnings allocation should be made to give a constant periodic rate of return on the lessor's net cash investment. This involves the use of an 'after tax' method of allocation; the two most common are the actuarial after tax method and the investment period method.[47]

5.5.2   Methodology

The actuarial after tax and investment period methods allocate gross earnings on a basis which takes the tax effect on cash flows into account. This approach is used because we are attempting to match the revenue recognised under the lease with the expenses incurred (which may be partly notional) in funding the lessor's investment in the lease.

At any time during the lease, the lessor's net cash investment will represent:

(a)   the original cost of the asset; less

(b)   cumulative cash flow receipts to date (rental income, grants received, tax relieved through both capital allowances and payment of interest, together with interest receivable during any period of negative net cash investment); plus

(c)   cumulative cash flow payments to date (interest payments and tax payable on both rental receipts and any interest receivable). This should also include an adjustment in respect of the profit the lessor takes out of the lease, because part of the rental receipts represents profit to the lessor over and above any interest he is estimated to be paying.

The interest payable/receivable is likely to be a notional figure using appropriate rates for the lessor as at lease inception to reflect an opportunity cost of funds raised or invested. Both interest payable/receivable and profit taken out should be calculated on the average net cash investment in any period. The profit taken out will be calculated at the percentage rate which results in a net cash investment at the end of the lease term of zero.

The actuarial after tax method and the investment period method differ in their use of the calculated net cash investment at each period end to allocate gross earnings. Under the actuarial after tax method, the estimated profit taken out in each period is grossed up for tax and estimated interest costs, to give a derived apportionment of gross earnings in each period.

In contrast, under the investment period method the estimated net cash investment at each period end is divided by the total of such figures over the lease term to give the fraction of total gross earnings allocated to each period. Whereas the actuarial after tax method is more accurate, the investment period method may be preferred (if resulting differences are immaterial) since it is arithmetically simpler.

The application of the actuarial after tax and investment period methods is illustrated in the following example:

Example 19.4

The terms of a lease are as in Example 19.2 above, i.e. a five year lease of an asset commences on 1 January 19X1. The rental is £2,600 p.a. payable in advance. The fair value of the asset at lease inception is £10,000 and it is expected to have a residual at the end of the lease of £2,372 (being its tax written down value at the time) which will be passed to the lessee. In addition, the lessee is responsible for all maintenance and insurance costs.

The lessor obtains writing down allowances on the leased asset at the rate of 25%. The rate of corporation tax is 35%. The lessor's accounting year end is 31 December and he pays or recovers tax in the following year. Interest on funds borrowed is assumed to be 10% p.a., payable on 31 December.

The lessor's net cash investment in this lease can be analysed as follows:

Year	(a) Net cash investment at start of year £	(b) Cash flows in year cost/tax £	(c) Cash flows in year rentals £	(d) Average net cash investment in year £	(e) Interest paid £	(f) Profit taken out of lease £	(g) Net cash investment at end of year £
19X1	—	(10,000)	2,600	(7,400)	(740)	(277)	(8,417)
19X2	(8,417)	224	2,600	(5,593)	(559)	(210)	(6,362)
19X3	(6,362)	(58)	2,600	(3,820)	(382)	(144)	(4,346)
19X4	(4,346)	(284)	2,600	(2,030)	(203)	(76)	(2,309)
19X5	(2,309)	(470)	2,600	(179)	(18)	(7)	(204)
19X6	(204)	204	—	—	—	—	—
		(10,000)	13,000		(1,902)	(714)	
		(384)					

Notes to table:

(a)   net cash investment at start of year: this is simply zero at the beginning of the lease and the previous year end figure in later years;

(b)   cash flows in year — cost and tax: the £10,000 outflow in 19X1 is the purchase of the asset which is, for simplicity, assumed to take place on the day the lease commences. All other amounts relate to tax payable/repayable.

The basis of taxation of the lessor was detailed above and tax payable/repayable relates to the previous year's rentals receivable, interest paid and writing down allowance. The tax repayable in 19X6 relates to 19X5's rental receivable, interest paid, writing down allowance and the deduction relating to the passing of the asset's sales proceeds of £2,372 to the lessee. This deduction should actually enter the table in 19X7, as that is when the tax repayment would arise from the sale in 19X6, but is included in 19X6 for simplicity. The sales proceeds and payment to the lessee are not shown as their net effect on the cash flows is nil;

(c)   cash flows in year — rentals: the annual rentals received at the beginning of each year;

(d)   average net cash investment in year: this is the sum of columns (a) to (c). For the purposes of this example, all cash flows are assumed to arise on 1 January of each year;

(e)   interest paid: calculated at 10% of the average net cash investment in year shown in column (d);

(f)   profit taken out of lease: this represents the amount required by the lessor to give a return on the lease over and above tax and interest costs. It is the percentage of the average net cash investment in year shown in column (d) which results in a net cash investment at the end of the whole transaction of zero. It can be found by trial and error but computer programs are usually used to do this. In this example the annual rate is 3.75%;

(g)   net cash investment at end of year: this is the sum of columns (d) to (f). It can be seen that this is zero at the end of the whole transaction.

The above analysis is performed under both the actuarial after tax and investment period methods. However, these methods then differ in their use of the table to give gross earnings allocated to the years of the lease.

The actuarial after tax method merely grosses up the profit taken out of lease figure for each year by the tax rate of 35% and adds interest paid to give gross earnings allocated to each year as follows:

Year	Profit taken out of lease £	Tax (35/65ths) £	Profit grossed up for tax £	Interest paid £	Allocated gross earnings £
19X1	277	149	426	740	1,166
19X2	210	113	323	559	882
19X3	144	77	221	382	603
19X4	76	41	117	203	320
19X5	7	4	11	18	29
	714	384	1,098	1,902	3,000

In contrast the investment period method allocates a portion of total gross earnings (of £13,000 — £10,000) to each year in the proportion of the net cash investment at the relevant year end to the total of such net cash investments as follows:

Year	Net cash investment at end of year £	x	Total gross earnings ÷ Sum of net cash investments	=	Allocated gross earnings £
19X1	8,417 }				1,167
19X2	6,362 }				882
19X3	4,346 }	x	3,000 ÷ 21,638	=	603
19X4	2,309 }				320
19X5	204 }				28
	21,638				3,000

It can be seen that the differences between the gross earnings allocated to each year by each method in this example are negligible. Under the assumption of 35% tax and 25% writing down allowances, both methods give similar results. The reason for this is that the lease never goes into surplus. If different assumptions are made about rates of tax and allowances, cash surpluses may arise in certain periods, and in these circumstances the actuarial after tax method and the investment period method yield different results. Using the former method, the interest received on the cash surplus (the re-investment income) is brought back and recognised in the periods when the lessor has funds invested in the lease, rather than taken to income when it arises. Thus no profit is recognised in the period when the lease is in surplus. Because of this effect, the lessor may be in an exposed position in this period in the event, for example, of early termination of the lease by the lessee. If this method is used, it may therefore be necessary to make an appropriate provision for early termination losses so that the net investment in the lease does not exceed the termination value at any time. Under the investment period method, any re-investment income is recognised when it arises; that is, it is not brought back and recognised in the periods in which the lessor has funds invested in the lease. Thus, where cash surpluses arise, the investment period method is more conservative than the actuarial after tax method.[48]

The above example is a simplified one, in that all cash payments and receipts have been assumed to have occurred on either the first or last day of the year. In practice, the calculations would have to reflect the actual timing of the cash payments and receipts; for example, if the rentals were received monthly then the calculations would be performed at monthly rests.

5.5.3 Assumptions

Although they differ in the way gross earnings are allocated, both the actuarial after tax and investment period methods use the same assumptions and process to calculate the net cash investment at the end of each relevant period (quarter/year etc.).

The major assumptions used in this calculation of net cash investment are as follows:

(a)   sufficient taxable capacity will exist to relieve any tax deductible expenses and capital allowances in the forecast period;

(b)   borrowing and re-investment interest rates and levels of taxation will be as predicted;

(c)   defaults or termination of the lease will not occur;

(d)   administrative costs will be negligible.

If any of these assumptions ceases to hold, and the effect on the calculated allocation of gross earnings to accounting periods is material, then the calculations should be reperformed from the date when the change in assumptions takes place.

5.5.4   Other methods

Many variations of the actuarial after tax and investment period methods are found in practice due to differences in treatment of certain elements, e.g. re-investment income. Further, other methods exist of allocating gross earnings, e.g. the net earnings sum of the digits method allocates gross earnings to each period using the usual sum of the digits arithmetic (i.e. the balance is allocated to a period in proportion to the number of periods remaining).

5.5.5   Net investment or net cash investment

A lessor is concerned with both his net cash investment in a lease for allocating gross earnings to accounting periods and, also, his net investment for calculating the finance lease receivable in his balance sheet. These amounts are quite different in their calculation and use. As is explained at 5.6 below, owners under hire purchase contracts use the net investment in the contract for both of the above purposes.

The difference between net cash investment and net investment can be illustrated by way of the actuarial after tax figures in Example 19.4 above. The gross earnings given are deducted from total rentals in the year to give the reduction in net investment in that year. The opening net investment is simply the cost of the asset. This is shown as follows:

Example 19.5

Year	Total rentals £	Gross earnings £	Reduction in net investment £	Net investment at year end £
19X0	—	—	—	10,000
19X1	2,600	1,166	1,434	8,566
19X2	2,600	882	1,718	6,848
19X3	2,600	603	1,997	4,851
19X4	2,600	320	2,280	2,571
19X5	2,600	29	2,571	—
	13,000	3,000	10,000	

The net investment at each year end will be the finance lease debtor amount shown by the lessor in the balance sheet.

The use in SSAP 21 of both net investment and net cash investment for finance leases, but not hire purchase contracts, was explained by the less important tax effects of hire purchase contracts compared to finance leases for lessors; essentially because finance lessors receive capital allowances, but owners under hire purchase contracts do not. The Finance Act 1984 reduced the importance of these tax effects by lowering capital allowance and corporation tax rates. It is now arguable as to whether the extra complexity of the net cash investment approach of allocating gross earnings by finance lessors is warranted.

5.6   Allocation of gross earnings — hire purchase contracts

5.6.1   Introduction

As discussed above, the difference between the net investment and net cash investment in a lease relates to taxation and interest payable/receivable. SSAP 21 allows the use of a net investment method to allocate total gross earnings to accounting periods under those hire purchase contracts which are treated similarly to finance leases under SSAP 21 (the vast majority of them).[49] This is justified by the fact that capital allowances on an asset subject to a hire purchase contract usually accrue to the hirer. When SSAP 21 was introduced this meant that taxation was not such a major factor in the owner's evaluation of cash flows under a hire purchase contract as it was in the lessor's evaluation under a finance lease.

5.6.2   Methodology

There are two usual net investment methods of allocating gross earnings — the actuarial before tax method, and the sum of the digits ('rule of 78') method.[50]

The actuarial before tax method involves an analysis of the net investment in a contract for each period. The gross earnings percentage is then calculated such that when it is applied to the net investment figure in each period (to give a gross earnings allocation for each period) the net investment at the end of the lease/hire term is zero.

The sum of the digits method simply involves an apportionment of gross earnings over the hire purchase period in proportion to the number of future rentals receivable.

These methods usually ignore notional interest payments/receipts, with the result that the calculations are performed in exactly the same way as in Example 19.2 at 3.4 above in calculating the allocation of the finance charge for a lessee.

When considering hire purchase contracts it can be seen that the net investment in the lease/hire is used for both the allocation of gross earnings to accounting periods and the calculation of the lease/hire receivable in the owner's balance sheet. This contrasts with the position for finance leases (see 5.5.5 above).

5.6.3   Choice of method

The actuarial before tax method is the most accurate net investment method. Alternatives (the sum of the digits method or a simpler one, e.g. straight-line over the contract term) can be used where the differences in allocated gross earnings are immaterial.

6   DISCLOSURE BY LESSORS

6.1   SSAP 21 requirements

The following lessor disclosures are required by SSAP 21:

(a)   policies adopted for accounting for operating and finance leases and, in detail, the policy for accounting for finance lease income;[51]

(b)   aggregate rentals receivable in respect of the relevant accounting period from (i) finance leases and (ii) operating leases;[52]

(c)   if the provisions of SSAP 21 have not been applied retroactively to all leases existing at July 1, 1984, disclosure of the gross earnings from the finance leases and hire purchase contracts which have arisen under each of the methods used;[53]

(d)   net investment in (i) finance leases and (ii) hire purchase contracts;[54]

(e)   costs of assets acquired for the purpose of letting under finance leases and hire purchase contracts;[55]

(f)   gross amount of fixed assets held for use under operating leases, together with the related accumulated depreciation.[56]

6.2   Related Companies Act requirements

It is suggested in the Guidance Notes on SSAP 21 that the net investment in finance leases and hire purchase contracts should be included in current assets under the heading of debtors.[57] Accordingly, lessors who have to comply with Schedule 4 of the Companies Act, will have to comply with the requirement that 'the amount falling due after more than one year shall be shown separately for each item included under debtors'.[58]

There are a number of other disclosures required by the Companies Act which may affect lessors, and these should also be considered; e.g. details of fixed assets.[59] (This is relevant to assets leased under operating leases.)

6.3 Disclosure in practice

The following are examples of disclosures given in practice by lessors:

Extract 19.5: National Westminster Bank PLC[60]

NOTES TO THE ACCOUNTS

1 Accounting policies [extract]
(ix) Finance lease and operating lease assets
Amounts receivable under finance leases are included with other amounts receivable under 'Advances and other accounts', and the amounts attributable to assets held for use in operating leases are included in fixed assets.
Income from finance leases (including regional development grants grossed up to reflect their tax free nature) and instalment credit agreements is credited to profit and loss account in proportion to the funds invested.
Income from operating leases is credited to profit and loss account on a straight line basis over the period of the contract.

3 Group profit before taxation [extract] is stated after:	**1987** **£m**	1986 £m
(a) Income:		
(i) Aggregate amounts receivable under		
- finance leases, hire purchase and conditional sale contracts	**2,098**	1,844
- operating leases	**96**	89

12 Advances and other accounts [extract]
Group amounts include £2,983m (1986—£3,125m) receivable under finance leases and £1,697m (1985—£1,449m) in respect of hire purchase and conditional sale agreements.

16 Premises and equipment [extract]	Operating lease assets £m
The Group:	
Cost or valuation at 1 January 1987	**225**
Additions	**209**
Disposals	**(60)**
Cost or valuation at 31 December 1987	**374**
Accumulated depreciation and amortisation	**(97)**
Net book value at 31 December 1987	**277**
Net book value at 31 December 1986	154

The above accounting policy for recognising finance lease income is not as detailed as some other companies' policies, such as that of Barclays PLC as illustrated below:

Extract 19.6: Barclays PLC[61]

(h) Finance lease receivables
Finance lease receivables are included in advances and other accounts at the cost of the equipment less amounts charged against rentals to date. Net leasing income under finance leases is taken to profit using an actuarial method to give a constant periodic return on the net cash investment. It includes amounts in respect of regional development grants and certain tax credits grossed up at the average rate of corporation tax applicable to the particular period of each lease.

The reference under accounting policies in the above two extracts to grossing up regional development grants to reflect their tax free nature is now of less importance, as these grants have been substantially phased out. However, this was an attempt to take account of the fact that if a lessor received such a grant, the effect of it being ignored in calculating capital allowances for taxation purposes could be to give a pre-tax loss but post-tax profit on the lease for the lessor. Essentially, this procedure involved grossing up finance income and the tax charge in the profit and loss account.

The disclosure which SSAP 21 requires which is not given by National Westminster Bank PLC (presumably on the ground of materiality) is of the cost of assets acquired for the purpose of letting under finance leases and hire purchase contracts. A suitable note would be as illustrated below:

Extract 19.7:Barclays PLC[62]

15 ADVANCES AND OTHER ACCOUNTS [extract]

Assets acquired in the year for letting under finance leases amount to £1,138m (1986 £1,054m).

---

7   PROBLEM AREAS

7.1   Classification of leases

7.1.1   Current practice

The 90% test detailed in SSAP 21 (discussed at 2.1 above) appears to have been used in practice as a fairly definitive test instead of being one factor in deciding whether substantially all of the risks and rewards have been transferred to the lessee under a lease. It seems that the 90% test has been widely interpreted as a rule rather than a guide.

7.1.2   SSAP 21

The standard indicates that 'it should be presumed that'[63] substantially all the risks and rewards of ownership of an asset have been transferred to the lessee if the 90% test is met. However, this presumption may 'in exceptional circumstances be rebutted if it can be clearly demonstrated that the lease in question does not transfer substantially all the risks and rewards of ownership'.[64] 'Correspondingly, the presumption that a lease which fails to meet the [90% test] is not a finance lease may in exceptional circumstances be rebutted.'[65]

It is the use of the words 'in exceptional circumstances' which has resulted in the 90% test being taken as firm rule. Certain lessors have apparently used this to their advantage by structuring the lease to give a present value of minimum lease payments for the lessee which is just below 90%. It is then only in exceptional circumstances that the lease could be classified as a finance lease by the lessee.

7.1.3   *Technical Release 664*

The ICAEW published TR 664 — *Implementation of SSAP 21* — in an attempt to influence the practice of interpreting the 90% test as a firm rule.[66] It stated that any evaluation of a lease agreement should involve an overall examination of substantial risks and rewards as follows: 'Lease agreements give rise to a set of rights, rewards, risks and obligations and can be complex. The package must be analysed with greater weight given to aspects of the agreement which are likely to have a commercial effect in practice. In this way the substance of the transaction can be identified and then reflected in the financial statements in order to give a true and fair view. ... [The 90% test] does not provide a strict mathematical definition of a finance lease. Such a narrow interpretation would be contrary to the spirit of SSAP 21 and SSAPs generally.'[67]

TR 664 is indicative of good practice and is, therefore, to be supported; however, it does not have the same mandatory status as an accounting standard.

7.1.4   *Leasing as an off-balance sheet transaction*

Some lessees may prefer not to capitalise leased assets. This is because capitalisation of finance leases will affect the lessee's gearing and return on assets. Instances exist where leases are structured such that an operating lease treatment is permitted by SSAP 21 but, at least on certain interpretations, the substance of the lease is to provide a source of finance to the lessee.

Methods of achieving this typically involve use of the expected residual value of the leased asset because (based on our earlier outline of lease classification criteria) if this residual is significant and is not guaranteed by the lessee or a party related to him, then the lease is likely to be classified as an operating lease. Further, a lease may be structured such that the most likely outcome of events relating to the residual value indicates that no significant risk will attach to the lessee.

Example 19.6: A lease structured such that the most likely outcome is that the lessee has no significant residual risk.

Brief details of a motor vehicle lease are:

> Fair value — £10,000
> Rentals — 20 monthly @ £275, followed by final of £2,000
> At end of lease, lessee sells vehicle as agent for lessor, and if sold for
> > (i) more than £3,000, 99% of excess is repaid to lessee; or
> > (ii) less than £3,000, lessee pays deficit to lessor up to maximum of 0.4 pence per mile above 25,000 miles p.a. on average that the leased vehicle has done.

Therefore, as a result of (ii) above, this lease involves a guarantee of the residual value of the leased vehicle by the lessee of £3,000. However, the guarantee will only be called upon if both:

(a)   the vehicle's actual residual value is less than £3,000; and
(b)   the vehicle has travelled more than 25,000 miles per year on average over the lease term.

Further, the lessee is only liable to pay a certain level of the residual; namely, £100 for each 2,500 miles above 25,000 miles that the vehicle has done. It is arguable whether SSAP 21 intended that this guarantee should be treated similarly to a guarantee of £3,000 with no restrictions on when it will apply. One could argue that the guarantee should be assumed not to apply if experience or expectations of the sales price and/or the mileage that vehicles have done (and the inter-relationship between these) indicate that a residual payment by the lessee will not be made. On the other hand it could be said that the guarantee exists and therefore should be taken into account.

The treatment of the guarantee would obviously affect the 90% test and the overall consideration of factors which impinge on the risks and rewards of ownership.

One company which has entered into leases where residual risks have been passed to another party is British Airways Plc (BA).

BA have entered into a number of 'extendable operating leases', brief details of which were given in their privatisation document. The leases are structured such that BA can at certain times return the leased assets (aircraft or engines) to the lessors (a syndicate of banks) with resulting 'residual liabilities which are not expected to be material'.[68] The leases can be renewed on a broadly comparable basis for a number of years during which time BA can convert the leases into longer-term finance leases.

BA's financial statements for the period to March 31, 1988 indicate that none of the leases had been converted into finance leases. Their leasing commitments note discloses the following:

Extract 19.8: British Airways plc[69]

11 Tangible assets [extract]
f Leasing commitments

	Group		Company	
	1988 £m	1987 £m	1988 £m	1987 £m
The aggregate payments, for which there are commitments under operating leases as at the end of the year, fall due as follows:				
i) Fleet				
Within one year	**107**	113	**101**	113
Between one and three years	**53**	105	**52**	105
	160	218	**153**	218
Amounts payable within one year relate to commitments expiring as follows:				
Within one year	**34**	30	**31**	30
Between one and three years	**73**	83	**70**	83
	107	113	**101**	113

The fleet leasing commitments include the balance of the minimum three year rental obligations assumed under the operating leases for sixteen Boeing 737, three Boeing 747 and ten Boeing 757 aircraft. On completion of the three years the Company has a yearly option to renew the operating leases up to the sixth year or it has the option, at any time after three years, to convert the operating leases into finance leases for the period to 15 years from delivery of the aircraft.

If these options are not exercised, the Company may be required to meet a small share of any loss on resale.

7.2 Termination of leases

7.2.1 Lease classification

The expectations of lessors and lessees regarding the timing of termination of a lease may affect the classification of a lease as either operating or finance. This is because it will affect the expected lease term, level of payments under the lease and expected residual value of the lease assets.

Termination during the primary lease term will generally not be anticipated at the lease inception because the lessee can be assumed to be using the asset for at least that period. In addition, such an early termination will be unlikely because a termination payment is usually required which will give the lessor an amount equivalent to most or all of the rental receipts which would have been received if no such termination had taken place.

7.2.2 Operating leases

If a lease has been classified as an operating lease at its inception, then no major difficulty arises on a termination. Any termination payment due under the lease agreement will be accounted for as income when receivable by the lessor and as an expense when due by the lessee.

7.2.3 Finance leases — lessee

Early termination of a finance lease results in a disposal of the capitalised asset by the lessee. Any payment made by the lessee will reduce the lease obligation which is being carried in the balance sheet. If either a part of this obligation is not eliminated or the termination payment exceeds the previously existing obligation, then the remainder or excess will be included as a gain or loss (respectively) in calculating the total gain or loss arising on the disposal of the asset.

A similar accounting treatment is required where the lease terminates at the expected date and there is a residual at least partly guaranteed by the lessee. For the lessee, a payment made under such a guarantee will reduce the obligation to the lessor under the lease as the guaranteed residual would obviously be included in the lessee's finance lease obligation. If any part of the guaranteed residual is not called upon, then the lessee would eliminate it by transferring it to the calculation of gain/loss on disposal of the leased asset. The effect on the overall gain or loss will depend on the extent to which the lessee expected to make the residual payment as this will have affected the level to which the capitalised asset has been depreciated. For example, if the total guaranteed residual was not expected to become payable by the lessee, then he would have calculated the depreciation charge to give a net book value at the end of the lease term equal to the residual element not expected to become payable. If this estimate was correct then the remaining obligation will equal (and contra out) the net book value of the relevant asset.

Example 19.7

We can consider this in the context of Example 19.6 in 7.1.4 above, where there is effectively a guarantee of a residual of £3,000 dependent on the mileage done by the leased vehicle. Assuming that the lease is capitalised as a finance lease, if the lessee considers at the lease inception that the guarantee will not be called upon, then he will depreciate the vehicle to an estimated residual value of £3,000 over the lease term. In the event that his estimate is found to be correct, then the asset written down value will simply contra out with the lease obligation of £3,000. However, if, for example, £1,000 of the guarantee was called upon, whereas the lessee had estimated that it would not be, then the net book value of £3,000 and the unused guarantee of £2,000 will both be eliminated and a loss of £1,000 will be shown on disposal of the vehicle.

7.2.4 Finance leases — lessor

Any termination payment received by a lessor upon an early termination will reduce the lessor's net investment in the lease shown as a receivable. If the termination payment is greater than the previously shown net investment, then a profit on termination of the lease will be shown by the lessee. On the other hand, if the termination payment is smaller than the net investment, a loss will be shown. Such a loss is usually deducted from finance lease income unless exceptionally large, in which case it is separately disclosed.

Any loss on termination is unlikely to arise in most situations because a finance lease is likely to have termination terms such that the lessor is compensated fully for early termination and the lessor has legal title to the asset. Because he has title, the lessor can continue to include the asset in current assets as a receivable to the extent that sales proceeds or new finance lease receivables are expected to arise. If the asset is then re-leased under an operating lease, the asset may be transferred to fixed assets and depreciated over its remaining useful life.

To some extent, these two reasons for losses on termination of a finance lease not arising (full compensation and legal title remaining with the lessor) are complementary. If the termination payment is intended to give full compensation, then the asset may be retained by the lessee and sold with any proceeds going to him. On the other hand, if the termination payment is not structured in this way then the lessor will repossess the asset and sell or re-lease it.

7.3   Tax variation clauses

7.3.1   Introduction

The level of rentals in a lease are determined using the tax regime which exists at the time the lease terms are agreed. Tax variation clauses are common in finance leases and are designed to protect the lessor from any adverse changes in the capital allowance or corporation tax rates which the lessor has assumed will exist when the level of rentals are agreed. These may also apply where any tax changes operate to the lessor's benefit; this was the case after the Finance Act 1984.

7.3.2   Adjustments

Where a tax variation clause takes effect the rental adjustment may be made via:

(a)   lump sum payments as and when the lessor pays the new higher/lower tax charge for any period; or

(b)   the future rentals including stepped increases or decreases to reflect the changes; or

(c)   a new fixed rental being calculated to be paid over the remainder of the primary lease term.

7.3.3   Lessee

As regards the lessee, any change in total rentals payable represents an alteration to his remaining finance charges under a lease. These alterations should be accounted for by spreading the revised finance charges over the remaining lease term using the methods detailed at 3.4 above. However, in the possibly unusual circumstances of 7.3.2 (a) above, where the calculations of lump sum payments are not made until the relevant tax calculation is made by the lessor, then the altered rentals should be accounted for in the periods in which they arise. Although a constant rate of charge on the lessee's remaining liability will not result, this approach is justified because the lessee does not know what the future rentals will actually be.

Under either approach, if any reduction in rentals exceeds the finance charges which were expected to accrue, then the excess should be deducted from the capitalised cost such that future depreciation charges are lower than they would have been.[70] Negative finance charges are not permitted.[71]

7.3.4 *Lessor*

Any variations in taxation and rentals (due to a tax variation clause) which materially alter the lessor's analysis of net cash investment in the lease over its remaining term will alter the total of future gross earnings and also their allocation to accounting periods. This will therefore affect the reduction in net investment in the lease (shown as a receivable in the lessor's balance sheet) over its remaining term. The specifics of such an exercise are outside the scope of this chapter.

7.4 Sale and leaseback transactions

7.4.1 *Introduction*

Such transactions involve the original owner of an asset selling it (usually to a finance house or a merchant bank) and immediately leasing it back. These parties will be termed the vendor/lessee and purchaser/lessor respectively. Sometimes, instead of selling the asset outright, the original owner will lease the asset to the other party under a finance lease and then lease it back. Such a transaction is known as a 'lease and leaseback' and has similar effects. The term 'sale and leaseback' is taken to include such a transaction.

7.4.2 *Purchaser/lessor*

The purchaser/lessor will treat the lease in the same way as he would any other lease which was not part of a sale and leaseback transaction.[72]

7.4.3 *Vendor/lessee*

For the vendor/lessee there are further considerations which may apply if the transaction has certain characteristics. He must first decide whether the leaseback transaction gives rise to an operating or finance lease in the normal way, i.e. the fact that he has sold the asset to the lessor is irrelevant for this purpose. The accounting consequences depend on this categorisation.

7.4.4 *Leaseback under a finance lease*

Where the leaseback is of a finance nature and sales value is greater than written down value, then this apparent profit should not be taken to profit and loss account at the time of the sale and leaseback.[73] This is because it would be inappropriate to show a profit on disposal of an asset which has then, in substance, been re-acquired under a finance lease.

The apparent profit may be treated in either of two ways:

(a) the asset is treated as sold in the normal way except that the apparent profit should be deferred and taken to the profit and loss account over the lease term. The asset and the obligation under the lease are recorded at the sales value; or

(b)   the asset may remain in the vendor/lessee's books at the written down value with the sales value being treated as a creditor. This creditor balance represents the finance lease liability under the leaseback. When lease payments are then made, they are treated partly as a repayment of that creditor, and partly as a finance charge to the profit and loss account (in the usual way for a finance lease).

We consider that the second treatment better reflects the substance of the transaction whereby, effectively, a loan is being raised which is secured on the asset which was previously owned.

If sales value is less than written down value, the apparent loss arising on the sale should again not be taken to profit and loss account at the time of the sale and leaseback, but accounted for in the same way as for apparent profits as described above. However, if the low sales value demonstrates that a permanent diminution in value has occurred, this will result in an immediate write down in the profit and loss account.

Example 19.8

A company has machinery with a written down value of £5,000. The remaining useful life of the machinery is five years. A sale and leaseback is entered into on the following terms:

    Sales value: £8,000
    Rentals: five annual rentals of £2,000.

The machinery is expected to have negligible residual value at the end of the lease.

Such a lease will constitute a finance lease because the lessee is gaining use of the machinery for all of its useful life (the '90% test' would give a result of 100%).

Under method (a) above, the excess of sales value over written down value of £3,000 (£8,000—£5,000) will be deferred and amortised (credited) to the profit and loss account evenly over the five year lease term, i.e. at £600 p.a. The depreciation charge on the machinery capitalised under the finance lease will be £1,600 p.a.

Under method (b) above, the existing net book value is depreciated at £1,000 p.a.

In the case where the above machinery had been subject to a sale and leaseback on the following terms:

    Sales value: £4,000
    Rentals: five annual rentals of £1,000.

The machinery is expected to have a negligible residual value at the end of the lease.

Once again, the leaseback will constitute a finance lease under SSAP 21. We note that the lower sales proceeds result in lower rentals because the lessor requires less rental as a result of paying the lessee less for the machinery. Under method (a) above, the loss on disposal by the lessee of £1,000 (£4,000—£5,000) will be deferred and amortised (debited) to the profit and loss account evenly over the lease term (i.e. £200 p.a.). The depreciation on the machinery capitalised under the finance lease will be £800 p.a. Again, under method (b) depreciation would be £1,000 p.a. Where there is considered to have been a permanent impairment in the value of the machinery, the loss should not be deferred but be taken to the profit and loss account at the time of the sale of the machinery.

If an asset which is carried at a revalued amount is sold and leased back under a finance lease, then the relevant revaluation reserve should continue to be treated in the way it was prior to the sale and leaseback. If the revaluation reserve is being transferred to profit and loss reserve, this should now be over the shorter of the lease term and the asset's remaining useful life in order that the period of transfer matches the depreciation term of the leased asset.

An interesting anomaly seems to arise where there is a sale and 'hire purchase back', and the hire purchase contract term is shorter than the remaining useful life of the asset. If a profit is made on the sale it will (as we have just outlined) be deferred and amortised over the hire purchase term. If, however, method (a) above is used to deal with the apparent profit, then the asset will be capitalised at the sales value and, as it is a hire purchase contract, this amount will then be depreciated over the remainder of the asset's useful life, as required by paragraph 36 of SSAP 21. The result of this is that the profit is amortised over the hire purchase term, whereas the capitalised asset is depreciated over the life of the asset.

Example 19.9

An asset with a written down value and fair value of £100 has a remaining useful life of ten years. It is sold for £10,000 and repurchased under a hire purchase contract over a two year period with rentals of £6,000 p.a. The apparent profit of £9,900 (£10,000—100) will be deferred and amortised over the hire purchase period of two years. However, the asset is carried at £10,000 and depreciated over the useful economic life of ten years.

If this treatment (which appears to follow SSAP 21's requirements) was used, the vendor/lessee will show a massive gain over the first two years (because of the amortisation of the apparent profit of £9,900) but a large depreciation charge in the next eight years (because the asset is being carried at a cost of £10,000).

In such a case we believe that the treatment of an apparent profit, using method (b) above, should be used with the sales value of £10,000 being treated as a creditor to be eliminated over the hire purchase term and the asset retained at £100 to be depreciated over ten years.

In our view, the intention of paragraph 46 of SSAP 21 is to amortise the apparent profit or loss over the same period that the 'new' asset is depreciated, but has been drafted with only sale and *leaseback* transactions in mind. As assets capitalised under hire purchase contracts are required to be depreciated over their useful lives, the apparent profit or loss should be amortised over the same period.

7.4.5   Leaseback under an operating lease

Where a lessee enters into a sale and leaseback transaction which results in an operating lease then (1) the original asset should be treated as having been sold, and (2) the operating lease should be accounted for under the provisions of the standard (see 3.6 above).

Where the transaction is established at the fair value of the asset concerned, then any profit or loss on the sale of the asset should be recognised immediately.[74] Where the transaction is not based on the fair value of the asset, then the accounting treatment is best explained by the schedule, as shown below, which uses the following three amounts:

(a) WDV : the written down value of the asset prior to its sale by the vendor/lessee;

(b) SV : the sales value at which the asset is sold to the purchaser/lessor; and

(c) FV : the fair value of the asset, i.e. the price it would fetch if sold in an arm's length transaction to a third party (not as part of a sale and leaseback transaction).

Schedule of possibilities:[75]

1. SV<WDV<FV Loss (WDV—SV) recognised immediately unless lease rentals are below normal levels when it should be deferred and amortised.

2. SV<FV<WDV Loss based on fair value (WDV—FV) recognised immediately. Balance (FV—SV) should also be recognised immediately unless lease rentals are below normal levels when it should be deferred and amortised.

3. WDV<SV<FV Profit (SV—WDV) recognised immediately.

4. WDV<FV<SV Profit based on fair value (FV—WDV) recognised immediately. Balance (SV—FV) deferred and amortised.

5. FV<WDV<SV Loss based on fair value (WDV—FV) recognised immediately. Profit (SV—FV) deferred and amortised.

6. FV<SV<WDV Loss based on fair value (WDV—FV) recognised immediately. Profit (SV—FV) deferred and amortised.

Where any amounts are to be deferred and amortised, this should be done evenly over the shorter of the lease term and the period to the next lease rental review.

Transactions in categories 5 and 6 above are, essentially, dealt with in two stages. The asset is firstly written down to fair value because the asset is treated as having been sold for that amount; secondly, the excess of sales value over the fair value is treated as only an apparent profit, which is deferred and amortised.

The rationale behind the above treatments is that if the sales value is not based on fair values, then it is likely that the normal market rents will have been adjusted to compensate. Accordingly, the transaction should be recorded as if it had been based on fair values. However, this will not always be the case:

(a) where the fair value is above the written down value of the asset it is possible for the vendor/lessee to arrange for the sales value to be anywhere within that range and report a gain in the year of sale based on that sales value. Any compensation which the vendor/lessee obtains by way of reduced rentals will be reflected in later years;

(b)   where the sales value is less than fair value there may be legitimate reasons for this to be so, e.g. where the seller has had to raise cash quickly. In such situations, as the rentals under the lease have not been reduced to compensate, the profit or loss should be based on the sales value.

7.4.6   Creative sale and leaseback structures

Parties to a sale and leaseback transaction are given a certain level of flexibility such that the transaction may be structured to give a particular accounting treatment.

Firstly, the leaseback can be structured such that it is an operating lease within the terms of SSAP 21 for the vendor/lessee, with the purchaser/lessor being a controlled non-subsidiary as described in 2.1 and 2.2 of Chapter 5. In the present accounting environment, any profit made by the vendor/lessee on the sale will be taken to the group's profit and loss account in the normal way (unless sales value is greater than fair value as described above when an element of the profit would be amortised over a specified period of time). However, use of a controlled non-subsidiary as purchaser/lessor means that the asset will leave the group's financial statements. but is likely to remain under the control of the group. It would appear that such a scheme was used by The Burton Group PLC (although apparently no profit or loss was recorded on the transaction) as illustrated below:

Extract 19.9: The Burton Group PLC[76]

2 5 Related companies [extract]
High Street Property Investments Limited (HSPI)
In August 1986 the Group entered into sale and leaseback arrangements with HSPI (formerly Hall and Sons Ltd), in respect of properties with a book and market value of £100.1 million. HSPI has granted ten year options to certain Group companies to repurchase the individual properties at market value and pre-emptive rights over the properties for a period of 20 years. The Group has no obligations to repurchase the properties or in respect of the repayment of loans made to HSPI by its lending banks. The Group is entitled to, and accounts for, the retained profits of HSPI under the equity method of accounting, including any profit which may arise on the sale of properties to third parties.

Another example of structuring a sale and operating leaseback transaction in order to achieve a particular accounting result is found where a profit would arise on the sale if based on fair value. As indicated in 7.4.5 above, the transaction may be altered by reducing the sales value below fair value, compensated for by a lower level of lease rentals, so that a lower profit (or no profit) is recognised in the year of sale.

7.5   Manufacturers/dealers

7.5.1   *Introduction*

A manufacturer or dealer (M/D) in assets may offer customers the option of either outright purchase or rental of the assets. Where a rental agreement is such that it comes within the definition of an operating lease, then the M/D should not recognise a selling profit.[77] Where, on the other hand, a rental agreement is such that it comes within the definition of a finance lease (as substantially all the risks and rewards of ownership have passed), then there can be seen to be two elements of the M/D's overall profit or loss on the transaction. These are:

(a)   the selling profit or loss at the inception of the lease which is equivalent to the profit or loss that would arise on an outright sale made under an arm's length transaction; and

(b)   the gross earnings received by the M/D as lessor under the finance lease.

7.5.2   *Allocating the total profit of the manufacturer/dealer*

If the M/D is in the (relatively unlikely) position of incurring an overall loss because the total rentals receivable under the finance lease are less than the cost of the asset to the M/D, then the prudence concept dictates that this loss should be taken to profit and loss account at the inception of the lease. If an overall profit is made, then an allocation between the selling profit and lessor's gross earnings must be made.

In those situations where the customer is offered the choice of paying the cash price for the asset immediately or paying for it on deferred credit terms then, as long as the credit terms are the M/D's normal terms, the cash price can be used for determining the selling profit. However, in many cases such an approach should not be followed as the terms of the lease are often influenced by the M/D's marketing considerations. For example, a car dealer may offer 0% finance deals instead of reducing the normal selling price of his cars. It would be wrong in this instance for the dealer to record a profit on the sale of the car and no finance income under the lease.

It is not appropriate to take a 'normal' level of selling profit if the gross earnings under the finance lease would then be lower than normally expected, because the selling profit is taken to the profit and loss account at the lease inception and, if it is partly offset by lower than normal gross earnings under the lease, prudence dictates that this be taken into account. The correct practice is, therefore, to calculate gross earnings under the finance lease at the normal level, with any remaining element of the overall profit being taken as selling profit at the lease inception.

How then should the appropriate level of gross earnings under the finance lease be estimated? This clearly depends on the estimated interest rate implicit in the lease. In some situations the M/D will have a normal implicit interest rate based on his other leasing activity. However, in other situations where the M/D does not conduct other leasing business, an estimate will have to be made of the implicit rate for such leasing activity.

7.6 Sub-leases and back-to-back leases

7.6.1 *Introduction*

Situations arise where there are more parties to a lease arrangement than simply one lessor and one lessee. The discussion below relates to situations involving an original lessor, an intermediate party and an ultimate lessee. The intermediate party may be acting either as both a lessee and lessor of the asset concerned or, alternatively, as an agent of the lessor in the transaction.

Both sub-leases and back-to-back leases involve the intermediate party acting as both lessor and lessee of the asset. The difference between the two arrangements is that, for a back-to-back lease, the terms of the two lease agreements match to a greater extent than would be the case for a sub-lease arrangement. This difference is really only one of degree, and the important decision to be made concerns whether the arrangement is one of agency or, rather, the intermediate party is acting as both lessee and lessor in two related but independent transactions.

7.6.2 *The original lessor and the ultimate lessee*

The accounting treatment adopted by these parties will not be affected by the existence of sub-leases or back-to-back leases. The original lessor has an agreement with the intermediate party which is not affected by any further leasing of the assets by the intermediate party unless the original lease agreement is thereby replaced.

Similarly, the ultimate lessee has a lease agreement with the intermediate party. He will have use of the asset under that agreement and must make a decision, in the usual way, as to whether the lease is of a finance or operating type per SSAP 21.

7.6.3 *The intermediate party*

The appropriate accounting treatment by the intermediate party depends on the substance of the series of transactions. This turns on whether the intermediate party is acting either as an agent/broker for the original lessor or as a principal in both transactions. In the latter case, the intermediate party will act as lessee to the original lessor and lessor to the ultimate lessee.

In determining the role of the intermediate party, the question of recourse is important. If the ultimate lessee defaults on his lease obligations (for whatever reason), does the original lessor have recourse against the intermediate party for the outstanding payments under the lease?

Another important factor in the decision of how the intermediate party should account for the transaction is what happens if the original lessor defaults, e.g. through his insolvency. If the intermediate party is merely a broker/agent, then he will suffer no loss upon such default, and the ultimate lessee would only have a claim against the original lessor.

If these factors indicate that the intermediate party is acting merely as a broker or agent for the original lessor, he should not include any asset or obligation relating to the leased asset in his balance sheet. The income received by such an intermediary should be taken to profit and loss account on a systematic and rational basis.[78]

If, on the other hand, the intermediate party is taken to be acting as both lessee and lessor in two independent although related transactions, he should recognise his assets and obligations under finance leases in the normal way.

The recognition of income as lessor will be affected by the lease from the original lessor. Clearly, if the intermediate party had purchased the asset concerned outright, then his income recognition as a lessor would be on the usual net cash investment basis explained in 5.3 above. However, as he has obtained use of the asset under a finance lease, his income recognition will be based on the net investment in the lease. This is because the intermediate party's investment in the leased asset will be shown as the present value of the minimum lease payments, as reduced throughout the lease by the capital portion of total rental payable to the original lessor. In other words, there are no major tax consequences of the lease from the original lessor. The net investment approach to income recognition used for hire purchase contracts will therefore be appropriate (see 5.6 above).

It should not be inferred from the above discussion that all situations encountered can be relatively easily allocated as one of either a broker/agent or lessee/lessor in nature. In practice this is unlikely to be the case, as the risks and rewards will probably be spread between the parties involved. This is especially likely where more than the three parties discussed above are involved. In all cases, it is a question of judgement as to whether substantially all the risks and rewards from an asset attach to any party under the leases.

8   COMPARISON WITH US AND IASC PRONOUNCEMENTS

8.1   US

In most situations there are not major differences between accounting for leases in the UK and the US. This is because SSAP 21 is based on the same principles as SFAS 13 — *Accounting for Leases* — which became effective for leases entered into on or after January 1, 1977.[79] There are, however, some differences in detail between the two standards.

As regards lease classification, SFAS 13 gives four classification criteria. If any of these criteria are met, then the lease is a capital lease (which is equivalent to a finance lease in the UK). A 90% test, similar to that in SSAP 21, forms one of these four criteria, which means that the 90% test is more accurately described as a rule in the US. This is because if the 90% test indicates a capital lease under SFAS 13, then no other factors can change this classification. As has been discussed in this chapter, the 90% test in SSAP 21 gives a rebuttable assumption of a particular lease classification (as finance or operating). The other three criteria are:

(a)   the lease transfers ownership of the asset to the lessee at the end of the lease;

(b)   the lease contains a bargain purchase option (i.e. a provision allowing the lessee, at his option, to purchase the asset at a price sufficiently lower than the fair value at the exercise date, such that it is reasonably assured that he will exercise the option);

(c)   the lease term is equal to 75% or more of the estimated remaining economic life of the asset. However, if the lease term begins within the last 25% of the total economic life of the asset, then this criterion should not be used for the purpose of classifying the lease.

Another major difference between SSAP 21 and SFAS 13 relates to the method used by lessors to allocate gross earnings to accounting periods. The SFAS uses the net investment method, whereas the SSAP uses this only for hire purchase contracts, with the net cash investment method being used for finance leases.

Other requirements of SFAS 13 which are different from those of SSAP 21 include the following:

(a)   lessees with operating leases should disclose future minimum rental payments payable over each of the next five years and in aggregate thereafter;

(b)   specific rules are given for the classification of leases involving real estate although once this is done, accounting and disclosure are the same as for other leases;

(c)   lessor accounting for leveraged leases is based on additional specific rules, although the basic concept is the same as for other leases. Essentially, a leveraged lease is one that involves the lessor funding a large element of the purchase of the asset by nonrecourse debt under a long-term credit arrangement.

As in most areas, the FASB have issued more detailed and definitive guidance than the ASC.[80] This serves as a useful source of information in areas of lease accounting not specifically covered by SSAP 21 and its Guidance Notes.

8.2   IASC

IAS 17 was issued in September 1982 for accounting periods beginning on or after January 1, 1984.[81] Its basic requirements are similar to those of SSAP 21. A finance lease is defined as one that 'transfers substantially all the risks and rewards incident to ownership of an asset'.[82] Examples of situations where a lease would normally be classified as a finance lease are given, one of which is a 'present value test' which makes no reference to a specific percentage, such as the 90% mentioned in SSAP 21.

IAS 17 allows lessors accounting for finance leases to recognise finance income to reflect a constant periodic rate of return on either the net investment or net cash investment in the lease. The definitions of these terms are essentially the same as those in SSAP 21.

The IASC has recently issued an exposure draft, E32 — *Comparability of Financial Statements* — which proposes to amend, inter alia, the requirements of IAS 17. The main changes proposed are as follows:

(a)   for finance leases other than leveraged leases, lessors are to recognise finance income to reflect a constant periodic rate of return on the net investment in the lease; the present option of using the net cash investment in the lease (which is that required by SSAP 21) will no longer be available;[83]

(b)   leveraged leases are to be distinguished from other finance leases, and lessors are to recognise finance income on leveraged leases to reflect a constant periodic rate of return on the net cash investment in the lease during periods in which the net cash investment is positive.[84]

References

1 *Asset Finance & Leasing Digest*, April 1988, p. 32 and 33.
2 SSAP 21, *Accounting for leases and hire purchase contracts*, August 1984, para. 14.
3 *Ibid.*, para. 18.
4 ED 29, *Accounting for leases and hire purchase contracts*, October 1981.
5 Department of Trade, *Inspectors' Final Report on Court Line Limited*, p. 153.
6 *Ibid.*, Appendix J, p. 141.
7 *Ibid.*, p. 153.
8 ASC, *Guidance Notes on SSAP 21: Accounting for Leases and Hire Purchase Contracts*, August 1984.
9 SSAP 21, Introductory paragraph.
10 SSAP 21, para. 15.
11 *Ibid.*, para. 17.
12 *Ibid.*, paras. 15 and 16.
13 *Ibid.*, para. 25.
14 *Ibid.*, para. 24.
15 *Ibid.*, para. 20.
16 SFAS 29, *Determining Contingent Rentals*, FASB, June 1979, para. 11.
17 SSAP 21, para. 26.
18 *Ibid.*, para. 19.
19 *Ibid.*
20 *Ibid.*, para. 35.
21 Guidance Notes on SSAP 21, para. 20.
22 Further examples are given at paras. 21 to 36 of the Guidance Notes on SSAP 21.
23 SSAP 21, para. 37.
24 *Ibid.*, para. 57.
25 *Ibid.*, para. 55.
26 SSAP 21, para. 53.
27 *Ibid.*, para. 50.
28 *Ibid.*
29 *Ibid.*, paras. 51 and 52.
30 *Ibid.*, para. 56.
31 *Ibid.*, para. 54.

32 CA 85, Sch. 4, para. 53(6).
33 *Ibid.*, para. 8.
34 *Ibid.*, para. 50(5).
35 *Ibid.*, paras. 42 to 44.
36 *Ibid.*, para. 48.
37 British Telecommunications plc, Report and accounts 1988, pp. 31—47 *passim.*
38 Cadbury Schweppes p.l.c., Annual Report 1987, p. 58.
39 MEPC plc, Report and Financial Statements 1988, p. 39.
40 Walter Lawrence plc, Annual Report 1987, p. 26.
41 Coats Viyella Plc, Report and Accounts 1987, p. 38.
42 SSAP 21, para. 43.
43 *Ibid.*, para. 28.
44 *Ibid.*, para. 39.
45 *Ibid.*, para. 23.
46 L.C.L. Skerratt and D.J. Tonkin (eds.), *Financial Reporting 1987—88: A Survey of UK Reporting Practice*, London: ICAEW, 1988, p. 208.
47 Guidance Notes on SSAP 21, para. 92.
48 *Ibid.*, para. 121. See *Guidance Notes on ED 29: Accounting for Leases and Hire Purchase Contracts*, ASC, October 1981, paras. 81—86 for an illustration of the difference that can arise in such circumstances.
49 SSAP 21, para. 39.
50 Guidance Notes on SSAP 21, para. 116.
51 SSAP 21, para. 60.
52 *Ibid.*
53 *Ibid.*, para. 61.
54 *Ibid.*, para. 58.
55 *Ibid.*, para. 61.
56 *Ibid.*, para. 59.
57 Guidance Notes on SSAP 21, para. 124.
58 CA 85, Sch. 4, para. 8.
59 CA 85, Sch. 4, paras. 42—44.
60 National Westminster Bank PLC, Report and Accounts 1987, pp. 41—50 *passim.*
61 Barclays PLC, 1987 Report & Accounts, p. 30.
62 Barclays PLC, 1987 Report & Accounts, p. 38.
63 SSAP 21, para. 15.
64 *Ibid.*, para. 16.
65 *Ibid.*
66 Technical Release 664, *Implementation of SSAP 21.*
67 *Ibid.*, paras. 4 and 5.
68 British Airways Plc, Offer For Sale by Hill Samuel & Co. Limited on behalf of The Secretary of State For Transport, January 1987.
69 British Airways Plc, Report and Accounts 1987—88, pp. 45 and 46.
70 Guidance Notes on SSAP 21, para. 38.
71 SSAP 21, para. 34.
72 *Ibid.*, para. 48.
73 *Ibid.*, para. 46.
74 *Ibid.*, para. 47.
75 Adapted from para. 122 of Guidance Notes on ED 29.
76 The Burton Group PLC, Annual Report 1988, p. 54.
77 SSAP 21, para. 45.
78 Guidance Notes on SSAP 21, para. 165.
79 SFAS 13, *Accounting for Leases*, FASB, November 1976.
80 See the detailed US requirements relating to leasing in FASB, *Accounting Standards, Current Text, General Standards as of June 1, 1988*, FASB, 1988, Section L10, pp. 29141 — 29255.

81   IAS 17, *Accounting for Leases*, IASC, September 1982.
82   *Ibid.*, para. 2.
83   E32, *Comparability of Financial Statements*, IASC, January 1989, para. 76.
84   *Ibid.*, para. 81.

Chapter 20

Segmental reporting

1   INTRODUCTION

1.1   Historical background

Segmental reporting involves the reporting of disaggregated financial information, such as turnover, profits, capital employed etc., about a business enterprise. This information is generally analysed in two ways:

(a)   by industry segment. Industry segments are the distinguishable components of an enterprise each engaged in providing a different product or service, or a different group of related products or services, primarily to customers outside the enterprise;[1]

(b)   by geographical segment. Geographical segments are the distinguishable components of an enterprise engaged in operations in individual countries or groups of countries within particular geographical areas.[2]

Segmental reporting has been debated since the early 1960s; that period being significant for the rapid emergence and growth, especially in the US, of the multinational conglomerate business enterprise.

As enterprises became involved in a large number of distinct products, even industries, the readers of their financial statements found it increasingly difficult to analyse the effect of different segments' results on past performance and the likely effect on future performance. Clearly, there could be a wide range of levels of profitability, levels of growth and risk factors concealed within the consolidated financial statements of a diversified multinational business enterprise. Pressures grew, mainly from the investment analyst community, for disclosure of the results and resources of the different segments which comprised the whole business enterprise. As Mautz noted, 'The progress and success of a diversified company are composites of the progress and success of its several parts. The analyst must have some knowledge about each of these parts to have a basis for forecasting the future of the company. By definition the diversified company is subject to internally varying rates of profit, degrees of risk and potential for profit.'[3]

Since the early 1960s, most major industrialised countries have introduced segmental reporting requirements to varying degrees; by State legislation, accounting standard and Stock Exchange pronouncement. Similarly, supra-national bodies such as the OECD have developed guidelines for disclosure of segmental information in the financial statements of multinational business enterprises.[4]

The growth of the diversified, multinational business enterprise has continued to the present day; it is a predominant feature of modern business and there is no evidence that this status will change in the future, particularly with the move towards a single European market by the end of 1992. Recurring periods of merger and acquisition activity merely confirm that the justification for segmental reporting is as strong as ever.

1.2   The objectives of segmental reporting

1.2.1   *Introduction*

The objectives of segmental reporting derive from the fact that users need a greater level of detail of information about the results and resources of a business enterprise than is provided by its profit and loss account and balance sheet in order to make more informed economic decisions. There is, obviously, a vast amount of detail that could be given about a large business enterprise's financial activities. Nevertheless, it is presumably as a result of pressure from interested parties that this additional feature of financial reporting has developed and that there is a need, or a perceived need, for such information.

To understand the objectives of segmental reporting it is useful to discuss these in the context of a number of the user groups identified in Chapter 2. The user groups most likely to benefit from segmental information are:

1.2.2   *The shareholder group*

Shareholders are interested in assessing the potential profits and cash flows of the company. If they are provided with disaggregated data, it is presumed that they will be able to make more informed decisions. Research undertaken, both in the US and the UK, has indicated that segmental information does improve the ability of shareholders to predict an enterprise's future profits. Interestingly, it appears that the ability to predict future profits based on segmental sales information is not significantly improved by the additional disclosure of segmental profit information.[5]

Shareholders will also be interested in the stewardship of their funds in the past. Therefore they may regard relatively poor performance in one segment as an indication that their company has failed to use its resources in the most efficient manner.

1.2.3   *The investment analyst group*

The objectives of the investment analyst group are broadly similar to those of the individual shareholder. However, because they are more expert in the techniques of financial analysis, segmental information is, perhaps, even more useful to this group. This is reflected in the fact that much of the early pressure for segmental reporting came from the investment analyst group.

It would be likely that investment analysts would be supplied with more segmental information, if it were not for the fact that reporting enterprises have to bear both the costs of producing the information and the possible risk that some advantage may accrue to competitors having more detailed knowledge of their activities. Therefore, opposing pressures are likely to lead to a compromise solution, although the compromise solution may change over time.

1.2.4 The lender/creditor group

To the extent that segmental information improves the ability to predict future profits and cash flow, lenders and creditors will be similarly interested in having such information available. Improved ability to predict cash flows will assist lenders and creditors to make decisions regarding short-term liquidity and long-term solvency.

1.2.5 Government

There are a number of reasons why Governments would be interested in segmental information. It is likely that segmental information assists governmental bodies to collate statistics on macro-economic performance; for example, the investment in and the performance of various industries and products.

Geographical analysis of results and resources may be of significant interest to foreign Governments. They will be better able to assess the activities of the reporting company within their borders. This assessment may lead to a change in level of regulation, revision of tax status, amendment to amount of financial assistance and so on.

Government may also take the view that more detailed information will act as an aid to competition, thus resulting in benefits to the general economy.

2   THE UK POSITION

2.1   Legislative requirements

The Companies Act 1967 introduced the requirement that where a company carried on business of two or more classes which 'in the opinion of the directors, differ substantially from each other', turnover and profit before tax shall be disclosed split into those classes. This disclosure was to be made in the directors' report.[6]

The 1967 Act also required a statement of the value of goods exported from the UK to be included in the directors' report (unless turnover did not exceed £50,000). If none were exported a negative statement was required. If the directors were able to satisfy the Board of Trade that it was not in the national interest to disclose this export information the requirement could be waived.[7]

These requirements were extended by the Companies Act 1981. Firstly, the requirement to state the value of goods exported from the UK was replaced by a requirement to disclose turnover by export market.[8] Secondly, this disclosure and the disclosure of turnover and profit before tax split by class of business required by the 1967 Act were to be made in the notes to the accounts rather than in the directors' report.

The exemption from the requirement to disclose this information was also extended by the 1981 Act. Exemption was permitted 'where in the opinion of the directors, the disclosure . . . would be seriously prejudicial to the interests of the company.' However, the fact that the information had not been disclosed was required to be stated.[9]

These legislative requirements have been consolidated into the Companies Act 1985; and the relevant provisions are contained within paragraph 55 of Schedule 4 of the 1985 Act.

2.2   Stock Exchange requirements

The Stock Exchange requires listed companies to provide in their annual report a geographical analysis of both turnover and contribution to trading results of those trading operations carried on by the reporting enterprise outside the United Kingdom and the Republic of Ireland. This analysis should be by continent but if 50% of total overseas operations relates to one continent, a further analysis is required, for example, by country within that continent.[10] Similar requirements are imposed on USM companies.[11]

No analysis of the contribution to trading results is required unless the contribution to profit or loss from a specific area is 'abnormal' in nature. 'Abnormal' is defined as substantially out of line with the normal ratio of profit to turnover.[12]

An example of segmental reporting which complies with the requirements of the Companies Act 1985 and The Stock Exchange would be that of Reckitt & Colman plc as illustrated in the following extract:

Extract 20.1: Reckitt & Colman plc[13]

ANALYSIS OF SALES AND PROFIT BEFORE TAX BY AREA

	Sales 1987 £m	1986 £m	Sales 1987 % of total	1986 % of total	Profit before tax 1987 £m	1986 £m	Profit before tax 1987 % of total	1986 % of total
UK domestic	**300.47**	291.77	**19.8**	21.6	**33.95**	30.34	**20.5**	21.6
UK export	**70.32**	63.44	**4.6**	4.7	**16.62**	15.19	**10.0**	10.8
UK total	**370.79**	355.21	**24.4**	26.3	**50.57**	45.53	**30.5**	32.4
Europe (excluding UK)	**324.20**	299.66	**21.4**	22.1	**19.33**	16.16	**11.6**	11.5
North America	**422.85**	322.38	**27.8**	23.8	**29.18**	23.23	**17.6**	16.5
Australasia & Asia	**187.55**	185.77	**12.3**	13.7	**27.58**	22.75	**16.6**	16.2
Africa	**93.46**	80.11	**6.2**	5.9	**13.83**	12.12	**8.3**	8.6
Latin America	**119.30**	110.40	**7.9**	8.2	**25.48**	20.68	**15.4**	14.8
	1,518.15	1,353.53	**100.0**	100.0	**165.97**	140.47	**100.0**	100.0
Add/(deduct): UK export sales intra group	**(25.59)**	(24.18)						
Corporate interest & expenses					**1.64**	(1.01)		
	1,492.56	1,329.35			**167.61**	139.46		

ANALYSIS OF SALES AND PROFIT BEFORE TAX BY PRODUCT GROUP

	Sales 1987 £m	Sales 1986 £m	Sales 1987 % of total	Sales 1986 % of total	Profit before tax 1987 £m	Profit before tax 1986 £m	Profit before tax 1987 % of total	Profit before tax 1986 % of total
Household & toiletry	689.61	648.50	46.2	48.8	84.27	73.32	50.8	52.2
Food & wine	541.24	426.00	36.3	32.0	39.33	29.32	23.7	20.9
Pharmaceutical	134.34	123.97	9.0	9.3	26.07	23.87	15.7	17.0
Colours	43.36	38.15	2.9	2.9	11.49	8.89	6.9	6.3
Industrial cleaning	55.02	65.39	3.7	4.9	1.72	1.69	1.0	1.2
Fine art & graphics	28.99	27.34	1.9	2.1	3.09	3.38	1.9	2.4
	1,492.56	1,329.35	100.0	100.0	165.97	140.47	100.0	100.0
Add/(deduct): Corporate interest & expenses					1.64	(1.01)		
					167.61	139.46		

It will be noted that the above tables also provide some percentages in relation to the figures disclosed. While disclosure of such percentages is not required, it tends to aid understanding of the segmental information and is to be encouraged.

2.3 Accounting standards

At present there is no Statement of Standard Accounting Practice which deals with segmental reporting. However, an exposure draft has recently been issued by the ASC which deals with this issue. This exposure draft is discussed below.

The only requirements which potentially impinge on segmental reporting are contained within SSAP 14 — *Group accounts* and SSAP 6 — *Extraordinary items and prior year adjustments.*

SSAP 14 requires disclosure of an indication of the nature of the business of each of the holding company's subsidiaries.[14]

SSAP 6 refers to the concept of a business segment (see 2.2.1 of Chapter 8).[15] For example, costs of closure of such a segment may be regarded as extraordinary rather than ordinary or exceptional. However, it does not necessarily follow that the definition of a business segment in this context would be the same definition applied in the context of segmental reporting.

2.4   ED 45

2.4.1   *Introduction*

The ASC set up a working party on segmental reporting in 1986. This working party produced ED 45 which was issued in November 1988.[16] At the time of publication of this book it is not possible to determine what areas, if any, of the exposure draft will be amended in any subsequent standard.

2.4.2   *General principle*

ED 45 is based on the principle that, unless the financial statements of an enterprise contain segmental information, they do not enable the reader to make judgements about the nature of the different activities or of their contribution to its overall financial result.[17]

The exposure draft aims to contribute to improved segmental reporting in two ways. Firstly, by providing guidance as to how the reportable segments should be determined and, secondly, by specifying the information to be disclosed.

2.4.3   *Scope*

The proposed standard will apply to all financial statements intended to give a true and fair view of the financial position and profit or loss of an enterprise. However, it is intended that certain of the information required by the proposed standard to be disclosed (effectively that which is additional to the provisions of the Companies Act (see 2.1 above)) will only have to be given by:[18]

(a)   public companies (as defined in section 1 of the Companies Act 1985) or holding companies that have one or more public companies as a subsidiary; and

(b)   private companies (and other enterprises) which do not satisfy the criteria, multiplied in each case by ten, for defining a medium-sized company under the Companies Act.

At present, this means that enterprises with any two of the following will have to give the extra information:

(i)   turnover exceeding £80m,
(ii)   total assets exceeding £39m,
(iii) average number of employees exceeding 2,500.

This will be achieved by giving exemption to enterprises other than the above from certain of the disclosure requirements of the standard. These exemptions are dealt with in 2.4.10 below.

Where both parent company and consolidated financial statements are presented, segmental information is to be presented on the basis of the consolidated financial statements.[19]

Comparative figures for the previous accounting period are to be given. However, on the first occasion on which a company provides segmental information, comparative figures need not be given if the necessary information is not readily available.[20]

The exemption remains that where, in the opinion of the directors, the disclosure of any information required would be seriously prejudicial to the interests of the company that information need not be disclosed, but the fact that any such information has not been disclosed must be stated.[21] In practice very few companies choose to take advantage of the exemption under the Companies Act (see 2.1 above) and we believe that this situation will not change following the issue of an accounting standard containing a similar exemption.

2.4.4   *What is a reportable segment?*

Information can be segmented in two main ways — by class of business and geographically. ED 45 supports the provisions of the Companies Act 1985 which state that it is the directors' responsibility to determine the analysis of the segments.[22] The exposure draft does not seek to override these provisions; instead it aims to provide guidance on factors which should influence the definition of segments.

The basic guidance of the proposed standard is that directors should have regard to the overall purpose of presenting segmental information and the need for the readers of the financial statements to be informed where a company carries on operations in different classes of business or in different geographical areas that:

(a)   earn returns on investment that are out of line with the remainder of the business; or

(b)   are subject to different degrees of risk; or

(c)   have experienced different rates of growth; or

(d)   have different potentials for future development.[23]

In determining whether or not a company operates in different classes of business the directors should take into account the following:

(a)   the nature of the products or services;

(b)   the nature of the production processes;

(c)   the markets in which the products or services are sold;

(d)   the distribution channels for the products;

(e)   any separate legislative framework relating to part of the business.[24]

In determining whether or not a company operates in different geographical segments the directors should take into account the following:

(a)   expansionist or restrictive economic climates;

(b)   stable or unstable political regimes;

(c)   exchange control regulations;

(d)   exchange rate fluctuations.[25]

This may result in companies having to reassess the geographical segments which they are currently disclosing as in many cases this would appear to be based on geographical proximity; the proposed standard emphasises that 'although geographical proximity may indicate economic trends and risks, this will not always be the case.'[26]

In establishing segments for both classes of business and geographical areas, there is no single set of factors which is universally applicable nor is any single factor predominant in all cases.

It is noteworthy that there are no guidelines to help determine whether or not a reportable segment is sufficiently material to be disclosed. It is implied that materiality for disclosure of a reportable segment is dependent upon the directors' judgement.

2.4.5 *What is to be reported?*

The company should define each of the reported classes of business and indicate the composition of each of the reported geographical segments.[27] For each separate class of business and geographical segment, a company would be required to disclose:

(a) turnover;

(b) results;

(c) capital employed.[28]

Turnover should be analysed between sales to external customers and sales between segments. The basis of inter-segment sales pricing is to be disclosed.[29]

The geographical analysis of turnover is to be given with reference both to its source (i.e. where the products are manufactured) and to its destination (i.e. where the customers are located). However, only one of these analyses need be given if there is no material difference between them.[30]

Companies which prepare special category accounts under Schedule 9 of the Companies Act and are exempt from disclosing turnover because it is attributable to the business of banking or discounting will not be required to disclose such turnover segmentally. However, this fact should be stated.[31]

Results are the profit or loss before tax, minority interests and extraordinary items. Profit or loss may be before or after accounting for interest.[32] It is anticipated that in most situations the profit or loss before interest should be used. However, the profit or loss after interest is likely to be used in those companies where the earning of interest income or the incurring of interest expense is fundamental to the nature of the business; for example, companies in the financial sector.[33] In giving the geographical analysis of results it is considered that it will be more appropriate if it is based on the areas from which goods or services are supplied.[34]

Capital employed is not defined in the proposed standard. Generally it will be non-interest bearing operating assets less non-interest bearing operating liabilities. However, where interest income/expense has been included in arriving at the segmental results the related interest bearing assets/liabilities should be taken into account in determining the capital employed.[35] The aim should be to relate the definition of capital employed to the definition of results so that a 'return on investment' type calculation can be performed (it is unlikely that any comparison between companies of such returns will be meaningful, given the fact that some companies incorporate fixed assets at valuation and others do not). Operating assets and liabilities which are shared by more than one segment are to be allocated, as appropriate, to those segments.[36] Again, it is considered that it will be more appropriate for the geographical analysis to be based on the areas from which goods or services are supplied.[37]

It is highly unlikely that different companies will interpret capital employed in the same way. Perhaps the best that can be achieved is for companies to settle on one definition of capital employed that is meaningful for their own company, and apply it consistently. In view of the fact that no definition is given for capital employed, the proposed standard requires the method of calculating capital employed to be described.[38]

The total of the information disclosed by segmental analysis should agree with the related totals in the financial statements. If they do not agree, a reconciliation between the two figures is required.[39]

2.4.6   Disclosure in practice

One company which currently discloses the information which would be required to be disclosed in terms of ED 45 is Imperial Chemical Industries PLC. Perhaps it is not unexpected that a company which states that it 'manufactures in more than 40 countries and territories and sells to over 150'[40] should be particularly comprehensive in the area of segmental reporting.

While the full note is reproduced below it should be borne in mind that a number of the disclosure items given by Imperial Chemical Industries PLC would not be required under a future accounting standard based upon ED 45. These would include the segmental information given on capital expenditure and depreciation as well as average number of people employed.

Extract 20.2: Imperial Chemical Industries PLC[41]

2 SEGMENT INFORMATION

INDUSTRY SEGMENTS

The table below sets out information, on a worldwide basis, for each of the Group's industry segments. The Group's policy is to transfer products internally at external market prices. Certain product reclassifications have taken place, following the merger of the Group's interests in oil production and exploration with those of Enterprise Oil plc and the formation of ICI Chemicals and Polymers Group, in order to align the segmental information with revised management responsibilities. Oil activities, including continuing oil trading, are now included in the Industrial Products segment; methanol and related products, formerly in Agriculture, have been transferred to Industrial Products; biological products, formerly in

Agriculture, have been transferred to Consumer and Speciality Products; a number of other chemical products and catalysts and licensing have been transferred from Agriculture to the Industrial Products segment; and certain engineering plastics, formerly in Industrial Products, are now classed as Consumer and Speciality Products. Comparative figures for 1986 have been restated to reflect these changes; in particular, the results of the former Oil and Gas segment are shown in the comparative figures for that year within Industrial Products.

	Total assets less current liabilities		Turnover		Profit	
	1987 £m	1986 £m	1987 £m	1986 £m	1987 £m	1986 £m
Consumer and speciality products	1,955	2,062	4,332	3,668	574	507
Industrial products	2,207	2,547	5,170	4,942	595	458
Agriculture	1,217	1,084	1,744	1,657	48	7
Miscellaneous			199	166	20	5
			11,445	10,433	1,237	977
Net operating assets	5,379	5,693				
Inter-segment eliminations			(322)	(297)	(2)	(4)
Non-operating and miscellaneous assets	438	456				
	5,817	6,149	11,123	10,136	1,235	973
Royalty income and government grants					62	76
Trading profit					1,297	1,049
Share of profits less losses of related companies					157	95
Net interest payable					(142)	(128)
Profit on ordinary activities before taxation					1,312	1,016

Non-operating and miscellaneous assets include investments in related and other companies, current asset investments and short-term deposits and cash, less short-term borrowings.

	Capital expenditure		Depreciation	
	1987 £m	1986 £m	1987 £m	1986 £m
Consumer and speciality products	300	285	136	115
Industrial products	269	230	232	289
Agriculture	121	112	78	72
Other	18	16	18	15
	708	643	464	491

The basis of allocation of capital expenditure to industry segments was revised in 1987; comparative figures for 1986 have been restated.

GEOGRAPHIC AREAS

The information opposite is re-analysed in the table below by geographic area. The figures for each geographic area show the net operating assets owned by and the turnover and profits made by companies located in that area; export sales and related profits are included in the areas from which those sales were made.

	Net operating assets		Turnover		Profit	
	1987 £m	1986 £m	1987 £m	1986 £m	1987 £m	1986 £m
United Kingdom						
Sales in the UK			2,703	2,530		
Sales overseas			2,927	2,771		
	2,539	2,575	5,630	5,301	617	487
Continental Europe	713	810	2,539	2,238	184	134
The Americas	1,219	1,402	2,934	2,455	271	224
Australasia, Japan and the Far East	712	760	1,668	1,554	156	119
Other countries including Indian sub-continent	196	146	393	406	35	40
	5,379	5,693	13,164	11,954	1,263	1,004
Inter-area eliminations			(2,041)	(1,818)	(28)	(31)
			11,123	10,136	1,235	973
Royalty income and government grants					62	76
Trading profits					1,297	1,049

EMPLOYEES

	1987	1986
Average number of people employed by the Group in:		
United Kingdom	55,800	56,800
Continental Europe	15,500	15,000
The Americas	29,500	22,800
Australasia, Japan and the Far East	14,700	14,600
Other counties including Indian sub-continent	12,300	12,600
Total employees	127,800	121,800

GEOGRAPHIC MARKETS

	1987 £m	1986 £m
Turnover in each geographic market in which customers are located		
United Kingdom	2,732	2,545
Continental Europe	2,787	2,527
The Americas	3,048	2,561
Australasia, Japan and the Far East	1,881	1,794
Other countries including Indian sub-continent	675	709
Total turnover	11,123	10,136

It can be seen from the above extract that Imperial Chemical Industries PLC only analyse the information between four industry segments (consumer and speciality products, industrial products, agriculture and miscellaneous) in their note to the financial statements. Additional information is given in their directors' report in which the turnover and profit attributable to the first three segments is sub-divided into three, four and two sub-segments respectively.[42] It will be interesting to see whether they will re-define their reportable segments if ED 45 becomes a standard.

An additional feature of Imperial Chemical Industries PLC's segmental reporting is the presentation of five year record segmental information.[43] This additional information is a most useful aid to financial analysis and one which is to be encouraged.

2.4.7 *Associated companies*

A company should segmentally disclose, in its consolidated financial statements, the following information in respect of its associated companies:

(a) the company's share of the profits or losses of associated companies before accounting for taxation, minority interests and extraordinary items;

(b) the company's share of the net assets of associated companies (including goodwill to the extent it has not been written off) stated, where possible, after attributing fair values to the net assets at the date of the interest in each associated company.

This disclosure should be of the aggregate information for all associated companies and should be shown separately in the segmental report.[44]

The disclosure is only required if the results or assets of associated companies form a material part of the group's results or assets. For this purpose, associated companies form a material part of the reporting company's results if, in total, they account for at least 20% of the total results or at least 20% of the total capital employed by the reporting group (including the group's share of the results and net assets of the associated companies).[45]

It may commonly be the case that the associated companies do not come within the scope of the proposed standard and are therefore not disclosing segmental information in their financial statements. Where this is the case the investing company may be unable to obtain the necessary information to meet the requirement of the standard as it does not control the associated company. ED 45 recognises this problem by providing an exemption to the effect that the segmental information requirements do not apply where the company is unable to obtain the information.[46]

One company which presently discloses some segmental information about its associated companies (in this case synonymous with related companies) is Blue Circle Industries PLC as shown in the following extract:

Extract 20.3: Blue Circle Industries PLC[47]

2 Turnover and profit

	Parent and sub-sidiaries 1987 £m	Share of related companies 1987 £m	Total 1987 £m	Parent and sub-sidiaries 1986 £m	Share of related companies 1986 £m	Total 1986 £m
Geographical analysis						
(a) Turnover						
(by customer location):						
United Kingdom	530.8	—	530.8	533.4	—	533.4
United States	444.3	—	444.3	460.6	—	460.6
South America	31.1	—	31.1	30.8	2.3	33.1
Mexico	—	73.5	73.5	—	71.9	71.9
Africa	39.2	88.5	127.7	25.4	91.5	116.9
Australasia	12.7	7.2	19.9	36.8	60.5	97.3
Asia and other areas	10.6	57.7	68.3	11.0	69.3	80.3
	1068.7	226.9	1295.6	1098.0	295.5	1393.5
(b) Operating profit:						
United Kingdom						
Cement			45.6			28.8
Home products			12.3			10.5
Property			16.7			8.5
Other operations			4.6			3.7
			79.2			51.5
United States			35.9			49.4
Chile			11.7			10.7
Mexico			18.7			15.0
Africa			16.1			12.8
Australasia			3.4			18.4
Asia and other areas			5.0			7.7
			170.0			165.5
Class of business						
(a) Turnover:						
Cement and building materials	874.8	211.4	1086.2	925.1	282.9	1208.0
Home products	113.6	—	113.6	115.7	—	115.7
Property	31.7	1.5	33.2	21.6	2.9	24.5
Other operations	48.6	14.0	62.6	35.6	9.7	45.3
	1068.7	226.9	1295.6	1098.0	295.5	1393.5
(b) Operating profit						
Cement and building materials			136.2			144.1
Home products			12.3			8.6
Property			17.2			9.7
Other operations			4.3			3.1
Operating profit			170.0			165.5

It can be seen that Blue Circle Industries PLC has only shown separate segmental information in respect of its share of associated companies' turnover (which will not be required if ED 45 becomes a standard); their share of associated companies' profit being included with the rest of the group's profit in the segmental analyses of profit. Another approach taken by companies is to give segmental disclosure inclusive of their share of the associated companies' turnover and profit.[48]

It will therefore be necessary for these companies to give additional disclosure of the segmental analyses of their associated companies' profits if ED 45 becomes a standard.

2.4.8 Common costs

Common costs are defined as costs relating to more than one segment.[49] The exposure draft merely requires that they are treated in the way that the directors deem most appropriate with regard to the objectives of segmental reporting. Companies may, therefore, allocate common costs where they have a reasonable basis for doing so or may deduct common costs from the total of segment results.[50]

2.4.9 Methods of presentation

No examples of presentation of segmental information are provided in ED 45. In developing the exposure draft it was, at one point, suggested that a matrix format be encouraged. However, while many commentators felt that a matrix approach had some merit it was contended that a complex matrix of segmental information may confuse readers and give competitors valuable commercial advantage.

One company which does in fact present their segmental information for turnover in matrix form is The BOC Group plc as illustrated in the following extract:

Extract 20.4: The BOC Group plc[51]

1 Segmental information [extract]
a) Turnover by business — 1988

	Gases and related products £ million	Health care £ million	Special products and services £ million	Dis-continued £ million	Total by origin £ million	Total by destination £ million
Europe[1]	314.5	143.9	167.9	—	**626.3**	**612.5**
Africa	118.3	28.0	19.4	3.5	**169.2**	**173.3**
Americas[2]	450.3	369.3	63.4	118.7	**1001.7**	**963.9**
Asia/Pacific	635.4	44.9	84.7	—	**765.0**	**812.5**
Turnover, including related companies	1518.5	586.1	335.4	122.2	**2562.2**	**2562.2**
Less turnover of related companies						
BOC Group share	186.8	11.5	11.5	1.7	**211.5**	**211.5**
External share	206.4	11.5	11.5	1.8	**231.2**	**231.2**
Turnover	1125.3	563.1	312.4	118.7	**2119.5**	**2119.5**

Turnover by business — 1987

	Gases and related products £ million	Health care £ million	Special products and services £ million	Dis-continued £ million	Total by origin £ million	Total by destination £ million
Europe[1]	302.6	129.6	154.1	—	586.3	574.3
Africa	138.0	34.2	17.8	5.9	195.9	203.5
Americas[2]	392.9	301.2	58.7	167.6	920.4	869.3
Asia/Pacific	573.0	41.8	38.4	—	653.2	708.7
Turnover, including related companies	1406.5	506.8	269.0	173.5	2355.8	2355.8
Less turnover of related companies						
BOC Group share	164.0	14.4	7.3	2.9	188.6	188.6
External share	183.4	14.4	7.3	3.0	208.1	208.1
Turnover	1059.1	478.0	254.4	167.6	1959.1	1959.1

1 Turnover and operating profit relating to the UK amounted to £499.4 million
  (1987:£468.3 million) and £98.1 million (1987:£80.5 million) respectively.
2 The US turnover and operating profit were £923.8 million (1987:£856.2 million)
  and £120.8 million (1987:£111.8 million) respectively.

Such a presentation is fairly rare — however, it does provide a great deal of information; not only is the user given the level of turnover attributable to, say, health care (£563.1 million) and the level of turnover attributable to Africa (£169.2 million), but also the amount of turnover attributable to health care in

Africa (£28.0 million). They do not, however, use a matrix approach in giving their segmental analyses of operating profit, capital employed and capital expenditure.[52]

In practice, different companies adopt different methods of presentation. For example, some companies, such as The BOC Group plc and Imperial Chemical Industries PLC,[53] present the information within a note to the accounts. Others, such as Reckitt & Colman plc,[54] have a note to the accounts which merely refers to the pages where the relevant information is contained within a review of operations, or review of activities. These reviews will generally be located outwith the statutory accounts themselves. However, by virtue of the reference in a note to the review, the segmental information is effectively assumed into the accounts. Other companies, such as Trusthouse Forte plc,[55] present the information in the form of a separate statement, after the profit and loss account, balance sheet and statement of source and application of funds. The proposed standard, although requiring segmental information to be reported, does not prescribe where such information is to be presented and, therefore, any of the aforementioned approaches can be followed. However, it will be necessary for all such information to be audited and covered by the audit report.

2.4.10 *Exemptions from ED 45 requirements*

As indicated in 2.4.3 above, certain of the disclosure requirements of ED 45 do not apply to private companies (and other enterprises) with any two of the following:

(a)   turnover not more than £80m,

(b)   total assets not more than £39m,

(c)   average number of employees not more than 2,500.

The segmental information which it is proposed should not be given by such companies is as follows:[56]

(a)   split of turnover between external customers and other segments;

(b)   basis of inter-segment pricing;

(c)   geographical analysis of results (analysis by business segment is still required);

(d)   capital employed;

(e)   share of results and net assets of significant associated companies.

3   PROBLEM AREAS

3.1   How to define an industry segment

ED 45 has concluded that the initial definition of a segment can only be done by management of the reporting company. Guidance on how such segments are defined can be given but only in very general terms (see 2.4.4 above).

Use of the Standard Industrial Classification system has been advocated as a consistent method of grouping products and services. SFAS 14, however, noted that the FASB 'has examined several systems that have been developed for classifying business activities, such as the Standard International Classification and the Enterprise Standard Industrial Classification systems and has judged that none is, by itself, suitable to determine industry segments. Nonetheless, those systems may provide guidance for the exercise of the judgement required to group an enterprise's products and services by industry lines.'[57]

Similarly ED 45 concludes that 'determination of a company's classes of business must depend on the judgement of the directors'.[58]

The factors which provide guidance in determining an industry segment are often the factors which lead a company's management to organise its enterprise into divisions, branches or subsidiaries. This has the advantage that the information required for segmental reporting will be more readily available.

3.2   How to define a geographical segment

In the UK the definition of a geographical segment also rests with the reporting company's management. The factors which should guide their judgement have been set out already (see 2.4.4 above).

However, it is worth emphasising that geographical proximity may not be appropriate. For example, the 1987/88 ICAEW survey of published accounts notes that BTR PLC provides a geographical analysis of the Revenue Cash Flow and also a Regional Balance Sheet. The analysis comprises disclosure of information for three regions, Europe, West and East. The survey argues that the list of subsidiaries companies indicates that the East includes Australia, Japan, South Africa and Taiwan and that several different trends, prospects and risks lie behind the figures.[59]

3.3   Changes in definition of segments

We have seen in 3.1 and 3.2 above that the proposed standard leaves the definition of a segment up to the reporting company's management. The proposed standard recommends that the directors should review their definitions annually and redefine them when appropriate.[60] Where this is done, the comparative figures should be restated to reflect the change; disclosure of the nature of, the reasons for, and the effect of the change should also be made.[61]

3.4   Geographical analysis : source or destination?

Geographical analysis of financial information could, in theory, be given in two principal ways. Firstly, with reference to the countries in which the company operates and, secondly, with reference to the countries where the markets for its goods and services are located. The approach taken by ED 45 is to require analysis of financial information on the basis of the geographical segments in which the company operates. However, it is recognised that it would be useful to users of the accounts to be provided with information on the markets which the company serves. Thus, there is the additional requirement that turnover (but not revenue or capital employed) be analysed between geographical area to which goods or services are supplied (see 2.4.5 above).

In terms of the UK legislation an analysis of turnover by geographical area is required and this is generally considered to mean an analysis by destination.

We have seen in Extract 20.4 in 2.4.9 above an example of a company giving both types of analysis. One other company which also gives both, but does so in matrix form, is Allied-Lyons PLC as illustrated in the following extract:

Extract 20.5: Allied-Lyons PLC[62]

2 TURNOVER [extract]

Geographical distribution	United Kingdom £m	Rest of Europe £m	Canada £m	USA £m	Rest of the World £m	1988 Total £m	1987 Total £m
Sales by companies based						
in United Kingdom	2,543.3	119.6	23.1	12.7	45.1	2,743.8	2,566.7
Rest of Europe	29.0	446.0	7.1	4.8	21.8	508.7	515.3
Canada	—	0.7	98.7	11.0	9.0	119.4	43.8
U.S.A.	0.9	0.8	5.6	825.1	1.4	833.8	463.8
Rest of the World	0.2	—	—	0.4	29.8	30.4	25.2
1988 Total	2,573.4	567.1	134.5	854.0	107.1	4,236.1	3,614.8
% of total sales	60.7	13.4	3.2	20.2	2.5	100.0	
1987 Total	2,467.4	486.5	60.7	518.6	81.6		3,614.8
% of total sales	68.3	13.5	1.7	14.3	2.2		100.0

3.5 Inter-segment sales

The proposed standard requires that the turnover disclosed for each segment be split between sales to external customers and sales to other segments. Many companies currently do not disclose all such information; they either disclose the total turnover for each segment and deduct one figure for inter-segment sales (see Extract 20.2 in 2.4.6 above) or disclose sales to external customers only. As can be seen from Extract 20.1 in 2.2 above Reckitt & Colman plc uses the former approach in giving the analysis by geographical segment and uses the latter approach in giving the analysis by industry segment.

ED 45 also requires disclosure of the basis of transfer pricing; e.g. market value, full cost, marginal cost. However, no single basis of transfer pricing is prescribed by ED 45 for the purposes of financial reporting. SFAS 14 requires that the transfers be accounted for on the same basis as is used by the enterprise for its own internal purposes.[63] Although not required in the UK, we would expect almost all companies to follow this route. It has the practical advantage that the costs of re-pricing transfers for the purposes of external reporting will be avoided.

3.6 Common costs

Common costs will, normally, take the form of central administration overheads. However, in practice, there could be a wide range of categories of common costs.

ED 45 allows common costs to be treated as a separate item in segmental analysis or to be allocated to different segments on what the company's management believe is a reasonable basis (see 2.4.8 above).

As stated in the ICAEW survey of published accounts 'There is little point in making an artificial allocation of corporate expenses. It is preferable to deduct them as a separate figure from the total of segment profits or to treat the central companies as a separate segment.'[64]

However, the proposed standard emphasises that 'costs that are directly attributable to individual reportable segments are not common costs for the purposes of this statement and therefore should be allocated to those segments, irrespective of the fact that they may have been borne by a different segment or by Head Office.'[65]

3.7 Allocation of interest income and interest expense

ED 45 is not prescriptive as regards allocation of interest income and interest expense. It states that the directors should decide the appropriate treatment in the light of the particular circumstances. However, it does suggest that in the majority of companies the individual segments will be financed by interest-bearing debt and equity in varying proportions. The interest earned or incurred by the individual segments is, therefore, a result of the holding company's overall policy rather than a proper reflection of the results of the various segments. The proposed standard implies that in these circumstances the results should exclude interest as it states 'comparisons of profit between segments or between different years for the same segment are likely to be meaningless if interest is included in arriving at the result'.[66] This would seem to be the treatment adopted by most major companies in the UK.

However, where interest is fundamental to the nature of the business, the proposed standard suggests that interest should be included in arriving at the segment result. Such an approach would be relevant to those companies involved in the financial sector.

4   COMPARISON WITH US AND IASC PRONOUNCEMENTS

4.1   US

As discussed in 1.1 above, segmental reporting as a financial accounting and reporting issue began in the US in the early 1960s with the development of the multinational conglomerate business enterprise.

In 1969 the SEC issued requirements for reporting line-of-business information in registration statements. In 1970, those requirements were extended to annual reports filed with the SEC on Form 10-K and in 1974 they were extended to the annual report to security holders of companies filing with the SEC. The FASB responded with the issue of SFAS 14 — *Financial Reporting for Segments of a Business Enterprise* — which was issued in 1976 and currently forms the main basis for segmental reporting in the US (there have been a number of other US standards which have subsequently been issued which have made amendments to SFAS 14).[67]

4.1.1 SFAS 14

Basically the requirements of SFAS 14 (as amended) are very similar to those of ED 45 in that disclosure of turnover, profits and assets analysed by industry and geographical segments is required. The major differences are as follows:

A Scope

SFAS 14 applies to all enterprises (a) whose debt or equity securities trade in a public market on a foreign or domestic stock exchange or in the OTC market, or (b) which are required to file financial statements with the SEC.[68] ED 45 applies to all public limited companies, whether their securities are publicly traded or not, and to large private companies (and other enterprises). There is no exemption in SFAS 14 to allow companies not to disclose segmental information on the grounds that disclosure would be seriously prejudicial to the interests of the company.

B Profits

SFAS 14 requires the operating profit or loss of each reportable industry segment to be disclosed.[69] This will generally be the same as the results that are required to be analysed by ED 45. However, SFAS 14 specifically states that interest has to be excluded in arriving at the operating profit or loss (except in the case of industry segments whose operations are principally of a financial nature),[70] whereas ED 45 only implies that this is to be the case. SFAS 14 also requires that a company's share of profits or losses of associated companies are to be excluded.[71] ED 45 would allow such amounts to be included as long as separate segmental information about the associated companies' results were also given.

SFAS 14 also requires that where any unusual or infrequently occurring items have been added or deducted in computing operating profit or loss, the nature and amount shall be explained.[72]

C Assets or capital employed?

ED 45 requires segmental analysis of capital employed, i.e. operating assets less operating liabilities. SFAS 14, on the other hand, requires the aggregate carrying amount of identifiable assets to be presented for each reportable segment.[73] Identifiable assets of an industry segment are defined as those tangible and intangible assets (i.e. without deduction of operating liabilities) used exclusively by that segment and an allocated portion of assets used jointly by that industry segment and one or more other industry segments. Allocations should be made on a reasonable basis.[74]

D Reportable industry segments

SFAS 14 takes a similar approach to ED 45 in leaving the determination of the different industry segments of an enterprise to the management of the reporting company.

However, SFAS 14 then requires that each industry segment that is 'significant' to an enterprise as a whole shall be identified.[75] For this purpose, significance is established if one or more of the following criteria are met:

(a)   its revenue from both other segments and external customers is 10% or more of the total revenue of all the enterprise's segments;

(b)   its operating profit or loss is 10% or more of the greater of the following two amounts:

     (i)   the combined operating profit of all industry segments that did not incur an operating loss, and

     (ii)   the combined operating loss of all industry segments that did incur an operating loss;

(c)   its identifiable assets are 10% or more of the combined identifiable assets of all industry segments.[76]

Disclosure of the types of products and services supplied by each reportable segment is required.[77]

A further test is applied once the reportable segments are identified, in order to determine 'whether a substantial portion of an enterprise's operations is explained by its segment information'.[78] The total revenue from sales to unaffiliated customers of all *reportable* segments must constitute at least 75% of total revenue from sales to unaffiliated customers of all *industry* segments. If the 75% criteria is not met, additional industry segments must be identified as reportable until the 75% test is met. Though a limit is not set, ten reportable segments is given as an indication of a practical maximum.[79]

In circumstances where an enterprise has one industry segment or a dominant segment (i.e. revenue, operating profit or loss and identifiable assets each constitute more than 90% of the totals for all industry segments), disclosures required for reportable segments do not need to be made except that the industry must be identified.[80]

E   Reportable geographical segments

Again SFAS 14 takes a similar approach to ED 45 in leaving the determination of the different geographical segments of an enterprise to the management of the reporting company.

However, information is only required if either of the following conditions is met:

(a)   sales revenue generated by the enterprise's foreign operations is at least 10% of consolidated revenue as reported in the enterprise's income statement;

(b)   identifiable assets of the enterprise's foreign operations are at least 10% of consolidated total assets as reported in the enterprise's balance sheet.[81]

Foreign operations are defined as those revenue producing operations that:

(a)   are located outside the enterprise's home country; and

(b)   are generating revenue either from sales to unaffiliated customers or from intra-enterprise sales or transfers between geographic areas.[82]

If information is required and the enterprise conducts its foreign operations in two or more geographic areas, then that information is to be presented for each significant foreign geographic area and in aggregate for all foreign geographic areas not deemed significant. A foreign geographic area is deemed to be significant if its sales revenue to unaffiliated customers or its identifiable assets are at least 10% of related consolidated amounts.[83]

Foreign geographic areas are individual countries or group of countries as may be determined to be appropriate in an enterprise's particular circumstances.

F   *Export sales*

SFAS 14 does not require a geographical analysis of turnover by destination except for export sales to unaffiliated customers made by an enterprise's *domestic* operations. Where the amount of export sales revenue is at least 10% of total sales revenue to unaffiliated customers that amount shall be reported, in aggregate, and by such geographic areas as are considered appropriate in the circumstances.[84]

G   *Other related disclosures*

SFAS 14 requires disclosure of information which is additional to that required by ED 45 as follows:

(a)   for each reportable industry segment, disclosure shall be made of:

(i)   the aggregate amount of depreciation, depletion and amortisation,

(ii)   the amount of capital expenditure, and

(iii)   the enterprise's equity in the net income from and investment in the net assets of the unconsolidated subsidiaries and other equity method investees whose operations are vertically integrated with the operations of that segment;[85]

(b)   if an enterprise's sales to one customer (or a group of entities under common control) are 10% or more of its total revenue, that fact and the amount of revenue from each customer must be disclosed. The identity of the customer does not need to be disclosed but the industry segment making the sales must be disclosed.[86]

4.2   IASC

4.2.1   *Introduction*

The most significant international pronouncement on the issue of segmental reporting is IAS 14 — *Reporting Financial Information by Segment* — published by the IASC in August 1981, which became operative for financial statements covering periods beginning on or after January 1, 1983.

4.2.2   IAS 14

Basically the requirements of IAS 14 are very similar to those of ED 45 in that the definition of reportable segments is left to the management of the reporting company and that disclosure of turnover, profits and assets analysed by industry and geographical segments is required. The major differences are as follows:

A   Scope

IAS 14 applies to all enterprises whose securities are publicly traded and to other economically significant entities including subsidiaries. An entity is defined as economically significant if its levels of revenues, profits, assets or employment are significant in the countries in which its major operations are conducted.[87] ED 45 applies to all public limited companies, whether their securities are publicly traded or not, and to large private companies (and other enterprises). There is no exemption in IAS 14 to allow companies not to disclose segmental information on the grounds that disclosure would be seriously prejudicial to the interests of the company.

B   Assets or capital employed?

IAS 14 follows the approach of SFAS 14 in the US rather than ED 45 in that it requires segment assets employed to be disclosed. Segment assets include all tangible and intangible assets that can be identified with that particular segment, as well as an allocation of assets shared between that segment and one or more other segments. Unlike ED 45, liabilities are generally not allocated, either because they are considered to relate to the enterprise as a whole or because they are viewed as giving rise to a financing result rather than an operating result.[88] For the disclosure of information on segment assets this information may be expressed in money amounts or as percentages of the consolidated totals.[89]

5   CONCLUSION

As business enterprises have diversified into different markets and different locations, it has become increasingly necessary to analyse the impact of the different components, or segments, of an enterprise's activities on its performance and financial position. This need has resulted in the concept of segmental reporting. By disclosing financial information about the different segments of an enterprise it is intended that this additional information will enable readers to better assess the enterprise as a whole.

In the UK, the publication of ED 45 is an important step in the formalising of existing good practice and the development of new disclosure. Although it is unlikely to have any significant impact on major companies if it becomes a standard, it will lead to increased disclosure of segmental information relating to:

*   capital employed;

*   inter-segmental turnover; and

*   associated companies.

References

1 IAS 14, *Reporting Financial Information by Segment*, IASC, August 1981, para. 4.
2 *Ibid.*
3 R. K. Mautz, *Financial Reporting by Diversified Companies*, p. 94.
4 Organisation for Economic Co-operation and Development, *International Investment and Multinational Enterprises*, OECD, issued 1976, revised 1979.
5 T.A. Lee, *Developments in Financial Reporting*, p. 30.
6 CA 67, s 17.
7 *Ibid.*, s 20.
8 CA 81, Sch. 1, para. 55(2).
9 *Ibid.*, para. 55(5).
10 The Council of The Stock Exchange, *Admission of Securities to Listing*, Section 5, Chapter 2, para. 21(c).
11 The Council of The Stock Exchange, *The Stock Exchange Unlisted Securities Market, General Undertaking*, para. 10(c).
12 *Admission of Securities to Listing*, Section 5, Chapter 2, para. 21(c).
13 Reckitt & Colman plc, Annual Report 1987, p. 3.
14 SSAP 14, *Group accounts*, September 1978, para. 33.
15 SSAP 6, *Extraordinary items and prior year adjustments*, April 1974, para. 32.
16 ED 45, *Segmental reporting*, November 1988.
17 *Ibid.*, para. 1.
18 *Ibid.*, paras. 3 and 33.
19 *Ibid.*, para. 36.
20 *Ibid.*, para. 43.
21 *Ibid.*, para. 34.
22 *Ibid.*, para. 6.
23 *Ibid.*
24 *Ibid.*, para. 9.
25 *Ibid.*, para. 12.
26 *Ibid.*, para. 13.
27 *Ibid.*, para. 35.
28 *Ibid.*, paras. 37 and 38.
29 *Ibid.*, paras. 37(a) and 38(a).
30 *Ibid.*, para. 40.
31 *Ibid.*, para. 39.
32 *Ibid.*, paras. 37(b) and 38(b).
33 *Ibid.*, para. 20.
34 *Ibid.*, para. 21.
35 *Ibid.*, para. 23.
36 *Ibid.*, para. 24.
37 *Ibid.*, para. 25.
38 *Ibid.*, paras. 37(c) and 38(c).
39 *Ibid.*, para. 42.
40 Imperial Chemical Industries PLC, Annual report 1987, p. 4.
41 Imperial Chemical Industries PLC, Annual report 1987, pp. 36 and 37.
42 Imperial Chemical Industries PLC, Annual report 1987, pp. 6—16 *passim*.
43 Imperial Chemical Industries PLC, Annual report 1987, pp. 4 and 5.
44 ED 45, para. 41.
45 *Ibid.*, para. 27.
46 *Ibid.*, para. 41.
47 Blue Circle Industries PLC, Report & Accounts 1987, p. 15.
48 See AMEC p.l.c., Annual Report and Accounts 1987, pp. 26 and 31; Fisons plc, Annual Report and Accounts 1987, pp. 26 and 29; and Redland PLC, 1988 Report, pp. 28 and 32.

49   ED 45, para. 32.
50   *Ibid.*, para. 22.
51   The BOC Group plc, Report and Accounts 1988, p. 47.
52   The BOC Group plc, Report and Accounts 1988, p. 48.
53   Imperial Chemical Industries PLC, Annual Report 1987, pp. 36 and 37.
54   Reckitt & Colman plc, Annual Report 1987, p. 38.
55   Trusthouse Forte plc, Report and Accounts 1988, p. 27.
56   ED 45, para. 33.
57   SFAS 14, *Financial Reporting for Segments of a Business Enterprise*, FASB, December 1976, para. 91.
58   ED 45, para. 10.
59   L.C.L. Skerratt and D.J. Tonkin (eds.), *Financial Reporting 1987—88: A Survey of UK Reporting Practice*, p. 154.
60   ED 45, para. 7.
61   *Ibid.*, para. 44.
62   Allied-Lyons PLC, Report & Accounts 1988, p. 41.
63   SFAS 14, para. 23.
64   Skerratt and Tonkin, *op. cit.*, p. 151.
65   ED 45, para. 22.
66   *Ibid.*, para. 20.
67   Amending standards comprise: SFAS 18, *Financial Reporting for Segments of a Business Enterprise — Interim Financial Statements*; SFAS 21, *Suspension of the Reporting of Earnings per Share and Segment Information by Nonpublic Enterprises*; SFAS 24, *Reporting Segment Information in Financial Statements That Are Presented in Another Enterprise's Financial Report*; and SFAS 30, *Disclosure of Information about Major Customers*.
68   SFAS 21, *Segment Information by Nonpublic Enterprises*, FASB, April 1978, paras. 12 and 13.
69   SFAS 14, para. 24.
70   *Ibid.*, para. 10(d).
71   *Ibid.*
72   *Ibid.*, para. 24.
73   *Ibid.*, para. 26.
74   *Ibid.*, para. 10(e).
75   *Ibid.*, para. 15.
76   *Ibid.*
77   *Ibid.*, para. 22.
78   *Ibid.*, para. 17.
79   *Ibid.*, paras. 17—19.
80   *Ibid.*, para. 20.
81   *Ibid.*, para. 32.
82   *Ibid.*, para. 31.
83   *Ibid.*, para. 33.
84   *Ibid.*, para. 36.
85   *Ibid.*, para. 27.
86   SFAS 30, *Disclosure of Information about Major Customers*, FASB, August 1979, para. 6.
87   IAS 14, para. 2.
88   *Ibid.*, para. 18.
89   *Ibid.*, para. 22.

Chapter 21

Related party transactions

1 INTRODUCTION

In the UK, parties have been said to be related if one party has the ability to exercise either direct or indirect *control* or *significant influence* over the other party or over the assets or resources of the other party. A relationship is also considered to exist where parties are under common control or significant influence.[1]

A related party transaction is defined in ED 46 — *Disclosure of related party transactions* — as a transfer or granting of benefits or obligations between related parties, irrespective of whether the transactions are recognised in the accounting records or whether consideration passes.[2]

Related party relationships and transactions between related parties are a normal feature of business; many enterprises carry on their business activities through subsidiaries and associated companies and there will inevitably be transactions between the parties comprising the group.

1.1 The related party issue

The problem with such relationships and transactions is expressed in SFAS 57 — *Related Party Disclosures* — as follows:

'Reliability of financial information involves "assurance that accounting measures represent what they purport to represent." Without disclosure to the contrary, there is a general presumption that transactions reflected in financial statements have been consummated on an arm's-length basis between independent parties. However, that presumption is not justified when related party transactions exist because the requisite conditions of competitive, free-market dealings may not exist. Because it is possible for related party transactions to be arranged to obtain certain results desired by the related parties, the resulting accounting measures may not represent what they usually would be expected to represent.'[3]

A related party relationship can affect the financial position and operating results of an enterprise in a number of ways:

(a) transactions may be entered into with a related party which may not have occurred if the relationship did not exist, e.g., a company may sell a large proportion of its production to its parent company, where it might not have found an alternative customer if the parent company had not purchased the goods;

(b)   transactions may be entered into with a related party on terms different from those with an unrelated party, e.g., the terms under which a subsidiary leases equipment to another subsidiary of a common parent may be imposed by the common parent and might vary significantly from one lease to another because of circumstances entirely unrelated to market prices for similar leases; indeed, the terms may be such that no financial consideration passes between the parties;

(c)   transactions with third parties may be affected by the existence of the relationship, e.g., two enterprises in the same line of business may be controlled by a common party that has the ability to increase the volume of business done by each.

1.2   Possible solutions

1.2.1   *Remeasurement of transactions at fair values*

One solution would be to adjust the financial statements to reflect the transaction as if it had occurred with an independent third party and record the transaction at the corresponding arm's length price. However, as a study by the Accountants International Study Group states that 'it often is impossible to establish what would have been the terms of any non-arms' length transaction had it been bargained on an arm's length basis, because no comparable transactions may have taken place and, in any event, the transaction might never have taken place at all if it had been bargained using different values'.[4]

1.2.2   *Disclosure of transactions*

As a result of the above difficulty, accounting standards internationally have focused on the disclosure of related party transactions and relationships, rather than require adjustments to be made in the financial statements. This is the approach adopted by the IASC in their standard on related parties, IAS 24, and by the FASB in their standard, SFAS 57. The ASC in their recent exposure draft on the topic has similarly adopted this route (see 2 below).

The main issues which have to be considered in determining what information needs to be disclosed are as follows:

(a)   identification of related parties;

(b)   types of transactions and arrangements;

(c)   information to be disclosed.

1.3   Position in the UK

Financial reporting in the UK has been significantly affected by Department of Trade reports into the affairs of companies. Related party matters, particularly in respect of transactions with directors, have featured in many such reports, and this has been instrumental in bringing about the current position where, for example, directors' loans and transactions have to be disclosed by law (see Chapter 23).

Nevertheless, there is presently no UK accounting standard requiring general related party disclosures in financial statements, although the ASC has recently issued an exposure draft on the subject, ED 46 — *Disclosure of related party transactions*. The requirements proposed in the exposure draft are discussed at 2 and 3 below. However, the disclosure of some related party matters is specifically required by the Companies Act 1985. The statutory provisions are mainly concerned with group companies and with directors. These are discussed at 4.1 below.

It must be emphasised that there is an obligation, under section 228 of the Companies Act 1985, which overrides the provisions of Schedule 4 to the Act, for the balance sheet to give a true and fair view of the state of affairs of a company as at the end of the financial year; and for the profit and loss account to give a true and fair view of the profit or loss for the financial year. If the financial statements drawn up in compliance with the requirements of the Act do not contain sufficient information, any necessary additional information must be provided in the balance sheet, or profit and loss account, or in a note to the financial statements . Therefore, if a related party disclosure is necessary to give a true and fair view, it ought to be made.

In addition to the requirements of the Companies Act, The Stock Exchange imposes additional requirements on listed and USM companies which impinge on related party issues. These are discussed at 4.3 below.

2 ED 46

2.1 Introduction

The purpose of ED 46 is to propose standard accounting practice for the disclosure of information concerning a reporting enterprise's relationships, and for the disclosure of certain transactions between the reporting enterprise and its related parties.[5] At the time of publication of this book it is not possible to determine what areas, if any, of the exposure draft will be amended in any subsequent standard.

2.2 Identification of related parties

ED 46 defines related parties as those where for all or part of the financial period:

(a) one party is able to exercise either direct or indirect *control, or significant influence* (emphasis added), over the other party or over the assets or resources of the other party; or

(b) two or more parties are subject to common control or significant influence from the same source.

In deciding whether parties are related, it is necessary to consider the substance of the relationship. This is determined by identifying all its aspects and implications and by giving greater weight to those likely to have commercial effect in practice.[6]

Control comprises determination of, or the ability to determine, the financial or operating policies of an enterprise.[7] Significant influence involves participation in, or the ability to participate in, the financial or operating policy decisions of an enterprise but not necessarily control of them.[8] Two examples of relationships involving significant influence are illustrated in the following diagram:

Example 21.1

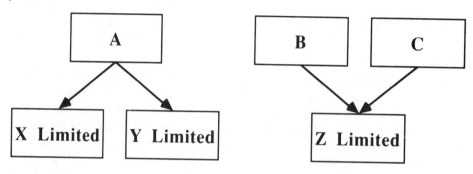

(a)   A significantly influences X Limited and Y Limited. A is, therefore, a related party of both companies. In addition, X Limited and Y Limited are considered to be related parties of each other.

(b)   B and C significantly influence Z Limited. B and C are, therefore, related parties of Z Limited. However, B and C are not considered to be related parties of each other merely as a result of them both significantly influencing Z Limited.

The exposure draft presumes that certain parties will be related parties of an enterprise, and these are listed at 3.1.5 below.

2.3   Types of transactions and arrangements

As indicated at 1 above, a related party transaction is defined in ED 46 as a transfer or granting of benefits or obligations between related parties, irrespective of whether the transactions are recognised in the accounting records or whether consideration passes. Such transactions would include sales, purchases and transfers of goods, other assets and services; transactions related to management, royalty and license agreements; and leases, guarantees and loans.[9]

Having defined what a related party transaction is, ED 46 then makes a distinction between two types of transaction; 'normal' and 'abnormal'. A normal transaction is defined as one which is undertaken by the reporting enterprise in the ordinary course of business on normal commercial terms, except where it is so material that it has a significant impact on the financial statements. Transactions entered into in the ordinary course of business are those which are usually, frequently or regularly undertaken by the enterprise.[10] Normal commercial terms are those which are no more or less favourable than it would be reasonable to expect if the transaction had not been with a related party.[11] An abnormal transaction is any transaction other than a normal transaction.[12] The reason for this distinction is that it is proposed that only abnormal transactions with related parties will be required to be disclosed, as users of an enterprise's financial statements are considered to be primarily interested in the existence or otherwise of related parties and any abnormal transactions that may take place between them and the enterprise.[13]

The distinction between normal and abnormal transactions is discussed further at 3.2.2 below.

2.4 Information to be disclosed

2.4.1 *Abnormal transactions*

ED 46 proposes that the following information should be disclosed about each abnormal transaction with related parties:

(a) the name of the related party;

(b) the relationship between the parties;

(c) the extent of any ownership interest (in percentage terms) in the related party or by it in the reporting enterprise;

(d) the nature of the transaction;

(e) the amounts involved, either in percentage or in monetary terms;

(f) the amount due to or from the related party at the balance sheet date;

(g) the basis on which the transaction price has been determined; and

(h) any other information necessary for an understanding of the commercial substance of the transaction and of its effects on the financial statements.[14]

In order to reduce the volume of disclosure, disclosure of individual transactions with an individual related party may be made on an aggregated basis unless disclosure of an individual transaction is necessary for an understanding of the impact of related party transactions on the financial statements of the reporting enterprise or is otherwise required to be disclosed by statute or by The International Stock Exchange.[15]

The degree of aggregation that is appropriate in particular circumstances will depend, for example, on the materiality of the individual transactions and the length of disclosure that would arise if all were to be separately reported. We believe that only similar types of transaction with the same related party should be aggregated, dissimilar types being separately disclosed. We also believe that it would be appropriate to aggregate similar types of transactions with similar types of related party (e.g. management charges from all fellow subsidiaries), rather than separately disclosing the management charges from each fellow subsidiary. However, the exposure draft would appear not to allow such aggregation.

2.4.2 *Controlling relationship*

The exposure draft proposes that the existence and nature of controlling related party relationships should be disclosed whether or not any transactions between the parties have taken place. Disclosure should include the name of the controlling enterprise and, if different, that of the ultimate controlling enterprise. If the latter is outside the United Kingdom and the Republic of Ireland, the name of the ultimate controlling enterprise in the United Kingdom or the Republic of Ireland should also be disclosed.[16]

The reason for such disclosure is that where control exists the financial position and/or results of an enterprise may be affected by such a relationship, even if transactions between the parties have not occurred. The mere existence of the relationship may be sufficient to affect the transactions of the reporting enterprise.[17]

2.4.3   *Economic dependence*

ED 46 proposes that where the transactions between an enterprise and another party, or other facts arising from a relationship with another party, have a pervasive influence on the enterprise, the identity of that party and a general indication of the nature and extent of the dependence should be disclosed.[18]

2.4.4   *Specific exemptions from reporting*

The exposure draft considers that in the following situations disclosures should not be required:

(a)   in consolidated financial statements of any transactions or balances between group companies which have been eliminated on consolidation;

(b)   in the holding company's own accounts where consolidated financial statements are presented at the same time; or

(c)   in the financial statements of wholly-owned subsidiaries (whether the shares are held directly by the reporting enterprise or indirectly by other group companies), of transactions with other group companies if the identity of the ultimate holding company is disclosed.[19]

The reasons for this last exemption are that there are no minority interests whose information requirements need to be taken into account,[20] and so long as it is known that the enterprise is under the control of another, readers will have been put on adequate notice that the financial statements may have been affected by the impact of related party transactions.[21] It is emphasised that such exemption does not apply to abnormal transactions with other related parties of the subsidiary.

2.4.5   *Examples of disclosure*

In order to illustrate the disclosure requirements of the exposure draft, the appendix to ED 46 contains a number of examples of disclosure in situations which an enterprise may meet in practice.

In the absence of an accounting standard which presently deals specifically with related party transactions, there is very little disclosure in financial statements in the UK of such matters other than that given to meet the requirements discussed in 4.1 to 4.3 below. Examples of disclosures in respect of transactions with directors are given in Chapter 23.

One company which discloses information about trading transactions between the group and related parties in its directors' report is Maxwell Communication Corporation plc as illustrated below:

Extract 21.1: Maxwell Communication Corporation plc[22]

Trading with related companies
Below are the significant trading relationships between the Group and related companies:
1. British Newspaper Printing Corporation plc, a wholly-owned subsidiary of the Company, prints on behalf of Mirror Group Newspapers Limited, the Daily Mirror, Sunday Mirror, The People and The Sporting Life, In London and Manchester, and the Daily Record and Sunday Mail in Glasgow.
2. The Company and Pergamon Holdings Limited incur certain charges on behalf of each other in respect of management services and occupancy costs. These charges are reimbursed at cost by the Company and Pergamon Holdings Limited to each other.
3. Pergamon Holdings Limited provides certain warehousing, financial and computer services to Pergamon Journals Limited in Oxford. Details of these arrangements are set out in a service agreement and two leases between Pergamon Journals Limited and Pergamon Holdings Limited. The service charges and rents payable by Pergamon Journals Limited in 1987 under these arrangements amounted to approximately £1,110,000. These arrangements have ceased with effect from 1st January 1988.
4. Pergamon Press Inc based in the USA provided accommodation and financial and computer services to Pergamon Journals Inc for an annual fee of $212,000. These arrangements have ceased with effect from 1st January 1988.
5. Three Pergamon companies collect on behalf of Pergamon Journals Limited journal subscriptions arising in a number of countries where Pergamon has representative offices including Germany, Australia, Japan, India and China. Pergamon Holdings Limited received £150,000 in 1987 for the provision of these collection services. These arrangements have ceased with effect from 1st January 1988.
6. The Company printed books on behalf of Pergamon Books Limited through 1987. The terms on which this printing was undertaken were agreed on a normal trade basis. With effect from 31st December 1987 the Company acquired the business (including assets and liabilities) of Pergamon Books Limited.
7. Prior to its acquisition in September 1987 from Hollis plc, The Aberdeen University Press Limited in Aberdeen and its subsidiary in Glasgow, provided typesetting and printing facilities for Pergamon Journals Limited on a normal trade basis.
8. Newport & Robinson Limited (trading under the name of Express Litho) and Nuffield Press Limited, subsidiaries of Pergamon Holdings Limited, provide typesetting and printing facilities for Pergamon Journals Limited on a normal trade basis.
9. In the normal course of trading, items of used printing machinery are bought and sold at market value from and to Milthorp Limited, a specialist printing machinery trader (which is a wholly-owned subsidiary of Hollis plc).
10. Professional fees totalling $2.5m were paid to Maxwell Communication & Information Corporation in respect of the acquisition programme in North America.

Although disclosure of such transactions is to be encouraged, it is unclear from the disclosures given the exact nature of the relationship of these related parties with the company, particularly as the directors' report also states that 'no director had any material interest in any contract of significance to the Group at any time during the year'.[23] However, it may be that the related parties are fellow subsidiaries or fellow associates of the company as the financial statements also disclose the following information:

Extract 21.2: Maxwell Communication Corporation plc[24]

6 NET INTEREST AND INVESTMENT INCOME [extract]

	1987 **£m**	1986 £m
Net interest received from Pergamon Holdings Limited	**6.4**	0.5

17 DEBTORS [extract]

	Group		Company	
	1987 **£m**	1986 £m	**1987** **£m**	1986 £m
Amounts due from fellow subsidiaries	**58.3**	27.0	**12.2**	3.3

19 CREDITORS — AMOUNTS FALLING DUE WITHIN ONE YEAR [extract]

	Group		Company	
	1987 **£m**	1986 £m	**1987** **£m**	1986 £m
Amounts due to Pergamon Holdings Limited (see (b) below)	—	20.6	**1.7**	23.4
Amounts due to other fellow subsidiaries	**20.2**	5.6	**15.3**	0.3
(b) Amounts due (from)/to Pergamon Holdings Limited				
— on current account	**2.9**	0.5	**4.6**	0.1
— on short-term funding	**(2.9)**	23.3	**(2.9)**	23.3
	—	23.8	**1.7**	23.4
Less due for group relief	—	(3.2)	—	—
	—	20.6	**1.7**	23.4

Pergamon Holdings Limited and the Company deposit surplus cash with each other at market rates of interest.

35 ULTIMATE HOLDING COMPANY
The Company's holding company is Maxwell Foundation (formerly named Pergamon Holding Foundation), a company incorporated in Liechtenstein.

3   PROBLEM AREAS

3.1   Identification of related parties

3.1.1   Control or significant influence

The question of whether or not one party is a related party to another depends on whether one has the ability to control or exercise significant influence over the other (or whether they are under common control or significant influence). The definitions of control and significant influence were indicated at 2.2 above.

ED 46 further explains control by stating that control usually results either from holding, directly or indirectly through subsidiaries, more than one-half of the voting power of the shareholders of the enterprise or from control of the composition of the board of directors. In certain circumstances, however, control may be granted to an enterprise which does not satisfy these criteria by long-term agreement or through the memorandum and articles of association of the controlled enterprise. It may also exist if the decisions of the board are controlled by directors' voting rights being weighted for the purpose of taking particular decisions. Further, the existence of call or put options concerning ownership of an enterprise may also give rise to effective control.[25]

The exposure draft also states that control or significant influence will often be, but need not be, exercised on an ongoing basis. Control or significant influence may be passive and not currently exercised but will nevertheless be real if key decisions can be made or influenced. Thus, an enterprise may have the right to take key decisions concerning a related party even though it is not controlling it or exercising significant influence on an ongoing basis.[26]

The definition of related parties contained in ED 46 means that an enterprise may have three types of related party:

(a)   parties over which the enterprise can exercise control or significant influence;

(b)   parties which can exercise control or significant influence over the enterprise;

(c)   enterprises under common control or significant influence.

These are considered in turn below.

3.1.2   Controlled or significantly influenced parties

One category of related party of an enterprise will be parties which it controls or has significant influence over; for example, subsidiary companies and related or associated companies.

A   Subsidiaries

In addition to subsidiaries of a company, any controlled non-subsidiaries of the company which are used for the purposes of off-balance sheet transactions will have to be considered as a related party.

B   Related or associated companies

Enterprises which are associated companies of a company in terms of SSAP 1 (or related companies in terms of the Companies Act) will be related parties in view of the fact that the company will have significant influence over them.

3.1.3   Controlling or significantly influencing parties

Another category of related parties of an enterprise will be those parties which control or have significant influence over it; such parties are generally either top management or shareholders.

A   Directors

Directors of a company are generally presumed to be related parties of the company. The directors of any holding company should also be considered to be related parties of a subsidiary company. This would be consistent with the disclosure requirements of the Companies Act in respect of transactions with directors (see Chapter 23). The exposure draft states that the term directors includes any person having the authority or responsibility for planning, directing or controlling the activities or resources of the reporting enterprise. Thus, in addition to those holding that title, it includes shadow directors, officers and other persons with similar authority or responsibility.[27]

Consideration has to be given as to whether or not past and/or future directors should be considered to be related parties. It could be argued that someone who is not a director of a company at the time the company enters into a transaction with him is not a related party as he is not at that time in a position to influence the company. However, this ignores the fact, particularly in the case of a past director, that the relationship may have had an impact on the transaction. The exposure draft, therefore, proposes that disclosures should be given in respect of transactions with parties that were related at any time during the financial year. In this context, it should be noted that the Companies Act requires disclosure of transactions with persons who were directors at any time during the financial year, even though the transaction may have taken place when the person was not a director (see 3.3 of Chapter 23).

In addition to directors being presumed to be related parties of an enterprise, certain family members of the directors are also generally presumed to be related parties. These family members are those whom the director might influence, or be influenced by, because of the family relationship.[28] This will obviously include the director's spouse and children under the age of 18 who are deemed to be 'connected persons' of the director for the purposes of the Companies Act (see 2.4 of Chapter 23). However, it could also include a parent, older child or brother or sister.

In some cases, directors of a company do not transact directly with the company, but do so through another company in which the director has an interest. Whether such a company is a related party is considered at 3.1.3 below.

B   Senior   management

Significant influence over a company is normally considered to mean significant influence over the whole of the company, its financial decisions etc. However, other management personnel may have influence over certain well defined aspects of the operations of the company.

Example 21.2

Ms. A is the purchasing manageress of Company X; however, she is not a director of that company. She arranges the purchase of a material amount of stock from Company Y, a company which she controls. Is Ms. A (and, therefore, Company Y) a related party of Company X?

The answer may depend on how much autonomy Ms. A has in choosing the suppliers of goods for Company X. If there is no involvement of a director in the process, then it could be argued that she is a related party.

As indicated at 3.1.2 A above, ED 46 considers the term 'director' to include officers of the company.

SFAS 57 regards a company's management as being a related party and states that 'management' will normally include persons 'in charge of principal business functions (such as sales, administration, or finance), and other persons who perform similar policy making functions'. In addition it emphasises that persons without formal titles also may be members of management.[29]

Similar considerations will also apply in group situations where a person is a director of a subsidiary but is not a director of the holding company. Clearly, such a person is a related party of the subsidiary, but is he a related party of the holding company so that disclosure might be required in the group financial statements?

Example 21.3

Suppose in Example 21.2, Ms. A had been a director of a subsidiary of Company X and the subsidiary had purchased the stock from Company Y. Is Ms. A (and, therefore, Company Y) a related party of the Company X group, such that disclosure should be made in the Company X group financial statements?

It could be argued that the answer should be no different to that in Example 21.2 above. However, in practice, disclosure is more likely to be made by a holding company of transactions between its subsidiaries and their directors than of transactions between the company itself and its senior management. This is probably a result of the fact that the information is more likely to be available regarding transactions and arrangements involving directors.

One company which currently discloses in its financial statements some information about transactions in which directors of subsidiaries are involved, even though the Companies Act does not require them to be disclosed, is Reed International P.L.C,. as illustrated below:

Extract 21.3: Reed International P.L.C.[30]

13   FIXED ASSET INVESTMENTS [extract]
Related Party Transactions
    The following transactions, which involved Directors of subsidiary companies, took place during the year and the Company's Auditors, Price Waterhouse, reported that in their opinion the terms of the transactions were fair and reasonable to the Company.
1   In June 1987 the Company acquired the whole of the issued share capital of Rinmed an unlimited company for £1,900,000 in cash and £823,500 in loan notes. Rinmed owned the business and assets of Carlton Publishing Group Limited which in turn provided editorial staff and consultancy services to Carlton Magazines Limited, a wholly-owned subsidiary of the Company. Included amongst the vendors of Rinmed's shares were Messrs T F Hornett, R H Pinny, M A Matthews and Miss S O'Sullivan who were also directors of Carlton Magazines Limited.
2   In November 1987 the Company acquired through a subsidiary the outstanding 25% of the shares it did not already hold in Daily News Limited, the publisher of the Birmingham Daily News. The shares were acquired from Bullivant Holdings Limited, a company controlled by Mr and Mrs C Bullivant who were also directors of Daily News Limited. The price paid for the shares was £1,140,000 and in addition an amount of £362,628 in respect of an outstanding loan by Bullivant Holdings Limited to Daily News Limited was repaid.
3   In January 1988, the Company, through its wholly-owned subsidiary Reed Overseas Corporation Limited, sold the entire issued share capital of Butterworth Publishers (Pty) Limited ('BPPL'), a company which publishes legal works and is based in Durban, South Africa, to Rand Merchant Bank Limited for R2,350,000 (£472,000). Following the sale, Rand Merchant Bank Limited transferred the business of BPPL to Professional Publishers (Pty) Limited, a company, the majority of whose share capital is held by Messrs C A Chisholm, G H Crews and U M Paladini. At the time of its sale by the Company, Messrs Chisholm, Crews and Paladini were all directors of BPPL.

Such transactions would appear to be Class 4 transactions in terms of The Stock Exchange requirements,[31] and it may be as a result of this that they have been disclosed. It can be seen that there are disclosures as to terms of the transactions from which it appears that the arm's length presumption has not been invalidated by the presence of related parties because the auditors are stated as having reported that in their opinion the terms of the transactions were fair and reasonable to the company.

C   Holding company

A holding company is presumed to be a related party in view of the fact that it can control the company. The relationship may not affect the day-to-day trading but may, for example, affect the way the subsidiary is able to do business by being under the financial umbrella of a large group, or not competing with another company in the group.

All holding companies, whether they be the ultimate or an intermediate holding company of a company, will be related parties of that company.

D   Significant shareholdings

A significant shareholding may be held by a person, another company or through a nominee (making the beneficial owner difficult to establish). Clearly, where a company has a shareholder which owns more than 50% of the voting share capital of the company, such a person can control the company and, therefore, will be a related party of the company.

However, what if the shareholder owns 50% or less of the shares of the company? Such a person would not normally be deemed to control the company (although he may have de facto control in view of the spread of the remaining shares amongst a number of other shareholders). Nevertheless, such a person may be considered to have significant influence over the company. What percentage holding is required to confer such influence? It could be argued that it should be 20%, which is the normal indication for determining whether an investment should be classified as an associated company. This would appear to be the view taken by IAS 24.[32] However, ED 46 takes the view that only a 10% interest in the voting rights is necessary for a shareholder to be presumed to be a related party.[33]

Furthermore, any family member whom a person owning 10% or more of the voting rights of an enterprise might influence, or be influenced by, because of the family relationship is considered to be a related party.[34] (See A above for examples of persons who could fall into this category.)

3.1.4 *Enterprises under common control or significant influence*

The third category of related parties of an enterprise are enterprises which are under the control or significant influence of a common party. As indicated at 2.2 above, where a company has a related party that exerts control or significant influence on another company the other company is regarded as a related party.

Example 21.4

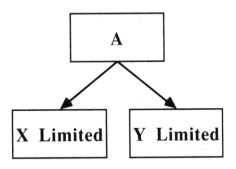

If A significantly influences X Limited and Y Limited (i.e. A is a related party of both), then X Limited and Y Limited are considered to be related parties of each other.

There may be practical problems, for the directors of a company such as X Limited, in identifying related parties, such as Y Limited, unless the controlling or significantly influencing party (here A) assists. Disclosures in the financial statements of A (if it is a UK company) may be useful, but may not be available on a timely basis or be presented at all if, for example, A's relationship or transactions with Y Limited are considered by A to be immaterial.

A   Fellow subsidiaries/associates

Where two companies are subsidiaries of the same company, then such fellow subsidiaries will be related parties of each other. This will be the case even if the two companies do not have the same immediate holding company, but are part of the same group as a result of having a common ultimate holding company.[35]

Similarly, where two companies are associates of the same company, then such companies can be presumed to be related parties of each other. Again, if the companies which own the shares are not the same, but are under the control of a common parent, then the associates will be deemed to be related parties of each other.[36]

Indeed, all subsidiaries and associates of a common ultimate holding company are likely to be presumed to be related parties of each other.

B   Other common shareholders

Certain shareholders are presumed to be related parties of the companies in which they own 10% or more of the voting rights. Where such shareholders (or members of their immediate family) control or can significantly influence another company (or enterprise), then that other company will be a related party of the company.[37]

C   Companies controlled or influenced by directors

Where a director (or a member of his immediate family) has an interest in another company such that he can control or significantly influence it, then such a company is presumed to be a related party.[38] This would include such companies that are considered to be connected persons of a director for the purposes of disclosing directors' transactions under the Companies Act (see 2.4 of Chapter 23).

D   Directors in common

Although directors of a company are presumed to be related parties of the company, if a person is a director of two companies, those two companies are not automatically considered to be related parties of each other. This principle is embodied in the Companies Act 1985[39] in relation to the disclosure of transactions in which a director has an interest.

This is the approach taken by ED 46, though if the common director is able to control or significantly influence the policy of one or both enterprises with regard to the relationship between them or to their mutual transactions then the parties would be related.[40] It will, therefore, be necessary for the facts of each double directorship to be established; where a director does have other directorships, it is important for the board to be aware of the degree of influence the director has on other companies in relation to their transactions or arrangements (if any) with the reporting company.

3.1.5   Economic dependence

It could be argued that although a company does not have a shareholding in another company such that it can control or significantly influence it, there may be a relationship between the two companies such that the other company is economically dependent on the company. A company that has a customer who takes a significant element of its sales may well be influenced by that customer, giving longer than normal credit terms or preferential prices and, in some cases, the viability of the company may depend on the continuance of the relationship. ED 46 considers that economic dependence exists where an enterprise is dependent on another person or entity either by virtue of the extent of transactions between them or due to some other agreement or relationship.[41] Economic dependence may arise because of relationships with a major customer, supplier, lender, franchisor, franchisee, agent, borrower, lender, etc. It could be argued that such economic dependence results in a related party relationship; however, ED 46 seems to suggest that in most cases the entities will not be related parties, although certain disclosures may be required about the relationship (see 2.4.3 above).

The IASC, when drafting IAS 24, took the view that the standard was to deal only with transactions (and the resulting balances), and, since the influences on a reporting enterprise generally are not required to be disclosed in financial statements, so neither are related party influences. Those who might be related parties only by virtue of economic dependence were deemed not to be related parties for the purposes of IAS 24.[42]

3.1.6 Conclusion

As can be seen from the above discussion, enterprises are likely to have many parties which could be considered to be related parties; it is therefore important that directors identify the enterprise's related parties and indicate whether or not control or significant influence is present. To this end, ED 46 lists those parties which are presumed to be related parties of an enterprise, unless there is evidence to the contrary. These are as follows:

(a)   its ultimate or intermediate holding company or companies, subsidiary companies, fellow subsidiaries, associated companies, related companies, and fellow associated and related companies;

(b)   companies controlled for voting purposes, in terms of votes exercisable by the shareholders or by the directors, by the same enterprise or person who controls the reporting company;

(c)   its directors and the directors of its holding company or companies and members of their immediate families;

(d)   a company or person owning, or able to exercise effective control over, 10% or more of the voting rights of the company, whether directly or through nominees, and members of the immediate family of any such person;

(e)   partnerships, companies or trusts or entities in which any person in (c) or (d) above has a controlling interest or which they have the ability to influence significantly;

(f)   the other party when a management contract exists and the reporting
       enterprise is either the managing or the managed party.[43]

It is emphasised that the above list is not intended to be an exhaustive list of
related parties.

3.2   Types of transactions and arrangements

3.2.1   *Introduction*

As previously stated, transactions between related parties are a normal feature of
business. ED 46 gives some examples of such transactions (see 2.3 above). Some
examples of common transactions between related parties are also given in IAS 24
as follows:[44]

(a)   purchases or sales of goods (finished or unfinished);

(b)   purchases or sales of property and other assets;

(c)   rendering or receiving of services, e.g., accounting, management,
       engineering or legal services;

(d)   agency arrangements;

(e)   leasing arrangements, e.g., allowing the use of an asset, whether for a rental
       or not;

(f)   transfer of research and development;

(g)   licence agreements;

(h)   finance (including loans and equity contributions in cash or in kind);

(i)   guarantees or collaterals;

(j)   management contracts.

3.2.2   *Normal/abnormal transactions*

It can be seen from the above that there are many different types of transactions
which can be carried out between related parties. Since ED 46 proposes that only
abnormal transactions are to be disclosed, it will, therefore, be necessary for
transactions to be categorised between normal and abnormal transactions.

A   Normal transactions

The definition of a normal transaction contained in ED 46 was given at 2.3 above.
A significant test for normalcy would be the existence of similar transactions on
the same terms with unrelated parties.

B   Abnormal transactions

Abnormal transactions are those transactions other than normal transactions.
Abnormal transactions between related parties are either entered into in the
ordinary course of business, but which are affected by the relationship (e.g. as to
terms, price etc.), or not entered into in the ordinary course of business. The

exposure draft considers that abnormal transactions are generally of the following types:

(a)   entered into in the ordinary course of business:

    (i)   transactions which, although entered into in the ordinary course of business, are of such size or nature in a particular accounting period that they have a significant impact on the financial statements,

    (ii)   transactions entered into in the ordinary course of business but on significantly different terms from those on which similar transactions are undertaken by the reporting enterprise with unrelated parties. The terms of the transactions may be either more favourable or less favourable than those applicable to unrelated parties;

(b)   not entered into in the ordinary course of business:

    transactions entered into other than in the ordinary course of business, irrespective of the terms on which they are undertaken. Such transactions would include those related to management charges or income.[45]

The distinction between the terms 'normal/abnormal' and 'in the ordinary course of business/not in the ordinary course of business' is important as the terms are not synonymous. Examples of the types of transactions which the exposure draft considers to be 'abnormal' are illustrated in the Appendix to ED 46.

4   OTHER REQUIREMENTS IN THE UK

Although there is presently no accounting standard which deals specifically with related parties, the disclosure of some related party matters is dealt with in the Companies Act 1985, existing standards and, for listed and USM companies, Stock Exchange requirements.

4.1   Legislative requirements

The Companies Act 1985 contains provisions for the disclosure in financial statements (or directors' report) of what might be considered to be related party matters in so far as the related parties are as follows:

(a)   directors;

(b)   non-director officers or senior employees; and

(c)   group companies (including associated companies).

The disclosures for other related party matters are only regulated by the overriding requirement for the financial statements to give a true and fair view.

The disclosure requirements relating to each of the above categories of related parties are outlined below.

4.1.1   *Directors*

In general, the Companies Act requires the following information to be disclosed in respect of directors of a company:

(a)   names of directors who have served during the year;[46]

(b)   interests of each director in the share capital or debentures of the company or
       of any other group company;[47]

(c)   information about directors' emoluments (see Chapter 24);

(d)   loans and other transactions with directors or persons connected with the
       directors (see Chapter 23).

4.1.2   Non-director officers

Currently, the Companies Act requires information to be disclosed about higher-
paid employees; this may not be required in the future as the recent Companies
Bill proposes to repeal the present provisions of the Act (see 3.2 of Chapter 24).
It also requires disclosure of information relating to loans and other transactions
with officers of the company other than directors (see 6 of Chapter 23).

4.1.3   Group companies

There are various disclosure requirements relating to group companies (including
related companies)[48] contained in the Companies Act; these are indicated below.

A   Ultimate holding company

If at the year end a company is a subsidiary of another body corporate, then the
name of the company's ultimate holding company and its country of incorporation
are required to be disclosed.[49]

B   Information about subsidiary and related companies

If at the year end a company has subsidiaries, then the following disclosures
should be made in respect of each subsidiary:

(a)   its name;

(b)   description and proportion of class of shares held; and

(c)   its country of incorporation (if outside Great Britain) or its country of
       registration (i.e. Scotland or England and Wales) if different from that of the
       company.[50]

Similar information is required about other companies in which the company
either holds more than 10% of any class of equity share capital or holds more than
10% of the allotted share capital.[51]

Further information about the subsidiaries and such investments may also be
required to be disclosed.[52]

C   Transactions with subsidiary and related companies

In addition to requiring the amounts in respect of shares in group companies and
shares in related companies to be separately disclosed, the balance sheet formats
also require separate disclosure of the following inter-company balances involving
group companies and related companies:

(a)   loans;

(b) amounts owing from;

(c) amounts owed to.[53]

The amounts involving group companies are required to be further split between (i) amounts relating to subsidiaries of the company and (ii) amounts relating to any holding company or fellow subsidiary of the company.[54]

The profit and loss account formats contained in the Companies Act require separate disclosure of:

(a) income from shares in group companies;

(b) income from shares in related companies;

(c) interest receivable from group companies; and

(d) interest payable to group companies.[55]

Unlike the balance sheet information, the amounts relating to group companies do not require to be split further between (i) subsidiaries and (ii) any holding company and fellow subsidiaries.

The Companies Act requires companies to disclose details of any guarantees and other financial commitments.[56] Where such guarantees or commitments are undertaken on behalf of or for the benefit of group companies then they are required to be separately disclosed from any other guarantee and financial commitment. Again, the information relating to group companies should be split between that in respect of subsidiaries and that in respect of any holding company and fellow subsidiaries.[57]

4.2 UK accounting standards

The only existing standards which impinge on the issue of related parties are SSAP 1 — *Accounting for associated companies* — and SSAP 14 — *Group accounts* — in that the following disclosures are required to be made in the financial statements of the investing company:

(a) the name, proportion of shares held and nature of business of associated and subsidiary companies;[58]

(b) loans to or from associated companies;[59]

(c) debtors and creditors resulting from trading with associated companies.[60]

These standards are essentially concerned with the financial statements of the investing company and, therefore, do not require any disclosures to be given in the financial statements of the associated or subsidiary companies.

4.3 Stock Exchange requirements

The Stock Exchange requires listed companies to disclose, in their annual reports and accounts, various information relevant to related parties, or which indicate the existence of related parties, in addition to that required by the Companies Act. Certain of the requirements are also imposed on USM companies. The specific disclosures relevant to related parties concern either the directors or the shareholders of the company.

4.3.1 Directors

A   Directors' interests in share capital

The requirements extend beyond those contained in the Companies Act 1985 in that they require disclosure of:

(a)   beneficial and non-beneficial interests, separately distinguished. For this purpose a holding is non-beneficial only if neither the director, nor his spouse, nor any of his children under 18 has any beneficial interest;

(b)   changes in interests between the balance sheet date and a date not more than one month before the date of the notice of the annual general meeting. If there has been no change, then that fact should be disclosed;

(c)   particulars of any duplication of directors' interests.[61]

B   Contracts of significance with directors

Particulars of any contract of significance subsisting during or at the end of the financial year in which a director of the company is or was materially interested are required to be disclosed by listed companies. If there has been no such contract, a statement of that fact is required.[62] (See 5 of Chapter 23 for a further discussion of these requirements.)

C   Directors' waived emoluments

Particulars of any arrangement under which a director has waived or agreed to waive any emoluments must be disclosed (see 2.6 of Chapter 24).[63]

D   Service contracts of retiring directors

Listed companies are required to disclose in the directors' report the unexpired period of any service contract of any director proposed for re-election at the forthcoming annual general meeting. If a director does not have a service contract of more than one year's duration, the directors' report must contain an appropriate negative statement.[64]

4.3.2 Shareholders

A   Substantial holdings of the company's shares

A statement is required to be given showing particulars, as at a date not more than one month prior to the date of the notice of the annual general meeting, of an interest of any person (other than a director), in any substantial part of the share capital of the company. A substantial holding is one which amounts to 5% or more of the nominal value of any class of capital carrying rights to vote in all circumstances at general meetings of the company. If there is no such interest, a statement of that fact is required to be made.[65]

Such disclosure will give an indication of possible related parties of the company.

B   Close company status

A statement is required to be given as to whether the company is a close company for tax purposes and whether the position has changed since the year end. If there is any doubt about the status, that uncertainty should be disclosed.[66]

The disclosure of close company status gives information about the concentration of shareholdings, and hence the possible existence of related parties.

C   Contracts with a corporate substantial shareholder

A corporate substantial shareholder means any body corporate entitled to exercise or control the exercise of 30% or more of the voting power at general meetings of the company or one which is in a position to control the composition of a majority of the board of directors of the company.[67]

Particulars of any contract of significance between the company, or one of its subsidiaries, and a corporate substantial shareholder are required to be disclosed by listed companies.[68]

In addition, particulars of any contract for the provision of services to the company or any of its subsidiaries by a corporate substantial shareholder are also required to be disclosed. Exceptionally, such a contract need not be disclosed, if it is a contract for the provision of services which it is the principal business of the shareholder to provide and it is not a contract of significance.[69]

D   Waived   dividends

Particulars of any arrangement under which a shareholder has waived or agreed to waive any dividends are required to be disclosed. In most cases, this is likely only to arise where the shareholder is a director or has some influence over the company.[70]

E   Purchase by the company of its own shares

The Companies Act contains provisions requiring disclosures of certain information where a company has purchased some of its own shares.[71] The Stock Exchange extends these for listed companies by requiring disclosure of, in the case of purchases made otherwise than through the market or by tender or partial offer to all shareholders, the names of the sellers of such shares purchased.[72] Again, in most cases, this is likely only to arise where the shareholder is a director or has some influence over the company.

5   COMPARISON WITH US AND IASC PRONOUNCEMENTS

5.1   IASC

The relevant international standard which deals with the disclosure of related parties and transactions between a reporting enterprise and its related parties is IAS 24 — *Related Party Disclosures* — which was issued in July 1984. The standard states that certain other international standards call for disclosures which may also be relevant in respect of related parties.[73]

5.1.1   IAS 24

Effectively, the requirements of IAS 24 are such that most related parties under ED 46 will be related parties under IAS 24, although IAS 24 does not appear to regard fellow associates and shareholders who own less than 20% of the share capital of the enterprise to be related parties of the enterprise.[74] The major differences between IAS 24 and ED 46 relate to the scope and the nature of disclosures required to be given and are as follows:

A   *Scope of the disclosures*

(a)   IAS 24 requires disclosure of *all* material transactions with related parties,[75] whereas ED 46 only requires disclosure of *abnormal* transactions;

(b)   IAS 24 only allows a wholly-owned subsidiary not to give related party disclosures if its parent is incorporated in the same country and provides consolidated financial statements in that country.[76] However, this exemption applies to all related party disclosures, whereas ED 46 only allows wholly-owned subsidiaries not to disclose information about transactions with other group companies;

(c)   IAS 24 does not require any disclosure about situations where the reporting enterprise is economically dependent on another.

B   *Nature of the disclosures*

IAS 24 does not specifically require disclosure of either the name of the related party or the extent of any ownership interest in either party as is proposed by ED 46; it only requires the nature of the relationship to be disclosed.[77]

5.2   US

The main accounting standard in the US dealing with this issue is SFAS 57 — *Related Party Disclosures* — which was issued in March 1982, as a codification of SAS 18. While SFAS 57 outlines general US GAAP in this area, there are a number of other pronouncements in the US which impact on the reporting of certain related party transactions. These include SFAS 68 — *Research and Development Arrangements* — and SFAS 13 — *Accounting for Leases* — as well as various Staff Accounting Bulletins issued by the SEC.

5.2.1   SFAS 57

Again, the requirements of SFAS 57 are such that related parties under ED 46 are effectively related parties under SFAS 57.[78] The major differences between the two pronouncements relate to the scope and the nature of the disclosures which are required, and are set out below.

A   *Scope of the disclosures*

(a)   Like IAS 24, SFAS 57 requires disclosure of *all* material transactions with related parties,[79] whereas ED 46 only requires disclosure of *abnormal* transactions;

(b)   SFAS 57 does not require disclosure in respect of compensation arrangements, expense allowances, and other similar items in the ordinary course of business,[80] whereas if these are considered 'abnormal' transactions in terms of ED 46 disclosure would be required;

(c) SFAS 57 requires disclosure of all material related party transactions in the financial statements of wholly-owned subsidiaries if these are produced,[81] whereas ED 46 does not require disclosure of transactions with group companies;

(d) like IAS 24, SFAS 57 does not require any disclosure about situations where the reporting enterprise is economically dependent on another.

B   *Nature of disclosures*

(a) Like IAS 24, SFAS 57 does not specifically require disclosure of the name of the related party and the extent of any ownership interest in either party as is done by ED 46; it only requires the nature of the relationship to be disclosed, although it does state that the name should be disclosed if necessary to the understanding of the relationship;[82]

(b) in addition to requiring disclosure of amounts due to/from the related party, SFAS 57 requires the terms and manner of settlement to be disclosed if not otherwise apparent;[83]

(c) SFAS 57 requires the monetary amount of the transaction to be disclosed[84] whereas ED 46 allows the amount to be disclosed in percentage terms;

(d) SFAS 57 does not specifically require disclosure of the basis on which the transaction price has been determined, although it does require 'such other information deemed necessary to an understanding of the transactions on the financial statements'[85] and 'the effects of any change in the method of establishing the terms from that used in the preceding period' to be disclosed.[86]

References

1   ED 46, *Disclosure of related party transactions*, para. 22.
2   *Ibid.*, para. 26.
3   SFAS 57, *Related Party Disclosures*, FASB, March 1982, para. 15.
4   Accountants International Study Group, *Related Party Transactions*, para. 15.
5   ED 46, Preface, para. 1.1.
6   *Ibid.*, para. 22.
7   *Ibid.*, para. 24.
8   *Ibid.*, para. 25.
9   *Ibid.*, para. 26
10 *Ibid.*, para. 27.
11 *Ibid.*, para. 28.
12 *Ibid.*, para. 29.
13 *Ibid.*, para. 12.

14　*Ibid.*, para. 32.
15　*Ibid.*, para. 33.
16　*Ibid.*, para. 35.
17　*Ibid.*, para. 16.
18　*Ibid.*, para. 36.
19　*Ibid.*, para. 34.
20　*Ibid.*, para. 18.
21　*Ibid.*, Preface, para. 1.12.
22　Maxwell Communication Corporation plc, 1987 Report and Accounts, p. 35.
23　Maxwell Communication Corporation plc, 1987 Report and Accounts, p. 34.
24　Maxwell Communication Corporation plc, 1987 Report and Accounts, pp. 43, 48, 49 and 54.
25　ED 46, para. 7.
26　*Ibid.*, para. 10.
27　*Ibid.*, para. 23.
28　*Ibid.*
29　SFAS 57, para. 24(d).
30　Reed International P.L.C., Annual Report 1988, pp. 39 and 40.
31　The Council of The Stock Exchange, *Admission of Securities to Listing*, Section 6, Chapter 1, para. 1.2.
32　IAS 24, *Related Party Disclosures*, IASC, July 1984, paras. 4 and 5(c).
33　ED 46, para. 23.
34　*Ibid.*
35　*Ibid.*
36　*Ibid.*
37　*Ibid.*
38　*Ibid.*
39　CA 85, Sch. 6, para. 5.
40　ED 46, para. 11.
41　*Ibid.*, para. 30.
42　IAS 24, para. 6(c).
43　ED 46, para. 23.
44　IAS 24, para. 19.
45　ED 46, para. 14.
46　CA 85, s 235(2).
47　*Ibid.*, Sch. 7, para. 2.
48　As discussed at 5.2.2 of Chapter 4, the term 'related company' used in the Companies Act and the term 'associated company' used in SSAP 1 can usually be regarded as synonymous.
49　CA 85, Sch. 5, para. 20.
50　*Ibid.*, para. 1.
51　*Ibid.*, paras. 7 and 8.
52　See *ibid.*, paras. 14 — 17 for the information to be disclosed and the possible exemptions from disclosure.
53　*Ibid.*, Sch. 4, para. 8, balance sheet formats.
54　*Ibid.*, para. 59.
55　*Ibid.*, para. 8, profit and loss account formats.
56　*Ibid.*, para. 50.
57　*Ibid.*, para. 50(6).
58　SSAP 1, para. 49 and SSAP 14, para. 33.
59　SSAP 1, paras. 27 and 28.
60　*Ibid.*, para. 29.
61　*Admission of Securities to Listing*, Section 5, Chapter 2, para. 21(h); The Council of The Stock Exchange, *The Stock Exchange Unlisted Securities Market*, General Undertaking, para. 10(h).
62　*Admission of Securities to Listing*, Section 5, Chapter 2, para. 21(k).

63 *Admission of Securities to Listing*, Section 5, Chapter 2, para. 21(n); *The Stock Exchange Unlisted Securities Market*, General Undertaking, para. 10(k).
64 *Admission of Securities to Listing*, Section 5, Chapter 2, para. 43(c).
65 *Admission of Securities to Listing*, Section 5, Chapter 2, para. 21(i); *The Stock Exchange Unlisted Securities Market*, General Undertaking, para. 10(i).
66 *Admission of Securities to Listing*, Section 5, Chapter 2, para. 21(j); *The Stock Exchange Unlisted Securities Market*, General Undertaking, para. 10(j).
67 *Admission of Securities to Listing*, Section 5, Chapter 2, para. 21(l).
68 *Ibid.*
69 *Ibid.*, para. 21(m).
70 *Ibid.*, para. 21(o); *The Stock Exchange Unlisted Securities Market*, General Undertaking, para. 10(l).
71 CA 85, Sch. 7, para. 8.
72 *Admission of Securities to Listing*, Section 5, Chapter 2, para. 21(p).
73 IAS 24, para. 18.
74 *Ibid.*, paras. 4 — 6.
75 *Ibid.*, para. 26.
76 *Ibid.*, para. 3.
77 *Ibid.*, para. 26.
78 SFAS 57, para. 24.
79 *Ibid.*, para. 2.
80 *Ibid.*
81 *Ibid.*, footnote 2.
82 *Ibid.*, footnote 3.
83 *Ibid.*, para. 2(d).
84 *Ibid.*, para. 2(c).
85 *Ibid.*, para. 2(b).
86 *Ibid.*, para. 2(c).

Chapter 22

Pension costs

1 THE DEVELOPMENT OF AN ACCOUNTING STANDARD IN THE UK

1.1 Background

Accounting for the costs of pensions in the financial statements of employer companies presents one of the most difficult challenges in the whole field of financial reporting. The amounts involved are large, the timescale is long, the estimation process is complex and involves many areas of uncertainty which have to be made the subject of assumptions; in addition the choice of matching principles to be applied is complicated and open to argument. It is not surprising, in the face of these difficulties, that this subject has taken some time to be dealt with, and that it is only recently that the ASC has succeeded in developing an accounting standard on the subject.[1]

Hitherto, generally accepted practice in the UK has been to charge pension costs in the profit and loss account on the basis of funding payments made to the pension scheme, which obviously means that the reported profit of the employer company is susceptible to fluctuations because of changes in the contributions made. In addition, most companies have given only very limited information in their financial statements about the obligations to pay pensions to which they are committed, and the assets which have been built up in their pension funds to meet these obligations. The ASC has spent several years trying to develop both a more sophisticated and systematic approach to the recognition of pension costs and a set of disclosure requirements which provides a comprehensive overview of pension arrangements.

1.2 Napier interim report

The first document on the subject to be published by the ASC comprised an assessment of the issues to be addressed, set out in a report by Christopher Napier of the London School of Economics in 1982.[2] This paper identified certain key characteristics of pension schemes which have subsequently formed the foundation of the ASC's thinking on the subject. These were that pensions should be seen simply as a form of deferred remuneration; that the application of the accruals concept would require that their cost should be matched against the benefits of the employees' services over their working lives; and that although the objective of funding the pension scheme was also to provide for the ultimate cost of the pensions, the pattern of funding payments depended on management decisions which were not necessarily a good basis for measuring the annual cost for accounting purposes.

The paper also drew a distinction between 'normal' costs of providing for pensions, and 'abnormal' or 'special' costs. Normal costs were described as those which would arise if (a) no credit was given by the pension scheme for service prior to the scheme's introduction, and (b) the assumptions of the actuary as to mortality, employee turnover, salary progression, investment returns etc. were borne out by subsequent events. Abnormal or special costs were therefore those costs which arose because of variations in the assumptions in (a) and (b) above. This distinction subsequently formed the basis for that used in SSAP 24 between the regular ongoing cost and the effects of variations, which are discussed in 2.5.1 and 2.5.2 below.

Napier also briefly touched on the need for disclosure of information about pension arrangements in company accounts, and stated his belief that the following disclosures should be considered:

(a)   the existence of pension schemes, including a description of the employee groups covered;

(b)   the amount charged to the profit and loss account in respect of pension provision (distinguishing between normal and special costs), and the contributions made to pension funds, where these differed from the amounts charged;

(c)   the rates at which the employer and employees contribute to the fund, and an indication as to whether it is expected that these rates will change in the foreseeable future;

(d)   a statement that the fund's actuaries regard the fund as solvent on both the following bases:

   (i)   that there are sufficient assets in the fund to secure the benefits of existing pensioners and to provide paid-up (i.e. preserved) pensions to present employees on the basis of present salaries and credited periods of service (the 'discontinuance' basis—SSAP 24 subsequently referred to this as a 'current funding level valuation');

   (ii)   that there are sufficient assets in the fund to secure the benefits of existing pensioners and to fund the appropriate proportion, based on credited periods of service, of projected pension benefits, based on salary levels projected to the year of retirement or earlier leaving (the 'projected benefit' or 'going concern' basis—SSAP 24 later called this an 'ongoing actuarial valuation');

(e)   in the event that the fund is not solvent on either or both of these bases, the amount by which the fund is in deficit, and a statement of the intentions of the employer as to the funding of this deficit;

(f)   the date of the latest actuarial valuation of the pension fund and the name and qualification of the person carrying out the valuation;

(g)   any other matters in relation to pension provision which are considered necessary in order that the employer's financial statements may disclose a true and fair view.[3]

Napier's interim report was a by-product of a research study commissioned by the Institute of Chartered Accountants in England and Wales in 1981, and his full report was finally published by the Institute in 1983.[4] This comprises a comprehensive and lucid exposition of the issues involved in accounting for pension costs, and is of particular value in explaining the mechanics of the actuarial valuation process and how they may be adapted to accounting use.

1.3   ED 32

At the time of publishing Napier's interim report, the ASC was already working on the subject of pension costs, and in 1983 they published the exposure draft of a standard on the subject, ED 32 — *The disclosure of pension information in company accounts*.[5] As the title reveals, the Committee had decided as a first stage to limit its strategy to one of ensuring better disclosure in financial statements about the details of company pension schemes, before proceeding towards the more difficult question of measurement in the profit and loss account. The main thrust of the proposals of the exposure draft were contained in a single, lengthy, paragraph, which read as follows:

'Disclosure should be made in financial statements of sufficient information concerning pension arrangements to enable users of the statements to gain a broad understanding of the significance of pension costs in the accounting period and of actual and contingent liabilities and commitments at the balance sheet date. Towards this general objective, the disclosures should include at least the following, subject to any necessary modifications in the case of employees paid abroad and to summarising to a reasonable extent in the case of individual companies or groups with a number of different pension schemes:

(a)   the nature of the pension schemes, (e.g. defined benefit or defined contribution), whether they are externally funded or internally financed and any legal obligations of the company (e.g. undertakings to meet the balance of cost);

(b)   the accounting policy, and the funding policy if different from the accounting policy, indicating the basis used for allocating pension costs to accounting periods;

(c)   whether the pension costs and liabilities are assessed in accordance with the advice of a professionally qualified actuary and, if so, the date of the most recent actuarial valuation;

(d)   the amount charged in the profit and loss account for pension costs, distinguishing between normal charges related to employees' pay and service in the accounting period and other charges or credits, (e.g. additional charges to cover the cost of post-retirement awards not covered by the normal charge, or reductions in the normal charge to take account of contribution holidays or a temporarily reduced contribution rate resulting from overfunding) with explanations of such charges or credits;

(e)   any commitments to change the rate of contributions or to make special contributions;

(f)   any provisions or prepayments in the balance sheet, resulting from a difference between the accounting policy and the funding policy;

(g)   the amount of any deficiency on a discontinuance basis actuarial valuation or on the requirements of the Occupational Pensions Board, indicating the action, if any, being taken to deal with it in future financial statements;

(h)   the amount of any material self-investment (i.e. investment by the pension fund in the employer company itself);

(i)   in the case of internally financed schemes, the amount of the provision at the balance sheet date and of any identifiable fund of assets representing the provision; and

(j)   expected significant effects on future financial statements of any changes which have occurred in the above, including the effects of any material improvements in benefits.'[6]

As can be seen from this list, ED 32 picked up a number of the requirements which Napier had suggested, but also introduced a number of new ones. The exposure draft drew attention to the Companies Act requirements to disclose pension costs and commitments (described in 4 below), but said that compliance with the ED would not necessarily ensure compliance with the legal requirements.

1.4   Statement of intent

In 1984, the ASC published a further document on the subject; this time it was a consultative Statement of Intent.[7] This revealed that the Committee had altered its strategy and was now ready to address the measurement of pension costs, rather than merely proposing disclosure requirements about pension arrangements. The broad principles which it outlined were consistent with those recommended by Napier, but were discussed in rather more detail than in Napier's interim report.

1.5   ED 39

Having received and considered the reaction to its statement of intent, the ASC proceeded to formulate an exposure draft based on the principles which the statement had outlined, and in May 1986 they published ED 39 — *Accounting for pension costs*.[8] The exposure draft dealt both with the measurement of pension cost for profit and loss account purposes and with fairly extensive disclosure requirements. Its main proposals were as follows:

(a)   Pension costs should be recognised on a systematic basis over the expected service lives of employees.

(b)   Total pension cost charged in the profit and loss account should be equal to regular cost plus variations arising from experience deficiencies and surpluses, changes in assumptions, etc. This broadly corresponded to the analysis made by Napier of 'normal' and 'abnormal' costs.

(c) For a defined benefit scheme, the regular pension cost should be a substantially level percentage of pensionable payroll. (For defined contribution schemes, the cost is simply the contribution payable, since that is the extent of the employer's commitment.)

(d) Variations from regular cost should generally be allocated over expected average remaining service lives of employees. The only exceptions would be if prudence dictated that a deficiency should be recognised over a shorter period, or if the variation were linked to an extraordinary item, in which case it would be recognised immediately as part of that item.

(e) A liability should be provided for if the cumulative pension cost charged against profits has not been completely discharged by contributions or directly paid pensions.

(f) Various proposals were made on how to account for the pension arrangements of an acquired company.

The exposure draft also proposed a fairly comprehensive list of disclosure requirements.

1.6 SSAP 24

In May 1988, the ASC finally issued SSAP 24[9] which was modelled on ED 39. The main amendments which were made from the exposure draft were to incorporate some exceptions to the basic rule that variations from regular cost should be spread over the average future working lives of the employees, to add transitional provisions, to soften the requirement to take account of expected discretionary pension increases, and to modify certain aspects of the disclosure requirements. In addition, the proposals concerned with accounting for the pension costs of an acquired company were deleted, since the subject was instead to be dealt with in the ASC's discussion paper on Fair Values (see section 6.4.3 E of Chapter 4). The standard is effective for periods beginning on or after July 1, 1988.

2 REQUIREMENTS OF SSAP 24

2.1 Scope

The standard is very broad in its scope. It applies to all pension arrangements, whether they arise from an explicit contractual commitment, or from custom and practice, or even if they are of an ex gratia nature; it applies to both funded and unfunded schemes; it applies to defined benefit schemes, defined contribution schemes and to those which are a hybrid mixture of the two; it applies equally to insured schemes (where all the investment is conducted by an insurance company) and self invested schemes (where the trustees themselves manage the fund's investments directly); it applies both to UK schemes and to foreign schemes (although when it is difficult to apply it to the latter, there is a hint of de facto relaxation of the requirements in the standard); it applies to schemes of all sizes; it is suggested even that the principles of the standard should be applied to any other post-retirement benefits, of which an example might be private health care. The only specific exclusions from the scope of the standard are in respect of state social security contributions and redundancy payments.

2.2   Accounting objective

The basic accounting objective which the standard sets is that the employer should recognise the cost of providing pensions on a systematic and rational basis over the period during which he receives benefit from the employees' services.[10] The standard explicitly distinguishes this from the funding objective, which is described as being to build up assets in a prudent and controlled manner in advance of the retirement of the members of the scheme, in order that the obligations of the scheme may be met without undue distortion of the employer's cash flow.[11] It is emphasised that the funding plan will not necessarily provide a satisfactory basis for the allocation of pension cost to accounting periods.

2.3   Definition of terms

The standard defines the terms which are used as follows:[12]

Accrued benefits are the benefits for service up to a given point in time, whether the rights to the benefits are vested or not. They may be calculated in relation to current earnings or projected final earnings.

An *accrued benefits method* of actuarial valuation is a valuation method in which the actuarial value of liabilities relates at a given date to:

(a)   the benefits, including future increases promised by the rules, for the current and deferred pensioners and their dependants; and

(b)   the benefits which the members assumed to be in service on the given date will receive for service up to that date only.

Allowance may be made for expected increases in earnings after the given date, and/or for additional pension increases not promised by the rules. The given date may be a current or future date. The further into the future the adopted date lies, the closer the results will be to those of a prospective benefits valuation method (which is defined below).

The *average remaining service life* is a weighted average of the expected future service of the current members of the scheme up to their normal retirement dates or expected dates of earlier withdrawal or death in service. The weightings can have regard to periods of service, salary levels of scheme members and future anticipated salary growth in a manner which the actuary considers appropriate having regard to the actuarial method and assumptions used.

A *current funding level valuation* considers whether the assets would have been sufficient at the valuation date to cover liabilities arising in respect of pensions in payment, preserved benefits for members whose pensionable service has ceased and accrued benefits for members in pensionable service, based on pensionable service to and pensionable earnings at, the date of valuation including revaluation on the statutory basis or such higher basis as has been promised. (This is sometimes called a 'discontinuance' basis, because it evaluates the scheme's ability to meet its obligations if it were to be discontinued.)

A *discretionary or ex gratia increase* in a pension or an *ex gratia pension* is one which the employer has no legal, contractual or implied commitment to provide.

A *defined benefit scheme* is a pension scheme in which the rules specify the benefits to be paid and the scheme is financed accordingly. (These are commonly referred to as 'final salary' schemes. This means that the employer promises to pay the member a pension which is related to (usually) his final salary at or near the date of retirement; a typical example might give the employee a pension which was calculated at one sixtieth of his final salary for each year in which he was an employee and a member of the scheme. Because various factors, notably the amount of the final salary, will not be known until many years have elapsed, the eventual cost of providing the pension will have to be estimated).

A *defined contribution scheme* is a pension scheme in which the benefits are directly determined by the value of contributions paid in respect of each member. Normally the rate of contribution is specified in the rules of the scheme. (These are commonly referred to as 'money purchase' schemes. In contrast to defined benefit (final salary) schemes, the employer has no obligation to provide a pension beyond that which is earned by the contributions which are payable under the scheme, so the cost of providing the pension is fixed and known from the outset.)

An *experience surplus or deficiency* is that part of the excess or deficiency of the actuarial value of assets over the actuarial value of liabilities, on the basis of the valuation method used, which arises because events have not coincided with the actuarial assumptions made for the last valuation.

A *funding plan* is the timing of payments in an orderly fashion to meet the future cost of a given set of benefits.

A *funded scheme* is a pension scheme where the future liabilities for benefits are provided for by the accumulation of assets held externally to the employing company's business.

The *level of funding* is the proportion at a given date of the actuarial value of liabilities for pensioners' and deferred pensioners' benefits and for members' accrued benefits that is covered by the actuarial value of assets. For this purpose, the actuarial value of future contributions is excluded from the value of assets.

An *ongoing actuarial valuation* is a valuation in which it is assumed that the pension scheme will continue in existence and (where appropriate) that new members will be admitted. The liabilities allow for expected increases in earnings.

Past service is used in SSAP 24 to denote service before a given date. It is often used, however, to denote service before entry into the pension scheme.

Pensionable payroll/earnings are the earnings on which benefits and/or contributions are calculated. One or more elements of earnings (e.g. overtime) may be excluded, and/or there may be a reduction to take account of all or part of the state scheme benefits which the member is deemed to receive.

A *pension scheme* is an arrangement (other than accident insurance) to provide pension and/or other benefits for members on leaving service or retiring and, after a member's death, for his/her dependants.

A *prospective benefits method* of valuation is a valuation method in which the actuarial value of liabilities relates to:

(a)   the benefits for current and deferred pensioners and their dependants, allowing where appropriate for future pension increases; and

(b)   the benefits which active members will receive in respect of both past and future service, allowing for future increases in earnings up to their assumed exit dates, and where appropriate for pension increases thereafter.

Regular cost is the consistent ongoing cost recognised under the actuarial method used.

2.4   Defined contribution schemes

2.4.1   *Accounting*

The accounting for defined contribution ('money purchase') schemes remains straightforward under SSAP 24. Since the employer has no obligation beyond payment of the contributions which he has agreed to make, there is no difficulty in measuring the cost of providing pensions; it is simply the amount of those contributions payable in respect of the accounting period.[13] If the amount actually paid in the period is more or less than the amount payable, a prepayment or accrual will appear in the balance sheet in accordance with normal accounting practice, but otherwise the payments made will simply be charged in the profit and loss account when made.

2.4.2   *Disclosure*

A   *Requirements*

The disclosure requirements of the standard for defined contribution schemes are also very simple, and add little to the requirements which already exist under SSAP 2 and the Companies Act. They are:

(a)   the nature of the scheme (i.e. the fact that it is a defined contribution scheme);

(b)   the accounting policy (arguably required already by SSAP 2);

(c)   the pension cost charge for the period (already required by the Companies Act — see 4.2 below);

(d)   any outstanding or prepaid contributions at the balance sheet date.[14]

B   Example

An Appendix to SSAP 24 gives an example of these disclosures which rolls all of these requirements into a single note, in the following terms:

Example 22.1: Disclosures relating to defined contribution scheme[15]

The company operates a defined contribution pension scheme. The assets of the scheme are held separately from those of the company in an independently administered fund. The pension cost charge represents contributions payable by the company to the fund and amounted to £500,000 (1986 £450,000). Contributions totalling £25,000 (1986 £15,000) were payable to the fund at the year end and are included in creditors.

In practice, while there is nothing to prevent companies disclosing all these details in a single note, it is likely that most companies will continue to deal with the different elements of the disclosure in different places. The policy and the nature of the scheme will often be dealt with together as part of the statement of accounting policies, the expense for the year will be included in the statutory staff costs note, and any prepayment or accrual will be shown on the balance sheet or in a note analysing the relevant balance sheet figure.

2.5   Defined benefit schemes

The accounting requirements for defined benefit ('final salary') schemes are very much more complicated. In this case the employer's commitment is open-ended, and in order to achieve the accounting objective mentioned at 2.2 above it is necessary to apply actuarial valuation techniques and use a large number of assumptions. The standard seeks to achieve this by drawing the distinction mentioned earlier in this chapter, between regular (ongoing) pension cost and variations from that cost. The essence of the standard's measurement rules is that the charge for pension cost in the profit and loss account should basically be the regular cost, but with adjustments for the effects of the variations from that cost which arise from time to time.

2.5.1   Regular pension cost

As stated at 2.3 above, regular cost is defined as the consistent ongoing cost recognised under the actuarial method used. The standard goes on to say that 'where a stable contribution rate for regular contributions, expressed as a percentage of pensionable earnings, has been determined, that rate will provide an acceptable basis for calculating the regular cost under the stated accounting objective so long as it makes full provision for the expected benefits over the anticipated service lives of employees'.[16] The actuary will be able to inform the company of the amount of the total cost which is to be regarded as the regular cost component.

Essentially, the regular cost is that amount which the actuary would regard as a sufficient contribution to the scheme to provide the eventual pensions to be paid in respect of future service, provided present actuarial assumptions about the future were borne out in practice and there were no future changes to the terms of the scheme. Even then, this amount will depend on the particular method which the actuary is using to attribute cost to individual years. (The standard does not stipulate that a particular actuarial method be used, provided that it meets the accounting objective of recognising the cost of pensions on a systematic and rational basis over the employees' working lives.)

2.5.2   *Variations from regular cost*

A   *Examples of variations*

The standard identifies four categories of variations from regular cost.[17] The first two are to do with the actuarial process and the methods and assumptions which it entails, while the second two are to do with changes in the scope or the terms of the scheme itself. The four categories are:

(a)   experience surpluses or deficiencies. These are surpluses or deficiencies which are identified in the course of an actuarial valuation of the scheme which have arisen because the assumptions which were made at the time of the previous valuation have not been fully borne out by subsequent experience. For example, an assumption will have been made as to the rate of return which was predicted to be earned on the scheme's investments. If this rate was in fact exceeded in practice, this will give rise to a surplus at the time of the next valuation, and this will be an experience surplus as the term is used in the standard. Similar variations may arise in relation to all the other main assumptions, such as those relating to salary inflation, the pattern of people joining and leaving the scheme, and so on;

(b)   the effects on the actuarial value of accrued benefits of changes in assumptions or method. Insofar as they relate to assumptions, these are similar to the previous category, except that they relate to the period beyond the date of the present valuation, rather than to the period since the previous valuation. Thus, a change in the assumption to increase the rate of predicted salary inflation in a final salary scheme would have the effect of increasing the total pension cost to be recognised and give rise to a variation. A change in actuarial method will have similar effects, in that it will give rise to a different present valuation of the scheme because of the particular way of attributing cost to particular years of service.

The wording of the standard is perhaps deficient in referring only to the effects on the value of the accrued *benefits*, which might be regarded as by implication excluding effects on the valuation of assets available to meet these benefits. We do not believe that any such distinction was intended, and we believe that the proper way to apply the standard is to regard changes affecting any part of the actuarial valuation of the scheme as variations and account for them as such;

(c)   retroactive changes in benefits or in conditions for membership. This might arise, for example, when the scope of a scheme is changed to include a class of employee which was previously excluded, and some credit is given for their past service with the company; alternatively, it might be an enhancement of the rights of existing members, say to give them an improvement in the terms of the formula under which their eventual pension will be calculated. These will generally entail an increase in the overall cost of pensions to the employer, and the past service element will give rise to a variation from regular cost;

(d) increases to pensions in payment or to deferred pensions for which provision has not previously been made. These are also treated as variations, provided that they were within the scope of the actuarial assumptions, which the standard says is the preferred position. However, where the increases are of a discretionary or ex gratia nature and if no allowance has previously been made for them in the actuarial assumptions, then they fall outside the scope of the valuation of the scheme and are not treated as variations under the standard but are dealt with separately (see 2.5.3 below);

B *Normally allocated over remaining service lives of current employees*

The basic rule set by the standard for all such variations from regular cost is that they should not be recognised immediately, but rather spread forward over the expected remaining service lives of employees in the scheme. There are, however, a number of exceptions to this basic rule, some of which in our view detract from the conceptual cohesion of the standard. These are discussed at C to F below.

The rationale for this basic rule merits some discussion. First of all it has to be looked at in the context of the standard's overall approach, which is orientated more towards the profit and loss account than towards the balance sheet. If actuarial surpluses and deficiencies were included in the balance sheet as soon as they were recognised, there would be enormous volatility in the amounts reported and, assuming the differences between the balance sheet figures were charged or credited directly in the profit and loss account, there could be a very significant effect on earnings in the years of actuarial valuation. The standard has instead opted for a smoothing approach, so that these effects are recognised in the profit and loss account gradually rather than immediately following a valuation.

Insofar as these variations arise from changes to do with the actuarial process, (categories (a) and (b) above), this treatment can be justified because of the high degree of uncertainty and subjectivity inherent in actuarial valuations; it would be wholly inappropriate to give immediate recognition to such changes, which are of a very long term nature and may easily be reversed at the time of the next valuation. However, at first sight it may seem more justifiable to give immediate recognition to the other broad class of variations — those reflecting changes in the scheme itself, described above under headings (c) and (d).

Broadly, the reason for not doing so is that such changes, even if they are expressed in terms which give credit for periods relating to the past, are made with a view to providing benefits for the future, not to meet any latent obligation which already exists. An improvement to the pension terms of an employee is only one of a range of possible improvements to his remuneration package; it may be decided on, for example, as an alternative to a future salary increase (or part of it). Accordingly it is thought appropriate to spread such increases forward over the employee's working life.

The standard does not specify exactly how variations are to be amortised. The relevant paragraph says that they should be amortised over the expected remaining service lives of the employees in the scheme, and that an average period may be used if desired.[18] Some of the possible methods available in practice are illustrated in the following example, which is based on the circumstances used in an example in the US accounting standard.[19]

Example 22.2: Methods of amortisation of variations

A company has 100 employees in its pension scheme, and predicts that 5 of them will withdraw from the scheme in each of the next 20 years. An actuarial valuation at January 1, 1987 identifies a variation of £750,000 to be spread over the working lives of the employees.

If companies do not use an average period, they will have to allocate the cost on the basis of the likely withdrawals from employment of their existing workforce until the date of the last employee leaving service; such an allocation is likely to involve a declining pattern of amortisation, as is illustrated in the first possible method as shown below.

METHOD A: If the amortisation is weighted in relation to the service years of the actual employees in the scheme at the time of the valuation it will produce the following result:

Year	Opening balance £	Amortisation rate (on £750,000)	Amount amortised £
1987	750,000	100/1050*	71,429
1988	678,571	95/1050	67,857
1989	610,714	90/1050	64,286
1990	546,428	85/1050	60,714
1991	485,714	80/1050	57,143
1992	428,571	75/1050	53,571
1993	375,000	70/1050	50,000
1994	325,000	65/1050	46,429
1995	278,571	60/1050	42,857
1996	235,714	55/1050	39,286
1997	196,428	50/1050	35,714
1998	160,714	45/1050	32,143
1999	128,571	40/1050	28,571
2000	100,000	35/1050	25,000
2001	75,000	30/1050	21,429
2002	53,571	25/1050	17,857
2003	35,714	20/1050	14,286
2004	21,428	15/1050	10,714
2005	10,714	10/1050	7,143
2006	3,571	5/1050	3,571

*The amortisation fraction is derived by using the sum-of-the-digits method, based on the predicted number of employees.

METHOD B: Another method of spreading the total cost of £750,000 would be to weight it for the effects of salary increases rather than charging it as a fixed sum amount. This method, taken in conjunction with Method A as shown above (which is shown alongside for purposes of comparison), would produce the following charge if salary inflation of 7% p.a. were assumed:

Year	Amortisation taking account of rising salaries £	Amortisation under Method A £
1987	43,997	71,429
1988	44,723	67,857
1989	45,335	64,286
1990	45,814	60,714
1991	46,137	57,143
1992	46,281	53,751
1993	46,220	50,000
1994	45,922	46,429
1995	45,357	42,857
1996	44,488	39,286
1997	43,275	35,714
1998	41,673	32,143
1999	39,636	28,571
2000	37,109	25,000
2001	34,035	21,429
2002	30,347	17,857
2003	25,977	14,286
2004	20,847	10,714
2005	14,871	7,143
2006	7,956	3,571

As can be seen from this example, this produces a much flatter charge for most of the period because the assumptions as to members leaving the scheme and as to the salary rate tend to offset each other. The amortisation profile is again obtained by use of the sum-of-the-digits method, based on the fractions used in Method A after introducing an escalation factor of 7% compounded.

If the salaries of all members of the scheme were equal, this method would produce a charge which was a level percentage of payroll for the employees in service at the time of the valuation. In practice they will not be equal; if the withdrawals from the scheme represented the retirement of senior employees with higher pay, then using a level percentage of payroll as the basis would tend to produce a profile of amortisation closer to Method A.

METHOD C: The US standard also gives an alternative based on straight-line amortisation over the average period, which is calculated as 10.5 years, which produces the following result:

Year	Opening balance £	Amount amortised £
1987	750,000	71,429
1988	678,571	71,429
1989	607,142	71,429
1990	535,713	71,429
1991	464,284	71,429
1992	392,855	71,429
1993	321,426	71,429
1994	249,997	71,429
1995	178,568	71,429
1996	107,139	71,429
1997	35,710	35,710

None of the methods shown above takes any account of interest, which, under the US standard, is charged as a separate component of the total pension cost. Since the variation identified in an actuarial valuation will implicitly be a discounted amount, it would be appropriate to account for interest on the amount identified, rather than simply amortising the amount itself. If this is not done, the interest which would otherwise have been charged will simply form part of the variation which will have to be accounted for following the next actuarial valuation.

When interest is taken into account, the amount amortised will be higher, because it will be equal (in this example) to £750,000 in present value terms, rather than as an absolute amount. The remaining three methods are variants of the first three methods shown above after modification to take account of the interest charge.

METHOD D: When the amount derived from Method A is combined with interest on the unamortised balance (at an assumed rate for the purposes of this example of 9%) the charge becomes even more heavily loaded towards the beginning of the period. This is illustrated in the following table:

Year	Opening balance £	Amortisation under Method A £	Interest on opening balance £	Total charge including interest £
1987	750,000	71,429	67,500	138,929
1988	678,571	67,857	61,072	128,929
1989	610,714	64,286	54,964	119,250
1990	546,428	60,714	49,179	109,893
1991	485,714	57,143	43,714	100,857
1992	428,571	53,571	38,572	92,143
1993	375,000	50,000	33,750	83,750
1994	325,000	46,429	29,250	75,679
1995	278,571	42,857	25,072	67,929
1996	235,714	39,286	21,214	60,500
1997	196,428	35,714	17,679	53,393
1998	160,714	32,143	14,464	46,607
1999	128,571	28,571	11,572	40,143
2000	100,000	25,000	9,000	34,000
2001	75,000	21,429	6,750	28,179
2002	53,571	17,857	4,822	22,679
2003	35,714	14,286	3,214	17,500
2004	21,428	10,714	1,929	12,643
2005	10,714	7,143	964	8,107
2006	3,571	3,571	322	3,893

METHOD E: The equivalent of Method B above would be to increase the amounts generated under that method by a constant ratio so that the present value of the amounts is £750,000, rather than adding interest on the unamortised balance in each year as was done under Method D above. This would produce the following charge:

Year	£
1987	87,204
1988	88,643
1989	89,856
1990	90,804
1991	91,445
1992	91,731
1993	91,609
1994	91,020
1995	89,899
1996	88,176
1997	85,772
1998	82,598
1999	78,560
2000	73,552
2001	67,457
2002	60,150
2003	51,488
2004	41,319
2005	29,474
2006	15,769

In fact something like this method will tend to be used in practice, because the actuary will tend to build these factors into his calculations when he is advising on the appropriate rate; rather than expressing the amount of the variation as a capital sum, he may present his conclusions on the valuation in a form which recommends a certain contribution rate as a percentage of payroll for the regular cost and an additional rate for the effect of variations, both designed, therefore, to result in increased contributions as salaries increase. This will not equate exactly to the calculation illustrated above, because Method E, like Method B, assumes that all employees are paid the same amount, which is unlikely to be the case.

METHOD F: The equivalent of the straight-line example shown as Method C above would be obtained by calculating the annuity for 10.5 years which equated, at an interest rate of 9%, to a capital value of £750,000. This would result in an annual charge of £113,368 for the first ten years and £56,684 for the final six months.

Since the standard does not specify the use of any particular method, it would appear that any of the above would be acceptable, but we would regard those methods that take account of interest (Methods D to F above) as preferable to those which do not. Whatever method is chosen should be applied consistently.

Although, as indicated above, it is both likely and preferable that factors such as interest cost and salary inflation will be built into the amortisation pattern in practice, these have been excluded from the worked examples shown in the remainder of this chapter for the purposes of simplicity. These examples also use an average period to represent the working lives of members in the scheme, and are therefore based on the application of Method C as shown above.

SSAP 24 does not provide any worked examples of the spreading treatment, but the forerunner of the standard, ED 39, contained two such examples, the second of which is reproduced below to illustrate the mechanics of the accounting process.

Example 22.3:   *Spreading variations from regular cost*[20]

The actuarial valuation at 31 December 1984 of the pension scheme of company B showed a surplus of £260m. The actuary recommended that B eliminate the surplus by taking a contribution holiday in 1985 and 1986 and then paying contributions of £30m p.a. for 8 years. After that the standard contribution would be £50m p.a.. The average remaining service life of employees in the scheme at 31 December 1984 was 10 years. B's year end is 31 December.

Assuming no change in circumstances, the annual charge in the profit and loss account for the years 1985 to 1994 will be:

$$\text{Regular cost} - \frac{\text{surplus}}{\text{average remaining service life}} = \pounds50\text{m} - \frac{\pounds260\text{m}}{10} = \pounds24\text{m}$$

The funding in these periods will be:

1985-86	Nil
1987-94	£30m p.a.

The difference between the amounts funded and the amounts charged in the profit and loss account will be recognised as a provision as follows:

	Funded £m	Charged £m	Provision £m
1985	—	24	(24)
1986	—	24	(48)
1987	30	24	(42)
1988	30	24	(36)
1989	30	24	(30)
1990	30	24	(24)
1991	30	24	(18)
1992	30	24	(12)
1993	30	24	(6)
1994	30	24	—

The example notes that in practice further actuarial valuations will occur, usually triennially, during the 10 year amortisation period and that these may reveal a surplus or deficiency which will require an adjustment to the charge and prepayment/provision in succeeding periods. However, it does not specify how this might be calculated. This point is considered below at 3.3.4.

C   *Reductions in employees arising from an extraordinary event*

The standard continues to follow the line taken by ED 39 that the spreading rule is overridden by the requirements of SSAP 6 where the variation is associated with an event which gives rise to an extraordinary item, such as the closure of a business segment.[21] SSAP 24 does not specifically say how such events are to be treated, but this can be adduced from SSAP 6. Where the company is accounting for the closure of a business segment, or some similar extraordinary event, it must provide for all the financial effects of that closure, perhaps including the costs of redundancy programmes and so on. If a variation of pension cost arises from the same event, it follows from the rules of SSAP 6 that this should be recognised as part of the overall effect of the closure; this will mean that it will be taken into account in that year and will therefore result in a departure from the normal spreading rule.

This may seem sensible in principle, but it could give rise to a further anomaly. Where a company decides on a programme of future closures and provides for the cost of the associated redundancies, it would appear that the question of whether it can take credit for the saving in pension costs at the same time depends on whether the closure is dealt with above or below the line. If they are treated as extraordinary losses, the provision may be offset by the effect of the reduction of pension obligations, whereas if they are not this would appear to be prohibited. It is difficult to see this disparity as logically defensible. Admittedly, the variation may qualify instead to be dealt with under the treatment described under D below, but as we explain in that section, we do not find that a very satisfactory treatment either.

The operation of this exception can be illustrated by the following example, which is based on the figures used in Example 22.3:

Example 22.4:Variations arising from an extraordinary event

The actuary advises that £50m out of the £260m surplus is attributable to the redundancy programme associated with the closure of a business segment which is treated as an extraordinary item in 1985. The accounting treatment in this instance will be to deal with this variation from regular cost immediately, as a credit to the extraordinary cost of the closure, and to deal with the remaining £210m by amortising it over the working lives of the employees in the scheme.

The effect of this amortisation on the amount charged will be as follows:

$$\text{Regular cost} - \frac{\text{surplus}}{\text{average remaining service life}} = £50\text{m} - \frac{£210\text{m}}{10} = £29\text{m}$$

The effect on the financial statements will therefore be:

	Funded £m	Charged (Credited) £m	Prepayment (Provision) £m
1985 – ordinary charge	—	29	
extraordinary credit		(50)	
		(21)	21
1986	—	29	(8)
1987	30	29	(7)
1988	30	29	(6)
1989	30	29	(5)
1990	30	29	(4)
1991	30	29	(3)
1992	30	29	(2)
1993	30	29	(1)
1994	30	29	—

D   *Where variations result from a significant reduction in number of employees then surplus should be taken when the reduced contributions occur*

The next exception from the general 'spreading' rule occurs where there is a significant change in the normal level of contributions in order to eliminate a surplus or a deficiency which results from a significant reduction in the number of employees in the scheme in circumstances which do not fall within the definition of an extraordinary event. The standard says that where these circumstances apply, the effect of the variation in cost should not be spread over the average working lives of the remaining employees, but rather recognised when the reduction in contributions occurs.[22] The rationale for this exception is probably that it makes little apparent sense to spread this effect over the working lives of those who remain, when it arises from those who have left. An illustration of the effect of the exception is set out below, again using the same figures as for Example 22.3 above:

Example 22.5: Variations arising from a significant reduction in employees

The actuary advises that £50m out of the £260m surplus is attributable to a major redundancy programme occurring since the date of the last valuation. Accordingly the accounting treatment will be to deal with this variation from regular cost in line with the adjustments made to the funding programme, and deal with the remaining £210m by amortising it over the working lives of the employees in the scheme.

The effect of this amortisation on the amount charged will again be as follows:

$$\text{Regular cost} - \frac{\text{surplus}}{\text{average remaining service life}} = £50m - \frac{£210m}{10} = £29m$$

However it is still necessary to decide when to recognise the effect of the £50m which is attributable to the reduction of employees, because in reality the contributions have been adjusted to eliminate the whole of the £260m surplus, not just the £50m. If the whole of the contribution holiday in the first year were designated as intended to deal with this part of the surplus, the effect would be as follows:

	Funded £m	Charged (Credited) £m	Prepayment (Provision) £m
1985	—	(21)	21
1986	—	29	(8)
1987	30	29	(7)
1988	30	29	(6)
1989	30	29	(5)
1990	30	29	(4)
1991	30	29	(3)
1992	30	29	(2)
1993	30	29	(1)
1994	30	29	—

The credit in 1985 is calculated in the same way as is shown in Example 22.4, although the whole effect is shown as part of the ordinary pension cost in this case. In fact the result is the same as in that example only because the contribution holiday in 1985 is large enough to deal with the whole amount of the surplus arising from withdrawals.

Clearly, this produces a rather extreme and, some may say, unfair result. It would be possible to arrive at different results by attributing the changes in the contribution rates to their underlying reasons in a different way. For example if the allocation were made in proportion to the changes in the contribution rate, the effect would be as follows:

	Funded £m	Charged £m	Provision £m
1985	—	19.2	(19.2)
1986	—	19.2	(38.4)
1987	30	25.2	(33.6)
1988	30	25.2	(28.8)
1989	30	25.2	(24.0)
1990	30	25.2	(19.2)
1991	30	25.2	(14.4)
1992	30	25.2	(9.6)
1993	30	25.2	(4.8)
1994	30	25.2	—

(The effect on the funding rate has been to reduce it by £50m in each of the first two years and by £20m in the remaining eight. Accordingly, the total surplus of £50m attributable to the redundancy programme has been apportioned over that period in the same way, to reduce the £29m charge (calculated as shown above) by £9.8m in the first two years and by £3.8m in the remaining eight years.)

This appears to produce a more sensible and consistent charge, and we prefer it for that reason. Nevertheless either allocation, or indeed any other reasoned allocation, would appear to be acceptable under the terms of the standard.

Overall, we do not believe that this exception stands up very well to closer examination. The standard requires that recognition be given to the effects of significant reductions in the number of employees in line with the consequential change in contributions which is an uneasy compromise between the basic spreading rule described at B above and the immediate recognition required in the circumstances of C. Moreover, this leaves the timing of recognition at the whim of management, who may take it in the form of a contribution holiday, by a longer term reduction of the contribution rate, or they may even decide to make no change in the contribution rate at all. As illustrated above, even when they have amended the contribution rate they will still have to decide how to allocate the change in rate against the various factors which have given rise to it. As a result, we believe that this exception is unlikely to improve comparability and consistency in financial reporting.

In any event, the general thrust of the standard is to treat variations of all kinds in the same manner, and to look at the workforce as a whole, rather than to focus attention on particular groups of employees. We therefore think it odd to make an exception for these particular circumstances.

E   *Refunds subject to tax may be taken in the period the refund occurs*

Another exception to the normal spreading rule which is allowed by the standard is where the company receives a refund from the scheme, subject to the deduction of tax. At present, this is governed by the rules of the Finance Act 1986, which are designed to prevent companies from making excessive funding payments to their pension schemes and, if necessary (and permitted by the trust deed), to remedy the situation by obtaining a refund from the scheme after deduction of tax at a rate of 40%.

The standard provides that, where such refunds are taken, the company is allowed (but not required) to credit the refund to income in the year of receipt, rather than spreading the effects of the variations which have given rise to the surplus forward.[23] In other words, it allows a cash basis to be used for this transaction if desired. It is very difficult to see any conceptual merit in this exception to the basic spreading rule. The only concession made by the standard to comparability is to require full disclosure of the treatment where a refund is taken.

F   *In certain circumstances material deficits may be recognised over a shorter period*

Finally, the standard provides that, in very limited circumstances, prudence may require that recognition should be given to the costs of making good a material deficit over a period shorter than the normal amortisation period. This exception applies only where significant additional contributions have been required, and where the deficiency has been occasioned by a major event or transaction which has not been allowed for in the actuarial assumptions and is outside their normal scope.[24] An example which is quoted in the standard is that of a major mismanagement of the scheme's assets (presumably resulting in their loss for reasons other than the normal risks of investment). Although this may be a justifiable exception in certain cases, it is expected to be only very rarely applied.

2.5.3   Discretionary and ex-gratia pension increases and ex-gratia pensions

As mentioned in 2.5.2 A (d) above, it is envisaged by the standard that allowance should preferably be made in the actuarial assumptions for pension increases of all kinds, even where these are not the result of any contractual obligation. Where this applies, any increases in pensions will simply be dealt with as giving rise to variations in regular cost, to be treated as discussed in the previous section.

However, where no allowance has been made for such awards, different rules apply. The standard requires that the full capitalised value of these is provided for in the year in which the grant is made, except to the extent that it is covered by an existing surplus. This would appear to mean that if there is a surplus in the scheme at the time of the grant then the cost can in effect still be spread forward (as a reduction of a variation which would otherwise have reduced future pension cost), but if there is no such surplus, or an insufficient surplus, then it must be charged against current profits.

It is not clear whether this applies only where it is possible in fact to use the surplus in the fund to meet this expense. This may be impossible if the provisions of the scheme do not permit the trustees to apply the funds for this purpose. It is arguable that even then the treatment may still be justifiable because the unrecognised gain in the fund provides sufficient reason to justify non-recognition of the unfunded liability for the discretionary or ex gratia award. However we believe that the standard intended the narrower interpretation, that the offset can be applied only when the surplus in the scheme is in fact applied to meet the cost of the new award.

2.5.4   Balance sheet

As explained earlier, the standard is orientated towards the profit and loss account rather than the balance sheet, and the asset or liability which will appear is literally the balancing figure. It is the cumulative difference between the amount which has been charged in the profit and loss account and the amount which has been paid as contributions, and it will appear as a prepayment or an accrual, representing the extent to which contributions have been paid either ahead of or behind the recognition of cost. Since companies will generally continue to have contributions allowed for tax when they are paid, this figure will also represent the cumulative timing difference which has to be taken into account for the purposes of deferred tax.

It might be thought that this balance has no definable meaning, particularly as there are circumstances where it appears to 'go the wrong way'. For example, as is shown above in Example 22.3, a company which takes a contribution holiday because there is an underlying surplus in the fund may end up showing a liability in its financial statements, which may seem incongruous. However, in reality the balance can be explained as being the combination of two figures; the most recently reported actuarial surplus or deficiency in the fund (as adjusted for subsequent contributions and regular costs), combined with the cumulative amount of unamortised variations awaiting recognition in the profit and loss account. This can be illustrated by reference to the figures shown in that example:

Example 22.6:   *Explanation of balance sheet figure*

	Fund			*Financial statements*	
	1	2	3	4	5
			Surplus/	Unamortised	
	Contribution	Regular cost	Deficit	variation	Balance
	£m	£m	£m	£m	£m
Actuarial surplus /variation			260	(260)	-
1985	—	50	210	(234)	(24)
1986	—	50	160	(208)	(48)
1987	30	50	140	(182)	(42)
1988	30	50	120	(156)	(36)
1989	30	50	100	(130)	(30)
1990	30	50	80	(104)	(24)
1991	30	50	60	(78)	(18)
1992	30	50	40	(52)	(12)
1993	30	50	20	(26)	(6)
1994	30	50	—	—	—

Columns 1 to 3 show the theoretical movements in the fund after the valuation resulting from the effects of contributions and regular costs; for the sake of simplicity the effects of interest and the time value of money have been ignored. Column 4 is the amount of the unrecognised variation, being the variation identified in the 1984 valuation, successively reduced by annual amortisation of £26m p.a. to the pension cost charged in the profit and loss account. Column 5 is the net of columns 3 and 4 and is the amount shown as a provision in the balance sheet. Although it may seem odd that a liability is shown when an underlying surplus exists, it simply reflects the fact that the effects of the surplus have been recognised more quickly in cash terms (by the contribution holiday) than for accounting purposes.

2.5.5 Disclosure

A Requirements

Although the standard does deal with calculation of pension cost, there is still a large degree of flexibility as to the measurement of the amounts to be recognised, partly because of the exceptions to the basic spreading rule mentioned above but also because there is a large degree of subjectivity inherent in the actuarial process, and because no single actuarial method has been specified. In this light, it is still possible to characterise the standard as being primarily a disclosure standard, because the new disclosure requirements which it has introduced are very extensive. These are as follows:[25]

(a) the nature of the scheme (i.e. the fact that it is a defined benefit scheme);

(b) whether it is funded or unfunded;

(c) the accounting policy and, if different, the funding policy;

(d) whether the pension cost and provision (or asset) are assessed in accordance with the advice of a professionally qualified actuary and, if so, the date of the most recent formal actuarial valuation or later formal review used for this purpose. If the actuary is an employee or officer of the reporting company, this fact should be disclosed;

(e)   the pension cost charge for the period together with explanations of significant changes in the charge compared to that in the previous accounting period;

(f)   any provisions or prepayments in the balance sheet resulting from a difference between the amounts recognised as cost and the amounts funded or paid directly;

(g)   the amount of any deficiency on a current funding level basis (a 'discontinuance' basis) indicating the action, if any, being taken to deal with it in the current and future accounting periods. Where there is more than one pension scheme, the standard emphasises that it is not permitted to set off a surplus of this type arising on one scheme against a deficiency on another;

(h)   an outline of the results of the most recent formal actuarial valuation or later formal review of the scheme on an ongoing basis. This should include disclosure of:

   (i)   the actuarial method used and a brief description of the main assumptions. This should include the assumption made regarding new entrants unless it is apparent from the description of the method used;[26] If there has been a change in the method, this fact should be disclosed and the effect quantified;[27]

   (ii)   the market value of scheme assets at the date of their valuation or review. (Note that this means the actual market value of the assets, which will not generally be the same as the value on the basis used by the actuary for valuing the scheme — see 3.1.5 below);

   (iii) the level of funding expressed in percentage terms. (This, taken with the previous requirement, will allow a reasonable estimate of the actuarial surplus or deficiency to be derived. It will only be an estimate because the previous requirement calls for the market value of the assets to be shown, rather than the value put on them for the purposes of the actuarial valuation);

   (iv)   comments on any material actuarial surplus or deficiency indicated by (iii) above;

   (v)   the effects of any significant post-valuation events.[28]

(i)   any commitment to make additional payments over a limited number of years;

(j)   the accounting treatment adopted in respect of a refund made under deduction of tax (see 2.5.2 E above), where a credit appears in financial statements in relation to it. (We presume that this means a credit in the profit and loss account rather than in the balance sheet, otherwise the last few words of the previous sentence add nothing to the requirement);

(k)   details of the expected effects on future costs of any material changes in the company's pension arrangements;

(l)   in the first year of implementing the standard, the way in which the transitional provisions have been applied.[29]

Many of these requirements are similar to those originally proposed in ED 32 (see 1.3 above), but SSAP 24 goes further in its requirements relating to actuarial information. Conversely, the Standard does not contain the requirement to disclose any material self-investment, which was one of ED 32's suggestions.

B   Example

Appendix 1 to the standard contains two examples of comprehensive notes which are designed to meet these disclosure requirements, one for a small company with a single pension scheme and the other for a large group with more complex pension arrangements. The second of these is reproduced below:[30]

Example 22.7: Defined benefit scheme disclosure

The group operates a number of pension schemes throughout the world. The major schemes, which cover 85% of scheme members, are of the defined benefit type. With the exception of the main scheme in Germany, the assets of the schemes are held in separate trustee administered funds.

The total pension cost for the group was £2,050,000 (1986 £1,585,000) of which £300,000 (1986 £285,000) relates to the overseas schemes. The pension cost relating to the UK schemes is assessed in accordance with the advice of a qualified actuary using the attained age method. The latest actuarial assessment of these schemes was as at 31 December 1985. The assumptions which have the most significant effect on the results of the valuation are those relating to the rate of return on investments and the rates of increase in salaries and pensions. It was assumed that the investment return would be 9% per annum, that salary increases would average 7% per annum and that present and future pensions would increase at the rate of 4% per annum. The cost has risen significantly as a result of the acquisition of ABC Limited at the beginning of the period and the resultant increase in group scheme members. Of the total cost, £350,000 (1986 £300,000) is attributable to amortisation of past service liabilities that are being written off over a ten-year period ending in 1988.

At the date of the latest actuarial valuation, the market value of the assets of the UK scheme was £32.1m and the actuarial value of the assets was sufficient to cover 85% of the benefits that had accrued to members, after allowing for expected future increases in earnings. This deficiency should be eliminated by 1991 at the current employer's contribution rate of 12% of pensionable earnings.

The element of the total pension cost relating to foreign schemes includes £280,000 (1986 £250,000) where the charge has been determined in accordance with local best practice and regulations in the Federal Republic of Germany.

A provision of £5,500,000 (1986 £5,000,000) is included in creditors, this being the excess of the accumulated pension cost over the amount funded. The major part of this relates to the unfunded German scheme.

As with Example 22.1 above, which dealt with defined contribution schemes, all of the disclosures have been combined in a single note. However, it will be equally acceptable, and probably more common, to spread a number of the disclosures around in the relevant parts of the financial statements.

3   PROBLEM AREAS

3.1   Actuarial methods

3.1.1   *Background to actuarial methods*

Actuarial methods have been developed not with the primary purpose of generating figures for the measurement of pension cost for accounting purposes, but with a view to valuing the fund and determining appropriate contribution rates. The focus of funding recommendations is to ensure that assets are set aside in a prudent and orderly way so as to meet the obligations of the scheme when they become due for payment; it is to do with cash flows, not with profit measurement.

Nevertheless, although the methods have been developed for funding purposes, they can provide a good basis for attributing cost to the years in which the employees render their services to the employer company. The difficulty is that, even if the actual amount of pensions which would eventually be paid to existing employees were known with precision, there is no particular method of attributing the cost of that pension to individual years of employment which is unarguably the best way of applying the matching concept. Different actuarial methods would approach this task in different ways.

To explain how different methods would attribute cost in a different way it is helpful to draw the distinction between the two main families of methods used by actuaries — 'accrued benefits methods' and 'projected benefits methods' (or 'level contribution methods' as they are sometimes called). These terms are defined in the standard as shown in 2.3 above, but the essential difference between the two can be explained, slightly simplistically, as follows: the accrued benefits approach seeks to build up the cost of providing the pension by putting a value directly on each incremental year's service so that it builds up towards the final liability which will arise on retirement; the projected benefits approach looks directly at the expected eventual liability and seeks to provide for it evenly over the whole period of service. The first method will tend to show a rising trend of cost over the employee's working life, while the second will tend to show a flatter charge. The methods, and some of their different versions, are described more fully in 3.1.3 and 3.1.4 below.

There are different possible accounting arguments as to why either of these might be a more desirable way of matching cost and benefits. For example, the accrued benefits method could be portrayed as an approach which tries more precisely to measure the cost of the pension which has accrued in any specific year, and therefore is a more faithful application of the matching concept than the projected benefits method, which seems to adopt more of a 'smoothing' approach. Conversely, it may be argued that the benefits from employees' services accrue over their whole working lives and that the total cost of their pensions should be spread evenly over these lives, as is achieved by the projected benefits approach, rather than weighting it towards the later years of their employment, as happens under the accrued benefits approach. A variety of further arguments could be summoned to support either side of the debate; but suffice it to say that there is no unanswerable point which seems to make either method conclusively the best.

The distinctions between the methods are in practice blurred when one moves from considering the cost of the pension of an individual employee to looking at the cost of a scheme comprising many employees, with a range of ages. For mature schemes where the age profile of the scheme remains steady through time, there will be comparatively little difference between the total cost calculated under either approach.

3.1.2   The approach taken by the standard

As has been explained already in this chapter, SSAP 24 does not prescribe a particular valuation method, and leaves it to the employer, with the benefit of actuarial advice, to ensure that the method chosen can fulfil the accounting objective set out in the standard, that cost should be recognised on a systematic and rational basis over the working lives of the employees in the scheme. Both of the broad categories of actuarial method described above could generally be said to meet that objective, although some of their variants may not, as discussed in the two sections which follow.

The standard says comparatively little about particular actuarial methods, but discusses them briefly in the following terms: 'In practice, it is common for actuaries to aim at a level contribution rate, as a proportion of pensionable pay in respect of current service. The contribution rate thus determined depends on the particular actuarial method used and the assumptions made regarding new entrants to the scheme. In broad terms, in projecting a stable contribution rate, accrued benefits methods rely on the assumption that the flow of new entrants will be such as to preserve the existing average age of the workforce; prospective benefits methods, on the other hand, normally look only to the existing workforce and seek a contribution rate that will remain stable for that group despite its increasing age profile until the last member retires or leaves. In a mature scheme both types of method may in practice achieve stable contribution rates, but the size of the fund under a prospective benefits method will tend to be larger than under an accrued benefits method because it is intended to cover the ageing of the existing work-force'.[31]

3.1.3   Possible actuarial methods — accrued benefit methods

As mentioned above, the accrued benefit approach focuses directly on the incremental liability which builds up year by year as pensionable service is recorded by the employee. It sees each year as giving rise to a further unit of pension entitlement, and values each unit separately to build up the total accrued liability.

Although the emphasis is on what benefits have been earned to date, this does not mean that the method is incapable of looking to the future, and in particular it is not necessarily the case that it does not anticipate future pay rate inflation (which is a vital factor in a final salary scheme). Admittedly some variants of the accrued benefits approach do not take such factors into account, but the most significant version, the projected unit method, is based on estimates of final salary rather than on present rates of pay. (Confusingly, the projected unit method is in the 'accrued benefit' family of valuations, not the 'projected benefit' family.) This method is discussed below.

A   Projected unit method

A description of the main features of this method runs as follows:

'Under the projected unit method, a standard contribution rate expressed as a percentage of earnings is obtained by dividing the present value of all benefits which will accrue in the year following the valuation date (by reference to service in that year and projected final earnings) by the present value of members' earnings in that year. An actuarial liability is calculated by summing the present value of all benefits accrued at the valuation date (based on projected final earnings for members in service). The recommended contribution rate expressed as a percentage of earnings is obtained by modifying the standard contribution rate to reflect the difference between the value placed on the scheme assets for valuation purposes and this actuarial liability.'[32]

A diagrammatic representation of the valuation of the fund using the projected unit method could appear as follows:

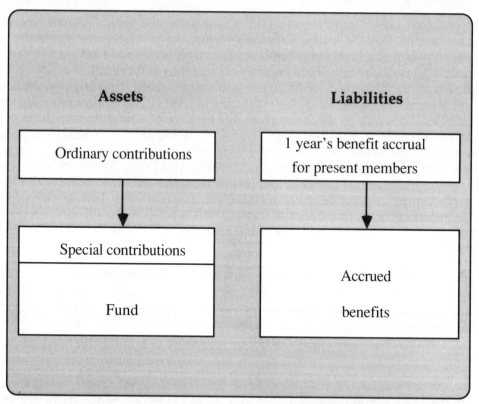

The 'special contributions' shown in the diagram are those that are needed to take account of a deficiency in the fund which may have arisen due to factors such as experience differences or benefit improvements. It is equally possible that a surplus might emerge, so that reduced contributions become an available option. In terms of SSAP 24, therefore, the 'special contributions' shown in the diagram is equivalent to variations, while the amount shown as 'ordinary contributions' represents the regular cost.

This method can result in a stable level of contributions provided the age profile of the workforce remains steady. In these circumstances it will generally form a suitable basis for the measurement of cost under SSAP 24. However, its use might have to be more critically considered if the characteristics of the scheme are likely to result in a more volatile contribution rate, and actuarial advice on this point may be necessary.

B   Current unit method

This method is essentially similar to the projected unit method, with the vital distinction that it looks at current, rather than projected pay rates. As a result, the effects of salary inflation have to be picked up in future years in an accelerating pattern, which means that the cost is likely to be heavily skewed towards the later years of employment. For this reason it is doubtful whether such a method could meet the accounting objective of SSAP 24, and we do not recommend its use.

C   Discontinuance method

This method, which is described in SSAP 24 as a 'current funding level' basis, is, as its name suggests, founded on the premise that the scheme is to be wound up immediately and the assets applied to meet the existing entitlements of the members. It therefore does not form an appropriate method for valuing the scheme on a forward-looking, going concern basis. Because of the objectives of the method, contribution rates are not calculated, and for all these reasons the use of a discontinuance approach could not provide an appropriate measure of cost under SSAP 24.

A variant of the discontinuance method, which is sometimes referred to as the 'discontinuance target method', is occasionally used to determine funding rates, and is quite commonly used by insurance companies. This involves funding for the discontinuance liability which would arise if the scheme were to be wound up at some specified time, say 20 years, in the future. The period chosen is referred to as the 'control period' in actuarial parlance. In principle this method would still not follow the accounting objective of SSAP 24, because it does not look through to the final salaries on which the pensions are expected to be paid. However, the greater the length of the control period, the nearer the method will become to one which is acceptable under the standard. Where the method is used, it will be necessary to obtain actuarial advice on whether it produces results which are materially different from one which is based on projected final salaries.

3.1.4   Possible actuarial methods — projected benefit methods

As discussed previously, these methods try to look at the eventual amount of pensions which are expected to be paid, and establish contribution rates which are designed to remain stable over the period of the employees' service. Usually, this means that they are designed to represent a level percentage of payroll costs, not a level figure in pounds, although the latter is also theoretically possible (although not an appropriate method for SSAP 24 purposes).

A   Aggregate method

The actuaries' description of this method reads as follows:

'Under the aggregate method, a recommended contribution rate expressed as a percentage of earnings is obtained by dividing the excess of the present value of all benefits which have accrued and will accrue (based on total service and projected final earnings for members in service) over the value placed on the scheme assets for valuation purposes by the present value of total projected earnings for all members throughout their expected future membership.'[33]

A diagrammatic view of this method would show:

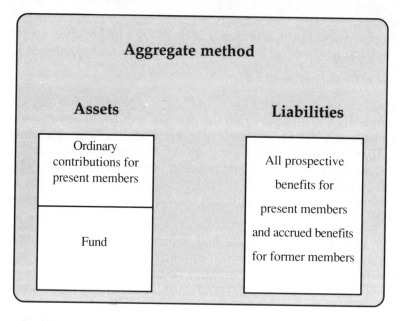

The 'Ordinary contributions' box represents the balancing figure in the valuation, and the method does not in fact identify either the surplus or deficit on the fund or the element of contributions which relates to variations from regular cost. This method of valuation is regarded by some as rather a simplistic one, and while it has been quite extensively used in the past in the UK, it is now much less common.

B   Attained age method

This method is described by the actuaries thus:

'Under the attained age method, a standard contribution rate expressed as a percentage of earnings is obtained by dividing the present value of all benefits which will accrue to present members after the valuation date (by reference to service after the valuation date and projected final earnings) by the present value of total projected earnings for all members throughout their expected future membership. An actuarial liability is calculated by summing the present value of all benefits accrued at the valuation date (based on projected final earnings for members in service). The recommended contribution rate expressed as a percentage of earnings is obtained by modifying the standard contribution rate to reflect the difference between the value placed on the scheme assets for valuation purposes and the accrued actuarial liability.'[34]

On a diagram, a valuation under this method looks like this:

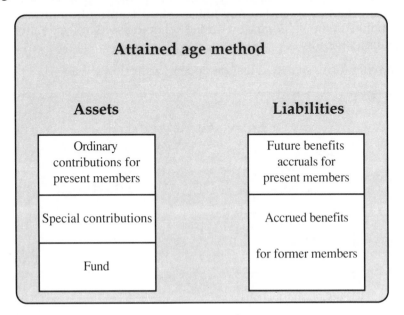

In concept, this is not dissimilar to the aggregate method, and if the 'special contributions' are paid as well as the ordinary contributions they will produce the same total contribution as under that method. The main difference is that the liabilities are split between those benefits which have already accrued and those which are projected to accrue in the future for existing members. By splitting it in this way, the amount of 'special contributions' can be identified which represents the amount needed to redress the deficit between the value of the fund and the accrued benefits. Again, this could be a negative figure if the scheme were in surplus.

For SSAP 24 purposes, the 'ordinary contributions' shown in the diagram again equate to regular cost, and the 'special contributions' to variations from that regular cost.

C   *Entry age method*

This method is comparatively rare in the UK, but has been more commonly used in North America. It is described as follows:

'Under the entry age method, a normal entry age is chosen which may be estimated from the actual membership records. A standard contribution rate expressed as a percentage of earnings is obtained by dividing the present value of all future benefits by reference to projected final earnings for a member entering at the normal entry age by the present value of total projected earnings throughout his expected future membership. An actuarial liability is calculated by deducting from the present value of total benefits (based on projected final earnings for members in service) the value of the standard contribution rate multiplied by the present value of total projected earnings for all members throughout their expected future membership. The recommended contribution rate expressed as a percentage of earnings is obtained by modifying the standard contribution rate to reflect the difference between the value placed on the scheme assets for valuation purposes and this actuarial liability.'[35]

In diagrammatic form, such a valuation appears as follows:

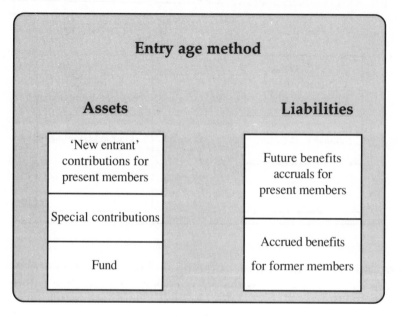

In this case the calculation of the liabilities is the same, but the amount of 'special contributions', which is the balancing figure (and could again be negative), is determined after calculating the ordinary contributions in a different way; rather than basing it on the actual contributions to be made by the existing members, it is calculated on the basis that existing members are at the age of the typical new entrant to the scheme. This creates a difficulty in theory at least, because the 'new entrant' contributions are calculated in such a way that they do not distinguish between past and future service (from the point of view of a new entrant, all service is future service). Accordingly, it might be argued that the split shown in the diagram does not follow the SSAP 24 approach that variations should deal with the past service elements of cost and the regular cost should deal with the ongoing cost related to future service. However, we expect that in practice such a split will be applied and will be regarded as acceptable.

3.1.5 *Actuarial valuation of assets*

Under any of the above methods chosen for valuing the accrued benefits of the fund, the actuary will also have put a value on the fund's investments. Practice in this area differs, but generally the investments will not be valued directly at their quoted market prices on the relevant day but rather at a value which takes a longer term perspective. A common method will be to value the investments on the basis of their projected dividend income.

When this approach is applied, it provides an effective cushion against short-term fluctuations in the securities markets. Thus, the market crash which occurred in October 1987 will not have had the devastating effect on the valuation of pension funds which might have been expected if the valuation were based directly on market values.

3.1.6 *Conclusion*

As discussed at 3.1.2 above, the standard does not specify that a particular actuarial valuation method be used, so long as the effect is to allocate the cost rationally and systematically over the period of the employee's services, and this means that the method must base its calculations on the final salaries which are expected to be paid. It would seem therefore that the only methods which have been discussed above which could *not* achieve that are those which do not try to take into account the value of the pension which will be paid on the basis of final salary — the current unit method and the discontinuance basis. As noted above, there may also be a difficulty, where the entry age method is used, in obtaining a sensible split between regular cost and variations.

For mature schemes, the remaining valuation methods seem likely in practice to produce broadly similar costs for recognition in the profit and loss account, and on that basis they are likely to be equally acceptable. In fact it is often the case that the effect of using different methods is much less significant than the effect of varying the amounts of the key actuarial assumptions. However, for schemes which are likely not to remain stable in terms of their age profile, companies should discuss the circumstances in more detail with their actuaries and we recommend that they should base their choice of method on that which can be predicted to show greatest stability of pension cost as a percentage of pensionable payroll in the future.

3.2 Actuarial assumptions and best estimates

The standard requires that the actuarial assumptions and method, taken as a whole, should be compatible and should lead to the actuary's best estimate of the cost of providing the pension benefits promised.[36] Frequently, the assumptions made by the actuary for funding purposes cannot be described as 'best estimates', because, for example, the company has consciously decided to fund the scheme strongly and has therefore deliberately asked that assumptions be made on a conservative basis. While this is entirely legitimate as the basis of funding decisions, it is necessary to reconsider the assumptions when they are to be used to measure cost for accounting purposes; if necessary it may lead to the use of two different sets of assumptions, one for accounting purposes and the other for the purposes of funding.

It is quite difficult to talk about 'best estimates' in the context of actuarial assumptions, because the matters which are the subject of estimation can be extremely uncertain and a wide range of possible estimates could be made. Nevertheless it is appropriate that, so far as possible, the choice is made sensibly around the middle of the possible range rather than at the extreme.

The standard talks about the assumptions 'taken as a whole': because of the way in which the various factors interrelate, it is possible to arrive at a similar overall result by flexing individual estimates in opposite directions so as to compensate for an optimistic estimate in one area by making a conservative assumption in another. In this way, it is also mathematically possible to make implicit allowance for factors which on the face of it are not provided for, such as increases in pensions.

In our view it is preferable that implicit offsetting allowances of this nature are not made, and that each assumption in isolation should seek to reflect a realistic view of what will happen in the future. We take this view partly because it makes the valuation process more explicit to those within the company who are involved in it, but also because the standard requires the key assumptions to be disclosed in the financial statements, and unless they are meaningful on a stand-alone basis, the reader of the financial statements may be misled as to the strength of the valuation on which the figures are based.

3.3   Variations from regular cost

3.3.1   Calculation of remaining service lives

The standard says that variations should normally be spread over the remaining service lives of employees currently in the scheme after making suitable allowances for future withdrawals, and that it is possible to apply this principle by using an average period relevant to the current membership if desired.[37] This issue is discussed at 2.5.2 B above. Where the average approach is taken, this will be determined by the actuary on the basis of the age profile of the workforce and the assumptions made about mortality, retirements and withdrawals. The period is usually likely to be shorter than might intuitively be assumed, and a range of 10 to 15 years might be typical.

3.3.2   What is a significant reduction in employees?

As discussed at 2.5.2 D above, one of the compulsory exceptions from the normal 'spreading' rule for variations is when there has been a significant reduction in the number of employees in the scheme. However although this exception is expressed as being mandatory, it only becomes so once it has been determined that the reduction of employees should be regarded as significant, and this term is not further defined.

In one sense the term could be thought of as meaning 'significant enough to make a measurable impact on the actuary's recommendations on funding rates', since the exception requires the accounting to follow whatever change in contributions results from the fall in the number of employees; if there is no measurable impact then clearly the provisions of this exception cannot be applied. In any event, we believe that the exception was intended to be applied relatively rarely, and should be used only where there has been a major scaling down of operations, rather than for every minor trimming exercise.

It should, however, be noted that the reduction need not result from one single closure — it could be the result of a series of redundancies over the period since the last valuation of the fund. Where it does relate to a single closure, and that event has been treated as giving rise to an extraordinary item, the treatment will again be different, as described in 2.5.2 C above.

3.3.3 *Allocation of experience differences to funding consequences*

Any surplus or deficit thrown up by an actuarial valuation will result from a number of different causes, and it will be necessary to ask the actuary to provide an analysis in order to allow the appropriate accounting to be applied. Since there are exceptions to the normal 'spreading' rule for variations, some choices may emerge, depending on how the individual experience differences are linked with the funding consequences. An example will illustrate this.

Example 22.8: Allocation of experience differences to funding consequences

As a result of an actuarial valuation, a surplus of £5m has been identified. The actuary reports that this is mainly due to experience differences concerning investment performance of the fund, but that £1.2m of the surplus resulted from the withdrawal of a significant proportion of the workforce in the course of a redundancy programme over the last two years. The company decides that it will reduce the surplus both by suspending contributions to the fund for the next two years and also by taking a refund from the scheme of £1m, which, in terms of the Finance Act 1986, will be subject to tax at 40%.

The standard permits taxed refunds to be taken to profit and loss account when received, regardless of the reason for the surplus arising. It also requires variations resulting from significant reductions in the number of employees to be accounted for in line with their effect on the funding of the scheme. Accordingly the company would appear to have the following options open to it:

(a)   to notionally link the refund to the reduction in the number of the employees rather than to the other experience differences. The effect of this would make it compulsory, rather than optional, to credit the refund to the profit and loss account immediately. That part of the contribution holiday which could be attributed to the remaining £0.2m surplus could also be recognised as affecting income in the year or years in which the holiday is taken. (There would appear to be a further choice between spreading it over the two years in which contributions were to be suspended and attributing it wholly to one or other of the years, although the latter would seem somewhat artificial.)

(b)   to notionally link the refund to the other experience differences rather than to the reduction in the number of the employees. The effect of this would be to leave the company with the option of recognising the refund in the profit and loss account immediately, but also to require it to give full recognition to the effects of the reduction in the workforce in the year or years of the related contribution holiday. The combined effect of this notional allocation would allow the company to report higher profits in the short-term than if the alternative allocation under (a) had been chosen.

No guidance can be offered on how to choose between these different approaches; either would be acceptable. This illustrates some of the anomalies which can arise because the various exceptions to the basic rule for spreading variations forward lack an adequate conceptual thread.

3.3.4 *How to account for the unamortised difference remaining in the year of the next actuarial valuation*

As mentioned at the end of 2.5.2 B above, no guidance has been given on how to account for the remaining part of previously identified variations, when a subsequent valuation is made and reveals fresh variations. Consider the situation, using the figures from Example 22.3, where a further actuarial valuation is conducted at 31 December 1987, and reveals a different surplus.

Example 22.9:Effect on unrecognised variations of subsequent valuations

The previous actuarial valuation at 31 December 1984 of the pension scheme of company B showed a surplus of £260m. The actuary recommended that B eliminate the surplus by taking a contribution holiday in 1985 and 1986 and then paying contributions of £30m p.a. for 8 years. After that the standard contribution would be £50m p.a.. The average remaining service life of employees in the scheme at 31 December 1984 was 10 years. As a result of the above, the financial statements for the next three years showed the following:

	Funded £m	Charged £m	Provision £m
1985	—	24	(24)
1986	—	24	(48)
1987	30	24	(42)

The next actuarial valuation at 31 December 1987 showed a surplus of £70m. The actuary this time recommended that B should maintain the contribution rate at £30m p.a. until 1990 and then raise it to £40m in 1991 and to £50m thereafter. The average remaining service life of employees in the scheme at 31 December 1984 was still 10 years The company intends to take account of this valuation in its financial statements for the year to 31 December 1988.

On the face of it, it might appear that there is a further £70m of surplus which will go to reduce the pension cost still further. However, on closer examination it is clear that there has in fact been a deterioration since the 1984 valuation, because a larger surplus would have been predicted based on that valuation. The valuation at that time showed a surplus of £260m, but contributions of only £30m have been made since then, compared with a regular cost requirement of £150m; the combination of these figures would have given rise to a predicted surplus of £140m (260+30-150), yet the surplus is now only £70m, which in fact represents a deterioration of £70m, not an improvement of that amount. There is therefore the equivalent of a new *deficit* of £70m to be accounted for over the future service lives of the employees. (NOTE: For the sake of simplicity, all these figures are presented ignoring the effects of interest and the time value of money. In practice these will form significant elements in the calculation.)

The question that then arises is how to combine the effect of this newly identified variation with the unamortised amount of the previously identified variation. Of the previously identified surplus of £260m, only 3 instalments, totalling £78m have so far been recognised and the remaining £182m is still to be recognised as an adjustment of future pension costs. Either it could be combined with the newly identified variation of £70m, and the net amount of £112m could be written off over 10 years, or the original amortisation period (a further 7 years) could be retained for the original variation, and the new variation written off separately over a new period of 10 years starting from 1988. The effects of these two possibilities are shown below.

Option 1: combining the elements:

	Funded £m	Charged £m	Provision £m
Opening provision			(42.0)
1988	30	38.8	(50.8)
1989	30	38.8	(59.6)
1990	30	38.8	(68.4)
1991	40	38.8	(67.2)
1992	50	38.8	(56.0)
1993	50	38.8	(44.8)
1994	50	38.8	(33.6)
1995	50	38.8	(22.4)
1996	50	38.8	(11.2)
1997	50	38.8	—

(The charge is calculated as the regular cost of £50m less the amortisation of £112m over 10 years (£11.2m).)

Option 2: keeping the elements separate:

	Funded £m	Charged £m	Provision £m
Opening provision			(42)
1988	30	31	(43)
1989	30	31	(44)
1990	30	31	(45)
1991	40	31	(36)
1992	50	31	(17)
1993	50	31	2
1994	50	31	21
1995	50	57	14
1996	50	57	7
1997	50	57	—

(The charge is calculated as the regular cost of £50m less the amortisation of £182m over seven years (£26m) plus the amortisation of £70m over ten years (£7m).)

In our opinion, option 1 is preferable as it is more in line with the general philosophy of the standard that the effects of variations should be smoothed forward on a rolling basis. However, option 2 is probably an acceptable method. Option 1 has the additional merit that it requires fewer detailed records and calculations; indeed the amount to be amortised can be identified directly following each valuation because it is the amount of the difference between the actuarial surplus or deficiency in the fund and whatever figure is in the employer's balance sheet; in the above case (£70m - (-£42m)) = £112m.

3.4   Hybrid schemes

Although the standard lays down separate rules for defined contribution schemes and defined benefit schemes, in some cases the scheme will not fall so neatly into one or other of these classifications. There is a growing practice within pension schemes of offering elements of both kinds of arrangement; for example, a final pay scheme may give its members the option to take benefits based on an alternative money purchase-based formula, to allow them to participate to some extent in the investment performance of the fund if it proves successful. It will therefore be necessary to decide how to account for such arrangements.

The standard acknowledges that this difficulty exists. Although no easy solution can be offered, the only possible response is to try to identify the true underlying nature of the scheme as accurately as possible. Is it in essence a final pay scheme, but with some money purchase features as a theoretical extra? Alternatively, is it principally a money purchase scheme, but with some benefits linked to final pay to provide a safety net against bad fund performance? Only by assessing the basis under which benefits are likely to be paid in practice will it be possible to determine to which category the scheme can be regarded as belonging in substance. It will also be necessary to re-evaluate this regularly, since changes in economic conditions (such as inflation rates) could alter the probability that benefits will be payable on one basis rather than another. In most cases, this evaluation should be conducted with the benefit of advice from the actuary, who will advise on the most appropriate accounting treatment to be adopted.

Since the distinction between the two accounting treatments depends on whether or not the employer's obligation is limited to the contributions payable, the amount of these contributions will generally represent the minimum measure of the pension cost to be charged, and it will be necessary to consider whether the existence of the defined benefit formula means that additional costs have to be provided for in addition to these contributions. It will also be necessary to disclose a more comprehensive description of the scheme than usual, in order to allow the reader of the financial statements to appreciate the nature of the obligations to which the employer is committed.

3.5   Foreign schemes

A group which operates in a number of foreign countries may well have a number of local pension schemes, in some cases imposed by legal requirements of the host country, which are of quite a different nature from that of the parent company. In principle all the rules of the standard still apply, and the group financial statements should contain consolidated information on these schemes which has been prepared using consistent policies and methods. However in certain cases this may prove impracticable, and it would be unrealistic to expect quite disparate arrangements to be treated in a uniform way.

The standard acknowledges this difficulty, and broadly says that while the measurement rules should be applied so far as possible, in certain instances it will be necessary simply to take the cost as determined for local purposes as the basis of the charge. Whether or not this provides an acceptable answer will obviously also depend on the materiality of the amounts involved. Where it is not possible to apply the rules of the standard completely, it will be necessary to explain the circumstances involved, stating the amount of the charge which is affected by this difficulty, and the basis on which it has been determined.[38]

3.6 Unfunded schemes

Unfunded schemes are relatively uncommon among private sector companies in the UK, although they do exist; they may also arise in respect of foreign subsidiaries which are dealt with in the consolidated financial statements of a UK parent. The standard says relatively little about them, but the same basic accounting rules apply. In essence, an unfunded scheme can be looked upon as equivalent to a funded scheme under which no contributions have yet been paid and which accordingly has no assets.

One issue which is of particular relevance to unfunded schemes is the need to recognise interest in the measurement of the cost of providing the pension. The provision which is set up in the balance sheet will be assessed on a discounted basis. This means that the amount to be added to the provision in each year can be looked upon as falling into two components; an interest charge on the unfunded liability (or amortisation of the discount) together with a charge for the year which would be equivalent to the contribution which would be made if the scheme were funded.

The question which then arises is whether that interest element is a finance charge or a component of pension cost. Although either treatment would be acceptable, it is arguable that it is more appropriate to treat it as a finance charge. This can be regarded as the finance cost which would have been incurred if the company had instead made funding payments to a scheme; the fact that it has not done so does not directly increase the cost of providing the pension itself. However there are also cogent arguments for treating it as part of the pension cost, and this is the treatment which is applied under the American accounting standard.[39]

3.7 Should interest be charged on balance sheet amounts?

Where an asset or liability emerges in the balance sheet because the cost charged in the profit and loss account is not the same as the funding payments made, it is a matter for consideration whether or not notional interest should be added to this amount thereafter. The standard touches on this issue in paragraph 40, but leaves it unresolved, since the question of discounting is not unique to pensions but requires to be answered more generally for many different accounting issues.

In principle, we believe that it would be right to attribute interest to this balance. Where it is a liability (because contributions have not kept up with cost recognition) it is in effect equivalent to the unfunded portion of the scheme and the principles which apply to unfunded schemes as discussed above therefore apply. Corresponding principles should be applied to the converse situation, where there is an asset recorded in the financial statements. However, as SSAP 24 notes, the amount of the asset or liability will frequently be small and its existence transitory, so on materiality grounds this aspect may usually be ignored.

3.8 Transitional provisions

3.8.1 Prior year adjustment or spread over remaining service lives

The standard offers a choice between two methods of implementing it in the year of adoption. Companies may look upon the actuarial surplus or deficiency in the scheme as equivalent to an experience surplus or deficiency which gives rise to a variation from regular pension cost, and accordingly spread it forward over the working lives of the members in the scheme. Alternatively they may incorporate the surplus or deficiency in the balance sheet by means of a prior year adjustment, as a pension prepayment or accrual, which means that the pension charge until the next valuation of the scheme will be solely the regular cost. Where the company has a surplus in its fund, it may therefore apply it either to subsidise its future earnings, by reducing the future pension costs to be charged, or to increase its assets and reserves immediately, which may be more attractive, say, for those companies whose borrowing powers are restricted by ratios based on these factors. The choice is illustrated by the following example, which uses the same figures as are used in Example 22.3.

Example 22.10:   *Illustration of transitional provisions*

A company is implementing SSAP 24 for the first time in their financial year to 31 December 1989. The most recent available actuarial valuation of the pension scheme, at 31 December 1986, showed a surplus of £260m. The actuary had recommended at that time that they eliminate the surplus by taking a contribution holiday in 1987 and 1988 and then paying contributions of £30m p.a. for 8 years. After that the standard contribution would be £50m p.a.. The average remaining service life of employees in the scheme at 31 December 1986 was 10 years.

It can be inferred from the above that the effect of the contribution holiday in the two years since the date of the valuation has been to reduce the surplus at the beginning of 1989 to £160m, on the assumption that no other changes have occurred. (This is based on the premise that the regular cost of £50m p.a. has depleted the surplus by £100m; as with previous examples, the effect of interest and the time value of money has been ignored for simplicity.)

The company may elect to apply the standard either (a) by treating it as equivalent to an experience surplus, to be amortised over the remaining service lives of the employees or (b) by incorporating the assumed £160m surplus as a pension prepayment in the balance sheet. The effect of each of these treatments is shown below.

The funding in these periods will be:

1989-96	£30m p.a.
1997-98	£50m p.a.

	Funded	Option (a)		Option (b)	
		Charged	Provision	Charged	Prepayment
	£m	£m	£m	£m	£m
Opening balance					160
1989	30	34	(4)	50	140
1990	30	34	(8)	50	120
1991	30	34	(12)	50	100
1992	30	34	(16)	50	80
1993	30	34	(20)	50	60
1994	30	34	(24)	50	40
1995	30	34	(28)	50	20
1996	30	34	(32)	50	—
1997	50	34	(16)	50	—
1998	50	34	—	50	—

$$\text{Regular cost} - \frac{\text{surplus}}{\text{average remaining service life}} = £50m - \frac{£160m}{10} = £34m$$

Arguably option (b) gives a cleaner start, in the sense that it produces a sensible charge against profits from the outset, but the standard expresses no preference, and management have a free choice between the methods. However, where companies have more than one scheme, we believe that they should be consistent in their choice of implementation method.

3.8.2 Restrictions on the choice of transitional method

The standard appears to limit the choice of transitional method in certain circumstances. In the explanatory section, it says that 'to the extent that the adjustment (i.e. the surplus or deficit) relates to a variation from regular cost that, in accordance with the provisions of paragraphs 81 and 82, would not be eligible to be spread over the remaining service lives it should be accounted for as a prior year item'.[40] These paragraphs deal with the exceptions to the normal treatment of variations which are discussed at 2.5.2 C and F above. Effectively this means, say, that if a surplus exists at the date of implementation and can be attributed to a significant reduction in the number of members of the scheme, it must be set up in the balance sheet as a prepayment, rather than spread forward as a quasi-variation from regular cost. This is illustrated in the following example:

Example 22.11: Transitional provisions where a significant reduction in employees has occurred

The circumstances are identical to that shown in Example 22.10 above, except that the actuary reported at the time of making the most recent valuation that £120m of the £260m surplus could be attributed to the fact that a significant number of members had left the scheme as a result of a major redundancy programme. The next question to be addressed in this particular example is whether the contribution holiday in the intervening two years should be linked to that part of the surplus, to the remaining surplus of £140m, or to be apportioned between the two. In our view this question can only be answered arbitrarily, so any of these options would be acceptable.

If the pension holiday were linked to the £140m surplus which had arisen for reasons other than the redundancy programme, £40m of that surplus would still remain at the time of the implementation of the standard, together with the whole £120m relating to the reduction in employees. The effect of applying the accounting options described in Example 22.10 which would then be available would be as follows:

		Option (a)		Option (b)	
	Funded £m	Charged £m	Prepayment (Provision) £m	Charged £m	Prepayment £m
Opening balance			120		160
1989	30	46	104	50	140
1990	30	46	88	50	120
1991	30	46	72	50	100
1992	30	46	56	50	80
1993	30	46	40	50	60
1994	30	46	24	50	40
1995	30	46	8	50	20
1996	30	46	(8)	50	—
1997	50	46	(4)	50	—
1998	50	46	—	50	—

(The amount charged under option (a) is the normal cost adjusted by the amortisation of the £40m surplus which does not relate to the redundancy programme.)

Alternatively, if the contribution holiday were attributed to the effects of the redundancy, so that only £20m of the remaining surplus were regarded as attributable to that cause, the options would become:

		Option (a)		Option (b)	
	Funded £m	Charged £m	Prepayment (Provision) £m	Charged £m	Prepayment £m
Opening balance			20		160
1989	30	36	14	50	140
1990	30	36	8	50	120
1991	30	36	2	50	100
1992	30	36	(4)	50	80
1993	30	36	(10)	50	60
1994	30	36	(16)	50	40
1995	30	36	(22)	50	20
1996	30	36	(28)	50	—
1997	50	36	(14)	50	—
1998	50	36	—	50	—

(The amount charged under option (a) is the normal cost adjusted by the amortisation of the £140m surplus which does not relate to the redundancy programme.)

It is not clear how far back to go in evaluating the reasons for a surplus or deficiency at the time of implementing the standard. If there had been a major redundancy programme five or even ten years before the date of implementation, some of its effects could still be regarded as inherent in an actuarial surplus at the implementation date. In principle we see no reason why an upper limit on this time period should be imposed, but in practice we expect that companies will generally look only at events close to the date of the most recent valuation, and we believe that this will be an acceptable approach.

3.8.3   *Comparative figures in the year of implementation*

The standard does not explicitly deal with how the comparative figures in the profit and loss account should be adjusted (if at all) in the year of implementation under either of the transitional options. However, we believe that it is preferable that an adjustment is made, so that the charge for the current and the previous year is calculated on a comparable basis using the same accounting policy. If this is not done, the company's earnings trend will be liable to distortion, particularly if a contribution holiday was being taken in the previous year so that under the old policy there was no charge to the profit and loss account for pension costs at all. This would have been the case in Example 22.10 above, where a charge of either £34m or £50m in the current year would have been compared with a charge of nil in the previous year.

We suggest that the most sensible approach is to calculate the figures as if the standard were being implemented at the beginning of the comparative year, even if they were not used as the basis of reporting in that year. This will be a relatively straightforward option on the assumption that the actuarial valuation being used is as of a date at or before the beginning of that year, and that the figures for the comparative year can thus be calculated with equal facility to those for the current year. However, if this is not the case, or if there have been significant events since the time of the last valuation which have affected its validity, it will be necessary to consult the actuary to see how a comparable charge for the previous year should be determined.

The calculation of the comparative figure is shown below, again using the figures of Example 22.10:

Example 22.12:   Calculation of comparative figure for first year of implementation

If option (a) is selected (treating the surplus as equivalent to an experience difference, to be amortised over the remaining service lives of the employees), one approach would be simply to start the amortisation at the beginning of the comparative year, effectively shifting the whole of the amortisation period back one year. This would produce the following result:

	Funded £m	Charged £m	Provision £m
1988	—	29	(29)
1989	30	29	(28)
1990	30	29	(27)
1991	30	29	(26)
1992	30	29	(25)
1993	30	29	(24)
1994	30	29	(23)
1995	30	29	(22)
1996	30	29	(21)
1997	50	29	—
1998	50	50	—

As can be seen, this approach produces a different charge from the £34m charged as shown in Example 22.10, because at the beginning of 1988 there is a bigger implicit surplus in the scheme (£210m) to be amortised. In addition, it results in the creation of a balance at the beginning of the year of implementation, which would be incorporated by a prior year adjustment, and this might be thought contrary to the general approach of the standard that the effects of implementing the standard should be recognised prospectively.

An alternative approach, which does not suffer from these defects, would be simply to take the charge for the current year and incorporate it in the profit and loss account of the comparative year, with an equal and opposite adjustment to the opening reserves of that year. However, it would be appropriate to discuss this with the actuary to ensure that the charge for the current year could be regarded as a suitable approximation to that which would have been reported in the previous year under the new policy. This approach would produce the following result:

	Funded £m	Charged £m	Prepayment (Provision) £m
Opening balance			34
1988	—	34	—
1989	30	34	(4)
1990	30	34	(8)
1991	30	34	(12)
1992	30	34	(16)
1993	30	34	(20)
1994	30	34	(24)
1995	30	34	(28)
1996	30	34	(32)
1997	50	34	(16)
1998	50	34	—

We would regard either of these methods as acceptable under the standard.

If option (b) is selected (incorporating the assumed £160m surplus as a pension prepayment in the balance sheet), the treatment is more straightforward; the company would make the prior year adjustment so as to adjust the comparative year as well, with a corresponding effect on the opening balance of the comparative year. The effect would be:

	Funded £m	Charged £m	Prepayment £m
Opening balance			210
1988	—	50	160
1989	30	50	140
1990	30	50	120
1991	30	50	100
1992	30	50	80
1993	30	50	60
1994	30	50	40
1995	30	50	20
1996	30	50	—
1997	50	50	—
1998	50	50	—

Ideally, similar retrospective adjustments would be made to any published table of five or ten-year trading results, but in practice this will almost always be impossible. Where the effect is material, it will be appropriate to indicate in such tables that the earlier years have not been put on to a consistent basis.

3.8.4 *Whether to use a special valuation on implementation*

The standard offers a further choice on implementation; whether to use the last available actuarial valuation (provided it is on a basis consistent with the requirements of the standard) or to commission a special one for the purposes of the implementation.

There are a number of reasons why obtaining a special valuation might be regarded as desirable. The last available one may be significantly out of date, particularly if there have been significant changes which would affect the valuation. However, even an updated valuation is likely to be as of a date which is some time (probably a year) before the date of the financial statements. The standard says that when the last available valuation is the one used, account should be taken of subsequent changes in contributions made in consequence of it and other major changes affecting the scheme. (This was illustrated in Example 22.10).

Another reason for commissioning a new valuation is that it may be decided to change the method or assumptions used to produce a result more compatible with the accounting objective. This will be particularly true where the valuation used in the past has deliberately been based on conservative assumptions in order to achieve a strongly funded scheme.

4 RELATED COMPANIES ACT REQUIREMENTS

4.1 Pension commitments

The Companies Act requires that particulars should be disclosed of:

(a) any pension commitments included under any provision shown in the company's balance sheet; and

(b) any such commitments for which no such provision has been made.[41]

The requirement goes on to say that separate disclosure should be given to any part of these commitments which relate to pensions payable to former directors of the company. There is also a requirement to disclose commitments undertaken for the benefit of other group companies.[42]

The Act offers no further interpretation of what constitutes a pension commitment for the purposes of this disclosure requirement. It would be possible to interpret it very broadly, so that disclosure of the commitment would require a full description of the obligation which the company had accepted in making pension promises to its employees; this would involve giving details of the terms of the pension scheme, together with a description of the arrangements which had been made to meet that obligation. This broad interpretation is supported by ED 32, which proposed quite extensive disclosure requirements described at 1.3 above, and went on to say that 'the disclosures required by this proposed standard have been framed having regard to the requirements in company legislation for the disclosure of pension information. Compliance with these proposals, however, will not necessarily ensure compliance with these legal requirements which must be considered in the light of each company's individual pension arrangements.'[43]

In practice, however, the general interpretation of the requirement has been much narrower. Many companies appear to have taken the view that as long as the pension scheme is adequately funded, there is no further commitment on the part of the company itself which has to be disclosed. Companies generally confine their disclosure to a relatively brief description of the pension arrangements in force and the fact that the funds were fully funded, as illustrated in the following extracts.

Extract 22.1: Storehouse PLC[44]

Note 19   Commitments (extract)

The group operates defined benefit pension schemes for its UK employees, the funds of which are administered by trustees or independent insurance companies and are fully funded based on recent actuarial valuations. Actuarial valuations on an on-going basis are prepared every three years and contributions are made in accordance with the actuaries' recommendations. The cost of these contributions is charged against the profits of the year in which they are made. The amount charged to the profit and loss account in respect of these pension arrangements is shown in note 2. The reduction in the pension cost reflects the benefit of reduced contributions as a result of actuarial surpluses arising on certain schemes.

(Note 2 shows that pension cost has fallen from £4.5 million in the previous year to £3 million.)

Extract 22.2 Norcros P.L.C.[45]

Note 23   Pension commitments
The Group has a number of pension funds for its employees, the largest of which was last revalued at 31st March 1986, by Clay & Partners, the fund's actuaries. They indicated that there were sufficient assets in the fund to secure the benefits of existing pensioners and to provide paid up pensions to employees in accordance with the rules of the fund.

Occasionally, however, there are details of unprovided liabilities to be disclosed:

Extract 22.3: Pilkington plc[46]

Note 23 Commitments and contingent liabilities (extract)

The Group has a commitment, amounting to £3.4 million (1987 £4.5 million) not provided for in the financial statements, to make up the pension payments of certain employees who have retired early. A subsidiary company has a commitment not provided for in the financial statements, to provide certain benefits to its retired employees. The cost in the year of such benefits was £11.3 million.

Following the introduction of SSAP 24, the disclosures given by employer companies will be much more extensive (see 2.4.2 and 2.5.5 above), and we believe that in almost all cases this will ensure compliance with the Companies Act requirement to disclose pension commitments.

4.2 Pension costs

The Act also requires disclosure of pension costs charged in the profit and loss account. This is one of three elements of staff costs which have to be disclosed, the other two being wages and salaries and social security costs.[47] The Act goes on to say that for this purpose pension costs 'includes any other contributions (i.e. other than social security costs) by the company for the purposes of any pension scheme established for the purpose of providing pensions for persons employed by the company, any sums set aside for that purpose and any amounts paid by the company in respect of pensions without being first so set aside.'[48]

Since companies have in the past generally measured their pension cost simply as the amount of contributions paid to the fund, that has generally been the amount disclosed under this heading. However, following the introduction of SSAP 24, the cost charged in the profit and loss account is not dependent on the amount funded; the SSAP 24 measure of cost will now be disclosed under this heading and the definition quoted above is broad enough to accommodate the alternative measurement of cost.

4.3 Directors' emoluments

There are detailed requirements in the Companies Act for the disclosure of directors' emoluments. These include both pensions paid directly by the company to directors and past directors, and contributions made to a pension scheme to secure a pension for a director in the future. These requirements are fully considered in Chapter 24 and not described more fully here; however it is worth noting that it is still required to include the amount of contributions paid to a fund on behalf of a director in the calculation of directors' emoluments, even if this may no longer be the amount charged in the profit and loss account because SSAP 24 requires the cost of a defined benefit scheme to be measured in a different way.

5 COMPARISON WITH US AND IASC PRONOUNCEMENTS

5.1 IASC

5.1.1 IAS 19

In January 1983, the International Accounting Standards Committee issued IAS 19 — *Accounting for Retirement Benefits in the Financial Statements of Employers*. In most respects it is similar in its approach to SSAP 24. The international standard discusses actuarial methods in a little more detail, and specifically says that either an accrued benefit valuation method or a projected benefit valuation method should be used. An Appendix gives examples of individual methods which fall under these classifications.

The treatment of variations under IAS 19 is rather different from that in SSAP 24, in that they may either be charged or credited to income as they arise or alternatively allocated systematically over a period *not exceeding* the expected remaining working lives of the participating employees.

5.1.2   E 32

In January 1989, the IASC issued an exposure draft, E 32, which made certain proposals to amend IAS 19. The most significant change is that it is proposed to make the use of an accrued benefit valuation method the preferable approach, although projected benefit valuation methods would still be permitted. Whichever method is used, an assumption regarding projected salaries must now be incorporated. It is also proposed to require variations to be spread over a period approximating the average remaining working lives of the employees in the scheme.

5.2   US

5.2.1   *Background*

There have been professional pronouncements in the USA dealing with accounting for pension costs for very many years. The subject was dealt with briefly in the compendium Accounting Research Bulletin (ARB) 43 which was issued in 1953 and subsequently in ARB 47 in 1956, but was given much more comprehensive treatment in APB Opinion No. 8 — *Accounting for the Cost of Pension Plans,* issued in November 1966. The FASB first got involved with disclosure issues, publishing SFAS 36 — *Disclosure of Pension Information,* in May 1980, and later dealt with related topics in SFAS 74 — *Accounting for Special Termination Benefits Paid to Employees* — and SFAS 81 — *Disclosure of Postretirement Health Care and Life Insurance Benefits.* (The question of how to account for such post-retirement benefits is now being addressed by the FASB, and is highly controversial, because of both the size of the amounts involved and the difficulty of estimating them in advance.)

The FASB's most recent pronouncements on pension costs have been the two statements published in December 1985, SFAS 87 — *Employers' Accounting for Pensions,* and SFAS 88 — *Employers' Accounting for Settlements and Curtailments of Defined Benefit Pension Plans and for Termination Benefits.* These last two statements have superseded all the earlier pronouncements on the subject.

5.2.2   *SFAS 87*

SFAS 87 requires a particular actuarial approach to be used for measuring cost, and in general prescribes tightly drawn rules as to the computation and disclosure of pension figures in the financial statements. It also breaks down the cost to be charged into six components, and has detailed provisions dealing with how these are to be calculated.

Under the standard, the pension cost to be attributed to a period is that which accrues in respect of the period under the terms of the pension scheme. That is to say, it applies an accrued benefit approach to the allocation of cost to periods (as discussed in 3.1 above). This means that for final salary schemes, the statement requires that the cost be calculated using the projected unit method (as we would call it in the UK — in the USA it would be described as the projected unit *credit* method).

For defined benefit schemes, the cost must be analysed into the following components:

- service cost

- interest cost

- actual return on plan assets, if any

- amortisation of unrecognised prior service cost, if any

- gain or loss (including the effects of changes in assumptions) to the extent recognised

- amortisation of the unrecognised net obligation (and loss or cost) or unrecognised net asset (and gain) existing at the date of initial application of the statement.

Each of these terms is further defined and the required accounting specified.

The standard requires that each of the significant assumptions made in valuing the scheme should be the best estimate, in relation to that individual aspect in isolation. In respect of discount rates, it departs from normal actuarial practice by requiring that these should reflect the rates at which the pension benefits could be effectively settled; this means that a market rate at each valuation date should be used, rather than a long term rate estimated by the actuary.

Among the disclosures which are specified are the analysis of cost under the headings discussed above and a reconciliation of the funded status of the scheme with the amounts which appear in the employer's balance sheet.

Although SSAP 24 follows the same broad approach as SFAS 87 in a number of respects, the American standard is very much more tightly defined; the major difference is the specification of an accrued benefit approach to the measurement of cost, but there are several other differences of detail as well. The more significant ones are as follows:

(a) As mentioned above, SFAS 87 requires settlement rates to be used to discount the pension liability. Under SSAP 24, a long term interest rate would be used which was compatible with the other assumptions made by the actuary in valuing the scheme.

(b) In general, SSAP 24's exceptions to the basic rule on spreading the effects of variations forward would not be permitted under SFAS 87. In particular, accounting for refunds from the scheme in the profit and loss account when the cash is received would not be allowed.

(c) SFAS 87 treats increases in pensions as a past service cost and accordingly amortises its effects over the working lives of the members after the increase is awarded; SSAP 24 encourages expected increases to be provided for in advance by being built into the actuarial assumptions.[49]

5.2.3   SFAS 88

This statement requires immediate recognition of certain previously unrecognised amounts when certain transactions or events occur. It prescribes the method for determining the amount to be recognised in the profit and loss account when a pension obligation is settled (i.e. when the employer takes action to relieve himself of responsibility for a pension obligation), or curtailed (i.e. when defined benefit accruals for the future services of present employees have been eliminated or significantly reduced). There is no direct equivalent of this standard in the UK. However, the circumstances mentioned at 2.5.2 D above, where a significant number of employees leave the scheme, would probably fall within the definition of a curtailment. Under SFAS 88, the effect of this would be recognised immediately, whereas under SSAP 24 it would be dealt with in the periods in which contributions to the scheme were adjusted as a result of the curtailment.

6   CONCLUSION

The introduction of SSAP 24 represents a major stride forward in the presentation of meaningful information about pension costs in the financial statements of UK companies. It takes the subject from a low base, where the measurement of cost could only be described as unsophisticated, to a level where serious attempts must now be made to account for that cost on a systematic basis. Nevertheless, it may not achieve a high measure of standardisation between one company and another, because there is still a considerable amount of flexibility in the standard, in terms of the choice of actuarial method, the setting of actuarial assumptions, and the selection between optional accounting treatments which the standard either explicitly or implicitly allows.

It would, however, be wrong to be over-critical of the standard because of that flexibility. Moreover, although the standard may not achieve complete comparability between one company and another because of the freedom of choice which remains, it will at least achieve a much higher degree of consistency of treatment in the financial statements of any individual company between one year and another, since earnings trends will no longer be distorted by the effects of funding decisions. It is partly for this reason that the standard provides a significant step forward.

In the end, however, the standard is arguably still more of a disclosure standard than a measurement standard, and it is in this light that its main contribution should be recognised. The disclosure requirements are now extensive, and go a long way to compensate for the weaknesses that might follow from any excessive flexibility in the measurement rules; even if a company can still decide to make relatively conservative assumptions in measuring its pension cost, the disclosure requirements will help the reader to identify that that is the case.

The standard is still in its infancy, and it remains to be seen how it will fare in practice, but it is clear that it must provide significantly better information for the users of financial statements than they were accustomed to receiving before SSAP 24 was introduced.

References

1   SSAP 24, *Accounting for Pension Costs*, May 1988.
2   Christopher J. Napier, *Accounting for pension costs — An interim report*, ASC, February 1982.
3   *Ibid.*, para. 23.
4   Christopher J. Napier, *Accounting for the Cost of Pensions*, ICAEW, 1983.
5   ED 32, *The disclosure of pension information in company accounts*, May 1983.
6   *Ibid.*, paragraph 38.
7   *Accounting for pension costs*, ASC, November 1984.
8   ED 39, *Accounting for pension costs*, May 1986.
9   SSAP 24, *Accounting for pension costs*, May 1988.
10 *Ibid.*, para. 16.
11 *Ibid.*, para. 12.
12 *Ibid.*, paras. 56 to 72.
13 *Ibid.*, para. 78.
14 *Ibid.*, para. 87.
15 *Ibid.*, Appendix 1, para. (a).
16 *Ibid.*, para. 20.
17 *Ibid.*, para. 21.
18 *Ibid.*, para. 80.
19 SFAS 87, *Employers' Accounting for Pensions*, FASB, December 1985, Appendix B, Illustration 3.
20 ED 39, Appendix 2, Example 2.
21 SSAP 24, para. 81.
22 *Ibid.*, para. 81.
23 *Ibid.*, para. 83.
24 *Ibid.*, para. 82.
25 *Ibid.*, para. 88.
26 *Ibid.*, para. 48.
27 *Ibid.*, para. 18.
28 *Ibid.*, para. 49.
29 *Ibid.*, para. 92.
30 *Ibid.*, Appendix 1, para. (b)(ii).
31 *Ibid.*, para. 14.
32 Pension Fund Terminology — Specimen descriptions of commonly used valuation methods, The Institute of Actuaries and The Faculty of Actuaries, May 1986.
33 *Ibid.*
34 *Ibid.*
35 *Ibid.*
36 SSAP 24, para. 79.
37 *Ibid.*, para. 23.
38 *Ibid.*, para. 91.
39 SFAS 87, paras. 20 and 22.
40 *Ibid.*, para. 53.
41 CA 85, Sch. 4, para. 50(4).
42 *Ibid.*, para. 50(6).
43 ED 32, para. 40.
44 Storehouse PLC, Annual Report and Accounts 1988, p. 40.
45 Norcros P.L.C., Report and Accounts 1988, p. 41.
46 Pilkington plc, Annual Report for the year ended 31st March 1988, p. 49.
47 CA 85, Sch. 4, para. 56(4).
48 *Ibid.*, para. 94(2).
49 For a more detailed comparison of the UK and the US standards, see, for example, Cook and Ward, *'Countdown to Compatibility'*, Accountancy, September 1988, or Morgan and Arnold,

The New UK Accounting Standard for Pension Costs — SSAP 24 compared with FAS 87 and FAS 88, Benefits & Compensation International, August 1988.

Chapter 23

Directors' and officers' loans and transactions

1 INTRODUCTION

Company directors are treated as fiduciaries[1] and as such must not permit their personal interests and their duty to the company to conflict. In order to avoid such conflicts or potential conflicts arising, transactions between a company and its directors are restricted. Such transactions are regulated in a number of ways, in particular, by means of statutory prohibition, corporate approval and disclosure in the statutory accounts. In this chapter, attention is focused on the Companies Act requirements for disclosure in a company's financial statements of transactions involving directors (except for those relating to directors' remuneration which are dealt with in Chapter 24). The provisions determining the legality or otherwise of such transactions are discussed in outline in the Appendix to this chapter.

1.1 Outline of historical development in the UK

The Companies Act 1948 provided that a public company could not make a loan to any of its directors or directors of its holding company.[2] Loans to directors of exempt private companies (in essence, companies where the number of members was restricted) were permitted.[3] However, it became apparent over the years that directors could circumvent the restrictions on loans by carefully structuring transactions with their company. Thus, a company could make payments in respect of a director's personal expenditure and seek reimbursement from him without contravening the statutory prohibitions. In such cases, the director would be in substantially the same position as if he had been lent funds to pay off his debts. In an effort to close these loopholes, more extensive requirements were enacted by the Companies Act 1980;[4] for example, the types of unlawful transaction were extended to encompass quasi-loans and credit transactions (see respectively 2.7 and 2.8 below). The relevant legislation is now consolidated in the Companies Act 1985.[5]

2 DEFINITIONS

In order to promote a fuller understanding of this chapter, the following definitions have been included:

2.1   Director

This term includes any person occupying the position of director, by whatever name called;[6] i.e., it is a person's role and duties and not his title which determines whether or not he is a director. Thus, for example, a director's appointment may be defective because the procedure prescribed in the company's articles has not been followed; however, if he performs the functions associated with a person in such a position, he will be regarded as a director for the purposes of the legislation. Conversely, a person may be designated a director yet not be regarded as a director for statutory purposes; for example, it is common for companies to recognise senior managers by conferring titles such as divisional director[7] on them. These persons usually only exercise limited managerial power and hence are unlikely to be subject to the restrictions on directors' transactions, although the disclosure requirements relating to officers may be of relevance (see 2.5 and 6 below).

2.2   Shadow director

This is a person in accordance with whose directions or instructions the directors of the company as a whole (i.e. the board as a collective unit) are accustomed to act.[8] However, if the directors' reason for following a person's advice is that it is given in a professional capacity, that person is not regarded as a shadow director.[9] Clearly, a professional adviser might fall to be treated as a shadow director if the advice which he gives to the board is not given in a professional capacity.

A holding company is not deemed to be a shadow director of a subsidiary even though the directors of the subsidiary act as the holding company directs.[10]

2.3   Alternate director

Broadly, an alternate director is a person who is nominated by another director to act in that director's place during his absence from the company.[11] Alternate directors may only be appointed if the company's articles expressly so provide; for example, Table A[12] provides that: 'any director (other than an alternate director) may appoint any other director or any other person approved by resolution of the directors and willing to act, to be an alternate director and may remove from office an alternate director so appointed by him'.

2.4   Connected person

If the restrictions on directors' transactions solely extended to directors, they could easily be circumvented by the company making, say, a loan to the director's spouse or a company controlled by him. The concept of the connected person seeks to close this loophole.

A person is connected with a director if, (not being a director himself), he is:

(a)   that director's spouse, child or step-child (legitimate or otherwise) under the age of 18;[13] or

(b)   a body corporate with which the director is associated.[14]

Broadly speaking, a company is associated with a director if the director and his connected persons are either interested in at least 20% of the company's equity share capital or are entitled to exercise or control more than 20% of the voting power in general meeting.[15]

The director's interest may be direct (i.e. he personally owns the shares or controls the votes) or indirect (i.e. a company that he controls owns the shares or controls the votes). In this latter context, a director will have control of a company (X) if:

(i)   he and his connected persons are interested in X Co.'s equity share capital or are entitled to exercise voting power at X Co.'s annual general meeting (AGM); and

(ii)   he, his connected persons and fellow directors are together interested in more than 50% of X Co.'s share capital or are entitled to exercise more than 50% of the voting power at its AGM.[16]

In order to determine whether or not a company is associated with or controlled by a director, another company with which the director is associated is only deemed to be connected with him if connected by virtue of (c) or (d) below; similarly for these purposes, a trustee of a trust, the beneficiaries of which include another company with which the director is associated, is not thereby deemed to be connected with the director;[17]

(c)   a person acting as trustee of any trust, the beneficiaries of which include the director or his family or a company with which the director is associated.[18] In addition, where the director or his family or an associated company is the object of a discretionary trust, the trustee thereof is also deemed to be a connected person.[19] Trustees of employee share or pension schemes are excluded;[20]

(d)   a partner of the director or any person connected with him by virtue of (a) — (c) above;[21]

(e)   a Scottish firm in which the director or a connected person is a partner, or in which a partner is a Scottish firm in which the director or a connected person is a partner.[22]

These provisions are complex and may be illustrated in the following example:

Example 23.1

Mr. A owns 40% of the equity capital of Company X, and his wife and his daughter, aged 17, each hold 6% of the company's equity capital. Company X holds 12% of the equity capital of Company Y. Mr. A's partner, Mr. B, holds 13% of Company Y's equity capital.

Company X is clearly a connected person of Mr. A; he and members of his family are interested in more than 20% of the company's equity capital.

The position of Company Y is more difficult. In order to determine whether Company Y is connected with Mr. A, Company X's interest in Company Y's equity capital must initially be disregarded.[23] However, Mr. A, by virtue of his family's holdings in Company X, is deemed to control the company (i.e. the total holding of Mr. A and his connected persons is 52% of Company X's equity capital).[24] Company Y therefore, is connected with Mr. A because he is deemed to have an interest in 25% of the company's equity capital (since Mr. B's 13% stake in Company Y is added to Company X's holding of 12%).[25]

2.5   Officer

The statutory definition of officer encompasses directors, managers and company secretaries.[26] This definition is not, however, exhaustive and it would appear that the term extends to any person who exercises a significant degree of managerial power; for example, a financial controller of a company is likely to be an officer, whereas a branch manager of a bank is not.

2.6   Loan

There is no statutory definition of a loan for the purpose of the legislation. However, the term has been judicially defined as 'a sum of money lent for a time, to be returned in money or money's worth'.[27] It is crucial to this definition that the parties to the agreement intend that the amount will be repaid. Recurring problems in this context arise where a director draws remuneration on account or expense advances. Such drawings may constitute a loan depending on the particular circumstances. There is no litmus test which can be applied in determining whether, say, a salary advance is in fact a loan;[28] it is necessary to examine each transaction to decide whether in light of all the facts the director is really receiving an interest free loan. The example below illustrates this problem:

Example 23.2

Mr. A, a director of Company Y, draws an expense advance of £9,000, on January 1, 19X0. By the end of the financial year (December 31, 19X0), the director has only incurred business expenditure of £2,500 and the outstanding sum is then repaid. Ordinary expense advances would not normally fall within the scope of the legislation because such advances are made on the understanding that the director will apply the funds in performance of his duties to the company. However, in these circumstances the funds have remained outstanding for an unusually long period and, prima facie, the advance appears to have taken on the nature of a loan.

2.7   Quasi-loan

This is a transaction under which one party (the creditor) pays a sum on behalf of another (the borrower) or reimburses expenditure incurred by a third party for the borrower, in circumstances:

(a)   where the borrower (or a person on his behalf) will reimburse the creditor; or

(b)   which gives rise to a liability on the borrower to reimburse the creditor.[29]

A quasi-loan will only arise where the borrower is under an obligation to reimburse the expenditure incurred by the company. Quasi-loans commonly arise where a director is permitted to use a company credit card to pay for private and business expenditure and he undertakes to reimburse the company in respect of personal expenses charged to the card. Likewise, if a company pays a director's household bills on the understanding that the expenses will be recouped by making a deduction from his monthly salary, a quasi-loan will arise.

The following example shows the distinction between a loan and a quasi-loan:

Example 23.3

A director of Company X wishes to buy a painting for £2,000 which is coming up for sale, but will not have the money at that time. If he draws a cheque for £2,000 from the company made payable to himself so that he can buy the painting then, assuming he intends to repay this sum, this will constitute a loan as it is 'a sum of money lent for a time, to be returned in money or money's worth'. If, however, he arranges for the company to pay for the painting on his behalf in the meantime, with the intention that he will repay the company at a later date, then this will be a quasi-loan.

2.8 Credit transaction

This is a transaction whereby a person either:

(a) supplies any goods or sells any land under a hire-purchase agreement or a conditional sale agreement; or

(b) leases or hires any land or goods in return for periodical payments; or

(c) otherwise disposes of land or supplies goods or services on the understanding that payment (whatever form it may take) is to be deferred; i.e. repayment need not be made by means of instalment but could be made by means of a single lump sum.[30]

In this context, services are defined as anything other than goods or land.[31]

The examples below indicate two of the many forms which a credit transaction may assume:

Example 23.4

A property company leases a residence to a director in return for monthly rental payments. This constitutes a credit transaction under (b) above, irrespective of whether the rental payments are made in advance or arrears. Consideration should also be given to whether this arrangement gives rise to a benefit-in-kind which requires disclosure (see 2.3.2 of Chapter 24).
If, however, the lease was rent-free then it would not be a credit transaction as there are no periodical payments.
Alternatively, if the company had granted the director a one year lease but he had made a lump sum payment covering the term of the lease at the outset, then again the transaction would not have constituted a credit transaction, as there would have been no periodical payments.

Example 23.5

A director of a company which repairs motor vehicles has his motor car serviced by the company and payment is to be effected by a single deduction from his following month's salary. The company normally requires payment immediately after the work has been done. This constitutes a credit transaction under (c) above, as payment has been deferred.
However, what if the company's normal procedure was to invoice customers for work done and request payment 30 days after the date of invoice, and the date the amount is to be deducted from the director's salary falls before the date the invoice would be due for payment?
It is unclear whether or not this would constitute a credit transaction, since the legislation does not define what is meant by 'deferred'. It could be argued that this is not a credit transaction as payment is not deferred beyond normal credit terms. However, the legislation makes no reference to normal credit terms and the service would thus appear to require disclosure as a credit transaction.

There is, however, a degree of overlap between credit and material interest transactions and, therefore, those transactions referred to in the above examples which are not credit transactions might require disclosure as material interest transactions (see 3.5 below).

3   DISCLOSURE REQUIREMENTS

3.1   Introduction

A director (including a shadow director) of a company who is interested in a contract with the company must declare the nature of that interest to the board.[32] In this context, transactions include loans, quasi-loans and credit transactions[33] (see E of the Appendix below).

A considerable level of disclosure is required in the notes to both group and individual company financial statements in respect of transactions with directors (including shadow directors).[34] Even where the holding company is not required to produce group accounts by virtue of one of the statutory exemptions (for example, because it is itself a wholly-owned subsidiary or it would involve expense and delay out of proportion to the value to the company's members), these requirements still apply in full,[35] and therefore, for example, require disclosure of transactions between the directors and subsidiaries.

If the notes to the financial statements do not disclose the required details of directors' transactions, it is the auditors' duty to include the relevant information in their audit report 'so far as they are reasonably able to do so'.[36]

3.2   Scope

A company's financial statements must disclose transactions between the following:[37]

(a)   the company and its directors and their connected persons;

(b)   the company's subsidiaries and its directors and connected persons thereof;

(c)   the company, its subsidiaries and the directors (and their connected persons) of any holding company of the company.

A company need not disclose details of transactions entered into between the company or its subsidiaries and directors (and their connected persons) of the subsidiaries (provided the director is not also a director of the company or its holding company).[38] Such information should be disclosed in the financial statements of the subsidiaries.

The multiplicity of disclosures which may ensue from a single transaction are detailed below:

Example 23.6

Assume the following group structure:

Company X

Company Y

Company Z

Companies Y and Z are both wholly owned subsidiaries of Company X. Company Z undertakes to guarantee a loan made by a bank to Mr. A, a director of company X. The guarantee will be disclosed as follows:

(a)   in the financial statements of Company Z as a guarantee of a loan to a director of its holding company;

(b)   in the financial statements of Company Y as a guarantee of a loan by a subsidiary to a director of its holding company;

(c)   in the financial statements of Company X as a guarantee of a loan by a subsidiary to a director;

These requirements do not apply to institutions authorised under the Banking Act 1987, which are subject to separate disclosure provisions (see 4 below).[39]

3.3   Transactions requiring disclosure

Broadly, the legislation[40] requires disclosure of two types of transaction involving directors, namely:

(a)   loans, quasi-loans, credit transactions, related guarantees,[41] assignments and arrangements (section 330 type transactions); and

(b)   transactions (other than section 330 type transactions) in which a director has a material interest.

The disclosure provisions apply irrespective of whether:

(a)   the transaction was lawful;[42]

(b)   the person for whom the transaction was made was at the time of its execution a director or a connected person;[43] or

(c)   the company was a subsidiary at the time the transaction was executed.[44]

For example, details of the following transactions would need to be disclosed in a company's financial statements:

(a)   a loan made to an employee who later in the financial year becomes a director, for example:

Extract 23.1: Blue Circle Industries PLC[45]

23 Directors and employees [extract]

An amount of £25,000 was outstanding in respect of an interest free housing loan made to Mr. A. M. M. Spurr following his transfer to the United Kingdom from Australia in 1981, but prior to his appointment as a Director (which loan is now secured on a freehold property wholly owned by Mr. Spurr).

An amount of £9,039 was outstanding in respect of an interest–free loan made to Mr. D. A. Simpson upon his relocation prior to his appointment as a Director.

(b)   a contract entered into with a director who retired during the financial year, for example:

Extract 23.2: The Plessey Company plc[46]

6 Directors and senior employees [extract]

Since his retirement W. J. Dalziel has been paid at the rate of £100,000 per annum under a consultancy agreement which will expire twelve months after his date of retirement.

(c)   a credit transaction entered into with a director of another company which then becomes the reporting company's parent.

3.4   Section 330 transactions

3.4.1   Introduction

Details of these transactions must be disclosed in both group[47] and individual company[48] financial statements (subject to various exemptions: see 3.6 below).

Thus, disclosure must be made where any company:

(a)   makes a loan or a quasi-loan to, or enters into a credit transaction with, or enters into a guarantee or provides any security in connection therewith for one of its directors, a director of its holding company or a connected person thereof;

(b)   arranges for the assignment to it, or the assumption by it, of any rights or obligations or liabilities under a transaction that would have contravened section 330 if the company had originally entered into it (see B.3 of the Appendix below);

(c)   takes part in any arrangement such that another person enters into a transaction that would have contravened section 330 had the company entered into it (see B.4 of the Appendix below);

(d)   agrees to enter into any of the above transactions or arrangements.

3.4.2 Disclosure requirements

The particulars to be disclosed are the principal terms of the transaction, arrangement or agreement.[49] The principal terms must include, as a minimum:

(a)   a statement of the fact that the transaction was made or existed during the financial year;[50]

(b)   the name of the person for whom it was made and, if this person is connected with a director, that director's name;[51]

(c)   for loans (including agreements and arrangements relating thereto):[52]

    (i)   the principal and interest at the beginning and the end of the financial year,
    (ii)   the maximum amount outstanding during the year,
    (iii)   the amount of any interest due but unpaid,
    (iv)   the amount of any provision in respect of non-payment of the loan;

(d)   for guarantees and security:[53]

    (i)   the potential liability of the company (or its subsidiary) at the beginning and the end of the financial year,
    (ii)   the maximum potential liability of the company (or its subsidiary),
    (iii)   any amount paid and any liability incurred by the company in fulfilling the security or discharging the security;

(e)   for quasi-loans and credit transactions, it is necessary to disclose the value of the transaction.[54] The value of a quasi-loan is defined as the maximum amount which the person to whom the quasi-loan is made is liable to reimburse the creditor.[55] In the case of a credit transaction, value is defined as the price which it is reasonable to expect could be obtained for the goods, land or services to which the transaction or arrangement relates if they had been supplied in the ordinary course of business and on the same terms (apart from price) as they have been supplied, under the transaction or arrangement in question.[56] Although, the legislation does not specify the extent of disclosures, given that details of any transaction subsisting during the year must be disclosed, it would be relevant for the disclosures to be similar to those for loans (see (c) above).

In addition to the above, it may be necessary to disclose other principal terms of the transaction; for example, the repayment term in the case of a loan or the credit limit for credit transactions and quasi-loans.

The following extracts illustrate a variety of section 330 type transactions:

A   Loans

Extract 23.3: The Plessey Company plc[57]

6 Directors and senior employees [extract]
At 1 April 1988 there were outstanding interest-free loans to V Butler £65,000, W Gosling £30,000, K B Huntbatch £5,000 and A W Jones £25,000, all of which were made before their appointment as directors and were unchanged from the end of the previous financial year.
An interest-free loan which was made prior to appointment as director of £46,500 to A D Mayes which had continued unchanged since the end of the previous financial year was reduced to £7,012 on 30 November 1987.
An interest-free loan which was made prior to appointment as director of £30,000 to D Dey which had continued unchanged since the end of the previous financial year was repaid on 19 January 1988.

It can be seen from the third paragraph of the above extract that, even though there is no amount outstanding at the year end, disclosure is required; this is because the transaction *existed* during the period. This is also the case where there are no amounts outstanding at either the beginning or the end of the year, as the following extract shows:

Extract 23.4: B.A.T Industries p.l.c.[58]

Other transactions with Directors
Overdraft facilities were provided by Dunbar Bank plc on its standard commercial terms to Sir Mark Weinberg.

Amount of overdraft:	
1 January 1987	Nil
31 December 1987	Nil
Maximum overdraft during 1987	£10,725

B   Guarantees and security

Extract 23.5: British Aerospace Public Limited Company[59]

7 DIRECTORS [extract]
(b) Transactions
(2) Under a Housing Loan Scheme operated by the Company, Mr. I. R. Yates and Mr. S. Gillibrand have bank loans, bearing interest at 5% per annum, incurred in buying their respective houses and entered into prior to their becoming Directors of the Company as a result of relocating at the Company's request. Mr. Yates' loan is secured on his house and certain insurance policies; Mr. Gillibrand's loan is secured by a mortgage on his house. For the duration of each loan the Company maintains with the bank a deposit equal to the amount outstanding under the loan; such deposit bears interest at $3^{1}/_{4}$% per annum and is available as additional security for the loan. Mr. Yates and Mr. Gillibrand have each agreed to indemnify the Company against any liability to the bank by reason of their respective loans. Mr. Yates' loan is repayable not later than 18th May, 1997 and Mr. Gillibrand's not later than 9th February, 2002.
The amounts of principal and accrued interest outstanding under these loans were as follows:

	At 31st December, 1987		At 1st January, 1987	
	Principal	Interest	Principal	Interest
	£	£	£	£
Mr. Yates	**45,000**	**111**	45,000	105
Mr. Gillibrand	**78,425**	**193**	80,393*	88*
			(* at 1st July, 1987)	

The maximum amount of principal and accrued interest outstanding at any time during 1987 under each loan was as follows:

	£
Mr. Yates	45,604
Mr. Gillibrand	80,481

All interest which has become payable under the loans has been paid.

C   Credit transactions

Extract 23.6: National Westminster Bank PLC[60]

25 Transactions involving directors and others [extract]
(b) Loans, quasi-loans and credit transactions made by companies, other than authorised institutions, within the Group for directors of the Bank and their connected persons are as follows:

Name of borrower	Relationship of director	Nature of agreement	Date of agreement	Term of agreement	Total cost of assets	Rentals payable at commercial rates
Lord Boardman & Son	Lord Boardman Partner	Lease	1987	3 years	£10,250	£11,940
West Midland Timber Treatment Co.	Lord Boyne Partner	Lease	1986	5 years	£20,800	£24,478
Butler Farms (Halstead)	Sir Richard Butler Partner	Lease	1985	3 years	£46,040	£46,040

3.5   Material interest transactions

3.5.1   Introduction

The group[61] and individual company[62] financial statements must disclose details of transactions or arrangements in which any person who was a director of the company, its holding company or a connected person thereof had a material interest (subject to various exemptions: see 3.6 below). Section 330 type transactions are excluded from this category.[63]

It is for the directors to determine whether a transaction is material.[64] For these purposes, a transaction is not material if the directors of the reporting company (or at least a majority of them), excluding the director whose interest is under review, decide that it is not.[65] However, if the directors do not consider the question of materiality, it cannot be presumed that the interest was immaterial.[66] In these circumstances, the materiality of the transaction will be regarded as a matter of fact.

3.5.2   Definition of material interest

The definition of 'material' has proved to be one of the more problematic issues in this area of the law. There are two widely accepted interpretations namely, that 'material':

(a)   should be judged by what is relevant to the users of the financial statements (the relevant view). Rumbelow[67] suggests that the rationale for this disclosure requirement is to ensure that shareholders are better informed about their directors and better able to take any decisions they may have to take as shareholders (particularly as regards those directors). Consequently, he reasons that to decide what is material, one must look to see if the interest is such that its disclosure would be likely to influence a reasonable shareholder in making those decisions;

(b)   means substantial in relation to the individual transaction in which the director is interested (the 'Mars Bar' view). Proponents of this view claim that the wording of the provision points to this interpretation.

However, as the following example illustrates, the 'Mars Bar' view may give rise to curious results:

Example 23.7

A director arranges a £50m contract on behalf of his company; the agreement provides for an arrangement fee of 1/2% of the value of the contract (i.e. commission of £250,000). The director will not need to disclose his interest if the 'Mars Bar' approach is adopted because his interest in the transaction is insignificant in relation to that transaction. However, if a director purchases a bar of chocolate for himself in the staff restaurant, the 'Mars Bar' view would demand disclosure of this transaction (subject to the de minimis exceptions: see 3.6.3 below); in this instance, he has a 100% interest in the transaction.

There is a third possible interpretation, albeit not widely held; namely, that material must be determined by reference to the director's financial position. Proponents of this view argue that if a transaction is not material vis-à-vis the director's personal position, there will be no conflict of duty and interest.

However, the jurisprudence in this area makes it clear that the courts will not look into the merits of a transaction but adhere strictly to the rule that the possible conflict of interest and duty must not be allowed to arise, hence this rationale is somewhat spurious. On a practical note, if this view were adopted curious results could arise, as shown in the following example:

Example 23.8

Mr. M, a director of ABC plc, has amassed a personal fortune of £10m. The latest audited accounts of ABC plc show net assets of £50,000 and turnover of £200,000. XYZ plc, a company of which Mr. M is the majority shareholder, enters into a contract to buy goods worth £20,000 from ABC plc. Arguably, if the foregoing basis of assessing materiality is used, the transaction would not require disclosure.

On balance, we prefer the relevant view since its application is most likely to satisfy the needs of the users (or potential users) of the accounts, by keeping them informed of the types of dealing between a company and its directors which impact upon investment, credit and other decisions which they may be required to take. Clearly, this test involves the making of a qualitative judgement, that is, whether disclosure of the transaction might make a difference to a business decision. In practice, as Swinson argues,[68] this qualitative assessment may often be answered by establishing whether a director's interest is material in quantitative terms. If an interest is immaterial in quantitative terms, it may be irrelevant to the users of the accounts and vice-versa.

3.5.3 Disclosure requirements

The principal terms of material interest transactions must be disclosed;[69] in particular:

(a) the name of the director who has the material interest and the nature thereof;[70]

(b) the value of the transaction.[71]

The types of transaction in which a director may have an interest are diverse as the following extracts demonstrate:

Extract 23.7: Continental Microwave (Holdings) PLC[72]

23. Directors' interests [extract]
During the year payments of £193,000 (comprising £165,000 for materials purchased at cost from third parties and £28,000 for engineering consultancy fees) have been made by Group companies in the ordinary course of business to Lancom Associates of which D.R. Lance is the proprietor.

Extract 23.8: S. & W. Berisford plc[73]

5. DIRECTORS' REMUNERATION AND INTERESTS [extract]
c Directors' interests in contracts and other transactions with the Company:
On 22 July, 1987 pursuant to a covenant of even date the Company paid to Mr P Aaronberg
the sum of £280,000 to compensate him for relinquishing the rights which he then enjoyed as
a partner with Arthur Andersen & Co.

Extract 23.9: The Plessey Company plc[74]

6 Directors and senior employees [extract]
During the year ended 3 April 1987 4 cars were sold by the Company to retiring directors for
an aggregate consideration of £30,750 (market value £40,970).
In order to enable M W Clark to discharge his executive functions, the Company made
premises in London available to him at nil rental. The benefit on which he is assessed is
included in the emoluments shown above, and the market rental is £50,000 per annum.
For the year ended 3 April 1987, the firms of Satterlee & Stephens, Attorneys and Patterson,
Belknap, Webb & Tyler, Attorneys in which W J Sinsheimer was successively a partner,
rendered fees to the Group of US$44,735 and US$1,655,805 respectively and M W Clark
rendered fees of £5,200 to the Company in respect of enjoyment of rights over land.

Extract 23.9 highlights the fact that the value of the transaction is not necessarily
the amount at which the transaction is transacted, but is the amount which could
have been obtained in the ordinary course of business.[75]

Where the value of the transaction cannot be expressed as a specific amount of
money, then it is deemed to exceed £50,000,[76] as the following extract shows:

Extract 23.10: British Aerospace Public Limited Company[77]

7 DIRECTORS [extract]
(b) Transactions
(1) Until 30th September, 1987 Sir Raymond Lygo continued to occupy a leasehold house in
London purchased by the Company (as to nine-tenths) and him (as to one-tenth) in 1983 to
assist him to fulfil his duties as Chief Executive. As noted in previous accounts, the house
was held by the Company and Sir Raymond on the terms of a trust deed dated 3rd March,
1983, whereunder Sir Raymond was entitled to occupy the house without payment of any rent
to the Company (but subject to the payment of the rent due to the freeholder and other normal
outgoings). The Companies Act 1985 requires accounts to state the 'value' of any such
arrangement and provides that, if such value cannot be expressed as a specific sum of money,
it is deemed to exceed £50,000. The Directors consider that Sir Raymond Lygo's right to
occupy the property in accordance with the provisions of the Trust Deed cannot be expressed
as a specific sum of money; however, they believe that the real value of this right during
1987 was smaller than £50,000. On 30th September, 1987, Sir Raymond purchased from the
Company its nine-tenths interest in the house for a consideration of £207,000 pursuant to
shareholders' approval given at the last Annual General Meeting.

Extract 23.9 above would appear to be an example of a company adopting the
'Mars Bar' approach. This can be contrasted with the following statement

(contained in the company's directors' report) which suggests that the relevant view has been adopted, as no disclosure is included as a note to the financial statements:

Extract 23.11: Trusthouse Forte PLC[78]

Directors [extract]
None of the Directors had a material interest during the financial year in a beneficial capacity in any contract which was significant in relation to the Company's business. In the ordinary course of business Ryde Farm Estate, in which Lord Forte and Mr. Rocco Forte have an interest, sold to the Company farm produce at a substantial saving to the Group and Mr. G. F. L. Procter is a consultant with Paisner & Co., which undertook legal work during the year on behalf of the Group.

One company which explicitly states that the director's interest is not material is Storehouse PLC, as illustrated below:

Extract 23.12: Storehouse PLC[79]

Directors [extract]
Sir Terence Conran has interests in several companies which trade from time to time with the Company and its subsidiaries on terms which are negotiated on an arm's length basis. These interests have been reported to the Directors who have concluded that none of them is material.

The Stock Exchange imposes additional disclosure requirements for listed and USM companies (see 5 below).

3.6   Exemptions from disclosure

The following transactions involving directors do not require disclosure.

3.6.1   General

(a)   Transactions between companies in which a director is interested only by virtue of his being a director of both companies;[80]

(b)   directors' service contracts.[81] However, details of service contracts of directors of listed companies may require disclosure (see 1.4 of Chapter 24);

(c)   transactions which were not entered into or which did not subsist during the year.[82] However, transactions which were entered into after the year end will require disclosure if at the year end there was an agreement between the parties to enter into the transaction.[83] In addition, material transactions involving directors post year-end may fall to be disclosed as post balance sheet events in accordance with the provisions of SSAP 17 (see Chapter 16).

3.6.2   Section 330 transactions

(a)   Credit transactions and related guarantees, arrangements and agreements where the aggregate amount outstanding for the director and his connected persons did not at any time during the financial year exceed £5,000;[84]

(b)   there is a reduced level of disclosure for intra-group loans and quasi-loans,[85] although relief has not been granted for guarantees, credit transactions etc. The only details to be disclosed in respect of such transactions are:

   (i)   a statement that the transaction etc. was made or subsisted during the financial year;
   (ii)   the name of the person for whom it was made and in the case of a loan or quasi-loan to a connected person, the name of the director.

This exemption only applies if there are no minority interests involved.

Brown[86] has criticised this partial exemption on the ground that it is too narrow in its application and argues that even though the exemption helps to relieve the burden of disclosures, the number of disclosable transactions could still be unmanageable in certain group situations.

3.6.3   Material interest transactions

(a)   Transactions in which the director's interest is not material (as decided by a majority of his fellow directors);[87]

(b)   transactions in which a director has a material interest which are entered into at arm's length in the ordinary course of business.[88] This exemption has given rise to particular difficulty. It is sometimes argued that the exemption, as presently drafted, only applies if each party to the transaction is a member of the same group. The explanatory note to the statutory instrument[89] which introduced the exemption indicates that there is no need for the counterparties to the transaction to be group companies. Given that one of the aims of introducing the exemption was to reduce the level of disclosure, it seems logical to interpret the provision as exempting all arm's length material interest transactions involving directors. This view, however, is not universally held.[90]

The uncertainty surrounding this provision has been highlighted by the Institute of Chartered Accountants of Scotland (ICAS) which has called for the provision to be redrafted;[91]

(c)   any material interest transaction between members of a group of companies which would have been disclosable only because of a director being associated (see 2.4 above) with the contracting companies, provided that no minority interests in the reporting company are affected.[92] A higher level of disclosure is required where there are minority interests since minorities can be affected by transfers of value within a group. The wording of this exemption is arcane and the drafting is considered to be defective;[93]

(d)   transactions in which a director had a material interest where the value of each transaction (with no reduction in the amount outstanding) in the financial year and the value of transactions in preceding financial years (less the amount by which the director's liabilities have been reduced) did not at any time during the financial year exceed £1,000 or, if more than £1,000, did not exceed £5,000 or 1% of the value of the net assets of the reporting company.[94] Net assets is defined as the aggregate of the company's assets, less the aggregate of its liabilities.[95] It is not clear how this provision interacts with the other exemptions for material interest transactions (see (b) and (c) above). Unless these provisions are discrete, the exemptions are likely to be rendered ineffective.

4   INSTITUTIONS AUTHORISED UNDER THE BANKING ACT 1987

An institution authorised under the Banking Act 1987 (or its holding company) is subject to different disclosure requirements in respect of section 330 type transactions to which the institution is a party.[96] Material interest transactions involving directors of authorised institutions must be disclosed as for other companies (see 3.4 above).[97]

In brief,[98] authorised institutions must maintain a register of section 330 type transactions for the current and preceding ten financial years.[99] A statement of such transactions must be:[100]

(a)   made available for members to inspect; and

(b)   examined and reported on by the institution's auditor.

4.1   Disclosure of transactions by authorised institutions

The financial statements must disclose:

(a)   the aggregate amount of loans, quasi-loans, credit transactions and related transactions outstanding at the end of the financial year;[101] and

(b)   the number of persons for whom the transactions were made.[102]

In this context,[103] amount outstanding means the outstanding liabilities of the person for whom the transaction was made and as respects a guarantee or security, the amount guaranteed or secured.

Extract 23.13 provides an illustration of the disclosures of transactions between an authorised institution and its directors.

Extract 23.13: National Westminster Bank PLC[104]

25 Transactions involving directors and others [extract]
(a) The aggregate amounts outstanding at 31 December 1987 under transactions, arrangements and agreements made by recognised banks within the Group for persons who are, or were directors of the Bank during the year or who are, or were, connected with a director of the Bank during the year, relating to loans, quasi-loans and credit transactions were:

	Number of directors	Number of connected persons	Amount £000
Quasi-loans	4	—	210
Loans	26	38	2,247
Credit transactions	—	—	—

It must be emphasised that these disclosures only apply to section 330 type transactions with the authorised institution. The disclosure requirements outlined in 3.4.2 above still apply to any such transaction with other companies within the group (see Extract 23.6 above).

5   REQUIREMENTS OF THE STOCK EXCHANGE

In addition to the disclosure provisions imposed by the Companies Act 1985, The Stock Exchange imposes additional requirements in respect of transactions involving directors of listed[105] and USM companies.[106] There are no additional requirements for Third Market companies.

5.1   Listed companies

Capital transactions involving directors, past directors and their associates (similar to connected persons) may constitute Class 4 transactions.[107] To this end, full particulars of the transaction must be given[108] including:

(a)   the name of the director concerned, and, where applicable, the associate's name; and

(b)   the nature and extent of the director's or his associate's interest in the transaction.

Normally these particulars should be circulated to the company's shareholders prior to obtaining their approval[109] and The Stock Exchange must also be notified of the proposed transaction.[110] However, in practice, The Stock Exchange often waives these requirements, especially for smaller companies, provided that the company's accountants express the opinion that the terms of the transaction are fair and reasonable.[111]

The annual report and accounts of listed companies must also disclose particulars of any contract of significance in which a director of the company is or was materially interested. If there has been no such contract, a statement of this fact must be made.[112] A contract of significance is defined as one which represents in amount or value, a sum equal to 1% or more of:

(a) in the case of a capital transaction or a transaction the principal purpose of which is the granting of credit, the net assets of the company; or

(b) in other cases, the total purchases, sales, payments or receipts, as the case may be, of the company.

In most cases, companies which have disclosable items under the Companies Act refer to the disclosure of those items in giving this disclosure, even though the transactions do not appear to meet the definition of 'significant', along the following lines:

Extract 23.14: British Aerospace Public Limited Company[113]

Directors [extract]
The Board is not aware of any contract of significance (other than service contracts or as disclosed in note 7 to the accounts) in relation to the Company or its subsidiaries in which any Director has, or has had, a material interest.

It is likely, however, that in most cases the transactions which are disclosed to meet the requirements will not be contracts of significance (as defined) and therefore a completely negative statement can be given to meet The Stock Exchange requirement. This was done, for example, by Imperial Chemical Industries PLC.[114]

5.2   USM companies

Transactions involving a director or an associate thereof are required to be approved by the company in general meeting and details published in an explanatory circular.[115] The Stock Exchange may waive these requirements in appropriate circumstances (see 5.1 above). However, there are no additional requirements relating to disclosures to be made in the financial statements of such a company.

6   TRANSACTIONS INVOLVING OFFICERS

6.1   Introduction

The Act requires certain details of transactions between a company and its officers to be disclosed.[116] To this end, group[117] and individual company[118] financial statements must contain particulars in the notes[119] of transactions entered into by officers. A holding company's financial statements must take into account transactions between the company and its subsidiaries with officers of the company;[120] however, transactions between the subsidiaries and their directors do not need to be included in the holding company's financial statements.[121] If a company does not produce group financial statements by virtue of one of the statutory exemptions, these requirements still apply in full.[122]

6.2   Disclosure requirements

The financial statements must disclose the following details in respect of transactions with officers (which, for these purposes, in order to avoid duplication of disclosure excludes directors):[123]

(a)   the aggregate amount of loans, quasi-loans, credit transactions, guarantees and arrangements outstanding at the end of the financial year;[124] and

(b)   the number of officers for whom the transactions were made.[125]

For these purposes, the amount outstanding is defined as the outstanding liabilities of the person for whom the transaction was made and in the case of a guarantee or security, the amount guaranteed or secured.[126]

Disclosure of such transactions is not, however, necessary:

(a)   for a particular officer if the aggregate amount outstanding under the transactions at the end of the financial year for that officer does not exceed £2,500; or

(b)   for officers of authorised institutions (see 4 above).[127]

The following extracts illustrate the disclosure of transactions involving officers:

Extract 23.15: GKN plc[128]

22 Share capital [extract]
At 31st December 1987 there was a loan of £3,568, made under an established scheme to provide supplementary finance for house purchase, and secured by a mortgage, to one officer of the parent company.

Extract 23.16: Lucas Industries plc[129]

Note 23: Directors' emoluments [extract]
At 31 July 1988, there was a loan to a United Kingdom employee who is an officer of the company amounting to £7,593 (1987 — £9,619).

---

7   CONCLUSION

Various professional bodies have made representations to the DTI suggesting that the legislation be clarified and simplified. For example in 1983, the Law Society and the CCAB proposed an amendment to the legislation in an effort to clarify the meaning of material interest.[130] In addition, the ICAS claimed in a memorandum[131] submitted to the DTI that the complexity of the disclosure requirements led to difficulty in interpretation. It argued that simplifying the provisions would make compliance easier and thus make the rules more effective. The memorandum also called for the meaning of material interest to be clarified.

The provisions governing the disclosure of transactions between a company and its directors and officers are generally regarded as unsatisfactory. The provisions do not appear to form a coherent whole whereby a director's contractual freedom can be meaningfully regulated; for example, there are de minimis exemptions from disclosure of credit and material interest transactions yet no parallel provisions for loans and quasi-loans. In addition, aspects of the legislation are difficult to comprehend, for example, the material interest transaction exemptions. We believe that the objectives of the legislation could be more readily attained if the law were to be simplified and rationalised. As the Companies Act is presently being amended for other matters, in our view this would be the ideal opportunity to clarify the legislation in this regard. However, the Companies Bill only proposes minor amendments relating to this area, although it remains to be seen whether any significant changes are introduced at a later stage in the legislative process.

APPENDIX: LEGAL REQUIREMENTS

A   INTRODUCTION

Although the primary objective of this chapter is to discuss how transactions with directors should be disclosed in a company's financial statements, a brief exposition of the statutory provisions determining the legality of such transactions is considered necessary in order to place the disclosure requirements in context.

B   PROHIBITED TRANSACTIONS

The Companies Act 1985 contains complex provisions[132] which prohibit or restrict many transactions involving directors (and shadow directors).[133] The legality of a transaction is determined at the time of its execution. Therefore, a loan to a person who subsequently becomes a director is legal because the recipient was not a director at the time of its making.

The basic prohibitions are dealt with in B.1 to B.4 below and the exemptions therefrom are dealt with in C below.

B.1   Loans

A company may not make a loan to its directors or those of its holding company.[134] In addition, a relevant company[135] (i.e. a public company or a company which is part of a group which includes a public company) may not make a loan to a connected person thereof.[136] Likewise, a company may not enter into a guarantee[137] or provide any security in connection with a loan made by another person to its directors or those of its holding company[138] and, in the case of a relevant company, a connected person thereof.[139]

B.2   Quasi-loans and credit transactions

A relevant company may not make a quasi-loan nor enter into a credit transaction with its directors, the directors of its holding company or a connected person thereof.[140] There is a similar restriction on the provision of guarantees or security in connection with such transactions.[141]

B.3   Assignment/assumption of rights, obligations or liabilities

A company may not arrange for the assignment to, or the assumption by it, of any rights, obligations or liabilities in respect of transactions which, if undertaken by the company in the first place, would have been unlawful,[142] for example:

Example 23.9

A bank makes a loan to a director of Company X and thereafter assigns its rights to Company X. The company will have entered into an unlawful assignment.

Example 23.10

The facts are as above, but the loan from the bank is guaranteed by a friend of the director. Subsequently, Company X becomes the guarantor of the loan releasing the director's friend from his obligations. The assumption of the guarantee by Company X is unlawful.

B.4 Arrangements

Schemes whereby a third party enters into an arrangement which if entered into by the company would have been unlawful, in circumstances where the company (or a fellow group company) provides a benefit to the third party, are not permitted,[143] for example:

Example 23.11

Company X arranges for a bank to make a loan to one of its directors on favourable terms in return for which the company places business with the bank. This series of transactions constitutes an unlawful arrangement whereby the bank enters into an arrangement forbidden to Company X and receives a benefit for so doing.

C   EXEMPTED TRANSACTIONS

C.1   Loans of small amounts

A loan to a director of a company or its holding company is not illegal if the aggregate of the sums advanced to the director does not exceed £2,500;[144] in computing the sum of £2,500, amounts already advanced to the director must be taken into account.[145] It should be noted that this exemption does not extend to loans of small amounts to connected persons of directors of a relevant company.

C.2   Short-term quasi-loans

Quasi-loans by a relevant company are permitted if made on the condition that the director reimburses the company within two months and where the aggregate of the sums outstanding under quasi-loans does not exceed £1,000.[146] Again, this exemption does not extend to quasi-loans made to connected persons of directors of a relevant company.

C.3   Minor or business credit transactions

A relevant company may enter in a credit transaction for a person if:

(a)   the aggregate of such amounts does not exceed £5,000;[147] or

(b)   the transaction is entered into by the company in the ordinary course of its business on terms which the company would have extended to a person of the same financial standing unconnected with the company.[148]

C.4   Inter-company transactions

A relevant company is not prohibited from making loans and quasi-loans to a group company where a director of one company is associated with another.[149] Likewise a company may make a loan or quasi-loan to or enter into a credit transaction as creditor for its holding company.[150]

Furthermore, a holding company may make a loan to a director of its subsidiary or a connected person thereof; similarly, a subsidiary may make a loan to a director of a fellow subsidiary (provided in both cases that the director is not on the board of the company or the holding company and that the other group company does not thereby obtain some benefit (see B.4 above)).

C.5   Directors' business expenditure

A director can be placed in funds to enable him to properly perform his duties as a corporate officer.[151] However, funds may only be advanced:[152]

(a)   if prior approval of the company in general meeting has been obtained; or

(b)   where approval is not obtained at or before the next annual general meeting, the loan is to be repaid within six months of the conclusion of that meeting.

Furthermore, relevant companies may only advance an aggregate of £10,000 to the director for these purposes.[153]

C.6   Money-lending companies

A money-lending company (namely one whose ordinary business includes the making of loans or quasi-loans)[154] may make loans or quasi-loans or enter into related guarantees to its directors, directors of its holding company and connected persons.[155] However, such transactions are only permitted if made by the company in the ordinary course of its business on terms which are no more preferential than are available to persons who have no connection with the company.[156] In addition, relevant companies (excluding authorised institutions: see 4 above) may only make loans up to a £50,000 limit.[157]

Loans made for the purpose of facilitating the purchase of or improving a director's house may also be made by money-lending companies if the facility is ordinarily available to employees of the company on equally favourable terms; this exemption is again subject to a £50,000 limit for all companies.[158]

There is some doubt as to the interaction between the monetary limit on housing and 'other' loans to directors of relevant money-lending companies (which are not authorised institutions under the Banking Act 1987: see 4 above). This problem is compounded by what appears to be a drafting error[159] in references in section 339(1) which impacts upon how previous loans, etc, made by money-lending companies are to be aggregated with amounts already advanced to directors and their connected persons. On balance, we believe that the intention of the legislation is that the aggregate value of all loans, whatever their nature, made by money-lending companies to any given director and his connected persons, must not exceed £50,000.

C.7   Companies registered overseas[160]

The following transactions entered into by an overseas company are not subject to the statutory restrictions; transactions entered into by an overseas incorporated subsidiary:

(a)   with a director of its UK incorporated parent; and

(b)   of a UK incorporated parent with a director of the UK parent's overseas incorporated holding company.

D   SANCTIONS

D.1   Civil remedies

A prohibited transaction is voidable at the company's option unless:

(a)   restitution is impossible, for example, where the proceeds of an illegal loan have been used to build an extension to the director's house;[161] or

(b)   the company has been indemnified for the loss suffered by it;[162] or

(c)   rights have been acquired by a bona fide purchaser for value who does not have notice of the contravention.[163]

The director, any connected person for whom the transaction was made and any director who authorised the transaction is liable:

(a)   to account for any gain which he has made; and

(b)   to make good any loss made by the company.[164]

However, where the transaction is made for a person connected with a director, then that director will not be liable if he can demonstrate that he took all reasonable steps to secure the company's compliance with the legislation.[165]

The person connected with the director and any other director who authorised the transaction will not be liable if he can demonstrate that at the time the transaction was entered into he did not know the circumstances constituting the contravention.[166]

D.2   Criminal penalties

A director of a relevant company who authorises or permits the company to enter into a transaction knowing or believing that the transaction was illegal is guilty of an offence and is liable to imprisonment and/or a fine.[167] A relevant company entering into an illegal transaction is also guilty of an offence[168] unless it did not know the circumstances at the time of the transaction.[169] A person who knowingly procures the transaction or arrangement is also guilty of an offence.[170]

E   INTERESTS IN CONTRACTS

A director must, upon pain of a fine,[171] declare any interest (direct or indirect) in a contract with the company at a board meeting.[172] In this context, an interest in a section 330 type transaction requires disclosure[173] (see generally 3 above). If the contract is merely proposed, the director must declare his interest at the board meeting at which the contract is under consideration.[174] The Court of Appeal held in *Guinness plc v Saunders & Ward* [175] that this duty cannot be fulfilled by disclosure to a sub-committee of the Board; only disclosure to a properly convened meeting of the full Board will suffice. If the director was not interested in the contract at the time it was made, disclosure should be made at the first board meeting after the director becomes interested.[176] For these purposes, a general notice of interest in specific types of contracts given to the board suffices.[177]

Example 23.12

Mr. A, a director of Company X is the majority shareholder in Company Y. Company X purchases quantities of stock from Company Y. Mr. A must disclose his interest in such contracts to the board of Company X.

These requirements also apply to shadow directors who are required to make disclosure of interests in contracts by means of a written notice addressed to the board.[178]

In addition to the statutory restrictions, the company's articles may amplify the director's ability to enter into contracts. Thus, Table A, provides that: 'Subject to the provisions of the Act, and provided that he has disclosed to the directors the nature and extent of any material interest of his, a director notwithstanding his office

(a)　may be a party to, or otherwise interested in, any transaction or arrangement with the company or in which the company is otherwise interested;

(b)　may be a director or other officer of, or employed by, a party to any transaction or arrangement with, or otherwise interested in, any body corporate promoted by the company or in which the company is otherwise interested; and

(c)　shall not, by reason of his office, be accountable to the company for any benefit which he derives from any such office or employment or from any such transaction or arrangement or from any interest in any such body corporate and no such transaction or arrangement shall be liable to be avoided on the ground of any such interest or benefit.'[179]

F　　SUBSTANTIAL PROPERTY TRANSACTIONS

A director or connected person may not acquire from or sell to the company a non-cash asset[180] above the requisite value unless the transaction has been approved by the company in general meeting.[181] If the transaction occurs between the company and a director or connected person of its holding company, the holding company's approval is also required.[182]

In this context, the requisite value of transactions is the lower of 10% of the company's net asset value or £50,000.[183] This is subject to a de minimis threshold of £1,000, below which property transactions do not require approval.[184]

There are a number of exemptions from the requirement to obtain approval;[185] for example, an acquisition of an asset of the requisite value:

(a)　by a director from his company which is a wholly owned subsidiary of another company,[186] and

(b)　by a person from a company of which he is a member[187] (i.e. a shareholder in his capacity as member), and

(c)　by one group company from another, provided there are no minority interests involved,[188] do not require approval.

A transaction entered into without the necessary approval is voidable at the company's option[189] unless:

(a)   restitution of the property is impossible;[190] or

(b)   rights to the property have been acquired by a bona fide purchaser for value who does not know that approval has not been obtained;[191] or

(c)   the arrangement has been affirmed by the company (and if appropriate its holding company) in general meeting within a reasonable period.[192]

The director, any connected person for whom the transaction was made and any director who authorised the transaction is liable:

(a)   to account for any gain which he has made; and

(b)   to make good any loss made by the company.[193]

However, where the transaction is made for a person connected with a director, and that director can demonstrate that he took all reasonable steps to secure the company's compliance with these provisions,[194] he will escape liability.

The person connected with the director and any other director who authorised the transaction will not be liable if he can demonstrate that at the time the transaction was entered into he did not know the circumstances constituting the contravention.[195]

G   TRANSACTIONS INVOLVING OFFICERS

Officers, other than directors, are not subject to any statutory restrictions on their ability to transact with their company. A company's articles may address the contractual position of its officers, although Table A[196] is silent on this issue.

References

1 A person who holds anything in trust. A fiduciary relationship arises where a person has rights and powers which he is bound to exercise for the benefit of another. Hence he is not allowed to derive any profit or advantage from the relationship between them, except with the knowledge and consent of the other person: J. Burke, *Jowitt's Dictionary of English Law, Volume I A—K*, p. 788. If a director breaches this duty, a range of remedies are available to the company. The company may, inter alia, seek an injunction, claim damages or compensation, require the director to account for profits made or rescind contracts entered into with him.

2 CA 48, s 190(1).

3 *Ibid.*, s 190(1)(a).

4 CA 80, ss 49—50.

5 CA 85, ss 330—346, Sch. 6.

6 *Ibid.*, s 741(1).

7 Companies should ensure that they do not allow persons described as divisional directors to hold themselves out as being members of the board. Otherwise there is a danger that contracts entered into by such persons, in excess of their managerial authority, may be binding on the company.

8 CA 85, s 741(2).

9 *Ibid.*

10 *Ibid.*, s 741(3).

11 The position of the alternate director is discussed in more detail in R. Pennington, *Company Law*, p. 628, and C.M. Schmithoff (ed.), *Palmer's Company Law Volume I*, p. 879.

12 The Companies (Tables A—F) Regulations 1985 (S.I. 1985 No. 85), Table A, Article 65.

13 CA 85, s 346(2)(a), (3)(a).

14 *Ibid.*, s 346(2)(b).

15 *Ibid.*, s 346(4).

16 *Ibid.*, s 346(5).

17 *Ibid.*, s 346(6).

18 *Ibid.*, s 346(2)(c).

19 *Ibid.*

20 *Ibid.*, s 346(3)(b).

21 *Ibid.*, s 346(2)(d).

22 *Ibid.*, s 346(2)(e).

23 *Ibid.*, s 346(6)(a)

24 *Ibid.*, s 346(7) and Sch. 13, para. 5.

25 *Ibid.*, s 346(8).

26 *Ibid.*, s 744.

27 *Champagne Perrier - Jouet SA v H.H. Finch Ltd* [1982] 1 WLR 1359.

28 If a director draws remuneration on account, the Inland Revenue may treat the director as having received a beneficial loan and thus raise an assessment if the notional interest is deemed to exceed £200: Taxes Act 1988, s 160. In the case of a close company, advance corporation tax may be payable which can only be recovered when the loan is repaid: Taxes Act 1988, s 417 et seq. These difficulties may be surmounted if the company accounts for PAYE and NIC on all withdrawals by directors.

29 CA 85, s 331(3).

30 *Ibid.*, s 331(7).

31 *Ibid.*, s 331(8).

32 *Ibid.*, ss 317(1), (8).

33 *Ibid.*, s 317(6).

34 *Ibid.*, ss 232(1)—(3).

35 *Ibid.*, s 232(4).

36 *Ibid.*, s 237(5). A discussion of the procedures which the auditor should adopt in relation to directors' emoluments can be found in A. Brown and D. Foster, *Directors' loans, other transactions and remuneration,* pp. 5—7.

37 *Ibid.*, s 232 and Sch. 6, paras. 1—2.

38 *Ibid.*, Sch. 4, para. 63(b).

39 *Ibid.*, s 234.

40 *Ibid.*, s 232 and Sch. 6, paras. 1—2.

41 This includes indemnities: *ibid.*, s 331(2).

42 *Ibid.*, Sch. 6, para. 6(a).

43 *Ibid.*, para. 6(b).

44 *Ibid.*, para. 6(c).

45 Blue Circle Industries PLC, Report and Accounts 1987, p. 24.

46 The Plessey Company plc, Report and Accounts 1987, p. 30.

47 CA 85, s 232(2) and Sch. 6, paras. 2(a), (b).

4 8 *Ibid.*, s 232(2) and Sch. 6, paras. 2(a), (b).
4 9 *Ibid.*, Sch. 6, para. 9(1).
5 0 *Ibid.*, para. 9(2)(a).
5 1 *Ibid.*, para. 9(2)(b).
5 2 *Ibid.*, para. 9(2)(d).
5 3 *Ibid.*, para. 9(2)(e).
5 4 *Ibid.*, para. 9(2)(f).
5 5 *Ibid.*, para. 14(c).
5 6 *Ibid.*
5 7 The Plessey Company plc, Report and Accounts 1988, p. 31.
5 8 B.A.T Industries p.l.c., Annual Report and Accounts 1987, p. 26.
5 9 British Aerospace Public Limited Company, Annual Report and Accounts 1987, p. 39.
6 0 National Westminster Bank PLC, Report and Accounts 1987, p. 54.
6 1 CA 85, s 232(1) and Sch. 6, para. 1(c).
6 2 *Ibid.*, s 232(2) and Sch. 6, para. 2(c).
6 3 *Ibid.*, Sch. 6, paras. 1(c) and 2(c) refer to any 'other transaction or arrangement'.
6 4 *Ibid.*, Sch. 6, para. 3(2). Materiality for these purposes should not be confused with the materiality level calculated for the purposes of the audit of the financial statements. This is clearly illustrated in Extract 23.9 where The Plessey Company plc have disclosed fees of £5,200 paid to the director for rights over his land.
6 5 *Ibid.*, Sch. 6, para. 3(2). Assuming the directors' opinion is formed in good faith and is not perverse, their view should prevail. However, in extreme circumstances the directors' opinion may need to be overridden in order for the accounts to give a true and fair view: A. Brown and D. Foster, *op. cit.*, p. 17.
6 6 *Ibid.*, Sch. 6, para. 3(2).
6 7 C. Rumbelow, 'When Directors Must Tell', *The Law Society's Gazette*, Wednesday 3 November 1982, pp. 1390—1392.
6 8 C. Swinson, 'Director's "Material interest" — just how do you measure it', *Accountancy*, October 1983, p. 110.
6 9 CA 85, Sch. 6, para. 9(1).
7 0 *Ibid.*, para. 9(2)(c).
7 1 *Ibid.*, Para 9(2)(f).
7 2 Continental Microwave (Holdings) PLC, Annual Report and Account 1988, p. 23.
7 3 S. & W. Berisford plc, Report & Accounts 1987, p. 40.
7 4 The Plessey Company plc, Report and Accounts 1988, p. 31.
7 5 CA 85, s 340(6).
7 6 *Ibid.*, s 340(7).
7 7 British Aerospace Public Limited Company, Annual Report and Accounts 1987, p. 38.
7 8 Trusthouse Forte PLC, Report and Accounts 1988, p. 23.
7 9 Storehouse PLC, Annual Report and Accounts 1988, p. 22.
8 0 CA 85, Sch. 6, para. 5(a).
8 1 *Ibid.*, para. 5(b).
8 2 *Ibid.*, para. 5(c).
8 3 *Ibid.*, paras. 1(b) and (2)(b).
8 4 *Ibid.*, para. 11.
8 5 *Ibid.*, para. 10.
8 6 A. Brown, 'New exemptions from disclosure of directors' transaction', *The Accountant's Magazine*, February 1985, pp. 66—67.
8 7 CA 85, Sch. 6, para. 3(2).
8 8 *Ibid.*, para. 7.
8 9 SI 1984 No 1860.
9 0 B. Johnson and M. Patient, *Accounting Provisions of the Companies Act 1985*, p. 270.
9 1 The Institute of Chartered Accountants of Scotland, *Current Problem Areas in Company Law*, p. 4.

92 CA 85, Sch. 6, para. 8.
93 The Institute of Chartered Accountants of Scotland, *loc. cit.*, has criticised the wording of this provision.
94 CA 85, Sch. 6, para. 12.
95 *Ibid.*, para. 12.
96 *Ibid.*, s 234 and Sch. 6., para. 4.
97 *Ibid.*, Sch. 6, para. 4.
98 See generally CA 85, ss 343—344.
99 *Ibid.*, s 343(2)
100 *Ibid.*, s 343(5)—(6). A pro forma audit report is contained in A. Brown and D. Foster, *op. cit.*, p. 23.
101 CA 85, Sch. 6, para. 19(a).
102 *Ibid.*, para. 19(b).
103 *Ibid.*, para. 21.
104 National Westminster Bank PLC, Annual Report and Accounts 1987, p. 54.
105 The Council of The Stock Exchange, *Admission of Securities to Listing*, Section 5, Chapter 2, para. 21(k) and Section 6, Chapter 1, paras. 6.1 — 6.3.
106 The Council of The Stock Exchange, *The Stock Exchange Unlisted Securities Market*, General Undertaking, para. 1(d).
107 *Admission of Securities to Listing*, Section 6, Chapter 1, paras. 6.1—6.3.
108 *Ibid.*, para. 6.3.
109 *Ibid.*, paras. 6.1 and 6.2.
110 *Ibid.*, para. 6.1.
111 *Ibid.*, para. 6.2. The report by the company's accountants is known as a Class 4 waiver.
112 *Ibid.*, Section 5, Chapter 2, para. 21(k).
113 British Aerospace Public Limited Company, Annual Report and Accounts 1987, pp. 25 and 26.
114 See Imperial Chemical Industries PLC, Annual Report 1987, p. 30. P. 51 disclosed loans to directors which are clearly not contracts of significance in view of the amounts involved.
115 *The Stock Exchange Unlisted Securities Market*, General Undertaking, para. 1(d).
116 CA 85, s 233.
117 *Ibid.*, s 233(1).
118 *Ibid.*, s 233(2).
119 *Ibid.*, s 233(4).
120 *Ibid.*, s 233(1).
121 *Ibid.*, Sch. 4, para. 63(b).
122 *Ibid.*, s 233(5).
123 *Ibid.*, s 223(1).
124 *Ibid.*, Sch. 6, paras. 15 and 16(1)(a).
125 *Ibid.*, paras. 15 and 16(1)(b).
126 *Ibid.*, para. 17.
127 *Ibid.*, para. 16(2).
128 GKN plc, Report & Accounts 1987, p. 42.
129 Lucas Industries plc, 1988 Report to shareholders, p. 39.
130 The Law Society's Standing Committee on Company Law and the Consultative Committee of Accountancy Bodies *'Material interest'* — *Proposed Amendments to S.54*, October 1983.
131 The Institute of Chartered Accountants of Scotland, *op. cit.*, pp. 3—4.

Appendix

132 CA 85, ss 317, 320, 330—346.
133 *Ibid.*, ss 317(8), 320(3), 330(5).
134 *Ibid.*, s 330(2).
135 *Ibid.*, s 331(6).

136 *Ibid.*, s 330(2)(b).
137 This includes indemnities: *ibid.*, s 331(2).
138 *Ibid.*, s 330(2)(b).
139 *Ibid.*, s 330(3)(c).
140 *Ibid.*, ss 330(3)(a),(b), 330(4)(a).
141 *Ibid.*, ss 330(3)(c), 330(4)(b).
142 *Ibid.*, s 330(6).
143 *Ibid.*, s 330(7).
144 *Ibid.*, s 334. S 339 determines how the threshold of £2,500 is to be calculated.
145 *Ibid.*, ss 334, 339.
146 *Ibid.*, s 332.
147 *Ibid.*, s 335(1). See also s 339.
148 *Ibid.*, s 335(2).
149 *Ibid.*, s 333.
150 *Ibid.*, s 336.
151 *Ibid.*, s 337(1)—(2).
152 *Ibid.*, s 337(3).
153 *Ibid.*, s 337(3). See also s 339.
154 *Ibid.*, s 338(2).
155 *Ibid.*, s 338(1).
156 *Ibid.*, s 338(3).
157 *Ibid.*, s 338(4). See also s 339.
158 *Ibid.*, s 338(6).
159 If the pre-consolidation legislation is to be reproduced accurately, the reference in s 339(1) to s 338(4) should actually be a reference to s 338(1).
160 The legislation applies to companies; that is, an entity formed and registered under the various Companies Acts: *ibid.*, s 735. This definition applies unless the contrary intention appears: *ibid.*, s 735(4). Since no contrary intention is expressed, a body incorporated overseas is not a company for the purposes of the directors' transactions provisions.
161 *Ibid.*, s 341(1)(a).
162 *Ibid.*
163 *Ibid.*, s 341(1)(b).
164 *Ibid.*, s 341(2).
165 *Ibid.*, s 341(4).
166 *Ibid.*, s 341(5).
167 *Ibid.*, s 342(1).
168 *Ibid.*, s 342(2).
169 *Ibid.*, s 342(5).
170 *Ibid.*, s 342(3).
171 *Ibid.*, s 317(7).
172 *Ibid.*, s 317(1).
173 *Ibid.*, s 317(6).
174 *Ibid.*, s 317(2).
175 [1988] 1 W.L.R. 863.
176 *Ibid.*
177 *Ibid.*, s 317(3).
178 *Ibid.*, s 317(8).
179 The Companies (Tables A—F) Regulations 1985, *op. cit*, Article 85.
180 CA 85, s 739(1).
181 *Ibid.*, s 320(1).
182 *Ibid.*
183 *Ibid.*, s 320(2).
184 *Ibid.*
185 *Ibid.*, s 321.

186 *Ibid.*, s 321(1).
187 *Ibid.*, s 321(3).
188 *Ibid.*, s 321(2)(a).
189 *Ibid.*, s 322(1).
190 *Ibid.*, s 322(2)(a).
191 *Ibid.*, s 322(2)(b).
192 *Ibid.*, s 322(2)(c)
193 *Ibid.*, s 322(2).
194 *Ibid.*, s 322(5).
195 *Ibid.*, s 322(6).
196 The Companies (Tables A—F) Regulations 1985, *op. cit.*

Chapter 24

Directors' remuneration

1 INTRODUCTION

This chapter focuses primarily on the disclosure requirements in respect of directors' remuneration. However, preparers of company financial statements should possess an awareness of the law governing the remuneration of directors and their service contracts. Accordingly, a brief exposition of these requirements has been included (see 1.1 to 1.4 below).[1]

Professor Gower reasoned that the need to disclose directors' remuneration was because 'it is too obvious that the system [of remunerating directors] tends itself to abuse, since directors will be encouraged to bleed the company by voting themselves excessive salaries and expense allowances. The latest Act [the Companies Act 1948] attempts to minimise these dangers by providing for full disclosure of the total emoluments received by directors ... '.[2] This requirement is simply a feature of the principle that a fiduciary should not allow his personal interests and duty to the company to conflict.[3]

1.1 Remuneration

Remuneration paid to directors may assume any form and its amount will depend on the terms of the directors' service contracts (if any) and the company's articles of association; for example, Table A[4] provides that 'the directors shall be entitled to such remuneration as the company may by ordinary resolution determine ... '. Accordingly, if the directors do not have service contracts and the articles are silent on this issue, the directors are not *entitled* to receive anything.[5]

Remuneration may not be paid to a director (in whatever capacity he acts) free of income tax nor may a company pay him remuneration of an amount such that, after paying income tax, it will leave a specified sum in his hands.[6] Any provision in a company's articles, or in any contract, or in any resolution for payment to a director of remuneration free of income tax takes effect as if it provided for payment of the gross amount subject to income tax payable by the director.[7]

1.2 Pensions

Pensions are only payable to former directors if the company is authorised to do so by its memorandum or articles of association. Table A[8] contains an express power to provide benefits to former directors and for any member of his family or any dependant and to make contributions to secure such benefits.

1.3   Compensation for loss of office

Payments to a director for loss of office, or as consideration for or in connection with his retirement from office, must be disclosed to and approved by the company in general meeting.[9] It is unclear whether payments to directors in respect of compensation for loss of other offices, for example, the company secretaryship, require approval. Pennington[10] believes that this rule applies irrespective of the office lost, although this view is not universally held. This requirement does not apply to 'any bona fide payment by way of damages for breach of contract or by way of pension in respect of past services'.[11] Thus, for approval purposes, a payment is only treated as compensation for loss of office if the company is under no legal obligation to make it.

Although outside the scope of this book, other contentious aspects of the provisions dealing with payments to directors for loss of office include:

(a)   whether ex-gratia payments are related to the lost office and thus constitute compensation requiring approval;[12]

(b)   whether payments made after a director has resigned (i.e. to past directors) are covered by the approval requirement;

(c)   whether the payment of non-monetary compensation, e.g. company motor cars, requires approval.

1.4   Service contracts

In outline, the provisions of the Companies Act 1985 relating to service contracts are as follows:

(a)   a copy or memorandum of the terms of directors' service contracts must be kept at an appropriate place, e.g. the company's registered office, and be available for inspection. The level of information required for directors who discharge their duties wholly or mainly outside the UK is reduced. These requirements do not apply where the unexpired portion of the contract is less than 12 months or where the company is able to terminate the director's contract without payment of compensation within the ensuing 12 months;[13]

(b)   terms incorporated into a director's service contract for a period of more than five years during which time his employment either cannot be terminated or can only be terminated in special circumstances are void unless approved by the company in general meeting. The resolution is only valid if a written memorandum setting out the proposed agreement is available for inspection for 15 days before and at the meeting itself.[14]

The Stock Exchange imposes additional requirements[15] in relation to service contracts of directors of listed companies. Copies or written memoranda of the terms of all directors' service contracts of more than 12 months' duration must be available for inspection from the date of the notice covering the annual general meeting (AGM). The notice of the AGM must specify when and where such information will be available for inspection or state that there are no such contracts. In addition, the directors' report must state the unexpired portion of any service contract of any director proposed for re-election at the forthcoming AGM (where details are required to be available for inspection) or that there are no such contracts. The disclosures required in the directors' report are illustrated below:

Extract 24.1: THORN EMI plc[16]

Directors [extract]
The directors due to retire at the Annual General Meeting on 10 September, 1987 are as follows:

a. Sir Graham Wilkins and Mr. R.H.H. Nellist retire by rotation pursuant to Article 92 and, being eligible, each offers himself for re-election;

b. Mr. J.D.F. Barnes and Mr. T. Mayer retire pursuant to Article 98 and, being eligible, each offers himself for re-election.

Sir Graham Wilkins has a service agreement which is due to expire on 22 January, 1989 and Mr R.H.H. Nellist and Mr. T. Mayer each has a service agreement which provides for a three year notice period by the Company.

There are no special Stock Exchange requirements in respect of service contracts of directors of USM or Third Market companies.

2   DISCLOSURE OF REMUNERATION

2.1   Introduction

It is the duty of each director to give notice to the company of his emoluments.[17] Details of directors' emoluments (including emoluments waived), pensions and compensation for loss of office must be disclosed by way of note to the company's financial statements.[18] In group financial statements, these requirements only extend to directors of the holding company.[19] If these disclosures are not made in the financial statements, it is the auditors' duty to include in their report, so far as they are 'reasonably able to do so', a statement giving the required particulars.[20]

2.2   Disclosure of aggregate emoluments

2.2.1   *Legal requirements*

The aggregate amount of the directors' emoluments must be disclosed.[21] This amount includes emoluments:

(a)   in respect of services as director of the company;

(b)   in respect of services as director of any of the company's subsidiaries (whilst a director of the company);

(c)   in connection with the management of the affairs of the company or any of its subsidiaries.[22]

In this context, the definition of subsidiary is extended to include the situation where the director of the reporting company is nominated by that company to act as its representative on the board of another body corporate (whether or not it is actually a subsidiary of the reporting company).[23] This extended definition applies for the purposes of all the disclosures discussed in 2.3 to 2.8 and 3.2 below, and is illustrated in Examples 24.1 and 24.2 below:

Example 24.1

Company X has an investment in company Y. Company X appoints one of its directors, Mr. A, to the board of company Y. Mr. A receives fees of £10,000 in respect of this appointment. The financial statements of company X must include the fees receivable by Mr. A in respect of his services as director of company Y, in the relevant disclosures.

Example 24.2

Company A is a debenture holder of a non-group company, company B. The trust deed entitles company A to appoint one of its directors to the board of company B. The emoluments of the appointee from company B must be included in the relevant disclosures in company A's financial statements.

The figure for emoluments must distinguish between emoluments in respect of services as director (which will include fees) and other emoluments.[24] Generally speaking, 'emoluments in respect of services as director' will, in the main, represent fees paid for attendance at board meetings and similar duties which are specifically related to the office of director. In most companies therefore, executive directors will receive only 'other emoluments' in the form of salaries and benefits under their service contracts and non-executive directors (if any) will receive only fees.

In practice, this distinction is denoted in a variety of ways, for example:

Extract 24.2: BICC plc[25]

3 Directors' emoluments [extract]	**1987**	1986
	£m	£m
The remuneration of directors of BICC plc was:		
Fees as directors	**·068**	·055
Other emoluments	**1·190**	1·095

Extract 24.3: Cadbury Schweppes p.l.c.[26]

5 DIRECTORS' REMUNERATION [extract]	**1987**	1986
	£	£
As directors	**61,667**	62,500
Management emoluments (including pension contributions)	**1,408,084**	1,314,284
	1,469,751	1,376,784

2.2.2 Problem areas

A Other services

The disclosures in respect of directors' remuneration relate to a person's services as director of a company and management services (see 2.2.1 above). In some companies, particularly small private companies, directors may also perform services unrelated to the above and for which they receive remuneration. Such remuneration should be excluded from the directors' emoluments disclosures (as illustrated in Example 24.3 below) but should be disclosed in the wages and salaries note (see 3.1 below).

Example 24.3

A journalist director of a small provincial newspaper is paid a fee for writing a weekly column. Since this fee is quite distinct from his directors' fees or management remuneration, it should be excluded from the remuneration disclosures. However, consideration should be given to disclosing this arrangement as a transaction in which a director has a material interest (see 3.5 of Chapter 23).

In practice however, it is often difficult to determine whether or not such services are, in fact, unrelated, since directors are often appointed as a result of the other services which they perform. In such cases where doubt exists, the remuneration for other services is often included with directors' remuneration.

B 'Golden hellos'

Recently, a number of companies have been offering payments (of varying kinds) as incentives for particular staff to join them (so-called 'golden hellos'). These payments made to directors do not relate to a person's services as director of the company; nor do they pertain to management services and thus do not require disclosure as part of directors' remuneration. However, such payments should be disclosed as a transaction in which a director has a material interest (see 3.5 of Chapter 23) as disclosed in the extracts below:

Extract 24.4: Beecham Group p.l.c.[27]

26 Directors' emoluments [extract]
In addition Dr. P. Jackson received the sum of £130,000 in order to compensate him for substantial losses or the risk of such losses relating to share options and other rights associated with his previous employment.

Extract 24.5: S. & W. Berisford PLC[28]

5. DIRECTORS' REMUNERATION AND INTERESTS [extract]
c Directors' interests in contracts and other transactions with the Company:
On 22 July, 1987 pursuant to a covenant of even date, the Company paid to Mr P Aaronberg the sum of £280,000 to compensate him for relinquishing the rights which he then enjoyed as a partner with Arthur Andersen & Co.

2.3   Definition of emoluments

2.3.1   *Legal requirements*

Emoluments are defined as including:[29]

(a)   fees and percentages;

(b)   any sums paid by way of expenses allowance (insofar as those sums are charged to UK income tax);

(c)   any contributions paid in respect of the director under any pension scheme. For these purposes, a pension scheme means a scheme for the provision of pensions in respect of services as director or otherwise which is maintained in whole or in part by means of contributions;[30]

(d)   the estimated money value of any other benefits received by the director otherwise than in cash (in particular, share options,[31] company cars, cheap loans (including mortgage subsidies) and cheap accommodation).

The aggregate emoluments disclosure should exclude employers' national insurance contributions as such sums are not paid in respect of a pension scheme. However, these contributions will need to be disclosed in the wages and salaries note as part of social security costs (see 3.1 below).

2.3.2   *Problem areas*

A   *Benefits–in–kind*

(a)   General

There is no universally accepted basis upon which the estimated money value of benefits received by directors is assessed; consequently, the valuation of such benefits is problematic. There are a number of possible methods whereby such benefits may be determined, in particular:

   (i)   market value of the facility provided for the private benefit of the director (less any personal contribution paid by him);

   (ii)   taxable values. Tax scale rates are often used as a yardstick whereby the values of benefits-in-kind can be readily determined. Indeed, in practice, this method is the most widely used thereby ensuring some degree of comparability between the relevant disclosure in the financial statements of different companies.
          However, as the Chancellor of the Exchequer's Budget Statement[32] of March 15, 1988 illustrated, the use of this method of determination has resulted in company motor cars being 'substantially undertaxed'. The Chancellor added that: 'independent studies, based on figures supplied by the AA, suggest that an employee with a typical company car may be taxed on only about a quarter of its true value'.
          The deficiencies of this method are illustrated by the anomalous situation where, as a result of the 1988 Budget, the money value of

       company cars included in the aggregate emoluments figure will have doubled, yet the benefit to directors will be the same;

(iii)   cost to the company. Proponents of this method argue that since the directors are appointed by the shareholders of a company to run the company on their behalf, they are entitled to be informed as to how much it is costing the company, and therefore ultimately themselves, for the directors to perform this stewardship function. However, this interpretation does not appear to be supported by the wording of the legislation, which refers to the *money value* of benefits received;

(iv)   perceived benefit to the director. It is sometimes argued that companies expect their directors to maintain certain appearances and thus provide them with, say, a particular motor car which they would not drive if they had to finance the transaction personally. In this particular example, the benefit to the director would be the cost of the make of car which he himself would have purchased, had he not been provided with a company car. This argument assumes that the company restricts the director's freedom of choice by imposing the particular benefit on him which, in practice, is unlikely.

We believe that given the wording of the legislation, the most appropriate basis for determining the money value of benefits-in-kind received by the director is by reference to the market value of the facility provided for his benefit, (i) above, notwithstanding computational difficulties inherent in using this basis. Where it is not practicable to use the market value basis, taxable values, (ii) above, should be used.

Based on our preferred approach, the method of determining the more common benefits might be as follows:

(b)   Motor cars

Where a company provides a director with a leased motor car, the market value of this facility could be calculated with reference to the lease payments and any additional running costs borne by the company. Likewise, if the company purchases a car for the use of the director, then the sum disclosed could be calculated by reference to the annual running costs, including depreciation, and associated interest costs. This may involve distinguishing between private and business mileage.

(c)   Share options

It is often difficult to make a meaningful determination of this particular benefit. Clearly, the grant of an option is beneficial to the recipient and thus must have a value. Arguably, the benefit derived by the director is the premium which a third party would be required to pay for a call option on the company's shares on the same terms as those granted to the director. However, in the case of many public and private companies, calculating the premium on a call option is a complex process. The directors should endeavour to make a reasonable estimate of this cost. If they omit to make an estimate, this should be stated in the financial statements and justified on the grounds of uncertainty as to what the proper value of the benefit is. In these circumstances, an explanatory note should be inserted at the foot of the directors' emoluments disclosures, detailing the existence and terms of the option, for example:

> During the financial year, an option to acquire shares in the company was granted to Mr. A. The option, which must be exercised before December 31, 19X9, provides that Mr. A may subscribe for 1,000 £1 ordinary shares of the company at a price of £1.10 per share. In the absence of a readily available market value for options on the company's shares, the directors are unable to arrive at an accurate assessment of the value of the option to Mr. A.

A more widely accepted basis of determination, however, is that the benefit should be valued as the difference between the mid-market price of the shares at the date that the option is granted, and the price at which shares may be acquired under the terms of the option. In the case of companies where a market price is not readily available, the directors will again have to make a reasonable estimate, and the considerations outlined in the preceding paragraph will apply.

It is worth noting that the Inland Revenue will only approve an executive share option scheme if the option price is not manifestly less than 90% of the market value of the shares at the date at which the option is granted.[33] The advantage of approved schemes is that the grantee is not liable to be taxed on the option. Accordingly, unless a scheme is unapproved, the benefit of an option to a director calculated under this approach is only likely to be nominal.

A good example of disclosure of director's share options under an approved scheme (albeit in excess of the statutory requirements in respect of directors' interests in the company's share capital) is illustrated below:

Extract 24.6: Imperial Chemical Industries PLC[34]

26 EMOLUMENTS OF DIRECTORS AND EMPLOYEES [extract]
Some directors and employees were also granted options to subscribe for Ordinary shares under the Company's share option schemes.

27 DIRECTORS' INTERESTS IN STOCKS, SHARES AND DEBENTURES [extract]
Options to subscribe for Ordinary shares granted to and exercised by directors during 1987 are included in the table below:

	At 1 January 1987	Options granted	Price £	Options exercised	At 31 December 1987
J D F Barnes	52,797			1,397	51,400
A W Clements	75,495			37,279	38,216
R C Hampel	61,566				61,566
D H Henderson	89,700	17,200	15.12		106,900
T O Hutchison	59,000				59,000
Sir Robin Ibbs	77,300				77,300
C H Reece	69,100				69,100

The options outstanding are exercisable at prices between £3.96 and £15.12.

There is no further requirement for amounts to be treated as emoluments in later years either when the value of the option increases or when it becomes exercisable or is actually exercised on the ground that any such gain is not related to the director's services to the company but is caused by external factors.

(d)   Cheap loans

The benefit derived by a director on a cheap loan (including a subsidised mortgage) could be assessed as the difference between the interest payable on the loan and the market interest payable on a like loan, calculated in accordance with a weighted average rate for the financial year.

Companies should ensure that any loans made to directors do not contravene the prohibitions on transactions with directors (see generally Chapter 23).

(e)   Cheap accommodation

Directors of companies are frequently permitted to reside in property owned or leased by the company. Where the company owns the property, the benefit derived by the director is the difference between the rent he pays and the estimated market rent for that property which the company would receive if it were to lease the premises on a commercial basis. If the company merely leases the property, the benefit could be assessed as the difference between the rent and other expenses paid by the company and that paid by the director.

Companies should ensure that any such arrangements do not contravene the restrictions on transactions with directors (see generally Chapter 23).

B   Pension contributions

Although pension contributions must be included in the aggregate emoluments figure (see 2.3.1 above), pensions paid or receivable under an adequately funded pension scheme (for example, an occupational pension scheme) do not require disclosure. If a company makes additional or top-up contributions to a pension fund (or returns surplus funds) as a result, say, of the actuaries reporting that the scheme is underfunded, it could be argued that this charge (or distribution) should be reflected in the directors' remuneration disclosures. However, contributions paid in respect of two or more persons do not require to be disclosed if the amounts paid in respect of each of them is not ascertainable.[35] These top-up payments are not usually related to past contributions paid in respect of ascertained individuals. Nevertheless, if these contributions are material, separate disclosure as an exceptional item may be necessary.

In addition, the notes to the financial statements must also disclose details of any pension commitments whether or not a provision has been made in the company's financial statements.[36]

2.4   Computing aggregate emoluments

2.4.1   *Legal requirements*

The amounts to be disclosed are the sums receivable in respect of a financial year irrespective of when paid.[37] Thus, a director's service contract may provide that he is to receive a bonus for the financial year of X% of the company's profits as disclosed in the statutory financial statements duly presented to the members in general meeting. This bonus should be accrued and included in the financial statements for the relevant financial year, notwithstanding that it is not payable until the financial statements are laid in general meeting. Any remuneration which is not receivable in respect of a period, should be disclosed in the financial statements when actually paid. Bonuses which are based on the company's results or the market performance of its shares over several years are arguably not receivable in respect of any given period, and thus fall to be disclosed when paid. An illustration of these types of bonus payments is provided by the extract below:

Extract 24.7: S. G. Warburg Group plc[38]

	1988 £000	1987 £000
1 PROFIT BEFORE INTEREST ON LOAN CAPITAL AND TAXATION [extract]		
Emoluments of directors of the Company:		
Fees	48	22
Other emoluments		
Remuneration excluding performance related payments	3,083	2,311
Performance related payments		
Annual	100	3,011
Non-recurring, long term	480	672
	3,711	6,016

In addition to the performance related payments charged in these accounts as shown above, which include annual payments arising under the Group's profit sharing schemes, provision has also been made for:

(a) Annual performance related payments which arise under senior executive bonus schemes in which there are 1,070 (*1987 1,126*) participants. Payments are made from time to time into employee trusts which, at the discretion of the trustees, are used for payment of bonuses to employees of the Group including directors of the Company. It is estimated that some £1,100,000 of the amount provided at 31st March, 1988 may be applied by the trustees in payments to directors of the Company at a later date.

(b) Long term performance related payments which arise under schemes enabling 145 (*1987 167*) participants, including certain directors of the Company, to benefit from upward movement in the market price of the Company's shares over an extended period. Provision is made for the future liability under these schemes and payments made during the year have been charged against the provision brought forward, as have payments to an employee trust which holds shares purchased in the market, thereby matching a substantial part of the future liability under the schemes. At the balance sheet date the future liability was £21,338,000 (*1987 £28,061,000*) which was £1,105,000 less (*1987 £10,898,000 more*) than the remaining balance on the provision plus the value of assets held by the trustees at that date. This difference has been credited (*1987 charged*) to the profit and loss account.

If a director is liable to repay the company for any amount paid to him (for example, a season-ticket advance) such payments do not require disclosure as emoluments.[39] However, if the director is subsequently released from the liability or any expense allowance is charged to tax after the end of the financial year, these sums must be:[40]

(a)   disclosed in the first financial statements in which it is practicable to show them; and

(b)   distinguished from other remuneration.

In order to prevent companies making indefinite loans to directors, any such amount which a director is liable to repay, which remains unpaid for two years or more after the due date, will require disclosure as above.[41]

The sums disclosed must include all sums paid by or receivable from the company, its subsidiaries or any other person.[42] Indeed, in group situations, where directors of the holding company also act as directors of subsidiary companies, it is common for the holding company to remunerate the directors in respect of their services to the subsidiary companies. The notes to the financial statements of those subsidiaries must include details of the emoluments paid by the holding company in respect of the directors' services. Where this is the case, the notes to the subsidiaries' financial statements should also explain that the charge for directors' remuneration has been borne by the holding company (although there is no requirement to do so). Similarly, a blanket management charge may be made by a holding company to its subsidiaries in respect of a variety of expenditure incurred by it on the subsidiaries' behalf including the emoluments of the subsidiaries' directors. The reporting company should seek to analyse the expenditure between types and thereby arrive at a figure for directors' emoluments. If such an exercise is not practicable, the notes to the reporting company's financial statements should state this fact, for example:

> A management charge of £100,000 in respect of administration costs has been made by Y Co. the company's holding company, which includes the directors' emoluments which it is not possible to identify separately.

In some groups, all contracts of employment and/or directors' service contracts are vested in one company. The company will provide the personnel requirements (including directors) of other group companies and in return will levy a management charge. In these situations, the considerations outlined above are equally applicable.

If it is necessary to apportion the emoluments received by a director (for example, where he acted as director for a number of group companies and was remunerated by a single composite sum from the holding company which requires analysis between the group companies), the directors may apportion these payments in such manner as they deem appropriate.[43] However, where the directors consider that they are unable to make an appropriate apportionment, the note to the subsidiaries' financial statements should reflect this fact. For example:

> The directors of the company are also directors of the holding company and fellow subsidiaries. The directors received total remuneration for the year of £120,000 (19X1: £105,000), all of which was paid by the holding company. The directors do not believe that it is practicable to apportion this amount between their services as directors of the company and their services as directors of the holding and fellow subsidiary companies.

2.4.2 *Problem areas*

A *Payments to consultancy companies*

It is not uncommon for a director's emoluments to be paid to a consultancy company/partnership of which the director and/or members of his family are shareholders/partners. In such situations the consultancy company/partnership levies a charge to the company preparing the financial statements for the services of the director. The sums remitted to the consultancy company/partnership should be disclosed in the reporting company's financial statements as remuneration receivable by the director in respect of management services provided to the company. In this connection, the Institute of Chartered Accountants of Scotland (ICAS) has highlighted this practice and argues that directors who provide other technical services to their company often circumvent the disclosure requirements by representing that these emoluments are not in connection with the management of the affairs of the company.[44]

These arrangements may also require disclosure as transactions in which a director has a material interest (see 3.5 of Chapter 23), and may also require disclosure of emoluments waived (see 2.6 below).

B   Services to holding company

Complications may also arise if the reporting company considers that emoluments paid by its holding company are purely in respect of a director's services to the holding company and not for services as director of the reporting company. It is sometimes argued that the emoluments do not need to be disclosed in the subsidiary's financial statements but should simply be disclosed in the financial statements of its holding company, assuming that:

(a)   the director is also a director of that company; and

(b)   the holding company is incorporated in the UK.

However, it is our view that if the director's services to the subsidiary company occupy a significant amount of time, an appropriate apportionment should be made and the relevant disclosures given. If the directors consider that they are unable to make an appropriate apportionment, the note to the subsidiary's financial statements should reflect this fact (see 2.4.1 above). If the director's services to the subsidiary company do not occupy a significant amount of time, it may be concluded that the director is not remunerated for them and that, therefore, the subsidiary's financial statements should reflect the director as not having received any remuneration. It will be necessary to review the particular facts in each case to ascertain whether disclosure is necessary.

However, in the case of a foreign holding company where the director works full-time in managing its UK subsidiary, disclosure of the emoluments for such work should be made in the subsidiary's financial statements for the director is clearly providing full-time management services to that company.

2.5   Bandings

For the purposes of the following disclosures, the definition of emoluments (see 2.3 above), excludes:

(a)   pension contributions;[45]

(b)   payments made in respect of compensation for loss of office (see 2.8 below).

The emoluments of the company's chairman, provided that his duties are wholly or mainly discharged within the UK, require disclosure. In this context, the chairman is the person (however designated) who chairs board meetings or whose functions are substantially similar to such a person. If more than one person has been chairman, the emoluments of each person who has occupied the position insofar as the remuneration relates to the period during which he was chairman must be disclosed (again provided that his duties were wholly or mainly discharged within the UK)[46] as shown in the following extract:

Extract 24.8: Hawker Siddeley Group PLC[47]

9 Emoluments of the Directors of Hawker Siddeley [extract]
The emoluments included above for the chairman were:

		1986	1985
Sir Peter Baxendall	1.5.86 – 31.12.86	**£50,671**	
Sir Arnold Hall	1.1.86 – 30.4.86	**£35,733**	£107,495

In addition, the emoluments of the highest paid director who worked wholly or mainly within the UK, must be disclosed if his emoluments exceed those of the chairman (or where two or more persons have acted as chairmen, the aggregate of their emoluments).[48] If the chairman is also the highest paid director, the notes should state this fact, for example:

Extract 24.9 : British Gas plc[49]

4 DIRECTORS AND EMPLOYEES [extract]
The emoluments, excluding pension contributions, of the Chairman, who was also the highest paid Director, were £183,674 (1987 £109,446).

The emoluments of all directors who discharged their duties wholly or mainly within the UK must be disclosed in bandings of multiples of £5,000 starting with the range £0—£5,000.[50] However, in order to avoid duplication of disclosures, the emoluments of the chairman and, where relevant, the highest paid director (see above) are often excluded from the bandings, with appropriate wording to reflect these omissions. This is illustrated in the following extract:

Extract 24.10: Cadbury Schweppes p.l.c.[51]

5 DIRECTORS' REMUNERATION [extract]
Emoluments (excluding pension contributions) in respect of duties wholly or mainly discharged in the United Kingdom:

	1987 £	1986 £
Emoluments of the Chairman	**119,887**	93,709
Emoluments of the highest paid director	**184,358**	157,494

Number of other directors whose emoluments (excluding pension contributions) were within the scale:

£			1987 No.	1986 No.
	Up to	5,000	**1**	1
5,001	—	10,000	**4**	4
15,001	—	20,000	**1**	1
20,001	—	25,000	**1**	—
65,001	—	70,000	**—**	1
75,001	—	80,000	**—**	2
90,001	—	95,000	**1**	—
95,001	—	100,000	**—**	1
100,001	—	105,000	**1**	—
115,001	—	120,000	**1**	1
120,001	—	125,000	**—**	1
130,001	—	135,000	**1**	1
140,001	—	145,000	**1**	—

If a chairman is appointed during the course of a financial year, during which period he was also a director, disclosure of his emoluments as chairman should be made as described above. His emoluments as director could be omitted from the bandings and disclosed by way of a note; alternatively, the total emoluments of the chairman/director could be reflected in the bandings (in which case, the chairman is not omitted from the bandings as illustrated above).

The bandings are fixed and may not be adjusted where the company's financial year is not a year. Thus, if a company's financial year[52] is 15 months, the bands remain as multiples of £5,000. However, some companies provide the bandings disclosures on an annualised basis as supplementary information.

The above disclosure requirements may be omitted:

(a)   in respect of a company which is neither the holding company nor the subsidiary of another body corporate (including overseas companies), provided the total emoluments for the company for the financial year did not exceed £60,000.[53] For the purposes of calculating this threshold, directors' pension contributions should be included. Given the restrictions on the application of this exemption, it is usually only of relevance to (i) small private companies and (ii) to non-group companies with a short financial year,[54] since the £60,000 threshold is fixed and is not pro-rated if the accounting reference period is less than 12 months;

(b) where the chairman and directors discharged their duties wholly or mainly outside the UK; it is always a question of fact based on the director's personal circumstances whether advantage can be taken of this provision. However, a number of companies disclose the exclusion of such directors as supplementary information, for example:

Extract 24.11: S. & W. Berisford PLC[55]

5. DIRECTORS' REMUNERATION AND INTERESTS [extract]
a Remuneration
2 Directors were wholly remunerated outside the United Kingdom (1987 2).

2.6 Emoluments waived

The number of directors who have waived rights to receive emoluments and the aggregate amount thereof must be disclosed;[56] for example:

Extract 24.12: S. & W. Berisford PLC[57]

5. DIRECTORS' REMUNERATION AND INTERESTS [extract]
a Remuneration
5 Directors waived commission amounting to £3,105,000 (1987 5 Directors waived £2,335,000.

In addition, listed companies and companies traded on the USM must disclose particulars of arrangements under which a director has either waived or agreed to waive any current or future emoluments (this applies in respect of emoluments from the company or any of its subsidiaries),[58] as is illustrated below:

Extract 24.13: The Plessey Company plc[59]

6 Directors and senior employees [extract]
By an Agreement dated 31 July 1986, Dolphin Consultants Limited makes available to the Company the services of Lord Brookes in an advisory capacity in consideration of a fee at the rate of £15,000 per annum. Lord Brookes has waived all director's fees during the continuance of this Agreement, which is terminable by three months' notice expiring on 1 August 1988 or at any time thereafter.

There are no additional disclosures in respect of companies traded on The Third Market.

2.7 Pensions of directors and past directors

The notes to the financial statements must disclose the aggregate amount of directors' or past directors' pensions (including pensions receivable by their dependants and their nominees) distinguishing between:

(a) pensions in respect of services as director of the company or any of its subsidiaries; and

(b)   other pensions, i.e., pensions receivable in respect of services in connection with the management of the affairs of the company or any subsidiary of it.[60]

In this context, pension includes any superannuation allowance, superannuation gratuity or similar payment.[61]

In most cases, pensions will only be payable to executive directors and would, therefore, fall within the 'other pensions' classification and would normally be disclosed in the financial statements along the following lines:

Extract 24.14: Allied–Lyons plc[62]

6 EMOLUMENTS OF DIRECTORS AND HIGHER PAID EMPLOYEES [extract]

	1988 £000s	1987 £000s
Pensions for directors and past directors	129	105

Extract 24.15: Hawker Siddeley Group PLC[63]

8 EMOLUMENTS OF THE DIRECTORS OF HAWKER SIDDELEY [extract]

	1987 £000	1986 £000
Pensions paid in respect of former Directors	23	162

These disclosures relate to pensions which are not funded out of the company's pension scheme.[64] In some companies, a pension fund may have been set up after a director retired. Any pension paid to such a director would not be payable out of the company's pension fund and this would require disclosure under this head. If a company is required to make additional contributions to its pension fund in order to continue financing the pensions of past directors, these amounts may not require disclosure for the reasons outlined in 2.3.2 B above.

Details of pension commitments in respect of past directors also require disclosure[65] (see 2.3.2 B above).

2.8   Compensation for loss of office

2.8.1   Legal requirements

The aggregate amount of any compensation payable to directors or past directors in respect of loss of office must be disclosed. In this context, compensation for loss of office includes sums paid upon a person's retirement from office[66] as the following extract illustrates:

Extract 24.16: BICC plc[67]

5 Directors' emoluments [extract]

	1986 £m	1985 £m
Compensation to former directors in respect of early retirement from executive office	—	·158

However, if a former director is paid a pension in respect of his loss of, or retirement from, office, this amount should be disclosed as a pension paid to a past director and not as part of compensation for loss of office (see 2.7 above).

These requirements extend to the loss of any office or otherwise in connection with the management of the affairs of the company or any of its subsidiaries[68] and apply whether or not the compensation requires company approval (see 1.3 above). For example, if the managing director of a subsidiary company ceases to act in that capacity but remains on the boards of both that company and its parent, any compensation paid by the subsidiary in respect of this loss of office should be disclosed in both the holding company's and subsidiary's financial statements.

These disclosures should distinguish both between:

(a)   compensation in respect of the office of director and other offices;[69] and

(b)   compensation paid by or receivable from the company, its subsidiaries and any other person.[70]

2.8.2   *Problem areas*

A   *Non-monetary   compensation*

It is often argued that non-monetary compensation, for example a motor car, does not require disclosure because the disclosure provisions only extend to sums of money paid to or receivable by the director. This potential loophole in the legislation has been highlighted in a memorandum issued by the ICAS.[71] Although it may be possible to adopt such an interpretation of the legislation, it is our view that the compensation disclosure requirements ought to be applied to non-monetary compensation. The recent Companies Bill would appear to close this loophole as it proposes that 'references to compensation include benefits received, or receivable, otherwise than in cash; and in relation to such compensation references to its amount are to its value of the benefit received'.[72]

A particular problem associated with non-cash compensation relates to the valuation of such benefits.[73] Ordinarily, the market value of the asset should be disclosed; however, if the book value of the asset is used, an explanatory note should indicate the asset's market value, for example:

Example 24.4

A director is given a motor car upon retirement from the company and the book value of the car is £2,000 and its market value is £3,000. The company should either disclose the market value of the car in the compensation for loss of office disclosure or use the book value of the asset and append an explanatory note to the directors' remuneration note to the following effect: 'the amount for compensation for loss of office includes the written down value of a [description of vehicle] the market value of which was £3,000'.

The following extract supports this view:

Extract 24.17: The Plessey Company plc[74]

6 Directors and senior employees [extract]
During the year ended 1 April 1988 4 cars were sold by the Company to retiring directors for an aggregate consideration of £34,175 (market value £45,260) and surplus furniture was sold to a retiring director at market value for an aggregate consideration of £9,628.

B   Ex-gratia payments

Ex-gratia payments which do not constitute compensation for loss of office and which are not in connection with a person's retirement need not be disclosed. In order to decide whether a payment is ex-gratia, regard should be had to the nature of and all the circumstances surrounding the payment. The donor company's classification of the payment is irrelevant. The following examples distinguish a disguised retirement payment from an ex-gratia payment:

Example 24.5

Mr. A retires from the board of company X. The following week, company X makes Mr. A an ex-gratia payment of £25,000. In these circumstances, the payment albeit described as ex-gratia, should be disclosed as compensation for loss of office for it would appear to be connected with the director's retirement from the board.

Example 24.6

Mr. A is a former director of company X. After leaving company X, Mr. A sets up his own business, which through no fault of his own, goes into liquidation. Company A learns of Mr. A's plight and gifts him the sum of £20,000. In these circumstances, the payment is unrelated to Mr. A's retirement from the board of company X and need not be disclosed in its financial statements as compensation for loss of office.

3   EMPLOYEE DISCLOSURES

The Companies Act contains disclosure requirements relating to employees' remuneration which may also impact upon directors, namely, the staff costs and higher-paid employee disclosures. These requirements are discussed below.

3.1   Director as an employee

Directors may have a contract of service with the company, in which case they should be included in the detailed employee disclosures. Accordingly, certain of their costs will require disclosure in the wages and salaries note[75] (in addition to the disclosures in the directors' remuneration note), as is illustrated below:

Extract 24.18: The Plessey Company plc[76]

5 Employees [extract]	1988 £m	1987 £m
Staff costs, including directors' emoluments were:		
Wages and salaries	388.3	397.4
Social security costs	37.1	38.4
Other pension costs	17.0	17.1
	442.4	452.9

In this context, the employer's national insurance contributions should be included as part of social security costs (that is, any contributions by the company to any state social security or pension scheme, fund or arrangement);[77] however, the value of benefits-in-kind must be excluded.

The emoluments of directors who have a contract only for services as director (i.e. most non-executive directors) should not be included in the wages and salaries note, since such persons are not employees of the company. However, details of their emoluments will be disclosed in the directors' remuneration note.

3.2   Higher-paid employees

The notes to the financial statements must also disclose the number of employees whose emoluments exceed £30,000 in bandings, rising in multiples of £5,000 (i.e. £30,000 — £35,000, £35,001 — £40,000 etc).[78] For these purposes:

(a)   directors of the company and

(b)   other persons who worked wholly or partly outside the UK (see 2.5 above)

are excluded from the disclosures.[79]

The definition of emoluments for the banding disclosures of directors applies (i.e. pension contributions are excluded).[80]

The amounts to be brought into account are such sums as are receivable in respect of an employee's services:

(a)   as a person in the employment of the company;

(b)   as a director of a subsidiary

irrespective of the payer;[81] in addition, the sums to be disclosed are amounts receivable in respect of the financial year (whenever paid) or any sums paid which do not refer to a particular period[82] (see generally 2.4 above).

Example 24.7

Mr. X is an employee of company A for which he receives emoluments of £40,500 and a bonus (payable post year end) of £2,000, and a director of its subsidiary company B for which he receives fees of £5,000, i.e. a total of £47,500. The notes to company A's financial statements should thus disclose Mr. X's emoluments in the £45,001 — £50,000 banding in the higher-paid employees' note.

If a director of a subsidiary company is not an employee of the holding company, it is not necessary for him to be included in the bandings for higher-paid employees.

In group financial statements, these disclosures are only required in respect of higher-paid employees of the holding company.[83] The ICAS[84] argues that these requirements should apply to the whole group, since the holding company often does not have any employees. In practice, as the following extract illustrates, group financial statements often contain these disclosures in respect of higher-paid employees of all group companies:

Extract 24.19: Cadbury Schweppes plc[85]

6 EMPLOYEES AND EMOLUMENTS [extract]
Employees of the group (other than directors) whose duties were wholly or mainly discharged in the United Kingdom received emoluments (excluding pension contributions) within the following scale:

£			1987 No.	1986 No.
30,001	—	35,000	63	29
35,001	—	40,000	43	12
40,001	—	45,000	11	9
45,001	—	50,000	12	13
50,001	—	55,000	9	12
55,001	—	60,000	9	2
60,001	—	65,000	7	6
65,001	—	70,000	3	3
70,001	—	75,000	9	4
75,001	—	80,000	3	1
80,001	—	85,000	3	—
85,001	—	90,000	2	—
90,001	—	95,000	2	—
95,001	—	100,000	1	—
105,001	—	110,000	1	—
110,001	—	115,000	1	—

It is likely that disclosure of information relating to higher-paid employees will no longer be required as the Companies Bill proposes to repeal the current provisions of the Companies Act.[86]

References

1 A more detailed exposition of the law governing directors' remuneration can be found in R. Pennington, *Company Law*, pp. 634—641 and C.M. Schmitthoff (ed.), *Palmer's Company Law (Volume 1)*, pp. 902—907.
2 L.C.B. Gower, *The Principles of Modern Company Law*, p. x.
3 See Chapter 23, footnote 1.
4 The Companies (Tables A—F) Regulations 1985 (SI 1985 No 805), Table A, Article 82.
5 *Hutton v West Cork Railway* (1883) 23 Ch.D. 654. For a discussion of the extent to which company law is able to control the level of directors' remuneration, see J.E. Parkinson, *Directors' Remuneration*, pp. 130—132, 142—143.
6 CA 85, s 311(1).
7 *Ibid.*, s 311(2).
8 The Companies (Tables A—F) Regulations 1985, (SI 1985 No 805), Table A, Article 87.
9 CA 85, s 312.
10 Pennington, *op. cit.*, p. 639.
11 CA 85, s 316(3).
12 The validity of gratuitous payments to directors, other employees and their dependants is discussed in D.W. Fox, *In House Gifts by Companies*, pp. 21—30.
13 CA 85, s 318.
14 *Ibid.*, s 319.
15 The Council of The Stock Exchange, *Admission of Securities to Listing*, Section 5, Chapter 2, paras. 43(a)—(c).
16 THORN EMI plc, Annual Report 1987, p. 36.
17 CA 85, s 231(4). This duty also extends to anyone who is, or has within the last five years been, an officer of the company.
18 *Ibid.*, ss 231(1), (2)(b). If the directors are entitled to deliver accounts to the registrar modified as for small companies, the modified accounts may omit these details.
19 *Ibid.*, Sch. 4, para. 63(a).
20 *Ibid.*, s 237(5). A discussion of the procedures which the auditor should adopt in relation to directors' emoluments can be found in A. Brown and D. Foster, *Directors' loans, other transactions and remuneration*, pp. 25—27.
21 CA 85, Sch. 5, para. 22(1).
22 *Ibid.*, para. 22(2).
23 *Ibid.*, para. 33(2)(a).
24 *Ibid.*, para. 22(2)(b).
25 BICC plc, Annual Report 1987, p. 26.
26 Cadbury Schweppes p.l.c., Annual Report 1987, p. 42.
27 Beecham Group p.l.c., Annual Report 1988, p. 53.
28 S. & W. Berisford PLC, Report & Accounts 1987, p. 40.
29 CA 85, Sch. 5, para. 22(3).
30 *Ibid.*, para. 33(3)(b).
31 A survey of the constituent companies of the Financial Times/Stock Exchange (FTSE) 100 index found that 87 thereof had some form of share option scheme: 'News: Share Option Schemes', *Accountancy*, November 1986, pp. 11—13.

A more recent survey into performance related bonuses for senior management concludes that the incidence of both share options and performance related bonuses is rising. Indeed 70% of survey participants had both types of incentive. The report notes that the fall in share prices in October 1987 has highlighted the limitations of the share option scheme as a measure of management performance and expresses the hope that this fall may encourage more companies to examine the benefit of long-term or deferred bonus plans: T. Vernon-Harcourt, *Performance Related Bonuses for Senior Management*, pp. 15—49 *passim*.

The Association of British Insurers (ABI) has announced revised guidelines for executive share option schemes. The ABI has stated that a company should not as a result of such schemes issue more than 5% of its issued ordinary capital in any ten year period. Subject to these restrictions, any one individual may receive options exercisable after three years, worth up to four times his emoluments subject to real growth in the earnings per share (eps) of the company over a three year period following the date of grant. Options of a further four times emoluments which are in excess of the 5% limit referred to above may be granted if exercisable five years from the date of the grant provided that the underlying growth in the eps of the company over a five year period is equal to that of the top 25 of the FTSE 100 companies: Association of British Insurers, Investment Committee, *Share Option and Profit Sharing Incentive Schemes Revised Guidelines to Requirements of Insurance Offices as Investors*, July 13, 1987.

32 Hansard, *Parliamentary Debates*, March 15, 1988, Column 1009.
33 Income and Corporation Taxes Act 1988, Sch. 9, para. 25.
34 Imperial Chemical Industries PLC, Annual Report 1987, pp. 49 and 50.
35 CA 85, Sch. 5, para. 33(3)(c).
36 *Ibid.*, Sch. 4, para. 50(4).
37 *Ibid.*, Sch. 5, para. 31(1).
38 S. G. Warburg Group plc, Annual Report 31st March 1988, p. 45.
39 CA 85, Sch. 5, para. 30(2).
40 *Ibid.*, para. 31(2).
41 *Ibid.*, para. 31(2).
42 *Ibid.*, para. 30(2).
43 *Ibid.*, para. 32.
44 The Institute of Chartered Accountants of Scotland, *Current Problem Areas in Company Law*, p. 5.
45 CA 85, Sch. 5, para. 26.
46 *Ibid.*, paras. 24(1)—(3).
47 Hawker Siddeley Group PLC, 1986 Annual Report and Accounts, p. 31.
48 CA 85, Sch. 5, paras. 25(3)—(5).
49 British Gas plc, Annual Report and Accounts 1988, p. 24.
50 CA 85, Sch. 5, paras. 25(1)—(2).
51 Cadbury Schweppes p.l.c., Annual Report 1987, p. 42.
52 CA 85, s 742(1)(d).
53 *Ibid.*, Sch. 5, para. 23.
54 *Ibid.*, s. 742(1)(d)
55 S. & W. Berisford PLC, Report & Accounts 1988, p. 42.
56 CA 85, Sch. 5, para. 27(1).
57 S. & W. Berisford PLC, Report & Accounts 1988, p. 42.
58 *Admission of Securities to Listing*, Section 5, Chapter 2, para. 21(n); The Council of The Stock Exchange, *The Stock Exchange Unlisted Securities Market*, General Undertaking, para. 10(k).
59 The Plessey Company plc, Report and Accounts 1988, p. 31.
60 CA 85, Sch. 5, paras. 28(1)—(3).
61 *Ibid.*, para. 33(3)(a).
62 Allied-Lyons plc, Report & Accounts 1988, p. 43.
63 Hawker Siddeley Group PLC, Annual Report and Accounts 1987, p. 35.
64 CA 85, Sch. 5, para. 28(2).
65 *Ibid.*, Sch. 4, para. 50(4).
66 *Ibid.*, Sch. 5, paras. 29(1), (3).
67 BICC plc, Annual Report 1986, p. 27.
68 CA 85, Sch. 5, para. 29(2)(a).
69 *Ibid.*, para. 29(2)(b).
70 *Ibid.*, para. 30(3).
71 The Institute of Chartered Accountants of Scotland, *op. cit.*, p. 7.
72 Companies Bill, Sch. 4, para. 8(3).

73 In Example 24.4, the director will be taxed on the market value of the vehicle: Income and Corporation Taxes Act 1988, s 187(3).

74 The Plessey Company plc, Report and Accounts 1988, p. 31.

75 CA 85, Sch. 4, paras. 56(4), 94.

76 The Plessey Company plc, Report and Accounts 1988, p. 29.

77 CA 85, Sch. 4, para. 94(1).

78 *Ibid.*, ss 231(1), (2); Sch. 5, para. 35(1).

79 *Ibid.*, Sch. 5, para. 35(2).

80 *Ibid.*, para. 36(2).

81 *Ibid.*, para. 36(1).

82 *Ibid.*, para. 36(3).

83 *Ibid.*, Sch. 4, para. 63(a).

84 The Institute of Chartered Accountants of Scotland, *op.cit.*, p. 7.

85 Cadbury Schweppes p.l.c., Annual Report 1987, p. 43.

86 Companies Bill, p. ii.

Specimen financial statements

This appendix contains the annual reports of two mythical UK companies; a private company which is not a member of a group — *Good Practice Limited* — and a listed public company with subsidiaries — *Good Group P.L.C.* These are designed to illustrate the form and content of typical financial statements of manufacturing companies in the UK, but they do not attempt to show all possible disclosures, and they should not therefore be used as a checklist of all the requirements in force. For a full understanding of these requirements, it is necessary to consult the relevant sources in accounting standards, the Companies Act and the Stock Exchange Yellow Book.

The specimen financial statements are supplemented by marginal annotations which refer to the requirements being illustrated. The following abbreviations have been used for this purpose:

SSAP 24(87)	Paragraph 87 of SSAP 24
s.228(6)	Section 228(6) of the Companies Act 1985
sch 4.48(1)	Paragraph 48(1) of the Fourth Schedule to the Companies Act 1985
YB 5.21(e)	Paragraph 21(e) of Section 5 of the Stock Exchange Yellow Book

Proposed requirements which have not yet been finalised, such as exposure drafts of accounting standards and the Companies Bill, are not illustrated in the specimen financial statements.

Good Practice Limited adopts format 2 (as specified in the Fourth Schedule of the Companies Act 1985) for the profit and loss account, while *Good Group P.L.C.* adopts format 1. Both companies use format 1 for the balance sheet.

GOOD PRACTICE LIMITED
REPORT AND ACCOUNTS
December 31, 19X8

GOOD PRACTICE LIMITED

Directors

J.N. Smith (Chairman)
F.R. Brown
J. Archer
P.A. MacBryde
M.C. Holman

Secretary

J. Harris

Auditors

Chartered Accountants & Co.
7 Moor Street, Edinburgh

Bankers

Bank Limited
George Street, Glasgow

Solicitors

Solicitors & Co.
7 Waverley, Edinburgh

Registered Office

11 Smithdown Lane, Edinburgh

GOOD PRACTICE LIMITED

DIRECTORS' REPORT

The directors submit their report and financial statements for the year ended December 31,   s 235, 239
19X8.

Results and dividends

The trading profit for the year, after taxation, amounted to £139,000 before charging an   s 235(1)(b)
extraordinary loss of £23,000 incurred when a factory building subsided as a result of uncharted
mine works. The directors recommend a final ordinary dividend amounting to £15,000,
making the total of ordinary dividends £30,000 for the year, which, after appropriation of
preference dividends of £9,000, leaves a profit of £77,000 to be retained.

Review of the business

The company's principal activity during the year continued to be the manufacture and   s 235(2)
installation of fire-prevention equipment.

Turnover has increased by 22% to £3,980,000 during the year and the directors believe that the   s 235(1)(a)
trend will continue. Particularly encouraging has been the growth in export sales to the United
States, which have more than doubled to £650,000 and now comprise 16% of total turnover
and the company is in a good position to take advantage of any opportunities which may arise
in the future.

Market value of land and buildings

The freehold properties were revalued at December 31, 19X8. The valuation of £550,000   sch 7.1(2)
which was £125,000 higher than the former net book value, has been incorporated in these
financial statements.

The market value of the short leasehold property at the year end was higher than the book
value. It has been sold since the end of the year and details of the sale are given in the
paragraph relating to events since the end of the year.

Fixed assets

The significant changes in tangible fixed assets during the year arose principally from   sch 7.1(1)
improvements to plant and machinery, totalling £415,000.

The company acquired for £75,000 the goodwill of an unincorporated business which had
developed a fire retardant fabric and also increased its shareholding in Southlands Limited from
2% to 15% of its issued ordinary share capital.

Research and development

The company has increased its commitment in the area of research and development. There are   sch 7.6(c)
now five employees working solely on research and development activities. Continuity of
investment in this area is essential if the company is to retain a competitive position in the
market.

Future developments

The directors aim to maintain the management policies which have resulted in the company's   sch 7.6(b)
substantial growth in recent years. They consider that 19X9 will show a further significant
growth in sales, particularly of the exports to the United States.

Events since the end of the year

The company sold its leasehold property in Berwick-upon-Tweed on March 10, 19X9 realising   sch 7.6(a)
a gain on disposal of £27,500.

GOOD PRACTICE LIMITED

DIRECTORS' REPORT

Directors and their interests

The directors during the year were as follows: s 235(2)

J.N. Smith (Chairman)
F.R. Brown
R.D. Dixon (resigned June 30, 19X8)
J. Archer
P.A. MacBryde (appointed July 1, 19X8)

In addition M.C. Holman was appointed a director on May 27, 19X9. P.A. MacBryde and M.C. Holman retire from the board at the Annual General Meeting and, being eligible, offer themselves for re-election. J. Archer retires by rotation and, being eligible, offers himself for re-election.

The only interests in the share capital of the company of directors at the year end were as   sch 7.2
follows:

	At December 31, 19X8 Ordinary shares	At January 1, 19X8 or subsequent date of appointment Ordinary shares
J.N. Smith	1,000	1,000
F.R. Brown	625	625
P.A. MacBryde	2,500	2,500

No director was interested in the preference shares at either date.

Political and charitable contributions

During the year, the company made a political contribution of £250 to the Conservative Party   sch 7.3 — 5
and various charitable contributions totalling £1,000.

Auditors

A resolution to reappoint Chartered Accountants & Co. as auditors will be put to the members at the Annual General Meeting.

By order of the Board.

J. Harris
Secretary.

July 25, 19X9

REPORT OF THE AUDITORS
to the members of Good Practice Limited

We have audited the financial statements on pages   to   in accordance with Auditing Standards.

In our opinion the financial statements give a true and fair view of the state of the company's affairs at December 31, 19X8 and of its profit and source and application of funds for the year then ended and have been properly prepared in accordance with the Companies Act 1985.

Chartered Accountants & Co.
Edinburgh

July 25, 19X9.

GOOD PRACTICE LIMITED

PROFIT AND LOSS ACCOUNT
for the year ended December 31, 19X8

s 227, 228
sch 4.8

	Notes	19X8 £'000	19X7 £'000	
Turnover	2	3,980	3,268	
Change in stocks of finished goods and in work in progress		15	(27)	
		3,995	3,241	
Other operating income		41	32	
		4,036	3,273	
Raw materials and consumables		1,518	1,179	
Other external charges		161	34	
		1,679	1,213	
		2,357	2,060	
Staff costs	4	1,344	1,210	
Depreciation and amortisation		146	98	
Other operating charges		632	648	
		2,122	1,956	
Operating profit	3	235	104	
Income from investments	5	12	10	
Interest payable	6	(38)	(14)	
		26	4	
Profit on ordinary activities before taxation		209	100	sch 4.3(6), SSAP 6(34)
Tax on profit on ordinary activities	7	70	40	
Profit on ordinary activities after taxation		139	60	
Extraordinary items after taxation	8	23	—	SSAP 6(34)
Profit for the financial year		116	60	SSAP 6(34)
Dividends	9	39	37	sch 4.3(7), SSAP 6(34)
		77	23	
Retained profit brought forward		357	334	
Retained profit carried forward		434	357	

Movements on reserves	Share premium account £'000	Revaluation reserve £'000	Profit and loss account £'000	
				sch 4.3(7)
				sch 4.46(1), (2)
				SSAP 6(35)
At January 1, 19X8	25	—	357	
On issue of shares during the year (see Note 19)	25	—	—	
Surplus on revaluation of assets (see Note 11)	—	125	—	
Retained profit for the year	—	—	77	
At December 31, 19X8	50	125	434	

The notes on pages   to   form part of these financial statements.

GOOD PRACTICE LIMITED

BALANCE SHEET
at December 31, 19X8

s 227, 228
sch 4.8

	Notes	19X8 £'000	19X7 £'000	
Fixed assets				
Intangible assets	10	60	—	
Tangible assets	11	1,045	731	
Investments	12	213	136	
		1,318	867	
Current assets				
Stocks	13	340	350	
Debtors	14	747	625	
Cash at bank and in hand		180	120	
		1,267	1,095	
Creditors: amounts falling due within one year	15	1,027	977	
Net current assets		240	118	
Total assets less current liabilities		1,558	985	
Creditors: amounts falling due after more than one year				
Loans	16	355	175	
Obligations under finance leases	17	67	—	
		422	175	
Provision for liabilities and charges				
Deferred taxation	18	19	13	
Accruals and deferred income				
Deferred government grants		70	40	SSAP 4(9)
		511	228	
		1,047	757	
Capital and reserves				
Called up share capital	19	438	375	
Share premium account		50	25	
Revaluation reserve		125	—	
Profit and loss account		434	357	
		1,047	757	

J.N. Smith   )
F.R. Brown   )   Directors

July 25, 19X9

SSAP 17(26)

The notes on pages   to   form part of these financial statements.

GOOD PRACTICE LIMITED

STATEMENT OF SOURCE AND APPLICATION OF FUNDS   SSAP 10(9), (11)
For the year ended December 31, 19X8

	19X8 £'000	19X7 £'000
Source of funds:		
Profit on ordinary activities before taxation	209	100
Adjustment for items not involving the movement of funds:		
Depreciation	131	98
Amortisation of goodwill	15	—
Loss/(profit) on disposal of tangible fixed assets	3	(4)
Release from deferred government grants	(10)	(8)
Profit on disposal of investments	(5)	—
Total generated from operations	343	186
Funds from other sources:		
Proceeds of share issue	88	—
Proceeds of disposal of tangible fixed assets	96	62
Proceeds of sale of investments	90	—
Government grants received	40	25
Additions to obligations under leased assets capitalised	90	—
Loans	205	—
	609	87
	952	273
Application of funds:		
Dividends paid	39	34
Extraordinary items (before taxation)	35	—
Purchase of tangible fixed assets	329	175
Leased assets capitalised	90	—
Purchase of investments	162	30
Purchase of goodwill	75	—
Tax paid	44	11
Current instalment due on loan	25	—
Current instalments due on lease commitments	23	—
	822	250
Working capital — increase	130	23
Components of increase in working capital:		
Stocks	(10)	14
Debtors	122	21
Creditors	1	(24)
	113	11
Movement in net liquid funds:		
Cash at bank and in hand	60	12
Current instalments due on loans	(25)	—
Current instalments due on lease commitments	(18)	—
	17	12
	130	23

The notes on pages   to   form part of these financial statements.

GOOD PRACTICE LIMITED

NOTES TO THE FINANCIAL STATEMENTS
at December 31, 19X8

1.   Accounting policies

sch 4.36
sch 4.10 — 15
SSAP 2(17), (18)

Accounting convention

The financial statements are prepared under the historical cost convention modified to include the revaluation of freehold land and buildings.

Goodwill

Goodwill is the difference between the amount paid on the acquisition of a business and the aggregate fair value of its separable net assets. It is being written off in equal annual instalments over its estimated economic life of 5 years.

sch 4.21(4)
SSAP 22(39), (41)

Depreciation

Depreciation is provided on all tangible fixed assets, other than freehold land, at rates calculated to write off the cost or valuation, less estimated residual value, of each asset evenly over its expected useful life, as follows:

SSAP 12(25)

Freehold buildings	— over 50 years
Leasehold land and buildings	— over the lease term
Plant and machinery	— over 5 to 15 years

The part of the annual depreciation charge on revalued assets which relates to the surplus over cost is transferred from the revaluation reserve to the profit and loss account.

Deferred government grants

Government grants on capital expenditure are credited to a deferral account and are released to revenue over the expected useful life of the relevant asset by equal annual amounts.

SSAP 4(9)

Grants of a revenue nature are credited to income in the period to which they relate.

Stocks

Stocks are stated at the lower of cost and net realisable value as follows:

SSAP 9(32)

Cost incurred in bringing each product to its present location and condition:

Raw materials and goods for resale	— purchase cost on a first-in, first-out basis
Work in progress and finished goods	— cost of direct materials and labour plus attributable overheads based on a normal level of activity

Net realisable value is based on estimated selling price less further costs expected to be incurred to completion and disposal.

Long-term contracts

Profit on long–term contracts is taken as the work is carried out if the final outcome can be assessed with reasonable certainty. The profit included is calculated on a prudent basis to reflect the proportion of the work carried out at the year end, by recording turnover and related costs (as defined in Stocks above) as contract activity progresses. Turnover is calculated as that proportion of total contract value which costs incurred to date bear to total expected costs for that contract. Revenues derived from variations on contracts are recognised only when they have been accepted by the customer. Full provision is made for losses on all contracts in the year in which they are first foreseen.

SSAP 9(32)

GOOD PRACTICE LIMITED

NOTES TO THE FINANCIAL STATEMENTS
at December 31, 19X8

1.   Accounting policies (continued)

Research and development

Research and development expenditure is written off as incurred.   SSAP 13(30)

Deferred taxation

Deferred taxation is provided on the liability method on all timing differences which are   SSAP 15(24) — (28)
expected to reverse in the future without being replaced, calculated at the rate at which it is
estimated that tax will be payable.

Foreign currencies

Transactions in foreign currencies are recorded at the rate ruling at the date of the transaction.   sch 4.58(1)

Monetary assets and liabilities denominated in foreign currencies are retranslated at the rate of   SSAP 20(59)
exchange ruling at the balance sheet date.

All differences are taken to the profit and loss account.

Leasing and hire purchase commitments

Assets obtained under finance leases and hire purchase contracts are capitalised in the balance   SSAP 21(57)
sheet and are depreciated over their useful lives.

The interest element of the rental obligations is charged to profit and loss account over the
period of the lease and represents a constant proportion of the balance of capital repayments
outstanding.

Rentals paid under operating leases are charged to income on a straight line basis over the
lease term.

Pensions

The company operates a defined contribution pension scheme. Contributions are charged to   SSAP 24(87)
the profit and loss account as they become payable in accordance with the rules of the scheme.

2.   Turnover

Turnover, which is stated net of value added tax, represents amounts invoiced to third parties,   sch 4.95, SSAP 5(8)
except in respect of long–term contracts where turnover represents the sales value of work   SSAP 9(32)
done in the year, including estimates in respect of amounts not invoiced. Turnover in respect
of long-term contracts is calculated as that proportion of total contract value which costs
incurred to date bear to total expected costs for that contract.

The turnover and pre-tax profit is attributable to one activity, the manufacture and installation   sch 4.55(1)
of fire-prevention equipment.

An analysis of turnover by geographical market is given below.   sch 4.55(2)

	19X8 £'000	%	19X7 £'000	%
United Kingdom	3,330	84	2,948	90
USA	650	16	320	10
	3,980	100	3,268	100

GOOD PRACTICE LIMITED

NOTES TO THE FINANCIAL STATEMENTS
at December 31, 19X8

3. Operating profit

(a)   This is stated after charging or crediting:

	19X8 £'000	19X7 £'000	
Auditors' remuneration	17	14	sch 4.53(7)
Depreciation of owned fixed assets	111	98	sch 4.8, SSAP 12(25)
Depreciation of assets held under finance leases and hire purchase contracts	20	—	sch 4.8, SSAP 21(49)
Amortisation of goodwill	15	—	sch 4.8
Operating lease rentals — plant and machinery	36	12	sch 4.53(6),
— land and buildings	12	12	SSAP 21(55)

The profit and loss account includes gains on translation of long-term monetary items. The inclusion of these gains represents a departure from the statutory requirement that only realised profit may be included in the profit and loss account. The directors consider that this accounting treatment, which is in accordance with SSAP 20, is necessary in order to give a true and fair view. The unrealised gains included for the year amounted to £10,000 (19X7 — £ nil) and the cumulative amount included at December 31, 19X8 is £10,000.

sch 4.15, s 228(6)
SSAP 20(65)

(b)   Directors' remuneration:

	19X8 £'000	19X7 £'000	
			sch 5.22
Fees	13	10	
Other emoluments (including pension contributions)	133	106	
Pensions to former directors	10	8	sch 5.28
	156	124	

The emoluments of the chairman, who was also the highest paid director, excluding pension contributions, were £50,000 (19X7 — £40,000). Other directors' emoluments, excluding pension contributions fell within the following ranges:

sch 5.24, 5.25

	19X8 No.	19X7 No.	
			sch 5.25
£nil — £5,000	1	1	
£5,001 — £10,000	1	—	
£15,001 — £20,000	—	2	
£25,001 — £30,000	2	—	

(c)   Senior employees:

Two senior employees received remuneration falling within the range £30,001 — £35,000 (19X7 — one employee).

sch 5.35

4. Staff costs

	19X8 £'000	19X7 £'000	
			sch 4.56(4)
Wages and salaries	1,094	987	
Social security costs	215	192	
Other pension costs	35	31	SSAP 24(87)
	1,344	1,210	

The average weekly number of employees during the year was made up as follows:

	19X8 No.	19X7 No.	
			sch 4.56(1) — (3)
Office management	38	34	
Manufacturing	76	76	
	114	110	

GOOD PRACTICE LIMITED

NOTES TO THE FINANCIAL STATEMENTS
at December 31, 19X8

5.   Income from investments

	19X8 £'000	19X7 £'000	
Unlisted	7	5	
Listed	5	5	sch 4.53(4)
	12	10	

6.   Interest payable

	19X8 £'000	19X7 £'000	sch 4.53(2)
Bank loans and overdrafts	18	14	
Other loans not wholly repayable within five years	10	—	
Finance charges payable under finance leases	10	—	SSAP 21(53)
	38	14	

7.   Tax on profit on ordinary activities

	19X8 £'000	19X7 £'000	sch 4.54 / SSAP 8(22), (23)
Based on the profit for the year:			
Corporation tax at 35%	61	36	
Tax credits attributable to dividends received	4	3	
Deferred taxation	6	2	SSAP 15(33), (38)
	71	41	
Corporation tax overprovided in previous years	(1)	(1)	
	70	40	

If full provision had been made for deferred tax for the year, the tax charge would have been SSAP 15(35)
increased by £11,000 (19X7 — £7,000), as follows:

	19X8 £'000	19X7 £'000
Capital allowances in advance of depreciation	14	7
Other differences in recognising revenue and expense items in other periods for taxation purposes	(3)	—
	11	7

8.   Extraordinary items

	19X8 £'000	19X7 £'000	sch 4.57(2) / SSAP 6(37)
Expenses connected with factory subsidence due to uncharted mine workings	35	—	
Corporation tax relief thereon	(12)	—	sch 4.54(3) SSAP 6(38)
	23	—	

GOOD PRACTICE LIMITED

NOTES TO THE FINANCIAL STATEMENTS
at December 31, 19X8

9. Dividends

		19X8 £'000	19X7 £'000	
Preference	— paid	9	9	sch 4.3(7)
Ordinary	— interim paid	15	13	
	— final proposed	15	15	sch 4.51(3)
		39	37	

10. Intangible fixed assets

	Goodwill £'000	sch 4.8, 4.42 SSAP 22(41)
Cost:		
At January 1, 19X8	—	
Acquired during the year	75	
At December 31, 19X8	75	
Amortisation:		
At January 1, 19X8	—	
Provided during the year	15	
At December 31, 19X8	15	
Net book value:		
At December 31, 19X8	60	
At January 1, 19X8	—	

11. Tangible fixed assets

	Land and buildings		Plant and Machinery	Total	sch 4.8, 4.42 SSAP 12(25)
	Freehold £'000	Short Leasehold £'000	£'000	£'000	sch 4.44
Cost or valuation:					
At January 1, 19X8	450	99	582	1,131	
Additions	—	4	415	419	
Surplus on revaluation	100	—	—	100	
Disposals	—	(10)	(220)	(230)	
At December 31, 19X8	550	93	777	1,420	
Depreciation:					
At January 1, 19X8	20	15	365	400	
Provided during the year	5	4	122	131	
Surplus on revaluation	(25)	—	—	(25)	
Disposals	—	(6)	(125)	(131)	
At December 31, 19X8	—	13	362	375	
Net book value:					
At December 31, 19X8	550	80	415	1,045	
At January 1, 19X8	430	84	217	731	

The net book value of plant and machinery above of £415,000 includes an amount of £70,000 in respect of assets held under finance leases. SSAP 21(49), (50)

GOOD PRACTICE LIMITED

NOTES TO THE FINANCIAL STATEMENTS
at December 31, 19X8

11.   Tangible fixed assets (continued)

For the freehold land and buildings included at valuation:		sch 4.33
	£'000	
Historical cost: At January 1, 19X8 and December 31, 19X8	450	
Depreciation based on cost: At January 1, 19X8 Charge for the year	20 5	
At December 31, 19X8	25	

The freehold properties were valued at their open market value for existing use on December   sch 4.43
31, 19X8 by Estate Valuers & Co., Chartered Surveyors.

12.   Investments

	Shares £'000	sch 4.8, 4.42
At January 1, 19X8	136	
Additions	162	
Disposals	(85)	
At December 31, 19X8	213	

	19X8 £'000	19X7 £'000	
Listed investments, dealt on a recognised Stock Exchange	39	39	sch 4.45(1)
Unlisted investments	174	97	
	213	136	
Valuation: Listed investments – market value	80	75	sch 4.45(2)
Taxation on potential capital gain if sold at valuation	12	11	SSAP 15(42)

The company owns 15% of the issued ordinary share capital of Southlands Limited, a   sch 5.7
company registered in England.

13.   Stocks

	19X8 £'000	19X7 £'000	sch 4.8, SSAP 9(27)
Raw materials and consumables	42	59	
Long-term contract balances	43	51	
Work in progress	168	143	
Finished goods and goods for resale	87	97	
	340	350	

Finished goods and goods for resale would amount to £107,000 (19X7 — £119,000) if valued   sch 4.27(3) — (5)
at replacement cost at December 31, 19X8.

Long–term contract balances consist of:			SSAP 9(30)
Costs to date less provision for losses	103	109	
Applicable payments on account	(60)	(58)	
	43	51	

GOOD PRACTICE LIMITED

NOTES TO THE FINANCIAL STATEMENTS
at December 31, 19X8

14. Debtors

	19X8 £'000	19X7 £'000	
			sch 4.8
Trade debtors	563	473	
Amounts recoverable on long-term contracts	122	100	SSAP 9(30)
Other debtors (see Note 24)	40	32	
Prepayments and accrued income	22	20	
	747	625	

Included in trade debtors is an amount of £38,000 which is payable after more than one year (19X7 nil).   sch 4.8(note 5)

15. Creditors: amounts falling due within one year

	Notes	19X8 £'000	19X7 £'000	
				sch 4.8
Current instalment due on bank loan	16	25	—	
Loan from a former director		82	58	
Obligations under finance leases and hire purchase contracts	17	18	—	SSAP 21(51)
Payments on account on long-term contracts		95	75	SSAP 9(30)
Trade creditors		635	695	
Current corporation tax		37	29	sch 4.8(note 9)
Other taxes and social security costs		31	24	sch 4.8(note 9)
Other creditors		63	62	
Accruals		26	19	
Proposed dividend		15	15	sch 4.51(3)
		1,027	977	

Included within other creditors is £10,000 (19X7 — £5,000) relating to outstanding contributions payable to the pension scheme.   SSAP 24(87)

16. Loans

	19X8 £'000	19X7 £'000	
			sch 4.48(1), (2)
Wholly repayable within five years:			
Bank loan	75	75	
Not wholly repayable within 5 years:			
Bank loan at 13.25% per annum, repayable in annual instalments of £10,000 commencing August 17, 19X9	100	100	
US Dollar loan at 14% per annum, wholly repayable on December 31, 19Y4	205	—	
	380	175	

GOOD PRACTICE LIMITED

NOTES TO THE FINANCIAL STATEMENTS
at December 31, 19X8

16.   Loans (continued)

	19X8 £'000	19X7 £'000	
Amounts repayable after five years other than by instalments	205	—	sch 4.48(1)
Amounts repayable by instalments:			
within 5 years	125	115	
after 5 years	50	60	
	175	175	
	380	175	
Included in current liabilities	25	—	
	355	175	

The US Dollar loan is secured by a fixed charge on the freehold property and the bank loans   sch 4.48(4)
are secured by a floating charge on the assets of the company.

17.   Obligations under finance leases

The maturity of these amounts is as follows:

	19X8 £'000	19X7 £'000	
Amounts payable			SSAP 21(51), (52)
Within one year	21	—	
Over one year:			
In the second to fifth years inclusive	76	—	
Over five years	—	—	
	97	—	
Less: Finance charges allocated to future periods	(12)	—	
	85	—	
	£'000	£'000	
Finance leases are analysed as follows:			
Current obligations	18	—	
Non-current obligations	67	—	
	85	—	

18.   Deferred taxation

Deferred taxation provided in the financial statements and the amounts not provided are as
follows:

	Provided		Not Provided		
	19X8 £'000	19X7 £'000	19X8 £'000	19X7 £'000	SSAP 15(37), (40)
Capital allowances in advance of depreciation	23	15	74	60	
Other differences in recognising revenue and expense items in other periods for taxation purposes	2	4	—	3	
	25	19	74	63	
Less: Advance corporation tax	6	6	—	—	SSAP 15(29)
	19	13	74	63	
Taxation on valuation surplus	—	—	10	—	
	19	13	84	63	

GOOD PRACTICE LIMITED

NOTES TO THE FINANCIAL STATEMENTS
at December 31, 19X8

19.   Share capital

	Authorised		Allotted, called up and fully paid		
	19X8 No.	19X7 No.	19X8 £'000	19X7 £'000	
Ordinary shares of £1 each	500,000	375,000	313	250	
7% preference shares of £1 each	125,000	125,000	125	125	
	625,000	500,000	438	375	

sch 4.8(note 12)
sch 4.38(1)

During the year, 62,500 ordinary shares of £1 each, with an aggregate nominal value of £62,500, were issued fully paid for cash of £87,500, in order to help finance the purchase of plant and machinery.   sch 4.39

20.   Post balance sheet events

The company sold its leasehold property in Berwick-upon-Tweed on March 10, 19X9 and realised a gain on disposal of £27,500. No tax liability will arise due to rollover relief.   SSAP 17(23) — (25)

21.   Capital commitments

	19X8 £'000	19X7 £'000	
Contracted	335	163	sch 4.50(3)
Authorised by the directors but not contracted	61	30	

22.   Pension commitments

The company operates a defined contribution pension scheme for its directors and senior employees. The assets of the scheme held separately from those of the company in an independently administered fund.   sch 4.50(4)
SSAP 24(87)

23.   Other financial commitments

At December 31, 19X8 the company had annual commitments under non-cancellable operating leases as set out below: sch 4.50(5)
SSAP 21(56)

	19X8		19X7	
	Land and Buildings £'000	Other £'000	Land and Buildings £'000	Other £'000
Operating leases which expire:				
Within one year	—	10	—	4
In the second to fifth years inclusive	—	20	—	18
In over five years	12	8	12	13
	12	38	12	35

GOOD PRACTICE LIMITED

NOTES TO THE FINANCIAL STATEMENTS
at December 31, 19X8

24.   Transactions with directors

Included in 'other debtors' (see Note 14) is a loan to a director, Mr J. Archer. It is an interest   sch 6. part 1
free season ticket loan repayable in monthly instalments.

	19X8	
	£	sch 6.9
Amount outstanding at end of year	820	
Amount outstanding at beginning of year	650	
Maximum outstanding during the year	910	

25.   Contingent liability

An overseas customer has commenced an action against the company in respect of equipment   sch 4.50(2)
claimed to be ineffective. It has been estimated that the maximum liability should the action   SSAP 18(18)
be successful is £35,000.

The company has been advised by Counsel that the action is unlikely to succeed and
accordingly no provision for any liability has been made in these financial statements.

GOOD GROUP P.L.C.
ANNUAL REPORT 19X8

GOOD GROUP P.L.C.

Directors

Sir Joshua Barraclough (Chairman) (Non-executive)
J.N. Smith
F.R. Brown
J. Archer
P.A. McBride
M.C. Holman (Non-executive)
N.O. Evans

Secretary

J. Harris

Auditors

Chartered Accountants & Co.
7 Moor Street, London EC2 1VQ

Bankers

Bank P.L.C.
George Street, London EC2 2LD

Solicitors

Solicitors & Co.
7 Scott Street, London WC3 4AB

Registrars

Registration Services Limited
45 Market Street, London W2 7JA

Registered Office

Homefire House, Ashdown Square,
London EC2 3AS

GOOD GROUP P.L.C.

CHAIRMAN'S STATEMENT

The year was one when strong foundations were laid for the future growth of Good Group.

As in the three previous years, the results showed the increased importance of the fire-prevention division, and your directors have continued to make decisions which will further develop this sector.

The group has discontinued its loss-making activities in Northern Ireland and this has led to an extraordinary charge for the year.

The group has continued to extend its North American activities and to this end has set up a new company, Sprinklers Incorporated, in Chicago. It is expected that by the summer of 19X9, Sprinklers will be manufacturing the group's newest fire-prevention products in the USA.

The acquisition of Extinguishers Limited, a company which has been established in Lincoln for many years, has further strengthened the fire-prevention division. This company has a well established research and development department, and will help ensure that the group's products remain 'state of the art'.

The electrical engineering division has shown a small overall decline in sales during 19X8, down by 2.5% to £20,750,000, although profit margins have held up well. Your directors believe that the group's research and development activities will ultimately lead to a resurgence of sales in this sector, but 19X9 sales are expected to continue at 19X8 levels.

The year's results would not have been possible without the enthusiastic participation of all our employees and I thank them all sincerely for their efforts.

We now look forward with confidence to a very busy and productive period for the group.

Joshua Barraclough

March 25, 19X9

GOOD GROUP P.L.C.

NON-EXECUTIVE DIRECTORS   YB 5.21(t)

Sir Joshua Barraclough, 64, joined the board of Good Group P.L.C. in 19X1. He is Lord Lieutenant of Borsetshire, non-executive chairman of the Pole Star Building Society and director of Antimony Holdings Plc, Northland Bank plc and Wessex TV PLC. Between 19X2 and 19X6, he was also Chairman of the Board of Governors of Wessex College of Management Science.

M.C. Holman has been a non-executive director of Good Group P.L.C. since 19X2. As well as being Professor of Business Studies at Wessex College of Management Science, he is director of St. James' Bank PLC and Sheen Palace Estates P.L.C. Until 19X5, he was also director of Ulster Extinguishers plc.

GOOD GROUP P.L.C.

DIRECTORS' REPORT

The directors submit their report and group financial statements of Good Group P.L.C. for the   s 235, 239
year ended December 31, 19X8.

Results and dividends

The group trading profit for the year, after taxation and minority interests, amounted to
£1,547,000 before charging extraordinary items of £178,000. Included in these results is a
profit of £95,000 earned by Extinguishers Limited from the date of acquisition on July 1,
19X8, and a loss of £38,000 suffered by Sprinklers Incorporated in the seven months from
incorporation on June 5, 19X8.

The directors recommend a final ordinary dividend of 7.9125 pence per share, amounting to   s 235(1)(b)
£199,000 making a total of 14.43 pence and £363,000 for the year, which with preference
dividends of £35,000 leaves a profit of £971,000 to be retained.

Principal activities

The group's principal activities during the year were electrical engineering and the manufacture   s 235(2)
and installation of fire-prevention equipment.

Review of the business

The group has had a satisfactory year with an increase in overall sales. There has been a   s 235(1)(a)
substantial increase in sales of fire-prevention equipment, which have grown by 23% during
the year. The growth has been in the home market, while sales to the United States have been
disappointing, showing a slight decline from 19X7 levels. However a new company,
Sprinklers Incorporated, has been set up to manufacture the group's new fire-prevention
system in the USA.

During the year the group acquired Extinguishers Limited, a company which has developed a
fire retardant fabric.

The loss-making factory in Northern Ireland was closed in October 19X8.

The group's electrical engineering activities have not shown any growth during the year
although profit margins in this area generally remain good.

Future developments

The directors consider that the current year will see a major increase in sales of new fire   sch 7.6(b)
protection products in the United Kingdom. Sprinklers Incorporated is expected to commence
production in June 19X9 and this will lead to an expansion in sales in the United States. The
group is looking for ways of making the electrical engineering business more profitable by
way of acquisitions and new product lines.

Market value of land and buildings

The group's investment properties were revalued on December 31, 19X8. The valuation of   sch 7.1(2)
£1,415,000, which was £210,000 higher than the former net book value, has been
incorporated in these financial statements. In the opinion of the directors, the market value of
the group's other properties was not materially different from the net book value.

Fixed assets

The changes in fixed assets during the year are summarised in the notes to the financial   sch 7.1(1)
statements. The most significant additions were £1,300,000 relating to the group's
production facilities in Chicago and £900,000 in connection with the acquisition of
Extinguishers Limited. Of these, assets worth £200,000 were subsequently sold.

Research and development

With the acquisition of Extinguishers Limited, the number of staff employed by the group on   sch 7.6(c)
research and development has more than doubled.

There are two main fire-prevention research and development projects: improved fire detection
and sprinkler systems and fire retardant fabrics for vehicles and aircraft.

Research and development in the electrical engineering business is concentrating on
developing new products capable of generating greater turnover.

GOOD GROUP P.L.C.

DIRECTORS' REPORT

Events since the end of the year

On February 14, 19X9 a short leasehold building with a net book value of £150,000 was   sch 7.6(a)
severely damaged by flooding. It is expected that insurance proceeds will fall short of the
costs of rebuilding and loss of profits by some £20,000. No provision has been made in these
financial statements for this loss.

Disabled employees

The group gives every consideration to applications for employment from disabled persons   sch 7.9
where the requirements of the job may be adequately covered by a handicapped or disabled
person.

With regard to existing employees and those who have become disabled during the year, the
group has continued to examine ways and means of providing continuing employment under
normal terms and conditions and to provide training and career development and promotion
wherever appropriate.

Employee involvement

During the year, the policy of providing employees with information about the group has   sch 7.11
been continued through the newsletter in which employees have also been encouraged to
present their suggestions and views on the group's performance. Regular meetings are held
between local management and employees to allow a free flow of information and ideas.
Employees are encouraged directly to participate in the success of the business through the
group's Profit Sharing Scheme.

Political and charitable contributions

During the year the group made a political contribution of £5,500 to the Social and Liberal   sch 7.3 — 5
Democrats and various charitable contributions totalling £10,000.

Directors and their interests

The directors at December 31, 19X8 and their interests in the share capital of the company (all   s 235(2)
beneficially held except those marked with an asterisk which are held as trustee) were as   sch 7.2
follows: YB 5.21(h)

	At December 31, 19X8 Ordinary shares	At January 1, 19X8 or subsequent date of appointment Ordinary shares
Sir Joshua Barraclough (Chairman)	35,000	35,000
J.N. Smith	40,000	40,000
F.R. Brown	25,000	25,000
	9,000*	9,000*
J. Archer	—	—
P.A. McBride	10,000	10,000
M.C. Holman	250	250
N.O. Evans	3,000	3,000

No director was interested in the preference shares or debentures of the company, or in the
shares or loan stock of any subsidiary company.

During the period from the end of the financial year to March 18, 19X9, M.C. Holman   YB 5.21(h)
acquired 1,000 ordinary shares in the company. In all other respects, the interests of the
directors were unchanged.

In addition to the directors listed above, R.P. Jones served as a director until May 31, 19X8
when he resigned.

N.O. Evans, who was appointed a director on May 31, 19X8, retires from the board at the   YB 5.43(c)
Annual General Meeting and, being eligible, offers himself for re-election. J.N. Smith and
P.A. McBride retire by rotation and, being eligible, offer themselves for re-election. The
service contracts of J.N. Smith and P.A. McBride expire on June 30, 19Y0 and that of N.O.
Evans on May 31, 19Y2.

GOOD GROUP P.L.C.

DIRECTORS' REPORT

Directors and their interests (continued)

The company has a share option scheme by which directors and other executives are able to subscribe for shares in Good Group P.L.C. The interests of the directors at the year end were:

sch 7.2
YB 5.21(h)

J. Archer	— 35,000 ordinary shares at £3.80 each, exercisable before January 1, 19Y0
P.A. McBride	— 20,000 ordinary shares at £3.85 each, exercisable before January 1, 19Y2
F.R. Brown	— 15,000 ordinary shares at £3.85 each, exercisable before January 1, 19Y2

Details of directors' material interests in contracts are given in the notes to the financial statements.

YB 5.21(k)

Substantial shareholder

On March 8, 19X9, International Fires P.L.C. held 791,670 ordinary shares of £1 each (31.48% of the ordinary share capital) in the company. During the year, group companies made sales totalling £1,395,000 in the ordinary course of business to International Fires P.L.C. No other person has reported an interest of 5% or more in the ordinary shares of the company, requiring to be recorded in the register under S.211 of the Companies Act 1985.

YB 5.21(i)
YB 5.21(l)

Close company status

The company is not a close company within the provisions of the Income and Corporation Taxes Act 1988.

YB 5.21(j)

Auditors

A resolution to reappoint Chartered Accountants & Co. as auditors will be put to the members at the Annual General Meeting.

By order of the Board,

J. Harris

March 25, 19X9

REPORT OF THE AUDITORS

to the members of Good Group P.L.C.

We have audited the financial statements on pages   to   in accordance with Auditing Standards.

In our opinion the financial statements give a true and fair view of the state of affairs of the company and the group at December 31, 19X8 and of the profit and source and application of funds of the group for the year then ended and have been properly prepared in accordance with the Companies Act 1985.

Chartered Accountants & Co.
London.

March 25, 19X9.

GOOD GROUP P.L.C.

GROUP PROFIT AND LOSS ACCOUNT
for the year ended December 31, 19X8

s 229, s 230
sch 4.8

	Notes	19X8 £'000	19X7 £'000	
Turnover	2	38,700	36,000	
Cost of sales		30,825	28,900	
Gross profit		7,875	7,100	
Distribution costs		3,061	2,866	
Administration expenses		2,860	2,429	
		5,921	5,295	
		1,954	1,805	
Other operating income		125	130	
Share of profits of associated companies		500	250	SSAP 1(19)
Operating profit	3	2,579	2,185	
Income from investments	5	50	40	
Bank interest receivable		185	119	
Interest payable	6	(288)	(274)	
		53	115	
Profit on ordinary activities before taxation	2	2,526	2,070	sch 4.3(6), SSAP 6(34)
Tax on profit on ordinary activities	7	928	605	
Profit on ordinary activities after taxation		1,598	1,465	
Minority interests		51	5	SSAP 14(35)
Profit before extraordinary items	8	1,547	1,460	
Extraordinary items after taxation	9	178	—	SSAP 6(34)
Profit attributable to members of the holding company	10	1,369	1,460	SSAP 6(34)
Dividends	11	398	297	sch 4.3(7), SSAP 6(34)
Retained profit for year	24	971	1,163	
Earnings per share — basic	12	67.13p	71.25p	SSAP 3(14)
— fully diluted		54.57p	57.23p	SSAP 3(16)

A statement of the movement on reserves can be found in note 24.   SSAP 6(35)

The notes on pages to form part of these financial statements.

GOOD GROUP P.L.C.

GROUP BALANCE SHEET
at December 31, 19X8

s 229, 230
sch 4.8

	Notes	19X8 £'000	19X7 £'000
Fixed assets			
Intangible assets	13	412	337
Tangible assets	14	6,066	5,300
Investments	15	798	801
		7,276	6,438
Current assets			
Stocks	16	5,225	4,020
Debtors	17	3,267	1,727
Cash at bank and in hand		1,994	2,257
		10,486	8,004
Creditors: amounts falling due within one year	18	4,986	5,024
Net current assets		5,500	2,980
Total assets less current liabilities		12,776	9,418
Creditors: amounts falling due after more than one year	19	2,444	1,812
Provision for liabilities and charges			
Deferred taxation	22	5	23
		2,449	1,835
		10,327	7,583
Minority interests		55	9
		10,272	7,574
Capital and reserves			
Called up share capital	23	3,015	2,500
Share premium account	24	100	100
Revaluation reserve	24	663	486
Other reserves	24	950	—
Profit and loss account	24	5,544	4,488
		10,272	7,574

SSAP 14(34)

J. Archer   )
P.A. McBride   )   Directors

The notes on pages   to   form part of these financial statements.

GOOD GROUP P.L.C.

BALANCE SHEET
at December 31, 19X8

s 227, 228
sch 4.8

	Notes	19X8 £'000	19X7 £'000
Fixed assets			
Tangible assets	14	3,042	2,585
Investments	15	3,422	1,295
		6,464	3,880
Current assets			
Stocks	16	2,314	1,425
Debtors	17	2,320	2,255
Cash at bank and in hand		1,415	1,840
		6,049	5,520
Creditors: amounts falling due within one year	18	2,304	1,829
Net current assets		3,745	3,691
Total assets less current liabilities		10,209	7,571
Creditors: amounts falling due after more than one year	19	1,944	1,812
Provision for liabilities and charges			
Deferred taxation	22	2	19
		1,946	1,831
		8,263	5,740
Capital and reserves			
Called up share capital	23	3,015	2,500
Share premium account	24	100	100
Revaluation reserve	24	553	486
Other reserves	24	1,250	—
Profit and loss account	24	3,345	2,654
		8,263	5,740

J. Archer   )
)   Directors
P.A. McBride)

The notes on pages to form part of these financial statements.

GOOD GROUP P.L.C.

GROUP STATEMENT OF SOURCE AND APPLICATION OF FUNDS   SSAP 10(9), (11)
for the year ended December 31, 19X8

	19X8 £'000	19X7 £'000
Source of funds:		
Profit on ordinary activities before taxation		
less minority interests	2,475	2,065
Extraordinary items before taxation less minority interests	(289)	—
	2,186	2,065
Adjustment for items not involving the movement of funds:		
Minority interest in retained profits of the year	46	5
Depreciation	494	416
(Profit)/loss on disposal of fixed assets	(255)	170
Amortisation of development expenditure	35	10
Amortisation of goodwill	13	12
Share of profits before tax of associated companies	(500)	(250)
Dividends received from associated companies	318	130
	151	493
Total generated from operations	2,337	2,558
Funds from other sources:		
*Proceeds of share issues	1,785	—
Proceeds of disposal of tangible fixed assets	2,065	793
Proceeds of disposal of investments	260	—
Receipt of long-term loan	932	900
Exchange differences	37	—
	5,079	1,693
	7,416	4,251
Application of funds		
Dividends paid	330	297
*Purchase of tangible fixed assets	2,070	1,200
Purchase of investments	93	46
*Purchase of Extinguishers Limited	1,750	—
Development expenditure incurred	115	202
Current instalments due on loans	300	100
Current instalments due on finance leases and hire purchase contracts	40	37
Tax paid	581	316
Share issue costs	20	—
Exchange differences	—	40
	5,299	2,238
Working capital — increase	2,117	2,013

The notes on pages   to   form part of these financial statements.

GOOD GROUP P.L.C.

GROUP STATEMENT OF SOURCE AND APPLICATION OF FUNDS
for the year ended December 31, 19X8

	19X8 £'000	19X7 £'000
Components of increase in working capital:		
*Stocks	222	512
*Debtors	1,052	149
*Creditors	707	9
	1,981	670
Movement in net liquid funds:		
Bank and cash	(263)	1,312
Bank overdraft	602	131
Current instalments due on loans	(200)	(100)
Current instalments due on capitalised leases and hire purchase contracts	(3)	—
	136	1,343
	2,117	2,013

*Analysis of the acquisition of Extinguishers Limited		SSAP 10(5)
Net assets acquired:		
Tangible fixed assets	900	
Stocks	983	
Debtors	434	
Creditors	(867)	
	1,450	
Goodwill	300	
	1,750	
Discharged by:		
Proceeds of shares issued	1,750	

The notes on pages   to   form part of these financial statements.

GOOD GROUP P.L.C. AND SUBSIDIARIES

NOTES TO THE FINANCIAL STATEMENTS
at December 31, 19X8

Events relating to the year ended December 31, 19X8, which occurred before March 25, 19X9,   SSAP 17(26)
the date of approval of the financial statements by the board of directors, have been included in
the financial statements to the extent that it is required by Statement of Standard Accounting
Practice No. 17.

1.   Accounting policies

sch 4.36
sch 4.10 — 15
SSAP 2(17), (18)

Accounting convention

The financial statements are prepared under the historical cost convention modified to include
the revaluation of certain land and buildings.

Basis of consolidation

The group financial statements consolidate the financial statements of Good Group P.L.C. and   s 228(7)
all its subsidiaries made up to December 31 each year. No profit and loss account is presented   SSAP 14(15)
for Good Group P.L.C. as provided by S.228(7) of the Companies Act 1985.

The group profit and loss account includes the results of Extinguishers Limited for the   SSAP 23(22)
6 month period from its acquisition on July 1, 19X8. The purchase consideration has been   SSAP 14(15), (18)
allocated to each class of asset on the basis of fair value at the date of acquisition.   SSAP 22(39)

Advantage has been taken of the merger relief offered by S.131 of the Companies Act 1985 in   sch 4.75(1)
respect of consideration received in excess of the nominal value of the shares issued in   SSAP 23(21)
connection with the acquisition of Extinguishers Limited. However, although the transaction   SSAP 14(15)
qualifies for merger accounting, the directors have decided to account for the combination as an
acquisition.

The group profit and loss account also includes the results of Sprinklers Incorporated for the   SSAP 14(15),(19)
seven month period from its incorporation on June 1, 19X8.

Companies in which the group has an investment comprising an interest of not less than 20%   SSAP 1(18), (26)
in the voting capital and over which it exerts significant influence are defined as associated
companies. Such companies are also related companies as defined in the Companies Act 1985
and there are no other related companies. The group financial statements include the
appropriate share of these companies' results and reserves based on audited financial statements
to December 31, 19X8.

Goodwill

Individual elements of purchased goodwill are either written off directly against reserves or are   sch 4.21(4)
amortised through the profit and loss account over the directors' estimate of their useful   SSAP 22(39)
economic lives.

Properties

Certain of the group's properties are held for long-term investment and, in accordance with
SSAP 19:

(i)   Investment properties are revalued annually and the aggregate surplus or deficit is   SSAP 19(11), (13)
         transferred to a revaluation reserve, and

(ii)   no depreciation or amortisation is provided in respect of freehold investment   SSAP 19(10)
         properties and leasehold investment properties with over 20 years to run.

Depreciation

Depreciation is provided on all tangible fixed assets, other than investment properties at rates   SSAP 12(25)
calculated to write off the cost or valuation, less estimated residual value, of each asset evenly
over its expected useful life, as follows:

Leasehold land and buildings   — over the lease term
Plant and machinery   — over 5 to 15 years

Government grants

Government grants on capital expenditure are deducted from the cost of the related assets.   SSAP 4(9)
Other grants are released to revenue over the life of the project to which they relate.

GOOD GROUP P.L.C. AND SUBSIDIARIES

NOTES TO THE FINANCIAL STATEMENTS
at December 31, 19X8

1. Accounting policies (continued)

Stocks

Stocks are stated at the lower of cost and net realisable value as follows:

SSAP 9(32)

Cost incurred in bringing each product to its present location and condition:

Raw materials	— purchase cost on a first-in, first-out basis
Work in progress and finished goods	— cost of direct materials and labour plus attributable overheads based on the normal level of activity.

Net realisable value is based on estimated selling price less further costs expected to be incurred to completion and disposal.

Research and development

Research and development expenditure is written off as incurred, except that development expenditure incurred on an individual project is carried forward when its future recoverability can be foreseen with reasonable assurance. Any expenditure carried forward is amortised in line with the sales from the related project.

sch 4.20(2)
SSAP 13(30)

Deferred taxation

Deferred taxation is provided on the liability method on all timing differences to the extent that they are expected to reverse in the future without being replaced, calculated at the rate at which it is estimated that tax will be payable. Advance corporation tax which is expected to be recoverable in the future is deducted from the deferred taxation balance.

SSAP 15(24) — (28)

Foreign currencies

Company

Transactions in foreign currencies are recorded at the rate ruling at the date of the transaction. Monetary assets and liabilities denominated in foreign currencies are retranslated at the rate of exchange ruling at the balance sheet date. All differences are taken to the profit and loss account with the exception of differences on foreign currency borrowings, to the extent that they are used to finance or provide a hedge against foreign equity investments, which are taken directly to reserves together with the exchange difference on the carrying amount of the related investments.

sch 4.58(1)
SSAP 20(59)

Group

The financial statements of overseas subsidiaries are translated at the rate of exchange ruling at the balance sheet date. The exchange difference arising on the retranslation of opening net assets is taken directly to reserves. All other translation differences are taken to the profit and loss account with the exception of differences on foreign currency borrowings to the extent that they are used to finance or provide a hedge against group equity investments in foreign enterprises, which are taken directly to reserves together with the exchange difference on the carrying amount of the related investments.

Leasing and hire purchase commitments

Assets obtained under finance leases and hire purchase contracts are capitalised in the balance sheet and are depreciated over their useful lives.

SSAP 21(57)

The interest element of the rental obligations is charged to profit and loss account over the period of the lease and represents a constant proportion of the balance of capital repayments outstanding.

Rentals paid under operating leases are charged to income on a straight line basis over the term of the lease.

GOOD GROUP P.L.C. AND SUBSIDIARIES

NOTES TO THE FINANCIAL STATEMENTS
at December 31, 19X8

1.   Accounting policies (continued)

Pensions

The group operates two defined pension schemes, both of which require contributions to be   SSAP 24(88)
made to separately administered funds. Contributions to these funds are charged to the profit
and loss account so as to spread the cost of pensions over the employees' working lives
within the group. The regular cost is attributed to individual years using the projected unit
credit method. Variations in pension cost, which are identified as a result of actuarial
valuations, are amortised over the average expected working lives of employees in proportion
to their expected payroll costs. Differences between the amounts funded and the amounts
charged to the profit and loss account are treated as either provisions or prepayments in the
balance sheet.

2.   Turnover and group profit

Turnover represents the amounts derived from the provision of goods and services which fall   sch 4.95, SSAP 5(8)
within the group's ordinary activities, stated net of value added tax.

Turnover and group profit on ordinary activities before taxation were contributed as follows:

Turnover

	19X8 £'000	%	19X7 £'000	%	sch 4.55(1)
Area of activity					
Electrical engineering	20,750	52	21,279	57	
Fire-prevention equipment	19,400	48	15,741	43	
	40,150	100	37,020	100	
Less: Inter-divisional sales	1,450		1,020		
	38,700		36,000		
Geographical area					
United Kingdom	26,600	69	23,040	64	sch 4.55(2)
USA	12,100	31	12,960	36	YB 5.21(c)
	38,700	100	36,000	100	

Profit on ordinary activities before taxation

	£'000	%	£'000	%	sch 4.55(1) YB 5.21(c)
Area of activity					
Electrical engineering	1,800	51	1,798	62	
Fire-prevention equipment	1,730	49	1,102	38	
	3,530	100	2,900	100	
Less: Unallocated administrative expenses and interest	1,004		830		
	2,526		2,070		

GOOD GROUP P.L.C. AND SUBSIDIARIES

NOTES TO THE FINANCIAL STATEMENTS
at December 31, 19X8

3. Operating profit

(a) This is stated after charging or crediting:

	19X8 £'000	19X7 £'000	
Auditors' remuneration	85	77	sch 4.53(7)
Depreciation of owned assets	457	382	sch 4.8, SSAP 12(25)
Depreciation of assets held under finance			
leases and hire purchase contracts	37	34	sch 4.8, SSAP 21(49)
Research and development expenditure written off	389	182	SSAP 13(31)
Amortisation of deferred development expenditure	35	10	sch 4.8, SSAP 13(31)
Amortisation of goodwill	13	12	sch 4.8
Employees' profit sharing scheme	35	—	sch 4.57(3)
Operating lease rentals — land and buildings	10	68	SSAP 21(55)
— plant and machinery	35	26	sch 4.53(6)
Net rental income	(125)	(130)	sch 4.53(5)
Exceptional item — professional expenses incurred			sch 4.57(3)
in respect of unsuccessful proposed acquisition	119	—	SSAP 6(36)

(b) Directors' remuneration   sch 5.22

	19X8	19X7	
Fees	20	15	
Other emoluments (including pension contributions)	267	211	
Pensions to former directors	25	20	sch 5.28
	312	246	

	19X8	19X7	
Emoluments (excluding pension contributions) of the chairman	£15,000	£10,000	sch 5.24
Emoluments (excluding pension contributions) of the highest paid director	£53,000	£50,000	sch 5.25

The emoluments (excluding pension contributions) of the other directors fell within the following ranges: sch 5.25

	19X8 No.	19X7 No.
£Nil — £5,000	1	1
£30,001 — £35,000	2	2
£35,001 — £40,000	2	1
£40,001 — £45,000	1	1

During the year options were granted to P.A. McBride to subscribe for 20,000 £1 ordinary shares and to F.R. Brown to subscribe for 15,000 £1 ordinary shares, in each case at £3.85 each before January 1, 19Y2. No estimated money value of the options is included in the above figures.   sch 5.22(3)

(c) Senior employees

The numbers of senior employees of Good Group P.L.C. who received remuneration falling within the ranges below were: sch 5.35

	No.	No.
£30,001 to £35,000	4	2
£35,001 to £40,000	2	1

GOOD GROUP P.L.C. AND SUBSIDIARIES

NOTES TO THE FINANCIAL STATEMENTS
at December 31, 19X8

4.   Staff costs

	19X8 £'000	19X7 £'000	
Wages and salaries	4,158	3,564	sch 4.56(4)
Social security costs	408	349	
Other pension costs	530	455	SSAP 24(88)
	5,096	4,368	

Other pension costs includes £10,000 (1987 — £9,000) arising from variations in pension   SSAP 24(88)
cost which were identified by the most recent actuarial valuation. These are being written off
over 11 years, the average remaining service lives of employees.

The average weekly number of employees during the year was made up as follows:

	19X8 No.	19X7 No.	
Office management	37	37	sch 4.56(1) — (3)
Manufacturing and installation of fire prevention equipment	348	321	
Research and development	33	15	
Electrical engineering	122	113	
	540	486	

5.   Income from investments

	19X8 £'000	19X7 £'000	
Listed	30	20	sch 4.53(4)
Unlisted	20	20	
	50	40	

6.   Interest payable

	19X8 £'000	19X7 £'000	
Bank loans and overdrafts and other loans wholly repayable within five years	209	195	sch 4.53(2)
Debentures	72	72	
Finance charges payable under finance leases and H.P. contracts	7	7	SSAP 21(53)
	288	274	

GOOD GROUP P.L.C. AND SUBSIDIARIES

NOTES TO THE FINANCIAL STATEMENTS
at December 31, 19X8

7. Tax on profit on ordinary activities

The taxation charge is made up as follows:

	19X8 £'000	19X7 £'000	
			sch 4.54
			SSAP 8(22), (23)
Based on the profit for the year:			
Corporation tax at 35% (19X7 35%)	778	498	
Tax credits attributable to dividends received (excluding associated companies)	15	12	
Deferred taxation	(29)	20	SSAP 15(33), (38)
	764	530	
Double taxation relief	(215)	(187)	
	549	343	
Overseas taxation	215	196	
	764	539	
Taxation overprovided in previous years:			
Corporation tax	(11)	(34)	
	753	505	
Associated companies	175	100	SSAP 1(20)
	928	605	

The effective tax rate for the current year is higher than normal as a result of disallowable professional expenses in connection with a proposed acquisition (see Note 3). If full provision had been made for deferred tax for the year, the tax charge would have been increased by £1,000 (19X7 — £25,000), as follows:

sch 4.54(2)
SSAP 15(35)

	19X8 £'000	19X7 £'000
Capital allowances in advance of depreciation	(3)	22
Other differences in recognising revenue and expense items in different periods for taxation purposes	4	3
	1	25

8. Profit before extraordinary items

The profit before extraordinary items but after taxation includes the results of Extinguishers Limited from the date of acquisition.

Extinguishers Limited earned a profit of £204,000 in the year ended December 31, 19X8, of which £95,000 arose in the period from July 1, 19X8, the effective date of acquisition, to December 31, 19X8.

SSAP 14(30)
SSAP 23(22)

On October 31, 19X8, fixed assets of Extinguishers Limited valued at £200,000 were disposed of, realising a profit of £15,000.

sch 4.75(2)

GOOD GROUP P.L.C. AND SUBSIDIARIES

NOTES TO THE FINANCIAL STATEMENTS
at December 31, 19X8

9. Extraordinary items

	19X8	
	£'000	sch 4.57(2)
		SSAP 6(37)
Profit on disposal of investment property	(10)	
Profit on disposal of long-term investments	(165)	
Expenses of cessation of operations in Northern Ireland	469	
Extraordinary loss	294	
Taxation on the above:		SSAP 6(38)
Corporation tax	(97)	sch 4.54(3)
Deferred tax	(14)	SSAP 15(34), (38)
	111	
	183	
Minority interests	5	SSAP 6(37)
	178	

10. Profit attributable to members of the holding company

The profit dealt with in the financial statements of the holding company was £1,056,000   s 228(7)
(19X7 — £1,260,000).

11. Dividends

		19X8	19X7	
		£'000	£'000	sch 4.3(7)
Preference	— paid	35	35	
Ordinary	— interim paid	164	131	
	— final proposed	199	131	sch 4.51(3)
		398	297	

12. Earnings per ordinary share

The calculation of earnings per ordinary share is based on earnings, after deducting preference   SSAP 3(15)
dividends, of £1,512,000 (19X7 — £1,425,000) and on 2,252,500 ordinary shares, being the
weighted average number of ordinary shares in issue during the year (19X7 — 2,000,000).

The fully diluted earnings per share is based on 2,902,500 (19X7 — 2,600,000) ordinary   SSAP 3(16)
shares, allowing for the full conversion of the convertible preference shares and the full
exercise of outstanding share purchase options (see Note 23), and adjusted earnings of
£1,584,000 (19X7 — £1,488,000). Earnings before the preference dividends have been
adjusted, in connection with the share options, by adding interest deemed to be earned from
$2^{1}/_{2}$% Consolidated Stock on the proceeds of such share issue.

GOOD GROUP P.L.C. AND SUBSIDIARIES

NOTES TO THE FINANCIAL STATEMENTS
at December 31, 19X8

13. Intangible fixed assets

Group	Goodwill £'000	Development expenditure £'000	Total £'000	
				sch 4.8, 4.42
				SSAP 22(41)
				SSAP 13(32)
Cost:				
At January 1, 19X8	50	302	352	
Increase during the year	—	115	115	
At December 31, 19X8	50	417	467	
Amortisation:				
At January 1, 19X8	5	10	15	
Provided during the year	5	35	40	
At December 31, 19X8	10	45	55	
Net book value at December 31, 19X8	40	372	412	
Net book value at January 1, 19X8	45	292	337	

Goodwill arising on the consolidation of Bright Sparks Limited is being amortised over the directors' estimate of its useful economic life of 10 years. sch 4.21(4) SSAP 22(40), (41)

Goodwill on the acquisition of Extinguishers Limited during the year has been written off directly to reserves (see Note 24). SSAP 22(40)

14. Tangible fixed assets

Group	Land and buildings £'000	Plant and machinery £'000	Total £'000	
				sch 4.8, 4.42
				SSAP 12(25)
Cost or valuation:				
At January 1, 19X8	3,720	3,620	7,340	
Exchange adjustment	10	155	165	
Additions	495	1,575	2,070	
Arising on acquisition of a subsidiary	510	390	900	
Surplus on revaluation	210	—	210	
Disposals	(925)	(1,650)	(2,575)	
At December 31, 19X8	4,020	4,090	8,110	
Depreciation:				
At January 1, 19X8	335	1,705	2,040	
Exchange adjustment	—	110	110	
Provided during the year	85	409	494	
Disposals	(100)	(500)	(600)	
At December 31, 19X8	320	1,724	2,044	
Net book value at December 31, 19X8	3,700	2,366	6,066	
Net book value at January 1, 19X8	3,385	1,915	5,300	

GOOD GROUP P.L.C. AND SUBSIDIARIES

NOTES TO THE FINANCIAL STATEMENTS
at December 31, 19X8

14.   Tangible fixed assets (continued)

Company

	Land and buildings £'000	Plant and machinery £'000	Total £'000
Cost or valuation:			
At January 1, 19X8	1,620	1,705	3,325
Additions	455	580	1,035
Surplus on revaluation	100	—	100
Disposals	(125)	(800)	(925)
At December 31, 19X8	2,050	1,485	3,535
Depreciation:			
At January 1, 19X8	190	550	740
Provided during the year	50	153	203
Disposals	—	(450)	(450)
At December 31, 19X8	240	253	493
Net book value at December 31, 19X8	1,810	1,232	3,042
Net book value at January 1, 19X8	1,430	1,155	2,585

The net book value of land and buildings comprises:

	Group		Company		
	19X8 £'000	19X7 £'000	19X8 £'000	19X7 £'000	sch 4.44
Investment properties:					
Long leasehold	1,415	1,320	575	600	SSAP 19(15)
Other properties:					
Long leasehold	1,145	198	639	198	
Short leasehold	1,140	1,867	596	632	
	3,700	3,385	1,810	1,430	

Investment properties were valued on an open market value for existing use basis on December 31, 19X8 by Chartered Surveyors & Co. No depreciation is provided in respect of leasehold investment properties with over 20 years to run. The directors consider that this accounting policy results in the financial statements giving a true and fair view. Depreciation is only one of the factors reflected in the annual valuation, and the amount which might otherwise have been shown cannot be separately identified or quantified.

s 230(6)
sch 4.43
SSAP 19(10), (12)

The historical cost of investment properties included at valuation is as follows:

sch 4.33

	Group £'000	Company £'000
At December 31, 19X8	752	22
At January 1, 19X8	834	114

GOOD GROUP P.L.C. AND SUBSIDIARIES

NOTES TO THE FINANCIAL STATEMENTS
at December 31, 19X8

14. Tangible fixed assets (continued)

Included in the amounts for plant and machinery above are the following amounts relating to   SSAP 21(49), (50)
leased assets and assets acquired under hire purchase contracts:

	Group and Company £'000
Cost:	
At January 1, 19X8	200
Additions	—
At December 31, 19X8	200
Depreciation:	
At January 1, 19X8	50
Depreciation provided during the year	37
At December 31, 19X8	87
Net book value at December 31, 19X8	113
Net book value at January 1, 19X8	150

15. Investments

Group

Associated Companies	Share of net tangible assets £'000	Goodwill £'000	Total £'000	
				sch 4.8, 4.42
				SSAP 1(26)
At January 1, 19X8	361	30	391	
Share of profits of associated companies	7	—	7	SSAP 1(22)
Amortisation of goodwill	—	(8)	(8)	
	368	22	390	
At December 31, 19X8				

Goodwill is being amortised over the directors' estimate of its useful economic life of five   sch 4.21(4)
years.   SSAP 22(41)

The group's share of retained profits of associated companies at December 31, 19X8 is   SSAP 1(31)
£90,000 (19X7 — £83,000)

Other fixed asset investments

	Listed £'000	Unlisted £'000	Total £'000	
				sch 4.8, 4.42
				sch 4.45(1)
Cost:				
At January 1, 19X8	155	420	575	
Additions	93	—	93	
Disposals	—	(95)	(95)	
At December 31, 19X8	248	325	573	
Amounts written off				
At January 1, 19X8 and December 31, 19X8	—	165	165	
Net book value				
At December 31, 19X8	248	160	408	
At January 1, 19X8	155	255	410	

The market value of listed investments dealt with on a recognised stock exchange at December   sch 4.45(2)
31, 19X8 was £437,000 (19X7 — £243,000) and if they had been sold at this value there   SSAP 15(42)
would have been a liability to tax of £39,000 (19X7 — £10,000) on the capital gain arising
from the sale.

GOOD GROUP P.L.C. AND SUBSIDIARIES

NOTES TO THE FINANCIAL STATEMENTS
at December 31, 19X8

15.   Investments (continued)

Total

	19X8 £'000	19X7 £'000
Associated companies	390	391
Other fixed asset investments	408	410
	798	801

Company

	Subsidiary companies £'000	Associated companies £'000	Other investments £'000	Total £'000
Cost:				
At January 1, 19X8	750	135	575	1,460
Additions	2,182	—	—	2,182
Exchange difference	40	—	—	40
Disposals	—	—	(95)	(95)
At December 31, 19X8	2,972	135	480	3,587
Amounts written off:				
At January 1, 19X8				
and December 31, 19X8	—	—	165	165
Net book value:				
At December 31, 19X8	2,972	135	315	3,422
At January 1, 19X8	750	135	410	1,295

Other investments include investments listed on a recognised stock exchange at a cost of £155,000 (19X7 — £155,000). The market value of listed investments at December 31, 19X8 was £274,000 (19X7 — £243,000) and if they had been sold at this value there would have been a liability to tax of £19,000 (19X7 — £10,000) on the capital gain arising from the sale.

The group holds more than 10% of the equity of the following companies:

Name of company	Country of registration (or incorporation) and operation	Holding	Proportion held	Nature of business	
Subsidiary companies:					
Extinguishers Limited	England	Ordinary shares	100%	Fire-prevention equipment	sch 5.1 SSAP 14(33)
Bright Sparks Limited	England	Ordinary shares Preferred shares	85% 45%*	Electrical engineering	YB 5.21(d)
Wireworks Inc.	USA	Common stock	90%	Electrical engineering	
Sprinklers Inc.	USA	Common stock	100%	Fire-prevention equipment	
Lightbulbs Limited	England	Ordinary shares	100%	Dormant	
Associated companies:					
Power Works Limited	England	Ordinary shares	25%*	Electrical engineering	sch 5.7, 5.8 SSAP 1(49)
Showers Limited	England	Ordinary shares	33%	Fire-prevention equipment	YB 5.21(e)
Others:					
Drains Limited	England	Ordinary shares	15%		sch 5.7
Shamrocks Limited	Eire	Ordinary shares	12%		

* held by a subsidiary company.

                                                                                    sch 5.2

GOOD GROUP P.L.C. AND SUBSIDIARIES

NOTES TO THE FINANCIAL STATEMENTS
at December 31, 19X8

15. Investments (continued)

On July 1, 19X8 the group acquired 500,000 ordinary shares of £1 each in Extinguishers   sch 4.75(1)
Limited being 100% of its nominal share capital.

16. Stocks

	Group		Company		
	19X8 £'000	19X7 £'000	19X8 £'000	19X7 £'000	sch 4.8, SSAP 9(27)
Raw materials and consumables	1,513	1,275	631	460	
Work in progress	2,168	1,685	943	625	
Finished goods and goods for resale	1,544	1,060	740	340	
	5,225	4,020	2,314	1,425	

The replacement cost of raw materials of the group is approximately £1,720,000 (19X7 —   sch 4.27(3) — (5)
£1,410,000) and for the company £717,000 (19X7 — £508,000). For other stocks, the
difference between purchase price or production cost and replacement is not material.

17. Debtors

	Group		Company		
	19X8 £'000	19X7 £'000	19X8 £'000	19X7 £'000	sch 4.8
Trade debtors	2,852	1,426	1,017	820	
Amount owed by subsidiaries	—	—	980	870	sch 4.59
Amount owed by associated companies	46	29	—	—	SSAP 1(29)
Other debtors	286	208	249	506	
Prepayments and accrued income	83	64	74	59	
	3,267	1,727	2,320	2,255	

Included within prepayments and accrued income for both the group and the company, is   SSAP 24(88)
£30,000 (19X7 — £15,000) in respect of pension contribution payments made in advance of
their recognition in the profit and loss account.

Amounts falling due after more than one year and included in the debtors above are:

	Group		Company		
	19X8 £'000	19X7 £'000	19X8 £'000	19X7 £'000	sch 4.8(note 5)
Other debtors	200	200	—	—	
Advance corporation tax recoverable	55	1	73	25	

18. Creditors: amounts falling due within one year

	Notes	Group		Company		
		19X8 £'000	19X7 £'000	19X8 £'000	19X7 £'000	sch 4.8
Current instalments due on loans	21	300	100	300	100	
Bank overdraft (see below)		152	754	—	—	
Obligations under finance leases and hire purchase contracts	20	40	37	40	37	SSAP 21(51)
Trade creditors		3,138	2,771	948	602	
Current corporation tax		625	492	338	292	sch 4.8(note 9)
Other taxes and social security costs		30	84	12	19	sch 4.8(note 9)
Other creditors		399	544	399	593	
Accruals		103	111	68	55	
Proposed dividend		199	131	199	131	sch 4.51(3)
		4,986	5,024	2,304	1,829	

The bank overdraft is secured by a floating charge over certain of the group's assets.   sch 4.48(4)

GOOD GROUP P.L.C. AND SUBSIDIARIES

NOTES TO THE FINANCIAL STATEMENTS
at December 31, 19X8

19. Creditors: amounts falling due after more than one year

	Notes	Group 19X8 £'000	Group 19X7 £'000	Company 19X8 £'000	Company 19X7 £'000	
Loans	21	2,372	1,700	1,872	1,700	sch 4.8
Obligations under finance leases and hire purchase contracts	20	72	112	72	112	SSAP 21(51)
		2,444	1,812	1,944	1,812	

20. Obligations under leases and hire purchase contracts

Group and company

	19X8 £'000	19X7 £'000	
Amounts payable within one year	48	45	SSAP 21(51), (52)
Over one year:			
In the second to fifth years inclusive	86	134	
Over five years	—	—	
	134	179	
Less finance charges allocated to future periods	(22)	(30)	
	112	149	

Finance leases and hire purchase contracts are shown as:

	Notes	19X8 £'000	19X7 £'000
Current obligations	18	40	37
Non-current obligations	19	72	112
		112	149

The commitments under non-cancellable operating leases are as follows:

Group

	19X8 Land and Buildings £'000	19X8 Other £'000	19X7 Land and Buildings £'000	19X7 Other £'000	
Operating leases which expire:					sch 4.50(5)
Within one year	—	10	—	6	SSAP 21(56)
In the second to fifth years inclusive	—	20	—	15	
Over five years	12	8	12	14	
	12	38	12	35	

Company

	19X8 Land and Buildings £'000	19X8 Other £'000	19X7 Land and Buildings £'000	19X7 Other £'000
Operating leases which expire:				
Within one year	—	4	—	3
In the second to fifth years inclusive	—	18	—	9
Over five years	12	2	12	8
	12	24	12	20

GOOD GROUP P.L.C. AND SUBSIDIARIES

NOTES TO THE FINANCIAL STATEMENTS
at December 31, 19X8

21. Loans

	Group		Company		
	19X8 £'000	19X7 £'000	19X8 £'000	19X7 £'000	sch 4.48(1)
Not wholly repayable within five years	1,872	900	1,372	900	
Wholly repayable within five years	800	900	800	900	
	2,672	1,800	2,172	1,800	
Amount due within one year (included in current liabilities)	300	100	300	100	
	2,372	1,700	1,872	1,700	
Instalments not due within five years	640	630	540	630	

Details of loans not wholly repayable within five years are as follows:

	Group		Company		
	19X8 £'000	19X7 £'000	19X8 £'000	19X7 £'000	sch 4.48(2)
8% debentures repayable in annual instalments of £90,000 commencing December 31, 19Y0	900	900	900	900	
9½% secured loan repayable in annual instalments of £100,000 commencing December 31, 19Y0	500	—	—	—	
10¼% secured dollar loan repayable on May 31, 19Y5	472	—	472	—	
	1,872	900	1,372	900	

Amounts due at December 31, 19X8 are repayable as follows:

	Group		Company		
	19X8 £'000	19X7 £'000	19X8 £'000	19X7 £'000	sch 4.48(1) YB 5.21(f)
Bank loans					
After five years	572	—	472	—	
Between two and five years	600	500	200	500	
Between one and two years	300	300	300	300	
	1,472	800	972	800	
Within one year (included in current liabilities)	300	100	300	100	
	1,772	900	1,272	900	
Debentures					
After five years	540	630	540	630	
Between two and five years	270	270	270	270	
Between one and two years	90	—	90	—	
	900	900	900	900	
Total	2,672	1,800	2,172	1,800	

The long-term loans are secured by fixed charges over various of the group's properties. sch 4.48(4)
Included in both the group and the company loans wholly repayable within five years is £300,000 (19X7 — £300,000) which is secured by a floating charge over the company's assets.

GOOD GROUP P.L.C. AND SUBSIDIARIES

NOTES TO THE FINANCIAL STATEMENTS
at December 31, 19X8

22.   Deferred taxation

Deferred taxation provided in the financial statements and the amounts not provided are as follows:

Group

	Provision		Not provided		
	19X8 £'000	19X7 £'000	19X8 £'000	19X7 £'000	SSAP 15(37), (40)
Capital allowances in advance of depreciation	35	64	254	257	
Other differences in recognising revenue and expense items in other periods for taxation purposes	—	—	16	12	
	35	64	270	269	
Less: Advance corporation tax	30	55	—	—	
	5	9	270	269	
Taxation on valuation surplus	—	14	50	36	
	5	23	320	305	

No provision has been made for deferred tax in respect of earnings which are retained overseas.   SSAP 15(44)

Company

	Provision		Not provided		
	19X8 £'000	19X7 £'000	19X8 £'000	19X7 £'000	
Capital allowances in advance of depreciation	14	36	127	129	
Other differences in recognising revenue and expense items in other periods for taxation purposes	—	—	14	11	
	14	36	141	140	
Less: Advance corporation tax	12	31	—	—	SSAP 15(29)
	2	5	141	140	
Taxation on valuation surplus	—	14	40	36	
	2	19	181	176	

23.   Share capital

	Authorised		Allotted, called up and fully paid		sch 4.8(note 12) sch 4.38(1)
	19X8 No.'000	19X7 No.'000	19X8 £'000	19X7 £'000	
Ordinary shares of £1 each	3,500	3,000	2,515	2,000	
7% convertible cumulative preference shares of £1 each	500	500	500	500	
	4,000	3,500	3,015	2,500	

During the year the authorised share capital was increased to 3,500,000 ordinary shares of £1   sch 4.39
each. Shares were allotted as follows:

On July 1, 19X8, 500,000 ordinary shares were issued at £3.50, in consideration of the   sch 4.75(1)
acquisition of Extinguishers Limited for £1,750,000. Advantage has been taken of the merger   SSAP 23(21)
relief offered by S.131 of the Companies Act 1985.

On October 25, 19X8, 15,000 ordinary shares in the company were allotted at £2.33 each to
the trustees of the Profit Sharing Scheme.

The company has a share option scheme under which options have been granted to certain   sch 4.40
executives which offers 100,000 ordinary shares at £3.80 each, exercisable before January 1,
19Y0, and 50,000 ordinary shares at £3.85 each, exercisable before January 1, 19Y2.

GOOD GROUP P.L.C. AND SUBSIDIARIES

NOTES TO THE FINANCIAL STATEMENTS
at December 31, 19X8

23. Share Capital (continued)

The 7% convertible cumulative preference shares are convertible into a like number of ordinary sch 4.38(2) 4.40 shares of £1 each on January 1, 19Y1, 19Y2 or 19Y3 and any preference shares not converted are redeemable at par on December 31, 19Y7.

24. Reserves

Group	Share premium account £'000	Revaluation reserve £'000	Other reserves £'000	Profit and loss account £'000	
At January 1, 19X8	100	486	—	4,488	sch 4.46(1), (2) SSAP 6(35) SSAP 19(15)
Exchange differences on retranslation of subsidiaries	—	—	—	92	SSAP 20(60)
Exchange difference on loans	—	—	—	(40)	SSAP 20(60)
Surplus on revaluation of assets	—	210	—	—	
Realised revaluation surplus on sale of property	—	(33)	—	33	
Reserves arising on share issues	20	—	1,250	—	
Goodwill on acquisition of Extinguishers Limited written off	—	—	(300)	—	
Share issue costs	(20)	—	—	—	
Retained profit for the year	—	—	—	971	
At December 31, 19X8	100	663	950	5,544	

Company	Share premium account £'000	Revaluation reserve £'000	Other reserves £'000	Profit and loss account £'000	
At January 1, 19X8	100	486	—	2,654	
Exchange difference on investment in subsidiary	—	—	—	40	SSAP 20(60)
Exchange difference on loan	—	—	—	(40)	SSAP 20(60)
Surplus on revaluation of assets	—	100	—	—	
Realised revaluation surplus on sale of property	—	(33)	—	33	
Reserves arising on share issues	20	—	1,250	—	
Share issue costs	(20)	—	—	—	
Retained profit for the year	—	—	—	658	
At December 31, 19X8	100	553	1,250	3,345	

25. Post balance sheet events

On February 14, 19X9 a short leasehold building with a net book value of £150,000 was SSAP 17(23) — (25) severely damaged by flooding. It is expected that insurance proceeds will fall short of the costs of rebuilding and loss of profits by some £20,000. No provision has been made in these financial statements for this loss.

26. Capital commitments

Amounts contracted for but not provided in the financial statements amounted to £900,000 for sch 4.50(3) the group and £350,000 for the company (19X7 — £850,000 and £200,000 respectively). Amounts authorised by the directors but not contracted for were £150,000 for the group and £50,000 for the company (19X7 — £60,000 for both).

27. Contingent liability

The company has guaranteed the bank overdraft of a subsidiary to the extent of £152,000 sch 4.50(2) (19X7 — £75,000). SSAP 18(18)

GOOD GROUP P.L.C. AND SUBSIDIARIES

NOTES TO THE FINANCIAL STATEMENTS
at December 31, 19X8

28. Pension commitments

The group operates two defined benefit pension schemes, both of which are funded by the payment of contributions to separately administered trust funds.   sch 4.50(4) SSAP 24(88)

The contributions to these schemes are determined with the advice of independent qualified actuaries on the basis of triennial valuations using the projected unit credit method. The most recent valuations were conducted as at December 31, 19X6, using the following main assumptions:

Real rate of return on investments   3.5% per annum

Real rate of salary increases   2% per annum

Pensions will be increased in line with inflation.

These valuations showed that the market value of the schemes' assets at that date amounted to £2,000,000 and the actuarial value was sufficient to cover 90% of the benefits that had accrued to members, after allowing for the effect of future increases in their earnings. Further contributions, in addition to the current employer's contribution rate of 12%, are being made in order to eliminate this deficiency by 19Y1.

Since the date of these valuations, the group has acquired Extinguishers Limited and closed down its operations in Northern Ireland. The group's actuarial advisers have confirmed that neither of these events is likely to have had a significant effect on the position of the fund.

29. Directors' interest

During the year, payments of £509,000 have been made by group companies in the ordinary course of business to UK Gnome Industries Limited, of which P.A. McBride is a director and controlling shareholder.   sch 6, part 1 YB 5.21(k)

F.R. Brown was interested throughout the year, through his 25% equity interest in Welsh Home Fires Limited, in a contract for the supply of fire extinguishers to that company. During the year the company supplied extinguishers to Welsh Home Fires Limited to a value of £225,000, at normal market prices.

There are no other interests in contracts which are required to be disclosed under the Companies Act 1985.

30. Director's loan

At the Annual General Meeting held on July 15, 19X8 approval was given for an interest free loan up to a maximum of £10,000 to be made as necessary to F.R. Brown to enable him to meet expenditure to be incurred in his capacity as sales director at marketing exhibitions and tours in the United States of America. During the year £6,500 was advanced to him for this purpose and at December 31, 19X8 £2,432 was outstanding and is included in debtors.   sch 6, part 1 YB 5.21(k)

GOOD GROUP P.L.C. AND SUBSIDIARIES

FIVE YEAR SUMMARY

1964 letter from
Stock Exchange

Years ended December 31	19X8 £'000	19X7 £'000	19X6 £'000	19X5 £'000	19X4 £'000
Turnover	38,700	36,000	34,200	25,900	29,160
Profit before interest **and taxation**	2,814	2,344	1,907	1,446	1,617
Interest	(288)	(274)	(201)	(245)	(183)
Profit on ordinary activities **before taxation**	2,526	2,070	1,706	1,201	1,434
Tax on profit on ordinary activities	(928)	(605)	(575)	(546)	(491)
Minority interests	(51)	(5)	—	—	—
Extraordinary items	(178)	—	—	104	—
Dividends	(398)	(297)	(258)	(224)	(195)
Retained profit	971	1,163	873	535	748
Employment of group capital					
Fixed assets	7,276	6,438	6,371	5,490	4,400
Net current assets (less deferred tax)	5,495	2,957	940	1,048	1,703
	12,771	9,395	7,311	6,538	6,103
Group capital employed					
Loans falling due after more than one year	2,444	1,812	900	1,000	1,100
Capital and reserves	10,272	7,574	6,411	5,538	5,003
Minority interests	55	9	—	—	—
	12,771	9,395	7,311	6,538	6,103
Net borrowings					
Cash at bank and in hand	1,994	2,257	945	1,189	1,006
Bank overdraft	(152)	(754)	(885)	(637)	(205)
Current instalments due on debenture and bank loans	(300)	(100)	—	—	—
Loans falling due after more than one year	(2,372)	(1,700)	(900)	(1,000)	(1,100)
	(830)	(297)	(840)	(448)	(299)
Statistics					
Earnings per ordinary share of £1	67.13p	71.25p	54.80p	31.00p	45.40p
Dividends per ordinary share of £1	14.43p	13.10p	11.15p	9.45p	8.00p

GOOD GROUP P.L.C.

NOTICE OF ANNUAL GENERAL MEETING

NOTICE IS HEREBY GIVEN that the thirtieth annual general meeting of the company will be held at Homefire House, Ashdown Square, London EC2 3AS on May 15, 19X9 at 11.00 a.m. for the following purposes:

1. To receive and, if approved, adopt the directors' report and financial statements for the financial year 19X8 and the auditors' report thereon.

2. To re-elect N.O. Evans as a director.

3. To re-elect J.N. Smith as a director.

4. To re-elect P.A. McBride as a director.

5. To reappoint Chartered Accountants & Co. as auditors.

6. To authorise the directors to fix the remuneration of the auditors.

7. To transact any other business which may be transacted at an annual general meeting.

By order of the board,

J. Harris
Secretary,

April 14, 19X9.

A member entitled to attend and vote at the above meeting is entitled to appoint one or more proxies to attend and vote instead of him. A proxy need not also be a member of the company.

Forms of proxy must be deposited at the company's registrars, Registration Services Limited, 45 Market Street, London W2 7JA, not less than 48 hours before the time fixed for the meeting.

A statement or summary of transactions of directors (and their family interests) in the share capital of the company and copies of their service contracts will be available for inspection at the company's registered office during usual business hours on any weekday (Saturdays and bank holidays excluded) from the date of this notice to May 14, 19X9 inclusive, and during the meeting.   YB 5.43(b)

Index

Leases — *contd.*
  substance over form, 69–70
  tax position, 767–8
  tax variation clauses—
    adjustments, 798
    introduction, 798
    lessee, 798
    lessor, 799
  termination—
    finance leases by lessee, 797
    finance leases by lessor, 797–8
    lease classification, 796
    operating leases, 796
  type determination—
    current practice, 793
    ICAEW TR 664, 794
    90 percent test, 769–72, 806
    other factors, 772–3
    SFAS 13, 806–7
    SSAP 21, 794
    US practice, 806–7
  US practice, 806–7
Lee, Tom, 34
Liabilities—
  assets and liabilities statement, 58
  contingent, 250–1
  defined by ED 42, 254
  in SFAC No 6, 50–1
  valuation, 57–8
Liability method *see* Taxation
Licence receipts, 97–8
Licensed premises non-depreciation, 457–8
LIFO (Last-in, First-out), 388, 398–9
Littleton, AC, 24
Lloyd Cheyham & Co Ltd v *Littlejohn & Co*, 5
Loan arrangement fees, 99
Loans to directors *see* Directors, loans
Local currency *see* Foreign currencies
Long-term contracts—
  approved variations and claims, 432
  definition, 393–4
  IAS 11, 428–9
  inclusion of interest, 433
  profit amount, 429–30
    short-term contracts, 432
  SSAP 9, 419–28
  turnover, 419, 420, 430–1
  US practice, 428
  see also Stocks and long-term contracts
Losses—
  earnings per share and, 274
  financing loss-making companies, 238–40
  in SFAC No 6, 52–3
  see also Post-acquisition losses

McKinnon Report, 3
MacNeal, Kenneth, 33
Macve, Professor Richard, 39
Macve Report, The, 39–40
Maintenance, property non-depreciation and, 457–8

Majority-owned subsidiary, 117
Making Corporate Reports Valuable, 55–60, 64
  additional information, 59–60
  background to study, 55–6
  literature survey, 58
  proposed new information package, 58–9
  users and their needs, 56–7
  valuation of assets and liabilities, 57–8
Management—
  related parties, 846–8
  unified, 116
Market value of land and buildings, 467
Marking to market, 83, 416–18
Matching concept *see* Accruals concept
Material interest transactions, 5
  definitions, 926–7
  disclosure requirements, 927–9
Materiality, 48–9, 69–70
Merger accounting, 149, 50
  EC Seventh Directive, 153–4
  for demergers, 213
  optional, 153
  qualifying conditions, 151
    see also Mergers
Merger relief, 150–2, 206
  compulsory, 151
  disclosure, 198–9
Merger reserve, 151
  goodwill write-off, 159
    immediate, 175
Mergers, 149–54, 190–4
  basic principles, 190
  disclosure, 197–8
  dividends of subsidiary, 194
  equity eliminations, 191–2
  expenses of, 192
  incorporation as new holding company, 193
  new entity method, 190
  non-coterminous accounting periods, 192–3
  share issue for, 271–2
  vendor rights or placings, 153
  see also Business combinations
Minority interests *see* Group financial statements
Monetary items—
  fair value of consideration, 157
  fair value of net assets acquired, 164
Moonitz, Maurice, 25
Mortgages—
  of freehold properwty, 237–8
  securitisation, 244–7
Most, KS, 43, 62

Napier, Chirstopher, 863
Napier interim report, 863–5
Negative goodwill, 174
Net liquid funds, 584, 587
Net realisable value, 404, 413–16
Netting off of transactions, 600
New entity method, 190
Non-aggregation principle, 68